AUSTRALIA IN THE WAR OF 1939-1945

SERIES ONE
ARMY

VOLUME VI
THE NEW GUINEA OFFENSIVES

AUSTRALIA IN THE WAR OF 1939-1945

SERIES 1 (ARMY)
    I. To Benghazi. *By Gavin Long.**
    II. Greece, Crete and Syria. *By Gavin Long.**
    III. Tobruk and El Alamein. *By Barton Maughan.*
    IV. The Japanese Thrust. *By Lionel Wigmore.**
    V. South-West Pacific Area—First Year. *By Dudley McCarthy.**
    VI. The New Guinea Offensives. *By David Dexter.**
    VII. The Final Campaigns. *By Gavin Long.*

SERIES 2 (NAVY)
    I. Royal Australian Navy, 1939-42. *By G. Hermon Gill.**
    II. Royal Australian Navy, 1942-45. *By G. Hermon Gill.*

SERIES 3 (AIR)
    I. Royal Australian Air Force, 1939-42. *By Douglas Gillison.*
    II. Air War Against Japan, 1943-45. *By George Odgers.**
    III. Air War Against Germany and Italy, 1939-43. *By John Herington.**
    IV. Air Power Over Europe, 1944-45. *By John Herington.*

SERIES 4 (CIVIL)
    I. The Government and the People, 1939-41. *By Paul Hasluck.**
    II. The Government and the People, 1942-45. *By Paul Hasluck.*
    III. War Economy, 1939-42. *By S. J. Butlin.**
    IV. War Economy, 1942-45. *By S. J. Butlin.*
    V. The Role of Science and Industry. *By D. P. Mellor.**

SERIES 5 (MEDICAL)
    I. Clinical Problems of War. *By Allan S. Walker**
    II. Middle East and Far East. *By Allan S. Walker.**
    III. The Island Campaigns. *By Allan S. Walker.**
    IV. Medical Services of the R.A.N. and R.A.A.F. *By Allan S. Walker and others.**

* Published.

The writers of these volumes have been given full access to official documents, but they and the general editor are alone responsible for the statements and opinions which the volumes contain.

THE NEW GUINEA OFFENSIVES

by

DAVID DEXTER

The Naval & Military Press Ltd

Published by
The Naval & Military Press Ltd
5 Riverside, Brambleside, Bellbrook
Industrial Estate, Uckfield, East Sussex,
TN22 1QQ England
Tel: +44 (0) 1825 749494
Fax: +44 (0) 1825 765701
www.naval-military-press.com
www.military-genealogy.com

In reprinting in facsimile from the original, any imperfections are inevitably reproduced and the quality may fall short of modern type and cartographic standards.

CONTENTS

	Page
Preface	xv
List of Events	xix

Chapter		Page
1	THE HOLDING WAR	1
2	MARKING TIME	20
3	DEFENCE OF LABABIA RIDGE	55
4	RENDEZVOUS AT NASSAU BAY	84
5	THE CAPTURE OF MUBO	107
6	THE STRUGGLE FOR THE RIDGES	137
7	THE FIGHT FOR KOMIATUM	179
8	THE PACIFIC FRONT	217
9	BENA BENA AND TSILI TSILI	233
10	BEFORE LAE	264
11	THE SALAMAUA MAGNET	285
12	ASSAULT ON LAE AND NADZAB	326
13	THE FALL OF LAE	347
14	PURSUIT	393
15	FROM THE MARKHAM TO THE RAMU	414
16	SCARLET BEACH TO THE BUMI	444
17	THE BATTLE FOR FINSCHHAFEN	480
18	EASY STREET AND THE SATTELBERG ROAD	501
19	THE JAPANESE COUNTER-ATTACK	527
20	IN THE RAMU VALLEY	561
21	ROUND SATTELBERG AND PABU	602
22	TORPY SITS ON SAT.	634
23	THE WAREO-GUSIKA ADVANCE	656
24	TOEHOLD ON SHAGGY RIDGE	680
25	ON TO SIO	714
26	KANKIRYO SADDLE	738

Chapter		Page
27	THE PURSUIT TO MADANG	763
28	TO MOROTAI AND THE PALAUS	790
	APPENDIX: Abbreviations	818
	INDEX	821

ILLUSTRATIONS

	Page
Salamaua isthmus and the coastline to Nassau Bay	12
General Sir Thomas Blamey and Lieut-General Sir Iven Mackay	13
Major-General F. H. Berryman with Brigadier M. J. Moten	13
A "biscuit bomber" dropping supplies at Goodview	44
Natives gathering supplies at Goodview dropping ground	44
Looking towards Salamaua along the Francisco River	45
Looking north along Komiatum Ridge to the Francisco	140
The Francisco River and Arnold's Crest	141
Native carriers crossing the kunda bridge near New Bobdubi	156
A native carrier line setting out from Mubo area	156
A 2/3rd Independent Company machine-gun pit on Ambush Knoll	156
Sergeant G. R. C. Ayre and Private W. O. W. Johnson	156
Private F. W. McVicar, 2/5th Battalion, at Mount Tambu	157
The 2/5th Battalion in the Mount Tambu area	157
A three-man weapon pit manned by the 2/5th Battalion in the Mount Tambu area	157
Brigadier H. H. Hammer with officers of the 15th Brigade	157
Men of the 2/3rd Independent Company preparing for the attack on Timbered Knoll	172
The attack on Timbered Knoll	172
The 2/3rd Independent Company on Timbered Knoll	173
Major G. R. Warfe and officers of the 2/3rd Independent Company	173
Lieutenant R. H. Dawson firing a captured mountain gun	204
Major-General S. G. Savige and Brigadier M. J. Moten at a 2/6th Battalion observation post	204
Salamaua isthmus after its capture by the 5th Division	205
Brigadier W. J. V. Windeyer and Major B. V. Wilson at the embarkation of the 20th Brigade at Cairns	348
General Blamey, with Major-General Vasey and Brigadier Eather, inspecting the 2/33rd Battalion	348
The scene after the crash of a Liberator bomber into the marshalling area at Jackson's airfield	348
Men of the 2/4th Field Regiment prepare for the parachute landing at Nadzab	348
Lieut-Colonel J. T. Lang's force from Tsili Tsili crossing the Markham River on the way to Nadzab	349
The landing of the 503rd American Parachute Regiment at Nadzab	349

	Page
Transport aircraft at Nadzab airfield on 21st September 1943	364
Crossing at the mouth of the Buso River on 5th September	365
Troops of the 7th Division entering Lae on 16th September 1943	365
Kaiapit village	428
Men of the 2/16th Battalion arrive by plane at Kaiapit	428
The Markham-Ramu divide	429
Brigadier I. N. Dougherty, commanding the 21st Brigade	460
Brigadier F. O. Chilton, commanding the 18th Brigade	460
Lieut-General Sir Edmund Herring, Lieut-General Sir Leslie Morshead, Major-General G. A. Vasey and Lieut-Colonel J. A. Bishop	460
Sappers of the 2/6th Field Company bridging the Gusap River	461
Troops of the 7th Division in the Ramu Valley	461
Chimbu and Bena Bena carriers	508
The 2/16th Battalion on Johns' Knoll, 17th October 1943	508
An L.S.T. landing troops of the 9th Division at Scarlet Beach	508
General Morshead with Major-General G. F. Wootten, Brigadier B. Evans and Colonel A. R. Garrett	508
A jeep negotiating mud and slush in the Finschhafen area	509
Men of the 2/24th Battalion and the Papuan Infantry in the Sattelberg area	509
The 2/48th Battalion moving forward to attack Coconut Ridge	509
The attack on Coconut Ridge, 17th November 1943	509
Horace the Horse	652
The Sattelberg Road, 27th November 1943	653
Shaggy Ridge	684
Troops of the 21st Brigade in the foothills of the Finisterres	685
Natives carrying food and ammunition through the Mosa Gorge	685
The 2/16th Battalion on the Pimple, Shaggy Ridge	700
A wounded man of the 2/16th Battalion	700
The 2/9th Battalion on Shaggy Ridge	700
Looking towards Madang from Shaggy Ridge, 22nd January 1944	700
American marines boarding L.S.T's, bound for Cape Gloucester	701
The landing of the 126th U.S. Regimental Combat Team at Saidor	701
Men of the 2/2nd Commando Squadron crossing the Ramu River after patrolling to Jappa	701
Australians climbing the muddy slopes of the Finisterres	701

	Page
Australian troops on the way to Japanese-held Bogadjim	748
A weary soldier rests on a track in the Finisterres	748
The road from Bogadjim to Yaula built by the Japanese	749
Lieut-General S. G. Savige, Major-General A. H. Ramsay and Brigadier C. E. Cameron at Alexishafen	780
Aerial view of Finschhafen Harbour	780
Hollandia airfield, April 1944	781
The Allied invasion convoy in Humboldt Bay, April 1944	781

MAPS

	Page
Bobdubi Ridge area	27
The Territories of Papua and New Guinea, and Bougainville in the northern Solomons	28
Australian and Japanese dispositions Wau-Salamaua-Lae area, 30th April 1943	32
The 17th Brigade's attack on Mubo, 7th-13th July	108
Operations of the 29th Brigade and 162nd U.S. Regiment, 26th August-10th September	293
The advance on Lae-Nadzab, 1st to 5th September	327
Huon Peninsula	396
Australian and enemy dispositions Finschhafen area, 16th-17th October	528
Australian and Japanese redispositions Finschhafen area, last light 18th October	545
The 4th Brigade's advance to Fortification Point, 5th-20th December	717
Capture of Kankiryo Saddle by the 18th Brigade, 19th January-1st February 1944	740
Across the Finisterres to Madang	773
The Allied offensive in the Pacific, April 1943 to September 1944	814

SKETCH MAPS AND DIAGRAMS

Extent of Japanese conquest to April 1943, and Allied Areas of Command	5
Australian dispositions and area of Militia Bill	15
Lababia Ridge-Pimple-Green Hill area	25
Encirclement of Tatterson's company, 2/7th Battalion, 9th-11th May	39
Hote-Cissembob area	48
2/6th Battalion patrols to Nassau Bay, 2nd-9th June	62
Lower Markham River Valley area	68
Hogan's patrol to Nadzab, 14th-18th June	69
Defence of Lababia Ridge, 20th-23rd June	76
Morobe to Duali	85
Nassau Bay landing, 29th-30th June	92
58th/59th Battalion attack, 30th June	109
Ambush Knoll, 6th-7th July	116
The 2/3rd Independent Company at Goodview Junction, 8th-10th July	131
Tambu Bay area	141
The 2/5th Battalion's toehold on Mount Tambu, 16th-19th July	146

	Page
Action at Buang River mouth, 21st July	156
Capture of Old Vickers by 58th/59th Battalion, 28th July	170
Defence of Old Vickers by 2/7th Battalion, 2nd-4th August	174
The capture of Roosevelt Ridge, 13th August	183
The 2/7th Battalion's attack on Coconuts, 14th August	190
Allied and enemy dispositions, Salamaua area, 15th August	194
The capture of Komiatum and Mount Tambu by 17th Brigade, 16th-19th August	196
The attacks by 2/7th Battalion and 2/3rd Independent Company on Bench Cut-Bobdubi track junctions, 17th-18th August	204
Japanese raids on Allied artillery positions, August 1943	212
Burma-China	218
The Solomons	224
The Central Highlands	235
Maululi-Wesa-Waimeriba area	248
Tsili Tsili-Nadzab area	252
24th Battalion patrol from Sunshine to Markham River, 7th-26th May	254
Area of Mosstroops' operations	258
Mosstroops' staging camps on the Sepik and Yellow Rivers	262
Some Allied landing craft	273
Australian and American dispositions, Salamaua area, 25th-26th August	290
Whitelaw's company of the 24th Battalion on the Hote-Malolo track	291
Operations of the 15th Brigade north of the Francisco River, 26th August-10th September	301
Arnold's Crest, 27th August	302
The fall of Salamaua, 11th-13th September	319
Landing diagram, Red Beach	331
Landing diagram, Yellow Beach	331
Initial objectives of the 9th Division, 4th September	333
The landing of the 503rd Parachute Regiment at Nadzab, 5th September	339
Battalion emplaning procedure diagram	340
The 24th Battalion at Markham Point, 4th September	342
The 2/23rd Battalion action in the Singaua Plantation area, 6th September	348
The 9th Division's advance to the Busu River, 8th September	350
Crossing of the Busu River by 2/28th Battalion, 9th September	352

	Page
Last opposition before Lae to the 9th Division, 14th September	369
The 7th Division's advance to Heath's, 13th September	375
Last opposition before Lae to the 7th Division, 15th September	383
The fall of Lae, 11.30 a.m., 16th September	388
Routes of withdrawal of the *51st Japanese Division* across the Huon Peninsula	394
The attack on Kaiapit by 2/6th Independent Company, 19th September	418
The capture and defence of Kaiapit, 20th September	420
Key points and route as set out in *Nakai Force* operation order	424
The upper Ramu and Markham River Valleys	427
The 2/14th Battalion action near Wampun, 4th October	441
The landing at Scarlet Beach, 22nd September	452
Scarlet Beach-Bumi River area	461
Hopoi to Scarlet Beach coastline	467
From the Bumi to Finschhafen	485
The 2/13th Battalion's attack on Kakakog to 3 p.m. 1st October	494
Approaches to Jivevaneng and Kumawa	501
Tami Islands	508
Japanese seaborne attack on Scarlet Beach, 17th October	531
Dumpu-Shaggy Ridge area	562
The holding of Guy's Post, 7th-8th October	568
The capture of Pallier's Hill by 2/14th Battalion, 11th October	577
Defence of Trevor's Ridge and Johns' Knoll by 2/27th Battalion, 12th October	581
Reproduction of sketch of Shaggy Ridge in war diary of 2/16th Battalion for October 1943	588
Dumpu-Bogadjim area	591
Clearing the track to Jivevaneng, 2nd November	606
26th Brigade offensive, 17th-21st November	617
The 2/32nd Battalion on Pabu, 20th November	631
The Japanese counter-attack on the 24th Brigade, 22nd-23rd November	635
The capture of Sattelberg, 16th-25th November	639
Sattelberg, 24th November	647
Capture of Wareo-Gusika position, 27th November-15th December	660
Western patrol area	684
Dispositions 2/6th Commando Squadron and "B" Company, Papuan Battalion, in the Kesawai area, 8th December	690

	Page
Attack on "A" Company, 2/25th Battalion, night 12th-13th December	699
The 2/16th Battalion assault on Shaggy Ridge, 27th-28th December	708
Shaggy Ridge area	710
The 20th Brigade pursuit to Sio, 21st December 1943 to 15th January 1944	726
The American landing at Saidor	731
Sio to Bogadjim	734
Capture of Spendlove Spur by 24th Battalion, 24th January	757
The 57th/60th Battalion in the Orgoruna-Kesa area, 30th January	759
The 8th Brigade's pursuit along the Rai Coast, 20th January-4th February	765
The 8th Brigade's advance to Saidor, 4th-10th February	768
The 57th/60th Battalion's attack on Bridge 6, 10th-11th April	783
American operations in the northern Solomons, New Britain and the Admiralty Islands, December 1943-March 1944	793
The attack on Los Negros, 29th February to 4th March	796
Operations along the north coast of New Guinea	799
Aitape-Babiang	807
Madang-Wewak	808
Area of Merauke Force operations	811

PREFACE

THIS volume chronicles the operations of the Australian Army in New Guinea from April 1943 until mid-1944. Mainly it is the story of four Australian divisions—two A.I.F. and two militia. It tells how the army, after emerging from the holding war towards the end of the Salamaua campaign, surged forward in a great offensive which cleared the *XVIII Japanese Army* from Lae, the Huon Peninsula, the Ramu Valley and in fact most of Australian New Guinea. The theme is thus one of triumph, though still against all sorts of odds. The British-Indian operations in Burma and the American operations in the Pacific are only briefly recorded, except where American units in New Guinea are serving under Australian command.

I have tried, as have writers of other volumes in this series, to tell the story of the front line—if operations along a gloomy jungle track, or on a rain-drenched razor-back, or in the stifling kunai can be so described. Inevitably it is a story of individuals and small sub-units on patrol, in ambush, in attack or defence; this was not a war of massed battalions but of the forward scout, the section, the platoon and the company. Thus the supporting arms—artillery, signals, engineers, supply and the like—probably receive less attention than is their due except when, as sometimes happened, they shared the fierce excitement of battle with their infantry comrades. Similarly the vital and increasingly powerful support by the Allied air and naval forces is mentioned only briefly as part of the background to the army's operations.

The detail in this volume has been drawn principally from the war diaries of units in action—thirty-six infantry battalions (including the Papuan Infantry Battalion), five Independent Companies, plus the supporting arms such as artillery regiments and engineer companies; together with war diaries and reports of eleven brigades, five divisions, two corps and other organisations such as Angau, New Guinea Force, Land Headquarters and General Headquarters. The scale of these basic sources varies from the one which describes a minor patrol action in several pages to that which dismisses a splendid attack or a resolute defence with "had a bit of a bash today". Whenever there has been controversy about what actually happened at a given place and time I have accepted the version of the man on the spot—often written by a private, N.C.O. or junior officer on a scrap of paper. I have benefited from interviews recorded by Mr Gavin Long in New Guinea and elsewhere in 1943-44, from my own interviews with commanders after the war, and from letters, diaries and other personal papers gladly lent by many. For the account of strategic planning I have had access to Australian War Cabinet papers, to Field Marshal Blamey's files, and to a wealth of reports and memoirs by American and British leaders. Several Allied histories (national and unit) have been studied. Unfortunately, memoirs by Australian leaders in this period are non-existent, and published Australian unit histories are disappointingly few.

Where a man is first mentioned in the text a footnote gives brief biographical details, but people who have appeared in earlier Pacific volumes of the series are not footnoted again in this one.

In whole or in part the draft of this book has been read by more than 200 participants. Generally, except where operations tailed off towards the end, I have aimed at giving the opportunity to comment to at least two key figures from virtually every front-line unit and to commanders and others who were with the higher formations. They have responded most generously. While these readers have seldom been able successfully to challenge the facts as set forth, the drafts have stimulated memories: old forgotten far-off things have come crowding back in the form of a name or two, a little added colour, an interpretation of a moment in time.

As a member of that green-clad fighting machine—the Australian Army of 1943-44—I tramped or flew over much of the country described; I fought over some of it as a platoon commander in the 2/2nd Independent Company on the Bena Plateau, in the Ramu Valley and in the aptly named Finisterre Mountains; and I was borne on a stretcher for several days over some of the worst of it by our devoted and compassionate New Guinea carriers.

Any soldier who fought the Japanese cannot but have respect for them as fighters, even though, with the tide turning against them, they did not fight it out to the last, as on the Papuan beaches. It has been difficult to present a satisfying picture of the enemy side because the *XVIII Army* later destroyed many records, but I have tried to piece the story together, mainly from the multitude of documents captured by the Australians. The individual Japanese soldier was an inveterate diarist, he carried his unit badge in the front line, and his commanders carried operation orders and future plans in the forward area. The story derived from these basic documents has been amplified with the help of post-war Japanese reports and interviews, and books written by Japanese war-time leaders.

The task of writing this book has been with me for more than a decade. I have written it, appropriately enough, in both Australia and Asia—in Canberra, in Colombo and on a tea estate in Ceylon's high country; the finishing touches were put to it in New Delhi and at a Himalayan hill station. At many midnights over the years I had perforce to leave Private Smith and his patrol in danger along the jungle track—and yet as often as not I went on with him through the night. To the men who fought, this book is dedicated.

Separated as I was so often from War History headquarters, I had to rely on several people to help me. I am grateful to Dr C. E. W. Bean who pioneered the master-diary method of arranging extracts from the sources. I would not have been able to write this volume without the wise guidance, serene encouragement and gentle nudging of Gavin Long who has been my *guru* over all these years, and who has thought nothing of helping me out by drafting occasional pieces himself. I have been most fortunate in having efficient and dedicated literary assistants—Jim Brill till the end of 1955 and Mary Gilchrist thereafter—who have cheerfully and without complaint borne many heavy burdens. I am indebted to Mr Hugh Groser's experience and skill in military map-making, to Miss Elaine Oates who helped him; and to my brother Barrie who read the final drafts.

D.D.

New Delhi,
2nd July 1959.

LIST OF EVENTS
FROM APRIL 1943 TO SEPTEMBER 1944
Events described in this volume are printed in italics

1943	23 Apr	*Kanga Force dissolved and Headquarters 3rd Division takes over direction of Salamaua campaign*
	11 May	American forces land on Attu in Aleutian Islands
	13 May	Campaign in Tunisia ends
	11 June	British forces capture Pantelleria
	30 June	Main American landings on New Georgia, in Central Solomons
		Nassau Bay landing
	10 July	Allies invade Sicily
	14-24 Aug	First Quebec Conference
	19 Aug	*Japanese abandon positions on Mount Tambu and Komiatum Ridge*
	26 Aug	*Headquarters 5th Division takes over direction of Salamaua campaign*
	3 Sept	Allies invade Italy
	4 Sept	*9th Division lands at Red Beach, east of Lae*
	5 Sept	*American parachutists land at Nadzab*
	11 Sept	*Salamaua falls*
	16 Sept	*7th and 9th Divisions enter Lae*
	19-20 Sept	*Independent Company troops capture Kaiapit*
	22 Sept	*Troops of the 9th Division land at Scarlet Beach*
	2 Oct	*Finschhafen village and harbour falls to 9th Division*
	4 Oct	*Elements of 7th Division capture Dumpu*
	27 Oct	New Zealand troops land on Stirling and Mono Islands in the Treasury Group
	1 Nov	Americans land on Bougainville in northern Solomons
	20 Nov	American forces invade Makin and Tarawa in Gilberts
	25 Nov	*Sattelberg falls to the 9th Division*
	28-30 Nov	Teheran Conference
	15 Dec	Americans land on New Britain
1944	2 Jan	American Sixth Army task force lands at Saidor
	9 Jan	Allied forces overrun Maungdaw on Arakan front in Burma
	23 Jan	*Troops of the 7th Division clear Shaggy Ridge*

1944	31 Jan	Americans invade Marshall Islands
	10 Feb	*Australian troops link with Americans at Saidor*
	15 Feb	3rd New Zealand Division invades Green Islands
	29 Feb	American forces land on Los Negros in Admiralty Islands
	8 Apr	Soviet forces open offensive in the Crimea
	13 Apr	*Australians enter Bogadjim*
	22 Apr	Americans land at Hollandia and Aitape
	24 Apr	*Australians enter Madang*
	26 Apr	*Australians occupy Alexishafen*
	27 May	Americans land on Biak Island
	4 June	Allies enter Rome
	6 June	Allies invade Normandy
	15 June	Americans invade Saipan in Marianas
	19-20 June	Naval battle of Philippine Sea
	2 July	Americans land on Noemfoor
	21 July	Americans invade Guam
	30 July	Japanese begin withdrawal from Myitkyina, Burma
	4 Aug	British Eighth Army reaches Florence, concluding campaign for central Italy.
	7 Aug	Russian summer offensive halts, having advanced over 400 miles from the Dneiper to the Vistula
	15 Aug	Allies invade southern France
	12-16 Sept	Second Quebec Conference
	15 Sept	Americans land in Palau Islands and on Morotai in Halmaheras

CHAPTER 1

THE HOLDING WAR

IN the south-western Pacific in April 1943 the tide was turning against the Japanese. Their thrust towards Wau in New Guinea had just been defeated, and in the Solomons in February they had abandoned Guadalcanal. They still held, however, a vast arc stretching from the Aleutians, through the western Pacific, New Guinea and the Indies to Burma, and had held it for about a year.

After many setbacks in the west the Allies were meeting with some success against the Germans and Italians. The British victory at El Alamein in November 1942 had been followed by Allied landings in North Africa. In April 1943 the British Eighth Army advancing west across North Africa linked with the British First Army, supplemented by an American corps. Tunis fell to the British and Bizerta to the Americans on 7th May. About 250,000 prisoners were taken and the German Army of Africa was destroyed. With the loss of North Africa the spirit and power of Italy were broken.

In November 1942 the Russians had startled the Germans by suddenly going over to the offensive. All along the line the Germans were pushed back. On 31st January 1943 the commander of their *Sixth Army* surrendered at Stalingrad; nearly 90,000 prisoners were taken. In the same month the Russians broke the investment of Leningrad. Like the British victory in Libya and the Allied victory in Tunisia, the Russian victories could not be measured wholly or even mainly in terms of ground gained. The British, American and Russian armies had won a moral ascendancy over the Germans and had inflicted vast human and material damage.

President Roosevelt, Mr Churchill and the Combined Chiefs of Staff[1] had met at Casablanca in January to decide Allied policy for 1943. The American Joint Chiefs of Staff, to whom direct control of the war against Japan had been entrusted, considered it opportune to prepare for a large-scale offensive in the Pacific. Before the Casablanca Conference there was no comprehensive plan for the defeat of Japan.[2] Faced by the Germans across the Channel, the British Chiefs of Staff still emphasised the importance of beating Germany first, and containing Japan in the Pacific until the defeat of Germany should make larger Allied forces available.

---

[1] The Combined Chiefs of Staff was the term given to the Chiefs of the American and British Services sitting in conference together. The American Chiefs alone were known as the Joint Chiefs of Staff. The Combined Chiefs who met at the Casablanca Conference comprised the Americans (General George C. Marshall of the Army, Admiral Ernest J. King of the Navy, General H. H. Arnold of the Army Air Force); and the British Chiefs of Staff (General Sir Alan Brooke, Chief of the Imperial General Staff; Admiral of the Fleet Sir Dudley Pound, First Sea Lord; Air Chief Marshal Sir Charles Portal, Chief of the Air Staff). Roosevelt's Chief of Staff, Admiral William D. Leahy, was unable to go to Casablanca because of illness. Mr Harry L. Hopkins accompanied the President. Field Marshal Sir John Dill, head of the British Staff Mission to Washington, and Vice-Admiral Lord Louis Mountbatten were also present.

[2] The Joint Chiefs' directive of 2nd July 1942 had given three localised tasks: 1. Occupation of Santa Cruz and Tulagi by South Pacific forces assisted by South-West Pacific Area forces. 2. Occupation of north-eastern New Guinea and the northern Solomons by SWPA forces. 3. Reconquest of New Britain by SWPA forces.

At the first meeting of the Combined Chiefs at Casablanca on 14th January, before the arrival of the two main figures next day, the American naval chief, Admiral King, criticised the small dimensions of the Allied effort against Japan. In December 1942 he had made an estimate of the percentage of the total war effort (men, ships, planes, munitions) of all the Allies, including China, then used in the Pacific. His conclusion was that only 15 per cent of the total Allied resources then engaged was being used there. The remaining 85 per cent was being used in Europe, Africa, the Battle of the Atlantic and in the build-up of forces in Britain.[3]

It is not easy to see how King arrived at these figures in view of the fact that, in December, the greater part of the United States Navy was in the Pacific; nine infantry divisions and two Marine divisions were also there, whereas there were only eight American infantry divisions in the United Kingdom and North Africa. There were, however, more American air groups in the western than the eastern theatre—34 against 25.[4] King's statistics were indicative not so much of the actual situation as of his determination to spare no efforts to have larger forces allotted to the Pacific.

At Casablanca not only Admiral King but General Marshall, although agreeing that Germany must be defeated first, urged that the hard-won initial successes in the Pacific must be followed up promptly and that Japan must not be allowed to build up her strength and launch fresh offensives.

Marshall informed the British Chiefs that the Americans wished to strike the Japanese defences in the rear and on the flanks (for example, in Burma). The American Chiefs thought that the Japanese were establishing a strong defensive line from the Solomons to Timor. King stated that the fighting in the Solomons and eastern New Guinea was designed to secure the approaches to Australia "and the key to the situation is Rabaul". After the capture of Rabaul, which, in the Casablanca planning, was almost taken for granted, King urged that the Philippines be attacked across the Central Pacific, using stepping stones in the Marshalls, Carolines and Marianas.

The British Chiefs were not keen yet to take any large-scale initiative against Japan. They were apprehensive lest a large effort even in Burma should reduce the strength of the main attack on Germany, although they agreed on the desirability of reopening the Burma Road. Nor were they enthusiastic about attacking Truk or the Philippines before the fall of Germany.

---

[3] The account of high-level planning in this chapter is largely based on the official histories of the United States Navy, Army and Air Force, and the memoirs or biographies of Churchill, Brooke, King, Leahy, Arnold and others.

[4] See M. Matloff and E. M. Snell, *Strategic Planning for Coalition Warfare 1941-1942* (1953), a volume in the official series *United States Army in World War II*.
The American Army divisions in the Pacific were:
Central Pacific: 24th, 27th, 40th.
South Pacific: Americal, 25th, 37th, 43rd.
South-West Pacific: 32nd, 41st.

There were 346,000 American troops overseas in Pacific commands, including Hawaii, and 347,000 in Great Britain and North Africa, or on the way thither.

President Roosevelt, however, regretted that so little attention appeared to have been paid by the Combined Chiefs to China. He said that "island hopping strategy" promised to be too lengthy and "that some other method of striking at Japan must be found". As American submarines were reputed to have sunk 1,000,000 tons of Japanese shipping (one-sixth of the Japanese merchant marine) in the first year of the war, Roosevelt suggested that submarine warfare be intensified and supplemented by air attacks on Japanese shipping from Chinese airfields. Mr Churchill made it evident that he was mainly interested in operations in the Mediterranean.

A lively discussion ensued between the Combined Chiefs on 17th and 18th January when the Americans reaffirmed their desire to keep the initiative in the Pacific, and Marshall stated emphatically that the American people would not tolerate "another Bataan". In a warning which must have shaken the British Chiefs of Staff, Marshall stressed that enough forces must be kept in the Pacific because "a situation might arise in the Pacific at any time that would necessitate the United States regretfully withdrawing from the commitments in the European Theatre".[5] King supported Marshall and informed the British that many of the demands in the Pacific came from Australia—a British country.[6]

By 18th January the Combined Chiefs had finished their recommendations for Pacific objectives in 1943. After the Americans had offered to provide some ships and landing craft for Burma, the Combined Chiefs agreed that the recapture of Burma should begin in 1943, but that they would discuss it again later in the year. The Americans considered that the Japanese forces must remain under continual, powerful and extensive pressure. Because the Japanese were operating on short interior lines, the Allies could keep the initiative along their 12,000-mile line and prevent the Japanese consolidating only by attacking areas important enough to draw "counter-action" which would be defeated and would result in whittling away the enemy's strength, particularly at sea and in the air. The Americans therefore considered that these operations were necessary:

1. Seizure of the Solomons, of eastern New Guinea as far as Lae and Salamaua, and of the New Britain-New Ireland area;
2. Seizure of Kiska and Attu in the Aleutians;
3. After Rabaul, seizure and occupation of the Gilberts, Marshalls, and Carolines through Truk and extension of the occupation of New Guinea to the Dutch border;
4. Operations in Burma designed to keep China in the war and increase the employment of China-based aircraft against shipping.

---

[5] Quoted in J. Miller, Jr, *Cartwheel: The Reduction of Rabaul* (1959), p. 7, a volume in the official series *United States Army in World War II*.
[6] In his diary of the Casablanca Conference, Brigadier Ian Jacob (Assistant Military Secretary to the United Kingdom War Cabinet) wrote on 13th January: "Apparently the operations in the Pacific are planned exclusively by the Navy Department, who in their turn leave the rest of the world to the War Department. There is little or no collusion, so that the allocation of resources as between the Pacific and the rest of the world is inevitably a hit and miss affair, or perhaps one could better describe it as a game of grab. The Navy have their ships and the Army have theirs. The Navy control the landing-craft, so that the Army finds it difficult to squeeze out what they want for their own projects. On the other hand, the Navy is apt to find itself in difficulty on the administrative or logistical side of their Pacific operations, as they often do not bring the Army into the picture early enough. This happened at Guadalcanal, where the U.S. Marines were thrown ashore and then it was found that there was no follow-up, no maintenance organisation, and no transport. The Army was then called in to help—very nearly too late." Quoted in A. Bryant, *The Turn of the Tide 1939-1943* (1957), p. 540.

The British Chiefs feared that the number of operations envisaged by the Americans in the Pacific might jeopardise success against Germany, and therefore suggested that the operations in the Pacific for 1943 should be limited to operations against Burma and Rabaul.

Finally the Combined Chiefs of Staff agreed that in the Pacific the Allies were to retain the initiative and prepare for a full-scale offensive when Germany had been defeated. At the outset the Allies would take Rabaul, make secure the Aleutians, and then advance from east to west across the Pacific through the Gilberts and Marshalls towards Truk and the Marianas.

With strategic plans for the war against Japan settled, the Americans now gave the British a statement of how they intended to carry them out. The Combined Chiefs noted a memorandum from General Marshall, Admiral King and General Arnold that the Allies in 1943 would "work towards positions from which land-based air can attack Japan". The Joint Chiefs' memorandum continued that "assault [by ground troops] on Japan is remote and may well not be found necessary".

For the final top-level meeting on 23rd January the Combined Chiefs produced an eleven-page paper covering their proposals for the conduct of the war in 1943.

> It is interesting to note that as a result of eleven days of deliberations they gave top priority to "security of sea communications". This meant that they considered the Atlantic Ocean the most important battlefield of the war and that the shortage of escort vessels was the first need to be met. Second on the priorities list—and closely involved with the first item—was "assistance to Russia in relation to other commitments". Third on the list was "Operations in the Mediterranean"—the plan for the capture of Sicily, giving as the target day "the favourable July moon". . . . Fourth on the list was "Operations in and from the United Kingdom"—provisions for the continued build-up of American forces. . . . Fifth on the list was "Pacific and Far East Theatre"—operations in the Aleutians, from Midway towards Truk and Guam, advances in the East Indies and the reconquest of Burma. The three final items on the list were provisions for a study of the Axis oil positions—for naval and air command in West Africa—and a provision that "all matters connected with Turkey should be handled by the British".[7]

Thus, in theory, the Pacific war theatre came only fifth on the list. To attain even this degree of priority the American Joint Chiefs had been forced to abandon their opposition to a Mediterranean offensive in 1943 and had accepted postponement of the invasion of France until 1944. When he saw the paper of the Combined Chiefs at the conference on 23rd January Harry L. Hopkins scribbled a pencilled note to Field Marshal Dill: "Jack, I think this is a *very* good paper and damn good plan."[8] The paper and plans certainly were good as far as the war against Germany was concerned; but about the Pacific war, particularly in the South and South-West Pacific Areas, the American Joint Chiefs of Staff and through them the Combined Chiefs were less realistic and less well informed. It was one thing to capture Sicily in July; another to capture Rabaul in May.

---

[7] R. E. Sherwood, *The White House Papers of Harry L. Hopkins*, Vol II (1949), p. 688.
[8] Sherwood, p. 688.

Prospects in Burma were even less promising. In the whole vast Burma-India-Ceylon theatre Field Marshal Wavell, at the beginning of 1943, commanded 14 divisions and 24 independent brigades, of which 5 divisions

Extent of Japanese conquest to April 1943, and Allied Areas of Command

were deployed in eastern India and Assam; but most of Wavell's formations were under-equipped and under-trained. The Japanese *Burma Area Army,* formed in March 1943, contained 4 well-trained divisions. Wavell had opened a limited offensive against Akyab in December 1942, but by March it was evident that it was doomed, and "by the start of the monsoon, our forces in Arakan were back approximately in the positions from which the advance had begun five months earlier".[9]

Wavell had originally planned to assist the reconquest of Burma by allowing Brigadier O. C. Wingate's specially trained jungle force, known as the "77th Indian Infantry Brigade", to penetrate into central Burma and thus assist the Allied campaigns in north and south Burma. Because

---
[9] A. P. Wavell, *Despatch on Operations in the India Command, from 1st January 1943 to 20th June 1943,* para. 14.

of restricted resources, however, he had then decided to help a possible advance from the north by Chinese forces commanded by the American, Lieut-General Joseph W. Stilwell, by sending Wingate into upper Burma to cut the enemy's line of communication to Myitkyina, Bhamo and Lashio. When Wavell heard from Stilwell that the Chinese had no intention of advancing, he decided to let Wingate's force go ahead for the sake of gaining experience.

On 7th February Wingate's men left Imphal in seven columns to cut the main north and south railway between Mandalay and Myitkyina, harass the enemy in the Shwebo area, cross the Irrawaddy, and cut the railway line between Maymyo and Lashio. By 18th February the main body had crossed the Chindwin although two columns were ambushed and dispersed. The railway line was successfully blown and Wingate then crossed the Irrawaddy in March, but, because of many difficulties—the climate, the health of the men and animals, the lack of water, and the danger of arranging dropping of supplies from the air when large numbers of Japanese were about—operations against the Mandalay-Lashio railway were abandoned, and Wingate retraced his steps. When the Japanese opposed a crossing of the Irrawaddy at Inywa, Wingate broke up his force into dispersal groups most of which returned to India by June.

Describing this operation Wavell wrote:

> The enterprise had no strategic value, and about one-third of the force which entered Burma was lost. But the experience gained of operations of this type, in supply dropping from the air, and in jungle warfare and Japanese methods, was invaluable. The enemy was obviously surprised and at a loss, and found no effective means to counter the harassment of our columns.[1]

The Japanese occupation of Burma during 1942 had isolated China except for a tenuous air supply route over 500 miles of the Himalayan "hump" between Assam and Yunnan. By early 1943 China's position was serious, with the 39 divisions of the Japanese *Kwantung* and *China Expeditionary Armies* controlling strategic areas. Theoretically China had about 300 divisions but most of these were well below brigade strength and of dubious quality.

It was not long before the salient but unpalatable fact that the war against Japan would take second place began to be placed before the Australians. Broadcasting on 18th April the Prime Minister, Mr Curtin, spoke of the Casablanca decisions and made Australia's position clear.

> To the people of Australia I say that the holding war imposed on Australia by the decisions of the Casablanca Conference . . . means that our resources will be used up in many cases, worn out in many instances, and strained to a serious extent in others. . . . To our Allies I say that the Australian Government accepts global strategy insofar as it conditions Australia's employment as an offensive base until Hitler is beaten, but it does not accept a flow of war material, notably aircraft, which does not measure up to the requirements of a holding war.

---

[1] Wavell, despatch, para. 28.

Five days before the beginning of the Casablanca Conference the American Joint Chiefs of Staff had requested General Douglas MacArthur, Commander-in-Chief of the South-West Pacific Area, to submit plans for the capture of Rabaul. MacArthur had replied that his forces would be unable to take part in any further operations without a long period of rest and preparation; the 7th Australian and 32nd American Divisions were being withdrawn for "reconstruction" after the Papuan campaigns, the 1st Marine Division was recuperating after Guadalcanal, and the 9th Australian Division was just returning from the Middle East.[2]

The "beat Hitler first" strategy was the cause of intense chagrin to MacArthur who did not accept it with the same resignation as Curtin and who repeatedly complained of the paucity of forces at his disposal. At Casablanca it was clear that General Marshall would not take undue risks in the Pacific, that General Arnold was convinced that daylight bombing of Europe was the quickest way to break down Axis resistance, but that Admiral King on the other hand was primarily interested in the Pacific war. King's support, naturally, meant support for the predominantly naval Central Pacific Command of Admiral Chester W. Nimitz, whose orders up to date had been to hold the island positions necessary to secure lines of communication between America and the South-West Pacific Area, prevent the Japanese from further expansion in the Central Pacific, defend North America, protect essential sea and air routes, and support MacArthur's forces.

On the day when the Casablanca Conference ended Admiral Nimitz met Admiral William F. Halsey, commander of the South Pacific Area, at Noumea, to discuss their next objective after Guadalcanal. The two admirals believed that they would receive no substantial naval reinforcements during the period of the fight for Tunis and the projected invasion of Sicily, or while submarines remained a grave threat in the Atlantic. They had already rejected any plan to assault Rabaul as being too costly. It was indeed strange that the Combined Chiefs at Casablanca should have based most of their Pacific plans on the early capture of Rabaul, at a time when the three Pacific commanders (MacArthur, Nimitz and Halsey) realised and stated the impracticability of capturing this great Japanese base with their existing forces. Nimitz and Halsey considered that their next move should be a northward advance in the Solomons to Munda on New Georgia where the Japanese had built a good airfield; and Nimitz insisted that this central Solomons operation should be conducted by the navy. Here he collided with MacArthur who was equally firm that Halsey's command should be under his wing. MacArthur's stand was backed by the Joint Chiefs' directive of July 1942, under which the three tasks were primarily the responsibility of the South-West Pacific Area, but the admirals felt that, as MacArthur had his hands full in New Guinea, the navy should run the central Solomons operations.

---

[2] The components of the third veteran Australian division—the 6th—were at this time scattered in New Guinea, eastern Australia, and the Northern Territory.

The growing concept that the main advance against Japan should be made across the vast reaches of the Central Pacific was strongly resisted by MacArthur, who considered that the quickest way to Japan was by a series of hops along the coast of New Guinea and on to the Philippines.

It was too early for such thoughts as what follows shows. On 28th February MacArthur and his staff completed an outline plan for the achievement of the second and third tasks set in the Joint Chiefs' directive of July 1942. It was very tentative and no fixed dates were set for the five operations which it outlined. The first of these would be the capture of Lae by an airborne force landing in the Markham Valley cooperating with an amphibious force moving along the coast in small craft; Salamaua would be bypassed but important bases in the Huon Peninsula-Vitiaz Strait area such as Finschhafen would be captured, and a combined airborne and amphibious attack would finally be launched against Madang. The second operation, after the capture of the Huon Peninsula-Vitiaz Strait area, would be the capture of New Georgia in the Solomons by the South Pacific Command. The South-West Pacific and South Pacific Commands would then launch amphibious assaults on New Britain and Bougainville. The fourth and fifth operations would be the capture of Kavieng and Rabaul respectively.

MacArthur believed that in order to carry out his part of this ambitious plan he would need to be reinforced by five infantry divisions, and about 3,200 combat and transport aircraft. He considered that, with this extra strength, his command and the South Pacific Command, which, he suggested, needed no reinforcement, would be able to drive the Japanese back to Truk and Wewak during 1943. Even Rabaul might be captured.

After MacArthur had asked permission to send staff officers to Washington to explain his plans, the Joint Chiefs called a conference of representatives of the three Pacific commanders beginning in Washington on 12th March. MacArthur sent Lieut-General George C. Kenney, the commander of the Fifth Air Force; Major-General Richard K. Sutherland, his Chief of Staff; and Brigadier-General Stephen J. Chamberlin, his senior Operations Officer. Halsey was represented by Captain Miles R. Browning, his Chief of Staff, and others; and Nimitz by his deputy, Rear-Admiral Raymond A. Spruance and others. After much discussion, during which the navy insisted that the Pacific was and would continue to be "a naval problem as a whole" and should be unified under a naval command, Marshall suggested a solution which he admitted "skirted" the question of combining the commands. Under this proposal Halsey would retain control of operations in the Solomons but would be subject to general directives from MacArthur, while naval units attached as task forces would remain under Nimitz's control. King said that as the Joint Chiefs had undertaken to prevent difficult situations developing between MacArthur and Nimitz, he would agree with Marshall, provided that control of the fleet remained "in a fluid state".

When the Joint Chiefs announced the maximum reinforcements for the Pacific in 1943 it was obvious that the plan would have to be considerably modified. Two infantry divisions would be sent to MacArthur in the second and third quarters of the year; by December the aggregate number of American-manned aircraft in the South and South-West Pacific Areas would have been increased from 1,476 to 2,663. Additional naval units requested would be supplied, if available, by the Pacific Fleet.

On MacArthur's behalf Sutherland suggested, therefore, that the scope of the plan be much reduced and that the tasks for 1943 be limited to the capture of the Solomons, the north-east coast of New Guinea as far as Madang, and western New Britain. He also suggested that airfields should be constructed on Kiriwina and Woodlark Islands, 115 and 165 miles respectively north and north-east of Milne Bay, to provide bases for medium bombers and fighters to attack New Britain and support Halsey's operations in the Solomons. These practical recommendations were approved by the Joint Chiefs of Staff, and the plan with which the destinies of the Australian forces were to be so intimately linked was set out in a cabled directive from Marshall dated 28th March.

Under the heading "Command" the directive stated:

(a) The operations outlined in this Directive will be conducted under the direction of the Supreme Commander, South-West Pacific Area.
(b) Operations in the Solomon Islands will be under the direct command of the Commander, South Pacific Area, operating under general directives of the Supreme Commander, South-West Pacific Area.
(c) Units of the Pacific Ocean Area, other than those assigned by the Joint Chiefs of Staff to task forces engaged in these operations, will remain under the control of the Commander-in-Chief, Pacific Ocean Area.

The tasks were then outlined:

(a) Establish airfields on Kiriwina and Woodlark Islands.
(b) Seize Lae-Salamaua-Finschhafen-Madang area and occupy western New Britain.
(c) Seize and occupy the Solomon Islands to include the southern portion of Bougainville.

The intentions were, in the words of the directive, "to inflict losses on Japanese forces, to deny these areas to Japan, to contain Japanese forces in the Pacific theatre by maintaining the initiative, and to prepare for the ultimate seizure of the Bismarck Archipelago". MacArthur was finally instructed to submit to the Joint Chiefs of Staff his plan, including the composition of the forces to be used and the sequence and timing of the operations.

Thus, MacArthur was in strategic command of the South-West and South Pacific Areas, but Halsey retained tactical control in his area. Subject only to directives from the Joint Chiefs, Nimitz allocated ships and aircraft from his fleet as he saw fit. Early in April Halsey flew from his headquarters in Noumea to Brisbane to see MacArthur. Later, he described the meeting thus:

I had never met the General. . . . Five minutes after I reported, I felt as if we were lifelong friends. I have seldom seen a man who makes a quicker, stronger, more favorable impression. He was then sixty-three years old, but he could have passed as fifty. His hair was jet black; his eyes were clear; his carriage was erect. If he had been wearing civilian clothes, I still would have known at once that he was a soldier. The respect that I conceived for him that afternoon grew steadily during the war. . . . I can recall no flaw in our relationship. We had arguments, but they always ended pleasantly. Not once did he, my superior officer, ever force his decisions upon me. On the few occasions when I disagreed with him, I told him so, and we discussed the issue until one of us changed his mind.[3]

These then were the general Allied plans in April 1943 when both sides paused for a breathing space after the bloody battles for Papua and Guadalcanal. Until March 1942 the information available to the Allies about the Japanese Army had been disturbingly scanty. It was supplemented considerably as a result of the capture of documents and prisoners in the Papuan campaign, and the Australian Intelligence staff became a main source of new information about the opposing army, but still far too little was known.[4]

A fortunate incident early in March 1943, however, transformed the situation. At that time the 47th Australian Battalion was garrisoning Goodenough Island. On 7th March and for the next few days groups of Japanese—survivors of the convoy dispersed or sunk in the Bismarck Sea battle of 2nd to 5th March—landed on the island. Between the 8th and the 14th Australian patrols killed 72 Japanese, captured 42 and found 9 dead on a raft. One patrol, under Captain Pascoe,[5] stalked a group of eight Japanese, who had landed in two flat-bottomed boats, killed them all, and found that the boats contained large quantities of documents in sealed tins.

This important-looking discovery was hurried back to the headquarters in Brisbane where the documents were found to include a complete Army List showing the names of all Japanese officers and their units. Examination and collation provided a complete and detailed picture of the Japanese Army and revealed the existence of many units hitherto unknown.[6] Soon afterwards Intelligence officers from all Allied headquarters attended a conference at Washington at which the new information was re-examined and a system of interchange arranged which resulted

---

[3] W. F. Halsey and J. Bryan, *Admiral Halsey's Story* (1947), pp. 154-5.

[4] The extent to which the Australian Intelligence staff at this stage was influencing Intelligence staffs farther afield is perhaps illustrated by the following occurrence. On 23rd September 1942 the staff at Allied Land Headquarters (L.H.Q.) had prepared a paper on Japan's war policy. It reached the conclusions that Japan's air strength would not permit her to undertake the offensive against Russia, India or the SWPA simultaneously, or even against two of these. Her immediate aim would be to secure the East Asia sphere. This would involve creating a strategic barrier north of Australia, completing the occupation of New Guinea and "thereafter possibly Darwin and the north-east coast of Australia". Generally she would build up her strength so that, should Germany be defeated, she could defend her sphere against the Allies and rely on their exhaustion and war weariness to secure a negotiated peace. On 8th November the Combined Intelligence Committee at Washington prepared a paper for the Combined Chiefs of Staff which reached General Blamey's headquarters a few days later. It reproduced the Australian paper almost word for word (without acknowledgment), one difference being that the Washington paper said (in the telegraphic version which reached Australia), "in particular unlikely at present attempt occupy Australia, British Joint Intelligence Committee consider occupation Darwin is possibility".

[5] Capt J. C. Pascoe, VX112201; 47 Bn. Grocer; of Wonthaggi, Vic; b. Violet Town, Vic, 27 Jan 1909.

[6] Captain A. W. McWatters who was in charge of mopping-up along the coast later described the result of Pascoe's action thus: "When it was over the badges showed some of the Japanese dead were in the brass-hat class and had some official looking boxes. . . . They were immediately shoved back to battalion and quickly sent away. . . . We gradually learned the show had picked up the stud book and all the box and dice, etc."

in all partners thenceforward having an extensive and accurate knowledge of the Japanese Army's composition and deployment.[7]

The time had gone when the Japanese had hoped to cut the American supply route to Australia by capturing New Caledonia, Fiji and Samoa. When the Japanese realised that this was beyond them, they had concentrated on preparations to hold a line running from Timor across the Arafura Sea to Wewak, Lae and Salamaua, thence along the south coast of New Britain to Rabaul and south to New Georgia in the Solomons.

Since the early days of the war Field Marshal Count Terauchi's *Southern Army Headquarters* at Saigon had controlled the *XIV Army* in the Philippines, the *XVI Army* in the Netherlands East Indies and the Japanese forces in Burma and Malaya.[8] A new army—the *XIX*—was established in January 1943, under the *Southern Army,* to take over from the *XVI* in Timor, the Arafura Sea, Dutch New Guinea, Ceram, Ambon, Halmahera and Morotai. The troops in New Guinea and the Solomons comprised the *Eighth Area Army,* commanded by Lieut-General Hitoshi Imamura, who was under the direct control of *Imperial General Headquarters.* Under Imamura were Lieut-General Haruyoshi Hyakutake's *XVII Army* in the Solomons and Lieut-General Hatazo Adachi's *XVIII Army* (*20th, 41st* and *51st Divisions*) in New Guinea. In the area about 400 combat aircraft were available. Japanese naval forces based on Truk were estimated to consist of 6 battleships, 2 aircraft carriers, 15 cruisers, approximately 40 destroyers and 27 submarines.

Arrayed against Imamura's *Eighth Area Army* in April 1943 were the forces of the South and South-West Pacific Areas. Under his command Halsey had the 2nd Marine Division and two American infantry divisions (25th and Americal) which had taken part in later fighting on Guadalcanal, three fresh American divisions (the 3rd Marine, the 37th from Fiji and the 43rd from New Zealand and New Caledonia), and the 3rd New Zealand Division. He also had a powerful fleet, consisting of 6 battleships, 2 aircraft carriers, 3 escort carriers, 13 cruisers, approximately 50 destroyers, and numerous smaller ships and submarines; 350 carrier-based aircraft and 500 land-based aircraft of the Thirteenth American Air Force and the Royal New Zealand Air Force completed Halsey's force, described by the American naval historian as "a well-oiled fighting machine, strong in all three elements".[9]

---

[7] The Australian representative was Lieut-Colonel R. R. Lewis who had specialised in this field with great success.

In May 1943 LHQ Intelligence estimated that there were 347,000 troops in Japan; 1,161,000 in China, Manchukuo and neighbouring areas; 82,000 in Burma; 117,000-119,000 in the Indies; 100,000-106,000 in New Guinea and the Solomons. When other garrison forces were added the total strength of the Japanese Army was estimated at 2,169,000-2,176,000.

[8] The Japanese Army in the field was organised into army groups, area armies, and armies. There were four groups of armies (*Japan Defence, Kwantung, China Expeditionary* and *Southern*) which were each the equivalent of an Allied command of a theatre of operations. An area army (e.g. *Eighth Area Army,* Rabaul) was the equivalent of a British or American army, while a Japanese army was the equivalent of a British or American corps. A Japanese division, containing three regiments, each of three battalions, was approximately equal in numbers to an Australian division.

[9] S. E. Morison, *Breaking the Bismarcks Barrier 22 July 1942-1 May 1944* (English edition 1950), p. 95, a volume in the series *History of United States Naval Operations in World War II.*

In the S.W.P.A., MacArthur had two American infantry divisions (32nd and 41st), but the 32nd and one regiment of the 41st were tired and depleted as a result of the Buna campaign. The 1st Marine Division was recuperating in Australia. His main infantry force comprised the Australian Army of twelve divisions (ten infantry and two armoured). About half of the 1,400 aircraft of the Fifth Air Force under the command of General Kenney were R.A.A.F. planes of a variety of British, American and Australian types. It was in his naval forces that MacArthur suffered most by comparison with Nimitz and Halsey. In March MacArthur's naval force had been renamed the Seventh Fleet.[1] Thus

by a stroke of Admiral King's pen (wrote the American naval historian) the impoverished Southwest Pacific Force achieved fleet status. On its birthday, however, the new Seventh Fleet was still measured in tens rather than thousands. On paper it made a brave showing with seven task forces composed of strangely assorted surface, air and underwater craft scattered between northern Papua and south-western Australia, under three different flags (Australian, American and Netherlands), but most of its strength was still listed as "upon reporting", which meant assigned ships en route or still in American waters. Planes, corvettes, minelayers and destroyers . . . were busy searching for Japanese submarines in Australian waters. Vice-Admiral Crutchley's cruisers (H.M.A.S. *Australia* and *Hobart*, U.S.S. *Phoenix*) waited for their services to be required. There were a few tenders, only two tankers and but one transport; freight to New Guinea was hauled by the "Army's Navy" of small chartered Australian vessels, or the Dutch ships that had survived the Buna campaign. Most skeletal of all was the Amphibious Force, commanded by Rear-Admiral Barbey.[2]

The paucity of the naval forces of the South-West Pacific was due not only to lack of ships and beaching craft, but to the rivalries between the American Services. Believing that the Pacific war was primarily a naval problem, the American Navy was reluctant to place substantial numbers of naval ships at the disposal of an American military commander; a fact which not only complicated MacArthur's planning but caused him to look around for an alternative naval force.

As the decisions of the Casablanca Conference descended from the high places in Washington to the Allied commanders in the Pacific, it became obvious that any military offensive in the South-West Pacific in 1943 would have to be carried out mainly by the Australian Army, just as during the bitter campaigns of 1942.

As Commander-in-Chief of the Australian Army and Commander of the Allied Land Forces in the South-West Pacific, General Sir Thomas Blamey had the dual task of controlling operations and administration. His main administrative problem early in 1943 was how to obtain enough men to sustain the Australian part of his army.

As a result of the expansion of the army in the critical months of 1942 and the subsequent heavy losses, chiefly because of tropical diseases, a struggle for manpower had begun between each of the three Services, and

---

[1] Each American fleet could be further subdivided into task forces which could be shuffled for each different operation. In these task forces the first digit was the number of the fleet. Task forces were divided into task groups with numbers following a decimal point, and the groups into task units, with numbers following a second decimal point.

[2] Morison, p. 130.

Salamaua isthmus and the coastline looking south to Nassau Bay.

General Sir Thomas Blamey and Lieut-General Sir Iven Mackay at New Guinea Force headquarters.

(Australian War Memorial)

(Australian War Memorial)

Major-General F. H. Berryman, Deputy Chief of the General Staff (left), with Brigadier M. J. Moten, commander of the 17th Brigade.

the munitions and aircraft factories. In March 1943 the War Cabinet noted that the army's actual strength was 79,000 below the establishment and that it required a monthly intake of 12,500 men. "If this manpower is not forthcoming," said a War Cabinet Minute, "it will be necessary either to reduce the striking force or to reduce the number of other formations to maintain it. This is a critical question of supreme importance." On 30th January the War Cabinet had ordered a review of war production programs and of plans for the expansion of the Services. Now, in March, it directed that such a review be expedited, and "that the personal attention of the Commander-in-Chief, A.M.F., be again drawn to this matter in regard to the delay that has arisen".

Already, after the Papuan operations, Blamey had carried out a fairly far-reaching reorganisation of the army "partly", as he wrote afterwards, "as a result of experiences in New Guinea and the general need for saving manpower and partly as a result of my desire to simplify the administration of the Army". It provided that the First and Second Armies should take over certain responsibility from the three eastern lines of communication areas with consequent saving of manpower; the coast-defence units were reduced by 3,630, and further reduction was planned. Five infantry divisions—5th, 6th, 7th, 9th and 11th—were being organised as "jungle divisions" with reduced transport, artillery, etc. The 2nd Motor Division was being disbanded and the men thus released were to be used to bring to full strength an armoured force to consist of the 1st and 3rd Armoured Divisions, 4th Armoured Brigade, and 3rd Army Tank Brigade.

On 30th April the War Cabinet had before it Blamey's views on the problems. It had to bear in mind the advice of the War Commitments Committee that 10,000 persons a month were the maximum available for the three Services, and for munitions and aircraft production. Blamey said that any reorganisation was limited by the need (*a*) to prepare a force of three infantry divisions for offensive operations in accordance with General MacArthur's plans, and (*b*) to maintain adequate forces to defend the mainland of Australia and Australian territory in New Guinea, and to provide a reserve for relieving units in New Guinea. He assessed the total at nine infantry divisions, two armoured divisions, one armoured brigade, one army tank brigade with proportionate non-divisional and base units. Three infantry divisions (apart from those required for offensive operations) would be required for New Guinea.

Blamey added:

This requirement insofar as the defence of Australia is concerned is based on the altered strategic situations since the submission of the C-in-C's last appreciation in Sep 42, when Japanese Naval and Army units were concentrated in great strength in the South-West Pacific, and the position was one of extreme gravity. Since then, however, the recent successful campaigns in the Solomons and New Guinea areas, and the effectiveness of air attack on Japanese invasion convoys have improved our position considerably by forcing the enemy front farther to the north and seizing the initiative. This has not removed the danger of invasion since the enemy's reaction has been to increase his land and air forces to a very great degree. It is obvious that he does not intend to accept his defeats without a great effort to wrest the initiative from us.

In these circumstances it is a justifiable and indeed an unavoidable risk to weaken our defensive forces in areas most remote from the enemy in favour of concentrating such forces in areas in which they are most likely to be required. With this in view the forces in Australia are now in course of being disposed as follows:

> *Queensland*—Torres Strait Force (approximately one battalion group), one armoured division, and brigades in movements to and from New Guinea (in addition the offensive force of three divisions and ancillary units is en route to or in training in the Atherton area).
>
> *Darwin*—One infantry division and ancillary units.
>
> *Western Australia*—One infantry division, one armoured division and ancillary units.
>
> *New South Wales*—One infantry division (mainly under-age personnel) and ancillary units, one armoured brigade and one army tank brigade.
>
> *Other States*—Miscellaneous units but no field formations.

The allocation of three infantry divisions for the defence of New Guinea is based on the need for holding areas of strategic importance, and the provision of a small force for reinforcing such areas or other points that may be threatened. The areas in question are Milne Bay-Goodenough Island, which requires a minimum of one division, Buna which requires another division, Wau which requires at a minimum two brigades, and Moresby for which there remains one brigade as a general reserve and for Moresby's defence. . . . In addition to the A.M.F. formations, arrangements have been made to retain 158 U.S. Regiment for garrison duties in New Guinea, whilst the remainder of the U.S. forces in Australia are being trained as a Task Force for special operations.

In view of increased Japanese interest in the Arafura Sea area, the garrison at Merauke is being increased from one battalion group to a brigade group less a battalion. Any serious Japanese threat in the direction of Merauke would have to be met from the force being prepared in Australia for future offensive operations.

Blamey stated that he was disbanding some ancillary units, reducing base units and replacing army men by men of the Volunteer Defence Corps in the coast defences. The reduction so achieved would not exceed 20,000, and further field formations would have to be disbanded if the intake into the army—now 4,000 a month, and gradually decreasing—was not increased. The monthly wastage rate as soon as major operations began again was estimated at 11,800, leaving a deficiency of 7,800 a month.

If further releases from industry could not be made, Blamey advised that "the force being prepared for offensive operations should be reduced by one infantry division (with ancillary units) for the reason that the Australian New Guinea and mainland defensive component has been reduced to the barest minimum". The War Cabinet decided that the Minister for Defence should discuss the matter with MacArthur; and that a force of three divisions must be maintained for major offensives.

In this appreciation the size of the forces required for purely defensive roles in Australia and New Guinea seems, in retrospect, to have been estimated on a lavish scale, particularly in view of the naval and air losses Japan had suffered: there were to be three divisions in New Guinea, three (one armoured) in northern and western Australia, and three (including one armoured) in eastern Australia, in addition to the three A.I.F. divisions retraining in north Queensland.

Thus Australia, with a population of 7,000,000, was maintaining twelve divisions and now had in the army nearly 500,000 men, about 7 per cent of the population. The number of divisions was greater in proportion to population than was being maintained, for example, by Britain or the United States. At the same time Australia was engaged on a relatively big munitions program. Some reduction of the army was inevitable.

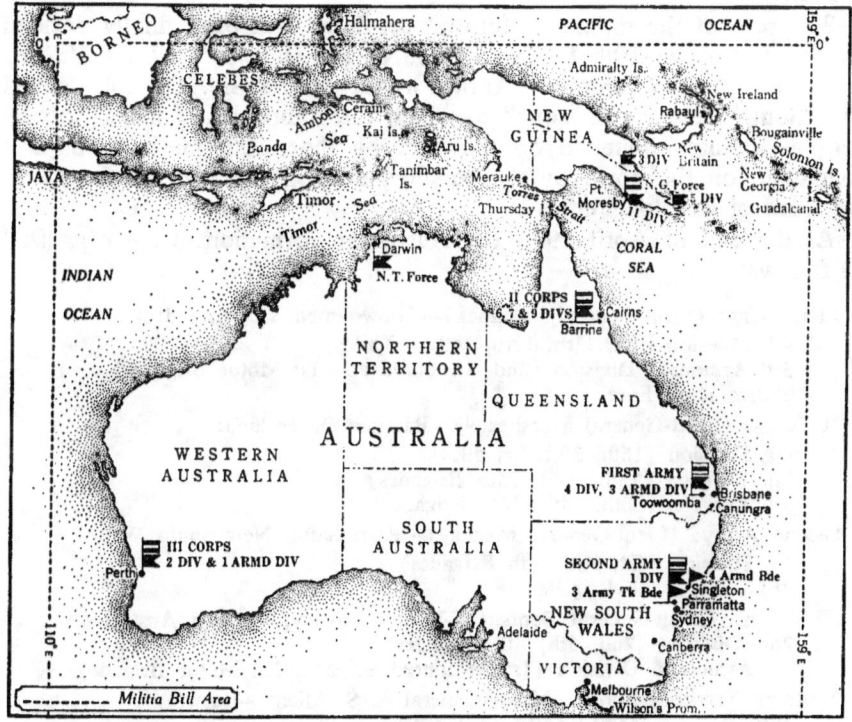

Australian dispositions and area of Militia Bill

On 24th April the A.M.F. actually numbered 466,901 (not including 22,823 women[3]) of whom 285,931 were in the A.I.F., including 125,912 who had enlisted in that force from the militia. On the same date there were 128,197 members of the R.A.A.F., including 16,746 serving overseas; and 30,658 members of the R.A.N. including 17,199 afloat.[4]

In New Guinea there were 54,809 Australian troops of whom 40,534 were in operational units. The largest part of the Australian Army (141,650) was in Queensland; 35,033 troops were stationed in the North-

---
[3] These were 2,997 AANS, 15,678 AWAS and 4,148 AAMWS.
[4] Mr Curtin on 22nd June 1943 announced that at the end of March 1943 the gross enlistment figures were 820,500, and of these 530,000 had volunteered.

ern Territory; and 60,970 in Western Australia. The American Army in the Australian area numbered 111,494 including 40,023 round Brisbane and 30,058 in New Guinea; but only 18,124 of the American troops in New Guinea were in operational units. MacArthur also had 48,961 members of the American Army Air Force, making a grand total of 160,455 American troops.

Militia units as a whole could now become part of the A.I.F. if 75 per cent of the unit's actual strength or 65 per cent of the authorised "war establishment", whichever was the greater, had volunteered to join the A.I.F.

The role of the militia in future operations had been finally decided by the passing on 19th February 1943 of the *Defence (Citizen Military Forces) Act 1943* commonly known as the Militia Bill. The bill defined the "South-West Pacific zone" to which the militia could henceforth be sent as an area bounded on the west by the 110th meridian of east longitude, on the north by the equator, and on the east by the 159th meridian of east longitude.[5]

At the end of April 1943 the Australian formations were organised as follows:

First Army: (Lieut-General Lavarack)—Toowoomba, Queensland:
    4th Division (6th, 11th, 12th, 14th Brigades)
    3rd Armoured Division (2nd Armoured and 1st Motor Brigades)
    Torres Strait Force

II Corps: (Lieut-General Morshead[6])—Barrine, Queensland:
    6th Division (16th, 30th Brigades)
    7th Division (18th, 21st, 25th Brigades)
    9th Division (20th, 24th, 26th Brigades)

Second Army: (Lieut-General Mackay)—Parramatta, New South Wales:
    1st Division (1st, 9th, 28th Brigades)
    3rd Army Tank Brigade

III Corps: (Lieut-General Bennett)—Mount Lawley, Western Australia:
    2nd Division (2nd, 5th, 8th Brigades)
    1st Armoured Division (1st Armoured Brigade, 3rd Motor Brigade)

Northern Territory Force: (Major-General A. S. Allen)—Darwin:
    12th Division (13th, 19th, 23rd Brigades)

New Guinea Force: (Lieut-General Mackay, acting[7])—Port Moresby:
    3rd Division (17th Brigade)
    5th Division (4th, 29th Brigades)
    11th Division (7th, 15th Brigades)

L.H.Q. Reserve:
    3rd Brigade—Adelaide
    4th Armoured Brigade—Singleton, New South Wales

---

[5] One Australian territory—Norfolk Island—lay in the South Pacific Area, and, appropriately, was garrisoned by New Zealand troops from October 1942 until February 1944. See O. A. Gillespie, *The Pacific* (1952), a volume in the series *Official History of New Zealand in the Second World War 1939-45*.

[6] Lt-Gen Sir Leslie Morshead, KCB, KBE, CMG, DSO, ED, NX8. (1st AIF: 2 Bn and CO 33 Bn 1916-19.) Comd 18 Bde 1939-41; GOC 9 Div 1941-43, II Corps and NGF during 1943-44, I Corps 1944-45. Branch manager, shipping line; of Sydney; b. Ballarat, Vic, 18 Sep 1889. Died 26 Sep 1959.

[7] Lieut-General E. F. Herring, commander of NGF, was on leave.

Major-General S. G. Savige's 3rd Division headquarters was, in April, establishing itself at Bulolo, Major-General E. J. Milford's 5th was at Milne Bay, and Major-General C. A. Clowes' 11th at Port Moresby.

Just across the Dutch border on the southern coast of New Guinea the 62nd Battalion (Lieut-Colonel Haupt[8]), assisted by a Netherlands East Indies company, was garrisoning Merauke. The battalion had arrived between December 1942 and February 1943 and was given the task of defending the airfield and docks area. Between New Guinea and Australia was Torres Strait Force (Colonel Langford[9]) responsible for the defence of the islands in the strait.

American forces under the control of New Guinea Force at this time included the 158th Regiment attached to the 11th Division in Port Moresby and the 41st Division (162nd, 163rd and 186th Regiments) in the Oro Bay area. Back in Rockhampton Lieut-General Robert L. Eichelberger's I American Corps controlled only one division—the 32nd (126th, 127th, 128th Regiments) at Brisbane.

Of the nine A.I.F. and eighteen militia infantry brigades comprising the army in April, only one A.I.F. brigade (the 17th) and four militia brigades (4th, 29th, 7th, 15th) were in New Guinea. With such a large and vulnerable coastline and with such a comparatively small force in New Guinea, the army was finding increasing use for the Independent Companies,[1] the first seven of which had carried out infantry tasks along Australia's vast defence arc from Timor to New Caledonia.

By April 1943 15 A.I.F. and 8 militia battalions had gained battle experience in New Guinea. The militia battalions belonged to the 7th Brigade (9th, 25th, 61st Battalions) which had taken part in the successful defence of Milne Bay; the 30th Brigade (3rd, 39th and 55th/53rd Battalions) which had fought over the Kokoda Trail, and, in company with the 14th Brigade (now 36th and 49th Battalions) had joined the 4 A.I.F. brigades attacking Gona and Sanananda. In July 3 of these 8 battalions—the 3rd, 39th and 49th—would be disbanded and their officers and men distributed among the units of the 6th Division as reinforcements, leaving only 5 battle-tried militia infantry battalions.

As mentioned, two armoured divisions (Major-General H. C. H. Robertson's 1st and Major-General W. Bridgeford's 3rd), the 4th Armoured Brigade and the 3rd Army Tank Brigade were being maintained in Australia. There had been 185 tanks in Australia in April 1942; there were now, in April 1943, 1,672, and 775 more had been ordered in Australia.[2]

---

[8] Lt-Col A. G. K. Haupt, ED, SX1475. 2/1 MG Bn 1940-42; CO 62 Bn 1943-44, 2/1 MG Bn 1944-45. Industrial chemist; of Renown Park, SA; b. Adelaide, 31 Jan 1910.

[9] Col H. R. Langford, OBE, MC, QX53209. (1914-18: 1 LH Regt and Lt RFA.) Comd Tps Thursday I 1942, Torres Strait Force 1942-43, 1 Beach Gp 1943-44. Grazier; of Brisbane; b. Waverley, NSW, 18 May 1895.

[1] An Independent Company in 1943 included 18 officers and 277 other ranks, organised into three platoons each of three sections, and with a headquarters including signallers and engineers.

[2] In July 1943, however, the War Cabinet decided that manufacture of tanks in Australia would cease.

For most of the volunteers who had enlisted in the 1st Armoured Division in 1941 believing that they would be serving in the Middle East early in 1942 the past year had been one of frustration. By the spring of 1942 Robertson had trained the division to as near perfection as a formation is likely to achieve without being in action; and sprinkled through it were a considerable number of officers who had served in North Africa and Syria, chiefly in the mechanised cavalry. In retrospect it seems unfortunate, for a variety of reasons, that a more sanguine view of the possibility of invasion of Australia was not taken in the summer of 1942-43 and that this fine division was not transferred to Africa, perhaps in the transports which brought the 9th Division home, to play a part in the coming campaigns there and in Europe.

Around the arc embracing the Japanese conquests there was, in April, little actual fighting between opposing ground forces. Indians and British were withdrawing in Burma after the failure of the Chindit operation and the operations in Arakan; the Chinese were now in the eighth year of their dogged resistance to the Japanese. In New Guinea Brigadier M. J. Moten's Kanga Force was patrolling against the Japanese among the jungle-clad precipitous ridges of the Mubo area.[3]

The men of Kanga Force knew nothing of the great plans for the future; only that they had saved Wau, that they were now held up near Mubo and that they presumed their objective was Salamaua. It seemed to these Australians, fighting in such primitive conditions, that the Japanese sun was still at its zenith; and that it would be an immense and arduous task to fight from Wau to Salamaua, let alone from Wau to Tokyo. Soldiers and civilians alike had watched the bitter campaigns of attrition in Guadalcanal and Papua with anxiety and foreboding. What alternative was there to this slogging, exhausting fighting where gains were to be measured almost by the yard stick of trench warfare? It was a grim and gloomy future and none could foresee the end of the war if similar battles had to be fought for all islands along the route to Tokyo.

The operations in New Guinea were now under the control of Lieut-General Mackay, who, since January, had been acting commander of New Guinea Force. Mackay, a sage, exacting and resolute commander, had led the 6th Division in the campaigns in North Africa and Greece early in 1941, and from September 1941 to April 1942 had commanded the Home Forces in Australia. Since then his substantive appointment had been that of commander of the Second Army. On 24th March Major-General Savige, another former officer of the 6th Division, now commanding the 3rd Division, arrived at Port Moresby to take command in the only active battle zone in the South-West Pacific. At this time few commanders of his rank had had more varied active service: a junior infantry officer on Gallipoli and in France in 1914-18, commander of an independent force in Kurdistan in 1918, and of an infantry brigade—

---

[3] Kanga Force consisted of: 17th Brigade (2/5th, 2/6th, 2/7th Battalions), three Independent Companies (2/3rd, 2/5th, 2/7th), one battery from the 2/1st Field Regiment and one section from 1st Mountain Battery.

the 17th—in operations in North Africa, Greece and Syria in 1940-41. In order to see his new area, and to renew his acquaintance with his old brigade which, it so happened, was to be his main fighting force, Savige visited the battle areas between 30th March and 13th April. He returned to Wau six days later, and on 23rd April moved with his divisional headquarters to Bulolo. On the same day he took command of all troops in the area and Kanga Force ceased to exist.

CHAPTER 2

MARKING TIME

"I AM anxious to increase the garrison at Wau-Bulolo as soon as possible by flying in approximately 1,500 troops," wrote General Mackay on 18th April to General Kenney, the commander of the Allied Air Forces in the South-West Pacific Area. "After these have arrived," he continued, "about 600 troops will be relieved and brought to Port Moresby, leaving the garrison of Wau-Bulolo approximately 6,500. . . . The total number of plane loads required to carry the above personnel with their weapons, ammunition and limited stores is 103." These words emphasised the dependence of the Allied Services on one another in New Guinea. Merchant ships, guarded by the navy, carried troops and war materials to Port Moresby but, without the use of air transport, the Wau-Bulolo area could not have been held in January 1943. Against great difficulties engineers were building a road to Wau from Bulldog on the Lakekamu River but this would not be ready for some time. In the meantime the only practicable way to reinforce and maintain the Australians in the Wau-Bulolo area was over the Owen Stanley Range in American air transports guarded by Allied fighters. Possession by the Allies of the DC-3 transport aircraft was thus a big factor in enabling the Australians to hold their positions in the forward area against the Japanese who had more accessible bases at Lae and Salamaua.

Mackay's Intelligence staff estimated that enemy strengths in New Guinea included between 9,000 and 11,000 men at Wewak, between 6,000 and 8,000 at Madang, about 5,500 in the Lae-Salamaua area, with smaller detachments at Vanimo, Aitape, Bogia, Saidor and Finschhafen. Mackay thought that the Japanese were determined to strengthen their grip on the north-east coast of New Guinea by using the divisions stationed in the Wewak, Madang and Lae-Salamaua areas, and by preparing airfields for bombers at Wewak and for fighters at Madang and Saidor. He believed that they would now try to build up the Lae-Salamaua area by developing the old coastal route from Wewak to Lae with barge staging points between the main areas, and that, when their communications and airfields improved, they would attack in the area south of the Markham or against the Australians' forward positions in the Mubo and Missim areas.

Mackay therefore on 20th April directed General Savige to keep the enemy away from the airfields at Wau, Bulolo, Bulwa and Zenag; to prevent them from entering the Wau-Bulolo-Partep 2 area from the east, north and west; and to deny them a secure base for developing operations south of the Markham River particularly in the Wampit and Watut River Valleys. He also made Savige responsible for developing the Wau-Bulolo area into "an active operational zone for mobile defence in such a manner as to facilitate offensive operations". Mackay finally warned Savige that "Salamaua is a strongly defended area and no attempt is to be made at present to capture it by siege tactics".

One of the most difficult and unpleasant areas ever to confront troops lay before the Australians. It posed an immense supply problem. Endurance and determination in generous quantities were needed from the troops themselves, while a high degree of ingenuity was required from those responsible for planning and organisation. The troops found it difficult to find enough unpleasant adjectives to describe the country, which, for the most part, consisted of rugged mountains clothed with dense, almost impenetrable jungle, and in the higher areas with moss forest. Occasionally hills covered with kunai grass, such as those in the Snake Valley, stood out against the jungle background. Gloom and eerie stillness, clouds which frequently descended upon the mountains, rain, towering trees and drooping vines, which shut off the sunshine when it did eventually break through the clouds, sodden earth and rotting vegetation, all combined to add a touch of the primaeval to the battlegrounds of this part of New Guinea. When the wind blew it raised a sour unclean smell of decay from the vegetation which, season after season, rotted in the all-pervading damp. Clothing was perpetually wet with rain and perspiration; the ravages of insect pests, notably mosquitoes and leeches, were enough to call out the blasphemous superlatives of the sorely-tried Australian soldier.

The tropical rains of many centuries had cut deep ravines and, as a result, any movement entailed constant negotiation of watercourses and steep descents on tracks hardly meriting the name, with correspondingly steep ascents to follow. After many bitter and exhausting experiences the troops learnt to measure distance in hours not miles. Time taken in one direction might be far different from time taken in another, depending on the lie of the land. The soldier's life was governed by the tracks around and along which all operations took place. Mostly they led through the jungle of trees and undergrowth, but sometimes through moss forests or the stifling kunai. As the track became worn the troops had to wallow along in mud up to the knees and perhaps over them, stumbling now and then over hidden rocks and roots, and for support clutching vines and branches which often broke off rotten in their hands.

The report of the 3rd Australian Division said:

Such conditions of rain, mud, rottenness, stench, gloom, and, above all, the feeling of being shut in by everlasting jungle and ever ascending mountains, are sufficient to fray the strongest nerves. But add to them the tension of the constant expectancy of death from behind the impenetrable screen of green, and nerves must be of the strongest, and morale of the highest, to live down these conditions, accept them as a matter of course, and maintain a cheerful yet fighting spirit.[1]

The Japanese shared such opinions. A company commander of the *115th Regiment* wrote of the overpowering jungle: "One advances as if in the dark." A senior staff officer on the headquarters of the *51st Division* described the characteristics of the jungle thus:

---
[1] Report on Operations of 3 Aust Div in Salamaua Area 22 April 43 to 25 August 43.

All the tall trees are entwined by vine-like plants, which make them either die or fall. There are many fallen trees which frequently become an obstacle to movements. During the rainy season they collect water on the moss, and the vines grow luxuriantly in every direction, twisting among withered trees. As for the surface of the ground, it is covered with leaf-mould, and moss grows on the network of exposed roots. No matter to what high place one climbs, the eye can penetrate only a short distance, and since one cannot depend on this to see the form of the mountains of the vicinity, it is difficult to orient the actual terrain with maps. One can rarely see more than 100 metres through the jungle, so, when one is crawling up on the enemy, it is not difficult to come within 20 metres. Consequently when perceiving the approach of the enemy, it goes without saying, one must be alert for any rustling of foliage, and must make good use of one's ears, just as at night.

In these conditions the human element played a big part for it was important to keep the fighting soldiers fit and cheerful. They were wet most of the time, and tended to become depressed and ill. Brigadier Moten had already decided that the main way to keep them interested and fit was to place rest camps where they could sleep dry, have a hot meal or two, and wash themselves and their clothing, close behind the forward positions. He established such a camp at Edie Creek, where it was cold enough at night for four blankets, and there the men gained appetite amazingly and even put a little weight on lean frames.

The main route from Wau to Mubo was via Summit, which as its name implied was the highest point on this track, 6,400 feet above sea level, and Guadagasal. After leaving the kunai-covered spurs to the south of Wau the track entered mountainous jungle. To Mubo the track was reasonably well graded. The Mubo Valley in this region was a deep wedge-shaped cleft in the jungle-covered mountains with Observation Hill rising sharply to the north. East of Mubo lay Lababia Ridge—an unbroken almost perpendicular wall of jungle. North of Lababia Ridge were the precipitous enemy strongholds of Green Hill[2] and the Pimple[3] while north again and across the Bitoi River was the jungle clad Bitoi Ridge running west to Buigap Creek. North again was the mass of Mount Tambu which could only be approached along narrow razor-backs with almost perpendicular drops on each side. Stretching out like three fingers to the north-east, north and north-west of Mount Tambu were three large ridges; only one was yet named—Komiatum Ridge, a long sprawling feature separating Buirali and Buiwarfe Creeks and finishing at their junction. West of Mount Tambu lay the Komiatum Gap separating it from the Pioneers Range at whose northern extremity lay Bobdubi Ridge. Goodview Junction, on Komiatum Gap, was the watershed between Buigap and Buirali Creeks. The main Salamaua-Komiatum-Mubo track, after leaving the valley of the Francisco River, travelled up the valley of the Buirali east of Bobdubi Ridge and on to Komiatum Ridge where it ran mainly through open kunai patches. It then went over Goodview Junction and down the valley of the Buigap to the Mubo area.

---

[2] So named because, among all the greenness on Vickers Ridge, it appeared greenest.
[3] Named by the NGVR because it looked like a pimple among other mountains.

From the Saddle another track ran along the crest of Lababia Ridge and then down the eastern slope of the ridge at an angle of very nearly 60 degrees to Napier at the junction of the Bitoi and Buyawim Rivers, whence the low-lying delta of the Bitoi spread eastwards towards the coast at Duali and Nassau Bay.

The Missim area was dominated by Bobdubi Ridge which rose from the U-shaped curve of the Francisco River. Its whole length was cut and broken into many smaller features; an area described in the 3rd Division's report as "a country of razor-backs and panoramas of Salamaua". To the west Uliap Creek ran north to join the Francisco; some conception of the nature of the country could be gained from the fact that the main north-south track in this area ran in the bed of the stream itself. In the Missim area two main routes led west towards the interior. From Malolo, north along the coast from Salamaua, a track led to Hote and thence via Bobadu and across the Kuper Range to the Bulolo Valley. The other route branched from the Salamaua-Mubo track to cross Bobdubi Ridge and follow the Francisco River inland to Missim. As this track was under observation from the Salamaua area in many places, when the 2/3rd Independent Company arrived in January they covered it with a post known as Meares' Camp,[4] and cut a concealed route eastwards from Missim along the south side of the Francisco. This track crossed a series of ravines and ridges and the going was very rough. It passed through Base 3,[5] Jeffery's O.P., Vial's O.P.[6] and finally Namling on Bobdubi Ridge.

When General Savige with the headquarters of the 3rd Division took command of the Wau-Bulolo-Mubo-Missim-Markham area he inherited dispositions and the tactical situation from Brigadier Moten, who had been commanding the troops in this area since January. Before going to Wau Moten had received instructions from the Commander-in-Chief, General Blamey. He wrote later:

> At that time the C-in-C also gave me a forecast of future events which included the capture of Lae by a combined amphibious and land move. . . . The C-in-C stressed that to assist the Lae operations Kanga Force would, in addition to its main role of the defence of the Bulolo Valley, threaten the approaches to Salamaua with a view to drawing Japanese troops from Lae into the Salamaua area.

The Japanese withdrawal from Wau ceased when they reached the Mubo area. Moten had then decided not to drive them out of Mubo, but to control the area by offensive patrolling forward from a line running

---

[4] After Captain W. A. Meares, 2/3rd Independent Company.

[5] Lieutenant S. G. Jeffery of the 2/3rd Independent Company had established three bases as he pushed his men and supplies slowly forward towards Komiatum. Base 1 and Base 2 fell into disuse but Base 3 became a regular staging point.

[6] When the 2/3rd Independent Company came into the area the natives explained that a Master "Wells" had been in the area before and had set up this tree-top observation post. They were undoubtedly referring to Flying Officer Leigh Vial who, armed with a radio transmitter and assisted by loyal natives, had done valuable Intelligence work in the early days of the Japanese occupation. Vial's O.P. should not be confused with the more important Wells O.P. south of Namling and about 1½ miles west of Komiatum across the Buirali, also named after Vial.

between Guadagasal and Waipali, thus maintaining a threat to Salamaua without prejudicing his main role of protecting the approaches to Wau from Mubo. His main force was the veteran 17th (Victorian) Brigade, engaged recently in the defence of Wau. After the Japanese retreat Moten had decided that the danger of attack on the Wau-Bulolo valley had shifted from the Mubo to the Markham area. He had therefore sent the 2/6th Battalion to cover the approaches from the Markham while the 2/5th Battalion faced the Mubo area, and the 2/3rd Independent Company, which had joined in the fight for Wau after having been part of the garrison of New Caledonia, went to the Missim area. Early in April the 2/7th Battalion had relieved the 2/5th and was supported by a section of the 1st Mountain Battery.[7] The 2/5th and the 2/7th Independent Companies were on their way out and the first battalion of the 15th Brigade, the 24th (from Victoria), was on its way in towards the end of April.

Moten had been worried about his right flank and had attempted to gather information about the area stretching from his main forward positions east towards Nassau Bay. On 12th April a patrol from the 2/5th, which included Sergeant Saunders,[8] an aboriginal member of the 2/7th, had left Napier to reconnoitre about Duali and raid enemy positions there. As a result of this and further reconnaissance the company at Napier was ordered to clear up the villages south of Duali on Nassau Bay. When moving towards Duali on 21st April, however, the force was ambushed and, although no casualties were sustained, it withdrew to the river junction at Napier. A Japanese Intelligence report described the action thus:

> The patrol of 9 men that set out at 0750 hrs on the 21st on a reconnaissance in the vicinity of Buyawim River encountered 30 or 40 enemy troops about 1,300 m. west of the river mouth. The patrol was immediately reinforced by 22 men, and repulsed the enemy.

Moten then ordered the commander of the 2/7th, Lieut-Colonel H. G. Guinn, to place a senior officer in charge at Napier. Major St E. D. Nelson took charge but reported that no Japanese had been in the area "since Adam was a boy". On 23rd April Guinn was ordered to make and maintain contact with the enemy in the Bitoi junction-Duali-Nassau Bay area, patrolling to the coast if necessary; and he was also asked for a new plan for clearing the enemy from this vicinity.

The main Australian defensive line ran through the Saddle-Waipali-Buibaining area. Company positions at Napier, Lababia Ridge and Mat Mat were outpost bases from which continuous aggressive patrolling was

---

[7] In 1942 in an effort to obtain light guns for tropical warfare the army sought 3.7-inch howitzers but could obtain only four which had been made in England in 1923. These were bought from New Zealand in 1942 and were used to equip the 1st Mountain Battery. The MGRA at Army Headquarters, Major-General J. S. Whitelaw, then suggested, and Blamey agreed, that three regiments be armed with heavy mortars. Meanwhile encouraging progress was made with a lightened 25-pounder, originally suggested by Lieut-Colonel A. E. Arthur and Lieutenant R. Gamon, both formerly of the 2/2nd Field Regiment. This gun weighed 2,500 pounds compared with 4,000 pounds for the normal 25-pounder equipment. On 10th December 1942 one of these guns was tested and proved remarkably accurate. The first 12 light guns were completed in January 1943.

[8] Capt R. W. Saunders, VX12843; 2/7 Bn. 3 Bn RAR Korea 1950-52. Sawyer; of Portland and Cheltenham, Vic; b. Purnim, Vic, 7 Aug 1920. (Saunders was the first aboriginal to gain commissioned rank in the Australian Army.)

carried out against the enemy positions. No-man's land included the southern slopes of Observation Hill, Garrison Hill, Mubo Valley, including the airfield, Vickers Ridge and a small area on Lababia Ridge between the Australian company position and the Japanese positions on Green Hill and the Pimple. Since their retreat from Wau the Japanese had dug themselves in well on the Pimple, Green Hill and Observation Hill, but otherwise they were quiet. They did little patrolling but were apparently content to allow the Australians to control no-man's land.

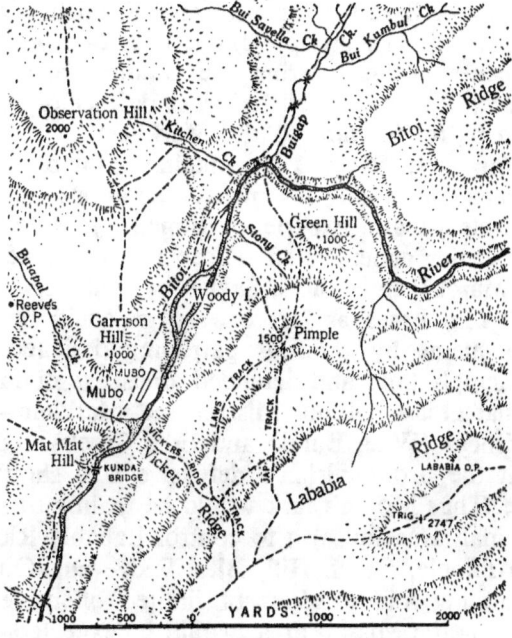

Soon after taking over the Mubo area Guinn was working on a plan whereby a company, supported by artillery, mortars, machine-guns and aircraft, would destroy the Japanese in the Green Hill-Pimple area. On 22nd April Moten informed Guinn that his plan was approved. "You will attack and consolidate Green Hill," Guinn ordered Captain F. B. Pringle, the company commander on Lababia Ridge.

Thus, when General Savige arrived to command all troops in the area, arrangements were ready for an attack by the 2/7th Battalion on the Pimple and for extensive patrolling to the east. From divisional headquarters there was telephone and wireless communication to all units except the 2/3rd Independent Company, the Lae observation post,[9] and Bena Force,[1] which were connected by wireless telegraphy only.

---

[9] The Lae observation post, known as "Tojo", was situated on a spur of the Hertzog Range about 6 miles west of Lae. The observation post had been established by the NGVR and manned in succession by the NGVR, 2/5th Independent Company and 24th Battalion, with the aid of signallers of the New Guinea Air Wireless Warning Unit and Angau police and cook boys. The view of Lae was excellent, the only obstruction being mist or fog rolling in over the Labu swamps from the Huon Gulf and Mount Lunaman which obscured the buildings of Chinatown. One of the main worries was the noise made by the battery charger (for the wireless) and charging was therefore done when the wind was strong enough to drown the noise. The wireless room was prepared for instant demolition and was linked to the actual observation post 120 yards away where a 24 hours' watch was kept. Fires could not be lit by day, and care had to be taken not to let the sun glint on the binoculars and naval telescope used by the spotters who were ever ready to summon the air force to attack enemy aircraft, barges or troops in the Lae area.

[1] Bena Force at this stage consisted of an infantry platoon and an MMG section of the 2/7th Battalion. See Chapter 9.

On 25th April Savige issued his first operation instruction from his headquarters at Bulolo.[2] He instructed the 17th Brigade to prevent the Japanese from entering the Bulolo Valley from the Mubo area, secure the Mubo-Guadagasal-Waipali area, and gain control of the coastal area immediately south of the Bitoi River. The 2/3rd Independent Company (Major G. R. Warfe) was to prevent the Japanese from entering the Bulolo Valley through the Missim area, and secure the Missim-Pilimung area as a base for raids towards Komiatum and Salamaua. Lieut-Colonel F. G. Wood's group (2/6th and 24th Battalions) was to prevent the Japanese from entering the Bulolo Valley through the Markham and Partep 2 areas, establish a close defence of the Bulolo and Bulwa airfields, and patrol forward to the Markham.

Strangely, Savige knew nothing of the plan for the big offensive although Moten did. Using his own observations, but also relying largely on the knowledge and experience gained by Moten and Lieut-Colonel Wilton,[3] his senior general staff officer (who had been attached to Kanga Force in March) and others, Savige by 29th April decided that he must establish firm bases as far forward as could be maintained and also harass the enemy by vigorous patrolling designed to open the way for raids on supply lines and defended areas. He divided his area into three operational areas—Mubo, Missim and Markham—and three areas with fixed defences (Wau, Bulolo and Edie Creek). To all his units he emphasised that the 3rd Division's defensive role should nevertheless be an active one. Thus Moten's task would be mainly to secure the Mubo-Guadagasal-Waipali area but also to control Lababia Ridge, Mat Mat, and ultimately the Pimple, Green Hill, Bitoi Ridge and Observation Hill, by aggressive patrolling and a series of limited offensive actions. Warfe, as well as holding the Missim area, would be expected to raid the Komiatum Track, and Wood to patrol aggressively to the Markham River.

Facing the four battalions and one Independent Company of the 3rd Australian Division was Lieut-General Hidemitsu Nakano's *51st Japanese Division*, also under strength. Lae and Salamaua were still occupied at the beginning of 1943 by the *7th Naval Base Force* approximately 2,500 strong. The Japanese force actually arrayed against the Australians in the Salamaua area on 23rd April consisted of the remnants of the 1,500 troops from *I* and *II Battalions* of the *102nd Regiment* which had arrived in the Lae-Salamaua area in January 1943, attacked Wau, and then withdrawn to Mubo. At the end of February *III/102nd Battalion* was dispatched to Nassau Bay to secure the left flank against either a seaborne or coastal attack. With headquarters at Komiatum Major-General Teru Okabe commanded this force.

Aboard 8 transports and 8 destroyers which had been attacked by Allied planes in the Bismarck Sea at the beginning of March had been part of the *51st Division*, principally the *115th Regiment* and the *14th Field Artillery Regiment*. All ships were sunk with the exception of four destroyers, but about 1,600 sur-

---

[2] The principal appointments on the staff of the 3rd Division in April 1943 included: *GOC* Maj-Gen S. G. Savige; *GSO1* Lt-Col J. G. N. Wilton; *LO* Capt A. S. Sturrock; *AA&QMG* Lt-Col E. A. Griffin; *DAAG* Maj R. C. Tomkins; *DAQMG* Maj D. J. Breheny; *ADMS* Col N. H. W. Saxby; *LSO* Maj R. R. Marsh; *ADOS* Lt-Col G. McA. Pont; *DAPM* Capt R. K. McCaffrey; *CRA* Brig W. E. Cremor; *CRE* Lt-Col T. A. Symons; *CO Sigs* Lt-Col L. W. Fargher; *CASC* Lt-Col F. W. MacLean.

[3] Maj-Gen J. G. N. Wilton, CBE, DSO, NX12337. BM Arty 7 Div 1941; GSO1 3 Div 1942-43; Aust Mil Mission, Washington 1943-45. Comd 28 British Commonwealth Bde, Korea 1953. Regular soldier; of Sydney; b. Sydney, 22 Nov 1910.

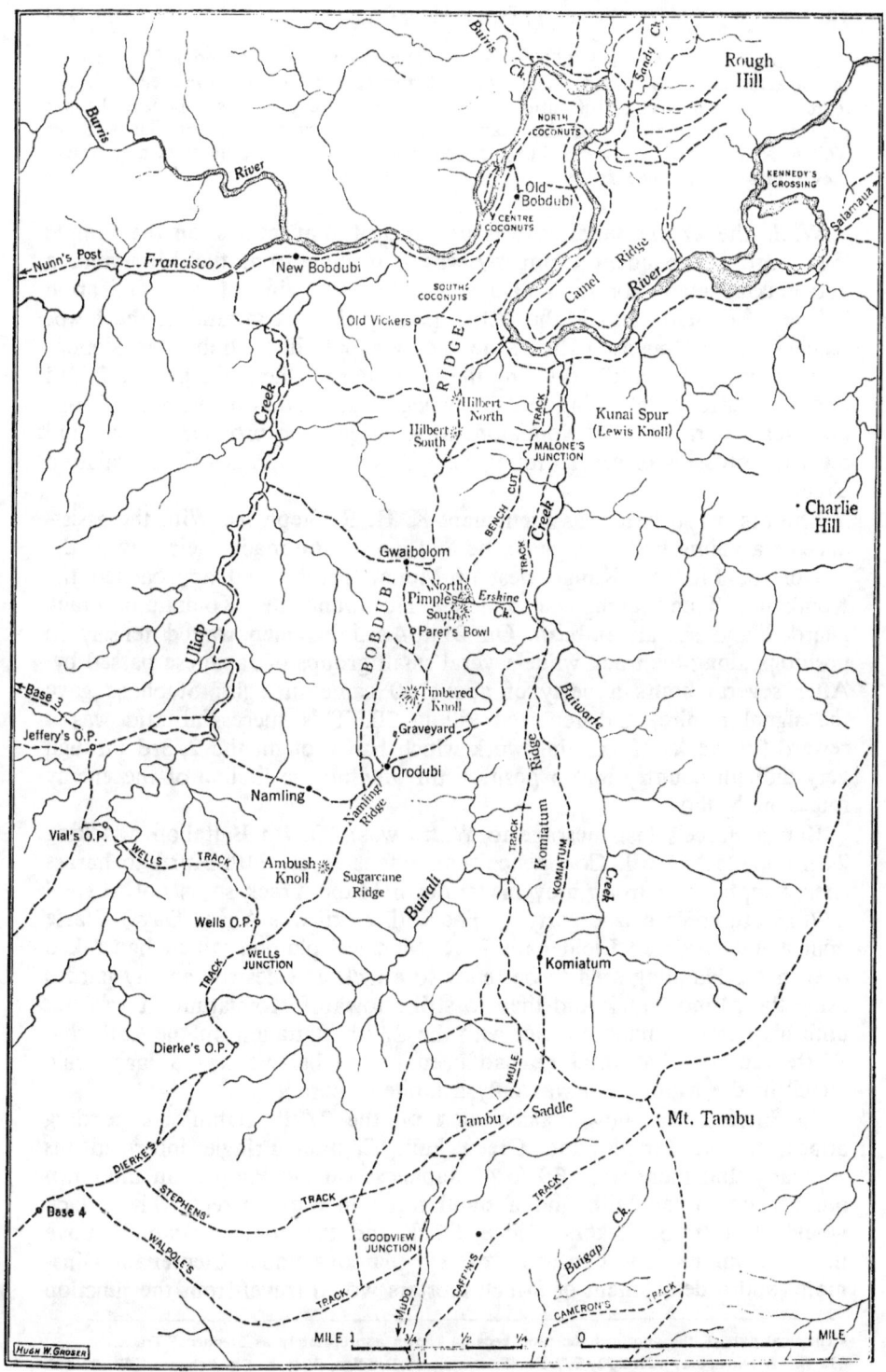

Bobdubi Ridge area

vivors reached Rabaul and 2,000 reached New Guinea out of about 7,000 troops of the *51st Division* aboard. The *115th Regiment* appears to have been reduced temporarily to a strength of little more than one battalion. This Japanese disaster prevented another attack on the Wau area, possibly by way of the Snake River Valley. Many of the survivors, however, were sent to the Lae-Salamaua area where they reinforced Okabe's force.

While the 2/7th Battalion was preparing for an attack on the Pimple the 2/3rd Independent Company was patrolling from the Missim area and making ready for raids against the Japanese line of communication between Salamaua and Mubo. After leaving the flat ground at the lower reaches of the Francisco River, the enemy supply line climbed up Komiatum Ridge to the saddle dividing the Buirali from the Buigap. The 2/3rd already controlled Namling but this village was located on Bobdubi Ridge and was separated from Komiatum by a gorge. The problem was to find means of crossing or getting round this obstacle to approach the Komiatum Track.

The first to succeed was Lieutenant K. H. R. Stephens. With the assistance of a young native as guide, he and his section made their way to the top of the Pioneers Range west of Mount Tambu and approached the Komiatum Track along the saddle.[4] He found the Komiatum Track guarded and set an ambush. On 21st April his men waited tensely in positions along the track while several small groups of Japanese passed by. After several hours a party of about 60 came in sight; Stephens gave the signal to fire, and reported killing 20. This successful raid was a reward for weeks of exacting work which had brought the 2/3rd through very difficult country into a position threatening the lifeline of the enemy forces in Mubo.

Kanga Force's last message to Warfe was: "2/7th Battalion attacking 24th and 25th April. Commence your offensive on 24th April to harass enemy supplies or troop movements down Mubo Track so as not to spoil 2/7th Battalion's Anzac party." (The 25th April was Anzac Day.) Warfe immediately ordered Lieutenant J. R. Menzies' platoon which had taken over in the Namling area to be ready to attack and destroy enemy parties using the Mubo Track and then to strike towards Komiatum. It was not until his wireless made contact with the 2/7th Battalion on the 25th that Warfe realised that what he had been led to believe was a large-scale attack in the Mubo area was only a limited operation.

All interest was now concentrated on the 2/7th Battalion's pending attack on the Pimple and Green Hill. Captain Pringle informed his company that there were 30 to 40 Japanese on the Pimple, an unknown number on Green Hill, and a small force in Stony Creek. The attack would start from Vickers' Ridge Track and the company would move in two columns: one consisting of two platoons under Lieutenant Dinsmore[5] and a detachment of 3-inch mortars would travel from the junction

---

[4] The final part of the approach he used became known appropriately as Stephens' Track.
[5] Lt B. M. Dinsmore, VX10322; 2/7 Bn. Salesman; of Bendigo, Vic; b. Christchurch, NZ, 22 Feb 1913. (Changed name by deed poll in January 1944 to W. B. Dinsmore.)

The Territories of Papua and New Guinea,

and Bougainville in the northern Solomons.

of the Jap, Vickers and main Lababia Tracks along the Jap Track towards the Pimple; the second, consisting of the third platoon and company headquarters, would move north from the junction of Vickers and Laws' Tracks, along Laws' Track—a difficult and almost unknown trail —to encircle the Pimple from the west. The first attack would be made astride the Jap Track.

A message of good luck to the company and an injunction to "remember Anzac" were Colonel Guinn's final words before the attack to capture the objective of Phase One—the Pimple[6]—began at 10.30 a.m. on 24th April when four Boston aircraft began a twenty minutes' attack on Green Hill, Stony Creek, Observation Hill and Kitchen Creek. At this time patrols from Captain Tatterson's[7] company at Mat Mat began a move designed to deceive the enemy by crossing and recrossing the kunda[8] bridge; patrols also investigated the approaches to Observation Hill. One patrol crossed Buiapal Creek and climbed Observation Hill to a position previously occupied by the enemy. Ahead they saw a clearing in which was a tree with a platform. This observation post probably accounted for the fact that each time a patrol had left Mat Mat, a shot had been fired from Observation Hill.

After the air strike the two columns set off, covered by sporadic mortar fire, and with the signalmen keeping up the telephone line along the Jap Track. By 1 p.m., however, all concerned realised that the steep and precipitous Pimple was a natural fortress which could be held by a few good troops. Dinsmore's forward platoon under Lieutenant Worle,[9] after advancing to within 100 yards of the Pimple and firing twelve grenades from a discharger, was pinned down by the enemy's machine-guns in front. These were guarded on the flanks by light machine-guns which were in turn guarded on their flanks by snipers. Worle's right section was out of contact and nothing was seen or heard of Pringle. Guinn then sent Major Nelson along the Jap Track with an extra platoon at 1.40 p.m. Nelson reported that he thought the situation was under control. As there was still no news of the left column, however, the adjutant, Captain Dixon,[1] went forward and at 3.25 p.m. he found it pinned down about 400 yards from Dinsmore's position and west of the northern end of the Pimple. Here Pringle was forced to remain for the rest of the day. During this period a Japanese called out: "I can control you from here. I have got you surrounded. Surrender at my terms."

At 4.30 p.m. Guinn ordered an "all in show" to drive out the enemy. Nelson reported half an hour later that Pringle was still held but that the remainder of the force was making good progress towards surrounding the Japanese machine-gun positions; he decided to attack with one platoon

---

[6] Green Hill was the objective of Phase Two.
[7] Capt L. V. Tatterson, MC, VX5660; 2/7 Bn. Butcher; of Newry, Vic; b. Newry, 25 Nov 1915. Killed in action 4 Aug 1943.
[8] A type of very strong vine commonly found in the mountains of New Guinea. It is the rattan of commerce.
[9] Lt H. J. Worle, VX4741; 2/7 Bn. Labourer; b. Melbourne, 31 Aug 1913.
[1] Maj R. F. Dixon, MC, VX10378. 2/7 Bn; BM 23 Bde 1945. Shop assistant; of Brim, Vic; b. Warracknabeal, Vic, 21 Jul 1916.

along the track and one on each flank. Unfortunately the platoon in the centre broke into two columns, both of which swung too far to the right and left where they joined up with the flanking platoons. As darkness was coming on Dinsmore, who had suffered some casualties, reported the confusion to Nelson who ordered him to hold the ground he had gained until next morning. The situation report for that day described the Japanese ambush position as being 400 yards in depth with the enemy well dug in. Seven Australians had been wounded and all that could be said for certain was that two Japanese had been killed.

After dusk on 24th April cries for assistance were heard. Sergeant Russell,[2] the medical N.C.O. attached to the company, immediately moved through the undergrowth and discovered one of the Australians lying seriously wounded close to the enemy machine-gun position. Russell found it impossible to move the wounded soldier before attending to his wound. Returning to the undergrowth he lit a cigarette and hiding it from the enemy he returned and successfully stitched the soldier's wound by its glow, then lay with him throughout the night, thus saving the wounded man's life.

On the morning of 25th April Guinn, who had come forward to Lababia, advised Pringle to make more use of artillery and mortars. In the morning three Bostons again strafed and bombed Green Hill, and at 12.45 p.m. the mountain battery fired on the Pimple. Artillery support was necessarily limited, as Moten had been forced, because of scarcity of ammunition, to limit the artillery support to 50 rounds a gun. The forward observation officer, Lieutenant Colless,[3] directed the firing of 74 shells into the Pimple area during the day. Taking a telephone almost up to the Pimple he remained ahead of the infantry directing fire for an hour, while the enemy was firing in his direction and he was in grave danger from his own shells.

The situation report at midday said that "owing to strong enemy defences and dense undergrowth in ambush area impossible to dislodge enemy with company weapons". Acting in this spirit Pringle sent his Intelligence man, Lance-Corporal Robertson,[4] along Laws' Track with instructions to tell Lieutenant Tyres[5] to withdraw his platoon from the west side of the Pimple. Robertson was killed before he could inform Tyres, who had seen Japanese moving towards the Pimple from Green Hill at first light. Tyres was forced to withdraw when he ran low in ammunition after about 60 Japanese from Green Hill had attacked and tried to encircle his position. He fought a delaying action and then reported to Pringle that the Japanese in the Pimple area were being reinforced.

---

[2] Sgt W. C. Russell, MM, VX37523; 2/7 Bn. Grocery manager; of East St Kilda, Vic; b. Fitzroy, Vic, 26 Aug 1905.

[3] Capt J. M. Colless, MC, NX14722. 2/13 Fd Regt, 1 Mtn Bty. Printer's reader; of Sydney; b. Sydney, 19 Jan 1916.

[4] L-Cpl D. J. Robertson, NX111730; 2/7 Bn. Barman; of Sydney; b. Dungog, NSW, 13 Sep 1919. Killed in action 25 Apr 1943.

[5] Lt B. W. E. Tyres, VX16557; 2/7 Bn. Labourer; of Auburn, Vic; b. South Yarra, Vic, 8 Apr 1922. Died 5 Jun 1951.

By 6 p.m. it was obvious that the attack had failed and that the enemy had even gained some ground, through no fault of the attacking troops but simply because the difficulties in attacking such a position as the Pimple had been underestimated. Flaws in planning were also apparent. Reconnaissance before the attack had not been of the intensive nature required to pinpoint enemy positions. Lack of intercommunication by telephone line or wireless between the two attacking columns had resulted in lack of coordination and that hopeless feeling of impotence caused by plans going wrong and no one knowing where they had gone wrong. Runners were too slow and very vulnerable. With proper intercommunication Robertson would not have been used as a runner, or, if it had been necessary to use him, he would have been warned of the strong enemy force approaching from Green Hill. This lesson was well learnt: the hard-working signallers accompanied most patrols in future, and more attention was paid to the detailed aspects of intercommunication in any planned attack. Another flaw was the lack of ammunition dumps well forward, and this was partly responsible for Tyres' withdrawal. Another lesson which the Australians were gradually learning was that only direct hits by the supporting aircraft and artillery were of much value. Australian casualties were 7 killed and 11 wounded, while it was possible to claim only 3 Japanese killed for certain. The password for the Anzac operation happened to be "Calamity".

On the morning of the 26th Moten arrived in Guinn's area from Wau to see for himself the country in which his troops were fighting. He believed it was too costly to assault positions like the Pimple, which should be bypassed. While he had been commander of Kanga Force, Moten had decided that his vast area and the time it would take to carry out extensive reconnaissance of it would preclude his leaving Wau. Bearing in mind his main task of preventing enemy movement into the valley of the Bulolo he had decided to watch three known approaches from Mubo. Having now seen the Skindewai Track he was satisfied that it was adequately covered. He was not happy about his left flank at Waipali which could be easily bypassed. The 2/5th Battalion was therefore retained at Wau and patrolled along the two approaches (Jap Track and Black Cat Track) from Waipali. Moten remained convinced that the best position for his headquarters was still at Wau. Savige, however, thought differently, and by declaring Wau a defensive area, endeavoured to influence a move forward of the 17th Brigade headquarters.

Meanwhile in the northern area Lieutenant Menzies was ready to strike at the Komiatum Track. Leading a patrol on 25th April he headed north from Namling (the opposite direction from that which Lieutenant Stephens had taken) and boldly followed the remains of an old graded track reputed to have been cut in the days of the German occupation (the Bench Cut Track). Reaching the river flats near the junction of the Francisco River and Buirali Creek he found the enemy's supply line and began to lay an ambush. It was successful and he reported that he had killed 18 of a Japanese party of about 60. Warfe immediately ordered

Lieutenant Crawford[6] to repeat "the tea party" farther south. Coming soon after Stephens' success Menzies' ambush gave added confidence to the 2/3rd Independent Company. This was the type of fighting for which they had been especially trained and they were delighted at the opportunity to exercise their skill.

An Intelligence report from General Nakano's headquarters, captured later, stated that "at the north end of Komiatum the *Provisions Transportation Unit* . . . encountered enemy of unknown strength armed with automatic rifles". Reinforced by 20 men from Salamaua, the Japanese, according to the report, repulsed the Australians, who left 44 dead, while the Japanese lost 5 killed and 5 wounded.

This mendacious report which claimed more casualties than there were attackers was typical of the Japanese tendency to exaggerate the number of casualties inflicted in jungle warfare.

Crawford had been patrolling along the southern heights of Bobdubi Ridge and had established Dierke's O.P. (named after a native boy) overlooking the Komiatum Track. On the 28th he set out to find a new way of crossing the valley separating Bobdubi Ridge and Komiatum Ridge. No route seemed feasible and he was obliged to continue south to Stephens' Track on the saddle of the Pioneers Range. The enemy supply line was accessible at this point but, as Crawford feared, precautions had been taken as a result of Stephens' ambush. Near the junction of Stephens' Track with the Komiatum Track he made contact with an enemy position.

Leaving the remainder of his section twenty yards behind, Crawford, Sergeant Carr,[7] Corporal McRae[8] and Private Taylor[9] moved forward to investigate. The Japanese opened fire, killing Taylor instantly. Carr escaped back to the section. McRae was hit in the leg and fell down a steep bank, and Crawford jumped over the bank where he found that McRae had a broken leg. Corporal Lamb,[1] who had been left in charge of the remainder of the section, then moved forward with a sub-section and the medical N.C.O., Corporal Good,[2] to investigate. Firing his Tommy-gun from the hip, Lamb led his men in an attack which killed four Japanese who were examining Taylor's body. After finding Taylor dead, Lamb withdrew to a pre-selected ambush position to avoid being outflanked by the Japanese.

Crawford, leaving his Tommy-gun and rations with the wounded McRae, set off to find his section and return with more men to carry McRae out. Unable to find his section he returned to where he thought he had left McRae only to find that the wounded corporal had disappeared. A

---

[6] Capt A. W. Crawford, VX65517. 2/3 Indep Coy, and staff and training appointments. Salesman; of Camberwell, Vic; b. Melbourne, 13 Jun 1917.
[7] Lt J. W. Carr, QX35259. RAAF 1940-41; 2/3 Indep Coy, 2/10 Cdo Sqn. Forest overseer; of Moggill, Qld; b. Brisbane, 12 Dec 1916.
[8] Cpl K. McRae, VX58938; 2/3 Indep Coy. Herd tester; of Camperdown, Vic; b. Camperdown, 17 Jul 1917.
[9] Pte J. Taylor, VX109417; 2/3 Indep Coy. Laundry hand; of Mount Macedon, Vic; b. Woodend, Vic, 24 Jun 1923. Killed in action 28 Apr 1943.
[1] Cpl B. A. Lamb, WX2212. 2/11 Bn, 2/3 Indep Coy. Miner; of Coolgardie, WA; b. Foster, Vic, 17 Nov 1918.
[2] Sgt R. R. S. Good, VX90284. 2/3 Indep Coy, 2/3 Cdo Sqn. Medical student; of Geelong, Vic; b. Young, NSW, 8 Oct 1919.

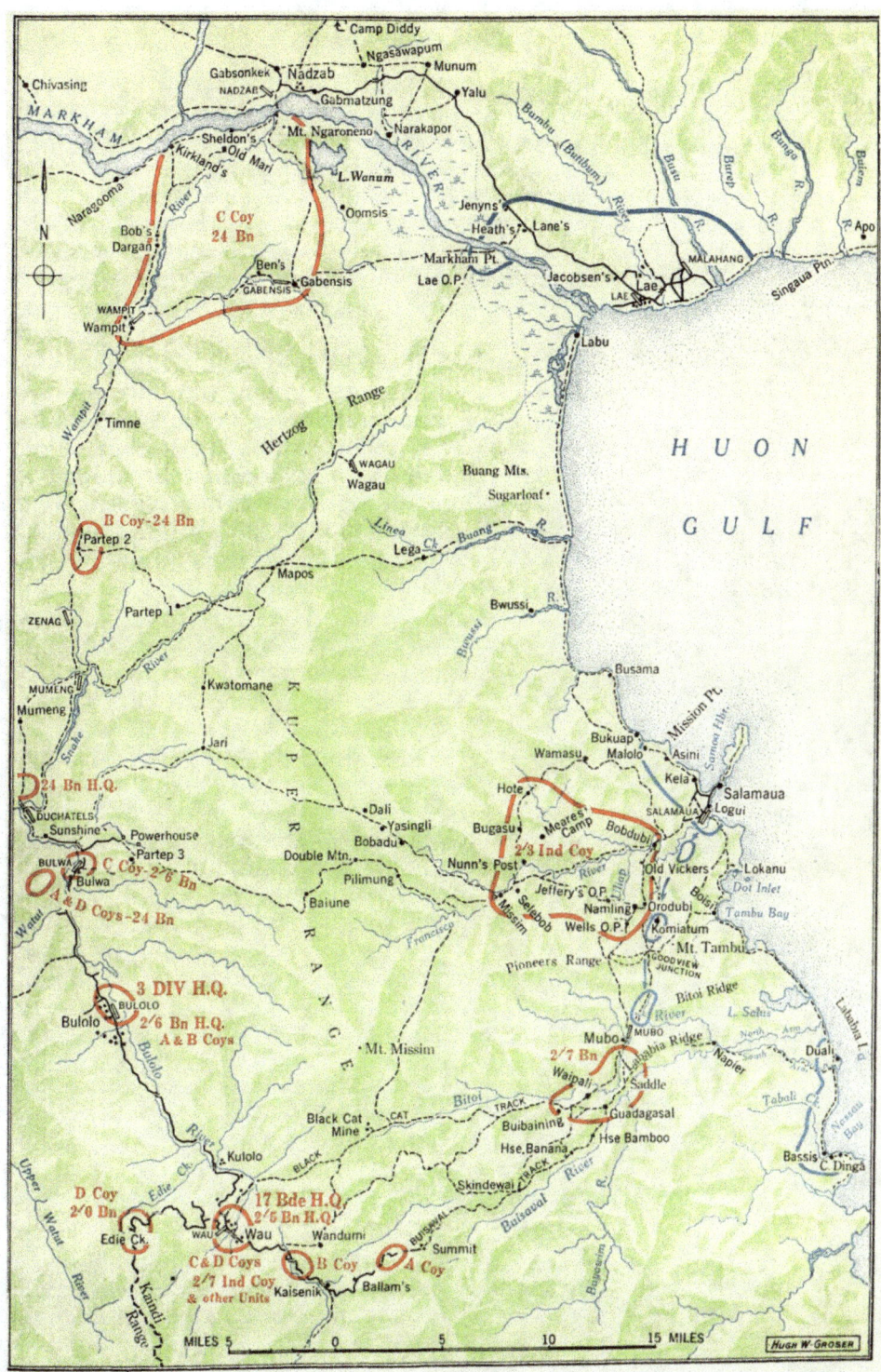

Australian and Japanese dispositions Wau-Salamaua-Lae area, 30th April 1943

long burst of Tommy-gun fire followed by a long burst of Japanese light machine-gun fire was assumed to have been his farewell note. Warfe, however, ordered that a search be made for McRae, and Crawford's men set out again from Wells O.P. They had reached a patch of sugar-cane near Namling when they heard a familiar voice suggesting they need not take life so seriously as there were no Japanese for miles around. McRae had rigged up a splint for his leg and had worked his way backwards in a sitting position, using the palms of his hands and the seat of his pants for propulsion—a remarkable 80 hours' feat of endurance and determination.³

By the end of April the Independent Company was spread over a large area with two platoons forward probing the north and south ends of Bobdubi Ridge, and the third in reserve in the Missim area. Warfe had soon realised that the force holding Bobdubi Ridge virtually controlled the Salamaua-Komiatum-Mubo track from the west during daylight. Information from his reconnaissance patrols and from natives led him to believe that Bobdubi Ridge was held only lightly by the enemy. Therefore on 27th April he obtained permission to "bash Bobdubi" in order to protect his lines of communication from Missim to Namling—a rather flimsy excuse as the Japanese held only the northern part of the ridge near the bend in the Francisco and in the southern or Namling part Menzies and Crawford had the run of the area. Bobdubi Ridge was a tempting target and the thrustful Warfe could not resist the opportunity to stir up trouble. Savige was aware of the great effect that the capture of Bobdubi Ridge would have on the Japanese, and eventually granted the request, but forbade heavy casualties and stated that not more than one platoon must be used at a time.

In the coming attack Menzies' platoon would secure the Namling area; Lieutenant J. S. Winterflood's would secure the Hote and Missim areas and form the company reserve; and Captain Meares' platoon would capture Bobdubi Ridge. At Savige's suggestion Crawford was kept in a suitable position to ambush enemy movement between Mubo and Komiatum, which might take place as a result of a forward move of the 2/7th Battalion, due to attack Green Hill and the Pimple again on 2nd May.

In the Mubo area on the morning of 28th April an Australian patrol found the Japanese positions on the Pimple unoccupied and moved in, at the same time sending a runner back with the information. Unfortunately the Japanese returned in strength and forced the patrol to withdraw but not before some of the patrol reached the top of the Pimple and observed the location of weapon-pits and machine-gun positions and the accuracy of the bombing, shelling and strafing. Guinn deduced from this episode that the Japanese must have anticipated an air strike at the usual time and withdrawn, returning when they realised that no strike was to be made.

Casualties in the forward company, now commanded by Lieutenant Dinsmore, had been increased by faulty bombing by Allied planes when,

---
³ McRae, under the nose of the enemy on the Komiatum Track, set his leg so well that it did not need to be re-set.

on 27th April, a stick of bombs killed one and wounded five. By 30th April Captain Tatterson's company had relieved Dinsmore's, and Captain Barr's[4] company had taken Tatterson's place on Mat Mat. The fourth company, now led by Captain Baird,[5] was on the Saddle.

On 1st May Guinn gave Tatterson's company an opportunity to dispose of the Pimple when he ordered it to "attack and consolidate Pimple area". Guinn estimated that there were 40 Japanese there with at least three machine-guns. A plan for air support was carefully worked out whereby aircraft would bomb the Pimple every day until 2nd May when, instead of bombing the Pimple, they would make deceptive passes over it, dropping bombs on Green Hill well ahead of the attacking infantry. The mountain battery would complete the deception by firing smoke concentration on the Pimple each day. It was hoped that the Japanese would have vacated the Pimple on 2nd May just as they had done on 27th April.

Shrewdly conceived though it was, the plan went astray. At 10.25 on the morning of the 2nd six Bostons strafed Green Hill and the junction of the Bitoi and Buigap Creek and, as a further deception and a signal for Tatterson to advance, the mountain battery fired four rounds on to the Pimple area. Tatterson's company left its start-line but soon afterwards the right-hand platoon was fired on. It became apparent that the Japanese had indeed vacated the Pimple during the air strike, but had moved not back but forward on to the southern slopes. The men were forced to withdraw after two had been killed and three wounded.[6] In spite of the failure of the attack at least one Japanese staff officer was impressed for he wrote in his diary:

> Enemy's use of combined strength of air and land, especially on 2nd May, is well organised.[7]

As the result of this second failure to capture the Pimple, Moten on 4th May received from divisional headquarters a statement of policy for operations in the Mubo area with which he entirely agreed. It said that the securing of the Mubo-Guadagasal-Waipali area and the implication that Lababia Ridge, Mat Mat and ultimately Observation Hill must be controlled, called for aggressive patrolling and a series of minor limited

---

[4] Capt F. A. Barr, VX39195; 2/7 Bn. Clerk; of Camberwell, Vic; b. Kew, Vic, 7 Oct 1913. Died of wounds 14 Aug 1943.

[5] Capt V. C. Baird, MC, VX35458; 2/7 Bn. Traveller; of Caulfield, Vic; b. Drysdale, Vic, 4 Jan 1910.

[6] On 22nd May an extraordinary feat of endurance was completed when Private D. Smith, 2/7th Battalion (of Ballarat, Vic), reached Dinsmore's forward positions, having been missing since the attack on the Pimple on 2nd May. He had managed to survive on three operational rations, berries, and water. The greater part of the 20 days for which he was lost had been spent behind the enemy lines in the Stony Creek and Green Hill areas. Still carrying his Tommy-gun, magazines and equipment, he had at last reached the slopes of Vickers Ridge where he followed an Australian track to the Bitoi. Attempting to cross the river he was almost swept away when he was rescued by one of Dinsmore's men. "Although physically weak, he is still strong in spirit," proudly wrote the 2/7th Battalion's diarist.

[7] The 3rd Division's policy on requests for air support, set out on 3rd May, was designed to conserve air power so that when occasions arose for its use the maximum effort compatible with the importance of the target could be employed. Requests for indirect air support such as air strikes of a harassing nature not immediately followed by ground action were to be submitted to divisional headquarters for confirmation. Air strikes giving direct support for attacks by infantry would only be approved if the target could not be engaged by the mountain battery. If the request for direct air support were approved, efforts would be made to provide an air strike of sufficient magnitude to saturate the target, instead of small strikes. Expenditure of air effort on small or doubtful targets to support patrol action was not considered worthwhile. The Fifth Air Force air support control at Wau was to be the channel of communication.

offensives. Attacks should not be made against prepared enemy positions in circumstances under which heavy casualties would be incurred without commensurate results. Such positions should be outflanked, neutralised and isolated from sources of supply and water, and the enemy should be constantly harassed by raids, ambushes and fighting patrols.

Shortly before the 2/7th's attack on the Pimple on 2nd May Warfe warned his company that the attack on the northern part of Bobdubi Ridge would begin on the 3rd. Meares' platoon concentrated in the Bobdubi area and Warfe joined them with a small headquarters. Meantime Stephens was moving with his men from Namling down the Bench Cut Track to cut off the enemy on north Bobdubi Ridge from the rear.

On 3rd May Lieutenant Lillie's[8] section moved forward along the main track to Salamaua and Meares with the rest of his troops headed for the high ground farther south. Lillie found New Bobdubi occupied and moved towards Old Bobdubi—two huts near Centre Coconuts—but in the afternoon he was stopped by fire from Centre Coconuts, where the main Missim-Salamaua track crossed the north end of Bobdubi Ridge. The Japanese then withdrew towards the crest of the ridge at Centre Coconuts. Warfe reported that the attack was "proceeding according to plan".

By 1 p.m. on the 4th May Corporal Muir's[9] section occupied a position about 50 yards south of South Coconuts and set up a Vickers machine-gun on a position later known as Old Vickers. Five hours later his men attacked and gained South Coconuts, about 200 yards from Centre Coconuts. Old Vickers was the key position on the northern portion of Bobdubi Ridge; from it Muir could see Salamaua, the mouth of the Francisco and part of the track to Mubo. That afternoon the Vickers kept up harassing fire on any enemy movement. Signs of the enemy's determination to hold the ridge were apparent in the evening when 21 Japanese reinforcements were observed approaching Bobdubi Ridge from the direction of Salamaua. Before dawn on the 5th a counter-attack forced Muir's men to withdraw from South Coconuts but they held Old Vickers.

Lieutenant Erskine's[1] engineer section, armed with a Vickers gun, was operating along the Bench Cut behind Stephens, and at midday on the 5th fired on about 60 Japanese moving towards Salamaua from Komiatum and killed about a dozen. At 2.30 p.m. Warfe, with whom was the company's medical officer, Captain Street,[2] set up a Vickers near Gwaibolom[3] where they could observe about 250 yards of the Komiatum

---

[8] Lt J. C. Lillie, WX8576; 2/3 Indep Coy. Station overseer; of Mount Lawley, WA; b. Perth, 19 Oct 1916.

[9] L-Sgt A. S. Muir, VX57539; 2/3 Indep Coy. Auctioneer and stock and station agent; of Kerang, Vic; b. Kerang, 12 Aug 1915. Killed in action 29 Jul 1943.

[1] Lt D. D. Erskine, VX52975; 2/3 Indep Coy. Mounted policeman; of Melbourne; b. Scotland, 22 Feb 1915. Died of wounds 26 Jul 1943.

[2] Capt F. N. Street, MC, NX34858. RMO HQ AIF ME; 2/3 Indep Coy, 2/3 Cdo Sqn; AIF Reception Camp UK. Medical practitioner; of Vaucluse, NSW; b. Sydney, 19 Jun 1916.

[3] Gwaibolom received its name when in April, in preparation for the Bobdubi attack, Captain R. N. Hancock was in the Namling area. Gwaibolom was the name of a very frightened native who acted as guide. On the way Hancock asked the name of a hut which could be seen farther south along Bobdubi Ridge. Gwaibolom gave some explanation but no actual place name emerged, so Hancock decided to name it after the boy. The Namling tribesmen derived great amusement from hearing Gwaibolom constantly on the lips of the troops as a place name.

Track from a distance of 700-800 yards, and opened fire on a party of about 80 Japanese moving south along the Komiatum Track, probably killing 15. The Japanese, dismayed by this long-distance fire, blazed away wildly, obviously thinking that they were being ambushed by troops close at hand.

Although it seemed that the enemy firmly occupied the Coconuts, Warfe remained confident that he could gain his objective without costly frontal attacks. The need to establish contact with Stephens and to cut the enemy from their base was, however, becoming urgent if the attack was to succeed. Accordingly, on 6th May, the second-in-command, Captain Hancock, accompanied by Private Pinney,[4] reconnoitred the enemy's rear. They found Lieutenant Stephens in position commanding the enemy's approach from Salamaua ready to attack any Japanese using the track. On the way along the bank of the Francisco they found an approach to high ground at the northern extremity of the ridge. Next day Hancock led a patrol along this position. Finding that North Coconuts was unoccupied and commanded the enemy positions in Centre and South Coconuts, Hancock established Lieutenant Leviston[5] there. As Lieutenant Egan's[6] signals section linked Leviston and Stephens by telephone cable to headquarters, the enemy was virtually surrounded and coordinated pressure could be brought to bear from four directions.

Early on the 7th Erskine ambushed Japanese moving along the Komiatum Track and killed ten. At 8 a.m. Meares began a heavy mortar bombardment of Centre Coconuts. Under cover of this fire Corporal Muir led his section forward, found the Japanese had withdrawn because of the fire and immediately occupied Centre Coconuts. An hour later the Japanese, thoroughly aroused, counter-attacked three times, but were driven back, losing seven killed. It was not until 10 a.m. that they were able, with the aid of mortars, to force Muir to withdraw. Next day, however, the enemy received a severe blow from Stephens' men, who had been waiting for several days in trying conditions—in the unrelieved gloom of dense forest, on flat marshy ground, heavy with mosquitoes, and in earshot of the enemy. At dawn about 60 reinforcements for the Centre and South Coconuts positions were seen approaching from Salamaua. The Australians went into action, killing about 20 and wounding many before the affray was over.

Warfe, who was fast becoming a legendary figure, was now at his full tide of success and confidence and, according to Savige, was "ready and willing to fight the whole Jap force". So ambitious were his plans at this time (they included a raid through Malolo to Mission Point), that Savige felt constrained to warn him: "You must appreciate that your

---

[4] Cpl P. P. Pinney, MM, NX38335. 2/9 Fd Regt, 2/3 Indep Coy, 2/8 Cdo Sqn. Student; of Bowral, NSW; b. Epping, NSW, 10 Jun 1922. Author of *Road in the Wilderness* (1952), a book about experiences in the Bougainville operations, and other works.

[5] Lt G. W. Leviston, VX50489. 2/3 Indep Coy, 2/3 Cdo Sqn. Fibrous plasterer; of Ballarat, Vic; b. Enfield, Vic, 18 Dec 1915.

[6] Lt H. L. Egan, VX59445; 2/3 Indep Coy. Radio engineer; of Moonee Ponds, Vic; b. Melbourne, 8 Sep 1918. Killed in action 21 Jul 1943.

troops must conform to a wider plan governing the whole area. Premature commitments in the Salamaua area could not be backed at present by an adequate force."

On 5th May Major Smith[7] of the 2/6th Battalion was appointed to command the 24th which had its first action the same day. A four-man patrol led by Corporal Gray[8] crossed Deep Creek, a slow-moving stream 40 feet wide, along an 18-inch wide log. The route was then over hilly country, and down a spur to the Markham. Following the river to the east the patrol came to a small clearing. Gray crossed it safely but as a second man crossed the enemy fired from a spur on the right and wounded him—the 24th Battalion's first blood. The remainder of the patrol covered the two men's withdrawal. This was the first of many patrols by the 24th Battalion towards Markham Point—a timbered spur descending from the Hertzog Mountains through the swampy river flats to overlook the Markham River.

Away on the right flank of this tangled and heart-breaking battlefront, Lieutenant Troon's[9] platoon of the 2/7th Battalion and Lieutenant R. Watson of Angau were patrolling on 3rd May towards the coast from Napier. In an old native garden east of Napier they met two natives—the doctor boy and tultul[1] from Duali. Watson learnt from them that the Japanese were now occupying the shores of Nassau Bay to Cape Dinga and were in strength on both sides of the Bitoi overflow near its mouth. The Japanese were short of food and were supplied by pinnace from Salamaua. After learning that 20 Duali and Salus natives had left for Salamaua via Lokanu to carry cargo for the Japanese from Salamaua to Mubo, and Japanese wounded from Mubo to Salamaua, Watson sent the tultul to bring the natives to him. When they arrived Watson proposed to the luluai a plan of evacuation protected by an Australian patrol. The natives agreed and the withdrawal of the people of the two villages was completed without incident on 5th May; 105 natives who might otherwise have assisted the Japanese were quartered in the Guadagasal area. This was typical of the valuable work of Angau. In this case, besides playing a humanitarian role, Watson had gathered the first definite information, admittedly second-hand, of enemy movements and dispositions in the swampy malarial lands round the Bitoi's mouths and along the coast.

The stalemate in the Mubo area caused General Mackay on 6th May to send General Savige a letter in which he stated that, without altering the role of the division as set out on 20th April, the situation required further examination. The Australian force was small for the large area in which it was operating; it was difficult to supply even this force, entailing as it did a four-day carry for native parties or precarious air dropping; and the problem of reinforcement depended on the availability

---
[7] Lt-Col G. F. Smith, DSO, ED, VX185. 2/6 Bn 1939-43; CO 24 Bn 1943-44; Comd AIF Reception Camp UK 1944-45. Bank officer; of Colac, Vic; b. Nhill, Vic, 20 Apr 1905.
[8] Cpl H. D. Gray, VX109116; 24 Bn. Faller; of Healesville, Vic; b. Beulah, Vic, 26 Jun 1920. Killed in action 4 Sep 1943.
[9] Capt J. Troon, VX18511; 2/7 Bn. Clerk; of Ascot Vale, Vic; b. Stawell, Vic, 9 Apr 1914.
[1] The luluai and tultul are administration appointments of head man of a village and his assistant. The role of a tultul is principally that of interpreter.

of transport and fighter planes, the weather, and the condition of the landing strips. "Japanese forces in and around Green Hill, Duali, villages to south of Duali, Komiatum and other places seem to be tenacious and stout fighters," wrote Mackay, "and . . . appear to hold their own with our troops." He added that the Australians seemed to have no advantage at present in the forward Mubo area in number and use of light machine-guns, medium machine-guns, mortars and small arms, although they possibly had a slight advantage in the presence of a section of 3.7-inch howitzers and a distinct advantage in aircraft. This, however, was offset by the fact that targets such as infantry posts were very difficult to find and hit in the exceedingly rough country. "Unless our attacks, raids and skirmishes are properly organised, supported by fire superior to that of the enemy, and fully driven home in a determined manner, they fulfil no useful military purpose," he added. "Unsuccessful attempts against the enemy tend to lower our own morale and raise his." Mackay then directed that patrolling should continue forward of the Guadagasal-Waipali area, but positions in strength forward of this line neither could nor should be maintained; small enemy parties should be harassed and destroyed.

After receiving Mackay's letter Savige called for an appreciation of the situation in the Pimple area by Guinn. On 7th May Guinn reported that the enemy's strength in the Mubo area was approximately one battalion with one company in the Green Hill-Pimple area, part of a company on Observation Hill and the remainder in the Kitchen Creek area and north along the Buigap. The enemy had established himself on commanding ground with well-dug and concealed ambushes on the main approaches and a strongly-defended position on the Pimple, and had lightly cleared fire lanes to enable his machine-guns to prevent rush tactics and the use of grenades by the Australians. Guinn pointed out that the Jap Track was the only feasible approach to the Pimple as Laws' Track was a very rough bush track cut by patrols. He proposed a company attack supported by aircraft and artillery; in other words, the same sort of attack which had failed twice before.

The outline plan was again based on the classical approach by two platoons forward and one platoon in reserve. On the morning of the 7th bombing and strafing straddled the Pimple east and west—a useless procedure as hits not directly on the target did little damage—and then one mountain gun shelled the Pimple to cover the movement of Captain Tatterson's company to an attacking position. Forty yards from the enemy position in dense jungle the right flank platoon was held up by sniper fire. A section sent to neutralise this opposition was confronted by precipitous slopes with enemy fire positions overlooking the only line of approach, and was pinned down, as were the remaining two sections. The left platoon was held up by enfilade fire 35 yards from the enemy position. Tatterson then sent the third platoon in a wide encircling move to the left, but the Japanese pinned it down by enfilade fire 30 yards from its objective. To complete the mortification and discomfiture of the company heavy rain began at 2.30 p.m. and developed into a tropical downpour. The position was hopeless and the men were withdrawn after dusk.

"The Pimple is now a Carbuncle", ruefully signalled Guinn to Moten. The 2/7th Battalion had lost 12 killed and 25 wounded in attacks on the Pimple. It was indeed strange that these pointless attacks should continue, despite the views held and orders given by force, division and brigade commanders.

The unsatisfactory state of affairs in the Mubo area was exacerbated by the rate of medical evacuations, about 70 a day, largely with dysentery and malaria; this called for rigid anti-malarial precautions and hygiene measures. It was also reflected in a message from Moten on 8th May: "Essential that your patrols be imbued with a determination to find the enemy and then keep him under constant observation." Moten suggested that patrols should continue until the enemy was contacted, after which standing patrols of three to four men should be left in the area to maintain observation. Ten minutes later, Guinn, ever-mindful of his battalion's honour, replied "patrols fully realise responsibilities".

At 8.15 a.m. on 9th May a booby-trap suddenly exploded in front of the defensive perimeter of Tatterson's company, 400 yards south of the Pimple on the Jap Track. A reconnaissance patrol investigated while the company stood to. It was 15 minutes before movement was noticed and another 15 before the enemy opened up on the company's right flank. At first Tatterson thought that the shooting came from a Japanese patrol, but as it increased he realised that this was a strong attack; the enemy made no attempt to conceal his movements and seemed to be feeling for weak spots. Most of his fire was inaccurate and struck the trees up to 12 feet from the ground.

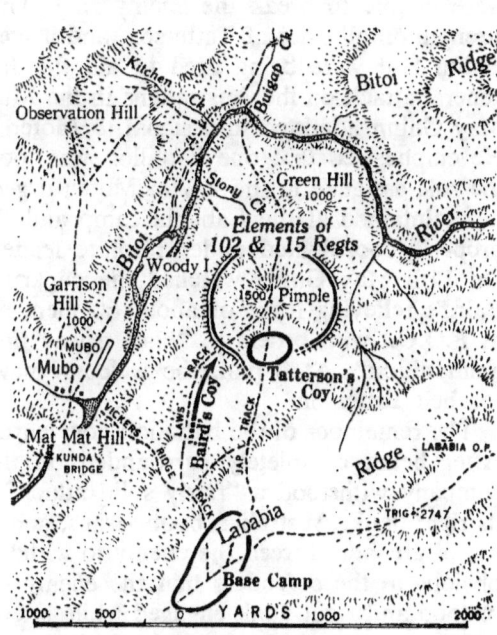

Encirclement of Tatterson's company, 2/7th Battalion, 9th-11th May

Guinn and his runner, carrying 1,000 rounds of 9-mm ammunition forward, arrived at Tatterson's rear platoon. Realising that the Japanese were trying to encircle the company Guinn rang Tatterson and instructed him to send a small force back along the track to keep it open. Japanese progress was slow and steady. While

Guinn was talking to Tatterson by telephone at 3.30 p.m. the enemy cut the track and severed the telephone lines to the rear.[2] As a result a platoon under Sergeant Hubble[3] was sent forward to assist the encircled company and occupy a defensive position in its rear, thus bridging the dangerous gap. However, an enemy force astride Tatterson's line of communication pinned down Hubble's patrol. Lieutenant Newton's[4] platoon was sent out to extricate Hubble. Major M. P. O'Hare's 1st Mountain Battery then shelled the Pimple area which was as near as the guns dared shoot because the forward company had been close to the Pimple and might have moved since losing communication. The battalion's medical officer, Captain Peterson,[5] who had been with Tatterson, was retiring up the track towards the Lababia camp when he was fired on and forced to return to the embattled company.

As speedily as possible all available troops concentrated in the Lababia camp area. That night Guinn signalled Moten that he was confident of restoring the position in the morning. Next morning, however, two fighting patrols sent out by Captain Baird, who was in charge at the Lababia camp, were unable to break the enemy ring. The Japanese appeared to be in strength on all sides of Tatterson, and it seemed that the enemy on Observation Hill were being used to aid the Japanese from the Pimple in a general attack on the Australians in the Mubo area. At 8.15 p.m. on 10th May Guinn admitted in a signal to Moten that the situation was "grim". He emphasised that one battalion was too small to carry out effectively the role assigned to the 2/7th. Moten urged that a strong position should be maintained at the Lababia camp and that relieving parties should be properly coordinated under resolute leaders with good communications. On 11th May Guinn watched the departure from the track junction of Baird's relieving force of about 60 men, accompanied by Major O'Hare as F.O.O., with orders to "blast a way through even if it takes all your ammunition". At 2 p.m. the welcome news was received that they had reached Tatterson.

The remainder of the battalion now learnt the story of the gallant stand. After being completely surrounded on the afternoon of 9th May the company withstood a "fairly solid attack" (as Tatterson called it) from its right flank. Australian booby-traps, good fire control, and the judicious use of grenades forced the enemy to withdraw with casualties. It was now obvious to the defenders that the enemy plan was to keep their forward platoon and right flank engaged while attempting to crush the Australians with a stronger force from the high ground to the right rear. By 4.50 p.m. the Japanese had set up two medium machine-guns (known to the troops as "Woodpeckers") in this area. At dusk the forward platoon laid

---

[2] In addition to the company telephone wire along the track the mountain battery's FOO, Lieutenant R. D. W. Caterson (of Liverpool, NSW) had a duplicate line to his headquarters. Thereafter Caterson and his team of technicians fought as infantry during the siege.

[3] Sgt C. E. Hubble, WX13342. 2/28 and 2/7 Bns. Compositor; of Bridgetown, WA; b. York, WA, 22 Jun 1907.

[4] Lt T. E. Newton, VX12682; 2/7 Bn. Farmer; of Narre Warren North, Vic; b. Wangaratta, Vic, 13 Mar 1914.

[5] Capt B. H. Peterson, MC, NX77377; RMO 2/7 Bn. Medical practitioner; of Strathfield, NSW; b. Greenwich, NSW, 21 Sep 1918.

telephone lines to company headquarters. "This proved to be a great help," wrote Tatterson in his report, "as movement especially to the forward platoon in daylight was not healthy." Next morning the enemy fired machine-guns and mortar-type grenades, but most of the machine-gun fire was more than head high and many of the grenades failed to explode because they struck trees, forcing the ignitor set out of alignment and causing the firing pin to jam. During the morning an attack from the rear was beaten off. In the afternoon of the 10th the enemy made his most determined attack, again from the rear. Using all his weapons and increasing the din by loud orders, yelling and screaming, he poured in heavy fire for an hour and a half. Only his riflemen got in close and the entrenched defenders drove them back. The next attack, later in the day, was beaten off by steady and accurate fire on a slightly smaller scale from the same position. No more fighting occurred until, at 7 a.m. on 11th May, the Japanese fired heavily into a section area on the right flank, but made no attempt to follow on. Just before this five mortar bombs had been fired by the enemy to the east and west and into the centre of the Australian position. These may have been a signal for withdrawal, while the firing on the right flank section may have been used to cover the withdrawal.

The relieving force found the men in the best of spirits and full of fight. There was great jubilation in the battalion and elsewhere. Tatterson, slightly wounded, had carried on throughout the defence and inspired his men to remain steadfast. A typical example of the resolute courage of the surrounded troops was supplied by Private Waters,[6] a Number 1 Bren gunner. His position had been subjected to some of the fiercest enemy fire during the action. On the afternoon of 9th May three enemy machine-gunners engaged in a shooting match with the Australian Bren gunner and, in spite of damage to themselves, they managed to shoot away one of the Bren's bipod legs and the sights, but this did not prevent Waters from continuing to inflict casualties until on the morning of 10th May enemy fire damaged his flash eliminator and wounded him in the arm, forcing him to hand over to his Number 2. Another Number 1 Bren gunner from the same platoon, Private Bowen,[7] during the morning of the 9th, kept firing his Bren from an almost untenable position after his Number 2 had been wounded. Two enemy light machine-guns tried to silence Bowen and his Bren, but this determined infantryman killed both enemy machine-gun crews instead. Even the cook, Private Tyrer,[8] from his cookhouse weapon-pit shot a Japanese who thrust aside a bush and peered at him. Guinn reported that a conservative estimate of Japanese casualties was 100, including 50 killed. Australian casualties were about 12.

Guinn now reorganised his forward positions. Tatterson's company was to occupy a position in depth on the Jap Track, while Baird's, with

---
[6] Pte L. J. Waters, MM, NX142762; 2/7 Bn. Gardener; of Hornsby, NSW; b. Wyong, NSW, 6 May 1920.
[7] WO2 L. Bowen, MM, QX27980; 2/7 Bn. Stove moulder; of West End, Qld; b. Melbourne, 9 Nov 1920.
[8] Pte W. A. Tyrer, VX30611; 2/7 Bn. Assistant foreman; of Northcote, Vic; b. Liverpool, England, 12 Jul 1903.

an additional platoon, was to occupy the track junction and Lababia camp area. The two-company defensive position was planned by Guinn in the light of all the lessons learned. Cleared fields of fire were developed, trees of all sizes being felled; section positions were sited and given mutual fire support, and were fully dug with connecting crawl trenches. Artillery defensive fire plans were coordinated with O'Hare.

The wounded were still coming out along the Lababia Track. Corporal Allen[9] of Angau had been of great assistance during the operations, controlling native stretcher bearers and carriers with a coolness which maintained order among the natives.

When the Australians had been halted at Mubo after their advance from Wau the Japanese commander, Major-General Okabe, thought that his Australian opponent had reached the end of his tether and was unable to keep his troops adequately supplied. He therefore determined to build up his forces until he thought that the time was ripe to deliver a counter-attack with the object of regaining the initiative and perhaps having another crack at Wau. In late April and early May Okabe moved more troops and supplies up the Komiatum Track towards Mubo to prepare for an attack which was launched on 9th May by troops from *I* and *II Battalions* of the *102nd Regiment* and parts of the *115th Regiment* against Tatterson's company; 440 men from the *102nd Regiment's* total of 1,070 were available for the attack. General Nakano in an address stated: "In the fighting near Mubo, *7 Company* of the *102nd Infantry* and a part of *8 Company* of the *115th Infantry* penetrated the enemy's positions, but the others did not rush in after them, and in spite of the great success *3 Company* of *115th Infantry* was having in breaking up enemy reinforcements, the others lacked the spirit to take advantage of this, and as a result there was no great victory to celebrate."

Tatterson's defence raised the spirits of the 2/7th Battalion, but the lack of success in operations round the Pimple was discouraging to the troops and worrying to the leaders. The failure caused a natural shuffling of responsibility between division, brigade and battalion commanders, none of whom at this stage fully understood the difficulty of attacking Japanese in entrenched positions concealed by the jungle. Irritation was evident when Savige urged Moten to move his headquarters forward from Wau to a position where he could be more thoroughly in the picture. Savige stated that the recent repeated attacks on the Pimple indicated that his instruction was either not understood or that Moten was not complying with it. "It is obvious," he wrote, "that any aggressive action by patrols decided on should be directed towards the 'soft spots' rather than against a position which is known to be strongly defended such as the Pimple." Moten, as already indicated, agreed with this principle. When Savige signalled him asking him where his headquarters would be to control his forward operations, Moten replied, "Wau". Such relations could not continue. Moten went to Savige's headquarters at Bulolo where the two officers had a frank but friendly discussion. Savige made it clear that Moten was no longer responsible for the defence of the Wau Valley itself but only had to prevent enemy entry into the valley from Mubo, as stated in Savige's order of 25th April. Moten moved his headquarters forward

---

[9] Sgt W. Allen, NG2325. NGVR and Angau. Sawyer; of Wau, TNG; b. Rabaul, TNG, 24 Sep 1912.

to Skindewai. Differences of temperament did not prevent the two men from working thereafter in harmony and mutual confidence.

On 12th May Moten made his plan based on his belief that the Japanese (who, he thought, numbered 700-800 in Mubo-Komiatum, 500 round Nassau Bay and 1,500-1,800 in Salamaua) would probably maintain a defensive role round Salamaua and Mubo. He decided that he would continue to use one infantry battalion forward while one company would secure control of the coastal area south of the Bitoi to Nassau Bay by raids. The other battalions would be retained in reserve.

Both Savige and Moten were concerned about the right or southern flank. There were persistent reports of enemy activity in the Duali-Nassau Bay area but, so far, patrols from the 2/5th and 2/7th Battalions had been unable to provide any real information except that the area was very swampy. At this time Moten did not contemplate any operations at Nassau Bay but he wanted to check on enemy movement and maintain control south of the Bitoi River. He therefore chose from the 2/6th Battalion a company which had gained skill in reconnaissance while patrolling the Markham area from January until April, and ordered its commander, Captain W. R. Dexter, to establish a patrol at Napier. On 12th May the company came under command of Guinn who received permission to station one of its platoons at Napier and use the other two to strengthen his carefully-dug positions in the Lababia area where Tatterson's company was relieved by Captain Barr's from Mat Mat.

Major Takamura, the Japanese commander of *III/102nd Battalion* in the Nassau Bay area, was equally concerned at the lack of any real information about the Australians in the Napier and Lababia areas. To coincide with the main attack on 9th May, he was ordered to "capture the high area on the right bank of the Buyawim River fork" on the same day. The battalion left early on the 9th to "advance to the neighbourhood of the native village 5 kilometres west of the Bitoi River mouth, and reconnoitre the enemy's situation and terrain in front". By 1 p.m. Takamura reached the village, but was worried about rumours of Australian movement ahead. "It seems," he said, "that a small enemy force is advancing." He again ordered his battalion to "reconnoitre the enemy's situation and terrain in front of them", but "early tomorrow morning" would do. The next morning he was undecided. "Putting together various information," he wrote, "it seems there is evidence that some of the enemy have sneaked to the area east of the fork at the mouth of the Bitoi." He now decided that it would be better to "hold firmly the important points on the right bank of the Bitoi mouth".

Takamura's battalion had been turned back by rumours of the small Australian patrol which was daily moving along the track from Napier. It was extraordinary that the Australians and Japanese did not meet along the track in this period. Australian positions in the Lababia area might well have been endangered had *III/102nd Battalion* been urged forward by a more resolute commander. By 19th May Takamura recorded that his battalion's role would be "to continue its present mission as Nassau Bay guard". He now had fresh anxieties for "on the sea at our guard sector before dawn on 16th May two boats like armoured M.L.C. entered Nassau Bay and reconnoitred an area some 100 metres off shore". Again on the 17th and 18th a craft of the same type was seen off shore.

Major Warfe, meanwhile, had been tempted to make an all-out assault on north Bobdubi Ridge, but his orders were to avoid casualties, and indeed, the diversion of native carriers to man stretchers would have placed an impossible strain on his already-stretched supply line. He was content, therefore, to keep the enemy under constant pressure by harassing fire from Vickers, Brens and 2-inch mortars, and occasionally to carry out grenade and sub-machine-gun raids. On the night of 9th-10th May Lieutenant Egan carried out a "terror" raid on the enemy, using flares, screaming and yells. On 11th May the enemy seemed unnaturally quiet and a patrol found the entire Coconuts vacated. It was promptly occupied. The 2/3rd Independent Company now held Bobdubi Ridge, if extremely lightly, from the Coconuts in the north to Namling in the south. Determined to make the most of the situation Warfe turned his attention to the Komiatum Track. Late on 11th May parties of Japanese were observed moving south towards Mubo. Lieutenant Erskine's Vickers gun accounted for five of them. The enemy was better prepared this time, however, and retaliated with heavy machine-gun fire from Komiatum Ridge. Warfe promptly moved the sappers under cover of darkness to a new position near Gwaibolom. Next morning, when they opened fire on 80 Japanese moving south along the Komiatum Track, the enemy retaliated with a mountain gun. A new weapon in the experience of the 2/3rd, its distinctive sound effects were a little disconcerting. The sappers duly reciprocated with their Vickers. Eventually these broadsides across the ravine between Komiatum Ridge and Bobdubi Ridge subsided—in both cases probably for lack of ammunition.

The men of the Independent Company now thoroughly appreciated their Vickers medium machine-guns, which were not on the establishment of an Independent Company but which they had acquired in New Caledonia. Warfe had four of them in action—one at North Coconuts, one at Old Vickers, one at Gwaibolom and one at Graveyard;[1] the two latter, about 1,200 and 2,000 yards away respectively, dominated Komiatum Ridge. As the enemy seemed to have two mountain guns, a heavy mortar and two medium machine-guns against the Independent Company Warfe brought forward two more Vickers and arranged to have a 3-inch mortar and ammunition dropped from aircraft.

From 3rd till 12th May the company had performed outstanding work. It became obvious, however, that the Japanese, at grips with the main Australian force in the Mubo area, could not tolerate such an impudent threat to their flank. Lieutenant S. G. Jeffery's section east of Bobdubi Ridge astride the Missim-Salamaua track repulsed sharp Japanese attacks on the 12th and 13th. At 9 a.m. on 14th May, the Japanese, roused in the extreme, sent a reconnaissance plane over Bobdubi Ridge, and at 12.15 p.m. began heavy shelling and mortaring of the Independent Company's positions on the ridge. The counter-attack was on in earnest when, at 12.20, the Japanese, advancing along the Salamaua-Bobdubi track, ran into Jeffery's booby-traps. The section engaged the enemy, numbering between 100 and 200, but overwhelming odds forced the Australians to withdraw step by step to South Coconuts.

---

[1] So called because some curious circles of stones and canna lilies growing suggested a cemetery.

(Australian War Memorial)

During the Salamaua operations troops in the forward areas were largely dependent on air droppings for food and ammunition. Here a "biscuit bomber" is shown dropping supplies to the Australians at Goodview, 600 yards from the Japanese lines, on 1st August 1943.

(Australian War Memorial)

Natives gathering supplies at the Goodview dropping ground.

(R.A.A.F.
Looking eastward towards Salamaua from the junction of the Dulam and Francisco Rivers.

Between 12.45 and 4 p.m. the length of Bobdubi Ridge was heavily engaged by an 8-inch gun, sited east of Kela Hill and known to the troops as "Kela Kitty", and mortars near the junction of the Salamaua-Bobdubi-Komiatum tracks. By 4 p.m. fighting was taking place at numerous points from the north foot of Bobdubi Ridge to Gwaibolom, a distance of 2,300 yards. The remainder of the Japanese force, estimated at one battalion, fanned out after passing the track junction. At 3.30 p.m. Lieutenant Stephens' section was ordered to try to outflank the enemy's left flank, while a section under Sergeant Carr was ordered to attack the enemy's right. Before this movement began Captain Meares' headquarters on Old Vickers was overrun by about 200 Japanese advancing from a southerly direction and withdrew to the flat ground south of New Bobdubi, covering approaches from the south. Carr's attempt to move downstream along the Francisco River and turn the enemy's right flank was frustrated when he encountered a large enemy force which caused him to withdraw and secure the track at the foot of the north end of Bobdubi Ridge. Stephens was withdrawn to Warfe's headquarters at New Bobdubi to guard the kunda bridge and cover any withdrawal.

When it became apparent that the Japanese were moving north down the ridge from Old Vickers and would probably then attack towards the kunda bridge, Warfe decided that retention of his positions would cause heavy casualties, and that he would probably have to withdraw his five attacking sections across the bridge, knowing that his third platoon around Namling and Wells O.P. remained in a good position to harass the enemy's supply route to the south. At 5 p.m. he ordered the withdrawal of all valuable stores from the Bobdubi area west across the kunda bridge.

As the Australians would have to fight until dusk to get their stores across the Francisco, Captain Hancock, at 5.30 p.m., led sections commanded by Lieutenants Leviston and Allen[2] into a counter-attack from north to south up Bobdubi Ridge. Meeting severe small arms fire at close range and heavy mortar fire from the south, the sections were unable to move forward and Hancock held them at Centre Coconuts with the other two sections (Lieutenants Jeffery and Barry[3]) now concentrated there. This force held its ground until nightfall, and suffered casualties. Enemy pressure was severe and the position could only have been held longer at serious cost. Warfe therefore ordered the withdrawal of the company to the kunda bridge area. By 8.30 p.m. all sections and valuable stores had been extricated.

A feature of the fighting had been the comparison between the enemy's inaccurate small arms and artillery fire and his very accurate mortar fire. Warfe estimated the Japanese casualties at 72 against 3 Australians killed and 8 wounded. It was disappointing that the forces available and the difficulties of supply had prevented further advantage being taken of the

---

[2] Capt P. H. Allen, VX34170. 2/3 Indep Coy, 2/3 Cdo Sqn. Clerk; of Melbourne; b. Clifton Hill, Vic, 8 Sep 1914.

[3] Lt E. J. Barry, WX12436; 2/3 Indep Coy. Fibrous plasterer; of Mount Lawley, WA; b. Perth, 2 Sep 1915. Killed in action 17 Aug 1943.

daring capture of Bobdubi Ridge, particularly as the next attempt to capture the ridge would undoubtedly meet far stiffer opposition.

Late that night Warfe again received instructions from Savige to avoid casualties. If necessary the company might be withdrawn to a firm position. Savige warned that an unknown number of aircraft had landed at Lae during the afternoon of 14th May and might be used against the company next day. At the same time Savige asked New Guinea Force for an air strike on the aircraft at Lae on the night 14th-15th May or at first light on the 15th. At 6.30 a.m. on the 15th the Independent Company, except for the platoon at Namling, withdrew to Meares' Camp.

As anticipated, at 8.45 a.m. on 15th May, 20 Japanese dive bombers gave the Independent Company a grandstand view when they bombed and strafed the kunda bridge and Bobdubi village, causing neither damage nor casualties. An hour later 10 dive bombers and 20 fighters attacked the same area, and three dive bombers attacked Hote and killed three natives. At 3.30 p.m. to the great delight of the Australians 34 twin-engined bombers and 30 Zero fighters attacked in error Japanese positions from the mouth of the Francisco to Kela.

The 2/3rd Independent Company had indeed worried the enemy and had given them what Savige described as a "salutary lesson". Captured documents indicated the Japanese fear of guerilla attacks. The 2/3rd Independent Company was proving that a small, mobile, well-trained force was as necessary in jungle warfare as the battalions with their heavier equipment and hitting power. Its exploits and the fact that it was commanded by an officer from 17th Brigade were helping to raise the brigade's opinion of Independent Companies in general. Realisation of the fact that more compactness and mobility were necessary was evident on 9th May when Savige received a signal from New Guinea Force that General Blamey had approved the reorganisation of infantry battalions on a new tropical war establishment.[4]

All the Japanese commanders from Adachi himself to Nakano and Okabe considered it essential to recapture Bobdubi Ridge. When the Australians got their first real foothold on the ridge on 7th May about 40 men under Lieutenant Gunji of the *102nd Regiment* were opposing them. One Japanese diarist noted on 9th May that the "trend of battle situation is turning to worse". Reinforcements were sent to the Bobdubi area. By 10th May 70 naval men from Salamaua reached the area east of Bobdubi Ridge and 10 men from the ill-starred *115th Regiment*. Lieutenant Ogawa of the *115th* was then rushed forward with about 70 men from Markham Point and Captain Okura of the *102nd Regiment* led forward from Salamaua one infantry company, one infantry gun platoon and one machine-gun platoon to reinforce Bobdubi. Altogether about 400 men (330 infantry and 70 navy) were finally available to attack the Independent Company, which the Japanese estimated at 300-400 men. The whole attack was under the command of Lieut-Colonel Sekine with Ogawa commanding the northern flank and Okura the south; on 11th May the date for the attack was fixed for 14th May. That day the main Japanese body attacked from its left flank on to the higher southern slopes of Bobdubi Ridge while Ogawa at 8.30 a.m. led his company plus a platoon

---

[4] In effect this resulted in a reduction from 36 officers and 812 other ranks to 32 officers and 745 OR's.

on the right flank with orders to capture Coconut Ridge and advance towards the kunda bridge. The naval contingent held the front.

General Nakano was not particularly pleased with the efforts of his troops, and, in his "address of instruction" on 17th May, stated: "In the attack at Bobdubi, although a certain group was advancing on a height on the enemy's flank, instead of really carrying out the attack in such a way as to prepare the way for an assault by our main force, they went no further than a vain firing at the enemy with their weapons. The spiritual and physical strength which was worn down in the Wau campaign is at the present time still lower, but I believe it can easily be restored if the officers will take the initiative, set an example and command as leaders of their men."

The *51st Division* was reorganised into three groups as from 16th May: Salamaua Defence Force, Mubo Defence Force and Nassau Defence Force under Major Komaki, Lieut-Colonel Maruoka and Major Takamura respectively.

From 15th May the 17th Brigade concentrated more on aggressive patrolling in all sectors than on actual attacks. Strong patrols daily harassed the Pimple and the area north of the Pimple. On Observation Hill constant patrolling combined with intelligent siting of booby-traps almost paralysed movement by the Japanese outside their positions. By the time brigade headquarters opened at Skindewai on 17th May the enemy was getting little respite and was closely confined.

All was quiet on the Mubo front except for this patrolling, and by 18th May Major Dexter's company of the 2/6th was linked with Captain Barr's of the 2/7th on the Jap Track. Considerable boat activity near Lababia Island and Duali aroused interest among the newcomers in view of their role in that direction. On the same day Lieutenant Urquhart's[5] platoon established a standing patrol at Napier. During this change-over period booby-trap accidents increased in number and caused Guinn to signal all sub-units instructing them that there must be greater care and supervision.[6]

As with his southern flank Savige was also anxious about his northern flank in the Hote area. Therefore early in May a company (Captain Whitelaw's[7]) had been detached from the 24th Battalion and placed under divisional command. Two of its platoons were to guard the lines of communication between Powerhouse and Pilimung and the third (Lieutenant Looker's[8]) was to take over in the Cissembob-Bugasu area to provide left flank protection for the 2/3rd Independent Company. One section was detached from this platoon at Pilimung where it came under command of the Independent Company. On 17th May the platoon took

---

[5] Capt R. D. Urquhart, VX38096; 2/6 Bn. Commercial traveller; of Essendon, Vic; b. Moreland, Vic, 2 Oct 1915.

[6] Booby-traps were a double-edged weapon unless great care was taken with them. Several casualties were caused by lack of supervision. Sometimes traps were laid without a plan being made or were not collected before the troops responsible left the area; sometimes incoming units were not informed of booby-trap positions. The lethal effects of indiscriminate and irresponsible booby-trapping soon impressed themselves on the troops, and booby-trap discipline became rigid and efficient.

[7] Maj S. H. Whitelaw, VX104144; 24 Bn. Bank officer; of St Kilda, Vic; b. Bendigo, Vic, 17 Oct 1905.

[8] Lt L. W. A. Looker, MC, VX41023; 24 Bn. Timber sawyer; of Ballarat, Vic; b. Dunkeld, Vic, 18 Jun 1916.

over a position established by a section of the Independent Company at Cissembob. A Vickers machine-gun crew with their gun remained under Looker's command. From this post the whole track along the ridge to Hote, 1,000 yards away, could be observed.

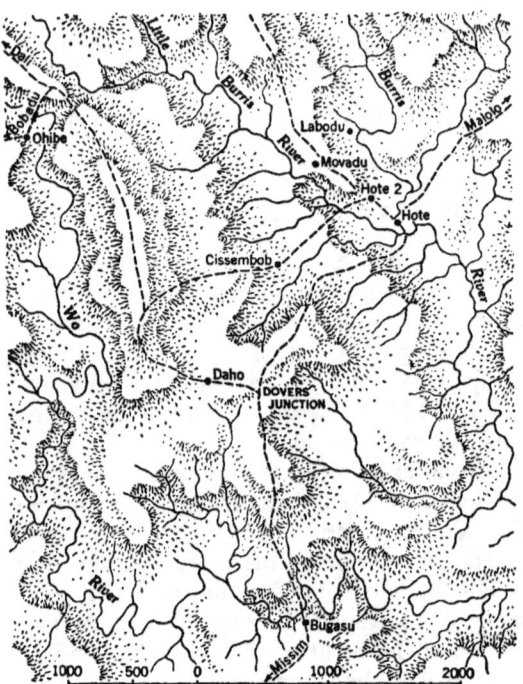

There had previously been no contact here, and for the first two days the platoon patrolled uneventfully to the east. Early on the 19th, however, a patrol was ambushed when moving up a steep kunai-covered ridge about 500 yards beyond Hote along the track to Malolo. When the patrol returned about 10.30 a.m. and reported one man missing, Looker immediately led another patrol to the scene of the ambush where he found the missing man unscathed. Looker returned to Cissembob at 4.30 p.m. and soon afterwards counted 170 Japanese moving into Hote from the east.

Before dark the enemy could be seen moving around in Hote and preparing a meal. That night the Australians in Cissembob, keyed for what they knew would be their first action, spent an eerie, sleepless night. Fifty yards forward along the Hote Track Looker set a booby-trap consisting of a grenade in a jam tin attached to a string across the track. At 3.30 a.m. on the 20th a runner arrived from Missim with orders from Warfe to send two men with a Bren to cover Dovers' Junction. Looker also sent three men to cover a track leading from Daho about 900 yards along the same ridge as Cissembob. To defend Cissembob against 170 Japanese he now had 24 men. The core of his defence was the experienced Vickers gun team which was guarding the main Hote Track. Looker and an Owen gunner were with the machine-gunners, and two depleted sections watched the flank.

The booby-trap exploded at 5.30 a.m. About 10 minutes later, when light was dawning, Japanese could be seen creeping up the main track about 700 yards away. The Vickers gunners and riflemen opened up on them and swept them from the track, the Vickers knocking out three Japanese machine-guns. "Things were pretty lively for a while and we fired on all movement," reported two of the gunners, Privates Crossley[9] and May,[1] after the action. It was not long before the Japanese pinpointed the Vickers, and, after working out its arc of fire, they rapidly moved large forces with machine-guns to the right and left flanks and kept another force maintaining pressure along the track. The Vickers, however, continued to inflict casualties and, among the riflemen who were in a position to shoot, Private Gibson[2] killed three Japanese and George, a native, two.

At 9 a.m. Looker and Private Hetherington[3] of the Vickers crew were observing through a telescope with Private Greene[4] of the 24th Battalion on the left, when an enemy machine-gun opened up from a distance of 25 yards and wounded Hetherington and Greene. "We think he must have got through early in the piece," reported the other Vickers gunner. Looker immediately silenced the Japanese gun with a grenade, remarking to Greene as he did so, "That cleaned out the bastards, Danny."

By 1 p.m., when the position was becoming desperate, the Japanese were seen moving up a razor-back to the left and were occupying ground overlooking Cissembob. Threatened with encirclement, Looker heeded the general instructions to avoid being committed to heavy action if casualties were likely. He therefore ordered a withdrawal and instructed the gun crew to render the gun useless. Crossley and May removed the lock, slides and firing pin, and then withdrew with the men of the 24th Battalion. The gunners had fired over 6,000 rounds and were estimated by Looker to have killed at least 30, his own men killing another 20. Once the withdrawal began, some of the men moved off so quickly that the four men carrying the unconscious Hetherington on a stretcher found themselves left behind except for a small rearguard, including Looker, and the Vickers and Bren gunners. Progress was slow and the carriers exhausted as they struggled on towards Ohibe. "During this running fight," reported Looker, "all men were under very heavy fire, but once again it was brought out what rotten shots the Japanese were. Not one of our boys were hit, and believe me things were hot."

About 500 yards along the exposed track the enemy began firing heavily from Cissembob. When it seemed that they would pursue the Australians, and that no more men were available to carry the stretcher, Crossley and May took it down the side of the razor-back ridge into the concealment of the jungle 50 feet below. Looker was reluctant to leave the gunners, but decided that it would be best if they hid until dark when he would send back a carrying party from Ohibe. He did this, but in

---

[9] Tpr A. E. G. Crossley, VX39603. 2/1 AA Regt, 2/3 Indep Coy, 2/3 Cdo Sqn. Grazier; of Shepparton, Vic; b. Shepparton, 26 Dec 1907.
[1] Tpr H. F. C. May, NX78180. 2/3 Indep Coy, 2/3 Cdo Sqn. Metal worker; of Sydney; b. Sydney, 22 Dec 1921. Died 18 Oct 1956.
[2] Pte J. D. Gibson, VX139857; 24 Bn. Bank officer; of Glen Iris, Vic; b. North Brighton, Vic, 9 Aug 1917. Killed in action 26 Aug 1943.
[3] Pte O. T. Hetherington, MM, VX36692; 2/3 Indep Coy. Agent; of Wycheproof, Vic; b. Sea Lake, Vic, 18 Mar 1914. Died of wounds 30 May 1943.
[4] Pte D. M. Greene, VX138491; 24 Bn. Tobacco worker; of Dandenong, Vic; b. Ballarat, Vic, 20 Nov 1922.

the meantime Corporal Dovers[5] of the 2/3rd Independent Company, who was stationed with Looker's third section at Dovers' Junction, decided to investigate what all the firing was about. Along the track to Cissembob he met the watchful gunners, returned to his base, collected six men from the 24th Battalion and carried Hetherington out, reaching Ohibe at 5 a.m. on the 21st. This carry was typical of the many arduous and selfless journeys performed by devoted men, white or black, throughout the battlefields of New Guinea.

Warfe had already sent Stephens with his section from Bobadu to take command in the area. Patrols from the combined force found Cissembob deserted on the 22nd and Hote on the next day, when Looker promptly reoccupied it. Within five minutes of arriving there the Vickers was once again usable. Other stores which had been abandoned and were now recovered included seven days' rations, the wireless set and the telescope.

Early in May the Japanese estimated that there were 150 Australians in the Hote area. Nakano believed that he must guard this northern flank and on 11th May portion of Major Nishikawa's *III/115th Battalion* was warned to prepare for an attack.

The 20th May was a hectic day also for the divisional staff as they tried to plug the gaps caused by the Japanese advance to Hote. General Savige feared that the enemy might advance to Sunshine through Ohibe, Dali and Jari. Although supply difficulties were considerable, he decided to send forward two platoons from the 24th Battalion—one along the track from Powerhouse to Pilimung and another from Sunshine via Jari and Dali to secure the tracks leading to Jari, Kwatomane and Yasingli. Both came under Warfe's command on 24th May. On 23rd May Savige decided to rest the Independent Company in preparation for future raids against the track to Mubo, and in order to lull the enemy on Bobdubi into a false sense of security. At 7 p.m. that day Warfe received a message ordering him to reorganise and rest his force "with a view to more active operations in future".

In the latter part of May Guinn was both driving and nursing his tired battalion. In a signal on patrolling issued to his companies on 23rd May he expressed his disappointment that "recent patrol reports in some cases have not been sufficient to plan future operations". One patrol which refuted this opinion was led to the Observation Hill area by Corporal Ericson[6] to cover Corporal Naismith[7] on a booby-trap expedition. Naismith had a reputation as a booby-trap expert and was keenly interested in his gadgets.[8] In the upper approaches to Kitchen Creek he

---

[5] Cpl R. Dovers, WX38115. 2/1 Survey Regt, 2/3 Indep Coy, 2/3 Cdo Sqn. Surveyor; of Wollongong, NSW; b. Wollongong, 6 May 1922.

[6] Sgt A. H. Ericson, VX14546; 2/7 Bn. Woodworker; of Fitzroy, Vic; b. Fitzroy, 12 Mar 1917.

[7] Sgt A. K. Naismith, DCM, VX4838; 2/7 Bn. Tobacco grower; of Gunbower, Vic; b. Bendigo, Vic, 10 Mar 1915.

[8] One of Naismith's most valuable inventions was a booby-trap which would only explode when walked into from the enemy side. A man who tripped over the wire when moving out from the Australian lines would not set the trap off.

found an enemy tent where he set five traps. Twenty-five more were set on all tracks leading into the area. At dawn the first of these was heard to explode and later a whole series of explosions was heard.

On the same day as Guinn issued his patrolling signal Savige decided to restore the 2/6th Battalion to Moten's command to relieve the 2/7th. The staff estimated that the relief would take 10 days as the track could maintain only two companies travelling at one time. The forward move of the 2/6th began on 27th May, the day on which 15th Brigade headquarters and the first company of the 58th/59th Battalion arrived in Wau. The arrival of the 15th Brigade had been delayed because of the shortage of aircraft and rations. It was an example of how the supply problem dictated the scope of operations.

Before the 2/6th moved into action again Colonel Wood informed the men in his standing orders what they were to wear and carry. These orders were based on a divisional instruction of 29th April and were the result of the pooling of ideas and experiences by the various units which had fought in the jungle against the Japanese. The term "tropical scale" meant to the troops that they wore their jungle green uniform (boots, socks, gaiters, underpants, trousers, shirt), also "hat fur felt" as the famous Australian hat[9] was officially known, clasp knife, identification discs, webbing equipment, field dressing in the right hip pocket and a tin of emergency rations in the left, water-bottle on the right-hand side, haversack on the left-hand side and pack. The haversack contained one tin of emergency rations, one field operation ration, one day's ordinary ration (usually bully beef and biscuits), mess gear, towel, anti-mosquito cream,[1] toilet gear including shaving gear, and six atebrin tablets. The pack held a spare pair of boots, two pairs of socks, one singlet, one shirt, one pair of underpants, one pair of trousers and a mosquito net. One blanket in a groundsheet was wrapped outside and over the top of the pack and a steel helmet was strapped on to the pack. Fifty rounds were carried by each rifleman, 100 rounds in magazines by each Tommy-gunner,[2] and 100 rounds in magazines for each Bren gun. Eighteen bombs of high explosive and six bombs of smoke were carried for the 2-inch mortar. Six No. 36 grenades with 7-seconds fuses were carried for the grenade discharger while all ranks carried one No. 36 grenade with a 4-seconds fuse (usually carried hooked on the webbing belt by the lever). Anti-tank rifles and Bren tripods were not carried unless ordered. Such

---

[9] General Mackay, who had seen much of the hat in two wars, condemned its use as unsuitable, especially in New Guinea. At a later date he wrote of the hat: "Enshrouded in sentiment by Australians ever since the South African war of 1899, it does not compare for comfort, serviceability and general usefulness, especially while sitting in vehicles or sleeping at night, with the soft, peaked cloth caps issued by the armies of France, Germany, United States and Japan."

[1] Later, the less messy mosquito repellent—a liquid with the consistency of water—was used.

[2] At this time a few Owen sub-machine-guns were sent forward from LHQ accompanied by a memorandum saying that they were to be tested in the forward areas. It was not considered by LHQ that the OSMG would be as popular as the TSMG. Deeming that the men were the best judges, Savige distributed the Owens among the forward sections. He was surprised when all sections testing the Owen preferred it to the Tommy-gun. The men's reasons were that the Owen was handier to use, it had fewer working parts and, above all, 130 rounds of 9-mm ammunition represented the same weight as 100 rounds of .45 ammunition for the Tommy-gun. Thus the Owen came into its own and rapidly superseded the Tommy.

were the possessions of the Australian soldier as he battled with the Japanese in the murky jungle and precipitous hills of the backbreaking areas round Mubo and Bobdubi.

The last important patrols of the 2/7th took place on 27th May, when Lieutenant Mackie[3] with fifteen men left at midday to reconnoitre the Pimple area. When approaching Tatterson's old position he heard a rattle of tins. A shot followed and Private Pincott[4] fell to the ground. The patrol moved off the track and Private Sanders,[5] while taking aim from behind a tree, was shot in the back by a Japanese who immediately ran back to his own troops after firing the shot. Mackie, trying to move forward, was shot in the shoulder seven yards from Sanders. A runner was then sent to Barr's company, and Lieutenant Fietz[6] with 10 men reinforced Mackie's position, but attempts to advance were frustrated by enemy fire. A Bren set up to draw the enemy fire was successful, but jungle echoes made it impossible to tell whence the fire came, even though it was estimated to be not more than 25 yards away. At this stage Pincott called out to his comrades to wait until dark before attempting rescue. Late in the afternoon the patrol saw a Japanese moving towards Pincott, who threw a grenade which killed the Japanese. After dark the patrol reached Pincott and Sanders but found them both dead. Other patrols from Barr's company into the Pimple area heard the usual Japanese sounds—talking, rattling tins, chopping—but no enemy was seen.

From the Lababia Ridge-Napier area two patrols from the company of the 2/6th Battalion already there departed for the east on 23rd May, after the bombing and strafing of Duali and Nassau Bay by six Bostons and six Beaufighters. The Duali patrol under Corporal McElgunn[7] returned two days later, having heard Japanese in the dense undergrowth leading to the Duali area. Sergeant Ellen[8] and Privates Arnott[9] and Shadbolt,[1] three very experienced scouts, comprised the other patrol which blazed a difficult route as far as the dry creek bed, then scrub-bashed east to the last ridge overlooking Bassis and looking across Nassau Bay. They found evidence of previous Japanese occupation of the ridge, and, in the distance, Japanese seemed to be camped on the shores of Nassau Bay.

In the north of Savige's divisional area the 24th Battalion—the first militia battalion to fight in the area—after a month was beginning to settle down. There was now no rushing to slit trenches when enemy aircraft flew overhead, nor was there any dearth of volunteers for patrols.

---

[3] Lt J. W. S. Mackie, NX105195; 2/7 Bn. Ice carter; of Weston, NSW; b. Scotland, 25 Nov 1916.

[4] Pte G. A. Pincott, VX36939; 2/7 Bn. Farmer; of Warragul, Vic; b. Drouin, Vic, 6 Dec 1918. Died of wounds 27 May 1943.

[5] Pte J. A. Sanders, VX34545; 2/7 Bn. Truck driver; of Chiltern, Vic; b. Chiltern, 18 Apr 1911. Killed in action 27 May 1943.

[6] Lt W. H. Fietz, MC, VX7125; 2/7 Bn. Labourer; of Albury, NSW; b. Peak Hill, NSW, 10 Aug 1918.

[7] Sgt J. T. McElgunn, MM, VX9016; 2/6 Bn. Labourer; of Warrnambool, Vic; b. Warrnambool, 13 Jul 1915.

[8] Sgt L. G. Ellen, MM, VX12571; 2/6 Bn. Mill hand; of Woori Yallock, Vic; b. Korumburra, Vic, 7 May 1916.

[9] Pte K. G. Arnott, VX2931; 2/6 Bn. Moulder; of Collingwood, Vic; b. Carlton, Vic, 18 Sep 1916. Killed in action 8 Jul 1945.

[1] Pte L. G. Shadbolt, MM, TX5382; 2/6 Bn. Salesman; of Ulverstone, Tas; b. Ulverstone, 30 Apr 1922.

Hidden physical disabilities, particularly of the older men, were soon found out by the mountains and swamps, and it became necessary to change three company commanders because of their physical condition. Major Smith was sure that a militia battalion could successfully take over the operational role of an A.I.F. unit provided it cut its teeth in a quiet area and he was determined that the 24th Battalion would be able to play its part.

Captain Peck's[2] company bore the brunt of the battalion's patrolling during May. As the company's front was 30 miles long by 10 miles deep, it was only possible for the troops to be spread thinly on the ground. One platoon was responsible for watching and patrolling along the Markham River between Mount Ngaroneno and Naragooma some 15 miles to the west; another covered an area of 10 miles from Ben to Markham Point, while the third remained at Wampit with company headquarters, changing fortnightly with forward platoons. By good discipline the incidence of malaria was being reduced. A second company during May occupied positions at Partep 2 dug by the 2/6th Battalion. The third company (Captain Kennedy's[3]) was sent to the Missim line of communication at the specific request of Savige who was worried about getting the 58th/59th Battalion over Double Mountain—one of the worst tracks in New Guinea. Savige depended on Kennedy to erect rest areas and provide hot meals at the end of each day's march.

The 24th Battalion was learning fast. One outstanding patrol under Corporal Bartley[4] reached the coast between Lae and Salamaua at the mouth of the Buang River. Bartley, accompanied by Privates Milne[5] and Hillbrick,[6] a native guide and a native carrier, left Partep 1 on 17th May to reconnoitre the mouth of the Buang River and the Sugarloaf area for signs of enemy activity and to glean information from natives. His five-day patrol was typical of many being carried out in the New Guinea battle areas by troops who needed the fitness of mountain goats, the endurance of bulldogs, and the courage of lions.

The patrol's route from Partep 1 through Mapos and Lega to the mouth of the Buang lay along an ill-defined and overgrown track, in parts boggy, in parts very rocky, and most of it infested with leeches. Dense jungle crowded in on all sides and obscured the sun overhead. The remainder of the patrol's experiences resembled those of other reconnaissance patrols—enemy footmarks; planes overhead, seen or heard, Allied or enemy; broken-down huts; no natives; patrol of 12 Japanese moving north along the beach track; torrential rain; jungle; foul track; excellent guide; patient carrier; an object out to sea which might have been a submarine but the patrol had no binoculars; fireless meals; mos-

---

[2] Capt D. V. Peck, VX88146; 24 Bn. Accountant; of East Kew, Vic; b. Melbourne, 29 Jul 1913.
[3] Maj E. M. Kennedy, VX104153; 24 Bn. Commercial traveller; of Surrey Hills, Vic; b. Flemington, Vic, 14 Jul 1908.
[4] Sgt G. T. Bartley, VX122364; 24 Bn. Packer; of Trafalgar, Vic; b. Traralgon, Vic, 7 Apr 1912.
[5] Cpl R. A. Milne, VX137828; 24 Bn. Textile worker; of Montrose, Vic; b. Richmond, Vic, 21 Mar 1919.
[6] Cpl R. G. Hillbrick, VX123361; 24 Bn. Dairyman and contractor; of Berwick, Vic; b. Melbourne, 16 May 1917.

quitoes; incessant damp. Bartley arrived at the river mouth on 19th May and left it soon after seeing a Japanese patrol, arriving back on the 21st. He concluded that there was little Japanese movement inland from the Buang mouth, that the enemy patrol was in all probability the Lae-Salamaua patrol which, according to the Angau representative at Mapos, Warrant-Officer Sherlock,[7] split at the mouth of the Bwussi River, one half moving inland to Bwussi village in search of food and one patrolling to the mouth of the Buang. He concluded his patrol report with a tribute to his guide Olum without whose knowledge of the area the patrol would have been unable to negotiate the country to the coast via the Buang. Similar tributes had been paid to many a Papuan or New Guinea guide during the campaigns. Patrols such as Bartley's found it difficult to send back messages about their progress. To overcome this lack Major Smith suggested to divisional headquarters that pigeons should be used, but three weeks were needed to orient pigeons and in that time the tactical situation might have changed.

Between the time Savige took command in the battle area and the end of May his headquarters estimated that the Japanese had suffered 380 casualties—323 killed and 57 wounded. The 3rd Division in that period had lost 20 killed and 58 wounded.

During April and May Japanese reinforcements had arrived in the Lae-Salamaua area to join the *102nd Regiment,* naval troops, and survivors of the Bismarck Sea convoy already there. About 1,000 troops of Colonel Katsutoshi Araki's *I/66th* and *II/66th Battalions* formed the bulk of the new arrivals. About 200 more men from the *115th Regiment* also arrived; 200 gunners from the *14th Artillery Regiment,* 150 sappers from the *51st Engineer Regiment,* and 200 others made up the total of 1,750. Thus, by the end of May, three regiments (*66th, 102nd* and the depleted *115th*) of the *51st Division* were available to oppose the 3rd Australian Division. Large convoys were now out of the question and about 400 of these troops had been landed at Lae by submarine, 40 being landed from each vessel at a time. Other troops from Rabaul were taken by barge or destroyer to Cape Gloucester whence they went in barges to Finschhafen. From Finschhafen some went by barge to Lae while others marched overland. By 23rd May General Nakano had ordered Araki to work out a plan for assembling supplies and ammunition in the Mubo area in preparation for another attack.

---

[7] Lt J. H. Sherlock, NX151481; Angau. Commercial traveller; of Kalgoorlie, WA; b. Subiaco, WA, 19 Jul 1917.

CHAPTER 3

DEFENCE OF LABABIA RIDGE

LATE in 1942 General Blamey had been contemplating action against Lae and Salamaua. After the victory at Oivi-Gorari, north of the Owen Stanley Range, he had hoped to reach Buna and Sanananda quickly, and had even arranged for supplies to be sent by ship to Oro Bay to enable him to make a quick attack on Salamaua and Lae. This hope had been disappointed, and it was not until late in January 1943 that the Japanese had been finally cleared from the Papuan beaches. The price of the Papuan victory was the exhaustion of four of the six brigades of the 6th and 7th Divisions. Experience had shown that the A.I.F. brigades must be the spearhead of the next offensive as their training and battle experience had made them by far the most efficient troops in the South-West Pacific. Until the 6th and 7th Divisions could be rehabilitated in Australia and until the returning 9th could be trained for jungle warfare the period was, of necessity, one of marking time and planning for an offensive.

The Japanese, after their defeats in Papua, at Wau, and in the Solomons, had also paused for regrouping and replanning in the South-West Pacific and South Pacific Areas. Blamey was sure that the Japanese were embarking in New Guinea on a long-range plan involving first, the establishment of a land route from Madang to Lae; secondly, the defeat of the Australians in the Wau-Salamaua area; and thirdly, a southward move against Port Moresby.

By the end of the Papuan campaign Blamey and his New Guinea Force commander, Lieut-General E. F. Herring, were emphasising the complementary nature of air and ground action in operations in New Guinea. "Each forward move of air bases," they wrote in their respective reports, "meant an increase in the range of our fighter planes and consequently an increase in the area in which transport planes supplying our troops could be operated. To get airfields further and further forward was thus the dominant aim of both land and air forces." Obviously the next suitable area for airfields was the valley of the Markham River whence the Vitiaz Strait, between New Guinea and New Britain, could be controlled. Gradually, ideas took a more definite form and resulted in an outline plan to capture Lae and the Markham Valley. Lae would provide a land base to which supplies could be transported by sea, while the Markham Valley was flat and would provide excellent areas for airfields particularly in the Nadzab area.

On 7th May General MacArthur had issued an instruction based on his orders from the Joint Chiefs of Staff in Washington, outlining the offensive which the forces of the South-West Pacific and South Pacific would carry out in 1943. As part of these operations New Guinea Force was given the task of seizing the Lae, Salamaua, Finschhafen and Madang areas. Provision was made for an operation in the Salamaua area to take place as a "feint" on 30th June when other operations were due to take place on Kiriwina and Woodlark Islands and on New Georgia in the Solomons. Further details of MacArthur's order will be given later.

General Herring had left New Guinea for leave late in January. On 10th May he returned to Brisbane and there conferred with staff officers of Blamey's Advanced Land Headquarters and with Rear-Admiral Daniel E. Barbey, the commander of the American Amphibious Forces. Blamey arrived in Brisbane on the 15th and next day he and Herring had a long conference with a model of the Salamaua and Lae areas before them. Blamey explained his plan, which provided for two phases; the first entailing the capture of Lae and the Markham Valley and its airfields, and the second exploitation round the coast to Finschhafen and Madang. To capture Lae a seaborne landing would be necessary. "This in turn," wrote Blamey in his report, "demanded the prior seizure of a shore base within 60 miles of Lae, this being the maximum range of the landing craft which would carry the troops by night to the assault. Nassau Bay was selected as the area most suited for the purpose since its capture would also enable a junction to be made with our forces operating at Mubo and consequently reduce the problem of maintenance of their supplies. I instructed G.O.C., New Guinea Force, to carry out a preliminary operation for the seizure of Nassau Bay and for its protection as a base to assist the larger operation. With this latter end in view he was directed to seize the high ground around Goodview Junction and Mount Tambu and the ridges running down therefrom to the sea. Beyond this, however, he was not to go."[1] As it seemed essential that Nassau Bay should be captured as soon as possible, Blamey intended that his "preliminary operation" should take the place of MacArthur's "feint". "We realised we had to do something more," wrote Herring later. "We had to capture Nassau Bay and hold it and this being so, we thought that quite conveniently it could be fitted into the operation that we had in mind for 3 Div."

In discussion with Herring Blamey pointed out that the preliminary operation to capture Nassau Bay would not only enable a junction to be made between the landing force and the Australians at Mubo, but would increase the threat to Salamaua and perhaps draw enemy reinforcements from Lae to Salamaua. This idea, so fundamental to the success of the offensive, was described by Blamey in his report:

> If the enemy's attention could be concentrated on the operations for the capture of Salamaua there was every chance that he would drain his strength from Lae by reinforcing his forces south of Salamaua and that any discovery of further preparation on our part might lead him to believe that we were preparing for heavier action against the latter area. Thus the operations round Salamaua might have a decisive part in the capture of Lae.[2]

Herring summed up the matter more picturesquely when he wrote later that Blamey "wanted the operation against Salamaua to serve as a cloak

---
[1] Commander Allied Land Forces, Report on New Guinea Operations 23 Jan 1943 to 13 Sep 1943.
[2] Report on New Guinea Operations 23 Jan 1943 to 13 Sep 1943.

for our operations against Lae, and to act as a magnet drawing reinforcements from Lae to that area".

Blamey's opponent in New Guinea, General Adachi, later stated that the object of the Japanese was to hold Salamaua in order to delay the advance of the Australians and Americans as long as possible. He considered Salamaua "a very strategic position" which was to be held at all costs and was to be defended to the last man. Adachi considered that, should Salamaua fall, Lae would definitely be lost as its security depended on the Salamaua defences. The strength of the Salamaua garrison was accordingly built up to about 5,000 troops with troops from Rabaul, New Ireland, Lae, and Wewak.

Blamey's instruction of 17th May was handed to Herring in Brisbane. It was addressed to Herring by name and the distribution list was very limited. Herring took this written instruction with him when he returned to Port Moresby on 22nd May. Next day he resumed command of New Guinea Force and General Mackay returned to the command of the Second Army in Australia. At this time Herring was the only Australian in New Guinea who knew the plan. He was now beginning his second period in command of the force in New Guinea, having commanded the I Corps and New Guinea Force in the later stages of the fighting in the Owen Stanleys and on the Buna coast until the end of January.

New Guinea Force at the end of May numbered 53,564 Australian soldiers and 37,200 Americans. In addition there were about 9,000 men of the R.A.A.F. and 19,100 of the American Army Air Force in New Guinea. The Australians estimated early in May that between 31,600 and 34,200 Japanese troops were deployed in Australian New Guinea with a further 38,000 in Dutch New Guinea and the Banda Sea islands. As mentioned earlier General Savige had a brigade headquarters with four battalions and an Independent Company in the battle area, and another brigade headquarters (the 15th) and another battalion—the 58th/59th —were moving in. Major-General Milford's 5th Australian Division (4th and 29th Brigades) garrisoned Milne Bay and Goodenough Island. The 41st American Division was in the Buna-Oro Bay area; and in Port Moresby Major-General Clowes' 11th Division included the 7th Brigade and the remaining battalion—the 57th/60th—of the 15th Brigade. New Guinea Force also controlled the Papuan Infantry Battalion in Port Moresby and Bena Force, far off in the Bena-Mount Hagen plateau.

In the actual Lae-Salamaua battle area the Intelligence staff of New Guinea Force estimated early in June that Japanese strength had grown to about 7,025. Of this total 1,500 were thought to be round Mubo, 400 in the Bobdubi area, 250 in the Duali-Nassau Bay area and the remainder in Lae and Salamaua. It was also estimated that the Japanese had 105 aircraft (50 bombers, 50 fighters and 5 float planes) on New Guinea airfields. General Kenney's Fifth Air Force deployed far more aircraft than that. In the whole South-West Pacific Area (in April) there were some 690 serviceable aircraft in the Australian squadrons and 770 in the American. In New Guinea were nine American and two Australian fighter squadrons; a third Australian fighter squadron arrived in June.

Three days before General Herring's return, General Savige had received a note from New Guinea Force stating that "our forces are to occupy Kiriwina and Woodlark Islands for the establishment of airfields thereon", and that New Guinea Force would cooperate in this operation. Savige was warned to be ready by 15th June to "threaten Salamaua by aggressive overland operation from the Wau-Bulolo valley and by threats along the coast from the Morobe area". This warning was based on MacArthur's instruction of early May, but it was ill-framed, for Savige then had no troops on the coast to advance from Morobe. An instruction to "threaten" Salamaua could be construed as giving the green light for an attack on Salamaua—an event which would strike at the very basis of the plot being hatched by Blamey. The note continued that New Guinea Force hoped to transport to Wau most of Savige's units still in Port Moresby (110 officers and 2,447 men) within 14 days. Based on the assumption that he would have two Australian brigades each of three battalions and at least one Independent Company, Savige jotted down his preliminary thoughts on this instruction and noted: "We must get clarification of the words 'threaten Salamaua'. It may mean 'secure' Salamaua or continue our present tactics on a bigger scale."

On 18th May New Guinea Force had ordered that Colonel Wilton be sent to Port Moresby to be given "special information" based presumably on the General Headquarters' order. At this time Wilton was absent in the Cissembob area and it was not till the 23rd May that he arrived at Port Moresby. Herring gave an outline of forthcoming operations to Wilton and to Colonel Kenneth S. Sweany, the chief staff officer of the 41st American Division at Morobe. On the 27th Wilton returned with a copy of an operation instruction[3] issued to the commanders of the 3rd Division, 41st American Division, Fifth Air Force, and American P.T. (Patrol Torpedo) Boats.

The object of the pending operations was "to bring about offensive overland action against Salamaua from the Wau-Bulolo area and along the coast from Morobe, without jeopardising the defence of our bases in New Guinea". Savige's task was defined as ultimately to drive the enemy north of the Francisco River by aggressive action as soon as practicable; and immediately to establish a beach-head at Nassau Bay in order to open a sea line of communications into the Mubo area and enable American forces to operate in conjunction with the Australians. The task of Major-General Horace H. Fuller, commanding the 41st Division, would include ensuring the security of New Guinea east of the Owen Stanleys from Oro Bay to Morobe, moving a battalion group to secure the Lasanga Island-Baden Bay area three days before D-day as a base for operations northwards along the coast, and arranging for the landing of the battalion group at Nassau Bay whence it would cooperate in driving the Japanese north of the Francisco.

---

[3] Generally an operation order was issued for such operations, but in circumstances when other Services were involved, or for some other special reason, commanders resorted to the use of the more diplomatic operation instruction. In this case the role of the air force and navy were defined by informing all concerned of their cooperation in the operations as directed by GHQ.

The Fifth Air Force, now gaining control in the air, would defend New Guinea bases against the enemy air force; carry troops and supplies and maintain them; prevent reinforcements or supplies reaching Salamaua by sea; reconnoitre and attack targets in the Lae-Salamaua-Sachen Bay area; and directly support the ground forces. The American P.T. group would attack enemy sea forces in the Huon Gulf in cooperation with the air force, protect the ground forces whilst seaborne and during movement along the coastal area from Oro Bay to Salamaua. All were warned to be ready by 15th June and it was plainly indicated that command of ground forces in the battle area would be exercised by Savige.

Mackay's warning order of 20th May was now cancelled by Herring's instruction of 27th May, but both served to make Savige all the surer that his objective was Salamaua. On 29th May he issued his own orders in which his intention was "to destroy the enemy forces in the Mubo area and ultimately to drive the enemy north of the Francisco River". He considered that the enemy forces in the Mubo area must first be destroyed in order that the line of communication from Nassau Bay to Mubo might be successfully opened. The operation for the capture of Mubo would take place in three phases. First, on the night before D-day, an American battalion group would land at Nassau Bay. Secondly, the newly-arriving 15th Australian Brigade would capture Bobdubi Ridge on D-day while small forces raided the Malolo and Kela Hill areas, north-west of Salamaua, to distract the enemy's attention from the Bobdubi attack. After the capture of Bobdubi Ridge this brigade would advance south to Komiatum and prevent the escape of the enemy northwards from Mubo. Thirdly, a battalion of the 17th Brigade and the American battalion group would attack the Japanese forces in the Mubo area—preferably not later than six days after the Bobdubi attack—and, after the capture of Mubo, would advance north towards Komiatum and north-east towards Lokanu. While these main operations were proceeding the 24th Battalion would harass Markham Point and provide a strong fighting patrol to move to the mouth of the Buang River and establish an ambush position on the coastal track one day before D-day to prevent enemy movement along this track in either direction.

The 17th Brigade was given the task of reconnoitring the shores of Nassau Bay to confirm whether any enemy defences existed and also to decide whether the beach was suitable for an unopposed landing. "It is essential," said Savige in his order, "that the movements of this recce party be not observed by the enemy." The 17th Brigade would also send a patrol along the south bank of the south arm of the Bitoi, and, three days before D-day, would establish a strong company patrol base as close as possible to the coast. On the day before D-day this patrol would create a diversion at Duali and on the night of the landing would provide a beach party to establish signal lights facing seawards. Moten was also ordered to detail a liaison officer (Savige suggested Captain McBride[4] of the

---

[4] Capt D. A. McBride, VX3707. 2/5 Bn. and staff appointments. Bank officer; of Echuca, Vic; b. Kyneton, Vic. 25 Apr 1915.

2/5th Battalion) to move with the American battalion group. After establishing a beach-head in the Nassau Bay area at a spot selected after detailed reconnaissance by the Australians, the Americans would destroy enemy forces at Duali and Cape Dinga, and then move to Napier and come under Moten's operational command.

General Herring's concern was now to tie up the operations of the 3rd Australian and 41st American Divisions for the landing at Nassau Bay. After outlining plans to the two senior staff officers—Colonels Wilton and Sweany—he summoned the two generals—Savige and Fuller—for a conference at Port Moresby on 31st May. Savige and Fuller rapidly reached agreement on the main points. On the question of beach lights, Savige had planned to have red lights on the flanks and a white light for signalling in the centre, but when Fuller wanted them the other way round, Savige agreed. Most discussion centred on the size of the Australian force to cover the landing at Nassau Bay. Savige was startled to find that Fuller had been pressing Herring to have a battalion on the beach. This was obviously impossible, for not only did Savige not have a battalion available for such a task, but, even if he had, he could not move it or supply it across the terrible country which he called the "Unspeakables". Savige believed that a platoon was adequate for the job but he did not say so. When Fuller persisted in his request for a battalion, Savige countered by saying that he would not be able to scrape together a full battalion, but that he would guarantee an "adequate force".

After the discussion, Fuller drafted "notes on agreement" between the two divisional commanders. Savige agreed with these, which set the tentative date for opening the operations as the night 16th-17th June, requested that the Australian liaison officer should know the country, that guides from 17th Brigade should lead the Americans to an assembly area preparatory to the Mubo action, and that the Australians should make a demonstration on the afternoon before the landing. The lights would be lit only if the beach was clear, and finally the Australians would "block approach to beach from both ends with adequate force".

Considerable reorganisation was taking place in Savige's area at this time. In the Mubo area the relief of the 2/7th Battalion by the 2/6th was completed on 2nd June, when Colonel Wood opened his headquarters at Guadagasal. By 28th May the 2/7th Independent Company had been flown into Bena Bena, and Bena Force now came under Herring's direct command. Between 25th and 31st May 49 officers and 784 men of the 15th Brigade headquarters and the 58th/59th Battalion were flown from Port Moresby to the Bulolo area.

The 3rd Division had originally consisted of the 4th, 10th and 15th Brigades. The 4th had been detached to the 5th Division and the 10th broken up. The 15th was an amalgamation. The original battalions of the 15th Brigade stationed at Seymour in 1941 had been the 58th, 59th and 57th/60th. In 1942 the brigade trained at Casino in New South Wales and later at Caboolture in Queensland. Here the 24th Battalion had joined it from the 10th Brigade and the 58th and 59th were merged to form the 58th/59th. Brigadier Hosking,[5] chosen by Savige, had also come from the 10th Brigade to command the 15th. Changes in unit identity—a proud possession of soldiers—and late changes in command had an adverse effect on the brigade, particularly on the 58th/59th. The brigade had arrived in Port Moresby in January 1943. Brigadier Hosking and Lieut-Colonel P. D. S. Starr (the former commander of the 2/5th Battalion at Wau) who had been chosen by Savige at Mackay's suggestion to command the 58th/59th after its arrival in New Guinea, prepared at the end of May to move to the Pilimung and Missim areas respectively.

West of Bobdubi Ridge the 2/3rd Independent Company was in reserve, enjoying the bracing climate and hot mineral springs of Missim, with a company of the 24th Battalion at Pilimung under command. Manned by men of the Independent Company, Wells O.P. was paying full dividends. On 5th June it reported that during the past five days there had been a continual procession of Japanese and carriers, thought to be Chinese coolies, passing north and south along the Komiatum Track mainly between the hours of 2 and 3 p.m. For instance, on this day 208 Japanese had moved south towards Komiatum from Salamaua while 110 had moved north towards Salamaua.

To the north the remainder of the 24th Battalion was given the task of preventing the Japanese from entering the Bulolo Valley, defending Zenag and Bulwa airfields, and patrolling to the Markham. To ease the ever-present problem of supply, not more than two companies were to move beyond the jeep-head at Sunshine without reference to divisional headquarters. After a patrol skirmish near the Markham on 3rd June, the 24th reported that the Japanese had reoccupied their old camp site at Markham Point. Another patrol attempting to set booby-traps near the Japanese camp was fired on and forced to withdraw. On 9th June, after the forward observation post had heard explosions and seen fires from the direction of Nadzab, Savige ordered that a small patrol should cross the Markham to obtain information of Japanese movement in the Nadzab area and, in particular, of any activity on the airfield.

In the Mubo area, which the 2/7th Battalion had vacated, one company of the 2/6th was on Lababia Ridge with a platoon at Napier, a second company was at Mat Mat, a third at Summit, and the fourth at the Saddle. Both the 2/5th and 2/7th Battalions were in the Wau area.

The company commander on Lababia Ridge, Major Dexter, changed the Lababia defensive position by withdrawing it to the higher ground at the junction of the Lababia and Jap Tracks where he considered it would be less difficult to counter another enemy attempt at encirclement. One of the company's first patrols along the Jap Track towards the Pimple on 2nd June heard voices and chopping in the position previously occupied by Captain Tatterson's company of the 2/7th. Moten was concerned at

---

[5] Brig F. Hosking, ED, VX108279. Comd 10 Bde 1942, 15 Bde 1942-43. Civil engineer; of South Yarra, Vic; b. Middle Park, Vic, 19 Sep 1904.

this movement by the enemy south of the Pimple, and told Wood that the Australian positions were too far removed from the Pimple either to restrict or to observe the enemy movement, and it would be possible for the Japanese to move a force from the Pimple and cut the Lababia Track, "which action would be detrimental to the success of POSTERN" (the code name for the offensive). On 4th June he ordered Wood to place a small force near the south end of the Pimple from which enemy movement could be seen or heard, and to patrol constantly to both flanks so that the enemy could not move in force from the Pimple without being detected. Dexter carried out this direction by placing a semi-circle of listening posts south of the Pimple.

Moten's order to Wood coincided with reports from the Independent Company's observation posts, particularly Wells O.P., of considerable activity along the Komiatum-Mubo track. Dexter's patrols were busy for the next few days to the south, east and west of the Pimple, and, although no shots were exchanged, the usual talking, coughing, chopping and rattling of mess tins suggested that the Japanese were still in the area south of the Pimple. So dense was the jungle that on 5th June a patrol stayed within 30 yards of the enemy position during the day, hearing voices but not seeing any Japanese.

In other areas occupied by the battalion patrols which may have seemed routine were in fact preparing for the offensive designed to end the stalemate.

Detailed plans for action before and after the American landing were now being formulated by Moten, his brigade major, Eskell,[6] and his staff captain, I. H. McBride. But the plans of force, division, brigade and battalion hinged on information as yet unknown. For the task of reconnoitring the beach at Nassau Bay and a track through the area of swamp and foothills along the lower reaches of the Bitoi, Lieutenant Burke[7] was chosen. Burke set out with Sergeant Ellen and three others from Napier on 2nd June with instructions to return to Napier and submit a report by 5th June. Sometimes moving along the track running along the south arm of the Bitoi and sometimes breaking bush over and round the foothills and spurs, Burke's patrol finally came to the last of the spurs running in a north-easterly direction down to the Bitoi about two miles from the

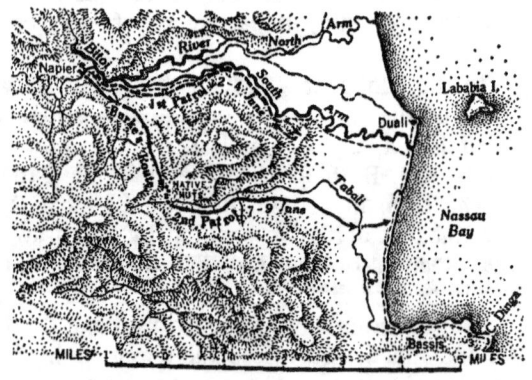

---

[6] Brig S. L. M. Eskell, DX853, 2/3 Fd Regt; BM 17 Bde 1943-44; and various staff appointments. MLC (NSW) since 1958. Regular soldier; of Sydney; b. Melbourne, 4 Jan 1918.

[7] Capt D. B. Burke, MC, VX20415. 2/6 Bn and Provost Corps. Physical culturist; of East St Kilda, Vic; b. Hobart, 14 Oct 1916.

coast. From the spur the men could see Nassau Bay, although the shape of the spur prevented them from seeing Duali and Lababia Island. As it was then 2.30 p.m. on 4th June the patrol returned to Napier, where Burke reported that it was doubtful whether a proposed signal fire on Lababia Ridge could be seen from the beach. (At this stage it was intended that the arrival of the Australians at the beach on D-day should be signalled with bonfires.)

Moten ordered Burke to carry out his original task after a day's rest and to return to Napier by 13th June. Burke, accompanied this time only by Ellen, set out again from Napier at 8 a.m. on 7th June.

The two men followed the route blazed by Ellen and his two companions in April. After travelling along the dry creek bed for an hour Burke and Ellen set off southward following a native pad up a re-entrant and into the range of hills to the south of the Bitoi. Continuing in a southeasterly direction, they crossed a mountain range at a saddle about 2,500 feet high, and five hours after leaving the Bitoi reached Tabali Creek where they camped on the night of 7th-8th June. In the morning they crossed Tabali Creek, which at this point was steep with a hard stony bed. A faint native pad which they followed on the other side disappeared after three hours in a dry creek bed which continued in an easterly direction for 300 yards until dense swamp and jungle prevented further movement except by cutting a track. Hacking their way east, Burke and Ellen four hours later again reached the winding Tabali where they camped for the night of 8th-9th June surrounded by swarms of mosquitoes and drenched by heavy rain. Next morning they swam the Tabali which had flooded overnight and at this point was 40 yards wide, slow-moving, overgrown and about 10 feet deep close to the banks. After marching for an hour and a half through swamp country the two weary men reached a clearing 100 yards from the coast.

This clearing was about 400 yards long and 100 yards wide and went right to the water's edge. There were signs of a camp near the shore and abandoned weapon-pits with the revetting timber rotting. An indistinct track wound north and south. They considered the flat beach an excellent one for landing flat-bottomed craft. The beach bank was about 10 yards from the water's edge and 6 feet above sea level. They estimated that there would be good cover for the landing craft provided an Australian platoon held the beach. They returned to Napier in nine hours arriving there at 6 p.m. on 9th June. "We reached the bay, had a very quick look round then got to hell out of it," wrote Ellen later. A high degree of determination and pioneering ingenuity had enabled the two men to carry out their difficult task.

Burke's conclusions, on which Moten could now base his detailed orders, were that the route was a good one, the beach was suitable for the landing, protection would be available for the landing party, the enemy did not occupy the area although they may have patrolled it regularly, and the strip of coast from the mouth of the south arm of the

Bitoi to Nassau Bay could quickly be made suitable even for motor transport.

When the time element had prevented Burke's first patrol from reaching the coast, Moten had decided to make sure that at least one patrol would reach the Nassau Bay area. He had therefore sent out another two-man patrol from the 2/6th Battalion—Lieutenant Gibbons[8] and Corporal Fisher[9]—on the same day as Burke's second patrol. Leaving Napier, Gibbons and Fisher followed the track along the south arm of the Bitoi towards the coast. At 11 a.m. on 8th June, Dexter, who was then visiting the Lababia O.P., sent an ominous report to Wood of heavy mortar and machine-gun fire coming from the direction taken by Gibbons' patrol. Twenty-four hours later Fisher wearily returned to the junction camp alone.

He said that after bivouacking the first night about a mile and a half from the sea, whence they could clearly hear the surf, they set off slowly at 6.30 a.m. on 8th June along the well-defined track and followed it for 45 minutes. They then saw fresh Japanese footprints on the track for another 10 minutes. Gibbons who was five yards in front of Fisher suddenly stopped, turned round, said "Jap" and moved back towards Fisher, who saw the Japanese behind a banana tree on the north side of the track about five yards from Gibbons. The Japanese fired and Gibbons fell. Fisher fired and thought that he killed the Japanese. After Gibbons had waved him back Fisher broke bush on the south side of the track about 100 yards back. He waited and saw Gibbons staggering back along the track. Gibbons then disappeared, and, as Japanese were now moving west along the track firing machine-guns and mortars indiscriminately, Fisher zigzagged back along the track for 300 yards, fell into a fresh weapon-pit, crossed to the north side of the track and reached the south arm of the Bitoi. From the firing he gathered that the Japanese were now ahead of him on the track.

Suffering that hopeless hunted feeling when the future seems black, Fisher struggled back through the great loneliness of the jungle towards Napier. After being swept downstream by the Bitoi and lost in a pit-pit swamp he finally rediscovered the track and returned to Napier in a shocked condition.

Major Takamura, commander of the *III/102nd Battalion*, was very pleased with Superior Private Koike who shot Gibbons. In a letter of commendation Takamura wrote on the same day: "While on sentry duty at a point 300 metres in front of the patrol at the banana plantation, he sighted an enemy patrol of 3 men, each armed with an automatic rifle at around 0940 hours. Signalling to the neighbouring sentry, he coolly prepared to fire, and awaited the approach of the enemy. The enemy approached step by step carrying their automatic rifles in readiness. He waited until they approached within 10 metres, and then fired, killing one man and causing the other two to retreat in haste. He captured one automatic rifle, 4 magazines, a sketch map and a pocketbook, etc., which were of great value to future operations."

---

[8] Lt E. N. Gibbons, MM, VX2525; 2/6 Bn. Paper machinist; of Ivanhoe, Vic; b. Richmond, Vic, 2 May 1920. Killed in action 8 Jun 1943.

[9] Sgt J. C. Fisher, VX56144; 2/6 Bn. Linesman; of Northcote, Vic; b. Swan Hill, Vic, 9 Feb 1921.

The map captured by Koike was the Mubo 1:25,000 sheet which was the main map used in the Australian area. Takamura realised that plans for an offensive were being prepared for in a special order issued on 11th June he said: "On 8th June in the battle in the area on the right arm of the Naka River [south arm of Bitoi] a captured sketch map together with records from enemy who were killed and secret activity of natives all indicate that the enemy is planning and in a position to attack."

During early June two important and successful patrols were carried out by other members of Dexter's company in preparation for the coming offensive. Corporal McElgunn and Private Rose[1] patrolled from Napier, intending to reach the coast by a route north of those taken by Burke and Gibbons. After moving through extremely difficult country on the outward journey McElgunn reached the beach about half way between Duali and the mouth of the north arm of the Bitoi. He returned along the north arm with information that no enemy activity was taking place along the coast north of Duali. Sergeant Hedderman[2] led a patrol which pioneered a route to Bitoi Ridge in readiness for the advance of the Americans towards Mubo, and managed to reach a point from which he could overlook the Mubo-Komiatum track along Buigap Creek. Both McElgunn's and Hedderman's patrols were the first to reach these objectives. From 5th June Lieutenant Johnson[3] and Sergeant Gibson[4] were detached from their platoon on Lababia Ridge and stationed with Lieutenant Urquhart's platoon at Napier whence they would prepare two suitable routes on to Bitoi Ridge. Sergeant Daniel[5] from the Pioneer platoon was also sent to Napier to build shelters for the Americans.

Throughout Savige's area the troops were supplied by native carriers, or "cargo boys", who transported ammunition, rations and supplies from the airfields and dropping grounds to various units. It was largely the skilful and careful planning of his senior administrative officer, Lieut-Colonel Griffin,[6] and the devotion of the native carriers that made it possible for the mountain-based Australians to continue the fight against the sea-based Japanese.[7] As far as possible the natives were kept away from the area where the bullets were flying; there the supplies were carried by their white employers and friends. On return journeys the

---

[1] Cpl A. D. Rose, VX57347; 2/6 Bn. Pastrycook; of Cobram, Vic; b. Beechworth, Vic, 13 Aug 1920.

[2] Lt J. W. Hedderman, DCM, MM, VX12728; 2/6 Bn. Travelling salesman; of North Brighton, Vic; b. Uralla, NSW, 25 Jun 1916.

[3] Capt L. C. Johnson, TX6054; 2/6 Bn. Commercial traveller; of Hobart; b. Waratah, Tas, 3 Nov 1914.

[4] Sgt J. S. Gibson, VX3858; 2/6 Bn. Teamster; of Alexandra, Vic; b. Orkney Islands, Scotland, 13 Dec 1904. Died 21 Jul 1951.

[5] Sgt J. H. Daniel, DCM, MM, VX9453; 2/6 Bn. Shearer; of Holbrook, NSW; b. Yass, NSW, 20 Dec 1916.

[6] Col E. A. Griffin, OBE, ED, VX108122. AA&QMG 3 Div 1942-44, 5 Div 1944-45. Building contractor; of East Malvern, Vic; b. Perth, 18 Jan 1907.

[7] The aim was to maintain 14-20 days' reserve of rations and ammunition in the area and this was achieved in May following the visit of the DAQMG of New Guinea Force, Brigadier V. C. Secombe (relieved by Brigadier R. Bierwirth on 20 June). Stocks dwindled to 12 days in early June and thereafter average holdings were from one to five days. "Reserves of rations reached and remained on an extremely dangerous level," wrote Savige later. "It was not uncommon for troops in the outlying areas to have to subsist for a time on native sweet potatoes and other native foods."

natives acted as stretcher bearers for wounded and sick Australian soldiers, an arduous task which they performed with great solicitude.

An organisation which played a major role in maintaining this lifeline of supplies was the Australian New Guinea Administrative Unit—or Angau. In the field the Angau officers and N.C.O's assisted commanders in the control of native labour, advised on matters peculiar to New Guinea, and gathered information. They were responsible for the local allocation and marshalling of native carriers, organisation of carrier lines between staging points, and the administration of punishment to natives for pilfering. Quite soon Savige saw trouble brewing in the "boy lines" mainly because of the fact that control was in the hands of the combatant officer while the Angau officer or N.C.O. was relegated to a subordinate position. On 9th June he issued a clarification designed to avoid clashes of temperament between some local commanders who considered they knew how to control natives and some Angau officers who considered they knew how to command troops. Members of Angau on the lines of communication were to be subject to direction by senior local commanders at each staging point concerning the duties to be performed by native labour, but they were to be responsible directly to Angau headquarters for the internal economy and administration of allotted native labour. Attached to his headquarters Savige had Major D. H. Vertigan of Angau, while Captain H. McM. Lyon was with the 17th Brigade and Lieutenant G. K. Whittaker with the 15th. All were old New Guinea hands whose advice was much respected.

An example of the value of Angau was provided on 11th June when, between 7.25 and 7.40 a.m., four Beaufighters strafed Wood's headquarters on Guadagasal Ridge instead of Green Hill and the Pimple. Two natives were wounded, but the calamitous aspect of the mistake was that 300 native carriers went bush. Angau assembled them again, but without Angau it might well have proved impossible to round them up and get them back to the carrier lines.

Because of what he called "unavoidable inactivity" in the Missim area, General Savige on 10th June ordered Brigadier Hosking to harass the Japanese supply route between Salamaua and Mubo but not in such a way as to indicate the main objectives of the coming offensive nor the area from which it was to be launched. He suggested that a force from the 2/3rd Independent Company, now included in Hosking's command, should be employed, but that the Independent Company should be relieved of all its present commitments by a company of the 58th/59th Battalion which had now arrived at Selebob after a gruelling march from Bulwa. Two days later, in accordance with this order, Major Warfe ordered Captain Menzies to attack between Komiatum and Mubo by raid or ambush at a point no farther north than Stephens' Track and to make every attempt to take prisoners.

Menzies at once began to concentrate his men, who were widely scattered on patrols, and to organise his supplies. Setting off from Wells

O.P. with a strong raiding party, he moved south over the Pioneers Range and worked his way towards the enemy supply line over rough, disused tracks. On 16th June Warfe received word that the party had run into a booby-trap, Menzies and three others being wounded. Menzies had travelled for some time and must have reached the scene of earlier operations in the Mubo area. The booby-trap encountered was made with Australian grenades and Australian trip wire. Once again the Australians learnt from tragic experience the effectiveness of their own grenades. Thirty-two native stretcher bearers were required to carry the wounded to Missim. The medical officer, Captain Street, met the party on its way in and gave the men what attention he could during an overnight halt at Base 4. Medical orderlies accompanied the party for the rest of the journey. Menzies and two others recovered, but Private McDougall,[8] a boy of only 17, died soon after reaching Missim.

The disabling of Menzies left the platoon without a commander and Captain Hancock took over. The platoon had not had any respite since their arrival in the Missim area and the 22 men who were still fit for duty were very tired. However, days had passed since the order had been received to strike at the Komiatum-Mubo track south of Stephens' Track, and to take prisoners if possible.

Hancock decided to approach by the quickest route. He moved with Sergeant Tomkins[9] and a small party along the ridge of the Pioneers Range in the general direction of Mount Tambu. Guided by Corporal Lamb, who had spent many weeks patrolling in this area, he continued directly along the ridge not far south of the junction of Stephens' Track and the Komiatum Track leading to Goodview Junction. The ridge descended steeply to the enemy track but provided a definite means of access and the terrain permitted an almost "text book" ambush position. There was flat ground near the track with a line of undergrowth along the track and a small hill near by which gave a view over short stretches of the enemy track in each direction. On 20th June the party took up position—the plan was to capture the last man of any enemy party which passed and to shoot the remainder. A long jungle vine was laid between the ambush party and the supporting party on the hill in order to transmit signals between them. Just as Hancock was completing the siting of the supporting party three Japanese appeared from the direction of Mubo. Hancock gave the pre-arranged signal and, as the Japanese passed, Lamb rushed forward on to the track closely followed by the rest of the party. Unfortunately the scrub beside the track was thick enough to give the enemy warning and the Australians were forced to shoot it out with them. The Japanese were killed, dragged off the track and relieved of their arms and equipment. The loot included official papers and diaries, which were immediately sent to Missim. Later the unit learnt that the papers gave parade states and other useful information about the enemy in the

---

[8] Pte W. J. McDougall, NX38916; 2/3 Indep Coy. Coal miner; of Swansea, NSW; b. Wickham, NSW, 29 Nov 1925. Died of wounds 18 Jun 1943.

[9] Sgt A. V. Tomkins, WX14528. 2/3 Indep Coy, 2/3 Cdo Sqn. Carpenter; of Perth; b. Perth, 28 Mar 1920.

Mubo area: the three men had been members of the *II/102nd Battalion* probably returning to Salamaua after their unit had been relieved by the *66th Regiment*. On the 21st June a listening post established above Goodview Junction heard sounds of running, dropping of tins, shouted orders, cursing and general commotion; it was clear that the bodies had been discovered and that the raid was causing a due amount of consternation.

Meanwhile, the newly-arrived 15th Brigade headquarters began to scent action; and on 15th June it issued its first operation instruction, signed by the brigade major, Travers.[1] The brigade's tasks on entering the Missim area would be to prevent the enemy from entering the Bulolo Valley through its area of responsibility; to secure the Missim-Pilimung-Hote area as a firm base to enable offensive raids to be carried out towards Komiatum and Salamaua when ordered; to plan the capture of Bobdubi Ridge and exploitation to Komiatum; and to reconnoitre and plan for a diversion against Salamaua in the Malolo area. The 2/3rd Independent Company, with a company of the 24th Battalion and one of the 58th/59th under command, was allotted the task of controlling the main tracks and establishing defensive positions in the Cissembob-Daho area to protect the brigade's left flank and provide a base for patrols towards Salamaua along the Hote-Malolo track.

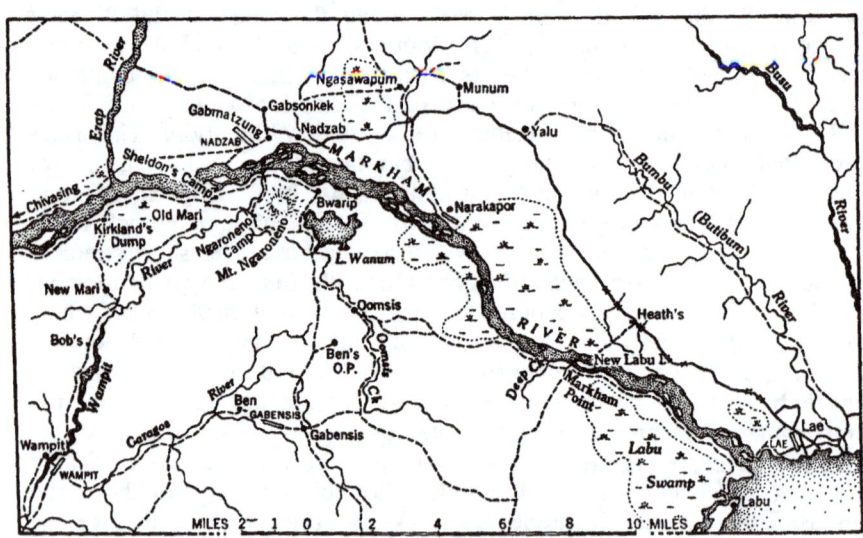

Lower Markham River Valley area

In the Markham area a daily patrol moved forward to observe the Japanese camps at Markham Point and on Labu Island in the Markham, half an hour's walk beyond. When first discovered the Markham Point camp had been deserted and had consisted of 12 weapon-pits on a sharp rise, almost a cliff face, 40-50 feet high, running at right angles to the

---

[1] Lt-Col B. H. Travers, OBE, NX17. 2/2 Bn 1939-42; ADC to GOC 6 Div 1940-41; BM 15 Bde 1943-44; GSO2 (Ops) II Corps 1944-45. Student; of Kirribilli, NSW; b. Bondi, NSW, 7 Jul 1919.

river. By 11th June the Japanese were protected by ambush positions 150 yards west of the cliff-face position, while the huts were let into the side of the ridge of the precipice like blast bays of an airfield.

In pursuance of Savige's order that a small reconnaissance patrol from the 24th Battalion should go to the Nadzab area, Sergeant Eaton[2] with two men and a native left at 5.30 p.m. on 11th June to cross the Markham. During the crossing one boat swamped causing the two other members of the patrol to spend the night uneasily on a sandbank and return to Old Mari the next morning. Eaton and a native guide reached the north bank of the Markham, but returned at 8.30 p.m. next day after their boat had capsized on the return trip. Major Smith obtained permission for Eaton's patrol to be repeated.

Sergeant Hogan,[3] Lance-Corporal McInnes[4] and Private O'Connor[5] set out on the second Nadzab patrol on 14th June, and returned four days later. The patrol crossed the Markham by moonlight in rubber boats which they hid in the reeds, and then moved east along the north bank of the river and north to Gabmatzung across what the natives called "Big Road", and on to Gabsonkek. As the natives were very friendly, Hogan stayed there during the night 17th-18th June and gathered information. "Natives say," Hogan wrote in his report, "that the Japs come to the village every day between 1000 and 1200 hours tak-

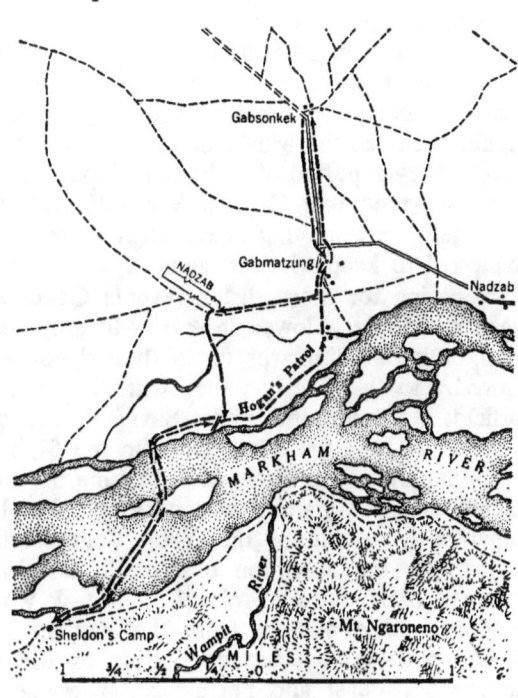

14th-18th June

ing everything in sight—pigs, fowls, fruit, etc., without paying; they take native girls back to Lae if they can catch them." The guides would not proceed farther to Ngasawapum because "Japan man come up Big Road, cut us off", and they would not go to Narakapor because they claimed there were "too many Japs and two big guns". Native information gathered by

---

[2] Lt N. E. Eaton, VX104430; 24 Bn. Warehouse employee; of Lilydale, Vic; b. Warrnambool, Vic, 22 Feb 1920.
[3] Lt D. A. Hogan, VX104452. 24 and 58/59 Bns. Public servant; of Bendigo, Vic; b. Bendigo, 21 Jun 1917.
[4] L-Cpl L. M. McInnes, NX128919; 24 Bn. Labourer; of Lismore, NSW; b. Lismore, 9 Sep 1922.
[5] Pte W. S. M. O'Connor, NX145724; 24 Bn. Labourer; of Stockton, NSW; b. Stockton, 13 Nov 1920.

Hogan from the Gabsonkek "boss boy", who had been forced to carry cargo to Lae, was that 300 Japanese had recently crossed the Markham with the intention of going to Oomsis; 200 Japanese patrolled daily from Heath's Plantation where "Jap dig hole"; 100 to Gabmatzung and 100 to Chivasing; one kiap [European official] and five police boys had been killed by the Japanese; and natives would not cross the river now unless with a patrol. At 6 a.m. on 18th June Hogan's patrol retraced its steps while the Gabmatzung natives obliterated all traces of them in the village and on the track. Moving west along the disused motor road the patrol came to the Nadzab airfield which was overgrown by kunai three to six feet high. Hogan finally reached the south bank of the Markham at 10 p.m. after an exceptionally fine patrol.

After Hogan's return Captain Kyngdon[6] of Angau questioned Markham natives who were nervous about patrols crossing the Markham because they feared reprisals by the large numbers of Japanese there who, they said, were being reinforced by submarine. The natives pleaded that patrols should not cross the Markham, and promised to obtain information themselves. They reported also that the Japanese, by means of radio location, had discovered that Captain Howlett[7] and Warrant-Officer Ryan,[8] both of Angau, were moving in the Urawa area. Kyngdon asked that they be requested to keep wireless silence.

Preparing for more distant events General Herring on 8th June had warned General Clowes in Port Moresby and General Savige that the 57th/60th Battalion was on 24 hours' notice to move by air from Port Moresby to the Watut Valley with the task of defending the Marilinan airfield; it would come under Savige's command on arrival.

By 20th June two platoons from the 57th/60th were patrolling in the Marilinan area. On 18th and 19th June the commander of the 57th/60th, Lieut-Colonel Marston,[9] was informed that his task was to prevent the Japanese from entering the Watut Valley sufficiently far to interfere with or hamper the operation of aircraft on airfields selected in the valley between Marilinan and Wuruf. This task would be done by an infantry platoon and a platoon from the Papuan Infantry Battalion based on Pesen, with reconnaissance patrols to the north and standing patrols to the north-east and north-west. The main defensive position of two companies would be constructed in the Wuruf area while the Marilinan airfield would be protected by two companies and American anti-aircraft guns.

How to supply his augmented force was one Savige's major problems. The air force did its best, but bad weather caused delays and throughout June the troops often went hungry or were down to their last meal.

---

[6] Maj L. G. R. Kyngdon, PX162; Angau. Patrol officer; of Bena Bena, NG; b. Bowral, NSW, 6 Jun 1911.

[7] Capt L. F. Howlett, NGX45. 2/4 Bn and FELO. Patrol officer; of Scottsdale, Tas; b. Sydney, 13 Dec 1913. Killed in action 21 Jun 1943.

[8] Lt P. A. Ryan, MM, VX128541. Angau; Instr School of Civil Affairs LHQ 1945. Clerk; of Glen Iris, Vic; b. Melbourne, 4 Sep 1923. Author of *Fear Drive My Feet* (1959).

[9] Lt-Col R. R. Marston, DSO, ED, VX108132. HQ 3 Div; CO 57/60 Bn 1943-45. Building contractor; of Kalgoorlie, WA, and Melbourne; b. Perth, 20 Oct 1902.

Inaccurate dropping of supplies and lack of carriers also helped to keep the cupboard bare. An example of this combination of circumstances had occurred on 10th June when, after some days of adverse weather in the 15th Brigade's area, the aircraft approached the steep-sided Selebob Ridge (the dropping ground) at right angles instead of making their run as requested along the ridge; they also dropped too high and too fast. This necessitated the commandeering of a boy-line of 90 leaving Powerhouse on 11th June for rations. Such was the shortage in this area that Lieut-Colonel Refshauge,[1] commander of the 15th Field Ambulance, considered that fighting troops would be unable to maintain their strength. The 11th of June was an exasperating day also for the troops at Guadagasal: to the insult of bad supply dropping by four Douglas aircraft bringing supplies was added the injury of mistaken strafing by the Beaufighters. One transport emptied nearly all its packages in heavy timber off the clearing and another continued to throw out packages after passing the clearing.

In mid-June General Herring decided to see something of the forward area and to hold a final coordinating conference there. On 13th June he flew to Bulolo accompanied by the Deputy Chief of the General Staff, Major-General F. H. Berryman. That day Savige signalled Brigadier Moten to be at Summit at midday on 15th June. Herring, Savige and Berryman, accompanied by Colonels Wilton, Griffin, Sweany and Archibald R. MacKechnie (the commander of the landing force), jeeped to Summit on the 15th. After assembling in a large tent specially erected for the conference Savige called on Moten, who would actually control the ground operations, to explain his plan for covering the landing at Nassau Bay and the capture of Mubo.

While the three senior commanders sat on one side, Moten explained his plan to this distinguished audience. He said that he thought that the enemy in the Mubo-Komiatum area was approximately 1,100, comprising the *I* and *II Battalions* of the *102nd Regiment*; and in the Duali-Nassau Bay area there were about 200. His appreciation of enemy dispositions had led him to believe that the Japanese were in strength along the line of Buigap Creek with forward positions at Observation Hill, Kitchen Creek, Green Hill and the Pimple. The Salamaua garrison, believed to be about 2,600 with a further 500 in the Bobdubi Ridge area, would have their hands full countering the attack of the 15th Brigade and be unable to reinforce the Mubo area, although it would be possible to bring reinforcements from outside by submarine and barge. His brigade's object was to "clear the enemy from Mubo area and drive forward to Mount Tambu with a view to exploiting via tracks of access to Lokanu to the line of Francisco River".

Moten envisaged the operation being carried out in five phases. In phase 1, MacKechnie's battalion group (the I/162nd Battalion) would establish a beach-head at Nassau Bay where they would come under Moten's command and would be assisted by a company of the 2/6th Battalion; after

---
[1] Maj-Gen W. D. Refshauge, CBE, VX220. CO 15 Fd Amb 1943-44, 2/8 Fd Amb 1944-45, DGMS 1955-60. Medical practitioner; of Hawthorn, Vic; b. Parkville, Vic, 3 Apr 1913.

clearing the enemy from Duali and the other villages of Nassau Bay, the Americans would push forward to the assembly area at Napier. In phase 2, the 2/6th plus a company of the 2/5th would capture Observation Hill and the ridge between Bui Savella and Kitchen Creeks and exploit along both these creeks to Buigap Creek and along the track through the Mubo Valley to the Archway; at the same time the Americans would capture Bitoi Ridge and exploit to Buigap Creek. Phase 3 would consist of the capture of Green Hill and the Pimple by the Americans and the 2/6th. With the object of exploiting towards Komiatum and Lokanu, the 2/5th in phase 4, would advance from Mubo through the 2/6th, occupy Mount Tambu, link up with the 15th Brigade at Komiatum, and patrol towards Lokanu. Phase 5 would consist of the capture of Lokanu and Boisi and the clearing of the enemy from south of the Francisco by troops yet to be allotted. Four days previously D-day had been advanced to 30th June.

When Moten had finished Herring said: "That seems all right, Moten." Savige and Berryman agreed, and so did the Americans. There was then some general discussion to elucidate a few points, among which was a request by the Americans to have red lights on the flanks and a white light in the centre on the landing beach. Savige agreed to this with a smile. MacKechnie and Moten agreed that the officer commanding the beach party (Lieutenant Burke) would meet the landing force commander (MacKechnie) at the white light, and guides at each red light would lead the landing parties to where detachments from the 2/6th would be guarding the flanks 300 to 400 yards from each red light. The Allies agreed that Captain E. P. Hitchcock's company of the seasoned Papuan Infantry Battalion, which had served in the Papuan campaign and which had arrived at Morobe on 7th June in a schooner, would delay its movement from Buso (which it had reached overland and by canoe on 15th June) until D-day in order to retain the element of surprise. After arriving at Nassau Bay it would be used by MacKechnie for mopping-up operations and right flank protection in the coastal area north of the south arm of the Bitoi, and later would move north along the coast. The Summit conference also decided that the time of the landing would be between 11 p.m. and midnight on the night before D-day.

Moten gave MacKechnie a copy of Burke's report and also some notes about projected movements for the seven days from the day before D-day. These indicated that on 29th June Burke's party would arrive, the bombing and strafing of Duali would begin, and two Australian platoons would demonstrate near the mouth of the south arm of the Bitoi so as to entice the Japanese inland. On 30th June Burke, with the latest information, would have guides ready to lead MacKechnie's troops to Napier. The Americans would consolidate the beach-head next day, patrol forward and to the flanks, and use their artillery to engage suspected Japanese positions. On 2nd July the Americans would begin the move to Napier, improve the track for artillery, and finish the mopping up at Nassau Bay. After arriving at Napier Australian troops would be withdrawn, leaving only guides. Three days after D-day the Americans would complete their move to Napier and would bring their artillery forward; on 4th July the artillery would register targets while the infantry established observation posts and prepared for a forward movement to Bitoi Ridge. In his notes Moten expressed the hope that the Americans would begin to move from Napier on to Bitoi Ridge five days after the landing.

Dexter on 14th June outlined the role of his men for D-day, when they were to create a diversion and draw the enemy inland from the position reached by Gibbons. He allotted portion of Urquhart's platoon to Burke as a beach guiding party. One of the other platoons was given the task of establishing a base camp half way between Napier and the last spur, and drawing the enemy back from the coast. The third platoon was allotted the less exciting but no less vital task of carrying supplies forward from Napier for the remainder of the company. Later action would depend on the situation but the company would try to remain in contact with the enemy until a junction was established with the Americans. The troops were warned of the similarity of Japanese and American helmets.

The conferences at Port Moresby on 31st May and Summit on 15th June had discussed an offensive whose objectives were Nassau Bay, Mubo and Bobdubi Ridge. Nothing was said about the ultimate objective—the capture of Lae and the Markham Valley—nor of the vital fact that Salamaua must not fall before Lae. This was doubtless done for security reasons, but later misunderstandings might have been avoided had Savige been told of the bigger plan. He remained convinced that he should capture Salamaua as soon as possible. There appeared to him to be no ambiguity about his orders to drive the enemy north of the Francisco, and Salamaua was immediately north of the mouth of the Francisco. The position was all the more anomalous in that Moten knew of the bigger plan. General Blamey himself was not satisfied that New Guinea Force fully understood his intentions and on 15th June he wrote to Herring:

> I note one divergence from the plan I had approved for future operations. You will remember that it had been decided that Salamaua should not be seized; it should be bypassed. . . . This has been ignored and the outline of plan indicates that Salamaua would be first seized. If this is done of course all hope of obtaining any degree of surprise at Lae will disappear. Whereas any build up south of Salamaua will tend to draw forces into the latter area. I hope to go north again at the end of this week and will discuss the matter further with Berryman, but so far I do not see any valid reason for changing the plan already agreed upon.

Herring explained that a misunderstanding had occurred because New Guinea Force had been referring to the preliminary operation for the seizure of the Komiatum Ridge as the Salamaua operation. "It was never intended," he wrote, "to depart from the plan you approved, nor should I think of doing so without your approval. . . . We hope and intend to get guns forward to shell Salamaua but further than this we did not intend to go."

One day before the Summit conference Wood had informed Moten that reports from patrols and listening posts led him to believe that the Japanese were in the area previously occupied by Tatterson's company. Between 7th and 11th June they were more active than usual and were sending out small reconnaissance patrols towards the Australian position on Lababia Ridge and the Lababia O.P.

Moten was anxious about persistent reports from Wells O.P. of Japanese moving south along the Komiatum Track and about Wood's reports of increased enemy activity round Mubo. He could not be sure whether a large-scale attack was intended round Mubo or whether the Japanese were reinforcing their defensive positions fearing an Australian attack. It did not seem improbable to the Australians that the enemy might know of the planned landing, for even the native carriers knew something of it.

Preparations for D-day continued. Lieutenant Swift[2] of the 2/1st Field Regiment had left Lababia on 13th June to look for suitable artillery positions and to find out whether guns could be moved inland from the coast. On the 15th Lieutenant Johnson and Sergeant Gibson again left Napier for Bitoi Ridge reconnoitring the route to be taken by the Americans. They returned five days later and reported that the journey from the river junction to the top of Bitoi Ridge would take a few lightly-equipped troops about eight hours and a larger number approximately ten. By the time of the Summit conference Sergeant Daniel had supervised the construction of 16 large huts for the incoming Americans. Across the Bitoi Sergeant Sachs[3] from Reeve's O.P.[4] found a route for troop movement to Observation Hill without meeting any signs of Japanese beyond blood spots and fresh excreta on Observation Hill. Tracks were cut from Reeve's O.P. to Buiapal Creek and assembly areas were prepared north of the creek at the foot of Observation Hill. As with the patrols to Bitoi Ridge, these patrols were carried out without exciting the enemy's suspicion. The series of two-man listening posts and daily reconnaissance patrols north of Lababia Ridge had located Japanese positions where little security was being observed. On the night of 16th June Private McGrath[5] and Private Hurn[6] volunteered to raid the position. They moved stealthily along the Jap Track, no mean task at night, and had a pleasant evening's sport when they located about a dozen Japanese squatting round a camp fire without a sentry. Each Australian fired 20 shots at the silhouetted targets causing many screams; a delay of two minutes ensued before the Japanese reached their weapon-pits and started firing wildly in all directions.

In the next few days patrols from the 2/6th Battalion's forward companies on Lababia Ridge and Mat Mat kept close watch on the Pimple

---

[2] Capt P. W. Swift, NX58982; 2/1 Fd Regt. Station overseer; of Killara, NSW; b. Wollstonecraft, NSW, 14 Dec 1911.

[3] Lt J. Sachs, MM, NX9629. 2/6 Bn, "Z" Special Unit. Oil company representative; of Double Bay, NSW; b. Chatswood, NSW, 4 Oct 1913. Executed by Japanese 5 Apr 1945.

[4] Named after Lieutenant E. R. Reeve, 2/5th Battalion.

[5] Pte L. R. McGrath, MM, NX36229; 2/6 Bn. Moulder; of Yarraville, Vic; b. Seddon, Vic, 13 Apr 1918.

[6] Pte E. G. Hurn, NX84293; 2/6 Bn. Grocer; of Waverley, NSW; b. Semaphore, SA, 23 Jul 1913.

and Observation Hill areas respectively. The mountain battery periodically fired on the Bitoi crossing and air strikes on the Stony Creek and Kitchen Creek areas were made on 18th June. On the previous day four enemy aircraft had bombed Wood's headquarters at the Saddle, obviously attempting to silence the mountain gun about 400 yards away. Skirmishes between small Australian patrols and Japanese listening posts or standing patrols occurred near the Jap Track. Normally the Japanese had been content to sit in their defences and let the Australians control no-man's land, but now they were unusually active.

Information about enemy movement poured in from Wells O.P. On the 15th 486 Japanese were counted moving south along the Komiatum Track. At 6 a.m. on the 16th Wells O.P. reported that three heavily laden launches had arrived at Salamaua from Lae the previous evening; at midday that 80 Japanese were seen moving south along the Komiatum Track. Between 3 and 5 p.m. the men at the observation post saw 173 Japanese and 60 heavily laden carriers moving south towards Komatium and 58 Japanese moving north towards Salamaua.[7]

Thus Savige and Moten felt fairly certain by 20th June that the Japanese intended to strike hard at the forward Australian positions in the Mubo area. From 10.20 a.m. that day Japanese aircraft dive-bombed and pattern-bombed Guadagasal, Mat Mat and the Mubo Valley. In the day 83 enemy aircraft were overhead. The bombing caused some casualties and damage, particularly to the 2/6th's "Q" store at the Saddle but the most serious outcome was the dispersal of the brigade's native carriers. They went bush, and by 4.30 p.m. next day only three had returned and about 578 were missing. It took three days for Angau to gather them together, and this caused a commensurate delay in moving forward rations, stores and ammunition.[8] With D-day 10 days away this time could ill be spared. Angau officers who were rounding them up—Major N. Penglase and Lieutenant Watson—said that more Japanese air attacks in the near future would make it impossible to hold the carrier lines; in consequence, Moten suggested that frequent fighter sorties be made over the forward areas.

Dexter's company at this grave moment was divided between the Lababia camp, Napier, and the Lababia O.P. Lieutenant Roach's[9] platoon and Sergeant Hedderman's were slightly forward on the left and right respectively of the Jap Track, just north of its junction with the Lababia Track. Their rear near the track junction was guarded by Lieutenant Exton's[1] platoon from another company. West of these three platoons across a small saddle Dexter established his headquarters guarded to the north by

---

[7] Between 22nd May and 18th June Wells O.P. counted a total of 1,472 Japanese moving south and 528 north along the Komiatum Track.

[8] Fortunately the Lababia camp was well stocked with ammunition, and brigade headquarters' orders to send back ammunition thought to be unserviceable had hardly begun to be implemented on 19th and 20th June.

[9] Lt L. S. Roach, MC, NX113462; 2/6 Bn. Bricklayer; of Port Kembla, NSW; b. Auburn, NSW, 8 Feb 1920.

[1] Capt E. G. Exton, MC, NX129161; 2/6 Bn. Railway porter; of Lismore, NSW; b. Boston, England, 14 Jan 1919.

Lieutenant Smith's[2] anti-tank platoon working as riflemen. Lieutenant Urquhart's platoon was at Napier. Five men from the battalion Intelligence section and the forward company were at Lababia O.P. About 200 yards north of Roach's platoon an entrenched section listening post was manned night and day.

At 1 p.m. on 20th June a patrol led by Private Watt[3] moving north along the Jap Track about 50 yards forward of the listening post noticed

Defence of Lababia Ridge, 20th-23rd June

a few Japanese moving up the track towards the listening post. After firing on them and killing the leader, who was giving hand signals to those in the rear, the patrol withdrew under fire. Soon afterwards the Japanese began firing indiscriminately from both sides of the track. The Jap Track at this point was very steep with re-entrants on either flank. Corporal

---
[2] Capt R. J. H. Smith, NX54942. 2/6 Bn, 3 NG Inf Bn. Bank officer; of Warrawee, NSW; b. Sydney, 28 Feb 1921.
[3] Cpl A. J. Watt, MM, VX53894; 2/6 Bn. French polisher; of Northcote, Vic; b. Northcote, 12 Jan 1919. Died of wounds 16 Sep 1943.

A. J. Smith,[4] commanding this forward section, was reinforced and although the Japanese made several attempts during the afternoon to get round to the section's flanks they were at a disadvantage for they were on lower ground. Enemy pressure continued, however, with the result that Smith was withdrawn to the forward platoon position. Private Watt ran forward and, with machine-gun fire, covered Smith's withdrawal. After inflicting heavy casualties Watt saw six Japanese in dead ground on the flank and killed them with two grenades. In the withdrawal he re-set four booby-traps. At 4.30 p.m. the Japanese withdrew and half an hour later all was quiet. No movement was seen or heard during the night. Learning that about 50 Japanese had been engaged, Dexter concluded that they were probably a strong patrol sent out to find the main Australian positions before launching a large-scale attack. The Japanese had moved up the track in a very open way and had appeared surprised to stumble across the outpost; according to Corporal Smith the Japanese leader had smiled at him. They were well camouflaged, wearing greenish uniforms with packs on their backs to which were strapped boughs and green foliage. During the afternoon when they were held up they had made a great deal of noise and had held many consultations. Whistles blown before the firing of automatic weapons had helped to indicate Japanese positions to the defenders and to facilitate the killing of 9 and wounding of 11 while only one Australian was wounded.

Next morning at 6.30 a small Australian patrol moved 500 yards up the track to the Lababia O.P. and found all quiet. An hour later the telephone line to the observation post cut out. A patrol accompanied by linesmen had barely left the company perimeter when firing broke out from enemy positions north of the observation post track. This continued intermittently throughout the morning during which time the Japanese were apparently moving to the flanks in small groups of two and three and assembling for an attack. This movement was harassed by the defenders' fire which scattered several small groups, and by booby-traps. At 11 a.m. a large body of Japanese, advancing on either side of the Jap Track, was dispersed by fire from the grenade discharger, Brens, rifles and Tommy-guns. Both the grenade with a 7-seconds fuse fired from a discharger attached to the muzzle of the .303 rifle and the grenade with a 4-seconds fuse thrown by hand were supporting Savige's contention that units experienced in jungle warfare were unanimous in their praise of the grenade as the Number 1 jungle weapon. In the morning Corporal Smith set out with a patrol to hunt the enemy. Coming upon 25 Japanese he hit five before his rifle was shot from his hands. Grasping the rifle of a wounded comrade he kept the Japanese at bay until he was able to pick up the wounded man and carry him back. Up to 2 p.m. probably 25 Japanese were hit by small arms fire from Roach's and Hedderman's platoons, exclusive of those killed by the supporting weapons, and the booby-traps which were continually being sprung.

---

[4] Cpl A. J. Smith, DCM, VX54565. 2/14, 2/6 and 2/9 Bns. Labourer; of South Yarra, Vic; b. Ulverstone, Tas, 21 Sep 1919.

Sensing that a dangerous situation was about to develop, Moten at 1.17 p.m. sent a message to Wood who had left his headquarters at the Saddle to visit Mat Mat: "POSTERN prejudiced by enemy occupation of Lababia Ridge. Take immediate aggressive action to drive enemy back to former location in Pimple area." In order to reinforce Dexter's company, Moten, eight minutes later, ordered Lieut-Colonel T. M. Conroy of the 2/5th Battalion to send part of one company from Banana to the Saddle to relieve Captain Cameron's[5] company of the 2/6th which would then move to Lababia Ridge.

An hour earlier Lieutenant Smith's platoon reported slight movement well round on the left flank but forward of his position covering the Lababia-Saddle track. At 2 p.m., however, the Japanese began a heavy attack on Hedderman's position between the Jap Track and the Lababia O.P. Track. The attack quickly spread to Roach's and Exton's front. Pouring automatic and mortar fire into the two forward platoons the Japanese pressed harder and harder. A bayonet attack along the Jap Track was halted within 10 yards of the forward Australian position; another one on the right flank brought some of the Japanese to within 20 yards of the Australian positions before they were stopped. During the attack Hedderman and his runner, Private G. L. Smith,[6] found time to carry two badly wounded men to comparative safety where Captain Scott-Young[7] attended to them. At 3 p.m. Hedderman's left flank was endangered by a determined enemy assault supported by mortar fire. Moving to the threatened spot he silenced the mortar and dispersed the enemy attack by using the grenade discharger. Private Smith meanwhile was distributing ammunition to the weapon-pits and joining in the fight where it was hottest. Desperate attacks were then launched against Roach's troops, who fought back with fierce determination although it seemed that so few men could not hold back the large enemy force much longer. When all but three of his section had been killed or wounded Private Ryan[8] took command and coolly held off the attack with Bren-gun fire. When another machine-gunner was hit Private McGrath picked up his gun, ran to another pit where all the occupants were casualties, and drove off the attackers.

With the enemy massing for another assault Dexter decided to use part of his small reserve—a few men from his company headquarters—to reinforce Roach's platoon. The reinforcements arrived just as Corporal A. J. Smith and his remaining riflemen, with fixed bayonets, were meeting a Japanese bayonet attack up the Jap Track. The determination and courage of Corporal Smith's gallant band were too much for the attackers, who wilted. Every Japanese in this attack was killed by the bayonets of these men or by fire from the weapon-pits.

---

[5] Maj W. J. Cameron, VX5015; 2/6 Bn. Labourer; of Barwon Heads, Vic; b. Connewarre, Vic, 21 Nov 1915.

[6] Cpl G. L. Smith, MM, VX4436; 2/6 Bn. Printer; of Melbourne; b. Melbourne, 22 Aug 1919. Killed in action 28 Mar 1945.

[7] Capt N. R. Scott-Young, NX77345. RMO 2/6 Bn, and 2/3 Cdo Sqn. Medical practitioner; of Lane Cove, NSW; b. Sydney, 8 Jan 1917.

[8] Pte R. W. Ryan, DCM, SX13321; 2/6 Bn. Labourer; of Adelaide; b. Adelaide, 27 Sep 1921.

The edge of the Japanese attack had now been blunted; it received a large dent when, at 3.15 p.m., Sergeant Mann[9] used the 3-inch mortar for the first time, from a clearing near company headquarters. The second bomb caught in a small branch and exploded. The head native climbed up the tree and cut down the limb although bullets were flying through the trees. Firing throughout the remainder of the afternoon on the Jap and Lababia O.P. Tracks the mortar caused the Japanese to break on several occasions. One of Dexter's main concerns was to conserve his ammunition. Whenever he heard any prolonged bursts from the defenders he was forced to warn his platoon commanders to "keep your bloody fingers off the triggers".[1] The problem of supplying ammunition to the weapon-pits of the perimeter was solved by the troops with typical ingenuity. They took off their socks, put the ammunition in them, and threw them to the various weapon-pits.

The Japanese continued to attack Roach's, Hedderman's and Exton's positions throughout the late afternoon, and, although suffering heavy casualties, it seemed that they might break through Exton's position where their shouting and determined attacks appeared to unnerve one post. Exton and Corporal Martin[2] ran forward and rallied the men, who, encouraged by their example, waited until the enemy were within 30 yards before firing. It was with some relief that Dexter welcomed Cameron and his company who arrived at Lababia Ridge between 5.15 and 6.15 p.m. along the Lababia-Saddle track which the enemy had not reached. Cameron's men dropped their packs at company headquarters and were sent forward immediately to reinforce Roach and Exton.

Towards dusk the Japanese attack gradually decreased in intensity. Throughout a night of sleepless expectancy the Australians could hear sounds of the Japanese moving dead and wounded, the eerie howling of a dog, and much moaning and groaning. These melancholy cries of the wounded contrasted with the arrogant calls of the Japanese at the height of the fight: "We are Japan; we will win," or "Come and fight you conscript bastards." The Japanese attackers had lost about 100 men killed and wounded during the day while Australian casualties amounted to 9 killed and 9 wounded.

Desultory fire from both sides began about 6.30 a.m. on 22nd June. From 8 a.m. onwards small parties of Japanese were observed moving round to the Australian left flank and, Dexter feared, to the Lababia-Saddle track. These parties were effectively sniped; while the grenade dischargers and 3-inch mortar, always great morale builders or morale lesseners depending on which end of them the troops happened to be, continued to have great effect down the Jap Track judging from the squeals and sounds of stampeding. Movement during the morning was

---

[9] Sgt W. Mann, VX35080; 2/6 Bn. Carpenter's labourer; of Richmond, Vic; b. Richmond, 8 Aug 1906.

[1] In the defence of Lababia Ridge 6 Tommy-guns were put out of action with split or burst barrels—probably caused by faulty ammunition. The Tommy-guns were also difficult to fire when they became dirty.

[2] Cpl G. Martin, MM, VX11341; 2/6 Bn. Farmer; of Hopetoun, Vic; b. Williamstown, Vic, 18 Feb 1913.

confined to the Australians' left flank and the right flank beyond the Lababia O.P. Track, where Australian sniping was most effective. Here the Japanese were climbing trees and firing down into the Australian weapon-pits, but they reckoned without Exton, a crack shot. Dexter was telephoning Exton's platoon sergeant, who said suddenly: "Just a minute —there's a Nip getting up a tree about 100 yards away—Exton's going to have a shot—he's got him and he's bouncing."

At 2.10 p.m. heavy fire poured this time into Lieutenant R. J. H. Smith's position just north of the Lababia-Saddle track. Fire from the Australian defenders, however, again proved too powerful and after five minutes the attack died out. Five minutes later a Japanese mountain gun began shelling embattled Lababia. At first the shells landed to the west but soon started to arrive within the company perimeter. One severed the line to battalion headquarters, but it took the hard-pressed signallers only half an hour to fix it.

That afternoon two patrols tried to find the whereabouts of the Japanese attackers. One moved east from the Lababia camp to the south of the Lababia O.P. Track but was forced to withdraw after running into the enemy before reaching the track. Another patrol, led by Lieutenant W. T. Smith[3] from the 2/5th Battalion left the Saddle to try to make contact with the enemy west of Dexter's position and north of the track from Lababia Ridge to the Saddle. It reached the track leading to Vickers Ridge but was unable to find any enemy. Japanese casualties for 22nd June were thought to be between 50 and 60, excluding those killed by supporting weapons. One Australian died of wounds and 3 others were wounded making a two-day total of 10 killed and 12 wounded, mostly caused by light mortar fire or tree snipers. During the night the weary Australians heard the Japanese again moving their dead and wounded.

The Japanese attacks seemed to the defenders to have been in three phases. In the first, the Japanese moved up the track until fired on, when they deployed to either flank and pressed on. In the next phase they concentrated for the attack on the right flank which was probably carried out by moving a force of from 50 to 60 up to the vicinity of the track to Lababia O.P. during the early hours of 21st June and building up this force by the movement of groups of three or four from the Pimple. Later investigation showed signs of much movement and occupation on both sides of the observation post track by approximately 200-300 troops. The third phase was the attempted encirclement on the left flank which was carried out in the same manner as on the right flank but without a force in position before small groups began to move. To reach their positions on the left flank the Japanese cut a new track from the Jap Track to meet the Vickers Ridge Track. A feature of the attack which amazed the defenders was that the Japanese never closed their enemy's line of communication—the Lababia-Saddle track—although they encircled the perimeter to within 50 yards on the north side. Because of this failure reinforcements went forward without interference and supplies were kept

---
[3] Capt W. T. Smith, VX41104; 2/5 Bn. Insurance agent; of Ballarat, Vic; b. Ballarat, 10 Jul 1916.

up. The Japanese failure to cut the track to the Saddle was all the more remarkable because of the presence of a track leading from the position formerly occupied by Tatterson's company to the Lababia-Saddle track.

After a miserable night with heavy rain a series of booby-trap explosions were heard at first light on 23rd June. The few available men, from the company commander to the company clerk, manned the perimeter but no attack developed. Soon afterwards ineffective firing along the Jap Track came from the enemy's positions. As on the previous day this firing seemed designed to draw the Australian fire and so to enable the tree snipers to operate: on both days four or five tree snipers had been shot from the trees soon after first light. Automatic fire continued from the Jap Track until 9 a.m. by which time the 3-inch mortar was proving effective in breaking up enemy movement. Between 9.45 and 11 a.m. the mountain guns joined in the punishment and shelled the Jap Track and Pimple area north of Lababia with great effect. Major O'Hare had used two 3.7-inch howitzers throughout the fight and at this stage was O.P.O. (observation post officer) himself, but shortage of ammunition had reduced firing to times when the Japanese were actually attacking. The mountain guns with their 21-lb shells and extreme accuracy were more decisive than the 3-inch mortar which could not shoot close to the perimeter. The screams of the bombarded Japanese and the excellent shooting caused the 2/6th Battalion war diarist to exult, "the morale of our troops which has always been high was raised to the highest pitch by the excellent shooting of the mountain battery". At midday when the intermittent Japanese fire from the front and the right and left flanks suddenly increased in volume the 3-inch mortar again caused the Japanese to disperse. Wood now rang Dexter and said: "I've got a surprise packet for you. Stop the arty." Soon afterwards the delighted troops watched Beaufighters spread their "whispering death" up and down the Jap Track. By 1.30 p.m. the enemy had withdrawn and firing had ceased.

While the enemy was receiving his final *coup de grâce* Lieutenant W. T. Smith's patrol moved up the Lababia Track to the observation post which he reached at 2.45 p.m. without sighting the enemy, although the telephone wire was cut in many places. Smith's platoon relieved a seven-man patrol which Moten had ordered Urquhart to lead to the observation post during the Lababia attack. Urquhart had left Napier at 7 p.m. on 22nd June in total darkness, climbed 2,500 feet up the steep track and arrived at 2 o'clock in the morning. After their relief Urquhart's men returned to Napier.

Documents containing Japanese plans for the attack were found on a dead Japanese who had died with his hand in the air as though in salutation to his victors, who returned his grisly greeting and waved to him.

With the Japanese mortaring Mat Mat in the late afternoon of 23rd June Dexter's force for the first time in four days had a respite from fighting. While Corporal A. J. Smith re-occupied the listening post, other troops reconnoitred the battle area and found many Japanese dead. Their own comrades buried the Australian dead on Lababia Ridge after a moving service conducted by Padre O'Keefe.[4] The enemy dead were buried by the Pioneer platoon which Wood sent forward for that task. Soon after darkness had fallen an enemy 75-mm gun opened fire on Guadagasal[5] and Mat Mat. This was the first time during the Japanese attack that the gun had fired. The shelling ceased at 7 p.m. by which time the attack had been defeated.

Congratulatory messages were received by Wood from Herring and other senior commanders. To Herring, Savige and Moten the defeat of the enemy meant that subsequent re-grouping and concentration of units for the offensive could proceed unhindered; it also meant that for the first time in the bitter nerve-racking fighting since April the Australians had scored a notable success. The action underlined a development in Australian defensive tactics. Previously the teaching had been to camouflage defensive positions and conceal the defenders. The Lababia defences, however, had been based—first by the 2/7th and then by the 2/6th—on positions which to some extent sacrificed concealment to the clearing of fields of fire. Approached from the enemy side, however, there was little to be seen for the enemy had to come up hill and could see nothing until he was on a level with the diggings, and the fire lanes were cleared from the ground up, only leaves, twigs and small shrubs being removed to a height of about four feet.

"This engagement is noteworthy," wrote Moten, "and is a classic example of how well-dug-in determined troops can resist heavy attacks from a numerically superior enemy. Our troops in Lababia Base totalled 80 and when joined by C Coy 2/6 Aust Inf Bn totalled 150. It is conservatively estimated that 750 Japs attacked our perimeter. Our casualties were 11 killed and 12 wounded. Enemy casualties were estimated as 200."

The Australian estimate of the Japanese strength was too low—more than 1,500 not 750 took part in the attack. The estimate of enemy losses was a little high but not very: the Japanese recorded that 41 were killed and 131 wounded.

Documents captured at Lababia Ridge identified the *66th Infantry Regiment* (less *III Battalion*) under Colonel Araki. The *I Battalion* was 687 strong, the *II* was 552. The *66th Regiment* had been shipped from Rabaul to Finschhafen and had marched down the coastal track to Lae, leaving Finschhafen on 13th April. General Adachi said after the war that the Japanese forces engaged were about 1,500 strong. The two battalions engaged had recently relieved *I* and *II Battalions* of the *102nd Regiment* which had been in the area during May. Including technical troops there were about 2,000 Japanese in the Mubo area.

On 23rd May General Nakano, the commander of the *51st Division*, had been confident of his ability to clear the Lababia-Guadagasal-Waipali area. He had directed that ammunition and rations be accumulated at Mubo between 25th May and 20th June ready for the attack on Waipali which should be successfully completed by 22nd June. Preparations for the attack had included the repairing of the main track for about 5,500 yards north and 2,500 yards south of Komiatum.

Following Nakano's instructions, Araki, on 27th May, had issued an order that the *66th Regiment* would carry out a surprise attack on the Australians' "key point" at Lababia and annihilate them. "Immediately after this," continued the

---

[4] Chaplain Rev P. G. O'Keefe, MBE, VX90116; 2/6 Bn. Catholic priest; of Camperdown, Vic; b. Koroit, Vic, 31 Jan 1907.

[5] The 2/6th Battalion headquarters was about to have its evening meal when the shelling started. Wood immediately sent one of his staff to tell the Salvation Army officer to put out the fires in his coffee stall for fear of "drawing the crabs". In fact, captured maps always showed the Saddle area marked as "cooking fires".

order, "advance to Waipali with lightning speed and mop up enemy in the vicinity. After succeeding in these objectives, quickly concentrate in already established position in vicinity of Mubo." The leading battalion commander, Lieut-Colonel Matsui of the *1/66th,* on 19th June, informed his troops that "tomorrow at dawn we will start mopping up with entire strength and will destroy the enemy. We will then continue on to Guadagasal." "The enemy appears not to be aware of our plans," noted Araki, "he is sunbathing at Guadagasal."

As the Japanese learnt to their cost, the Australians were prepared and fought what Savige described as "one of the classic engagements of the war". Early Japanese reports from the battle area complained that "piano wires are set up everywhere". By 22nd June the enemy reports stated that the *66th Regiment* was enveloping the Australians but that there were a great number of positions linking together in the rear. The optimistic tone rapidly disappeared from Japanese reports as the stubborn defenders held on until the attack was abandoned.

CHAPTER 4

RENDEZVOUS AT NASSAU BAY

BECAUSE of the successful Australian resistance on Lababia Ridge, planning for the offensive was not hampered. As mentioned, it was to take place in three phases: first an American battalion group would establish a bridgehead round Nassau Bay on the night 29th-30th June; second, a battalion of the 15th Brigade would capture Bobdubi Ridge while small forces would raid the Malolo and Kela Hill area to distract attention from the attack at Bobdubi; third, a battalion of the 17th Brigade and the American battalion group would attack Mubo, not later than 6th July.[1]

The American battalion chosen to carry out the first phase was the I/162nd Battalion (Lieut-Colonel Harold Taylor), one of three comprising Colonel MacKechnie's 162nd Regiment. This would be the 162nd's first action. It had landed at Port Moresby from Rockhampton in February 1943 and later relieved the 163rd in the Buna-Sanananda area. At the end of February it began leapfrogging up the coast using mainly surfboats and trawlers, and looking for any Japanese who had survived the Buna fighting. By 4th April Taylor had established a defensive position at Morobe. Soon afterwards the I/162nd Battalion was relieved by the III/162nd and moved south to the Waria River for intensive training. To help the Americans in their baptism of fire Captain Hitchcock's company of the Papuan Infantry Battalion was attached to MacKechnie Force, which included detachments of artillery, signals, etc.

On 9th June Captain D. A. McBride, liaison officer from the 17th Brigade, arrived at MacKechnie's headquarters. He was informed that planning was in abeyance pending advice about the availability of landing craft and a unit known then as the 2nd Engineer Amphibian Brigade whose task would be to handle all transport between Morobe and the beach-head.[2]

> The 2nd Engineer Special Brigade was born on the sandy shore of Cape Cod, Massachusetts, on 20 June 1942. . . . Everything was "secret". Announcement of the event was proclaimed only by the roar of motors and the sight of queer looking landing craft splashing through the choppy waters of Nantucket Sound. . . . Although training of the new unit was veiled in secrecy, it was not long before the local residents of that picturesque cape showed keen interest in the "boys with the boats". . . . Gradually they began to refer to the new Amphibians as "Cape Cod Commandos". . . . The name stuck. It followed them across the United States and the Pacific Ocean to Australia, New Guinea, New Britain and the Philippines.[3]

---

[1] The main sources for the account of American operations in the Salamaua campaign are: Colonel H. Haney, Report of Operations of the 162nd Infantry, June 29-September 12 1943, in Morobe-Nassau-Bitoi Ridge-Mount Tambu-Tambu Bay-Salamaua Area of New Guinea; W. F. McCartney, *The Jungleers: A History of the 41st Infantry Division* (1948); *History of the Second Engineer Special Brigade* (1946); J. Miller, Jr, *Cartwheel: the Reduction of Rabaul*; and Australian situation reports, orders, telegrams and sundry reports.

[2] In July 1943 the name was changed to 2nd Engineer Special Brigade and the regiments became "Boat and Shore Regiments". The substitution of "Special" for "Amphibian" was probably done for security reasons.

[3] *History of the Second Engineer Special Brigade*, p. 1.

The "Amphibs", as they were known, were specially selected from men with maritime or other relevant experience. Eventually three brigades of "Amphibs", the 2nd, 3rd and 4th Engineer Special Brigades, served in the Pacific. The establishment of a brigade was 360 officers, 7,000 men and 550 landing craft; each brigade included three Boat and Shore Regiments.

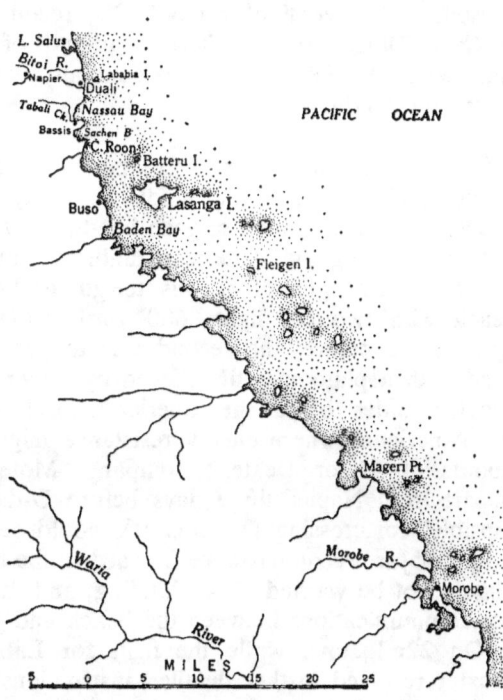

The training of the I/162nd Battalion had included the loading of 70 men on each of three patrol torpedo boats and their transfer at sea into L.C.V's (Landing Craft, Vehicle). Morobe Harbour, a deep land-locked bay protected to seaward by several high coconut-covered islands and surrounded from shore to foothills by mangrove, provided an excellent base. It was regularly bombed by the enemy, but good hideouts were available near by for P.T. boats, trawlers and barges. North of Morobe the coast was indented with large bays, while heavily timbered mountain spurs extending to the sea precluded the possibility of any land advance along the coast and dictated that all movement must be by water. Even the natives in this area were canoe-borne.

After the Summit conference MacKechnie had decided on 16th June to change the staging base for the landing from Lasanga Island to Mageri Point, an excellent sandy beach 12 miles north of Morobe with good cover for troops and ample hideouts for landing craft among the mangrove-lined inlets.

Uncertainty about the number of landing craft that would be available caused great difficulty. MacKechnie originally believed that 35 L.C.V's, 3 L.C.M's (Landing Craft, Mechanised) and 9 salvaged Japanese barges would be available. Four days before the landing, however, he was informed that there were available only 20 L.C.V's, 1 L.C.M. and 3 Japanese barges, together with 3 P.T. boats to pilot the landing waves and carry 70 men each. With these craft MacKechnie carried out a practice landing on 27th June at Mageri Point. The exercise was not a success but valuable lessons were learnt by the infantry and the amphibious engineers.

The Papuan company reached Buso by 15th June.[4] Although they were not to move north from Buso for the present this did not prevent the native soldiers from carrying out long-range patrols, at which they were adept. For example, Lance-Corporal Tapioli went overland to Tabali Creek, and Lance-Corporal Bengari joined an enemy carrier line and spent two nights and a day with the enemy at Nassau Bay. Hitchcock himself, with several of his N.C.O's, reconnoitred the track from Buso to Cape Dinga—the southern headland of Nassau Bay—and decided that he could safely conceal his company behind Cape Roon on the day before the landing.

Brigadier Moten informed Colonel Wood on 21st June that Lieutenant Burke would arrive at the Saddle next day and would be supplied with direct communication to brigade headquarters until the completion of his task of assisting the American landing. Much depended on Burke. He had four tasks. The first was to guide the Americans to the landing beach with two red lights 600 yards from one another with a white light in the centre; the second was to protect the flanks of the beach-head with a platoon until relieved by American troops; the third was to provide guides to lead the Americans to Napier; and the fourth to inform the Americans where enemy resistance might be met and of the whereabouts of Major Dexter's company. Moten also instructed Burke to depart from Napier three days before D-day; ordered that "boats, collapsible" for crossing Tabali Creek would be carried; that there would be no premature reconnaissance forward to the beach in order that the enemy should not be warned of the landing; and that six runners would be used for communications between the beach and Napier.

On 22nd June, while the fight for Lababia Ridge was still raging, Dexter received further detailed instructions from Moten about his company's role. The company could anticipate no respite until it had drawn the enemy inland to the last spur and had been relieved by the Americans on their way to Napier where tracks had been cut to newly-built bridges over the Bitoi and on to Bitoi Ridge. On the day after the landing a small detachment from Napier would climb Bitoi Ridge to select a vantage point from which the Japanese lines of communication to Komiatum could be overlooked. Dexter's company, plus an additional platoon, marched from Lababia Ridge to Napier on 25th June. Left at Lababia was Captain Cameron's company reinforced by a platoon from each of two others. On 24th June Moten's headquarters closed at Skindewai and opened at Guadagasal.

At this time the supply problem was again causing concern. Too much weather and too few aircraft often meant that the troops felt the pinch. Even one inaccurate drop could endanger the build-up of supplies and so threaten to disrupt the plan for the offensive. For example, at

---

[4] The strength of "A" Company, Papuan Infantry Battalion, was 5 officers (Australians), 18 NCO's (Australian and native) and 119 native other ranks. The PIB was smaller than an Australian battalion, its establishment being 20 officers and 421 other ranks.

Guadagasal on 27th June Mitchells came in too fast and flew across the dropping ground instead of along it; only 6 of about 40 parachutes landed on the dropping ground. One aircraft dropped supplies on Buisaval Ridge, some 4,000 yards south-east of the dropping ground, and many packages were lost in inaccessible gorges. Moten's vigorous protest that a continuation of such dropping would have a ruinous effect on maintenance for the coming operations was immediately passed on to General Herring. The supply position worsened, particularly in the 15th Brigade's area. By 27th June there were no rations for natives in the whole Missim area, and troops and natives round Hote were without food. This unfortunate situation was not likely to improve the spirits or stamina of troops who were to go into action three days hence, most of them for the first time. Complaints and entreaties brought their reward, and on 27th June 13 aircraft dropped rations and ammunition, 12 at Selebob and one at Hote; and a further 20 dropped supplies on 28th June.

It was natural for troops in the forward areas to believe that the irregularity and scarcity of rations were caused by New Guinea Force's lack of interest. Nothing could have been further from the truth. Herring and his staff knew only too well that the fate of the offensive depended on their ability to get supplies forward by air to the right place at the right time. The problem of supplying the Salamaua battle area was no easy one. All supplies had to be flown from Port Moresby. The mountains themselves were a serious enough obstacle for transport aircraft, but when the clouds built up over the mountains flying was impossible. Another hazard for the Allied supply dropping planes was the presence of Japanese fighters only a short distance away at Lae, while the nearest Allied fighters were at Dobodura some 200 miles away. To overcome this difficulty the Fifth Air Force adopted the practice of using bombers to carry supplies. The high speed of the bombers over the targets led to bad dropping, but bad dropping was better than none at all. Another important factor was later described by Herring: "The dropping had to take place in the shadow of high mountains and not only is it bad for aircraft to run into high mountains but there are a large number of air currents about which make flying in the vicinity somewhat hazardous and raw pilots found it very difficult at first to avoid these and get their runs over the dropping places just right."

On 22nd June Colonel Guinn,[5] now in temporary command of the 15th Brigade, issued the brigade's first operation order which had been drawn up by Brigadier Hosking. The 58th/59th Battalion received the premier role of capturing Bobdubi Ridge from Orodubi to the Coconuts on the north end of the ridge—a very onerous task. Other tasks included

---

[5] Guinn, who enjoyed walking, was tramping the Bulldog-Wau road when a police boy arrived with a letter demanding his presence at divisional headquarters. He arrived 26 hours late and, after being reprimanded in language that "if put to print would scorch the best of parchment", he was instructed to proceed to 15th Brigade at Pilimung, hand a sealed envelope to Brigadier Hosking, take temporary command of the brigade and carry on with the planning and execution of the forthcoming operation. Guinn made up for lost time and did the journey in one day— normally a two days' trip. He took over the 15th Brigade on 21st June. The next time he saw Savige his opening remark was: "Well, I made up that day you stirred me up over."

raids by the 2/3rd Independent Company on Malolo and Kela and the establishment of ambush positions by the company of the 24th Battalion forward of Hote.

On 23rd June Colonels Guinn and Starr and Major Travers arrived at Missim and later left with Major Warfe for the Meares' Creek area. Next day they arrived at Nunn's Post[6] where Warfe, from his detailed and intimate knowledge of the wild country, oriented the other two commanders. As a result of this reconnaissance Guinn decided that Old Vickers and Gwaibolom (the highest feature on the ridge) were the keys to Bobdubi Ridge. He therefore instructed Starr that these two places would be his objectives, and ordered Warfe to send patrols to investigate Gwaibolom and Orodubi.

The bulk of the 2/3rd Independent Company had been resting during early June in the Missim area. Canteens and the Y.M.C.A. and even the Salvation Army were still unknown in this part of New Guinea. Missim was not equipped for large concentrations of troops and huts had to be hastily erected to accommodate them. Books and other means of recreation were lacking but two luxuries were available: the men could bathe in the swirling pools of the Francisco and wash at the hot springs. Most important of all, however, was the opportunity to relax after months of tension.

To prevent the enemy from discovering his lines of approach to Goodview Junction (Stephens' and Walpole's Tracks) against which danger he had been warned by Warfe, Captain Hancock decided not to strike again in that direction but to coordinate any further strike with the coming offensive. His decision was also influenced by a message from the surprisingly erudite Warfe, who had no wireless time left in which to encode a message after Private Hemphill's[7] arrival with information about the miscarrying of Captain Hancock's prisoner raid but who wished to inform his second-in-command of the arrival of the 58th/59th: *"Major opus multi populi iam Missim sunt."*[8] Other activities of the Independent Company included two successful patrols led by Lieutenant Erskine and Sergeant Tomkins to reconnoitre the routes south from Base 4 to the 17th Brigade area and thus to prepare the way for the move north by the 17th Brigade.

In the Markham area a patrol led by Lieutenant Baber[9] (of the 24th Battalion) was surprised by the Japanese on 19th June near Markham Point. As a result of this action Corporal Giblett[1] was officially posted as

---

[6] Named after Corporal C. W. Nunn, 2/3rd Independent Company.

[7] Pte E. C. Hemphill, NX14216. 2/3 Indep Coy, 2/3 Cdo Sqn. Poultry farmer; of Coolgardie, WA; b. Ravensthorpe, WA, 31 Oct 1909. (His correct name was Hampel. He enlisted in November 1939 and served as WX829 Pte E. C. Hampel with the 2/11th Battalion until March 1940 when he was discharged medically unfit. He re-enlisted under the name of Hemphill and served until the end of the war.)

[8] Warfe was confident that Hancock would translate this as: "A major operation is about to take place; many troops are now at Missim."

[9] Lt E. C. Baber, NX6612; 24 Bn. Store manager; of Brighton-le-Sands, NSW; b. Carlton, NSW, 12 Nov 1912. Killed in action 11 Sep 1943.

[1] Cpl A. R. Giblett, VX135886; 24 Bn. Commercial traveller; of Burwood, Vic; b. Warrnambool, Vic, 30 May 1908. Missing, presumed killed in action, 19 Jun 1943.

missing and became the 24th Battalion's first loss in action. The first news of further casualties in the Markham area filtered in on 22nd June when the police boy of Captain Howlett and Warrant-Officer Ryan (of Angau) reached Kirkland's Dump and reported that the Japanese had attacked the party at the Chivasing crossing. At dusk Ryan arrived at Kirkland's with the news that Howlett had been killed the previous day. Ryan in his report told of a hazardous long-range patrol he had conducted with Howlett in areas to the north of the Markham which they had crossed on 25th April. He told of reconnaissances carried out in the Japanese-infested area north of the river, of close misses with the Japanese, of sicknesses, of Japanese movements (including two patrols which left Boana for Kaiapit on 18th April and 30th May) and of new tracks. On 21st June Howlett and Ryan and one native, on being assured by the local natives that there were no Japanese in the area, entered Chivasing before re-crossing the Markham. As the three men entered the centre of the village a volley of rifle shots and a burst of machine-gun fire came from a row of huts. As Ryan jumped down into a creek Howlett was shot dead.

The Japanese who had ambushed Howlett and Ryan consisted of 10 military police who had left Lae on 10th June "to ascertain the condition of the enemy and to conciliate natives in the coastal region of the Markham River". On 21st June, according to the leader's report which was subsequently captured, the Japanese attacked "an enemy reconnaissance patrol which had broken into the village of Chivasing", killed one of the two Australians, and captured some ammunition and equipment. "This enemy reconnaissance patrol," reported the Japanese, "had crossed the Markham River from the direction of Marilinan. They had been sent to relieve a reconnaissance patrol which had been detailed to Finschhafen."

Ryan blamed the Markham natives for the betrayal and stated that as the Japanese patrol had been waiting at least three weeks for the patrol's return the natives of Chivasing, had they so desired, could have warned Howlett. "Instead they chose to assist the Japanese in every possible way and for that reason, in my own mind, I look upon Captain Howlett not as a battle casualty but as the victim of a cold-blooded murder by these treacherous Markham natives," wrote Ryan.

Such behaviour contrasted strangely with the treatment accorded Sergeant Hogan's patrol by the Gabmatzung people, who also belonged to the Markham tribes. The Australian soldier had a considerable understanding of and sympathy for the natives in spite of derogatory opinions about his handling of them by those considered more expert in native affairs. He had come to the conclusion that natives in enemy territory should not be blamed too harshly for helping the enemy. Living very close to the bare existence level the natives knew well that enemy depredations against their crops and livestock would reduce them to starvation. If the natives refused to carry or spy for the enemy their villages would be burnt, their food taken, and they themselves perhaps killed. Commonsense dictated to the natives—logical and practical people—that it would be prudent to serve Japanese or Australians, whichever happened to control the areas in which they lived. Thus it became the exception for natives to refuse to obey the enemy. Many fled from enemy territory and many others served the Japanese with their hands and the Australians with their hearts.

Angau capitalised on the natives' genuine affection for the Australian soldier. News of good treatment, regular food and tobacco and care of the carriers' families soon spread, with the result that principal Allied formations usually had numbers of carriers who had come from enemy-occupied territory. During the fluctuating fighting for Bobdubi Ridge the natives found themselves carrying for both sides in turn, usually for the Japanese first. The Australians, at least, did not blame or punish the natives for their actions. Some who were on Angau's black list were undoubtedly pro-Japanese from choice; but on the whole they were amiable, likeable and cooperative and helped enormously to win the war in New Guinea.

Angau officers wished to punish the Chivasing natives and destroy their canoes. Savige decided, however, that the punitive expedition should consist only of an Angau representative and police boys, as an expedition by soldiers might turn the natives against the Australians. The Angau officer, moreover, was to sink the canoes but only address the natives. The Chivasing natives, pre-warned, or armed with the intuition which so often enabled a native to avoid trouble, did not wait to be harangued and left only three canoes.

On 26th June Savige informed Major Smith of the 24th Battalion that Captain J. A. Chalk's company of the Papuan Infantry Battalion, less one platoon, would move forward from Wau to Sunshine where it would come under Smith's command and patrol along the Markham. While the Papuans were moving up, a 3-inch mortar team from the 24th Battalion under Sergeant Christensen[2] bombarded Markham Point on the 27th and again on 29th June. On the second occasion Lance-Corporal McInnes' covering party inflicted 12 casualties on Japanese who came out to look for the troublesome mortar.

Final preparations were now being made for the landing of Mac-Kechnie Force. It was the first time that so large a force would land in enemy-occupied territory in the South-West Pacific Area. By 28th June all troops were assembled at Mageri Point except for the 210 who were to travel on the three P.T. boats. From the reconnaissance of his own scouts and of Hitchcock's Papuans MacKechnie believed that there were about 75 Japanese near the mouth of the south arm of the Bitoi, an outpost or two along the beach at Nassau Bay, and about 300 on Cape Dinga with an outpost on the ridge near the east end of the Cape Dinga peninsula. On the night of 28th-29th June three small detachments from the I/162nd Battalion were posted on Batteru, Lasanga and Fleigen Islands between Mageri Point and Nassau Bay. Their task was to flash signal lights each night from 29th June until 5th July to guide landing craft and supply boats. MacKechnie's planning was again complicated

---

[2] WO2 G. H. Christensen, VX104419; 24 Bn. Salesman; of Camberwell, Vic; b. Auburn, Vic, 21 Jan 1920.

on 29th June itself when he learnt that he now had 28 L.C.V's, three L.C.M's, one salvaged Japanese barge, and four P.T. boats, three of which would carry troops and guide the barges. In these craft he decided to move three infantry companies, two artillery batteries, one anti-aircraft platoon, and five days' rations during the two nights 29th-30th June and 30th June-1st July. Radio silence was imposed until midnight on 29th-30th June.

At dusk on 29th June three P.T. boats loaded 70 men each at Morobe and set off north to their rendezvous off Mageri Point with the main body of MacKechnie Force, about 770 strong, loaded into about 30 craft manned by boatmen of the 532nd Engineer Boat and Shore Regiment.[3] The landing force was divided into three waves each of which was to rendezvous with a P.T. boat outside Mageri Point. The boats moved off in twos with an interval of 20 minutes between waves. When they reached the open sea they encountered a heavy swell about 15 feet high, which added to the discomfort already caused by driving rain. So dark and stormy was the night that it was difficult for the boats to see the wakes of those in front of them, and more than half an hour was spent in finding lost boats. The first two waves met their P.T. boats but the third wave failed to do so and proceeded without a guide.

The other main groups of actors in the drama were also on the move on 29th June. The Papuans left Buso in canoes and arrived at Cape Roon whence they moved overland to Sachen Bay. Here Hitchcock set up his headquarters and during the dark night the native soldiers moved stealthily towards Cape Dinga.

Dexter's company of the 2/6th Battalion, together with Burke's small party, had arrived at Napier from Lababia late on the afternoon of 25th June. Next day the troops assembled in the largest hut where the company commander put them all in the picture. Towards evening Burke, with Urquhart's platoon, left Napier on the first stage of their vital task. That night the patrol camped at the hut in a native garden along the Bitoi Track ready to push on next day.

At last light on the 27th Dexter marched east with the remainder of his company and camped at the hut. All movement was by night because the track along the Bitoi was exposed and a large force might have been noticed by enemy patrols. On the 28th the company was dug in at the last spur ready to withstand the Japanese whom it was planned to entice up the track, and ready to link up at this position with the vanguard of the Americans. At the same time a section led by Corporal McElgunn moved off as a guerilla force along the north side of the Bitoi's south arm, hoping to capture the mortar used against Lieutenant Gibbons' unfortunate patrol.

---

[3] It is difficult to decide exactly how many landing craft set out from Morobe and Mageri Point. The report of the 162nd Regiment says that there were 4 PT boats, 28 LCV's, 3 LCM's and one captured Japanese barge. The report of MacKechnie Force mentions 35 LCVP's and 2 LCM's. A "narrative of events" prepared by the headquarters of the 3rd Australian Division on 10th July 1943 from various conflicting reports and signals mentions "three waves each consisting of 12 boats". The historian of the 2 ESB says that 29 LCVP's and 2 captured Japanese barges were escorted by 3 PT boats.

At 1.30 p.m. on the 29th Lieutenant R. J. H. Smith's platoon moved out to try and draw back the Japanese from the position where Gibbons had been killed, about 400 yards from the coast. So far this part of the plan was working smoothly and when Private Trebilcock[4] arrived from Burke to say that the beach patrol had reached Tabali Creek, Dexter was able to telephone this news to Moten. For about two hours in the late afternoon the men listened contentedly to sounds of an Allied air attack on Duali and Nassau Bay. At various times late at night and early

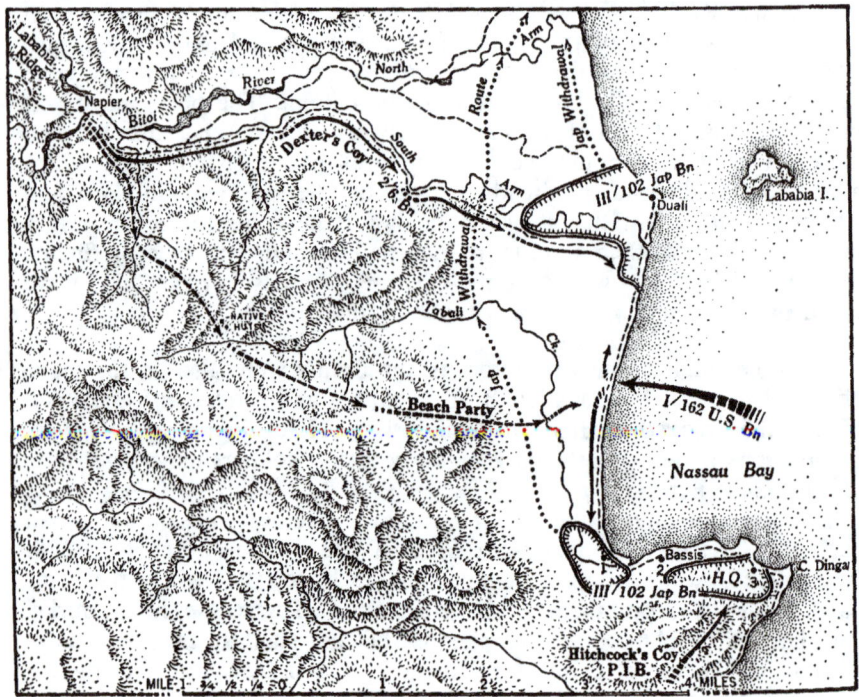

Nassau Bay landing, 29th-30th June

next morning the Australians at the last spur could hear engines throbbing out to sea.

At first light on 28th June Burke had departed from the hut along the route which he and Ellen had blazed. The patrol spent the night in the jungle just off the track. Early on the 29th they moved off again and in the afternoon arrived at the edge of a swamp which was described feelingly by Urquhart as "the worst bastard I'd ever struck". For two hours the men waded and staggered through the swamp, laboriously dragging out their feet, sinking now ankle deep, now up to their loins in the foul slime; dragging out their hindquarters by slapping weapons crosswise on the reeds and getting a purchase on them. After about 1,000 yards of

[4] Pte T. G. Trebilcock, MM, SX13732; 2/6 Bn. Gardener; of Montacute, SA; b. Payneham, SA, 16 Nov 1921.

swamp the men reached firmer ground just after dusk and flung themselves down to rest near the dark and deep waters of the Tabali, which was said to be crocodile-infested. They hoped that the familiar jungle noises would drown the wheeze and whistle as they inflated their rubber boat. In pitch darkness Ellen and Private Molloy[5] crossed the Tabali in the rubber dinghy which was then hauled back for the next load and so on. Before the last men were ferried across rain was pouring down. Burke, however, wished to reach the beach not more than one hour before the scheduled landing time because he believed that the actual site chosen for the landing might be occupied and it would be unwise to have a fight before the landing. Moreover, Moten had ordered no forward reconnaissance before the landing. He therefore paused for a short period despite Urquhart's advice to press on.

At 9.45 the 26 men began moving towards the beach. It was soon apparent that they had under-estimated the difficulties of the night and jungle. Linking themselves together by each man grasping the bayonet scabbard or shoulder strap of the man in front, they set out towards the beach which was only 500 yards away. Creepers, vines, trees, undergrowth and hidden logs impeded progress, and the patrol blundered too far south; in Burke's opinion the considerable amount of metal carried by the troops caused a southing pull on the compass bearing worked out on the previous reconnaissance. "Try to imagine it," wrote one participant soon afterwards, "only 500 yards between us and the sea, no more than the distance from Spencer Street to the Town Hall, from the Woolshed to Cassidy's Creek, and we couldn't do it. There we were . . . a stumbling, straining, cursing serpent of men, lured on by the distant rumble of the ocean, and never getting any nearer to it. It became evident we were moving in a circle. We all stopped and listened—the croaking of frogs, the sullen drum-drum of the rain on our shoulders and always the rumble of invisible breakers."[6]

Time was slipping away and it began to appear that the patrol could not reach the beach in time. The troubled moment produced the man. Corporal G. L. Smith went to the front and began hacking at the tangled jungle growth. At intervals he shone back a torch to guide the remainder of the patrol and was in turn guided left or right by Corporal Stephens[7] holding a compass on a bearing of 90 degrees.

Progress was less frustrating as the men moved up to Smith before he advanced again. Burke realised that this procedure was risky but he knew there was no alternative if he was to reach the beach on time. As the men followed Smith and the flashlight the sound of the surf became stronger. After navigating a patch of thick jungle in this slow but sure manner the leading men about 11.15 p.m. reached a semi-cleared area whence they could hear the waves breaking on the beach. "Then of a sudden," wrote Stephens, "Smithy gave a loud cry, the scrub relinquished

---
[5] Cpl J. W. Molloy, NX85507; 2/6 Bn. Public servant; of Gundagai, NSW; b. Wagga Wagga, NSW, 1 Mar 1923.
[6] J. F. Stephens, "Rendezvous at Nassau Bay", *Khaki and Green* (1943), p. 150.
[7] Sgt J. F. Stephens, VX57226; 2/6 Bn. Schoolteacher; of Beeac, Vic; b. Beeac, 29 Aug 1915.

us and slipped quietly out of the game and, as we topped a low sand-dune, the ocean opened up with a million-horsepowered roar and swallowed us and the whole world in the noise of it."

Burke now made straight for the beach with Ellen, Smith and four others. These seven men had become separated from the rest of the patrol when the movement through the jungle had accelerated but Urquhart knew the general plan. The smaller group found themselves well south of the landing beach and raced north along the sand without worrying about the enemy, in order to get into their signalling positions as soon as possible. Breathless and soaked, the seven men set up the signalling lights (five minutes late according to the plan), red lights 600 yards apart on the flanks and a white light in the centre. The lights were positioned on a high bank of sand whence they could be seen from the sea even taking account of the height of the waves which Burke estimated was about 10 feet. For about half an hour the men waited tensely for some movement from the sea. They then saw figures moving rapidly up the beach and believed they were Japanese approaching from Bassis. Burke had already withdrawn his men from the lights and now they returned to the shelter of the jungle. The "Japanese" were actually Urquhart and the rest of the party who had reached the beach too far south and had moved rapidly north where they had also begun to signal with two lights. At the same time as Burke's men saw the group approaching from the south (about 12.30 a.m.) they heard the throb of engines in the bay. "It was at this psychological moment," wrote Burke later, "that the first of the landing craft hit the beach—and I really mean hit."

The convoy of landing craft had experienced great difficulty in finding the beach. The leading and central boat of the first wave, carrying two key figures, Colonel Taylor and Captain D. A. McBride, as well as 29 troops, had an unfortunate experience. After two hours the lieutenant in charge of the first wave and leading boat informed Taylor that he was doubtful whether his craft was capable of reaching its destination. He suggested that the more important members of the boat should transfer to the next craft, called to the next craft to come alongside, waved the remainder on and began the trans-shipment—no easy task in the rain, the darkness and the high sea. By the time that five had trans-shipped the first wave had disappeared and the second wave had passed through. The lieutenant, who had also transferred, took the lead of the third flight which automatically followed. The boat led the wave on until 2 a.m. on 30th June, over two hours after the scheduled time of landing, when all began to be smitten with sickening doubts about their whereabouts.

At 3 a.m. Taylor ordered the wave to turn south. After milling about in what McBride considered was Lokanu Bay, the boats again headed for the open sea and proceeded south for two hours. McBride recognised Lasanga Island and suggested to Taylor that he could navigate to Nassau Bay. At this stage it was noticed that eight of the boats that had been following closely had disappeared. As always with men trying to reconcile their fears with their duty, there was now some vacillation. An opinion was advanced and eagerly seized upon that it was doubtful if the landing had taken place. Making the best of a bad job the remaining three boats put into Buso where men at Hitchcock's rear headquarters stated that the landing had indeed taken place. McBride, a bewildered passenger, classed the transfer as a "complete mystery", particularly as the first boat, minus the lieutenant, landed on the first night. The other boats of the third wave returned to Mageri Point.

Except for McBride's report there is naturally no Australian account of what happened in the landing craft at the actual landing. Both the American infantry and American boatmen have left accounts which vary in detail although they coincide in general.

> Everything went wrong during the landing at Nassau Bay (wrote the historian of the 41st Division). The leading PT boat overshot the beach; in turning back, several of the boats carrying the first wave were lost and much time passed before they could be located. By this time the second wave was moving ashore and crossed in front of the first wave, almost causing a collision. As the boats approached shore they found a ten to twelve-foot surf pounding the beach. Utter confusion reigned throughout the landing. Boats of the first and second waves attempted to land at the same time in an interval between two lead lights which covered only half of the landing beach. There was a great deal of congestion and, due to the high surf, many of the craft were rammed onto the beach and were unable to get back to sea. Later boats ran into these beached craft or over the open ramps. Of eighteen boats which landed only one made it off the beach and back to sea. All others broached and filled with water as the high surf pounded against them. Despite the rough sea, beaching of the landing craft, confusion and congestion, no men were lost or injured and the only equipment lost were some Aussie radios, which made communications somewhat limited thereafter. . . . The leading elements discovered, after they landed, that the Australian platoon had been lost and had arrived at the beach only in time to establish two lead lights, instead of the three that had been planned.[8]

The historian of the 2nd Engineer Special Brigade thus described the voyage and landing:

> Escorted by only three PT boats, the convoy inched northward a few miles off the enemy-held coast through the inky darkness and into ever increasing rain, wind and heavy seas. . . . The PT boats were too fast even at their lowest speed for the convoy and could not effectively guide it. Their craft cruised at twenty-five knots, ours at eight. One wave of boats got off the course entirely. . . . The main group of boats finally located the landing beach. An Aussie patrol from the mountains had infiltrated through the Jap lines to the objective beach and flashed recognition signals to the convoy. They were barely visible in the murky, rainy darkness. . . . The Amphibs . . . directed their boats straight toward the lights of the Aussie patrol and pulled their throttles wide open. It was obvious to the experienced boatmen that the barges could not be beached successfully in the churning surf, which was now running twelve feet high, but orders were to land that night. So land they did, an hour after midnight,[9] even though the boats were

---

[8] W. F. McCartney, *The Jungleers: A History of the 41st Infantry Division*, p. 53.

[9] The various accounts left of these exciting minutes make it impossible to determine with any certainty the actual time of the landing. For instance, Burke's report and the war diary of the 2/6th Battalion state that the first wave landed at 12.30 a.m. MacKechnie puts the time at 12.15 a.m., Urquhart and the history of the 2 ESB say about 1 a.m., while Japanese Intelligence reports mention 2 a.m. as the landing time. It would seem probable, however, that the first landing occurred between 12.15 and 12.30. Similarly it is impossible to know which lights (Burke's or Urquhart's) guided the Americans to the landing beach. The 41st Division history mentions seeing two lights; this would seem to indicate that they were guided by Urquhart's two, but they landed opposite Burke's three lights.

tossed about like match sticks as they approached the shore. Much equipment, weapons and ammunition were lost in the landing but every soldier was put safely ashore. Most of the boats were unable to retract and twenty-one of them were left swamped on the beach, twisted in every direction while the surf pounded them into distorted shapes within a few minutes.[1]

The confusion of the landing was accentuated by the absence of the battalion commander on whom MacKechnie was relying to look after operations while he himself would concentrate on establishing a base. Despite the confusion and mishaps, the fact that a landing did take place at all was a remarkable feat. As Burke wrote later: "It was a great effort on the part of the troops and the inexperienced navigators in the landing craft, that they ever managed to reach the beach in one piece."

Between the landing of the two waves Burke moved all lights 200 yards farther north to prevent the boats from bunching—the boats of the first wave had mostly made for a position from the centre light to the south light when 8 of the 11 boats had broached. It had been intended that Captain George's company of the I/162nd Battalion would move about 300 yards north of the northern landing light and Captain Newman's a similar distance south of the southern light. As the landing craft had broached, the company in the P.T. boats could not be trans-shipped for landing and returned to Morobe.

Unfortunately both regimental and battalion headquarters, portions of three infantry companies, the hospital, the engineers, the men manning the landing craft and other service detachments were dumped together in a very small area where the sub-units became intermingled. The inexperience of the Americans was apparent to the small Australian party on the beach from the way several smoked and many spoke in loud voices. Urquhart sent his men moving among the Americans to urge them off the beach and into cover, and by dawn the two flanking companies had been guided to their positions and had been assisted in fixing their defences. About three hours after the landing Burke met MacKechnie who was dismayed at the mishaps suffered by the craft and upset that so few of his troops had landed.[2] Although no contact was made with the enemy that night several recently-abandoned weapon-pits were found immediately inland.[3]

Nor was all well with the Japanese in the Nassau Bay area. Major Takamura had been relieved of his command of *III/102nd Battalion* by Major Oba. Speaking to his officers on the eve of his departure Takamura said: "There is still insufficient understanding and zeal in execution. It is a regrettable fact that with a lack of clearness of understanding, there have been many instances of failure to get any practical results. To be specific: there is a lack of quick, reliable transmission of orders; slowness and lack of comprehension in carrying out plans; leaders are lacking in eagerness to serve; they are not strict in supervision of their subordinates; and there are those whose sense of responsibility cannot be relied upon. Reports are

---

[1] *History of the Second Engineer Special Brigade*, pp. 37-9.

[2] By daylight 770 officers and men had landed, including "A" Company (Captain George), 5 and 91; "C" Company (Captain Newman), 6 and 160; "D" Company, 4 and 106.

[3] There are reports from American sources that the Japanese attacked the perimeter on the night of the landing but they are not verified by Australians who were there. There were some firing and some casualties and there may have been a patrol brush but there was no attack.

greatly delayed, some are not straightforward and frank, and there has been much carelessness and many mistakes in the various investigations; hence, opportunities to advance our objective are lost."

General Nakano was anything but pleased with the showing of his force at Nassau Bay. He issued a severe lecture to his senior and middle grade divisional officers about their lack of willpower, their poor leadership, their prevalent whines, their feeble morale, their lost prestige, and their lack of attention to detail. He said that they had "forfeited their trust and confidence because of the contradiction of their words and deeds".

Other changes were occurring in the Japanese area. On 29th June Nakano ordered Major-General Chuichi Muroya, commander of the infantry of the *51st Division*, to protect and fortify Salamaua. Under command Muroya would have the *III/66th Battalion* and two battalions of the *102nd Regiment*, together with artillery and ancillary troops. The new command would be established from noon on 30th June.

As MacKechnie's wireless sets had been submerged during the landing Savige and Moten knew nothing about what had happened at the beach. A reconnaissance aircraft reported at 1.15 p.m. on the 30th that 19 barges (actually 21) were lying on the beach at Nassau Bay and that troops were clustered along the foreshore. As all landing craft were to be clear of Nassau Bay by dawn to avoid air attacks, Savige and Moten knew that something must be wrong. Moten had telephone communication to the last spur, but his patrols thence had not yet made contact with the Japanese or the Americans.

At 7 a.m. on the 30th the platoon sent out by Dexter the previous afternoon returned and reported having gone beyond the suspected Japanese position without making contact with the enemy. As a second patrol was unable to ascertain if the track to the coast was clear, Lieutenant Roach's platoon was sent east at 11 a.m. in an attempt to attract the enemy. It returned at 5.30 p.m. and reported being fired on about 400 yards from the coast. The platoon engaged the enemy for about 30 minutes and withdrew when a gun opened fire from north of the Bitoi. Roach occupied an ambush position 300 yards farther back for an hour but the enemy refused to fall into the trap.

Dexter telephoned this information to Moten and was ordered to move forward early next morning and destroy the enemy at the mouth of the south arm of the Bitoi by 9 a.m. It was a wild rainy night and the Victorians were soaked to the skin. In Dexter's opinion his company, which had received no let-up since 19th June, was exhausted; men were falling asleep on their feet and were in no condition for fighting. The voice of Moten came over the wire emphasising that the task must be done and Dexter, having given his assurance that it would be, sent for a section from his reserve platoon at Napier to take over the last spur position. Success or failure was to be indicated by pre-arranged Very light signals. MacKechnie Force would then attack the enemy position at 11 a.m. Savige told Fuller about this, and the orders were sent to MacKechnie in a message dropped by a Wirraway and carried by P.T. boat from Morobe.

On the morning after the landing Captain George's company of the I/162nd Battalion began patrolling towards the mouth of the Bitoi while Captain Newman's patrolled towards the mouth of Tabali Creek. Urquhart was requested to move with George's company towards Duali, assisting and advising him where possible. The Allied patrol advanced north along the coastal routes in the general direction of Duali. After half a mile Urquhart's forward scout, Corporal G. L. Smith, shot a lone Japanese on the inland track. Hearing the firing George moved his company to the inland track, after which Urquhart decided to leave the Americans there and advance along the coastal track. Soon afterwards the Australians were pinned down by machine-gun fire coming from the direction of Duali. Private Shadbolt with his Bren, assisted by Private Skuse,[4] ran forward and cleared the track. Soon afterwards Private Barwise[5] noticed two Japanese setting up another machine-gun on the beach ahead and, with grenades from his grenade discharger, killed them both and destroyed the gun. George's company meanwhile had gone to ground. American mortars were fired indiscriminately in the direction of Duali.

MacKechnie ordered Newman's company north from the Tabali to help George's company. Leaving one platoon in a defensive position 200 yards north of the Tabali, Newman joined George in the early afternoon and slowly advanced towards the south arm of the Bitoi. At 4.30 p.m. the platoon near the Tabali reported that the enemy had crossed the river near its mouth and were moving inland towards the American flank. The platoon was ordered to move north and establish a defensive position from the beach to the swamp at the south edge of the actual beach-head area. While moving to this position it was attacked, at 4.45 p.m., and had to fight its way back towards the beach-head, losing its leader and four men killed. To support it the two northern companies were now moved back to the beach-head.

Indiscriminate firing continued, and after dark the Americans apparently thought that they were being attacked from all sides. They reported that the enemy were using machine-guns, mortars, grenades and rifles with tracer ammunition, and at the same time calling out names and English phrases. Because the night was so dark physical contact was necessary before the outline of a body could be seen and the Americans believed that several Japanese infiltrated their positions. As a result of the firing throughout the night 18 unfortunate Americans were killed and 27 wounded. Of this night, which the Australians dubbed "Guy Fawkes night", Urquhart commented: "My blokes went to ground and stayed there. Not one man fired a shot." Even in experienced units "itchy finger" often led to accidental casualties at night. In this case the night was pitch black, the noises of the jungle appeared magnified by the noises of the surf until the hearers were sure that the enemy was upon them, and the nerves of the Americans were on edge because of their skirmishes to the north and south of the beach-head during the day. There was a little mortar fire and the enemy sent over some tracers, evidently with the object of getting the Americans to fire back and dis-

---

[4] Cpl E. E. G. Skuse, NX96350; 2/6 Bn. Station mechanic; of Rockdale, NSW; b. Bristol, England, 8 Apr 1919.

[5] Pte H. C. Barwise, VX44503; 2/6 Bn. Orchard worker; of Port Melbourne; b. Geelong, Vic, 14 Sep 1912.

close their position. Undoubtedly the enemy had been prowling around at night and some small attacks were possibly made, as reported, but it is improbable that any large attack took place. It was a relief to all concerned when morning came.

On this second night, when the Americans were again concentrated in a small area on the beach-head, three landing craft, one of which contained Colonel Taylor and Captain McBride, attempted to land. Although the boats approached to within 150 yards of the shore and moved up and down, with much signalling and shouting, there was no reply from the shore. It is possible that the boats approached the wrong shore, for there are no reports of such signalling and shouting by any of those ashore. The three boats returned to Buso.

On 30th June reports of the landing began to reach Japanese headquarters. Major Kimura of the *III/66th Battalion* was immediately ordered to send about 150 men south from Salamaua to reinforce the fight of Major Oba's *III/102nd Battalion* against the invaders and to halt them, if possible, north of the Salus area. Colonel Araki ordered the remainder of his *66th Regiment*, in the Mubo area, to be prepared to cooperate with Oba. The Japanese commanders estimated that about 1,000 men had landed.

By dawn on 1st July Dexter's company was ready to move forward. After a strafing attack by Beaufighters at 9 a.m. the company went straight through the enemy position which had obviously just been abandoned, and reached the coast. Dexter sent back a runner to the last spur with a telephone message for Moten (he had been unable to fire the Very lights as arranged because they were too damp), and at 10.40 a.m. Moten learnt that the route to the coast was clear. Patrols pursued the enemy, who fled north without seeking an engagement. On receiving the telephone call Moten, who was very worried at the non-appearance of the Americans at the last spur, instructed Dexter to make contact with MacKechnie, give him details of the situation, hand over responsibility for defence of the area at the river mouth and then proceed to Napier.

The force dispersed from the mouth of the Bitoi consisted largely of a machine-gun company from Oba's battalion. This company had lost two of its platoons when the *Heiyo Maru* was sunk off New Britain in January 1943. In January a force from the *102nd Regiment*, including machine-gunners, had been sent to Mambare but with the advance of the Americans through the Mambare and Morobe areas the force was gradually withdrawn to the Bitoi area.

At the same time that MacKechnie Force was being tossed ashore, the leading Papuan platoon took up a position along the ridge at Cape Dinga overlooking the Bassis villages. On 1st July a patrol under Sergeant Beaven[7] drew the Papuans' first blood in the Nassau Bay area when three Japanese were killed in foxholes. Although a strong patrol led by Lieutenant Bishop[8] was forced to withdraw from the Japanese positions near

---

[7] Sgt B. V. Beaven, VX72687; Papuan Inf Bn. Labourer; of Carlton, Vic; b. Berrigan, NSW, 18 Sep 1904.
[8] Lt C. E. Bishop, QX55306; Papuan Inf Bn. Farmer; of Beenleigh, Qld; b. Beenleigh, 16 Nov 1919.

the coast after striking strong opposition, the company continued to keep pressure on the enemy in the Cape Dinga area. MacKechnie had no means of communication with the Papuans but Captain Hitchcock arrived on 1st July with news that two enemy outposts on Cape Dinga had been deserted, but that a few Japanese were still in Bassis No. 3. Hitchcock was then sent to make contact with the American platoon near the Tabali before continuing with his task of attacking the enemy on the north coast of the Cape Dinga peninsula and blocking any escape inland along the track leading to a saddle at the west end of the peninsula.

Early on 1st July Newman's company again moved south but dug in 1,000 yards north of Tabali Creek. During the 600 yards' advance the company reported finding about a dozen dead Japanese and meeting several stragglers. The rest of the force remained concentrated on the beach-head. The Australians on the beach-head did their utmost to instil confidence into the Americans. Burke remained with MacKechnie while Urquhart and his platoon helped with the re-establishment of defensive positions and Major Hughes,[9] a liaison officer from N.G.F., tried to organise communications. Soon after midday the three barges containing the missing battalion commander and McBride arrived at the beach. When MacKechnie informed McBride that his force was the victim of "considerable misfortune", McBride, who had been briefed by Moten and Wilton and who was the only Australian present fully acquainted with the whole plan, suggested that it would be a good idea to send George's company north to the Bitoi and Newman's company south to the Tabali. The arrival of Dexter and a small party of the 2/6th Battalion who had walked unhindered from the mouth of the Bitoi lent point to McBride's suggestion and induced MacKechnie to issue orders to this effect.

Dexter reported to MacKechnie who was sitting in a tent surrounded by his men in foxholes. The Americans had done little patrolling to find the enemy's whereabouts but now MacKechnie asked that Dexter should lead Urquhart's platoon and some Americans south to clear the mouth of the Tabali. The Australian instead urged MacKechnie to move towards Napier. The American, however, decided that his troops were too inexperienced and tired to move and that their supplies were inadequate. Dexter then returned to the mouth of the Bitoi after Burke and Urquhart had emphasised that no one should approach the American perimeter at night and that the Australians should take no notice of any shooting from the beach-head. Only mosquitoes attacked the Australians at the mouth of the Bitoi that night, and all was quiet except for some shots from the American perimeter.

Next morning Dexter returned to the beach-head and arranged for MacKechnie to have a company ready at midday to be escorted to Napier. The Australians were now without rations and received MacKechnie's permission to retrieve broken cases of food from a foundered ration

---

[9] Col R. L. Hughes, DSO, DX852. GSO2 I Corps and NGF 1943, I Corps 1943-44 and 1944-45. CO 3 Bn RAR Korea 1952-53. Regular soldier; of Strathalbyn, SA; b. Adelaide, 17 Sep 1920.

barge; needless to say several "broken" cases were found. Towards midday MacKechnie walked to the mouth of the Bitoi and here agreed with Dexter's suggestion that the Bitoi Track should be protected by establishing one platoon at the river mouth, one platoon at the former enemy camp 400 yards inland and one platoon at the last spur. With this protection the engineers would be able to begin work on the jeep track.

Dexter had already sent Moten a message suggesting the company's recall. MacKechnie appeared reluctant to lose the services of the Australians but, just as he was trying to apply pressure, Private Trebilcock arrived, wet through, with a message from Moten instructing Dexter that his task was now finished and that all responsibility for the area should be handed over to MacKechnie. Trebilcock had set out from the last-spur camp accompanying two line-laying signallers but had met a party of Japanese. The signallers retraced their steps towards Napier, but Trebilcock ran into the jungle, dived into the Bitoi, and swam down towards the coast, thus getting the message through. MacKechnie, now realising that the Australians were bent on moving westward, asked that they should clear the track back to the last spur. Dexter agreed and left Lieutenant R. J. H. Smith and two men to guide the American platoon.

The main body of Australians had hardly settled in at the last-spur camp when they heard firing from down the track. They waited on the alert and presently Smith and his two companions accompanied by the American platoon commander arrived. They had been fired on by a small Japanese party and had been cut off from the American platoon which had decided to move back to the beach. Dexter immediately sent out a patrol which found the missing Americans who were told what was expected of them. They were given a position in the perimeter with instructions not to fire without orders. The telephone line was then taken through to the beach-head. At the last-spur camp troops had a peaceful night and no shots were fired.

Lieut-Colonel Matsui, the commander of *1/66th Battalion*, in an Intelligence report on 1st July stated that the Australians were "assembling in the coconut groves 2½ kilometres from the coast opposite Lababia". Other units listed as soon due to arrive in Salamaua were the *1/80th Battalion* (*20th Division*) 400 strong on 2nd July, and *I Battalion* of the *14th Field Artillery Regiment*, consisting of 146 men and six mountain guns, next day.

Savige now ordered Moten to instruct MacKechnie that the Papuan company should as soon as possible advance along the coast north of the Bitoi with the tasks of maintaining contact with the retreating enemy, mopping up pockets of resistance, and ultimately reconnoitring for a secure bridgehead for landing barges in Dot Inlet. Time should not be wasted by operations against any Japanese in the Cape Dinga area as these could be contained with a minimum force and dealt with at leisure. Already irritated with events at the beach, particularly the lack of decision and the concentration of troops which invited air attack, Savige told Moten by telephone to issue orders to MacKechnie as to one of his own battalion commanders, and to report any failure on the American's part to obey orders. Savige also urged General Fuller, commanding the 41st Division, to send the remainder of his engineers and artillery to Nassau Bay as soon as possible and to instruct MacKechnie that his forward elements must begin to move from the beach-head to the assembly area.

The scanty reports received by Savige and Moten under-emphasised the actual confusion at the beach-head. Moten had attempted to ring MacKechnie at Nassau Bay on the night of 1st July. A long conversation had ensued with the American signaller at the end of the line, the gist being that he could not fetch MacKechnie because anyone who moved would be shot and in any case he was closing down about 9 p.m. as soon as he had heard the B.B.C. news.

MacKechnie was convinced that his force had received a severe mental and emotional shock. By 2nd July a headquarters and supply dumps had still not been organised and no orders were being issued except those covering affairs of small importance. At dawn a further 10 boats arrived, carrying mainly the fourth infantry company, and two P.T. boats accompanying the landing craft bombarded enemy positions at Cape Dinga.[1] Troops and supplies remained concentrated at the beach-head making ideal targets for air attack. At 1 p.m. 10 Japanese medium bombers bombed and strafed Nassau Bay and both sides of the mouth of the south arm of the Bitoi, some of the bombs falling near Corporal McElgunn's patrol which had returned to the Bitoi mouth and reported that Duali seemed empty. At 3.10 p.m. a further 8 bombers and about 15 fighters attacked. The only damage was done by a direct hit on one of the broached landing craft.

Hitchcock reported that the enemy outposts on Cape Dinga peninsula had been evacuated and late on 2nd July the Papuan company began skirmishing with enemy remnants in Bassis 2. Newman's company reached the Tabali late on the 2nd but had not yet made contact with the Papuan company advancing west along the coast. It began to seem that the enemy had evacuated the Cape Dinga area because Newman's men found between 50 and 60 Japanese packs abandoned near the Tabali.[2] Later reports from farther north that a similar number of Japanese had been seen moving north across the Bitoi added weight to this belief.

Early on the 3rd the Americans began moving towards Napier. They were slow mainly because they were not used to hard jungle marches and carried too much gear. Helped by the 2/6th, Colonel Taylor's headquarters and three infantry companies moved inland. The Australians returned in the afternoon and by 5 p.m. were at Napier, whence they would move to the Saddle next day. The example of determination, efficiency and coolness shown by these experienced soldiers had helped the Americans to reorganise and proceed with their task.

---

[1] Commenting on the failure of the third wave to land on the first night the historian of the 2 ESB wrote: "This proved most fortunate, for the boats of this wave were the only ones available for several days to run resupply missions to Nassau Bay."

[2] From these packs documents and maps were taken giving details of the strength of the III/102nd Battalion (350), the small defensive posts which had been established between Duali and Cape Dinga, and the regular weekly patrol to Salus.

To Savige's disappointment MacKechnie was at least one day late by 3rd July. The position was improved, however, by the arrival at Nassau Bay that day of one battery of the 218th Field Artillery Battalion, an engineer company and other detachments. The artillery lifted the spirits of the Americans at the beach-head and along the Bitoi Track and the Australians in the distant Mubo hills when from 1.35 p.m. its four 75-mm guns shelled for 50 minutes the mouth of the Tabali Creek, Cape Dinga, Lababia Island and the area from the mouth of the south arm of the Bitoi to Duali.

By 4th July 1,477 troops of MacKechnie Force had been landed at Nassau Bay.[3] At 3.30 p.m. on the 4th Taylor's battalion was spread out between its assembly area at Napier and the beach. Headquarters and two companies were at Napier and another was in the dry creek bed east of Napier. To keep this force supplied all available men including gunners and sappers carried supplies to Napier on 5th July. This supply train was ambushed about three miles inland but the enemy scattered and fled across the Bitoi after killing three Americans. At this time the jeep track running west from the mouth of the south arm of the Bitoi was open to traffic for half a mile along the river. The gunners as well as 150 natives were assisting the American engineers in its construction. Unfortunately the tractors and bulldozers were out of action either through being stuck in the stream or bogged in the mud, and in order to keep to the program Savige told Moten to set the Americans working on the track with picks and shovels.

MacKechnie had different ideas. In a letter to Moten on 4th July he said that loss of over half his landing craft and his inability to get his guns, troops and supplies in as originally scheduled had materially delayed him. He considered that it would not be tactically sound to leave his base, with Japanese about, in order to concentrate all his troops 8 to 10 miles inland with no supplies. It would take, he thought, three weeks, not two days, to construct the artillery road; troops at the assembly area would be out of rations tomorrow, and there were no native carriers. "To be very frank we have been in a very precarious position down here for several days and my sending the rifle troops inland was contrary to my own best judgment." Troops had gone inland "stripped to the bone", he wrote, and without heavy weapons and mortar and machine-gun ammunition. "Therefore, these troops who are up there now are in no position to embark upon an offensive mission until we are able to get food, ammunition and additional weapons up to them." General Fuller had advised him not to embark on offensive operations unless adequately supported by artillery and heavy weapons. "In short I must advise you at this time that it will be impossible for me to comply with the orders as they now stand." MacKechnie concluded by suggesting that the plan be changed, that he would not and could not sacrifice lives to meet a time

---

[3] The total strength of MacKechnie Force was 109 officers and 1,648 enlisted men.

schedule and that he did not plan to leave the beach until the position was secure and supplies adequate.⁴

Moten informed Savige of the letter and suggested that pressure would be necessary if operations were to proceed as now planned for 7th July. Moten then informed MacKechnie that arrangements had been made to drop supplies to Taylor on 5th July and that Bitoi Ridge was not occupied by anyone except Australian patrols waiting for the Americans to take over. He advised MacKechnie that heavy machine-guns could not be used on Bitoi Ridge but mortars would be useful. In Moten's opinion casualties to MacKechnie Force would be unlikely and one or at most two companies resolutely led could capture and hold the objective. Best news for Moten was that, with MacKechnie's consent, he could now deal direct with Taylor, who was willing and anxious to carry out the attack as planned but hampered by lack of supplies and ammunition. Moten arranged for the delivery to Taylor of 100 boy-loads of ammunition from the beach on 6th July and 1,000 rations from 17th Brigade.

Reports from the Australian liaison officers at the beach (Major Hughes, Captain McBride and Captain Rolfe⁵) caused Moten to suggest to Savige on 6th July that Fuller be asked to send an officer to take charge of and relieve MacKechnie of responsibility for beach organisation. Aware of the danger of delay to the plans for the attack on Mubo, Savige relayed this to Herring and informed Moten: "I have placed MacKechnie under your command and he must obey orders and instructions issued by you."

The dangers of dual command were already sensed by Savige. Although it was stated in operation orders emanating from N.G.F's instruction of 26th May that the Americans were under Australian command, and although it had been confirmed at the Summit and Port Moresby meetings, the question who really commanded the Americans was not really settled. MacKechnie thought that he had to serve two masters—Savige and Fuller. Back in Port Moresby Herring understood the delicate nature of the problem and felt that Fuller might protest to MacArthur if the Americans were placed under the command of an Australian several mountains away from the coast. Herring decided that one of his main tasks was to ensure smooth cooperation between Americans and Australians and for this reason he was diffident about placing the Americans completely under Savige's command. In Savige's own mind, however, there was no doubt that Herring's written and oral orders clearly placed the Americans under Australian control.

---
⁴ Later events helped to make MacKechnie's attitude more understandable. In the light of this later knowledge Savige wrote: "MacKechnie, as regimental commander, came forward with his first echelon of troops apparently . . . to supervise the establishment of his base. Although we were not aware of it at the time, he was ordered by Fuller not to make any forward movement of troops until the base was fully established and protected. MacKechnie, I think, relied on Taylor to fulfil the tactical requirements in protecting his beach-head and, when Taylor failed to land, he was overwhelmed with the unexpected added responsibility. . . . In my view, he should have appointed his senior company commander to command the weak battalion while he went on supervising the establishment of his base and his temporary battalion commander."

⁵ Capt C. B. N. Rolfe, NX43. 2/4 Bn and 17 Bde. Bank officer; of Hunter's Hill, NSW; b. Adelaide, 21 Sep 1913. Killed in action 8 Aug 1943.

Because of this uncertainty both the Australian and American divisional commanders were apt to misinterpret each other's actions. An example was contained in an exchange of signals following MacKechnie's landing. On 1st July Moten advised Savige that planes were attacking Duali and that, if they were Allied planes, they would "endanger our troops and . . . prevent attack planned". Savige replied that the attack was arranged without his concurrence and promptly changed the bomb-line. At 10 a.m. he signalled Fuller: "Air attack arranged by you for 8 a.m. on targets Duali-Bitoi mouth should have been coordinated at this HQ. This attack may endanger troops of the 17th Bde who were in target area at time of attack . . . requests for air attacks by you direct from MacKechnie must be referred here for coordination to avoid repetition today's attack." Late that night Herring asked who had altered the bomb-line and, on being told that Savige had done so to avoid danger to his own troops, signalled that he "would be glad if you would communicate your regrets to 41 U.S. Div". About midday on the 3rd Savige signalled Fuller that "attack not arranged by me or Air Support Party here. Assumed arrangements had been made through you as MacKechnie had no communication with us. Took prompt action to alter bomb-line to avert certain danger to our troops."

Late on the 3rd Savige received Fuller's reply (dated 1st July) to his first message. Fuller said that he had not arranged the air attack but that a request for an air support mission had been received at 41st Division headquarters and had been relayed to 3rd Division headquarters, which had received it at 9.25 p.m. on 30th June, and to First Air Task Force. Clearance for the mission had been given by the Fifth Air Force during the night of 30th June. Fuller concluded that "all requests for air attacks will be forwarded to your headquarters as was done in this case". On examination it appeared that the Americans had acted on an information signal between Air Support Parties at the two divisional headquarters and had not used the proper procedure to obtain coordinated attacks. On receipt of Fuller's delayed signal Savige replied late that night: "Your signal now clarifies whole matter and emphasises difficulties in communications leading to misunderstandings and assumptions by reader not contemplated by sender. You have my regrets for either as may be applicable to me."

This incident has been fully described in order to show how dual command could lead to much unnecessary work, worry and misunderstanding. Whenever the allocation of command is deliberately or unconsciously left vague, there is trouble. This incident might well have served as a warning to prevent further such incidents. But for the sane attitude of the commanders and the genuine friendship between the Australian and American troops in the front line, relations between the two commands might have been strained at this time. Give and take was necessary on both sides.

Order very gradually came to the congested beach-head. Hughes assisted with the organisation of American headquarters. Captain Wilson,[6] an

---

[6] Maj R. H. M. Wilson, NX34739. 2/1 Pnr Bn; OC 2/8 Fd Coy 1944-45. Architect; of Cremorne, NSW; b. Mosman, NSW, 9 Jan 1916.

engineer officer sent by Moten, assisted the American engineers in the construction of a jeep track. Rolfe and D. A. McBride were hard at work urging the gunners to attempt to manhandle their guns. Communications remained the most unsatisfactory feature, as American signallers appeared reluctant to do night work.

On 4th July Savige informed Moten that the attack against Mubo would open on 7th July. Moten then advised MacKechnie and Taylor that Taylor's move from the assembly area at Napier to his objective on Bitoi Ridge would also begin on the 7th, and that this move would be coordinated with attacks by 15th Brigade to the north and 2/6th Battalion to the west. Adopting a persuasive tone, Moten informed the American commanders that it would be desirable but not essential for MacKechnie Force guns to be in position by 6th or 7th July.

While Taylor was moving west, Oba was moving north. General Nakano's headquarters on 7th July estimated that 4,000 had landed at Nassau Bay.

Most of the Japanese from Nassau Bay escaped to the north to join in the fight again. Small detachments, particularly those whose foxholes the Americans found soon after landing, scattered into the jungle and moved north; they either starved or helped themselves to American rations. One of these more resourceful Japanese was Sergeant Taguchi who left the following entries in his diary: "About 0230 hours (30th June) there was a sudden enemy landing at Nassau Bay and 6 of us—Sergeant Taguchi, Leading Private Shimada, Pfc Takata, Takano, Ohata, Superior Private Ishijima—escaped to the jungle according to company orders. I was not able to walk by myself so Pfc Takata helped me and we went deep into the jungle. Due to my condition, both of us were determined to die at that place. The Hori Company arrived at the place at 0730 and engaged the enemy."

Three weeks later Taguchi and Takata were still in the area and Taguchi wrote: "As it grew darker, advanced closer to enemy voices. Moved slowly on all fours since it was too dangerous to walk. This stealing is a difficult proposition. Got lost on the way. Was so dark I could not see anything and had to feel my way.... Wish they would hurry up and go to sleep. Mosquitoes are coming at my outstretched legs. I am getting sleepy too but I cannot do that. About [10 p.m.] it suddenly started to pour and I got soaking wet. Time has come. Moved out to the path and advanced cautiously. What an uncomfortable feeling! Moon came out. When they smoked their cigarettes I was watching for the direction and distance. ... There seemed to be no one in front, so I walked up and found a large barrel. I thought it was oil because it was still dark. I searched the place and found many ... large and small tins of canned foods and dry foods, which Pfc Takata would like to eat, and there seemed to be dozens of them. This joy could not be expressed. I took my bayonet and opened the can and ate the contents. The taste was never so good as this. We had been eating taro before this for over ten days."

Next day, 22nd July, Taguchi wrote: "Looking at the things which I brought last night, there were 29 small and large cans and 3 large loaves of bread and one extra large can. After segregating these, there were 11 cans of corned beef, 9 cans of milk, 3 cans of peaches and 7 cans with unknown contents."

CHAPTER 5

THE CAPTURE OF MUBO

IN the last days of June the 15th and 17th Australian Brigades were preparing for the operations that were to follow the American landing at Nassau Bay. The 15th Brigade was to capture Bobdubi Ridge beginning on the day of landing, while the 17th was to begin the capture of Mubo and Observation Hill a week later. The 17th Brigade would have the main task while the 15th Brigade would draw off some of the enemy forces and then close the escape route north from Mubo.

Brigadier Moten's orders issued on 2nd July (after the 15th Brigade's opening move) stated that the 2/6th Battalion supported by the 2/5th would attack the Mubo-Observation Hill area on 7th July and would then mop up the area south from the junction of Bui Savella and Buigap Creeks, and join the Americans from Bitoi Ridge at the footbridges across the Buigap. The orders continued that the I/162nd Battalion would capture Bitoi Ridge on 8th July and, a day later, the ridge between Bui Alang and Bui Kumbul Creeks and the small feature west of Bitoi Ridge between Bui Kumbul Creek and the Bitoi River overlooking the footbridges, where the Americans would make contact with the Australians and cut the Japanese lines of communication along Buigap Creek.

After receiving the 15th Brigade's operation order on 22nd June Major Warfe of the 2/3rd Independent Company and Colonel Starr of the 58th/59th Battalion issued their own orders four days later. Warfe's order covered two diversionary patrols designed to deceive the enemy as to the direction of the main attack. The first was to raid the Malolo and Bukuap areas on the coast and the second to make a demolition raid in the Kela Hill area.

Lieutenant J. E. Lewin led the Malolo patrol of 16 from Missim on 27th June and on the morning of the 29th they watched small enemy parties along the coast at Busama and Bukuap. At midday George, the plausible son of the local luluai, joined the patrol and later the luluai of the area arranged for the evacuation of all Wamasu natives. George, who had been absent for some time, returned at 4 p.m., stating that the natives would be moving to Hote that night. At 4.30 p.m. Lewin withdrew his guards and while he was issuing orders for the raids on the following morning about 30 Japanese attacked from two directions. The Australians managed to get a few shots at the encircling enemy, but they had only one course and that was to depart in a hurry. They split into three parties and rejoined at the rendezvous with the company of the 24th Battalion on the Hote Track. Unfortunately the patrol lost seven weapons, including its Bren gun. The loss of a weapon was always regarded seriously and this loss undoubtedly took a lot of explaining to Warfe. Often when there was the slightest relaxation of precautions by a patrol operating deep into enemy territory the Japanese were able to carry out a surprise attack. Their good fieldcraft and use of native intelligence was usually offset by their inaccurate shooting. In this case, although the foremost Japanese were only 10 yards away when first seen, they inflicted no casualties. Lewin had possibly been betrayed by George and the luluai.

The other diversionary patrol, consisting of Sergeant Swan[1] and five men, was moving forward to place demolition charges on the Japanese anti-aircraft guns at Kela Hill when, at midnight on the night 29th-30th June, it was challenged and fired on by a sentry. Machine-gun and mortar fire forced Swan to withdraw without being able to lay his charges. Although unsuccessful, both patrols probably helped to make the Japanese doubtful as to the direction from which the main attack might come and may have caused the enemy to delay sending his reserves to the Bobdubi and Mubo areas.

The 58th/59th Battalion had been moving forward throughout most of June. On 26th June Colonel Starr issued the operation order for the battalion's first action: "58th/59th Battalion will capture Bobdubi Ridge with a view to controlling Komiatum Track", it stated. Each company was allotted a detachment of 3-inch mortars. One company was to take Orodubi, Gwaibolom and Erskine Creek;[2] another was to take Old Vickers Position and the village west of it; a third was to take portions of the Government Bench Cut Track south-east of Old Vickers. The fourth company was in reserve, with the task of preventing encirclement along the New Bobdubi Track and guarding the river crossings and the kunda bridge area. The 2/3rd Independent Company was to supply three guides to each company.

On 28th June Colonel Guinn issued to the 58th/59th Battalion one of those rousing orders of the day of which he was so fond; it adequately summed up the importance of the battalion's task:

> Bobdubi Ridge which is your objective is the key to the situation extending south to Mubo area. Its occupation means that we will be placed in a position to prevent the enemy reinforcing or supplying their forward areas. Further, those forward will be trapped like rats in a trap—it will be your duty to see they are annihilated in attempting to get out. By your determination and courage to carry out the heavy task allotted you will win the day thereby adding your first battle honours to a unit with a fine tradition during the years 1914-18.

This Victorian battalion, young, inexperienced and inadequately trained through no fault of its own, needed all possible encouragement. After the battalion had moved forward at night, company by company, to Meares' Creek, Captain Millikan,[3] its medical officer, felt that the men were fatigued, as they had had little rest since the march forward over the gruelling Missim trail; prepared accommodation and rations were scarce at Pilimung and unsatisfactory hygiene, resulting from the troops'

---

[1] Sgt R. A. Swan, VX109898. 2/3 Indep Coy, "M" and "Z" Special Units. Clerk; of Melbourne; b. Broken Hill, NSW, 2 Oct 1917.
[2] Named after Lieutenant D. D. Erskine of the 2/3rd Independent Company.
[3] Maj H. R. Millikan, VX108490. RMO 58/59 Bn 1943; 11 Fd Amb 1944-45. Medical practitioner; of Glen Iris, Vic; b. Shepparton, Vic, 1 May 1911.

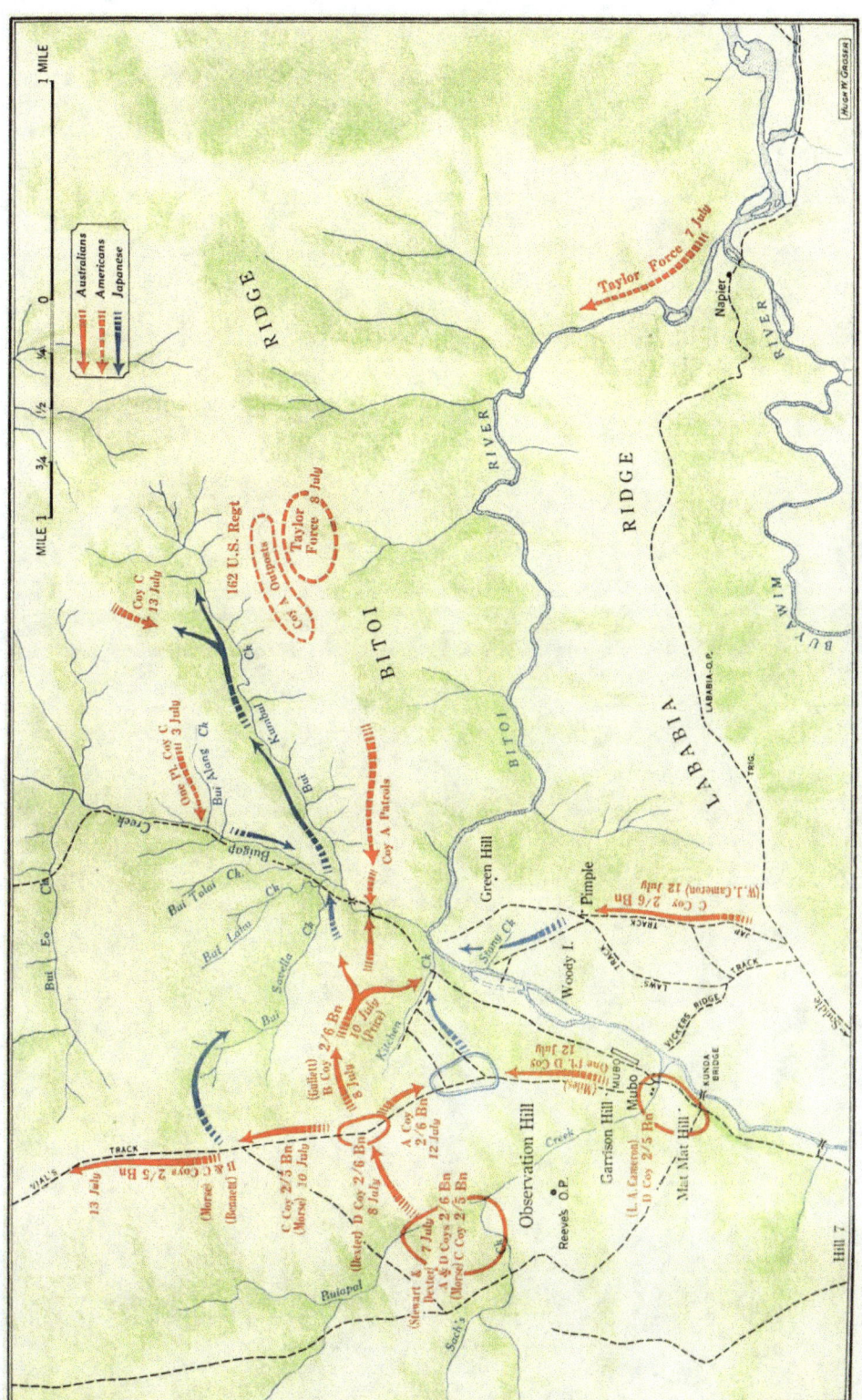

The 17th Brigade attack on Mubo, 7th-13th July

weariness in the arduous crossing of Double Mountain, had caused outbreaks of diarrhoea or dysentery, tropical ulcers and tinea.

On the same miserable night that MacKechnie Force landed at Nassau Bay the men of the 58th/59th crossed the Francisco River on a swinging kunda bridge erected by their Pioneer platoon, and early next morning plodded towards their start-lines in torrential rain. The bad weather hampered the air strike planned for 8.30 a.m. on Gwaibolom, Old Vickers and the Coconuts area. Only four aircraft got through low clouds to the target area, the remainder dropping their bombs on Salamaua.

The three attacking companies left their start-lines near Uliap Creek in the early morning of 30th June. Major Heward[4] in command of the southern company planned that Lieutenant Roche's[5] platoon would capture Orodubi, Sergeant Barry's[6] would move through to Gwaibolom and Lieutenant Houston's[7] would move through to Erskine Creek. A section sent north to Graveyard saw about 10 Japanese strolling round Orodubi and fired on them, causing them to jump into pits under the huts. Roche's platoon then attacked Orodubi at 12.30 p.m. Anticipating booby-traps the men left the Bench Cut Track 70 yards south of Orodubi, climbed a 40-foot kunai slope and joined the main track within 10 yards of the enemy. They could hear the Japanese but could not see them; in the firing which now broke out the Australians were at a disadvantage as they could be seen by the Japanese. Corporal Crimmins[8] was mortally

58th/59th Battalion attack, 30th June

---

[4] Maj H. M. Heward, VX102640; 58/59 Bn. Insurance clerk; of Kew, Vic; b. Richmond, Vic, 12 Jun 1909. Killed in action 13 Jul 1943.

[5] Lt F. J. Roche, NGX170; 58/59 Bn. Clerk; of Rabaul, TNG; b. Hobart, 19 Apr 1910.

[6] Capt H. W. K. Barry, VX89713; 58/59 Bn. Clerk; of Tatura, Vic; b. Seymour, Vic, 23 Feb 1921.

[7] Lt W. F. Houston, VX114248; 58/59 Bn. Railway employee; of Pascoe Vale, Vic; b. Pascoe Vale, 4 Nov 1913. Killed in action 15 Aug 1943.

[8] Cpl B. L. Crimmins, VX138112; 58/59 Bn. Draper; of Dookie, Vic; b. Cobram, Vic, 24 May 1915. Killed in action 30 Jun 1943. His brother, Corporal K. J. Crimmins, also from the 58th/59th Battalion, was accidentally killed on 12th August 1943.

wounded and three others wounded. After 20 minutes firing and grenade throwing at close range Roche withdrew with only 10 men unscathed. During the action Private Duncanson,[9] a stretcher bearer, went forward under fire and tended Crimmins and then, still under heavy fire, brought out the other casualties.

Heward then reconnoitred Orodubi from the Graveyard area to the north and from Namling to the south. By the time he had finished it was almost dusk and perhaps too late to attack. Rather than dig in where he was he withdrew to Namling, and decided to contain Orodubi with one platoon, a course which had been previously suggested by Starr. After telephoning at night to brigade headquarters (which was to retain control of the company until it had captured its objective) Heward was ordered to contain Orodubi with one platoon and move the rest to Gwaibolom and Erskine Creek next day.

Captain Jago's[1] company, which had the stiffest task, drove a Japanese outpost from the village west of Old Vickers in the early afternoon of the 30th, losing Lieutenant Pemberton[2] and Corporal Gibson,[3] killed, and capturing some documents. The company then had its first experience of meeting a well-entrenched and heavily-armed enemy when Lieutenant Griff's[4] platoon attacked Old Vickers. Griff's move up Old Vickers was hounded by bad luck. Two of his men accidentally discharged Owen guns and one fell and cut his leg on a machete. The Australians did not know that the Japanese had deep dugouts 40 feet down from the top. In these they would take shelter from Allied bombing or shelling only to reappear in their foxholes on the top before the attackers could take advantage of the bombardment. As the platoon reached the top of the ridge they were surprised to see about 20 Japanese approaching from the direction of the recently captured village. Corporal Anderson's[5] section on the right flank was pinned down by heavy fire from the top of Old Vickers after they had inflicted several casualties with accurate small arms fire. Suddenly to the left the other sections saw four Japanese run yelling from a foxhole towards a Woodpecker concealed in a clump of bamboos. A grenade thrown by Griff killed all four. A group of Japanese riflemen then attacked but were dispersed by fire from a Bren. Griff now sent his platoon sergeant (Clarke[6]) to instruct Anderson to withdraw. On his return Clarke was hit by fire from the Woodpecker in the bamboo clump but, although in great pain, managed to make his report to the

---

[9] Cpl R. G. Duncanson, MM, VX140229; 58/59 Bn. Wood machinist; of Brunswick, Vic; b. Zeehan, Tas, 3 Jan 1916.

[1] Capt E. O. Jago, VX102644; 58/59 Bn. Secretary; of Brunswick, Vic; b. Port Fairy, Vic, 6 May 1911.

[2] Lt R. G. M. Pemberton, NGX171; 58/59 Bn. Clerk; of Hobart; b. Westbury, Tas, 30 Jul 1915. Killed in action 30 Jun 1943.

[3] Cpl R. B. Gibson, NX116810; 58/59 Bn. Driver; of Leichhardt, NSW; b. Leichhardt, 26 Jun 1917. Killed in action 30 Jun 1943.

[4] Lt-Col E. M. Griff, MC, VX51665; 58/59 Bn. 3 Bn RAR Korea 1953. Foreman joiner; of Oakleigh, Vic; b. Oakleigh, 25 May 1918.

[5] Sgt A. R. Anderson, MM, VX102548; 58/59 Bn. Service mechanic; of Northcote, Vic; b. Wagga Wagga, NSW, 22 Jun 1917.

[6] Sgt J. T. Clarke, VX84607; 58/59 Bn. Bricklayer; of Yarrawonga, Vic; b. Corowa, NSW, 12 Feb 1918.

company commander and was then dragged back by Griff. During the fighting Sergeant Ayre[7] in charge of stretcher bearers did fine work going among and tending the wounded and arranging their evacuation. The platoon was now drawing fire from what Griff estimated to be one Woodpecker, six light machine-guns and one light mortar. Using the grenade discharger the Australians unsuccessfully tried to destroy the Woodpecker. Griff crawled forward to reconnoitre its position but, unknown to him, he was crawling along a fire lane thinking it was a track. Bursts of firing from several machine-guns induced him to roll rapidly down the hill to his platoon, which had now been rejoined by Anderson's section. As he could hear enemy on both flanks Griff withdrew about 100 yards to some high ground where he reported to Jago and was ordered to join the rest of the company in the village area. In the day's fighting the company had lost three killed and five wounded.

Early on the 30th Captain Drew's[8] company moved towards the track junction on the right flank of Jago's company. When Jago was held up, Starr ordered Drew to go to his objective, but the company did not reach the track junction by nightfall, mainly because its information about tracks was faulty and progress was barred by a sheer cliff face. It camped near Jago's position. The company might well have emulated Lieutenant Stephens' section in May by going straight east down to the Bench Cut via tracks leading from positions known later as the Hilberts[9] and thence north along the Bench Cut towards the Salamaua-Bobdubi track.

With orders direct from Guinn, Heward smartly set out for his objectives on the morning of 1st July. By 11.30 a.m. Roche's platoon occupied Gwaibolom and by 1 p.m. Houston's occupied Erskine Creek—both without opposition—while Barry's platoon "contained" Orodubi by setting up two Brens covering it. The Japanese did not need many troops at Orodubi as the crest of the ridge on which it stood would prevent more than one platoon attacking from the Bench Cut Track. From the Gwaibolom-Erskine Creek area Heward set up a Vickers gun to fire on the Komiatum Track.

Drew's company set out again at 9 a.m. on 1st July towards its objective but, after "scrub-bashing" for several hours, the men carrying the mortar and machine-gun and their ammunition were exhausted. The company then slowly followed a creek until Drew called a halt and sent two lightly-equipped volunteers forward to look for a suitable route. After an hour and a half they returned saying that the country ahead was impossible for loaded troops. Unfortunately the guides from the 2/3rd Independent Company did not know this particular area. Drew therefore had the distasteful task of leading back a "bloody-minded" company to

---

[7] Sgt G. R. C. Ayre, MM, VX89711; 58/59 Bn. Carpenter; of Shepparton, Vic; b. Bendigo, Vic, 29 Jun 1902.
[8] Capt F. A. Drew, VX102641; 58/59 Bn. Advertising representative; of Melbourne; b. South Yarra, Vic, 4 Aug 1907.
[9] Named after Captain H. H. Hilbert of the 58th/59th Battalion.

the Bobdubi Ridge Track. It was later found that Drew was within half an hour of the Bench Cut Track when he turned back.

Plans for Jago's company to attack Old Vickers again and for the reserve company to join in with an attack on the Coconuts were delayed on 1st July because 3-inch mortar ammunition had not arrived. Griff, however, led a patrol to the top of the ridge and sketched some of the defences of Old Vickers. The battalion learnt this day that documents captured by Jago's company on 30th June had identified the Japanese as part of the *115th Regiment*.

Jago's attempt to capture Old Vickers, quickly following the American landing, helped to cause consternation among the Japanese planners at Salamaua. On the previous day Major Komaki, in charge of the Bobdubi sector, had upbraided Lieutenant Ogawa stationed at Old Vickers for not reporting "approximately 100 of the enemy . . . seen moving towards Bobdubi through the grassy plain 9,000 metres south of the mountains". This approach by men of the 58th/59th Battalion had apparently been seen by artillerymen. On 1st July General Muroya's order read: "The enemy has made an opening in *No. 9 Company, 115th Infantry Regiment* (Ogawa's unit) at Bobdubi, and is infiltrating also along the Komiatum Track. *1 Battalion* commander *66th Infantry Regiment* (Colonel Matsui) will dispatch one infantry company to Bobdubi to relieve Ogawa on 2nd July. Be especially careful to conceal relief operations from the enemy. When the company is relieved it will immediately return to Salamaua and guard the area." Thus the attack drew off to the north a portion of the enemy force defending the Mubo area.

During the first two days of its operations the 58th/59th Battalion had seen very few Japanese. The Japanese were not in unexpected localities nor in large numbers, except in Old Vickers, but from their well-entrenched defensive positions they were able to drive back attacks which could not be supported by heavy weapons. Lack of battle experience and shortage of adequate rations (not an isolated event in this area) reacted on the young soldiers of the 58th/59th to the prejudice of efficient patrolling. Captain Newman[1] of the 15th Brigade staff, who investigated the shortage, found that a two days' patrol meant that those who stayed behind went hungry because rations had to be scraped together for the patrol.

In spite of heavy bombing of Salamaua and Kela Hill by Allied aircraft on 1st July considerable enemy activity was observed by the Salamaua O.P. in the area from the quarry to the township of Salamaua during the day. Savige warned Guinn that these movements possibly indicated a counter-attack from Salamaua on 2nd July. Hearing of this, Starr ordered Drew to leave one platoon on the right flank of Jago's company and move the remainder to join the reserve company. Guinn did not agree with this move and ordered Starr to reassemble the company and send it to its objective via Gwaibolom and Erskine Creek.

The unusual activity observed in the Salamaua area was caused by the arrival from Madang of the *1/80th Battalion*, which was sent to the Bobdubi area immediately.

To guard against a possible counter-attack on Bobdubi Ridge, Savige ordered Guinn to redeploy the 2/3rd Independent Company on 1st July

---

[1] Maj C. E. Newman, MC, VX112181. 58/59 Bn, and HQ 15 Bde. Barrister and solicitor; of Numurkah, Vic; b. Warracknabeal, Vic, 14 Jul 1912.

so that they could support or reinforce the 58th/59th Battalion. When the enemy counter-attack did not take place by 2nd July Savige signalled Guinn that the Independent Company's task would now be to prevent the escape of the Japanese from Mubo and he took the unusual step of instructing Guinn where he thought the three platoons should go. Despite the removal of the immediate threat Savige was still apprehensive about the northern flank, with the result that the company of the 24th Battalion patrolling the Malolo Track was ordered to prepare an ambush position on the New Asini Track as well. The forward patrol of this company on 7th July skirmished with the enemy on the Malolo Track about three miles from the coast.

Worried by the failure to reach the Bench Cut Track and so threaten the rear of the Japanese at Old Vickers as well as the supply route to Mubo, Starr sent the company, now commanded by Griff, through Gwaibolom and Erskine Creek towards its objective. Having at length found the elusive Bench Cut Track the company advanced and on 3rd July set up a patrolling base at Osborne Creek, to harass both the Salamaua-Bobdubi track to the north and the Salamaua-Komiatum track to the east. Of these tasks the more important would be the Salamaua-Bobdubi track and the approach to Old Vickers. The capture of Old Vickers was essential to the capture of Bobdubi Ridge as a whole and to an effective command of the Salamaua-Komiatum track. At 5 p.m. on 3rd July the leading platoon was attacked by a party of 20 Japanese moving towards Old Vickers. In hand-to-hand fighting the Australians killed half of them, including an officer.[2] Corporal Beaumont,[3] who had already escaped from Malaya, killed one Japanese with the butt of his rifle. As the area of the track junctions was in a flat densely covered swamp Griff withdrew after dark to high ground near Osborne Creek.

Living conditions in this area, about 400 yards above the Komiatum Track, were primitive and uncomfortable. The company was forced to live on field operation rations as cooking of dehydrated foods was impossible because smoke might indicate the position to the enemy. Supplies of solidified alcohol, however, enabled the troops to make hot drinks in the early stages but were soon being used instead to combat tinea. As the natives were reluctant to carry beyond Gwaibolom one platoon usually had to act as carriers for the other two. The men were not downcast, however. Events in New Guinea again and again proved that troops would cheerfully endure wretched conditions if they were enjoying good hunting.

The men of the 58th/59th Battalion would have been inspirited had they known the effect which their activities were having on the enemy. Colonel Araki, commanding the *66th Regiment*, issued orders on 2nd July to counter the northern moves of the Australians. "The enemy appears to have begun frontal resistance and is gradually increasing his strength at Nassau and Bobdubi. This morning there was an attack on the left front height by the enemy and the situation does not

---
[2] Probably Colonel Hungo, Chief of Staff of the *51st Division*.
[3] Cpl A. G. W. Beaumont, VX56605. 2/29 and 58/59 Bns. Timber worker; of Port Melbourne, Vic; b. Fitzroy, Vic, 9 May 1913. Killed in action 16 Jul 1943.

permit any optimism; all defence areas are being strengthened. The Mubo garrison will move immediately to Komiatum to strike a telling blow at the enemy on this front. The *II/66th Battalion* will hold the present position strongly and, if the situation permits, will dispatch some weapons to Komiatum tomorrow." In another order Araki directed the Mubo garrison, except for the *II/66th Battalion,* to move the Mubo ammunition stores and ration dump to Komiatum. By this time General Muroya expected the main attack to develop in the Bobdubi area. As well as Major Jinno's *I/80th Battalion,* he ordered Araki to dispatch the whole of Matsui's *I/66th Battalion* towards Bobdubi on 3rd July. Thus the 58th/59th Battalion was again drawing off more of the enemy force facing the 17th Brigade.

On 3rd July Brigadier Hammer[4] who had been at Savige's headquarters since 26th June arrived at Missim to take command of the 15th Brigade. Hammer, a dashing soldier, had been in action as a brigade major in Greece and battalion commander at El Alamein. After handing over to Hammer at midnight on the night of 3rd-4th July, Guinn reported to Savige that the ground situation was well under control and that the enemy in Old Vickers would be surrounded and attacked. He was disappointed with some of the leadership, but stated that the attack of Jago's troops on the village area west of Old Vickers was well done; the men had heard the Japanese run and squeal and had killed 20 out of the 40 enemy met in the area. Replying to Guinn Savige stated:

Your report on situation encouraging and verifies my faith in these boys. . . . Not surprised your assessment leadership values. A broom will be necessary later.

Now that Griff's company was in position Starr was free to concentrate on capturing Old Vickers and Orodubi. Patrols from the battalion's four companies were active during the next few days. Early in the morning of 4th July reconnaissance patrols from Captain Hilbert's[5] company approached the North Coconuts area where they "drew the crabs" (drew fire) from the enemy in Old Vickers Position and Centre Coconuts. As it appeared that the northern end of the ridge was only lightly held, Lieutenant Franklin's[6] platoon from this company set out at 5 p.m. to attack North Coconuts. Jago poured fire from machine-guns and mortars on to Old Vickers to keep the enemy there occupied. Partly covered by this fire Franklin reached North Coconuts and prepared to dig in for the night. Success was short lived, however, as his platoon was attacked next morning at 10.30 a.m. by about 100 Japanese. Unfortunately only Franklin and 10 men were present, the others having gone back for supplies. The Japanese came on with much noise and indiscriminate firing, and blew bugles and waved flags. The depleted platoon was forced to retire, but could have inflicted many casualties had it been at full strength and able to stand its ground.

---

[4] Maj-Gen H. H. Hammer, CBE, DSO, ED, VX24325. BM 16 Bde 1941; CO 2/48 Bn 1942-43; Comd 15 Bde 1943-45. Manufacturers' agent; of Ballarat, Vic; b. Southern Cross, WA, 15 Feb 1905.
[5] Capt H. H. Hilbert, VX117052; 58/59 Bn. Dairyman; of Essendon, Vic; b. Armadale, WA, 24 Apr 1907.
[6] Maj L. Franklin, MC, VX102646; 58/59 Bn. Salesman; of Ascot Vale, Vic; b. Moonee Ponds, Vic, 8 Dec 1918.

Franklin's attack had disturbed Colonel Araki who was now apparently responsible for the battle area from the Francisco to Mubo. "The enemy is gradually increasing his strength in the Bobdubi area," he wrote. "Strength is now about 500, a section of which has advanced to a height covered with coconut trees. Moreover it is feared that they will advance in the vicinity of the pass . . . at the southern foot of Komiatum [Goodview Junction]. The enemy forces which landed in the Nassau area are also increasing their strength and are cooperating with the enemy forces on the Mubo front and it is estimated that those advancing on the Komiatum area are numerous." Araki ordered the commander of *II/66th Battalion* to send a platoon to repel attacks from the west. At the same time he anticipated an attack from the south to the "Komiatum high ground".

On 5th July a patrol from Griff's company stationed near the junction of the Komiatum and Bobdubi Tracks saw 102 Japanese moving along Bobdubi Track towards Bobdubi Ridge. It did not fire on this force, which was apparently carrying out a relief as 120 Japanese were later observed moving along the same track towards Salamaua. Both Japanese patrols were well dispersed, and moved cautiously with weapons at the ready. Previous ambushes had surprised Japanese patrols moving in close order with weapons slung, but now they were on the alert. Casualties could undoubtedly have been inflicted on the Japanese but the numbers unharmed would have been sufficient to encircle the Australians. Griff therefore decided to reserve his hitting power for smaller parties with which he could deal adequately. Hammer was troubled, however, by what he considered was Griff's failure to attack the Japanese on the Bobdubi Track and instructed Starr that every movement on the track must be fired on and that the offensive spirit must be built up. Next day Lieutenant Bethune's[7] platoon ambushed a party of 20 Japanese coming from Bobdubi and killed 10.

During the 58th/59th Battalion's initiation Savige had kept the 2/3rd Independent Company in reserve in order to use it to plug any gaps caused by enemy infiltration. On 5th July he ordered Hammer to send the company towards Tambu Saddle and Goodview Junction where it would cut the Komiatum Track and prevent the enemy's escape north from Mubo.

Warfe's headquarters and two of his platoons arrived at Namling on the 5th while the third platoon arrived at Vial's O.P. from Base 3. Next day this third platoon (Captain Winterflood's) climbed to the head of the Pioneers Range and then went east along the ridge turning off at Walpole's Track to approach Goodview Junction, while the rest of the company left Namling for Dierke's, a three hours' march.

The column moved from Namling in the morning with Captain Meares' platoon in the lead followed by Warfe's headquarters, a carrier line of 85 natives with an engineer spaced at every tenth native, and the 16 men from Lieutenant Barry's platoon as rearguard. After half an hour the carrier line had just passed the feature known later as Ambush Knoll

---

[7] Capt J. F. Bethune, MC, VX112185; 58/59 Bn. Salesman; of Armadale, Vic; b. Rose Bay, NSW, 1 Jan 1921.

Determined that plans should not be thwarted by any untoward delay caused by the Japanese ambush of the 2/3rd Independent Company, Hammer on the night of 6th July ordered Warfe to leave a force to secure Wells Junction while the remainder of the company proceeded with its original role. Next day therefore Warfe moved on with two platoons (Winterflood's and Meares') to take up positions on Stephens' Track (Tambu Saddle) and Walpole's Track (Goodview Junction) respectively with the object of cutting the enemy's supply route from Komiatum to Mubo. The third platoon assumed a defensive role with parties at Base 4, Stephens' Hut and Wells Junction.

From 4th July the Japanese commanders could not make up their minds about the intentions of their enemy and, in fact, were now dancing to the Australian tune. Orders for the withdrawal of the main Japanese forces in the Mubo area were contained in an order from Araki on 4th July: "Tomorrow, 5th, at sunset, *II Battalion (66th Regiment)* will leave the battle line and proceed with the utmost dispatch to assemble at Komiatum." An hour later this order was cancelled "because of the situation" and all units were ordered to carry out their previous duties. This was because Araki thought on 3rd July that the Australians were about to attack from the west, and had decided to withdraw quickly, on 4th July, to guard his vulnerable centre and to prepare defensive positions on the high ground south of Komiatum and Mount Tambu. When no attack came he changed his mind and decided to stay round Mubo, particularly as the activity of Australian patrols on Observation Hill made him conclude that an attack on the Mubo area was imminent. Nakano was so uneasy at the progress of the fighting in the Bobdubi area that he moved from Salamaua on 2nd July to supervise operations personally. It was near Bobdubi that his chief of staff, Colonel Hungo, was killed on 3rd July while inspecting front line defences.

Portion of Matsui's *1/66th Battalion* and Jinno's *1/80th Battalion* were concentrated about a mile north of Komiatum by 3rd July, ready to attack in the Bobdubi area or defend in the Goodview Junction area. Araki sent portion of these battalions west to seek information about Australian intentions. At 11 a.m. on 6th July Matsui reported that his patrols had seen about 160 enemy and 60 natives on the track towards Wells Junction. A composite force from the two battalions attacked the Australian line at Ambush Knoll and captured the equipment mentioned above.

Meanwhile the three detached forces—the Papuans along the coast, the 24th Battalion in the Markham area, and the 57th/60th Battalion in the valley of the Watut—had been busy.

Hitchcock's Papuans, who had been skirmishing with the Japanese in the Bassis villages, learnt on 2nd July that they were to move overland from the Tabali Creek area to Salus. Hitchcock, who did not relish the overland movement when water transport was available, set out for MacKechnie's headquarters where he was successful in persuading MacKechnie to let him move by sea. On 3rd July, however, two attempts to land at Salus from launches failed because of heavy surf. At Hitchcock's request MacKechnie made four landing barges available, on which the company embarked that day. After a Japanese air attack had caused the company to disembark at Nassau Bay, Lieutenant Gore's[9] platoon was sent forward

---

[9] Capt R. R. St G. Gore, QX56645; Papuan Inf Bn. Student; of Port Moresby; b. Brisbane, 28 Aug 1917. Died 14 Mar 1949.

when the rear of the column was attacked by a Japanese force approaching from Orodubi. The natives, although not actually under fire, and despite the efforts of their escorts, "went bush" to Namling, leaving behind the stores including one 3-inch mortar, two machine-guns and a medical pannier containing, among its legitimate contents, the unit's war diary. This was indeed a calamity, for rations were again scarce, and Hammer had ordered a combing of the brigade's long lines of communication for supplies. Worse, however, was the loss of the mortar and machine-guns.

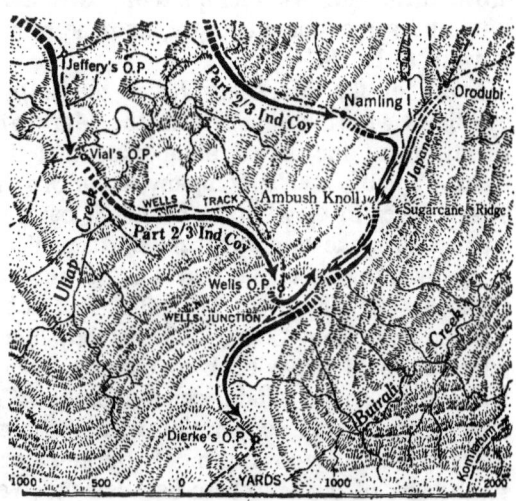

Ambush Knoll, 6th-7th July

Despite the confusion of the sudden attack and rapid disappearance of the natives, Barry immediately counter-attacked, killing eight Japanese for the loss of one killed and two wounded. To avoid being cut off from the main force Barry pushed on to Wells Junction collecting some stores as he went. Here he reorganised his two small sections—Lewin had not yet rejoined the platoon since his raid—and again unsuccessfully attacked the Japanese. Warfe, who had reached Dierke's, then had to weaken his force moving towards Tambu Saddle in order to clear Ambush Knoll and recover the stores. A section from Meares' platoon was sent during darkness to reinforce Barry while the native carriers were sent to Vial's to quieten down. It was not until the next evening that Barry's persistent pressure forced the Japanese to move back from Ambush Knoll to Orodubi. He retrieved the mortar and the two machine-guns.

From the beginning Hammer was uneasy at the lack of depth in the 58th/59th Battalion's positions especially as the Missim line of communication was on the extreme north. He considered that he might have to withdraw Heward's company to protect the north flank, but above all he strongly desired to capture Old Vickers Position. On 4th July he instructed Starr to plan an attack and two days later he visited battalion headquarters. Nor was he the only worried commander. According to the plan Bobdubi Ridge should now be in Australian hands and the 15th Brigade exploiting towards Komiatum.[8] On 6th July Savige pressed Hammer for his plan for the capture of Old Vickers Position and the Coconuts.

---

[8] On 8th July Colonel Wilton said in a letter to General Berryman: "When the armchair strategists visit Bobdubi Ridge later they will realise that 58/59 Bn have had the toughest proposition of the whole operation—a fact that is not fully realised just at present."

to reconnoitre the Salus area. In a skirmish at Lake Salus two men were wounded. Hitchcock then arranged artillery fire on the Japanese and drove them out. Another platoon patrolled along the south arm of the Bitoi and surrounding country, and the remainder of the company moved forward to Duali.

South of the Markham River the 24th Battalion had now clashed five times with the Japanese in the Markham Point area. To deceive the enemy about the actual numbers and activities of the troops opposing them, Captain Duell's[1] company, from 3rd July, sent patrols forward over kunai ridges in view from the north bank of the Markham River in an attempt to make any Japanese and hostile natives observing from north of the Markham believe that a large number of Australians were in the Chivasing crossing area. The relief to Deep Creek would move out over a kunai spur from Oomsis with its boy-line carrying rations, while those relieved would move back to Oomsis by a covered route. On 4th July Duell and Captain Chalk, commanding "B" Company of the Papuan Infantry Battalion, in cooperation with Captain Kyngdon of Angau, decided to tighten security arrangements by allowing no native movement on the south bank of the Markham between the Watut and Markham Point, and no unauthorised native crossing of the Markham. The natives on both sides of the Markham, however, were of the same tribe and they could not really be prevented from crossing if they wanted to do so by swimming or in darkness.

Ever since the success of Corporal Bartley's patrol to the mouth of the Buang River, Savige had toyed with the idea of establishing there a small force which would lead the Japanese to detach some of their strength from the main effort. The upshot was that on 27th June Major Smith of the 24th Battalion sent forward a platoon under Lieutenant Rayson[2] across the valley of the Snake River and along the rugged track through Mapos and Lega to the coast. The patrol, known as "Smoky Force", was to establish an ambush at the mouth of the Buang and observe Japanese movement between Lae and Salamaua along the beach, firing only on large enemy parties.[3]

The patrol reached the mouth of the Buang by 29th June.[4] Four days later Smith received a message by police boy from Smoky Force that it had seen no Japanese and was mainly concerned with settling in and reconnoitring the banks of the Buang back to the crossing 30 minutes from the beach. According to Rayson's native guides the Labu natives knew of the Australians' presence; it was therefore likely that the enemy also knew. On 4th July Smoky Force intercepted on the beach five

---

[1] Major A. R. Duell, VX51557; 24 Bn. Clerk; of Glen Iris, Vic; b. Aspendale, Vic, 22 Apr 1919.
[2] Capt M. W. Rayson, VX108126; 24 Bn. Clerk; of Hawthorn, Vic; b. Kew, Vic, 26 Aug 1912.
[3] Smoky Force was really Lieutenant P. R. ("Smoky") Dawson's platoon but he had been absent on another job and Rayson had therefore been given temporary command.
[4] It is interesting to note that, as early as 30th June, the Japanese estimated that there were 100 Australians in the Buang area. As an example of over-estimation this was in line with other Japanese estimates of Australian and American strengths early in July: 8,000 Australians in the Mubo area, 4,000 Americans round Nassau Bay, 500 Australians in the Bobdubi area, and 150 round Hote.

natives including an ex-Rabaul police boy who told the Australians of the presence of the enemy in Busama, Bukuap and Kela. In order to gain more information by skilled interrogation Rayson reported to Smith that he was sending the natives back under guard to the Angau representative at Lega. Aware of the danger to Smoky Force if the natives escaped or were released, Smith sent a warning not to let them go, but before this message arrived the natives were released, largely on Angau advice that they were apparently reliable and that the enemy would look for them unless they were let go. By setting free the Lega natives, Smoky Force had almost certainly prepared trouble for itself, even though Japanese activity past the mouth of the Buang was still conspicuous by its absence.

Far to the north-west Lieut-Colonel Marston's 57th/60th Battalion was gradually assembling in the Watut Valley. Twelve aircraft landed at Tsili Tsili and Marilinan on 1st July carrying battalion headquarters and portions of two companies. Six days later thirty-two aircraft brought to Tsili Tsili an American anti-aircraft battery, a detachment of Australian engineers and more of the 57th/60th. To help in patrolling, a platoon of Chalk's Papuan company went to the Watut Valley where it came under Marston's command. By 4th July a Papuan section had established a standing patrol at Pesen.

By 6th July Colonel Araki had come to the conclusion that the main blow was not to be in the Goodview Junction area after all, but that the enemy on the Mubo front was planning an attack. He directed the Mubo garrison to strengthen its defences, and ordered that the two platoons from *II/66th Battalion* previously sent north to guard the approaches to Goodview Junction be recalled. "All units to leave the present location will thoroughly consider counter-intelligence and burn every scrap of paper or document and must destroy all articles so that they will be of no use to the enemy," he ordered. This was one of the rare references to security in a captured document.

By 6.30 p.m. on 6th July the attacking companies of the 17th Brigade —Captain H. B. S. Gullett's and Captain H. McB. Stewart's from the 2/6th Battalion and Captain Morse's[5] from the 2/5th—arrived stealthily at their assembly area at Buiapal Creek ready for the assault on Mubo and Observation Hill. Another company of the 2/6th was on Lababia Ridge and the fourth arrived back at the Saddle on 4th July from its task at Nassau Bay. The remainder of the 2/5th was in areas from which the attack could be readily reinforced. The 17th Brigade was poised and ready to drive the Japanese from the area which they had occupied for so long. From 4 p.m. on 6th July synchronisation of watches began and continued at intervals throughout the night.

The Allied thrust against Mubo really began at 9.30 a.m. on 7th July when Mitchells bombed and strafed Kitchen Creek, Woody Island and the eastern slopes of Observation Hill. They were followed by Liberators and Fortresses bombing Kitchen and Buigap Creeks and Bostons heavily strafing Stony and Kitchen Creeks. An impressive spectacle was watched by the members of Moten's headquarters from a grandstand seat on

---
[5] Maj S. L. Morse, MC, VX5228. 2/5 Bn, 1 Parachute Bn. Butcher; of Bendigo, Vic; b. Devonport, Tas, 30 Mar 1919.

Guadagasal Ridge. The entire Mubo Valley was enveloped in thick smoke broken only by sheets of flame flashing across the valley as the heavy bombers dropped their loads. Most bombs seemed to be in the target area, and, even if the attack did not inflict many casualties on the entrenched enemy, it certainly helped to raise the spirits of the attackers and lower those of the defenders. Approximately 120 aircraft including fighter escorts were in the air over the Mubo area at one time and more than 100 tons of bombs were dropped. The bombing and strafing ceased at 10.40 a.m.

The air attack was the curtain-raiser for the attack by the 17th Brigade. In Colonel Wood's plan there were two objectives: first was Observation Hill, south of Kitchen Creek and on the general line of Vial's Track, and second was the high ground between Kitchen and Bui Savella Creeks.

At 8.40 a.m. on 7th July Stewart's company moved to its start-line south of Observation Hill. Towards the end of the air attack Morse's company, followed by Gullett's, moved north to their start-lines. When the end of the air attack was indicated by the dropping of signal flares, the mountain guns opened fire on Observation Hill, their isolated whines and bangs contrasting with the full-throated brazen roar of the bombing raid. After three-quarters of an hour's firing one of the guns blew up. Thirty minutes before zero hour—midday on 7th July—Morse's company set off in a north-easterly direction for Vial's Track. At zero hour Gullett's men moved west from the attacking companies' start-line running north and south through a fallen log on the track about 1,000 yards west of the kunai patches on Observation Hill. By 1.40 p.m. Gullett had reached his first objective—the kunai patch on the south-west slopes of Observation Hill—without opposition. Two hours later, when telephone communication was established with Wood's headquarters, Gullett reported that Morse was also in position about 1,000 yards to his north along Vial's Track. No opposition had yet been encountered, but by 3.45 p.m. Stewart's company, which was to capture the southern slopes of Observation Hill after passing through Gullett's company, was held up 300 yards south of Gullett by heavy automatic and rifle fire. Although Stewart captured one enemy position he was halted by another 40 yards farther south. As the time was now 5.30 p.m., and as he had lost one man killed, one missing and three wounded, Stewart decided to occupy a defensive position for the night. To the north also the enemy had been encountered when, at 4.30 p.m., one of Morse's patrols ambushed five Japanese. By dusk Savige and Moten considered that a splendid start had been made.

At 7.55 p.m. Stewart was ordered to make a dawn attack on the enemy position. When he held Observation Hill, Gullett's company would carry out the original plan of securing the high ground between Kitchen and Bui Savella Creeks. At midnight Morse was ordered to send a patrol up Vial's Track at first light next morning to make contact with the Independent Company.

This patrol set out along Vial's Track at 5.40 a.m. An hour later Stewart cancelled the dawn attack believing that a frontal attack would be hopeless and that a flanking attack would be more successful. When Wood learnt that this attack might take three hours he ordered Stewart to keep two platoons on the ridge to guard Gullett's flank and to find an outflanking approach with the other platoon. Wood then instructed Gullett to wait no longer for the clearing of the ridge but to set out for the high ground between Bui Savella and Kitchen Creeks.

By 8.30 a.m. Gullett's men were moving through Morse's position and swinging south-east down the ridge. Three times they were held up by a few riflemen and machine-gunners, but the opposition was rapidly shifted. By 2 p.m. Gullett was sure that he was on his objective. News of the company's success was eagerly awaited by Savige and Moten, as Gullett's was the key role in the Mubo attack. Eventually Moten telephoned and passed on Gullett's report: "I have fetched up with a creek on my right and a creek on my left which I hope to —— are Kitchen and Bui Savella Creeks."

While moving towards his objective Gullett had heard firing from the rear. He was anxious about this until Morse sent a message telling him that his company had been skirmishing with an enemy position up Vial's Track. Morse had attacked and inflicted casualties, but heavy automatic fire prevented him from capturing or outflanking the position.

Between 10.10 a.m. and 11 a.m. 46 Allied aircraft made a bombing and strafing attack, but it was hard for the troops to discover what they were aiming at, and they actually fired on Australian positions. One stick of bombs was dropped on Mat Mat, five Mitchells bombed the mountain-gun positions and made five strafing runs over the area during which one gunner was killed, the bridge over the Bitoi was destroyed, and the carrier lines were disrupted. "It is not understood," signalled Savige to Herring, "how our request as to type of attack and targets was altered." Such unfortunate accidents were always likely in this tangled area and it was most improbable that anyone would deliberately alter a bomb-line; the type of aircraft and the missiles to be used were of course the business of the Fifth Air Force.

Stewart was still held up. After mortar fire his company at 2 p.m attacked the stubborn enemy positions. The leading section under Private Moss[6] temporarily occupied two posts before withdrawing in the face of a strong encircling counter-attack. The Japanese followed their success by attacking the company's flanks, but were repulsed. In the day 10 Japanese were killed and 3 Australians wounded. Because of the company's inability to clear the ridge Wood was forced to use his fourth company (Dexter's). By 6 p.m. it arrived at Observation Hill and occupied Gullett's former position.

Out on the right flank in the Lababia area the fifth Australian company in the Mubo line-up had been patrolling the area south of the Pimple. It directed mortar fire on the Japanese positions, and afterwards a patrol found the Japanese still in occupation.

---

[6] Sgt R. K. Moss, DCM, SX20339; 2/6 Bn. Warehouseman; of Adelaide; b. Adelaide, 31 Mar 1923.

Meanwhile, early on 7th July, Colonel Taylor's I/162nd Battalion had begun to move forward from Napier on to Bitoi Ridge. Led by Captain George's company, the Americans crossed the swollen Bitoi using hand ropes. The tracks, prepared mainly by Lieutenant Johnson and Sergeants Hedderman and Gibson, were narrow, rough and winding and so precipitous and slippery that if a man fell he would keep going until stopped by a tree, roots or vines. One platoon with light packs climbed ahead of the main body which spent the first night at the foot of Bitoi Ridge. By 3.15 p.m. on 8th July battalion headquarters with most of Captain George's and Captain Robert E. Kitchen's companies had reached the upper southern slopes of the ridge, with patrols forward on the crest.

Many patrol clashes occurred on 9th July as the Australians moved deeper into Japanese territory in fulfilment of Wood's orders to "worry at" the enemy and to join up with the Americans. Early in the morning four patrols set out on various tasks: one under Lieutenant Trethewie[7] to make contact with the enemy between the two creeks, another under Lieutenant Lang[8] to join the Americans, a third under Sergeant Ellen to destroy the Japanese near the source of Kitchen Creek along which Wood anticipated that the Japanese facing Stewart would withdraw, and a fourth led by Private Moss to the rear of the enemy position on the ridge. Soon after the departure of these patrols two Japanese scouts disguised as bushes moved up the track towards Gullett's company. The bushes became stationary when observed and, after being fired at, one became permanently stationary.

Later in the morning Trethewie's patrol returned after moving about 600 yards towards Kitchen Creek and then encountering 30 Japanese with four machine-guns. In the ensuing skirmish the Japanese first scattered, but later counter-attacked and forced the Australian patrol back. Ellen's patrol returned at midday after climbing down the steep bank of Kitchen Creek without finding any trace of the enemy. Lang reported that he had reached the Bui Savella and was moving down it towards the Buigap. After midday, Private Moss, now acting as platoon sergeant because of casualties in his platoon, climbed to near the top of Observation Hill behind a Japanese position which he considered was not the one holding up Stewart's company. At 4 p.m. another runner from Lang reported strong opposition on the high ground in the area at the junction of the Bui Savella and Buigap Creeks. After killing four Japanese, Lang was forced to withdraw.

To the north the Japanese were seriously threatening Morse's company. Moving south along Vial's Track they poured in heavy fire and attempted to encircle the company from the west. Pressure continued for an hour and three-quarters until 5.45 p.m. when the firing ceased. As enemy success on Morse's flank would imperil Gullett's line of communication, Wood ordered Dexter to send a platoon north to clear that flank. At

---

[7] Lt E. C. Trethewie, VX3814; 2/6 Bn. Insurance clerk; of St Kilda, Vic; b. Longford, Tas, 6 Jun 1911.
[8] Lt A. B. Lang, NX89646; 2/6 Bn. Medical student; of Willoughby, NSW; b. Sydney, 6 May 1922.

6 p.m. the platoon, under the ever-willing Ellen, reinforced Morse. The Japanese attackers at this stage could be heard chopping and digging 40 yards to the north.

During the day artillery had become an important factor in the bitter hide-and-seek fighting. The remaining mountain gun, guided by mortar smoke, fired 40 shells in half an hour on to the stubborn Japanese position on the ridge but failed to shift them. Even more welcome and encouraging sounds for Australians and Americans were those from the American guns which, manhandled forward, had begun intermittent firing on the Pimple and Green Hill on 8th July.[9]

More inconclusive but intrepid patrol activity followed on 10th July as Wood's five companies increased their pressure on a stubborn enemy. Patrols from "B" Company, now led by Lieutenant Price[1] in place of Gullett[2] who had fallen ill with malaria, set out towards the two flanking creeks. One patrol towards Kitchen Creek met the Japanese 100 yards from Price's position. These were probably the Japanese who on the previous day and also on this morning had attempted unsuccessfully to draw fire from the company. Unfortunately for this enterprising Japanese band the mountain battery's forward observation officer, Lieutenant Cochrane,[3] was travelling with the patrol. Having fired at dawn on the Japanese area north of Morse's company and the Japanese position reported by Lang at the junction of the Bui Savella and Buigap Creeks, the gun now shelled the Japanese met by the patrol and drew forth many squeals. In the afternoon Price reported that the track to Kitchen Creek was clear.

North-west of Price's area Morse found no Japanese in his immediate vicinity although signs on Vial's Track to the north showed that his recent opposition had consisted of an enemy company. At 1.30 p.m. Dexter, in local control on the ridge, sent a platoon of Stewart's to attack the enemy position to the south. It was immediately pinned down by at least six automatic weapons and the forward scout was killed. In spite of a shoot of 28 mortar bombs on to the Japanese position, the platoon was unable to advance and finally withdrew at 3.15 p.m.

The Americans meanwhile had been drawing closer to the Australians. On 9th July the leading company reached the Bui Kumbul Creek, where Captain George left one platoon astride a track on the high ground between Bui Kumbul and Bui Alang Creeks to cut what was thought to be a

---

[9] Because of supply difficulties, ammunition for the support weapons in the Mubo operation was severely limited. A section of machine-guns on Mat Mat was to fire not more than 10,000 rounds a gun, with a further 10,000 rounds a gun reserved for defensive fire tasks. A section of machine-guns in reserve on Hill 7 was limited to 5,000 rounds a gun for defensive fire tasks. Six mortars only were to be used and not more than 70 bombs per mortar fired to support the attack, with 50 bombs per mortar reserved for defensive fire tasks. The mountain battery was limited to 100 rounds a gun on 7th July and 70 rounds a gun on the 8th.

[1] Capt E. W. A. Price, MC, VX4559; 2/6 Bn. Farm hand; of Red Hill South, Vic; b. Abbotsford, Vic, 22 Sep 1913.

[2] On 4th July a signal was received by the 3rd Division from New Guinea Force stating that the United Australia Party wished Captain Gullett to contest the Henty seat in the forthcoming Federal elections. The signal was answered on Gullett's behalf accepting nomination. Gullett left the 2/6th Battalion for Australia on leave without pay on 30th July and returned on 27th August. He was not elected, but in 1946 stood again, with success.

[3] Lt M. Cochrane, QX5903. 2/1 A-Tk Regt, 1 Mtn Bty. Surveyor; of Brisbane; b. Sandgate, Qld, 23 Aug 1917.

possible enemy escape route from the Buigap Creek area. Lieutenant Marvin B. Noble's platoon moved down the high ground between the two creeks to the Buigap intending to cut the Komiatum Track, while the remainder of the company advanced down the left bank of Bui Kumbul Creek to follow the left bank of the Buigap south to the footbridges and join the Australians attacking from the west. While these platoons were getting into position, Captain Kitchen's company went to the western tip of Bitoi Ridge where it set up the battalion's 81-mm mortars. One platoon, stationed on the Bitoi, patrolled south over rough and precipitous country towards Green Hill. By the afternoon of 9th July a third company reached the north side of Bitoi Ridge and the fourth guarded the guns of the 218th Artillery Battalion between Napier and the coast.

Before first light on 10th July Noble's platoon followed the Komiatum Track south-west until, at dawn, it found 10 Japanese asleep in a hut and killed them all. Continuing along the track the Americans were ambushed by about 70 Japanese. In the ensuing fight Noble lost over half his patrol killed and wounded before withdrawing. As he had no communication with his company commander he decided to move northeast along the Komiatum Track in an endeavour to join his company. At 6 p.m. he ran into what appeared to be the main Japanese defence just north of the junction of Bui Savella and Buigap Creeks. After suffering severe casualties, including Noble and his platoon sergeant, and heavily outnumbered, the remnants of the platoon withdrew to their overnight position. Next morning they moved back to the head of Bui Kumbul Creek now occupied by Captain Newman's company. This was the first news of the missing platoon since 9th July.

During Noble's fight patrols from George's and Kitchen's companies made contact with one another on 10th July but found no tracks leading up to Bitoi Ridge from the Buigap, although a patrol from Newman's company found a good track running east along the ridge. Twice during the day George reported sending patrols across the Komiatum Track in an attempt to meet the Australians. All he met was an enemy force near the southern footbridge, and at nightfall he established a strong outpost east of the northern footbridge.

Thus, across the Buigap, American patrols were watching for the Australians who were advancing against stiffer opposition. At 3.30 p.m. on 10th July Price sent out three men to meet the Americans at the southern footbridge, but they returned next day unable to reach their objective because of enemy positions along the Buigap. As reports filtered in from the two Allied forces it appeared to Savige and Moten that the Japanese had no alternative but withdrawal.

Warfe's Independent Company was already in position in the Komiatum-Goodview Junction area ready to attack any Japanese escaping from the Mubo area. To safeguard Warfe's flank and to clear a supply route Savige, on 10th July, ordered that an infantry company base be established at Base 4 for patrolling east and north-east, and Morse was given this task.

The next two days, 11th and 12th July, saw the beginning of the triumph of the persistent Australian patrol policy. On 11th July patrols from Wood's five companies were constantly seeking the enemy. In the area between Bui Savella and Kitchen Creeks, Price's patrols were very active, particularly towards the footbridges and the Bui Savella-Buigap Creek junction. A patrol to the north footbridge on 11th July was fired on and retired about 400 yards north of the Buigap-Kitchen Creek junction where it was again forced to withdraw by heavy fire from entrenched enemy positions. Forty 3-inch mortar bombs on to the razor-back and covering fire from one of Stewart's sections failed to prevent the Japanese from repulsing an attack by one of Dexter's platoons on the 11th. From the Lababia area a platoon, split into small patrols, tried to find the Japanese and draw their fire. One patrol actually managed to push into the Pimple clearing before drawing fire.

The enemy force in the Mubo area, disorganised and depleted before 7th July by Araki's vacillations, fought bitterly to retain Mubo after the Allied attack commenced. Lieutenant Usui's company of *II/66th Battalion* consisted of three officers and 87 men at the beginning of July. In the afternoon of 8th July Usui met an Allied patrol "at the three road junctions" and claimed to have repulsed it. Usui reported to his battalion commander at 6 a.m. on 9th July that "the enemy was already on the high ground and they are now being attacked to repel them". By the end of the day Usui's strength had decreased to three officers and 72 men. By 10th July the Japanese found that the Allies were astride the Mubo-Komiatum line of retreat, and by 6 p.m. next day the defenders of Mubo were retreating towards Mount Tambu, probably along Bui Kumbul Creek. At this time Usui had only three officers and 46 men left.

In an attempt to capture the stubborn Japanese position holding up Stewart's company on a razor-back to its south, Captain L. A. Cameron, of the 2/5th Battalion, was ordered to send a patrol from Mat Mat to attack the position from the south. Lieutenant Miles[4] led his platoon forward from Mat Mat early on 12th July, but, as he was crossing the Buiapal Creek at Mubo, suffered the unusual misfortune of being accurately bombed by a Japanese reconnaissance plane and lost one man killed and two wounded. After sending back the wounded the patrol began to climb the southern slopes of Observation Hill and successfully brushed aside opposition from a Japanese outpost. Further progress was prevented when the patrol came to the main enemy position which was causing such trouble to the 2/6th Battalion. Although heavy enemy machine-gun fire prevented much movement Miles went forward with the battalion's mortar sergeant, Robertson,[5] and Signalman Turnbull[6] with a telephone and wire. Only 50 yards from the enemy position and thus in a very dangerous position from his own ranging fire as well as enemy fire, Robertson directed 3-inch mortar and medium machine-gun fire from Mat Mat upon the Japanese. A slight slip by one Vickers gun actually sprayed the

---
[4] Lt C. H. Miles, MC, VX5382; 2/5 Bn. Farmer; of Mitiamo, Vic; b. Pyramid Hill, Vic, 14 Jan 1919.
[5] WO1 C. A. Robertson, MM, VX41331; 2/6 Bn. Brick drawer; of Oakleigh, Vic; b. Sea Lake, Vic, 29 Dec 1911.
[6] L-Sgt C. P. Turnbull, VX7544; 2/5 Bn. Timber-mill hand; of Yarram, Vic; b. Yarram, 10 Sep 1915.

forward position and wounded Turnbull. As soon as the bombardment finished, Miles' platoon arose and attacked the formidable position. The Japanese had had enough and fled before the determined advance of the small body of Victorians who completely cleared the area by 4.30 p.m.

Advancing steadily the platoon passed through innumerable defensive positions just abandoned. Three large bullet-riddled and blood-stained huts, hastily-buried corpses, tins of food opened that day, and a good lookout position in a large tree overlooking Mat Mat and the Saddle were passed before the patrol found a big Japanese camp, with accommodation for 700, freshly-cooked food and many bloodstains. Miles saw a path leading north-west, but as it was getting dark and his platoon could not occupy the abandoned Japanese battalion area he withdrew to the position which his platoon had captured. He then reported by telephone to L. A. Cameron who informed Stewart that the Japanese had left Observation Hill and that Miles had apparently dislodged their rearguard.

Events were also moving rapidly in Lieutenant Price's area on 12th July. Between Bui Savella and Kitchen Creeks his men were keeping up a relentless pressure. At 3 p.m. a runner reported to Price that a patrol under Corporal Martin had reached the junction of the Buigap and Bitoi without opposition and had met an American platoon whose commander, Lieutenant Williams, asked that the Australian company should come forward before he (Williams) crossed the Buigap. Price went forward and he and Williams joined forces and took up positions with two machine-guns commanding the track and the river junction.

South of the Bitoi W. J. Cameron's patrols were getting closer to the Pimple than the Australians had been before. At 8.30 a.m. on 12th July one platoon moved out to harass the Japanese position south of the Pimple. It probed forward and found 25 pill-boxes and 50 weapon-pits unoccupied. At 5.32 p.m. on 12th July the long campaign of attrition against the Pimple came to an end with its occupation by the forward platoon, led by Sergeant Longmore.[7] There was no opposition nor were there any signs of the enemy. Patrols sent forward along a well-defined track to Stony Creek could not make contact; the track to Green Hill had not been used for some time. As a result of the easy capture of the Pimple, Moten informed Taylor that the capture of Green Hill was no longer an American responsibility.

The Americans, meanwhile, were also finding evidence of Japanese withdrawal. Recently-deserted positions had been found near the junction of the Bitoi and Buigap on 10th July. Next day a patrol from George's company moved across the Buigap between the footbridges to meet the Australians, but again met instead a large enemy force withdrawing to the north-east, and retired across the Buigap at 2.15 p.m. The 81-mm mortars then fired 60 bombs into the enemy. With telephone line now laid to his forward positions, George was able to call down artillery fire also, and it produced loud cries and groans from the bombarded Japanese.

---

[7] Sgt J. R. Longmore, VX5162; 2/6 Bn. 3 Bn RAR Korea. Cafe proprietor; of Colac, Vic; b. Colac, 13 Nov 1904. Killed in action Korea 29 Oct 1950.

Kitchen now withdrew his platoon from the Bitoi, north of Green Hill, and advanced towards the junction of the Bitoi and the Buigap with the object of destroying any Japanese still remaining there and joining the Australians.

Captain Newman's company, which had been maintaining outposts on the east and north slopes of Bitoi Ridge, began to march north-west on 11th July, intending to cut the Komiatum Track north of the junction of Buigap and Bui Alang Creeks and reconnoitre towards Mount Tambu. This move was the outcome of a suggestion to Moten by Savige, who thought that the Americans were in a better position than the Australians to advance quickly towards the enemy's main supply route. The leading platoon camped during the night north of Bui Kumbul Creek with George's company. Next morning two platoons advanced north but soon ran into a strong enemy force on the ridge between the two creeks. They repulsed attacks until determined Japanese resistance forced them to withdraw to the overnight position. George meanwhile had found the track between the Bui Savella and Bui Talai honeycombed with weapon-pits. During the afternoon his patrols had followed an artillery barrage into the Bui Savella area where they found 40 to 50 Japanese killed by artillery fire. The remainder of the Japanese dispersed in confusion leaving their packs and equipment.

The constant pressure exerted by the attacking companies had its reward on the 13th when all companies advanced. Supported by the mountain battery, two platoons of Price's company moved south from the junction of the Bitoi and Buigap Creek towards Mat Mat. After reaching Garrison Hill the patrol returned, having found no Japanese although they saw many camps, one capable of holding about 300 troops. Another patrol reported camps "everywhere". The whole of the Observation Hill area was thoroughly searched without any Japanese being found. By dawn of 14th July the Mubo airstrip had been made ready for small ambulance aircraft, and Green Hill had been occupied.

The Americans arranged for an artillery shoot at 11 a.m. on 13th July at the Japanese occupying the high ground at the head of the Bui Kumbul. After their grim experience of the previous day the Japanese rapidly withdrew after the first few rounds. The Japanese fear of artillery fire enabled Newman's company to reach the Bui Alang early in the afternoon, when George's company advanced up the Buigap through abandoned pill-boxes and foxholes. "Literally hundreds of dead Japanese and fresh graves were seen," said this company's report. The area from Bui Alang south to the Bitoi was now cleared of organised enemy resistance. During Newman's and George's operations it became apparent that the enemy, fearful of using the Komiatum Track because of the Australians' marauding raids to the north, was using a route via Bui Kumbul Creek to Mount Tambu.

Reports from all the forward fighting units of the 17th Brigade indicated that the enemy had apparently escaped during the night by tracks unknown to the Allied troops in the area. The escape of the Japanese, however, could not dampen the jubilation of Moten's message to Savige: "Woody Island clean bowled 0900; Green Hill 1140; Yanks now batting on the Buigap; no further scores to luncheon adjournment."

Both the Allies and the Japanese were aware that the success of the 17th Brigade round Mubo had been helped greatly by the pressure exerted by the 15th Brigade to the north. The attacks by the 58th/59th Battalion had not been successful in clearing the Japanese from Bobdubi Ridge, but they had caused the enemy commanders to reinforce this area rather than the main Mubo battle area, and had eventually played an important part in causing the withdrawal.

The thorn in the side of the 15th Brigade during the success of the 17th had been Old Vickers Position. Conferring with Starr on 7th July Hammer outlined the battalion's essential tasks: the capture of Old Vickers, patrolling of the ridge track between it and Orodubi, and control of the Komiatum Track. That day another attack was launched on Old Vickers, after an hour's bombing and strafing by five Bostons and by mortars. The attack reached within 60 yards of the pill-boxes when it wavered before heavy fire. With one platoon Captain Jago covered the forward move of the other two platoons which had the unpalatable task of attacking up an incline swept by machine-guns tunnelled into the hill and thus not hit during the air strike. This machine-gun fire caused the Australians to withdraw with four casualties.

In the following days there were a few examples of the battalion's inexperience but, in spite of disappointments, the battalion was learning. On 7th July a platoon from Hilbert's company which was patrolling the north-west slopes of Old Vickers successfully held its ground against two attacks by 30 to 50 Japanese; on 8th July a patrol from Heward's company inflicted five casualties at the Graveyard; on 9th July one of Griff's platoons ambushed a party of about 30 Japanese on the Bench Cut Track north of Erskine Creek and killed nine.

After consultation with Hammer on 9th July, Starr's plan was that Jago's company would again attack Old Vickers after an air bombardment, Heward's and Griff's companies would attack enemy parties of any size on the Komiatum Track, and the whole battalion would make an all-out effort for the next three days. The attack on Old Vickers again failed. It was a difficult task because the knife-edged saddle had no cover on it and dictated a one-man front. In the two attacks on Old Vickers Position on 7th and 9th July the Australians lost 6 killed and 13 wounded.

Hammer came to the conclusion that when his troops had suffered more casualties they would be more successful. This was a reaction to be expected perhaps from a man who had recently commanded a battalion at El Alamein in a battle conducted on a European scale. He was also making a constant struggle to get accurate information. His signal wires ran hot checking back on what he described as "the most appalling reports". In the end he resorted to asking a series of set questions. "Times, map references, numbers, directions don't seem to mean a thing to these people," he wrote to Savige on 8th July, "but by constant reiteration we are making them learn." For their part the officers and men of the 58th/59th thought that the new brigadier had lots of drive but that, at this stage, did not realise the difficulties of the forward troops in the jungle. At brigade headquarters maps were available; in the platoons they often were not.

Many hard things were said about the failure of the 58th/59th Battalion to capture Old Vickers. The battalion was discovering, as the 17th Brigade had done in attacks on the Pimple, how sound were the enemy's prepared defences. Repeated attacks without adequate preparation or support helped to make the men think that they were facing a hopeless task. They had no artillery, air attacks were insignificant and inaccurate, and mortars and machine-guns had very limited ammunition.[8] Nothing was more demoralising to a small band of troops than an order to attack a strongly-defended position when they knew that there was little hope of success.

The attacks on the Old Vickers Position (wrote the historian of the 58th/59th Battalion) suffered from the same faults that so often foredoomed Australian attacks to failure—lack of effective support, insufficient preparation, and the use of too small an attacking force to crack a stronghold capable of resisting a force three or four times as strong. The policy of attacking a company position, first with a section, then with a platoon, then with a company, was costly in that unnecessary casualties were caused with each attack, and the enemy was encouraged by the persistence of the attacks to consolidate his defences. It also had unfortunate effects on morale, since repeated setbacks left the impression that the position was impregnable.[9]

From 10th July the Japanese showed increased interest in the Erskine Creek area, no doubt engendered by Griff's recent ambush activity on the Bench Cut and Komiatum Tracks, and their own desire to safeguard their withdrawal from Mubo. The first indication of this interest came

---

[8] Air support confronted the infantry with a dilemma. An accurate air attack with direct hits on prepared enemy positions raised the spirits of the infantry and lessened the opposition, but on the knife-edged spurs and crests where the Japanese usually built their defences bombs seldom hit the target. The safety margin required that the troops be withdrawn at least 600 yards from the target area. In precipitous country there was always a dangerous time lag between the end of the air attack and the launching of the infantry attack; and thus much of the value of the bombing might be lost. The Australians now knew that the enemy withdrew during an air strike and took cover either in alternative positions or in prepared underground shelters linked by intricate systems of tunnelling and dugouts. When it was over the forward positions were reoccupied immediately.

In Port Moresby General Herring was well aware of these difficulties. He also realised that, in spite of its good and courageous work, the air force had sometimes made such errors as the shooting up of the 17th Brigade on 8th July. Relations between New Guinea Force and the Fifth Air Force were very cordial and Herring made it his business to maintain daily personal contact with Generals Kenney and Ennis C. Whitehead. "We just had to be in one another's complete confidence," wrote Herring later, "we were always thinking ahead together." The air force had many responsibilities (e.g. Rabaul, shipping, airfields) and could only bring its full weight to bear on ground targets every now and again. On 9th July Herring signalled Savige that the Fifth Air Force was anxious to assist the 3rd Division's operations in every way but would be glad of guidance as to the method of employment on a large scale on tasks other than direct support. It was impossible for the full weight of air power to be felt if planes were restricted to half-hour operations. Kenney and Whitehead were ready to attack with seven squadrons over a period of 90 minutes to two hours and would require if possible 24 hours' notice of the strike.

Savige replied on 10th July by requesting an immediate visit by a senior air force officer to discuss details of targets and problems of both parties. He was emphatic that careful time limits, within which the air attack would begin and end, must be framed. The forward troops could not wait indefinitely, not knowing for certain whether the air attack would eventuate, and last-minute changes of heavy attacks were not feasible, as information, usually conveyed by runner, could not be sent to forward troops in time. There was also the grave danger of the enemy occupying positions vacated by Allied troops in order to be safe behind the bomb-line. Port Moresby was disappointed not to receive a more enthusiastic response.

[9] From the manuscript of the history of the 58th/59th Battalion by R. L. Mathews.

at 9.45 a.m. when the carrier supply line to Griff's company was ambushed on the Bench Cut Track. The carriers were bringing mail and tobacco as well as rations and ammunition.[1] They abandoned their cargoes and with their escorts, one of whom was wounded, fled back along the track. As Griff's only wireless was returning in the ambushed carrier line, and as the enemy cut the telephone so often that it was impossible to keep it in repair, little accurate information could be passed back to battalion headquarters. A patrol led by Lieutenant Hough[2] was sent to salvage the supplies but was ambushed on the Bench Cut near Erskine Creek, suffering 11 casualties, six of whom were missing but later returned. In order to let Starr know what was happening Griff sent out two experienced scouts to find battalion headquarters. They followed compasses on fixed bearing but were unable to get through until next day. Two hours after the ambush one of Heward's machine-guns on the Bench Cut near Erskine Creek was overrun, apparently by the same Japanese party. The section manning the gun withdrew after killing two Japanese and rendering the gun unserviceable. Having disorganised these two companies the Japanese party now sat down on the Bench Cut north of Erskine Creek. Two of Griff's platoons were withdrawn from the Bench Cut on 11th July and scrub-bashed their way to Gwaibolom while the third remained on the track north of the Japanese position. A combined attack planned for the two companies failed when faulty communications prevented Griff from receiving Starr's orders until too late to put in a coordinated attack with Heward, whose attack was unsuccessful.

The ambush position in the Bench Cut between the two companies had disorganised them and, until it could be removed, Australian operations there would be confused. The leading elements of Griff's company, moving to attack the ambush position on 12th July, recovered two machine-guns lost on the 10th. Griff found that the belt boxes had been shot through often—obviously during the fighting. He also found the machine-gun sergeant's body near the gun; the sergeant's legs were tied together with a webbing strap, apparently splinting the broken leg to the good one, and he had died from exposure or loss of blood.

Starr had now come forward and at 9.30 a.m. on 13th July he and Heward set out to see Griff. They came to a section posted on the track and asked for Griff. The corporal in charge said that he was away but would soon be back. Starr and Heward and Heward's orderly went on, thinking that Griff was ahead. The corporal did not mention that his was the forward post. Soon they saw two men a few yards away. Starr called to them thinking they were his own men, but they were Japanese and opened fire. Starr jumped aside and escaped but Heward, who was carrying a copy of Starr's operation order, was killed.

---

[1] The men had been without tobacco for a week. A soldier without his tobacco is a peevish fellow. Many of the men were smoking tea leaves wrapped in paper; a few managed to wheedle native carriers into parting with their "boong twist".

[2] Lt R. W. Hough, NX72454; 58/59 Bn. Solicitor; of Blayney, NSW; b. Inverell, NSW, 10 Feb 1917. Missing, believed killed, 1 Aug 1943.

It was a patrol from Jinno's *1/80th Battalion* which fired on the three men. The patrol's report stated: "*No. 1 Company* . . . destroyed an officers' patrol and captured materials; code book, map, operations order, etc." The Japanese translation of Starr's operation order was subsequently recaptured. In it all units of Savige's force were listed, but the Japanese concluded, probably with dismay, that "the presence of the 6th Division is now certain".

South of the 58th/59th Battalion, the 2/3rd Independent Company had been moving towards its objective after having driven the Japanese from Ambush Knoll. Determined to cut the Komiatum Track and gain the high ground to the east, Warfe had issued orders on the night 7th-8th July for an attack at dawn by two platoons down Walpole's and Stephens' Tracks. Hammer was constantly on the phone, the rain was incessant, and Warfe's temperature was 104. The adjutant put him to bed under a groundsheet. All were hungry and wet, but at dawn, after a cup of tea

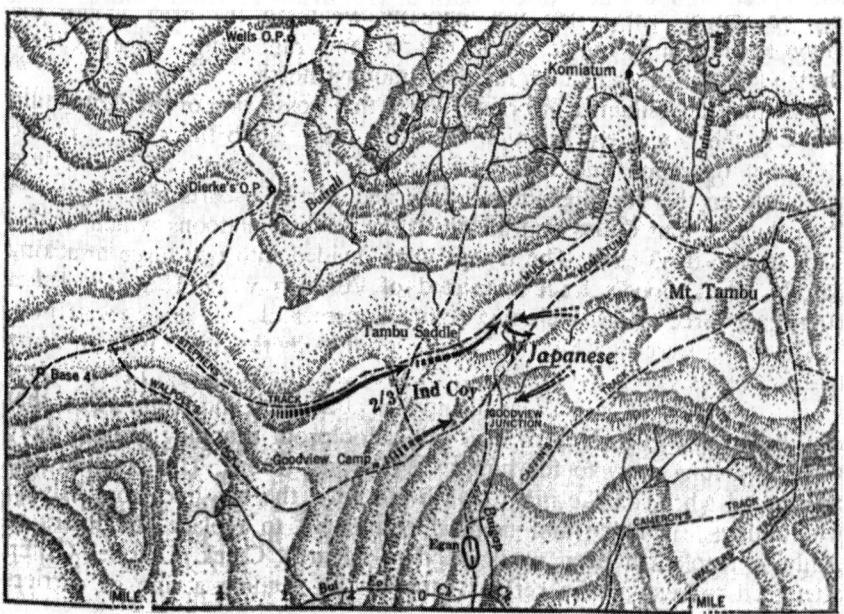

The 2/3rd Independent Company at Goodview Junction, 8th-10th July

and a meal of boiled rice, Winterflood's platoon advanced down the steep ridge along Walpole's Track and drove Japanese outposts from positions on Goodview Junction, killing 12 for the loss of one man wounded.

In the afternoon, however, the Japanese struck back; under cover of mortar and machine-gun fire, large numbers of Japanese attacked from both flanks. Twenty-five Japanese were killed but Winterflood found the hastily-dug positions among a thick bed of roots untenable and withdrew 300 yards west up Walpole's Track.

Captain Meares' reinforced platoon moving along Stephens' Track on 8th July unexpectedly encountered strong opposition from a Japanese position in the Tambu Saddle area at the junction of Stephens' Track and the Mule Track. One section engaged this position while three others bypassed the Japanese to the south and moved across the Mule Track to the Komiatum Track. After engaging another enemy position at the junction of Stephens' and Komiatum Tracks Meares attacked the first enemy position on the Mule Track from the east and killed 13 Japanese. At dusk he decided to withdraw to a holding position on Stephens' Track. His scouts had previously seen about 90 Japanese moving to reinforce the positions already encountered at the track junctions, and had heard a great deal of enemy activity on the slopes of Mount Tambu east of the Komiatum-Mubo track.

All this time Lieutenant Egan was harassing the enemy from his impregnable position about 800 yards south of Goodview Junction and overlooking the Buigap gorge. He was actually watching the area where the Mubo-Komiatum-Salamaua track entered and ran along Buigap Creek. On the 8th his men killed 11 Japanese moving north.

Late that day Hammer informed Warfe that possession of the Komiatum Track in the Goodview Junction area was essential to the success of the divisional operation and that all available troops must be thrown into the battle on the 9th. Signallers, cooks and carrier escorts were removed from their regular duties and added to the fighting platoons which at this stage averaged 63 each. The troops were divided into two large attacking patrols. Winterflood's force consisted of 70 men while Hancock led a composite force of 50, including some sappers and the transport section.

The plans were fine but, as Napoleon and others had found, an army marches on its stomach. On 8th July the forward units had no lunch except some native rice. Aircraft dropped supplies at Selebob and Nunn's Post that day, but even though Nunn's Post was a foolproof dropping ground there was still a long carry to the hungry and weary troops. The position was aggravated when, on the night of 8th-9th July, the boy-line from Missim with rations, signalling and medical equipment to replace the losses at Ambush Knoll had been misdirected to Meares' Creek. Colonel Griffin attempted to remedy the serious situation by sending a line of carriers with rations from Mubo to Base 4 by back tracks. An earlier line of rations from Missim, however, arrived providentially in the afternoon and all troops then had iron rations to last until the 10th.

Winterflood's men attacked frontally on 9th July but were pinned down by heavy fire, suffering four casualties. It took some time to assemble Hancock's composite force, which set out at 10 a.m. along Stephens' Track, across the Mule Track and into the track triangle area. Hancock advanced south parallel to the Komiatum Track but did not reach the vicinity of Goodview Junction until next morning (much too late to support Winterflood) because of the need for caution in the presence of large numbers of Japanese heard immediately east of Goodview Junction and Tambu Saddle. Twenty-four hours after setting out Hancock came across a party of Japanese digging in on the west side of the Komiatum Track at the southern corner of the track triangle. The Australians killed eight and dispersed the remainder, but as no rations were being carried because there were none to carry, action against the enemy east of the Komiatum-Mubo track could not be pursued. By dusk Winterflood's and Hancock's forces were holding positions on Walpole's and Stephens' Tracks respectively.

The plan for the Independent Company had been to harass the unprotected enemy supply line between Komiatum and Mubo. Instead, it now appeared that they had struck the considerable strength of the west flank of the Japanese defences on Mount Tambu, and there were indications that the Japanese might be using another supply route farther east. There was no movement either north or south along the Komiatum Track until 12th July when a party of 16 heavily camouflaged Japanese, moving stealthily from Goodview towards Mubo, was attacked, 14 being killed.

Sounds of chopping and digging from the Japanese positions as well as the fact that all Japanese encountered had been well clothed, well fed and lightly burdened, made it apparent that the enemy had a large fresh force available in the Mount Tambu area. The Americans had proved that the enemy escaping from Mubo were using a new route up Bui Kumbul Creek to Mount Tambu. By mid-July it was clear that, instead of hunting fleeing bands of enemy escaping from the south, the Independent Company was up against a new and powerful force well established to the east.

This force consisted mainly of Matsui's *1/66th Battalion,* which had been withdrawn from Mubo before Moten's attack was launched, and later the remnants of *II/66th Battalion* which escaped from Mubo after 7th July.

The northern unit of Hammer's force was Captain Whitelaw's company of the 24th Battalion in the Cissembob-Hote area. Its tasks as formulated by Hammer on 8th July were to defend that area as a base for operations against Salamaua, and establish control of the Hote-Malolo track. This was an enlargement of its previous role of establishing a defensive position on the left flank of Warfe's company and protection of the Missim supply route. The specific task of preventing the enemy approaching from Malolo was relatively simple for determined troops as the country was wild and rugged and ideal for defence.

It was troops from the *115th Regiment* who had attacked the Australians at Cissembob in May, before being withdrawn to the Heath's, Markham Point or Lae areas by the beginning of July. On 2nd July General Muroya ordered the commander of *102nd Regiment* "to furnish a platoon immediately, the main part of which will occupy the heights about 3 kilometres north-east of Hote".

During the operations early in July Savige's staff thought that Hammer, fresh from desert warfare, except for three months' training on the Atherton Tableland, was unduly worried about the insecurity of his flanks. On the other hand Hammer's front extended from Goodview Junction in the south to the Francisco River in the north and then through a gap of unoccupied country to Hote farther north. His troops were very thinly spread and with only one battalion and a quarter and an Independent Company available, his concern was understandable. The possibility of encirclement of his northern flank from the Buiris Creek area at the beginning of July had delayed the move of Warfe's company south. Enemy thrusts into the middle of the brigade area, which disorganised portion of the 58th/59th Battalion, underlined the two-mile gap between the southern area held by the 58th/59th Battalion at Namling and the Goodview Junction area for which the 2/3rd Independent Company was fighting. It would be possible for the enemy to drive a wedge into this gap and threaten the Base 3 and Uliap Creek supply routes. Hammer therefore telephoned Colonel Wilton on 11th July and asked that Warfe's company be relieved from Goodview Junction in order to fill the gap between Wells O.P. and Base 4 and to strengthen Starr's southern flank at Namling and Orodubi.[3] Savige and Wilton considered that gaps and lack of a continuous line must be accepted as a concomitant of jungle and mountain warfare, but in this case they agreed with Hammer that the gaps were unduly large and the dangers to the supply routes too acute.

By 10th July Colonel Conroy had already received orders for the movement north of two companies of the 2/5th Battalion, so that Wilton was able to inform Hammer that these would relieve Warfe's company which could then protect the southern flank of the brigade. Captain A. C. Bennett's company was sent north to join Captain Morse's at Base 4 on 13th July. The two companies, known as "Bennett Force", took over from the Independent Company on 14th July. Bennett was instructed to secure the Goodview area, prevent the Japanese escaping from Mubo, protect the line of communication to Base 4, patrol vigorously north to Komiatum, make and retain contact with the Japanese in that area, and patrol northeast to Mount Tambu. The remainder of the 2/5th moved up the Buigap as far as Bui Alang Creek on 14th July.

It will be recalled that the Papuan company at Nassau Bay had begun to move north into the Duali and Salus areas on 6th July. Next day Hitchcock received a message from MacKechnie to "move north sending out patrols east of Salus to mop up enemy"—a difficult task since to the east of Salus lay the sea; and to find suitable landing places for barges at Tambu Bay and Dot Inlet. In its progress north the company unearthed a Japanese machine-gun hastily buried in the sand near the mouth of the north arm of the Bitoi, and on 8th July a patrol from Lieutenant Bishop's platoon moving west along the Bitoi captured one badly wounded prisoner a mile from the coast.

By 9th July the Papuans were following traces of 150 Japanese who had apparently moved north from Lake Salus about four or five days before; Hitchcock reported to MacKechnie on 10th July that there was further evidence of the move north of the 150 Japanese along both sides of Lake Salus.

---

[3] Later Hammer wrote: "I was not really concerned about the right (northern) flank. What I was after was for the 17th Brigade to take more responsibility towards the north, thus allowing me to concentrate my force to deal with the Japs in the Bobdubi Ridge area."

These Japanese were the remnants of Major Oba's *III/102nd Battalion* which had been mainly in the Cape Dinga area when the Americans landed. On 7th July Oba's battalion was met north of Lake Salus by the *III/66th Battalion* which, as mentioned, General Nakano had sent south to help Oba. Oba's 250 remaining men reached Salamaua two days later.

North of the main battle area interest chiefly centred on the 24th Battalion's Smoky Force at the mouth of the Buang River. There is little doubt that the Japanese now knew of its existence, and early on 9th July an indeterminate skirmish occurred on the beach between forces of about section strength. Neither side pressed the affair with much enthusiasm and both withdrew.

Smoky Force then moved the ambush position north across the river 450 yards, and sited it between the beach, at this point 15 yards wide, and an old native pad 20 yards to the west. The firm base was moved 200 yards north-east of the old one to a position backed by swamp. On 12th July Lieutenant Dawson[4] took over the Buang area. He was not impressed with the ambush position because the narrow beach was not good "killing ground", and because foliage hanging over the beach and water reduced visibility, but in spite of reconnoitring the beach 1,000 yards to the north he was unable to find a better position. Smoky Force did have the consolation of seeing four Japanese aircraft on the 12th circle their old ambush position and dive-bomb it from a low level.

Early in June Australian patrols from the 24th Battalion across the Markham had caused General Nakano to prepare for the possibility of an Australian attack down the Markham Valley to Lae. The *115th Regiment* was therefore ordered to hold the area on a line from the high ground north of Heath's to Munum and Narakapor, with patrols to Nadzab. Markham Point was also occupied.

Even before the American landing at Nassau Bay Generals Adachi and Nakano had been worried about the possibility of an Allied landing on the coast between Lae and Salamaua. They could foresee the pattern in the advance of the Americans by water hops to Morobe. On 20th June Nakano planned to allocate a portion of the *115th Regiment* to the suitable landing area near the mouth of the Buang River. With fighting flaring up along the *51st Division's* front, Nakano, early in July, dissolved the *Mubo* and *Nassau Defence Forces* and concentrated all his forces under direct divisional control. On 6th July General Muroya issued Nakano's orders for the defence of the Buang mouth: "It is feared the enemy will land between Lae and Salamaua or use the Wagau-Buang track to intercept Lae and Salamaua." Muroya ordered Major Yamaguchi's *I/115th Battalion*, with artillery, to "occupy the Buang area and, while guarding against the Wagau area, thwart enemy plans to land". Two infantry companies and the artillery company left for the Buang mouth on 9th July. A patrol clash on this same day with Smoky Force convinced the Japanese commanders that a land threat by about 100 Australians along the Buang Track from the Snake River Valley was likely. By 10th July Yamaguchi's force was disposed north and south of the river mouth to meet the threat. Thus, one Australian platoon had managed to keep occupied a substantial enemy force, which might have been used in the main battle farther south.

After the loss of Mubo, Nakano issued an instruction describing how the Emperor had graciously "bestowed his Imperial solicitude upon the war situation in the Salamaua area". Nakano continued: "The Lae-Salamaua area is at the very limit of this decisive struggle, and upon the decision in this fight, the whole fate of our

---

[4] Capt P. R. Dawson, VX104426; 24 Bn. Clerk; of Toorak, Vic; b. Melbourne, 16 Nov 1918.

Empire depends. The strongholds of Lae and Salamaua must be defended to the death."

Such were the sentiments of the general. The feelings of the ordinary Japanese soldiers may have been different. A private from *1/80th Battalion* in the Bobdubi area wrote this entry in his diary on 14th July: "I am now living in a trench 5 kilometres from Salamaua and we are bombed incessantly. Enemy planes, on reconnaissance, increase daily over our heads. I had no idea that I would fall into such a miserable situation. We are sniped and shelled when we go to obtain water so badly needed by us. Our rations are compressed food only and I am sick in the stomach."

By 13th July the troops of the 3rd Division had inflicted a heavy defeat on the enemy. The Japanese had lost Mubo and their hold on Bobdubi Ridge was insecure and subject to increasing attack. The Australian division, aided by an American battalion, had defeated their enemy under appalling conditions which required the highest qualities of physical endurance, grit and determination.

CHAPTER 6

THE STRUGGLE FOR THE RIDGES

THE capture of Mubo enabled General Savige to press nearer Salamaua, which he regarded as his ultimate goal. The airfield, the isthmus and the peninsula could now be seen from several high points along the Allied front. But although the 17th Brigade had fulfilled its immediate task, the 15th Brigade had been unable to capture Bobdubi Ridge. Savige now ordered Brigadier Moten to exploit north towards Komiatum and north-east towards Lokanu; and Brigadier Hammer to carry out his original task.

As early as 3rd July Savige had warned his brigade commanders about a possible "exploitation phase" to follow the Mubo fight. A day later he sent General Herring a plan asking for an extra brigade which could be used to control the Wampit and Watut River Valleys in place of the 24th and 57th/60th Battalions which could then rejoin the 15th Brigade. He suggested that, "although it may not be intended to attack Salamaua . . . action should be taken to isolate the garrison and prevent them receiving further supplies or reinforcements by land". He considered that this could best be done by harassing the Lae-Salamaua coastal track from a battalion base west of Malolo.

Herring's view of all this forward planning was expressed later: "There is a great need in war as in other things for first things first and not worrying too much about the distant future. You cannot exploit until you have broken through." He decided that it was time to apply the brake, and on 11th July informed Savige that it was not considered desirable at that time to lay down a policy regarding Salamaua and that the role of the division remained "to drive the enemy north of the Francisco River". Politely, however, he did request an outline plan for the capture of Salamaua. Not knowing that Lae was to be a goal before Salamaua, Savige was at some disadvantage in framing the plan which he sent to Herring on 17th July. It provided that the Australians would attack from the north-west, west and south-west towards the airfield and Samoa Harbour, while the Americans secured the south bank of the Francisco River from Logui 2 to the first bend of the river. The combined force would then capture the isthmus and peninsula.

While Savige was busy with these plans, Herring was busy ensuring that Salamaua should be a means of helping the drive to the north. The problems of today, however, pressed more urgently upon the commanders and staffs of New Guinea Force and the 3rd Division than did the problems of the future. The main one was supply. Because of its distance from the coast, the 3rd Division had to be fed mainly from the air, an inaccurate and expensive method. The problem became more burdensome as it became necessary to build up reserve dumps for the operations against Lae. Herring considered that it would be very difficult, if not impossible, to maintain any further units in the Salamaua area unless they were based on the coast. Savige's outline plan for the capture of Salamaua, involving the use of an additional brigade, was therefore pigeon-holed in Port Moresby.

The immediate and practical problem facing Herring was how to establish a coastal base whence he could supply the main part of the 3rd Division and bring more artillery against the enemy. Early in July General MacArthur was in Port Moresby. Like other Australian leaders who had served in the Papuan campaign Herring had got to know MacArthur well. On 3rd July he had conferred with him at G.H.Q. and obtained permission to use at least one other battalion of the 162nd Regiment for the coastal move. Herring then summoned General Savige, and General Fuller of the 41st American Division, to Port Moresby, where on 5th July Herring discussed with them his plan to move a battalion of the 162nd Regiment along the coast to Tambu Bay and to instal guns there. Himself a gunner, Herring realised that Tambu Bay was the only possible site whence the guns could support the 3rd Division and shell Salamaua. They were of no use at Nassau Bay and they could not be dragged forward via Mubo. As Savige's headquarters were a long way from the coast and as Fuller was responsible for supplying both MacKechnie Force under Moten and the troops who would move up the coast, Herring decided that the coastal move should be under Fuller's command. This decision about command was apparently not clear to Savige, who made "brief notes" of the conference and wrote of the new troops from the 162nd Regiment who were soon to arrive at Nassau Bay: "These troops then under my command. . . ." Of the proposed move against Tambu Bay and the high ground overlooking it he wrote: "Operations would be directed by 3rd Aust Div."

On receipt of a signal from Moten that conditions at the Nassau Bay beach-head were chaotic, Savige signalled Herring after his return on the 6th suggesting that Fuller should consider replacing MacKechnie. On the same day the first company of the American III/162nd Battalion, selected to establish an area at Tambu Bay for the guns, arrived at Nassau Bay. Major Archibald B. Roosevelt, the battalion commander, arrived on the 8th with another company; the remainder of the battalion assembled at Nassau Bay by the 12th.

Fuller had no doubts about the decisions of 5th July. On the 11th he issued a "letter of instruction" to his artillery commander, Brigadier-General Ralph W. Coane, who had been chosen to lead the American advance up the coast. Coane would "have command of all troops in the Nassau Bay-Mageri Point-Morobe area,[2] exclusive of MacKechnie Force", and would "be prepared to conduct operations north as directed by G.O.C. New Guinea Force, through this headquarters". "Coane Force" would be created on 12th July. Thus, when the regimental commander, MacKechnie, returned from Napier to Nassau Bay on 14th July he found

---

[2] The troops listed by Fuller comprised mainly: II/162nd Battalion, a battery of 218th Field Artillery Battalion and "D" Troop, 2/6th Australian Field Regiment at Morobe; and the III/162nd Battalion and "A" Company, Papuan Infantry Battalion at Nassau Bay.

that two-thirds of his former command had been assigned to an artilleryman.

On 12th July Savige began to have misgivings about the command situation and repeated to Herring a signal from MacKechnie to Moten stating that Fuller had instructed MacKechnie that Roosevelt's battalion was no longer under MacKechnie's command but responsible directly to Fuller himself. This appeared absurd to Savige who was not yet even aware of the formation of Coane Force. Accordingly he asked for definite instructions clarifying the command of American troops in the Nassau Bay area and stated that dual control would cause confusion. Herring that day signalled "for clarification of all concerned all units Mack Force are under operational control of 3 Aust Div".

Savige chose to believe that this signal meant that the 3rd Division commanded all troops of MacKechnie's 162nd Regiment—not merely MacKechnie Force. Herring, however, obviously meant MacKechnie Force. Had the ambiguity been overcome at this stage, some disagreements and difficulties which temporarily marred Allied efficiency and the relationships between the Australian commanders in New Guinea would not have occurred.

Trouble soon began. Savige placed Roosevelt under Moten's command for his northward move, but, replying to a signal from Moten, Roosevelt signalled on 14th July:

> Regret cannot comply your request through MacKechnie Force dated 14th July as I have no such orders from my commanding officer. As a piece of friendly advice your plans show improper reconnaissance and lack of logistical understanding. Suggest you send competent liaison officer to my headquarters soon as possible to study situation. For your information I obey no orders except those from my immediate superior.

Having sent this *billet-doux* to the startled Moten, Roosevelt then reported to Fuller:

> I received orders by 17 Aust Bde that I was assigned to 3 Aust Div. I also received orders from 17 Aust Bde to perform a certain tactical mission and have informed them I am under command of 41 Div and will not obey any of their instructions. If you are not in accordance with this action request that I be relieved of command III Bn. In my opinion the orders show lamentable lack of intelligence and knowledge of situation and it is possible that disgrace or disaster may be the result of their action.

On 14th July Savige decided to bring matters to a head. He signalled MacKechnie and Roosevelt (and repeated the signal to Herring, Moten and Fuller) that New Guinea Force's latest instructions clearly indicated that Roosevelt's battalion was under the command of MacKechnie Force which was under command of Moten for the time being. Roosevelt replied: "I do not recognise this signature. I take orders only from my commanding general 41 US Div and will hereafter be careful to certify his signature."

Savige then wrote to Herring, stating that

> a confused and impossible situation has now arisen which makes it impossible to coordinate control of operations. . . . The position as understood at this head-

quarters is that the Roosevelt combat team has been placed under operational control of 3 Aust Div for employment on the coast north of Nassau Bay. . . . Roosevelt now refuses to obey the orders issued by MacKechnie. . . . It has now become a matter of most urgent operational necessity that clarification of operational command of Roosevelt combat team be made and that Roosevelt be informed accordingly by 41 US Div.

The next step in this confused situation was that on 15th July MacKechnie telephoned to Moten a message sent from Fuller to Coane on the previous day and stating: "Roosevelt is not part of Mack, is not under comd 3 Aust Div or 17 Aust Inf Bde. . . . Until such time as this HQ informs you to the contrary you will comply with letter of instruction given to you. Confusion due to 3 Aust Div and 17 Aust Inf Bde not having received copy of letter of instruction due to communication difficulties." MacKechnie also signalled Moten on the 16th apologising for Roosevelt's messages, speaking warmly of Australian cooperation and saying: "I trust you will recognise the difficult position in which Roosevelt has been placed due to confusion in command situation."[3]

In his earnest attempt to maintain cordial Australian-American relations and to seek a formula satisfactory to Australians and Americans Herring had the ill-fortune to have his orders misunderstood by his Australian divisional commander. The decision to establish the two commands in the battle area was a logical one in the circumstances but it was surprising that there should have been such a sorry period of doubt about who was commanding what. A report from his liaison officer at Nassau Bay, Major Hughes, finally convinced Herring that further clarification was necessary. Hughes signalled on 15th July: "Utter confusion exists as to command of III/162 Bn." On the same day therefore Herring signalled Savige that "with view to straightening out control US forces" he had conferred with Fuller's chief of staff, Colonel Sweany. The signal continued: "41 Div desires that MacKechnie retain control of American troops moving inland and agrees that this Force should operate under operational control of Moten as in past. 41 US Div has sent Brig Coane to control ops for coastwise operations. In view of rapid changing situation this force forthwith under operational control of 3 Div."

Fortified with this clarification Savige on 15th July signalled Coane, Moten, MacKechnie, Herring and Fuller concerning Coane Force's task. This would be to establish a secure bridgehead at Tambu Bay by moving companies north along the coast, to land the remainder of Roosevelt's battalion and the artillery when the bridgehead was secure, and to engage artillery targets in the Komiatum and Bobdubi areas. Coane's ultimate task would be to advance along the coast and secure the general line from Lokanu 1 to Scout Hill. Coane was ordered to maintain close liaison with Moten, and Captain Sturrock[4] of Savige's staff was sent to Coane's headquarters as liaison officer.

---

[3] That MacKechnie also did not understand the command situation was evident from his signal in which he said that Roosevelt's messages had been sent without his knowledge and that there would be no repetition.

[4] Capt A. S. Sturrock, VX108128; HQ 3 Div. Timber merchant; of Brighton, Vic; b. Brunswick, Vic, 14 May 1915.

Looking north along Komiatum Ridge to the Francisco River.

The Francisco River, looking north to Arnold's Crest. Much of the heavy fighting by the 15th Brigade took place in this area.

Savige again flew to Port Moresby on 19th July to confer with Herring's staff and the Americans about the use and control of artillery, the regrouping of forces, details of proposed operations, and the problem of supplies. In order to remove any lingering American doubts about who was in command in the operational area Herring on the 23rd issued an instruction which stated:

> 3 Aust Div has command of all troops north of inclusive Nassau Bay and inland from those places with the right to effect such regrouping of forces in this area as it may from time to time consider necessary.

Thus apparently ended a period of confusion of command, an unnecessary period, annoying particularly to those subordinate commanders who received conflicting orders from two sources. This conflict of command caused the very irritation which Herring was so anxious to avoid and which was so apparent in Roosevelt's remarkable signals.

Herring also ordered that "as soon as required by 3 Aust Div" Coane would become C.R.A., 3rd Division.[5] Until then Coane would make available to the 3rd Division Colonel William D. Jackson and such artillery staff as would be necessary to carry out artillery control and planning. Herring would provide a brigade major and a staff captain for Jackson. On his return from Port Moresby Savige had already offered Coane his choice. Coane had replied that he had been designated divisional artillery commander and would continue to command Coane Force.

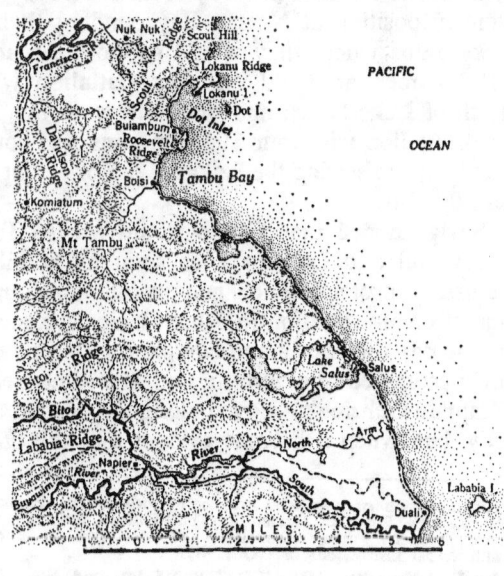

Meanwhile the advance up the coast continued. On 10th July an American patrol skirmished with the Japanese south of Lake Salus. Well ahead of the Americans two of Captain Hitchcock's Papuan platoons were patrolling between Lake Salus and the lagoon south of Tambu Bay while the third platoon patrolled west of Lake Salus.[6] MacKechnie had already instructed Hitchcock to push north, clear Japanese pockets of resistance, capture the high ground overlooking Dot Inlet by 15th July, and estab-

---

[5] Coane had already been appointed CRA 3rd Division when he was given command of Coane Force. As the result of the conference of 19th July it was left to him to decide whether he would accept the position or retain command of Coane Force.

[6] On 14th July a Papuan patrol saw four men swimming in the west end of Lake Salus. On receiving no reply when they challenged the swimmers, the Papuans fired a shot and then discovered that the four men were the crew from a crashed Mitchell bomber (B-25).

lish outposts on Lokanu Ridge and Scout Hill. On 12th July MacKechnie told Hitchcock that future operations depended on the results of his reconnaissance in the Lokanu 1 and Scout Camp areas. Again on 14th July MacKechnie signalled: "On arrival at Tambu Bay area you will recce the beach to ascertain a suitable exit for artillery and also to locate gun positions from which targets on Salamaua Isthmus and Komiatum can be reached."[7] Hitchcock was able to report on the same day that the natives said that Tambu Bay and Dot Inlet were occupied by the Japanese.

A company from the II/162nd Battalion landed unopposed on Lababia Island on 15th July and found there an Australian signaller, Sergeant Parmiter,[8] who had volunteered to establish a wireless spotting station and report enemy movement.

Next day, as Roosevelt assembled on the beach for the move north, Hitchcock reported that the Japanese had an observation post on the north side of the lagoon and another on Dot Island; and that natives reported 200 Japanese at Boisi and the remnants of the Japanese Nassau Bay force digging in on the ridge west of Lokanu 1. The advance to Tambu Bay began on the 17th when two companies, guided by the Papuans, were ordered north by an inland track known to the Papuans and a third by the coastal route.

Next day Major Thwaites'[9] battery of the 2/6th Australian Field Regiment arrived at Nassau Bay from Buna. By 20th July four 25-pounders were in position at Nassau Bay pending their movement to the north of Lake Salus where they would support the advance; two batteries of the 218th American Field Artillery Battalion with eight 75-mm guns were north of Lake Salus; and one battery of the 205th American Field Artillery Battalion with four 105-mm guns was south of the lake. The artillery was busy registering the Lokanu 1, Boisi, Dot Island and Buiambum areas on 20th July.

Savige hoped that Coane would secure Tambu Bay and then occupy Scout Hill and Lokanu 1 as soon as possible in order to provide the necessary protection for gun installations and to threaten the Japanese line of communication to Moten's area. Expecting to reach their objectives in one day the two inland companies (led by Captains Colvert and Kindt) underestimated the terrain and the time required. The third company (Captain Gehring's) moved along the coastal track on the morning of 18th July, but, when it became evident that the other companies would not be

---

[7] The confusion of command was here evident. The Papuan company had been working with MacKechnie Force at Nassau Bay but Fuller's order of 11th July listed the PIB as being a part of Coane Force, although it also said that the Papuans would operate "in accordance with verbal instructions of GOC, NGF".

[8] Sgt F. J. Parmiter, MM, VX12770. 2/5 Bn, and NG Air Warning Wireless Coy. Mechanic; of Coburg, Vic; b. Kalgoorlie, WA, 28 Apr 1910. Parmiter had landed on the island, assumed to be in enemy hands, on 31st May. Isolated from outside help, he had found that the island was regularly patrolled by the Japanese who had almost succeeded in finding him on 5th July. The alert signalman, however, had the best of an encounter with three Japanese, killing one and taking one prisoner. Four days later he had rescued the crew of a crashed American aircraft. He finally left the island on 24th August.

[9] Maj G. R. Thwaites, OBE, NX405; 2/6 Fd Regt. Bank officer; of Sydney; b. Melbourne, 6 Mar 1911.

in position by the end of the day, it halted half way between Lake Salus and the lagoon. By the next evening a Papuan platoon moved into position to attack a Japanese outpost south of Boisi. On the morning of the 20th the platoon killed four Japanese and then Gehring's men destroyed the outpost. With the Papuans scouting ahead the American company advanced to Boisi meeting no further resistance.

Gehring's advance was now harassed by Japanese guns and mortars from Roosevelt Ridge, 1,500 yards distant, and 12 men, including the company commander, were hit. American artillery began counter-battery work, while the company withdrew and dug in south of Boisi, where it was joined later that night by the two companies which had moved along the inland track. On 21st July the artillery supported the move of the remainder of the battalion into Tambu Bay, and that night, in the face of sporadic fire, more reinforcements, including two 25-pounders of the 2/6th Regiment, heavy machine-guns and anti-tank guns for beach defence, and Bofors anti-aircraft guns, arrived.

From information gathered by the Papuans Savige was convinced that the Japanese were lightly holding the eastern end of Roosevelt Ridge. As the map showed that the ridge rose to a greater height on the western flank, he considered that it would be wiser to go for this apparently undefended area and, after obtaining a footing, move east along the ridge and attack the Japanese from the high ground. Savige signalled Coane on 21st July about a track leading to this western flank, and informed him that it was essential to occupy the high ground to prevent the escape of the enemy from Mount Tambu along this route and to protect the American's western flank. As a result a Papuan platoon was sent by Coane on 22nd July to set up an ambush in this western area.

On the same day at 7 a.m. Kindt's and Gehring's companies attacked the eastern end of Roosevelt Ridge. The attack which reached to within 50 yards of the crest of the ridge was unsuccessful and the two companies withdrew to the original perimeter near Boisi. Savige then signalled Herring asking for permission to use the II/162nd Battalion also. Herring replied that the remainder of the regiment would be sent forward as soon as possible. The III/162nd Battalion made further unsuccessful attempts to dislodge the Japanese from Roosevelt Ridge that day.

After these failures Savige on the 23rd sent a strong signal to Coane reminding him that the task allotted him on 15th July of securing a bridgehead at Tambu Bay entailed occupying Roosevelt Ridge and also the high ground to the west. The signal continued:

> A frontal attack by you on ridge to north of bay has failed. No effort to outflank the enemy's west flank appears to have been attempted. The enemy opposing your advance is not strong and is numerically weaker than forces available to you. In addition you have sufficient artillery to support your operations. It is considered that determined action by your forward commander to carry out your original plan which included an outflanking move along ridge to west would have succeeded.

Coane was then directed to send one company to secure the high ground to the west where he had previously sent only a detachment of Papuans.

He was also ordered to maintain contact with the Japanese on Roosevelt Ridge, to dig in and consolidate any gains, and to prevent his troops withdrawing to a close perimeter on the beach each night. Savige felt sure that a coordinated attack from the south and west must succeed.

As a result Coane sent a company to the high ground west of Tambu Bay with orders to verify the existence of Scout Ridge Track and, if found, to patrol it southwards towards Mount Tambu until meeting the enemy, and northwards to the junction of Scout and Roosevelt Ridges. All other companies were still in perimeters surrounding the flat Boisi area although Papuan sections, attached as scouts, were eager to lead the Americans into the hills. Coane signalled Savige on the 24th that he would attack next day down the ridge and from the flat ground north-east to Roosevelt Ridge. "This force will be on the way towards securing the ridge north of Tambu Bay before dark 25th July," signalled Coane.

Artillery bombardments continued on both sides. Some of the Allied shelling was directed by Lieutenant Donald W. Schroeder of the American artillery. On 24th July Sergeant Makin[2] and three Papuan soldiers led Schroeder to high ground west of Tambu Bay whence he could bring down fire on the enemy on Roosevelt Ridge. After the shelling the patrol reached the base of the ridge where Schroeder was wounded by a patrol of about 10 Japanese. Moving to Schroeder's side Makin placed himself between the wounded man and the enemy. Emptying his sub-machine-gun into the Japanese he forced their withdrawal, dressed Schroeder's wound, telephoned for a stretcher and succeeded in withdrawing with the stretcher party.

Australian artillery officers were also in forward positions ready to direct the fire of their guns. By the time that the first two 25-pounders from the 2/6th Field Regiment landed at Boisi on the night of 21st-22nd July Lieutenants Dawson[3] and Lord[4] had already left to be observation post officers for the 15th and 17th Brigades respectively. Major Thwaites was disturbed on 23rd July when he found that his two guns were within 1,000 yards of the Japanese positions and were outside the perimeter to which the Americans had withdrawn for the night. He also was a victim of the confusion of command which still existed on 27th July, and signalled his headquarters in Buna that he was receiving conflicting and impracticable orders from several Australian and American sources.

The reports from Savige's liaison officer with Coane Force, Captain Sturrock, were not encouraging. As with the I/162nd Battalion in the early days at Nassau Bay, opposition caused the III/162nd to cluster in a close perimeter at night instead of holding the ground gained. This had been noticeable during the advance on 20th and 21st July. The attack on 22nd July was again followed by a withdrawal to the original perimeters

---

[2] Sgt F. Makin, MM, NX28029. 2/1 Pnr Bn and Papuan Inf Bn. Labourer; of Canberra; b. Macclesfield, England, 11 Jul 1909.

[3] Capt R. H. Dawson, MC, NX12463; 2/6 Fd Regt. Garage proprietor; of Gordon, NSW; b. Sydney, 6 Sep 1915.

[4] Capt C. R. Lord, NX34977; 2/6 Fd Regt. Trustee officer; of Chatswood, NSW; b. Nadi, Fiji, 10 Nov 1915.

even though the attacking companies had gained much valuable ground. "Am most unpopular over trying to get information re future operations and sitreps," wrote the liaison officer. Major Roosevelt resented suggestions and did not want Australian advice. "The only way I can get information is to remain within battalion headquarters area and listen in to phone conversations," continued Sturrock's report. His conclusion was that "the organisation at battalion headquarters stinks. . . . If the show continues as it is now going I can't see them getting very far."

The Japanese in the Tambu Bay area when the Papuan and American soldiers entered it were mainly members of Major Kimura's *III/66th Battalion* to which General Nakano of the *51st Division* had given the task of driving the Americans from Nassau Bay. Instead, Major Oba's *III/102nd Battalion* had been driven north from Nassau Bay and had passed through Kimura's position north of Lake Salus, on its way to Kela Hill. Kimura had been unable to accomplish his task and by mid-July he was on the defensive. Nakano was now very anxious about his southern coastal flank and the threat of the advance of the Allies' big guns capable of shelling Salamaua. On 21st July he sent south a reserve company which had marched hurriedly from Finschhafen and 250 men from the *115th Regiment*, thus seriously depleting Salamaua of reserves.

On the central front the 17th Brigade continued to push north after the capture of Mubo. By 14th July Bennett Force from the 2/5th Battalion relieved the 2/3rd Independent Company in the Goodview Junction area while the remainder of the battalion was moving up the Buigap as far as the Bui Alang Creek.

Savige informed Moten and Hammer on 13th July that the Japanese in the Komiatum-Mount Tambu area must be destroyed before his plan to exploit the Mubo success could be carried out. Moten was therefore ordered to clear the Japanese from south of Goodview Junction, contain them there and attack Komiatum from the western flank. He was permitted to use Colonel Taylor's American battalion to contain Goodview Junction so that Bennett Force could rejoin the 2/5th Battalion for the flank attack. Meanwhile Herring had written to Savige on 13th July suggesting that Moten might bypass Goodview Junction which now seemed of secondary importance to the vital Orodubi-Gwaibolom area which was really the key to Komiatum. He wrote:

At this distance I realise that it is hard to know exactly what is in your mind or how far troops are committed in any particular direction. I would however feel much happier about your future prospects if I knew you held the Orodubi-Gwaibolom area in strength as a base from which you can again control the Komiatum Track. . . . With this track controlled in this way you bottle the enemy at Komiatum as you have done at Mubo.

Savige replied that he already held the general locality of Goodview Junction which was the highest point on the track north towards Komiatum and south towards Mubo. He recognised the importance of Gwaibolom and Orodubi, but his views, "based on a mass of information at my disposal and a personal knowledge of this type of country", led him to believe that the best direction for an attack on Komiatum would be from the west. "With any luck," he wrote, "I can cut his line of communication from Lokanu-Komiatum. If so, Mubo will be repeated."

Moten's instruction, issued before receipt of Savige's signal, was to exploit northwards and destroy the enemy round Komiatum. The 2/5th Battalion, with a company of I/162nd, was ordered to clear the enemy from the area north of the Bui Alang Creek along the main Mubo-Komiatum track, secure Tambu Saddle and the line of communication to Base 4, and destroy the enemy in the Komiatum area.

When the 2/5th took up its position on the 15th, Captain Bennett's company was 500 yards south-west of Goodview Junction astride Walpole's Track with patrols to Stephens' Track; Captain Morse's was 500 yards south of the junction astride the Komiatum Track and on the high ground between Komiatum and Walpole's Tracks, and Captain Cameron's in reserve. Captain Walters'[5] company moved north-east up a new very steep track known as Walters' Track, intending to occupy Mount Tambu, and reached a point 500 yards from the top of a spur running south from the mountain.

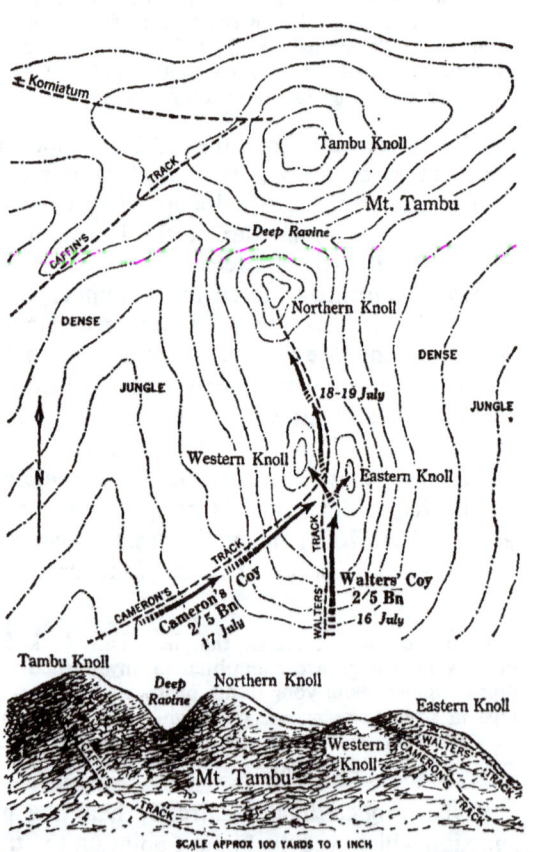

Next afternoon at 5 p.m. Walters' company (about 60 men) approached Mount Tambu from the south and attacked up a steep razor-backed spur heavily defended by enemy positions overlooking the rise. Lieutenant McCoy's[6] platoon attacked on the right but was pinned down. On the left flank Sergeant Tiller,[7] out in front of his men, wiped out an enemy machine-gun crew. After hand-to-hand fighting in which 20 Japanese were killed, Tiller captured enemy positions on the eastern of the two southern knolls or humps of the approach ridge to Mount Tambu. The third platoon led by Lieutenant E. R.

---

[5] Maj V. M. Walters, MC, TX708; 2/5 Bn and 1/West Yorkshire Regt. Bank officer; of Moonah, Tas; b. Hobart, 23 Aug 1918.

[6] Lt K. J. P. McCoy, QX19681; 2/5 Bn. Clerk; of Mitchell, Qld; b. Torbanlea, Qld, 23 Nov 1918.

[7] Sgt W. L. Tiller, DCM, VX4026; 2/5 Bn. Farmer; of Leongatha, Vic; b. England, 24 May 1907. Killed in action 24 Jul 1943.

Reeve then attacked and captured the western knoll. The Japanese remained on a northern and higher knoll, leaving about 100 yards of jungle-covered no-man's land between the two forces. Walters' attack finished at 6 p.m. when he consolidated the captured positions as well as he could before darkness. As the men had not carried digging tools it was fortunate that they had captured a Japanese position with pill-boxes and weapon-pits for 100 men.

Realising their tactical error in allowing the Australians to gain this toehold on Mount Tambu the Japanese counter-attacked eight times during the night. They crawled to within 10 or 15 yards of Walters' position before rushing the defences, firing and screaming. "Fighting was thick and furious during these counter-attacks and the small arms fire was the heaviest I've known," said Walters' report. His ammunition was used sparingly but even so the riflemen were down to five rounds each and the Bren guns to two magazines a gun by morning. The Japanese fired 120 mortar bombs into the company's position during the night. Mortaring, shelling by a mountain gun, and a hail of fire from light and medium machine-guns failed to shake the defenders' resolve. At 8.30 a.m. on the 17th Cameron's company with a detachment of 3-inch mortars moved up to support Walters along a new and better track discovered by Cameron himself—Cameron's Track. Walters' ammunition and supplies were replenished and the two companies prepared to face enemy attacks down the north-south razor-back. Cameron dug in on a knoll 300 yards back along the track to give depth to the defences.

Meanwhile Captain Newman's company of the I/162nd Battalion was at the junction of the Buigap and Bui Eo, and the remainder of the battalion farther back along the Buigap. A reconnaissance patrol from the mountain battery found suitable gun positions north-west of the junction of the Buigap and Bui Eo. With the assistance of 90 natives and 80 men from the 2/6th Battalion two guns were hauled over the precipitous track along the Buigap; by dusk on 17th July both guns were in position, and four guns of the American 218th Battalion were being hauled from the south arm of the Bitoi over Lababia Ridge to Green Hill.

The Japanese from Mount Tambu attacked Walters' company again at noon on the 17th, but with a fresh supply of ammunition, particularly 3-inch mortar bombs, Walters held the enemy at bay. During the afternoon enemy movement to the north enabled the crack shots among the defenders to do some sniping: Sergeant McCormack[8] killed eight Japanese and Private Kirwan[1] four. At 6 p.m. about 200 Japanese attacked Reeve's position, but, although outnumbered ten to one, the platoon repulsed the attack. After this attack had petered out little vegetation remained between the Japanese and Australians.

Supported by the mountain guns and 3-inch mortars Walters attacked north-west on 18th July to clean out a Japanese pocket and gained an

---

[8] Sgt F. J. McCormack, MM, VX3299; 2/5 Bn. Labourer; of Melbourne; b. Mathinna, Tas, 26 Sep 1904.

[1] Pte D. Kirwan, SX18952; 2/5 Bn. Clerk; of Quorn, SA; b. Quorn, 12 Apr 1922. Killed in action 18 Jul 1943.

extra 80 yards of toehold among the lower Japanese positions. This advance was made possible largely by the exploits of Lance-Corporal Jackson,[2] one of Sergeant Tiller's section commanders. Using three grenades he destroyed an enemy machine-gun post and then wiped out the three occupants of a pill-box with his Tommy-gun. With this extra ground Walters strengthened his position but could not advance farther because of the difficulty of encircling the Japanese on the razor-back to the north. As both companies were at only half strength, Cameron placed Lieutenant Martin's[3] platoon under Walters' control on the western flank. Water, ammunition and food were carried forward by the other two platoons in the afternoon. The battalion's medical officer, Captain Busby,[4] set up two large American tent flys for a forward post in the middle of Cameron's position.

It was now apparent that Conroy was faced with a stalemate similar to that which confronted Guinn during his attacks on the Pimple two months earlier. It was also apparent that the Japanese were determined to eliminate the Australian hold on the southern fringe of their Mount Tambu fortress. If the Japanese attacked the entrenched defenders the pattern of Lababia and not the Pimple might be repeated.

> The enemy at Tambu were temporarily repulsed (said the *51st Division's* Intelligence Summary on 18th July), but with the second attack we finally withdrew. Although the front-line company has counter-attacked, the enemy is not yet dislodged.

In the evening a severe earth tremor startled the troops. It rained heavily on the night 18th-19th July but this did not deter the Japanese from moving in darkness from Mount Tambu to the flanks of the two companies of the 2/5th. Despite the torrential downpour the guards of Cameron's rear platoon heard noises and reported to their platoon commander, Lieutenant Miles. At about 4 a.m. on the 19th a signaller woke Cameron to report that the telephone line was dead. Just then the Japanese charged out of the darkness. A defending Bren gunner, with a lucky burst into the darkness, knocked out the raiders' machine-gun which had been firing along the track into the centre of the Australian position. All enemy attempts to recapture their machine-gun resulted in their dead being piled up along the track. Confidence and steady defence by Miles' men kept out the Japanese who withdrew just before first light leaving 21 dead, including one officer and two N.C.O's.

The Japanese from Mount Tambu viciously attacked Walters' positions in the afternoon. In the company's forward section post only Private Friend[5] and a Bren gunner (Private Prigg[6]) were in occupation because

---

[2] L-Cpl J. J. Jackson, DCM, VX14220; 2/5 Bn. Truck driver; b. Brunswick, Vic, 5 Mar 1918.
[3] Lt H. H. Martin, VX4611; 2/5 Bn. Hairdresser; of Mildura, Vic; b. Mildura, 12 Feb 1916.
[4] Capt H. Busby, MC, NX100094. RMO 15 and 2/5 Bns. Medical practitioner; of Bathurst, NSW; b. Bathurst, 8 Feb 1918.
[5] Sgt P. J. C. Friend, MM, NX87971; 2/5 Bn. Bank officer; of Lane Cove, NSW; b. Narrabri, NSW, 15 Sep 1920.
[6] Pte J. R. Prigg, VX36052; 2/5 Bn. Labourer; of Colac, Vic; b. Colac, 30 Sep 1907.

the remainder of the section was away bringing up supplies and ammunition. With fire from Tommy-gun and Bren, Friend and Prigg managed to hold the section post for 20 minutes against fierce attacks until the section returned. When the enemy attack was at its most critical stage and ammunition was short, Tiller advanced towards the enemy throwing grenades and inflicting such casualties that the early attacks were beaten off.

Sporadic attacks on the forward company continued during the day but none had the intensity of the pre-dawn attack, although the battalion diarist described them as culminating in a "terrific battle". As usual the Japanese increased the din of battle with screaming and yelling, for example: "Come out and fight, you Aussie conscripts", and "Come out and die for Tojo." On several occasions the Japanese reached within 10 yards of the defenders' pits. All available men from Moten's headquarters and his two Australian battalions were used to carry ammunition and supplies forward day and night. In the end the determination and experience of a seasoned unit prevailed and the Japanese retired to Mount Tambu. Walters reported: "By 2.30 p.m. that day we knew we had him. Our men stood up in their trenches and sometimes out of them yelling back the Japs' own war cry and often quaint ones of their own. One of them knew a smattering of Japanese and had a great time, shouting out such things as 'Ten minutes smoko, lads'. It developed into absolute slaughter of the Jap and we literally belted him into the ground." The Australians considered an estimate that the enemy had suffered 350 casualties to be conservative while the two exhausted but undaunted companies had lost 14 killed and 25 wounded.

At 5.30 p.m. on the 19th Walters' company was relieved by Cameron's and withdrawn to the junction of Walters' and Cameron's Tracks, while Newman's Americans occupied the positions vacated by Cameron. The battalion's second-in-command, Major N. L. Goble, now took command of this force on the southern slopes of Mount Tambu.

The 129 rounds fired by the mountain guns and the supporting mortar fire had been invaluable in breaking up the attacks. True to the traditions of artillery forward observation officers, Lieutenant Cochrane, the mountain battery's F.O.O., had operated within 50 yards of the foremost Japanese positions.[7]

From 19th until 23rd July patrols probed the Japanese positions in the Mount Tambu and Goodview Junction areas. Bennett's men on 20th July made contact with a strong Japanese position down Walpole's Track. Morse's company found Japanese positions in the Goodview area and dug in within 100 yards of them. As usual the Australians did all the patrolling, the Japanese being content to sit tight. Patrols to the flanks of Mount Tambu found strong defensive positions on the Japanese right and left flanks, and disclosed that the track connecting Goodview Junction and Mount Tambu was well used by the Japanese. Another track

---

[7] Cochrane's observation post was close to the foremost Australian weapon-pit. Throughout the fight 25 yards of the 50 per cent zone rested on Australian troops without one shell dropping short. O'Hare wrote of his mountain guns: ". . . the 3.7 How was a miracle gun for accuracy and reliability."

—Caffin's Track[8]—was discovered leading to Mount Tambu from Bui Eo Creek. All indications were that the Japanese were extending and improving their defences. Savige informed Moten that artillery would be on the coast in a few days' time, and no advance was to be made without it.

On 13th July Savige ordered the 15th Brigade to secure Bobdubi Ridge from Namling in the south to Old Vickers Position in the north. This would prevent the Japanese escape from the Komiatum area by securing the Komiatum-Salamaua-Bobdubi track junctions, and support Moten's flank attack on Komiatum. Hammer next day issued orders which, he hoped, would enable him to regain the initiative. The 2/3rd Independent Company on 15th July would attack Ambush Knoll where the Japanese had been digging in for the past two days, and would then exploit to Namling Ridge. On the same day the 58th/59th Battalion would seize the northern track junctions where the Komiatum and Bench Cut Tracks met the Salamaua-Bobdubi track. These attacks would be followed on 16th July by a concerted attack by the Independent Company and a company from the 58th/59th on Graveyard and Orodubi.

After its relief at Goodview Junction, the Independent Company was again short of rations and was forced to borrow from the 2/5th. Most of the company's native carriers stationed at Vial's O.P. were sick and hungry. When the company moved to Wells Junction on 14th July in preparation for the attack on Ambush Knoll rations were scraped together from Base 4 and Vial's O.P. and arrangements made for future rations to come up Uliap Creek from Nunn's Post. Rations were barely sufficient for the attack on Ambush Knoll.

Warfe planned that one platoon (Captain Meares) would attack from the south while another (Captain Winterflood) went round the east flank and attacked from the direction of Orodubi. On 15th July Meares' platoon attacked Ambush Knoll at 1.45 p.m. after half an hour's supporting fire from two Vickers guns and a 3-inch mortar. The entrenched position was strongly held by the Japanese who flung Australian grenades at the attackers. In the centre six men under Corporal McEvoy[9] were the spearhead. Although under heavy fire McEvoy leaped over a bamboo barricade across the ridge. Only one of his men (Private Collins[1]) could follow him across the barricade as the others were wounded by a grenade. McEvoy had expected that the bombardment would have killed all the Japanese on the knoll. He wrote afterwards:

> When I got over that barricade with half my shirt ripped off my back by a machine-gun burst and four bullet grazes across my ribs, I realised it was no place for Mrs McEvoy's little boy and the first thought was to let the Nips keep the place, but then I noticed I had one man with me and he had the light of battle in his eye and was shouting above the din, "Come on Mac, let's go through the b——s."

---

[8] Named after Sergeant M. L. Caffin, 2/5th Battalion (of Canterbury, Vic), who discovered it.
[9] Cpl K. A. McEvoy, DCM, WX11335. 2/3 Indep Coy, 2/3 Cdo Sqn. Truck driver; of Grass Valley, WA; b. Northam, WA, 9 Nov 1918.
[1] Cpl R. F. Collins, WX17690. 2/3 Indep Coy, 2/3 Cdo Sqn. Labourer; of Northcliffe, WA; b. Northam, WA, 30 Sep 1918.

The dash of McEvoy and Collins enabled Meares' troops to occupy these positions 50 feet from the main barricaded pill-boxes. In this advance Private Wellings,[2] firing his Bren from the hip, destroyed one Japanese machine-gun. The adjutant, Lieutenant Harrison,[3] was killed and 9 others wounded. Meares was then reinforced by Lieutenant Egan's section, bringing his total assaulting force including casualties to 50, but by nightfall the Japanese, estimated at about 30, still held on.

While Meares was attacking Ambush Knoll, Winterflood led his platoon, reduced by casualties and sickness to 30, in an attempt to cut the enemy track from Orodubi to Ambush Knoll. He did this, and, after driving back an enemy party from Orodubi, made a spirited attack with hand grenades on Ambush Knoll, supported by covering fire.

The determined attacks by the two platoons made the position too unhealthy for the Japanese. At first light on 16th July patrols from the Australian platoons met on Ambush Knoll which the enemy (members of the *II/66th Battalion*) had vacated during the night. The Japanese defensive position which had two log pill-boxes and a perimeter with a circumference trench 100 yards long had been occupied by double the number previously estimated. In their haste to depart, the Japanese left 10 corpses on the knoll.

The 58th/59th Battalion meanwhile was preparing to carry out Colonel Starr's orders to "maintain offensive action" against the Japanese on Bobdubi Ridge north from Namling and to gain control of the Komiatum Track. One company (Lieutenant Griff's) was ordered to clear the Bench Cut and advance north down to the Salamaua-Bobdubi track; two others were to patrol Bobdubi Ridge; and the fourth (Captain Jackson's[4]) was to hold the Gwaibolom-Erskine Creek area against any attack from the south.

Unfortunately, the battalion's plans were upset when the Japanese drove one of Jackson's platoons from Erskine Creek on 14th July. Griff's company while moving to the Bench Cut met other Japanese who stopped any further advance and called down the fire of a mountain gun on the Australians. Griff was then ordered to recapture Erskine Creek in cooperation with Jackson. The two companies failed to meet, Erskine Creek was not recaptured, and the 58th/59th Battalion was not in a position to carry out its plan.

On the 16th Griff tried to find positions from which to attack the enemy flank in the Erskine Creek area. Concluding that the only means of progress was along the Bench Cut, he found that this track had been heavily reinforced and Japanese were encountered in four places along 600 yards of the track. Hammer then revised the plan: Jackson was ordered to capture Graveyard on 17th July with the assistance of Warfe

---

[2] Pte C. Wellings, MM, VX105917. 2/3 Indep Coy, 2/3 Cdo Sqn. Timber faller; of Warragul, Vic; b. Warragul, 1 Oct 1914.

[3] Lt F. B. Harrison, VX36927; 2/3 Indep Coy. Wool buyer; of Armadale, Vic; b. Sydney, 21 Jun 1917. Killed in action 15 Jul 1943.

[4] Capt A. C. Jackson, MC, VX102607; 58/59 Bn. Municipal clerk; of Corowa, NSW; b. Corowa, 22 Mar 1918.

from the south, Griff to attack the Japanese positions on the Bench Cut, and the other two companies to be ready to capture Old Vickers and the Coconuts in readiness to push on to the Komiatum Track. After assisting in the capture of Graveyard, Warfe would capture Orodubi. The 58th/59th had thus been given a huge area to capture—from Coconuts to Graveyard. It was too much for even the best trained troops.

The Independent Company fulfilled its small part in the plan. Lieutenant Barry with 10 men attacked Graveyard at 10.50 a.m. on the 17th and by 5 p.m. this small force, reinforced by six men, captured its objective, killed at least five Japanese and repulsed two counter-attacks. Barry was unable, however, to guarantee that he could hold his position against larger numbers of Japanese which he might have to face. Already on this day 119 Japanese had been observed moving north from Komiatum, probably to reinforce the Orodubi area, and no troops were available to reinforce Barry.

Jackson's company of the 58th/59th meanwhile encountered enemy positions 500 yards south of Gwaibolom on the morning of 17th July soon after it set out for Graveyard. Attacks on these on 17th and 18th July were repulsed. Worse still, it became apparent that the Japanese were gaining the initiative in this area, for Jackson found more Japanese in positions 400 yards north-east of Gwaibolom. He withdrew to Gwaibolom in face of the crowding enemy. Griff's patrols farther north established the fact that the Japanese were holding Erskine Creek area in strength. With no reinforcement available from south or north Barry was forced to withdraw from Graveyard to Namling Ridge on the morning of the 18th by superior numbers of Japanese.

The Japanese troops seen moving south on 17th July towards the area precariously held by Barry were probably members of Jinno's *1/80th Battalion* which was apparently in the Komiatum area with the *1/66th Battalion* and the remnants of *II/66th Battalion*. Since its arrival at the beginning of the month the *I/80th Battalion* had been in action at Bobdubi. On 17th July Jinno's order stated: "The battalion will assemble in strength at the present area and will attack the enemy in the Wells area."

North of the Francisco, a patrol from the 58th/59th investigated a report that Japanese had been heard crossing Buiris Creek on the night of the 17th-18th July. The patrol found positions occupied by 50 to 60 Japanese one hour's journey from the junction of the Francisco River and Buiris Creek. This report disturbed Hammer who was well aware of the weakness on his northern flank. The tactical position of his brigade on the night of 18th July was not satisfactory. Because of the failure of his plan, he decided to concentrate on capturing Graveyard and freeing Jackson's company for use as a reserve in the area north of the Francisco. To coordinate the attack on Graveyard and to ensure that the Namling-Dierke's track was sufficiently held, Hammer sent Travers to Namling.

At 8.15 p.m. on 19th July in bright moonlight about 60 Japanese overran the Independent Company's listening post south of Ambush Knoll on the ridge track to Wells Junction, and attacked the two sections led by Lieutenants Egan and Garland[5] on Ambush Knoll. At this stage Warfe's headquarters was at Namling where Winterflood's weary platoon returned in the afternoon of 19th July, Meares' platoon was occupying the area south from Ambush Knoll to Wells Junction, and Lewin's platoon was on Namling Ridge. Realising the threat to the divisional line if the enemy succeeded in recapturing Ambush Knoll, Warfe sent Winterflood with two of his sections to reinforce Ambush Knoll and take command there. The first Japanese attack on Ambush Knoll was repulsed; the Japanese attacked again at 9.30 p.m., five minutes before Warfe dispatched Winterflood's platoon. In the defence very effective use was again made of the Independent Company's Vickers guns. They were sited in the forward trenches—one directed along the ridge towards Wells Junction and one along the ridge towards Orodubi. Their targets were at hardly more than 30 yards' range.

Hammer now well realised that his forces were not sufficient to attack the enemy in the large area for which his brigade (only a battalion and an Independent Company) was responsible. The Japanese now had more troops available on the spot as their line of communication was not so long as it had been before the capture of Mubo. They were holding the high ground near Gwaibolom and appeared to be trying to seize the high ground in the Wells O.P. area. Captured documents led Hammer to believe that the Japanese line of defence was Mount Tambu-Goodview-Buirali Creek-Orodubi-Old Vickers. With his plans again frustrated Hammer informed his brigade on 19th July that its task was generally to continue offensive operations in order to maintain control of Bobdubi Ridge and gain control of the Komiatum Track.

Winterflood's platoon joined Egan on Ambush Knoll at 6.30 a.m. on 20th July. Soon after its arrival the Japanese gained the main ridge track, thus effectively sealing off supplies by the main route. Attacks by the enemy continued almost without let-up on this day, when 12 separate thrusts were repulsed by the tenacious defenders. Warfe wrote later that "the Japs attacked bravely and in large numbers and the fight for Ambush Knoll developed into a classic defence". The machine-gun crews put their guns on loose mountings and "hosed" the approaches whenever movement was seen. In Warfe's opinion "these guns undoubtedly saved the situation by their characteristic of sustained fire". From Namling Ridge Lieutenant Lewin could see the Japanese moving from Orodubi to Sugarcane Ridge which was their base and control area for the attack on Ambush Knoll. Warfe therefore placed a Vickers gun with Lewin at the junction of Namling Ridge and the main track. From here Lewin fired on enemy movement at a range of 700 yards across the deep re-entrant to Sugarcane Ridge.

Hammer had been hoping to reduce his front by encouraging the advance of the 17th Brigade along the Komiatum Track. "I felt that the greater weight of enemy was directed at Bobdubi and not towards Tambu," he wrote later, "as the Japs must have felt our pressure from the Bobdubi

---

[5] Maj R. S. Garland, MC, NX123781. 2/3 Indep Coy, 2/3 Cdo Sqn, 2 NG Inf Bn. Clerk; of Marrickville, NSW; b. Belmore, NSW, 18 Nov 1921.

area although we were not making good headway." From a long distance away it seemed to Hammer that the 17th Brigade was slow in reacting to the Japanese withdrawal particularly as he considered that the enemy had become defensive in the Tambu area "while they became offensive on the Bobdubi front which threatened to eat into their middle". He also thought that if the enemy established themselves in the Wells Junction area the advance of the 17th Brigade would be jeopardised. In Hammer's opinion he was trying to hold ground "vital to the whole operation".

He therefore signalled Savige suggesting that the 17th Brigade should take over responsibility for the area north to Namling. Savige agreed and explained the critical situation by phone to Moten, proposing as a matter of urgency that the 2/6th Battalion be sent immediately to the area south of Namling. Moten complied wholeheartedly even though it might mean upsetting his own plan. There was nothing except lack of supplies to stop a rapid move forward by the 2/6th Battalion, and Lieutenant Price's company set out from the Mubo area to establish a base at Wells O.P. and patrol east and north down Buirali Creek to prevent Japanese movement south. Savige signalled to Herring on 20th July that he had explored and put into action "every conceivable abnormal method" to supply the battalion with rations and ammunition and even then there had not been enough. "My ability to meet present situation and defeat Japs depends entirely on large and sustained droppings," he signalled.

At 3 a.m. and again an hour later on 21st July enemy night attacks on Winterflood's men on Ambush Knoll were repulsed. Again the Vickers guns played a vital part with Lewin's gun joining in by firing along a fixed line from daylight observation. Enemy attacks waned on the morning of the 21st although a heavy machine-gun firing from Sugarcane Ridge on to Namling caused a scatter at Warfe's headquarters just after breakfast.

The progress of the fight was followed anxiously at company headquarters, whence carrying parties worked constantly taking up supplies to Ambush Knoll. Every spare man, including some natives who would not normally have been so far forward, were pressed into service. As the attack intensified all regular approaches were cut, but for some unexplained reason the enemy left open one means of access up a western spur from Uliap Creek and the supplies got through. Of great value to the morale of the defenders were the dixies of hot tea and stew which were hauled up this precipitous route and carried from one weapon-pit to another during lulls in the fighting. Both sides used up ammunition at a fast rate. The enemy were supported sporadically by a mountain gun from Komiatum Ridge, by a heavy mortar from Orodubi, and by light mortars from Sugarcane Ridge. At 1 p.m. another fierce Japanese attack was beaten off by the stubborn defenders. They suffered a severe loss when one of their outstanding leaders, Lieutenant Egan, was killed by a mortar bomb explosion. Although very tired, Winterflood's men were in high spirits and answered the enemy's English phrases with other unprintable English retorts.

When Price's company, leading the move of the 2/6th Battalion, arrived at Wells Junction in the early afternoon of 21st July Major Travers met them. Price's written orders were to establish a base but not to fight; he did not know that the 17th Brigade was to take over the area south of Namling next day. Travers asked him to attack the Japanese on Ambush Knoll and relieve the pressure on Winterflood as soon as possible. "I explained the whole position to Price," wrote Travers later, "and Price had sense enough to see it was easy enough to help Warfe and guts enough to go against written orders." Price wrote later: "On arrival Major Travers told me that my instructions were two days old. As I had not been in touch with the battalion I had no reason to disbelieve him when he assured me that Brigadier Hammer had later orders from 17th Brigade for my company to attack Ambush Knoll." Although worried about attacking without being able to make an adequate reconnaissance Price attacked down the ridge from Wells Junction to Ambush Knoll at 2 p.m. and came in behind the enemy. He met heavy opposition, lost two killed and several wounded, and had to be content with digging in on the slopes of Ambush Knoll close to the enemy.

In his diary for the 21st Travers noted: "At 1630 hours I got an order from 17th Brigade to say that the attack would not be launched without reference to 17th Brigade or 2/6th Battalion headquarters. I spoke to Tack [Hammer] about it but he . . . said he agreed with my action. Anyway I am not especially worried about it except for a breach of etiquette. . . . Had this company not attacked the Ambush Knoll would have been lost. I have no doubt at all on this."

Hammer in a letter to Savige expressed his pleasure at "a bit of real stoush going on now". He explained that Ambush Knoll was higher than Namling, Namling Ridge and Orodubi. "That's why the Jap wants it." Referring to Gwaibolom and Old Vickers Position he wrote: "The situation is much the same with the Jap firmly planted on the Bench Cut Track and until they can be shifted we have no hope of getting on the Komiatum Track. . . . Strengths are getting low, 58th/59th Battalion about 460, 2/3rd Independent Company about 180."

With Winterflood holding stubbornly and Price maintaining pressure from the south the Japanese finally had had enough, and at 6 a.m. on 23rd July Warfe himself guided Lieutenant Maloney's[6] patrol from the 2/6th Battalion via the secret route to Ambush Knoll where they joined Winterflood and reported to the thankful defenders that there were no Japanese in between, although some were still on Sugarcane Ridge. The vacated position from which the Japanese had attacked consisted of three pill-boxes with tunnelled trenches and weapon-pits, sufficient for 70 men. By 1.30 p.m. the 2/6th Battalion relieved Warfe's troops of their responsibilities south of Namling-Orodubi and the weary Independent Company moved to Namling. During three days and four nights Winterflood's men had been subjected to heavy mortar and machine-gun fire from Sugarcane

---

[6] Capt V. N. Maloney, VX3497; 2/6 Bn. Schoolteacher; of Albert Park, Vic; b. Melbourne, 26 Apr 1914.

Ridge. Twenty separate assaults had been made using three different lines of approach. The chief thrust on all occasions came from the south-east with lighter attacks from Sugarcane Ridge and the ridge leading south towards Wells Junction. During the six heaviest attacks, all three approaches were used. The Japanese several times reached within a few yards of the Australian positions but on each occasion they were driven back. This successful defence of Ambush Knoll had accounted for 67 Japanese against 3 Australians killed and 7 wounded.

Savige breathed a sigh of relief when the Japanese finally withdrew. He had been apprehensive of an enemy breakthrough along Dierke's Track which might have prejudiced his entire operations by enabling the Japanese to establish themselves between his two brigades.

The 2/7th Battalion was now about to re-enter the battle area after a two months' spell in the Wau-Bulolo valley. On 22nd July Savige had received a message from Herring that recent information suggested the possible reinforcement of the enemy in the Salamaua area. Herring therefore authorised Savige to move the 2/7th from the Bulolo Valley immediately and Savige decided that the battalion would be attached not to its parent brigade but to the 15th to stiffen his force in the northern area.

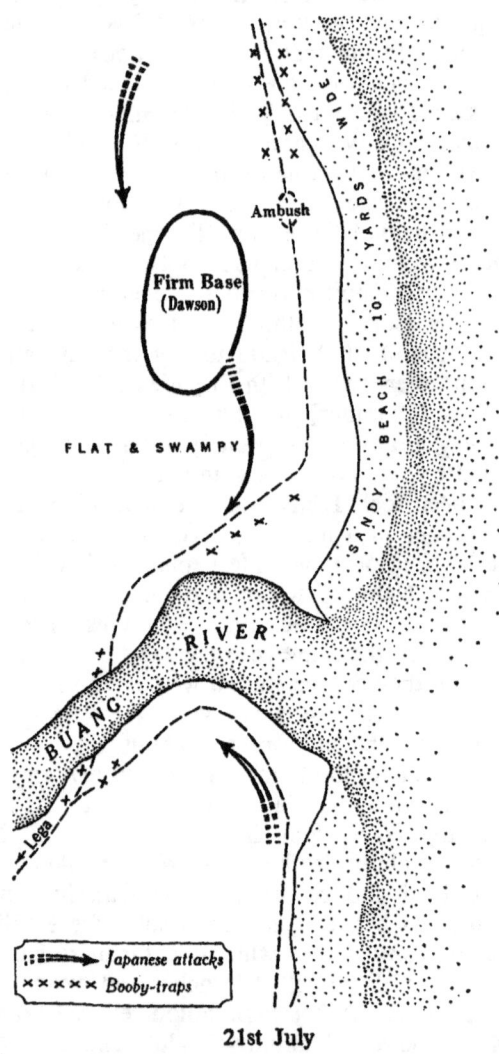

21st July

Along the Markham there were no clashes at this time. However, in the south-eastern portion of Lieut-Colonel Smith's huge domain of jungle, mountain, river and swamp Lieutenant Dawson's patrol of the 24th Bat-

(G. R. Warfe)

Native carriers crossing the kunda bridge over the Francisco River near New Bobdubi on the way forward to the 58th/59th Battalion, in June 1943. The two natives in the centre of the bridge are carrying a bush stretcher.

(Australian War Memorial)

A carrier line setting out from the Mubo area with supplies for the forward troops.

A 2/3rd Independent Company medium machine-gun pit on Ambush Knoll, July 1943. This gun-pit, commanding enemy movement along Komiatum Ridge, was typical of others in the area. The soldier in the bottom left-hand corner is using a rangefinder. Above him is Lieutenant H. L. Egan (killed in action on 21st July 1943), and on the right (pointing) is Private H. F. C. May.

Sergeant G. R. C. Ayre helps Private W. O. W. Johnson of the 58th/59th Battalion across a creek to an advanced dressing station. Johnson was wounded by a Japanese grenade during an attack on the Coconuts on 13th July 1943.

(Australian War Memorial)

A forward scout, Private F. W. McVicar of "D" Company, 2/5th Battalion, in the attack on Mount Tambu on 23rd July 1943. McVicar was killed next day. A dead Japanese soldier can be seen on the right of the picture.

(Australian War Memorial)

Corporal L. C. Allen of the 2/5th Battalion, N.C.O. in charge of stretcher bearers in the Mount Tambu area, giving 18 Platoon instructions on 24th July as to the signals they should give if wounded. On Allen's right is ~~Lieutenant~~ H. A. Bell, commanding the battalion's ~~machine~~-gun platoon.

(Australian War Memorial)
Three members of the 2/5th Battalion, equipped with Tommy-gun, Bren and .303 rifle, covering the track from captured Japanese positions in the Mount Tambu area, 24th July 1943.

(H. H. Hammer)
A conference of officers of the 15th Brigade at Gwaibolom on 25th July 1943. *Left to right*: Major G. R. Warfe (O.C. 2/3rd Independent Company), Brigadier H. H. Hammer (commanding the 15th Brigade), Lieut-Colonel P. D. Starr (C.O. 58th/59th Battalion) and Major B. H. Travers, Hammer's brigade major.

talion near the mouth of the Buang was preparing for trouble. On 15th July a native saw the patrol's sentry and escaped towards Labu. Next day the Australians found footprints leading to the old ambush position, and on the night 18th-19th July heard a great deal of barge movement along the coast. Of more intimate concern, however, was the explosion of the patrol's northern booby-trap along an old native track 100 yards north of the base. Next morning a small patrol found a large pool of blood, four field dressings with the anchor sign of the Japanese marines on them, and the marks of a four-man patrol. After a day of uneasy calm a booby-trap in the same place near the mouth of the Buang exploded at 8.30 a.m. on 21st July. Investigations showed signs of casualties and tracks of a large party of Japanese on the beach.

At 10.30 a.m. a six-man patrol acting as a protective force for Sergeant Lane,[7] who was re-laying the exploded booby-traps, found at least 12 Japanese field dressing covers, and pools of blood. While examining these signs the patrol heard Japanese talking and next moment was attacked by about 20 of them. Private Rowley[8] swiftly killed two with his Owen and Private Kleinitz[9] one, before the patrol was forced to withdraw to the ambush position while the Japanese moved south along the beach and also began an outflanking movement through the bush to the left of the ambush.

Dawson's position in thick jungle was not sited to withstand strong attacks from rear and flank. Heavy machine-gun fire and shells from a mountain gun soon forced him to withdraw to his firm base. Enemy pressure along the track continued, and when a party of more than 20 Japanese were seen crossing the Buang from south of the ambush position Dawson retired along the Lega Track without being able to carry out his stores, ammunition and rations. The Australians set another ambush one hour farther west but as very little ammunition and rations were left Dawson withdrew to Lega by 5.30 p.m., thus losing contact.

Kleinitz, who had been missing since the first action, arrived at Lega an hour later and reported that the Japanese had swarmed into the ambush position from the beach and through the bush. He shot one more Japanese and heard and saw what he estimated was about 200 in the area. Being one against 200, Kleinitz returned to the firm base where he found no Australians. Private Murphy,[1] who was the last man to leave the ambush position before it was overwhelmed at 11.40 a.m., fired a full Owen magazine into a group of Japanese moving along the beach. Dawson estimated that 14 Japanese were killed during the action. The last missing man from the Buang action, Private Hillbrick, arrived at Lega on 22nd

---

[7] Lt G. R. Lane, VX23594. 24 and 58/59 Bns. Accountant; of East Coburg, Vic; b. Echuca, Vic, 19 Mar 1912. (He had been promoted to lieutenant in May but his unit was unaware of this.)

[8] L-Cpl E. R. Rowley, VX106361; 24 Bn. Farmer; of Glengarry, Vic; b. Traralgon, Vic, 15 Sep 1913.

[9] Cpl J. Kleinitz, VX143884; 24 Bn. Farm hand; of Newmerella, Vic; b. Bairnsdale, Vic, 9 Feb 1921.

[1] Cpl J. H. Murphy, VX143972; 24 Bn. Bread salesman; of Oakleigh, Vic; b. Oakleigh, 18 Apr 1917.

July and reported hearing two of the booby-traps on the southern end of the ambush position exploding before he left.

A reconnaissance patrol along the Buang on 22nd July did not reach far enough to establish whether the Japanese were still at the mouth of the river. Savige then ordered Smith to use Dawson's platoon as a "commando" force which would operate from a base east of Lega and harass and delay the Japanese force.

General Nakano's anxiety about an Australian thrust down the Buang River Valley or a landing at its mouth caused him to tie up a large part of his *102nd Regiment* there, plus detachments of the *115th*. Patrols between 17th and 20th July failed to meet the Australian enemy although one patrol which left at 8 p.m. on 18th July ran into Dawson's booby-traps. By 20th July about 100 men from the *102nd Regiment* and the marines were in occupation of the mouth of the Buang. Nakano's Intelligence report for 21st July stated that in the clash between the "naval party" and the Australians one Japanese officer was killed and 7 soldiers wounded.

General Adachi and his staff officer in charge of operations, Lieut-Colonel Tanaka, were also concerned about the intentions of the Australian force in the Buang Valley. After the war they said: "From the beginning of July onward an Australian force, which had been stationed at Wampit, pushed down in the direction of the Buang. It was considered at the time that the object of this manoeuvre was to secure Buang and facilitate a landing by Allied troops from the sea. In order to prevent this, about 150 men of the *102nd Infantry Regiment* attacked the Australian troops who had reached Buang from Wampit and occupied the position.

Savige on 23rd July appointed the American Colonel Jackson to command all American and Australian artillery units, and Major Scarlett[2] was allotted to Jackson as brigade major. The 205th American Field Artillery Battalion (105-mm guns) and the 218th Field Artillery Battalion (75-mm guns) less one battery were allotted to support Coane Force; one battery of the 218th Battalion and one section of the 1st Australian Mountain Battery to Moten's brigade; the 11th Battery of the 2/6th Australian Field Regiment to Hammer's brigade. Brigade and force commanders were ordered to deal directly with commanders of artillery units allotted to their brigades when support from those units only was required. When larger concentrations were required requests would be made to Jackson who would coordinate all requests.

On the right flank of the battle area success was still denied the Americans. Colonel MacKechnie had been relieved of the command of MacKechnie Force on 22nd July, and at Tambu Bay Lieut-Colonel Charles A. Fertig was now Brigadier-General Coane's infantry commander. The Americans were fortunate to have Captain Hitchcock's Papuan company to help them pinpoint Japanese positions and thus save them from trusting too much to the unreliable Komiatum map (1:25,000). Because of their natural bushcraft, the native soldiers were better fitted than those of most units to iron out by reconnaissance the numerous discrepancies between map and ground, and to lead the American companies to their

---

[2] Lt-Col G. Y. D. Scarlett, ED, NX134. 2/1 Fd Regt; BM HQ RAA 6 Div 1942-43, 11 Div 1943-44; and training appointments. Bank officer; of Greenwich, NSW; b. Sydney, 8 Jul 1910.

correct positions. On 23rd July two Papuan soldiers approaching from the east along a track made the first contact between Coane Force and the 17th Brigade when they met an American platoon below Mount Tambu.

Savige signalled Coane on 26th July that as the II/162nd Battalion, commanded by Major Arthur L. Lowe, was arriving at Tambu Bay Coane should get his troops moving to secure the line from Lokanu 1 to Scout Hill. This battalion, which was now to receive its battle initiation, assembled at Tambu Bay between 21st and 29th July, and was given the task of capturing Roosevelt Ridge. Roosevelt's battalion at the end of July was in the Boisi area with two companies on the slopes of Scout Ridge west of Tambu Bay.

On 27th July Captain Coughlin's company from the new battalion attacked Roosevelt Ridge from the south, inflicted casualties on the Japanese and gained a firm hold on a small ridge slightly below the crest. The American troops showed their appreciation of this aggressive leadership by tenaciously clinging to the first substantial gain made by Coane Force since its arrival at Tambu Bay. Aided by Captain Ratliff's company from the beach Coughlin's company again attacked Roosevelt Ridge on 28th July and advanced a little farther. The two companies were counter-attacked several times and were subjected to sniping and mortar fire, but held their ground. Two days later they tried unsuccessfully to improve their positions by attacking from the west. The Japanese were too well dug in along the steep narrow crest of the ridge; their defences were well camouflaged, mutually supporting, and often connected by underground tunnels. The reverse slope of the ridge was similarly organised and, during the Allied artillery and mortar bombardments, the Japanese took shelter in their tunnels, and after the fire lifted, again manned their defences, often as the result of a bugle call and usually as the Americans began to attack. The Americans were learning that it was futile to batter well-prepared positions and best to encircle them.

The III/162nd Battalion was now concentrating on cutting the enemy supply route along Scout Ridge to the west of Tambu Bay. On 27th July Captain Colvert's company destroyed a Japanese position south of the junction of Scout and Roosevelt Ridges, and next day made a substantial advance to a position 500 yards south of the junction where they withstood several attacks from the north. Meanwhile a patrol from Captain Kindt's company, aided by a Papuan platoon, moved south along Scout Ridge towards Mount Tambu and encountered an enemy patrol moving north towards Scout Hill. The Americans dispersed the patrol, but were then forced back by a larger enemy force.

So the skirmishing and patrolling continued in the last days of July and the first days of August. There was no real progress. In a signal to Savige on 28th July Coane had said that he was upset that the calibres of the guns had been divulged to the enemy by the shelling of Salamaua before he could provide anti-aircraft support for them.[3] "Both MacKechnie

---
[3] Actually the Japanese knew all about the Allied guns. A Papuan patrol had recently killed a Japanese officer who was carrying a sketch map accurately pinpointing the artillery positions in the Tambu Bay area.

and I assumed that it would take a full regiment plus two batteries of artillery to carry out our mission assigned," he stated; "events have proved that estimate to be conservative. We must have more troops if we are to complete our mission." Coane then requested an extra battalion and spoke of the threat to Savige's flank and line of communication "if we are overcome" particularly as "we are extended for miles with no reserves whatever". He concluded his signal with a statement which made Savige angry in view of all the trouble and time spent on this vexatious problem. "I wish to respectfully point out also that I have been placed in command of all American troops in this area by General Fuller including the Taylor battalion. This includes all American artillery as well as other troops."

Upon receipt of this signal Savige, who had already censured Coane that day for giving instructions to Colonel Jackson, sent a brief reply saying he would arrive at Nassau Bay by "Cub" on 30th July and wished to be taken to American headquarters to discuss the points raised in Coane's signal. Unable to secure a plane from Australian sources Savige asked Coane to send one. Released from his unpleasant duties at Tambu Bay Captain Sturrock guided the pilot of a Piper Cub sent to pick up Savige. Unfortunately the Cub crashed but Sturrock and the pilot escaped serious injury. Knowing that Coane had a second Cub, Savige asked him to send it across. This Cub landed at Bulolo and took Savige on 31st July through very bad weather to Nassau Bay. Four hours after landing he arrived at Coane's headquarters by barge.

Although discussions between the two men were conducted in a friendly manner, Savige was shocked at what he considered was lack of control and discipline in the force. Savige showed Coane copies of Herring's order of 23rd July and a directive from Fuller based on Herring's order. Coane had not seen these orders and was in the dark about his role beyond that of placing the guns at Tambu Bay. Savige emphasised that all Australian and American units including artillery were under the command of the 3rd Australian Division and that Jackson, not Coane, was responsible to him for control of the artillery. Regarding Coane's fear that the calibre of the guns had been disclosed Savige pointed out that the Japanese already knew of the existence of 75-mm and 105-mm guns in the area and were very worried about the shelling of Salamaua, which would be continued.

Finally Savige told Coane that he must push on immediately and capture Roosevelt Ridge and the high ground to the west in order to protect the guns and the base at Tambu Bay. When Coane protested that he must have the whole of his two battalions forward, Savige pointed out that it was neither necessary nor possible to hold a continuous line. He urged that the American troops must hang on to ground gained and dig in.

A signal from Coane to Savige and Fuller on 4th August was full of foreboding as to the fate of the Tambu Bay troops. Coane stated that his total infantry combat strength was 708, and was being lessened by the daily evacuation of about 50 sick and wounded. In four or five days his

strength would be so depleted as to make it impossible to hold the
Tambu Bay area. He considered that the Japanese must attack in order
to silence the guns, and that Allied reinforcements must arrive at once if
he was to hold Tambu Bay and not lose the guns. Savige's reply on 5th
August, drafted by Wilton, said:

> On all sections of divisional front units are depleted and in many cases are
> confronted with much greater difficulties and have been fighting continuously for
> a longer period. Your strength in men and weapons in proportion to your task
> is much greater than other sectors. Reports from your forward troops indicate
> that their morale is very high and their positions are secure. . . . GOC does not
> agree that the situation at Tambu Bay is as desperate as you indicate.[4]

In the central area, meanwhile, Moten was preparing for another attack
on Mount Tambu. On 22nd July 20 aircraft attacked enemy positions
on Komiatum Ridge completely baring parts of it. That day Moten signalled to Savige an outline of his plan to capture Mount Tambu on 24th
July with three companies of the 2/5th. Two other companies would
attack limited objectives at Goodview Junction at the same time.

Colonel Conroy's plan to capture Mount Tambu was issued on 23rd
July and called for an attack next morning by two companies—Captain
Cameron's left of the main track and Captain Walters' from the west
along Caffin's Track. The anti-tank platoon would establish a position
astride the Mount Tambu-Goodview Junction track from the west.

Covered by Corporal Smith,[5] Cameron crept forward before dawn on
the 24th to within 15 yards of Japanese pill-boxes on the left of the
track. Here he counted seven pill-boxes in two lines of defence on both
sides of the track. Steep slopes on both sides gave little hope of a reasonable approach by more than one platoon at a time, and sharpened bamboo pickets on the left flank led Cameron to believe that an attack
was expected there where it could be enfiladed from the west.[6] From his
reconnaissance and with the little time available to him Cameron had no
option but to order a frontal attack with platoons in echelon, although
he thought that a flanking movement wide to the right with two companies
would have cleared Mount Tambu.

For 15 minutes before the attack Australian and American artillery
fired on Mount Tambu. The two Australian mountain guns fired 90
rounds per gun while the four 75-mm guns of the American battery
on Green Hill fired 60 per gun. The mortars also helped. Cameron attacked
at 11.30 a.m. with Sergeant Williams'[7] platoon on the right and Lieutenant

---

[4] The establishment of an infantry battalion at this time was 33 officers and 772 men. The strengths of some infantry battalions in the 3rd Division in August were:

	Officers	OR's		Officers	OR's
2/5 Bn	34	605	58/59 Bn	28	521
2/6 Bn	38	639	15 Bn	40	665
24 Bn	35	657	47 Bn	32	640
57/60 Bn	40	721			

[5] Cpl J. Smith, MM, VX3491; 2/5 Bn. Wool classer; of Clifton Gardens, NSW; b. East London, South Africa, 11 Nov 1916. Died of wounds 26 Jul 1943.

[6] A captured Japanese Intelligence report on 23rd July indicated that the Japanese were expecting trouble: "Officer's patrol in Komiatum area reveals that enemy units are assembling south of Mount Tambu to attack."

[7] WO2 A. E. Williams, VX11866; 2/5 Bn. Farmer; of Lima South, Vic; b. Violet Town, Vic, 6 Jun 1920.

Leonard's[8] on the left. His intention was that they should drive a wedge into the two lines of pill-boxes and exploit to each flank, when Lieutenant Martin's platoon would come through to clear the top. Cameron had 59 men against an estimated 400 entrenched on Mount Tambu. The assault was supported by the battalion's Vickers guns from lower Tambu.

The Japanese let the two platoons reach almost the line of the forward pill-boxes before a storm of fire swept the advancing Victorians. Among the casualties on the right was Cameron who was moving with Williams' platoon. He was wounded and, as the platoon hesitated under the onslaught, he yelled, "Forward and get stuck into them." Williams, followed by Corporal Carey,[9] then led the depleted platoon forward, and, with great dash, soon swept through the outer ring of Japanese pill-boxes.

On the left Leonard's men captured two pill-boxes before the heavy enfilade fire from the left pinned them down. Cameron's wound prevented him from carrying on and he handed over the attack to Martin who placed Corporal J. Smith in charge of his own platoon and sent him forward to clear the left of Williams' successful advance. "Follow me," called Smith, and with bayonets fixed the small band headed up Mount Tambu. With three men behind him Smith gained the crest of Mount Tambu beyond a third line of pill-boxes, but lack of reserves and severe casualties (16 including 3 killed), caused Martin to order a withdrawal. The Japanese hurled grenades at Smith's gallant band in an attempt to stop their furious charge. Smith had literally to be dragged back semi-conscious but still full of fight. There were some 40 wounds in his body and he died later. During the assault Corporal Allen[1] carried out the wounded and dressed their wounds.

Meanwhile, on the left flank Walters' company had tried to cut the Mount Tambu-Komiatum track 600 yards west of Mount Tambu. While forming up off Caffin's Track the Australians saw 115 Japanese moving east towards the Mount Tambu perimeter. This meant a substantial increase in the fortress to be attacked, but Walters was not in a suitable position to attack them on the track. No sooner had the company crossed the track than it came under heavy fire from an unsuspected enemy position on a precipitous razor-back 300-500 yards west of Mount Tambu. During the bombardment of Mount Tambu the Japanese had come forward from their positions and were thus able to bring down this fire on the discomfited company. The steepness of the track and the fire from the pill-boxes ahead and the ridge to the west gave Walters no choice but to withdraw about 500 yards south-east to Caffin's Track.

During these attacks and in order to create a diversion a platoon from Captain Morse's company climbed through very difficult country and set an ambush on the Komiatum Track high up on Goodview Spur, where they waylaid a party of Japanese, killing three before being compelled to withdraw by a larger enemy force.

---

[8] Lt B. I. Leonard, NX47998; 2/5 Bn. Insurance inspector; of Yass, NSW; b. Yass, 8 Nov 1916.
[9] Cpl V. F. Carey, VX3603; 2/5 Bn. Process worker; of Footscray, Vic; b. Richmond, Vic, 16 Oct 1918.
[1] Cpl L. C. Allen, MM, VX12513; 2/5 Bn. Farm hand; of Ballarat, Vic; b. Ballarat, 9 Nov 1916.

The inability of the 2/5th to capture Mount Tambu emphasised again the danger of attacking frontally high features on which the Japanese were firmly entrenched, without allowing time for very thorough reconnaissance and detailed planning. Had the attacking company commanders been given this breathing space, they might have found a way to encircle the enemy, they would certainly have gained a more accurate appreciation of the enemy's strength and dispositions, and they might have been given a more adequate reserve. The pity was that, even so, Corporal Smith and his gallant band did reach the crest of Mount Tambu, only to be forced back again.

In this period the 2/7th Battalion had been marching forward. Savige had not exactly made up his mind where to use them and on 22nd July had signalled Herring that the enemy's determined thrust at the Buang ambush position and intensified patrolling in the Buiris Creek area indicated large reinforcements from Lae. "Consider most disconcerting enemy blow my left flank," he said, and added that he planned to move half the 2/7th to Hote-Missim. Believing that the principle of concentration of force was being departed from, Herring signalled that the dispersal of the 2/7th Battalion in the Hote area would involve keeping a fresh and well-trained battalion out of the "vital battle now impending Tambu Bay-Tambu Ridge". He considered that enemy action on the left was purely defensive and involved spreading his forces "which is most desirable from your point of view". He added: "Most desirable that you should not conform to what I believe is merely defensive action on his part but should concentrate your forces in the vital area. . . . Most desirable 2/7th Battalion should revert to its brigade earliest." Herring made it evident that Salamaua should continue to attract enemy troops from Lae, and that Savige should develop a sea line of communication to ease the general supply burden.

Savige replied on the 24th that his plan remained unaltered and that the "battle of Mount Tambu commenced this morning". He added that his "concentration of greatest force and fire power within vital area complete and adequate"; and that the 2/7th Battalion, which could not arrive in time to participate in the battle, would move as previously planned to be a reserve to the 15th Brigade. "Movement of enemy from Hote over the mountains never contemplated by me," he said. "Such luck not to be expected. I have defeated the enemy. I have inflicted heavy casualties on him. I have handled time and space better. I anticipate success equal if not greater than Mubo. I have the initiative and will retain it."

After receiving Savige's situation report in which the failure at Mount Tambu was noted, Herring sent a strong signal about the "failure your planned attack to capture Mount Tambu", and urged "most resolute action required". Savige replied on the same day that "yesterday's operations were of a limited nature, a necessary preliminary to subsequent operations which include action by Conroy and Taylor in Mount Tambu-Goodview area, by Wood towards Sugarcane Ridge, with Coane and Hammer exerting pressure on the flanks".

Herring was puzzled and worried at the apparent lack of frankness in these signals and at his difficulty in discovering exactly what was happening in the battle area. He was not to know that Savige's signal about the beginning of the battle for Mount Tambu should not have been taken too literally. He could assume only that the battle had begun on 24th July, particularly when he read this signal in conjunction with an air force signal that an attack was to be made on Komiatum after an air strike which had been requested for 24th July. When he learned that either the attack had failed or the battle had not in fact begun Herring sent forward his chief staff officer, Brigadier Sutherland,[2] who arrived at Bulolo on 26th July.

It seemed to Savige and his staff, however, that New Guinea Force did not fully understand the nature of his operations or the difficulties encountered in terrain, weather, supplies, the enemy; and that they lacked confidence in his conduct of the campaign. The air force signal had been sent without reference to divisional headquarters.

When Sutherland arrived at Bulolo he expressed N.G.F's concern that attacks on Komiatum and Mount Tambu had failed. Savige asked Wilton and Griffin whether any battle had been fought and they replied in the negative. Savige then repeated that the attack on Mount Tambu had the limited objectives of gaining information and, if possible, ground, while no attack had been made on Komiatum. The discussion then centred on Sutherland's doubts whether there was sufficient force available to capture Mount Tambu, and his desire to know exactly when Komiatum and Mount Tambu would be captured. Savige said that he had enough troops but that he could give no guarantee when the two objectives would be taken.

After detailed discussions about supply Sutherland passed on Herring's message urging that divisional headquarters should move forward from Bulolo in order to make the eventual supplying of the whole division from the sea more practicable.

While the 2/5th was preparing to attack Mount Tambu, the remainder of the 2/6th arrived in the Wells area, and Colonel Wood took over responsibility for the area south of Namling. He was ordered by Moten to maintain maximum pressure on the Japanese south of Namling-Orodubi, assist Hammer's operations and clear the Japanese from Sugarcane Ridge and Orodubi. On the morning of the 24th a patrol from the 2/6th cleared the forward slopes of Sugarcane Ridge, and for the next three days further patrols made a thorough reconnaissance of the enemy position which appeared to be the typical defensive position on a small steep-sided feature. From 26th July the Australian 25-pounders concentrated on shelling the ridge.

In the late afternoon of the 27th Wood received a message from Moten: "One company 2/6th Battalion will attack and capture Sugarcane Ridge 28th July." Wood selected Lieutenant Price's company, and Price

---
[2] Brig R. B. Sutherland, WX1570. (1st AIF: Lt 4 Div Engrs.) CRE I Corps 1940-41; GSO1 6 Div 1941-42; BGS HQ NT Force 1942-43, NGF and I Corps 1943. Regular soldier; of Kew, Vic; b. Murrumbeena, Vic, 24 Oct 1897. Killed in aircraft accident 28 Sep 1943.

decided to attack frontally with one platoon while the remaining two platoons moved round by the Bench Cut Track and attacked from the rear. Price had thoroughly reconnoitred the area and he had the benefit of the information gained by several patrols over the previous few days. From 12.40 to 1.30 p.m. the 25-pounders and mortars, machine-guns and grenade dischargers pounded the ridge.

At 1.30 p.m. Lieutenant Trethewie's platoon moved off from Ambush Knoll towards Sugarcane Ridge but was held up by machine-gun fire. Price now sent the other platoons, which had moved to the south of the ridge, up an extremely steep slope on the enemy's right. They clambered up in open formation and, on reaching the top, charged forward shouting and yelling, a habit learnt from the Japanese. Sergeant White's[3] platoon found itself in a position to bring heavy fire on the defenders who had moved forward towards Trethewie's men. This lessened the enemy fire on the third platoon—Lieutenant Exton's—which came in behind the Japanese and mopped up. By 2.30 p.m. Price's company occupied the Japanese position which was well sited and dug in but unprotected on the flanks, the Japanese apparently having thought that the slopes were too steep. They counter-attacked twice but could not dislodge the Victorians.

Moten, after sampling the rigours of the country at first hand, told Savige that the Mount Tambu area was "terrific" and rougher than Mubo. He was amazed how his troops had reached their present positions. The enemy positions, which he had viewed from 150 yards, were situated on a razor-back parallel to that held by his own troops who must cross a ravine to attack the enemy. Moten estimated that there were about two Japanese companies sitting tight among their mass of pill-boxes, which would need to be saturated with shells. The country was indeed an attacker's nightmare. Taylor's battalion (including L. A. Cameron's company of Australians) faced the rugged and precipitous Mount Tambu from the south. Conroy's battalion to the south of Goodview Junction was faced with a razor-back in the form of an elongated triangle with its base at Goodview Junction and its apex running north to the area east of Gwaibolom. The Komiatum Track ran along this rough razor-back. West of the track the Buirali Creek flowed through a precipitous gorge indented with numerous rough east-west valleys. Wood's battalion was west of the Buirali. Between Conroy's positions and Mount Tambu a similar gorge containing the headwaters of the Buigap prevented easy access to Mount Tambu.

At 2.45 p.m. on 28th July Moten, on his return from the battalion areas, informed Savige by telephone of his plan for another attack on Mount Tambu-Goodview Junction. He proposed that, on 30th July, the I/162nd Battalion would capture Mount Tambu, the 2/5th would then capture Goodview Junction, and next the 2/6th would capture Orodubi and exploit north-east to cut the Komiatum Track. Moten was anxious

---

[3] Lt S. G. White, VX4514. 2/6 and 2/2 Bns, 2 NG Inf Bn. Tractor driver; of Main Ridge, Vic; b. Dromana, Vic, 4 Jul 1918.

about his ration situation and Savige signalled Herring immediately that if rations were not supplied the effect on operations would be detrimental. Herring replied that 9 planes would drop at Goodview and 9 at Observation Hill on the 30th.

With five companies at his disposal Taylor already had Newman's American and L. A. Cameron's Australian companies forward on the southern slopes of Mount Tambu. On the morning of 30th July the artillery and mortars bombarded Mount Tambu until 9.5 a.m. when Newman's company left the start-line to attack the right flank of the enemy positions. The front lines were only about 30 yards apart on the razor-back. The two forward platoons dashed through heavy fire but were pinned down near the Japanese positions. Attempts by the third platoon and by a platoon from the reserve company to outflank the enemy were unsuccessful.[4] A determined American attack had been unable to breach the Japanese fortress and had been beaten back with 40 casualties. Among these were 12 wounded who owed their lives to the devotion of Corporal Allen of Cameron's company. Twelve times he advanced through heavy fire and carried back a wounded man.

Because the American attack had failed, attacks by the 2/5th and 2/6th Battalions did not take place. As with the Pimple it was proving impossible to capture Mount Tambu by direct assault.

On 29th July Herring wrote to Savige and for the first time took him into his confidence about the offensive which was being prepared on Lae.

> It is most important for future operations that are now being planned (Herring wrote) that the Air should be relieved of its supply obligations in your forward area at the earliest possible moment. These operations for your own private ear only involve an attack on Lae from both east and west. George Wootten will come in from the east transported and supplied by sea and George Vasey will come in from the west transported and supplied by air. The latter part of this combined operation requires relief of the Air as early as possible, so that Tsili Tsili airfield can be quickly developed and the air freed for a maximum effort in support of George Vasey. It is hoped that this operation will be under way before the end of August. There has been a lot of planning to be done for this pending operation, so I trust you will understand why I haven't been up to see you since your operation commenced. Your role is still first of all to drive the enemy north of the Francisco River. The capture of Salamaua is of course devoutly to be wished but no attempt upon it is to be allowed to interfere with the major operation being planned. . . . The role of 3 Aust Div during the main op will be to hold in the Salamaua area, if not already in your hands, the maximum number of the enemy.

In Moten's fertile brain the seed of a plan to drive the enemy from Mount Tambu and Komiatum was germinating. On 30th July he wrote to Wood, referring to a patrol by the 2/6th from Ambush Knoll to Buirali Creek:

---

[4] In *The Jungleers* (p. 57), the remainder of the day was described thus:

The Nips continued to pour in troops and weapons and shortly after noon all units were pinned down by automatic and small-arms fire and were being severely pounded by mortars and grenades. Several minutes later a withdrawal was ordered, this being covered by machine-gun fire and smoke grenades. . . . Our casualties were heavy, one-third of the attacking force having been either killed or wounded. By [6 p.m.] silence reigned over bloody, enemy-held Mount Tambu.

Your patrol to Buirali. . . . If we could only get a company (or two) on to the Komiatum Spur and supply them by the same route as they went in, it might be the answer to a lot of our problems. It would isolate both Mount Tambu and Goodview. Let me have your views.

Orodubi. The photos seem to indicate that this can be better tackled from the north as you suggest. I am of opinion that its capture at this stage will not materially assist us—hence my signals to limit your operations to offensive patrolling. If you can clean out the two knolls (Price and Exton) without undue casualties, go ahead. Especially so if you think the capture of these two knolls will help us in our subsequent operations towards Komiatum.

On the evening of 1st August Savige approved Moten's tentative plans and allotted him a company of the 2/7th as a reserve. For the next few days Moten's three battalions patrolled extensively. The 2/6th usually had three or four patrols out at one time searching the re-entrants of Buirali Creek, seeking ways up Komiatum Ridge and probing the Japanese positions in front of them. Few of them clashed with the enemy although Lieutenant Sachs and another man crept through the kunai grass to the Japanese position on Price's Knoll and threw grenades into the occupied weapon-pits.

As the idea of placing a force astride the Komiatum Track north of Mount Tambu grew, Moten ensured that a particular company would be available to carry out the arduous and detailed reconnaissance necessary to find suitable routes for the movement of large bodies of troops on to Komiatum Ridge and to obtain information about Japanese dispositions in the area. On 30th July he had specifically asked Wood to retain "D" Company of the 2/6th, now led by Captain H. L. Laver, as brigade reserve, at Base 4; and on 3rd August he called the company forward. Soon after Laver arrived at Drake's O.P.[5] at midday on 4th August two small patrols led by Lieutenant Johnson and Sergeant Hedderman were ordered to move off on 5th August. While these patrols were out Wood was ordered to bring forward his battalion to the Stephens' Track area.

The 2/5th Battalion meanwhile had tried to capture limited objectives south of Goodview Junction. On 4th August Bennett's and Walters' companies attacked Hodge's Knoll, a small steep knoll where Walpole's Track met the Mule Track, and a spur leading to Goodview Junction. Lieutenant Hodge's[6] platoon surprised the Japanese and got a foothold on the knoll while Lieutenant Lind's[7] platoon moving along Walpole's Track could make no headway against Japanese pill-boxes even after being reinforced. At 4.30 p.m. the enemy heavily counter-attacked Hodge's platoon from three sides and forced it to withdraw. In the fighting, which lasted most of the day, 28 Japanese were killed for the loss of 7 Australians killed and 10 wounded. The companies finally withdrew to their original positions south-west of Goodview Junction. It seemed that the enemy was firmly resolved to hold the Mount Tambu and Goodview Junction areas which were being extended and strengthened. Reconnaissance

---

[5] Named after Lieutenant L. R. Drake, 2/5th Battalion.
[6] Capt B. Hodge, QX21235; 2/5 Bn. Bank officer; of Biloela, Qld; b. Biggenden, Qld, 28 Mar 1921.
[7] Lt W. A. T. Lind, VX3358; 2/5 Bn. Clerk; of Kew, Vic; b. Armadale, Vic, 9 Feb 1919.

patrols and observation posts also lent colour to this belief. On 31st July Wells O.P. had observed 300 Japanese moving south along the Komiatum Track. Lieutenant Robinson[8] and two men from the 2/5th Battalion whose task was to observe Japanese movement on the Komiatum Track stayed on the ridge for a night and reported on 4th August much Japanese movement along the Komiatum Track at the top of the Komiatum Spur.

On 5th August a patrol of the I/162nd Battalion from south of Mount Tambu reconnoitred the north-south ridge, subsequently known as Davidson Ridge,[9] lying between Komiatum and Scout Ridges, and found it unoccupied.

At the end of July General Nakano had the *I* and *II Battalions* of Araki's *66th Regiment* in the Komiatum-Mount Tambu-Goodview Junction area. Major Kimura's *III/66th Battalion* was still detached from the regiment and was in the Roosevelt Ridge-Scout Ridge area after its unprofitable coastal excursion farther south. Araki's total strength, exclusive of Kimura's battalion, was 743. Engineers and other headquarters troops accounted for 192 of these; 25 were in an ambush position on Scout Ridge east of Mount Tambu, 112 were on Mount Tambu, 85 on Tambu Saddle, 89 on Goodview Junction and Spur, 63 at the junction of Walpole's and Tambu Tracks, and 177 on Komiatum Ridge.

On 31st July Herring signalled that he was considering moving a battalion of the 29th Brigade into Nassau Bay or Tambu Bay as a reserve for the Tambu operations or for the possible relief later of the 17th Brigade. The 29th Brigade led by Brigadier Monaghan[1] comprised three battalions of Queenslanders—15th, 42nd and 47th—which had reached Buna on 17th July from the Milne Bay area where they had spent the previous six months. Following up his signal Herring wrote on the 31st: "Your fellows seem to be frightening the very devil out of the Jap Command in Salamaua"; and he warned Savige not to let Monaghan become bogged down in battle against prepared positions but to establish him on the Tambu ridges in order to isolate Komiatum and force the Japanese to fight on ground of Savige's choosing. Savige should follow the policy of encircle and destroy and, with his guns, should be able to give the Japanese "a dreadful sickener in his forward positions". In Savige's absence at Coane's headquarters Wilton asked that the new battalion should arrive at Tambu Bay as soon as possible to operate against Mount Tambu from the north-east thus relieving Coane Force of that commitment and assisting the 17th Brigade.

Herring's letter also expressed the hope that divisional headquarters would soon move to the Mubo area, thus moving closer to the coast and easing the supply problem.[2] By 4th August preparations for a forward

---

[8] Lt B. L. Robinson, VX28106; 2/5 Bn. Clerk; of Dimboola, Vic; b. Glenferrie, Vic, 15 Sep 1918.
[9] Named after Lieut-Colonel C. W. Davidson, CO of the 42nd Battalion.
[1] Brig R. F. Monaghan, DSO, QX6152. CO 2/2 A-Tk Regt 1940-42 (Admin Comd 2/33 Bn, 2/2 Pnr Bn in 1941); Comd 29 Bde 1942-45. Regular soldier; of Brisbane; b. Goulburn, NSW, 28 Nov 1898.
[2] Savige wrote later: "A change in location for HQ of a division is not so easy as it looks, as, for one thing, it requires a new set up in communications. Already my overworked linesmen had erected something like 2,000 miles of line. In the first phase, Moten occupied the only possible site for HQ of a Div at Guadagasal. . . . Once he was able to move forward, I could take over his communications which would not only link up with his new HQ, but the link up with Hammer would be easy too. The coast itself for a site for Div HQ was still out of the question as Nassau Bay was too far away, and the Jap still barred the way to Tambu Bay."

move of divisional headquarters to Guadagasal were complete and Savige opened his headquarters there on 6th August. Moten had closed his headquarters at Guadagasal on 2nd August and reopened it at the junction of the Bui Eo and Buigap Creeks within 500 yards of the Japanese at Goodview Junction.

On 24th July Hammer had called his commanding officers to a conference at Gwaibolom. He was happier now that Moten had assumed responsibility north to Namling and Orodubi and felt that his brigade was concentrated enough to guarantee more security on Bobdubi Ridge and allow attacks to be made elsewhere. Because of Moten's pressure from the south the enemy position at Graveyard was not as important as previously and could be "contained". For the 27th Hammer planned that the 58th/59th Battalion would attack Erskine Creek and Old Vickers. On 26th July Starr received not only his orders for these attacks but a letter from the vehement Hammer in which a salvo of criticism of Starr's unit, some of his officers, and, by implication, Starr himself, was delivered. The criticism was based largely on the ground that the officers, Hammer considered, lacked adequate knowledge of the whereabouts of neighbouring units and the enemy. The criticism was almost certainly too sweeping. The 58th/59th had entered the operations less well trained than it could have been but, under Starr's leadership, was gaining confidence and skill, as later events were very soon to show.

All was not well with the Japanese in the Bobdubi area.

> This is our 71st day at Bobdubi (wrote Sergeant Kobayashi of the *115th Regiment* on 23rd July), and there is no relief yet. We must entrust our lives to God. Every day there are bombings and we feel so lonely. We do not know when the day will come for us to join our dead comrades. Can the people at home imagine our suffering. Eight months without a letter. There is no time even to dream of home.

Since the Gwaibolom conference patrols of the 58th/59th, assisted by detachments from the Independent Company, were gaining all possible information for the attack on Erskine Creek. Just as preparations were almost completed, Hammer at 5.30 p.m. on 26th July received a signal from Savige postponing the attack until it could be coordinated with an attack by the 2/6th on Orodubi. Hammer therefore ordered Starr to concentrate immediately on attacking Old Vickers.

The battalion's mortars and the artillery battered Old Vickers on 27th July. The artillery scored several direct hits. This cheered Starr's men and the battalion diarist, in lauding the shelling, recorded that "troops had completely lost faith in air strikes as a means of paving the way for attack". The attack on this troublesome and obstinate Japanese fortress took place on 28th July. A company, led by Lieutenant Franklin, and Lieutenant Proby's[3] platoon from another company, were to be the attacking force, with another platoon guarding Franklin's base south of Old Vickers. For weeks the assaulting company had been vigorously recon-

---

[3] Lt L. S. Proby, MC, VX102654; 58/59 Bn. Salesman; of Essendon, Vic; b. Mornington, Vic, 20 Jul 1919.

noitring Old Vickers and planning its capture. As the artillery fire on the previous day had been so effective it was decided to attack under cover of another artillery and mortar barrage.

From 2.45 to 3 p.m. the 25-pounders fired 102 shells per gun. Then two machine-guns fired 10 belts on to enemy positions on Coconut Ridge while two detachments of mortars fired 60 bombs per mortar. By 3 p.m. Franklin's four platoons, having made intelligent use of the artillery bombardment and smoke provided by the mortars, approached close to the target. Proby led the direct assault with Sergeant Hammond's[4] platoon on the right flank and Lieutenant Evans'[5] on the left. The task of the fourth platoon (Sergeant Anderson's) was to create a diversion to the right. During the bombardment and smoke Proby approached Old Vickers Position. As the smoke lifted his platoon came across three bunkers which were grenaded "just in case". Proby wrote later: "This was the first good support we had had from arty and it was most effective indeed. I don't blame Nippon for keeping his head down. The mortar and MMG covering fire was also a big help." So effective was it that by the time the platoon reached the crest the Japanese were just emerging from their dugouts. Proby, leading his men along a narrow ridge, was the first on to Old Vickers. Amid exploding grenades the Australians pressed forward throwing their own grenades and fighting with such spirit that some of the defenders disappeared in the direction of the Coconuts. Others remained, and severe fighting ensued as the Australians struggled to enlarge the breach in the fortress. Proby killed the crew of a 70-mm gun before being wounded by a grenade. Dazed by the explosion he was grabbed

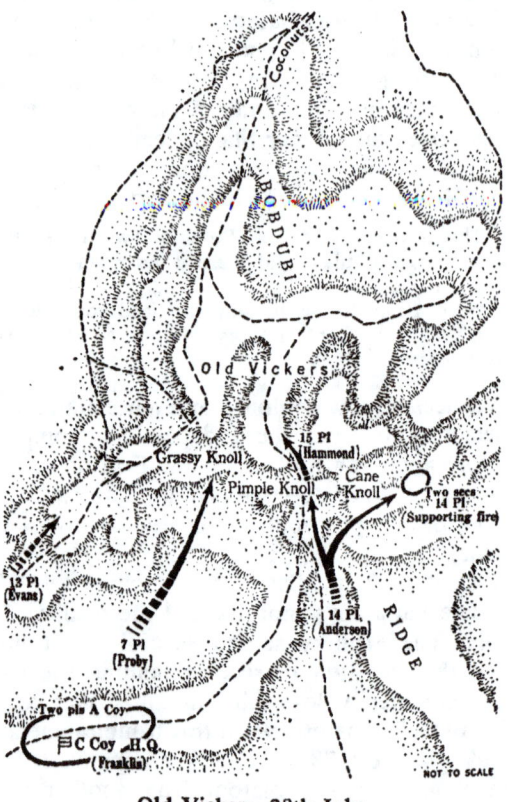

Old Vickers, 28th July

---

[4] S-Sgt V. W. Hammond, VX140443; 58/59 Bn. Farmer; of Murchison, Vic; b. Murchison, 17 Dec 1908.

[5] Lt J. Evans, VX112186; 58/59 Bn. Schoolteacher; of Wangaratta, Vic; b. Ballarat, Vic, 28 Mar 1915. Killed in action 28 Jul 1943.

by a medical orderly who started to bandage him. Coming to, he charged back into the fight with yards of bandage trailing from him.

Aided as they had been by the supporting fire and inspired by Proby's example, the 58th/59th was not to be denied, and after an hour and a half most of the remaining Japanese scrub-bashed towards the Coconuts pursued by the platoon's bullets. Proby and Sergeant Farrelly[6] meanwhile used grenades to wipe out Japanese still lurking in the defences on Old Vickers. The flanking platoons helped with the mopping up.

The 58th/59th Battalion had gained a notable success and had captured the key to Bobdubi Ridge. This might have been achieved earlier had the assaulting troops been properly supported. The success was a spirited reply to the criticism—some justified and some unfair—which had pursued the battalion since it had joined in the fight. Among the 16 Australian casualties were two platoon commanders, Evans killed and Proby wounded; and Franklin himself was wounded by the last enemy weapon to be silenced. Sergeant Farrelly then organised the company's defence preparations against the expected counter-attack until Captain Jackson arrived. Besides abandoning 17 dead on Old Vickers, the Japanese left a large amount of booty, including the 70-mm gun, and 300 shells which Lieutenant Dawson gladly appropriated, four light machine-guns, one medium machine-gun, 28 rifles and one light mortar.

Next day the victorious company was relieved by one from the 2/7th. The outgoing company was only 31 strong and there were no officers left at all. All three liaison officers from brigade headquarters had been sent to replace officer casualties in the companies. Captain Newman was the last spare officer on brigade headquarters, and he took over Franklin's company, which he divided into three platoons with strengths of 8, 8 and 7 and a company headquarters of 8.

Warfe now decided to add to the good tidings by attacking Timbered Knoll. On the night of 28th-29th July a listening post reported no sounds from the knoll, but at dawn a patrol towards the knoll was fired on. At 4 p.m. Lewin's platoon prepared to attack Timbered Knoll supported by the Independent Company's mortars and the Tambu Bay battery of the 2/6th Field Regiment which, during the night, brought four extra 25-pounders from Nassau Bay to a position 3,000 yards north of Lake Salus. Two sections assaulted the knoll from north to south but were pinned down by machine-guns. Lewin, however, took Lieutenant Read's[7] section south along the Bench Cut, down the east side of Timbered Knoll and then attacked from south to north. Advancing up this steep razor-back the party came under heavy fire from the Japanese pill-boxes and weapon-pits. Using grenades and his Tommy-gun with deadly effect Private Dawson[8] assaulted these positions and inflicted such heavy casualties

---

[6] Lt R. P. Farrelly, VX111772; 58/59 Bn. Storeman; of Porepunkah, Vic; b. Bright, Vic, 17 Jul 1920. Killed in action 30 May 1945.

[7] Lt S. Read, NX114931. 2/3 Indep Coy, 2/3 Cdo Sqn, 1 NG Inf Bn. Welder; of Manly, NSW; b. London, 19 Nov 1913.

[8] Pte W. H. Dawson, MM, VX50665. 2/3 Indep Coy, 2/3 Cdo Sqn. Junior chemist; of Caulfield, Vic; b. Yarraville, Vic, 13 Oct 1915.

that the Japanese began to withdraw. Once again a determined attack from the flank had demoralised the enemy, who made off from their extensive defences on Timbered Knoll after severe close-quarters fighting, and allowed the Australian party attacking from the south to join the two sections pinned down to the north. Lewin's men received a surprise when buns freshly baked by the cooks and cups of tea were brought up during the attack. Damien Parer,[9] a photographer who had already made some famous films of Australian fighting men, took time off from his filming of this fight to take round the buns and tea, and to help Meares' men carry up ammunition; Parer's Bowl, 250 yards from Timbered Knoll, was named after him.

By 5.45 p.m. Lewin's men were entrenched on Timbered Knoll and were able to look down on other enemy positions towards Orodubi. The victors had lost three N.C.O's killed, including the intrepid Sergeant Muir, and three men were wounded; they found 15 Japanese bodies on the knoll as well as two machine-guns, two 2-inch mortars, rifles and documents; next day they killed three more Japanese hiding in the entrenchments. The enemy position as usual was well dug in with weapon-pits, trenches and pill-boxes. Some of these defences had been destroyed by the supporting fire, but hand grenades had been responsible for most of the success. Again and again the grenade had proved the most effective weapon at close quarters whether in attack or defence. Warfe's troops had learnt that the first and vital object was to gain and occupy at least the enemy's outer weapon-pits and so place the fight on a more even footing. At Timbered Knoll a successful assault had been made from the flank, and, one hour after contact, the troops held several weapon-pits in the rear of the main defences. The rest of the position was cleared in half an hour. Warfe's men had also learnt from the Japanese the value of battle cries or shouting and yelling—but only after the attack was launched; and learnt that the most valuable natural cover for movement was not moonlight but rain.

With Old Vickers Position and Timbered Knoll in his hands and three companies of the 58th/59th Battalion available for further action, Hammer on 29th July allotted new tasks. The 58th/59th would hold positions on the Bench Cut between Erskine Creek and Osborne Creek, cut the Komiatum Track north of Osborne Creek and capture the Coconuts. Starr allotted Newman's company the task of getting astride the Bench Cut between the two creeks, Jackson's the task of cutting the Komiatum Track, and Griff's the task of capturing the Coconuts. By evening Newman's and Jackson's companies were in position, and for the next few days they skirmished with the enemy in the rugged area between the two creeks and between the Komiatum and Bench Cut Tracks. "Your show going great guns. Keep it up," signalled Savige to Hammer.

Starr planned that Griff would be supported by the 25-pounders of the 2/6th Regiment. When he reached his start-line near Old Vickers, Griff

---

[9] Damien P. Parer. Official war photographer, Department of Information 1940-43, with Americans 1943-44. Photographer; of Sydney; b. Malvern, Vic, 1 Aug 1912. Killed in action 17 Sep 1944.

(Australian War Memorial)
Men of the 2/3rd Independent Company moving into the assembly area for the attack on Timbered Knoll on 29th July 1943.

(Australian War Memorial)
Forward troops occupying weapon-pits during the attack on Timbered Knoll.

(Australian War Memorial)

The 2/3rd Independent Company at Timbered Knoll, 29th July 1943. Corporal R. R. S. Good about to dress the wounds of Private H. W. Robins with the assistance of Private R. S. Wood (left) and Sergeant K. M. MacLean.

(G. R. Warfe)

On the summit of Timbered Knoll, July 1943. *Left to right*: Major G. R. Warfe, Lieutenants E. J. Barry, J. E. Lewin and S. Read of the 2/3rd Independent Company, waiting for the mist to clear before making a visual reconnaissance of Graveyard and Orodubi.

rang Starr to check about his support, and was told that the guns within range were out of ammunition and those with ammunition were out of range. His only artillery support was 30 shells fired from the captured Japanese mountain gun by Lieutenant Dawson, but Dawson could sight the gun only by looking through the barrel and it did not do much damage.

At 2.30 p.m. on the 30th Griff's company moved down the ridge from Old Vickers on a one-man front. About 80 yards from South Coconuts the company came under fire. Griff tried to get a platoon up either flank but both were greeted by grenades thrown by the Japanese from above. The Australians then occupied part of the Japanese trench system just below the crest of South Coconuts and dug in for the night. The enemy counter-attacked at dusk but were driven back. It was an eerie night for the Australians as the Japanese infiltrated among their weapon-pits; before dawn Griff sent back seven men with stab wounds inflicted by the prowling Japanese. About first light, when the Japanese again attacked, Griff pulled back his forward platoon, now only 10 strong, to his main company position 50 yards behind. He was then ordered to withdraw to the village west of Old Vickers to give depth to the 2/7th Battalion, now occupying Old Vickers, in the face of more expected attacks on the vital position.

After Griff's company withdrew on 31st July Captain Cramp's[1] company of the 2/7th Battalion, now established on Old Vickers, noticed enemy movement to the east. Documents captured by Franklin's men on 28th July revealed that Old Vickers was one of the main key points on the enemy's perimeter for the defence of Salamaua. Counter-attacks were therefore to be expected.

At 6.15 a.m. on 1st August the enemy began to fire on Cramp's company. Half an hour later the telephone line was cut but, after communications had been re-established by means of a Lucas lamp, a patrol from the 58th/59th pioneered a route into the position. Although the Japanese expended much ammunition in spasmodic firing at Old Vickers no actual assault was made on 1st August.

As on each occasion when their hold on Bobdubi Ridge was threatened the Japanese reacted violently. Nakano seemed unable to anticipate where the next blow of his Australian adversary would fall. Believing that his main threat would come from Tambu Bay he had sent the remainder of Jinno's *1/80th Battalion*, which arrived at Salamaua from Madang on 22nd July, to join the first contingent of the *1/80th* and the other units and sub-units already sent to the south. In the diary of Lieutenant Matsuda of Jinno's battalion the subsequent change in orders was described:

"27th July: Prepared to attack Lokanu. Division's plan to attack American forces which landed at Lokanu is to destroy heavy artillery positions. It is a novel plan.

28th July: The high point at Bobdubi is occupied by the enemy, therefore battalion changed the plan and departed at 5 p.m. to destroy them. We advanced under darkness in the jungle."

"The enemy concentration at Bobdubi plateau is estimated to be about 200," stated Jinno in orders issued a day after Old Vickers Position had fallen to the

---
[1] Capt S. M. Cramp, VX4717; 2/7 Bn. Radio agent; of Mildura, Vic; b. Mildura, 3 Aug 1914.

58th/59th. "Artillery units will cooperate in full force with the battalion in the attack. Battalion will raid the enemy positions at dawn tomorrow, the 30th, and will recapture Bobdubi plateau with one blow." Jinno's battalion, having been used at the southern end of Bobdubi Ridge a fortnight previously, was now to be used again at the northern end.

The Japanese had the worst of the exchanges of fire on 1st August. At 9 a.m. a mortar bomb registered a direct hit on *1/80th Battalion* headquarters wounding Jinno, one of his company commanders, and a sergeant.

At dawn on the 2nd Japanese attacked Old Vickers Position from Grassy Knoll west of the main Bobdubi Ridge. The attack was determined but so was the defence. Soon the notes of a bugle were heard and the Japanese broke off. In the afternoon they intermittently sniped at Old Vickers and heavily and accurately engaged Lieutenant Anderson's[2] platoon (strength 9) which Griff had placed on Cane Knoll south-east of Old Vickers in response to a request by Cramp. The main difficulty about Anderson's position was the provision of food and water, but after collecting from the rest of the company Anderson had enough for three days, a fortunate occurrence as he was cut off in the initial attack. A composite force from both battalions was advancing to aid Anderson when it also was heavily

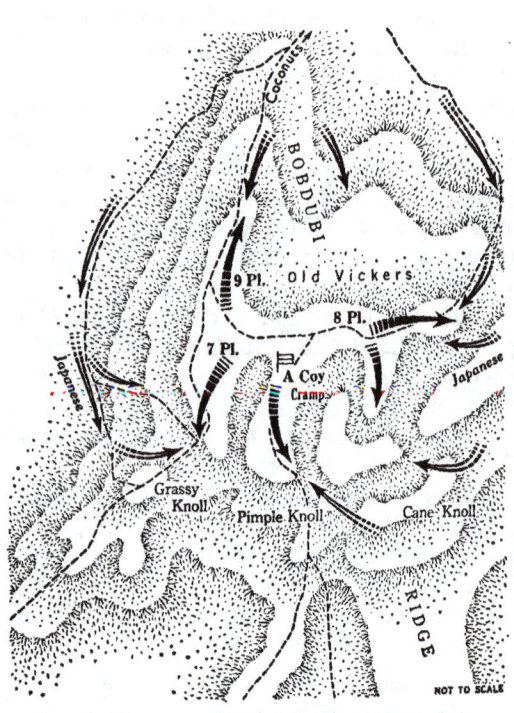

Defence of Old Vickers by 2/7th Battalion, 2nd-4th August

attacked and forced to withdraw. In the withdrawal two men fell wounded within full view of the enemy, only 70 yards away. Private Forst[3] of the 2/7th Battalion crawled out twice under intense fire and rescued both men. The afternoon was enlivened for the defenders by Sergeant Naismith's performance in crawling forward and killing with grenades four Japanese who were priming their weapons. In the two days 25 Japanese had been killed and only two Australians wounded.

---

[2] Lt H. K. Anderson, VX40132; 58/59 Bn. Factory employee; of Warrnambool, Vic; b. Warrnambool, 28 Aug 1912. Killed in action 22 Aug 1943.

[3] Pte H. C. Forst, MM, SX18856; 2/7 Bn. Hairdresser; of Port Adelaide, SA; b. Exeter, SA, 20 Jun 1909.

During the 3rd Cramp's men noticed that the Japanese seemed very busy on Grassy Knoll, and persistent sniping occurred towards Naismith's position. At 9.15 p.m. Major Picken,[4] in command of the 2/7th Battalion since Guinn had become ill on 26th July, received a message from Cramp that a determined attack was under way. Covered by the sniping the Japanese had moved forward until they were in a position to attack quickly. In the dark and with steady rain falling the Australians could yet hear the sound of the enemy crashing through the undergrowth, and were alert. Hysterical chanting and screams heralded the attack which was greeted with grenades as the sounds came closer. Although the Japanese attacked the whole perimeter the area in front of Naismith's platoon was the scene of the most bitter fighting. Lit by flashes of exploding grenades the Japanese came with fixed bayonets in a final assault to recover their coveted ground. Against the roar of grenades and the din of machine-guns the fighting grew in intensity. Their bayonet charge, although covered by the darkness, broke before the defenders' fire, and they fled leaving many dead, some even in the forward weapon-pits. The remainder of the night was quiet.

In this violent attack the company sergeant-major, "Jock" Sym,[5] gave the troops a great feeling of confidence as he crawled to the section pits to distribute the grenades with which his shirt bulged and to pass on news from other positions and words of encouragement. Private Finn[6] in a forward weapon-pit was the first to hear the Japanese rushing forward. With grenades and then a Bren Finn broke up the attack and enabled the remainder of the platoon to join in. During the enemy attack Naismith managed to be where the fighting was stiffest, moving among his men and using captured Japanese grenades as well as his own. As each attack was repulsed Naismith moved forward under fire and collected grenades from enemy dead and dumps in the area. By this means he collected 200 grenades for his 12 men.

By 4th August the Japanese had had enough of frontal attacks but they were still determined to regain Old Vickers. Picken received a message from Cramp stating that the enemy from the east had encircled Old Vickers and were digging in astride the beleagured company's line of communication in spite of harassing mortar fire. Captain Tatterson, leading an attack from the perimeter, was unable to dislodge the Japanese astride the supply route and was killed by a sniper. Major K. R. Walker, recently returned from Australia, moved out with a patrol guided by Private Briggs[7] to find a way into the perimeter. Japanese prevented the patrol getting very far but Walker and Briggs broke bush and eventually reached the perimeter by a subsidiary spur. The company was glad to

---

[4] Lt-Col K. S. Picken, DSO, VX48. 2/6, 2/7 Bns; CO 2/27 Bn 1943-45. Clerk; of East Geelong, Vic; b. Warragul, Vic, 20 Oct 1907.

[5] WO1 J. Sym, MBE, VX4670; 2/7 Bn. Building contractor; of Dareton, NSW; b. Dalmeny, Scotland, 12 Jan 1905.

[6] Cpl B. D. Finn, MM, VX111577; 2/7 Bn. Labourer; of Kinglake, Vic; b. Scotsburn, Vic, 13 Aug 1918.

[7] Cpl H. G. Briggs, VX68436; 2/7 Bn. Truck driver; of Cardinia, Vic; b. Brunswick, Vic, 10 Jun 1922.

see its commander back at such a critical time and the telephone line which had been cut by the Japanese was relaid along Briggs' route.

The Australians were determined to get rid of the surrounding Japanese and Griff's company was given the task of breaking the ring. He was given Lieutenant Murphy's[8] anti-tank platoon to reinforce his own depleted company, now only the size of a platoon. Griff planned to attack at 3.45 p.m. with two platoons—Lieutenant McDonald's[9] on the right and Murphy's on the left, after a concentration of 30 mortar bombs. The light began to go and, as the mortar fire was slow because of the proximity of Cramp's company, Griff stopped the fire and attacked up the slope. Just before dark when Griff made contact with Lieutenant Anderson for the first time in three days and a half, the attackers had managed to throw a circle around the enemy position. Darkness came and the mopping up was left until next morning. In the night several Japanese tried to break out but were killed or wounded.

At first light on the 5th Griff's runner, returning to his reserve platoon, met a Japanese officer and two soldiers trying to escape and killed them; he returned with a sword, a light machine-gun and a rifle. At dawn the mopping up began. Several Japanese in their defences seemed to call for mercy, but each time the Australians demanded surrender they replied with machine-gun fire. The line of communication to the 2/7th was now clear.

Old Vickers Position was sited for all-round defence and all likely approaches were covered. This siting was very sound as the 2/7th's casualties were only 2 killed and 11 wounded, while 87 dead Japanese were buried by the Australians, the largest number of bodies yet found by any unit of this brigade, and the actual casualties must have been much higher as the Japanese had removed all casualties from the area whence they launched the first 12 of their 14 attacks. The brigade staff reckoned that, between 30th June and 6th August, the brigade had inflicted 800 casualties of whom 400 were killed. In the same period 46 of the 15th Brigade were killed and 152 wounded.

Hammer now redisposed his troops and ordered the more experienced but smaller 2/3rd Independent Company to change places with the 58th/59th, which would then be responsible for the area from Gwaibolom to Namling, regarded by Hammer as less vulnerable than the area to the north. By 6th August the 2/7th Battalion was responsible for the area north from Old Vickers Position, the Independent Company for the area south from Old Vickers to Griff's Track, and the 58th/59th for the area south from Griff's Track to the Namling-Orodubi area.

With the redisposition of the troops a phase in the operations of the 15th Brigade concluded. By the capture of Old Vickers and its retention against a week of counter-attacks the brigade had really gained control

---

[8] Lt B. M. Murphy, VX102653. 58/59 and 4 Bns. Storeman and packer; of Essendon, Vic; b. Moonee Ponds, Vic, 8 Jul 1918.

[9] Lt R. L. McDonald, VX114247; 58/59 Bn. Cost accountant; of Essendon, Vic; b. Stawell, Vic, 8 Feb 1919.

of the vital position on Bobdubi Ridge. It was now ready to prepare a firm base from which future operations could be maintained.

The Independent Company and the 58th/59th Battalion were in need of rest as they had been fighting over the exhausting ridges in close contact with the enemy for 38 days. Hammer therefore ordered each of his units to establish rest camps (similar to those already established by Moten) where tired and keyed-up men could have a day or two in which to relax, wash and eat good meals. The units were in need of reorganisation as well as rest. The 58th/59th, for example, had lost 32 killed, 100 wounded and 9 missing; the Independent Company 12 killed and 38 wounded.[1] Reinforcements were hard to find. By 28th July Herring's staff had noticed a falling-off in the numbers arriving since the end of May. Checking against the holding of reinforcements for New Guinea at Sellheim and Oonoonba in Queensland they found no undue accumulation there. It was then apparent to Herring that units which were beginning to leave Australia destined for the northern offensive had priority of reinforcements and had brought their actual strengths up to their war establishments. In early August, however, 82 reinforcements arrived for the 58th/59th and 30 for the 2/3rd Independent Company.

In late July and early August the 24th Battalion, assisted by Chalk's Papuan company, was patrolling the area south along the Markham River, particularly to Markham Point. Patrols spread thinly over this area caused the enemy to over-estimate the size of the force opposing him. Almost daily the Australians and Papuans reported sounds of motor launches across the Markham near New Labu Island, which suggested that this route might be an alternative to the main crossing between Lae and Salamaua at Labu. One Papuan patrol near the Markham was unlucky enough to have four 1,000-lb bombs dropped near by from American aircraft. The bombs cleared an expanse of jungle 340 yards by 100 yards and killed one of the native soldiers. Another Papuan patrol saw fresh footprints along the track from Deep Creek towards Markham Point and followed them cautiously, but was nevertheless ambushed. While the patrol withdrew, Corporal Undariba camouflaged himself and returned to the scene of the ambush where he fired three Owen magazines into the Japanese, killing two.

In the distant Buang area Lieutenant Dawson of the 24th Battalion carried out his orders to "act offensively" to the east and set up a firm base forward of Lega. He established a base east of Linea Creek, which he manned himself, with 13 men and the police boy. At Linea Creek he kept a 6-man standing patrol; a mile and a half west of Lega 2 he based 15 men; and 1,200 yards west again at Lega 1 he placed the signallers and R.A.P. On 24th July Dawson led a patrol in an attempt to reach the coast at Sugarloaf but the dense jungle and swamp prevented it from reaching its destination in the two days available. While the patrol was out, however, the police boy reported that at midnight on 24th-25th

---

[1] Unit strengths at this time were: 58th/59th Battalion, 20 officers and 460 men; 2/3rd Independent Company, 13 and 185.

July he heard motor-driven craft, coming south from the direction of Lae, stop at the Buang River mouth and then return north. This lent weight to the growing belief that the enemy was fearful of a thrust down the Buang to cut his Lae-Salamaua line of communication or that he intended to push up the Buang himself towards the Snake and Bulolo Valleys. After the return of the Sugarloaf patrol Colonel Smith of the 24th Battalion sent Lieutenant Robinson's[2] platoon to relieve Dawson's.

Both opposing forces in the Buang Valley now began patrolling towards one another. On 30th July Corporal Langford[3] led an eight-man patrol north round the Japanese ambush position encountered seven days previously. As he was moving north of the island in the river he saw seven Japanese wading to the west. Langford went quickly back and set up an ambush into which the enemy patrol walked but escaped, unscathed, because the Bren gunner fired prematurely—the gun's legs collapsing in the burst. On 5th August Robinson led a patrol from Linea Creek towards the beach and next day clashed with a Japanese outpost about a quarter of a mile from the beach.

By the beginning of August four Australian and three American battalions, an Australian Independent Company and a Papuan company, supported by two Australian artillery batteries and five American batteries, were drawing the ring tighter round the enemy's position at Salamaua. The enemy's outer defences had been breached and they were fighting desperately to retain their positions on Roosevelt Ridge, Scout Ridge, Mount Tambu, Komiatum Ridge and the eastern slopes of Bobdubi Ridge. To the north two other Australian battalions and another Papuan company were forcing the enemy to detach large forces from the main battle area farther south.

Early July had seen the real beginning of the New Guinea offensive. The American landing at Nassau Bay, followed by Moten's success at Mubo, had carried the fight closer to Salamaua. The remainder of the month and the beginning of August had seen much bitter fighting during which the Allies had captured vital knolls and ridges, had withstood counter-attacks, and then prepared to attack the enemy's main defences.

---

[2] Capt E. R. Robinson, MC, VX104160; 24 Bn. Farmer; of Wandin, Vic; b. Subiaco, WA, 24 Jul 1919.

[3] Cpl D. A. Langford, VX106352; 24 Bn. Clerk; of Balwyn, Vic; b. Melbourne, 8 May 1923.

CHAPTER 7

THE FIGHT FOR KOMIATUM

ALTHOUGH there seemed little chance of the Japanese seizing the initiative again in the Salamaua campaign they were defending their natural fortresses stubbornly. By costly and frustrating experience the Australians had learnt that it was easy enough to pin the enemy down but quite another problem to shift them, and that frontal attacks on high features like Mount Tambu were unprofitable. The Australians had also realised that to surround an enemy force did not mean its extermination because small parties could filter through gaps in the positions occupied by the besiegers who could not possibly maintain a continuous line in the dense jungle. Severing the various lines of communication, however, did lead to disorganisation of the defenders and would probably cause their withdrawal and the abandonment of equipment.

By early August plans were already well advanced for the encirclement of Komiatum and Mount Tambu. In order to achieve Brigadier Moten's intention to place the 2/6th Battalion on Komiatum Ridge north of Mount Tambu and thereby to cut the main Salamaua-Komiatum track, patrols from the 17th Brigade were seeking the most suitable route to Komiatum Ridge. Moten realised that he must block not only Komiatum Ridge but also the other two ridges which led north and north-east from Mount Tambu. On the northern ridge—Davidson Ridge—he intended to use a company of the 2/5th Battalion and he hoped that Coane Force which was responsible for blocking the north-eastern ridge—Scout Ridge—would in fact do so.

On 6th August General Savige walked to Moten's headquarters on the Bui Eo Creek. He agreed with Moten's tentative plans but told him that the incoming battalion from the 29th Brigade could be used on Davidson Ridge in place of the company from the 2/5th. Moten's pleasure at this unexpected addition to his fighting strength was increased when Savige gave him the first call on Colonel Jackson's Allied artillery. Moten said that he would require 10 days' reconnaissance before the attack could begin. Savige returned that night up the steep track to Guadagasal and issued an outline plan by which Komiatum Ridge would be secured and Mount Tambu isolated by an encircling movement of the 17th Brigade, Davidson Ridge occupied by the new battalion, and Roosevelt Ridge secured by Coane Force before the attack on Komiatum Ridge. The 15th Brigade would support the 17th by "offensive operations within their area".

A letter from Herring to Savige written on the 4th was carried by Colonel MacKechnie who had been at Herring's headquarters. In the course of it Herring wrote about the role of the new battalion and said that the use which Savige planned for it "would appear to make possible the further development of a line of communication from Tambu Bay. Its presence in the area should encourage Coane to make sure of getting Roosevelt Ridge, control of which is vital really to such line of communication and also to the proper deployment and effective use of your guns." Herring then urged Savige to "drive Coane on to the capture of Roosevelt Ridge even if the cost is higher than he cares about", adding:

> The question is whether you want me to make representations to higher authority with regard to any or all of the personalities concerned.

In his reply, on 7th August, Savige requested that Coane and Major Roosevelt be relieved. Savige now had confidence in MacKechnie if his health remained good, and also in the American "Executive Officer"—now Lieut-Colonel Harold G. Maison. On the 8th Savige sent a signal to Coane stating: "Our early occupation and control of Roosevelt Ridge of utmost importance irrespective of difficulties in achieving this vital objective . . . you will plan for this operation forthwith." He emphasised that the incoming battalion was not available for the attack on Roosevelt Ridge.

The 42nd Battalion (Lieut-Colonel Davidson[2]) was the one chosen from the 29th Brigade to move to Tambu Bay, and on 6th August the first flight of that battalion with a company of the 15th Battalion left Morobe for Nassau Bay in American barges. Already Captain Leu's[3] company of the 15th had moved from Morobe to Nassau Bay to relieve the remaining company of II/162nd Battalion, and by 6th August had moved to the Tambu Bay area where it took up a position on the left flank of the III/162nd Battalion on Scout Ridge.

After landing at Nassau Bay the men of the 42nd had a hot meal and a sleep, and began moving north at 1 p.m. Major Hodgman,[4] one of Savige's staff officers whom Colonel Wilton had sent hot foot to intercept the 42nd, was sitting on the track with his runner near the south arm of the Bitoi when the battalion came in sight. He informed Davidson that the battalion was on Coane's ration strength but under Moten for operations. Seeing the possibility of misunderstanding, Davidson asked Hodgman to suggest that the position be made clear to Coane.

On the way to Tambu Bay the 42nd passed Coane's headquarters at Salus. The meeting between Coane and Davidson at noon on the 8th was not over-cordial.[5] Coane had planned to use the Australian battalion to assist in the assault on Roosevelt Ridge. In justification of this he had Savige's signal of 1st August stating that the battalion "will be placed under your operational control". Savige, however, had undoubtedly been influenced by a portion of Herring's letter of the 4th which said: "I do not like putting the battalion under Coane in view of the stickiness which has been apparent in his command. Stickiness as you know is something that is catching especially by troops who haven't yet been engaged in battle." He had therefore sent Coane a signal at 11.55 a.m. on the 8th

---
[2] Lt-Col Hon C. W. Davidson, OBE, QX33882. (1st AIF: Lt 42 Bn.) CO 42 Bn 1942-44. MHR since 1946. Postmaster-General since 1956, and Minister for the Navy 1956-58. Sugarcane farmer; of Mackay, Qld; b. Brisbane, 14 Sep 1897.
[3] Capt R. S. Leu, QX50119; 15 Bn. Department manager; of Brisbane; b. Toowoomba, Qld, 22 Oct 1908.
[4] Lt-Col S. T. Hodgman, OBE, TX2003. 2/12 Bn; GSO1 (Ops) I Corps 1944-45. Bank officer; of Hobart; b. Burnie, Tas, 18 Nov 1907.
[5] A lively account of this meeting and the battalion's reception at Tambu Bay is contained in S. E. Benson, *The Story of the 42 Aust Inf Bn* (1952), pp. 48-9.

stating that "troops of 29th Aust Inf Bde are not repeat not available to you for operational purposes". Because he was moving his headquarters forward to Tambu Bay at this time Coane did not receive this signal, and another similar one sent late that night, until the next day. Savige had to send two more signals on the 9th requesting an acknowledgment of the change in orders before he heard anything from Coane who, even late on the 9th, had not received any of Savige's signals. Coane at length replied to Savige's several signals on 9th August that he would do everything possible to accomplish his mission, but because all high points on Roosevelt Ridge were heavily fortified each one would have to be taken in turn by coordinated artillery and infantry attack and this would be a slow process. However, he did intend to attack one strongpoint on 11th August if the 42nd Battalion was then in position to protect the left flank.

Marching overland and also conveyed by barge the 42nd Battalion arrived at Boisi on 10th August. On 9th August Moten placed a company of the 15th Battalion under Davidson's command, and also one medium machine-gun platoon and one infantry company of the 2/5th (Captain Cameron's) to assist the 42nd "in patrol activities, defensive preparations and the routine matters which troops usually acquire in the bitter school of practical experience". He emphasised that occupation of the ridge due north of Mount Tambu must be done secretly and defensive preparations carefully concealed and camouflaged. No patrolling was to proceed farther west than Buiwarfe Creek.[6] Aggressive action would be taken by offensive patrolling. With this letter came a copy of Moten's operation instruction of the same date, from which Davidson learnt that his battalion would defend "ridge east of Komiatum Ridge and line of communication Mount Tambu to Boisi".

At 3 p.m. on the 10th Davidson learnt that it was essential for his forward companies to be on the vital Davidson Ridge by the morning of 11th August. At dawn on the 11th the battalion was on the move. The climb from Boisi to the summit of Scout Ridge was a hard introduction to the battle area. Davidson ordered his troops to "travel light" with the result that tin hats and respirators were discarded, blankets and towels were cut in halves and all extra clothes (except a pullover and socks) were dumped;[7] the men's packs were still heavy because three days' rations were carried. By 12th August the battalion was dug in with two companies near the junction of Davidson and Scout Ridges, and two on Davidson Ridge.

Opposite Moten in the Mount Tambu-Goodview Junction-Komiatum area Colonel Araki, the commander of the *66th Regiment*, was dissatisfied with two of his battalion commanders. Early in August he relieved Lieut-Colonel Matsui and Major Kimura of their commands of *I* and *III Battalions* respectively; their places were taken by Captain Numada (*I/66th Battalion*) and Captain Okamoto (*III/66th Battalion*) both from *Eighth Area Army Headquarters* at Rabaul. By 8th August the *III/238th Battalion* of the *41st Division* had landed at Salamaua from small craft,

---
[6] Named after Lieut-Colonel G. R. Warfe.
[7] Remarkably enough respirators were still carried together with tin hats and gas capes. Troops usually rapidly discarded tin hats and respirators but kept the gas cape which gave better protection against the weather than the groundsheet.

a month after leaving Wewak. Thus the *51st Division* had now been reinforced with one battalion of the *20th Division (1/80th)* and one of the *41st*.

"I am terribly anxious to ease the air commitment as quickly as possible," wrote Herring to Savige early in August, "and I know you will do all you can in this regard. Plans for future operations are proceeding and I hope they will be able to get under way on time. Meanwhile you are assisting mightily by drawing reinforcements into your area." The only alternative to air dropping was the development of a supply route from Tambu Bay to the battle area, and this was becoming more and more a vital necessity as the air force began to concentrate on its task in the rapidly approaching offensive.

The plan for the big offensive in the Lae-Markham Valley area was issued to the relevant commanders on 9th August in the form of an operation order. The intention was that New Guinea Force in conjunction with the Fifth Air Force and U.S. Naval Task Force 76 would seize the Lae-Nadzab area with a view to establishing airfields. Savige found the tasks of the 3rd Division listed under "subsidiary operations". He would continue operations for the capture of Salamaua, patrol in the Markham area, and transfer control of the Watut Valley to the 7th Division at a time to be notified.

On 9th August Savige signalled Herring that he was anxiously awaiting a reply to his signal about Coane. Herring discussed the problem with General Sutherland, MacArthur's Chief of Staff, and next day Herring signalled MacArthur "now that guns under central control with Jackson as CRA Coane merely sits as an extra link between Savige and Maison who virtually commands 162nd U.S. Regiment less one battalion". Herring continued that this was most unsatisfactory and dangerous, and that he endorsed a request from Savige that MacKechnie relieve Coane. He emphasised that "new commander should feel completely free from all control 41 U.S. Div in operational matters".

At Savige's headquarters Colonel Jackson heard rumours of possible changes. "Say, General, that's highly political and mighty explosive," he said. The situation did indeed have such possibilities, but MacArthur supported the Australian leaders, and ordered that Coane should report to General Fuller at Rockhampton to resume his normal duties, and MacKechnie should resume command of the 162nd Regiment, which would be detached from the 41st Division and henceforth be under operational control of New Guinea Force.[8]

---

[8] On 22nd July Fuller had relieved MacKechnie of his command, a serious outcome for a regular army officer with 26 years' service. Fuller had charged MacKechnie with ordering the 1/162nd Battalion inland from Nassau Bay before clearing out all enemy forces there; relinquishing command of his force and so failing to protect American interests; returning from Napier without Fuller's knowledge; reporting that there was confusion in the command status, whereas in Fuller's opinion there was no such thing; and finally with permitting the Australians to "euchre" him out of his command and carry out orders without reference to Fuller.
All Fuller's charges could be answered by MacKechnie's belief that he was actually under Australian command, a not unreasonable assumption in the circumstances. After a more dispassionate talk with his irate general, MacKechnie found the charges against him reduced to three: failure or inability to keep Fuller advised of all details of operations, carrying out Savige's instructions to the letter without questioning them or objecting to them and without reference to Fuller, and finally an undiplomatic and facetious signal MacKechnie had sent to Fuller about the numerous conflicting orders he had received. As a result of their discussions Fuller had agreed at the end of July to send MacKechnie to be Executive Officer of Coane Force.

Savige's plan for the encirclement and capture of the Komiatum-Mount Tambu-Goodview Junction area involved movement on the entire divisional front. First move would be made by the Americans on 13th August —the capture of Roosevelt Ridge. On D-day the 17th Brigade would capture the Komiatum-Mount Tambu-Goodview Junction area, and next day the 15th Brigade would attack the Erskine Creek area and advance east to the Komiatum Track to prevent enemy movement north or south along the track.

Since the failure of the attack on Roosevelt Ridge at the beginning of August the II and III Battalions of the 162nd Regiment, assisted by the Papuan company, had been observing and patrolling south and west of Roosevelt Ridge. The II/162nd Battalion was clinging to positions on the southern slopes of Roosevelt Ridge and the III/162nd Battalion was on the eastern slopes of Scout Ridge about 500 yards from the ridge junction. Patrols found plenty of evidence that the Japanese were extending their defences. An observation patrol post near the western end of Roosevelt Ridge saw an officer wearing white gloves visit the Japanese lines at the ridge junction. The Japanese came to attention at his approach, and thereafter increased the number of barricades in front of their positions. Another patrol from Scout Ridge found the Japanese building more machine-gun pill-boxes near the ridge junction.

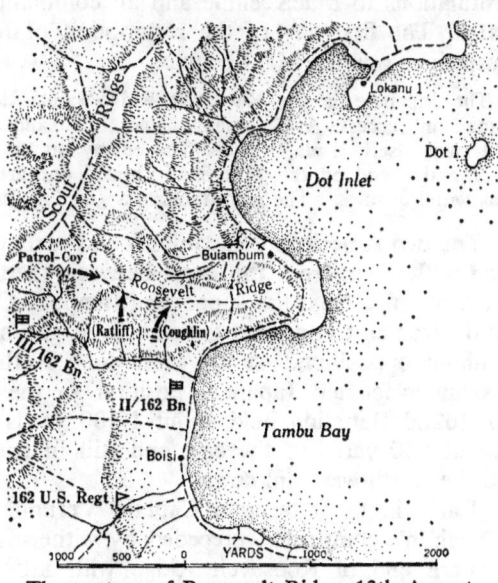

The capture of Roosevelt Ridge, 13th August

On 12th August Lieut-Colonel Maison issued orders for the attack on Roosevelt Ridge: the II Battalion, under Major Lowe, on the right flank would make "the main effort", while the III Battalion on the left, now under Major Jack E. Morris, who had replaced Roosevelt, would support II Battalion. On gaining the crest of the ridge the Americans would exploit to the east and north-west to its junction with main Scout Ridge. Zero hour would be 9 a.m. on 13th August.

A preliminary move began on 12th August when a patrol from the II Battalion penetrated enemy defences on Roosevelt Ridge and established an outpost position on the crest of the ridge about 2,000 yards northwest from Boisi. Between 6 p.m. on 12th August and 8 a.m. next day the enemy made several attacks from the west, but the Americans clung to their position.

At 7 a.m. on 13th August the artillery opened on the enemy positions in front of the attacking companies of the II Battalion (Captain Coughlin's on the right and Captain Ratliff's on the left). Two hours later it shifted to the right and left flanks of these companies. Ratliff's company then made the main attack on the left towards the enemy position on the crest east of the ridge junction, while Coughlin's company made a diversionary attack towards the next high ground to the east. Soon after the attack started the men in the outpost attacked the enemy opposing Ratliff's company and assisted it to reach the crest of the ridge. Boxed in on the flanks by the artillery barrage both companies reached their objectives. Enemy opposition during the attacks came from bunkers and well dug in but isolated positions. By nightfall the two companies were occupying high knolls about 500 yards apart and commanding a small Japanese force on a knoll between them. Coughlin's company was about 800 yards from the coast, and the enemy were still occupying the north-west position of the ridge from Ratliff's position to the ridge junction. During the day 39 Japanese were killed, and there were 25 American casualties. The Americans' success on 13th August delighted Savige who sent his congratulations to MacKechnie and all commanders and troops who participated. The first day of the resumption of his command was indeed an auspicious one for MacKechnie.

The Japanese in the Roosevelt Ridge-Scout Ridge area were worried by this American success. At Salamaua General Nakano's commander of the defence of Salamaua itself, Ikeda, wrote: "The enemy on the Boisi front have for some days been active and on the 13th finally seized our artillery positions. The army force has withdrawn. . . . The navy mountain gun unit has become the front line."

The two American companies found early on the 14th that the Japanese had withdrawn from the knoll between them during the night. Preceded by heavy fire from the supporting weapons Coughlin was able to advance 300 yards east and seize the next high ground after a 20-minute advance without opposition. At the same time Ratliff was advancing through a hastily evacuated Japanese position to the north-west. By midday the II/162nd Battalion held about 1,100 yards of Roosevelt Ridge, leaving about 500 yards of the east end still in enemy hands and the situation to the north-west unknown.

Early in the afternoon Captain Vernon F. Townsend's and Captain Coughlin's companies, preceded by withering supporting fire, reached the eastern end of Roosevelt Ridge with little opposition. By 3 p.m. the battalion controlled all Roosevelt Ridge from the sea inland to Ratliff's forward patrol, still advancing to the north-west about 2,000 yards inland from the seaward end of Roosevelt Ridge. This patrol was forced to halt at 4 p.m. by what MacKechnie's sitrep termed "extreme over-extension". While it was digging in it reported that the enemy was in a position about 200 yards farther up the ridge. Captain Colvert's company from the III/162nd Battalion was then sent to hold the position gained by the patrol, but after a short advance was pinned down by heavy fire and at 5.30 p.m. dug in for the night.

A day of triumph for the Americans, particularly the II/162nd Battalion, saw the capture of Roosevelt Ridge and the killing of about 120 Japanese, mainly by fire from supporting weapons. An accurate count, however, could never be made as many Japanese had perished in the holes, tunnels and underground caves which the artillery and other supporting weapons had blasted. The stench from the whole area was terrible. A feature of the attack had been the use made of the Bofors anti-aircraft guns in the Boisi area during the infantry's approach march before the attack. The guns had poured accurate and sustained fire on the enemy positions and had proved most effective against pill-boxes.

> At about 1315 (wrote the 41st Division's historian) the jungles north, south and west of Roosevelt Ridge shook and shivered to the sustained blast. The mountains and ridges threw the echo back and forth, down and out, and the quiet whitecapped sea to the east, ringing the outer third of Roosevelt Ridge, grew dark as it received the eruption of earth and steel on that stricken shoulder of land. Scores of guns—75-mm howitzers, Aussie 25-pounders, 20-mms, Bofors, light and heavy machine-guns, even small arms—had opened up simultaneously on the enemy-held ridge. A score or more Allied fighters and bombers had swooped low to strafe its dome and tons of bombs released from the B-24's and B-25's fell straight and true, to detonate, shatter, rip and tear and to deliver certain death at that moment on an August afternoon. Those who watched from the beach saw the top fourth of the ridge lift perceptibly into the air and then fall into the waiting sea. In a scant twenty minutes all that remained of the objective was a denuded, redly scarred hill over which infantrymen already were clambering, destroying what remained of a battered and stunned enemy.[9]

On 15th August MacKechnie reported to Savige that he would try to capture the ridge junction, but did not consider an advance north or west possible or advisable until the third battalion rejoined the regiment; the effective fighting strength of his two battalions was 55 officers and 620 men with an average daily evacuation of 26. Savige agreed and on 15th August ordered that the present American positions should be held and the forces regrouped to place one company in reserve. To MacKechnie he wrote:

> I have implicit faith in your judgment as well as that of Maison and Taylor. I hope, and believe, that we shall push the Jap beyond Komiatum within a few days. This will give you Taylor Battalion for your command and will achieve my aim in placing all US troops under American command which you know is my desire. Keep contact with 42 Aust Bn on your left flank.

For the success of the attack on Mount Tambu much depended on the patrols of the 17th Brigade to Komiatum Ridge. From patrol reports and interrogations of native carriers recently deserted from the enemy Moten deduced that the Japanese were in the habit of supplying their Mount Tambu defences every third day. He hoped that, if he could block this supply route, the Japanese position would become desperate by the

---

[9] W. F. McCartney, *The Jungleers: A History of the 41st Infantry Division*, p. 63.

third day and force them to abandon their defences. He would therefore try to hem in the Japanese on Mount Tambu on the day when their rations arrived, give his troops time to consolidate, and then expect the hungry Japanese to break out on the third day.

Much reconnaissance, however, had to be carried out before the dim outlines of the plan could be filled in. As mentioned, two three-man patrols from the 2/6th Battalion led by Sergeant Hedderman and Lieutenant Johnson had set out on the 5th. Hedderman's patrol had returned at 2 p.m. on 7th August having moved east from Coconuts[1] and across the Komiatum Track about 600 yards south of Komiatum, where the men spent a day observing a large amount of enemy movement. Hedderman reported that the country was very rugged and steep but not impassable. Johnson's patrol returned at 4 p.m. next day having reached the Komiatum Track near the old village of Komiatum about 250 yards north of the junction of the Komiatum and Mount Tambu Tracks. After crossing very rough and dense country, which he also reported was passable, Johnson found two positions suitable for occupation by troops: one an open kunai knoll, commanding the Mule Track and capable of accommodating two companies, and another, commanding the Komiatum Track, capable of accommodating a battalion. On his second day out Johnson had been ambushed on a spur to the west of the Mule Track but had escaped without casualties. Like Hedderman he reported much enemy movement. Komiatum Ridge near the old village had been bared by bombing, and thus had fields of fire already cleared. Savige now resolved to see the country for himself and discuss plans with his local commanders. He spent the night of 9th-10th August at Moten's headquarters, and on the 10th the two commanders viewed the country from every vantage point on their way to meet Wood at Drake's O.P. There Wood told them of the difficulties encountered by his patrols in negotiating the gorge of the Buirali—only 1,200 yards wide as the bullet flies, but patrols setting out east finished up at all points of the compass. Wood sent for Captain Laver whose company was responsible for the patrolling. Laver explained on the ground just what his difficulties were but was hopeful that the tireless Hedderman would find a better route. Savige arranged to meet Wood at the same spot on his way back from the 15th Brigade's area in two days.

On 11th August Hedderman and the battalion Intelligence officer, Lieutenant Marsden,[2] left to make a thorough reconnaissance of the Coconuts area which had been finally selected as a suitable supply base and assembly area for the forthcoming operation. Next morning seven men from Laver's company at Drake's O.P. cut a track from the company area to the Coconuts, and the first carrier line went forward. That afternoon Hedderman set out yet again, to define more clearly the route from Coconuts to

---

[1] Not to be confused with the Coconuts features on the north end of Bobdubi Ridge.
[2] Capt H. McL. Marsden, VX7586; 2/6 Bn. Bank officer; of Melbourne; b. Bridgewater, Tas, 31 Dec 1915.

the area on Komiatum Ridge selected for occupation, known as Laver's Knoll.³

Moten's other three battalions were also busy patrolling and skirmishing. On 7th August the enemy had driven back the forward platoon of the 2/5th on Walpole's Track, but after an accurate mortar bombardment the position was reoccupied. The I/162nd Battalion was harassing enemy supply routes to Mount Tambu from the coast, preparing ambushes at known water points and mortaring enemy positions. The 42nd Battalion on Davidson and Scout Ridges exchanged its first shots with the enemy on 12th August.

Conditions on these ridges were worse than the troops of the 42nd had imagined. Lack of sleep and patrolling in enemy territory were new experiences. Water was scarce and at least half an hour away from each company—a normal problem for troops occupying ridges and knolls. It was more than a week before the battalion received rations in sufficient quantities to be barely adequate. The troops' thoughts turned continually towards food and their hunger was not alleviated by stories of steak and eggs being taken to the Americans on Roosevelt Ridge or by stories from Boisi about fresh potatoes, fruit, fruit juices and other tasties which the Americans were said to be enjoying there. After the first week a little tea, sugar, milk, margarine and jam arrived.

Early on the morning of 12th August an Australian sergeant in charge of a party of natives working for the I/162nd Battalion reported that one of his natives had noticed a fresh track crossing the track from Boisi to Mount Tambu on the lower eastern slope of Scout Ridge. A small patrol followed the new track to the south and south-east and saw a Japanese force which it estimated as a company, with weapons, full equipment and camouflage, moving along the track. Colonel Taylor then sent Lieutenant Messec and his platoon to follow the enemy force, which seemed to be making for Bitoi Ridge. Their experiences will be described later.

On the left flank the 15th Brigade was getting what rest it could. The 58th/59th Battalion and the 2/3rd Independent Company certainly needed a spell but they were lasting better than their enemy—the *I/80th Battalion*, parts of the *66th* and *115th Regiments* and some marines. Long service in the tropics had sapped the fighting spirits of such units as the *115th Regiment*, but even in the more recently arrived units disillusionment was apparent. Captured diaries indicated that the Japanese soldiers now doubted their invincibility. They complained of the food, the rain, malaria, bombing and their hopeless position. A private of the *I/80th Battalion* wrote:

> The only Unit Commander remaining went forward but no word from him in a week. We don't know whether he is dead or alive. Two section leaders, corporals,

³ At this stage most companies were about half strength. Platoons with good men in them and with leaders such as Hedderman got results. Average patrols produced casualties but often no worthwhile results. An experienced company commander who had led many patrols in this fight later described a regrettable but necessary method of achieving patrol results. "All of our patrols which were likely to run into trouble were made up time and time again with the few really good men at patrolling. As these men were killed, wounded or evacuated sick the numbers of men available became less and less and the 'pitcher' went to the well again and again."

were both killed. We are on half rations. After twilight we cover the trench so no light can show and cook our food. We eat in pitch darkness and don't know what we are eating. It's all gritty.

Patrols from the 15th Brigade probed the Japanese areas from 7th August. There were several skirmishes but patrolling, mainly defensive, was not Hammer's idea of winning the war. He planned to drive the enemy from Bobdubi Ridge and then harass the Komiatum Track. He considered that his first tactical move would be the capture of the Coconuts followed by the capture of the Salamaua-Bobdubi and Komiatum Track junctions. Then would come the capture of Kunai Spur south of the Francisco and of important features north of the river. On 9th August Hammer called his commanding officers together and issued his orders for the capture of the Coconuts and the track junctions. He had not then received Savige's order of 9th August that the 15th Brigade would attack the Erskine Creek area and exploit east to the Komiatum Track.

At Dierke's O.P. on the 10th Hammer met Savige and outlined his dispositions and plans. He pointed out that a successful attack would secure the north flank of the divisional area and release troops for operations elsewhere on the brigade front. Savige, however, considered that active operations in the Erskine Creek-Komiatum Track area on the day before the 17th Brigade's attack on Mount Tambu would help Moten in his difficult operations. Hammer stuck to his guns and pointed out the difficulties, largely of terrain, which would be caused by any regrouping to deliver his main attack in the Erskine Creek area. He doubted the physical possibility of regrouping in the south in the time available and considered that Savige's requirements would be met by the capture of the Coconuts and subsequent exploitation to the Komiatum-Salamaua-Bobdubi track junctions.

Savige heeded the brigadier and deferred his decision until 11th August after he had completed a reconnaissance from Ambush Knoll and Mortar Knoll. Finally he decided that any regrouping of Hammer's units might result in a half-cocked attack on the southern flank, whereas there was every chance of success on the north. He approved Hammer's plan for an attack on the Coconuts two days before Moten's attack, provided some pressure was applied to the Erskine Creek area not later than two days after Moten launched his attack.

This trip by Savige into the forward area was an arduous one for a man of 53. He had undertaken it not only to see the country for himself but also to renew his acquaintance with his old brigade—the 17th—and to have a close look at the 15th Brigade, particularly the 58th/59th Battalion about which he had received so many critical reports. The sight of the well-loved general toiling along the rugged tracks with his pack up and observing the battle area from the forward observation posts gave a great boost to the spirits of the men. As he moved through the units tin pannikins of tea were offered in such numbers that he could drink no more. He was pleased with the appearance of the 58th/59th, of which he was Honorary Colonel, and told them of the great value of their effort. "When I met Wood on my return journey next day, the 12th," wrote Savige later, "he had a grin on his face like a Cheshire cat and I knew he had taken the trick. He then informed me that the way had been found, the route had been blazed, and work had started on cutting a track along which to carry stores to the start-line."

As the result of the excellent work performed by his patrols Moten was able to issue his orders on 12th August: the 17th Brigade would drive the enemy north of the general line Davidson Ridge-Komiatum-Ambush Knoll; D-day would be 15th August (but was subsequently changed to 16th August). The 17th Brigade would encircle and destroy their enemy by capturing Komiatum Ridge, and at the same time maintaining a constant pressure on the enemy from the south and holding Davidson Ridge. Moten hoped by these means to cut the enemy's line of communication and thus prevent his supply, reinforcement or escape.

The main task of attacking and capturing the south end of Komiatum Ridge was allotted to the 2/6th. The 42nd Battalion, assisted by companies from the 2/5th and the 15th, would hold Davidson Ridge, prevent the enemy being reinforced or supplied from the east, support the 2/6th with machine-gun fire, and protect the track from Boisi to Mount Tambu. The I/162nd Battalion would harass the enemy on Mount Tambu and, "at the appropriate time", destroy them. The 2/5th would also harass the enemy and would attack and destroy them in the Goodview Junction area "at the appropriate time when the enemy is weakened by encirclement". One company (from the 2/7th Battalion) would contain the enemy in the Orodubi area.

Hammer, on 11th August, issued his final orders for the attack on the Coconuts on 14th August, and the Salamaua-Bobdubi-Komiatum track junctions two days later. To precede the attack he requested an hour and a half of heavy bombing, which would be supplemented by 600 rounds from the Australian 25-pounders, 600 mortar bombs and eight belts each for six machine-guns. Captain Barr's company of the 2/7th Battalion—a total of 88 men—would attack North Coconuts from the west; a composite company of 60 men led by Major Walker would attack South Coconuts from the east and south; and Lieutenant Lewin's platoon of the 2/3rd Independent Company—now reinforced to 47 men—would cut the enemy line of communication along the Salamaua-Bobdubi track and prevent reinforcement or withdrawal.

Barr and his platoon commanders on 12th August climbed unobserved almost into North Coconuts and were able to form their plan for the attack with simplicity. To the south Captain Rooke,[4] on a stealthy patrol, found a track which led him and his section leaders to within 10 yards of the enemy positions on the Coconuts. At a conference with his commanders on 13th August Major Picken estimated that not more than an enemy company was holding Coconut Ridge.

At 9.20 a.m. on 14th August nine Liberators began circling Coconut Ridge. The artillery immediately began registering the targets and 10

---

[4] Capt A. N. Rooke, VX42593; 2/7 Bn. Accountant; of Ivanhoe, Vic; b. Heidelberg, Vic, 9 Mar 1915.

minutes later the first three Liberator aircraft released their bombs. These bombs, accurately dropped by the Liberators which were soon joined by 13 more Liberators and 7 Fortresses, had an annihilating effect. Through the dust which cloaked the ridge, trees, logs and rubbish could be seen erupting into the air. As the big bombers droned away an ominous report to the effect that 100 Japanese were standing to in South Coconuts, was received from an observation post.

Forty minutes after the beginning of the aerial bombardment, the artillery, mortars and machine-guns began to plaster Coconut Ridge to cover the forward move of the attacking troops who, during the air strike, had been 600 yards from the ridge. At 11.40 a.m. the artillery switched to the area of the Salamaua - Bobdubi - Komiatum track junctions.

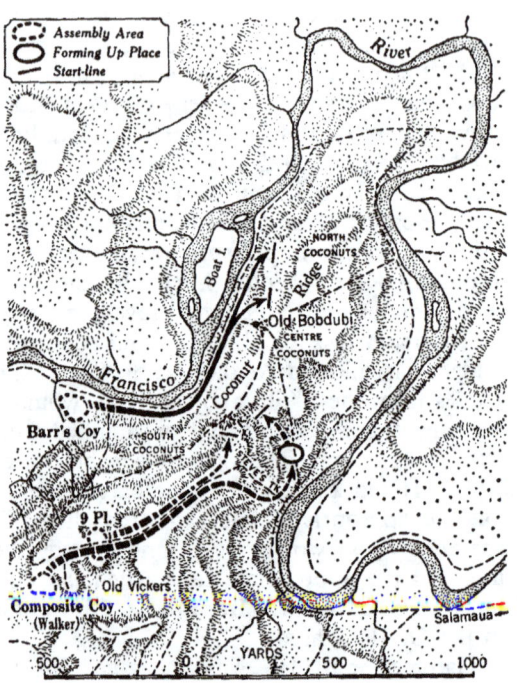

The 2/7th Battalion's attack on Coconuts, 14th August

Under cover of well-laid mortar smoke, Barr's company formed up with two platoons forward. Ahead, Barr found that the air strike had blown away all cover and previously reconnoitred lines of approach. The slope was now a cliff face of loose earth and rubble up which the troops had to crawl on hands and knees. The leadership of Barr and his platoon commanders and the determination of their men enabled the two platoons to reach the crest of the ridge at the positions previously planned. Sharp fighting ensued before they finally cleared out the Japanese by 2.45 p.m. The position captured consisted of two pill-boxes connected to weapon-pits by an intricate system of underground crawl trenches. Enemy fire from South Coconuts which had not yet been captured was responsible for most of the Australian casualties. Barr, moving throughout the action with his forward platoon, was mortally wounded by this fire. Lieutenant Walker[5] and Sergeant Tennant[6] were killed. Lieutenant Fietz

---

[5] Lt L. G. Walker, VX5870; 2/7 Bn. Farm worker; of Briagolong, Vic; b. Maffra, Vic, 12 Apr 1917. Killed in action 14 Aug 1943.

[6] Sgt D. A. Tennant, VX34000; 2/7 Bn. Forest ranger; of Launching Place, Vic; b. Berwick on Tweed, England, 21 Nov 1905. Killed in action 14 Aug 1943.

then took command and continued mopping up and exploiting to Centre Coconuts where most of the defenders had been buried by the air strike.

Meanwhile Major Walker's force had been unsuccessful. Rooke's platoon approached from the east, struggling over a mass of branches and trees smashed by the bombardment. When below South Coconuts it came under heavy machine-gun fire from three machine-guns only a few yards away. Rooke sent the left forward section led by Corporal Berry[7] round the left flank. It advanced up the steep slope swept by very heavy enemy fire until within 20 yards of the crest where it was showered with grenades. All except two men were wounded or killed, but Berry, although wounded, clung to the ground he had gained and sent a request to his platoon commander for more grenades. As the position gained by the section was untenable it was withdrawn. At this stage Rooke was wounded by a grenade.

A second platoon of Walker's group, attacking from Old Vickers, was pinned by heavy fire from earthwork bunkers. During the two operations, crowned on the north with success and on the south with failure, the 2/7th had lost 9 killed and 17 wounded.[8]

While this attack was in progress Lewin's platoon moved down Steve's Track, dug in by 11.30 a.m. astride the Bobdubi Track on the enemy line of communication to the Coconuts, and cut their signal wire. At 1.15 p.m. the platoon killed one Japanese out of a party of five moving towards Salamaua; half an hour later two Japanese out of seven were killed going the same way, and at 4.15 p.m. one more Japanese was killed from a party of four travelling towards Bobdubi. Those who escaped Lewin's ambush panicked and went bush, leaving weapons and equipment behind. Although the numbers were not great this action could not but have a very unsettling effect on the enemy on both sides of the ambush. During the next two days pressure by patrols and harassing mortar fire were maintained against the enemy in South Coconuts, and early in the morning of 17th August patrols found it unoccupied.

Again and again in the jungle it was found that encirclement did not mean destruction for those encircled. Dense growth and dark nights were the allies of those seeking to escape. So it happened on this occasion. Later investigations showed that the enemy had laid signal wire due east to the Francisco and, using the wire as a guide, had withdrawn from South Coconuts after darkness on the night of 16th-17th August. The whole of Coconut Ridge and the northern portion of Bobdubi Ridge were now in Australian hands.

Meanwhile, in the main battle area, the 2/6th was almost ready for the attack. Colonel Wood's plan allotted the task of capturing the selected spot on Komiatum Ridge (Laver's Knoll) to Captain Laver's and Captain Edgar's[9] companies under Laver's command. Another company was to

---

[7] Cpl C. S. Berry, MM, TX5314; 2/7 Bn. Orchard worker; of Exeter, Tas; b. Supply Bay, Tas, 25 Sep 1912.
[8] Lieutenant R. H. Dawson had supported the southern attack by again using the captured Japanese mountain gun to shell South Coconuts from Old Vickers.
[9] Maj A. G. S. Edgar, VX5140; 2/6 Bn. Jackeroo; of Hamilton, Vic; b. Melville Forest, Vic, 27 Nov 1914.

guard the line of communication and the fourth to carry supplies to the knoll. Reducing equipment to a minimum the troops would wear the clothes in which they stood, and each would carry his weapon and ammunition, pack, water-bottle filled, groundsheet or gas cape, pullover, spare pair of socks, mosquito lotion, four days' operational rations and half a mess set. The attacking companies and the one protecting the supply route would each carry 7 picks, 14 shovels and 10 machetes, while the company carrying supplies forward would carry 10 machetes. Each rifleman would carry 150 rounds, each Bren gunner 200 rounds and each Tommy-gunner 200 rounds. All troops would carry two 4-seconds grenades, and twelve 7-seconds grenades would be carried for the grenade discharger.

By 3 p.m. on the 15th Laver Force and Price's company were in position due west of Laver's Knoll near the Mule Track. Since they were in danger of being observed by the Japanese on Komiatum Ridge Laver decided not to cross the Mule Track until early on the 16th.

On 13th August Colonel Jackson had issued the artillery's operation order stating that the guns would support the operations of the 162nd Regiment, 17th Brigade and the 15th Brigade with timed concentrations, harassing fire and defensive fire.[10] Separate arrangements for the attack on Roosevelt Ridge had been made between MacKechnie and the commander of the American artillery in the Tambu Bay area. Most artillery units were suffering from accurate counter-battery fire, particularly Thwaites' battery of the 2/6th Field Regiment which was shelled on 12th August. The five observation posts manned by members of Thwaites' battery—Captain McElroy[1] and Lieutenants Lord, Dawson, Halstead[2] and Scotter[3]—extending from Old Vickers south to Wells O.P. and east to the western extremity of Roosevelt Ridge, did their best to support the infantry and arrange the salvation of their own and the American batteries by directing counter-battery fire. These observation post officers formed a pool and were allotted on call to guns not already committed to a task. For the attacks by the Australian brigades Dawson would be forward observation officer with the 15th Brigade, Lieutenants Melvin and Nelson from the 218th American Artillery Battalion would be with the 2/6th and 2/5th Battalions respectively, while Halstead would be with the 42nd Battalion. As usual the mountain battery had played its part. Heavy artil-

---

[10] The artillery units now under command of RAA 3rd Division were:
  205 US FA Bn (105-mm howitzer)
  218 US FA Bn (75-mm howitzer)
  11 Aust Fd Bty (25-pdr)
  1 Aust Mtn Bty less 1 section (3.7-inch howitzer)
  209 US CA(AA) Bn (40-mm Bofors)
  162 Lt AA Bty (40-mm Bofors)

[1] Capt J. L. McElroy, NX12395. 2/6 Fd Regt; Spotter 1 Naval Bombardment Gp 1944-45. Clerk; of Neutral Bay, NSW; b. Picton, NSW, 11 Apr 1917.

[2] Lt T. T. Halstead, NX79766; 2/6 Fd Regt. Company secretary; of Double Bay, NSW; b. Sydney, 21 Aug 1911.

[3] Lt G. K. Scotter, NX17903; 2/6 Fd Regt. Bank officer; of Sydney; b. Drummoyne, NSW, 13 Apr 1917.

lery support was the more necessary because the air strike planned for 15th August was cancelled because of bad weather.[4]

By nightfall on 15th August Moten's four battalions were ready. At 6 a.m. on 16th August Laver Force, with Laver's own company leading, crossed the start-line. Ten minutes later the guns began to fire on Komiatum Ridge and Laver's Knoll, and in half an hour they fired over 500 shells. Then the forward troops scrambled up the precipitous slope of Komiatum Ridge and arrived at their objective. The enemy, about a platoon, was surprised and fled leaving only one of their number dead. Laver Force immediately dug in and Laver sent Lieutenant Johnson's platoon to occupy Johnson's Knoll 150 yards to the south where the Japanese again fled leaving four killed.

Price's company soon arrived, breathless but laden with ammunition and supplies. Sergeant White's team carrying the heavy 3-inch mortar and ammunition actually followed Laver's leading platoon to the objective, and the mortar was soon in action. After dumping their loads Price's men set out down the steep rugged slope for the Coconuts which they left with their second load at 2 p.m., arriving at Laver's Knoll again at 5 p.m.

Meanwhile Laver's patrols had been active to the east, north and south seeking enemy positions, cutting signal wire, and trying to find the troublesome mountain gun.[5] By 11.15 a.m. the Komiatum Track for 300 yards

---

[4] The artillery plan formulated by Colonel Jackson and Major Scarlett to suit Brigadier Moten's convenience called for the following program:

DAY		KOMIATUM			GOODVIEW			MOUNT TAMBU		
	Time	Guns	Rounds	Time	Guns	Rounds	Time	Guns	Rounds
D minus 1	1100-0400 D-day	105-mm	100(a)	0900-0500 D-day	75-mm	50	1600-1630	105-mm 75-mm 3.7 howitzer	300 120 60
	1200-0100 D-day	75-mm	50(b)						
D-day	Z plus 10 to Z plus 40	105-mm 75-mm 3.7 howitzer	300(c) 120(e) 100(d)	Z plus 55 to Z plus 75	75-mm	200	0800-1900	105-mm	200
	Z plus 40 to 1700 hrs	105-mm 75-mm	150(f) 150(g)						
	1700-0400 D plus 1	3.7 howitzer	100(j)						
D plus 1				0800-2200	75-mm	50	0815-0845	105-mm 75-mm 3.7 howitzer	300 100 60

(a) South end
(b) North end
(c) South end
(d) Centre
(e) North end; 75-mm slightly east of objective
(f) South end
(g) North end

DEFENSIVE FIRE

	Number of Rounds Each Call	Total Calls Available Each Day
Komiatum North	25	7
Komiatum South	28	7
Goodview	30	3

[5] This Japanese mountain gun and another which had both been harassing the 2/6th on Ambush Knoll and Sugarcane Ridge had actually been knocked out by 3-inch mortars a few days previously after the crews had boosted the secondary charges to get the necessary range. After the war Colonel Tanaka, staff officer in charge of operations of the *XVIII Army*, said that 10 bombs landed very close to the guns, destroyed them both and killed the artillery commander.

The gunners of the MMG's which were at Wells had been told by Price (then at Ambush Knoll) that some enemy officers dressed in white were moving among the Japanese positions. Machine-guns had fired on them. Again Tanaka confirmed that the Australian machine-guns from 200-300 yards killed two senior naval officers inspecting the forward positions.

north of Laver's Knoll was clear of enemy although areas south and south-east were still under sniper fire.

East of Laver's Knoll the 42nd Battalion had suffered its first casualties as it prepared for its part in the encirclement of the Japanese on Mount Tambu. On the night before the capture of Laver's Knoll the enemy had

Allied and enemy dispositions, Salamaua area, 15th August

occupied a position just below Captain Greer's[6] company on Scout Ridge. The track from the company position crossed a saddle then led up Mount Tambu through an enemy perimeter to other enemy positions farther up the mountain. An Australian patrol probing along this track was climbing the mountain slope when the Japanese fired on it. The Bren gunner,

---

[6] Capt F. R. M. Greer, DX907. 42 and 35 Bns. Schoolteacher; of Enoggera, Qld; b. Sydney, 12 Oct 1913.

Private Eddlestone,[7] answered the fire until he was killed. Private Read[8] from the "fostering" company of the 2/5th Battalion rolled into Eddlestone's place but fired only a few shots before he also was killed. Cursing and yelling Private Greene,[9] 6 feet 3 inches tall, charged from the patrol's position up the ridge into the Japanese position. With his Owen he killed several of the enemy before he himself was killed by machine-gun fire. In its first action the 42nd had lost three men killed but had killed at least ten Japanese.

During the morning of 16th August the 42nd had observed Laver Force digging in. In the late afternoon enemy movement to the west and south of Johnson's Knoll led Laver to expect an attack. When the tense and expectant machine-gunners on Davidson Ridge saw Laver's Very lights soaring into the air at 6.45 p.m., they immediately placed a curtain of defensive fire south of Johnson's Knoll. In this task the eight Vickers guns were aided by three 3-inch mortars.[1] Half an hour later Moten rang Davidson to say: "I've just had word from Laver. Your defensive fire came down immediately, it was right on the spot and completely broke up the Jap attack."

Soon after 7 p.m. more enemy movement was heard in the darkness to the west and south of Johnson's Knoll, but 40 minutes later Johnson repulsed the attack 30 yards from his position by using grenades and small arms fire. During the night intermittent firing and enemy movement continued south of Johnson's Knoll until, in the darkness at 4 a.m. on the 17th, Johnson's men dimly saw a large Japanese force moving straight down the track from the south and west. As with the first attack, this third attack was dispersed by the prompt reply of the 42nd to a call for defensive fire.

As Laver Force had been harassed by an enemy mountain gun, Moten asked Taylor to use his 81-mm mortars in an attempt to silence it. Observation was made by an infantry officer (Captain Cole[2]) on Davidson Ridge, fire was directed by phone through Colonel Taylor's switchboard over at least 25 miles of wire, and apparently not only the gun but a large ammunition dump was destroyed by the American mortars. The machine-gunners of the 42nd had the best hunting for the day when they picked off Japanese trying to put out a kunai fire started by mortar smoke bombs.

After dusk on the 17th the Japanese came again for the fourth time from south and west against Johnson's Knoll. This attack and three subsequent ones between 7 and 8.15 p.m. were all launched with great determination but stubborn defence and very accurate supporting fire broke up all the attacks.

---

[7] Pte G. H. Eddlestone, QX24758; 42 Bn. Mill worker; of Cordelia, Qld; b. Cordelia, 26 Jul 1922. Killed in action 16 Aug 1943.

[8] Pte L. H. Read, VX53096; 2/5 Bn. Farm hand; of Cobden, Vic; b. Terang, Vic, 4 Jul 1919. Killed in action 16 Aug 1943.

[9] Pte J. H. Greene, QX31358; 42 Bn. Truck driver; of Mount Christian, Qld; b. Cootamundra, NSW, 23 Aug 1910. Killed in action 16 Aug 1943.

[1] During this firing an enemy mountain gun fired on the 42nd but, apart from blowing Sergeant T. H. Schulze (of Rockhampton, Qld) into a trench, it did little damage.

[2] Maj R. B. Cole, MC, QX34023; 42 Bn. Bank officer; of Gladstone, Qld; b. Coolah, NSW, 25 Apr 1910.

The 18th was a quiet day for Laver Force, which was strengthened when a Vickers gun was carried up from Coconuts. At 3.35 p.m. a patrol from the 42nd Battalion arrived at Laver's Knoll, having encountered no enemy on the way. With the occupation of Laver's Knoll the enemy was surrounded in the Mount Tambu and Goodview Junction areas. His attempts to break out along Komiatum Ridge had been unsuccessful;

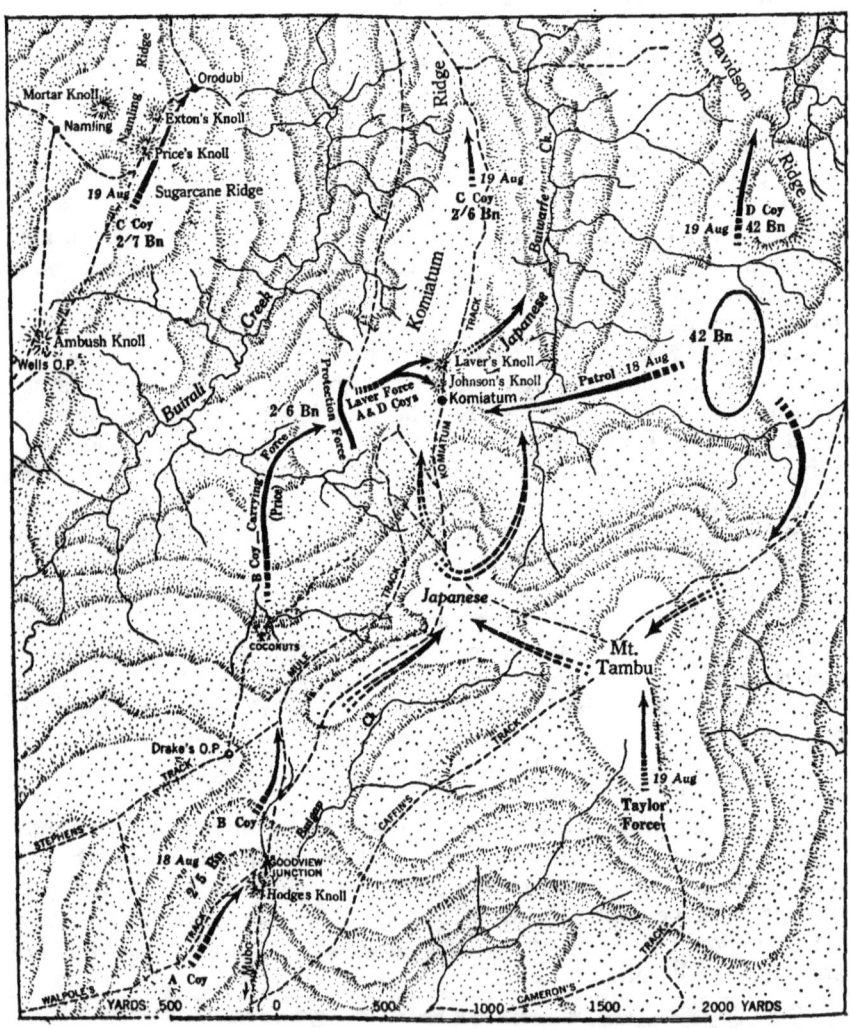

The capture of Komiatum and Mount Tambu by 17th Brigade, 16th-19th August

his position was growing desperate as pressure was maintained from all sides and artillery, mortars and machine-guns pounded his positions.

Meanwhile, the 2/5th Battalion had been ordered to capture the pillbox area south of Goodview Junction two nights before Laver's attack.

The task was allotted to Captain Bennett's company which set out a night late (on 16th-17th August) after Laver's Knoll had been captured. The attacking platoon followed tapes for a while but then became lost. Towards dawn it found itself on a ridge below which were a large number of the enemy. About 18 of them were killed but it was now light and the company withdrew under heavy fire.

At 4.30 p.m. on 17th August the stubbornly-defended Hodge's Knoll was found deserted and was immediately occupied by Bennett's company. To the north the junction of Stephens' and Mule Tracks was found unoccupied but the enemy was 40 yards along the track leading from the junction to Komiatum Spur. During the night a patrol from Bennett's company set out through Hodge's Knoll down to the Mule Track, then climbed a very steep track towards Mount Tambu where fire from pill-boxes stopped it. At first light another patrol moving cautiously up the Komiatum Track was also stopped by fire from the pill-boxes. During the day the Australians were unable to encircle the razor-back and could make no headway frontally. East of the junction of Stephens' and Mule Tracks another platoon found a Japanese position on a razor-back similar to the one confronting Bennett, and could make no progress.

At Port Moresby in mid-August, important decisions about the future of the command in the forward area were being made. On 15th August the Commander-in-Chief, General Blamey, with his Deputy Chief of the General Staff, General Berryman, arrived at General Herring's headquarters from Australia.[3] Blamey sent Berryman forward to see Savige and report on the situation at the distant front.

When he received a signal from Herring at 4 p.m. on 16th August saying that Berryman proposed visiting the divisional area Savige foresaw trouble. Were the senior commanders dissatisfied with the way things were going? Herring asked Savige to meet Berryman at Moten's headquarters on the 19th, and stated that Lieut-Colonel Daly[4] would travel with Berryman to relieve Wilton who had been selected for an appointment on the Military Mission at Washington. Berryman arrived at Tambu Bay by landing craft on 17th August, and next day moved through Taylor's headquarters near Mount Tambu to Moten's headquarters, 24 hours before Savige expected him.

After Moten had described how the Japanese were surrounded and would probably try to break out the next morning, Berryman realised that he had walked into one of the decisive battles of the Salamaua campaign. By the night of the 18th Moten's four battalions were pressing in on the enemy from all directions. It was obvious that the Mount Tambu area could not be held much longer; indeed the Japanese had

---

[3] Major-General Berryman was Deputy Chief of the General Staff at LHQ from September 1942 to January 1944. From December 1942 to February 1943 and from August 1943 to January 1944 he also held the appointment of MGGS at New Guinea Force.

[4] Maj-Gen T. J. Daly, CBE, DSO, SX1436. BM 18 Bde 1940-41; GSO1 5 Div 1942-43; CO 2/10 Bn 1944-45. Comd 28 British Commonwealth Bde, Korea, 1952-53. Regular soldier; b. Ballarat, Vic, 19 Mar 1913.

already given evidence of their intention to evacuate when an American patrol in the late afternoon of the 18th worked its way to near the crest of Mount Tambu and reported indications of at least partial evacuation.

Among the surrounded Japanese was Lieutenant Shimada who wrote a report to his company commander:

> The two men defending No. 6 position were killed. The enemy has penetrated in this area. We went out to meet this attack but were unsuccessful. At present we are face to face with the enemy. With the four men at No. 5 position, we will again try to counter-attack. As the enveloping enemy is quite strong, attack or retreat is difficult. Our strength is platoon commander and 18 men (two dead, and the 4 who went for fuel have not returned). Our telephone lines have been cut by the enemy. We will die in defence of our positions and drive back the enemy. . . . It will be extremely useful if you will press the enemy, who have penetrated No. 6 position, from the right rear flank.

Captured in the Mount Tambu area was a notebook belonging to Private Hamana of the battered *115th Regiment* whose attitude was less zealous than Shimada's. Against the date 18th August he wrote:

> Living in the mountains in front of Mount Tambu I wonder why they don't send things up to the front line? This is the reason the company's faces are pale, their beards long and bodies dirty with red soil from the ground. We are just like beggars. Because of the scarcity of men, to continue duty is to weaken the body. Everyone is longing for a full stomach. The higher officials should give a little more consideration and quickly replace the *51st Division* with the fresh *41st Division* or the *51st* will become decrepit.

From first light on the morning of 19th August Laver Force was very active. At 6.30 a.m. Sergeant Harrison[5] led a patrol north from Laver's Knoll about 100 yards and found a new track leading to the east. This track had been much used by the enemy and it seemed as though they may have withdrawn during the night. At 7.30 a.m. a patrol south from Johnson's Knoll found many enemy text books and papers. Two knolls north of Laver's Knoll were then occupied by Edgar's company; one of them had sheltered a mountain gun position. A patrol from Laver's company, moving back to Davidson Ridge with the 42nd Battalion patrol, found a track six feet wide on the eastern slopes of Komiatum Ridge. Along this track also there had been considerable movement to the north during the night. Further evidence of a general withdrawal was the attempt of small enemy parties to cross the Australian line of communication to Coconuts during the day.

Early on 19th August patrols of the 2/5th found enemy positions at Goodview Junction and on Goodview Spur deserted. As a stream of reports began to flow in to the brigade headquarters from Conroy indicating that the Japanese were withdrawing, Moten realised with satisfaction that the battle was being fought as he had planned it. After waking Berryman he ordered Conroy to advance along the Komiatum Track and join Laver. Captain Bennett's company led the advance and Berryman and Moten joined in. For a time they were with Bennett and his leading

---
[5] WO1 W. J. C. Harrison, MM, VX6858; 2/6 Bn. RSM 3 Bn RAR Korea. Cartage contractor; of Kerang, Vic; b. Wellington, NZ, 27 Aug 1909.

platoon commander, and just behind the leading section. Major-generals and brigadiers are likely to be an embarrassment to a patrol commander, and, after a time, the exasperated Bennett prevailed on Berryman and Moten to move farther back.

With opposition from enemy stragglers only, Bennett's company advanced to the junction of the Komiatum and Mount Tambu Tracks. Here Moten reminded Berryman that he was to meet Savige at midday. On their way back to Bui Eo Creek the two leaders met the signallers laying line. Moten telephoned his brigade major, Eskell, at brigade headquarters and told him to get the Americans moving. He was convinced that the Japanese had vacated their positions on Mount Tambu because Bennett had been able to reach the track junction, and therefore ordered that Taylor should clear Mount Tambu and join the 2/5th Battalion at the track junction as soon as possible.

Meanwhile, Savige was walking along the track towards Moten's headquarters. For the most part he was silent as he made up his mind how to handle his talk with Berryman. He then discussed his plan with Wilton, knocked it into shape, and stuck to it in his later discussions. The two men arrived a little before midday and Eskell informed them that Berryman and Moten were in the forward area. He then made tea for them and they were drinking it when Berryman arrived at Moten's office. After saying good morning to Berryman, Savige asked Moten, "How's she going?" and up went Moten's thumb. Savige then asked Moten to outline the situation.

After Moten had done this Savige ordered him to exploit north along the Komiatum Track and to get the 42nd Battalion moving towards Nuk Nuk along the high ground of Scout Ridge; he also warned that Hammer would exploit towards Komiatum Ridge from the direction of Orodubi and Erskine Creek. Savige asked Moten to send Taylor's battalion back to join the rest of the 162nd Regiment in accordance with his promise to MacKechnie. Turning to Wilton Savige ordered him to "issue the necessary orders to get things going". Savige, Berryman and Moten then went to the mess where, after a drink and a chat, Berryman handed Savige a letter signed by Herring on the 16th. This began:

> The Commander-in-Chief has directed that the time has arrived for the relief of Headquarters 3rd Australian Division and that it be relieved by Headquarters 5th Australian Division as early as possible. Major-General Milford is en route from Australia (ex leave) and should report to your Headquarters within the next seven days. The command of the forces now operating under your command in the Salamaua operations will pass to him as and when mutually agreed upon by yourself and him.

The letter also dealt with the need to establish divisional headquarters at Tambu Bay, and to organise a supply system whereby "your forces can be maintained from the sea and without air droppings as from 28 Aug at the latest". The letter concluded: "Am glad your plans have worked out so well; aggressive action should enable you to shorten your supply lines in the next day or two."

After reading the letter Savige turned to Berryman and said, "Frank, I have had rather a difficult and trying time but as you see we have got away with it." Savige had indeed "got away with it". He was a successful general in an operation which he later described as the "toughest operational problem I ever faced" in experience covering campaigns in four continents.[6]

While the generals were meeting at the Bui Eo Creek reports from all sectors confirmed the departure of the Japanese from positions which had previously seemed impregnable. They were no longer on the ridge east of the junction of Stephens' and Mule Tracks; two platoons from the 2/5th followed Walpole's Track unmolested to the Komiatum Track. Captain Walters' company then advanced along the Komiatum Track, passed through Bennett's position and moved north towards Laver's Knoll.

It was no surprise when an American platoon from Captain George's company reached the crest of Mount Tambu without opposition late in the morning of 19th August. The platoon mopped up enemy stragglers before two companies from the I/162nd Battalion moved on to Mount Tambu from the east. A platoon then advanced along the Mount Tambu Track and met the 2/5th Battalion at the track junction.

> After four long weeks of artillery and mortar pounding and three direct assaults Mount Tambu was at last in Allied hands (wrote the historian of the 41st American Division). Jap positions were found, in many instances, to be ten feet underground with a complete system of tunnels and connecting trenches. At least a full battalion, with virtually perfect organization underground, had occupied the position. Artillery and mortar fire had done little damage to the position but apparently had broken the morale of the garrison.[7]

After his talk with Berryman a thoughtful Savige accompanied by Wilton set out immediately after lunch to visit the conquerors of Laver's Knoll. On the way they passed through part of the 2/5th Battalion. Some stray bullets were flying as the two officers arrived on Laver's Knoll. Laver was then busy counter-attacking to the north and did not notice Savige in a slit trench until, with a startled look, he came along and said, "Sir, you shouldn't be here—it's too hot." "To hell with you," said Savige, "get on with your battle and forget us."

Walters' company from the 2/5th Battalion arrived at Laver's Knoll soon after 2 p.m. thus completing the link-up of Wood's, Conroy's and Taylor's battalions. Moten then ordered Davidson to patrol to the Americans on Mount Tambu. Lieutenant Stevenson[8] led this patrol, which soon began to run into the Japanese retreating from Mount Tambu. Seeing eight Japanese approaching Stevenson set an ambush which killed five of them, the others going bush. When a large Japanese force approached,

---

[6] On 22nd August Blamey signalled MacArthur: "Battle for Komiatum Ridge has resulted in complete success. . . . Berryman reports Savige's tactical plan of attacking from south-west and south excellently conceived and admirably carried out."
[7] McCartney, p. 59.
[8] Lt J. G. Stevenson, QX36389; 42 Bn. Engine driver (refrigeration); of Rockhampton, Qld; b. Yeppoon, Qld, 18 Jun 1919.

Stevenson fell back to await it. On the way Lance-Corporal Miller[9] met a lone Japanese to whom he said affably, "Good day; going some place?" and then dispatched him irrevocably towards it. The enemy force disappeared, probably down the gorge between Komiatum and Davidson Ridges. Captain Greer then led a patrol to clear the track, and, just on dusk, he rang from the American positions to say that the track was clear.

As on previous occasions many of the enemy had slipped through the Allied cordon, but they had been forced to desert defences which had proved a stumbling block to the 17th Brigade's advance. The splendid planning for the Komiatum offensive was matched by near faultless execution by the troops. "This little battle has been the perfect action. Everything went exactly according to plan," wrote Wilton that night. General Adachi said later that, as a result of Australian infiltration and bypassing, Komiatum was endangered; therefore, about the middle of August, the garrison withdrew to "Grass Mountain" (Charlie Hill[1]).

After the capture of Roosevelt Ridge Colonel MacKechnie's advance had been stopped to the west and north-west. On the east and north-east the Americans were faced with a series of ridges running to Dot Inlet. During Moten's attack on Mount Tambu American patrols had maintained pressure on the known Japanese positions near the junctions of Roosevelt and Scout Ridges and Roosevelt and "B" Ridges. They had been unable to make any gains and by 17th August the III/162nd Battalion was stationary, pinned down by enemy fire from the junction of Roosevelt and Scout Ridges. On 18th August MacKechnie told Savige that his total fighting strength was down to 791 and that, with 30 evacuations a day, he had insufficient troops to guard Tambu Bay. He added, "We will continue to do our best but insufficient numbers and resulting exhaustion may lose us golden opportunities or result in failure at critical time." Savige replied:

> Will send you one of Taylor's coys within forty-eight hours. With luck remainder should follow thirty-six to forty-eight hours later. . . . Can you lay hands on any sub-unit such as cannon company? Can you organise further detachments from people in rear not otherwise fully employed? This will provide some measure of rest for tired troops in forward areas.

On the 19th Captain Pawson,[2] the divisional liaison officer with the Americans, signalled Savige that the Americans' morale was high and they were determined to beat the enemy. Pawson stated that MacKechnie was worried that he may have given the wrong impression about the morale of his troops. "Point he wished to make was that troops were in need of rest from continual strain of shell and mortar fire in forward area," continued the signal. "There is definitely no suggestion of troops breaking in

---

[9] Cpl D. A. Miller, Q113687; 42 Bn. Meatworker; of Rockhampton, Qld; b. Rockhampton, 21 Dec 1920.

[1] The Christian name of the commander of the 42nd Battalion, Colonel C. W. Davidson.

[2] Maj J. H. Pawson, VX155. 2/3 Fd Regt, 2/6 Bn, 2 NG Inf Bn. Medical student; of Brighton, Vic; b. Caulfield, Vic, 27 Sep 1920.

any sector." Realising the need for improvisation MacKechnie streamlined his headquarters, and formed a provisional battalion, consisting of the anti-tank company, cannon company and regimental band.

When he learnt that the track between the I/162nd and 42nd Battalions was clear, Savige was able to redeem his promise to release the first of Taylor's companies within 48 hours. With the occupation of Mount Tambu the I/162nd Battalion had finished its task under Moten's command and by 21st August it returned to MacKechnie.

The 42nd Battalion meanwhile investigated a reported enemy position north of the junction of the Boisi and Scout Ridge Tracks. A patrol led by Lieutenant Cameron[3] set out to investigate on 18th August. As he and two men were creeping towards the enemy position a sentry fired and hit the youthful Cameron who fell into a narrow gully. One of the men (Corporal Stevens[4]) sent back for the patrol while he himself dressed Cameron's wounds and then carried him through the jungle for 500 yards in an easterly direction towards where he thought he would find Scout Ridge. Here the two men waited in vain for the patrol until Cameron ordered a reluctant Stevens back to return next morning with help. Stevens put Cameron beside a log, covered him with leaves and set off using Cameron's compass. At dusk he arrived back on the track junction where he found the patrol.

Davidson's plan to attack the Japanese perimeter north of the track junction was postponed while patrols set out on 19th August to find Cameron. In the early morning Stevens accompanied a searching patrol but returned baffled unable to find the log. Major Crosswell,[5] the battalion second-in-command, then led a large search party towards the enemy position. Disregarding the wild Japanese firing the patrol followed Stevens' attempt to retrace his route and finally found Cameron in high spirits and beginning to crawl back to safety despite a compound fracture of the left thigh. He was one of the few soldiers who had ever had an attack postponed for him.

After the capture of Mount Tambu the 42nd Battalion turned north and north-east and intercepted enemy parties escaping from Mount Tambu between Komiatum and Davidson Ridges. At dusk on 19th August Captain Cole's company overlooking the track down Davidson Ridge watched 20 Japanese walk into its ambush before firing on them. Next morning 12 dead Japanese were counted.

On 20th August Davidson ordered the capture of what he thought were only two knolls to the north of the battalion's positions on Davidson Ridge. The smaller knoll was occupied without opposition and Lieutenant Ramm's[6] platoon seized the second knoll against slight opposition.

---

[3] Lt S. A. Cameron, NX138179; 42 Bn. Regular soldier; of Dalveen, Qld; b. Dalveen, 5 Apr 1924.
[4] Sgt G. V. Stevens, MM, QX52469; 42 Bn. Carter; of Rockhampton, Qld; b. Rockhampton, 16 Jun 1921.
[5] Maj C. N. Crosswell, QX34022; 42 Bn. Schoolteacher; of Bundaberg, Qld; b. Mount Perry, Qld, 2 Aug 1905.
[6] Lt J. W. L. Ramm, QX45073; 42 Bn. Grazier; of Upper Ulam, Bajool, Qld; b. Upper Ulam, 1 Jan 1919.

Next morning Cole reported that there was another feature (Bamboo Knoll) about 600 yards farther north of the one occupied by Ramm. Davidson ordered him to capture it immediately and this was done with little opposition. From the kunai clearing on top of the knoll Cole's men could see Salamaua and shells from the Allied artillery landing there. They could not see the airstrip because another hill was in the way. Before actually seeing this hill (Charlie Hill), Davidson's Intelligence men thought that it was the one they had reached. The inaccuracies of the map had deluded them. Often from now on the battalion diarist recorded "these orders not put into effect due to our position not being as far north as we thought"; or "due to inaccuracies in the Komiatum sheet, these map references later found to be misleading and companies actually moved" to other positions.

Meanwhile the 15th Brigade on the left flank had not been idle. Even before patrols from the 2/7th Battalion had found the South Coconuts unoccupied on the 17th, Hammer's troops were moving towards their next objective, the Salamaua-Bobdubi-Komiatum track junctions. On the 15th Hammer had called together his three unit commanders, Major Picken of the 2/7th, Major Warfe now commanding the 58th/59th and Captain Hancock of the 2/3rd Independent Company, and issued his plan. A company of the 2/7th (Baird's) and two platoons from the Independent Company (Lewin's and Winterflood's) would be used in the attack while the 58th/59th created a diversion in the Erskine Creek-Graveyard area and set an ambush on the Komiatum Track east of Newman's Junction. As a preliminary move Winterflood would secure the high ground east of Middle Spur and north of Hilbert North, while Lewin's would capture the area between the track junctions suspected to be a Japanese staging camp, and link up with Winterflood's platoon. Baird's company would then move through and capture the two track junctions.

It was obvious that the enemy was occupying the track junctions and the northern corridor between the Komiatum and Bench Cut Tracks in strength. On 15th August Lewin's platoon successfully withstood a bayonet attack on its ambush position near the junction of Steve's and Bobdubi Tracks by a party of 30 Japanese from the east, and Lieutenant Allen's patrol next day skirmished with about 40 entrenched Japanese just south of the Bobdubi-Salamaua track in the corridor between the Komiatum and Bench Cut Tracks.

The attacking force—100 men from the Independent Company and 66 men from the 2/7th Battalion—were faced with a heavy task. A panoramic view from a bomb crater on Coconut Ridge as well as patrol reconnaissance showed that an unusually thick belt of jungle ran across the proposed line of advance. As he sat on the side of the bomb crater on 16th August pointing out targets to the artillery observation post and mortar and machine-gun officers Hancock regarded his task distastefully. It was apparent that observation would be restricted to a few yards, thus making it extremely difficult to travel off the main Bobdubi Track. The flat ground provided no natural and solid cover from fire and gave promise of increasing the effectiveness of the enemy's small arms. Hancock and Baird hoped that these disadvantages might be offset by an air strike which would not only have a physical effect on the defenders and dampen their enthusiasm, but would thin out the jungle, lay bare the enemy's positions, and dig craters which would provide some cover from fire. These points had been emphasised by the experience of one of Hancock's patrols which, although moving with the utmost caution, had unwittingly walked into the midst of the enemy's defences and had experienced great difficulty in extricating two wounded men. The dank gloom of the jungle flats also had its effect in depressing the men who arrived back on the ridge blinking at the light and sighing with relief at leaving this jungle dungeon. It was with foreboding that Hancock and Picken learnt late in the evening of 16th August that no aircraft would be available for strikes on 17th and 18th August. The attack, however, would go in as planned.

During 17th and 18th August the troops watched big fleets of American heavy and medium bombers flying north-west, and wondered. They were on their way to Wewak, where, Intelligence had learned, more than 200 Japanese aircraft were concentrated on four airfields. More than half the Japanese aircraft were either destroyed or badly damaged, and the Japanese Air Force in New Guinea was greatly reduced. There was little doubt that the Japanese air fleet was intended to support Japanese operations in the Lae-Salamaua area.

Between 10 and 11 a.m. on the 17th artillery, mortars and machine-guns opened up on the green carpet of tree tops. The attackers hoped that a proportion of the missiles would reach their destination. Moving cautiously along the Bobdubi-Salamaua track, Lewin met opposition from Japanese strongly entrenched east of a small creek bed which crossed

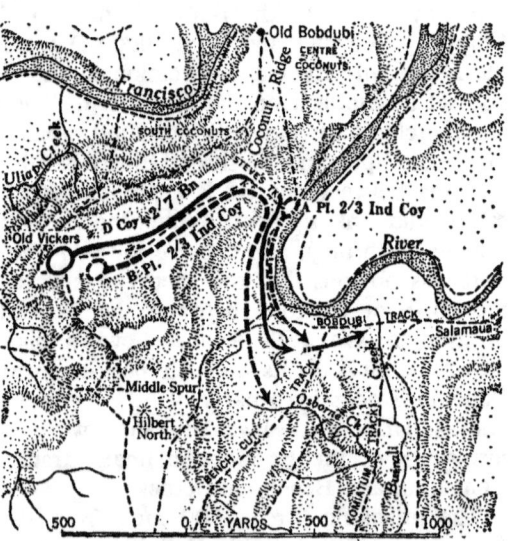

The attacks by 2/7th Battalion and 2/3rd Independent Company on Bench Cut-Bobdubi track junctions, 17th-18th August

the track. Meanwhile, Winterflood on Lewin's right moved round the foot of spurs leading up to Bobdubi Ridge and clashed with the enemy on their line of communication to the Hilberts and Middle Spur. His platoon killed five Japanese, but as he was about to push on to the main defences he was attacked from behind by another enemy force moving down the Hil-

(G. R. Warfe)

Lieutenant R. H. Dawson of the 2/6th Field Regiment firing a captured mountain gun on to Japanese in the Coconuts area on 30th July 1943, watched by a member of his observation post party, Gunner W. G. Pengelly.

(Australian War Memorial)

A 2/6th Battalion forward observation post in the Goodview Junction area, 10th August 1943. *Left to right*: Sergeant J. W. Hedderman, Captain H. L. Laver, Lieut-Colonel F. G. Wood (farthest from camera), Brigadier M. J. Moten and Major-General S. G. Savige, with binoculars.

Salamaua isthmus after its capture by the 5th Division on 11th September 1943.

(*Australian War Memorial*)

berts spur. Between two fires he was forced by 2 p.m. to withdraw to the next high ground to the north.

The attack was thus stationary, but Lewin's patrols began to probe to the flanks in an endeavour to find any weak spots in the enemy defences. About 150 yards to the south one of his patrols found a place whence the Japanese had unaccountably withdrawn leaving large quantities of equipment. Major Picken, in charge of the attack, then decided that a reinforced platoon, under Lieutenant Jeffery of the Independent Company, would drive straight through to the Japanese staging camp area and consolidate there, ready for the following troops to pass through to the Komiatum Track junction.

Jeffery found the staging camp unoccupied, but Baird, following with the remainder of his company, could find no signs of the spearhead force. He was faced with a problem, which he solved by deciding that his present area was too valuable to lose. He therefore dug in and sent out a patrol to find Jeffery. Visibility was about five yards and the area was covered with the densest jungle yet encountered by these troops. The patrol could find nothing and withdrew. Lewin's company attacked only to find the opposition along the creek stronger. At 6.30 p.m. he repelled a vicious Japanese counter-attack, although his casualties were heavy—5 killed including Lieutenant Barry, and 11 wounded. By dusk the Australian attacking force was thrust like a wedge into the enemy positions: Lewin on the left, Baird forward and centre, Winterflood on the right. Jeffery's strong patrol was out of touch although firing in the jungle ahead at 6.30 p.m. gave a clue that it was in trouble.

The mystery of Jeffery's disappearance was not solved until dawn on the 18th when Lieutenant P. C. Thomas and Sergeant Clues,[7] who were both wounded, and five men from Jeffery's patrol arrived exhausted at Old Vickers. It was then learnt that on reaching the staging camp and finding it empty the patrol, allowing enthusiasm to outrun discretion, had pushed on in an attempt to find the Japanese. Advancing east through the dense jungle, it had encountered concealed enemy positions near the Komiatum Track junction. In the ensuing fight the patrol had been at a disadvantage as it had cover only from the trees and none from the lie of the land. After suffering heavy casualties Jeffery had sent runners back to tell Baird what was happening but they could not get through because the area seemed suddenly alive with Japanese. Withdrawing, Jeffery had run into another ambush astride his route back to the staging camp, and more men were hit. On the evening of the 17th a group of wounded men under Thomas had tried to reach Baird's position. Being unable to find the staging camp, and realising how risky it would be to approach it in darkness, the wounded men had remained in the bush until the early morning, when they had found themselves at the foot of the spur leading to Old Vickers.

---

[7] Sgt W. J. Clues, VX25825. 2/6, 2/7 Bns. Process worker; of Albion, Vic; b. Gisborne, NZ, 24 Feb 1911.

Thomas' fit men, after a good meal, returned to Baird's position to act as guides. Lieutenant Fleming[8] then led a patrol into the dense jungle, and, as a result of shouting, another group of Thomas' men materialised from the jungle and were sent back to the west. Trying to find the remainder of the patrol Fleming found the enemy instead. Two parties of about 40 and 20 Japanese respectively were trying to cut off this patrol, but by moving wide Fleming managed to return safely about 10 a.m. with the enemy following.

On the left flank Lewin's platoon resolutely withstood strong Japanese attacks for three hours from 3 a.m. The strongest attacks were on his right but the enemy were unable to dislodge his platoon. The attacks ceased at dawn but began again with increased violence soon after Fleming's return. The diarist of the 2/7th Battalion described the fights thus:

> The enemy launched himself on all points of the line held by the force. The fire exchanged was tremendous and the observers in the command post were at a loss to know where the enemy were. The noise of small arms and the thumping of 36 grenades grew to a roar as though the Japs were attempting to scare the troops out by an impressive demonstration of fire. A call for defensive fire brought the mortars in play and the crash of bombs added to the noise. Finally the MMG opened up on their defensive lines and their chatter just completed the din.

During the remainder of the 18th patrols cautiously investigated the wall of jungle ahead. Although they were not successful in either pinpointing Japanese positions or in extricating Jeffery's men, they did have the effect of gradually forcing the enemy back to the line of the Komiatum Track.

To the south the 58th/59th Battalion was busily playing its part in attracting Japanese attention. During 17th August its patrols were active and aggressive. For the loss of 18 casualties, including one company commander, Captain Blackshaw,[9] wounded, 23 Japanese were killed, 10 of them at Erskine Creek. Next day there were signs that the Japanese were thinning out.

With the enemy being driven back on the north and with signs of his impending withdrawal on the southern sector opposite the 15th Brigade, it appeared to Savige that the enemy intended to hold with a strong rearguard the area from the track junctions along the line of the Hilberts-Erskine Creek-Graveyard-Orodubi-Exton's Knoll, with the intention of withdrawing from the Mount Tambu-Komiatum-Goodview Junction area and then from the southern portions of his line opposite the 15th Brigade. Events on 19th August gave added weight to this belief.

It was not until 2 p.m. on the 19th that a patrol at length found the missing men of Jeffery's patrol—all wounded and exhausted. Jeffery himself died next day. A platoon occupied the area where Jeffery had been found, and saw no enemy there; Lewin also found that the enemy had withdrawn.

---

[8] Lt W. A. Fleming, WX8970; 2/7 Bn. Clerk; of South Perth; b. Youanmi, WA, 16 Jul 1913.
[9] Capt J. R. Blackshaw, VX102649; 58/59 Bn. Cargo classifier; of Essendon, Vic; b. Prahran, Vic, 3 Nov 1918.

On the morning of the 19th Hammer warned his units that the enemy were withdrawing from the Mount Tambu-Komiatum area, and told them to watch for the Japanese and engage them with mortars and machine-guns. Lieutenant Fietz's company on North Coconuts could observe the Komiatum Track, and in the late afternoon enjoyed the sight of retreating Japanese groups being battered and harassed by mortars and machine-guns. Warned to harass the enemy retreating north from Mount Tambu, the 58th/59th Battalion had been largely responsible for providing this spectacle. Without opposition several of the positions which had proved such obstacles in the past were occupied by the 58th/59th: the Erskine Creek area, North and South Pimples and Orodubi.[1]

The unpleasant tasks of the 2/7th Battalion and 2/3rd Independent Company in fighting the entrenched enemy around the flat track junctions were now being rewarded. The turning of the enemy's flank by the attack along the line of the Bobdubi-Salamaua track from 17th August onwards had hastened the enemy's withdrawal from Mount Tambu and the Orodubi "pocket" area.

Just before midnight on 19th August Savige phoned Hammer's headquarters, and, in the absence of the brigadier, instructed Travers to secure Kennedy's Crossing and patrol the line of Buiris Creek north of the Francisco. As enemy resistance had collapsed in the Mount Tambu area, Savige ordered that every effort should be made to close the enemy's avenue of escape between Komiatum and Bobdubi Ridges. When Travers said that Hammer was worried about his northern flank, Savige replied that the 15th Brigade would be relieved of responsibility for the area south of Erskine Creek.

Hammer prepared to take advantage of the enemy withdrawal but it was necessary for his men to move cautiously through booby-trapped areas and clear up the area before setting off in full pursuit. At 4 a.m. next morning all units of the brigade had a hot meal, and an hour later they were on the move. Two companies of the 2/7th Battalion (Baird's and Cramp's) attacked where the Bobdubi-Salamaua track crossed the Buirali, captured some pill-boxes, and then withdrew for a mortar shoot on the remaining pill-boxes. Fighting stubbornly the Japanese hung on. By nightfall the two companies were still attacking the junction area. Another company (Captain Arnold's[2]) advanced north along the Bench Cut Track, the fourth company (Major Dunkley's[3]) gathered at the north end of Bobdubi Ridge, and a platoon crossed the Francisco and reconnoitred the area north and west of Buiris Creek. A platoon of the 2/3rd Independent Company found the Hilberts-Middle Spur area abandoned and moved

---

[1] "Looking back," wrote the company commander, Captain C. E. Newman, who occupied Orodubi, "it is laughable to think a platoon was sent to capture it on 30th June. It is a steep, partly kunai hill giving perfect fields of fire to defenders. The Japanese had deep dugouts and well sited weapon-pits giving cross fire." Soon after the occupation of Orodubi one of Newman's men stood on a landmine in the middle of Orodubi and had both feet blown off. After that the men walked like cats on hot bricks until they thought of the simple remedy of moving at the sides of the tracks.

[2] Capt E. Arnold, VX4621; 2/7 Bn. Hawker; of Mildura, Vic; b. Perth, 30 Apr 1909.

[3] Lt-Col H. L. E. Dunkley, DSO, MC, VX5174. 2/6 and 2/7 Bns; CO 7 Bn 1944-45. Schoolmaster; of Geelong, Vic; b. Creswick, Vic, 22 Dec 1911.

along what had been the enemy line of communication before reaching the 2/7th Battalion near the track junctions. By nightfall on the 20th the Independent Company had thrust from Malone's Junction to the Buirali, thus effectively cutting the Komiatum Track also. On the 20th the 58th/59th also reached the Komiatum Track in several places. One company was astride the Komiatum Track half way between Erskine Creek and Newman's Junction; another deloused 60 booby-traps along the Bench Cut in the same area. Major Rowell's[4] company from the Graveyard area was fired on as it approached the Komiatum Track. Lieutenant Mathews[5] then led his platoon round the east flank and, after an exchange of fire lasting for about an hour, he withdrew and led the company round the west flank after cutting a track. Late in the afternoon the company reached the enemy's main Erskine Creek Track and moved down it towards its junction with the Komiatum Track. Near the junction of the Erskine and Buirali Creeks the company again encountered a Japanese position.

Newman's company later met heavy resistance at the junction of the Komiatum and Orodubi Tracks where the Buirali joined Buiwarfe Creek. The company then attacked from the south but, like Rowell's from the west, they could not see the enemy, nor could they find suitable cover from enemy fire which swept the flat ground. The Japanese position was a well-chosen one in a bottleneck and commanding the ground east of the track. Nevertheless the two companies were beside and across the Komiatum Track, and a patrol to the south met the forward company of the 2/6th Battalion at the northern extension of Moten's advance.

By nightfall on the 20th the enemy had been pushed back to the general line of the Komiatum Track and beyond. Hammer now had freedom of movement along the Bench Cut from Ambush Knoll to Osborne Creek. His ambushes along the Komiatum Track, however, had not trapped the retreating Japanese. This fact supported his belief that the Japanese line of communication now led from the Komiatum-Orodubi track junction up Charlie Hill to Salamaua.

North of Brigadier Hammer's main area Captain Whitelaw's company of the 24th Battalion had been patrolling the tracks east towards the coast from its forward base without incident until 19th August, when a three-man patrol from Lieutenant Barling's[6] platoon was ambushed about a mile along a track which left the Hote-Malolo track and led south-east towards Buiris Creek. One man—Private Mathews[7]—was killed.

Still farther north Colonel Smith, on 7th August, received an interesting and encouraging signal from Savige:

---

[4] Maj F. A. Rowell, VX159. 2/5 and 58/59 Bns; 7 Bn 1944-45. Bank officer; of Canterbury, Vic; b. Canterbury, 19 Aug 1919.

[5] Capt R. L. Mathews, VX106327; 58/59 Bn. Accountant; of Balwyn, Vic; b. Geelong, Vic, 5 Jan 1921. Author of the history of the 58th/59th Battalion. Professor of Commerce at University of Adelaide since 1958.

[6] Maj D. R. Barling, NX68094; 24 Bn. Grazier; of Casino, NSW; b. Casino, 17 Jun 1918.

[7] Pte N. L. Mathews, VX104474. 2/5 and 24 Bns. Labourer; of Wangaratta, Vic; b. Geelong, Vic, 14 Apr 1915. Killed in action 19 Aug 1943.

Documents captured at Old Vickers Position reveal that our tactics at Buang River have succeeded in tying down a force of about one enemy battalion. Enemy fears an attack from west down Buang Valley. Intention is to keep as large as possible an enemy force occupied in this area. You will employ Warfe's tactics to harass the enemy wherever he can be found in the Buang Valley and river mouth. Operating from a firm base small patrols strong in firepower should be sent to find the enemy, hit him hard and pull out to strike again elsewhere. The enemy is there and must be kept there. You cannot be allowed for this job a force larger than that already allotted for this area.

In fulfilment of these orders Lieutenant Robinson led a patrol on 11th August from his base near the western end of the island in the Buang towards the coast, intending to cut the coastal track between Lae and Salamaua. That night he bivouacked north of the Buang about one mile from the coast near the south-eastern slopes of Sugarloaf, and next day reached the beach about a mile north of the previous Buang base. Two unarmed Japanese were immediately killed but the strong Japanese force in the area then fired on the patrol, forcing it to withdraw to near the old base. On the morning of the 13th the Japanese forced Robinson to withdraw to his own base in the Buang Valley.

A patrol on the 14th found an enemy barricade about half a mile from the coast near the south bank of the Buang. On 15th August Sergeant Fox[8] led a patrol to booby-trap, ambush and harass the enemy near the barricade. The patrol ran into heavy enemy fire which killed Fox and wounded two others. A small party led by Corporal Dybing[9] then covered the withdrawal of the patrol from the ambush and the evacuation of casualties.

In the Markham area Captain Chalk's Papuan company, under Colonel Smith's command, regularly patrolled the south bank of the Markham and watched the river from observation posts which reported that New Labu Island, immediately east of Markham Point, was being used as a crossing place. On 9th August a patrol led by the native Corporal Gabriel watched 10 natives fishing on the north side of the Markham about a mile west of Markham Point. When they crossed to the south bank, they were apprehended by Gabriel in accordance with orders; they said that there were about 40 Japanese at Markham Point.

Gabriel was now ordered to cross to the north bank between Markham Point and the area where he had caught the fishermen. It was impossible to cross the turbulent stream in the northern channel of the Markham and an instruction from Smith on 12th August had warned that the river west from Narakapor to Chivasing must not be crossed because of Australian weakness in that area and fear of reprisals. Smith's instructions may or may not have reached Gabriel's men who left at 6 a.m. on 12th August and paddled two canoes along the river to Bwarip. At 5 p.m. the canoes crossed the river. Leaving two natives to guard them Gabriel and his men crept up a creek bed to a small village where they caught three

---

[8] L-Sgt W. P. Fox, VX104437; 24 Bn. Tile layer; of Box Hill, Vic; b. Belfast, Ireland, 3 May 1907. Killed in action 15 Aug 1943.

[9] Cpl R. A. Dybing, VX144195; 24 Bn. Storeman; of Kew, Vic; b. Thornbury, Vic, 7 May 1919.

natives from Chivasing who worked for the Japanese. Three native soldiers guarded the captives while Gabriel and Lance-Corporal Kori followed a track from the village to the Markham Valley Road which they followed to the west for about a mile and a half. Returning to the village and the north bank of the Markham the canoes crossed the river to a small kunai-clad island near the south bank, where the Papuans decided to spend the night. Next morning Gabriel's canoe was being paddled along the north side of the island when it was fired on by a large party of Japanese and natives from the north. Kori and another native were killed but Gabriel held up the enemy advance across the river by killing two Japanese and one native. Although his canoe was wrecked and five weapons were lost, he and the two other surviving natives swam to the south bank. The two natives manning the second canoe managed to paddle it to safety. The bravery of Gabriel and his natives and their determination to find out what was happening along the north bank of the Markham, knowing the enemy was there, resulted in gaining important information about the Markham Valley Road and confirming that the enemy was alert and using natives.

By 13th August General Savige learnt from Herring that "as the major role of 3 Aust Div is the conduct of operations against Salamaua, the responsibility for the protection of areas not directly connected with the Salamaua area is to be transferred". The instruction then outlined the duties of two new forces: Wampit Force and Tsili Tsili Force.

Wampit Force, consisting mainly of the 24th Battalion (less Whitelaw's company) and Chalk's Papuan company (less Lieutenant Stuart's[1] platoon in the Watut Valley) came under the command of New Guinea Force from 9 a.m. on 17th August. Its role was to prevent the enemy from penetrating the Wau-Bulolo valley by routes leading into it from the area between the Buang and Wampit Rivers, to secure observation posts on the south bank of the Markham between Markham Point and the Wampit River, and to continue the construction of a road to the Markham.

Included in Tsili Tsili Force were Lieut-Colonel Marston's 57th/60th Battalion and the Papuan platoon. Marston was responsible for the tactical protection of Tsili Tsili airfield, under the command of the 2nd Air Task Force, and on the 18th he was given an additional task of preventing enemy movement from Onga to Pesen and the airfield.

While the battle of Komiatum was being fought other exciting events had occurred in the rear coastal areas. These had been caused by the enemy force of about company strength observed by the three-man patrol from the I/162nd Battalion on 12th August, and subsequently followed by Lieutenant Messec's platoon from that battalion. Savige instructed Colonel Jackson to warn all artillery units along the coast and in the Buigap Valley of the possibility of attack.

---

[1] Capt D. B. Stuart, NX23956; Papuan Inf Bn. Accountant; of Hunter's Hill, NSW; b. Lismore, NSW, 8 Oct 1909.

Messec at first thought that the Japanese were seeking the gun positions at the south end of Tambu Bay but he soon found that they were heading for Bitoi Ridge and Lake Salus. Taylor then dispatched another 16 men to join Messec, and at midday on the 13th the 45 Americans encountered and dispersed four Japanese south-east of Mount Tambu. The trail of the Japanese led south-east over very tortuous country towards a feature north of Bitoi Ridge, and it seemed that they were being guided by natives along an indistinct track which passed through some deserted villages. The chase continued on the 14th south-east to the main Bitoi Ridge, and finally to the south-western end of Lake Salus. During their pursuit the Americans discovered enemy bivouac areas with as many as 85 sleeping places. By this time the patrol was not in contact with Taylor because its line had run out after about six miles. Early on 15th August the patrol heard much firing towards the north-western end of the lake.

Captain Hitchcock's Papuans were also preparing to meet the Japanese raiders. On 12th August Lieutenant Gore with 34 Australians and Papuans left to guard an American battery on the south side of Tambu Bay. Two days later Lieutenant Green[2] with 35 men from the Papuan Battalion departed from Tambu Bay to join Gore.

Farther south the troops of the 29th Brigade were entering the battle area. The 47th Battalion, led by Major Watch,[3] had arrived at Nassau Bay on 9th August. Brigadier Monaghan arrived at divisional headquarters the next day, and his brigade major (Ross[4]) went to Tambu Bay to choose sites for brigade headquarters and the 47th Battalion. By 12th August the 47th Battalion and two companies of the 15th were defending Nassau Bay and the remainder of the 15th was at Morobe. Late at night on 12th-13th August Savige arranged for the 47th to provide a fighting patrol of platoon strength to reconnoitre the spur north of Lake Salus and search for any sign of Japanese movement. The route would be north along the coast to the north arm of the Bitoi, north-west around the west of Lake Salus, east to the coast, and back south along the coast by 15th August. While the remainder of the brigade marched north to Tambu Bay between 12th and 14th August, a company of the 47th, under Captain Stewart,[5] was left behind at Nassau Bay to carry out Savige's special reconnaissance. Lieutenant Hoffman's[6] platoon moved out as the fighting patrol desired by Savige at 8 a.m. on the 13th.

The next information about the elusive Japanese force came on 13th August when Messec reported seeing the Japanese at midday moving along a track towards Lake Salus. Savige passed this information on to Nassau

---

[2] Lt H. R. Green, NX31005. Papuan Inf Bn, and NG Inf Bn. Clerk; of Westmead, NSW; b. Gulgong, NSW, 1 Dec 1919.

[3] Lt-Col J. R. Watch, NX12394. 2/13 Bn 1940-42, 47 Bn 1943-45. Employment registrar; of Killara, NSW; b. Sydney, 4 Jul 1916.

[4] Maj J. A. Ross, QX40811. 42 Bn; BM 29 Bde 1943. Senior clerk; of Rockhampton, Qld; b. Mount Morgan, Qld, 24 Oct 1910.

[5] Capt W. D. P. Stewart, QX34726; 47 Bn. Postal assistant; of Dirranbandi, Qld; b. St George, Qld, 16 Feb 1912.

[6] Lt W. N. Hoffman, QX34728; 47 Bn. Metal gate maker; of Maryborough, Qld; b. Maryborough, 24 Jun 1920.

Bay and instructed that the fighting patrol of the 47th should establish an ambush on the high ground north-west of Lake Salus half way between the lake and the lagoon astride any track which appeared to come from the north-west. The patrol set the ambush on the 14th. On the same day

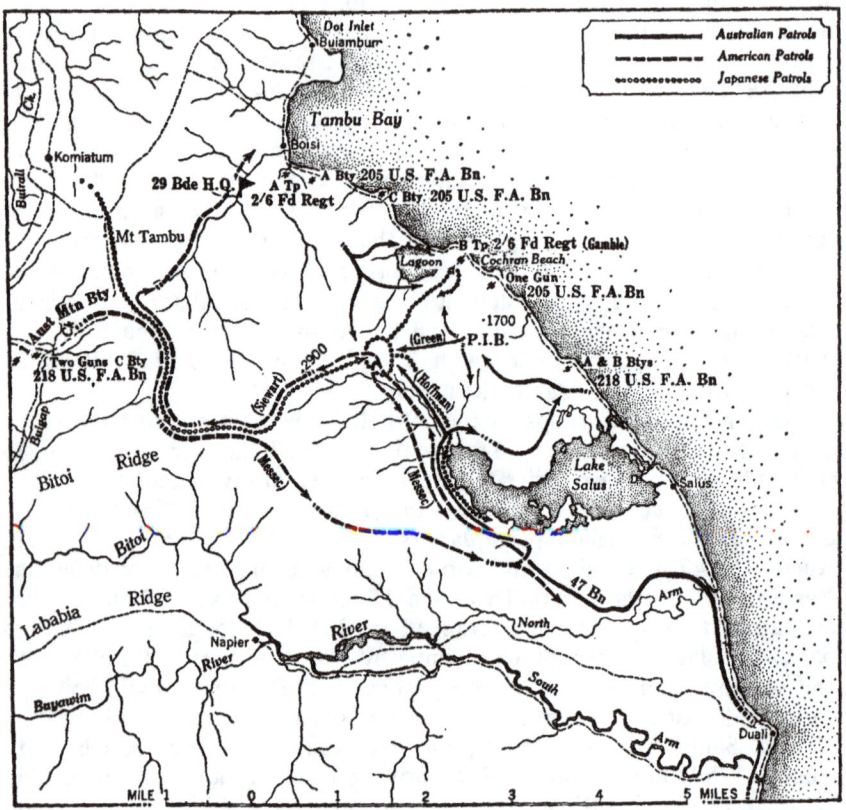

Japanese raids on Allied artillery positions, August 1943

Monaghan was ordered to defend the guns at the south end of Tambu Bay and the remainder of Stewart's company set out to defend the guns immediately north of Lake Salus. Along the shore and in the artillery positions all was tense expectancy as none knew where the enemy raiding force would strike.

At 10 a.m. on the 15th Monaghan received a report from the 218th American Artillery Battalion that Hoffman's platoon of the 47th had been ambushed north-west of Lake Salus at dusk the previous evening, that 15 survivors had reached the coast near an American battery south of Cochran Beach,[7] and that 15 were still missing. By 2 p.m. Hoffman, who

---

[7] Named after Lieut-Colonel G. P. Cochran, commander of the American artillery in the Tambu Bay area.

was wounded, reached the coast and reported that his platoon had been ambushed by about 50 Japanese west of the lake's northern tip the previous evening and that he had again encountered about 50 Japanese on the spur north-west of Lake Salus on the morning of 15th August. The patrol had been surprised and overrun and had dispersed leaving most of its weapons and equipment. Six men were still missing.

After hearing firing early on 15th August Messec divided his patrol; one detachment of 16 men departed for Nassau Bay, and the main body under Messec headed north. Striking the trail left by the Japanese, Messec came on the scene of Hoffman's ambush, and found six dead Australians, two dead Japanese, a Japanese machine-gun, an Australian Owen gun, Japanese rice and biscuits and tins of Australian field operational rations and bully beef. Speaking of this scene two days later Sergeant Siewart of Messec's patrol said:

> Two men had apparently been under or near mosquito nets and a reconstruction was that one man, whose body was riddled by automatic fire, had disposed of a Jap near by with a grenade. There was ample evidence of strong resistance having been offered.

Not only were the infantry in action against the raiders and the artillery ready for them, but the ubiquitous signallers were, as usual, playing their part. Accompanied by a linesman Lieutenant Hodson[8] on 15th August was restoring the telephone between Boisi and Nassau Bay where it had been cut by the Japanese, two miles north of Lake Salus. At 1 p.m. an enemy patrol fired on the two signallers, who jumped into prepared holes and returned the fire. The enemy soon withdrew and the signallers resumed their task.

Just north of Cochran Beach at 4 a.m. on 16th August the men of Lieutenant Gamble's[9] troop of the 2/6th Field Regiment and Lieutenant Grove's[1] platoon of the 47th Battalion—about 20 altogether—heard Japanese orders given in the darkness.[2] Immediately afterwards between 30 and 50 Japanese who had come from the west through swamp attacked. The attack began with automatic fire forward of the guns and then a second attack developed in the living area in the rear of the gun positions. This area was lightly held and the attack here made progress when the enemy got through to the beach between the guns and Gamble's unloading party, who were prevented from getting back by a machine-gun which the Japanese sited on the beach. The frontal attack, however, was driven off. The gunners and infantry defended the guns in hand-to-hand fighting but were unable to prevent the Japanese destroying their tents, damaging radio and other equipment and taking packs and personal effects, including

---

[8] Capt C. P. Hodson, MC, VX1559; 3 Div Sigs. Waterman; of Werribee, Vic; b. Healesville, Vic, 27 May 1910.

[9] Lt I. E. Gamble, MC, NX16462; 2/6 Fd Regt. Regular soldier; of Naremburn, NSW; b. Culcairn, NSW, 8 Jul 1915.

[1] Lt L. B. Grove, NGX175; 47 Bn. Clerk; of Crookwell, NSW; b. Crookwell, 13 Sep 1915. Killed in action 16 Aug 1943.

[2] Gamble's stores and ammunition had been landed from barges about 600 yards down the beach earlier in the night. In order to get this out of sight of the Japanese gunners on Lokanu before daylight, Gamble had detailed as many men as possible to do carrying duties.

a copy of the ammunition state and a map reference code. No damage was done to the guns. After three-quarters of an hour the Japanese withdrew leaving the bodies of two officers, bloodstained American rifles, and a trail of blood and discarded equipment along the line of their retreat. Demolition charges were found in front of the guns. Lieutenant Grove and Gunners George[3] and Johnson[4] were killed, while Lieutenant Bryant,[5] four artillerymen and two infantrymen were wounded in the determined and successful defence of the guns. By 9.30 a.m. Gamble's guns were in action.

During the morning of 16th August Stewart's company of the 47th repulsed three small attacks near the American artillery positions north of Lake Salus. To aid in hunting and destroying the raiders Savige placed Hitchcock's Papuan company under Monaghan's command. Soon after midday, on their way from the coast to an ambush position west of the 1,700-foot feature near Cochran Beach, the Papuans killed three Japanese of the *102nd Regiment* and a native guide. By the afternoon Lieutenant Green had 44 men from the Papuan company and 17 from the 47th at the ambush position.

That morning Messec's patrol followed the Japanese trail, strewn with discarded equipment, towards the 1,700-foot feature. One unfortunate Japanese had evidently not been woken by his comrades, for he was found asleep. As Messec approached the 1,700-foot feature he at last caught up with the enemy rearguard—about 20 Japanese in prepared positions. After inflicting about seven casualties Messec withdrew to the west of the feature where he established a perimeter. Quite unknown to one another, Green had chosen for his ambush position the identical map area chosen by Messec for his perimeter. Though both gave the same map reference for their areas, the patrols strangely enough did not meet.

The Japanese raiders were now hunted men. Finding Australians and Papuans to the east they made a break to the west. On the night 16th-17th August they came down the track towards Messec's position, chattering loudly. When they encountered the American patrol they encircled it and attacked vigorously. Using the Owen gun to supplement its own fire power, the patrol repulsed the attacks, killing several Japanese, until Messec decided that his position was desperate. Dividing his patrol once more into two forces, one under himself and the other under Siewart, he ordered them to break through the Japanese ring and make for Nassau Bay and Tambu Bay respectively. At 6 p.m. on the 16th the 16 men who had left the patrol on the western shores of Lake Salus arrived at Nassau Bay, accompanied by three of Hoffman's men found on the way. A day later Siewart's 15 men arrived at Tambu Bay, after an arduous march on half rations. Messec led the remainder of the patrol to Nassau Bay on the

---

[3] Gnr F. S. George, NX79982; 2/6 Fd Regt. Packer; of Lakemba, NSW; b. Sydney, 27 Apr 1922. Killed in action 16 Aug 1943.

[4] Gnr H. W. J. Johnson, NX80422; 2/6 Fd Regt. Bank officer; of Kingsford, NSW; b. Lithgow, NSW, 20 Mar 1918. Killed in action 16 Aug 1943.

[5] Lt J. R. Bryant, MC, NX13783; 2/6 Fd Regt. Stock clerk; of Gladesville, NSW; b. Haberfield, NSW, 21 Mar 1919.

18th, exhausted and footsore, after being practically without food for the last two days. By 21st August the three portions of the patrol rejoined the I/162nd Battalion, having played a resourceful and determined part in obstructing the raiders.

Between 17th and 20th August small parties of Japanese, disorganised and starving, tried to return to their base on Mount Tambu; but this was now in Allied hands. Some attempted to filter through to Salamaua via Davidson Ridge where they were killed by the 42nd. To clear the area finally Monaghan on 18th August gave the task of guarding the Tambu Bay gun positions to the 47th Battalion, now commanded by Lieut-Colonel Montgomery.[6] Captain Yates[7] had the task of protecting the guns in the coastal area between Lake Salus and Tambu Bay, and seeking out and destroying the Japanese in the area north of Lake Salus. Skirmishes occurred west of the 1,700-foot feature on the morning of 18th August, when the Papuans dispersed about 20 Japanese. Late on the 18th Gore's Papuans reported "many Japanese farther to the west". Monaghan then instructed Yates "to go in right away . . . as Japanese are apparently passing out of the area". At 9.10 a.m. on 19th August the last real contact was made with the remnants of the raiding force south-east of Mount Tambu, where a small patrol from Lieutenant G. N. Matthew's[8] platoon of the 15th Battalion and an American ration party intercepted about a dozen Japanese crossing the track towards the west. Of the five Japanese killed most were carrying Australian or American packs, and they were without food except for a few ounces of rice and scraps.

The enemy raid had proved a courageous failure. They had not succeeded in destroying any guns and had lost almost their entire force. As if to emphasise the futility of the raid an enemy 75-mm gun on 18th August scored direct hits on the No. 1 gun of Gamble's troop, putting it out of action and wounding three gunners. It had not been necessary to divert any of Savige's forces engaged on forward operational roles, except for Messec's platoon, which was in reserve. The gunners themselves were responsible for the protection of their guns but, with the infantry of the 29th Brigade passing through the raided area at the time, it would indeed have been folly not to use it to drive off the raiders.

Savige was therefore astonished to receive a signal from Herring on 17th August criticising him for making major alterations in his dispositions at the expense of getting on with the main battle because of the presence of small raiding parties. "Desire you cancel your order 29 Bde relative to local protection gun positions and concentrate Bde for main battle."

Savige replied explaining his action, saying:

---

[6] Lt-Col K. H. Montgomery, OBE, ED, NX94. 2/4 Bn; CO 8 Bn 1942-43, 47 Bn 1943-44; and training appointments. Bank officer; of Orange, NSW; b. Kogarah, NSW, 12 Dec 1904.

[7] Capt W. H. Yates, ED, QX36383; 47 Bn. Tally clerk; of Maryborough, Qld; b. Maryborough, 9 Oct 1905.

[8] Lt G. N. Matthew, VX5315. 2/5 and 15 Bns. Grocer; of St Kilda, Vic; b. Swan Hill, Vic, 15 Sep 1916. He and his brother, Lieutenant D. H. Matthew—killed later in this campaign—had enlisted together as privates and served in the Middle East with the 2/5th Battalion; both were commissioned in the 15th Battalion on the same day in 1942.

As my patrols move to and behind enemy positions so can the enemy also. Our complete domination this phase warfare has denied such enemy patrolling less this one. It is most difficult envisage nature of country from maps or air photos. This can only be known by personally walking it. . . . This episode like many others inseparable from jungle fighting did not nor will it interfere in any shape whatever with my general control of my forces for offensive ops. It caused neither a major nor minor alteration to my dispositions at any expense whatever in getting on with main battle.

While the 29th Brigade's headquarters was being established in the Erskine Creek area on 23rd August Captain Strom[9] (the brigade's Intelligence officer) led a patrol up the creek and captured a Japanese survivor from the Japanese raiding and demolition patrol—Sergeant Takahashi of *III/102nd Battalion*. From him it was learnt that the raiding force, which consisted mainly of Captain Arai's company and engineers attached for the demolition of the guns, was led by the battalion commander, Major Oba, who knew the coastal country well after his experiences during the retreat from Nassau Bay.

Oba's raiders were given their instructions on 2nd August. They "must be resolved to die as martyrs, burn with sincerity, especially brave and calm, see an opportunity and act quickly and passionately". It took a week to organise the raiding unit, which carried food for 9 days, and left Salamaua on 7th August 180 strong. It took one week to go from Salamaua to Lake Salus by way of Komiatum. The group bivouacked one night at Komiatum and one night at Tambu, and took the track to the east of Tambu. Towards the coast the unit divided into three groups—one reserve and two attacking. The next phase has been described above. On returning to their assembly area they found 30 or 40 Americans waiting. One attack group and the reserve group fought there while Major Oba and the remainder went towards Lake Salus; 16 Japanese were killed, including Arai and another officer. On the way back, this group encountered their enemies on a mountain which had a bamboo forest on it; three or four Japanese were killed in this encounter. Soon the force was broken up and scattered.

The splintering of the *51st Japanese Division* was a measure of the success of the 3rd Australian Division. A victory had been won at Komiatum. Salamaua was in sight as the Allies looked down from the vital ridges for which they had battled so long and so strenuously—Bobdubi Ridge, Komiatum Ridge, Mount Tambu, Davidson Ridge, Scout Ridge and Roosevelt Ridge. And still the Japanese sent to Salamaua large parties of reinforcements which could have been used to infinitely better effect elsewhere had they had an inkling of the Allied plan.

General Savige's task was nearly done by 20th August when he and his divisional staff, accompanied by General Berryman, and escorted by a platoon because Japanese raiders were in the area, arrived at Brigadier Monaghan's Tambu Bay headquarters. Walking along the track Berryman outlined Blamey's plan. At Tambu Bay advanced divisional headquarters was established. Late in the evening General Milford and his staff arrived at Tambu Bay and General Savige began to hand over his command.

---

[9] Maj G. F. Strom, VX5369. 2/5 and 15 Bns. Estate agent; of Bendigo, Vic; b. Castlemaine, Vic, 16 Jun 1916.

CHAPTER 8

THE PACIFIC FRONT

IN mid-1943 the Allied leaders in London and Washington were considering ambitious proposals for accelerating the defeat of Japan. Thus, on 6th April President Roosevelt discussed with his Chief of Staff, Admiral William D. Leahy, the Joint Chiefs, and Harry L. Hopkins, his adviser and assistant, the possibility of a campaign in Burma to open a road into China. Leahy later described the outcome:

> Great Britain apparently did not wish to undertake a campaign against the Japanese in the Burma area, and it was certain that Japan would interrupt our air transportation to China if its forces in Burma were not fully occupied in resisting Allied ground troops. . . . President Roosevelt appeared determined to give such assistance as was practicable to keep China in the war against Japan.[1]

On the other side of the Atlantic Mr Churchill, aware of the Americans' high estimate of the military importance of China, had no doubts about what the Americans were thinking concerning Burma. The advance on Akyab had failed and its capture before the monsoon was now impossible. No advance had been made from Assam. There had been some increase in the air transport available for the China route, but the full development of the air route and the requirements for a land advance towards central Burma had proved utterly beyond British resources. Churchill wrote later:

> It therefore seemed clear beyond argument that the full "Anakim" [reconquest of Burma] operation could not be attempted in the winter of 1943-44. I was sure that these conclusions would be very disappointing to the Americans. The President and his circle still cherished exaggerated ideas of the military power which China could exert if given sufficient arms and equipment. They also feared unduly the imminence of a Chinese collapse if support were not forthcoming. I disliked thoroughly the idea of reconquering Burma by an advance along the miserable communications in Assam. I hated jungles—which go to the winner anyway—and thought in terms of air-power, sea-power, amphibious operations and key points. It was, however, an essential to all our great business that our friends should not feel we had been slack in trying to fulfil the Casablanca plans and be convinced that we were ready to make the utmost exertions to meet their wishes.[2]

On 20th April Roosevelt received a message from Churchill suggesting that he and his full military staff should come to Washington for consultation early in May. The date was fixed for 12th May.

Meanwhile, on 28th April, the Joint Chiefs' planning staffs, possibly influenced partly by the Navy's desire to press on against Japan and partly by the President's interest in China, recommended the establishment of a large number of air bases in China, the maintenance of which would require, first the opening of a port such as Hong Kong, and secondly the reopening of the Burma Road. The port to be opened on

---
[1] W. D. Leahy, *I Was There* (1950), p. 186.
[2] W. S. Churchill, *The Second World War*, Vol IV (1951), p. 702.

the China coast could best be maintained by a direct drive across the central Pacific from Pearl Harbour to the Philippines. Although they recommended a simultaneous advance from the South-West Pacific Area they considered that MacArthur's proposed line of advance from New Guinea to the Philippines would follow the long way in and would have a vulnerable right flank.

When on 2nd May Roosevelt discussed the impending conference at Washington with Hopkins, Leahy and the Joint Chiefs, the Army Chief of Staff, General Marshall, declared that without an immediate offensive in northern Burma the air-ferry service to China would be destroyed by Japanese attacks on the landing fields. And at the Joint Chiefs' final pre-conference meeting with the President on the 8th it was agreed that, although the principal American objective at the conference would be to pin the British down to a cross-Channel invasion of Europe as soon as possible, the Americans should also press for some action in Burma.

On their way to Washington on 5th May Churchill and his staff prepared a paper on the situation in the Indian and Far Eastern spheres. Largely in order to seize the initiative at the conference his plan contemplated landings on the Andaman Islands, Mergui with Bangkok as the objective, the Kra Isthmus, Sumatra and even Java. Churchill would no doubt have been the first to admit that these proposals were merely conference tactics. He sent a frank signal to Marshal Stalin in Russia on 8th May: "I am in mid-Atlantic on my way to Washington to

settle further exploitation in Europe after Sicily, and also to discourage undue bias towards the Pacific, and further to deal with the problem of the Indian Ocean and the offensive against Japan there."[3]

The "undue bias" was causing deep concern to Churchill's advisers. For example, on 6th May the British Chief of the General Staff, General Brooke, wrote in his diary:

> There is no doubt that, unless the Americans are prepared to withdraw more shipping from the Pacific, our strategy in Europe will be drastically affected. Up to the present the bulk of the American Navy is in the Pacific and larger land and air forces have gone to this theatre than to Europe in spite of all we have said about the necessity of defeating Germany first.[4]

---

[3] Churchill, p. 705.
[4] Quoted in A. Bryant, *The Turn of the Tide 1939-1943*, p. 607.

Indeed, there were, in June, 13 American divisions in the Pacific, and 10 in the United Kingdom or Mediterranean.

At the Washington conference, which lasted from 12th until 25th May, the main decision was to fix the date for the cross-Channel invasion of Europe (OVERLORD) by an initial force of 29 divisions beginning on 1st May 1944. If the forthcoming assault on Sicily—it opened on 10th July—did not cause Italy to surrender, General Dwight D. Eisenhower, Allied Commander-in-Chief in North Africa, would be authorised to proceed as he thought fit to bring about the elimination of Italy from the war.

Turning to the Pacific the Combined Chiefs resolved "upon defeat of the Axis in Europe, in cooperation with other Pacific powers, and, if possible with Russia, to direct the full resources of the United States and Great Britain to force the unconditional surrender of Japan". They added: "If, however, conditions develop which indicate that the war as a whole can be brought more quickly to a successful conclusion by the earlier mounting of a major offensive against Japan, the strategical concept set forth herein may be reversed."[5]

In other words the conference did nothing to reconcile the variety of the opinions canvassed by the various leaders. These opinions were tartly summed up by General Brooke in his private diary on 24th May:

May 24th. Washington. Today we reached the final stages of the Conference, the "Global Statement of our Strategy". We [concluded] with a long Combined Meeting at which we still had many different opinions which were only resolved with difficulty.

Our difficulties still depended on our different outlook as regards the Pacific. I still feel that we may write a lot on paper, but that it all has little influence on our basic outlooks which might be classified as under:

(*a*) King thinks the war can only be won by action in the Pacific at the expense of all other fronts.

(*b*) Marshall considers that our solution lies in a cross-Channel operation with some twenty or thirty divisions, irrespective of the situation on the Russian front, with which he proposes to clear Europe and win the war.

(*c*) Portal considers that success lies in accumulating the largest Air Forces possible in England and that then, and then only, success lies assured. . . .

(*d*) Dudley Pound on the other hand is obsessed with the anti-'U' boat warfare and considers that success can only be secured by the defeat of this menace.

(*e*) Alan Brooke considers that success can only be secured by pressing operations in the Mediterranean to force a dispersal of German forces, help Russia, and thus eventually produce a situation where cross-Channel operations are possible.

(*f*) And Winston? Thinks one thing at one moment and another the next moment. At times the war may be won by bombing, and all must be sacrificed to it. At others it becomes necessary for us to bleed ourselves dry on the Continent because Russia is doing the same. At others our main effort must be in the Mediterranean directed against Italy or the Balkans alternately, with sporadic desires to invade Norway and "roll up the map in the opposite direction Hitler did". But more often than all he wants to carry out all operations simultaneously, irrespective of shortage of shipping.[6]

---

[5] Minute from JCS approved by CCS on 20th May. Quoted in W. F. Craven and J. L. Cate (Editors), *The Pacific: Guadalcanal to Saipan, August 1942 to July 1944* (1950), p. 134, a volume in the American official series *The Army Air Forces in World War II*.

[6] Quoted in Bryant, pp. 625-6.

There were no representatives of the South-West or South Pacific Areas at the Washington conference to state their case as the commanders in the China, Burma and India theatres had been able to do.[7] So far as the Pacific theatre was concerned the upshot of the conference was that "General MacArthur and Admiral Nimitz were directed to move against the Japanese outer defenses, ejecting the enemy from the Aleutians and seizing the Marshalls, some of the Carolines, the remainder of the Solomons, the Bismarck Archipelago, and the remainder of New Guinea".[8]

The Australian Army in June 1943 still included 10 infantry divisions and two armoured divisions. MacArthur's American formations now included or would soon include the Sixth Army Headquarters, under Lieut-General Walter Krueger, I Corps Headquarters, and four divisions: the 32nd and 41st; the 1st Marine from Guadalcanal; and the 1st Cavalry, to arrive in Queensland in July.

In the South Pacific Area Halsey still had seven divisions. The 2nd Marine Division had returned to New Zealand in February to recuperate after Guadalcanal. The 3rd Marine at the end of June sailed for the Solomons, where also the Americal, 25th, 37th and 43rd were established. The 3rd New Zealand Division, formed in 1942, garrisoned New Caledonia from late in 1942 until August and September 1943.

After receiving the Joint Chiefs' directive of 28th March MacArthur's planning staff had set to work to produce a plan for operations in the S.W.P.A. and South Pacific in 1943. Much of the preliminary planning had already been done, and, indeed, merely required what the American military historian has called a "revamping". The plan (ELKTON III) was ready by 26th April and with certain changes was approved by MacArthur and Halsey in Brisbane.

As previously indicated, MacArthur issued a warning instruction for the forthcoming operations on 6th May. "The general scheme of maneuver," it said, "is to advance our bomber line towards Rabaul; first by improvement of presently occupied forward bases; secondly, by the occupation and implementation of air bases which can be secured without committing large forces; and then by the seizure and implementation of successive hostile airdromes."[9] Describing the direction of attack the instruction stated that

the general lines of attack will proceed along two axes. In the west, along the north-west New Guinea coast to seize Lae and secure airfields in the Markham River Valley, thence eastward to seize western New Britain airdromes. The advance along the New Guinea coast will continue to the seizure of Madang to protect our western flank. In the east, north-westward through the Solomons to seize southern Bougainville, including the airdromes of the Buin-Faisi area, neutralising or capturing airdromes on New Georgia. Later occupy Kieta and neutralise hostile airdromes in the vicinity of Buka Passage. All operations are preparatory to the eventual capture of Rabaul and the occupation of the Bismarck Archipelago.

---

[7] Lieut-General Stilwell, Commanding General US Forces in China-India-Burma; Major-General Chennault, Commander Fourteenth American Air Force; and the three British area commanders: General Wavell, Admiral Somerville and Air Chief Marshal Peirse.

[8] *The War Reports of General of the Army George C. Marshall, General of the Army H. H. Arnold, Fleet Admiral Ernest J. King* (1947), p. 158.

[9] GHQ SWPA Warning Instruction No. 2 of 6 May 1943.

With regard to the Australian operations MacArthur's order stated:

The New Guinea Force, supported by Allied Air and Naval forces will:
(a) By airborne and overland operations through the Markham Valley and shore-to-shore operations westward along the north coast of New Guinea, seize Lae and Salamaua and secure in the Huon Peninsula-Markham Valley area, airdromes required for subsequent operations.
(b) By similar operations, seize the north coast of New Guinea to include Madang; defend Madang in order to protect the north-west flank of subsequent operations to the eastward.

While Halsey would occupy the Solomons including the southern part of Bougainville, the Sixth Army would:

(1) Occupy, by overwater operations, and defend Kiriwina and Woodlark Islands; establish airdromes thereon.
(2) Assume the responsibility for the defence of the island groups to the north of south-eastern New Guinea. Replace Australian ground troops on Goodenough Island by United States troops.
(3) Occupy western New Britain to include the general line Gasmata-Talasea by combined airborne and overwater operations and establish airdromes therein for subsequent operations against Rabaul.

By this stage General MacArthur had ensured that General Blamey would henceforth be the commander of "Allied Land Forces" only in name. Between February and April 1943 the headquarters of the Sixth American Army, mentioned above, arrived in Australia, although there were then only three American divisions in the area. General Blamey later wrote that "at no stage" was he given "any information as to the proposals [for the arrival of new American formations including the Sixth Army] or the development of the organisation". Blamey considered that at this stage MacArthur "took upon himself the functions of Commander, Allied Land Forces" and his own functions were limited to command of the Australian Military Forces. This position was arrived at, beyond doubt, on 26th February when, with the object of placing Sixth Army, and thus the American corps and divisions, directly under the command of G.H.Q., Sixth Army was named "Alamo Force" and was given the status of a "task force" under MacArthur's direct command. For this purpose MacArthur reconstituted "United States Army Forces in the Far East" (U.S.A.F.F.E.), his command when in the Philippines, with himself as its commander, and orders went directly from U.S.A.F.F.E. to the American formations.

In 1954 Major-General Charles A. Willoughby, MacArthur's senior Intelligence officer in the S.W.P.A., wrote:

The reasons for letting the Sixth Army operate in the field as the Alamo Force were never communicated to Krueger, but they were obviously bound up with international protocol: special task forces could undertake specific missions without complex inter-Allied command adjustments.[1]

Krueger's own comments were:

---

[1] C. A. Willoughby and J. Chamberlain, *MacArthur: 1941-1951* (1954), p. 124.

The reasons for creating Alamo Force and having it, rather than Sixth Army, conduct operations were not divulged to me. But it was plain that this arrangement would obviate placing Sixth Army under the operational control of C.G., Allied Land Forces, although that army formed part of those forces. Since C.G., Allied Land Forces, likewise could not exercise administrative command over Sixth Army, it never came under his command at all.[2]

MacArthur did not consult the participating governments about this change as he should have done under the terms of his directive, nor did Blamey then raise the question with his own government, as he was entitled to do. Whether the procedure—or lack of it—was right or wrong, the new arrangement was probably the only one that, in the circumstances that had developed, would have been politically acceptable in Washington. The direction of the operations in the Pacific had been allotted to the U.S. Joint Chiefs of Staff. Although a majority of its troops were Australian, MacArthur's headquarters was not an Allied but an American organisation, although it received extensive specialist assistance from Australian staffs and individual officers. There were practical and psychological obstacles in the way of leaving an Australian commander in control of the Allied land forces in the field now that they included a substantial American contingent; and the Americans evidently considered that, if separate roles could be found for the Australian and the American Armies, difficulties inseparable from the coordination of forces possessing differing organisation and doctrines could be avoided.

When the Japanese entered the war General Krueger, the new army commander, had been in command of one of the four American armies—the Third—and from it he had drawn most of his staff for the Sixth Army.[3] That staff had trained for a short period in Texas near Fort Alamo, which had gained fame in an American war with Mexico—hence "Alamo Force". One of America's most senior generals, Krueger was 62, German-born, cautious, tenacious and unexcitable. His previous war record included experience in the ranks during the American-Spanish war of 1898, as a junior officer in the Philippines insurrection of 1899-1903 and on the Mexican border in 1916, and as a staff officer in France in 1918.

Krueger set up his headquarters on 20th June at Milne Bay. On the same day Rear-Admiral Barbey flew in and hoisted his flag. Although there were many ribald tales about reconnaissance parties[4] having a good time with the comely Trobriand girls, the American troops were not informed that there was little likelihood of any opposition on the islands of Kiriwina and Woodlark; Krueger wished his men to have the experience of carrying out the landings, the first big amphibious operation in the S.W.P.A., under full combat conditions. And General Kenney, Vice-Admiral Carpender and Rear-Admiral Barbey did not expect that the landings would be undetected and intended to be ready at least for air

---

[2] W. Krueger, *From Down Under to Nippon: The Story of Sixth Army in World War II* (1953), p. 10.

[3] From August until December 1941 Krueger's Chief of Staff was Brigadier-General Dwight D. Eisenhower.

[4] In May small reconnaissance parties slipped ashore on Woodlark and Kiriwina to report on airfield sites, beach and defence conditions.

and naval reaction. As D-day was fixed for 30th June, however, it seemed that the landings would escape heavy opposition because of the more important landings at Nassau Bay and in the central Solomons, scheduled for the same day.

An advanced party of the 112th Cavalry Regiment made the landing on Woodlark Island from two destroyers on the night of the 22nd-23rd June. Ashore was Lieutenant Mollison,[5] a coastwatcher of the Australian Navy, who had not been informed of the operation. Natives saw the invading force and warned Mollison who formed them up into a "skirmish line" about 100 yards inland. Hearing the landing troops speaking in American accents, however, Mollison joined the shore party without any accidents.

The same destroyers landed the advanced party of the 158th Regimental Combat Team on Kiriwina on 24th June. Again the landing might have been opposed by Australian troops who were stationed on Kiriwina to protect a radar station. The Australians had been told that the island would subsequently be occupied by United States troops but were not told when. Seeing only two destroyers they feared that the enemy had arrived to put off troops to oppose the American landing.

The main bodies of both forces landed on the night 30th June-1st July. On 16th July an R.A.A.F. aircraft landed on the newly constructed airstrip on Woodlark and by 23rd July the American 67th Fighter Squadron began operations from Woodlark. Four days later the Japanese bombed Woodlark for the first time and followed this by another raid on 1st August. The construction of an airfield on Kiriwina was delayed initially because of heavy rains, unexpected difficulties with roads, and the slow arrival of heavy constructional equipment, but by 19th August No. 79 Squadron, R.A.A.F., was ready to begin operations from the island.

Kiriwina and Woodlark, however, never really paid dividends on the investment of effort. Although "planning was so thorough and comprehensive that the plans for movement of troops, supplies, and equipment in amphibious shipping became standing operating procedure for future invasions",[6] by the time the air bases were established the war had moved on and they were little more than "fixed carriers"[7] too far behind the fighting front to play an impressive part in the battle.

During his conference with MacArthur in Brisbane Halsey had explained his plan for moving north in the Solomons. New Georgia loomed as the next obstacle. MacArthur accepted Halsey's view that the invasion of New Georgia should take place at the same time as the occupation of Kiriwina and Woodlark rather than after the establishment of bases on the Huon Peninsula as MacArthur's staff had been advocating, and D-day was set at 15th May (later postponed to 30th June) to coincide with the Nassau Bay and island landings. Halsey was already building two

---

[5] Lt P. J. Mollison, RANVR. Coastwatcher, AIB. Patrol officer; of Melbourne and New Guinea; b. Melbourne, 17 Apr 1914.

[6] J. Miller, Jr, *Cartwheel: The Reduction of Rabaul*, p. 50.

[7] S. E. Morison, *Breaking the Bismarcks Barrier, 22 July 1942-1 May 1944*, p. 134.

airfields on the Russell Islands, which had been taken unopposed on 21st February 1943 by the 43rd Division.

In March and April 1943 the 37th Division from Fiji had relieved the Americal Division on Guadalcanal, and at the end of May the division's 148th Regiment had relieved the 43rd Division on the Russells. On the north-west tip of New Georgia the Japanese had hacked out Munda airfield; and on circular Kolombangara was Vila airstrip. Munda and Vila were among the bases from which the Japanese attacked Guadalcanal and Allied shipping in the Solomons area. Farther north was the enemy stronghold of Bougainville, the final objective, with its surrounding islands, Buka, the Treasurys, the Shortlands, and Ballale, all sheltering airfields and anchorages manned by large garrisons.

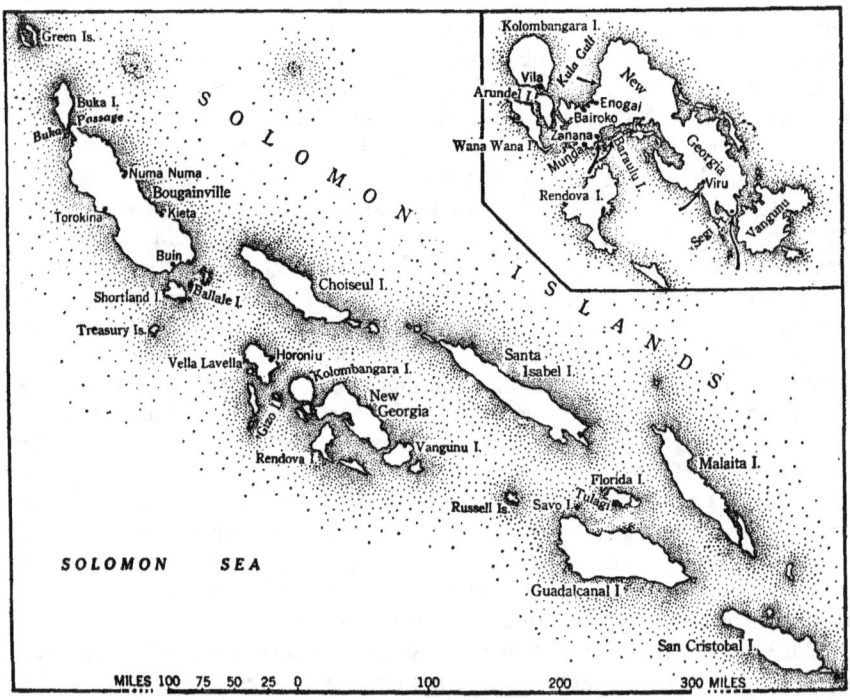

As a curtain raiser to the main attack on New Georgia and to aid a coastwatcher, Major Kennedy,[8] who was being pressed by the Japanese, two companies of marines landed unopposed at Segi Point on New Georgia on 20th-21st June after receiving a cheerful "O.K. here" from Kennedy. Next day two companies of the 43rd Division landed. Six miles east of Munda in the rainy pre-dawn of 30th June (soon after other Americans had landed far to the west at Nassau Bay) a destroyer-transport and

---

[8] Maj D. G. Kennedy, DSO. British Solomon Is Protectorate Defence Force 1941-45. District Commissioner. British Solomon Is; of Invercargill, NZ; b. Springhills, NZ, 12 Mar 1898.

minesweeper disembarked two companies on Sasavele and Baraulu Islands. At sunrise the 172nd Regiment landed on Rendova. Assisted by a party of Solomon Islanders under Major M. Clemens (of the British Solomon Islands Protectorate Defence Force) the 172nd killed about a quarter of the Japanese garrison of 300 and chased the remainder inland.

Rendova was a stepping-stone for Munda. Without opposition on 2nd July the 169th and 172nd Regimental Combat Teams landed on New Georgia at Zanana ready to attack west towards Munda. To prevent the Japanese garrison on Kolombangara from reinforcing the Munda garrison, it was decided to land a force on the north coast of New Georgia with orders to secure Enogai Inlet, block the Munda-Bairoko trail and later to secure Bairoko harbour. For this task a force consisting of a battalion of marines and two battalions from the 37th Division (a total of 2,600 men) landed unopposed early on 5th July. Here they were greeted by a coastwatcher, Flight Lieutenant Corrigan[9] (R.A.A.F.), who had organised a carrying party of 200 natives to help carry supplies inland. After some severe fighting the force captured Enogai on the 10th at a price of 51 dead and 76 wounded.

In the main battle area the 43rd Division was faring badly. By 9th July the 169th and 172nd Regiments were slowly advancing west against developing defences. To shorten the supply routes the 172nd secured a new beach-head 4,000 yards west of Zanana while the 169th struggled along the Munda trail. Stubborn resistance by the Japanese, who seemed to the Americans both elusive and ubiquitous, stopped the advance. Worse still the enemy infiltrated behind both regiments and cut the thinly held supply routes from Zanana. Under these circumstances, the hungry and sleepless division was in danger of defeat and urgently needed reinforcing.

The American commanders were becoming anxious. They controlled the air and sea and outnumbered the Japanese on the ground. "Rugged as jungle fighting is," wrote Halsey later, "by now we should have been within reach of our objective, the airfield. Something was wrong."[1] On the 15th Major-General Oscar W. Griswold, the commanding general of XIV Corps, was placed in command. The original plan had allotted about 15,000 men to wipe out the 9,000 Japanese on New Georgia; by the time the island was secured, the Americans had sent in more than 50,000. "When I look back on ELKTON, the smoke of charred reputations still makes me cough," wrote Halsey.[2]

When, on 11th July, the enemy drove a wedge between the two regiments of the 43rd Division, two regiments of the 37th Division—the 145th and 148th—were ordered to relieve the 169th Regiment and strengthen the tenuous American line. The 145th landed at Zanana on 16th July and the 148th on the 18th.

Fierce fighting continued throughout July, but after a long struggle the Japanese began to yield. On 1st August the 43rd Division reported

---
[9] F-Lt J. A. Corrigan, 273074. Coastwatcher, AIB. Mine manager; of Wewak, NG; b. 14 Nov 1904.
[1] W. F. Halsey and J. Bryan, *Admiral Halsey's Story*, p. 161.
[2] Halsey and Bryan, p. 161.

thankfully, "The going is easy." All along the front on 2nd August the Americans advanced, and next day the Japanese commander ordered an evacuation. Enemy remnants still resisted but on the same day leading troops of the 43rd and 37th Divisions converged on the eastern edge of Munda while the 148th Regiment cut the Munda-Bairoko trail thus preventing the enemy troops withdrawing along it. On the 5th organised resistance lessened and American infantry and tanks moved into Munda unopposed. By the time four New Zealand aircraft landed on Munda airfield on 13th August the enemy remnants had fled from the island.

To seize Arundel Island, the stopper in the bottom of Kula Gulf, Griswold landed the tired 172nd Regiment on 27th August. Reinforced from Vila the Japanese fought back and it was not until 20th September that the 172nd, reinforced by 2 battalions and 13 tanks, captured Arundel for the loss of 44 dead and 256 wounded.

In order to isolate Kolombangara, Nimitz had suggested to Halsey on 11th July that he should land troops on Vella Lavella to the north-west and thus bypass it. Until this time neither side had been much interested in Vella Lavella, but with the capture of New Georgia both began to cast eyes in its direction. On 15th August the 35th Regimental Combat Team (25th Division) landed unopposed. The Japanese regarded the landing on Vella Lavella as a threat to the evacuation of Kolombangara. On 19th August a mixed army and navy force of about 390 men from Buin landed at Horoniu on the north-east of Vella Lavella where a barge base was established. On 4th September, the Americans, slowly advancing towards Horoniu, first skirmished with the Japanese and captured a plan of the defences. Ten days later the barge depot was captured and, on 18th September, Major-General Barrowclough's[3] 3rd New Zealand Division relieved, with one brigade, the 35th Regiment. It completed the destruction of the enemy on Vella Lavella by 9th October.

"The Central Solomons campaign ranks with Guadalcanal and Buna-Gona for intensity of human tribulation," wrote the American naval historian. "We had Munda, and we needed it for the next move, toward Rabaul; but we certainly took it the hard way. The strategy and tactics of the New Georgia campaign were among the least successful of any Allied campaign in the Pacific."[4] New Georgia had indeed been a lengthy and costly affair. It was planned to capture the island with one division but elements of four divisions were eventually used. American casualties totalled 1,094 dead and 3,873 wounded. A count of enemy dead, not including Vella Lavella, totalled 2,483. But on Vella Lavella and New Georgia four airfields brought all Bougainville within range of Allied fighters.

Meanwhile, in May, the Americans had opened an offensive against the Japanese northern flank in the Aleutians where, in June 1942, the

---

[3] Maj-Gen Rt Hon Sir Harold Barrowclough, KCMG, CB, DSO, MC, ED. (1914-18: CO 4 Bn NZ Rifle Bde.) Comd 6 NZ Bde 1940-42; GOC 1 NZ Div 1942, 2 NZEF in Pacific and 3 NZ Div 1942-44. Chief Justice of New Zealand since 1953. Barrister-at-law; of Auckland, NZ; b. Masterton, NZ, 23 Jun 1894.

[4] Morison, p. 224.

Japanese had placed garrisons on the islands of Attu and Kiska. The 7th American Division was landed on Attu on 11th May and after 20 days of fighting, in which about 600 Americans and 2,350 Japanese were killed, they secured the island.

Planning immediately began for an attack on the more formidable base of Kiska where the enemy had built roads, submarine pens, a seaplane base and a modern airfield. American submarines and the Eleventh Air Force maintained a continual attack on the island until August. On 22nd July the air force and a task force heavily bombarded the island. Next day a dense arctic fog-bank descended for a week. Realising the hopelessness of their positions on Kiska after the capture of Attu, Japanese transports sneaked into Kiska and removed the garrison (about 10,000) by 28th July. When a powerful force, consisting of three American regimental combat teams and the 13th Canadian Brigade, landed on 14th August they found only an abandoned base, and insults scribbled on the walls.

Meanwhile the Australian Army was entering upon the largest offensive operation yet undertaken by the Allies in the Pacific (having regard both to the size of the opposing forces and the area to be involved). That army was still having difficulty, however, in maintaining its strength. On 13th July the War Cabinet reaffirmed that three divisions must be maintained for the offensive operations planned by MacArthur, and also that there must be "adequate forces" for the defence of Australia and New Guinea. At the same time the army was receiving only 4,000 male and 1,000 female recruits a month, and General Blamey had already pointed out that this was not enough to maintain the existing formations.[5] The War Cabinet also decided in July that the force on the mainland should be reduced by one infantry division within the next six months and, if the A.I.F. corps was employed in an offensive role for a period of 12 months, by the equivalent of a further division. In the event, as already narrated, the 2nd Motor Division ceased to exist, leaving the 6th, 7th, 9th, 2nd, 3rd, 4th, 5th, 11th and 12th Divisions (and the 1st, a purely training division), the 1st and 3rd Armoured.[6]

The army's commitments had now been increased in the Torres Strait-Merauke area. On 6th May MacArthur had ordered Blamey to "augment

---

[5] At the end of August 462,725 men were in the AMF, a decrease of 4,176 on the figures of four months previously; 312,285 of these were members of the AIF. Comparative figures for the RAAF and RAN at this time were, respectively, 139,726 (an increase of 11,529 in four months) including 19,812 serving overseas; and 33,408 (an increase of 2,750) including 18,074 serving afloat.

At the end of August MacArthur had 173,091 American soldiers under his command. There were also 67,215 members of the American Air Force and anti-aircraft units, making a grand total of 240,306—an increase of 79,851 in four months.

[6] At 31st August the 1st Armoured Division included the 1st Armoured and 3rd Motor Brigades; the 3rd Armoured Division included only an armoured brigade and divisional troops. The 4th Armoured Brigade still had its four regiments, and there were two "battalion groups" equipped with heavy tanks. In September both armoured divisions ceased to exist.

To complete the story of the disbanding of the armoured forces during 1944: the two tank battalion groups were disbanded in February, two armoured regiments in May, and then the 3rd Motor Brigade. By August there remained the 1st Armoured Brigade Group (2/6th and 2/10th Regiments) and the 4th Armoured Brigade Group (1st, 2/4th, 2/5th and 2/9th Regiments). Two regiments had now been in action—the 2/6th at Buna in 1942 and the 1st round Sattelberg in 1943.

the Torres Strait garrison by one brigade group and such divisional troops as are necessary to bring the strength of this area, including Merauke [in Dutch New Guinea] to approximately one composite division". In accordance with this instruction the 4th Division, consisting now of two brigades, provided the troops for York Peninsula, Torres Strait and Merauke. Japanese aircraft attacked the remote garrison at Merauke fairly frequently and long-range patrols had some clashes with Japanese patrols, as will be described later.

It was evident that for the remainder of the war the Australian Army would be used entirely against the Japanese in the Pacific. In order to prevent any repetition of the mistakes of sending inadequately trained units to fight in New Guinea the Australian Army was now being trained in a common mould. As mentioned in the previous volume, the Atherton Tableland in northern Queensland had been selected as a training ground for divisions destined to fight in the islands to the north. When Blamey first ordered a reconnaissance of the Atherton Tableland in November 1942 with a view to locating three divisions plus hospitals and convalescent depots there he had in mind the desirability of being able to bring troops forward to New Guinea more rapidly than hitherto, and the fact that rugged jungle country suitable for training was available on the tableland. Four officers made a thorough examination of the area, where already more than 5,000 troops were located, and selected a number of sites in the relatively dry western belt of the tableland. They recommended that only two divisions be placed on the tableland in view of the limitations imposed by the wet season, water supply and communications, and the third in the Townsville-Charters Towers area. Finally, however, accommodation was provided for more than 70,000 troops. From the point of view of the troops a big disadvantage of Atherton was its distance from the pleasures of the city. (The Americans were treated more kindly in this regard. In December 1942 when the 1st Marine Division from Guadalcanal arrived at Brisbane they found their camp there too uncomfortable and were moved to Mount Martha near Melbourne.) From early in 1943 when the 7th Division and the 16th Brigade began to arrive at Atherton, nearly all malaria-infected units returning from service in New Guinea were sent there for anti-malarial treatment before going on leave, and after leave the units usually returned to Atherton for training.

While these units returning from New Guinea were stationed at Atherton, new recruits were trained under rugged conditions at Canungra in the Macpherson Ranges, where the climate was less hospitable, but where jungle conditions were available near by. On 3rd November 1942 Army Headquarters had ordered the formation of an "L.H.Q. Training Centre (Jungle Warfare)" at Canungra. At this time it was decided that Canungra would consist of a reinforcement training centre, an Independent Company training centre, and a tactical school. With the establishment of Canungra the Independent Company training centre on Wilson's Promontory, where much money had been spent on camps and training facilities during 1941 and 1942, was abandoned.

The first troops to arrive at Canungra, on 27th November 1942, were the advanced party of the Independent Company troops from Wilson's Promontory. On 3rd December the first draft of infantry reinforcements arrived for training. At the end of December there were 96 officers and 1,279 men in training, and the first draft of 218 trained men marched out to units. By the end of April there were 164 officers and 3,320 men in camp.

By May 1943 the Canungra training centre consisted of an advanced reinforcement training centre for jungle warfare, a Commando Training Battalion, and any Independent Company that was re-forming or refitting.[7] The infantry training centre was training reinforcements for all combat units except signals. Men trained to a "normal draft priority 1 standard" (known as D.P.1's) were received at Canungra from Australian training camps, and were given an extra four weeks' training in jungle warfare before being sent forward. There were 2,000 reinforcements organised in eight training companies; 500 were received each week and 500 sent forward each week. The Commando Training Battalion trained reinforcements for the seven Independent Companies.

Canungra training was tough and realistic in the extreme. The concept was that the men should live and train under conditions as near as possible to those of active service. The reinforcements were ruthlessly disciplined, put through a hard physical fitness test, and given confidence in themselves and their weapons. With practically no amenities except for a canteen day and picture night once a week, and no leave except compassionate, the men were rigorously trained for 12 hours on each of six days and six nights each week for three weeks. For the fourth week they were sent into the deep and rough Macpherson bush, which closely resembled that of New Guinea, on a six-day exercise in which they carried their own food. If the men qualified on this final test they were passed out as fit for jungle warfare. The training for the Independent Company reinforcements was even more strenuous and covered a period of eight weeks in much the same way.

Canungra also trained 60 new officers from the Officer Cadet Training Unit (O.C.T.U.) each six weeks in the duties of a platoon commander in jungle warfare. Many of the instructors had seen service in the Middle East and South-West Pacific. It was made plain to the instructors that no man would move forward until he had reached a satisfactory standard of training. The test of a trainee's suitability would be, "If you were in the firing line and needed a reinforcement would you have him?" Canungra, commanded from January 1943 by Lieut-Colonel "Bandy" MacDonald,[8] helped enormously to create a finely trained army.

---

[7] Canungra was not equipped for this task. Early in 1943 three tired and experienced Independent Companies (2/2nd and 2/4th from Timor and 2/6th from New Guinea) gathered at Canungra after leave, and an attempt was made to treat them in the same manner as the reinforcements. This treatment did not last for long, mainly because all three companies were soon in action again. Thereafter Independent Companies usually returned to Atherton from service in the islands.
[8] Col A. B. MacDonald, SX4539. CO 2/16 Bn 1941; various training appointments including DDMT LHQ 1945. Regular soldier; of Walcha, NSW; b. Walcha, 13 Apr 1898.

After receiving MacArthur's warning order of 6th May Blamey issued his own plan which he described thus in his report:

> On 17th May 1943, from my headquarters in Brisbane, an order was issued giving in brief detail the method by which the task allotted New Guinea Force would be conducted. The seizure of the airfields in the Markham Valley involved, as a primary stage, the capture of the enemy base at Lae and this was to be carried out by two divisions: 9 Aust Div by a landing from the sea; 7 Aust Div by an overland advance down the Markham Valley. Planning for the operation was to be carried out conjointly by the Staff at my Advanced Headquarters in Brisbane and by the Headquarters staff of New Guinea Force at Port Moresby. Plans were to be completed in time to enable the launching of the operation on 1 August 1943 and arrangements were to be made for the move to New Guinea of portion of my Advanced Headquarters about fourteen days before the operation was to begin. On its arrival, the Commander of New Guinea Force was to establish a forward headquarters from which to control the activities of the Australian Corps, while I personally exercised command over the complete operation with my headquarters located at Port Moresby.[9]

Blamey arrived in Brisbane on 15th May and on the 16th he and Generals Herring and Berryman had the long conference mentioned earlier. It was because they had contemplated at this time that the 9th Division would be carried in the small craft of the 2nd Engineer Special Brigade that Nassau Bay, about 60 miles from Lae, had been selected as a staging point. Thus the present plans for the 3rd Division had been tied in with future plans for the 9th. As already narrated Herring carried Blamey's orders with him to Port Moresby on 22nd May.

In the new phase the acquisition and accommodation of adequate shipping would obviously be a major problem. To relieve congestion at Oro Bay where stores for the American air squadrons at Dobodura were accumulating, Herring decided to open a port at Buna for handling Australian requirements. Delays were caused because of the difficulty in obtaining a ship suitable for the transport of long piles for building a wharf. Attempts to obtain landing craft to unload the ships at anchor in the roadstead were unsuccessful in June because the craft were being used at Woodlark and Kiriwina. By 22nd July, however, when the first ship arrived at Buna, a few landing craft had been collected. Supplemented by some amphibious trucks (DUKWS), which arrived on the next ship, the Buna port boasted 22 landing craft on 21st August. With the completion of the wharf, shallow-draught coastal vessels unloaded there, while Liberty ships were unloaded into the landing craft until sufficiently reduced loads enabled them to tie up at the wharf. Morobe was also prepared as a base for the Americans who were to invade New Britain.

At the end of July Blamey asked MacArthur to begin the offensive on 27th August when the phase of the moon would be most suitable. MacArthur agreed and directed that the requirements of the offensive should receive first priority. Admiral Carpender took control of the water transportation system north of Buna; landing craft were withdrawn from Woodlark and Kiriwina for use along the north-east coast; small craft

---
[9] Commander Allied Land Forces, Report on New Guinea Operations, 4 September 1943 to 26 April 1944.

and amphibious trucks from Milne Bay were moved to Oro Bay and Buna; more troops were used for unloading; ships for maintaining Merauke Force were diverted; and the convoy system was revised to increase the speed of transport.

Describing this period Blamey wrote:

> These measures effected considerable improvement but as the target date approached it became obvious that complete readiness for the operation would not be obtained. The strategic position was such, however, that to delay the operation until the administrative position was entirely complete, would have granted the Japanese the time necessary to reinforce his forward troops and improve his general situation. I therefore decided to begin the offensive early in September when the administrative position would be capable of supporting the initial stages of the operation and of rapid expansion immediately afterwards.[1]

Blamey counted on a close association between the two A.I.F. divisions assigned to capture Lae and the Fifth Air Force. "The fulfilment of the offensive plan," he wrote, "contemplated the establishment of air superiority, the softening of enemy resistance by continued air attacks on the successive objectives of the land forces, and, by attacking enemy shipping, forward bases and airfields, the interruption to reinforcement and supply of enemy forces." The main enemy bases at Rabaul, Wewak, Madang and western New Britain were within range of medium bombers. In order to give fighter protection to these bombers and to provide close support in the early stages of the movement into the Lae-Markham Valley area, airfields had to be developed in the Watut Valley and an emergency landing ground established on the Bena Bena plateau.

Early in 1943 *Imperial General Headquarters* in Tokyo had decided to pursue a policy of "active defence" in the Solomons and to reinforce New Guinea for an "aggressive offensive". General Imamura in Rabaul therefore ordered General Adachi of the *XVIII Army* to strengthen Lae, Salamaua, Wewak and Madang, and in January and February the *20th* and *41st Divisions* were sent to Wewak from Palau. The Japanese were determined not to yield "an operational route for the proclaimed Philippines invasion". Imamura had emphasised to Adachi in April the importance of Lae and Salamaua, the building of a road from Madang to Lae and the establishment of coastal barge services from New Britain to Lae and Salamaua. In June Adachi was ordered to strengthen Finschhafen and prepare to capture Australian outposts and patrol bases at Wau, Bena Bena and Mount Hagen, as well as infiltrating up the Ramu and Sepik Rivers. The general idea was to prepare for an offensive in 1944. Without control of sea and air, however, and in the face of the gathering momentum of the Allied offensive, this resolve was bound to be but a pipe dream.

In New Guinea Adachi's army was then distributed thus—the *51st Division* in the Lae-Salamaua area, the *41st* in the Wewak area and the *20th* in the Madang-Wewak area. The main role of the force at Madang was to build the road through the upland valleys to Lae. Across the border in Dutch New Guinea the *XIX Army* was occupying positions along the coastline from the Vogelkop Peninsula to Hollandia. In the Solomons the *XVII Army*, consisting now mainly of the *6th Division*, was responsible for Bougainville; the *38th Division* and, from September, the *17th* were in New Britain under Imamura's direct control. While the Army was responsible for the northern Solomons the Navy—*South Eastern Fleet* (*XI Air Fleet* and *Eighth Fleet*)—under command of Vice-Admiral Jinichi Kusaka was responsible

---

[1] Report on New Guinea Operations, 4 September 1943 to 26 April 1944.

for the central Solomons where the *8th Combined Special Naval Landing Force* (*6th Kure* and *7th Yokosuka S.N.L.F's*) was garrisoning New Georgia, and the *7th* Santa Isabel Island. The naval troops on New Georgia were later reinforced by army troops—the *South-Eastern Detachment*.

The slow but sure Allied advance in New Guinea and the Solomons around mid-1943 compelled the Japanese leaders to take some counter-action. They decided to reinforce the area with another air division. Accordingly the *7th Air Division* in the Netherlands East Indies was transferred from the *Southern Army* to the *Eighth Area Army*. From June onwards its aircraft began to arrive in New Guinea. To coordinate the operations of the *6th* and *7th Air Divisions* a *Fourth Air Army Headquarters* (under Lieut-General Kumaichi Teramoto) was established at Rabaul on 6th August. The *6th Air Division* was to operate from Rabaul, the Admiralties, Wewak and Hansa Bay, while the *7th* would develop rear bases at But, Boikin, Aitape and Hollandia. The tasks of the two air divisions were to cooperate directly with the *XVIII Army* and to a lesser extent with the *XIX Army* in the Banda Sea area. About a fortnight after Teramoto's command was established, and just as a substantial number of planes were arriving in New Guinea, he lost practically the lot when, as mentioned, Allied air armadas attacked airfields in the Wewak area with devastating effect on 17th and 18th August.

CHAPTER 9

BENA BENA AND TSILI TSILI

IN the hinterland of New Guinea south of the towering Bismarck and Wahgi Ranges lies a huge plateau of grasslands. It begins near Kainantu about 100 miles west of Lae by the imperceptible watershed whence the Markham and Ramu Rivers run in opposite directions, and continues through Bena Bena, Garoka, and Chimbu to Mount Hagen, a distance of about 130 miles. Beyond, it goes on to the Star Mountains and the Dutch border, a total distance from Kainantu of roughly 350 miles. The plateau, criss-crossed by many small streams and broken into numerous valleys, is seldom wider than 20 miles. Lying at about 5,000 feet, it has a bracing temperate climate, and is free from mosquitoes.

Before the war relatively few white men were established on this plateau, so strangely different to the tropical jungle mainly encountered elsewhere in New Guinea. To protect the large but untamed population from exploitation, the administration had declared the Bena Bena-Mount Hagen plateau a closed area. The natives were smaller than the Papuan and Melanesian natives already so well known to Australian soldiers. Like many primitive peoples they fought tribal wars, but they were primarily gardening folk. And what a garden they lived in! To the first band of Australian soldiers who arrived there the Bena plateau seemed like an Eden.

The Mount Hagen area had been thoroughly penetrated in 1933 by a patrol led by an Assistant District Officer, J. L. Taylor. In the next year Roman Catholic and Lutheran missionaries established themselves in the area, and other missionaries followed. Patrolling continued and, by 1941, roads had been built in the Chimbu area, where 31,000 natives had been counted, and a post established at Mount Hagen, where 22,000 natives had been counted within a 10-mile radius.

Farther west the mountain country in which the Sepik rises had been visited by relatively few expeditions. The German explorer, Dr Thurnwald, had led a party to the headwaters of the Sepik in 1914. In 1926-1927 C. H. Karius and Ivan Champion, two officers of the Papuan administration, had crossed the island from south to north, travelling up the Fly River, across the Hindenburg Range and down the Sepik.[1] In 1936 and 1937 a party of seven under J. Ward Williams made a mining investigation of the upper Sepik area. This group made a landing ground in the Telefomin country on which was landed an amphibian aircraft, and, for the next five months, largely air-supplied, explored, on foot and from the air, the country round the headwaters of the Sepik.[2]

---

[1] See I. F. Champion, *Across New Guinea from the Fly to the Sepik* (1932).
[2] Stuart Campbell, "The Country between the Headwaters of the Fly and Sepik Rivers in New Guinea", *Geographical Journal*, September 1938. Flight Lieutenant (later Group Captain) S. A. C. Campbell was the pilot of the aircraft.

In March 1938 J. L. Taylor, J. R. Black and four other Europeans with about 250 natives set out from Mount Hagen towards the Dutch border. In the next 15 months this expedition covered the central highlands from Mount Hagen to Telefomin in the west and from below the Papuan border in the south to the Sepik in the north. They were supplied by parachute at one stage and made extensive aerial reconnaissances.

Thus, in miniature, several methods being used in 1943 on a larger scale had been employed in this area: supply by air transport, the dropping of supplies, and reconnaissance by land-based aircraft and flying-boat.

At the beginning of 1943 the natives in the Bena Bena-Mount Hagen country were a responsibility of J. R. Black (now a captain in Angau and the district officer for the Ramu area), and his staff of 4 officers and 9 N.C.O's. Black was able to recruit large teams of native carriers, mainly from the Chimbus who formed the largest numerical group of the population, but these carriers could safely be used only in the high non-malarious plateau and not in lower areas where they were likely to die from malaria. Payment for native services was made with sea shells.

At Bena Bena itself was a crude pre-war airstrip about 1,200 yards long, a fact known to the Japanese. The plateau would be strategically valuable to either side: for the Allies occupation of the plateau would help them to outflank the main enemy positions in the Huon Peninsula and Finisterre Mountains and provide emergency or advanced airfields; for the Japanese, occupation would place them on the high ground on the flanks of the main route through upland New Guinea, the Markham-Ramu valley. Early in 1943, however, both sides were recuperating after the fierce battles of the previous six months, and their resources were strained by the Wau-Mubo campaign.

Realising how close the Japanese had come to establishing themselves at Wau, and how much more difficult it would be to expel them from the interior of New Guinea than from the periphery, the Australians decided that they must occupy the plateau before the Japanese did so, even though only a small force could be employed. The Americans were interested in the plateau's potentialities, particularly since August 1942 when Lieutenant Hampton of the Fifth Air Force landed four American technicians on the rough Bena strip to collect parts from a crashed Mitchell near by, and picked them up four days later.

Thus New Guinea Force on 22nd January 1943 had ordered the 6th Australian Division to dispatch a small force by air from Port Moresby to Bena Bena next day. Lieutenant Rooke and 57 men of the 2/7th Battalion landed at the Bena Bena strip on 23rd January from six Douglas transport aircraft.[3] An operation instruction stated that the task of this small band (known as Bena Force) would be "to secure Bena Bena drome against enemy attack; to deny the enemy freedom of movement in the

---

[3] The force comprised Rooke's own platoon—17 Platoon—and 3 men from each of "A", "B" and "C" Companies, plus one section of machine-gunners (10 men and 2 Vickers guns), 2 signallers, a medical officer and a medical orderly. Rooke was joined later by one of the Air Wireless Warning companies.

Bena Bena Valley; to harass and delay any enemy movement in the area between Bena Bena and Ramu River".

Kanga Force was made responsible for the Bena detachment and Rooke was placed in charge of all troops on the Bena plateau. Besides his own troops these consisted of the small Angau detachment under Captain Black, a detachment of the R.A.A.F's Rescue and Communication Flight,

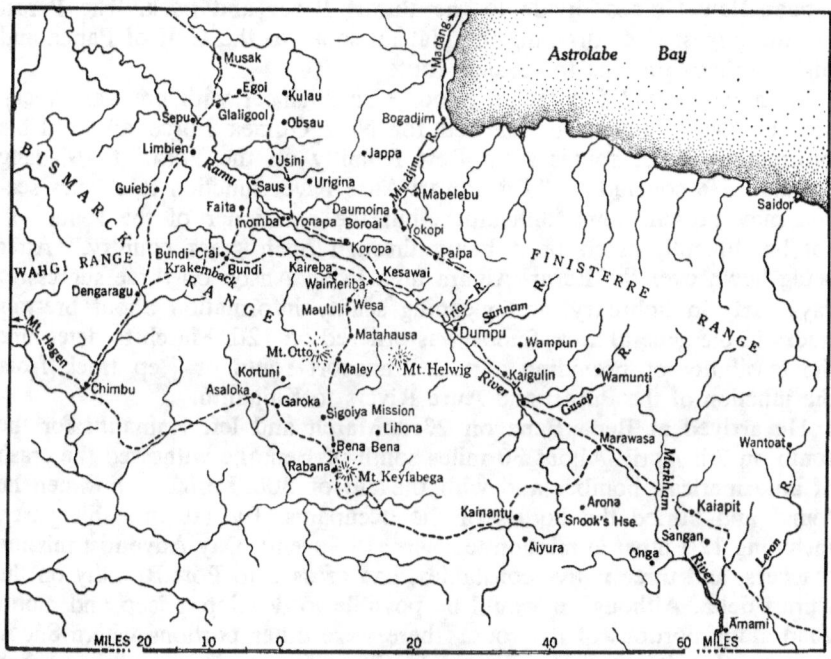

The Central Highlands

and "special New Guinea Force patrols" which were operating from Bena Bena. Information about the Japanese was scanty, but it was estimated that a Japanese force of about 1,000 was in Madang and was sending patrols south and south-west towards the Ramu; on 20th January about 100 Japanese were reported to be at Dumpu while a smaller patrol had attempted to cross the Ramu south of Kesawai. Not wishing to stir up the enemy across the river and invite reprisals, Brigadier R. N. L. Hopkins, then senior staff officer of New Guinea Force, instructed that "patrols of Bena Force will not cross Ramu River".

The tiny Bena Force could hardly be expected to hold the plateau against a determined Japanese thrust, but they might delay it long enough for reinforcements to be flown in as had been done recently at Wau. For the present, however, even if more troops could be found it would be difficult to spare the aircraft to fly them in, let alone supply them. It was apparent too that it would be easier for the Japanese to supply a base on the

Bena plateau by a land route from their north coast bases than for the Allies to do so by air from their south-eastern bases.

Just as the Bulldog Road was designed to provide an overland route to Wau, so New Guinea Force had been looking for an overland route from the south coast to the Bena plateau (and thence to Lae and Madang). For instance, in September and October 1942 Lieutenant Bloxham[4] of Angau had patrolled through uncontrolled areas from Kainantu across the Papuan-New Guinea divide to the Purari River and back. The Purari was the largest river draining the plateau south to the Gulf of Papua and might perhaps provide the easiest route.

In January 1943 Lieutenant Snook,[5] an engineer with pre-war experience in New Guinea, summarised for New Guinea Force all available information about routes from Port Romilly on the Purari to Madang and Lae. He concluded: "The Purari-Aure River junction to Aiyura section may present some difficulties, but the remainder of the route will not be difficult, much of it being through open grass country." After being flown over the Purari-Aiyura area in an Anson on three successive days early in February, and gleaning scanty information about pre-war tracks in the general area, Snook was ordered on 12th March to determine the feasibility of providing a pack transport route or jeep track from the junction of the Purari and Aure Rivers to Kainantu.

He arrived at Bena Bena on 23rd March and left Kainantu for the south on 7th April. About 30 miles south of Bena he witnessed the crash of an American bomber and with the aid of 300 Kesikena bowmen he found and buried the bodies of the occupants. By 1st June his party, including 12 Lutheran mission teachers, 13 Seventh Day Adventist mission teachers, and three native constables, had crossed to Port Romilly on the Purari delta. Although it would be possible to develop a jeep and motor road along portions of the route, there were other portions where Snook thought that it would be extremely difficult even to establish a pack transport route. Meanwhile, the Japanese were preparing to build a road south from Bogadjim to the Ramu over the rugged Finisterre Mountains.

As soon as Rooke's small band arrived in January 1943 it had begun digging defences around the Bena Bena airstrip, and soon Corporal Berry led a patrol towards Kainantu where he arrived on 28th January. The force rapidly became acquainted with the people of Bena Bena and the Chimbu carriers and, as ever, the natives seemed to appreciate the Australians' sense of humour. Soon they were helping them to build huts, chop timber for pill-boxes, and clear the kunai and crotelaria for fields of fire. By the end of January the Bena Force diarist stated that the natives were "working like tigers", patrols were reconnoitring all approaches, and four observation posts were established watching the tracks into Bena Bena

---

[4] Maj A. A. Bloxham, NGX454; Angau. District officer; of Lae, NG; b. Birmingham, England, 29 Jun 1906.

[5] Lt E. R. Snook, NX65877; RAE I Corps Troops. Recruiter of native labour; of Neutral Bay, NSW; b. Sydney, 17 Feb 1912.

with telephone communication to Bena airfield. One was in the Rabana area and the others close to the airfield. Attempts were made to conceal the Australian positions from the air, the airstrip was burnt in patches to resemble the surrounding partially burnt grasslands, the three-feet-deep gutters running down each side of the strip were filled in and grass allowed to grow to merge in with the airfield.

On 8th February four men left to reconnoitre the most direct route across the Bismarcks from the Ramu Valley into the plateau: the Waimeriba-Wesa-Matahausa track. Eight days later the patrol returned. "Tough trip" was the diarist's laconic comment describing the tortuous crawl over the range between Mounts Helwig and Otto towards the river flats. A patrol to Lihona in March found a native war raging along the route.

During the first two months Rooke was supplied by air, 12 transport loads arriving between 5th and 23rd February. To augment the ordinary army rations, already supplemented by native fruits and vegetables, a herd of mission cattle from Kainantu was driven to Bena Bena by two ex-stockmen in Bena Force.

Towards the end of March, when native rumours suggested that the Japanese were in Kaiapit and Sangan, Rooke moved his headquarters into the Kainantu area closer to Kaiapit. Before this there had been rumours that, in January or February, three Japanese patrols, totalling about 150 troops, had made the trip along the old trade route from Bogadjim across the Finisterres and down the great river valleys to Lae. On 2nd April Sergeant Cavalieri,[6] who had left Bena on 10th March to establish a teleradio station at Onga, reported that 90 Japanese were in the Kaiapit-Sangan area. As this enemy party had not been seen in the Ramu Valley it was assumed that it came from Lae, although it would not be hard for 90 men, moving under cover of darkness or weather along the river flats, to escape observation from the few and scattered observation posts overlooking the Ramu. "The Japs having decided to return to Lae and Madang," wrote the Bena Force diarist on 9th April, "our forward headquarters has decided to return to its base at Bena Bena."

Native reports indicating renewed enemy interest in the Ramu area soon began to reach Angau and Air Wireless Warning posts stationed along the Bismarcks, and were radioed back to Bena. From 20 to 30 Japanese with a carrier line of 50 natives were reported at Musak some miles west of Bogadjim on 26th April; four days later they were at Sepu on the Ramu. About the same time Japanese patrols were reported to be mapping the Koropa and Kesawai areas, directly north of the main route into the Bena plateau, and to have three native working parties cracking stones, presumably for the Bogadjim to Ramu road.

Throughout May the enemy showed increased interest in the three main approaches to the plateau. Native rumours made it appear that a limited enemy offensive against the Chimbu-Bena area, using the approaches through Guiebi, Bundi and Wesa might be imminent. It seemed definite

---

[6] Lt C. Cavalieri, NGX388. NGVR and Angau. Miner; of Merri Creek, TNG; b. Lugano, Switzerland, 22 Jul 1920.

that on 4th May a large Japanese force visited Kaigulin where it actually crossed the Ramu River. On 9th May a watching police boy saw two Japanese cross the river at Waimeriba. Next day Captain Rooke's watching post was surprised by a party of about 15 Japanese led in by hostile natives and had its supplies captured although it suffered no casualties. On 19th May Bena Force suffered its first casualty when an Australian was killed by natives.

At Port Moresby and Brisbane Australian planners by May 1943 were anxious about the frequent reports that the Japanese were interested in the plateau. New Guinea Force estimated that the Japanese now had at least 10,000 troops at Madang with about 500 at Bogadjim, and camps in the Egoi area 30 miles west of Bogadjim. For the first time the Japanese air force began to take an interest in the plateau and six attacks were made in May over Bena Bena and the old emergency landing strips at Asaloka and Garoka. As it now seemed possible that the Japanese intended to make a road from Madang to Bogadjim and across the Finisterres to the Ramu Valley and thence to Lae, it was decided that Rooke's tiny force must be reinforced.

As a battalion would be too difficult to supply, Major T. F. B. MacAdie's 2/7th Independent Company was withdrawn to Port Moresby from Wau and preparations made to send it to Bena Bena. The Independent Company, which had served in the Wau area for seven months, was tired and needed a rest but no other troops were immediately available.

On 27th May MacAdie received instructions from General Herring (who had returned to command of New Guinea Force on the 23rd) to move his company by air to Bena Bena and take command of all troops on the plateau. His tasks were the same as those originally given to Rooke in January, but he was to be directly responsible to New Guinea Force and not the 3rd Division. He would not, "except when attack is imminent or in progress interfere with the general tasks of Angau and special detachments". On 29th May the 2/7th was flown in, and Bena Force was then about 400 strong. MacAdie found that Angau was maintaining watching posts at Onga, Kainantu, Bundi, Lihona and Matahausa, but "these were not very effective as all information was from native sources and much of it unreliable". As he became acquainted with his area during June he noted that there were four main lines of approach to Bena Bena which the enemy might follow: first, from Lae through Kaiapit, Aiyura and Kainantu; secondly, from Bogadjim over the Finisterres, and through Lihona; thirdly, from Bogadjim through Kesawai, Wesa and Matahausa; and fourthly, from Bogadjim through Glaligool, Bundi and Asaloka. He therefore directed that observation posts should be established well forward and with good communications to give the greatest possible warning; that patrol bases should be dug on each of the approaches, and that delaying positions should be prepared along the lines of approach to inflict the greatest possible delay and so enable him to concentrate at the right place once the main threat was clear. Terrain difficulties would delay a Japanese advance on Bena Bena for several days after crossing the Ramu and MacAdie reasoned that if he had some mobility he would be in a better position to beat off an attack. He got permission to build a motor road from Bena Bena to Kainantu, to enable him to move his scanty reserves laterally and quickly.

In June he sent out patrols to test the native rumours; built huts for the troops and bomb-proof shelters for stores; recruited labour through Angau; proceeded with "extensive mapping, as existing maps hopelessly inaccurate";[7] reconnoitred the proposed vehicle route from Bena to Kainantu; and constructed a vehicle road from Bena to Garoka to link the Bena airfield with a proposed new airfield at Garoka.

There had been several pre-war airstrips besides Bena Bena dotted on the plateau from Mount Hagen to Kainantu. The small emergency strip at Garoka could not be extended, but near by there was excellent flat land for a large airstrip. Seeking an adequate fighter strip which could support raids against the enemy's north coast bases, and divert the enemy's attention from more important construction in the Watut Valley, the Fifth Air Force became interested in Garoka. General Kenney "didn't care about making anything more than a good emergency field, but . . . wanted a lot of dust raised and construction started on a lot of grass huts so that the Japs' recco planes would notice". He also ordered his air force commanders "to be sure to explain to the natives that we were playing a good joke on the Japs, that we were trying to get them to send some bombers over".[8]

The Japanese made aerial reconnaissances of the general area on the 1st, 2nd and 5th June, and their aircraft began attacks on 8th June when 7 bombed Chimbu, 5 bombed Asaloka, and 8 bombed Kainantu. Further reconnaissances of the Bena-Garoka-Kainantu area on the 9th and 10th were followed on the 14th by heavy raids on the Bena Bena, old Garoka, Asaloka, Kainantu and Aiyura airstrips by 27 bombers and 30 fighters. Next day 6 bombers and 6 fighters attacked Kainantu and Aiyura, and on the 16th 18 bombers and 22 fighters attacked Bena Bena.

The attacks from the middle of June apparently pleased Kenney.

> As I had hoped (he wrote later), the Jap reccos spotted the dust we were raising and the new grass huts we were building around Garoka and Bena Bena and evidently decided we were about to establish forward airdromes there. Beginning on the 14th they attacked both Garoka and the Bena Bena almost daily, burning down the grass huts and bombing the cleared strips, which looked enough like runways to fool them. The natives thought it was all a huge joke and when the Japs put on an attack they would roll around on the ground with laughter and chatter away about how we were "making fool of the Jap man".[9]

To those who were actually the recipients of the Japanese bombs there seemed little reason for such mirth. In these raids three natives were killed and three Australians wounded. Force headquarters and a stores

---

[7] This statement did not refer to Rooke's track maps which formed the basis for later maps of the area.
[8] G. C. Kenney, *General Kenney Reports* (1949), p. 253.
[9] Kenney, pp. 262-3.

dump at Bena Bena, the Seventh Day Adventist mission at Asaloka, and several native huts were demolished or damaged.

Despite Kenney's pleasant fiction MacAdie was given no instructions about the wider deception strategy in his original briefing; although he had been carefully briefed by General Herring who subsequently went to the trouble of keeping MacAdie in the general picture—usually by means of a weekly hand-written letter. Very soon after his arrival, however, MacAdie realised that his whole tactical operation would have to be based on deception. If he could convince the Japanese that he was much stronger than he really was it might help to discourage them or cause them to delay an attack across the Ramu. His first deception measures, if his widespread dispositions are disregarded, were taken without reference to New Guinea Force and were designed to draw enemy air action away from Bena Bena airfield and confuse the enemy regarding the Australian intention to build an airfield at Garoka.

At this early stage it was vital for MacAdie not only to keep Bena Bena airfield in his hands but to keep it serviceable. In the first air attacks heavy bombs had cratered it and there were no resources but Chimbu labour with picks and shovels to repair it. MacAdie feared that repeated bombing might so crater it as to render it too dangerous for loaded transports, and his force would then be really isolated.

The building of the Garoka airfield required a very large labour force of Chimbus organised by Major Black's successor, Captain H. L. R. Niall.[1] If the Japanese air force were to attack Garoka while work was in progress, it would not need many Chimbu casualties to make the entire labour problem acute because the whole force was entirely dependent on Chimbu carriers.

MacAdie therefore determined to use Asaloka for deception, and to a lesser extent Aiyura. There were old emergency landing fields at both places. At Asaloka his men cut strips of kunai along the airfield as though it were about to be enlarged, kept fires burning, put up tents around the Mission building, hung out many clothes to dry, and tramped Chimbus up and down to make fresh tracks.

Early in June when MacAdie learnt that he was to be reinforced he established force headquarters at Sigoiya Mission and handed over control of the company to Captain F. J. Lomas. MacAdie decided to concentrate on the main route, and Lieutenant Byrne's[2] section was sent on 1st June over the Bismarcks toward Wesa to occupy the area. Byrne sent back a disturbing native rumour that the enemy would soon make a drive through Wesa to Bena Bena, and reported that Wesa and Waimeriba were occupied in strength and natives under Japanese direction were

---

[1] Bena Force used Chimbu labour almost exclusively; first, because they were better workers than the more indolent people of Bena Bena, and secondly, because the Bena Benas and, later, other tribes between Bena Bena and Kainantu were needed to grow kau kau (sweet potatoes—their staple food) for the Chimbus. Native labour was enlisted on a three months' contract and then paid off in shell and sent back to Chimbu to recuperate. At one stage between 3,000 and 4,000 Chimbus were enlisted.

[2] Capt E. F. Byrne, MC, NX58832. 2/7 Indep Coy, 2/7 Cdo Sqn. Clerk; of Campsie, NSW; b. Campsie, 23 May 1920.

burning the kunai and scrub on both sides of the Ramu. He added that natives had disclosed the position of the patrol to the enemy.

The native problem was indeed a serious one along the river front. "It should be realised," wrote MacAdie early in June, "that the country between the Ramu River and Bena Bena is uncontrolled, unexplored and unmapped. No definite information of roads or tracks can be gained even from Major Black of Angau, who knows this area better than any man. The area is vast, and the quickest recce on foot would require months." He considered that the natives north of the Bismarcks and south of the Ramu were "treacherous".

Even on the plateau difficulties were being experienced with the natives. The Angau representative at Chimbu, Captain Costelloe,[3] wrote at this time:

> There is a spirit of unrest throughout the whole of this district and this is mainly due to the unsettled state of mind existing amongst the natives which tends to disorganise their general outlook. It is not really an "anti-British" feeling so much as a distorted and disturbed mental reaction. . . . This area seems likely to become a centre of military operations in the very near future. All military activities are bound up with the amount of native labour available. The main source of native labour is the Chimbu area. At present recruits are coming forward willingly enough and are sticking to their jobs despite enemy aerial activity, but to maintain this we must keep a firm hold on the Chimbu natives and endeavour to keep them settled and controlled.

The supply of the outposts in the low area north of the Bismarcks presented a complex problem. The Chimbus were free from malaria and intended to remain so; remembering that many of those taken into the low country some years before had died from malaria the Chimbus refused to leave the high ground. Along the main route over the Bismarcks they would carry only to Matahausa, two days' carry from the Ramu. They were not rice-eaters and needed to carry from 10 to 12 pounds of native food for each day's ration. Thus on a four days' carry they would be fully loaded with their own food even before they began to strive to lift cases of bully beef or ammunition. Consequently Angau brought in some lowland carriers from the Waria and Sepik Rivers to carry north of the Bismarcks to the Ramu Valley.

With its knowledge of the Chimbus' refusal to leave the high ground, it was surprising that Angau headquarters in Port Moresby should have ordered on 13th June that 300 plateau natives be held ready to help construct airfields in the comparatively low-lying Watut Valley.

Reports now arrived of enemy patrols in Dumpu, Kaiapit, Onga and Boana, and of patrols moving south from Bogadjim across the Finisterres, from the Rai Coast across the Saruwageds, and from the north-east coast by pinnace along the Keram River to a point opposite Annanberg. New Guinea Force, however, was not impressed, and on 9th June stated that "in spite of recent native rumours, there seems to be no good reason, tactical or otherwise, why the Japanese should try to open up a track

---
[3] Maj J. A. Costelloe, NGX395. NGVR and Angau. Public servant; of Belmore, NSW; b. Armidale, NSW, 5 Aug 1906.

across the Saruwaged and Finisterre Ranges which are over 11,000 feet high". At this time it was thought at Port Moresby that it would be quicker for enemy troops to move to Lae along the coastal route via Sio and Finschhafen. In the middle of June natives reported a large enemy force apparently awaiting reinforcements before crossing the river near Sepu. From Dengaragu Lieutenant Toole's[4] section of the 2/7th Independent Company reconnoitred towards Sepu and Lieutenant Davis'[5] section at Chimbu moved to Dengaragu whence the route to Guiebi and Bundi could be controlled; on 26th June the Allied air force attacked Sepu and burnt the huts.

From the Kainantu to the Sepu area both sides were now investigating the Ramu Valley. Towards the end of June Captain McKenzie's[6] Independent Company platoon relieved Captain Rooke's infantry platoon in the Kainantu area, Lieutenant Reddish's[7] platoon was defending the Garoka area and Lieutenant Byrne's was divided between the Matahausa, Bundi and Dengaragu areas. MacAdie had little reserve to reinforce the troops who might meet any Japanese advance over the mountains before the completion of the vehicle road and his hold on the vast and pleasant plateau was therefore very tenuous.

At the beginning of June General Herring suggested to Generals Blamey and Kenney that Bena Force should consist of a battalion and an Independent Company, with light anti-aircraft guns to protect the area so that fighters could be brought forward, but when Kenney decided that he could not maintain a force of more than 1,000 on the plateau Blamey decided to send in another Independent Company—the 2/2nd. The 2/2nd was already on the move from Canungra to the II Australian Corps area on the Atherton Tableland where the 2/2nd, 2/4th and 2/6th Companies would come under command of a newly created headquarters for Independent Companies known as the 2/7th Australian Cavalry (Commando) Regiment, originally the 7th Divisional Cavalry.[8] Six months exactly since returning emaciated from a year-long guerilla fight in Timor, the company, under the command of Major G. G. Laidlaw, set sail for Port Moresby where it arrived on 20th June. A week later Laidlaw's headquarters and one platoon were loaded into 10 transports and escorted by Lightnings over the swamp and meandering rivers of the southern Papuan coast, across the towering mountains of central New Guinea, and over the rolling grasslands of the plateau. Company headquarters moved to Garoka at the end of June, to be greeted three days later by a bombing attack which killed one native and wounded two others. On 8th July a

---

[4] Lt W. R. Toole, NX70117. 2/7 Indep Coy, 2/7 Cdo Sqn. Clerk; of Orange, NSW; b. Mosman, NSW, 15 Aug 1920.

[5] Maj S. E. Davis, MC, NX59724. 2/7 Indep Coy, 2/7 Cdo Sqn. Jackeroo; of Crookwell, NSW; b. Young, NSW, 15 Nov 1922.

[6] Maj N. B. McKenzie, MC, QX24484. 2/7 Indep Coy, 2/7 Cdo Sqn. Clerk; of Auchenflower, Qld; b. Brisbane, 7 Sep 1921.

[7] Maj N. G. Reddish, MC, VX80059. 2/7 Indep Coy, 2/7 Cdo Sqn, "Z" Special Unit. Merchant; of Melbourne; b. London, 10 Aug 1904.

[8] To the mystification of the Independent Companies the terms "Cavalry" and "Commando" were now often being used to describe them.

second platoon and others landed at Garoka and Bena Bena at the same time as enemy bombers and fighters appeared in the area.

During the landing (wrote the company's diarist) escorting Lightnings drove off nine enemy bombers and some fighters attempting to raid the aerodromes. . . . At Bena Bena, while transport planes were circling preparatory to landing, one enemy recce plane, by mistake, joined the formation. It was last seen heading east at high speed with three Lightning fighters in pursuit.

Captain Rooke's small force returned to Moresby in the transports. The remainder of the 2/2nd Independent Company had arrived by 1st August, by which time it numbered 20 officers and 274 men.

On 29th June construction work on the new Garoka airfield began under the supervision of the engineer sections of the 2/2nd and 2/7th Independent Companies; anti-aircraft, wireless and radar positions had been established soon after the arrival of a party of Americans under Major Homer Trimble on 12th June. With the assistance of Angau and 1,000 natives, the engineers built the airfield—6,000 feet long with dispersal bays—in seven days.

Meanwhile, MacAdie ordered Laidlaw to defend the new Garoka airfield, occupy the Chimbu and Asaloka airstrips as "anti-paratroop bases", build a road from Asaloka to Chimbu, oppose any enemy crossing of the Ramu between Sepu and Yonapa, and patrol across the Ramu into the area bordered by Sepu-Glaligool-Usini-Urigina in an attempt to secure more reliable information about the enemy than was being provided by native reports. On 7th July Laidlaw informed his company that they would operate to the west of a north-south line through Sigoiya; the 2/7th would operate to the east. He instructed Captain T. G. Nisbet's platoon to occupy Dengaragu and Bundi, Captain C. F. G. McKenzie's platoon to occupy Chimbu, Asaloka and Kortuni, and Captain D. St A. Dexter's platoon to remain in the Bena Bena area in reserve.

There was now a sudden increase in Japanese activity south of the Ramu. A message was received by a native police runner that the observation post at Lihona had been overrun by the Japanese before dawn on 7th July. Two days later an enemy patrol overran another of the 2/7th's observation posts in the Sepu area. Two Australians were wounded including Private Rofe.[9] Reports of 100 Japanese at Marawasa on the same

---

[9] Pte B. R. Rofe, SX15558; 2/7 Indep Coy. Farmer; of Balah, SA; b. Gulnare, SA, 26 Oct 1921.
Rofe displayed extraordinary fortitude. In the first burst of fire one bullet went through his left biceps, across his chest between skin and ribs and stopped on the right side. Another pierced him behind the left knee and another went through his left buttock. The Japanese officer leading the attackers then pounced and hacked at Rofe with his sword, severed his left deltoid muscle twice, gashed the left side of his head, stabbed him between the neck and left shoulder, cut the back of his left wrist, almost severed the left index finger, gashed the inner side of his right arm above the elbow and cut the inner side of his right elbow. "This," wrote Rofe later, "happened in a very brief space of time with no opportunity for resistance on my part and the blow on the head disabled me considerably. I came out of a daze to find my attacker standing a few feet away and out of sheer desperation I attempted to tackle him. I advanced unsteadily, abusing him in a rather ungentlemanly manner, while he drew a long-barrelled pistol and aimed it at my chest. Fortunately it misfired and while he was still gaping in amazement I seized the opportunity to retire hastily to the cover of the jungle. A few badly aimed shots followed me, but I managed to keep clear and, although I had not progressed far by nightfall, felt that I at least had some hope of getting back to the ambush at Limbien. (They had attacked about mid-day on 8th July.) I bathed my wounds as best I could and propped myself up against a tree for the night. My only hope of finding my way seemed to be on a track which we had carefully avoided on the way down. The next morning I was able to find this track by taking direction from the sun and followed it at a respectable distance reaching, by nightfall, a point

day, other patrols at Bumbum and Arona, and an enemy attack on "Snook's House" where two Australians and four Japanese were killed, caused MacAdie (now a lieut-colonel) to warn all posts to take precautions against surprise, particularly when the kunai grass along the Ramu was burning. By 11th July a patrol to Lihona established that two Australians had been killed and mutilated and two Japanese killed. The police boy, Woisau, who had been captured on the 7th but escaped, told the patrol that 16 Japanese and 9 Kaigulin natives had made the attack. It was apparent that the Japanese were being aided by the riverside natives; not otherwise could they have exhibited such accurate knowledge of the Australian positions and such skill at finding them by dark after advancing through the bush.

Other reports of native cooperation with the enemy were brought back by Corporal Merire who arrived exhausted at Bundi on 12th July from a memorable patrol into the heart of enemy territory near Madang. A stretcher party was sent out for his companion, Constable Kominiwan, who had been wounded and hidden by Merire. Merire made a full and convincing report of having seen a motor road from Bogadjim to Mabelebu, a "coolie track" thence to Boroai, 4,000 "coolies" constructing the road, 1,000 carrying supplies, 60 motor vehicles, and supply dumps. He reported that the Japanese were treating the natives very liberally and with good effect. This underlined one of MacAdie's main worries—the labour problem. "Stocks of trade [mainly shells and salt] are at present nil," wrote MacAdie to General Herring on 21st July, "and we are compelled to beg reluctant natives for credit for food supplies and labour—a deplorable situation when we are compared with the powerful and open-handed Nippon soldier, and until M.T. is functioning (on roads which the native is building) we are essentially dependent on the generosity of a population which owes the 'Allies' little or no allegiance."

The Japanese now left their newly-captured positions south of the Ramu and Lieutenant Byrne established two small five-man patrols at Wesa and Waimeriba. At 1.30 on the morning of the 17th, however, the Japanese recrossed the river, and, led in by natives, surprised the Waimeriba patrol. The five Australians escaped but two natives were killed and three wounded. Byrne then realised the vulnerability of the Waimeriba flats and established his section of 24 men on the higher ground near Wesa.

---

where we had camped overnight on the outward trip. Clad only in shorts and boots I spent a most uncomfortable night in pouring rain trying to keep some of the weather off (unsuccessfully) with leaves. The third day was the most difficult as the only water to be had was what had been caught in fallen leaves the night before. Apart from a few bites of green paw-paw I had not eaten since before the attack. The going on the third day was all uphill but I managed to reach Limbien by nightfall and much to my relief found that we were still in possession of that point. The natives soon organised a kunda vine and sapling stretcher and a message of my survival was radioed to Bena (or Garoka) from where the 2/2 Coy MO, Capt McInerney, immediately set out to render aid. The next morning I was moved off [by stretcher] from Limbien toward Guiebi where we spent the night. It was there on re-dressing my wounds that [it was] discovered my head wound was fly-blown. Having seen these pests successfully removed from sheep with kerosene and having no other medication to effectively attack them some kerosene was found and duly applied with apparently good result. By midday on 12 July we reached a point where R.A.P. Cpl Alf Monsen took over. He removed the bullet which was still between my skin and ribs on my right chest, inserted some stitches in other places and generally attended to my well-being until 17 July when Capt McInerney arrived. The top of the left index finger which had become infected was then removed and it must have been on the following day that we set out for Bena where, according to my service records, we arrived on 28th July."

The next message from this front—that a carrier line had been ambushed between Matahausa and Wesa—caused uneasiness at Sigoiya. MacAdie decided to use his reserve and instructed Laidlaw to send Dexter's platoon to take control in the Matahausa-Wesa area on 20th July.

Just as the platoon left Bena Bena early on 20th July enemy bombers and fighters attacked the airstrip and burned most of the huts. From this time on there was much activity in the air. Fleets of Allied bombers and fighters used the river valleys as their main landmarks, giving Australians north of the Bismarcks a grandstand view, while smaller groups of Japanese bombers and fighters worried the airstrips on the plateau. Often aircraft were heard but could not be seen because of lowering clouds. MacAdie's deception tactics were certainly causing the enemy air force to waste a considerable amount of effort in sporadic air attacks on the plateau.

With two of Laidlaw's platoons moving to the river front MacAdie sent a progress report to Herring in which he reasoned that

> there would seem little doubt that the enemy assess the size of Bena Force as well in excess of the actual figures. The constant building activities and rapidity of road construction as seen by his recce aircraft coupled with the fact that he has encountered our troops at four points on a line over eighty miles long is bound to affect his estimate considerably. It seems probable that he will regard this force as a definite threat to his new road.

By the evening of 21st July Dexter's platoon and the 150 Chimbu carriers had reached Matahausa after climbing over the Bismarcks. A diarist described this climb:

> Mount Helwig on right, Mount Otto on left—absolute bastard of a climb—dank, dark, dripping, rain forest—ancient moss covered trees looking like beeches—leeches—very cold—no natives—black mud and roots—awfully graded track—mist—up and then down terrible track—track beyond description.

It seemed to the incoming platoon that, if this was the most direct route from the Ramu to the plateau, Bena Force was reasonably safe. Captain Nisbet's climb over the Krakemback into the Bundi area was no less onerous.

By 24th July Nisbet relieved the detachment of the 2/7th in the western area and established his headquarters at Bundi-Crai with sections at Bundi, Guiebi and Dengaragu. Dexter, aided by Byrne, was reconnoitring Wesa and Waimeriba. It seemed that bases nearer the river must be established to prevent the Japanese getting a foothold on the Bismarck tracks. Matahausa in the rain forest, whence patrols had previously operated, was two days march from the Ramu, and had no fields of fire or good observation posts. The half-way camp now known as Maley[1] was better but still too far back. At the end of the month a new site, Maulu#[2] was selected near the northern tip of the Matahausa spur which ran towards the Ramu between Mounts Helwig and Otto. Here

---

[1] Named after Corporal J. L. Maley, 2/2nd Independent Company, who constructed a reasonably comfortable rear base there.

[2] After the platoon commander's Timor creado (boy).

on the verge of the jungle a strong defensive position commanding approaches from the Ramu and affording good observation posts was established.

Trouble with the natives began to flare up, but fortunately an experienced Angau representative, Captain O'Donnell,[3] now came forward to look after native affairs in the Wesa area.

> The history of the Matahausa-Wesa area had been one of bad management and some tragedy (wrote O'Donnell later). The pre-war history of the natives was of truculent groups with some experience of European plantation ways, very infrequently patrolled or visited by Government officers and, consequently, contemptuous of the authority of the Administration.

Soon after the Japanese invasion of the north coast of New Guinea a large cargo including rifles and ammunition had been carried from Madang by Sergeant Burnet[4] and hidden at Wesa, where there was a tiny overgrown airstrip and where houses were erected. Early in 1943 Sergeant Golden[5] and two men from the 2/6th Independent Company had taken over a watching brief in the area from men of the New Guinea Volunteer Rifles. In face of a native warning in May that a large enemy force was approaching, Golden withdrew from Wesa. During his absence the local natives raided the dump, stole the rifles and ammunition, and burned the huts. After attempting to salvage some stores despite enemy opposition Golden withdrew to his signals post not far from Wesa. Very ill, he and his police boy were in a lean-to near Wesa when they were awakened by four Japanese who had been led there by the local natives. Golden was killed but the police boy escaped to Matahausa.

It was the attitude of the riverside natives as well as the unfortunate experiences of Byrne's patrols and others that caused MacAdie to suggest firm action against the natives. Hearing many shots on the Helwig and Otto spurs, obviously fired by natives, and exasperated by the cutting of his telephone line, Dexter cleared the area, when necessary, by shooting first and asking questions afterwards. After several arduous and perilous patrols, including one by Captain O'Donnell (with bare feet) and three police boys, the natives were brought sufficiently under control, at least to the extent of keeping well clear of the Australians.

Early in August Australian patrols were watching the three main approaches to the plateau from the Kainantu, Wesa and Bundi areas. A huge area was patrolled: for instance, on the right flank Lieutenant Danne's[6] patrol of the 2/7th Independent Company investigated the activities of a Japanese patrol at Snook's House, while 100 miles away on the left flank Lieutenant C. D. Doig's section from the 2/2nd patrolled the Sepu area where there were periodic reports of Japanese activity.

---

[3] Capt G. C. O'Donnell, MC, PX144; Angau. Patrol officer; of Swan Hill, Vic; b. Leksand, Sweden, 17 Aug 1912.

[4] Lt J. W. Burnet, PX157; Angau. Public servant; of Dee Why, NSW; b. Burwood, NSW, 21 Aug 1909.

[5] Sgt J. A. Golden, N40133. NG L of C Sigs and Angau. Railway porter; of Tempe, NSW; b. Woolbrook, NSW, 12 Feb 1923. Killed in action 19 May 1943.

[6] Lt R. V. Danne, VX114271. 2/7 Indep Coy, 2/2 Cdo Sqn. Linotype engineer and salesman; of Hawthorn, Vic; b. Melbourne, 13 Jun 1915.

At this time obstructions were placed on the Mount Hagen and Ogelbeng airstrips. The enemy was thought to have paratroops in New Guinea, and MacAdie was warned that they might use them to seize Bena Bena and Garoka airstrips as a prelude to the landing of airborne troops. MacAdie did not regard the warning very seriously but took normal precautions and issued a plan for dealing with paratroop landings.

It was now quite apparent from air photographs that the "Bogadjim Road" had been rapidly built by the Japanese as far as Daumoina, and it seemed that the enemy intended to drive the road up the valley of the Mindjim and not, as at first thought, across the dividing range at Boroai and down to Kesawai on the Ramu. The pilot track had apparently been constructed as far as Paipa. Should the route then follow the Uria Valley a considerable amount of bench cutting would be necessary as both banks of the Uria were precipitous for 7 miles beyond Paipa, but from there on the gradient would be easy. On 1st August it was estimated at New Guinea Force headquarters that the Bogadjim Road could reach Dumpu in six to eight weeks. Although the route from Dumpu to Lae would then lie along the flat valleys of the Ramu and Markham Rivers, at least seven rivers would require bridging or ford construction before a motor road through to Lae would be possible, and three of these—the Surinam, Gusap and Leron—were wide, deep, swift-flowing streams. As little timber was available, the Japanese engineers faced a big task. In August 1943, however, the Bogadjim Road was regarded as a growing threat.

On 8th August a small patrol led by Lieutenant Hawker[7] of the 2/7th arrived at Wesa to reconnoitre the Bogadjim Road. Early on the 11th Corporal Merire, who had been reconnoitring the Waimeriba crossing, met some truculent river natives some of whom he shot with the revolver concealed under his lap lap. He was not happy about the Bogadjim Road trip and did not think the patrol would get through. During the night 11th-12th August the Australians at Matahausa, Maley and Maululi heard firing from the direction of Wesa.

On the evening of the 11th-12th the usual guards were posted at Wesa by Lieutenant Beveridge[8] and a moonlight patrol searched the area until the three-quarter moon set soon after 2 a.m. At 2.15 a.m. Lance-Corporal Marshall[9] and Lance-Corporal Monk[1] relieved the guards on the track leading up to the Wesa perimeter from the main Waimeriba-Maululi track. Fifteen minutes later Monk heard a rustling about five yards away. As such sounds were not unusual he whispered to Marshall that he thought it was a wild pig, but a few seconds later the men heard whispering. Monk silently moved from his position by a log on the side

---

[7] Lt W. E. Hawker, SX?05. 2/3 and 2/8 Fd Regts, 2/7 Indep Coy, 2/7 Cdo Sqn. Grazier; of Clare, SA; b. Mount Lofty, SA, 31 Jan 1910.

[8] Lt A. R. Beveridge, NX106299. 2/2 Indep Coy, 2/2 Cdo Sqn. Shop assistant; of Hamilton, NSW; b. Newcastle, NSW, 15 Aug 1916.

[9] Cpl A. Marshall, WX13399. 2/2 Indep Coy, 2/2 Cdo Sqn. Farmer; of Broomehill, WA; b. Broomehill, 21 Apr 1922.

[1] L-Sgt K. J. Monk, VX63724. 2/2 Indep Coy, 2/2 Cdo Sqn. Farmer; of Athlone, Vic; b. Cheltenham, Vic, 4 Aug 1921.

of the track to the cover of the roots of a big tree. Peering over the roots, he saw, against the eerie blackness of the night, a whitish figure crawling up the hill on hands and knees about a yard from where he had been sitting on the log. Monk trained his rifle on the ghost-like figure. Marshall called "shoot" and threw a grenade, while Monk squeezed the trigger and saw the figure disappear with a muttered groan as though hit. Both men then took aim down the track, fired a shot each and then threw grenades at a spot where they assumed others would be following the forward scout. They shouted to their section above to be prepared and streaked up the hill to where the men had already entered their fire pits. Then there was stillness punctuated two minutes later by a lone pistol shot. In the morning a dead Japanese officer and a dead sergeant, both well-conditioned men, were found at the foot of the Wesa hill. The officer, who had a neat bullet hole in his forehead, was wearing two shirts, the top one with a white square sewn on it.

After these discoveries a police boy accompanied a patrol led by Corporal Foster[2] which followed blood trails towards the Wei River where Foster reported hearing the enemy whistling. A patrol was sent out to repair the telephone line, which had been cut. From Maululi Corporal

---

[2] Lt T. A. Foster, WX13202. 2/2 Indep Coy, 2/2 Cdo Sqn. Station manager; of Geraldton, WA; b. Ararat, Vic, 1 Aug 1920.

Maley's[3] sub-section set out to reinforce Wesa and to find out what had happened.[4] Soon after he arrived at Wesa, Maley left his sub-section with Foster at the camp and went on to report to Beveridge who was with Hawker at the section's observation post manned by two men. While the five men were yarning at the observation post they heard a machine-gun open up from the direction of the camp soon after 11 a.m.

Maley's sub-section had walked rapidly and the men were out of breath when they arrived at Wesa. They gathered round Foster's men who were busy improving their weapon-pits and discussed the night's activities while the inevitable brew of tea was being prepared. Someone called "Come and get it".

As though this were a challenge an enemy machine-gun opened up on to the huts from about 30 yards. Everybody dived for cover. Several of the newcomers, not being familiar with the defences, slid down a steep 40-foot slope behind the huts where they were unable to take any part in the fighting.

The moment chosen by the Japanese for the attack could not have caught the Wesa defenders less prepared. One sub-section was on patrol; the reinforcing sub-section was out of the picture; and of the remainder the section commander and some of his men were at the observation post. Foster's sub-section numbered eight, but four who were nearing the cookhouse for a cup of tea when the first shots were fired found themselves at the foot of the steep slope with the newcomers. Foster dropped to the ground near the signals hut where he had been winding cable from a reel and, armed only with a pistol, crawled three yards to his fire pit where his Owen was. As he moved to the pit he saw about a dozen Japanese rushing towards the cookhouse from the direction of the observation post track. Simultaneously, Private Palm,[5] who had been yarning in the section headquarters hut, ran past Foster, picked up a Bren left by the incoming sub-section and charged the Japanese with the Bren at the hip. Unfortunately the gun was not cocked and the speed at which Palm was moving in the few yards separating the cookhouse from the other huts did not permit him to cock it. At the last moment before colliding with the Japanese he veered over the cliff.

Meanwhile, Foster was in position to make a lone stand. The Japanese justifiably thought that they had surprised the Australians but erroneously thought also that they had captured their objective. As they gathered near the cookhouse Foster from a distance of about 15 yards fired a full magazine from the hip into their midst and saw at least five fall. The survivors made off into the undergrowth.

At this stage "there seemed to be some confusion in the attack, with much shouting and blowing of umpires' whistles and shooting from the vicinity of ammo dump". For a short time the covering fire supplied by

---
[3] Cpl J. L. Maley, WX11488; 2/2 Indep Coy. Farmer; of Woongoondy, WA; b. Boulder, WA, 22 Nov 1909. Killed in action 12 Aug 1943.
[4] Not only was the telephone line cut but the 208 wireless set was, as usual, ineffective.
[5] Tpr N. Palm, QX42838. 2/2 Indep Coy, 2/2 Cdo Sqn. Stockman; of Duaringa, Qld; b. Beaudesert, Qld, 12 Dec 1923.

a mortar and a machine-gun ceased, but soon these weapons opened up from a new position towards which Foster hurled grenades. Then the Japanese attacked again towards the cookhouse and near-by sub-section hut this time with fixed bayonets and led by an officer brandishing a sword. Obviously they thought that the Australian defences, like their own, would be under the huts. This attack was more sustained than the first but again the cool young corporal drove them back after firing three magazines from his Owen and hurling a number of grenades.

There was now a short lull while the exasperated Japanese regrouped and Foster tried to rally his scattered sub-section. When the next attack was launched Private Giles[6] from the guard post along the main track was alongside him and Private Sharp[7] had wormed his way into the other sub-section trench near the cookhouse. For a third time the Japanese were driven back, unable to withstand the concentrated sub-machine-gun and rifle fire and grenades of the three defenders.

Disorganised by this gallant stand the Japanese frantically attacked the cookhouse area again, and, shouting among themselves, dragged away their casualties under cover of machine-gun and grenade fire. They attacked twice more before they finally withdrew towards Mount Otto about 40 minutes after the first attack, carrying their wounded, several of whom were found dead in succeeding days.

While Foster was writing a note to the platoon commander and Captain O'Donnell was rounding up the natives, Private Timmins[8] returned to the camp along the track from the observation post and reported how the five men from the observation post had tried to return to the camp in open formation along the axis of the track. When they reached the edge of the kunai they crossed the saddle between the observation post and Wesa. As they began to climb the Wesa hill, Maley, who was bursting through the scrub in front, was killed by machine-gun fire. Hawker met a Japanese on the track but his carbine jammed, his revolver misfired and the Japanese escaped—only temporarily, however, because a grenade hurled by Lieutenant Beveridge dispatched him. The five men had probably stumbled into the rear of the Japanese attack and had caused the confusion that occurred between the first and second attacks. Hawker was shot in the back and, unable to break through the Japanese ring, the two other men retired to the head of a near-by gully while Private Timmins became separated from them and returned to the observation post. When he returned to the section Lieutenant Beveridge decided to withdraw to Maululi because his ammunition was too low to withstand another attack, he had a wounded man, and, as he stated in his report, the Japanese "are able to get right up to us without our knowledge".

---

[6] Cpl T. B. Giles, WX37231. 2/2 Indep Coy, 2/2 Cdo Sqn. Cinematograph operator; of Mullewa, WA; b. Mullewa, 27 Dec 1922.

[7] Tpr W. Sharp, VX122794. 2/2 Indep Coy, 2/2 Cdo Sqn. Farmer; of Numurkah, Vic; b. Numurkah, 12 Aug 1924.

[8] Tpr E. Timmins, QX40318. 2/2 Indep Coy, 2/2 Cdo Sqn. Storeman packer; of Brisbane; b. Brisbane, 25 Oct 1922.

By 14th August, however, patrols found Wesa clear. By 17th August the track taken by the Japanese raiding party from Waimeriba up the Wesa Track to the Marea River, then up the Marea, Wei and Dhu[9] Rivers to the rear of Wesa, had been followed by patrols.

Patrolling was intense in August. Sergeant Davies[1] led his section from Asaloka via Kortuni and Mount Otto to Maululi, an almost intolerable week-long trip. To replace Lieutenant Hawker on the patrol to the Bogadjim Road Lieutenant C. J. P. Dunshea of the 2/7th arrived at Maululi on 18th August; he set out alone on the 21st, crossed the Ramu, but was fired on, and returned next day. Corporal Harrison[2] of the 2/2nd led a three-man patrol on the 23rd through Sepu and then along the Glaligool Track for about a quarter of a mile before contacting the Japanese. Private Smyth[3] and another man of the 2/2nd were 200 yards beyond the Ramu crossing on 25th August when they encountered about 10 Japanese and withdrew after having felled six of them. One of the main obstacles to successful patrolling in this area was the Ramu River—about 200 yards wide and flowing fast. The crossing of the river by small patrols in log canoes and rafts unsupported by fire power and little knowing whether they would be under observation by the enemy known to be in the area was in itself an achievement.

MacAdie now decided to see the direct route for himself and visited Maululi on 28th August. While he was climbing the Bismarcks, action was taking place at each end of his huge domain. A patrol led by Captain N. B. McKenzie from his platoon of the 2/7th in the Kainantu area, having discovered that an enemy patrol from Arona 1 visited Arona 2 daily, ambushed it on 27th August and killed six Japanese without loss. Far to the west, the boot was on the other foot, when an enemy patrol surprised Captain Nisbet's observation post at Faita early on the morning of the 27th and killed three men.

All the Japanese activity along the north bank of the Ramu and sometimes on the south bank was part of a pattern. General Adachi intended to capture Bena Bena, and, as secondary objectives, Kainantu and Chimbu. He planned that the *238th Regiment* based at Dumpu (and less the detachments round Lae) would capture these areas early in September, supported by a battalion of mountain artillery, engineers and perhaps paratroops. The main enemy attacks would be made from Kesawai and Dumpu along the Wesa-Matahausa track and along the Lihona-Mount Keyfabega track. Smaller detachments would attack from Kaireba along Sergeant Davies' route over Mount Otto to Asaloka, while the third battalion would attack Kainantu from Marawasa. When the Bena Bena and Kainantu areas were captured the regiment would exploit to Chimbu.

Further indications of the Japanese intention to attack the plateau were contained in a captured document in which the *20th Japanese Division* was depicted in Lae with an arrow pointing up the Markham Valley with a note "to Bena Bena". As late

---

[9] Named after Lance-Corporal R. C. Dhu, 2/2nd Independent Company, wounded at Maululi on 14th August.

[1] Sgt R. M. Davies, VX36786. 2/2 Indep Coy, 2/2 Cdo Sqn. Bank officer; of Melbourne; b. Kerang, Vic, 20 Dec 1909.

[2] L-Sgt P. J. Harrison, NX53272. 2/2 Indep Coy, 2/2 Cdo Sqn. Motor mechanic; of Peria, NZ; b. Rawene, NZ, 4 Jun 1911.

[3] Sgt R. N. Smyth, WX19098. 2/2 Indep Coy, 2/2 Cdo Sqn. Clerk; of Claremont, WA; b. Claremont, 8 Oct 1917.

as August Adachi intended to move into the Bena Bena plateau, but the troops required for this task (*20th Division*) were soon needed urgently elsewhere. As far back as 17th June an "Imamura Force Order" had stated that "a great enemy air force is located in the Bena Bena-Mount Hagen area. Our air force in close cooperation with the army is striving to break down the enemy positions."

The Australians would not have been surprised had the Japanese crossed the river in force. The enemy may have gained some initial success, perhaps in the more accessible Kainantu area, but from the choice of his routes for the main task he would be inviting another such disaster as befell him at Wau. Sergeant Davies particularly might have been inclined to advise that the detachment crawling over Mount Otto should be left

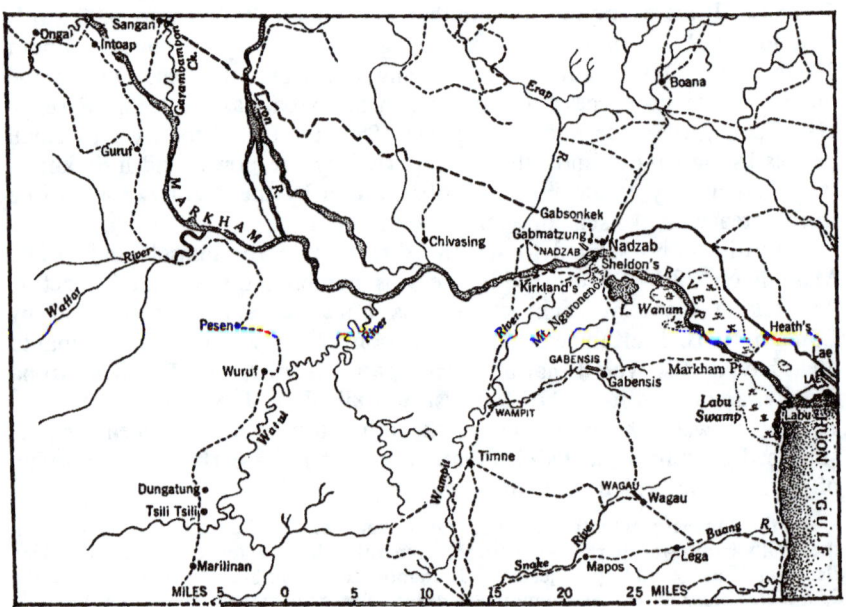

Tsili Tsili-Nadzab area

to its fate. The Australians, indeed, would have found a Japanese attack a change from their arduous patrolling. The real noises of battle would then have replaced the rush of the cassowary through the scrub, the startling machine-gun rattle of the hornbill, the crashing of falling limbs and trees, and the noises of wild pigs, Goura pigeons, flying foxes and birds of paradise.

East of the Bena plateau in the valley of the Watut, preparations to support the Australian offensive into the Markham Valley were being pushed forward rapidly. When the plans for the Lae and Nadzab offensives were first mooted the Allied commanders realised that it would be necessary, as a preliminary, to knock out the enemy's air force. As Wewak had become the enemy's main air base in New Guinea, an area from which escorting fighters could operate to protect the Allied attacking bombers was needed.

General Kenney later described his efforts to secure such a base:

> Ever since we first began to talk about capturing Lae and Salamaua, back during the Buna campaign, we had been looking for a place to build an airdrome close enough to Lae so that our fighters could stay around to cover either an airborne or seaborne expedition to capture those important Jap holdings. . . . Whitehead finally located a flat spot along the upper Watut River, about 60 miles west of Lae and near a native village marked on the maps as Marilinan. It was a pretty name, the site looked good, and it was ideally located to support operations to capture Lae, Salamaua and Nadzab.[4]

Early in May 1943, General Savige, conscious that one of his tasks was to guard the Wau-Bulolo area from all directions including the north-west via the Watut and Wampit Valleys, had flown along the Wampit Valley and then west to the junction of the Watut and Markham Rivers and south to Sunshine. He was impressed by the apparent ease with which aircraft could land in the Watut Valley and by the excellent track on the western edge of the wide, flat valley. This track had been improved soon after the Japanese invasion by Warrant-Officer Lumb[5] who had penetrated to the coast near Madang, rounded up cattle, and overlanded them across New Guinea to Edie Creek.

Anxious to find out what the track and valley were like and whether the Japanese were infiltrating or patrolling the valley, Savige ordered the 24th Battalion which had been in his area for about a fortnight to supply a patrol. Lieutenant Robinson was chosen to lead it—a section of eleven men, a police boy, and native carriers. They set out from Sunshine on 7th May. The Angau officer who was to act as interpreter was ill and could not go, and, with but a rudimentary knowledge of pidgin, Robinson pressed on across country not yet entered by the army; on the third night he entered Wowos and next day crossed the Watut over Lumb's cattle bridge.[6] From the top of the ridge at the end of the upper Watut the men gazed down into the broad valley of the lower Watut with its kunai plains, villages, creeks and swamps. They entered Marilinan that evening.

As this was the first patrol to enter the Watut area since the Japanese landed Robinson decided to "show the flag", and next day entered the villages of Tsili Tsili, Dungatung and Wuruf in military order and with fixed bayonets, to be greeted by the village dignitaries with the offer of the milk of green coconuts to drink. Next day Robinson met Lumb at Pesen, and he spent two days in the area reconnoitring to the junction of the Markham and Watut and collecting information.

Private Langford of the battalion's Intelligence section used a camera, a valuable forethought on the part of the Intelligence officer, Lieutenant

---

[4] Kenney, p. 251.

[5] WO2 H. Lumb, NG2062. NGVR and Angau. Goldminer and prospector; of New Guinea; b. Featherstone, Yorks, England, 9 Oct 1900. Killed in action 7 Jun 1943.

[6] Lumb's natives had built the bridge from gear salvaged from various mines and government dumps. It was suspended high across the Watut gorge by steel cables, was completely decked with timber, and wide and strong enough to take a jeep.

Bunsell,[7] to take snapshots of the Watut area. Having finished its task, Robinson's patrol returned with maps and photographs by the same route to Sunshine where it arrived on 26th May. Three days later an American air force reconnaissance party consisting of Major Cox, Captain King and Lieutenant Everette E. Frazier arrived at Sunshine. They were looking for an operational or staging fighter airfield north of Wau and had been unable to find anything suitable in the Wampit Valley. At battalion headquarters they heard about the Watut Valley's possibilities and Lieutenant Robinson was summoned to enlarge on sections of his report dealing with Marilinan and Tsili Tsili. The upshot was that Robinson took Frazier on a quick reconnaissance of the area. By travelling light they arrived at Marilinan on 2nd June after two days and a half. Frazier decided that the old overgrown airstrip, although blocked on one end by a mountain, would be able to take transport planes and fighters. Robinson organised the local natives to prepare the airstrip by cutting the kunai and filling

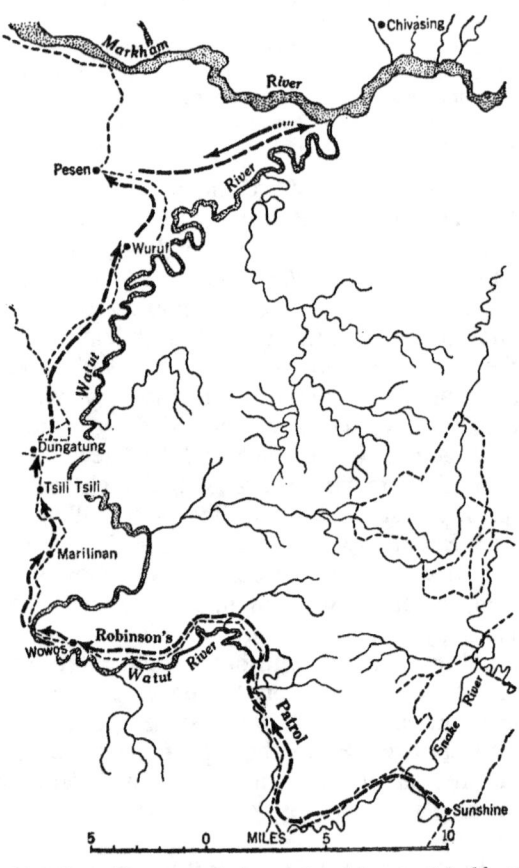

24th Battalion patrol from Sunshine to Markham River, 7th-26th May

in the holes. On 6th June Cox and King arrived on foot and after reconnoitring the general area decided that Tsili Tsili was the more suitable spot for an air base. Natives were then set to work cutting and burning the six-feet-high kunai in a 100-foot wide swathe for about 1,200 feet while Robinson and Frazier returned to Sunshine.

Next day Savige sent Robinson with Frazier to Port Moresby to assist the American air force with his knowledge of the country and in any other way possible. Frazier stated that Marilinan and Tsili Tsili could probably be used only until heavy rains began in September, and

---

[7] Maj A. W. C. Bunsell, ED, VX104151; 24 Bn. Public servant; of Kew, Vic; b. Boulder, WA, 10 Jan 1912.

all equipment would then have to be taken out or abandoned until the end of the rainy season. "But it could be anticipated that by that time the Allied advance ... would have reached Nadzab, a site already selected on the advice of Australians familiar with New Guinea as ideal for a permanent air base. The schedule would be tight, but it was believed that preparations could be completed at Nadzab in time to make the transfer before the rains made the move from Marilinan impossible."[8]

As a result General Paul B. Wurtsmith and Lieutenant A. J. Beck landed two aircraft on the Marilinan strip on 13th June. Wurtsmith agreed that, although Marilinan could be lengthened a little more, it would be able to take nothing larger than Dakota cargo aircraft. He agreed with Cox and King, however, that Tsili Tsili was an excellent site, which could be made into an airfield with double runways 7,000 feet long and with plenty of room for dispersal areas. In order to act as guide, Lieutenant Robinson flew to Marilinan with the advanced party soon after Wurtsmith's and Beck's experimental landings. There he remained for three weeks assisting in locating camp sites and dispersal areas.

Construction began at Marilinan on 16th June when American engineers and a platoon of the 57th/60th Battalion were landed. By 20th June the Marilinan airfield had been sufficiently enlarged to land transports and a road had been constructed to Tsili Tsili where the engineers began work on the real air base. By 1st July Dakotas were able to land there. Within 10 days these dependable planes flew in a company of airborne engineers with miniature bulldozers, graders, carry-alls and grasscutters. Before the end of July the new base was capable of handling 150 Dakotas a day.

On 26th July the first fighters landed at Tsili Tsili; on 5th August Lieut-Colonel Malcolm A. Moore (replaced on 27th August by Colonel David W. ("Photo") Hutchison) assumed command of the Second Air Task Force in the Watut Valley where, by the 11th, there were about 3,000 Allied troops; on 17th August Herring established Tsili Tsili Force under the command of Lieut-Colonel Marston of the 57th/60th Battalion.[9]

Herring had made it clear to Marston in June that the Australian commander would be operationally responsible for the Tsili Tsili area. By using tact and commonsense, and with the cooperation of the American commanders, Marston worked out his defensive plan so that the exceedingly liberal armament of every American air and construction unit would be used to the best advantage. One supply squadron had so many weapons that the American commander did not know what to do with them. It soon became obvious to Marston that "if someone didn't coordinate and prepare a fire plan, if the necessity arose for the use of this plethora

---

[8] W. F. Craven and J. L. Cate, *The Pacific: Guadalcanal to Saipan, August 1942 to July 1944*, p. 176.

[9] Kenney (p. 253) wrote of this: "General Herring . . . gave me a battalion of 1,000 Aussies and some machine-guns. They liked the idea, too, for while at Marilinan and attached to the Fifth Air Force they would get American rations, which were better than their own." Australian troops, however, soon tired of American rations.
In June the Australian force consisted of one company of the 57th/60th Battalion; from 1st July until late in August of two companies, portion of HQ Company and Battalion HQ; and from 25th August till 28th September the full battalion.

of weapons, a proper hellzapoppin would be the result". When the Americans knew what was wanted they set about implementing it in typical style. Moore lent Marston his Piper Cub aircraft for reconnaissance; Lieut-Colonel Murray C. Woodbury of the 871st U.S. Airborne Engineer Battalion whose task was to construct the strips on a 24-hour schedule working at night under arc lights set his dozers and graders to work cutting fire lanes and fields of fire.

It would appear that the Japanese were deceived as to the relative importance of the airfields in the Bena Bena and Tsili Tsili areas. At least, they had no firm plan to capture Tsili Tsili as they did Bena Bena. Thus MacAdie's deceptive tactics were successful, as was also Kenney's idea that "if the Nip really got interested in the Bena Bena area, he might not see what we were doing at Marilinan".[1] Camouflage and clever flying by pilots also helped to hide the full significance of Tsili Tsili from the enemy until their two raids in mid-August, despite Tokyo Radio's warning that Tsili Tsili would be bombed on 25th July. "My fingers by this time were getting calluses from being crossed so hard," wrote Kenney, "but the Japs still showed no signs of knowing that we were building a field right in their back yard."[2]

Before the establishment of Tsili Tsili Force on 17th August Australian and Papuan troops had not occupied positions forward of the Waffar River. To protect the Tsili Tsili airfield and to prevent the enemy using the tracks between Tsili Tsili, Pesen and Onga, Marston now decided to move his battalion forward. In its two months' sojourn in the Watut Valley, patrols from the 57th/60th had seen no Japanese between the Watut and Onga, although natives reported sporadic enemy patrolling into the Chivasing, Kaiapit and Sangan areas.

The Amami-Onga area now claimed Marston's attention. In August, at Amami where the high mountain spurs gave way to kunai flats, Lieutenant Frazier, Warrant-Officer Ryan of Angau and a small party of natives had made a small airstrip soon used by both American Piper Cubs and the R.A.A.F. Tiger Moths—the only means of supplying troops in the area. From Amami to Onga the flat country was suitable for the establishment of a jeep track, and at Onga tracks to Kainantu, Kaiapit and Pesen converged. Marston considered that an enemy force would have little difficulty following the track Onga-Amami-Pesen-Tsili Tsili. He therefore redisposed his force to meet this threat.[3] Early in September one company was in the Amami-Onga area, where they improved the strip

---

[1] Kenney, p. 253. Although Kenney preferred the name Marilinan to Tsili Tsili because "Tsili Tsili might have suggested to some people that it was descriptive of our scheme of getting a forward airdrome", Tsili Tsili was a name that deserved to stick and stick it did, despite Kenney's instruction at the end of July that it should be known as Marilinan. "I still didn't like the other name," he wrote. "In case the Nips should take us out, somebody might throw that Tsili Tsili thing back at me." (Kenney, p. 271.)

[2] Kenney, p. 271.

[3] At this stage a patrol of the 57th/60th, contrary to instructions, crossed the Markham and had a look at Kaiapit. Lieutenant L. S. Talbot's platoon was posted at Intoap on the southern bank of the Markham with the job of reconnaissance. Talbot was not to cross the Markham or seek contact with the enemy. Talbot, however, was anxious to test whether the Markham could be forded. With three natives he waded and swam across, and walked to the edge of Kaiapit, where they heard sounds of chopping. They recrossed the river some miles upstream and returned to Intoap.

to make it capable of taking transport aircraft; this solved the supply problem particularly when a jeep was landed to carry supplies forward to the platoon at Intoap, five hours' walk away. This company also patrolled to join up with a patrol from the 2/7th Independent Company. A second company was in the Waffar-Markham-Pesen area, while the other two were disposed round Tsili Tsili and Marilinan.

Throughout 1943 several Intelligence groups were operating behind the Japanese lines in the areas with which this volume is chiefly concerned. A few examples will illustrate the type of work carried out by these groups and the dangers confronting them in hostile territory.[4]

Behind Finschhafen two coastwatchers, Captain L. Pursehouse (Angau) and Lieutenant McColl[5] (R.A.N.V.R.) had in March 1943 witnessed the battle of the Bismarck Sea. A month later McColl, when walking down a path from their hut, was surprised by enemy fire from a near-by clump of bamboos. He fired a magazine from his Owen into the bamboos and then doubled back to the hut. In his haste he slipped and fell whereupon several Japanese rushed in firing to finish him off. Regaining his feet and still clutching his empty Owen he reached the jungle where he watched the Japanese surround the house and capture it empty. McColl rejoined Pursehouse at their rendezvous and, as it was obvious that their position had been given away to the Japanese by the natives, they were ordered to Bena Bena.[6]

To the west Lieutenant L. J. Bell (R.A.N.V.R.) and Sergeant Hall[7] were watching the enemy along the Rai Coast near Saidor. A party led by Captain Fairfax-Ross[8] was in the process of relieving the two men in February when natives led Japanese to the Australians' camp at Maibang. In the ensuing mêlée Fairfax-Ross was wounded but the two parties managed to fight their way out. Natives then led the Japanese to the supply hide-outs and killed Bell and two others. The remainder of the men then made the arduous journey back over the forbidding Saruwageds to Bena Bena.

At the beginning of 1943 Lieutenant Greathead's[9] party had clashed with Japanese patrols near the lower Ramu and had withdrawn to Bena

---

[4] For an account of the work of the coastwatchers see E. Feldt, *The Coast Watchers* (1946); and G. H. Gill, *Royal Australian Navy 1939-1942* (1957), a volume in the naval series of this history.

[5] Lt K. H. McColl, RANVR. Coastwatcher, AIB. Stock and station agent; of Chimbu, NG; b. Newcastle, NSW, 20 May 1907.

[6] By July 1943, with several "hush hush" parties in the field, General Herring charged Angau with the control, coordination, direction, maintenance and movement of these parties within New Guinea.

[7] Lt B. W. G. Hall, DCM, PX191. Coastwatcher, AIB; Angau. Planter; of Madang, NG; b. Sydney, 6 Apr 1912.

[8] Maj B. Fairfax-Ross, NGX8. 2/12 Bn, and "M" Special Unit. Plantation inspector; of Rabaul, TNG; b. Springwood, NSW, 4 Apr 1910.
    The members of his party were: Lt L. K. Searle, Lt D. A. Laws, Cpl J. B. Ranken, his brother Pte H. B. Ranken, and L-Cpl R. H. McLennan.

[9] Maj G. Greathead, VX80561. "M" Special Unit and Angau. Patrol officer; of Bundaberg, Qld; b. Bundaberg, 2 Feb 1909.
    The members of his party were Lt R. C. Cambridge, Capt D. G. N. Chambers and Sgt F. P. Mitchell.

Bena. By mid-March the party had arrived again on the Ramu about 60 miles from its mouth. Supply difficulties were aggravated when a plane guided by Flying Officer Leigh Vial crashed in the mountains killing all aboard. Greathead was then ordered back to Mount Hagen to hold the airfield if Bena Bena was lost.

A difficult and hazardous patrol by Private Curran-Smith,[1] accompanied by Private Hunt[2] and Warrant-Officer England[3] of Angau had left Bundi in March 1943 for Atemble, Mugunsif, Josephstaal, Apowen, Mosapa and Wasambu areas. Living in this area until August among

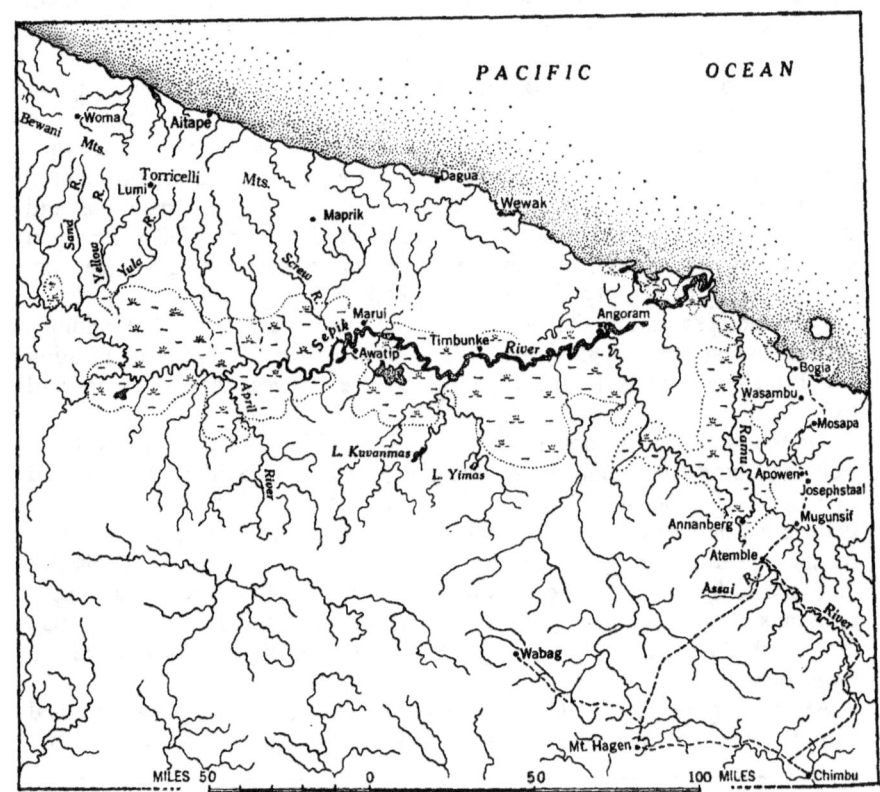

Area of Mosstroops' operations

natives of whose feelings they were not certain, the men were a prey to the many rumours which any man who has been isolated in enemy territory will readily remember. The patrol gathered much valuable information but it lived on its nerves, as for most of the period each member

---

[1] Pte J. W. Curran-Smith, VX79344. 2/6 Indep Coy, 2/6 Cdo Sqn. Labourer; of Essendon, Vic; b. Carlton, Vic, 17 Mar 1921.

[2] Pte H. H. Hunt, WX17564; 2/6 Indep Coy. Miner; of Ravensthorpe, WA; b. England, 27 Oct 1921.

[3] Lt P. R. N. England, PX192; Angau. Plantation manager; of Bogia, NG; b. Llanishan, Wales, 11 Dec 1904.

was in a separate area from the others and was accompanied only by police boys. Persistent reports of the enemy's intention to occupy Atemble culminated on 12th August when a party of about 20 Japanese attacked Curran-Smith in the Josephstaal area. He escaped across the Assai River, was lost for three days in the jungle, and suffered from malaria before finding Greathead's camp at Mount Hagen.

Far in advance of the battle areas and scattered round the periphery of New Guinea most of these small parties were, naturally enough, experiencing difficulty with the natives. Captain Ashton's[4] party had been flown to the Sepik at the end of February and had headed for Wewak until the men learnt from friendly natives that other natives, not so friendly, were leading two parties of Japanese from Wewak to look for them. Ashton then retraced his steps endeavouring to get far enough from Wewak to deter the enemy from following. Early in April while they were changing their sweat-drenched clothes in a native village and while Lieutenant J. McK. Hamilton was adjusting his transmitter, there was suddenly a yell and a fusillade of shots poured into the hut. Half dressed the party dashed out the back door just as a grenade came in the front. Hamilton became separated from the others and followed the first creek he found towards the Sepik. He waded through the mud by night and at dawn rolled in the mud as a protection against mosquitoes as he slept. Four days later he reached Marui on the Sepik and was fed and clothed by Father Hansen, a day before the other three members of the patrol reached this haven, having travelled without equipment, boots and food. The party was evacuated by Catalina at the end of April.

The Sepik and Wewak areas about which the Allies were anxious to obtain information were proving trouble spots. A party led by Lieutenant Fryer[5] and accompanied by a Dutchman, Sergeant H. N. Staverman of the Netherlands Navy, and an Australian, Sergeant Siffleet,[6] arrived in the well-populated Lumi area south of the Torricellis in July. After reaching Lumi, Fryer and Staverman parted, Fryer to remain in the general Sepik area and Staverman to penetrate across the border into the hills behind Hollandia. Once again the unreliability of the natives led to failure. Fryer's party was trapped by apparently friendly natives a few miles south of Lumi. The Australians managed to beat off the attack, but in the process their carriers deserted and seven weapons were lost. The party escaped south and joined Lieutenant Stanley's[7] party at Wamala Creek, a tributary of the Yula River. Fryer and Stanley then sent a signal asking for retaliatory action against the offending villages. After some delay a strafing attack was carried out in mid-September by two Lightnings on empty bush and near a friendly village.

---

[4] Maj L. E. Ashton, NGX256. NGVR; "Z" and "M" Special Units. Gold miner and prospector; of Wau, NG; b. Bowen, Qld, 14 Mar 1901.
[5] Capt H. A. J. Fryer, MBE, VX102690. "Z" and "M" Special Units. Engineer, surveyor and planner; of New Guinea and Willoughby, NSW; b. Canterbury, Vic, 6 May 1910.
[6] Sgt L. G. Siffleet, NX143314. "Z" and "M" Special Units. Shop assistant; of Enmore, NSW; b. Gunnedah, NSW, 14 Jan 1916. Died while prisoner of Japanese 24 Oct 1943.
[7] Lt-Cdr G. A. V. Stanley, DSC, RANVR; AIB. Geologist; b. Sydney, 26 Jul 1904.

Meanwhile Staverman and Siffleet with two Indonesian soldiers had crossed the Torricellis early in July. Learning of the Japanese patrols searching for Fryer they warned him by radio before setting out for the Dutch border. During August and September little was heard from them but at the beginning of October Siffleet, who had been left with one Indonesian at Woma, signalled that Staverman and the other Indonesian had been killed by Japanese guided by unfriendly natives. Siffleet stated that he and his companion would destroy their codes and withdraw south across the Bewani Mountains. He was instructed to proceed to the Wamala Creek base but nothing further was heard of him until it was learnt that he had been captured.

From the hills behind Finschhafen across the Saruwageds to the Rai Coast near Saidor, south across the Finisterres to the Ramu, west to the Sepik and outside the Japanese strongholds of Wewak, Aitape and Hollandia, these brave men gathered what information they could. Information useful for the air attacks on the Wewak area and the assault on the Huon Peninsula was gathered at the cost of several lives. These parties were often dogged by ill fortune and handicapped by the unreliability of the natives, but a share in the success of the Allied armies in New Guinea was their reward.

Enemy activity and intentions in the Sepik area were of great interest to both General MacArthur's and General Blamey's headquarters and both were keen to find out more. To General Herring on 28th June Blamey wrote:

> It is extremely important that we should get further information concerning enemy activities in this area, and do everything possible to enlist the natives on our side, or at least draw them away from the Japanese. . . . One thing may need to be watched with these . . . patrols, and that is, that the Japanese have very considerable forces along the coast in the area in which they will be working. Small patrols of ours, essential for the purpose of getting information, may get away with it, but if we make a show of force at all, with say, 20 or 30 men, the enemy could very easily and quickly bring a force of several hundreds or more against them. This would not only make it difficult for us to maintain observation in that area, but it could, with the superior force of the enemy, have the very effect on the natives that we want to avoid, and that is, that they would give allegiance to the stronger force.

By 13th July a memorandum was produced in MacArthur's headquarters recommending the establishment of a base on Lake Kuvanmas in the Sepik area for the purpose of obtaining Intelligence, gaining meteorological information, favourably influencing the natives, reconnoitring for possible airfields, and protecting Intelligence parties operating in uncontrolled areas. As 500 Japanese had been reported 40 miles north-west of Lake Kuvanmas, and as the Japanese were believed to have at least 20,000 troops in the Wewak area and 5,000 in the vicinity of Hansa Bay, it was important that the position should not be discovered. If it was discovered, it could not be defended. The chances of success therefore seemed less than 50 per cent, but, as the author of the memorandum (Colonel Van S. Merle-Smith) wrote:

Even partial success over a short period will yield benefit enough. G.O.C., N.G.F. and L.H.Q. are keen to take the chance, the risk to our planes is real. However, the risk at any one time is real—I would recommend that the project be backed.

Two days later G.H.Q. approved a plan for the establishment of a guerilla column on the Sepik. The force under the command of Major Farlow[8] would be known as "Mosstroops"[9] and would be flown in and supplied by air. The main task of Mosstroops would be to protect the special patrols operating in the area. At this time these patrols comprised, as well as the A.I.B. patrol of Fryer, the F.E.L.O. patrol of Stanley and the A.I.B.-N.E.F.I.S.[1] patrol of Staverman, Lieutenant Barracluff's[2] patrol on the April River, Lieutenant Boisen's[3] patrol between the April River and Lake Kuvanmas and Captain J. L. Taylor's Angau patrol near Lake Kuvanmas itself. Taylor had long been the district officer in this area, and, as mentioned, had been in a party which explored the Mount Hagen area in 1933 and had led a patrol thence to the Sepik in 1938-39.

In the month after the issue of the order by General Headquarters, 71 men were recruited in Australia for Mosstroops. An advanced party of four officers and one signaller under Captain Blood[4] ("Blood Party") was landed by Catalina at Lake Kuvanmas on 9th August; five days later Blood was informed by a local luluai that two Japanese patrols were on their way to the lake. Next day the enemy patrols approached nonchalantly, making no attempt to seek cover. They received a warm reception. "Native constables stood firm using their 303's like veterans," reported Blood. It was only when, after a 50 minutes' fight, the Japanese brought up mortars and sent a third party to cut off the Australians that Blood retired to a sago swamp with weapons, ammunition and codes intact. After great hardships in very rough country the party arrived exhausted at Wabag on 23rd September.

Meanwhile, Captain McNamara[5] and Sergeant Parrish,[6] after being cut off from Blood's party during the attack on Lake Kuvanmas, had hidden in a sago swamp. They decided to remain in the general area because they knew that Taylor's and Boisen's parties were heading for the lake. On 20th August six Japanese and a dozen armed natives attacked again but the two Australians fired on them as they fanned out, causing the natives and then the Japanese to panic and withdraw. By this action McNamara held the position until the arrival of Taylor.

---

[8] Maj R. M. Farlow, NX22678. 2/1 Pnr Bn; Angau (OC Mosstroops 1943-44). Asst District Officer; of Rabaul, TNG; b. Coburg, Vic, 5 Apr 1901. Died 19 Dec 1955.

[9] A moss-trooper was "one of the freebooters who infested the mosses (peat bogs) of the Scottish border in the middle of the 17th Century" (*Shorter Oxford English Dictionary*).

[1] NEFIS was the Netherlands East Indies Forces Intelligence Service.

[2] Lt J. T. Barracluff, NGX48. 2/1 A-Tk Regt and Angau. Medical assistant; of Milson's Point, NSW; b. Sydney, 2 Dec 1916. Missing believed killed on or after 15 Aug 1943.

[3] Capt F. N. Boisen, MC, NGX13. 2/1 A-Tk Regt and Angau. Schoolteacher; of Rabaul, TNG; b. Kingaroy, Qld, 22 Feb 1910.

[4] Capt N. B. N. Blood, PX169; Angau. Policeman; of Wewak, NG; b. Dublin, Eire, 12 Aug 1907.

[5] Capt D. W. McNamara, VX80879. "Z" Special Unit; OC 35 Sqn Air Liaison Section 1945. Commercial traveller; of Balwyn, Vic; b. Abbotsford, Vic, 3 Aug 1918.

[6] Lt D. J. Parrish, NX142834; Angau. Clerk; of Concord West, NSW; b. Chatswood, NSW, 4 Jun 1921.

During August Farlow and a small number of his officers and men reached Mosstroops' advanced headquarters at the junction of the Yellow and Sepik Rivers. On 5th September Farlow and Captain Grimson[7] reconnoitred Lake Yimas and next day Captain Cardew[8] with 5 men and 6 native constables were landed on the lake. That afternoon the enemy, with good warning from the natives, attacked this party forcing it to abandon its stores and withdraw south after inflicting 9 casualties. In his withdrawal south Cardew was entirely dependent on air droppings for supplies. The party reached Wabag on 29th October.

At one stage Farlow had plenty of worries. Not only were Blood's, McNamara's and Cardew's parties missing, but nothing had been heard from Barracluff since he and Father Hansen had been left at the April River early in August when Taylor and his party marched to Lake Kuvanmas. Boisen was therefore instructed to send out police patrols to search for him and Blood. Air reconnaissances early in September disclosed that Barracluff's camp was intact but empty and that the launch *Osprey* was missing. On 10th September Squadron Leader Coventry[9] who had previously found Cardew's missing party, picked up the beginning of a radio signal "To Cov from Joe . . ." which then faded out. The only "Joe" known in the area was Barracluff. Nothing was subsequently heard of Barracluff.

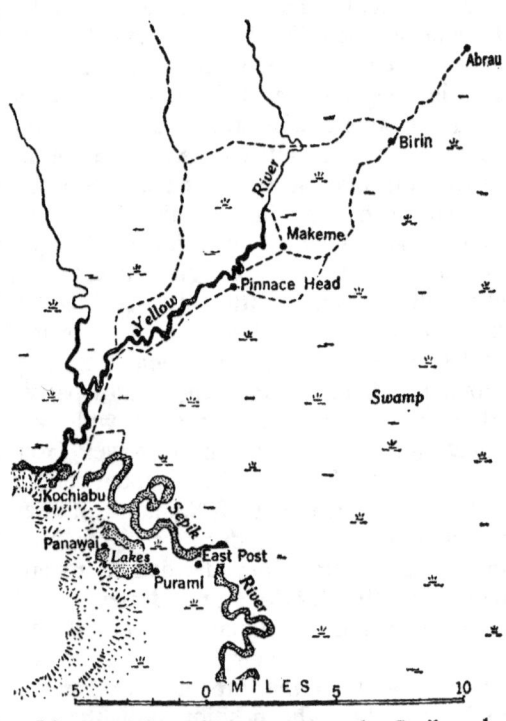

Mosstroops' staging camps on the Sepik and Yellow Rivers

In spite of this unfortunate start and although the enemy was now aware that something was happening along the Sepik, it was decided to insert the balance of Mosstroops into the Sepik-Yellow River area. On 10th September Captain Milligan[1] landed from a Catalina and

---

[7] Capt J. E. Grimson, NGX10. 2/1 MG Bn, "Z" Special Unit. Recruiter; of Rabaul, TNG; b. Armidale, NSW, 19 Jul 1900. Died of wounds 22 Aug 1944.

[8] Maj R. H. C. Cardew, NGX38. 2/8 Bn, "Z" Special Unit. Clerk; of Madang, NG; b. Sydney, 12 Apr 1918.

[9] Sqn Ldr G. W. Coventry, 457, 9 and 11 Sqns. Clerk; of Port Augusta, SA; b. North Adelaide, 15 Feb 1917. Missing, believed killed in action 2 May 1944.

[1] Maj J. S. Milligan, PX151; Angau. Public servant; of East Malvern, Vic; b. Glenferrie, Vic, 26 Jul 1908.

established a base on the Sepik but on the same day the river became swollen making Catalina landings dangerous. A temporary base was then established at Lake Panawai, and the remainder of Mosstroops and stores were flown in. By the beginning of October the movement was complete and the work of establishing a line of communication up the Yellow River and staging camps at Makeme, Birin and Abrau was begun. Advanced headquarters moved early in October from Lake Panawai to Pinnace Head.[2] The Catalina unloading point for supplies was at Kochiabu just downstream from the Sepik-Yellow River junction. Thus for a few weeks after their disastrous start Mosstroops had a chance to establish themselves.

News now arrived that Staverman had been killed and the remaining members of his party would cross the mountains to the head of the Yellow River. Lieutenants Fryer and Black[3] went out to find this party but returned on 23rd November having failed to do so.

On 20th October a strong party of Japanese in two pinnaces landed at East Post, forcing the five men at the base there to withdraw. Next day a group under Captain Fienberg[4] arrived from Panawai and found that the enemy had gone, after having taken the wireless set and other gear. East Post was again attacked on 20th November but the Japanese were driven off with losses.

Captain McKenzie and 23 of the 2/7th Commando Squadron arrived by air on 21st November and were posted at Purami, whence they patrolled.

General Blamey was apparently convinced that Mosstroops were doing a good job because on 6th December he wrote to General MacArthur to say that New Guinea Force and Allied Air Forces were discussing the withdrawal of Mosstroops but that he was not willing to withdraw them unless ordered to do so. General Chamberlin, however, advised MacArthur that the original purpose of Mosstroops was not being accomplished, air transport requirements had been increased, and a fighter airfield was no longer required in the area. Blamey now decided that it was advisable to withdraw Mosstroops.

Japanese aircraft attacked Kochiabu on 8th December. At this stage Major Farlow was informed that maintenance by aircraft could no longer be guaranteed and on 14th December he was instructed that all parties would be removed. Between the 16th and 19th aircraft took out the whole force of 102 Europeans and 127 natives—20 plane loads.

Bena Force and Tsili Tsili Force, as well as Mosstroops and the special parties, by harassing the enemy and by letting him know that Australian troops were spread from one end of New Guinea to the other, helped to cause uncertainty in his mind and forced him to dissipate strength which he might have conserved to meet the gathering storm round Lae.

---

[2] So called because it was the limit of navigation up the Yellow River.
[3] Capt G. B. Black, MC, NGX55. 6 Div Fd Cash Office; "Z" and "M" Special Units. Public servant; of Rabaul, TNG; b. Longreach, Qld, 24 Oct 1914.
[4] Capt D. M. Fienberg, MC, WX17501; Angau. Patrol officer; of Shenton Park, WA; b. Subiaco, WA, 24 Mar 1916.

CHAPTER 10

BEFORE LAE

THROUGHOUT the early months of 1943 two experienced A.I.F. divisions—the 9th and the 7th—were preparing for their roles in the coming offensive. As early as 2nd December 1942 General Morshead had cabled to General Blamey from Palestine: "Having regard to our future employment is there any particular form of training you wish us specially to practise?" Blamey had replied: "Re training. One. Combined training and opposed landings. Two. Jungle warfare." This briefest and clearest of signals accurately forecast the 9th Division's future.

After a triumphal review by General Alexander in Palestine, the 9th Division returned to Australia in February 1943. It was given three weeks leave, after which units of the division marched through the mainland capitals and received just acclaim from huge crowds; it re-formed in the Kairi area of the Atherton Tableland in April.

Soon after his return General Morshead was promoted to command of II Australian Corps, concentrated on the Atherton Tableland and consisting of the 7th and 9th Divisions and a brigade of the 6th. Here the jungle training of the 9th Division was intensified. Teams from the other two A.I.F. divisions, each consisting of one officer and four or five men, were attached to each brigade of the 9th, while officers from the 9th were attached to the 6th and 7th for periods of about four weeks. The units began to "learn quickly the methods of applying the principles of war to jungle conditions".[1]

After the promotion of Morshead Brigadier G. F. Wootten was appointed to command the 9th Division. It would be no easy task for anyone coming from outside the division to step into the shoes of the man who had led the 9th through two arduous and honourable campaigns. Wootten brought to the 9th Division, however, not only some experience of the kind of fighting the 9th had been through in North Africa—his 18th Brigade had for a time formed part of the division in the siege of Tobruk—but much experience of the tropical warfare it was now entering, having led the 18th Brigade in the Milne Bay and Buna-Sanananda fighting. He was by far the senior infantry brigade commander in the A.I.F. having succeeded Morshead in the 18th Brigade in February 1941.

The 9th Division, home after more than two years, took some time to settle down. Seldom had that elusive quality morale been higher in any division than in the 9th after El Alamein. For them it was St Crispin's Day. As part of the Eighth Army they had seen fighting on a majestic scale—tanks deployed in hundreds, men in tens of thousands and great bombardments by hundreds of guns—and they had shared the great exhilaration of victory that comes from participation in a massive battle. And now the bottom seemed rather to have fallen out of things. To a feeling

---

[1] Report on Operations of 9 Aust Div in the Capture of Lae and Finschhafen—4 Sep-2 Oct 1943.

of anti-climax and reaction after return home from the Middle East was added other more material troubles. In one brigade, for instance, about 5 per cent were absent without leave at the end of May. There were many influences at work and some were listed by a brigade commander: lack of amenities, contrast with the conditions enjoyed by militia units farther south and civilian employees in war industry, domestic worries including a number of unhappy matrimonial cases, reaction after home leave, discontent with the apparent unreality of some parts of Australia's war effort, and contact with industrial unrest in New South Wales. In general, however, the majority of the men who were A.W.L. were old offenders. The senior officers of the division soon discovered also that one of the penalties of service on their native soil was that they were subjected to frequent requests by Federal Ministers and others to do favours for this individual soldier or that.

The special problems of the period were soon left behind, however, although the special dog-barking or "Ho Ho" cry which characterised this phase remained with the 9th thereafter.[2] Although it is probably quite true that the 9th never quite recaptured the *élan* of the El Alamein period, the division soon began to recover from what one brigade commander later described as "this tremendous, sudden and almost frightening drop in morale". The 9th Division was fortunate that it was not required, as the 6th and the 7th had been in 1942, to transfer large batches of officers and N.C.O's to militia units, which now and until the end of the war were led chiefly by former officers of the 6th and 7th Divisions.

As plans for the coming offensive took shape the 9th began amphibious training, a new and fascinating experience for Australian soldiers, even though some of the officers and N.C.O's had attended a British school of amphibious warfare on the shores of the Bitter Lake in the Suez Canal area. On 27th May, only three weeks after General MacArthur had issued his orders for the New Guinea offensive, Major-General Wootten conferred with Brigadier-General William F. Heavey, the commander of the American 2nd Engineer Special Brigade, about amphibious training. After further conferences with General Morshead and his senior staff officer, Brigadier Wells,[3] three liaison officers from the boat and shore battalions of Colonel John J. F. Steiner's 532nd Engineer Boat and Shore Regiment were attached to the 9th Division for amphibious training. This engineer amphibian force was equipped to move one infantry brigade at a time in shore-to-shore operations over a distance not exceeding 60 miles, and to establish, protect and maintain a beach-head.

---

[2] There are many and varied versions of the origin of the "Ho Ho" cry and of its meaning. A senior officer later wrote of it as follows:

"This 'dog barking' was a curious and for a period a somewhat disconcerting matter. It needed to be dealt with wisely. . . . 'Ho Ho' became later a kind of battle cry which the Japs were to hear more than once. It was a kind of tribal call of the other ranks of the division. It could be insubordinate and disrespectful. It could be playful. It could be—for example, when Morshead visited the 9th Division at Finschhafen—a very warm greeting, a form of cheering really. Today when Morshead comes to 9th Division reunions in Sydney on El Alamein Day it is a form of mass acclaim by the men which precedes the enthusiastic drinking of his health."

[3] Lt-Gen Sir Henry Wells, KBE, CB, DSO, VX15120. Snr LO I Corps 1940-41, GSO1 9 Div 1941-43; BGS II Corps 1943-44, I Corps 1944-45. C-in-C British Commonwealth Forces, Korea, 1953-54; CGS 1954-58; Chairman, Chiefs of Staff Committee, 1958-59. Regular soldier; b. Kyneton, Vic. 22 Mar 1898.

The first Australian troops to undertake amphibian exercises—the 24th Brigade—arrived at Deadman's Gully near Trinity Beach north of Cairns on 16th June for a fortnight's training in shore-to-shore operations. Describing this training the 2nd Engineer Special Brigade's historian wrote:

> When the Amphibs heard that they were going to work with the famous 9th Australian Division (the "Rats of Tobruk") in impending amphibian operations in New Guinea, they took hold with renewed vigor and determination. These veteran AIF troops who had performed so admirably in the defense of Tobruk against Nazis, Fascisti, and desert sands had won every Amphib's confidence long before actual training began.[4]

The 20th Brigade took over from the 24th on 4th July. Unfortunately there was no time for the 26th Brigade to practise amphibious operations effectively, because, when its turn came at the end of July, the division was on its way north.

The mishaps to the small landing craft in the Nassau Bay operation, and the loss of surprise likely to result from the assembly of about 400 landing craft within 60 miles of the objective, caused Blamey and Herring to seek better means of transporting a whole division and at the same time maintaining the element of surprise. By 21st May Blamey's misgivings were such that he discussed the problem with MacArthur, emphasising the need to provide sufficient craft to move the whole 9th Division at once. Because this task was beyond the capacity of the E.S.B., and because of the hazards apparent in the use of Nassau Bay as the starting base, the Australian and American planners, now meeting weekly, began to contemplate using also the larger vessels of the Amphibious Force of the Seventh Fleet.

MacArthur's staff had planned that the main attack would come from the Markham Valley with a secondary one (by one brigade only) from the coast east of Lae. The Americans now found that Blamey's idea was that the main effort should be the landing of a whole division east of Lae, followed by an overland and airborne movement into the Markham Valley. Blamey therefore requested, in addition to the Engineer Special Brigade, 17 L.C.I's and 3 L.S.T's, or 15 L.C.T's. If this was agreed to there would be two forces—one from the army and one from the navy—with much the same sort of equipment, operating in the same area. After a careful evaluation of advantages and disadvantages, the planners of the "G3" section of G.H.Q. recommended to MacArthur on 25th May that, for the sake of simplicity of command, the E.S.B. should be placed under the operational control of the Amphibious Force, but for the Lae operation only.[5] For later shore operations along the coast the Commander of the Allied Naval Forces would be authorised to pass elements of the 2nd Engineer Special Brigade to the command of New Guinea Force. The naval commander would be responsible for the amphibious training of the 9th Division.

---

[4] *History of the Second Engineer Special Brigade*, p. 29.
[5] On an American staff G1 was concerned with Personnel, G2 with Intelligence, G3 with Operations and Training, G4 with Supply, Construction, Transportation and Evacuation.

In Brisbane on 27th June Blamey was assured by Admiral Carpender that the whole of Barbey's Amphibious Force planning staff would soon move to New Guinea so that joint planning could take place. On 11th July in Port Moresby Blamey discussed with Herring, Barbey and Wootten his outline plan for the movement of the 9th Division in the larger craft of Barbey's task force.

"This," wrote Herring later, ". . . involved a complete change in plan. As a result of the conference the following outline plan was submitted for the approval of the appropriate commanders. 9 Aust Div was to be brought to Milne Bay for training and rehearsal with Amphforce craft. On the appropriate date the assaulting brigades were to go direct from Milne Bay to the landing beach, while the reserve brigade, having done its training at Milne Bay was to be transferred some days before the operation to Buna and held there ready to be moved on the night of D + 1/D + 2."[6] In Herring's plan "the task of the 2 E.S.B. was . . . limited to the transport of one shore battalion in their small craft from the base in the Morobe area. The craft carrying the shore battalion to the landing beach were to remain there and come under command of 9 Aust Div, for movement of men, equipment and supplies along the coast." The main result of the change in plan was to render unnecessary any further development of staging bases along the coast. With its larger craft Amphforce needed only one port between Milne Bay and Lae. Buna was selected as the most suitable port and was speedily developed.

At the Port Moresby conference Wootten and his principal staff officer, Lieut-Colonel Barham,[7] learnt that the division would land on a beach east of Lae to be selected by Wootten and out of gun range of Lae. A joint planning headquarters (9th Division and Task Force 76—the naval force in support) would be established at Milne Bay where the planning staffs of the three Services would live together. Wootten's planning headquarters flew to Milne Bay on 20th and 21st July but because the naval staff remained on their headquarters ship, *Rigel,* eight miles away, intimate cooperation was not achieved, naval representation being spasmodic and uncertain at planning conferences.[8]

Between 26th July and 12th August the brigades of the 9th Division followed one another to Milne Bay in American and Australian ships, in the order in which Wootten had already decided they would land east of Lae—20th, 26th, 24th. "All ranks will immediately shave under the armpits and hair on heads will be close cropped", ordered the routine orders of one battalion; another's warned "the natives do not like being

---

[6] Report on Operations of NG Force and I Aust Corps in New Guinea from 22 Jan 43 to 8 Oct 43.

[7] Brig R. J. Barham, DSO, OBE, WX1560. HQ 9 Div 1941 and 1942; CO 2/15 Bn 1942-43; GSO1 9 Div 1943-44; Col GS (Ops) Adv LHQ 1944-45. Regular soldier; of Parramatta, NSW; b. Berry, NSW, 18 Jan 1908.

[8] Principal appointments on the staff of the 9th Division in August 1943 included: *GOC* Maj–Gen G. F. Wootten; *GSO1* Lt-Col R. J. Barham; *GSO2* Maj R. J. Hamer; *Senior Liaison Officer* Maj T. G. Trainor; *AA & QMG* Col B. R. W. Searl; *DAAG* Maj N. W. Lockyer; *DAQMG* Maj W. R. Kent; *ADMS* Col B. S. Hanson; *LSO* Maj A. G. Allaway; *ADOS* Maj J. H. Chinner; *DAPM* Maj R. I. Stone; *CRA* Brig S. T. W. Goodwin; *CRE* Lt-Col D. O. Muller; *CO Sigs* Lt-Col A. J. Campbell; *CASC* Lt-Col L. A. Withers.

called 'George'. The correct term to use is 'Boy' "; while a third stated "a certain number of men inadequately trained are still expressing the opinion that taking of atebrin will result in loss of manhood. . . . No case of loss of virility from taking atebrin has yet been recorded in scientific circles."

In its period of general training and re-forming in the Ravenshoe area of the Atherton Tableland the 7th Division had faced different problems from those confronting the 9th. The 7th needed no introduction to jungle warfare. When he returned from leave and sickness to resume command on 18th April Major-General Vasey found the division greatly below strength because of battle casualties in the Papuan campaign and recurring malaria. The 21st Brigade, for instance, had only 57 officers and 1,066 men whereas its war establishment was 119 officers and 2,415 men. As late as June the 18th Brigade had only 44 per cent of its authorised strength and was considered unfit for service without further training and reorganisation. By 10th July this brigade had absorbed 51 officers and 1,239 men from the 1st Motor Brigade then being disbanded. During April, May and June the brigades trained hard and in mid-July took part in a divisional exercise.

Camped at Gordonvale was Colonel Kenneth H. Kinsler's 503rd American Parachute Regiment. As early as 11th May Kinsler had provided a demonstration and inspection of equipment for Vasey and the three infantry brigadiers. MacArthur's headquarters on 19th June authorised Kinsler's parachute regiment to train with the II Corps and several exercises were carried out. Wishing to discuss the lessons of the Crete campaign with Brigadier I. N. Dougherty, who had commanded a battalion in the successful defence of Heraklion against German paratroops, Kinsler adopted the unusual method of arriving by parachute on the Ravenshoe golf links.

For the attack on Lae Blamey intended that the 7th Division would play second fiddle to the 9th which would actually capture Lae. He wrote later:

> The introduction of a force simultaneously into the Markham Valley was primarily to prevent reinforcement of the Japanese garrison at Lae. This would be carried out by interposing a force of sufficient size across the enemy's overland line of communication between Madang and Lae. When this had been done, an offensive operation would be carried out against Lae from the north-west to assist that which was to be made along the coast by the 9 Aust Div. Then, with a port and airfields in our possession, 7 Aust Div would be free to expand towards the north of the Markham Valley to secure or construct airfields.[1]

Blamey hoped that the 7th Division would be based early in the Bulolo Valley. Its advance from there into the Markham Valley would involve crossing the Markham River, no easy task, and a "serious defile" as he termed it. It would be necessary therefore to establish an air base north of the Markham as soon as possible after the launching of the offensive.

---

[1] Commander Allied Land Forces, Report on New Guinea Operations, 4 September 1943 to 26 April 1944.

There were many sites in the extensive Markham flats, and there were also a number of small overgrown pre-war landing grounds. Seizure of one of these would reduce the effort and accelerate the preparation of an airfield suitable for large transport aircraft. About 20 miles north-west of Lae was the old landing ground at Nadzab, which Blamey decided to seize.

The concentration of the 7th Division in the Bulolo Valley would involve movement of troops and supplies into an area which had no land or sea line of communication with Allied bases. As maintenance of the 3rd Division already made large demands on the limited number of transport aircraft available for crossing the mountains, it was hoped to use the Bulldog-Wau road to move troops and supplies into the Bulolo Valley and a road from Sunshine to move them thence to the Markham. Delays caused by equipment shortages and the rugged nature of the country led Blamey on 21st May to inform MacArthur that his ability to launch the 7th Division's offensive was dependent on the completion of the Bulldog Road.

On 17th June MacArthur agreed to provide an American parachute battalion to capture Nadzab after which an Australian brigade would move into the area either in air transports or overland from the Bulolo Valley. Blamey's outline plan provided that, in addition, an infantry brigade group would move overland through the Bulolo Valley to reach the Markham River before the airborne landing and would be available as a reserve.

On 8th July the 25th Brigade was warned to be ready for movement. By 20th July most of the brigade had sailed, in troopships well known to Australian soldiers moving to and from New Guinea—*Duntroon, Taroona* and *Canberra*. The remainder arrived at Port Moresby on 26th July aboard the *Katoomba*. The 21st Brigade followed at the beginning of August, and the 18th had arrived at Port Moresby by the 12th.

By the time his advanced headquarters arrived in Port Moresby on 25th July, Vasey already expected that it would be necessary for his entire division to be transported north of the Markham by air.[2] On 25th July he attended a conference at New Guinea Force. There Blamey outlined the plan and Barbey and Wootten said they would be ready by 27th August. Blamey had ascertained that the airfields in the Watut Valley would be capable of accommodating two fighter squadrons in early August, and that twin-engined fighter groups would be established at Dobodura by mid-August. Air support for the Nadzab operation would thus be assured, but as air operations depended so much on weather a firm date such as that suggested for the seaborne assault could not be guaranteed. Blamey was now convinced that two infantry brigade groups must be used at Nadzab, but because of delay in opening the Bulldog-Wau

---

[2] Principal appointments on the staff of the 7th Division in August 1943 included: *GOC* Maj-Gen G. A. Vasey; *GSO1* Lt-Col W. T. Robertson; *GSO2* Maj I. H. Lowen; *Senior Liaison Officer* Maj A. S. Mackinnon; *AA & QMG* Lt-Col L. G. Canet; *DAAG* Maj H. A. Solomon; *DAQMG* Maj P. S. Smith; *ADMS* Col F. H. Beare; *LSO* Maj J. W. Nash; *ADOS* Lt-Col F. B. Robertson and Maj C. S. McKay; *DAPM* Maj J. W. Ogden; *CRA* Brig T. C. Eastick; *CRE* Lt-Col R. A. J. Tompson; *CO Sigs* Lt-Col G. E. Parker; *CASC* Lt-Col D. J. A. Nelson.

road, he thought that it might be necessary to fly the second brigade into the Bulolo Valley.³

Already Vasey was capturing the imagination of the men of the A.I.F. as perhaps no other commander was to do. Lean, highly-strung and learned, he now had more experience as a field commander than any of his contemporaries in the regular officer corps. Like Wootten, Vasey would have close association with a particular American unit—in his case the 503rd Parachute Infantry Regiment; like Dougherty, Vasey had served against German paratroops in Crete. At the Port Moresby conference on 25th July Vasey had said that he doubted whether one parachute battalion was sufficient to seize and prepare landing strips capable of taking two brigades, which he considered the minimum force required for his task. On 31st July he suggested to Colonel Kinsler the use of the whole regiment (2,000 men) because of the nature of the Nadzab flats and the extensive front which the parachutists would have to cover; and on 2nd August he wrote to Herring asking that the strength of the paratroops be increased from one battalion to one regiment, that Australian engineer paratroops be attached to the American regiment for the operation, and the greatest possible number of gliders be made available and used (to carry engineers and their equipment).⁴ By 23rd August the entire parachute regiment had been transported with great secrecy to Port Moresby.

Vasey, however, was still not convinced that the regiment, by itself, could secure the Nadzab strip against possible opposition and then develop it. He therefore proposed that one of his brigades should be flown to Bulolo or Tsili Tsili some days before the operation, cross the Markham just after the airstrip had been seized by the paratroops, and assist in its preparation.

He immediately set about finding suitable crossings of the Markham. Thus, at the end of July, parties led by Captain K. Power of the 2/33rd Battalion and Captain D. L. Cox of the 2/25th reconnoitred north from Tsili Tsili and Sunshine respectively to the Markham.

To help the paratroops construct the airstrips Vasey now decided to move the 2/2nd Pioneer Battalion and 2/6th Field Company overland from Tsili Tsili and across the Markham to Nadzab on the day of the landing. On 6th August he ordered Lieut-Colonel Lang⁵ of the 2/2nd Pioneers to provide a patrol to reconnoitre the track Marilinan-Babwuf-Waime-Naragooma-Kirkland's Dump. The patrol's tasks would include finding a suitable crossing of the Watut near Tsili Tsili; reconnoitring a track east of the Watut to Kirkland's which could be used by about 2,000 troops; finding a suitable concealed area near Kirkland's to hide the troops, and recommending a suitable crossing of the Markham as well as the best means of crossing.

---

³ The road was opened for some single-way traffic on 31st August.
⁴ The gliders were actually brought from Australia to Dobodura, but, in the event, technical reasons prevented their use.
⁵ Lt-Col J. T. Lang, OBE, MC, QX6067. (1st AIF: Capt 53 Bn; and Indian Army.) 2/2 Pnr Bn (CO 1942-43); Comd Buna Base Sub-Area 1943-44. Mechanical and electrical engineer; of Brisbane; b. Dunedin, NZ, 15 Sep 1896.

The patrol was led by Major Kidd[6] of the Pioneers and included old New Guinea hands as well as representatives of the Pioneers and 2/6th Field Company. Kidd reached Kirkland's Dump on 15th August and later submitted a report on which subsequent movement of the overland force was based.[7]

Meanwhile, between 3rd and 5th August, Lieutenant Merry[8] of the 2/6th Field Company had floated in an assault boat down the Watut from Tsili Tsili to the junction of the Markham and Watut Rivers. He reported that the river was navigable in spite of sandbanks and snags, and provided the load in each boat did not exceed 2,000 pounds.

Damage caused to stores and equipment by careless handling and weather had been experienced by both the 9th and 7th Divisions in their movement from Australia to New Guinea. Stop-work meetings and go-slow tactics by the Cairns wharf labourers had delayed and confused the move of the 20th Brigade late in July. The 26th Brigade's stores had been dumped in confusion on Stringer Beach early in August in pouring rain and with insufficient time for unloading ships. At Port Moresby unloading was carried out by troops no better than the loading at Cairns. During the unloading of the 21st Brigade's stores at Port Moresby such delicate equipment as anti-tank guns, anti-aircraft guns and wireless equipment were dropped the last few feet on to the wharf. Crates burst open, and when the brigade officer detailed to prevent pilfering asked that more care be taken in the unloading of crates whose contents were valued at £2,000 each, the reply was "Righto, Mate", and another crate slipped from the sling and crashed into the lighter below. No care was taken to place generators and predictors upright, as requested, in the lighters. Before the last of the 21st Brigade's stores had been unloaded the holds were battened down and the ship sailed. Conditions were better at the bases on the north-east coast of Papua from which the attack would be launched—"one cannot say too much about the splendid planning, the speed with which those plans were put into effect and the spirit with which everyone set to work".[9]

While the 24th Brigade was moving to Buna the 20th and 26th Brigades prepared for a practice landing from Barbey's craft on two beaches on Normanby Island as similar as possible to those chosen east of Lae. The diarist of the 2/32nd Battalion, preparing to leave for Buna, wrote: "Should Jupiter Pluvius continue in his present vein, our camp will become

---

[6] Maj K. B. Kidd, SX8590. 2/3 and 2/2 Pnr Bns. Clerk; of Adelaide; b. Glebe, NSW, 1 Apr 1905.

[7] 3rd Division Headquarters, through whose area these patrols were taking place, were naturally curious but their curiosity went unsatisfied. Referring to Power's Watut patrol Savige had signalled Herring that the patrol "will gain most value by following route suggested by us"—west of the Watut. Regarding Cox's patrol, Savige suggested that "you allow us to advise him best route to carry out his mission". NGF had replied that "Party B knows best route is west of Watut River. . . . Party A will reconnoitre as instructed by its divisional headquarters."
That Kidd's patrol had kept its secret well was apparent from an entry in the diary of the 24th Battalion through whose territory the patrol passed: "No information was obtained of their mission, route out and in, or of their start and finishing points."

[8] Maj E. O. Merry, NX12713; 2/6 Fd Coy. Regular soldier; b. Seddon, Vic, 28 Nov 1905.

[9] Report on Operations of NG Force and I Aust Corps in New Guinea from 22 Jan 43 to 8 Oct 43.

an ideal spot to conduct amphibious operations." The real practice, however, took place, on 20th and 21st August and many valuable lessons were learned. The majority of the craft used were those actually to be employed for the real landing and consisted of "Assault Personnel Destroyers" (A.P.D's), L.C.I's, L.S.T's and L.C.T's of Barbey's Task Force and the 532nd Engineer Boat and Shore Regiment.

The craft which would carry the Australians to the landing beaches would be manned by the Americans, but, although probably few of the crews or the troops they carried realised it, the prototypes of many of these craft and others that were to land Americans and Australians on coast after coast northward towards Japan had been designed in Britain.

In the nineteen-thirties Japan led the Powers in the development of landing craft; from 1937 in China she used them on a scale not to be attained by any other Power until 1943. In Britain, in the 'thirties, work on the design of landing craft was accelerated; and, when war broke out, a modest number of L.C.A's (Landing Craft, Assault) and L.C.M's (Landing Craft, Mechanised) were being built there. The operations in Norway severely tested British landing craft and British staff work for combined operations; and the overrunning of France and the Low Countries compelled her to press on with improving the design and increasing the output of the landing craft without whose help her troops could not strike back against the Germans.

By 1941 some hundreds of "assault" and "mechanised" landing craft were being built, more than 100 larger L.C.T's (Landing Craft, Tank) were built or building, a number of L.S.I's (Landing Ships, Infantry—liners able to carry landing craft at their davits) were in use. Also L.S.T's (Landing Ships, Tank, vessels capable of landing through their bows 500 tons or more of tanks, vehicles and stores), had been built and tested, and other specialised craft were on the way. When the Pacific war began Britain gave large orders for these ships and craft in the United States, where the designs were adopted and mass production soon began on a scale unattainable in Britain, although in America some Service Chiefs had been "dubious about the need for landing ships and craft before Pearl Harbour".[1] In 1942, at the request of Admiral Mountbatten for a vessel able to carry about 200 men across the Channel and land them on a beach, a new and important type, the L.C.I. (Landing Craft, Infantry) was designed. The Americans, faced with the need for craft which could run ashore on the coral-fringed beaches and swampy shores of the Pacific —problems not encountered in Europe—developed amphibian vehicles: for example, the L.V.T. (Landing Vehicle, Tracked) and the D.U.K.W. (a lorry with a hull and propellers). A large number of other specialised types of ships and small craft for landing operations were developed by them as the war went on.

Rapid progress had been made in the planning and execution of amphibious expeditions as well as in their equipment since the experimental British seaborne raids by Independent Companies in 1940 and

---
[1] L. E. H. Maund, *Assault from the Sea* (1949), p. 91.

1941. In August 1942 a force equal to a small division had been put ashore at Dieppe; in November there were the North African landings by large forces but against a defender who was not expected to offer a very sturdy or well-organised resistance; and in July 1943 came the invasion of Sicily, the largest seaborne operation so far.

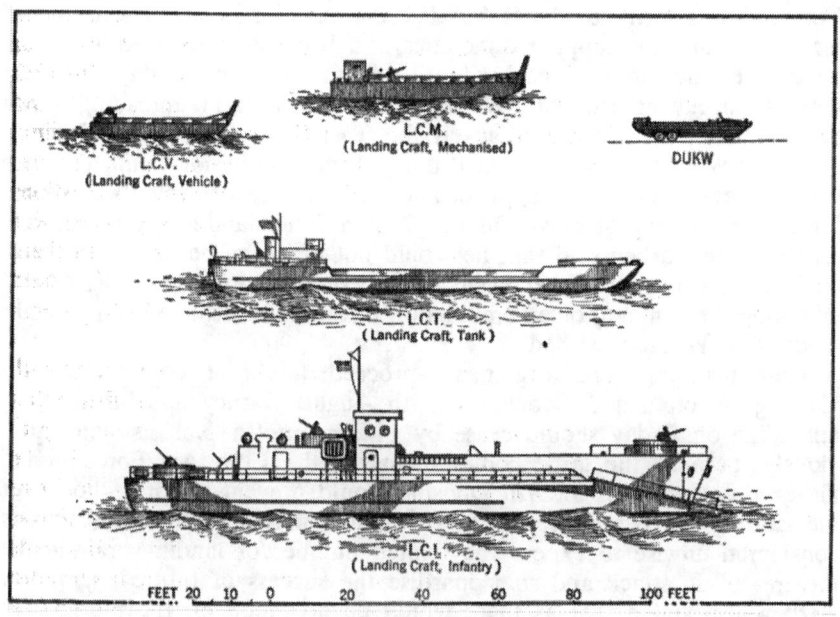

Some Allied landing craft

In the Pacific the landings had generally been on a smaller scale. At Guadalcanal in August 1942 the 1st Marine Division had put more men ashore than were in the British-Canadian force which landed at Dieppe in the same month, but on a far less strongly defended shore. In June 1943 the Americans had landed on New Georgia. In the S.W.P.A. there had been the rehearsal landing of two regimental combat teams on Woodlark and Kiriwina in June, and the landing of one battalion combat team at Nassau Bay on a beach occupied by a party of Australian troops. The landing of the 9th Division east of Lae would be the largest amphibious operation yet undertaken in the South-West Pacific.

General Blamey's instruction for the capture of the Lae-Nadzab area was issued on 30th July, and was followed on 9th August by General Herring's orders. These stated that "New Guinea Force, in conjunction with 5 A.F. and U.S. Task Force 76, will seize the area Lae-Nadzab with a view to establishing airfield facilities therein". To carry out this order the 9th Division would capture Lae after landing east of Lae, while the 7th Division would "establish itself in the Markham Valley by overland and airborne operation".

At Milne Bay Wootten continued his efforts to iron out the vital points of his plan with Barbey. For instance, when the two commanders lunched on *Rigel* on 2nd August, Wootten emphasised the necessity for carrying 10 days' reserve rations on D-day, and also the need for a full-scale rehearsal. At another conference five days later (attended by Herring, Wootten, Barbey, Colonel M. C. Cooper of the Fifth Air Force and Air Commodore Hewitt[2] of the R.A.A.F.) the date for D-day was postponed mainly because of shipping difficulties and because Barbey requested air cover over the landing beaches until at least noon on D-day. On 13th August Barbey agreed with Wootten that landing and unloading would proceed if enemy aircraft attacked the Task Force during the landing. Naturally Wootten was determined not to have his division dumped ashore inadequately loaded and supplied, and he therefore contested suggestions for doing the job quickly. On the 21st a long-standing argument was settled when Barbey said that he would not insist, as he had up to then, on L.S.T's being completely vehicle loaded. Bulk loading, which would take longer to unload, or a combination of bulk and vehicle loading might be used, as Wootten wished.

Thus planning—and argument—proceeded. At a conference with Herring, Wootten and Cooper on 19th August Barbey had insisted that unloading on D-day should cease by 11 a.m., not 1 p.m. as stated previously, because the large commitments of the Fifth Air Force in the airborne operation of the 7th Division would prevent air protection over the landing beaches for more than a limited period, and because it was considered unwise to expose the limited number of landing craft in the theatre to air attack and so jeopardise the success of future operations. Barbey also stated that as there would be no moon on the morning of 4th September, which had now been designated D-day, he would be unable to guarantee landing on the correct beaches until 20 minutes after sunrise at 6.30 a.m. "The time span for the landing was thereby reduced to 4½ hours," commented Wootten later, "which meant that after forward troops had been put ashore there would be a maximum time of three hours for unloading stores."[3]

At this conference on the 19th Barbey insisted on an "air umbrella" all the way, and the air force stated that aircraft could not be kept aloft indefinitely but that radar would enable them to reach the spot quickly. Because the air force could not provide close support over the beaches until 7.15 a.m. on D-day, Wootten decided to dispense with bombing and strafing of the beaches immediately before the landing. As continuous a fighter cover as possible, however, would be provided during the approach to the landing beaches, during the landing, and during the return of the amphibious craft.

Wootten's staff estimated that there were about 7,250 enemy troops, including 5,100 field troops in Lae, that the enemy had a large amount

---

[2] AVM J. E. Hewitt, CBE. Deputy Ch of Air Staff 1941-42; Dir Allied Air Intell SWPA 1942-43 and 1944; AOC 9 (Ops) Gp 1943; Air Member for Personnel 1945-48. Regular air force officer; of Toorak, Vic; b. Tylden, Vic, 13 Apr 1901.

[3] 9th Division report.

of artillery, and that most defences were in and around Lae itself. By the time Wootten issued his operation order on 26th August, his brigadiers and battalion commanders were well acquainted with their tasks. The 9th Division's landing would be preceded by a six-minute naval bombardment by five destroyers and would be carried out in three main groups. First, the 20th Brigade, supported by the 26th, would begin landing at 6.30 a.m. on 4th September on Red Beach. The 2/13th Battalion would land at the same time on Yellow Beach to the east to protect the eastern flank and secure an alternative beach-head if necessary. In this group of 7,800 troops, the first assaulting wave would be carried in the four A.P.D's—capable of carrying assault landing craft as well as troops to man them. On arrival near the landing beaches the A.P.D's would launch the craft carrying the first wave of infantry. The second group consisting of some 2,400 troops—rear details of the two brigades—with vehicles and bulk stores would land at 11 p.m. on 4th September, and the third, comprising the reserve brigade group, some 3,800 troops, would land on the night 5th-6th September. The boat and shore regiment would travel in their own craft from Morobe to join the first group, but all other troops and stores would be transported in and landed from Barbey's larger landing craft.

The area chosen for the landing was in the vicinity of the Bulu Plantation, and on 19th August Lieutenant W. A. Money of Angau, the owner of that plantation, gave Brigadier Windeyer[4] of the 20th Brigade and his battalion commanders a detailed description of the country. The area through which the 9th Division would advance consisted of a flat coastal plain averaging three miles in width before rising to the rugged foothills of the Rawlinson Range. West of the Burep River this plain broadened into the valleys of the Busu, Bumbu and Markham Rivers. About two miles and a half north of Lae the Busu and Bumbu were divided by the Atzera Range which dominated Lae. Dense jungle, interspersed with patches of kunai 8 to 10 feet high and mangrove swamps near the coast, covered the coastal plain. Between Red Beach and Lae, 16 miles away, the advancing division would have to cross five rivers and a large number of small streams. Swollen by the daily downpours of the rainy season[5] the rivers were now fast-flowing, but, except for the Busu, which might present a problem, they were narrow with shallow banks and stony bottoms. There were no roads in the area, only native paths. The two landing beaches were about 20 yards wide and of firm black sand, but behind them was a swamp through which were few exits.

In Port Moresby Vasey was better situated than Wootten to maintain close liaison with the Americans, and during August he constantly conferred with them about details of the Nadzab landing. American cooperation enabled him to fly low over the Nadzab area in a Superfortress bomber on 7th August.

---

[4] Maj-Gen Sir Victor Windeyer, KBE, CB, DSO, ED, NX396. HQ 7 Div 1940; CO 2/48 Bn 1940-42; Comd 20 Bde 1942-45; Admin Comd 9 Div 1945-46. Barrister-at-law; of Sydney; b. Hunter's Hill, NSW, 28 Jul 1900.

[5] The average rainfall in the Lae area was about 177 inches and September was usually the wettest month.

Meanwhile the units of the 7th Division were concentrating on acclimatisation and specialist training. The 2/2nd Pioneer Battalion, for example, practised with folding assault boats in the Laloki River, while the infantry battalions rehearsed the speedy loading and unloading of aircraft, assisted by a training film, "Loading the Douglas C-47". Between 8th and 21st August Brigadier-General Ennis C. Whitehead, Deputy Commander of the Fifth Air Force, made five planes available each day at Ward's and Jackson's airfields for Vasey's units to practise loading and unloading. Detailed movement tables were prepared and a great deal of research went into the operational loading of aircraft, particularly by Lieut-Colonel R. A. J. Tompson, the division's Chief Engineer, and Lieut-Colonel Blyth[6] of the 2/4th Field Regiment.

On 16th August Vasey wrote to Herring expressing his anxiety at the little equipment available to Tompson—one scoop, one ripper and one tractor on loan from New Guinea Force. By 26th August, however, Vasey was informed that the 871st United States Aviation Engineer Battalion would be placed under his command from that day. When the engineers of the 2/6th Field Company (Captain Dunphy[7]) saw the equipment of the 871st Battalion, their diarist was moved to write: "Their equipment (light mechanical earth moving equipment for air transport) was the envy of the company."

In order to reduce any interruption due to bad weather Vasey decided to use Tsili Tsili as a forward staging field to which the leading elements of the airborne brigade would be moved the day before Z-day.[8] Here also the 2/2nd Pioneer Battalion and 2/6th Field Company arrived by air on 23rd and 24th August.

Vasey's Intelligence staff estimated that there were about 6,420 enemy troops in Lae, including 4,780 field troops, slightly lesser numbers than those estimated by the 9th Division. This number, side by side with the 7,000 Japanese estimated by Herring's staff to be in the Salamaua area, made understandable Vasey's anxiety to have his fighting troops at Nadzab as soon as possible.

Vasey issued his plan on 27th August. Z-day would be 5th September, a date proposed by Vasey and Whitehead after taking into consideration the availability of fighter cover and the weather. The paratroops would jump over Nadzab at 10.30 a.m. under cover of a preliminary air attack and smoke screens placed by aircraft. The pioneers and engineers from Tsili Tsili would make a covered approach to the Markham on the previous day and cross to coincide with the paratroop attack. Vasey's forward headquarters and the first troops of Brigadier K. W. Eather's 25th Brigade would land at Tsili Tsili on 6th September and await the preparation of the Nadzab airfield before being ferried across by aircraft. When the airfield was ready, the 21st Brigade would move direct to Nadzab

---

[6] Lt-Col A. J. Blyth, DSO, ED, NX12326. 2/6 Fd Regt 1940-41; CO 2/4 Fd Regt 1942-45. Estate agent; of Bellevue Hill, NSW; b. Hobart, 12 Aug 1908.

[7] Maj W. J. Dunphy, NX19563; 2/6 Fd Coy. Civil engineer; of Cremorne, NSW; b. Petersham, NSW, 5 Apr 1912.

[8] Used by the 7th Division to distinguish it from the D-day of the 9th Division operation.

from Port Moresby. Immediately after landing Eather would relieve Kinsler of his protective tasks, and, when a sufficient force had been landed to block the Markham Valley from the west, he would begin the advance towards Lae.

The Markham Valley runs north-west of Lae for about 80 miles. Gradually rising from sea level at Lae, it is about 1,200 feet above sea level at the Markham's headwaters near Marawasa where the divide between the Markham and Ramu Valleys is so gradual as to give the impression that the two valleys are one. It was believed that in geological times the Markham and Ramu Valleys were beneath the sea, thus dividing New Guinea into two islands. Through the ages the Markham plains, varying in width from 6 to 12 miles, had been formed by rivers washing down huge quantities of alluvial gravel from the high ranges and then forming the Markham River on the extreme southern edge of the valley. The valley, being almost completely gravel, is infertile and covered with a stunted form of kangaroo grass, except where silt, deposited by smaller streams failing to reach the Markham, enables tall kunai to grow. It presents few obstacles east of Nadzab, although to the west there are Garambampon Creek and the Leron, Rumu and Erap Rivers, which could form natural obstacles during the rainy season. Militarily the Markham and Ramu Valleys were very important for they formed the easiest land route whereby Japanese reinforcements and supplies could reach Lae and Salamaua from Wewak and Madang, and were also suitable for the development of air bases needed to control Vitiaz Strait and to provide air cover for the land advance.

In a signal to Lieut-Colonel Smith of the 24th Battalion on 23rd August Herring had given an inkling of pending operations: "Essential for success our future plans that enemy Markham Point area be contained there and also any Japs withdrawing from Salamaua be prevented from joining this force."

Captain Chalk, whose company of Papuans was patrolling northward from the Wampit towards the Markham, had been summoned to Port Moresby where he received his orders from Vasey on 25th August. Before Z-day the Papuan company would patrol the south bank of the Markham from Mount Ngaroneno to the junction of the Watut and Markham to prevent natives seeing Australian activity on the track between Babwuf and Kirkland's Dump surveyed by Kidd's patrol. On Z-day Chalk would cross the Markham and ensure adequate warning of any enemy movement towards Nadzab from the west or north. To preserve secrecy Chalk was instructed not to discuss operations in the hearing of his native soldiers but to tell them that a Japanese crossing of the river was feared. When Chalk returned from Port Moresby on 27th August he carried also secret instructions for Smith to attack Markham Point with at least one company at first light on Z-day with the object of destroying the enemy south of the Markham and preventing any Japanese from the Salamaua area using the river crossings near Markham Point.

Meanwhile the air and naval forces were playing their parts in weakening the enemy. During August the air force attacked Lae, Salamaua and Finschhafen as well as flying deep into enemy territory to attack Wewak and Madang. Along the coast they hunted Japanese barges. Whitehead informed Kenney at the end of July that over 100 barges had been sunk that month, that the pilots were becoming expert at finding them in spite of elaborate camouflage, and that he expected good hunting in August. The tempo was set for the month when, on the 2nd, 23 Mitchells claimed 13 barges along the Rai Coast and the coast of the Huon Peninsula.

Kenney pointed out to MacArthur that, as he did not have enough air strength to handle the Japanese air forces at both Wewak and Rabaul, he proposed concentrating on the airfields in the Wewak area until the landing of the 9th Division. This policy culminated in the pulverising raids on 17th and 18th August which crippled the Japanese air force in New Guinea for the time being. Although barge hunting was not quite so profitable in the last two weeks of August, the aircrews reported the destruction of 57 and damage to about 60 others.

Barbey's patrol torpedo boats, from their forward base at Morobe, took over the barge hunting from the airmen at sunset each day. They were particularly active in Vitiaz Strait and in ambushing the Finschhafen-Lae supply line. These small venomous craft became so expert at finding the enemy barges that a Japanese diarist at Finschhafen wrote that on 29th August he had made the only trip "when barges were not attacked by torpedo boats"; his barge was sunk on its return journey. However, in spite of the vigilance of the P.T's (as the torpedo boats were known) seven Japanese submarine missions managed to land, in July, 195 men and 238 tons of supplies, while on 2nd and 5th August two destroyer-transports landed 1,560 troops and 150 tons of supplies at Cape Gloucester, a good springboard for New Guinea.

MacArthur informed Blamey on 20th August that there was evidence that the Japanese were planning to reinforce Salamaua, using landing barges that had recently arrived at Finschhafen, and that he had ordered the naval forces to make a sweep through the Huon Gulf. That day Vice-Admiral Carpender ordered Captain Jesse H. Carter to take four destroyers to "make a sweep of Huon Gulf—during darkness 22-23 August and follow this with a bombardment of Finschhafen".[9] For the first time in the New Guinea ground fighting a naval bombardment was scheduled. Although any damage caused by 540 shells fired by Carter's destroyers into Finschhafen was not observed, one of Carpender's staff remarked: "It will be worthwhile to prove the Navy is willing to pitch in, even if we get nothing but coconuts."

The Japanese were now becoming more active in the air, and since the beginning of September their planes had been met in substantial numbers over Wewak and Cape Gloucester. At noon on the 3rd 9 enemy bombers and 6 fighters attacked Morobe, but without damage and with only one casualty. Because Lae and Cape Gloucester had been heavily bombed

---

[9] S. E. Morison, *Breaking the Bismarcks Barrier, 22 July 1942-1 May 1944*, p. 259.

that day, the Allied air force was mystified as to where these aircraft came from. Kenney would have been surprised had he known that, in spite of what he termed "a farewell slugging with 23 heavy bombers, unloading 84 tons of bombs" on Lae, 3 bombers and 6 fighters had slipped undetected into Lae that afternoon and remained there for the night, apparently destined for Morobe next day.

Final discussions between the navy and the air force, hampered by the absence from Milne Bay of any air force representative with sufficient authority to make definite decisions, centred on Barbey's desire for an "air umbrella" or continuous coverage. Kenney undertook "to place the maximum number of fighter aircraft in the Lae vicinity on a continuous wave basis", and promised that reserve aircraft would be held on ground alert to support Barbey. Pressed further by the navy, Kenney finally agreed to provide a 32-plane cover over the task force as continuously as possible through daylight hours.

The two fighter control sectors, based on Dobodura and Tsili Tsili, did not have a complete radar coverage of the seas through which the convoy would proceed. It was believed that enemy aircraft could fly behind the mountains from Wewak and Madang towards Lae and others could fly across Vitiaz Strait from New Britain without being picked up until too late. To cover this gap the R.A.A.F. suggested that a destroyer, equipped with radar and radio, should be posted between Lae and Finschhafen to give adequate warning. This suggestion was adopted and the American destroyer *Reid* sailed to take up its station 45 miles south-east of Finschhafen.

In preparation for the coming offensive the machinery for the command of the forces in New Guinea was overhauled. Early in August the main part of New Guinea Force headquarters had been at Port Moresby with an advanced headquarters at Dobodura. On 25th August Blamey separated the two headquarters. Herring would remain at Dobodura, but now as commander only of I Corps, which would comprise the 7th, 9th, 5th and 11th Divisions, the 4th Brigade, and Wampit Force.[10] The command of New Guinea Force would pass to Blamey himself. It would control, in addition to I Corps, the 3rd Division, Bena Force, Tsili Tsili Force, the Port Moresby and Milne Bay bases, the advanced base ready to move into Lae, and Angau.

Blamey evidently decided that it would not be advisable for the Commander-in-Chief, Allied Land Forces, to act also as commander of New Guinea Force and soon again brought forward the veteran Mackay as "temporary G.O.C. New Guinea Force",[1] and revived the device of ap-

---

[10] By September the principal appointments on the staff of I Corps included: *Comd* Lt-Gen Sir Edmund Herring; *BGS* Brig R. B. Sutherland; *GSOI (Ops)* Col A. R. Garrett; *GSOI (Int)* Lt-Col L. K. Shave and Lt-Col E. Mander-Jones; *GSOI (Liaison)* Lt-Col I. T. Murdoch; *DA & QMG* Brig R. Bierwirth; *AAG* Lt-Col M. Ashkanasy; *AQMG* Lt-Col T. H. F. Winchester; *DDMS* Col G. B. G. Maitland; *DDOS* Lt-Col C. M. Gray; *CCRA* Brig H. B. Sewell; *CE* Brig A. G. Torr; *CSO* Col A. D. Molloy and Lt-Col A. E. Cousin; *DDST* Col E. A. Coleman; *DDME* Lt-Col R. W. C. Campbell; *APM* Maj A. E. Forster; *CLO* Lt-Col B. J. Dunn.

[1] Mackay, whose temporary re-appointment to New Guinea Force was dated 28th August, remained nominally commander of the Second Army, whose headquarters were at Parramatta, NSW.

pointing his own Deputy Chief of the General Staff, General Berryman, to be also Mackay's Chief of Staff.

Under the new organisation General Morshead, recently returned from the Middle East, remained at Atherton commanding II Corps which had originally comprised the three A.I.F. divisions but now consisted of little more than two brigades of the 6th Division. Meanwhile at Toowoomba another senior commander—General Lavarack of the First Army—and his staff still languished. The First Army had been established in April 1942. Its responsibilities, like those of the Second Army, had steadily diminished.[2]

However, these changes in organisation were not the outcome of sudden decisions. A big offensive was looming and it was natural that Blamey should choose Mackay and Herring who had experience of New Guinea conditions rather than Morshead and Lavarack who had no such experience. Herring wrote later that, early in 1943, during his leave in Australia, Blamey had made it clear that "the best way of handling things would be for me to carry on with operations to a certain stage and then when my staff had borne their share of the heat and burden of the day Morshead and his staff would relieve me and my staff and take over the next phase of ops and I would go back to Atherton and get on with the reconditioning and training job there. . . . The division of responsibility and time of change over was only roughly worked out, but it was contemplated quite

---

[2] The Australian Army, and the American formations nominally under Blamey's land headquarters, were now organised as follows:
   First Australian Army (Lt-Gen Lavarack): Toowoomba, Qld.
     11th Brigade—Merauke (Dutch New Guinea).
     Torres Strait Force—Thursday Island.
     4th Division (3rd Brigade)—Dick's Creek, Townsville (Qld).
     3rd Armoured Division (2nd Armoured Brigade)—Murgon, Manumbar (Qld).
   II Australian Corps (Lt-Gen Morshead): Barrine, Qld.
     6th Division (16th, 19th Brigades)—Wondecla, Qld.
     2/7th Cavalry (Commando) Regiment—Wongabel, Qld.
   Second Australian Army (Lt-Gen Mackay): Parramatta, NSW.
     1st Division (1st, 9th, 28th Brigades)—Burwood, Wahroonga, Wollongong, Rutherford (NSW).
   III Australian Corps (Lt-Gen Bennett): Mount Lawley, WA.
     1 Armoured Division (1st Armoured Brigade, 3rd Motor Brigade)—Walebing, Moora, Dandaragan (WA).
     2nd Division (5th, 8th Brigades)—Moonyoonooka, Mount Fairfax, Mingenew (WA).
   Northern Territory Force (Maj-Gen Allen): Darwin.
     12th Division (12th, 13th, 23rd Brigades)—Darwin area, 66½ mile camp.
   New Guinea Force (Lt-Gen Mackay): Port Moresby.
     3rd Division (7th Brigade)—Port Moresby.
     14th Brigade—Milne Bay.
   I Australian Corps (Lt-Gen Herring): Dobodura.
     5th Division (15th, 17th, 29th Brigades, 162nd US Regiment)—Salamaua battle area.
     7th Division (18th, 21st, 25th Brigades, 503rd US Parachute Regiment)—Port Moresby.
     9th Division (20th, 24th, 26th Brigades)—Milne Bay, Buna.
     11th Division (6th Brigade)—Dobodura, Hironda.
     4th Brigade—Milne Bay.
   LHQ Reserve
     2nd Brigade—Royal Park, Vic (en route Northern Territory).
     4th Armoured Brigade—Toorbul Point, Qld.
   Sixth US Army (Lt-Gen Krueger)—Camp Columbia, Qld.
     1st US Cavalry Division (5th, 7th, 8th, 12th Cavalry Regiments)—Strathpine, Toorbul Point (Qld), Port Stephens (NSW).
     158th US Regiment—Kiriwina.
     112th US Cavalry Regiment—Woodlark.
   I US Corps (Lt-Gen Eichelberger): Rockhampton, Qld.
     24th US Division (19th, 21st, 34th Regiments)—Rockhampton (arrived in Australia Aug-Sep 1943).
     32nd US Division (126th, 127th, 128th Regiments)—Camp Cable, Qld.
     41st US Division (163rd, 186th Regiments)—Rockhampton, Qld.

early that I Corps would carry on till Salamaua, Lae and Finschhafen were taken and II Corps would then carry on to Madang." This division was well understood by those concerned (Blamey, Herring and Morshead) by the time that Herring flew into Atherton on his way back to Port Moresby in May, and it was on this basis that Herring had invited Morshead to look around New Guinea in June.

When Herring left Port Moresby for Dobodura on 28th August he received his final instructions from Blamey's headquarters. As well as capturing Lae and Nadzab and establishing airfields, he would "without diverting means from the above role, threaten Salamaua and if opportunity occurred, occupy it and establish aerodrome facilities therein"; deny the enemy use of the Markham Valley in the Sangan area and the plain north of the Markham and east of the Leron, and prevent enemy penetration into the Wau-Bulolo valley by routes from the Buang or the Wampit Rivers. Herring's own operation order of 9th August had been followed by an amplifying instruction on 25th August.

It was during August that certain differences in doctrine and temperaments between the Australian and American planning staffs became evident. General Chamberlin in particular was very critical of Australian planning and it was largely due to his activities that a serious controversy between MacArthur and Blamey manifested itself in an exchange of letters four days before the invasion of Lae. In letters and notes to MacArthur, Sutherland, Kenney and Barbey, Chamberlin had criticised the Australian planning staff as "undoubtedly new to the game".

Anxious about the lack of detail apparently supplied by the Australian planners Chamberlin had conferred with Berryman on 4th August. Reporting this conference to Sutherland, Chamberlin wrote that "G3 was given the impression that the Chief of Staff, Allied Land Forces, knew nothing of the progress of the detailed planning of this operation". Berryman who got on well with Chamberlin noted the result of the conference.

> He [Chamberlin] wanted to know our detailed plans for "Postern" and arrangements for coordination. . . . I explained our system was to allow commands concerned to work out plans together with Air and Navy on the spot in accordance with the general outline plan. . . . The difference is we work on a decentralised basis whilst G.H.Q. have a highly centralised one.

In this last remark Berryman had summed up the difference in a nutshell. Chamberlin's desire to know every detail led to pungent criticism of the two long Australian orders of 9th and 25th August. Summarising his criticisms in a memorandum for his superiors on 28th August Chamberlin wrote: "The missions omitted are more numerous than those covered. In addition, there are numerous defects . . . varying in importance." Referring to the basic Australian order of 9th August he wrote:

> Judged from our standard of the preparation of combat orders it is elementary and incomplete. . . . It is extremely lacking in vision of the function this force is to perform. It decentralises control along with execution. Generally speaking, only the initiation of the operation is covered. The most serious defect is the total lack of appreciation of the logistic problem. . . .

This outburst was all the more remarkable in that it was directed at men with at least as much academic staff training as their American opposite numbers and vastly more battle planning experience than the officers at G.H.Q., and was written at a time when the two Australian divisional commanders were working out detailed logistical plans in cooperation with their American colleagues.

As the result of Chamberlin's worries MacArthur wrote to Blamey on 30th August about "three items of major importance which are not clear to me and which should, I believe, be clarified". The first point was the silence of New Guinea Force's orders of 9th and 25th August regarding the consolidation of the Huon Peninsula and the seizure of Finschhafen as ordered in a General Headquarters' instruction of 13th June. Secondly he asked for information about the means to be employed and the specific agency to be charged with the "arrangement of overwater transportation for elements of the Allied Air Forces and Lae— U.S.A.S.O.S. Advance Base Command and, by inference, Australian lines of communication elements which are to follow into Lae to activate airfields and port areas". MacArthur's third point was that only the Commander-in-Chief himself was in a position to coordinate the activities of New Guinea Force, Allied Naval Forces and Allied Air Forces, and that therefore it was not right for the New Guinea Force order of 25th August to delegate to the Commander of I Australian Corps "the authority to arrange details of air support and naval support for the operation".

Blamey replied next day. Referring to the first point he wrote: "The resources and facilities available do not permit of a simultaneous action against Lae, Markham Valley and Finschhafen. The Lae and Markham Valley areas have therefore been selected as the primary objective and the order was designed to secure the capture of these areas. . . . On the other hand Commander I Corps . . . has been warned to be prepared to take advantage of any early opportunity to seize Finschhafen should one arise."[4]

Regarding the other two points Blamey pointed out that his orders had in fact provided for the transport of the rear elements mentioned by MacArthur; and (with regard to command) that "it was not intended, nor could it be read, by an Australian commander, to mean that the arrangement of details in any way affected the 'coordination' of the work of the three Services on the level of the higher command".

There was no time for further argument as the invasion was pending. To the American staff it had seemed that the Australians were following a faulty staff procedure and resented inquiries about details: the Australian staff on the other hand was following principles employed with success

---

[4] Writing of this matter later Herring said: "TAB (Blamey) did believe in decentralisation, and so much of what we did in New Guinea was worked out in conversation or by correspondence between TAB and myself, and then later an order would be issued from his Headquarters setting it all in proper form, an order that would merely confirm what had already been arranged or agreed upon. . . . The decentralisation that operated as between TAB and NGF . . . also operated as between NGF and both 7 and 9 Divisions. Here Wootten and Vasey talked things over with me just as I talked things over with TAB in the larger sphere. I left them free to work things out in the one case with Barbey and in the other with Whitehead."

in many campaigns and thoroughly understood at every level of the force which would actually carry out the offensive.

This misunderstanding underlined the weakness whereby since April 1942 an American general headquarters on which there was quite inadequate Australian representation reigned from afar over a field army that was, for present purposes, almost entirely Australian, and whose doctrines and methods differed from those of G.H.Q. It was evidence of the detachment of G.H.Q. that, after 16 months, its senior general staff officers had little knowledge of the doctrines and methods of its principal army in the field.

It is interesting that only a few days before the Australian orders were written, Major-General S. F. Rowell, a former commander of New Guinea Force now Australian liaison officer in the Middle East, was writing a letter to General Morshead in which he set out some lessons of the landings in North Africa and Sicily, and confirmed two principles by which the Australian commanders were now standing. He wrote from Cairo on 25th July:

(a) *Planning*

It is essential that the people who carry out the operations should do the detailed planning. There will always be the tendency for those above to try and work out the plans, but I'm sure that this is wrong. Alexander gave Montgomery and Patton the broadest outline plan and the two Army Staffs then broke it down for Corps, Divisions, and Brigades to do the details.

(b) *Mixture of Allies in Task Forces*

The outstanding lesson of the original North African landings was the failure of mixed task forces. Had the French really fought, there would have been a hell of a mess. That lesson was applied to the full in Sicily where the two Armies were completely self contained right down to personnel for manning landing craft. For example U.S.N. looked after 7 U.S. Army and R.N. after 8th Army. This gives the freest rein for national characteristics. In your case, a lot will depend on the confidence you and your people have in the Allied organisation which is to transport you to battle and look after your shore organisation. But I'm convinced the principle is basically unsound and, as this war develops, I feel sure that we will see an ever-increasing tendency for us and the Americans to work in our own boxes. I'm talking, naturally, of land forces, as the problem is by no means so acute in the case of naval and air forces.

(c) *Beach organisation*

Closely allied to (b) is the thorny problem of the beach organisation. In the early stages here, this was found to be the greatest weakness, but, by dint of intensive training and frequent rehearsals, the beach organisation was brought up to a high standard. I think its worth has been proved in Sicily. As I see it, the vital period on a beach is the first few hours, the period when the enemy has the advantage. Again it is all a question of the Australians having confidence in the capacity of the Americans to deliver the goods on the beaches and I feel that no number of liaison officers, with no executive capacity or authority, can replace our own administrative organisations which have trained with assault brigades and have lived with them until they have come to be regarded as part of the brigades themselves.

I don't want to labour this point, or appear anti-American. Such is far from my mind. But it's much easier and more effective to lay down the law to our own people than to an Ally.

On 31st August, the day on which he had replied to MacArthur's complaint about Australian planning, Blamey wrote again to MacArthur criticising a proposal in G.H.Q's forward planning. Blamey had just received an outline plan from G.H.Q. which provided for an advance to Madang before the seizure of western New Britain. He thereupon sent MacArthur a four-page memorandum in which it was "strongly urged" that "since the capture of western New Britain is already decided upon, every advantage, and no disadvantage, appears to be on the side of capture of this area prior to the capture of Madang". Blamey's covering letter concluded: "It seems to me . . . that the Land Forces might anticipate much more vigorous assistance from the Naval Forces if we control Vitiaz Strait from both sides." Inevitably the events of the next few weeks would show whether Blamey's misgivings about naval support were justified.

CHAPTER 11

THE SALAMAUA MAGNET

AFTER the success of the 3rd Division round Komiatum and Mount Tambu in mid-August the *51st Japanese Division* fought back stubbornly and limited the Allied advance. On 23rd, 24th and 25th August the Japanese launched unsuccessful counter-attacks against the Americans at the junction of Roosevelt and Scout Ridges and at the junction of Roosevelt and "B" Ridges. The Americans tried hard to push along Scout Ridge to secure Scout Hill and Lokanu headland, but their advance slowed down.

On 24th August Brigadier Monaghan's 29th Brigade took over from Brigadier Moten's 17th which gathered at Nassau Bay before returning to Australia in September. Patrols of the 47th Battalion next day killed their first two Japanese in the Komiatum area.[1] By 23rd August most of the 15th Battalion (Lieut-Colonel Amies[2]) arrived at Tambu Bay, where it was retained as divisional reserve.

Meanwhile Captain Cole's company of the 42nd Battalion had repulsed attacks on Bamboo Knoll on 22nd August. The Japanese were mown down by the entrenched defenders who saw 20 bodies outside their perimeter. Cole and Private Deal[3] crept outside the perimeter to hunt snipers and killed three more Japanese. When the artillery shelled the attackers the Japanese decided they had had enough and withdrew. The company had a welcome reward when a transport aircraft mistaking Bamboo Knoll for another dropping ground, showered the incredulous troops with rice, powdered milk, custard powder, tinned fruit, prunes, jam, margarine, dehydrated potatoes and onions, fresh bread, buns and tobacco.

Under Lieut-Colonel Davidson's plan for the drive north along Davidson Ridge after the enemy evacuation of Mount Tambu, Captain Pattingale's[4] company became responsible for the battalion's rear and for flanking patrols. On the morning of the 22nd two platoons from this company were on patrol and only about 20 men were at company headquarters receiving stores and tightening up the defences. Suddenly they were attacked by about 40 Japanese making their way from the direction of Mount Tambu between Davidson and Scout Ridges. Pattingale and two men were killed immediately, and Lieutenant Friend[5] with 16 men concentrated in the south-east corner of the defences and attempted to hold off the charging

---
[1] The 47th Battalion had received a luckless introduction to the battle area. Casualties suffered in its clashes with the enemy raiding party and by Japanese shelling brought the total to 11 killed and 7 wounded before the battalion entered the Komiatum area.
[2] Brig J. L. Amies, CBE, ED, QX6007. 2/31 Bn 1940-42; CO 15 Bn 1942-44. Public accountant; of Brisbane; b. Sydney, 14 Dec 1913.
[3] L-Sgt F. S. Deal, MM, QX56274; 42 Bn. Sugar worker; of Gordonvale, Qld; b. Cairns, Qld, 25 Aug 1921.
[4] Capt E. J. Pattingale, QX34024; 42 Bn. Bus proprietor; of Rockhampton, Qld; b. Mount Morgan, Qld, 14 Jul 1912. Killed in action 22 Aug 1943.
[5] Capt G. C. Friend, QX34025; 42 Bn. Clerk; of Gladstone, Qld; b. Gladstone, 24 Mar 1917.

enemy. With his ammunition running low, Friend sent Private Brown[6] and then Private Ricks[7] to battalion headquarters to ask for assistance. Both got through but no help was available. Late in the afternoon the Japanese ceased trying to break the resistance of Friend's small band and disappeared leaving 10 dead inside the defences.

They had also been unable to stomach the fire from the machine-gun platoon of the 2/5th still with Davidson's battalion on a hill overlooking Friend's position. These Japanese, believed to be remnants of the gun raiding force, blundered into Captain Jenks'[8] company and rapidly retired in face of heavy fire leaving eight dead.

The 42nd now had only Charlie Hill between it and the flat country round Nuk Nuk. On 24th August, as Jenks' company began to advance towards Charlie Hill, it could see that the hill was separated from Davidson Ridge by a deep gorge through which rushed a creek. After slithering down the precipitous slope to the creek, the men began to climb the hill. Towards dusk they reached a part of the hill where it was possible to move without clinging to the foliage. Here the company camped for the night and Jenks reported that he would probably capture Charlie Hill next day.

On the left flank the 15th Brigade prepared for the pursuit. Brigadier Hammer ordered that his troops should move by night, that supplies should be pushed forward by day and night using all available resources, and that the enemy should be harassed. He hoped to strike before the Japanese could reorganise and consolidate their rear defences.

Although the enemy returned Hammer's harassing fire during the night 20th-21st August and engaged in a fire fight at the Orodubi-Komiatum track junction, the strong points at the northern track junctions and at the Komiatum-Orodubi track junction were vacated by first light on 21st August. In spite of the 15th Brigade's pressure the enemy had succeeded in breaking off action after a skilful withdrawal. One pocket in the area of the track junctions contained the bodies of a Japanese captain, two lieutenants and 20 men who had fought to the death.

It was now obvious that, to hold Salamaua, the Japanese must occupy Scout Ridge, Charlie Hill and Kunai Spur south of the Francisco and the Rough Hill-Arnold's Crest area north of the river. Hammer's previous action north of the river had been limited to patrols designed to ensure that the enemy was not encircling his northern flank. He intended now to gain the high features shown on captured maps as part of the inner defences of Salamaua, before the enemy could establish himself there. However, after learning that Salamaua must not fall before the invasion of Lae, Savige restricted Hammer to securing the Camel Ridge area north of the Francisco and patrolling from it.

---

[6] Pte A. C. Brown, Q36614; 42 Bn. Labourer; of Gladstone, Qld; b. Gladstone, 23 Mar 1921.
[7] Pte E. C. R. Ricks, QX47961; 42 Bn. Shop assistant; of Rockhampton, Qld; b. Rockhampton, 6 Nov 1920.
[8] Capt A. E. Jenks, QX40807; 42 Bn. Schoolteacher; of Yeppoon, Qld; b. Mount Morgan, Qld, 5 Nov 1911.

Knowing that he held the initiative Hammer was anxious to press on. Before dawn on 21st August his sub-units set out in pursuit. North of the river the leading platoon of the 2/7th climbed the razor-back to Rough Hill, but was pinned down. Major Dunkley then brought up the rest of his company and drove out the Japanese from the position which they had been occupying only about 12 hours.

South of the river a platoon from the 2/7th on the trail of the Japanese retreating from the track junctions was ambushed. All five men of the leading section were wounded and forced to remain within twenty yards of the enemy ambush. Hearing of these casualties the medical officer of the 2/3rd Independent Company, Captain Street, moved quickly north and under heavy fire gave first-aid and helped to carry them out. By evening Captain Cramp's company of the 2/7th Battalion was astride Buirali Creek while the enemy was holding a line south from the Francisco up Kunai Spur. At 3.30 p.m. on the 21st Lieutenant Bethune's company of the 58th/59th Battalion advanced up Kunai Spur along the ridge which was 40 yards wide and heavily timbered. Near the north end Bethune was fired on from north and east. With one flank on the Francisco and the other on Charlie Hill the Japanese were in a splendid defensive position and Bethune, with eight casualties, withdrew.

On 22nd August the attempt to prevent the enemy from organising his defences continued. Bitter fighting prevented the 2/7th from breaking the enemy line from the Francisco to Kunai Spur; Dunkley climbed farther up Rough Hill but was stopped by an enemy position near the top; Captain Arnold's company routed two small Japanese forces on the lower slopes of Arnold's Crest. Hammer now decided not to worry about his sub-units becoming entangled but to preserve the momentum of the pursuit by urging on companies and platoons wherever they happened to be. He therefore created two special forces: "Picken Force", comprising all troops north of the river,[9] and "Warfe Force", comprising all troops south of it.[1]

As it was now apparent that the Japanese had used another escape route from Mount Tambu, the Komiatum Track ceased to be the important life-line it had been throughout the year, and Hammer could move his troops north to the Kunai Spur area and on both sides of the Francisco. With the pursuit so rapid Hammer received a message from Savige on 22nd August stating:

> Situation most satisfactory but on no account undertake any operation which may influence the enemy to evacuate Salamaua.

Having sent this message in accordance with higher policy, Savige considered that it would be a shame to ease the pressure which Hammer was applying so skilfully to the disorganised enemy. Savige knew that Hammer would be unable to keep up the pace, and therefore sent another message on the 23rd that "in view of apparent demoralisation of enemy

---
[9] "B", "C", "D" Companies 2/7th Battalion, "C" and "D" Companies 58th/59th Battalion.
[1] "A" and "B" Companies 58th/59th Battalion, "A" Company 2/7th Battalion and 2/3rd Independent Company.

on your front pursue your advance to the fullest extent possible without jeopardising the security of your force".

For three days the troops of the 15th Brigade had kept the Japanese on the move. The men, though very tired, had maintained a remarkable speed of movement in such wretched country by moving at night. Hammer had ordered moonlight advances, but even he was unable to make the moon shine when it should. The men then moved under cover of darkness using torches, although one company commander commented later that "the cursing that was maintained constantly should have lit up the area".[2] While the Japanese were sleeping the Australians were moving. Caught above ground the Japanese did not stay to fight.

The next two days were a repetition of the previous three. South of the river the 2/7th[3] was still bogged down east of the track junctions, but across the river the battalion met with some success. On the 23rd Dunkley, aiming for surprise, grouped his Brens forward in pairs. Covering the Bren gunners with Owen gunners he arranged for supporting fire from his mortars and sent his attacking sections round the flanks. The Japanese were overwhelmed by this fire and by such individual acts of bravery as that performed by Corporal Hare[4] who charged the enemy's forward weapon-pits and killed the occupants with his Bren gun. It required only the use of grenades by the flanking sections attacking up precipitous slopes to rout the enemy, who left nine killed. Arnold's company on the 24th occupied Kidney and Steak after the enemy had vacated their ambush positions.[5]

Lieutenant Egan's[6] platoon of the 24th Battalion, attached to Captain Newman's company of the 58th/59th north of the Francisco, moved up Sandy Creek for about 600 yards on 23rd August and ran into a dozen Japanese who disappeared too quickly to be engaged. On the same day Captain Baird's company of the 2/7th moving up Sandy Creek through Newman's firm base found the enemy's signal and kai line running east and was then attacked by a force of about 60 Japanese. After a short fight the enemy withdrew, and later in the day a patrol from Arnold's company got through to Baird and reported that there were no enemy in between. Egan patrolled east towards Rough Hill along the course of the enemy's signal wire which had been cut and rolled up by Baird. Suddenly coming upon about 30 Japanese cleaning their rifles and rolling their tents Egan's men accelerated the enemy's preparations for striking camp.

---

[2] The moon rose at suitable times on 19th August—9.32 p.m.—and on the 20th and 21st but on the 22nd-23rd it did not rise until just after midnight.

[3] On 23rd August the 2/7th was delighted when two of Baird's men and one of Hancock's from the ill-fated spearhead patrol led by Lieutenant Jeffery six days previously returned. Private J. R. Fisher (of Amherst, Vic) of the 2/7th had been severely wounded in the abdomen and like his companions had been without rations for the whole period. Doctors were amazed at Fisher's endurance and fortitude and considered that any normal man would have succumbed two days previously.

[4] Cpl L. D. Hare, DCM, VX55687; 2/7 Bn. Farm hand; of Camperdown, Vic; b. Camperdown, 13 Mar 1917.

[5] All unnamed features were named by Hammer "Kidney", "Steak", "Hand", etc., mainly because of their shape on the maps.

[6] Maj C. J. Egan, MC, NX57168; 24 Bn. Farm hand; of Glen Innes, NSW; b. Armidale, NSW, 13 Aug 1917.

Captain Hancock's patrols from the Independent Company on 23rd August found two more tracks to the north running parallel with the Francisco. The most northerly of all had signal cable laid along it and was thought to be the main Salamaua Track. At 10 a.m. Lieutenant Allen's platoon, astride this track, drove back a party of 30 Japanese towards Salamaua, killing 7. At 6 o'clock the next morning two Japanese patrols, each about 15 strong, met in front of Lieutenant Lineham's[7] section on the main Salamaua Track and had a chat. Eight were killed before the remainder dispersed into the jungle.

Meanwhile, two companies of the 58th/59th Battalion were concentrating for an attack up Kunai Spur from the west. Kunai Spur rose like a cliff-face from the Buirali and the logical way of approach was from north or south along the razor-back. Yet this way would draw the heaviest fire. On the 23rd there were three separate attacks. First Cramp's company of the 2/7th Battalion unsuccessfully attacked from the west up precipitous slopes on the north end of the spur. Then one of Bethune's platoons also attacked unsuccessfully from west to east. The third attack was made by Captain Jago's company of the 58th/59th from east to west. Although the Japanese defences were not pierced, Lieutenant Mathews' platoon actually reached the crest and engaged in a fierce grenade fight until the Australians' grenades were all used. When probing for a weakness to the south Corporal McFarlane[8] was killed and Mathews wounded. As it was obvious that the platoon could not capture the strongly entrenched position on Kunai Spur, Mathews withdrew.

"Harass the Jap day and night," signalled Hammer to his troops, "spoil his sleep, lower his morale, keep him jittery and when you strike hit with all your strength." The momentum of the pursuit, however, was now petering out because of the wear and tear on the pursuers and stiffening enemy resistance. Determined to keep the enemy unsettled even to the extent of pushing his men to the limit of endurance, Hammer asked Savige to relieve his brigade of all responsibility south of the Francisco. Savige agreed and ordered Monaghan to take over responsibility south of the Francisco and east of the Komiatum Track.

When General Milford relieved General Savige at one minute before midnight on the 25th-26th August he knew that his task was to "continue offensive operations against Salamaua with the object of drawing maximum enemy strength away from Lae", but not to carry the threat to such an extent as to cause the enemy to withdraw to Lae. As soon as operations against Lae were begun by the 7th and 9th Divisions Milford was to capture Salamaua and destroy its garrison.

Milford was now on active service in the field for the first time since the war began. Four years younger than Savige, he was a regular soldier.

---

[7] Capt D. J. F. Lineham, VX51663. 24 Bn, 2/3 Indep Coy, 2/3 Cdo Sqn. Rubber worker; of Abbotsford, Vic; b. Abbotsford, 30 Mar 1917.

[8] Cpl L. M. McFarlane, VX135704; 58/59 Bn. Salesman; of Port Melbourne, Vic; b. Port Melbourne, 2 Oct 1912. Killed in action 23 Aug 1943.

He had graduated from Duntroon in 1915 and had been a major on the staff when the first war ended. Between the wars he had gained high qualifications as an ordnance and artillery expert and his special training had led to his recall from a command in the Middle East in 1940 to become Master-General of the Ordnance. In the crisis of early 1942 he

Australian and American dispositions, Salamaua area, 25th-26th August

was appointed to command the 5th Division then deployed in north Queensland and preparing for a possible invasion. The headquarters of the 5th Division had been at Milne Bay since January 1943.

The day after his arrival at Tambu Bay on 21st August Milford, a great walker of the Guinn class, set out to see the 15th and 29th Brigade areas, where he soon came to the same conclusion as his predecessor, namely, that planning purely from a map would be impractical in such difficult country.

The tasks set (he wrote in his report) were tempered by first hand knowledge of the effort and of the difficulties which might be encountered. At the time of taking over, a visit from Divisional HQ to HQ 15 Aust Inf Bde required two days each way—a total of four days. Unless traversed in person this would scarcely be believed, but it was unquestionably so in fact; a true appreciation of such difficulties was essential to successful planning.

The country surrounding Salamaua was shaped in the form of a rough bowl with Salamaua as the centre and the enemy holding the lip, but as the enemy's defence line became shorter, it became more difficult for the attackers to infiltrate and encircle his positions, as they had done earlier in the campaign. The Japanese were bitterly defending these inner defences.

Milford's resources were dwindling. His units, with the exception of those of the 29th Brigade, had been engaged in severe operations for periods varying from two to six months. The strength of the American battalions was about 33 per cent of their normal establishment and was continuously falling away because of illness. The units of the 15th Brigade were at about half strength. The 29th Brigade was fresh, but untried except for the brief experience of the 42nd Battalion. Many of the native carriers were very tired, having been carrying since the Owen Stanleys campaign, and the sickness rate averaged about 25 per cent. The line of communication from Tambu Bay led over Mount Tambu and down the Komiatum Track, thus entailing a two-day carry to the 29th Brigade. The 15th Brigade was still being supplied by air.

Charlie Hill, midway between Scout Ridge and the Komiatum Track was, in Milford's opinion, "obviously the keystone of the enemy's defence structure". If he could capture it, he would have a downhill run to the Francisco and Salamaua. He believed that a determined thrust by the fresh brigade might bring results. Thereupon he gave the main task to the 29th Brigade, which was ordered to "exert pressure along its entire front in order to ascertain the enemy's strength and location with a view to finding the best means to break through in this area and exploit down into Salamaua". Hammer would maintain his present positions, and patrol towards Kela Hill. This, it was hoped, would deceive the enemy as to the ultimate direction of the main drive and would induce him to reinforce his right flank to the detriment of his left and centre. Hammer would also conserve his strength and prepare plans for a drive towards the coast as soon as a break-through appeared imminent. Captain Whitelaw's company of the 24th Battalion would prepare to seize a position astride the Lae-Salamaua track when ordered. The 15th Battalion was retained as divisional reserve at Tambu Bay. Monaghan was upset

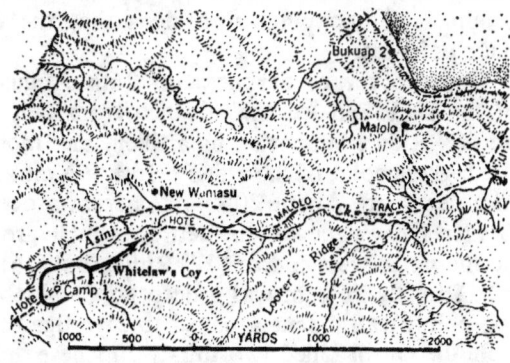

because he was "deprived" of its services but Milford, as well as having to keep a reserve, doubted his ability to keep up supplies to any more battalions west of Scout Ridge.

As the day for the offensive approached it became the more necessary to reduce air supply droppings. With the withdrawal of surplus troops from the Bulolo Valley and the firm establishment of the Tambu Bay line of communication, General Herring hoped that the 5th Division could soon be supplied almost entirely from the sea. Between 24th and 28th August the kai bombers dropped enough supplies to keep the division fighting for another five days. Milford knew that after 28th August he would be supplied by sea, except that the most inaccessible forward troops would still have supplies dropped to them. He decided that a new line of communication, which would avoid the tortuous crawl over Mount Tambu, must be established direct from Tambu Bay to the two brigades. The task of preparing this track was given to Major Colebatch[9] and the 11th Field Company and by 3rd September the new track was open.

In Colonel MacKechnie's area preparations were being made by the II/162nd Battalion to break the enemy's defences north of Roosevelt Ridge. This battalion, now led by Major Armin E. Berger, had been successful in capturing Roosevelt Ridge. After being relieved on Roosevelt Ridge by a Provisional Battalion of various sub-units, it was now ordered by MacKechnie to cut the Scout Ridge Track at the junction of Scout and "C" Ridges and to establish there a "trail block" on what appeared to be the enemy's line of communication. Companies from Major Morris' III/162nd Battalion were established on both sides of the enemy positions at the junction of Roosevelt and Scout Ridges and near the junction of Roosevelt and "B" Ridges; while Colonel Taylor's I/162nd Battalion was south and west of the junction of Roosevelt and Scout Ridges. In most enemy areas from 26th August MacKechnie's patrols heard sounds of digging and chopping, sure signs that the Japanese were strengthening their defences.

Under cover of darkness on 26th August Captain Ratliff's company of the II/162nd led the advance from Dot Inlet to a position half way up "C" Ridge. Supported by artillery and mortar fire the company reached the highest point of the ridge before 9 a.m. and found that the ridge came to a dead end. About 200 yards across a deep re-entrant to the right was Berger Hill, while on the left was high ground which first appeared to be the north-west end of "B" Ridge, but was later found to be a separate hill. Directly in front was a deep gorge which contained a Japanese watering point. Ratliff sent a patrol to investigate Berger Hill. Near the waterhole the patrol killed two thirsty Japanese and spotted defences on Berger Hill. Later in the day another patrol met an enemy party near the water-hole and claimed to have killed eleven before withdrawing under heavy fire.

---

[9] Lt-Col G. T. Colebatch, OBE, TX2095. I Corps Engrs 1940-41; SORE HQ NGF 1942-43; CRE 3 Div 1943-45. Civil engineer; of Hobart; b. Semaphore, SA, 10 Jul 1910.

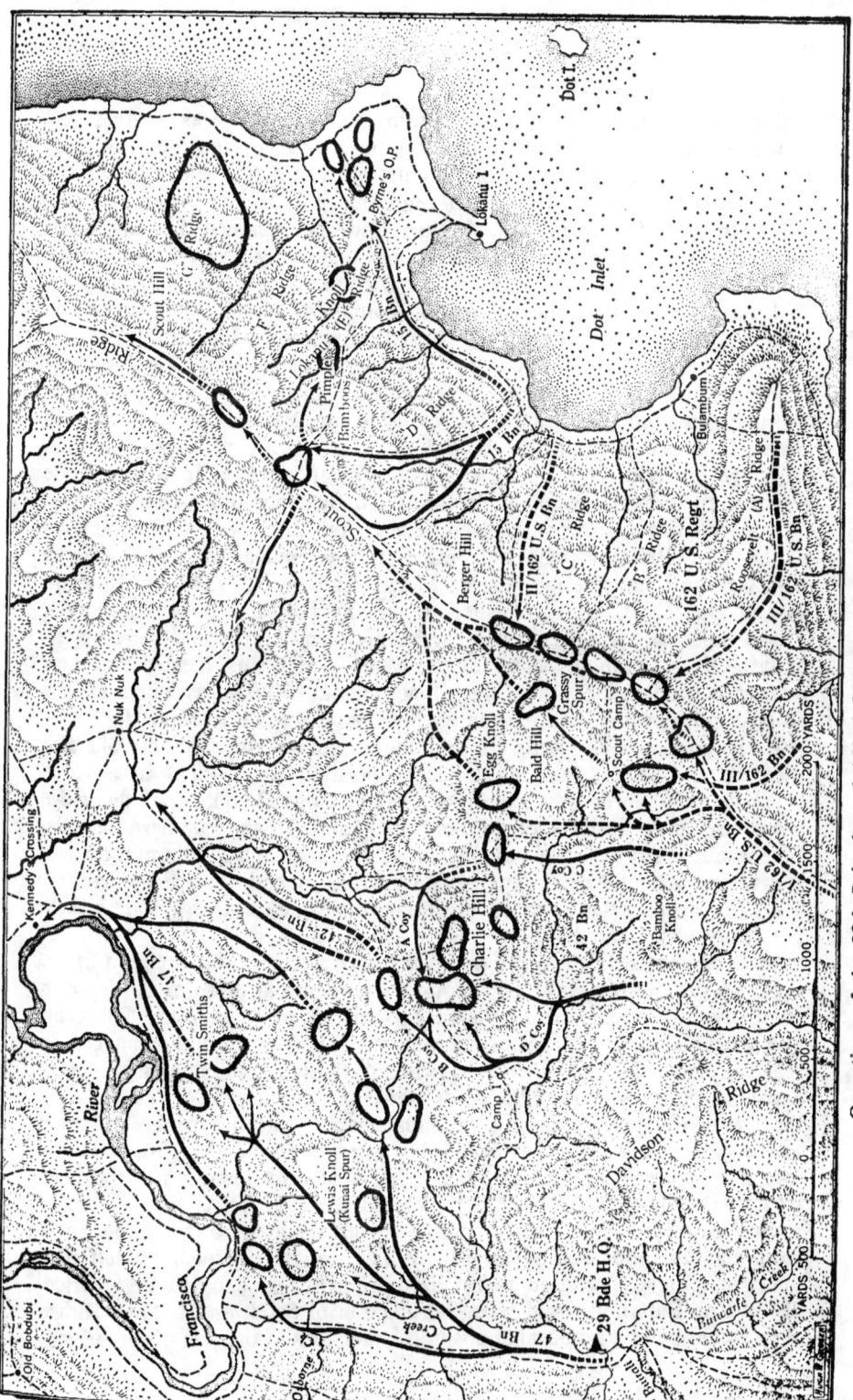

Operations of the 29th Brigade and 162nd U.S. Regiment, 26th August-10th September

For the next three days the battalion continued to patrol from "C" Ridge towards the two hills confronting it. As there was a great deal of surmise about the strength and location of Japanese positions on these two hills Colonel Daly, Milford's chief staff officer, who was on the spot, persuaded Major Berger to send out a patrol to examine them. The patrol, led by Lieutenant Munkres and accompanied by Daly, penetrated to the southern knoll and discovered a strongly-held enemy position. In the centre a patrol from Morris' battalion moving up "B" Ridge on 27th August found an enemy position containing about 50 Japanese and after a fight returned convinced that 24 Japanese had been killed.

Taylor's job on the left was to help Morris clear Scout Ridge but the enemy at the ridge junction prevented any progress. Taylor then sent two companies to the west to encircle these positions, but they were held up by Japanese positions on Bald Hill, a spur running north-west from the ridge junction. One of the companies (Captain George's) now made a wider encircling movement to the north through jungle-clad and precipitous country. After making contact on the 27th with two companies of the 42nd Battalion who were attempting to find a way round Charlie Hill, George found the main Scout Ridge Track about 1,000 yards north-east of Bald Hill, and ambushed an enemy patrol, killing about eight. These Japanese were fresh and carried new equipment and were apparently marines—ominous signs for the weary Americans. Next day George dug in astride the Scout Ridge Track about 300 yards north of the ambush position thus cutting the enemy's supply route to Bald Hill.

Early on the 29th patrols found the Japanese position on Bald Hill vacated, and later found an adjacent position unoccupied in an area of about 500 yards just south of Scout Ridge Track near the ridge junctions. Each position could hold 150 men. In the southern one the Japanese had left quantities of rifles, machine-guns and a 70-mm mountain gun. There were 80 dead Japanese in the area, mostly buried by artillery. Thus the strong ridge junction position which had held up progress since 24th July was cleared.

Milford now decided to put in fresh troops to harass the enemy further. First he ordered Captain Hitchcock to send a patrol from the Papuan company, now under direct divisional command, to reconnoitre "D" Ridge and Lokanu Ridge. A patrol set out on 28th August and managed to reach Lokanu Ridge, where they heard talking and shouting from a Japanese position about 100 yards down the south side of the ridge on the western slopes. After this reconnaissance Milford felt able to agree to the plan which Daly had been advocating—to send the 15th Battalion into the American area; Milford felt that a blood transfusion in the form of a fresh Australian battalion might aid the Americans to make more speedy progress. He was also anxious to divert the attention of the Japanese from the fast approaching assault on Lae and to establish himself in a good jumping off position to hit hard when the Lae operations started. If the 15th Battalion could seize the junction of Scout and Lokanu Ridges they would be in a favourable position either to join the rest of the brigade to the west or press along the ridges towards Salamaua. The 15th Battalion, if on Scout Ridge, could be supplied along a very short route from Dot Inlet.[1]

North of Davidson Ridge, the 42nd Battalion was stalled before Charlie Hill. Captain Jenks' company was unable to make any headway on 25th August and suffered several casualties. Realising that it was futile to adopt battering-ram tactics against the well-defended Charlie Hill, Monaghan and Davidson decided to try encirclement. They also had another motive for at 9.6 a.m. on 25th August Savige had signalled his commanders:

> Three heavily laden vessels reported leaving Salamaua 0900K/25 in direction of Lae. All units will intensify patrol activity to ascertain if any indication of general withdrawal.

Major Crosswell was therefore ordered to lead two companies of the 42nd to the south and east of Charlie Hill to ascertain if the Japanese were evacuating, and to cut their supply route to Charlie Hill if they were not.

On 26th August the artillery kept pounding Charlie Hill, and patrols of Jenks' company tried to pinpoint the enemy's positions. One patrol led by Corporal Hogan[2] saw six Japanese robbing the bodies of two Australians, killed the previous day too close to the enemy position to be carried out, and killed four of them.

A more detailed map of the area had recently been received. On it was marked a track running from Scout Ridge north down the next main ridge east of Davidson Ridge, then to the east of Egg Knoll and down towards Nuk Nuk and the Francisco. Another track from the top of Charlie Hill ran east along a saddle connecting Charlie Hill with Egg Knoll and joined the first one near Egg Knoll. Monaghan and Davidson recognised this track junction as a key point. Crosswell was therefore ordered to seize it as part of the plan to isolate and capture Charlie Hill, and also to assist Captain George's Americans dug in south of the track junction along the track to the east.

Crosswell's men experienced unpleasant conditions. At 6 a.m. on 26th August they set out from Bamboo Knoll along a very poor track which ran along the steep southern slope of Charlie Hill. After hanging on to the sides, dodging miniature landslides and crawling round jutting rocks for several hours, they descended to a creek junction south of Charlie Hill and then moved east up the main creek. Here a few shells, probably destined for Charlie Hill, landed near them. To avoid the artillery fire, and as darkness was approaching, the companies turned south-east up a steep spur and, almost exhausted, reached the top, where they dug in and had their meal of bully beef and water.

---

[1] Militia battalions could write AIF after their names if they had enough volunteers—75 per cent—and they were urged to aim for this status. Of the six battalions, however, only the 24th was in a position to do this during the Salamaua campaign. As with the others the 15th did not have anything like the required percentage. For example, on 7th August although all the officers and nearly all the NCO's were "AIF" only 212 of 541 privates were.

[2] Sgt P. E. Hogan, QX35897; 42 Bn. Carpenter; of Rockhampton, Qld; b. Rockhampton, 2 Dec 1915.

Soon after 8 a.m. on the 27th the two companies set out north-east. At 10.30 a.m. they met a patrol from George's company in the wild and rugged country between Charlie Hill and Scout Ridge. The telephone wire connecting the companies with Davidson's headquarters, now on Bamboo Knoll, had been severed by Allied artillery, and Davidson did not know what was happening to his two companies until news of the meeting was sent along the chain of communication from George to MacKechnie, to Milford, to Monaghan, to Davidson.

After parting from the Americans the two companies, about 3 p.m., came to a series of ridges running down to a creek east of Charlie Hill. Lieutenant Ramm's platoon approached a Japanese track, waited until six Japanese with full packs passed to the south-east and then moved on to the track and cut the signal wire. Platoons from the two companies then crossed the track in succession. During the move shots were fired by the Japanese from above and below. The troops went to ground and wriggled like eels into defensive positions, a not very difficult procedure, according to the historian of the 42nd Battalion, as they were moving through soft mud.[3] Digging holes in mud in a prone position was a backbreaking and filthy job, but by dusk the men were established astride the track 400 to 500 yards south of Egg Knoll and the track junction which was their objective. The position was actually between two Japanese posts which had been holding up the Americans. The enemy mortared the Australians and wounded seven.

After a night of tension and expectancy, and a breakfast of bully and water, Crosswell sent a patrol to find the track junction. It found vacated Japanese positions on the southern slopes of Egg Knoll 150 yards from the two companies' perimeter. Near by was the track junction, which Crosswell considered unsuitable for occupation because it was dominated by the enemy on higher ground. The telephone line had now been mended, and Davidson was thus able to order Crosswell to occupy the vacant Japanese position, place a standing patrol at the track junction during daylight and withdraw it that night.

That day Milford, Monaghan and Davidson were conferring on Bamboo Knoll. From patrol reports and experience of previous attempts to take Charlie Hill Davidson was convinced that it could not be taken by frontal assault from the south. He therefore proposed that a company should be sent round the western slopes of Charlie Hill to occupy a position on the northern slopes, thus isolating the Japanese, as had been done at Mount Tambu. Milford, however, decided on a frontal attack and promised Davidson 2,000 rounds from the 105-mm guns for the attack. As a result, Davidson warned Jenks that his company would attack Charlie Hill from the west on the 29th, and Crosswell, that one of his platoons would attack up the track from the east towards Charlie Hill in support of Jenks. Zero hour would be 3.20 p.m., and from 11.30 a.m. until that time the artillery would fire nearly 2,000 rounds, the mortars 450 bombs, and the machine-guns 6,000 rounds. The object of this lengthy fire program

---

[3] S. E. Benson, *The Story of the 42 Aust. Inf. Bn.*, p. 91.

was to accustom the enemy to the concentration so that he might be off guard at 3.20 p.m.

From 11.30 a.m. on the 29th the concentration came down on Charlie Hill. In the morning Crosswell sent Lieutenant Winter's[4] platoon to reoccupy the track junction. On the way to its objective the platoon was attacked by about 15 Japanese on its right flank astride the east-west ridge. The platoon killed six, but in doing so lost two killed, and was unable to make further progress. Until this position could be cleared Crosswell held back Lieutenant Steinheuer's[5] platoon which had been selected for the attack on Charlie Hill from the east.

Just on zero hour an American patrol, led by Lieutenant Williams, met Crosswell's men, and informed them that the Japanese had evacuated the knoll to the south, that resistance confronting the Americans about 800 yards south-east had disappeared, and that he had advanced unimpeded through several Japanese perimeters to meet the Australians. The Americans had pushed north to join with the Australians as the result of a telephone call from Monaghan to Daly asking that an American fighting patrol occupy Scout Camp and test out the knoll south of Crosswell's position.

On the western side of Charlie Hill as zero hour approached and while the artillery concentration was at full blast, the padre held a moving but unheard service for the assaulting company. Jenks then said quietly: "It's time to go up lads." Lieutenant Garland's[6] platoon led the attack, but was fired on after moving only 100 yards. Jenks sent his other two platoons to the right and left flanks but after going only a few yards each platoon found itself faced by precipitous slopes. The approach to Charlie Hill from the west was up a very steep thickly clad razor-back. Without seeing any enemy Garland had five men hit. Two hours after the attack began Jenks signalled Davidson that he could make no progress because of the gorges on either side; the hill was as "steep as side of house" and "every move brings fire which cannot be seen". Realising that it was useless to batter at Charlie Hill from this side, Davidson recalled Jenks to his original position.

With the brigadier ordering that Crosswell's two companies must be "pushed hard and fast" with the "utmost aggression", Davidson at dusk on the 29th issued orders that they move next morning to positions immediately north and north-east of Charlie Hill. Davidson himself set out next morning and arrived at Crosswell's headquarters soon after 10 a.m.

The decision that Monaghan's brigade would take over responsibility south of the Francisco and east of the Komiatum Track involved the 47th Battalion. Having relieved the 2/5th Battalion on 24th August the 47th next day took over the positions occupied by Warfe Force. Before the relief, however, sub-units of Warfe Force made further determined efforts

---

[4] Lt R. B. Winter, QX43158; 42 Bn. Labourer; of Mount Morgan, Qld; b. Mount Morgan, 3 Jan 1913.

[5] Lt P. E. Steinheuer, QX51619; 42 Bn. Storeman; of Annerley, Qld; b. Rockhampton, Qld, 29 Jun 1918.

[6] Lt B. J. Garland, VX54197; 42 Bn. Labourer; of St Kilda, Vic; b. Sydney, 25 Jun 1916.

to shift the stubborn enemy from Kunai Spur and the northern track junctions.

For the attack on Kunai Spur Warfe placed two companies from the 58th/59th under Hancock who had to decide whether to mix the two forces or to keep them independent. He decided to mix them under his own commanders. On 25th August he sent out two forces led by Lieutenants Allen and R. S. Garland of the 2/3rd Independent Company to attack Kunai Spur from the east.

Allen made repeated attempts for two hours and a half to reach the crest of Kunai Spur but heavy fire from the flanks forced his withdrawal to a position forty yards below the crest of the ridge where he dug in after inflicting seven casualties. Garland, attacking farther north, encountered two Japanese forces, each about 50 strong, one moving north and the other south; the Australians killed about 20 but were unable to reach the crest of the ridge because of heavy fire from both flanks. Garland tried again farther north but found stronger defended positions, and dug in 30 yards from the crest of the ridge on the line of his original approach. In these actions two were killed, including Sergeant Sides[7] killed while leading an assault up the steep slope. The two forces withdrew and Hancock sent out a reserve force under Lieutenant Lineham to attack from the south-west; but this attack met the same fate as the others: heavy enemy fire, precipitous slopes, untenable ground and inability to make any progress.

On the same day Cramp's company of the 2/7th Battalion made its last attack on the enemy position near the Komiatum-Salamaua track junction. One platoon succeeded in outflanking the enemy and shot three Japanese but when the enemy strongly counter-attacked the platoon was unable to hold its ground. Finally the whole company was forced to withdraw to its original line. During the withdrawal the enemy launched several counter-attacks from the high ground in an attempt to cut off the company's retreat. Two Bren gunners, Privates Finn and Bayliss,[8] decided to hold off the enemy attacks. While Finn took up a suitable position Bayliss ran to an ammunition dump and filled his shirt with grenades. For over an hour the two courageous Bren gunners held off the enemy attacks and enabled the company to withdraw intact. By the time the company was safe Finn had 12 rounds left and Bayliss 15, and all the grenades had been used. With about 50 Japanese casualties to their credit the gunners withdrew. After the failure of these two attacks the sub-units of Warfe Force began to move north and the 47th Battalion began to occupy their positions in the area of Kunai Spur and the track junctions. On 26th August Warfe and Picken Forces ceased to exist.

That day the two forward companies of the 47th began patrolling and probing the enemy's defences, and both had their first successful

---

[7] Sgt F. W. Sides, QX15400; 2/3 Indep Coy. Clerk; of Julatten, Qld; b. Mackay, Qld, 15 Dec 1913. Killed in action 25 Aug 1943. (Sides, a left-hander, played for Queensland and later Victoria in Sheffield Shield cricket before the war.)

[8] Pte W. A. Bayliss, MM, QX28150; 2/7 Bn. Dairy farmer; of Drillham, Qld; b. Yarram, Vic, 27 Oct 1905.

encounters with enemy pill-boxes. A patrol led by Lieutenant Barnett[9] climbed to within 40 yards of the main enemy position on Kunai Spur before being seen by the enemy in a forward pill-box. Barnett's Bren gun team now came into action, but because ferns and tall grass prevented good observation, the Number 2 gunner, Private Domin,[1] stood up and allowed the Number 1 gunner, Private Tobin,[2] to use his shoulder as a rest. From this human bipod four magazines were fired into the opening of the pill-box; several Japanese ran from it and five casualties were inflicted. Disregarding the bullets which whistled about them, Domin and Tobin coolly kept their unusual position until Barnett withdrew the patrol unscathed.

On the morning of 28th August Barnett was reconnoitring the right flank of the enemy-held spur where he found a large pill-box. He informed his company commander, Captain McWatters,[3] who sent forward a field telephone with which Barnett was able to direct accurate fire on to the pill-box. At 5.10 p.m. two platoons led by Barnett attacked the strong Japanese pill-box area from both flanks. One platoon on the right flank advanced north along the eastern side of the spur, and, climbing the crest, got in among the pill-boxes out of which swarmed yelling Japanese. Hand-to-hand fighting ensued. Seizing a machine-gun from a Japanese gunner, Barnett hurled it over a cliff. As his last grenade was faulty because the pin was too widely splayed he rushed a trench and clubbed a Japanese to death. Unable to reload his own weapon because of the fierce fighting Barnett grabbed a rifle held by a Japanese. In the tug-of-war he was wounded when the Japanese pulled the trigger, but this Japanese was clubbed to death also. Under such "cave-man" leadership the platoon killed 31 Japanese for the loss of 4 men wounded before being forced to withdraw. The platoon on the left flank was unable to make any headway up the precipitous slope because of intense fire, and after suffering four casualties it withdrew.

After the failure of this frontal assault, Colonel Montgomery ordered a company to occupy the track junction north-east of Kunai Spur and immediately south of the Francisco River by first light on 30th August. By dusk, however, it was stalled about 800 yards south of the track junction although one patrol did actually reach the junction at 4.30 p.m. and fired on the enemy there. Montgomery ordered Major Leach[4] to take command of the company and press on with the task next morning.

In Hammer's areas as in Monaghan's the enemy were now fighting back from well-sited and heavily-defended positions. North of the Francisco the 2/7th Battalion was attempting to keep the enemy on the run. Major Dunkley's company, after harassing Rough Hill during the previous

---

[9] Lt L. A. Barnett, MC, QX34736; 47 Bn. Engine driver; of Doolbi, Qld; b. Gympie, Qld, 22 Sep 1906.

[1] Pte R. J. Domin, MM, Q135032; 47 Bn. Dairy farmer; of Gympie, Qld; b. Gympie, 31 Mar 1917.

[2] Sgt T. Tobin, QX40681; 47 Bn. Pastrycook; of Gympie, Qld; b. Gympie, 13 Nov 1919.

[3] Capt A. W. McWatters, QX36382; 47 Bn. Journalist; of Maryborough, Qld; b. Maryborough, 26 Sep 1905.

[4] Maj I. A. Leach, SX10194. 2/48 and 47 Bns. Master butcher; of Sandwell, SA; b. Port Adelaide, SA, 8 Oct 1905. Killed in action 30 Aug 1943.

night, attacked the Japanese position on 25th August, but found it too extensive and well-sited. Pelted with grenades as it lay in unfavourable ground, and unable to reach the pill-boxes, it withdrew. From Captain Arnold's company Lieutenant Herrod's[5] platoon occupied Steak; while Lieutenant Edwards'[6] platoon, accompanied by three of Herrod's men who were to return next morning, occupied the feature named after its platoon commander. Captured Japanese documents and maps of the area north of the Francisco showed their anxiety about this area. In orders to the Japanese *No. 2 Sentry Group* at Arnold's Crest (Calabash Mountain) the Japanese commander stated:

> The enemy is in Bobdubi, Komiatum and Grass Hill [Charlie Hill] and apparently 20 enemy are in the upper reaches of the Buiris Creek. Our troops will soon arrive at the position. There is now a sentry group of ours in Ogura Mountain [Camel Ridge-Rough Hill]. About 300 metres to rear of this group is a larger sentry group. About 600 metres behind that is *No. 1 Sentry Group*.

Later orders to *No. 2 Sentry Group* stated:

> Main enemy body appears to be attacking from track leading to Buiris Creek whilst a portion are attacking from the direction of Mount Ogura. Defend the present position to the death while the main body counter-attacks on left flank and rear.

On 26th August Hammer planned the redisposition of his brigade. The 2/7th Battalion would occupy an outer perimeter extending from Savige Spur-Hand-Edwards' Spur-Kidney Hill-Steak, with a reserve on Swan's O.P.; the 58th/59th would occupy an inner perimeter extending from Camel Ridge-Rough Hill-Sandy Creek area-Arnold's Crest; and the Independent Company would be brigade reserve and protect Bobdubi Ridge in the Bench Cut-Coconuts area. For the first time in two months Hammer felt able to afford the luxury of a substantial reserve. While the units were on the move the kai bombers arrived over the area and distributed ammunition and rations over the countryside, mainly among the Japanese. Soon afterwards a company of the 2/7th was mortared with Australian 3-inch mortar bombs collected by the Japanese after the dropping, but the Japanese did not know of the disarming measures taken when dropping mortar bombs and none exploded.

Colonel Picken began to have misgivings next day that his troops were not actually in the positions reported, and eventually Dunkley found that his company was not on Savige Spur as reported previously and had not passed Rough Hill; the rugged nature of the country and the unreliability of the map made it extremely difficult to pinpoint positions accurately. It was evident from the appearance of Japanese in clean clothes that the enemy, who had been off balance since 20th August, were now being reinforced in an attempt to push back the weary Australians.

---

[5] Lt J. E. I. Herrod, NX68151; 2/7 Bn. Student; of Northwood, NSW; b. North Sydney, 17 Sep 1920.

[6] Maj O. L. Edwards, NX101652; 2/7 Bn. Student; of Mosman, NSW; b. Sydney, 22 Jun 1919.

Indeed, the Japanese were suddenly becoming very active north of the Francisco, and at 4.40 p.m. on the 27th Baird's company in Sandy Creek was heavily attacked by a large and determined enemy force attempting to move round his flanks. The Australians gave the enemy a hot reception. Taking up a position between the two forces Sergeant Sinclair[7] directed mortar fire on to the Japanese and thus helped to take the sting from their attack. In order to keep the troops supplied with ammunition Private Blythe[8] moved back and forth carrying boxes of ammunition to the hard-pressed troops. During one of his trips forward Blythe noticed an enemy force gathering on a spur to the left of the forward platoon. Completing his journey with the ammunition he returned with the grenade discharger and accurately grenaded the enemy, causing them to disperse. Enemy pressure continued, how-

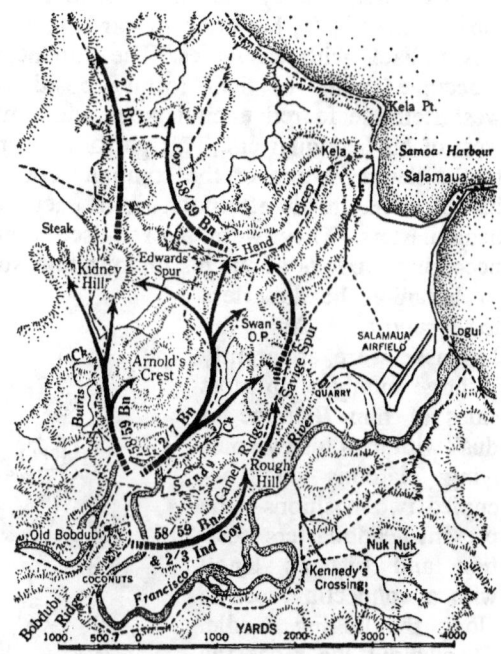

15th Brigade operations, 26th August-10th September

ever, and after a telephone conversation in which Baird, Warfe, Picken and Hammer were all on the line together, Baird extricated his company.

By dusk on 26th August the 58th/59th Battalion had occupied their positions as ordered by Hammer. Three companies were in the Camel Ridge area and Lieutenant Bethune's was on Arnold's Crest. At 9 a.m. on the 27th the carrier line to Bethune's company was ambushed south of Arnold's Crest and Bethune was out of communication. Relieving patrols from the 58th/59th were ambushed by strong Japanese forces. Bethune's first intimation that anything was wrong came at 6.15 a.m. on 27th August, fifteen hours after he had taken over, when he heard firing from the direction taken by a patrol sent to find why the telephone line between his company and Arnold's had been severed. An hour later his men saw Japanese moving along the track 100 yards south of company headquarters. At the same time line communication with battalion headquarters was cut. Arnold's Crest was a triangular-shaped feature. In

---

[7] Sgt B. T. Sinclair, MM, VX5583; 2/7 Bn. Hosiery employee; of Melbourne; b. Ceylon, 10 Dec 1916.

[8] Sgt S. G. Blythe, MM, VX90214; 2/7 Bn. Process worker; of Ascot Vale, Vic; b. Kensington, Vic, 8 Oct 1920.

the centre company headquarters was established with one platoon. The other two platoons were situated on the northern right and left hand spurs, about 400 yards from headquarters and from each other.

To counter enemy movement seen to his south Bethune sent out six men to investigate, but after 75 yards they met heavy opposition and were driven back with casualties. The Japanese, under cover of night, had reoccupied some of their former positions. Noticing movement to the west Bethune feared encirclement and sent five men to occupy a knoll west of his headquarters. This patrol met opposition on the knoll but, due to the determination of the company cook—Corporal Fisher[9]—it gained its objective. In the afternoon small enemy parties tried to stalk company headquarters. They were all repulsed, but by 1.30 p.m. Bethune was becoming anxious about his ammunition supply and sent three men west to battalion headquarters to report. As the Japanese were apparently in large numbers on most sides of him Bethune at dusk withdrew his two outlying platoons and occupied two positions—the present headquarters position and Fisher's Knoll with a connecting section along the linking saddle. Throughout the night the noise of enemy movement, voices, and harassing fire convinced Bethune that the Japanese were being reinforced.

At 5.30 a.m. on the 28th the Japanese attacked strongly from east, south and north. Using fixed bayonets, throwing grenades, and yelling they came on in greatest strength from the east. Here the Victorians, fighting stubbornly, were forced back. Determined enemy attacks continued, and when it became obvious that his ammunition would not last another quarter of an hour Bethune reluctantly decided to withdraw. By 7 a.m. when the company reached a creek junction west of Arnold's Crest, Bethune tapped the

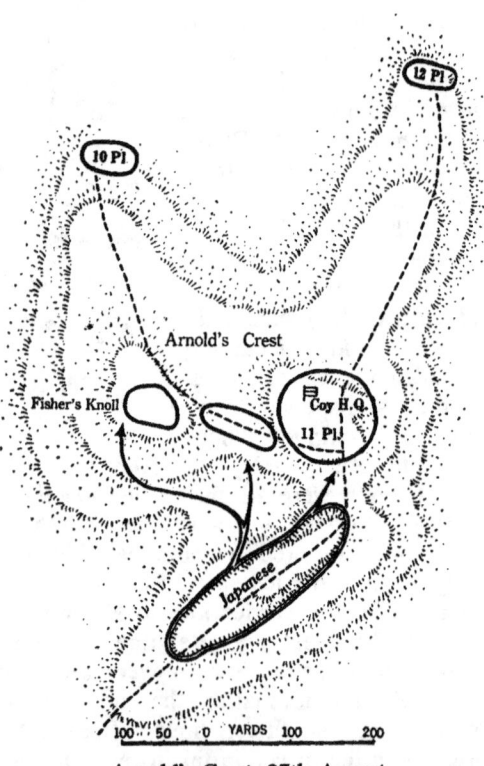

Arnold's Crest, 27th August

---

[9] Sgt M. Fisher, VX149937; 58/59 Bn. Farmer; of Carboor, Vic; b. Wangaratta, Vic, 23 Jun 1911. Died of wounds 17 Jun 1945.

signal wire and reported to Warfe. In this fighting Bethune had 8 casualties and estimated that his men killed at least 40 Japanese. Had sufficient supplies been available Bethune was sure he could have held the feature.

It would probably be fair to say that the enthusiasm of the forceful Hammer had led him to outreach himself. On 29th August he decided on a less ambitious plan—the holding of a line Rough Hill-Savige Spur-Arnold's Crest-high ground west of Buiris Creek. The 2/7th Battalion would occupy the area from Sandy Creek through Arnold's Crest to the high ground west of the Buiris; and the 58th/59th the Camel Ridge-Rough Hill-Savige Spur feature. Before carrying out this plan Arnold's two forward platoons were extricated from their scattered forward positions behind the enemy on Edwards' Spur and from Hand. Both platoons had remained in their areas until lack of food and ammunition forced them to return through enemy territory.

The Japanese were aggressive in their patrolling but they were unable to surpass the patrolling skill of the active Australians who, on the narrowing front, actually began running into one another. Reconnoitring ahead of a patrol Corporal Webster[1] saw 57 Japanese moving down the track with picks and shovels. Soon afterwards 20 returned and half an hour later they came back again carrying picks and shovels. Webster had just returned to his men when unexpected and heavy fire forced the patrol to take cover. Later it was found that a patrol led by Corporal Gibbons[2] was also watching the track. Gibbons and his men had taken up a favourable position behind a log on the side of the track. Six Japanese came up the hill puffing and sweating, and carrying full packs. Thankfully they sat down on the log. Politely allowing the panting Japanese to slip off their packs Gibbons' incredulous men arose from behind the log, killed five Japanese, sent the other down the track at high speed, and put Webster's patrol to ground.

North of the main theatre of operations Captain Whitelaw's company of the 24th Battalion was meeting stiffer resistance along the Hote-Malolo track. Moving south, to link up with the 2/7th in the Buiris Creek area, Lieutenant Looker's platoon on 26th August ran into an enemy position defended by about 50 Japanese astride the track and lost three men including one killed. The next day Looker unsuccessfully but persistently attacked the enemy, who had been reinforced during the night. It now appeared that the Japanese were holding a western defence line from New Wamasu south to Looker's Ridge, but this did not prevent Corporal Leslie's[3] patrol from killing eight Japanese washing in a small creek about three-quarters of a mile from Malolo.

By 29th August eight Allied infantry battalions, one Independent Company and one infantry company were struggling bitterly to gain the last

---

[1] WO2 J. V. Webster, VX33822; 2/7 Bn. Labourer; of Bentleigh, Vic; b. Towong, Vic, 26 Apr 1906.

[2] Cpl C. F. Gibbons, VX13484; 2/7 Bn. Labourer; of Walbundrie, NSW; b. Walla Walla, NSW, 27 May 1913.

[3] Capt J. B. Leslie, MC, VX109130; 24 Bn. Clerk; of Kew, Vic; b. Melbourne, 27 Nov 1922.

high semi-circle of ground before Salamaua. On all the key features—Scout Ridge, Charlie Hill, Kunai Spur, Rough Hill, Arnold's Crest—the enemy was fighting a desperate last ditch battle with skill and determination and some success. Both sides had some fresh troops but the majority were battle-worn and tired. In an endeavour to crack the Japanese defences General Milford brought his ninth infantry battalion into the line. On 30th August he ordered Colonel Amies to move the 15th Battalion round the right flank of the Americans and penetrate the enemy's main line of defence at all costs and with the least possible delay. On reaching the top of Scout Ridge one company would advance north-east to seize Scout Hill, while the remainder of the battalion would be ready to advance to Nuk Nuk. If strong resistance was met Amies would encircle the position and not commit his battalion to a frontal attack.

At first light on 31st August the leading platoon (Lieutenant Matthew[4]) of Captain Provan's[5] company struggled up the precipitous slopes and at 11.45 a.m. reached the Bamboos, a kunai patch with a clump of bamboos on a razor-back at the junction of "D" and Lokanu Ridges. There the advance was detected by the enemy and Matthew was halted by mortar and machine-gun fire. To Milford, hoping that surprise would enable the battalion to reach the crest of Scout Ridge, this check seemed the missing of a golden opportunity. He considered that "the enemy was given time to occupy strong positions on the crest of the ridge overlooking the Bamboos".[6]

At midday Daly obtained permission from Milford to go forward and try to push things along. Milford and Daly had hoped that the battalion would "go hell for leather" up the ridge with at least one company, and were certain that a swift punch would have got astride Scout Ridge before the Japanese could reinforce that particular position. The enemy obviously could not be strong all along the ridge.

This was a normal enough reaction from divisional headquarters, but the fact was that Matthew, who had learnt his soldiering with the 2/5th Battalion, knew the value of surprise and the effect of determined action when surprise is lost. He had no artillery or mortar support because the American signallers had been outstripped in the rapid advance and did not reach the forward area until late in the afternoon. He had been warned to avoid frontal attack and therefore tried to encircle the enemy. The precipitous slopes of "D" and Lokanu Ridges at their junction with Scout Ridge, however, rendered movement impossible on more than a one or two-man front. Despite heavy opposition Matthew did manage to advance another 75 yards, but at 12.50 p.m. was met with a shower of grenades from the enemy on a crest above. He therefore decided to await the arrival of some added fire support for an attack straight up the ridge.

---

[4] Lt D. H. Matthew, VX5316. 2/5 and 15 Bns. Storekeeper; of Swan Hill, Vic; b. Kyneton, Vic, 18 May 1915. Died of wounds 1 Sep 1943.

[5] Maj D. Provan, MC, ED, QX34106; 15 Bn. Schoolteacher; of Brisbane; b. Cairns, Qld, 25 Jun 1905.

[6] 5 Aust Div Report on Operations Leading to Capture of Salamaua, 26 Aug-21 Sep 43.

Provan arrived with the rest of the company soon after 1 p.m. and organised a company attack, which, however, could only be on a one platoon front. There was still no artillery or mortar support as Matthew's platoon led the attack up the slope. The Japanese, well entrenched in heavily timbered country, reacted violently and inflicted 11 casualties, including Matthew who was mortally wounded. By 4 p.m., however, Provan secured a precarious foothold and dug in for the night about 150 yards from the main Japanese positions on Scout Ridge. Captain Proctor's[7] company dug in 300 yards down the slope to support and supply Provan.

During the night Allied artillery shelled the Japanese above the Bamboos. At first light a detachment of mortars and a section of machine-guns were sent from the beach and manhandled into position at the Bamboos. In the morning the enemy above Provan's position made two determined attacks on the company which were repulsed by the defenders aided by artillery fire. Provan suffered heavy casualties: 21, including three officers wounded—himself, his second-in-command, Captain Struss,[8] and one of his two remaining platoon commanders, Lieutenant Rattray.[9] A stretcher bearer, Private Sallaway,[1] although wounded himself, tended the wounded men and arranged their evacuation to the beach.

The ranks of Provan's battered but still defiant company, now led by the remaining platoon commander, Lieutenant Thirgood,[2] were so depleted that Proctor moved his company late on 1st September and combined with Thirgood's men who were still clinging to the ground gained the previous day by Matthew's platoon. The rest of the battalion, blocking up behind, was kept busy bringing up supplies. At 6.55 p.m. the enemy made his third attack for the day but was again repulsed. Ten Japanese were seen to have been killed during the day and several others were seen falling down the steep sides of "D" Ridge. The defenders also captured three enemy L.M.G's and ammunition, which they used that night.

At first light on 2nd September patrols sought routes to Scout Ridge across the precipitous ravines to pinpoint the flanks and the depth of the enemy position. Lieutenant Best's[3] platoon climbed to the east and then approached the enemy from the north-east. After artillery fire they reached the Japanese defences and found them smashed by the fire, but discovered that the real crest of Scout Ridge was one ledge above this position. They were forced to withdraw, but not before 12 Japanese were killed. Artillery and mortars immediately registered the new Japanese positions, while the area of the false crest became no-man's land. On 3rd September the mortar platoon sergeant, Whitlam,[4] crawled to within 100 yards of the

---

[7] Capt P. C. R. Proctor, QX33742; 15 Bn. Schoolteacher; of Brisbane; b. Brisbane, 7 Oct 1916.
[8] Capt A. L. Struss, QX40852; 15 Bn. Overseer; of Beaudesert, Qld; b. Beaudesert, 20 Nov 1922.
[9] Lt K. C. Rattray, NX6390. 2/33 and 15 Bns. Motor driver; of Paddington, NSW; b. Sydney, 12 Jan 1921.
[1] Pte E. L. Sallaway, MM, Q31503; 15 Bn. Shearer; of Townsville, Qld; b. Gympie, Qld, 1 May 1917.
[2] Capt L. R. Thirgood, NX70167. 2/18 and 15 Bns. Salesman; of Balmain, NSW; b. Sydney, 16 May 1917.
[3] Lt L. D. Best, VX61868; 15 Bn. Store manager; of Devonport, Tas; b. Beaconsfield, Tas, 14 Mar 1914.
[4] WO M. J. Whitlam, MM, QX50487; 15 Bn. Clerk; of Annerley, Qld; b. Brisbane, 10 Jul 1913.

crest to register his mortars on to the enemy position. In the afternoon he led a small patrol up a re-entrant to the west; it reached the real crest of Scout Ridge, and reported that the enemy positions were a smoking ruin and that the crest of the ridge was a small plateau about 100 yards deep.

Expecting no opposition a platoon led by Lieutenant G. N. Matthew (brother of D. H. Matthew) followed the same route with another platoon in support. Matthew negotiated the almost perpendicular climb and had reached the lip of the plateau when his 24 men were heavily attacked by Japanese with mortars, grenades and machine-guns. The enemy was strongly established on the plateau, some of the barricades being made of trees felled by the artillery, and could only be reached on a one-section front. As it was obvious that further artillery preparation was necessary Matthew returned to the Bamboos.

Meanwhile Amies was paying attention to Lokanu Ridge, which, if occupied by the enemy, would command and threaten the battalion's right flank and supply route to the forward companies. As the entire Lokanu Ridge, as well as Dot Inlet and the battalion's beach-head were dominated by the eastern end of Lokanu Ridge Amies decided to seize it. He gave the task to Lieutenant Cavenagh's[5] company which had been patrolling to Lokanu Ridge since its arrival in Dot Inlet. On 3rd September Cavenagh sent Lieutenant Byrne[6] to occupy the eastern end of the ridge.

Byrne set out with three men, Privates Rose and Dehne[7] (of the 2/6th Battalion who were experienced scouts) and Private Kane,[8] up a spur to the north of Lokanu village. Scouting ahead of the other two, Rose and Dehne noticed, about 20 yards ahead along the track, a broken limb hanging from a tree and partly obscuring the track. Both leapt for cover as Japanese machine-guns opened up. Moving through the jungle the two men crept up to a pill-box into which Rose threw three grenades and Dehne fired his Owen. Inside they found three dead Japanese marines. Under cover of artillery fire Byrne's men crept up towards the knoll near the east end of the ridge hoping that the Japanese would vacate their positions during shelling. About 100 yards from the knoll the artillery ceased and Byrne dashed to grab the knoll before any Japanese could return. As anticipated he found freshly dug trenches, weapon-pits and foxholes, which had been recently occupied. As soon as the four men had occupied the position as adequately as they could Byrne sent Kane back for reinforcements.

The fresh Japanese marines encountered by the Americans and Australians on Scout Ridge were members of the *5th Sasebo Special Naval Landing Force*. Commander Takeuchi, in charge of these marines, had landed at Salamaua on 1st July. On 17th August two large M.L.C's landed some of his marines at Salamaua and

---

[5] Capt T. J. D. Cavenagh, QX40878; 15 Bn. Schoolteacher; of Brisbane; b. Brisbane, 5 Dec 1915.

[6] Capt L. W. Byrne, MC, QX4234. 2/31, 15 and 42 Bns. Farmer; of Brisbane; b. Brisbane, 27 Jul 1917.

[7] Pte A. E. Dehne, VX53469; 2/6 Bn. Served Korea. Buttermaker; of Barham, NSW; b. Toora, Vic, 24 Feb 1922.

[8] Pte F. Kane, DCM, QX33906; 15 Bn. Meatworker; of Brisbane; b. Blair Athol, Qld, 3 Aug 1917. Died of wounds 10 Jul 1945.

four others landed the remainder at Lae. On 28th August Takeuchi, now apparently commander of the Salamaua garrison, recorded that a naval force was defending the Lokanu positions. The army force there had been reinforced with fresh troops and was counter-attacking: Takeuchi ordered the marines to organise raiding units and attempt to wipe out the enemy in one week.

On 4th September reports began to come in from observation posts about the Allied landing fleet east of Lae. This landing, however, did not lead to any immediate lessening of the enemy's resolve to defend the ridges and knolls he was occupying.

In the early afternoon of the 5th Byrne, whose booby-traps had already claimed several victims, repulsed two attacks from the east and northwest. By this time patrols had found three Japanese positions on Lokanu Ridge—the Pimple, the Knoll and a pocket east of Byrne's O.P. Amies ordered Lieutenant Farley's[9] company to wipe out the Japanese opposition at the Pimple which threatened the rear of Proctor's company. About 2 p.m. a platoon attacked south down Lokanu Ridge from Proctor's position, but heavy machine-gun fire commanding the razor-back approach gave little hope of success and the platoon withdrew.

The enemy really tried to remove Byrne on 6th September. Several small attacks from first light were repulsed with the aid of the mortars. The platoon was in an arrow-shaped perimeter with the forward gun-pit at the tip of the arrow pointing down the narrow precipitous ridge towards the sea. Soon after 4 p.m. a booby-trap exploded. The Queenslanders, alert, waited. Suddenly screaming Japanese charged up the ridge with fixed bayonets. From the forward gun-pit, Private Troughton[1] and Private Gill[2] greeted the charging enemy with rapid Bren gun fire. Many of the Japanese fell but the charge continued and some reached within five to ten yards of the pit. One Japanese threw a grenade which landed on a mound in front of Troughton, showering him with earth and dazing him for a few seconds. The Japanese could not take advantage of this lull in the fire from the deadly Bren because of fire from other members of the platoon and because Gill hurled grenades which kept them at bay until Troughton recovered and fired the Bren again. The fight lasted about half an hour before the Japanese withdrew leaving 20 to 30 dead near the Bren gun-pit. Four of the dead Japanese were dragged into the Australian perimeter before dark and proved to be marines. After this seventh attack had been repulsed by the platoon, the remainder of Cavenagh's company joined Byrne in the Byrne's O.P. area.

Patrolling continued on the 7th and 8th when Amies probed enemy positions on Scout Ridge and Lokanu Ridge. Artillery and mortars softened up the Japanese positions. By 9th September Amies felt able to carry out a two-pronged attack on the crest—Proctor's company from the Bamboos and Captain Leu's company by an outflanking movement from the enemy's right rear along a newly-discovered track. Both attacking forces

---

[9] Capt A. W. Farley, QX33507; 15 Bn. Carton machinist; of Ascot, Qld; b. London, 17 Apr 1919.
[1] Pte H. J. Troughton, MM, QX31091; 15 Bn. Labourer; of Mareeba, Qld; b. Mareeba, 23 Mar 1923.
[2] Pte R. A. Gill, QX62603; 15 Bn. Stockman; of Cannon Hill, Qld; b. Brisbane, 19 Feb 1916.

were limited by confined approaches to a one platoon front; Best's from the Bamboos and Thirgood's round the flank. Thirgood set out at 10.10 a.m. and reached the crest of Scout Ridge without opposition at 2.40 p.m. One section remained at the track junction in the old Japanese perimeter at the false crest while the remaining two sections moved north-east up the crest of Scout Ridge. At 3.35 p.m. Thirgood reached the south-west edge of the Japanese position facing the Bamboos. After an artillery bombardment arranged by Lieutenant Johnson,[3] the O.P.O. for the 25-pounders, and mortar concentrations, Thirgood and Best attacked the position simultaneously. The enemy fired a green flare and withdrew. After minor skirmishes Thirgood and Best met in the enemy perimeter which contained many dead and much equipment. The Australians patrolled north-east up the track without encountering any opposition.

On Lokanu Ridge Lieutenant Turner's[4] platoon, with artillery and mortar support, attacked east towards the last Japanese strongpoint at the eastern tip of the ridge overlooking the sea. The Japanese hastily evacuated the position, fleeing into the jungle below and leaving their dead and equipment. Patrols from the Bamboos completed the happy picture when they found the Pimple and the Knoll on Lokanu Ridge unoccupied. Perhaps the Japanese had withdrawn from both positions when the green flare was fired. After a successful 10-day initiation in the battle area Amies was able to signal Milford late on 9th September that the 15th "now holds line of (Lokanu) Ridge complete from sea at Lokanu to crest of Scout Ridge".

To the left of the 15th Battalion the 162nd Regiment's II and III Battalions now concentrated on the enemy pocket between them on Scout Ridge, while Captain George's company from the I Battalion occupied Grassy Spur on the main Scout Ridge Track, thus completing the encirclement. George's company on Grassy Spur killed 20 Japanese on 29th and 30th August, most of them escaping north-east from the evacuated perimeters at the ridge junction. This aroused the enemy, who established strong positions east and west of George's company and severed his connection with battalion headquarters. Patrols were unable to break through to the beleaguered company on the 31st, and it was not until the afternoon of 1st September that George's runner, who had wormed his way out, was able to tell Colonel Taylor that during the previous day and night the Americans had repulsed nine determined bayonet attacks on Grassy Spur. The 84-man garrison estimated that it had killed 80 of 250 attacking Japanese for the loss of 8 casualties. The defenders' ammunition was almost exhausted as George awaited the rifle shot which was to be the signal to withdraw.[5] He then thinned out his troops, and managed to

---

[3] Lt A. T. Johnson, MC, NX34979; 2/6 Fd Regt. Electrical engineer; of Longueville, NSW; b. Geraldton, WA, 26 Mar 1916.

[4] Lt R. A. Turner, WX311. 2/11, 2/31, 15 and 42 Bns. Clerk; of West Perth; b. Midland Junction, WA, 12 Apr 1916.

[5] In order to make the hand grenades last as long as possible the men heaved mud balls when they heard a noise in the jungle. If the noise continued they concluded that it was a nocturnal animal, but if the noise ceased the men knew that it was made by Japanese and heaved grenades.

evacuate all, including his wounded, through the encircling Japanese to the I/162nd Battalion.

Meanwhile the II and III Battalions were trying to disperse the Japanese pocket. After a mortar bombardment two companies (Colvert's and Ratliff's) attacked the pill-boxes from two sides and by dusk their forward patrols were within 100 yards of each other, but were unable to make further progress. Patrolling and heavy bombardments by American mortars continued for the next few days.

> By 4th September Commander Takeuchi was more defensively minded about his southern flank than a few days previously when he had ordered his marines to defeat the Allies "in one week". Now he ordered his No. 1 company commander to "use one of his platoons to fill up the gaps between the army and the navy forces at Lokanu".

By 8th September the Japanese had begun to withdraw. The pill-boxes and also the ridge between the II and III Battalions were empty; and on 10th September it was found that the Japanese had withdrawn also from Berger Hill.

In the central area the enemy was grimly hanging on to Charlie Hill and Kunai Spur. East of Charlie Hill Davidson met Crosswell's two companies on the morning of 30th August, and instructed Crosswell to establish his force astride the track running along the saddle between Charlie Hill and Egg Knoll. When approaching the saddle Crosswell met strong enemy positions. Lieutenant Winter's platoon supported by Lieutenant Ramm's attacked but could not dislodge the Japanese before dark although they cleared several foxholes. Crosswell therefore withdrew to a perimeter position. During the fighting Captain Cole arrived to resume command of his company as Davidson required Crosswell as second-in-command. After dark the Japanese mortared the Australian position, wounding six men including Cole who remained on duty. The skirmishing continued on the 31st with the two companies unable to make any headway against strong well-camouflaged positions commanding both flanks.

At this time there was a race between Hammer and Monaghan to see who would reach Salamaua first. In idle "chipping" Hammer stated that Monaghan had come in at the death knock, and Monaghan told Hammer that he could relax and leave the battle to the 29th Brigade who would "clean it up for you". There was great rivalry between them about their brigades' performances and this tended to make them drive their men hard.

After the failure of Jenks' attack on 29th August Davidson decided to cut the enemy's supply route and try to encircle Charlie Hill by moving round the western flank of the hill instead of the east. This had been his original plan. Thinking of the tactics successfully employed at Mount Tambu he rang Captain Greer and said: "I want you to go around the other side of Charlie Hill and sit on the Nips' kai line." Artillery harassing fire was brought down during the day to keep the Japanese in their foxholes, and thus enable the company to move undetected.

On 2nd September at 3.45 p.m. Greer reported that he was north of Charlie Hill commanding a well-used track about 200 to 300 yards from the crest of the hill. He was jubilant about his position, from which he had a good view of Salamaua, but it was a three hours' job to fetch water. "Well done," signalled Monaghan to Davidson. "Now let him know you are there. Plenty of water on Charlie Hill."[6] Although he did not know it, Greer had dug in only 30 yards below the enemy perimeter on Charlie Hill. After he had completed his defensive preparations, the Japanese attacked three times but were repulsed each time with heavy casualties.

On 2nd September Captain Ross' company was ordered to establish contact and cut the remaining Japanese tracks running north-east from Charlie Hill. It had dug in on the saddle by 4.30 p.m., cut the enemy signal wire and set booby-traps. During this move Ross made contact with the I/162nd Battalion, and on 3rd September Davidson ordered him to link with Greer as soon as possible. After dispersing four Japanese examining their booby-traps, the company was preparing to move off about midday when the Japanese bombarded it with mortar bombs, among which were the usual percentage of duds. An attack followed, but after losing 15 killed in 10 minutes the Japanese withdrew.

The company then set off around the eastern slopes of Charlie Hill to link up with Greer who had already repulsed two enemy attacks that day. As soon as Ross' last section moved off, the Japanese moved in behind, occupied the position just vacated by the Australians and cut the Australians' communications. Moving slowly along the precipitous slopes of the hill Ross was forced to make an early halt for the night as his water supplies were getting low. A patrol obtained some from the bottom of the gorge at a stream obviously used also by the Japanese. As digging would have made too much noise the company perched for the night among the tree roots.

At 7.30 a.m. on 4th September Ross, still out of communication, continued his move. Searching for the main track, the leading platoon (Lieutenant Birch[7]) reached one Japanese supply track, and then crossed the main Japanese line of communication with signal wire running along it; 40 yards beyond this Birch met Greer's outposts. Only 500 yards separated the companies. Lieutenant Winter's supply train for Ross' company was fired on from the position at the saddle which the Japanese had reoccupied. The natives dropped their loads and went bush and Greer was instructed to supply Ross with rations from his own meagre store.

On 4th September Monaghan informed Davidson that he intended to visit the company position north of Charlie Hill to enjoy the view extolled by Greer and to watch an artillery bombardment on the 47th Battalion's area. Next morning Monaghan, accompanied by a British Army observer, Lieut-Colonel G. N. C. Smith, reached Greer's position just before midday. Soon afterwards misfortune again befell the ration train which this time was moving round the western slopes of Charlie Hill to supply

---
[6] So there was, whenever the boy-line carrying it could get through.
[7] Lt F. D. Birch, QX51119; 42 Bn. Clerk; of Rockhampton, Qld; b. Rockhampton, 2 Jun 1917.

Greer. From a newly-established position on a ledge commanding the supply route the Japanese fired on Lieutenant Harvey's[8] ration train with the same results as on the preceding day. Sergeant Blow,[9] leading the next ration train, decided to bypass the Japanese. Moving 100 yards down the ridge to the west, he travelled parallel with the track above and then turned east on to the track again. Unfortunately he came back too soon, and under enemy fire the carriers again went bush. Davidson then made arrangements for the ration train on 6th September to bypass the ambush more widely. Meanwhile the companies went hungry, and Monaghan and Smith were forced to spend the night in the perimeter.[1]

Soon after Birch's platoon met Greer's outposts, Ross and one of his men were mistaken for Japanese by Greer's men and wounded. The adjutant, Captain Frainey,[2] was then sent to take command. On the 5th Birch patrolled up Charlie Hill and reported that the enemy had a post 50 yards from the top. At 10.30 a.m. Corporal Dwyer[3] met a lone Japanese and shot him from the hip. To the delight of planners this Japanese was carrying a sketch of the defences of Charlie Hill. By the early afternoon the company had dug in between the old and new tracks. To the south-east Winter reported that the Japanese had a chain of positions 150 yards long astride the creek running north and south between Charlie Hill and Egg Knoll.

On the morning of 6th September, Davidson ordered Jenks to attack the ambush position and gather into a dump the rations discarded by the boy-line on the previous day. Monaghan also sent out Birch's platoon to try to clear the track. Under cover of these attacks a carrying party laboriously carried the dumped stores to the two hungry companies, bypassing the ambush position, and Monaghan and Smith returned with the carrying party, much to the relief of the various headquarters.

Although the night was cold and rainy and the platoon was miserably cold, Birch felt some compensation because his platoon had captured three maps during the afternoon's fighting. These were rushed to Boisi for interpretation; they showed three large Japanese perimeters on Charlie Hill.

In command of the Japanese defences on Charlie Hill was Lieutenant Usui of the *11/66th Battalion*. After fighting his way out of the Mubo trap up the Bui Kumbul Creek, Usui had fought on Ambush Knoll, whence he was forced to withdraw to Timbered Knoll. His disheartening series of withdrawals continued when Lewin drove him from Timbered Knoll at the end of July and reduced the effective strength of his company to 31. One of the captured messages said that the Japanese were planning to cut the supply and communication lines of the Australians at the

---

[8] Lt C. N. Harvey, QX44164; 42 Bn. Shop assistant; of Yeppoon, Qld; b. Yeppoon, 24 Dec 1920.
[9] Sgt M. W. G. Blow, Q36685; 42 Bn. Shop assistant; of Rockhampton, Qld; b. Rockhampton, 30 Dec 1919.
[1] Smith was impressed with the coolness of the men under fire. A few minutes after every "flap" he would see a few men produce a pack of cards and start a game of poker. "Amazing, positively amazing," he commented again and again. Naturally this quickly became "B" Company's retort to any occurrence.
[2] Maj J. F. Frainey, QX40809; 42 Bn. Asst Shire Clerk; of Mount Morgan, Qld; b. Mount Morgan, 20 Apr 1914.
[3] Cpl T. W. Dwyer, QX34531; 42 Bn. Farmer; of Yeppoon, Qld; b. Rockhampton, Qld, 9 Sep 1921.

rear of Charlie Hill as soon as reserves arrived, and were also planning to set fire to the kunai. In a second message written on the back of the first, Usui reported the disappearance of his line maintenance section after encountering the enemy on the way, the arrival of only one of his runners, and the killing or wounding of several others by the encircling Australians.

Unfortunately by the time the translation was received by Davidson the kai line had been cut and two of Greer's platoons had been forced to change their positions because of kunai fires.

At night on 6th September Monaghan warned Davidson to prepare for an attack on Charlie Hill in three days' time. The maps captured by Dwyer and Birch enabled the attackers to know exactly what they were up against. At 9.30 a.m. on the 9th after a mortar barrage, two of Frainey's platoons crossed their start-line on the northern slopes of Charlie Hill. Fifteen minutes later the first platoon occupied the first Japanese perimeter without opposition. The second platoon, passing through, occupied the other two Japanese perimeters. Charlie Hill was in Australian hands. The Japanese had moved out the night before leaving fresh uneaten food (including grapefruit), automatic weapons, mines and grenades. They had also dismantled and buried a mountain gun. The occupying platoons counted 30 dead Japanese mostly killed by artillery and mortar fire. The hill, as with most captured Japanese positions, was nauseatingly filthy and the stench overpowering. The habits of some Japanese soldiers in occupation were worse than those of many animals; and this poor sanitary discipline no doubt accounted for the enemy's high rate of sickness.

With Charlie Hill secured at the track junction between Egg Knoll and Charlie Hill and a link formed with the Americans, "B" Company, now led by Captain Ganter,[4] set off in pursuit towards Nuk Nuk at 10.20 a.m. and spent the night in an old Japanese position farther down the hill.

To the left of the 42nd Battalion, the 47th on 30th August was preparing for another attack on the Kunai Spur and pill-box area. Advancing over very rugged country Major Leach's company reached a position astride the main track west of the junction by 10.35 a.m. Here they were pinned down, and Leach and Sergeant Eisenmenger,[5] reconnoitring near the track junction, were killed by sniper fire. Patrolling to find the enemy's left flank continued but at 5.30 p.m. Captain Pascoe, having lost 9 casualties, reported that because of "intense enemy opposition" he was withdrawing to his firm base south-east of Kunai Spur.

After further skirmishes on the 31st Colonel Montgomery decided that the defences of Kunai Spur were known as well as they could possibly be from the outside, and he ordered Captain Lewis'[6] company to capture it. Next morning the artillery fired 600 rounds, mortars fired 120 bombs, and machine-guns 8,000 rounds. The platoons attacked vigorously, driving many of the panicking and screaming enemy from their positions. Others

---
[4] Capt A. G. Ganter, QX42360; 42 Bn. Grocer; of Rockhampton, Qld; b. Rockhampton, 23 Nov 1915.
[5] Sgt W. L. Eisenmenger, QX41363; 47 Bn. Farmer; of Murgon, Qld; b. Murgon, 6 Sep 1917. Killed in action 30 Aug 1943.
[6] Capt E. A. Lewis, MC, VX5145. 2/6 and 47 Bns. Watchmaker; of Colac, Vic; b. Colac, 7 Nov 1918.

who remained in their holes were killed with Owens and grenades. By 5.20 p.m. Lewis' men held positions facing the next Japanese defences on the north end of the spur.

Sound planning and determined execution by an untried company had resulted in a success equal to that expected from more experienced and battle seasoned men. For the loss of two casualties, including the leading platoon commander, Lieutenant Walters,[7] who was killed, Lewis' company counted about 60 dead Japanese on Kunai Spur, about 40 of whom had been killed by the artillery fire which had scored five direct hits on pillboxes.

Montgomery decided to make another attempt to cut the enemy's line of communication to the pill-box area north of Kunai Spur, now renamed Lewis Knoll. On 2nd September he ordered Captain Yates' company to occupy a base 500 yards east of the Salamaua Track junction which the battalion had previously been unable to capture. The company was held up by Japanese opposition ahead and on the flanks. A patrol cleared the enemy immediately ahead, killing five and sending the others fleeing into the dense jungle, but it was too late to go any farther that day; at 7.15 next morning the company again moved forward and managed to reach a razor-back running up to a strongly-held enemy position on Twin Smiths. Leaving their defences in an attempt to drive Yates off the spur, the Japanese lost 20 killed. Returning to their entrenchments they then waited for the Australians to advance. When the company did so, heavy fire and the difficulty of countering it from the Australians' precarious hold on the razor-back precluded the company from even digging in, and Yates withdrew. The Japanese resisted any further moves in this area and on 6th September drove back an attack by Lieutenant Edwards.[8]

After more reconnaissance by Lewis' and Captain Muston's[9] companies and small but successful ambushes, Montgomery ordered Lewis to capture the ridge north of Lewis Knoll on 8th September. For two hours the mortars and machine-guns fired on the Japanese positions and at 10.30 a.m. two platoons began to make their way up precipitous slopes to the Japanese position on the crest, through bamboo, undergrowth and timber felled by the mortars. Soon one of the supporting medium machine-guns was hit and put out of action, a light machine-gun was wrecked by grenades and another two developed stoppages at critical times. Japanese snipers on the left and heavy cross-fire from the pill-boxes helped to cause Lewis' withdrawal after getting within grenade and Owen range of the crest.

On the 8th, however, four pill-boxes on a knoll between Charlie Hill and Lewis Knoll were abandoned by the enemy. Indications of a general Japanese withdrawal from the area facing the 47th Battalion were still more apparent when, on the 9th, three forward companies found unoccupied pill-boxes facing them.

---

[7] Lt E. A. Walters, QX40800; 47 Bn. Storeman; of Gympie, Qld; b. Allora, Qld, 13 Sep 1916. Killed in action 1 Sep 1943.
[8] Lt N. Edwards, QX34731; 47 Bn. Clerk; of Bundaberg, Qld; b. Toowoomba, Qld, 17 Sep 1919.
[9] Capt P. C. Muston, QX34722; 47 Bn. Accountant; of Kingaroy, Qld; b. Kingaroy, 3 Feb 1914.

By the end of August any movement by 15th Brigade patrols aroused immediate and determined opposition from fresh and well-equipped troops —a readily understandable reaction in view of the 15th Brigade's close proximity to the enemy's most vulnerable areas. Japanese maps captured on 23rd August estimated that the brigade's strength was 4,000; actually it was only 1,227, not all of them fighting troops.

In his report Hammer summed up the brigade's feeling of dogged determination to see the job through:

> Our troops at this stage were magnificent, many sick refused to be evacuated— they knew the unit strengths were low and they preferred to remain and continue the fight. Gallant determined actions were fought day after day as our troops progressed on their encircling move along the high ground north of Salamaua but the strain of continual day and night moves and the heavy fighting over tortuous terrain began to tell. The needs of reorganising and the establishment of sound supply lines as well as rest forced a halt. . . . All troops were exhausted.

Tinea, recurrent malaria, general exhaustion and lack of fresh food were some of Hammer's main problems. Captain Millikan, the medical officer of the 58th/59th Battalion, stated that for his weary battalion "relief from the front line is necessary". With the campaign in its closing stages, however, relief was not possible. Examining the brigade's health at the end of August Lieut-Colonel Refshauge of the 15th Field Ambulance made an interesting comparison: from the 2/7th, between 19th August and 1st September, 137 men were evacuated sick, while the 58th/59th sent out only 59 sick in the same period. This was despite the fact that the 2/7th had enjoyed a good rest in the salubrious Bulolo Valley after its operations in the Mubo area, whereas the 58th/59th Battalion had been continuously in action for over two months. The 2/7th Battalion, however, had been longer in the tropics and malaria had taken a stronger hold.

From the end of August the brigade began a welcome period of less strenuous activity. This included harassing the enemy, discovering whether his intention was offensive or defensive, finding his strong and weak points, obtaining information regarding tracks and terrain, reconnoitring for future attacks on Rough Hill and Arnold's Crest, improving the line of communication, signposting the area, establishing fool-proof communications, building up supply and salvage dumps, and sending out to rest camps those who most needed rest. Patrolling never ceased, nor did the steady stream of casualties inflicted and received.[1]

---

[1] As mentioned earlier, on 25th August three men of Lieutenant Herrod's platoon of the 2/7th had been detached to Lieutenant Edwards' platoon on Edwards' Spur, whence they were to return next morning. They failed to do so but six days after they had disappeared the three men—Privates L. Ward (of Auburn, Vic), D. R. Knox (Dookie, Vic) and R. K. Wellam (Geelong, Vic)—reported to Arnold's headquarters where they told a story which reflected credit on their fortitude and endurance. After leaving Edwards' platoon they were ambushed and Wellam was wounded. From that time the small band had had several clashes with enemy patrols, during which Ward and Knox killed 10 Japanese. Although without rations they did not panic, but carefully nursed Wellam and travelled slowly in a westerly direction. On one occasion Allied artillery shelled an area near where they were sheltering, and, from the screams and squeals, it appeared that an enemy position had been hit. In the regimental aid post after their ordeal the three men gave valuable information to the Intelligence officer of the 2/7th, Lieutenant P. T. Gude (of Geelong, Vic).

On 1st September Hammer instructed Picken and Hancock to prepare for moonlight attacks on Arnold's Crest and Rough Hill respectively. Meanwhile two raids by sections of the 2/3rd Independent Company took place. The first, towards Rough Hill, was unsuccessful because surprise was lost. The second patrol of 13 men led by Lieutenant Garland established an ambush deep in enemy territory on the track linking the main Japanese position at Arnold's Crest with reserve positions farther north. After heavy diversionary fire from the 2/7th Battalion, a patrol of 12 Japanese, moving at intervals of five yards, without packs, with rifles at the trail, and wearing steel helmets covered with camouflage nets, approached the raiders' position. Garland's men killed 8 and after firing at the main Japanese positions withdrew. This skilful foray into enemy territory undoubtedly helped to confuse the enemy and make them wonder where next to expect the prowling Australians.

Patrol clashes continued throughout the brigade's area for the next few days. When it received no answering fire from a Japanese position ahead, a patrol on 3rd September advanced until it saw an Owen gun and an Australian slouch hat placed temptingly in front of it. Declining to fall for this old trick the platoon rapidly withdrew, but even so one man was wounded by an enemy sniper.

At 5 a.m. on 5th September Captain Dawson of the 2/6th Field Regiment directed artillery concentrations on Rough Hill and Arnold's Crest. A patrol from the 58th/59th and one from the 2/7th Battalion met heavy fire and were forced to withdraw. Thereupon Dawson arranged a further shoot of 240 rounds on to Rough Hill later in the morning.

On the 8th, for the first time in Australian areas, Hammer used an interpreter to suggest surrender to the enemy. After an hour's shelling of Rough Hill, Lieutenant Bowers, an American, issued an ultimatum to enemy troops 60 yards north-east from Lieutenant Griff's position south-west of Rough Hill. Escorted by Griff, Bowers carried out his task from a circular pit which the Japanese used as a forward machine-gun post at night and which was half way between the two lines and thus within grenade range of the enemy. Broadcasting in Japanese, Bowers told the Japanese that supplies, ammunition or relieving troops could never reach them because of the Allied grip on Lae. If they came forward between the hours of 10 a.m. and 5 p.m. in twos and threes with arms raised they would be assured of safe escort back to Australia where they would be given the opportunity of beginning a new life. No names would be submitted to Tokyo. During Bowers' address the Japanese made no response. Talking and muttering were heard when Bowers finished, but no Japanese came forward. When none had come forward by 5 p.m. Dawson guided 100 rounds from the 25-pounders on to Rough Hill.

After the launching of the assault against Lae on 4th September Hammer on the 7th ordered Captain Whitelaw of the 24th Battalion to send out a platoon to cut the Lae-Salamaua track in the Bukuap-Busama area. As the other two platoons were committed in forward positions along the Malolo Track and facing Looker's Ridge, Whitelaw was forced to use Lieutenant Looker's weary platoon which had just been withdrawn from the forward position for a brief rest. Looker left his base at 5.30 p.m. on the 7th. His route towards the Busama-Bukuap area would be north along the high spur to the north-west of the company's base, north-east to the high feature between Busama-Bukuap, and east to the coast.

Milford met his brigadiers at Davidson's headquarters west of Charlie Hill on 9th September. All reports indicated that there were only small centres of organised resistance south of a line from Lokanu Ridge to the Francisco. With the capture of Charlie Hill the enemy's main defences south of the river had been disorganised. Milford believed that it was now essential to speed the division's advance, allowing the enemy no respite to reorganise and occupy fresh positions. That afternoon he ordered a general advance at first light next morning. The 162nd Regiment would capture the area from the cape, previously known as Laupui Point and now known as Cape MacKechnie, to Logui 2; the 15th Battalion would capture the area from Logui 2 to Nuk Nuk; the 29th Brigade the area from Nuk Nuk to Kennedy's Crossing; and the 15th Brigade the area from Quarry to Kela.

Amies of the 15th sent Captain Proctor's company at first light on 10th September north-east along Scout Ridge. In a rapid pursuit of the fleeing enemy Proctor killed a few stragglers, occupied Scout Hill unopposed, and by nightfall secured the high ground overlooking the mouth of the Francisco. Patrolling south-west to Nuk Nuk, he linked with the 42nd Battalion. Lieutenant Farley's company set out for Nuk Nuk from the crest of Scout Ridge, but when the track shown on the map soon petered out the company was confronted with the unpleasant task of using a compass and cutting its way through dense jungle. By 4.30 p.m. it reached a well-made track leading to Nuk Nuk. At 4 p.m. the remainder of the battalion was relieved of responsibility east of Scout Ridge by MacKechnie's regiment moving up from the south. The fighting men of the 15th Battalion had left 107 dead Japanese in a brief 11 days of action. The battalion itself had suffered 57 casualties, including 10 killed. Along Scout Ridge the American battalions advanced without opposition.

Late on 9th September Monaghan ordered Davidson of the 42nd to occupy the area between Charlie Hill and Nuk Nuk, and Montgomery of the 47th the area between Lewis Knoll and Charlie Hill. Operations were proceeding as planned when the weather began to aid the enemy's withdrawal. Extremely heavy rain which had fallen continuously for 36 hours greatly hampered the advance; landslides swept away tracks; worse still, the Francisco was in flood and still rising. Neither battalion met any opposition but the flood prevented any crossing by the 42nd Battalion.

On the 9th Hammer rang his own headquarters at Artie Fadden and warned his units to be prepared to clear Kela Ridge, Savige Spur and Arnold's Crest. He thought that the enemy would probably try to hold the

Kela area long enough to evacuate his forces from the south and would probably begin to thin out from Rough Hill and Arnold's Crest. Estimating that his main thrust towards Kela could be launched on 11th September, he decided to test the enemy's defences on 10th September and contain them during the day while his main force moved up Sandy Creek to a forming-up place west of Swan's O.P. After an early morning reconnaissance and artillery bombardment Captain Jago's company of the 58th/59th attacked Rough Hill at 9 a.m. on the 10th. One platoon reached 50 yards from an enemy position where heavy fire forced its withdrawal. A second platoon then engaged the enemy who replied with heavy fire from formidable defences and forced the Australians to retire. The third platoon was also forced to withdraw after trying for two hours to drive out the enemy.

After this failure Lewin's platoon from the 2/3rd Independent Company fought its way up Savige Spur and dug in at 12.30 p.m. astride the enemy line of communication on the top of the ridge, thus isolating the Japanese on Rough Hill from those on Savige Spur. Lewin was subjected to heavy fire, which he returned, and counter-attacks from south-west and north-east, which he repulsed. During the night of 10th-11th September Lewin's and Jago's men kept pressure on Rough Hill where the enemy returned the Australians' harassing fire.

Elsewhere on Hammer's front Newman's company of the 58th/59th Battalion advanced 1,500 yards up Sandy Creek to secure the brigade's forming-up place. Just south of Kidney it came upon an enemy camp of fourteen huts. A platoon attacked and occupied the camp, capturing many documents. By darkness on the 10th six infantry companies and two Independent Company platoons were bivouacked in the Sandy Creek forming-up area ready for early movement on the 11th.

To the north Hammer ordered Whitelaw to drive the enemy from the Malolo Track and also from the position south of the track. Lieutenant Barling's platoon of the 24th advanced along the Malolo Track towards the coast until it ran into enemy booby-traps. While one section held the track the remainder of the platoon moved north-east and attacked from the east. Sergeant Wintle's[2] platoon attacked the southern position but heavy fire from this formidable enemy position, about 200 yards long, forced the attackers to withdraw.

By the evening of 10th September Japanese resistance had collapsed south of the Francisco, but north of it they were still fighting grimly to retain their last defensive positions before the Australians reached the flat country round Salamaua. Milford was now quite convinced that the Japanese did not intend to hold the river line. Whether they intended to evacuate Salamaua altogether or to fight to the last in the Salamaua peninsula or Kela Ridge area was not yet apparent. Heavy barge traffic

---

[2] Sgt E. B. Wintle, VX104543; 24 Bn. Insurance agent; of Kew, Vic; b. Collingwood, Vic, 3 Jan 1909.

heard on the night 9th-10th September caused Milford to ask Herring for naval intervention by the American P.T. boats.

On the 11th Herring informed Milford that the Japanese commander had possibly withdrawn from Salamaua to Lae. Wireless telegraphy between Lae and Salamaua by Japanese lower formations had been last heard at 10.21 p.m. on 10th September. Over the main Japanese lines no wireless traffic had been addressed to aircraft bases in New Guinea or New Britain since 1.5 a.m. on the 10th.

Milford now ordered MacKechnie's regiment to capture the area from the base of the Salamaua isthmus to the next track junction half way to Kela on 11th September. Thus the capture of Salamaua itself was allotted to the Americans, and the news travelled swiftly among the Australians. Milford, however, was not confident that the Americans would move quickly enough and, as a precaution, he ordered a company of the 15th Battalion (Proctor's) to bottle up any Japanese on the peninsula until the Americans arrived.

Milford hoped that Monaghan would thus be free to press on with the pursuit towards Lae without being diverted to his right flank. The 29th Brigade would capture the area from Bicep to Kela, while the 15th Brigade would reach the coast half way between Chinatown and Mission Point to isolate Kela. Milford gave his commanders authority to vary the boundaries in cases of urgency by agreement among themselves, and instructed them to contain and bypass enemy centres of resistance except where they constituted obstacles to the advance.

South of the river the pursuit was rapid on 11th September. Proctor's company crossed the flooded Francisco near its mouth at first light. There was no bridge and the crossing was made possible when a group of good swimmers led by Lieutenant Edwards[3] tested the river in darkness for depth and current and stretched a rope across to assist the remainder of the company, heavily laden with weapons and equipment. There were several anxious moments for the water was between 5 and 6 feet deep and the current was running a full flood rip. The crossing, undetected by the enemy, was completed just after first light and before the 42nd Battalion began crossing higher up the river. Proctor did not advance farther into the isthmus as his orders, given verbally by Daly, were to cross the river near its mouth and occupy a position from which he could dominate the isthmus by fire and protect the flank of other troops who were to move into the isthmus. The remainder of the 15th Battalion arrived at Nuk Nuk which was fast becoming a bottleneck. MacKechnie's two leading battalions, after crossing some very difficult country, spent the night in the Logui 2 area, but could not cross the flooded Francisco.

By 7.50 a.m. on the morning of the 11th Captain Ganter's company of the 42nd Battalion began to swim the river. Private Urquhart[4] crossed

---

[3] Lt E. C. Edwards, QX61062; 15 Bn. Letter machinist; of Brisbane; b. Brisbane, 9 Jun 1922.
[4] Cpl R. E. Urquhart, Q114049; 42 Bn. Assistant bottler; of Rockhampton, Qld; b. Rockhampton, 22 Aug 1921.

first, taking with him a signal cable which was used to help others across. At 9.30 a.m. they occupied the battered airstrip without opposition; 25 minutes later they occupied Logui 1 and at 11.40 a.m. followed the power line to Kela Radio Station which was occupied at 1.15 p.m. Here the patrol found in the side of the hill a heavy machine-gun and a mountain gun. While admiring its prize the patrol was fired on by its own artillery, a performance soon stopped by Captain McElroy who was with this company.

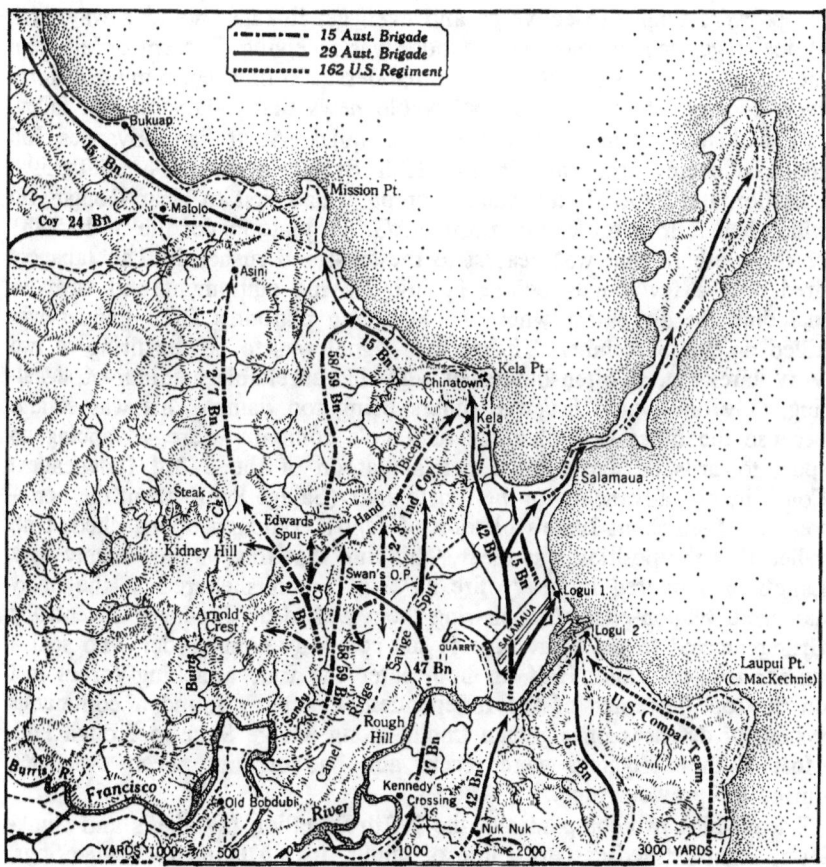

The fall of Salamaua, 11th-13th September

At 1.35 p.m. Ganter led a patrol of six men from Kela Radio Station for Logui 1 to join Proctor's company of the 15th. Proctor prepared to open fire thinking that the figures were Japanese, but when they turned out to be Australians he remained in position covering Ganter's patrol as it approached Salamaua. Ganter did not see Proctor's men hidden in the jungle and at 2.30 p.m. the patrol advanced along the south end of the isthmus, thus winning the race to the shattered town of Salamaua.[5] Half an hour later Ganter's men found a solitary and forlorn Japanese in a battered house on the isthmus. The rest of the company and second company of the 42nd then arrived on the isthmus followed at 6 p.m. by Proctor's company.

The 47th Battalion, after a difficult crossing of the flooded Francisco, advanced unopposed and, by nightfall, Lewis' company was exploiting along the crest of Bicep, and Muston's was at Swan's O.P. With so many Australians and Americans in the area and so few Japanese, the Allied troops were bound to converge and even get in one another's way, and, at one stage, one company commander was receiving different orders from the brigadier and two battalion commanders. No one really minded, however, because of the scarcely believable news that Salamaua had fallen.

The 11th September was a day of quick Australian advances and sporadic enemy resistance in the 15th Brigade's area. The 58th/59th Battalion and 2/3rd Independent Company had first to clear Rough Hill which had four spurs leading up to it. Griff's platoon (of the 58th/59th) on the southern spur was nearest to the crest and rushed it. The Japanese fired only a few bursts before fleeing, leaving equipment and weapons including the Bren lost when the attacking platoon's Bren gunner was killed on 5th September. The success signal was to be the firing of two Very flares but, as often happened with this unreliable medium of signalling, only one would fire, the others being too damp. This was serious because the other two platoons of Jago's company were advancing up spurs towards the crest and Lewin's platoon of the 2/3rd Independent Company was advancing up the fourth spur (Savige Spur) from the northwest. As Lieutenant Lane's platoon of Jago's company approached, Griff yelled that the position was clear. Thinking that this was an enemy trick Lane's men poured in heavy fire as Griff's men sheltered in the badly damaged weapon-pits, often sharing them with dead Japanese. Eventually Griff managed to get a message to his company commander who sent a runner to stop Lane. Half an hour later the four attacking forces met on the top. The men of the Independent Company found a continuous system of defences on eighteen knolls along Savige Spur to Rough Hill. Most of these diggings were recent and had certainly been evacuated during the previous night.

Meanwhile, two companies of the 2/7th Battalion (Walker's and Dunkley's) scrub-bashed east to a line of knolls linking Hand to Savige Spur, where they found the track and followed it towards Hand and a maze of unoccupied defences on a high knoll. Continuing the advance they

---

[5] Moving through the shattered buildings on the isthmus Sgt T. J. Smith (of Mackay, Qld) found a Japanese notebook with the first few pages covered with writing. On the first blank page he recorded the signatures of his companions in the patrol. The signatures of Ganter, Smith, Cpl G. V. Knudsen (of Milaa Milaa, Qld), Pte R. T. Moore (Rockhampton, Qld), Pte D. A. Staines (Coopers Plains, Qld), Pte C. P. Lawrence (Rockhampton) and Pte R. G. Walmsley (Malanda, N. Qld) appeared below the heading "Salamaua, 1500 hours, 11/9/43". Under the signatures appeared the following:

"This is to certify that the above members of 'B' Coy 42 Bn took possession of Salamaua for Australia on this date.

A. G. Ganter, Capt."

Overleaf Monaghan later wrote, "Good lads."

surprised a small enemy force which quickly dispersed. Moving towards Bicep Dunkley's company reached a kunai knoll which the Japanese rearguard was covering with machine-gun fire. Four unlucky men were killed and eight, including Dunkley, wounded on this day when Salamaua fell. Largely as a result of the efforts of Lance-Corporal Frawley,[6] who crawled forward under fire with telephone line from the unoccupied Japanese position to the area where the company was nearly encircled, Walker managed to extricate Dunkley's company. Combining the two companies into one force, he occupied the abandoned position near Hand. Other companies of the 2/7th occupied Arnold's Crest and Edwards' Spur.

On 12th September the 5th Division continued to clean up the Salamaua area. The 162nd Regiment, with orders to concentrate in the area between Cape MacKechnie, Logui and the airfield, crossed the Francisco one day after Monaghan's battalions had swum the turbulent river and had occupied Salamaua.[7]

MacKechnie's regiment now became divisional reserve.[8]

While the Americans were approaching the peninsula the 42nd Battalion established that there were no Japanese there and then occupied Chinatown. Patrols combing the peninsula found two naval and two antiaircraft guns (all without breech bolts), quantities of unused arms, medical supplies, a wireless transceiver and portable generator. Well-furnished huts

---

[6] L-Cpl T. I. Frawley, MM, VX17556; 2/7 Bn. Cheese maker; of Bayles, Vic; b. Lyndhurst, Vic, 22 Oct 1917.

[7] *The Jungleers* (p. 65) describes the capture of Salamaua somewhat inaccurately: "A small group of officers and men, deciding to test what the Japs would offer at Salamaua, walked into the Francisco River on 12 September and deliberately, although apprehensively, forded the stream. Not a shot greeted this group as it waded through the water and climbed out on the opposite bank. Just the previous day the Japs had been throwing out some heavy artillery fire but now the guns were silent. The Japs had fled. The 3d Battalion immediately crossed the river and Salamaua was in American hands. . . . The Aussies from the north poured into Salamaua on the heels of the Yanks and the 2d Battalion followed the 3d across the river."
It will be seen that the 162nd Regiment was mistaken in their belief that they had taken Salamaua. It was first entered by the 42nd Battalion at 2.30 p.m. on the 11th; the 162nd Regiment arrived a day later. The Americans encountered only a few stray Japanese and captured one member of the *Sasebo SNLF* in the Scout Ridge area. He had been ill in a shelter for a week, professed to know nothing of the evacuation, and would not at first believe it had taken place. He stated that a soldier passing by some days before said that he was going to Finschhafen.

[8] Like the Australian militia battalions, the 162nd Regiment, in its first campaign, had learnt the hard way. Inexperience, inadequate training, and command difficulties had accounted for slow progress in the coastal area. These restraints were not felt to the same extent by the I Battalion because of its close association with a veteran Australian brigade. Indeed, Taylor's battalion received a presidential citation "as public evidence of deserved honor and distinction" for its part in the Salamaua campaign.
The American soldier tried hard and learnt fast. He was equipped more lavishly, though not more effectively, than the Australian soldier. His *métier* was to capture enemy positions which had been flattened or blasted by a previous bombardment. The Australian jungle soldier, without the American's array of supporting weapons, had to rely more on his individualism, commonsense and stamina. That the Americans themselves understood the difference is evident from the following statement in *The Jungleers*: "The Australians and Americans fought entirely different campaigns. When the Aussie infantrymen lacked immediate artillery support they would storm the enemy and take the objective by sheer perseverance and bravery. . . . The Yank style of fighting was to wait for the artillery to come up and let the big guns blast the enemy positions as barren of all life as possible. It saved many American lives and got better results, although it took longer." (In fact the casualties of American battalions in this campaign were usually heavier than those of the Australian battalions involved.) Commenting on American tactics for the edification of the Japanese soldier, the author of a Japanese document wrote: "The American forces are slow and steady. They cannot attain a decision by one small test. Individually or sometimes in small units, sportsmanlike adventure will be attempted, but generally they are very steady and advance step by step and will not attack unless they are positive that they will not lose. . . . Once they attain confidence, however, they will display gallantry far beyond their expectations. It must be expected that when this is attained they will change to extreme caution as is the normal state of generally all foreigners."
The 162nd Regiment boarded LCT's for Oro Bay on 25th September, and on the 29th reached Rockhampton, where, when the American artillery returned, the 41st US Division was reunited.

apparently belonging to the Japanese headquarters, and food still on the table, indicated a recent and hurried departure; a notebook was found open on an office table. Further patrols reported that the main track along the peninsula ran around the western side with branch tracks running up to the high ground, and that bushes had been planted along the main track as a screen from sea and air observation. The enemy had built several camps on the steep shores of the peninsula along the water's edge. The fronts were on high stilts while the backs rested on ground-level posts sunk into the hill. Extra accommodation had been provided by digging caves into the hill. Finally the patrols reported that there must have been women in Salamaua; various items of female clothing were found and small quantities of lipstick and powder.

In the 15th Brigade's area there was no resistance on the 12th as Hammer sent his patrols hurrying north and east in an endeavour to bottle up the retreating enemy. A small patrol from the 58th/59th, stripped of all gear except weapons and machetes, was led by Warfe across the rugged country and through stinking swamps to the coast which was reached at 2.30 p.m., half way between Kela Point and Mission Point. On the Malolo Track on 12th September Looker's platoon, which had set out on 7th September to cut the Lae-Salamaua track, unexpectedly reported back. Its tale was a sad one of scrub-bashing through thick jungle shrouded by continuous rain and mist. Eventually the platoon reached "precipitous slopes down which it was impossible to move", and in weary frustration returned to base. It was unfortunate that circumstances, including the lack of a guide, prevented the platoon from breaking through, for Milford had no way of knowing whether the Japanese were using the coastal track for their withdrawal. Had the platoon managed to get through, the men would have had a grandstand view of the evacuation of Salamaua and would have been able to speed the retreat. By the time other patrols from the 15th Brigade reached the coast the enemy had gone.

The inability of this platoon to reach the coast was all the more unfortunate because of an ineffective attempt to cut the coastal track farther north. As mentioned, maintenance of an observation post and harassing base near the Lae-Salamaua track was rendered difficult by the strength with which the enemy held the mouth of the Buang. For one reason or another, attempts to cut a track from the Buang patrol's base to Sugarloaf and the Lae-Salamaua track were unsuccessful even when the patrol was reinforced to company strength. On 1st September the Japanese, who mostly remained passive within their Buang defences, showed that they were aware of Australian intentions by ambushing a patrol half way between the mouth of the Buang and Sugarloaf.

Two days before the 9th Division landed east of Lae Colonel Smith of the 24th ordered the patrol commander to occupy a position on the coast north of the Buang mouth by first light on 4th September to prevent the enemy's use of the Lae-Salamaua track. Smith then handed over charge of the Buang River operations to his newly-arrived second-in-command,

Major N. L. Fleay, and went forward to Markham Point. Another brush with the Japanese half way between the Buang mouth and Sugarloaf, a mortar shoot in the general area, and reports of much barge activity between Salamaua and Lae, were the only information received by the higher command of the progress of the attempt to block the coastal track. It was only on 9th September that it was discovered that the original signal ordering the patrol commander to establish the coastal block on 4th September had been received in a corrupt form giving the date as 11th September. The delay in discovering the error was caused by the fact that wireless had failed in this area, and an order given by telephone to Mapos had to be sent by runner to the Buang patrol—a two days' journey there and a similar one back. When the mistake was discovered patrols began probing towards the coast.[9]

On 11th September a strong patrol of 32 men set out towards the coast on the north side of the Buang. Next day Herring informed Smith's headquarters that the Japanese were evacuating Salamaua and were using the coastal track. Fleay passed this information to the patrol which was instructed to inflict casualties and delay enemy movement to the north. The patrol, however, found the country very difficult to penetrate and returned on 13th September after having failed to reach the coast; it fired 21 mortar bombs over an area of 2,000 yards of coastline north of the Buang. The flight of the main enemy force northward and the task of the rearguards left to fend for themselves was thus facilitated by the misfortune which overtook the two patrols sent to cut the Lae-Salamaua track. Many difficulties confronted the patrols, however: the terrain, weather, the condition of the men, the weight of the loads, inadequate communications, scarcity of rations.

By 13th September the Salamaua campaign was over for most of the 5th Division. In a signal to Herring that day Milford said:

Opposition now appears to have dwindled with rear elements numbering perhaps 250 and withdrawing north towards Lae. . . . My intention is to press on with one battalion with all speed to the Markham in order to destroy any of his troops still south of Lae and to mop up by degrees small parties cut off or left behind.

The only active role, apart from mopping-up, was now allotted to the 29th Brigade, which would provide one battalion for the pursuit up the coast. As the 15th Battalion had been in action for a shorter period than the 42nd and 47th, Monaghan gave it the task.

While the 29th Brigade was still technically the forward brigade the 15th Brigade thankfully accepted its role of divisional reserve. Except for the 15th Battalion, the men of both brigades luxuriated in hot meals, adequate medical treatment, rest, swimming and sunbathing. On the night of the 26th-27th the 2/7th Battalion moved to Milne Bay by barge on its way to Australia. The 2/3rd Independent Company joined it there and both sailed on 29th September.

---

[9] As mentioned, Colonel Smith had asked for carrier pigeons but the request had not been granted. Later in the war pigeons were used to good effect.

Throughout the period from 30th June when it began operations until 13th September the 15th Brigade lost 112 killed, 346 wounded and 12 missing.[1] In the same period 762 Japanese were actually killed by the brigade (287 by the Independent Company, 245 by the 58th/59th, 222 by the 2/7th and 8 by "D" Company of the 24th), not counting estimates for enemy wounded and casualties caused by supporting arms. The staff of the 3rd Division estimated the number of Japanese killed from April to August as 2,722 and the total casualties as about 8,100. The fighting qualities, the skill and the dogged stamina of the three Australian brigades had enabled the victory to be won.[2]

On 13th September the 2/7th Battalion had only 18 officers and 376 men, the 58th/59th 18 officers and 437 men, the 42nd 34 and 560, the 47th 30 and 591, and the 15th 31 and 569.[3] The 2/3rd Independent Company showed most markedly the wastage in officer casualties. A small unit, it had lost since it entered the Wau campaign 9 officers killed or died of wounds and another 6 wounded badly enough not to be able to rejoin the unit.

At one stage Salamaua was destined to become a big Allied base after its capture. When Herring arrived at Milford's headquarters on 14th September, however, one look at the insanitary shell of a township with its poor airfield and near-by swamp was enough for him to give a brief instruction to "wipe it" as a base. This discarded ruin, called by the Americans camped near the isthmus "a filthy, rat-ridden, pestilential hole", was the same Salamaua which had had something of a jewel-like radiance for the Allied troops as it lay below them throughout the long and weary months of the bitter campaign among the ridges. On 16th September Padre Sherwin[4] hoisted the Australian flag which was taken from Salamaua by the New Guinea Volunteer Rifles when the Japanese captured Salamaua in 1942. The troops could not get away from Salamaua quickly

---

[1] The unit casualties were:

	Killed	Wounded	Missing
2/7th Battalion	34	124	1
58th/59th Battalion	54	142	10
2/3rd Independent Company	20	69	—
"D" Company, 24th Battalion	4	11	1

[2] From 23rd April until 13th September the units of the 3rd and 5th Divisions had suffered casualties as follows:

	Killed		Wounded	
	Offrs	OR's	Offrs	OR's
17th Brigade				
2/5th Battalion	—	34	9	86
2/6th Battalion	1	37	6	88
2/7th Battalion	7	56	12	153
15th Brigade				
58th/59th Battalion	6	65	11	129
2/3rd Independent Company	6	31	2	74
24th Battalion	4	20	1	14
29th Brigade				
15th Battalion	1	10	4	46
42nd Battalion	2	27	2	51
47th Battalion	4	32	5	47
Papuan Infantry Battalion	1	7	—	17
Artillery	—	7	1	13
Engineers	—	—	2	3

From 29th June until 12th September the I/162nd Battalion lost 39 killed and 147 wounded; the II/162nd 22 and 128; the III/162nd 20 and 121.

[3] The War Establishment was 32 officers and 745 men.

[4] Chaplain Rev V. H. G. Sherwin, NGX433. NGVR and 2/7 Bn. Church of England clergyman; of Wau, NG; b. Gosport, Hants, England, 29 May 1895.

enough. It had served its purpose as a magnet drawing enemy troops from Lae.

"The capture of Salamaua marks the end of a campaign of 7 months duration," wrote General Herring on 13th September in a special order of the day when congratulating the 5th Division on its "magnificent job" in outfighting the enemy despite "difficult terrain and trying conditions". Herring addressed his message "primarily to all of you who have borne the heat and burden of the fighting, to the infantry first and foremost", but he did not forget the gunners, the sappers, the signallers, the medical services, the air force, and those who maintained the fighting troops.

General Adachi said after the war that after withdrawing from the Mount Tambu-Komiatum area, the Japanese formed a new line from Charlie Hill to the coast which was held until 4th September. Adachi and Nakano planned that, should it prove impossible to hold this line, they would shorten their defences by withdrawing to the north side of the Francisco River, where they would make a last stand. After the landing of the 9th Australian Division, however, Adachi realised that it would be impossible for his *51st Division* to hold Salamaua any longer; and he accordingly ordered Nakano to withdraw to Kiari on the north coast of New Guinea.

General Nakano considered two courses: to withdraw through the Markham and Ramu Valleys to Bogadjim or through the Finisterres to Kiari. He chose the mountain route because it offered concealment from air attack. The naval troops were to move first and then the army.

Until 4th September Nakano intended to defend Salamaua. On that date Takeuchi issued an order stating: "The main body of the Salamaua Peninsula unit will at once build and strengthen positions." From prisoners of war and captured documents, however, Allied Intelligence organisations learnt that 73 barge loads were allocated for the evacuation of the *51st Division* and the battalions of the *20th* and *41st Divisions* helping it. (These had been reinforced in August by 2,000 troops of the *115th Regiment* and *14th Field Artillery Regiment* from New Britain.) Each barge could carry 80 men. The size of the force evacuated by sea, starting on the 6th, could therefore be about 5,800. According to a prisoner, 5,000 went to Lae by barge just before the fall of Salamaua and 600 naval troops went by submarine to Rabaul. Another prisoner was a member of the rearguard, numbering somewhere between 50 and 250, which marched up the coast towards Lae.

CHAPTER 12

ASSAULT ON LAE AND NADZAB

ON the last day of August the commanders of the three battalions of the 20th Brigade, and of the 2/23rd Battalion which would also be under Brigadier Windeyer's command, issued their orders for the landing east of Lae, but, in the interests of secrecy, without specifying where the landing would take place. The 2/13th Battalion would land at and capture "Yellow Beach" on the right flank; the 2/15th Battalion would capture the right-hand half of the main landing beach—"Red Beach"; the 2/17th Battalion would capture the left-hand half; and the 2/23rd Battalion would land on Red Beach immediately after the other two and lead the advance to the west. Soon after landing, the 2/13th and 2/15th would send patrols to link up between Red and Yellow Beaches, while the 20th Brigade would proceed to capture their first, second and third objectives, known as "Bardia", "Tobruk" and "Benghazi".

On 1st September two battalions of the 26th Brigade—the 2/24th and 2/48th—were loaded into six L.S.T's together with bulk stores. Next morning reveille for Windeyer's battalions was at 5 a.m. Two hours later they moved in boat groups to Stringer Beach where all loading took place. It rained as the troops were leaving Milne Bay. "Standing there on the beach we must have looked like mobile sponges," wrote a diarist. A newspaper correspondent, describing the embarkation, wrote:

> Roads and tracks were swarming with green shirts. They resembled nothing so much as the long lines of chlorophyll-coloured ants that march up and around the trees of the rain-forests of New Guinea and North Australia. Packs that bristled with jungle knives, axes, and spades; MT bashing the mud under loads of ammo and HE, guns and gear, everything from a bullet to a bulldozer, it was all there, a perfect picture of the battle eve.[2]

At 9.30 a.m. eighteen L.C.I's were ready to embark the battalions and divisional headquarters. As each landing craft approached the shore the rain-soaked green-clad assemblage of troops reshuffled into another pattern. Webbing was slung on, then haversacks and blanket rolls. The usual badinage ensued and then the voice of authority took over and the troops detailed to travel in each approaching craft moved forward and embarked.

The 560 men comprising the two forward companies of the battalions which would form the first wave of the assault landing on both beaches then embarked on barges which would take them to the four A.P.D's. "We trundled aboard, somewhat in the fashion of overloaded donkeys, carefully picking our way lest our feet slip," wrote one participant. The assaulting troops were now told where they were going, and the hitherto-anonymous Red and Yellow Beaches of their training landings and the sand models became pinpointed as specific beaches east of Lae.

---

[2] A. Dawes, *Soldier Superb* (1943), p. 36.

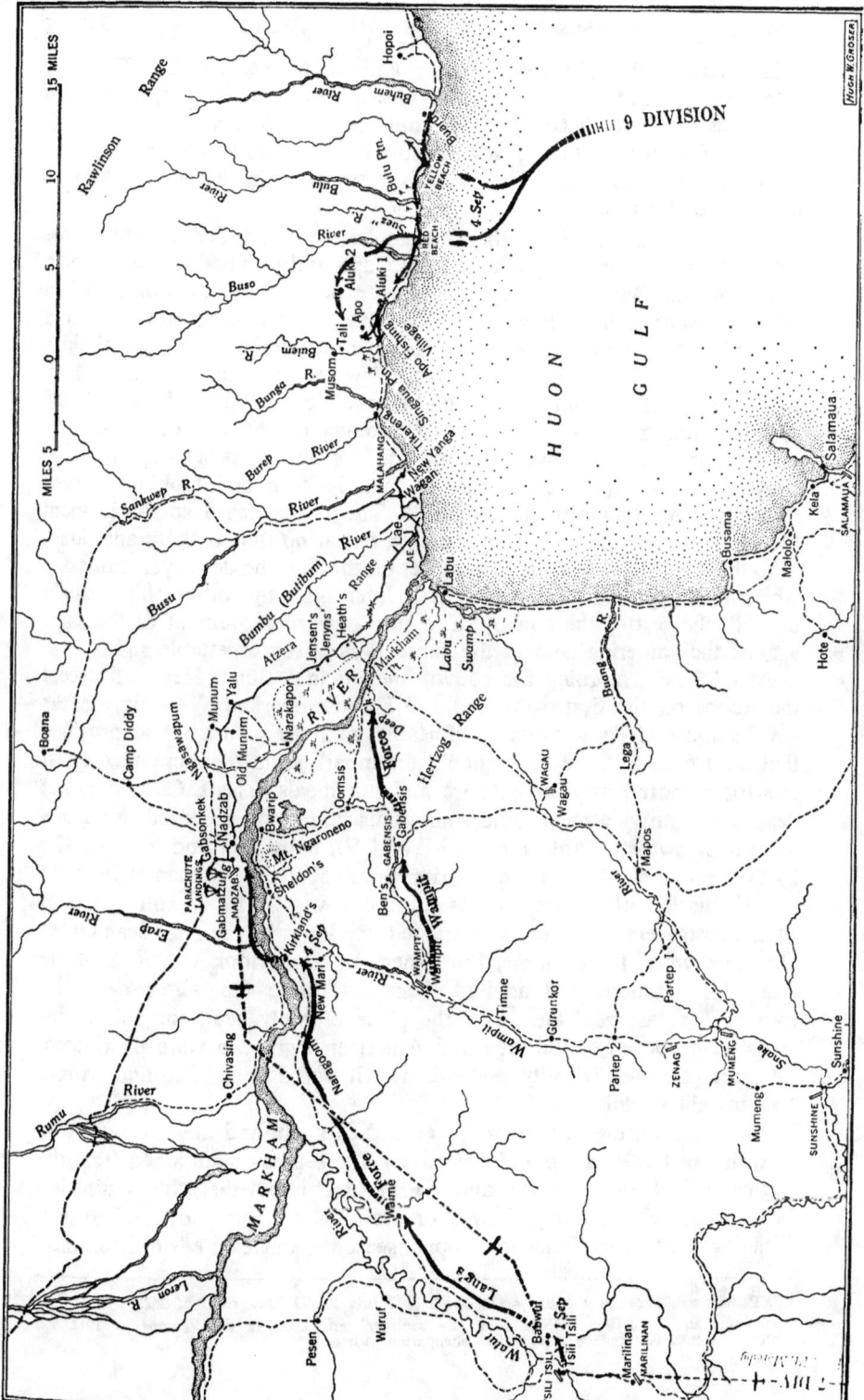

The advance on Lae-Nadzab, 1st to 5th September

Engineers and artillerymen mainly embarked on three L.C.T's. Bulk stores were loaded on 7 L.C.T's as well as the 6 L.S.T's carrying the two battalions of the 26th Brigade. The bulk tonnage loaded on each L.S.T. weighed 84 tons, including vehicles on the tank deck and anti-aircraft guns on the upper deck. The L.C.T's were each loaded with 120 tons of bulk stores and ammunition.

At 1 p.m. on 2nd September the convoy, in an order inverse to the speed of its components, rounded East Cape and steamed up the Papuan coast towards Buna and Morobe. "Never before had the Solomon Sea witnessed such a fleet; few waters had ever seen one so strange to old seamen's eyes," wrote the American naval historian.[3] "Long lines of ships formed a formidable but inspiring sight," wrote the diarist of the 2/13th Battalion, "giving complete feeling of confidence." The diarist of the 2/48th Battalion wrote: "All were heartened by the size of the convoy as destroyer after destroyer took up the position of protecting the huge convoy of the 9th Aust Div. Every man is keen and looking forward to the first meeting with the Japanese. They have heard so much about the enemy's methods—and they wonder, but at no time is there any doubt as to the result." An hour before sunset on the 2nd the destroyer-transports which had departed from Milne Bay later than the other ships caught up with the rest of the convoy. The sure onward movement of the ships against the gathering gold of the sunset was an unforgettable sight.

At 6.30 next morning the convoy moved into Buna. Here, all except the troops on the destroyers and L.S.T's disembarked. Voyaging in the L.C.I's and L.C.T's was not comfortable, and the planners had provided that the troops in these craft should disembark from their cramped quarters for a short period of exercise and hot meals. The L.C.I's were not designed to provide meals, and some units had come prepared to supplement their own standard rations—M. and V., bully beef and biscuits. The 2/23rd Battalion, for instance, had spent £160 from regimental funds to provide itself with canteen goods for the voyage. The assaulting troops on the destroyers, however, were treated like kings by the American crews. On the *Gilmer*, for example, the American cooks took one look at the Australians' rations and advised them to "dump the whole damn lot overside". Roast beef then took the place of bully beef; the ship's canteens were opened to the men and American cigarettes were distributed. "A more generous, friendly, goddam crew it would be hard to find," wrote an Australian soldier.

By 3 p.m. on the 3rd all troops embarked again and now all were told of their exact destination and objectives. The secrecy maintained from the beginning had been excellent and the furphies[4] about the 9th's destination being Salamaua, Madang, Wewak or even Rabaul were now laid to rest. Heading north from Buna the troops, seasoned but excited, cleaned their

---

[3] S. E. Morison, *Breaking the Bismarcks Barrier, 22 July 1942-1 May 1944*, p. 262.
[4] Rumours; the word was derived from the sanitary carts used in AIF camps in 1914 and later, and manufactured by Furphy, of Shepparton, Victoria.

weapons and repacked their gear, while maps of the area east of Lae were issued to officers and sergeants.

Two hours after dark the convoy was joined off Kakari Point by some 50 craft carrying the Shore Battalion of the 532nd E.B.S.R., commanded during the actual landing by Lieut-Colonel E. D. Brockett, which would provide amphibian scouts to land with the first wave of infantry, erect markers on both Red and Yellow Beaches and make a beach reconnaissance.

As the convoy steamed steadily north, the thoughts of this well trained and superbly fit division of Australians went crowding back to a similar night 28 years ago when another division of Australians was steaming towards a hostile shore. The simple words written by a private soldier typified the thoughts shared by all: "Not since our forefathers landed at Gallipoli had an Australian force made an opposed landing by sea. Could we the 2nd A.I.F. uphold the gallantry shown by those men?"

During this night men gathered on the decks of the destroyers to yarn and pass the wakeful hours sitting in groups, leaning over the rails or "spine bashing" (lying down). In the L.C.I's the excited anticipation of what the morrow would bring prevented many men from sleeping and there was much talk and laughter in the hot and sweaty holds. Although intercept wireless had picked up an enemy reconnaissance plane reporting the presence of the convoy in the Buna area, the voyage through the night to the landing beaches was uneventful. Towards the end of the voyage the headquarters ship *Conyngham* with Admiral Barbey and General Wootten aboard left the convoy and steamed ahead to identify the beaches. Difficulties expected in landing on the correct beaches during darkness had been the main reason why Barbey had considered impracticable Wootten's request to approach during darkness and land at dawn (5.15 a.m.); and had substituted a pre-landing naval bombardment to make up for lack of surprise.

Reveille on the 4th was at 4.30, when the assault troops were given hot tea or coffee and a meal. The first glimmerings of dawn revealed the convoy sailing west along the south coast of the Huon Peninsula. It was soon apparent to the infantry that the navy had not missed the mark. Soon after first light, about 5.50, *Conyngham* identified the beaches. "Clumps of coconut palms and a river bend were the main aids to identification," wrote Barbey later.[5]

Most of the soldiers in the destroyers were on deck when the dim outline of the hostile shore appeared in the pre-dawn. Even the old campaigners were suddenly quiet and the atmosphere was tense. Half an hour before the landing the ships' bells or horns sounded a warning to get ready and all troops were ordered below. The horns continued and slightly frayed the nerves of some until the 9th Division's own dog howl competed with the horns and relieved the tension. The assaulting waves donned their equipment and gave a final check to their weapons. Loaded as they were, there was scarcely room for them to move when they were standing

---
[5] Commander Seventh Amphibious Force, Report on Lae Operation.

waiting in the holds shoulder to shoulder with blanket rolls protruding from around the packs.

"Away the landing force" came the order through the amplifiers, and the assaulting troops climbed up the companion-ways, out from the murk and stench of the holds into the fresh air and grey light of dawn. Here the disciplined assembly waited while the destroyers changed course at 6.15 a.m. and made at full speed for the shore. Three minutes later two destroyers were in position off each beach and lowered their landing barges (eight L.C.P's to each beach), into which the troops clambered down cargo nets.

Five destroyers manoeuvred into position and at 6.19 began shelling the jungle-fringed beaches from two miles and a half out to sea. One soldier, going into action for the first time, asked an old soldier what the strange smell was. "Just cordite from the shells," replied the veteran, "you'll get used to that before long."

The bombardment consisted of dispersed fire. Wootten had felt all along that a swipe of fire like this would be more damaging to Japanese morale than a series of concentrations. During this bombardment the barges of the first assaulting waves, each carrying about 30 men, formed into line and roared off towards the beaches. In the barges the platoon commanders ordered the fixing of bayonets and the cold steel clipped on with an aggressive sound. Overhead the shells of the naval bombardment screamed and then thudded and exploded along the green fringe of the jungle. When there was no return fire from the shore many who had been crouching low beneath the gunwales gazing at the outline of their bayonets against the pale sky raised their heads to watch the shelling.

The naval bombardment ceased at 6.25 a.m. when the landing barges were 1,200 yards from the shore. As the barges revved their engines and moved towards the shore the machine-guns on each barge raked the jungle fringe. Then the barges bumped the shore and lowered their ramps. Down them rushed the green-clad men in single file. At the water's edge they spread into line and raced across the narrow strip of sand for the jungle's fringe.

From the deck of an L.C.I. in the third wave Brigadier Windeyer watched the scene and prepared to land 15 minutes after the assaulting troops. "Distinguished both as a scholar and a soldier—a combination not uncommon in the history of the Australian Army,"[6] Windeyer had risen to command the Sydney University Regiment by 1937, and in 1940 had been given the task of forming and commanding the 2/48th (South Australian) Battalion. He had led the battalion in the siege of Tobruk, and, in January 1942, had been appointed to command the 20th Brigade which he had led at El Alamein.

Describing the landing on Yellow Beach, the diarist of the 2/13th Battalion wrote:

> B and C Coys have been lowered in their barges from the A.P.D's and are heading off in perfect line and formation for the shore. Some miles to the west the

---
[6] "New Divisional Commanders", in *Stand To*, July 1950.

barges for Red mission appear to be the same distance from the shore as our barges. L.C.I's have spread out into their landing formation approximately 1,500 yards offshore and moving slowly in. First wave hits the far shore in correct formation and place. The gun crews on the barges rake the fringe of the jungle with fire a few seconds before landing. B and C Coys encounter no enemy opposition and move off their barges to their allotted tasks very quickly.

These leading troops of the 2/13th landed one minute after H-hour (6.30 a.m.). The leading troops of the 2/15th and 2/17th Battalions landed one minute later, and on this beach, too, there was no opposition. The battalions quickly moved off the beach towards their first objectives inland. Three minutes after landing with the first wave the American shore battalion erected beach markers on both beaches to guide the later waves. The assault troops from the A.P.D's were followed at approximately 15-minute intervals by waves of L.C.I's (15 to Red Beach and 3 to Yellow Beach), which landed 3,780 troops.

Half an hour after the initial landing, L.C.T's (3 on Red Beach and 2 on Yellow) began unloading Australian artillery and engineers. Five minutes later the fifth wave, comprising 7 L.C.I's, approached Red Beach. Suddenly, when these trim craft were about 100 yards from the shore, 6 Japanese fighters followed by 3 bombers, flying at 1,500 feet, strafed and bombed the L.C.I's, which had dropped their stern anchors. The bombers dropped 12 bombs, one of which exploded on the

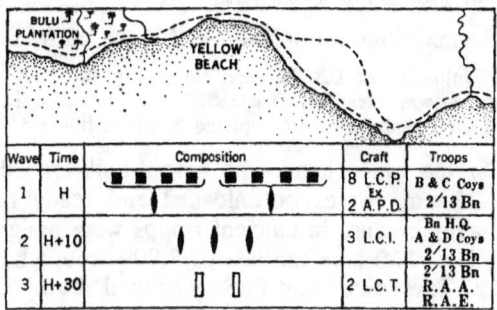

deck of *LCI-339* just forward of the bridge, killing the commander of the 2/23rd Battalion, Lieut-Colonel Wall,[7] a company commander, Captain Reid,[8] and 5 men, and wounding 28 including 6 officers. *LCI-341* received a near miss which blew a large hole in the ship's side and flooded two compartments. The L.C.I's were so crowded that men were unable to obey their first impulse and throw themselves flat, but could only crouch and hope for the best.

The captain of *LCI-341*, finding his ship listing to port because of the gaping hole through which the water was pouring, shouted "Every man to starboard." Under their weight the ship gradually righted itself and beached without further trouble. By the skilful handling and determination of Ensign James M. Tidball, *LCI-339* landed on time and disembarked the troops. Tidball radioed the flotilla commander, who ordered him to abandon ship. The crippled L.C.I. remained on the beach for a week, a target for Japanese airmen, before it was towed clear, and then it drifted on to a reef.

After the excitement of the fifth wave the American shore battalion, about 1,060 men, and its equipment were landed on Red Beach from L.C.V's, L.C.M's, and L.C.T's. From the first of the landing craft, tractors, road graders, wire mesh to make passable roads over sand and swamp, and power-driven saws to fell palm trees for corduroying roads, were unloaded. The unloading parties cleared stores from Red Beach and established dumps inland, while Australian and American engineers pushed the roads ahead.

At 8.14 a.m. the six L.S.T's began to unload. Describing the scene, the historian of the 2 E.S.B. wrote:

> As these ponderous hulks drove to the beach even the longshoremen working frantically in their unloading of the smaller craft stopped to view these monsters as they magically opened their bows and dropped immense ramps slowly to the edge of the surf. . . . Ton after ton of equipment was unloaded and, interspersed with the vehicles and materiel, companies of infantry filed out while artillerymen rode guns drawn by tractors.[9]

Commending the unloading of these craft, Barbey wrote later:

> Unloading of L.S.T's, each containing 400 men, 35 vehicles and 80 tons of bulk stores, was excellent. One L.S.T. was unloaded in 1 hour 42 minutes. Unloading of the remainder was completed within 2 hours 15 minutes.[1]

On the other hand, the seven bulk-loaded L.C.T's, which landed at 8.25 a.m., were not unloaded and ready to withdraw until 2.30 p.m., mainly because insufficient troops were assigned for unloading.

By 10.30 a.m. the last of 7,800 troops had landed, and when the last L.C.T. retracted and Barbey headed south, 1,500 tons of stores had been beached. Most of the landing craft of the 2 E.S.B., when unloaded, had

---

[7] Lt-Col R. E. Wall, ED, VX48254. 2/23 Bn (CO 1942-43). Security officer, insurance company; of Ivanhoe, Vic; b. Fitzroy, Vic, 27 May 1905. Killed in action 4 Sep 1943.
[8] Capt R. K. Reid, MC, VX46713; 2/23 Bn. Schoolteacher; of Terang, Vic; b. Malvern, Vic, 7 Jun 1916. Killed in action 4 Sep 1943.
[9] *History of Second Engineer Special Brigade*, p. 47.
[1] Seventh Amphibious Force report.

immediately retracted from the beach and set off to Morobe for extra supplies. About twenty, however, remained on the beach for use in emergencies and for moving supplies up and down the beach.

Ashore the infantry were expanding the beach-heads without opposition. In spite of the failure of wireless sets to function efficiently—the failures included a breakdown in communications between Wootten and Barbey—the battalions had been so well briefed and rehearsed that they pressed towards their objectives without hesitation.

On Yellow Beach, Lieut-Colonel Colvin's[2] companies of the 2/13th quickly moved inland and along the beaches. One patrol found signs at the southern end of the Bulu Plantation that about thirty Japanese had recently fled towards the hills. There were no further recent signs of the enemy, and at 2 p.m. patrols of the 2/13th and 2/15th met at an unnamed river known as Suez between the Bulu River and Red Beach. During the afternoon patrols advanced north and east without opposition. Everywhere the natives had departed from their villages, leaving their food and belongings and their fires burning. Two natives, captured later in the afternoon, stated that

Initial objectives of the 9th Division, 4th September

the only Japanese in the area had been at Ted's Point. The natives were told to send word to the villagers who had gone bush that they should return to their villages and bring some boys to headquarters in the morning to work.

From the main beach three miles to the west equally rapid progress, with no opposition, had been made. The 2/15th and 2/17th advanced through thick rain forest, mangroves and some patches of kunai as they quickly reached their objectives. While Lieut-Colonel Grace's[3] 2/15th Battalion protected the beach-head Lieut-Colonel Simpson's[4] 2/17th at 9 a.m. began to advance towards the Buso River in two columns. Two companies under Major Broadbent[5] advanced north and then west across the Buso to an area north of Aluki 2 and about four miles north of

---

[2] Lt-Col G. E. Colvin, DSO, ED, NX12217. 2/13 Bn (CO 1942-45). Manager; of Roseville, NSW; b. Melbourne, 22 Apr 1903.

[3] Col C. H. Grace, DSO, ED, NX457. HQ 7 Div 1940-41; 2/15 Bn (CO 1943-45). Office manager; of Sydney; b. Sydney, 17 Jul 1909.

[4] Maj-Gen N. W. Simpson, CBE, DSO, ED, NX12221. DAAG 7 Div 1941-42; CO 2/17 Bn 1942-44, 2/43 Bn 1944-45; Comd 29 Bde 1945, 23 Bde 1945-46. Bank officer; of Cremorne, NSW; b. Sydney, 22 Feb 1907.

[5] Brig J. R. Broadbent, DSO, ED, NX12225. 2/17 Bn (CO 1944-46). Solicitor; of Mosman, NSW; b. Manly, NSW, 24 Jun 1914.

the coast. The other companies were led by Simpson north-west through trackless and scorching kunai and dense rain forest across the Buso to a position about 1,000 yards east of Aluki 1.

Wootten was most anxious to speed the advance towards Lae to prevent the Japanese from preparing organised resistance east of the Busu River, particularly in the Singaua Plantation where there were excellent defensive positions. Because the 2/17th was farthest west on 4th September, Wootten placed it under the command of the 26th Brigade, whose task was to pass through the 20th Brigade and advance on Lae. Behind the 2/17th, the 2/24th and the 2/23rd moved through the hot coastal plain towards the Buso. By last light they had crossed the river and moved a short distance along the coast.

While the three leading battalions settled down for the night with sentries and standing patrols watching alertly to the west, General Wootten informed Brigadier Windeyer, and Brigadier Whitehead[6] of the 26th Brigade, of the plan for the 5th. Whitehead would secure a line from Tali in the north to the western side of Singaua Plantation by a double advance, along the coast and inland from Aluki 2 to the Musom-Tali area. The 2/17th Battalion would lead the advance to the Buiem River where the battalions of the 26th Brigade would pass through.

Japanese aircraft became active late in the afternoon. At 4.30 p.m. 4 bombers escorted by fighters attacked Yellow Beach without success. Over Red Beach about 5 p.m. 9 Japanese aircraft appeared, set fire to an ammunition dump, did further damage to the two stranded L.C.I's and inflicted 14 casualties on the American shore battalion. The Japanese commander in Lae meanwhile had asked Rabaul for help and had begun establishing defensive positions along some of the river banks east of Lae. At Rabaul General Imamura, the commander of the *Eighth Area Army*, sent 80 aircraft to help, but they were delayed by fog over New Britain. At 1 p.m. the radar of the destroyer *Reid*, stationed off Finschhafen with its fighter-director team on board, picked up three large groups of aircraft estimated at about 70 flying from New Britain. *Reid* directed 48 Lightnings to the scene, and 23 Japanese aircraft were believed to have been shot down for the loss of two Lightnings. *Reid*, which had already done such an invaluable job, shot down one of three planes which attacked her.

Although the air force provided an air umbrella over the convoys going to and coming from Red Beach, it could not prevent all enemy aircraft from breaking through towards Morobe. Four dive bombers attacked the destroyers guarding the retiring convoy, scoring near misses on two, including *Conyngham*. At 2 p.m., when the six L.S.T's of the second landing group were 25 miles off Cape Ward Hunt, Japanese torpedo and dive bombers attacked. Six dive bombers attacked *LST-473* and scored two

---

[6] Brig D. A. Whitehead, CBE, DSO, MC, ED, NX376. (1st AIF: CO 23 MG Coy 1917-18.) CO 2/2 MG Bn 1940-42, 2/32 Bn 1942; Comd 26 Bde 1942-45. Engineer; of Sydney; b. Leith, Scotland, 30 Sep 1896.

hits and two near misses. Eight Americans were killed and 11 Americans and 26 Australians wounded. *LST-471* was attacked by two torpedo bombers. One torpedo hit the port side, wrecking the ship's stern, killing 43 troops and sailors, and wounding 30. Among the casualties were 34 killed or missing and 7 wounded from the 2/4th Independent Company —a calamitous loss for a small unit. A vivid description of this attack was written by a man in a company of the 2/2nd Machine Gun Battalion, who was on *LST-471*:

1355. Some planes sighted very high and right in the sun. They're probably ours. No, they're peeling off. General alarm sounded; all men below deck. All AA opens up, with ship zig-zagging violently. With a shrill whine . . . dive bombers dive on the convoy with the sun behind them. In the distance two large explosions occur on the water, followed by clouds of black smoke; [it] appears as though our fighters have got in amongst them. The leading plane is now flattening out at about 300 feet, and you can see the red circles on the wing tips. The bombs are falling. . . . They are not going for our ship but further astern. Four bombs are falling directly down on *473*. The first two strike the water very close and the next two hit on the stern, with violent explosion and smoke can now be seen rising from her. Poor blighters—wonder what their casualties are? The other dive bombers miss the remaining L.S.T's, but bracket a little sub-chaser. She disappears behind columns of water and spray, but comes through unscathed. Spotters have now reported bombers only about 100 feet off the water on the starboard beam, and all guns open up on them as they approach. One is coming straight for this ship only 50 feet above the water. A torpedo seems to float down to the water and hits with a splash. The aircraft seems to rise a little and is just about on us. We are all expecting to be raked with MG fire but none comes. The AA fire seems to be hitting her everywhere, and as she roars over the L.S.T. the port wing dips slightly, exposing the belly. Every gun is on her and she just banks over on the starboard wing and hits the water 100 yards off the starboard beam of the ship, falling to pieces. . . . Just at this moment there is a terrific explosion . . . and the L.S.T. lurches violently, throwing everyone off their feet. We are hit! . . . Wounded are now staggering up from the after hatchways, covered in blood. Our mess orderlies, who had been in the kitchen, come out looking like niggers, and covered with white sticky dough, and such things as beetroot slices plastered about them. . . . An inspection of the crew's quarters aft revealed a most ghastly sight. All lights had been extinguished by the explosion, and in the pitch blackness, with the air like a furnace from escaping steam, the inspection party kept tripping over dead and wounded, who were quickly brought up on deck. On opening the bulkhead door a huge hole was seen in the stern of the ship, with the sea pouring in. The magazine had gone up when the torpedo hit. This deck was a mass of twisted, jagged steel plates strewn all around with most shockingly mutilated bodies and human remains. . . . The work of the ship's medical officer was beyond praise. He worked for hours on end in the sweltering heat, doing amputations, blood transfusions, and operations of all kinds, assisted only by medical orderlies.

The four remaining L.S.T's continued to Red Beach where they arrived at 11 p.m. The commanders of the two crippled L.S.T's, Lieutenants Rowland W. Dillard (*473*) and George L. Cory (*471*), were able to keep their craft afloat until L.S.T's *452* and *458*, returning from Red Beach, were diverted to their assistance and took them in tow. By what Barbey termed "excellent seamanship" the four L.S.T's reached Morobe where the cargoes and troops were transferred to the two undamaged L.S.T's, which waited to join the third landing group.

On the 5th the advance continued to east and west with no opposition from the enemy, though the going was very heavy. From Yellow Beach the 2/13th Battalion occupied Buaru. Leading the advance to the west, Simpson's southern column, when west of Aluki 1, found a track which was wet and boggy, but even so was infinitely better than the steaming kunai and jungle. Broadbent's northern column had lost communication with Simpson on the previous day when its wireless set had disappeared in the Buso and when the telephone line had been broken in several places by troops moving along the narrow track. A patrol, however, made contact with the southern column at Apo in the mid-afternoon. Broadbent reached the Buiem River near Tali and Simpson advanced through Apo Fishing Village to a position near the eastern end of the Singaua Plantation.

Behind the 2/17th came the 2/23rd and 2/24th following the 2/17th's signal wire. As the battalions were becoming mixed, Lieut-Colonel Gillespie[7] of the 2/24th let Major McRae[8] of the 2/23rd (now in command of the battalion) pass through and bivouacked south of Apo, where Whitehead had placed his headquarters. Late in the day the 2/23rd advanced cautiously from Apo past the 2/17th and along the beach to a position just west of the Buiem. Because of the difficult and boggy track the battalion had been unable to reach the Burep River as it had hoped. McRae therefore decided to send a small standing patrol forward to the mouth of the Burep while his three companies dug in west of the Buiem (the fourth having moved north to take over from Broadbent).

After a tiring march through the jungle all day Sergeant Lawrie's[9] platoon set out at dusk to establish a standing patrol at the mouth of the Busu River—about 4,000 yards west along the coast. At 2 o'clock in the morning a well-equipped company of about 140 Japanese passed by Lawrie's outpost heading east—to engage the 9th Division. Lawrie attempted to warn the battalion, but found that his wireless set would not work. The Japanese were now occupying his return route but it was imperative to send back a warning and Corporal Fairlie[1] and Lance-Corporal Schram[2] volunteered to take a message back. Stripping themselves of all arms and equipment, and accepting the grave risk of approaching their own battalion unexpectedly in darkness, the two men hurried east ahead of the enemy. To evade detection they waded in the sea for some time. Weary but determined, and still ahead of the enemy, they arrived at the 2/23rd's position in Singaua Plantation at 4.30 a.m. and gave the alarm.

---

[7] Lt-Col A. B. Gillespie, QX6408. 2/28 and 2/32 Bns; CO 2/24 Bn 1943-45. Oil company representative; of Gordonvale, Qld; b. Perth, 12 Jun 1904.

[8] Lt-Col B. H. McRae, VX8791; 2/23 Bn (CO Sep-Oct 1943). Bank officer; of Werribee, Vic; b. Bairnsdale, Vic, 9 Apr 1916.

[9] Lt D. C. Lawrie, DCM, VX7410. 2/5 and 2/23 Bns. Stockman and regular soldier; b. Pialba, Qld, 22 Nov 1917.

[1] Cpl D. J. Fairlie, MM, VX46231; 2/23 Bn. Labourer; of Holbrook, NSW; b. Holbrook, 19 Feb 1906.

[2] Cpl A. Schram, MM, VX20656; 2/23 Bn. Carpenter; of Lorne, Vic; b. Geelong, Vic, 22 Aug 1916.

Behind the advance of the infantry the engineers bulldozed a track from the Buso to Aluki, fit for three-tonners as well as jeeps, although it was understood that heavy rain would make the track impassable. After the landing of the second group there were 1,800 tons of stores in the area—enough for twenty days.

Back in Buna, now a very busy port full of landing craft and ships going and coming from the beaches, General Herring watched the 24th Brigade embarking on twenty L.C.I's at 8 a.m. on 5th September. Five L.S.T's, also proceeding towards Red Beach, were joined at Morobe by two more.

Soon after 11 p.m. the first wave of the 24th Brigade began to disembark. An hour later the second wave moved towards the shore. Unloading at night on to a tiny congested strip of beach was naturally confusing and difficult, but it was probably unjust for one battalion diarist to write of "scenes of indescribable confusion and brigade spread over half the countryside".[3] It was not long before the battalions had been led by their guides, who had accompanied the earlier waves, to assembly areas about 1,000 yards inland.

That night General Wootten issued his orders for the 6th. The 26th Brigade would secure crossings over the Busu from the mouth northward and would reconnoitre as far north as the kunda bridge; Brigadier Evans'[4] 24th Brigade would advance west and take over the coastal sector from the 26th Brigade, which would then "passage" to the north. Down on the coast McRae ordered Captain Dudley's[5] company to advance at first light along the track already taken by Lawrie's platoon and secure the track up to the Busu.

At the end of August there was much activity at Port Moresby and Tsili Tsili as General Vasey made his final preparations for the assault on Nadzab. Preparations were afoot for Lieut-Colonel Lang's group of 602 pioneers, 126 engineers, and 760 native carriers to leave Tsili Tsili on 2nd September and march for three days, over Major Kidd's route, to Kirkland's Dump. A small advanced party under Captain Dunphy of the 2/6th Field Company would set out on 30th August to improve the track. A third party, consisting of 90 engineers and 60 pioneers, would embark in Lieutenant Wegg's[6] 20 folding boats at Tsili Tsili on 4th September; 10 would sail by night from the junction of the Watut and the Markham Rivers to Kirkland's Dump where they would be met by

---

[3] Barbey wrote in his report: "Subsequent to the initial unloading on the morning of D-day all beaching and unloading was done at night. The rate of unloading was generally unsatisfactory. One cause was undoubtedly intermittent bombing of the beaches by enemy aircraft. . . . The need for supplies on the beach must be balanced with the period of exposure to air attack en route to and from the beach during daylight hours. Three hours appears to be the maximum time which LST's and LCT's should be permitted to remain on the beach."

[4] Brig B. Evans, DSO, ED, VX47819. CO 2/23 Bn 1940-42; Comd 24 Bde 1942-43; CI LHQ Tactical School 1943-45. Lord Mayor of Melbourne since 1959. Architect; of Melbourne; b. Manchester, England, 13 May 1905.

[5] Maj J. Dudley, VX5087. 2/6 and 2/23 Bns. Schoolteacher; of Sebastopol, Vic; b. Sebastopol, 25 Nov 1906.

[6] Lt C. H. Wegg, NX91233; 2/6 Fd Coy. Asst Shire Engineer; of Warren, NSW; b. Benoni, Transvaal, South Africa, 2 Apr 1914.

Lang's force. The remaining 10 would leave the river junction at H-hour on Z-day, when Lang's force would begin to cross the Markham.[7]

In Port Moresby the American paratroops were ready and eager. For eight months the regiment had been training for just such an operation as was now ahead. With his battalion commanders and some of his staff, Colonel Kinsler flew over the Nadzab area on 31st August. Information, maps, air photographs and the large and accurate model of the operational area kept in a big marquee by the Intelligence staff of 7th Division were closely studied, and meteorological reports were obtained to determine prevailing winds over the jump areas. These proved very accurate; they stated that the wind in the Markham Valley was peculiar in that until 11 a.m. daily, it blew down the valley and then suddenly changed and blew up the valley.

It was decided to use a formation of six planes in echelon right rear with thirty seconds between elements (Lieut-Colonel George M. Jones wrote in the 503rd's report). This formation was practised by the 54th Transport Wing on D-3, D-2 and D-1 days. As all pilots were veterans and knew each detail of the jump areas, main consideration was at this time given to the formation flying. As each battalion had a separate jump area, it was decided to fly in three battalion columns. The Fifth Bomber Command, who were to furnish our air support, and the Fifth Fighter Command, who were to furnish fighter protection and to lay smoke during the dropping, also practised their phase of the operation extensively as split timing was necessary between these two units.

At one stage it seemed that the paratroops would not have immediate artillery support. Then Lieut-Colonel Blyth of the 2/4th Field Regiment "submitted a revolutionary idea to the G.O.C. to use the new short 25-pounders in a paratroop landing".[8] The idea was accepted by Vasey and a note was sent to the three batteries calling for volunteers for an intensive physical training course, but saying no more than that. From 17th August these went through a tough course, and Blyth arranged with Kinsler for their further training with the newly-arrived parachute regiment. At the end of the course 4 officers and 30 men were selected to be placed under Kinsler's command, and on the 22nd Lieutenant Pearson,[9] of the 2/4th Field Regiment, who would lead the impromptu paratroop detachment, joined the Americans. Next day the other three officers (Lieutenants Ross,[1] Faulkner[2] and Evans[3]) and the men moved over to Kinsler's regiment where they were given specialised training by American jump-masters. When Kinsler found that the men had not volunteered as

---

[7] By 1st September 164 American inflatable rubber boats had arrived by air at Tsili Tsili to be used in the crossing if necessary. These boats were made available as a result of a recommendation by Herring to Advanced LHQ on 6th August that 200 ranger craft be provided for the 7th Division and 100 for the 9th Division.

[8] R. L. Henry, *The Story of the 2/4th Field Regiment* (1950), p. 206.

[9] Capt J. N. Pearson, MC, VX39725; 2/4 Fd Regt. Fire insurance officer; of Melbourne; b. Lindfield, NSW, 7 Oct 1920. Killed in action 1 Jul 1945.

[1] Lt F. E. H. Ross, NX138182; 2/4 Fd Regt. Regular soldier; of Wahroonga, NSW; b. Stanmore, NSW, 22 Mar 1922. Killed in action 14 Jul 1945.

[2] Capt F. A. Faulkner, VX39718; 2/4 Fd Regt. Manufacturer's representative; of Unley, SA; b. Kent Town, SA, 2 May 1914.

[3] Lt A. D. Evans, VX20423; 2/4 Fd Regt. Labourer; of Forrest, Vic; b. Geelong, Vic, 21 Jan 1916.

paratroops, he asked any man who wished to withdraw to take a pace forward. All stood still. On 30th August Vasey and Blyth watched the artillery paratroops carry out a practice jump with one of their guns at the Thirty-mile Strip. Evans and two men were injured in the jump. Lieutenant Clayton,[4] who replaced Evans, had his first jump on Z-day, an experience shared with some men who also missed the trial jump.

On 3rd September Kinsler issued his final orders. Major Britten's I Battalion and regimental headquarters would land on field "B" with the task of capturing the Nadzab airstrip, beginning work on it, and guiding the Australian pioneers and engineers to Nadzab where they would come under Kinsler's command; Lieut-Colonel Jones' II Battalion would land on field "A", capture Gabsonkek, and block all approaches from the north and north-west; and Lieut-Colonel J. J. Tolson's III Battalion would land on field "C", capture Gabmatzung, and prevent enemy penetration from the east. The artillery detachment, in four aircraft each with an American jump-master, would jump to field "F" one hour after the main landing, and establish gun positions. To create a diversion, 22 aircraft would drop dummies into the jungle south of Yalu six minutes after the authentic landing.

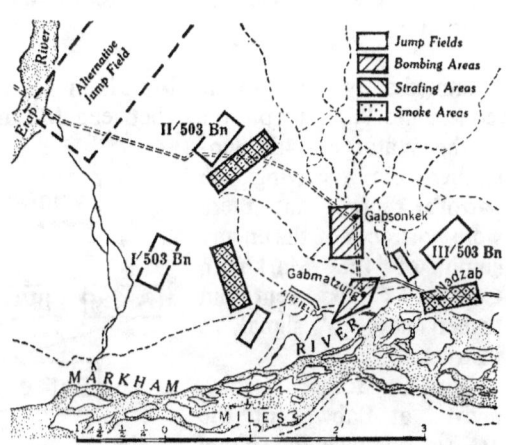

The landing of the 503rd Parachute Regiment at Nadzab, 5th September

On 31st August Brigadier Eather of the 25th Brigade issued his orders. Lieut-Colonel R. H. Marson's 2/25th Battalion would arrive in the first aircraft and would lead the advance on Heath's Plantation. Lieut-Colonel Cotton's[5] 2/33rd Battalion and Lieut-Colonel E. M. Robson's 2/31st would follow in that order and be ready to advance east. The 54th Battery would be prepared to engage targets east and north-east of Nadzab and the 2/5th Field Company would work on the Markham Valley Road.

Elaborate emplaning tables had been drawn up by Vasey's staff. Each aircraft had a serial number, and, as far as the infantry was concerned, each carried about 5,000 pounds, comprising 20 men and stores. The artillery faced complicated problems. With the meagre information that each plane-load would not exceed 5,000 pounds, it was left to the artillery-men to work out the details. Apart from their eight 25-pounders, five

---

[4] Lt A. C. Clayton, VX42706; 2/4 Fd Regt. Foreman; of Darling, Vic; b. Kooyong, Vic, 2 Sep 1910.

[5] Lt-Col T. R. W. Cotton, DSO, MC, WX299. 2/11 Bn; 2/33 Bn (CO 1943-45). Farmer; b. Dover, England, 14 Nov 1907.

jeeps and trailers, ammunition and heavy wireless gear, the gunners would travel light.

On 22nd August Vasey handed over the responsibility for emplaning the division to Brigadier F. O. Chilton of the 18th Brigade who appointed Captain Seddon,[6] his staff captain, as "chief controller". They arranged that units would assemble in "plane-loads" in company areas and be conveyed to battalion assembly areas by trucks on whose doors was marked the emplaning serial number of the occupants. As the loaded trucks arrived at the marshalling park they would be met by Seddon's staff, who would send them forward to airfield assembly areas. At the airfields they would be met by emplaning officers, who would send the trucks to individual dispersal bays for loading onto aircraft, as shown in the accompanying diagram.

Immediately south of the Markham all was in readiness. At Vasey's request the Papuans patrolled between Mount Ngaroneno and the mouth of the Watut on 4th September. On receiving the patrol's report that there were no traces of the enemy south of the Markham, Captain Chalk sent an "emergency ops" signal, as instructed.

Lang's force, which arrived at Babwuf on the 1st, set out next day along the track, now much improved by the efforts of the advanced party. It was an arduous trek but no one fell far behind, the men being spurred on by Lang's warning that anyone who dropped out would have to find his own way back. By 5.30 p.m. the last of the column arrived at Waime

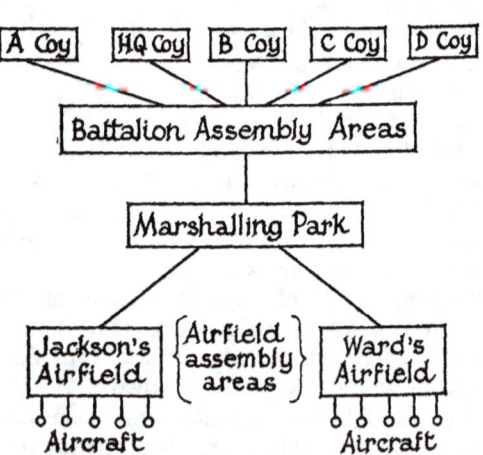

Battalion emplaning procedure diagram

where a camp was made. On the 3rd the column climbed steep kunai hills and then skirted the foothills on the south side of the Watut's eastern swamps to the camping ground previously reconnoitred. At 4 p.m. on the 4th the march ended at the Markham near Kirkland's Dump.

Preparations for the crossing, already begun by Captain Dunphy's engineers, were soon well in hand, and guides were stationed half a mile above Kirkland's to watch for the boats which had departed from Tsili

---

[6] Capt R. J. S. Seddon, SX1741; 2/10 Bn. Secretary; of Toorak Gardens, SA; b. Cleve, SA, 28 Nov 1917.

Tsili earlier in the day. Half an hour after midnight one boat, guided by Lieutenant Snook, arrived, followed in the next three-quarters of an hour by six others which had missed the right channel. One boat passed Kirkland's and landed about 400 yards below the crossing place, and the other two boats were sunk by snags on the trip from the mouth of the Watut. All occupants but one were rescued and transferred to other boats.

After months of patrolling and observing, occasionally enlivened with skirmishes, the 24th Battalion was at last to participate on 5th September in an all-out company attack on Markham Point which had long been a thorn in the side of the Australians. Originally it had been used as a dump for Japanese engineer stores for use in the construction of a road from the Markham to Wau. Several patrols of the 24th had reached the general area of Markham Point, but, even so, it was difficult to pin-point weapon-pits and gun positions.

Colonel Smith's planning for the attack had ill fortune from the start. At the end of August New Guinea Force had advised that 18 planes would drop rations and ammunition in the Wampit and Gabensis areas. Wampit Force was entirely dependent on air supply but the air dropping program in the few vital days before the attack was bewildering to the 24th Battalion. On 2nd September 9 planes dropped supplies without warning at Zenag, a four days' carry from Markham Point. Next day 3 planes dropped supplies at Wampit and 3 at Gabensis. As a result Smith had 2,200 boy-loads scattered over his wide area waiting to be lifted forward. A further blow was delivered when the Angau representative told Smith on the 2nd that, of the 150 Markham carriers promised, he could "rouse" up only 90 including "Marys"! Even this number was rapidly reduced when the carriers realised that Markham Point was the destination.

Smith planned to leave Wampit early on the 3rd to supervise preparations for the attack. Late on the 2nd he received a telephone call from Partep 1 where Major Fleay said that he had a message from Port Moresby which he had to deliver personally. Smith went back a half day's march to Timne where he met Fleay early on the 3rd and received the message that the date of the attack had been advanced from the 5th to the 4th. Smith rapidly set out for Markham Point and arrived exhausted at Deep Creek on the afternoon of the 3rd much too late to supervise any preparations for the attack.

Meanwhile, the company commander, Captain Duell, was disposing the four platoons which he had been allotted for the task of capturing Markham Point. New Guinea Force had forbidden concentration of the striking force in the area until the latest possible moment in order to prevent the Japanese from becoming suspicious. Lieutenant Childs'[7] platoon, however, had been reconnoitring the area while the other three platoons moved forward towards Markham Point. The original plan was that the platoons

---
[7] Capt F. H. Childs, MC, NX57501; 24 Bn. Clerk; of Dulwich Hill, NSW; b. Waratah, NSW, 21 Feb 1914.

would be in position by 3rd September, giving them the next day to survey the ground over which they would attack on the 5th. Now, however, this was changed and there was no chance of any reconnaissance of the area by the other three platoons.

Smith's late arrival led to a chain of events which denied the attacking platoons the control and coordination necessary for success. As instructed, Duell remained at Deep Creek to meet Smith. The assaulting platoons had already moved off incompletely briefed towards their start-lines when Smith arrived, and in the little daylight left there was no chance of the battalion and company commanders following them. Duell's plan was that Childs' platoon would capture Southern Ambush and advance to the Japanese camp, Lieutenant Young's[8] platoon would then pass through and capture the River Ambush, while Lieutenant Baber's platoon protected the company's base at Deep Creek and Sergeant Bartley's platoon guarded the mortars near the Golden Stairs. Because the guide got lost, the men did not reach their assembly areas south of the Japanese defences on the main spur, and camped at the junction of the main and kunai spurs some 40 minutes away. Smith and Duell moved forward towards the start-line in the early morning and arrived there after the first platoon had left its start-line.

At first light on the 4th, Sergeant Boyle,[9] who had the best knowledge of the area and was guiding the platoon, struck a land

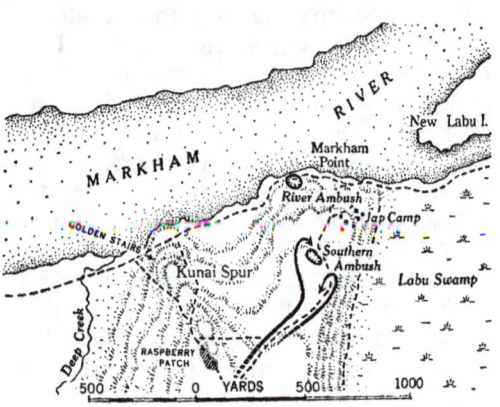

24th Battalion, 4th September

mine which wounded him and killed the leading scout. Swinging west to avoid any more mines, Childs and two of his sections advanced along the western slope of the main spur. Lack of opposition soon convinced Childs that he had gone too far, and, changing direction, he clambered up the hill with Sergeant Blundell's[1] section on the left and Corporal Gray's on the right. In extended line the two sections advanced upwards through areas cleared by the enemy above.

So silent had been the advance that several Japanese were still in bed when hit by the fire of the Australians as they scrambled into the outer defences, but soon the attackers were subjected to very heavy fire. Childs, wounded in both legs, and Gray's section, inside the enemy defences, fought gallantly, but were surrounded and cut off from the rest of the

---

[8] Lt M. J. Young, VX104167; 24 Bn. Salesman; of Surrey Hills, Vic; b. Surrey Hills, 15 Apr 1918. Killed in action 4 Sep 1943.
[9] Lt L. C. Boyle, VX117868; 24 Bn. Machinist; of Altona, Vic; b. Box Hill, Vic, 21 Feb 1918.
[1] Lt H. N. Blundell, MM, VX143592; 24 Bn. Regular soldier; of Glenhuntly, Vic; b. Abbotsford, Vic, 11 Aug 1917.

platoon.[2] On the left, Blundell was the first man to reach the outer defences. Killing two Japanese, he jumped into one of the inside trenches where he was cut off alone from the remainder of his section on the rim. For several hours the wounded Childs, the remnants of Gray's section and Blundell exchanged fire with the enemy. Their opponents seemed to number between 150 and 200. Unfortunately the third section had become detached from the others.[3] Unseen, it had reached within grenade-throwing range of the rear of the enemy busy firing at the other two sections, but took no action to relieve the pressure and returned to its start-line.

As no word had been received from Childs' platoon, Duell took Young forward to look for them. By skirting the western slopes of the spur they were able to enter the outer Japanese defences without being fired on. Here Duell met two of Childs' men who did not know where the rest of the platoon were. Duell decided that Young's platoon could enter the position by the same route and, leaving Young just outside the area cleared of growth, he sent the platoon forward to join him. The platoon could not find Young, whose body was discovered later.

Inside the Japanese defences the Australians were suffering such heavy casualties that Childs decided to withdraw. Corporal Stevens[4] covered his platoon commander's withdrawal to a spot where he was able to hear a message from Childs to fetch the third section. Disregarding enemy fire, Stevens ran back across the cleared ground to the start-line where he led Young's platoon towards the fight. All attempts to reinforce Childs were unsuccessful because of the enemy's enfilade fire, but they did manage to cover the withdrawal of Blundell and his section by 2 p.m.

The survivors of Gray's section and Childs held on until darkness when they began to creep back through the lines. Both badly wounded, Childs and Private Walker[5] assisted one another as they crawled painfully through the kunai. Twelve men had been killed or were missing; six were wounded. In return for these heavy casualties the remnants of the platoon estimated that they had killed at least 18 Japanese.

Duell was now ordered to "contain" the stubborn enemy at Markham Point. Before attacking again Colonel Smith decided to request an air attack, but he was surprised when the enemy positions were strafed by Allied aircraft on the 5th. He had not been informed of this attack and could not profit from it.

In Port Moresby, on the beaches east of Lae, and along the south bank of the Markham, all who had anything to do with the assault on Lae had early reveilles on 5th September. By 7.30 in the morning the American paratroops were loaded into 82 Douglas transports and the Australian

---

[2] The men were not equipped with bayonets which, over the months of patrolling, had been discarded as an encumbrance and as useless for digging. Thus they went handicapped into a hand-to-hand fight against a bayonet-carrying enemy.

[3] One more handicap was that signal wire for the operation had been dropped at Zenag. Duell had no telephones or wire to control his reserve and to guide his mortars.

[4] L-Sgt R. J. Stevens, DCM, V265240; 24 Bn. Farmer; of Genoa, Vic; b. Albury, NSW, 25 May 1922.

[5] Pte J. A. Walker, MM, V255944; 24 Bn. Sheet metal worker; of Box Hill, Vic; b. Bayswater, Vic, 26 Mar 1923.

gunners into five more; the bombers and fighters were warming up; the 2/17th Battalion was leading the 9th Division's advance on Lae; the pioneers and engineers at Kirkland's Dump were ready for the crossing; Chalk's Papuan company was concentrating near Sheldon's Crossing; and Duell's mortars were firing into Markham Point.

It took 45 minutes for the air armada to assume correct flight positions after the first C-47 rolled down the runway. Meeting the fighters over Thirty-mile Strip the transports flew to the north, crossing the Owen Stanleys at 9,000 feet, where the troops were intensely cold because the doors had been removed from the aircraft. About 10.15 a.m. Lang's men saw the aerial armada overhead.

General Kenney, who accompanied the paratroops (as did MacArthur) described the approach to Nadzab:

> Three hundred and two airplanes in all, taking off from eight different fields in the Moresby and Dobodura areas, made a rendezvous right on the nose over Marilinan, flying through clouds, passes in the mountains, and over the top. Not a single squadron did any circling or stalling around but all slid into place like clockwork and proceeded on the final flight down the Watut Valley, turned to the right down the Markham, and went directly to the target. Going north down the valley of the Watut from Marilinan, this was the picture: Heading the parade at one thousand feet were six squadrons of B-25 strafers, with the eight .50-caliber guns in the nose and sixty frag bombs in each bomb bay; immediately behind and about five hundred feet above were six A-20s, flying in pairs—three pairs abreast —to lay smoke as the last frag bomb exploded. At about two thousand feet and directly behind the A-20s came ninety-six C-47s carrying paratroops, supplies, and some artillery. The C-47s flew in three columns of three-plane elements, each column carrying a battalion set up for a particular battalion dropping ground. On each side along the column of transports and about one thousand feet above them were the close-cover fighters. Another group of fighters sat at seven thousand feet and, up in the sun, staggered from fifteen to twenty thousand, was still another group. Following the transports came five B-17s, racks loaded with 300-pound packages with parachutes, to be dropped to the paratroopers on call. . . . Following the echelon to the right and just behind the five supply B-17s was a group of twenty-four B-24s and four B-17s, which left the column just before the junction of the Watut and the Markham to take out the Jap defensive position at Heath's Plantation, about half-way between Nadzab and Lae. Five weather ships were used prior to and during the show along the route and over the passes, to keep the units straight on weather to be encountered during their flights to the rendezvous. The brass-hat flight of three B-17s above the center of the transport column completed the set-up.[6]

The three paratroop battalions landed on their assigned dropping grounds, met no opposition, and proceeded towards their assembly areas. This was a difficult task because the pit-pit and kunai were from six to ten feet high and very entangled, making walking difficult. The grass and the burning heat of the valley combined to delay the assembling of the battalions but, two hours after the jump, just as Lang's force was crossing Dunphy's bridge, the paratroops were in position, patrols were out along all approaches to Nadzab and work had begun on the strip.

In accordance with plans the five aircraft carrying the gunners of the 2/4th Field Regiment landed at Tsili Tsili. An hour later the artillerymen

---
[6] *General Kenney Reports*, pp. 293-4.

were again in the planes making the ten-minute flight to Nadzab. They barely had time to perceive Lang's force, spread out below on both sides of the Markham and along the sandbank in the centre, before they were coming in over the dropping grounds at 600 feet and the jump-masters called: "Stand to the door." "It was an exceptional man who did not get a sinking feeling in the stomach at that order," recorded the unit's historian.[7] Lieutenant Pearson was first out, quickly followed by the others in the first two aircraft. Equipment tumbling out of the next three aircraft was followed by the "pushers out" as the planes passed over for the second time.

The strong breeze along the valley, already noted by Kinsler, resulted in the gunners being landed too far west by the pilots who, in any case, overran the jumping ground. Some men landed in trees, including the only casualty—Gunner Lidgerwood,[8] who injured his shoulder. The scattering of the gunners and their equipment over a large area in tall kunai prevented the assembly of one gun until a detachment found a complete set of parts and selected a gun position on the edge of the kunai facing open country ahead. While the gunners were searching for the parts Lieutenants Faulkner and Ross, equipped with American portable wirelesses, joined the forward American platoons, but in order to maintain surprise they did not carry out their registration fire until next morning. At 3.15 p.m. two Fortresses, flying at great speed, dropped 192 rounds of ammunition. Although the aim was good, several of the boxes tore away from the parachutes. After all the hard work and courage of the gunners, their services were not required in the unopposed landing.

As the first planes flew over Kirkland's Dump at 10.15 a.m. a detachment of the 2/6th Field Company under Lieutenant Frew,[9] and Captain Garrard's[1] company of the 2/2nd Pioneers, which would establish the bridgehead, prepared to leave their hiding places under the trees. At the selected crossing place the Markham was about 400 yards wide and flowing in four channels. Three of these channels were fordable, but the fourth or main channel was about 210 feet wide, 15 feet deep and had a surface current of 7½ knots.

As the paratroops began dropping from the transports seven of Wegg's boats moved from their hiding places above Kirkland's Dump, picked up Garrard's party, deposited it on the north bank of the Markham and then moved down to the crossing place where they anchored after some difficulty in the fast stream. During the crossing by the leading company the remainder of the 2/2nd Pioneers waded through the Markham to a large sandbank by the main channel. The eighth boat ferried Lieutenant Frew's party across to erect sheer-legs on the opposite bank. Two parties

---

[7] Henry, p. 210.
[8] Gnr W. J. Lidgerwood, VX50125; 2/4 Fd Regt. Labourer; of Birregurra, Vic; b. Colac, Vic, 6 Jan 1917.
[9] Lt S. L. Frew, VX75221; 2/6 Fd Coy. Architect; of West Parkville, Vic; b. Auckland, NZ, 15 Feb 1914.
[1] Maj N. F. Garrard, NX77346; 2/2 Pnr Bn. Regular soldier; of Manly, NSW; b. Lewisham, NSW, 21 Oct 1910. Died 19 Apr 1957.

under Lieutenants Waterhouse[2] and Frew, working from opposite banks, lashed together sections of decking consisting of three poles each 3 inches in diameter and 35 feet long, and placed them across the folding boats. At the same time rubber boats were inflated ready to be dragged across by cable. This smaller rubber boat bridge could not be erected until the last eight boats from the junction of the Watut and the Markham passed downstream.

The folding-boat bridge was completed by 12.30 p.m. and, by 3 p.m., the engineers and Papuans had followed the pioneers across. The native carriers then crossed by 5 p.m. In the lead as the force marched towards Nadzab was Lieutenant Gossip[3] whose task was to lay out the Nadzab airfield. Captain Moorhouse,[4] of the 2/4th Field Regiment, had marched with Lang's force and now pushed on rapidly with telephones and wire for Pearson's jumpers. The trip took longer than expected because of the soft clayey mud on the north bank, and the head of the column did not begin to arrive until 5.45 p.m., when Lang immediately conferred with Kinsler whose paratroops had burned the kunai from the airstrip before dusk. The medical officer of the 2/2nd Pioneers, Captain Putland,[5] assisted the Americans by setting the broken legs of paratroops and treating several less severe injuries.

Chalk's Papuans, who had successfully carried out their task of picquetting the south bank of the Markham near the crossing places, moved up the Erap River after crossing the Markham. At 5.15 p.m. the company climbed from the stony bed and camped on the banks of the Erap, where they apprehended a local native for use as a guide to Chivasing and the western approaches to Nadzab.

By the night of 5th September the major Allied offensive of the New Guinea campaign was in full swing. South of Lae the 5th Division was closing in on Salamaua; east of Lae the leading platoon of the 9th was observing the first Japanese encountered by that division; west of Lae a mixed force of paratroops, pioneers, artillerymen, engineers and Papuans was in occupation of Nadzab and awaiting the arrival of the main body of the 7th Division. Under such pressure General Nakano's *51st Division*, already badly shaken, was likely to crack.

---

[2] Capt H. L. Waterhouse, NX86408; 2/6 Fd Coy. Schoolteacher; of Northmead, NSW; b. Casino, NSW, 13 Aug 1914.

[3] Capt R. D. Gossip, NX71146; 2/6 Fd Coy. Civil engineer; of North Bondi, NSW; b. Sydney, 16 Sep 1917.

[4] Capt D. Moorhouse, VX14115; 2/4 Fd Regt. Clerk; of Brighton Beach, Vic; b. Melbourne, 12 Dec 1916.

[5] Capt V. M. Putland, NX70384. 2/2 AGH; RMO 2/2 Pnr Bn; 2/5 and 121 AGH's. Medical practitioner; of Coonabarabran, NSW; b. Bourke, NSW, 4 Apr 1908.

CHAPTER 13

THE FALL OF LAE

EAST of Lae on 6th September the weather continued to favour the advance. On the right flank the 2/13th Battalion moved east from its base on Yellow Beach and, despite orders to stop at the Buhem River, Lieut-Colonel Colvin sent two companies across the river and along the coast towards the overgrown Hopoi airfield which he occupied without opposition that afternoon. On the main front west of Red Beach the 26th Brigade was about to receive its baptism of Japanese fire. The commander of this brigade, Brigadier Whitehead, was a former regular soldier whose restless and critical mind had led him to leave the army soon after World War I, in which he had commanded a machine-gun company. He had formed the 2/2nd Machine Gun Battalion in 1940, and commanded the 2/32nd Battalion in the El Alamein operations until September 1942 when he was promoted to his present appointment.

Just before the 2/23rd Battalion was about to move forward early on the 6th, Corporal Fairlie and Lance-Corporal Schram, wet and exhausted, arrived in time to warn that a Japanese company was approaching. The leading Australian company (Captain Dudley's) was warned to expect an ambush and, 100 yards along the beach, the company was fired on.

Dudley promptly attacked and drove the foremost enemy troops back about 40 yards through dense undergrowth. Major McRae next sent out Captain Thirlwell's[1] company to go north along the Buiem and then west for about 250 yards before turning south and closing in behind the enemy. While Thirlwell was cutting a track through the dense jungle and reporting his progress by means of three walkie-talkie sets placed along his route Dudley's men and the Japanese remained close to one another, both pinned down by heavy fire.

At 10.30 a.m., after enemy mortar fire had inflicted 16 casualties on the 2/17th Battalion behind McRae's position, Dudley sent Lieutenant Atkinson's[2] platoon into the attack. Effective use of grenades drove the enemy back another 40 yards and there the Japanese and Australians were again both pinned down. With the possibility of a stalemate developing, McRae sent in a third company to join in the assault, but the Japanese apparently guessed or heard the moves being made to encircle them and decided to withdraw. At 12.40 p.m. Thirlwell reported that he was in contact with about 80 enemy withdrawing to the west along the coast. Although some casualties were inflicted on them, the Japanese overran Thirlwell's southern positions and withdrew to the west across the little creek which the Australians were guarding. Not only had they

---

[1] Maj G. McA. Thirlwell, MC, VX27876; 2/23 Bn. 3 Bn RAR Korea 1950; served Malaya 1956-57. Clerk; of Elsternwick, Vic; b. Melbourne, 17 Apr 1917.
[2] Lt J. W. H. Atkinson, MC, VX42929; 2/23 Bn. Dairy farmer; of Timboon, Vic; b. Fairfield, Vic, 25 Jan 1920.

temporarily escaped, but they now pinned down the company from the flank.

Anxious to wipe out the remaining Japanese, McRae at 1 p.m. ordered the two encircling companies to advance south to the coast with the little creek as a boundary between them. At the same time Dudley advanced west for 200 yards until shortage of ammunition stopped him. His two platoons killed 20 Japanese during this advance, including two who committed suicide by clasping grenades to their chests.

There was a surprise in store for about 60 escaping Japanese. As they struggled back towards Lae they were intercepted about 2 p.m. by Sergeant Lawrie's lightly equipped platoon west of the mouth of the Bunga River. Between this time and last light on the 6th this courageous and determined N.C.O. inspired his men to resist six attacks by the frantic enemy who found they could not use the track which the tiny Australian force was holding so grimly. The Japanese attacks were heralded by bugle calls and shouts thus warning the Australians where and when to expect them. The fighting was close and fierce and the bayonet was used to eke out the Australians' slender ammunition supplies. Lawrie alone killed ten Japanese before the mauled enemy remnants infiltrated past his position towards the west. With four men dead and one wounded Lawrie waited until after dark before moving east to join his battalion, which he did half an hour before midnight.

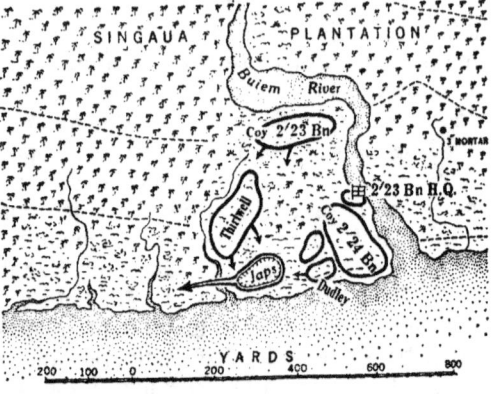

6th September

Meanwhile General Wootten had been urging his other troops west. His headquarters was established at Aluki 1 where the 2/48th Battalion remained in reserve. The three battalions (2/28th, 2/32nd, 2/43rd) of the 24th Brigade advanced west through the kunai, mangroves and jungle of the hot coastal plain, and camped between Apo and Aluki where the 2/32nd Battalion was detached as an additional divisional reserve. After conferring with Wootten, Brigadier Evans with his staff pushed on to Apo Fishing Village where they made arrangements for the 24th Brigade to take over the coastal advance and free the 26th for the northern advance in accordance with Wootten's orders on the 5th.

Brigadier Evans was a keen and able citizen soldier, and a Melbourne architect. He had been first commissioned in 1924, and by 1939 was commanding the 57th/60th Battalion. In 1940 he had helped to form "Albury's Own"—the 2/23rd Battalion—and had led it from its formation through

(Australian War Memorial)
Brigadier W. J. V. Windeyer with his brigade major, Major B. V. Wilson, at the embarkation of the 20th Brigade at Cairns on 26th July 1943, in preparation for the Allied offensive against Lae.

(Australian War Memorial)
Inspecting the 25th Brigade at Port Moresby on 28th August 1943 before their departure for the Lae operation. The colour patches on the men's puggarees have been obliterated by the wartime censor. *Left to right*: General Blamey, Major-General Vasey, Brigadier K. W. Eather and Lieut-Colonel T. R. W. Cotton (C.O. of the 2/33rd), whose battalion is being inspected.

(Australian War Memorial)

The scene after the crash of a Liberator bomber on the marshalling park at Jackson's airfield, Port Moresby, on 7th September 1943. The aircraft hit the tree shown in the left foreground and crashed into trucks carrying members of the 2/33rd Battalion and the 158th General Transport Company. Fifty-nine were killed or died of injuries and 92 were injured but survived.

(Australian War Memorial)

Men of the 2/4th Field Regiment checking over their equipment before taking off for the parachute landing at Nadzab on 5th September 1943. *Left to right:* Gunner I. G. Robertson, Lance-Bombardier W. D. Laurie, Lance-Bombardier W. G. Indian and Gunner T. A. Kettle.

Lieut-Colonel J. T. Lang's force of engineers, pioneers and Papuans crossing the Markham River on 5th September 1943 on the way to Nadzab, after their overland march from Tsili Tsili.

(*Australian War Memorial*)

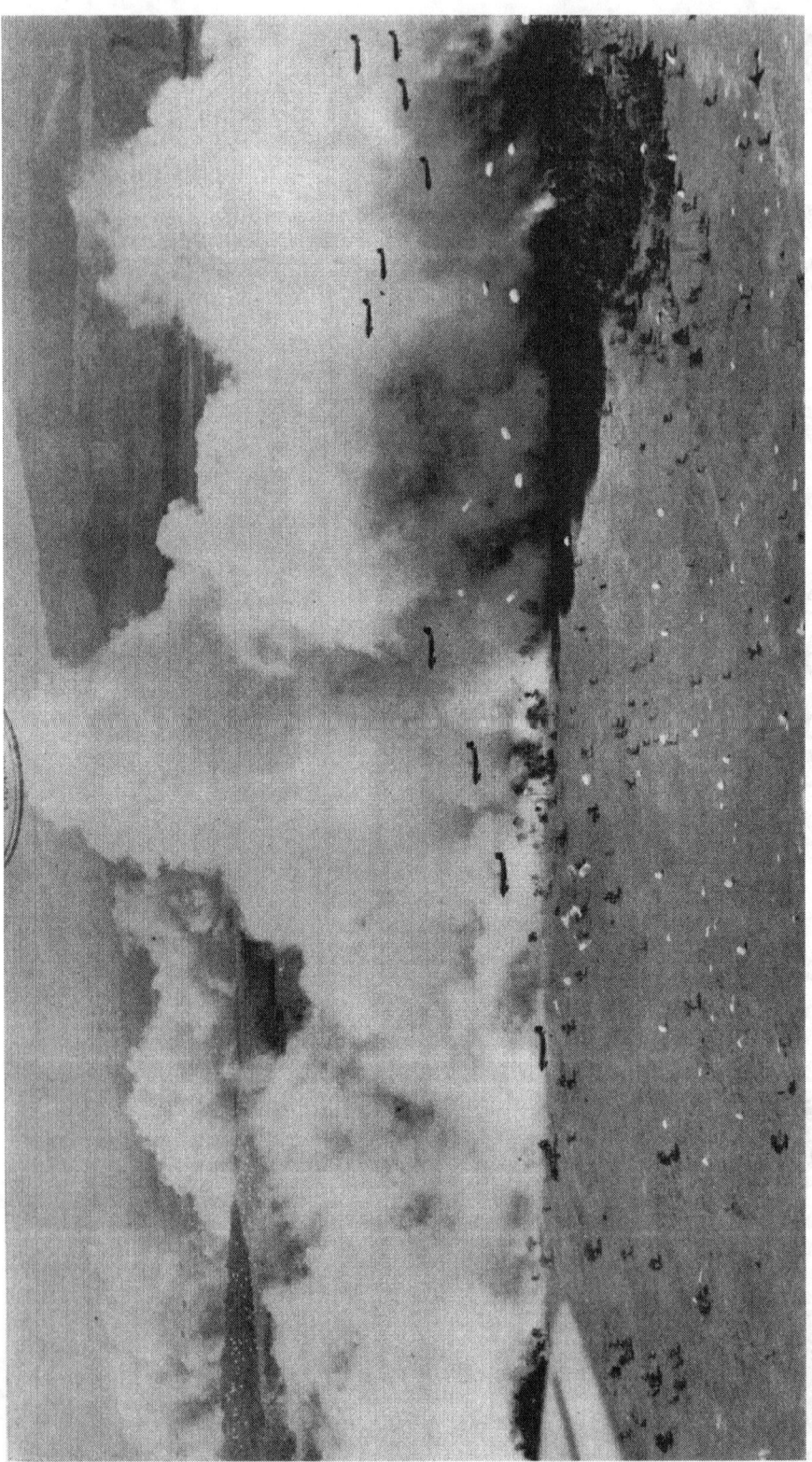

The landing of the 503rd American Parachute Infantry Regiment at Nadzab on 5th September 1943. One battalion is landing in the foreground and in the left background another battalion ringed by smoke can be seen dropping.

(*Australian War Memorial*)

the siege of Tobruk and part of the battle of El Alamein. He was appointed to command the brigade near the end of the El Alamein operations.

On both the 5th and 6th Japanese aircraft bombed Red Beach, the Aluki Track and the amphibian craft plying between the beaches, but this did little to hinder the movement of stores. Soon after midnight on the 6th-7th September 5 L.C.V's and 3 L.C.M's landed stores from Red Beach at Apo Fishing Village to alleviate the severe ration and ammunition shortage among forward troops and, by shortening the supply lines, to enable the advance to gather momentum. That night the rain poured down, soaking men and equipment, filling weapon-pits, and forcing the troops to perch like bedraggled fowls on logs or anything else above ground level. There were anxious thoughts about crossing the Busu.

Through mud and slush the advance continued on the 7th. Before dawn an L.C.V. and an L.C.M. landed stores on the beach south of Singaua Plantation where the 26th and 24th Brigades, each now with only two battalions, picked up supplies before moving west. Leading the advance the 2/24th Battalion reached the Burep at 11 a.m. followed by the 2/23rd, the 2/4th Independent Company and a Papuan platoon. A rumour that the Japanese were in Tikereng caused the 2/24th to advance cautiously until the cause of the rumour turned out to be Captain Cudlipp's[4] company of the 2/23rd awaiting the arrival of the remainder of the battalion. The 2/24th followed by brigade headquarters and the 2/23rd then moved rapidly north-west up the Burep and camped about five miles from the coast. Wootten had originally intended that the 24th Brigade would relieve the 26th after the Busu had been crossed, but opposition encountered at Singaua Plantation and expected at the Busu dictated relief farther east at the Burep where the 2/28th Battalion relieved the 2/23rd.

Orders for 8th September were that the two forward brigades should cross the Busu. Again heavy rain fell during the night until dawn, making marching very difficult. The two leading battalions—2/24th on the north and the 2/28th on the coast—advanced towards the Busu. The 2/24th had to cut a track, and to ensure the security of the advance and the compactness of his battalion, Lieut-Colonel Gillespie decided that companies should cut parallel tracks on each side of the main one. This reduced movement to a snail-like pace of about 300 yards an hour and prevented the battalion from quite reaching the Busu on 8th September. Captain Garvey's[5] 2/4th Independent Company, under Whitehead's command, passed through the 2/23rd Battalion that morning, followed the course of the Burep north to the foothills, and thence scrub-bashed through thick jungle to the west trying to discover whether it would be possible to make a jeep track from the Burep to a large kunai patch east of the Busu.

[4] Capt J. Cudlipp, VX38845; 2/23 Bn. Insurance clerk; of Brighton, Vic; b. Sydney, 29 Oct 1916. Died of wounds 18 Nov 1943.
[5] Maj K. B. Garvey, NX70709. OC 2/8 Indep Coy, 2/4 Indep Coy, 2/4 Cdo Sqn. Company secretary; of Bondi, NSW; b. Woollahra, NSW, 23 Feb 1910.

Along the coast the 2/28th reached the east bank of the Busu at 4 p.m. on the 8th. Towards evening two Japanese were seen on the other side. Lieut-Colonel Norman[6] of the 2/28th therefore expected that an attempt to cross the river would be opposed. Swollen by heavy rains the Busu was a formidable obstacle. Up from its mouth it was between 600 and 800 yards wide and flowing in several channels. In the main and westernmost channel the river was moving between 10 and 12 knots and was 5 to 6 feet deep. Wading seemed out of the question.

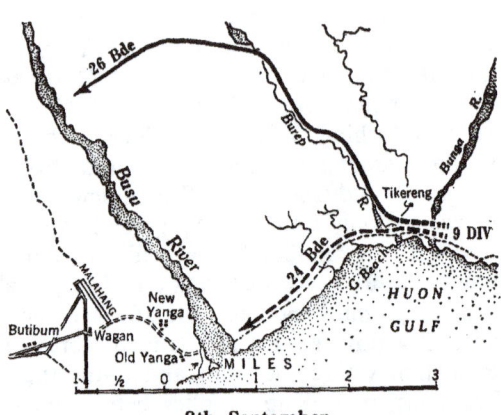

8th September

All activity on the 9th centred upon crossing the Busu. At 6 a.m. the leading platoon of the 2/24th Battalion arrived near the river. The battalion was not encouraged by what it saw even though no Japanese were seen on the opposite bank. The flooded river was flowing at 13 knots, much faster than at its mouth, and was divided into three channels 65 feet, 95 feet, and 40 feet wide, and varying in depth from one to seven feet. The strongest swimmers without clothes might be able to reach the other bank if they were not dashed against protruding rocks but naked they would not be much use against any Japanese awaiting them. While patrols reconnoitred for better crossing places Gillespie realised that bridging and ropes would be necessary.[7]

A patrol of the 2/23rd later in the day reported seeing an enemy patrol on the opposite bank north of the proposed crossing of the Busu. To the north again the 2/4th Independent Company reported that it would be "impossible" to make a jeep track to the kunai patch, and on the extreme north one of its platoons crossed the Sankwep River and moved north along the east bank of the Busu towards the kunda bridge.

Near the mouth of the swirling river the 2/28th received orders on the afternoon of the 8th to establish a base on the west bank at dawn

---

[6] Brig C. H. B. Norman, DSO, MC, WX3421. OC 24 A-Tk Coy 1940-41; 2/28 Bn (CO 1943-45). Administrator of Norfolk Island 1953-58. Grazier; of Perth; b. Sydney, 20 Feb 1904.
Norman was one of several battalion commanders in the Corps who had been first commissioned after the outbreak of war in 1939. Among the others were Robson of the 2/31st, Cotton of the 2/33rd, Sublet of the 2/16th. These rapid promotions had occurred in two West Australian battalions which had had exceptionally heavy casualties in earlier campaigns, and in the 25th Brigade which had been formed in England from reinforcements and technical troops and when few infantry officers were available.

[7] Whitehead soon realised that bridging was the only answer and that speed was essential because the enemy were then unaware of the presence of the 2/24th Battalion on the eastern bank and were not manning the opposite bank. He wrote later: "Had we obtained a small box girder when demanded there was every prospect of crossing unopposed." At that stage, however, the 9th Division was giving priority to the artillery build up on the Burep and, despite Whitehead's argument that the limited amount of bridging equipment necessary would not affect this build up, he was unable to secure his point.

on the 9th. Reconnaissance patrols before dawn on the 9th reported that there was no suitable crossing for 1,000 yards from the mouth.

After dawn Lieutenant Rooke's[8] patrol attempted to cross near the mouth and although it reached the large island in the centre of the Busu's mouth Rooke found that he could go no farther. About 8.40 a.m. Norman ordered Captain Lyon[9] to attempt the crossing by sending one platoon across via the sandbank at the mouth, while the remainder of the company covered the crossing with fire from Rooke's island. The platoon made the attempt at 9.15 a.m., but when one of the forward scouts was killed and another wounded by enemy fire Lyon withdrew the platoon while the Australians' mortars bombarded the western bank.

Wootten was disturbed at the unexpected delay and realised that, unless the crossings were quickly secured, "the Japs, knowing our situation will fortify banks and strongly oppose us". He therefore ordered Whitehead and Evans to seize bridgeheads over the Busu not later than first light on the 10th. These orders reached Norman at 12.50 p.m. on the 9th, and he determined that, as there was no other way of crossing, his battalion would walk from bank to bank.

Second in command of the 2/32nd Battalion was Major Mollard[1] who had lived in Lae for two years before the war. Early in the afternoon of the 9th Evans sent him to the 2/28th Battalion to answer any questions asked by Norman and his staff. The main question which Norman asked him was "Where do we cross?" Mollard pointed out that the natives always crossed at the mouth (or at the spot where the 26th Brigade was trying to cross). Norman decided against this advice and ordered a crossing higher up for reasons later described in a broadcast talk:[2]

> My personal reconnaissance indicated the best approach to be directly across from the island. Patrols had been unable to find anything better upstream within our right boundary and the bar could not be considered. Not only was it used by the Japanese, as indicated by footprints, but troops crossing there would be so strung out, on a front of one or two men, as to render them most vulnerable to enemy fire. . . . Owing to the island and a slight bend, there appeared to be a drift in the current towards the far bank, very little further down stream. Also, the far bank rose abruptly giving protection to anything below. This would permit some reorganisation before the troops went over the top.

Coolly Norman informed his company commanders that the battalion would assemble on the east bank, form up on Rooke's island, and cross the last channel of the Busu in four extended lines starting at 5.30 p.m. Norman chose this time because he believed it to be the enemy's "rice time". So, in the afternoon, the battalion waded to the island, keeping as well concealed as possible, although an alert enemy on the western bank could not have failed to observe the preparations. Half an hour before the starting time the artillery was used for the first time when

---
[8] Capt P. F. Rooke, MC, WX8402; 2/28 Bn. Farmer; of Katanning, WA; b. Perth, 14 Aug 1919.
[9] Maj L. H. Lyon, WX7500; 2/28 Bn. Regular soldier; of Merredin, WA; b. Moora, WA, 17 Nov 1912.
[1] Maj K. F. Mollard, DSO, VX48771. 2/24 and 2/32 Bns, "Z" Special Unit. Oil company representative; of Lae, NG; b. Melbourne, 20 May 1915.
[2] On 7th February 1953 from 6 WN Perth.

22 rounds from the troop of 25-pounders already at the Burep[3] were fired on to suspected enemy positions west of the mouth of the Busu.

Two minutes before time Lieutenant Hannah[4] led his company from the forming-up place on the island to the start-line on the island's far edge. As his men, in a long line and without hesitation, stepped into the swirling water the other companies moved one after another to the start-line at two-minute intervals. It was an incredible crossing. The men were swept off their feet by the fierce current, which snatched weapons from some of them, but most were swirled towards the west bank where they grasped overhanging boughs and kunai.

Meanwhile Lyon's company was stepping into the river, and the same story was repeated as the human

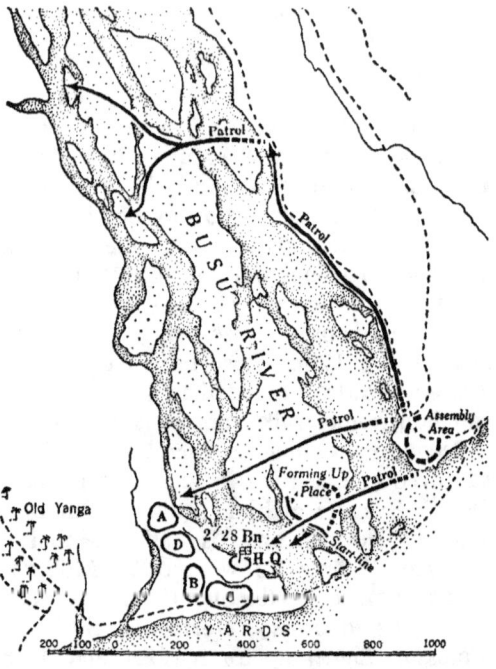

9th September

corks bobbed to the other side. Those who reached the far bank first turned to help their comrades, formed human chains out into the river, and held out branches and weapons to be grasped. It was harder for Norman's headquarters and the third and fourth companies because they saw men swept away in front of them, but the lines never faltered. Seeing the difficulties and the congestion ahead, the last company, followed by the main part of battalion headquarters, swung right incline, entered the river 100 yards higher up, formed a chain and reached the western bank north of the battalion's position. Describing the crossing Mollard wrote later: "It looked for all the world as though a giant hand was snatching them across to the far bank so fast did they travel the intervening distance."

The battalion had surprised the enemy who had not considered it possible for a crossing to be made except along the bar at the mouth.

---

[3] Wootten's artillery, consisting at this stage mainly of the 2/12th Field Regiment, had been deployed west of the Buso. In order to keep up with the advance and to avoid becoming bogged on the tracks which the rain had badly damaged the guns could be moved forward only by landing craft. Colonel Steiner sent 11 more LCM's from Morobe, making a total of 21 and increased the number of LCV's to 60. During the night of 8th-9th September six LCM's and five LCV's made two trips ferrying stores from Red Beach to a new beach-head west of the mouth of the Burep, known as "G" Beach. Among the stores landed at the new beach were a troop of 25-pounders, six jeeps, four trailers, one three-ton truck and two bulldozers.

[4] Capt J. F. Hannah, WX6881; 2/28 Bn. Bank officer; of Subiaco, WA; b. Menzies, WA, 22 Jun 1919.

Consequently, most of the enemy fire was directed there, and by the time they began firing on the lines of men it was too late as they were almost hidden beneath the high western bank. Great good fortune also favoured the 2/28th and indeed it was fitting that it should. Where the battalion hit the west bank there was a bend in the river, and it was this unexpected help from nature which probably prevented the battalion from being swept out to sea.

On the far bank Hannah was the first man across, and soon other bedraggled men were struggling up the western bank behind him to form the bridgehead. About 150 yards ahead Corporal May[5] saw an enemy machine-gun post 100 yards inland from the beach which was doing most of the firing along the bar. He advanced alone, hurling a grenade and firing his Owen, and wiped out the post, thus saving many Australian lives.

Describing the happenings on the far side a chronicler wrote:

> It was inevitable that there should be some confusion on the far bank. The companies had set out in orderly manner, but the river swept them into mixed groups along the bank. Darkness and heavy rain rendered difficult the task of reassembling and exploiting. . . . [Hannah] with numerous desert patrols in his record, had managed to keep most of his men together, as they were first across, and by orders shouted down to subordinate officers and men other company commanders were able to draw a large percentage of their troops together. Cries of "'A' Company here!" "Where's 'C' Company?" and so on were heard on all sides as men trampled countless paths through the kunai.[6]

Obviously such a crossing could not be made without cost, but for the results achieved, the cost was small. Thirty men had been carried towards the sea and did not make the crossing. Of these, 13 were drowned, and the remainder were saved by the bar where the water was only 3 feet deep. Under heavy enemy fire, these shivering men hid behind the scanty vegetation on the bar until they were rescued six hours later by their own Pioneers and Captain Buring's[7] company of the 2/43rd Battalion.

By 6.30 p.m. the company commanders had reorganised their scattered platoons and occupied a bridgehead 150 yards deep and 650 yards long. Swamps and darkness prevented Lyon on the north and Hannah on the south from advancing to the small creek west of the Busu. Then the rain came again and fell heavily throughout the night. "The reaction of the river crossing and the fact that the men had no protection of any kind might have reacted very unfavourably had they not been so fit and morale so high," wrote their commander in his report.

Twenty-five per cent of automatic weapons and about 80 rifles had been lost in the crossing and ammunition and signal equipment had been damaged. As it was imperative to re-establish communications with brigade

---

[5] S-Sgt N. May, DCM, WX8755; 2/28 Bn. Bogger; of Norseman, WA; b. Mt Yokine, WA, 27 Sep 1913.

[6] From "The Busu Crossing", by Corporal C. Ammon, 2/28th Battalion, in *Red Platypus—A Record of the Achievements of the 24th Australian Infantry Brigade 1940-45* (1946).

[7] Capt O. G. Buring, SX8899; 2/43 Bn. Clerk; of Black Forest, SA; b. Kensington, SA, 24 Jun 1914. Killed in action 12 Sep 1943.

headquarters, Norman's Intelligence sergeant, Crouchley,[8] although slightly wounded, swam back across the river and told Evans what had happened. Evans did his best to replace the lost weapons and sent up supplies of ammunition to the east bank where Buring was organising dumps ready to be sent across and attempting to establish telephone communication with Norman. By 11.30 p.m. Norman's battalion headquarters was connected with Buring's company largely due to the efforts of Private Trenoworth[9] of the 2/28th and Private Swift[1] of the 2/43rd, both of whom swam the river with telephone line. The achievements of Crouchley, Trenoworth and Swift were all the more meritorious because the torrential rain had caused the Busu to rise another foot.

Thus Norman had established his bridgehead before first light on the 10th. There were many individual acts of gallantry during the crossing. Most Australian soldiers who fought in the South-West Pacific would agree that they would rather face an aroused enemy than an angry Nature. It took a cold and calculated form of courage for the West Australians to walk into the raging Busu on 9th September 1943, particularly because, as in every unit, there were some men who could not swim.

Rain continued on the 10th, making the tracks unsuitable even for jeeps, and causing the 2/28th Battalion to wonder how it had ever crossed the flooded river behind it, and the 2/24th Battalion to wonder how it ever would. The diarist of the 2/32nd, which was marching along the coast to rejoin its brigade, described the men as "drowned rats" and eulogised the cup of tea and biscuits provided by the Salvation Army at the Burep crossing: "To this noble institution the battalion once again tenders its thanks for another demonstration of practical Christianity." Such an addition to rations was very welcome for most battalions were short of food. One battalion diarist described the ration situation as "totally inadequate and men are now definitely experiencing hunger all the time".[2]

This situation was not due to any omission on the part of Rear-Admiral Barbey's Task Force, which was regularly supplying the beaches, or to any want of enthusiasm on the part of the Shore Battalion, but to the general divisional shortage and to the difficulty of delivering rations to forward troops over long, sodden land supply lines. Canned heat issued to some battalions on the 10th helped to make the frugal meals more appetising and at least enabled the men to have a hot dish.

---

[8] Sgt J. Crouchley, MM, WX5090; 2/28 Bn. Labourer; of Busselton, WA; b. Milnrow, Lancs, England, 13 Apr 1913.

[9] Pte J. G. Trenoworth, WX7552; 2/28 Bn. Painter; of Leederville, WA; b. Perth, 5 Dec 1919.

[1] Cpl W. D. Swift, SX5808; 2/43 Bn. Transport driver and storeman; of Murray Bridge, SA; b. Waikerie, SA, 19 May 1921.

[2] The scanty meals on which men were existing each day at this stage comprised:
  biscuits: 1 packet per man
  sugar: 3 ozs per man
  coffee: 2 lb per 100 men
  margarine: 2 ozs per man
  rice: 20 lb per battalion
  bully beef: 4 men per tin
  beans: 6 men per tin
  sausages: 10 men per tin
  milk: 7 men per tin
  tea: 2 lb per 100 men.

See also A. S. Walker, *The Island Campaigns* (1957), pp. 274-9, a volume in the Medical series of this history.

Apart from shortages, the ration scale as laid down was inadequate for an operation which lasted as long as the Lae one. All brigades had protested when the ration scale had been outlined at Milne Bay. They were told, however, that it was the scale used by the 7th Division in its previous operations in New Guinea. "However," wrote Whitehead later, "the 7th Division had learned their lesson and the Division went into the Markham Valley operation with a ration scale completely different and much more adequate than that laid down for the 9th Division." The intention was that the scale should apply only for the first few days; in fact it lasted throughout the campaign.

An officer of the 2/23rd Battalion (Captain Lovell[3]) who was something of a cartoonist produced a comic strip about the battalion's experiences with rations and included one telling picture in which a Japanese was broadcasting the fact that there were 20,000 Australians lost and starving in the jungle around Lae. The cartoonist had added, "Who the Hell says we are lost?"

In spite of the weather and hunger the two forward brigades pressed on with their task on the 10th. In the northern foothills Lieutenant Hart's[4] and Lieutenant Cox's[5] platoons from the Independent Company bridged and crossed the Sankwep River near its junction with the Busu, while the third platoon remained south of the junction to carry rations. Advancing up the east bank of the Busu, Hart saw four Japanese moving up the west bank and sent two sections hurrying north to meet them, if they tried to cross the kunda bridge. Allowing them to cross the river Lieutenant Staples'[6] section then killed all four. Hart sent back the captured equipment, continued his advance and camped near Musom 2 in company with a Papuan section.

To the south Whitehead was urging the provision of engineer stores for bridging the Busu, the 2/24th Battalion was making unsuccessful attempts to cross the river, the 2/23rd Battalion was waiting, and the 2/48th Battalion was assisting the 2/7th Field Company to corduroy the jeep track from the Burep to the Busu as well as carry forward twelve miles of signal cable on mile reels each weighing 80 pounds.[7]

Heavy rain had caused the river to rise and render foolhardy any attempt by the 2/24th Battalion to wade across. When, at midday, a small party of engineers from the 2/7th Field Company arrived with rubber boats and rope, Sapper Amos[8] and another man swam the flooded river

---

[3] Capt F. K. Lovell, VX23475. Signals Corps and 2/23 Bn. Traveller-salesman; of Toorak, Vic; b. Windsor, Vic, 16 Jul 1916.

[4] Capt G. C. Hart, NX76250. 2/4 Indep Coy, 2/4 Cdo Sqn. Lithographer; of Carlton, NSW; b. St Peters, NSW, 17 Mar 1919.

[5] Capt W. M. Cox, VX75893. 2/4 Indep Coy, 2/4 Cdo Sqn. Clerk; of Moonee Ponds, Vic; b. Melbourne, 21 Jun 1921.

[6] Lt W. L. Staples, NX76307; 2/4 Indep Coy. Shipping clerk; of Kempsey, NSW; b. Manly, NSW, 26 Sep 1920.

[7] The bed of the Burep was a ready-made vehicle track. It was firm and gravelly and the many large stones did not prevent the passage of jeeps. Flooding was not a problem. Had it not been for this fortunate help from nature the problem of supplying the 26th Brigade from "G" Beach would have been very serious.

[8] Spr L. C. B. Amos, NX43296; 2/7 Fd Coy. Clerk; of Sydney; b. Lindfield, NSW, 28 Oct 1911. Killed in action 10 Sep 1943.

with a cable attached to a three-inch rope, but the cable broke.[9] Warrant Officer McCallum[1] then swam the river with another cable attached to the rope, and the three men secured it to the far bank. No sooner had they done so than the Japanese, who had received ample warning of the battalion's intention to cross, fired on them from a village on the western bank, killing Amos and forcing the other two men to hide. For forty minutes the 2/24th fired on the Japanese village. The hope of crossing unopposed had now vanished.

Several different methods of crossing were tried during the afternoon. Lieutenant Braimbridge[2] and one of his sections entered four of the engineers' boats which had been tied end to end and attached by loops to the rope across the river, but the current swamped the boats when 30 feet from the near shore. Other attempts to cross by towing boats containing equipment along the rope, and by crossing hand over hand along the rope, were abandoned because of enemy fire. McCallum and the surviving engineer finally swam back, McCallum reaching the east bank one mile downstream. As dusk came, a hold-fast was dug on the island in the Busu to facilitate swinging a boat across on the pendulum principle.[3] Again at night, it rained heavily.

In the swampy triangle formed by the western bank of the Busu and the small creek Colonel Norman issued his orders at 6 a.m. on the 10th for an attack on the Japanese who were sharing the triangle. Between 11 a.m. and midday small parties of enemy tried to infiltrate past Captain Newbery's[4] left flank positions on the coast. At midday the enemy fiercely attacked the left flank, using the beach as their line of advance and causing casualties with grenades. Largely because of the quick thinking of Sergeant MacGregor[5] who occupied the only slight rise from which the beach was fully visible, the enemy attack was beaten off. Although exposed to the enemy the gallant MacGregor refused to budge, even after he was mortally wounded, until the Japanese had been repulsed.

Hannah, meanwhile, was meeting no opposition in his advance down the west bank of the creek and at 2.20 p.m. reported that he was nearing the coast. Along the beach Newbery's company, particularly Lieutenant Brooks'[6] platoon, was under heavy fire from an enemy force in a swamp to the west. Brooks obtained permission to attack the Japanese ahead, and while the advance of the other companies was halted Brooks' platoon,

---

[9] The river was here at its narrowest and racing in three channels; the first between the east bank and a sandbank about 20 yards long, the second and main channel between the sandbank and an island 100 yards long with scrub on it, and the third between the island and the west bank.

[1] WO2 W. H. McCallum, VX47810; 2/24 Bn. Wood carver; of Fitzroy, Vic; b. Carlton, Vic, 15 Dec 1907.

[2] Lt F. Braimbridge, WX9693; 2/24 Bn. Schoolteacher; of Claremont, WA; b. Subiaco, WA, 9 May 1916.

[3] Known as a "flying bridge".

[4] Brig J. C. Newbery, ED, WX3391; 2/28 Bn. Chartered accountant; of Perth; b. Perth, 22 Jul 1911.

[5] Sgt A. C. MacGregor, WX6697; 2/28 Bn. Station hand; of West Perth; b. Cawnpore, India, 3 Aug 1907. Killed in action 10 Sep 1943.

[6] Lt J. W. Brooks, MC, WX5557; 2/28 Bn. Farmer; of Mount Barker, WA; b. Notts, England, 16 Jun 1904.

strengthened by a detachment from another platoon, advanced into the swamp. Waist deep, with tall tangled kunai and mangroves growing above, and heavily outnumbered, Brooks and his men attacked the enemy positions on several small islands. With great dash and determination the platoon overran these islands and almost annihilated the Japanese perched on them. For the loss of 4 men killed and 17 wounded Brooks' human amphibians killed 63 Japanese and captured much equipment including eight automatics. After this brief and severe clash the platoon withdrew and re-formed, and it was found that several men were missing. In near darkness the platoon returned to look for any wounded. It was already difficult to tell enemy casualties from their own in the swamp and with the light fading, but several were brought back. At one point, right on the beach line, Private Leonard[7] was lying, shot through the head, completely encircled by bodies of dead Japanese. Leonard had been a champion axeman, and it was almost as though he had been armed with an axe, not an Owen gun, so complete and so close was the circle of bodies.

As early as 7th August, General Herring had conferred with General Wootten about moving the 4th Brigade to take over the beach-head areas after the landing. On the 10th Admiral Barbey had agreed that he could transport another brigade, and now, on 5th September, the commander of the 4th Brigade, Brigadier C. R. V. Edgar, in Milne Bay received a warning order that his brigade was on six hours' notice to move by sea. In six L.S.T's and six L.C.I's the brigade left Milne Bay on the 9th, spent the night in Buna harbour, and arrived off Red Beach at 10.30 p.m. on the 10th. An hour after midnight headquarters and the three battalions—the 22nd, 29th/46th and 37th/52nd—were ashore.

North-west of Lae the Nadzab area was a hive of Allied activity. The diarist of the 2/6th Field Company wrote a terse and vivid description of the work on the vital Nadzab airfield:

> Work begins at 0700—an all-in go. Paratroops, sappers, pioneers and natives all cutting grass flat out. The cut grass is burned on the strip. At 0940 a Cub plane with Colonel Woodbury lands. The first three transport planes land at 1100 hours before the strip is quite completely cut, and nearly run down many of the motley throng. At 1400 planes start landing and continue until 1700—about 40 planes come in. Clouds of black dust everywhere and all concerned look like "Boongs". The C.R.E. arrives. . . . Still no sign of the enemy. One transport plane overruns end of strip and smashes a wheel on the stumps.

So the 6th passed at Nadzab in a swirl of black dust. The Douglas transports which landed among the workers on the rough airfield contained mainly American and Australian engineers under the command of General Vasey's chief engineer, Lieut-Colonel Tompson. Engineer equipment which arrived in the transports belonged mainly to Colonel Woodbury's 871st American Airborne Engineer Battalion from Tsili Tsili. Anti-aircraft guns were also carried on these first flights from Port Moresby

---

[7] Pte J. E. Leonard, WX19845; 2/28 Bn. Prospector; of Kalgoorlie, WA; b. Bridgetown, WA, 19 Nov 1902. Killed in action 10 Sep 1943.

By 8 a.m. that day the 2/25th Battalion resumed the advance towards Lae. Captain F. B. Haydon's company was 200 yards past the junction of the Markham Valley Road and the track to Jensen's Plantation when, at 1 p.m., it was fired on. Withdrawing to the track and road junction Haydon sent out three small patrols to try to find the enemy—one north to Jensen's and along the foothills to Jenyns' Plantation; a second along the left-hand side of the track; and the third along the right-hand side. When crossing a creek the leader of the middle patrol, Lance-Corporal Littler,[3] was wounded. Corporal Brockhurst[4] then led out five men to bring in Littler. While attending to the wounded man nine Japanese opened fire on Brockhurst's little band from behind and another enemy patrol fired from the front. Brockhurst attended to Littler's wounds while his party returned the fire. He then entered the fight and shot two Japanese, after which he found a safe route back to Haydon's perimeter.

South of the Markham, meanwhile, Wampit Force was attempting to pinpoint enemy positions at Markham Point, mainly round the area of the Southern, Central and River Ambushes. On the 8th Lieutenant Baber's patrol reached 100 yards south of the River Ambush where they heard enemy voices. Another patrol exchanged shots with the enemy near the River Ambush.

At 5.30 p.m. that day Lieutenant Childs and Private Walker crawled back to the Golden Stairs. Childs, who was wounded in both legs, and Walker, wounded in an arm and a leg, had been unable to rise from the ground. During their laborious and painful crawl through enemy lines from the evening of the 4th their wounds had become flyblown. Fortunately Childs had been able to use his hands to make detailed notes of enemy dispositions and to shoot with a pistol a prowling Japanese who attempted to strangle him. From information which the two men had gathered it seemed to Colonel Smith that the River Ambush might not now be occupied by the enemy. Patrolling for the next two days was therefore directed towards finding whether it would be possible to break the enemy lines near the river, but torrential rain and poor visibility prevented any worthwhile progress.

Herring now asked Vasey what assistance could best be rendered by Wampit Force. Vasey replied on the 10th that he considered that its best role would be to prevent the 200-odd Japanese at Markham Point from crossing the river to help the defenders of Heath's Plantation. Smith therefore received orders from Herring stressing the importance of preventing the enemy escaping across the river. As further frontal attacks on an alert and entrenched enemy at Markham Point would cause needless casualties Smith made several requests for an air attack on Markham Point, so that his men could attack "on its heels".

---

[3] L-Cpl J. W. Littler, QX20018; 2/25 Bn. Bank officer; of Brisbane; b. Brisbane, 2 May 1920.
[4] Sgt H. E. Brockhurst, MM, QX17700; 2/25 Bn. Stockman; of Pomona, Qld; b. Mount Mee, Qld, 31 Dec 1919.

East of Lae on 11th September the 4th Brigade began to relieve the scattered 20th; and the 2/17th Battalion was placed on an hour's notice to move to the Busu to form a firm base for the 26th Brigade when it eventually crossed the flooded river.

On the right flank of the division Hart's platoon of the 2/4th Independent Company in the Musom 2 area had explicit orders not to cross the Busu nor to go beyond Musom 2. At the kunda bridge itself Lieutenant Cox's platoon was guarding the crossing. On the 11th his sentries allowed a Japanese accompanied by two natives to cross the bridge from the west bank and then sent police boys to catch them. An hour later (at 3 p.m.) about 15 Japanese and 20 natives carrying rations approached the bridge. Cox held his fire until the Japanese began to cross. Although the Australians' opening bursts were not quite on the target, two Japanese fell into the river and two were killed near the bridge. Next day Cox's platoon noticed the Japanese digging in on the western bank. At 3.20 p.m. when another enemy party came up from the south and talked with the Japanese already there Cox opened up with his three Brens and caused casualties.

To the south the 2/24th Battalion, aided by Major Dawson's[6] 2/7th Field Company, continued their attempts to bridge the Busu. The battalion's Pioneer platoon began bridging the first stream of the Busu using logs placed on stone pylons. Later in the morning the engineers began preparations to cross by swinging one of the two recently-arrived folding boats from the hold-fast on the pendulum. Despite enemy mortar and small arms fire from the western bank during the afternoon, which caused seven casualties, the engineers launched the folding boat at 7 p.m. The first attempt with the empty boat was successful, but when it was being pulled back from the far shore it swamped. The hold-fast line then failed, and the boat, held only by the 3-inch rope attached to the bow, was brought ashore some distance downstream.

While the engineers made preparations to cross the third stream by "kedged raft", Colonel Gillespie and Dawson decided that the second stream must also be crossed by a log bridge. Alas, the river rose 2 feet 6 inches by midnight and washed away the Pioneers' first log bridge marooning on the island an infantry platoon and some sappers. These were rescued with difficulty and all attempts to bridge the river were abandoned for the night.

The 12th September was as frustrating as the 11th. The river was falling and the log bridge across the first stream was built again during the morning. The engineers persevered with the folding boat but eventually it sank. Using a tractor, which had arrived before the heavy rains made the jeep track from the Burep impassable, working parties hauled logs to the bank and manhandled them to the sandbank. The first log was too short and the second on being launched swung round, tearing away the pylon and part of the bank. When the log again swung round after

---

[6] Lt-Col B. F. Dawson, WX34. 2/1 Fd Coy; OC 2/7 Fd Coy. Engineering draftsman; of Newdegate, WA; b. Katanning, WA, 3 Jan 1915.

an extension had been fastened to it, and when it was apparent that there were no larger logs in the area, the disgusted workers gave up attempts for the night. Summing up the day's activities of his engineers Dawson noted: "Attempt at kedging fails—consider S.B.G. [small box girder] real answer for main river. Chase stores all day—no result except more [folding boats], so will attempt kedging again."

At 1 p.m. on the 12th a 2/23rd Battalion patrol found a likely crossing place about 3,000 yards north of the 2/24th where the river was between 70 and 100 feet wide. A large tree when felled might reach across the main stream, which flowed along the near bank, to an island in the centre whence the second stream could be waded. Whitehead then instructed McRae to send a company to cross there. The company arrived about dusk and felled the tree but it did not span the river.

Added to the frustration of being forced to halt for so long the troops in this area were hungry. Six L.C.M's were caught in a sudden storm on the unsheltered coast and were broached on the night 11th-12th September, but the remainder helped to establish dumps at the new "D" Beach west of the mouth of the Busu. Attempts to build up supply dumps at "D" and "G" Beaches and at the jeep-head on the Burep were handicapped by what Wootten later described as a "most distinct reluctance on the part of the Navy to put into 'G' Beach".[7] Stores hastily dumped ashore at Red Beach had therefore to be carried forward to the new beaches. It was only because the hard-working small craft made three trips a night from Red Beach that supplies, though inadequate, were kept up to the forward brigades. Under battle conditions novel to it, the "Q" side of the 9th Division tried its hardest to supply the forward troops. One error which would not have been committed in a more experienced jungle formation was the failure to send forward the mosquito nets and groundsheet rolls of the 2/17th Battalion "despite every effort and repeated requests by Brigade and its staff". The medical officer of the 2/23rd Battalion, Captain Davies,[8] scribbled a note to McRae on the 11th that rations were "quite inadequate considering the strenuous physical exertion involved". Continuing, he wrote: "Symptoms of malaria and vague dyspepsia are frequent and men are constantly complaining of weakness and inability to stand up to the work. Unless the quantity of food is increased the men will not be able to carry on under existing conditions."

The company of the 2/23rd which had been in the ill-fated landing craft at the landing was again the butt of misfortune on the 12th when a lone enemy shell burst in a tree killing Lieutenant Triplett,[9] and wounding 11, including Lieutenant Hipsley[1] (who remained on duty as company commander) and Captain Davies, who died later. Farther to the east the

---

[7] Report on Operations of 9 Aust Div in the Capture of Lae and Finschhafen—4 Sep-2 Oct 1943.
[8] Capt J. F. Davies, VX66289; RMO 2/23 Bn. Medical practitioner; of South Yarra, Vic; b. Melbourne, 1 Jan 1917. Died of wounds 12 Sep 1943.
[9] Lt L. C. Triplett, VX5343. 2/5 and 2/23 Bns. Truck driver; of Deniliquin, NSW; b. Carlton, Vic, 24 Mar 1909. Killed in action 12 Sep 1943.
[1] Capt J. W. Hipsley, VX51872. 2/23 and 29/46 Bns. Engineer; of Wollstonecraft, NSW; b. Wollstonecraft, 7 May 1917.

gun area on the Burep was attacked by 12 enemy bombers which inflicted 21 casualties.

On the coast Brigadier Evans had more cheerful news, although he was disappointed when informed that he must not let the 2/32nd Battalion pass through the 2/28th and resume the coastal advance. Wootten was unwilling that this battalion, until recently his divisional reserve, should be committed so soon. A clash of temperaments between Wootten and Evans was now becoming evident. Wootten was urging Evans on faster, and Evans felt that the services of one of his battalions was being denied him and the others were doing all humanly possible in the face of a stubborn enemy and a turbulent Nature. Evans believed that, if he could have only two small landing craft to move his troops in bounds along the coast and so avoid the slogging march along the coastal flats, the advance would be expedited. Wootten, however, had to reserve his few small craft for the movement of supplies for both brigades. Evans had been forced to strip the 2/43rd Battalion of weapons and ferry them over the Busu on the afternoon of the 11th by rope and punt to the 2/28th Battalion at a time when the better course would have been to use an L.C.V.P. Evans, however, arranged with the American boatmen to lend him an L.C.V.P. for a few trips which enabled him to equip the 2/28th Battalion properly again and get the 2/43rd moving inland. "If I could have used two boats under Brigade command," wrote Evans later, "our advance would have been faster and I would have been first into Lae." Wootten wrote later: "Had supplies been landed by the Navy on forward beaches as desired by me, small craft could probably have been made available to Evans."

The 2/32nd Battalion (Lieut-Colonel Scott[2]) began to cross on 12th September. The river rose and carried away the steel cable and the ferry ceased for six hours. Three L.C.V's took over the ferrying. One of these, commanded by Lieutenant Henderson E. McPherson (2 E.S.B.), kept shuttling troops across for 48 hours although it had its rudder shot away and had to improvise another. By the afternoon of the 12th the 2/32nd was ready to take over the bridgehead.

At dawn on the 12th the 24th Brigade was advancing towards Lae in the form of a prong—the 2/43rd on the right towards Old Yanga and the 2/28th along the coast towards Malahang Anchorage. While Captain Catchlove's[3] company of the 2/43rd Battalion patrolled towards New Yanga, Captain Gordon's[4] advanced along the road towards Old Yanga. During the morning both these companies met and dispersed enemy standing patrols, and at 2.30 p.m. a patrol reported that New Yanga appeared unoccupied.

---

[2] Brig T. H. Scott, DSO, ED, SX10309. 2/48 Bn 1940-42; CO 2/32 Bn 1942-45. Purchasing officer; of Glenelg, SA; b. Broken Hill, NSW, 16 Sep 1907.

[3] Maj W. E. L. Catchlove, MC, SX9947; 2/43 Bn. Salesman; of Camberwell, Vic; b. Adelaide, 25 Dec 1913.

[4] Lt-Col J. D. Gordon, MC, SX9822; 2/43 Bn. Warehouseman; of Grange, SA; b. London, 15 Apr 1918.

At 3.35 p.m. Catchlove was organising his company on the outskirts of New Yanga ready for an attack, when unexpected and heavy firing came from the direction of a hut. The surprised South Australians were unable to make any impression on the Japanese defenders. They bombarded New Yanga with mortars and many of the 525 shells fired by the two batteries of 25-pounders at the Burep landed on New Yanga. In spite of this a second infantry attack by Captain Siekmann's[5] company of the 2/43rd met the same reception as Catchlove's and both crestfallen companies, having suffered 22 casualties, were withdrawn to an area half way between Old Yanga and New Yanga.

By the 12th Brigadier Goodwin's[6] artillery was increasing its volume of fire. Targets on this day included the Lae and Malahang airfields. There were now fourteen 25-pounders of the 2/12th and 2/6th Regiments in action along the east bank of the Burep, and the 14th Field Regiment had arrived at Red Beach on the night 10th-11th September. A troop of two 155-mm guns (1917 model) from the 2/6th Regiment arrived at "G" Beach at 2 a.m. on 13th September and both guns were ready for action by 3 p.m. on the 15th.[7]

On 11th September, for the third day running, aircraft were unable to land at Nadzab, and thus the 25th Brigade still lacked its third battalion and the advance proper could not begin. While the remainder of the 2/25th Battalion moved along the Markham Valley Road, Captain Haydon's company was patrolling the area between Jensen's and Jenyns' Plantations, and brushed with the enemy occupying Jenyns' Track. Advancing along the north bank of the Markham from Narakapor, roughly parallel with the 2/25th Battalion, the 2/2nd Pioneers met little serious opposition. In the afternoon Lieutenant Hulse's[8] platoon dispersed a small enemy patrol and enabled the advance to continue without interruption to a position opposite Markham Point.

South of the Pioneers, across the river, Colonel Smith decided that Wampit Force would prevent the enemy crossing from Markham Point by attacking simultaneously the River and Southern Ambushes. At 4.30 p.m. the 24th Battalion's mortars fired 126 bombs including 8 rounds of smoke. When the mortar fire ceased the leading platoon attacked the River Ambush position, but the Japanese had moved forward during the bombardment, the mortar smoke was behind them, and they had little difficulty in repulsing the attack. Against the Southern Ambush the leading platoon commander had arranged for the M.M.G's to fire a short burst when in position whereupon he would fire his Owen as a signal for

---

[5] Capt D. C. Siekmann, MC, SX8896; 2/43 Bn. Salesman; of Kensington Gardens, SA; b. Adelaide, 29 Dec 1915.

[6] Brig S. T. W. Goodwin, DSO, VX11. (1st AIF: 6 Bty, AFA.) CO 2/12 Fd Regt 1940-43; CRA 9 Div 1943. Regular soldier; b. Ballarat, Vic, 6 Feb 1894. Killed in action 25 Oct 1943.

[7] Commenting on the experiences of the battery of 155-mm guns (1941 model) in the Salamaua and Lae campaigns the acting battery commander, Captain J. W. Hutton, wrote: "It is believed that this is the first time that artillery heavier than field has been used in active operations by the A.I.F. during the present war—excluding captured medium weapons."

[8] Lt T. Hulse, MC, QX4249; 2/2 Pnr Bn. Windmill expert; b. Warrington, Lancs, England, 15 Jun 1911.

Transport aircraft at Nadzab airfield on 21st September 1943. After its capture on 5th September the airfield was rapidly developed into one of the largest air bases in New Guinea.

(*Australian War Memorial*)

(Australian War Memorial)
Crossing at the mouth of the Buso River on 5th September 1943 after the 9th Division's landing at Red Beach.

(Imperial War Museum)
Troops of the 7th Division entering Lae on 16th September 1943 along a road littered with debris from air and artillery bombardments.

the troops to move forward and for the M.M.G's to give supporting fire. The platoon commander waited on the signal from the M.M.G's who waited for the signal from the platoon commander; and so time went on, the impetus petered out, and the attack was postponed.

For the 12th Vasey ordered Eather with the 2/2nd Pioneer Battalion under command to advance on Lae. On this day, when the 2/31st Battalion at length arrived in many of the 130 planes which landed on the two Nadzab airfields, the 25th Brigade began to meet stiffening opposition. By the time the rest of the 2/25th Battalion joined Haydon at 10.10 a.m., the company had inflicted 37 casualties in its three days of skirmishing with the enemy. Colonel Marson at 1.10 p.m. sent Robertson's company, accompanied by an observation post officer (Lieutenant Stokes[9]) from the 54th Battery round the left flank to attack the enemy company reported on Jenyns' Track. At 3 p.m. it crossed the creek, and advanced through Jenyns'.

An hour later Robertson reached Jenyns' Track behind the main enemy position after dispersing a small patrol. Cut off from the next plantation (Whittaker's) by Robertson's company, the encircled Japanese attacked fiercely but were repulsed by the Australians, who suffered eight casualties. The enemy suffered about 30 casualties, some caused by the artillery. At dusk Robertson established a perimeter defence near the junction of the main track and Jenyns' Track with Captain Gow's[1] company in support.

On the 12th a patrol of the 2/2nd Pioneers reached Heath's Track where it crossed the Narinsera Waters; a second, trying to cut a track towards Jenyns', found the tangled growth almost impenetrable, and a third along the Markham found four folding boats and a new outboard motor near Markham Point. As Colonel Lang's men watched the Markham racing east in a 600-yards-wide flood they marvelled that they had ever been able to cross it. The fate of Lae might well have been different had Z-day been delayed. As it was, the much smaller but flooded Busu was holding up one division while adverse weather had delayed a build up of supplies for another for three days.

On the 12th Smith's four platoons round Markham Point made another attempt to capture their objective. The force was now commanded by Captain Bunbury,[2] who decided to capture some of the Southern Ambush's pill-boxes as a "leg in for future grenade exploitation". Soon after first light the leading platoon used log frames to traverse the minefields but it was caught in heavy cross fire from the enemy who had heavily reinforced the position. The attack was repulsed and two men were killed, including the leading platoon commander, Lieutenant Richards.[3] "It is considered," wrote the battalion diarist with some justification, "that a

---

[9] Lt W. E. Stokes, MC, VX18177; 2/4 Fd Regt. Grazier; of Echuca, Vic; b. Echuca, 20 Aug 1908.
[1] Maj G. A. T. Gow, QX6339; 2/25 Bn. Bank officer; of Stanthorpe, Qld; b. Perth, Scotland, 4 Apr 1912.
[2] Maj C. R. Bunbury, NX150345. 24 and 2/6 Bns. Regular soldier; of Melbourne; b. Melbourne, 20 Feb 1919.
[3] Lt B. W. Richards, TX5359; 24 Bn. Baker's assistant; of Campbelltown, Tas; b. Devonport, Tas, 13 May 1920. Killed in action 12 Sep 1943.

further ground attack without support will not be successful and application has again been made for a synchronised air and artillery attack." With an abundance of air support available to the two A.I.F. divisions, a small modicum might well have been spared to soften up an elaborate defensive position before Wampit Force was asked to advance over cleared fields of fire to attack the strong position. It was not until Smith visited Vasey and asked for his aid that air and artillery support were arranged.

Wootten's main anxiety was how to keep his troops supplied. Signalling Herring on the 13th he protested against the dumping of stores at Red Beach instead of his forward beaches, pointing out that an L.C.T. (carrying field guns) had already safely beached on "G" Beach.

> Under these circumstances (he added) it is considered practicable to beach 3 LCT's on each of G and D Beaches. ESB craft available for forward maintenance from Red Beach are only 3 LCM's and 7 LCV's that arrived night 12/13. All others broached by heavy surf and badly damaged. Land maintenance impossible. Therefore for successful conduct of operations LCT's with re-supply must repeat must discharge on forward beaches as required.

Despite these supply difficulties Wootten ordered the 26th Brigade to cross the river and advance on a two-battalion front, one towards Kamkamun and Malahang Mission and the other through the sawmill to the north end of the Malahang airfield and Malahang Mission. On the southern front the 24th Brigade would advance with one battalion through New Yanga and Wagan, another along the coast towards Malahang Anchorage, and a third would "mask" the south end of Malahang airfield.

Even high in the mountains the Busu was difficult to cross, despite the fact that local natives informed the 2/4th Independent Company that it was possible to wade across when it had not rained for 24 hours beforehand. At dawn on the 13th Lieutenant Hart sent Lieutenant Staples' section to attempt to wade across upstream from the kunda bridge. As Staples led his men into the river at first light he was dragged in by the current and whirled out of sight, but finally managed to clamber out 300 or 400 yards downstream; while lying exhausted on the left bank he was wounded by a sniper. The remainder of the section were swept off their feet and scattered along the near bank of the river. Hoping that the Japanese had left the area, Hart then ordered Lieutenant Trevaldwyn's[4] section to cross the river on the kunda bridge, while the rest of the platoon gave covering fire. The Japanese now did what the Australians had done to them previously and allowed some of the section across before opening fire. Before this heavy fire cut the frail bridge to ribbons seven men, including the badly wounded Lance-Corporal Haly,[5] were marooned on the far side; others, including Trevaldwyn, were knocked off the bridge into the river and three men were killed.

---

[4] Capt D. E. Trevaldwyn, MC, VX117267. 2/4 Indep Coy, 2/4 Cdo Sqn, "Z" Special Unit. Rubber planter; of Malaya; b. Cheltenham, England, 14 Feb 1917.
[5] L-Cpl A. R. Haly, QX26815. 2/4 Indep Coy, 2/4 Cdo Sqn. Grocer; of Wooloowin, Qld; b. Nambour, Qld, 27 Feb 1919.

This desperate situation for the seven men would have been worse but for the cool courage of Private Jaggar[6] who attacked and destroyed two enemy machine-gun nests and a mortar post, killing several Japanese and capturing much equipment. Thereafter the small group was forced to crouch all day by the western bank.

Hart attempted to aid his beleaguered men by sending out patrols to cross upstream or downstream, but they were unsuccessful. A message was therefore fired to the stranded party in a hand grenade fired from a rifle cup discharger telling them to try to return under cover of darkness. After dusk the men destroyed the captured enemy equipment (including two L.M.G's, one mortar and one rifle) or threw it into the river, and then tried to swim across. Jaggar was an excellent swimmer and managed to get Haly across, but two men were swirled away and disappeared. The other men crossed after being swept down the river. The platoon had lost six killed or drowned and several wounded. The pity was that, if allowed to, the platoon could have crossed without opposition on the 10th and 11th and possibly early on the 12th. It was not until the enemy had dug in on the far bank that Hart was given orders to cross. Also, if permitted to patrol extensively beyond Musom 2 on these three days, when they were chafing on the bit, Hart's men would almost certainly have found the main enemy crossing of the Busu; and long-range patrolling was the specialty of an Independent Company.

On the 13th the sappers and the 2/24th Battalion worked very hard attempting to bridge the river for the 26th Brigade, but once again luck and the Busu were against them. By 4 in the morning another attempt at kedging had failed, but at "G" Beach an S.B.G. and more folding boats arrived an hour later and were sent along the Burep and jeep track towards the Busu. Soon after dawn timber-cutting parties began searching for bigger logs to bridge the second stream, but although two 90-foot logs were felled and dragged to the river they were not long enough.

At 11 a.m. the sappers, supported by artillery and small arms fire, prepared to make a crossing with the small box girder and a kedge of two folding boats. Unfortunately the S.B.G. missed the far bank by three feet, the nose twisted and the girder was washed away and lost. The S.B.G. was retained by a tail line although the raft collapsed in midstream. At 4 p.m. more girders, which now had top priority in movement from the beaches, arrived and the sappers prepared for a more deliberate effort at night using an extra box section and counterweight.

By 11.15 p.m. the S.B.G. was across the second stream and was being secured and decked, despite casualties caused by fire from the far bank. Reconnaissance parties from the sapper platoons led by Lieutenants Rushton[7] and Kermode,[8] who had been working continuously on

---

[6] Maj B. K. Jaggar, MM, NX134066. 2/4 Indep Coy, 2/4 Cdo Sqn. Clerk; of Maroubra Junction, NSW; b. Long Ditton, Surrey, England, 21 Nov 1920.

[7] Capt R. A. Rushton, MC, WX1198. 2/3 and 2/7 Fd Coys; RAE 9 Div 1944-45. Road Board secretary-engineer; of Gosnells, WA; b. Rochdale, England, 17 Jul 1909.

[8] Capt R. G. Kermode, NX77385. 2/7 Fd Coy; LHQ 1944-45. Civil engineer; of Melbourne; b. Melbourne, 21 Nov 1916.

the crossing for about 36 hours, went over the bridge to seek a ford over the last stream and patrols returned soon after midnight to report that the third stream would need bridging by logs. The logs were dragged across the two streams while the S.B.G. was handrailed. "2/24th Battalion becoming very impatient," noted Dawson.

Doubtful whether a crossing would ever be made, Whitehead, early on the 13th, asked Wootten for permission to send about 120 men to cross the Busu at its mouth and advance north to secure the bank opposite the 2/24th Battalion. An hour later Lieut-Colonel Ainslie[9] of the 2/48th ordered a company back by the jeep road to the mouth of the Busu. The company crossed at the 24th Brigade's crossing at midday and began advancing north but jungle, kunai and swamp slowed progress, and communications were unsure.

Unlike the 26th Brigade, the 24th was in a position to attempt to carry out Wootten's orders for the 13th. The 2/43rd Battalion found New Yanga unoccupied and camped for the night about half way between New Yanga and Wagan. Along the coastal track between "D" Beach and Malahang Anchorage the 2/28th Battalion was encountering stiff resistance on the 13th. The Japanese infiltrated the forward positions of the battalion soon after midnight on the 12th-13th. When the advance resumed in the morning Lieutenant Connor's[1] platoon at 11.20 a.m. encountered an enemy force entrenched at the track junction 1,000 yards east of Malahang Anchorage. Connor and Corporal Torrent[2] went ahead of the platoon and attacked three foxholes. Torrent killed six of the enemy including an officer, but heavy fire prevented the platoon advancing. Because the platoon's grenades were damp and therefore ineffective Torrent dashed back to the company and brought forward all the grenades he could carry. When he returned he found that Connor had been killed and he then assumed command of the platoon. Aided by another platoon on the right flank Torrent's men killed twelve more Japanese. At 3.30 p.m. Torrent advanced to the track junction which the remaining enemy had abandoned, thus enabling the advance to continue.

As the division advanced the enemy hit back with his many guns stationed around Lae. On the 13th a stray 75-mm shell had killed two men including the artillery observer with the 2/23rd Battalion, Captain Henty;[3] on the 14th enemy shelling increased and the idea crossed the mind of one battalion's diarist that the Japanese might be using all their artillery ammunition in a final bombardment before withdrawing. As the enemy guns inflicted about 50 casualties on the 14th, mainly among the American amphibian engineers along the coast,[4] it would be reasonable to assume

---

[9] Brig R. I. Ainslie, DSO, WX20. 2/11 Bn; CO 23/21 Bn 1942-43, 2/48 Bn 1943-45. Solicitor; of Perth; b. South Perth, 14 Jun 1909.

[1] Lt E. M. Connor, WX5263. 2/28 and 2/43 Bns. Bank officer; of Crawley, WA; b. Wagin, WA, 19 Jan 1920. Killed in action 13 Sep 1943.

[2] Sgt A. Torrent, MM, WX4822; 2/28 Bn. Station overseer; of Busselton, WA; b. Busselton, 21 Sep 1903.

[3] Capt W. M. Henty, VX898; 2/12 Fd Regt. Accountant; of Malvern, Vic; b. Armadale, Vic, 21 Nov 1916. Killed in action 13 Sep 1943.

[4] In the Lae campaign 532nd EBSR lost 9 killed and 66 wounded. (*History of the Second Engineer Special Brigade*, pp. 49-50.)

that the 22 Australian field guns[5] now along the Burep would inflict equally heavy if not greater casualties.

As the 2/4th Independent Company had been unable to find a crossing north or south of the kunda bridge Captain Garvey sent his third platoon south to cross in the wake of Whitehead's brigade. Another report about Japanese moving north along the west bank of the Busu came from Private Mannion,[6] who, although wounded and marooned west of the kunda bridge on the 13th, had swum the river at its junction with the Sankwep and told of seeing 100 Japanese on the opposite track.

The troops and their leaders were understandably becoming exasperated. With Wootten urging him on from behind, Whitehead said that more attention should have been paid to his early request for an S.B.G., when he could have crossed without opposition. He considered that artillery was being pushed forward to do a job which could have been done with mortars. This, of course, was not an entirely just picture, but the S.B.G. could doubtless have been hurried forward earlier.

After five days of frustration, however, the 26th Brigade was at last able to cross the Busu when the sappers finished bridging the third channel at first light on the 14th. At 6.30 a.m. the leading company of the 2/24th

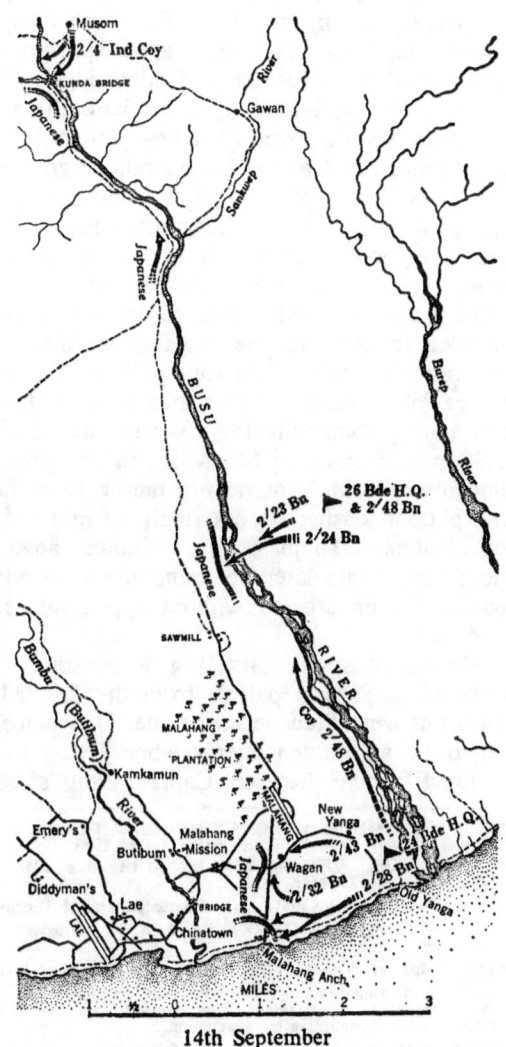

14th September

---

[5] Two days later 52 field guns and 2 medium guns were arrayed against the Japanese.
[6] Tpr F. Mannion, NX77965. 2/4 Indep Coy, 2/4 Cdo Sqn. Labourer; of St Peters, NSW; b. Avon Dam, NSW, 18 Aug 1920.

Battalion—Captain McNamara's[7]—crossed the log and girder bridges, and climbed the western bank, 30 feet high. As Lieutenant King's[8] platoon began to move upstream it saw the Japanese about to enter their weapon-pits after having apparently slept in a near-by village. At the edge of the jungle the platoon was fired on and King was wounded. Lieutenant Stevens'[9] platoon, moving to the south-west, was also fired on from the jungle fringe, but here the Japanese speedily withdrew in face of the Australians' advance. Lieutenant Braimbridge's platoon now went to the assistance of King's, intending to outflank the northern enemy position, but its advance was stopped when heavy enemy fire from the left flank wounded Braimbridge and forced his platoon to ground.

The task of Captain Finlay's[1] company, which began to cross the river, was more difficult than McNamara's, for the Japanese were now thoroughly alert. Supported by fire from one platoon Finlay sent the other two across; they suffered 12 casualties in doing so. Seventy yards down the third stream a signaller crossed and tied a cable to the other side. Finlay decided to continue the crossing at this point and Lieutenant Inkster[2] swam across with a light rope pulling a heavier one which he attached to a tree. While Finlay and six men were tightening the rope, a mortar bomb fell among them inflicting six casualties, including Finlay, wounded.[3] At 1.30 p.m. Signalman Mitchell[4] ran the gauntlet by taking a new signals line across to McNamara. For the next two hours the men of the supporting platoon dashed across singly to join the company, now commanded by Lieutenant Thomas.[5] When Thomas advanced against the enemy positions four hours later he found them abandoned. The remainder of the battalion then crossed without opposition, followed by the 2/23rd and 2/48th.[6]

On the coast the 24th Brigade continued to advance against stubborn opposition. Several patrols from the 2/43rd approached Wagan on the 14th but were fired on each time. One patrol lost its two forward scouts killed by an unseen enemy when trying to encircle the village. Lieut-Colonel Joshua[7] then sent Captain Grant's[8] company to capture the cross-

---

[7] Capt J. F. McNamara, MC, VX30994; 2/24 Bn. Auctioneer; of Yarrawonga, Vic; b. Yarrawonga, 25 May 1909. Killed in action 8 Dec 1943.

[8] Lt R. S. King, VX33868; 2/24 Bn. MHR since 1958. Farmer; of Warracknabeal, Vic; b. Warracknabeal, 22 Mar 1920.

[9] Lt K. W. Stevens, VX50311; 2/24 Bn. Salesman; of Thornbury, Vic; b. Thornbury, 22 Oct 1920.

[1] Capt J. T. Finlay, MC, VX40767; 2/24 Bn. Grazier; of Seymour, Vic; b. Melbourne, 16 Oct 1909.

[2] Lt J. J. Inkster, VX55630; 2/24 Bn. Warehouseman; of Melbourne; b. Carlton, Vic, 21 Apr 1920.

[3] Finlay had been wounded twice in the left leg—against the Italians at Tobruk and against the Germans at El Alamein; now wounded for the third time in the left leg he did not return to the battalion after evacuation.

[4] Sig R. Mitchell, VX67518; 2/24 Bn. Mail sorter; of Coburg, Vic; b. Stanhope, Vic, 27 Jun 1922.

[5] Lt G. E. Thomas, VX48726; 2/24 Bn. Carpenter; of Portland, Vic; b. Portland, 20 Apr 1910.

[6] Captain D. P. Hill's company of the 2/48th, meanwhile, had reached a position about 5,000 yards from the mouth of the Busu, in an abortive attempt to capture the bridgehead. Had permission been received earlier for this company to be dispatched on its task the crossing might not have been opposed.

[7] Lt-Col R. Joshua, MC, VX15117. 2/32 Bn 1941-43; CO 2/43 Bn 1943-44, 13/33 Bn 1944-45. MHR 1951-55. Bank officer; of Korumburra, Vic; b. Armadale, Vic, 6 Jun 1906.

[8] Maj E. C. Grant, MC, SX10270. 9 Div Ski School; 2/43 Bn. Regular soldier; of Woodville Park, SA; b. Rose Park, SA, 2 Jan 1910.

roads south-west of Wagan and thus cut the Japanese off from Lae, but the company met fire from a nest of machine-guns, and was unable to capture the track junction by a direct assault or by an encircling move through the dense undergrowth.

The 2/32nd Battalion entered the fight for the first time on the 14th. Relieved by the 2/17th early in the morning it set out along the coastal track. After hearing a report from Lieutenant Rice[9] of the Papuan company that one of his patrols had inflicted four casualties on the Japanese who were occupying a village about half way between Wagan and Malahang Anchorage, Brigadier Evans instructed Scott of the 2/32nd to capture the village. While issuing orders for the advance Scott's headquarters was shelled and Scott was slightly wounded. One and a half hours later Lieutenant Denness'[1] company preceded by a Papuan section met the Japanese south of the village.

"Fixing" the enemy with one platoon, Denness sent Lieutenant Day's[2] platoon round the right flank and his third platoon round the left. Sniped at from the tree tops and from an abandoned truck Day's platoon suffered heavy casualties, Day himself being shot through the spine. Warrant Officer Dalziel[3] tried to drag him out but was killed when success seemed near. Day was then killed by a grenade and Sergeant McCallum[4] took over. By this time Denness reported that the situation was "pretty warm", and requested mortar bombardment of the well-concealed enemy positions.

Denness withdrew for the mortar shoot and Captain Davies'[5] company prepared to capitalise on the twelve 3-inch and ten 2-inch bombs fired. Davies formed up his company and at 4.15 p.m. Lieutenant Scott's[6] platoon went straight in on a frontal attack, supported by machine-gun fire from the flanking platoons. Meeting heavy and sustained fire after 30 yards the platoon suffered six casualties including Scott, wounded, and was pinned down on the edge of the clearing. Davies then brought up the other two platoons on the flanks. Under their covering fire, the first platoon now led by Sergeant Bell[7] advanced again through the open. Seeing that an enemy machine-gun slightly to one flank was inflicting casualties Bell moved ahead of his men and coolly attacked and destroyed it.

The heavy enemy fire caused Davies to ask for support from Denness' company, which readily came forward and supported each of the forward

---

[9] Capt M. W. Rice, QX46961. 49 Bn and Papuan Inf Bn. Salesman; of Bardon, Qld; b. Brisbane, 19 Aug 1921.
[1] Maj A. P. Denness, MC, WX8667; 2/32 Bn. 3 Bn RAR Korea 1950-51. Butcher; of Fremantle, WA; b. South Fremantle, 26 Dec 1914.
[2] Lt D. P. Day, WX9248; 2/32 Bn. Bricklayer; of Albany, WA; b. Melksham, England, 28 Jan 1910. Killed in action 14 Sep 1943.
[3] WO2 G. A. Dalziel, NX6490; 2/32 Bn. Still hand; of Bankstown, NSW; b. Bankstown, 5 Jan 1922. Killed in action 14 Sep 1943.
[4] Sgt C. R. McCallum, VX35800. I Corps Sigs and 2/32 Bn. Salesman; of Auburn, Vic; b. Hawthorn, Vic, 24 Nov 1921.
[5] Capt H. G. Davies, MBE, QX37; 2/32 Bn. Truck driver; of Spring Hill, NSW; b. Toowoomba, Qld, 27 Jul 1915.
[6] Lt G. A. Scott, WX1884; 2/32 Bn. Farm worker; of Midland Junction, WA; b. Midland Junction, 20 Jun 1914.
[7] Sgt H. J. Bell, DCM, MM, VX29458; 2/32 Bn. Grocery salesman; of Northcote, Vic; b. Northcote, 3 Mar 1913.

platoons with one of its own. As the Japanese began to waver Bell's platoon pushed home the attack and pursued them through the village. Lieutenant Garnsey's[8] platoon on the left had been in a better position to support Bell's advance and the three Brens did valuable work. When Garnsey began to advance, his platoon ran into heavy machine-gun fire. Trying to silence the machine-guns Corporal Kendrick[9] went forward towards them firing, but before he could reach them he was mortally wounded. When one of the Bren gunners became a casualty Private Armitage,[1] who had only recently joined the battalion, took over the Bren and kept it in action. The platoon then advanced, mopping up snipers, as well as fowls destined for the cooking pot.

At dusk the two companies had captured the village and road to the west and dug in south of the road and track junction. In a very creditable introduction to jungle warfare the 2/32nd Battalion had killed at least 70 Japanese for the loss of 33 casualties, including 10 killed. "It would seem," wrote the battalion diarist, "that the rising sun has moved to the western sky insofar as Lae is concerned." He did not know how right he was.

Advancing towards Malahang Anchorage on the 14th Norman of the 2/28th planned to give the impression of continuing along the coast with one company (Newbery's) while the other three infiltrated to cut the road behind the Japanese. Patrols to find routes for the three company attacks set out soon after first light. At 9.15 a.m. Lieutenant Hindley's[2] patrol killed 12 Japanese without loss and at 12.40 p.m. it killed another 14. Lieutenant Hannah's company found two abandoned 75-mm dual-purpose guns north of the anchorage early in the afternoon. By 3.50 p.m. the two leading encircling companies (Hannah's and Lyon's) were in position after passing through difficult country and suffering a few casualties from sporadic enemy fire. Newbery's company edged forward to the eastern side of the anchorage against determined opposition at a bottleneck between the sea and a creek. As the company found it almost impossible to encircle this position, Norman ordered its withdrawal. North of the anchorage the other three companies were astride the road by dusk. By sheer tenacity they had infiltrated round the enemy positions through swamp and virtually sealed the anchorage's fate.

At Nadzab the aerial build-up continued; 165 planes arrived on the 13th and 106 on the 14th. General Vasey ordered Brigadier Eather to continue the advance on Heath's Plantation on the 13th. Eather gave his battalion commanders their tasks: the 2/25th would apply pressure to Whittaker's Plantation at daylight; the 2/33rd would move round the

---

[8] Lt K. A. Garnsey, MM, NX11889; 2/32 Bn. Farmer; of West Wyalong, NSW; b. Uralla, NSW, 14 May 1915.

[9] Cpl K. J. Kendrick, QX117; 2/32 Bn. Farm worker; of Toowoomba, Qld; b. Brisbane, 10 Aug 1918. Killed in action 14 Sep 1943.

[1] Pte H. L. W. Armitage, NX99971; 2/32 Bn. Mill hand; of Heron's Creek, NSW; b. Newcastle, NSW, 5 Jan 1920.

[2] Lt R. G. Hindley, WX10689; 2/28 Bn. Window dresser; of Subiaco, WA; b. Perth, 26 Apr 1916.

south, establish a road-block at Heath's and advance back towards Whittaker's; and the 2/31st would be prepared to lead the advance on Lae, once this opposition was overcome. By last light on the 12th Captain Gow's company of the 2/25th had moved round the left flank of Major Robertson's, at the track and road junction north-west of Whittaker's. Early on the 13th Colonel Marson ordered Gow's company followed by Captain W. G. Butler's to advance through the overgrown plantation on a compass bearing for Heath's and to hit the enemy with everything they had.

Half an hour later (8.30 a.m.) Robertson's company began to advance warily down the Markham Valley Road, and at 9.30 a.m. it met a strongly-entrenched enemy force at Whittaker's bridge. It was pinned down although Sergeant Jones'[3] platoon on the left of the bridge was able to report enemy movements. Robertson called for artillery support but Lieutenant Stokes, the forward artillery officer, protested that the Australians were too close to the Japanese and that artillery fire would be dangerous. Robertson replied, "We are well dug in; have a go at it, you'll do them more damage than you will us."[4] Several shells were fired but when one dropped short Stokes told Robertson that he would have to find some other way to knock out the enemy position. Robertson tried a mortar, but because he was so close to the bridge he found that even more dangerous than the gun.

The two northern companies moved slowly through difficult country cut by small streams. For the first time each company had walkie-talkie sets which enabled them to keep in touch with one another during their advance. Soon some well-beaten enemy tracks were crossed and the general air of tenseness reflected the knowledge that trouble might break at any moment. When the leading platoon (Lieutenant Howes[5]) reported that the going was becoming rougher, Gow reluctantly forsook the higher ground and swung down towards the Markham Valley Road through a re-entrant. A few minutes later Japanese voices were heard ahead. The platoon advanced for about 50 yards feeling very exposed in an avenue between cocoa trees. Soon after 10 a.m. two sections were pinned down by fire, having suffered casualties. The third section (Corporal Francis'[6]) then attacked but was held up. Francis seized the Bren from his mortally wounded gunner and relieved some of the enemy pressure before he too was wounded. With his whole platoon pinned down Howes requested assistance on his left flank where the opposition was heaviest.

Gow sent Lieutenant Burns'[7] platoon to attack on Howes' left. The leading section under Corporal Richards[8] fanned out in an extended line

---

[3] Sgt F. P. Jones, MM, QX16061; 2/25 Bn. Labourer-driver; of South Brisbane; b. Brisbane, 7 Oct 1919.

[4] Quoted in R. L. Henry, *The Story of the 2/4th Field Regiment*, p. 221.

[5] Capt J. F. Howes, QX14949; 2/25 Bn. Medical student; of Brisbane; b. Brisbane, 17 Aug 1920.

[6] Cpl M. J. Francis, QX20674; 2/25 Bn. Farm worker; of Kilcoy, Qld; b. Esk, Qld, 16 Mar 1915.

[7] Capt R. T. C. Burns, QX10366; 2/25 Bn. Clerk; of Toowoomba, Qld; b. Taree, NSW, 17 Jan 1915.

[8] Sgt W. H. Richards, MM, QX26271; 2/25 Bn. Master pastrycook; of Northgate, Qld; b. Brisbane, 30 Oct 1912.

while Burns' second section under Corporal Sawers[9] filled the gap between Richards and the platoon on the right. When both these sections met heavy fire Burns sent his third section (Corporal Duckham[1]) in on the left flank and adjoining the track which cut the Markham Valley Road. Soon this section also was pinned down.

Gow tried again and sent in his last platoon (Lieutenant Macrae[2]) on Burns' left, along a ridge from which the heaviest fire was falling on the two other platoons. Whereas the two leading platoons had struck the enemy's forward defences, Macrae entered through the "back door" and attacked what appeared to be the Japanese headquarters. Sergeant Hill[3] killed three Japanese as the platoon cleared the ridge and wiped out one machine-gun post. As Gow had now run out of troops Marson placed one of Butler's platoons (Lieutenant Howie[4]) under his command to move along the ridge to the right of Howes and clear out the enemy.

Meanwhile, the two pinned platoons were doing their best to wipe out the opposition ahead. Burns' platoon had suffered eight casualties including one section commander, Corporal Sawers, killed and another, Corporal Richards, wounded. Richards was lying out in front down the forward slope of a small rise and was doing his best to observe the enemy machine-guns and direct fire at them.

During this time Privates Kelliher[5] and Bickle[6] were lying in a dip. Kelliher said to his companion, "I'd better go and bring him [Richards] in." Hurling his and Bickle's last grenades at the machine-gun post he killed some of the enemy but not all. He then grabbed a Bren gun from a wounded gunner and dashed forward firing until the magazine was emptied. Returning he got another magazine, went forward again, fired it from a lying-down position and silenced the machine-gun post. Under fire from another enemy position Kelliher then carried the wounded Richards to safety.[7]

Entering the fight on Gow's right flank in the wake of Howie's platoon, Butler's company attacked down the ridge in a south-westerly direction towards the main track in the early afternoon. Against stiff opposition the company made only slight progress before being stopped; it dug in for the night in a plantation drain with one platoon about 50 yards from the Markham Valley Road. The two companies were about half a mile east of Robertson's company at Whittaker's bridge. The battalion had

---

[9] Cpl S. Sawers, QX20212; 2/25 Bn. Labourer; of Jambin, Qld; b. Miriam Vale, Qld, 26 May 1919. Killed in action 13 Sep 1943.

[1] L-Sgt J. Duckham, QX20162; 2/25 Bn. Horse breaker; of Nagoorin, Qld; b. Miriam Vale, Qld, 8 Jun 1914.

[2] Lt D. G. Macrae, NX113725; 2/25 Bn. Bank officer; of Grafton, NSW; b. Coraki, NSW, 8 Dec 1916.

[3] Sgt B. S. Hill, QX15433; 2/25 Bn. Surveyor; of Innisfail, Qld; b. Mourilyan, Qld, 28 Jul 1918. Died of wounds 19 Jul 1945.

[4] Capt T. M. Howie, MBE, QX10781; 2/25 Bn. Sawmill hand; of Nanango, Qld; b. Kingaroy, Qld, 5 Jun 1917.

[5] Pte R. Kelliher, VC, QX20656; 2/25 Bn. Labourer; of Brisbane; b. Ballybaggan, Tralee, Eire, 1 Sep 1910.

[6] Pte J. H. Bickle, QX20251; 2/25 Bn. Labourer; of Rockhampton, Qld; b. Rockhampton, 28 May 1913.

[7] Kelliher was awarded the Victoria Cross.

suffered 26 casualties on the 13th, including 10 killed, but it was estimated that the Japanese had lost about 100. Gow's wounded were carried out on stretchers at night by the light of lanterns.

During the afternoon while both companies were slowly inching forward it became evident that Macrae had overrun an important headquarters. In one hut was a wireless set, and other equipment captured included a machine-gun and a bullet-proof vest. More important, some documents and maps were captured. Macrae sent these to Gow who noted that one map of the Markham Valley and Lae showed markings which appeared to be enemy positions. From this he judged the documents to be important and sent them rapidly back through various channels to translators where "a most uninteresting paper in appearance", as Gow called it, caused no little excitement.

It was not until after midday when Macrae's platoon had captured the Japanese headquarters that Eather gave the 2/33rd Battalion the green light

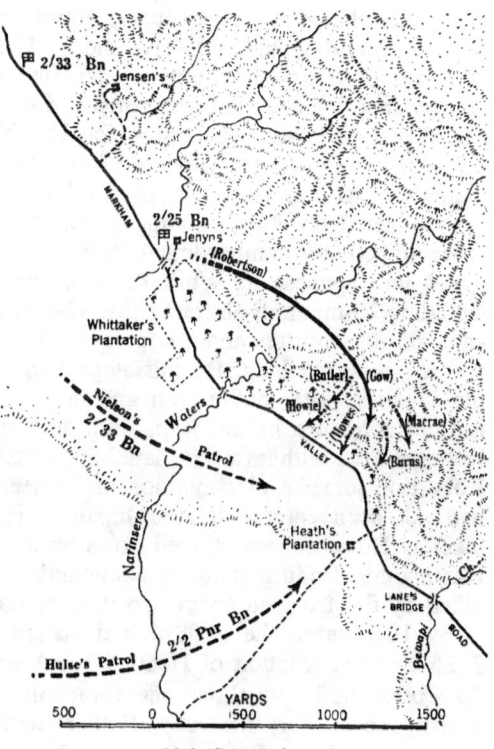

13th September

to find a route round the right flank into Heath's. Lieutenant Nielson[8] then led a patrol through the dense overgrown plantation seeking a suitable route, while the remainder of the battalion prepared to move forward.

Patrols from the 2/2nd Pioneers were very active on the 13th. One of them, led by Lieutenant D. O. Smith, cut a track north from the Markham towards the Markham Valley Road and near Edwards' Plantation. Another, led by Lieutenant Hulse, cut a track north towards Heath's. By 10.45 a.m. Hulse's patrol was close to Whittaker's, and at 3.30 p.m. it entered Heath's, deserted except for Nielson's patrol from the 2/33rd Battalion. Both patrols found Heath's devastated by aerial bombardment.

By 4 p.m. Nielson returned to his battalion having found a suitable route to Heath's while Hulse combed the area collecting documents.

---

[8] Lt R. H. Nielson, NX31139; 2/33 Bn. Clerk; of Arncliffe, NSW; b. Marrickville, NSW, 31 Oct 1919.

Hulse's patrol was followed into Heath's by Colonel Lang and three men. When he realised that the patrol had cut off the enemy who were bitterly defending the Whittaker's area against the 2/25th, Lang decided to occupy Heath's for the night and summoned Lieutenant Coles'[9] platoon. Before it could arrive Hulse's patrol was attacked by a small enemy force from the west. Largely due to the reports of Lance-Corporal Egan,[1] who climbed a tree in full view of the enemy, Hulse was able to repulse this enemy force surrounding him on three sides. The Japanese approached within 50 yards of Egan's tree but he emulated many Japanese snipers before him by shooting the leading enemy and driving the others to cover. Soon Coles' platoon arrived and occupied Heath's for the night.

For 14th September General Vasey ordered the capture of Edwards' Plantation. At 6 a.m. a patrol led by Corporal Duckham from Gow's company joined Robertson's company and reported no Japanese in between. After an artillery bombardment Robertson's company moved forward and found no Japanese at Whittaker's bridge. Much equipment was found, including 20-mm anti-aircraft guns, 37-mm anti-tank guns, heavy machine-guns, 85-mm mortars and a large quantity of ammunition and stores, some still in grease packing. By this stage Brigadier Eather was confident that the Japanese were pulling out and urged greater speed. He overtook the leading company in his jeep, and, finding the pace too slow, ordered Robertson to withdraw his flanking patrols and push on. By 8.30 a.m. Robertson joined Coles' platoon of Pioneers in Heath's Plantation, which had not been entered by the Japanese in their withdrawal from Whittaker's. Robertson continued to advance; half an hour after entering Heath's his leading platoon commander, Lieutenant Weitemeyer,[2] was killed by fire from an enemy position at Lane's bridge.

By 10.15 a.m. the 2/33rd had passed through the remainder of the 2/25th at the junction of Heath's Track and the Markham Valley Road. As Cotton had only three rifle companies because of the disaster to the fourth one at Port Moresby, Eather directed Lang to lend a company to Cotton. After relieving Robertson's company of the 2/25th near the bridge, Cotton decided to encircle the enemy position and sent one company to the right and one to the left. The third infantry company also moved round to the left in support; and Captain Garrard's company of Pioneers took over near the bridge. Soon after midday, as the companies began to close in, Lieutenant Carroll[3] of the 2/4th Field Regiment directed the shelling of the bridge position for 20 minutes. For the next 15 minutes Mitchells strafed the track ahead of the 2/33rd. It was difficult for artillery or aircraft to bombard accurately such a Japanese position which,

---

[9] Lt S. A. Coles, VX38716; 2/2 Pnr Bn. Salesman; of Carnegie, Vic; b. Coventry, England, 9 Apr 1915.

[1] Cpl P. K. Egan, MM, NX81212; 2/2 Pnr Bn. Carpenter; of Bega, NSW; b. West Wyalong, NSW, 2 Sep 1920.

[2] Lt H. W. Weitemeyer, QX13524; 2/25 Bn. Delivery superintendent; of Brisbane; b. Bundaberg, Qld, 28 Apr 1917. Killed in action 14 Sep 1943.

[3] Capt C. Carroll, VX50442; 2/4 Fd Regt. Estate agent; of Hawthorn, Vic; b. Melbourne, 2 Mar 1912.

like most defensive positions in the plantations area, was situated among the jungle-clad foothills of the Atzera Range.

The attacking companies helped to bring the Japanese casualties inflicted by the 25th Brigade to about 300. South of the road Lieutenant Johnston's[4] platoon was held up by machine-gun fire. When Johnston was wounded the company commander's batman, Private Burns,[5] dashed to his aid under heavy fire and dragged him to safety. On the northern flank another platoon commander, Lieutenant Scotchmer,[6] was wounded, but by 1.30 p.m. the Japanese were driven from their positions on the bridge.

Determined to maintain the pressure on the retreating enemy Cotton sent two infantry companies (Captains Weale[7] and H. D. Cullen) and Garrard's company of Pioneers to maintain contact. At 2.50 p.m. the leading portions of these three companies met another enemy force at the southern turn of the Markham Valley Road west of Edwards'. Mainly on the northern side of the road the companies fought a very heavy engagement watched by General Vasey who liked nothing better than to leave his headquarters and watch the fight from the front line. Again and again in New Guinea campaigns Australian troops were cheered by the sight of Vasey's conspicuous red cap in the front line with them.

A very troublesome machine-gun was holding up the Pioneers' advance until Corporal Hucker[8] moved ahead of his platoon and turned the tables on the Japanese by pinning them down with his Bren. Under cover of his fire his platoon found a more favourable position and was able to destroy the pocket of resistance. Weale's and Garrard's companies were now very heavily engaged. Cotton sent orders to Cullen to attack forthwith across the track to assist the other companies. Cullen led his company in a dashing attack to drive the Japanese from their point of vantage. By 4.15 p.m. the Japanese, yelling but unable to withstand the constant pressure, withdrew, leaving a large amount of equipment behind.

For 27 casualties, including three killed, the 2/33rd Battalion had made a good contribution to the defeat of the enemy. Two prisoners were captured, one of whom stated that Markham Point had been evacuated; during the night a large amount of motor-boat activity was heard between Markham Point and Tari by Wampit Force and the Pioneers.

At 5 p.m. on the 14th Eather learnt from divisional headquarters that one of the documents captured the previous day by the 2/25th was part of a Japanese operation order, dated 8th September, for the evacuation of Lae. To Vasey this exciting news meant that the enemy might have begun evacuating Lae six days ago. Like every member of his division

---

[4] Capt H. R. Johnston, SX547. 2/3 Fd Regt and 2/33 Bn. Stock agent; of Broken Hill, NSW; b. Broken Hill, 5 Mar 1920.

[5] Pte G. A. Burns, MM, NX36918; 2/33 Bn. Labourer; of Canberra; b. Isisford, Qld, 24 Sep 1914.

[6] Lt S. Scotchmer, NX101671; 2/33 Bn. Compositor; of Nowra, NSW; b. Nowra, 19 Nov 1916.

[7] Capt W. T. H. B. Weale, NX12473; 2/33 Bn. Public servant; of Canberra; b. Cairo, Egypt, 7 Dec 1919.

[8] L-Sgt S. J. Hucker, MM, VX74119; 2/2 Pnr Bn. Farmer; of Lake Bolac, Vic; b. Willaura, Vic, 8 Dec 1921.

he hoped to race the 9th Division to Lae, but he hoped also to prevent the enemy from escaping.

From a quick study of the translated document Vasey's staff concluded that the Japanese would probably attempt to withdraw up the Busu to Musom, Lumbaip and Boana, thence up the Sanem River to Mount Bangeta, Iloko, Ulap and Sio or Kiari. Vasey realised that it would be unwise to weaken Eather's assault on what he now realised were stubborn Japanese rearguards, for the memory of other Japanese rearguards in the Papuan campaigns was fresh in his mind. At the same time he must have some troops to attempt the severing of the enemy line of withdrawal to Boana. He therefore warned Brigadier Dougherty to prepare the 21st Brigade for movement by air from Port Moresby to Nadzab on the morning of the 15th ready for a possible role in the Boana area. Vasey ordered the 25th Brigade to "push on vigorously towards Lae". The American III/503rd Battalion would occupy the native gardens area near the headwaters of the Bumbu and would block any Japanese withdrawal up the river and the Papuans would move forward to the line of the Leron River and occupy Sangan.[9]

On the night of 14th September General Berryman was at the pictures in Port Moresby when Colonel K. A. Wills, his senior Intelligence officer, called him out to tell him about the captured Japanese evacuation order. Soon after midnight Berryman signalled Herring: "Captured order indicates enemy attempt break north through hills from Lae towards Sio. Imperative cut retreat. 9 Div will direct earliest not less one battalion to each Musom and Bungalumba. 7 Div not less one battalion Boana. Responsibility tracks 9 Div all east, 7 Div all west of Sanem and Busu Rivers. . . ." At 4 a.m. Herring rang Berryman objecting to N.G.F's interference. Blamey then stepped in and Herring was informed that, while it was not desired to interfere with his conduct of operations, it was at the same time necessary that energetic action should be taken to block the enemy's escape routes.

An hour and a quarter later Herring sent a "most secret", "most immediate" signal to Wootten and repeated it to Vasey: "Indications support your view that enemy may be aiming to withdraw northwards from Lae to Sio by routes leading through Musom and Boana. Vasey sending battalion to block Boana route. C-in-C considers it desirable you send one to Musom to block that route."

Like Vasey, Wootten now faced a double task: capture Lae, and prevent the Japanese from escaping. Both divisions knew by their experience since the 8th when the Japanese commander had apparently issued his evacuation order that there were at least strong rearguards prepared to make bitter stands east and west of Lae. Admiral Barbey had found that Lae was still occupied on the night 10th-11th September when four of his destroyers, in the course of a sweep of the Huon Gulf, "fired a total

---

[9] In *Fear Drive My Feet* Peter Ryan records that in mid-May two natives informed him that the Japanese had put a supply of food at Samanzing, and that they thought that the Japanese might be preparing an escape route from Lae. Ryan passed on this idea to headquarters but little notice seems to have been taken of it there.

of 158 rounds over a period of three minutes at 9,500 yards, but return fire . . . made it a bit uncomfortable and they withdrew without any apparent damage having been done".[1]

In order to cut the possible Japanese route of withdrawal up the Busu General Wootten ordered Garvey of the 2/4th Independent Company to hold the kunda bridge "at all costs". At this stage many native rumours were flooding into the Independent Company that Boana was an advanced base from which the Japanese were moving north in twenties and thirties. If the Japanese were using the kunda bridge route as their main line of withdrawal, Wootten realised that he would have to reinforce the lightly equipped Independent Company. As speed of movement was now the determining factor he decided to detach a battalion from Whitehead's brigade and send it to the kunda bridge area. At 11 a.m. the 2/24th Battalion, which had found 30 dead Japanese and a 20-mm pom-pom in the position from which the enemy had opposed the crossing for almost a week, was warned to prepare to move to the Musom-Gawan area, block all tracks and destroy the retreating Japanese. The battalion re-crossed the river during the afternoon.

Having made these arrangements Wootten replied at 2 p.m. on the 15th to Herring's early morning signal:

Consider impossible prevent enemy evacuating as cannot block the many unknown native paths nor prevent bypassing of our posts where established on tracks in jungle. Movement south by 26 Brigade will impede movement north enemy parties between River Bumbu and River Busu but not prevent. Enemy free to move from Jacobsen's Emery's N.W. along western side of River Bumbu. . . . Recommend 2/24th Battalion . . . move at first light 16 Sep to area Musom-Gawan and have issued orders to that effect. Two days journey. . . .

South of the crossing the 26th Brigade was now in a position to carry out Whitehead's orders issued three days previously—the capture of the sawmill, Kamkamun, the northern end of Malahang airfield and Malahang Mission. Wootten thought that the Malahang airfield would probably be occupied by the enemy in an attempt to keep open his evacuation routes. He therefore intended that both brigades would bypass the airfield and strike for the Bumbu, thus cutting all roads and tracks to enemy defences between the Busu and the Bumbu. During the day Wootten let his troops know that the enemy might be attempting to evacuate Lae by tracks to the north and north-east. The 24th Brigade was ordered to overcome all opposition between Wagan and Malahang Anchorage and advance to the Bumbu.

Early on the morning of the 15th, when the remaining troops of the 26th Brigade crossed the Busu, the 2/23rd Battalion began the advance. At first it cut tracks through kunai and jungle to a track junction about 1,000 yards west of the crossing, where it found three abandoned Japanese machine-guns. Then, preceded by Lieutenant Bruce's[2] Papuan platoon, it

---

[1] Commander Seventh Amphibious Force, Report on Lae Operation.
[2] Lt T. A. Bruce, QX55175; Papuan Inf Bn. Typewriter mechanic; of Sherwood, Qld; b. Brisbane, 15 Nov 1922. Killed in action 9 Nov 1944.

advanced south down the main track and at 11 a.m. reached the deserted sawmill. Soon after midday the 2/48th Battalion passed through down the main track to the airfield and the 2/23rd set off towards Kamkamun and bivouacked for the night about half way there.

During its advance the battalion encountered no Japanese, but was uncomfortably short of water, an ironical fact when the men thought of the flooded river which had been holding them up for so long. Late at night arrangements were made to carry 300 gallons of water to the battalion next morning. For many of the troops this campaign was one long carry. From the 2/2nd Machine Gun Battalion and the 37th/52nd Battalion 640 men were detailed to carry for the 2/24th in its march towards the kunda bridge.[3]

From the sawmill the 2/48th Battalion advanced down the road to Malahang airfield through a big coconut plantation on the right and jungle on the left, and occupied the north end of the airfield without opposition. At 5.35 p.m. Colonel Ainslie met Major Newcomb,[4] whose company of the 2/15th Battalion had arrived at the south end of the airfield soon after the 2/48th began digging in on the north end. The 20th Brigade had been ferried across the Busu at its mouth the previous night with the intention of taking over the Old and New Yanga areas from the 24th Brigade. By this time Wootten was receiving reports from his formations that they were passing through abandoned enemy positions. Concluding that the airfield would not be the difficult proposition he had anticipated he had ordered Windeyer to capture the south end of it.

On the right flank of the 24th Brigade the 2/43rd found the crossroads abandoned and recovered the bodies of its two forward scouts. Wagan also was unoccupied. At the crossroads and at Wagan the enemy had abandoned machine-gun positions of about platoon strength and near by the battalion found a damaged 75-mm gun. The battalion also received a report from the 2/17th Battalion that about 40 dead Japanese were clustered round mortar bomb craters near New Yanga, probably killed by the 2/43rd's mortars.

South of Wagan the 2/32nd Battalion counted 68 dead Japanese at the scene of its fierce fight on the previous day. Elated at its success the battalion set out to capture Malahang Mission. At 1.30 p.m. Captain Davies' company led the battalion towards the Mission on a compass bearing; 450 yards from the objective they found recently deserted diggings and two booby-traps. When at 5.15 p.m. a patrol reported hearing voices and sounds of woodchopping, Scott decided to postpone the attack until the morning.

Early on the 15th a patrol from the 2/28th moved through Malahang Anchorage with only sporadic opposition. While the battalion occupied the anchorage another patrol went along the coastal track. At 4.55 p.m.

---

[3] For the machine-gun battalion (Lieut-Colonel E. Macarthur-Onslow) and the 2/3rd Pioneers (Lieut-Colonel A. V. Gallasch) the Lae campaign was disappointing for they were used exclusively as guard or labour forces.

[4] Maj S. P. Newcomb, QX6238; 2/15 Bn. Clerk; of Graceville, Qld; b. Toowoomba, Qld, 3 Nov 1909.

they returned and reported that the country was all clear up to the east bank of the Bumbu River except for several pill-boxes on the beach at the eastern side of the river mouth. Along the entire divisional front these pill-boxes and the positions at Malahang were the only ones found occupied that day. It seemed likely that Lae would not be defended. Having reached the Bumbu, the 9th Division might have entered Lae on the 15th.

In these closing days of the Lae campaign the corps and the divisional commander exchanged "most immediate" signals which are of interest in underlining the attitude to air support at both levels. On 13th September Herring signalled Wootten: "Air Force prepared strike Chinatown dump area and Webb's forenoon 14 September. Have approved this strike unless you say no. Answer in clear Yes or No urgently." Never one to waste words Wootten replied, "No." Disturbed at this reply Herring signalled on the 14th: "Information so far received here reference your forward troops makes your refusal allow bombardment Lae 14 September most difficult to understand. My policy and desire is to hit the enemy as hard and as often as possible. Air force standing by to do it. I regard the air arm as one of our most potent weapons and desire to use it to the fullest. Experience at Salamaua has proved its efficiency. Propose ask air force strike Jacobsen's 15 September."

Wootten replied more fully to this signal on the same day: "Entirely agree your policy and desire. At last light 13 September enemy had withdrawn from Dump area. . . . As reports received of small parties enemy moving north from Lae considered possible enemy withdrawing in which case desired advance this morning to R. Butibum [Bumbu] with view crossing river. Orders to that effect had already been issued before receipt your message. Chinatown and Webb's very close river and near what appear possible crossings. Had quick advance been possible troops would have been endangered as not practicable warn forward troops after receipt your message. Forward troops only 2,000 yards from Webb's last night. Desire point out that owing inevitable time lag of information position forward troops advancing in dense jungle plus long notice requested by air force for preparation strikes bombing and strafing must be kept well back when infantry advancing as rate of advance not predictable. Close air support can only be given in coastal jungle when forward troops become static. Respectfully recommend you send liaison officers here."

While the 9th Division was advancing on the 15th against very little opposition, the 7th Division was continuing to meet fierce resistance from enemy rearguards supported by four 75-mm guns from the area of Jacobsen's Plantation. Eather ordered the 2/33rd followed by the 2/31st Battalion to move "with all possible speed" down the Markham Valley Road towards Lae. Having captured a Japanese position near the southern bend of the Markham Valley Road late on the 14th, the 2/33rd Battalion resumed the advance towards Edwards' at 7 a.m. next morning. A quarter of an hour later the leading company was fired on from the foothills north of the track. The stubborn Japanese were gradually pushed back. Eather then ordered Robson of the 2/31st to make a detour round the right flank to secure the high ground behind the Japanese and beyond the clearing near Edwards' House and overcome the Japanese at the bridge near by. Accompanied by an artillery team and the toiling signallers laying telephone line the 2/31st set out on a compass bearing of 166 degrees for 500 yards, then 89 degrees for 1,000 yards and finally 13 degrees to the road. As the men hacked their way through the bush with machetes, often up to their waists in water and mud, they could hear the noise of battle to the north and west.

Hoping to link with the 2/31st when it reached the high ground behind Edwards', Cotton sent two companies round the left flank along the high ground. They met fierce resistance but gradually pushed the enemy back. In a desperate endeavour to hold their position the Japanese used mortars, and snipers were active.

On the left flank the Pioneer company attached to the 2/33rd was unsuccessful in an attack on a machine-gun post lower down the ridge which they were occupying. Suffering casualties the company withdrew to the main track to reorganise, and Captain Cullen's company spread out to fill the gap. Deciding to deal with the machine-gun post himself, Cullen mounted a Bren on the shoulder of one of his men—the undergrowth was too thick for him to use the bipod—and, although he was wounded in the attempt, managed to wipe out the post. The company on Cullen's right flank were pinned down until Private Green[5] from Cullen's company found the machine-gun which was doing the damage and wiped its team out with grenades.

About the same time the 2/31st Battalion's leading company under Major Jackson[6] crossed the Markham Valley Road and moved to the high ground to the north where it was joined by Captain McKenzie's[7] company with platoons north and south of the road. While Captain H. F. Hayes' company prepared for a deliberate advance west along the road towards the 2/33rd, Captain Rylands'[8] company occupied a defensive position astride the road at the first bridge to the east. Hayes moved off at 3.15 p.m. with Lieutenant Sawyer's[9] platoon on the right of the road and Lieutenant Hamilton's[1] on the left of it. The men advanced through dense undergrowth. Soon the leading sections came under heavy fire from machine-guns situated near the bridge on the eastern side of Edwards' Plantation. About the same time Captain Power's company of the 2/33rd Battalion was advancing east along the Markham Valley Road from the

---

[5] Cpl D. K. Green, MM, NX91449; 2/33 Bn. Milk carter; of Rose Bay, NSW; b. Sydney, 14 Feb 1915. Died of wounds 11 Oct 1943.

[6] Maj J. G. Jackson, QX1506; 2/31 Bn. Jackeroo; b. Cheshire, England, 16 Nov 1910.

[7] Capt S. J. McKenzie, QX6535; 2/31 Bn. Insurance clerk; of Brisbane; b. Brisbane, 3 Sep 1918. Died 27 Jan 1945.

[8] Capt C. I. Rylands, QX2034; 2/31 Bn. Kangaroo shooter; of Hughenden, Qld; b. Westmoreland, England, 3 Jun 1912.

[9] Lt S. E. Sawyer, NX125454; 2/31 Bn. Clerk; of St Leonards, NSW; b. Sydney, 11 Jul 1918.

[1] Lt H. I. Hamilton, QX4161. 2/1 A-Tk Regt and 2/31 Bn. Bank officer; of Jackson, Qld; b. Maitland, NSW, 8 Jun 1910.

western side of the plantation. Fierce fighting ensued on both sides of the plantation as the trapped enemy fought back savagely.

In spite of the strong opposition Hayes' company advanced rapidly. The road was under hot fire and it was very dangerous to try to cross it. A number of men were hit when making such crossings. However, the direction of the attack evidently confused the Japanese, and Hayes' men captured a heavy machine-gun still pointing west—the original direction of the Australian advance.

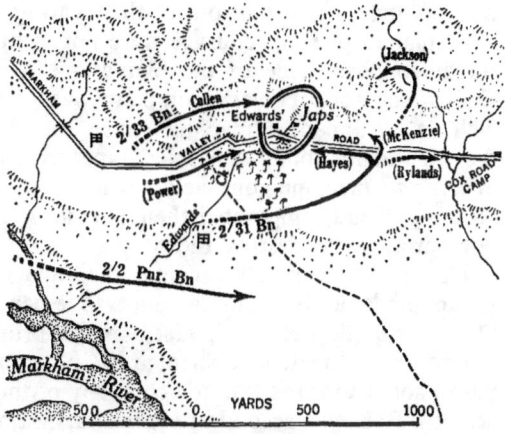

15th September

Soon Sawyer's platoon was pinned down by intense fire. Corporal Groundwater[2] then led his section through dense jungle farther to the right. Reaching a position where he thought he could attack the enemy's flank, he called to his men, "Right boys, into them." In the bitter close-quarters fight which followed, Groundwater and several of his men were wounded but the verve of the attack enabled the remainder of the section to kill 14 Japanese and clear the way for an advance by the platoon.

On the left of the road Hamilton's platoon was also pinned down by machine-gun fire from a Japanese post of ten men, Hamilton being wounded. Matching his section against this Japanese section Corporal Shervey[3] rushed straight at the machine-gun, firing his Owen with such effect that three of the Japanese including the gunner were killed. The remainder of the section following closely on their leader's heels then wiped out the post, and the platoon moved forward.

Both Hayes' leading platoons had suffered severe casualties. As usual, the Australian medical orderlies and stretcher bearers were not far behind the attack. In both leading platoons there were several men who owed their subsequent recovery, if not their lives, to these men. In the right-hand platoon Private Clark[4] had rescued and tended three men as well as Groundwater. In the left-hand platoon Private Rowe,[5] in an open clearing, had been badly wounded in the throat soon after the fight began and was

---

[2] Cpl R. J. Groundwater, MM, NX14353; 2/31 Bn. Lorry driver; of Condobolin, NSW; b. Condobolin, 4 Apr 1911.

[3] L-Sgt E. J. Shervey, MM, QX19277; 2/31 Bn. Labourer; of Cairns, Qld; b. Mudgee, NSW, 16 Mar 1906.

[4] Pte L. Clark, NX99016; 2/31 Bn. Labourer; of Gwabegar, NSW; b. Gwabegar, 6 Jun 1922.

[5] Pte L. G. Rowe, NX73569; 2/31 Bn. Property worker; of Bellata, NSW; b. Bellata, 16 Jan 1921. Killed in action 15 Sep 1943.

marooned from his comrades by a wall of enemy fire. Throwing off all his equipment except for his R.A.P. haversack Corporal Scott[6] dashed into the clearing. With bullets whizzing all round him he staunched the flow of blood by wrapping a field dressing hastily round Rowe's throat. The wounded man was hit again in the foot by a bullet as Scott picked him up and carried him out of the clearing to the cover of the trees.

Similar displays of courage were not lacking from the 2/33rd Battalion on the opposite side of the plantation. Advancing along the right-hand side of the road Power's company was delayed by the dense growth as well as by Japanese machine-guns. So thick was the undergrowth that the Australians found concealed Japanese foxholes within their own lines. When two machine-guns held up the company's progress Private Burns, scouting ahead, pinpointed their positions, thus enabling a 2-inch mortar bombardment to destroy the posts.

Under such constant pressure the Japanese began to draw back. One group made a desperate attempt to escape round the left flank. Here Shervey's section of the 2/31st bore the brunt of the Japanese attack until Robson sent Lieutenant Sheppard's[7] platoon to extend the left flank and patrol south towards Power's company of the 2/33rd. Ammunition parties sent by Robson's second-in-command, Major Byrne,[8] along the southern detour from the battalion's old position behind the 2/33rd were also sent hurriedly to the front to replenish the embattled company's ammunition; it had been a long advance and the enemy's strength had been underestimated.

At 4.50 p.m. Eather ordered the two forward battalions to meet at the bridge on the eastern fringe of the plantation. The plan was for Captain Garrard's company from the 2/2nd Pioneers to attack along the road west of the bridge and for Jackson's company of the 2/31st, on the high ground to the north, to prevent any enemy escape after the attack. By late afternoon the Japanese had had enough and began to withdraw up a spur running along the creek north of Edwards' bridge. At 5.35 Jackson's company counted 80 Japanese climbing this spur. Jackson had carefully concealed his men and surprise was complete. Fire was withheld until the most favourable moment and then it literally mowed down the enemy and 64 dead Japanese were later counted. In this one-sided action the Australians had no casualties. The artillery F.O.O., Lieutenant Kelly,[9] with this platoon could not fire the guns "owing to the complicated locations of our own troops".[1] Instead, he used his rifle against the Japanese.

In this day's successful "Battle of the Circle", as it was known locally, the 2/33rd had 19 casualties, including 2 killed, and the 2/31st 38, includ-

---
[6] Cpl A. Scott, DCM, VX4310. 2/1 MG Bn and 2/31 Bn. Labourer; of Fitzroy, Vic; b. Newcastle, NSW, 13 Nov 1915.
[7] Lt R. Sheppard, NX22082; 2/31 Bn. Clerk; of Woonona, NSW; b. Woonona, 2 Dec 1919. Killed in car accident 4 Feb 1949.
[8] Lt-Col J. H. Byrne, ED, QX6010. 2/31 Bn; CO 42 Bn 1944-45. Traveller; of Brisbane; b. Maryborough, Qld, 22 Oct 1913.
[9] Lt J. T. Kelly, VX16352; 2/4 Fd Regt. Grazier; of Briagolong, Vic; b. Briagolong, 13 Apr 1912.
[1] Henry, p. 226.

ing 13 killed; but they had inflicted well over 100 casualties on the enemy and had broken his resistance. Hayes' company, advancing without supporting fire, had driven out a stronger enemy force from a prepared position in which it had supporting weapons.

At last light a patrol which reached the bridge west of Cox Road Camp, saw only one Japanese but many signs of recent occupation. A quarter of an hour before midnight an enemy patrol of about 20 approached the company's standing patrol near the bridge from the east. The Australians fired on them, killing their officer and dispersing the others. For the two weary battalions the diarist of the 2/31st described the remainder of the night: "Apart from sporadic bursts of rifle fire at odd enemy troops, who endeavoured to pass through our lines, the night was without further incident."

Elsewhere in Vasey's area patrolling was extensive on the 15th. As the fourth company of the 2/2nd Pioneers had now been attached to the 2/25th Battalion, Eather's Intelligence officer—perhaps in earnest, perhaps not—sent a signal to the 7th Division that the 2/2nd Pioneers were advancing on Lae "less four companies". Actually Lang, a doughty veteran, did still have his Headquarters Company under command, and it was patrolling along the northern bank of the Markham in the Tari area towards the mouth, intending to set up a road-block along the track north of the mouth. North of the main advance a patrol from Lieut-Colonel Tolson's paratroop battalion met a strong enemy force of about 200 at the log crossing over the Bumbu south-east of Yalu. The Americans reported inflicting severe losses and forcing the Japanese to "withdraw to a new line of evacuation".[2]

Among the 117 plane loads deposited at the Nadzab airfields on the morning of the 15th was the headquarters of the 21st Brigade, the 2/14th Battalion, and a company of the 2/16th. Bad weather forced the remainder of the 2/16th to return to Port Moresby. Lieut-Colonel W. T. Robertson met Brigadier Dougherty at Nadzab and informed him of General Vasey's intention that the first battalion to arrive should attempt to cut the Japanese line of withdrawal. That afternoon Dougherty ordered Lieut-Colonel R. Honner of the 2/14th to go to Boana as soon as possible and secure it as a patrol base whence to destroy the retreating Japanese. Guided by Warrant Officer Bird[3] (Angau) the battalion set off towards Camp Diddy, which it reached the following afternoon. There Lieutenant Hall's[4] Papuan platoon came under their command and led the way north up Ngafir Creek. The remainder of the 2/16th Battalion arrived at Nadzab on the 16th.

At dawn on the 15th the leading troops of the 9th Division were about a mile and a quarter from Lae while those of the 7th Division were about

---

[2] Lt-Col G. M. Jones, Report on 503d Parachute Infantry, 31 October 1943.
[3] WO1 N. M. Bird, NG2394. NGVR and Angau. Sawmiller; of Wau, NG; b. Laurieton, NSW, 7 Jun 1900. Died 6 Feb 1959.
[4] Lt A. J. Hall, QX59258; Papuan Inf Bn. Shop assistant; of Bardon, Qld; b. Brisbane, 29 May 1919. Died 15 Jan 1944.

seven miles away. It appeared an odds-on bet that the 9th would reach Lae first. When the 9th met no opposition on 15th September and the 7th was delayed by some of the most bitter fighting of their advance, the result seemed to be all over bar the shouting. By dusk on the 15th the 9th Division had halted just before its objectives along the Bumbu, which was the boundary of Lae, while the forward troops of the 7th were at Cox Road Camp, about five miles from Lae.

The 16th September dawned with Wootten's northern troops in receipt of many native rumours. Moving north along the west bank of the Busu from the 26th Brigade's crossing place, Lieutenant C. D. Murphy's platoon of the 2/4th Independent Company reached a position opposite the other two platoons near the kunda bridge. Murphy reported that he had five Chinese who said that about 60 Japanese called at their village the previous night and inquired about tracks to Boana, Sio and Madang. Another Chinese stated that a submarine called nightly at Lae to evacuate generals and bring in fresh troops. Rumours from Chinese and natives, so familiar to Australians who campaigned in New Guinea, were often inventions, sometimes efforts to please their questioners, and sometimes not without a shred of truth. In this case the reports from the Chinese appeared credible. Along the east bank of the Busu the 2/24th Battalion by dusk reached the Sankwep River.

On the right flank the 26th Brigade met no opposition. The 2/23rd Battalion was greeted at first light by a providential shower which enabled water-bottles to be filled. A quarter of an hour before midday the leading company occupied Kamkamun and began to look for suitable crossing places over the Bumbu. To the south the 2/48th Battalion advanced southwest. Butibum was found unoccupied at 10.50 a.m. by Lieutenant Lewin's[5] patrol; a platoon then moved forward to the Bumbu.

On the right flank of the 24th Brigade the 2/32nd Battalion attacked Malahang Mission at dawn during the downpour which filled the water-bottles of the 2/23rd Battalion. It met some resistance but killed eight enemy stragglers. Entering such a Japanese living area for the first time, the 2/32nd, like many units before it, was astonished at the enemy's lack of security and disgusted at his deplorable lack of hygiene, particularly the sullying smell of putrefying corpses. While Colonel Scott was establishing his headquarters in the Mission church, Lieutenant Denness found three damaged 105-mm guns in a village 300 yards to the north-east. Patrols led by Lieutenants Buckley[6] and Gatward[7] then investigated the Chinatown bridge and the village of Butibum respectively. Buckley found that dense kunai fringed both banks of the Bumbu but there were no obstacles across the river as a native had reported. Gatward had reached Butibum some time before Lewin, and by 10.38 had returned to his company having killed six Japanese in Butibum. Of Gatward's patrol the

---

[5] Capt R. W. Lewin, WX6926; 2/48 Bn. Saddler; of Maylands, WA; b. Northam, WA, 15 Jan 1919.
[6] Lt W. M. Buckley, WX17028; 2/32 Bn. Cashier; of Gosnells, WA; b. Denmark, WA, 6 Jan 1914.
[7] Capt G. McG. Gatward, QX297. 2/9, 2/1 MG and 2/32 Bns. Gatemaker; of Brisbane; b. Brisbane, 14 Aug 1915.

battalion diarist wrote: "They left the village [Butibum] empty and, in view of the fact that Butibum was scheduled for a full scale attack by 26th Brigade this afternoon, the patrol's exploits occasioned great amusement at H.Q."

At 11.10 a.m. Scott issued his orders for the 2/32nd's assault on Lae across Chinatown bridge, supported by the 2/43rd Battalion on the left. The battalion was ready to advance at 1 p.m. Meanwhile the 2/43rd Battalion formed up to the south of the bridge, 500 yards east of the river, ready to support Scott's crossing.

All along the Bumbu River the two brigades were delighted by the bombardment and strafing of Lae by Fortresses, Mitchells, Bostons, Lightnings, Beaufighters and even Boomerangs. "There is no doubt that the Lae garrison is in an extremely desperate position," commented one diarist describing the results of the bombardment which another said was "a great tonic to tired troops". At 1 p.m., three-quarters of an hour after the last air strike, the 9th Division's artillery began to bombard Lae. The artillery ceased fire at 2.10 p.m. and five minutes later the leading company of the 2/23rd Battalion reported "approximately 100 Japs" across the Bumbu opposite Kamkamun.

At dawn on the 16th the 7th Division prepared for another fight with the enemy in the Edwards' Plantation area. The 2/33rd Battalion advanced down the Markham Valley Road towards the 2/31st. By 9 a.m. the last 10 Japanese, who had apparently remained in the surrounded pocket as a rearguard for the ill-fated 80 who had retreated the previous evening, were killed, and the 2/33rd pushed through to the position held by Captain Hayes' company of the 2/31st. Eather's orders for the two battalions had been to "press upon the enemy and annihilate him", while the 2/25th bypassed the other battalions and raced for Lae. At 8.35 a.m. when the 2/25th had already gone past, Eather signalled divisional headquarters: "Expect forward troops to be in Jacobsen's Plantation 0900/16. Request suspension further bombing Lae till called for. Enemy force in front of this brigade destroyed." The 2/25th, in fact, reached Jacobsen's at 10.15 a.m. after a rapid unopposed advance. While one company dug in at the junction of the Lae and Emery's Plantation roads the others advanced towards Emery's.

Eather considered that the advance was not speedy enough. He therefore went forward to urge the leading company to hasten. A vivid description of the final spurt for Lae on 16th September was written at the time by the 2/25th's leading company commander (Captain Butler):

> Up at daylight and off again. "C" Company leading the Brigade this time. Men are a bit nervous again and went pretty steadily. Sick Japs along track kept holding things up and we expected to run into something at any moment. Then along the track and into the middle of us came a jeep crowded with Brigade HQ. Passed me and up to the leading platoon. The old Brig jumped out and started urging the troops to hurry along. The troops weren't very impressed as they thought the Jap was in front. Finally the Brigadier, armed with a pistol, acted as leading scout, and the troops followed in column of route behind. . . . A brigadier is not an ideal

section leader. The whole reason for his action was that he wanted the brigade to be first onto the beach. He managed it O.K. I had to send a patrol down the beach and back so we have that honour—doubtful one—as there were no Japs. Unfortunately we advanced too quickly—due to no opposition—and the Yanks came over and strafed us.[8]

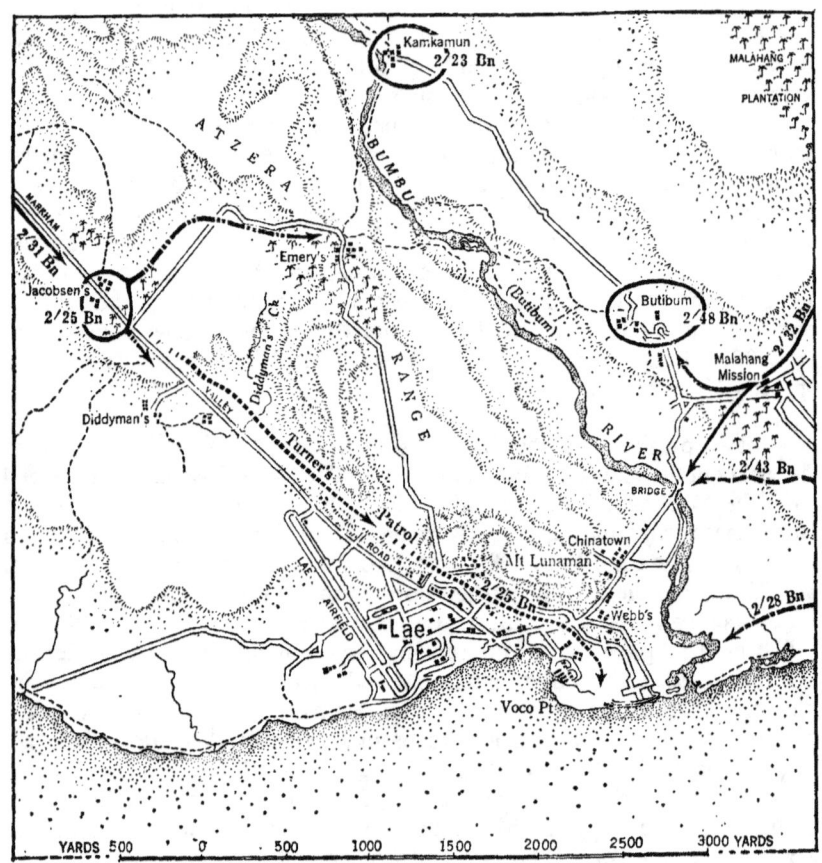

The fall of Lae, 11.30 a.m. 16th September

At 10.30 a.m., when the 9th Division was beginning to mass along the eastern bank of the Bumbu, Sergeant Turner[9] boldly led a patrol from Butler's company straight along the main road across Diddyman's bridge through the deserted town of Lae at 11 o'clock and reached Voco Point at 11.30. As this patrol, the first to enter Lae, arrived at Voco Point,

---

[8] Passing a fine looking motor-cycle and side-car on the track to Emery's, Colonel Marson put his hand on it and found that the motor was still warm. A man from the transport platoon found the distributor in the grass near by, filled up the tank with petrol from a drum, and half an hour later arrived at Emery's with the cycle in running order.

[9] Sgt C. A. Turner, QX11136; 2/25 Bn. Station hand; of Omanama, Qld; b. Glen Innes, NSW, 29 Dec 1916.

two Allied aircraft began strafing the track from Emery's to Lae. Each aircraft landed its first bursts in Captain Gow's company, and, between planes, the troops rushed out to a level spot with anything white to form first a large "X" (forward friendly troops) and then, after two men had been wounded, a "Y" (you are hitting our troops). The 2/33rd fired white flares to indicate to the aircraft that they were firing on their own troops but, as Eather later wrote, "the crews either did not see them or had left their books at home". After finishing strafing the aircraft dropped dozens of anti-personnel parachute bombs along the track.

When the strafing began Eather rang Robertson: "Am held up on outskirts of Lae by 5 U.S.A.F.; two casualties received from strafing; can some action be taken to stop." Robertson replied that "action has been taken to stop all air missions west of Bumbu River. Air missions were not asked for by 7 Aust Div."

On the Markham Valley Road the 2/31st passed through the 2/25th at the road junction and the leading company reached the north-west end of Lae airfield at 12.26.[1] At this time Turner had returned and informed Butler that the airfield was overgrown and adorned with wrecked aircraft. In mopping-up operations near the airfield the company killed 15 Japanese and captured one prisoner. By 1 p.m. Robson was in complete possession of the airfield, Marson was in occupation of Emery's, Cotton was at Jacobsen's, and Eather's headquarters was established at the north-east end of the airfield.

Just then the artillery of the 9th Division began to shell Lae from its new positions along the Busu as well as its old ones along the Burep. The battery commander of Vasey's only battery of artillery (Captain Thomas[2]) later reported: "This was my first—and I hope last—experience of being at the wrong end of a 25-pounder barrage. It started about 500 or 600 yards short of us but, fortunately, after a couple of lifts in range the Brig decided it wasn't good enough and retired to Jacobsen's."[3] Another unfortunate man was wounded; spurred on by the shelling the 2/31st rapidly dug in. After discussing the situation with Eather at Emery's, Marson had signalled to the 9th Division at 12.45 p.m. "25th Brigade in occupation Lae 1100 hours 16 September. Thanks for . . . support midday but please don't blow our ⎯⎯ down".

Encouraged by the same shelling the 2/32nd Battalion left the edge of the Mission plantation east of the Bumbu at 1 p.m. for the assault on Lae. Wootten had intended that zero hour would be when flares were dropped by aircraft to denote the last air strike. By 1 p.m. it was obvious that the aircraft which had last been over the target at 12.15 had forgotten to drop the flares and 1 p.m. became zero hour. With its objective Mount Lunaman the 2/32nd quickly crossed the river.

---

[1] While waiting for the 2/31st and 2/33rd to come up, Eather was moving among his troops at the road junction when it was reported to him that a Japanese was feigning death in the undergrowth. Eather arranged for him to be leg-roped and then had him questioned. The prisoner was cooperative.

[2] Maj J. H. Thomas, VX14104. 2/4 Fd Regt and 1 Naval Bombardment Gp. Accountant; of East Malvern, Vic; b. Melbourne, 3 Oct 1913.

[3] Quoted in R. L. Henry, p. 227.

Both divisions were now in Lae but the artillery continued shelling ahead of the 9th driving back the patrols of the 7th. Vasey tried every available channel to inform Wootten but it was not until 2.25 p.m. that Wootten received in clear Vasey's message sent through R.A.A.F. channels from "Air Nadzab" to "Air Hopoi": "Have occupied Lae. Prevent your troops engaging my troops." Wootten immediately stopped his artillery, fortunately for the 2/25th at Emery's which had been mistaken for Japanese by the 2/23rd across the river.

In Lae itself patrols from both divisions were coming closer to one another. As the 2/32nd crossed the river Lieutenant Anderson[4] led a patrol from the 2/25th at Emery's down the main track into Lae while a second patrol from the 2/25th was sent down the right bank of the Bumbu through Chinatown. After combing the town and killing four Japanese, Anderson's men moved down to the waterfront. Here they were resting when they met the 2/32nd Battalion. Patrols of the 2/31st and 2/32nd also met at 2.30 p.m. south of Mount Lunaman. Commenting on this meeting the diarist of the 2/32nd wrote: "2/31st Aust Inf Battalion is a member of our old brigade and was born at the same time and place as our unit—England in June 1940. Today's reunion is, therefore, a very historical event."[5]

At 3.30 p.m. the observation post of Wampit Force which had still not found whether Markham Point was abandoned, reported seeing troops haul down the large Japanese flag flying south of Mount Lunaman. These were Anderson's men. Later in the afternoon Eather hoisted an Australian flag over the devastated township.

With two divisions converging on the one objective from opposite directions, and with no limit of advance set by higher command for either division, it was remarkable that there were so few accidents. Careful control by the forward commanders and the good sense of the troops themselves were responsible.

Lae was a shambles. "It was in an indescribably filthy condition and had been very thoroughly wrecked," wrote Wootten.[6] Vast dumps of stores and discarded weapons littered the area. The airfield had not been used since just before the landing, the hangars were wrecked and about forty damaged planes were mute witnesses to the power of the Allied air force. The typical nauseating stench of an area occupied by the Japanese army pervaded Lae as it had Salamaua six days before.[7]

Lae had been captured but despite General MacArthur's communiqué of 8th September that "elements of four Japanese Divisions aggregating 20,000 at the beginning are now completely enveloped with their supply

---

[4] Lt J. R. Anderson, QX13661; 2/25 Bn. Health officer; of Wynnum, Qld; b. Bellata, NSW, 12 Apr 1910.

[5] The 2/32nd Battalion joined the 24th Brigade in Tobruk in May 1941, and the 2/25th Battalion, which had remained in Darwin when the other two battalions of the 24th Brigade sailed for the Middle East, joined the 25th Brigade just before the Syrian campaign in June 1941.

[6] 9th Division report.

[7] Mollard found the bachelors' quarters, where he had lived for two years before the war, still standing although riddled with holes from bomb splinters. He salvaged his bed, cane chair, cane desk and some china and crockery, and thus managed to live in comparative comfort in the shell of his old home town for a brief period.

lines cut", and Blamey's telegram to the Prime Minister on 16th September that "only battered remnant likely to have escaped", the main enemy garrison had escaped towards the north. Both Australian divisions had fought with their usual grim determination, but they had been handicapped by the same weather which had aided the escape of the Japanese from Salamaua. The enemy fighting units which escaped from the Lae trap were mainly those already battered by the bitter and deliberately prolonged fighting of the Salamaua campaign. The planners' excellent idea of using Salamaua as a magnet to draw troops from Lae had been successful. Great credit therefore is due to the 3rd and 5th Australian Divisions for their dogged part in the Salamaua operations which had facilitated the capture of Lae. Although the major Japanese bases of Lae and Salamaua, which had threatened Port Moresby and Australia for eighteen months, had been captured, together with a huge amount of equipment and stores, many Japanese soldiers, displaying great fortitude, had escaped to fight again.

The 9th Division had received a brief though in some cases a savage introduction to jungle warfare. Not all its units would have agreed with the opinion expressed by the diarist of one unit immediately after the occupation of Lae: "The enemy has done nothing to entitle him to our respect during the operation and his performance indicates that he is not as good as the Italian as a fighting soldier."

At the beginning of the Lae campaign Wootten's Intelligence staff estimated that there were 8,240 Japanese in Lae and 6,934 in Salamaua, while Vasey's estimated that there were 6,420 in Lae and 7,041 in Salamaua. It was now apparent that the two divisions had over-estimated the number of Japanese opposing them. Among the captured documents was an almost complete list of a medley of 47 enemy units in the Lae-Salamaua area.

The enemy decision to evacuate Salamaua from 6th September was caused not only by a realisation that Salamaua was doomed but by the urgent necessity to reinforce Lae where there were only about 2,000 troops comprising mostly base units, such as hospitals, engineers, fixed artillery and anti-aircraft.

The Japanese commanders made certain that the fighting units of the *51st Division* and the *238th Regiment* arrived in Lae in time for its defence. Opposing the advance of the 7th Australian Division down the Markham Valley were the remnants of the three ill-starred regiments of the *51st Division* reinforced by the *51st Engineer Regiment* and some naval troops. Opposing the advance of the 9th Australian Division east of Lae was a medley of units comprising mainly the *238th Regiment*, less a company of the *II Battalion* at Markham Point. On the east side of Lae too portions of the *51st Division* were used to stem the Australian advance. The Japanese with whom the 9th Division first made contact in the Singaua Plantation were from the *III/115th Battalion*, while the Japanese defending the mouth of the Busu were none other than Oba's experienced *III/102nd Battalion* which had received such a battering all the way north from Nassau Bay. There must have been more than the usual fog of war, panic and confusion in Lae as the exhausted units from the Salamaua fighting arrived. The first arrivals must barely have had time to come ashore before being sent to the battle fronts. As in the Salamaua campaign Nakano again broke up the organisation of his fighting units by sending companies of the same unit in different directions.

The total number of Japanese in the Lae-Salamaua area early in September was about 11,000. Casualties inflicted by the two Australian divisions were at least 2,200. In return the Japanese had inflicted 547 casualties on the 9th Division, including 77 killed, 397 wounded and 73 missing. The 7th had suffered 142 casualties—38 killed and 104 wounded.[8] About 2,000 Japanese were killed in the final drive on Salamaua.

The badly led and often beaten fighting units of the *51st Division*, together with portions of other fighting units, had carried out a creditable defence of Lae in face of the onslaughts of two of the finest divisions on the Allied side. Had the flooded Busu not delayed the 9th Division for such a period the enemy would in all probability not have escaped. Fortune and Nature, however, favoured a valiant defender despite the equally valiant striving of the attackers.

An *XVIII Army* report captured later shows that the strength of the *51st Division* and attached units at Kiari late in October when the retreat thither had ended was 6,417 of whom 1,271 were sick. It seems certain that nearly all of these came from Lae. The strength of the infantry regiments at that time was: *66th*, 759; *102nd*, 564; *115th*, 654; part of *80th*, 536; part of *238th*, 518. There were 1,416 naval troops, evidently mainly of the *2nd Maizeru, 5th Sasebo* and *5th Yokosuka Special Naval Landing Forces,* and other units of the *82nd Naval Garrison*.

---

[8] The total number of casualties suffered by the 7th Division in the Lae campaign was 9 less than the casualties suffered by the 2/33rd Battalion in the disastrous air crash at Port Moresby.

CHAPTER 14

PURSUIT

ROUND Salamaua the 5th Division rested after its final efforts to trap the retreating Japanese. Only the 15th Battalion was now required to chase the fleeing enemy rearguard. It advanced rapidly along the coast hoping to catch up with the remaining Japanese south of the Markham River. Two companies, under the command of Major Jenyns,[1] left the area north of Busama by barge on 14th September, landed between the Buang mouth and Sugarloaf, and there found signs of a hasty evacuation not one hour old. The attempt to speed up the chase and get ahead of the retreating enemy had apparently just failed.

Struggling ahead from the knoll west of Bukuap, which they had reached the previous evening (13th September), the other two companies under Major Lack[2] found the map hopeless. Gorges and razor-backs predominated; the track had not been used for a year and was overgrown by ferns and lawyer vine which had to be cut away; the numerous weapon-pits had been dug by the enemy before the last seasonal growth. Finally Lack decided that he could not adequately feed his 173 men who were already having only one meal a day. Accordingly, he sent one company back to the coast and gave the few remaining emergency rations to the other one, which continued along the mountain route before being forced to return.

Advancing along the coast Jenyns passed many weapon-pits and much equipment. The Japanese as usual had tunnelled and dug like rabbits. The country was ideal for defence and the enemy's choice of ground and siting of defences were excellent. Offsetting this, however, the battalion noticed practically no improvements to roads and ports. The enemy's living quarters along the coast were filthy.

Coastal natives who were now coming in from the hills said that the Japanese had left the area by barge, and the Bukuap natives stated that the Japanese, when evacuating Salamaua, walked to Busama and the Buang mouth where they were picked up by barges and taken to Lae. There was no other information available to Milford because no Allied troops were established on the coastal track during the Japanese evacuation.

On the 15th General Milford instructed Lieut-Colonel Smith, of the 24th Battalion, to send his Buang patrol to the coast. After finding signs of a recent evacuation of the Japanese position at the Buang mouth, a patrol from the Buang base joined Jenyns' force which had earlier met its first opposition between Sugarloaf and the coastal lake and had killed seven Japanese. The 24th Battalion's Buang patrol took no further part in the

---

[1] Maj J. R. T. Jenyns, ED, QX45102; 15 Bn. Business manager; of Brisbane; b. Beaudesert, Qld, 24 Aug 1900.
[2] Maj H. H. Lack, OBE, QX33887; 15 Bn. Bank officer; of Brisbane; b. Maryborough, Qld, 16 Sep 1907.

fighting. Colonel Smith described the joining of forces—"Thus weakly ended the unhappy Buang period."

Between the mouth of the Buang and Sugarloaf, and indeed as far north as Labu, the enemy had abandoned very strong positions which commanded the narrow coastal strip and were protected from the land-

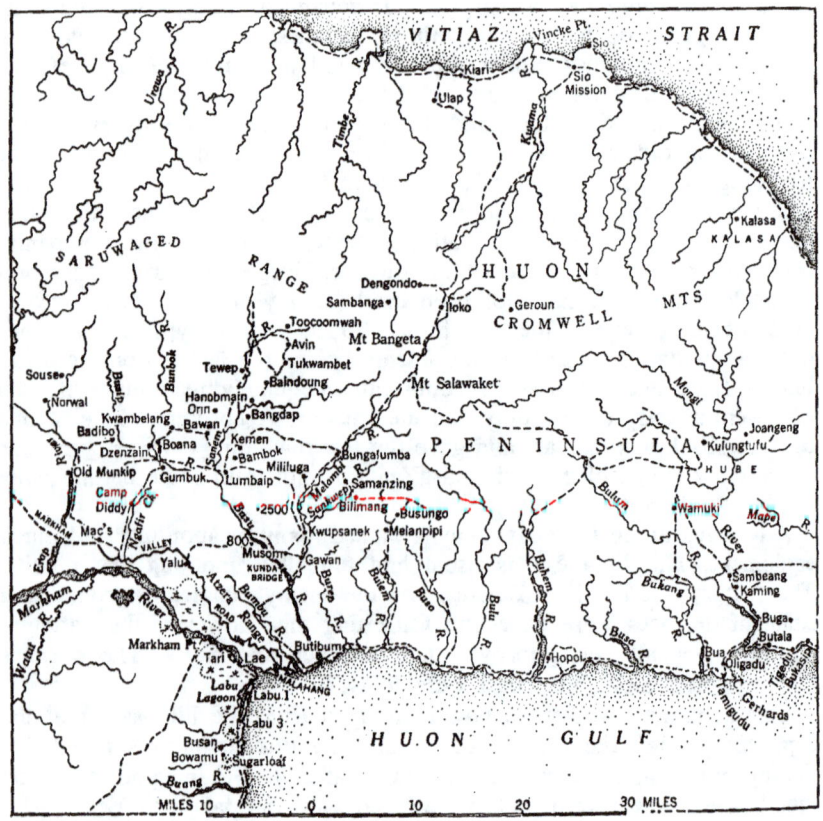

Routes of withdrawal of the *51st Japanese Division* across the Huon Peninsula

ward side by swamp. Throughout its series of frustrating attempts to reach the coastal track the Buang patrol had been forced to cut its way through the jungle, thus giving itself away to the Japanese, who were always able to reinforce a threatened spot. Having plenty of barges the Japanese could land or evacuate at will. It was seen later that the Buang patrol had been outnumbered nine to one. Therein lay its measure of success: it had managed to tie up a large enemy force which could have been used more effectively elsewhere.

Interrogation of a prisoner indicated (wrongly) that the enemy had abandoned his positions at Markham Point on the night of 13th-14th

September, and General Milford ordered Colonel Amies of the 15th to advance rapidly to the Markham, destroy any enemy along the way, and link with the 24th Battalion at Markham Point. The 15th Battalion, however, was not to cross the wide Markham River. By 17th September the battalion was in occupation of Labu 1, Labu 3, Busan, and Sugarloaf, and thus was deployed in one large ambush covering all likely approaches to the coast.

Before dawn on the 18th Captain Proctor's company at Labu 1 saw a party of at least 30 fully-armed Japanese trying to escape in folding boats across Labu Lagoon. When fired on the Japanese rowed to the shore and disappeared into the jungle. At 5.10 a.m. these Japanese attacked Proctor's company in an attempt to break out of the ring. Three attacks were made in the next hour, the third reaching the edge of Proctor's perimeter where it was stopped by the Australians' bayonets in hand-to-hand fighting, some of it in the defenders' weapon-pits. After this fierce fighting the enemy were driven off leaving 13 killed, including a captain and a lieutenant. One prisoner was taken—a man of the *II/238th Battalion,* who stated that he had withdrawn from Markham Point with about 100 other Japanese on the night of 16th September, hoping to reach Salamaua, as their supplies were no longer arriving from Lae. They had received no information that either Lae or Salamaua had fallen.

It thus became increasingly apparent that the Japanese from Salamaua had escaped and that the force being pinned by the 15th Battalion was the Markham Point garrison. All attempts to capture the strongly-dug Markham Point position had failed, and it was not until the 18th that Captain Bunbury's four platoons of the 24th Battalion found it abandoned —probably from late on the 16th. By the very persistence of its attacks, however, the 24th Battalion had prevented the Japanese—of the *II/238th Battalion*—from hampering the advance of the 7th Division towards Lae.[3] After the war General Adachi said that only two men of the company of the *II/238th* detailed to make a stand at Markham Point escaped to Finschhafen.

During the morning of the 18th Lieutenant Farley's forward platoon fired on about 20 enemy troops, believed to be the remnants of the force which attacked Proctor, killed nine of them, and sent the remainder fleeing into the jungle. After patrols north of Labu Lagoon had seen small enemy patrols heading south on the morning of 19th September Lieutenant Edwards led a patrol across the mouth of the lagoon to the north where it found 7 Japanese in some huts and killed 6 of them. An Owen gun was recaptured, and maps showing the enemy positions from Madang to Lae and estimates of the positions of the 7th and 9th Australian Divisions were found.

---

[3] Examining the formidable position at Markham Point, the troops of the 24th Battalion saw that there was room there for 250 men with air-raid shelters built 12 feet underground, well-laid-out administrative areas, pill-boxes and communication trenches. Hygiene was better controlled than in most Japanese camps. Smith reported that the position "had clean and tidy lines which would have done credit to a crack Australian battalion", that "fresh straw was in the weapon-pits", and that "the place was distinguished by absence of smell". During its attacks on Markham Point the 24th Battalion had lost 13 killed, including 3 officers, and 8 wounded; and in return it had inflicted 20 casualties and taken 2 prisoners.

When natives reported 53 Japanese at Bowamu on 24th September patrols of the 15th led by Lieutenants Tewksbury,[4] Oxley[5] and McCullough[6] approached Bowamu from the north, east and south respectively, hoping to surprise the hungry and exhausted Japanese. With visibility only six feet, one patrol fired into the village before the others were ready, with the result that only the Japanese trail leading west from Bowamu was found. On 25th September the three patrols, now known as Hunt Force, set about their task of finding the vanished enemy, but without catching them. By 25th October the 15th Battalion was in Lae except for one company in the Markham Point-Tari area.

Lieutenant Smith's[7] Papuan platoon had deduced by 15th October that the enemy had doubled back on his tracks. When the Papuans arrived at Markham Point on the 16th they killed five Japanese. Three days later they saw a dead Japanese floating down the Markham. Two patrols to the west and north-west found Japanese tracks converging on the south bank of the Markham where there were signs of a rough camp used by about 30 Japanese. Four dead were found at this spot and a one-man raft was found on the river bank. Across the river was another raft capable of taking four or five men. Here Japanese tracks headed to the north-east. Doubtless some few remaining Japanese may have joined the general flight of the *51st Division* over the mountains.

By 16th September two units of the 9th Division were on the trail of the Japanese escaping from Lae. The 2/4th Independent Company, in the kunda bridge area with two platoons on the east bank of the Busu and one on the west, had been ordered to hold the bridge. As mentioned, information from five captured Chinese indicated that about 60 Japanese had camped on the west bank the previous evening and inquired the way to Boana, Sio and Madang. By dusk on the 16th the 2/24th Battalion reached the Sankwep and made contact with the rearguard of the Independent Company.

On the 17th, when the 2/24th Battalion was strung out between the kunda bridge and the junction of the Busu and the Sankwep, some of Lieutenant Hart's men of the 2/4th Independent Company were reconnoitring north along the west bank of the Busu. From the natives the men learnt that many Japanese had passed north into the mountains on the preceding days. They saw the usual signs and smelt the usual smells of a Japanese trail and towards the end of the day they saw a band of enemy troops disappearing to the north apparently in a weak condition. The men of the Independent Company were at this stage inclined to think that the Japanese were little worse off than themselves for the 2/4th were at the end of a difficult supply line and were subsisting mainly on

---

[4] Lt A. R. Tewksbury, NX68328; 15 Bn. Grazier; of Scone, NSW; b. Temora, NSW, 3 Aug 1910.
[5] Lt-Col P. H. G. Oxley, NX138176; 15 Bn. Served Malaya 1955-57. Regular soldier; of Brisbane; b. Cairns, Qld, 17 Mar 1923.
[6] Capt J. B. McCullough, QX43412; 15 Bn. Clerk; of Yeerongpilly, Qld; b. Brisbane, 14 Mar 1916.
[7] Capt G. L. Smith, VX148599; Papuan Inf Bn. Regular soldier; of Black Rock, Vic; b. Brunswick, Vic, 18 Sep 1916.

Huon Peninsula

captured Japanese rice, and vegetables from the villages. On the 18th Hart, with a fourth section added, prepared to wipe out the enemy party, now estimated at about 100. This estimate was doubled next day when Hart counted 200 climbing a saddle at the 800 Feature. Because of the rugged terrain it was impossible either on the 18th or the 19th to get near enough to engage the enemy.

The two leading companies of the 2/24th Battalion on 18th September reached Musom 1 and 2, and Gawan, where the leading company reported finding a well-sited and concealed enemy position for about 50 men on the Gawan razor-back. This position, if manned, could have held up an advance. A Japanese straggler captured next day at Gawan said that it had been occupied by 50 Japanese until a few days before. The pursuit grew closer on the 20th and 21st. A platoon of the 2/24th attacked some Japanese at Kwupsanek and wounded three although all escaped into the undergrowth. In order to bring heavier fire power into the area where the Independent Company had seen the enemy rearguard of 200, Captain Mackenzie's[8] company of the 2/24th was sent north to reinforce Hart. All day on the 20th Hart's reconnaissance patrols followed the trail and gathered information about the enemy. They discovered that the Japanese were suffering from dysentery and that they had a number of wounded and sick with them.

By 5 p.m. on 21st September, when Mackenzie's company joined Hart's platoon on a spur leading to the 800 Feature, the Independent Company had counted 329 Japanese ahead of them. The main body of enemy, heavily loaded and substantially armed, had been moving slowly during the day following a small stream towards a saddle, leaving a rearguard camped beside the creek overlooked by Hart's position. In between these two enemy parties the sick and wounded were progressing laboriously. Hart deduced that after passing the saddle the Japanese would probably go down a creek to the Busu, move upstream to the crossing, and thence to Boana. He thought it possible, however, that they might, as an alternative, advance up the west bank of the Busu to its headwaters, or bridge the Busu north of the crossing before making for Boana.

To assist the 2/24th with deep patrolling Lieutenant Bruce's platoon was detached from the Papuan company destined for the Finschhafen landing and sent north. Bruce's orders were to occupy Gawan with two sections and patrol to Mililuga; the third section, stationed at Musom, would patrol the Boana Track.

At the same time units of the 7th Division were also trying to prevent the enemy's escape. On 15th September a patrol of paratroops from the III/503rd U.S. Parachute Battalion met a large enemy force withdrawing up the Bumbu River north of Lae and engaged it with sporadic fire. Natives reported that large bands of Japanese had passed north along the river valley earlier on the 15th. Because of the difficult terrain communica-

---
[8] Capt I. S. Mackenzie, VX40762; 2/24 Bn. Grazier; of Avenel, Vic; b. Trawool, Vic, 26 Apr 1918.

tions had to be by runner, with the result that it was not until 4.10 a.m. on the 16th that divisional headquarters learnt that the enemy was in greater strength than at first thought and that the Bumbu route might well be the main Japanese line of withdrawal.

By 9.30 a.m. one of Vasey's liaison officers, Major Mackinnon,[9] had raced orders to Dougherty to move to the Yalu area and take under command the III/503rd Battalion. Leaving instructions for the 2/16th to follow, Dougherty and two of his staff jumped into a jeep and bumped rapidly towards Yalu. Accompanied by an escort, Major Owens[1] immediately left Yalu on foot to cross the Atzera Range and find out what was happening on the Bumbu. That ubiquitous Angau guide, Major Duchatel,[2] led the 2/16th into the area and then left Yalu for the range to discuss matters with the Angau officer in the area, who stated that no Japanese had been seen in the Atzera Range itself.

At 3 p.m. Dougherty was led by paratroops along the track running north-west across the range, and by 6.30 p.m., when he met the returning Owens on top of the range, Dougherty had learnt from the natives that many enemy troops had passed along the valley before the arrival of the paratroops on the 15th. They seemed to think that the Japanese were heading for Boana and would probably use the three log crossings across the Busu farther north. When Owens reported all quiet on the Bumbu, Dougherty decided to move forward on the 17th to the III/503rd and also to send the 2/16th north-east in a final attempt to intercept the enemy. If the situation allowed, and if it appeared that the enemy had successfully bypassed the Americans, Dougherty would send Tolson's battalion back to Yalu.

By 10.30 a.m. on the 17th Dougherty had ascertained from Tolson that the Americans were not in contact with the Japanese and did not know their whereabouts in the Bumbu Valley. An American patrol was accordingly sent down the valley towards Lae to find whether that part of the route was clear. After a mile and a half the patrol met a small enemy party and dispersed it, losing one man killed. As this appeared to be the last of the stragglers Dougherty felt that no good purpose would be served by keeping the paratroops in the area, and ordered them to Nadzab.

Throughout the 17th the 2/16th Battalion followed a track along Munum Waters. Guided by Duchatel, Lieut-Colonel F. H. Sublet reconnoitred ahead of his battalion but saw no enemy. As the natives also reported no enemy in the area it seemed futile to go farther. At 5.15 p.m. Owens rang Sublet to inform him that the Western Australians had been allotted another task in the Markham Valley. Brigade headquarters arrived at Mac's Camp in the Nadzab area on the 18th and the 2/16th a day later.

---

[9] Maj A. S. Mackinnon, ED, NX325. 2/3 Bn 1939-42; HQ 7 Div 1942-44. Bank officer; of Sydney; b. Crow's Nest, NSW, 28 May 1907.

[1] Lt-Col E. S. Owens, NX55592. HQ 25 Bde 1941-43; BM 21 Bde 1943-44; GSO2 "G" Bch LHQ 1944; DAQMG 6 Div 1945. Chartered accountant; of Balgowlah, NSW; b. Armidale, NSW, 22 Sep 1916.

[2] Maj C. F. Duchatel, MC, NX151300. (1st AIF: Maj 13 MG Coy.) Angau. Mining engineer and New Guinea explorer; of Leura, NSW; b. Albury, NSW, 2 Apr 1892. Died of scrub typhus 21 Nov 1943.

While the 2/16th Battalion had been attempting to trap an enemy who had already escaped along the tracks north of Lae, the 2/14th was attempting a similar task along the tracks north of Nadzab. Resuming their advance on 16th September, the Victorians marched steadily north up Ngafir Creek all day. It was the same story on the 17th, except that the track into the Saruwaged mountains was steeper and signs of the enemy's hasty and recent use of it were more numerous. For the night the battalion camped on a kunai ridge one and a half miles south-east of Gumbuk.

At 9.55 a.m. on the 18th, Lieutenant Simmons'[3] platoon forded the Busip River west of its junction with the Bunbok. Approaching the Bunbok the platoon was fired on from three directions by what was obviously a Japanese rearguard covering the site of a wire-rope bridge which they had destroyed, and one man was killed. Supported by covering fire the platoon was extricated. Even without enemy opposition it would have been impossible to cross the raging Bunbok; both rivers were in flood and the Bunbok was unfordable. Colonel Honner kept a standing patrol on another of the Busip crossings about 300 yards west of its junction with the Bunbok while two companies prepared to cut tracks north from the crossing along the east bank of the Busip, keeping the west bank of the Bunbok under observation for a likely crossing place. Enemy could be seen on the far bank of the Bunbok as the companies explored trails to its west bank.

By the afternoon of 19th September a patrol led by the adjutant, Captain S. Y. Bisset, discovered a likely crossing place about a mile and a half north of the river junction where the Bunbok was fordable for half its width and the other half could be bridged by the trunk of a tree. By 6.30 p.m. a tree overlooking the river had been felled but it failed to bridge the gap, and thus there was no crossing on the night of the 19th and the Japanese were able to get farther ahead of their pursuers.

During the battalion's advance into the northern ranges wireless communications had failed and the laying of telephone cable had not kept pace with the battalion's advance. Dougherty felt that there was need to occupy Boana as soon as possible and, once there, patrol to the east. At 1 p.m. on the 18th therefore he sent a liaison officer, Captain Holley,[4] to order the 2/14th, after the occupation of Boana, to cut the probable enemy route of withdrawal through Lumbaip, Bambok or Kemen. After a rapid trip Holley arrived with his message at 5 p.m. on the 19th, shortly before the abortive attempt to cross the Bunbok. At this stage natives reported large numbers of enemy in Boana.

While Holley was racing north Dougherty was having misgivings about the wisdom of using the 2/14th in a pursuit role particularly as it, like the 2/16th, was required for a more important role up the Markham Valley. The maintenance of the battalion was also a problem, as the supply of native carriers was limited in the Nadzab area. Vasey signalled to Herring

---

[3] Lt T. McC. Simmons, VX48739; 2/14 Bn. Truck driver; of Port Melbourne; b. Port Melbourne, 15 Apr 1915.

[4] Maj V. H. Holley, WX3173; 2/16th Bn. Clerk; of Cottesloe, WA; b. Fremantle, WA, 28 Jan 1913.

on the 19th: "Track Ngafir to Boana up to Owen Stanley standard and is 17 hours march at least. Water is scarce. Would be glad permission to withdraw this battalion." Herring replied: "2/14th Battalion may be withdrawn your discretion. Should leave what you consider sufficient detachment give warning any approach your flanks by enemy forces. Will arrange relief earliest possible by units based Lae."

By 10.30 a.m. on the 20th the 2/14th succeeded in getting a bridge across the deep channel of the Bunbok. As the main body of the battalion was crossing Dougherty's signal cancelling the battalion's present role and ordering its return to Nadzab was received. During the recrossing of the Bunbok one man slipped and was drowned in the swift torrent. By 3.30 p.m. on 21st September the battalion was back at Camp Diddy. The 2/14th Battalion had been hotter on the trail than any other unit engaged in the pursuit and, had it continued through Boana, it might have caught the retreating enemy.

When Lae and Salamaua fell an immediate problem was the redistribution and reallocation of the troops and the creation of a great Allied base at Lae where stores could be accumulated for further blows against the enemy. During the final assault on these Japanese bases 25 Australian battalions, 3 American battalions, and 2 Independent Companies, with their quota of supporting troops, had been used. The administrative problem was a heavy one. Tentative plans had been made for the 9th and 7th Divisions to exploit their success at Lae by further assaults round the coast and up the Markham Valley, respectively. *Ad hoc* plans were also ready for the 5th Division to mop up in the Salamaua and Lae areas. Even so the initial task of pursuing the enemy north from Lae and Nadzab had fallen to the 7th and 9th Divisions and this meant that, as far as the pursuit north from Nadzab was concerned, the chase had to be abandoned when it was most promising.

When Herring visited Milford by motor torpedo boat at Salamaua on 14th September and found that the town would be quite useless as the site of the huge base which the Allies had in mind, he decided to concentrate on Lae and to leave only a small garrison at Salamaua.

At a meeting on the 18th Herring warned Milford to prepare for a move to Lae where he would supervise the establishment of the base. Milford welcomed this task. Signalling Herring on 20th September he outlined his understanding that he would be responsible for the layout of the base but not for the American portion of it. He also warned that the Americans intended to use their equipment solely for their half of the base, leaving the Australian side a series of camps connected by muddy tracks. Milford concluded his signal:

> The acceptance of stores until some roads are available will be extremely difficult. There is practically no Australian engineer mechanical equipment now available at Lae. . . . The need for Australian engineer units with heavy mechanical equipment is therefore extremely urgent especially tip-trucks, gravel loading equipment and graders. The construction of access roads to . . . depots involves a very large road construction program.

Lae was a small place with few port facilities. Several attempts had been made before the war to make a wharf in the little cove but the sea bed sloped steeply and always the Markham eventually came down in flood and the wharf slipped into the sea. Only after several failures did the American engineers manage to make a pile wharf which stayed put.

At the outset the road to Nadzab was usable only by jeeps and the Malahang-Butibum track was soon churned into deep mud. Along the Bumbu was a mere jungle track. First priority was given to a direct road to Malahang where many combat units were situated.

Some weeks passed before the engineer units with heavy mechanised equipment arrived, and in the meantime Milford had to struggle along with the few pieces of mechanical equipment held by the 59th Field Park Company. Until port facilities were developed everything had to be landed on the open beach from landing craft of the Engineer Special Brigade. Their orders forbade them to be within 20 miles of Lae at dusk and dawn, and on some nights there was not enough time to unload the few craft that were serving the base and they would depart with urgently-needed stores still on board. Each night the arrival of the landing craft marked the beginning of a few hours of intense activity. Stores were loaded on to trucks, hurried off the beach to a near-by area for sorting and thence sent to temporary depots concealed in the jungle. By dawn or soon afterwards the area round the beach was completely clear.

Milford and his headquarters moved to Lae on 22nd September. On the 23rd General Blamey returned to Brisbane, and General Mackay arrived in Port Moresby to take charge of New Guinea Force. In order to avoid any repetition of the confusion caused by divided Allied command during the advance on Salamaua, Herring clearly specified Milford's tasks. Lae Fortress would be established under Milford's command and would control all Australian and American base installations, the port at Lae, and the Lae and Malahang airfields. Milford would also have operational control over all military forces within the fortress area, although he would not disturb the execution of the general plan of local commanders of Allied air and naval forces and the American base, nor would he have authority over the "striking forces" proceeding through his area. The western boundary between Lae Fortress and 7th Division would be a line running north and south through Nadzab. The eastern boundary was at present unspecified but the southern boundary was as far south as Nassau Bay. As well as the 15th and 29th Brigades Milford would also have under command the 4th Brigade.

Milford was warned that he would later be responsible for delivery of supplies and stores to places determined by I Corps. "The situation that will obtain," stated Herring's instruction, "will be similar to that existing in the Buna area." Buna had of course been one of the main Allied bases from which the invasion of Lae had been launched. Milford's chief task would therefore be the development of the Australian base while the near-by American U.S.A.S.O.S. (United States Army Services of

Supply)[5] commander would be responsible for the development of the port, airfields and the Markham Valley Road.

With their formidable mechanical and earth-moving equipment the Americans of the "USASOS Advanced Base Lae" had the main engineering tasks to perform. The rough boundary between the American base and the Australian "Lae Base Sub-Area" was the Bumbu River with the Australians looking after the eastern sector.

In a final report the work of the American engineers in the Lae-Nadzab area was described thus:

> The airborne engineers who landed at Nadzab on 5 September 1943 had cleared the kunai grass and done a little grading; 2 days later the first transport strip was ready for use. By the end of the month three dry-weather runways were finished and the two airborne engineer battalions had begun work at Gusap, up the Markham River Valley. More U.S. Engineer and R.A.A.F. troops arrived shortly to commence the permanent improvement of these facilities. At Lae another 2-day record had been made, for, on 18 September, the Army Engineers had repaired the runway and lengthened it to 5,000 feet.[6]

Describing the port construction and road building finally achieved, after some months, the report stated:

> Two Liberty ship wharves, one petroleum pier, and one small ship wharf were built at Lae.... The principal road project was the one connecting Lae and Nadzab where troops were dependent for supplies on air shipments. An engineer aviation battalion began improving the primitive track and jungle trail late in September. The project was completed in record time on 4 October, but unfortunately the same drainage oversights that had earlier plagued the airfield workers now haunted the road crews. Stretches of the road were already impassable on the completion date. Two days later, with the road closed, work was resumed; on 15 December it was opened to all-weather traffic, this time in operational condition.[7] Considerable engineer effort was expended on access roads in the Lae-Nadzab region.[8]

---

[5] Commenting on the task of the engineers and USASOS the report issued by the Chief Engineer, General Headquarters, Army Forces Pacific (Major-General Hugh J. Casey), stated: "On the basis of all available intelligence information, the engineer mission became increasingly more specific. It was to embrace construction of an airdrome for one group of fighters at Nadzab, improvement of the airfields at Bena Bena and Lae, and development of port facilities at Lae and Salamaua. These activities were to be expedited, under fire if necessary. The engineers were also to improve the Lae-Nadzab road and extend it to the Leron River Valley; they were to provide oil storage and oil distribution facilities for airdromes in the Markham River Valley. Goodenough, Woodlark, and Kiriwina Islands were each to have an immediate emergency airfield with dispersal facilities. Port facilities here were to be expanded on a high priority basis to allow for unloading of ships and subsequent progressive development, with fixed shelter and storage construction kept to a minimum.... The complexities of the engineer mission were actually dwarfed by the administrative entanglements which the rapidly changing tactical situation and the demands of the campaign in Papua had made inevitable. During 1942, despite various reorganizations, there had been no unit in the Southwest Pacific Area charged with general administrative responsibilities. With the Papuan Campaign well over and plans being made for the continued offensive, GHQ and its subordinate United States Army Services of Supply (USASOS) were still burdened with administrative duties in addition to their basic functions. To remedy this situation the United States Army Forces in the Far East (USAFFE) was reconstituted on 26 February 1943 and given administrative control over USASOS, Fifth Air Force, and newly organized Sixth Army which had established its headquarters the previous week near Brisbane." (See *Engineers in Theater Operations* (1947), pp. 90-91, a volume in the official series *Engineers of the Southwest Pacific 1941-1945*.)

[6] *Engineers in Theater Operations*, p. 122.

[7] Vasey's Chief Engineer, Lieut-Colonel Tompson, had estimated as early as 14th September that it would take a mechanical equipment company, two field companies and 500 natives seven weeks to prepare the Markham Valley Road between Lae and Nadzab for use by an estimated 50 three-ton lorries per day as incidental traffic.

[8] *Engineers in Theater Operations*, pp. 127-31.

Each morning Milford would meet his engineer commander—Lieut-Colonel Bell[9]—to discuss the day's work. To overcome the problem of mud and slush Milford decided to build a road about seven miles long looping northwards between the Bumbu and Malahang. Offshoots from this looped road led to huge store depots tucked into the jungle. The building of the road was quite a feat. Usually Bell would have about 1,000 natives clearing the undergrowth, more clearing the big trees, more clearing the final strip, before the bulldozers put the finishing touches to levelling and draining. In order to conquer the mud it was necessary in some places to corduroy the road on top of three feet of gravel.

The building of this road and the huge store depots to supply the inland operations were among Milford's main tasks in Lae, just as the port and the airfields were the principal tasks of the Americans. By the time Milford handed over command of the "Lae Fortress" to his artillery commander, Brigadier Moriarty,[10] on 3rd November to assume duty as the senior general staff officer of New Guinea Force, the base at Lae was on the way to becoming one of the principal storehouses for present and future operations.

In the meantime troops had to be provided to continue the pursuit of the fleeing enemy and to guard all approaches to Lae. For the present General Wootten would continue to operate in the Gawan-Musom area. On the western flank General Vasey requested the "immediate release responsibility defence of Nadzab area", so that the 2/2nd Pioneer Battalion then at Camp Diddy could then move west. Vasey concluded that the only course would be to dispatch the 18th Brigade to Nadzab. As General Kenney had already pointed out that he would be unable to supply by air any more troops in the Nadzab area and Markham Valley it was decided that the 18th Brigade would not move forward until the Nadzab-Lae road was finished. After the completion of this road, supply of the three divisions in the Lae-Nadzab area by sea would be a relatively simple task. The making of the road took much longer than was expected and, in the meantime, the 7th Division continued to be supplied by air and the 9th by sea direct from Buna.

To enable Vasey to advance farther west it was decided that Milford would take over the Nadzab area in the near future, and ultimately control the whole Lae-Nadzab area from the Erap to the Mongi, largely by use of the Papuan Battalion and a system of observation posts. In the immediate future, however, it would still be necessary to cover the approaches from Gawan-Musom-Boana, while the feasibility of actually occupying Boana was still being considered. Some of the scattered units of the 15th Brigade were the most readily available for the task in the Nadzab area, and units of the 29th Brigade were given the task round Lae.

---

[9] Brig A. T. J. Bell, OBE, VX41. RAE 6 Div 1939-41; BM 19 Bde 1941, and various staff appointments in RAE. Regular soldier; of Melbourne; b. Melbourne, 10 Oct 1913.
[10] Brig G. V. Moriarty, CBE, MVO, MC, VD, QX36344. (1st AIF: Capt 3 Div Arty.) CRA 5 Div 1942-44. Chief trains clerk, Qld Railway Dept; of Brisbane; b. Bethania, Qld, 25 Mar 1894.

Wampit and Tsili Tsili Forces now ceased to exist. The 24th Battalion was ordered to Nadzab, and the 57th/60th gathered at Tsili Tsili. By 30th September a company of the 24th had relieved the 2/2nd Pioneers at Camp Diddy and the remainder of the battalion began to gather in a new camp on Ngafir Creek. Sub-units of the battalion, which were reunited for the first time since May, had assembled by launch, native canoe, aircraft and foot. At the same time the 57th/60th had been flown from Tsili Tsili to Nadzab and guarded the western approaches to Nadzab until it concentrated at Moresby on 21st October.

From the captured evacuation order of 8th September and other evidence, Milford knew that the enemy who had escaped from Lae were attempting to cross the mountains of the Huon Peninsula towards Sio on the Rai Coast. The general direction of the retreat was shown by the places named in the Japanese order as those where medical facilities would be available—Melambi River, Boana, Melanpipi, Iloko and Ulap. The first main stage of the journey would be either to Musom or Boana and thence to Kwambelang, Dengondo and the Rai Coast. There had already been ample evidence that Boana and Musom had been used.

Milford's Intelligence staff estimated that, at the end of September, there were about 200 scattered and disorganised Japanese north of Gawan-Musom, 300 in the hills between Musom and Boana and about 50 south of the Markham. Milford decided to establish standing patrols at Hopoi, Musom, Gawan, Boana and Camp Diddy and to patrol the tracks Yalu-Musom, Nadzab-Camp Diddy-Boana, Erap River-Boana, Musom-Lumbaip-Kwambelang-Boana, Gawan-Bungalumba-Bilimang, Busungo-Gawan.

From 21st September the 2/24th Battalion and 2/4th Independent Company, with the platoon of Papuans, were pursuing the 329 Japanese counted by the Independent Company's patrol. On the 22nd the Independent Company could not find the main enemy force although one section shot four Japanese along a mountain track leading west from the Busu. On the 23rd the pursuing troops again missed the main enemy body although 20 stragglers were killed. The Australians were astride the enemy escape routes from Yalu but the mystery of the disappearance of more than 300 Japanese seen two days previously was not partially solved until a patrol from the Independent Company found a newly constructed bridge across the Busu two miles up from the regular crossing.

As there were indications that the enemy had been across the saddle separating the 800 Feature from another feature Lieut-Colonel Gillespie sent a platoon from the 2/24th Battalion across it on the 23rd while the remainder of his force advanced west along a creek running into the Busu south of the 800 Feature. The route along the creek had signs of large enemy encampments. Next day the patrol from the 2/24th reported seeing a log bridge upstream from the main crossing—the one discovered the previous day by the 2/4th Independent Company. Gillespie then ordered Captain Monotti's[6] company and Lieutenant Hart's platoon of

---

[6] Capt F. R. Monotti, VX48808; 2/24 Bn. Articled law clerk; of Bendigo, Vic; b. St Arnaud, Vic, 15 Feb 1917.

the 2/4th Independent Company to advance up the west bank of the Busu, across the 800 Feature, and clear the area to the new bridge.

On the 25th Monotti and Hart advanced to the bridge through deserted enemy camps. Five Japanese stragglers were shot by Hart's platoon making its total 24 for this patrol and 51 since the landing. At 10 a.m. the troops reached the bridge which consisted of two spans each of an 18-inch log with a 6-inch log pinned on each side with bayonets to provide a foothold. Hand rails were attached on each side. From it, on the east bank, was a well defined track leading north-east up a creek and then steeply up the 2,500 Feature. Three natives who were apprehended at the Japanese bridge stated that they had been carrying for the Japanese, who had crossed the bridge a week earlier; the natives had deserted three days ago because they were not fed. The Japanese force for whom they had been carrying numbered over 200, and although the Japanese had only about two days' rice and were suffering from dysentery, they were still clinging to their machine-guns and lighter weapons. The bridge had apparently been built about a month before. As there was no reason for all the troops to remain in an area from which the Japanese had escaped a week before, and as supply was a great difficulty, Monotti and Hart withdrew, leaving a platoon to cover the bridge.

North from Nadzab patrols from the 2/2nd Pioneers had been guarding the approaches to Camp Diddy along the Boana Track and on 23rd September one patrol actually penetrated as far as Boana. One of the first men to arrive there after the Japanese had left was Warrant-Officer Bird of Angau. Soon after the 2/14th Battalion was relieved Bird continued along the trail right into Boana itself. Describing his lone patrol he wrote:

> Boana by the way is in a hell of a mess. Nippon pulled out not later than Monday last [20th September]—a hell of a party of him. It rained here Sunday night and he left after the rain cutting down bridge at Gumbuk on his way. If the battalion had gone to Boana Sunday it would have had a warm welcome. Gun positions of very strong construction commanding road and ambush positions about wherever he could put them. At the mission a big gun position being built—one finished—an excellent job. . . . Have posted a few notices here and there in good pidgin that we have Lae and that the Kiap is walking his bloody legs off looking for them. May help a bit when they are found by kanakas and when they pluck up enough courage to go near enough to read them.

By the end of the month the 24th Battalion relieved the 2/2nd Pioneers. Thus, by 30th September, the guarding of the approaches to Lae was in the hands of the 2/24th Battalion, while the 24th Battalion was guarding the Nadzab approaches.

At the beginning of October the main activity in the 2/24th's sector centred on the Papuan patrol's attempt to harass and destroy stragglers moving north along the Lumbaip-Kemen track. It reached the track junction near Lumbaip where a broad much-used track ran north to Kemen. A feature of the terrain was the bare rocky slopes of the hills which enabled the patrol leader to observe the track through binoculars for several miles in each direction. He could even see parties of Japanese moving into Kemen and occupying buildings there. The patrol then prepared an ambush at the track junction and in two days killed 23 Japanese.

The enemy had no fight left in them and invariably scattered when fired on, abandoning packs and equipment. The withdrawal in this area did not appear to be well organised and consisted mainly of parties of 10 to 60, usually led by an officer and without flank or any other protection. The Japanese were careless about lighting fires at night even when they knew their pursuers were close. Very little rice was carried by the hunted men who were living mainly on native foods, occupying the native villages along their route until they had eaten all the food. Little ammunition was carried and only one man in six had a rifle, although each carried grenades.

According to the natives the Japanese were making for Madang north along the Sanem River Valley and thence across the Saruwaged Range. This route did not accord with the one laid down in the captured withdrawal order. The supply dumps at Melanpipi, Iloko and Ulap were not along this route which would emerge on the north coast a long way from Sio. It seemed that the Japanese who were now apparently heading up the Sanem Valley had been prevented by the Australian occupation of the kunda bridge area from using the route via the kunda bridge, Musom, Melambi River and thence across the mountains to Iloko.

By 14th October it was clear that any further operations against the enemy remnants would take place in the Sanem River Valley. The 26th and 15th Brigades were therefore given the tasks of mopping up in the Kemen area as far north as the line Baindoung to Orin, with the inter-brigade boundary being the Sanem River. Gillespie's intention was to mop up in the Lumbaip-Baindoung area. To do this he sent one company to Kemen and established his headquarters at Musom 1. No sooner had he done this than the 26th Brigade was given 30 hours' notice to move. By 16th October the advanced party of the 42nd Battalion arrived and the relief of the 2/24th Battalion began.

When fresh reports from Angau that the Japanese were in the Sanem Valley reached Brigadier Hammer, he ordered Colonel Smith to send a company of the 24th Battalion into the Boana area to destroy the enemy.[7] On 8th October Captain Whitelaw's company set out along the muddy track to Boana.

Supplies were dropped on the old Boana airstrip on the 11th. After this Lieutenant Thomas[8] collected three days' rations and set out that day for Bawan where natives and Angau reported a strong force of Japanese. The platoon, guided by a Wampagnan native, approached Bawan by moonlight. Climbing hand over hand up a rocky cliff face which led to a small plateau on which Bawan was built, the men reached the top at 4.30 in the morning and saw a fire burning.

---
[7] On 1st October the 24th Battalion became 24th Battalion (AIF). Actually the percentage of volunteers for service with the AIF had exceeded the required percentage (75 per cent) since July 1943 when the battalion's application for reclassification as an AIF unit had first been made.

[8] Capt J. C. Thomas, VX43140; 24 Bn. Salesman; of Glenhuntly, Vic; b. Adelaide, 31 Jan 1917.

Silently half the platoon covered the northern entrance to the village and half the southern. The moon had set. The platoon waited for first light and the signal to attack. At 6.10 Thomas gave the signal—a solitary shot—and the Australians poured a heavy fire among the awakening Japanese. Despite the surprise, the Japanese fought with spirit, using mainly grenades. They had no chance. Fourteen were killed in a few minutes, and one killed and one captured in the pursuit. The prisoner was a private of the *III/238th Battalion*, who stated, probably fairly accurately, that about 7,000 survivors of the *41st* and *51st Divisions* had left Lae for Sio about 14th September. In the next three days patrols of the 24th killed 30 stragglers and found 6 dead.

Whitelaw's company now became the sole spearhead of the 5th Division. Other units in the northern hills were mere garrisons whose daily patrols sometimes found some unfortunate Japanese straggler who had been left far behind by the main body which, by mid-October, had largely arrived in Sio and Kiari.

Whitelaw's men resumed the chase on 16th October. As distances lengthened so supply and communication problems became more pressing but these were partly overcome by recruiting natives from each village to act as porters to the next. On the 16th a patrol killed five Japanese found in a native garden, and another two in a hut. Local natives reported that some 18 Japanese were in Tewep; the platoon poured a deadly fire into the huts and killed 17. Since arriving in the Sanem Valley the 24th Battalion had killed 80 Japanese and taken 3 prisoners. At this stage Smith pointed out to Hammer how difficult it was to satisfy the demands of various southern headquarters for prisoners:

Have impressed Whitelaw necessity taking prisoners. However, two men have been wounded in approaching huts in this endeavour and some Japanese have invariably escaped when party held up at point-blank range. Only hope is sick.

The dearth of prisoners ceased on 21st October when Whitelaw's headquarters encountered a Japanese sergeant who was able to speak and write perfect English and was used to capture four other Japanese in the vicinity. Standing on a high position he called out to his companions to come and surrender and be well treated, or stay where they were and be shot. Four Japanese quickly surrendered. Voluntary surrender such as this had not previously happened in the Australian Army's campaign against the Japanese.

The sergeant stated that the Japanese were in four groups. He was in the second as was General Nakano himself. The Japanese had moved along a very rough and steep track running along the east side of the Atzera Range, the object being to move overland to Sio and thence by barge to Madang. It was planned that the trip would take twenty days, but because of the weight only ten days' rations were carried, mainly rice and tinned food. All troops were consequently on half rations.

At one stage the Japanese were halted for three days while the sergeant's company built a bridge across the Busu. Soon afterwards he became ill; he could not state definitely the route taken by the first and third groups. The route taken by the second and fourth groups, however, was via Hanobmain, Baindoung and Avin and thence across the mountains to Sio. As the climb became more difficult the weaker men began to discard weapons, shovels, blankets. Each man retained one grenade, however, with which he was to take his own life rather than be captured by the Australians who were stated by Japanese officers to be cruel torturers.

On 27th October Captain Bunbury's company relieved Whitelaw's which began the journey to Ngafir Creek where rumours that they had many trophies of the chase spread like wildfire among the free-spending Americans. The spirits of the outgoing company were high. Since the mopping-up campaign began the battalion had killed 155 Japanese, taken 13 prisoners and found 115 dead. Of these Whitelaw's company had killed 145, taken 12 prisoners and found 115 dead. The thirteenth prisoner was taken by Bunbury's company on the 27th when the fittest Japanese yet encountered was found asleep under a hut in Bangdap.

Whitelaw ascribed much of his success to the cooperation of the natives. In the early stages his platoons cleared each village after careful reconnaissance and movement by night. In the later stages, however, natives would quickly guide the Australians to the enemy's hideouts. On the approach of patrols many of the Japanese would hide and come back on to the track after they had passed. Several Japanese were thus killed by Australian rearguards moving well back. Lieutenant Thomas' platoon killed 46 Japanese in this manner, against 49 by Sergeant Jackson's[9] and 47 by Lieutenant Robinson's.

"The area can now be considered clear of all but a few stragglers," stated an Intelligence summary of the 5th Division at the beginning of November, referring to the Sanem Valley. Thus Bunbury's task was merely to garrison the Sanem Valley and Boana and the chase was nearly at an end except for the interest of the 24th and 42nd Battalions in finding the Japanese tracks over the northern mountains.

On 29th October Bunbury was instructed to send a patrol along the Sio Track in the wake of the Japanese. Lieutenant Barling was chosen for the task and was accompanied by Sergeant Brack[1] from his platoon, Sergeant Cowen[2] from the signallers and Corporal Langford from the Intelligence section. The patrol's specific objects were to ascertain how far it was possible to proceed along the Avin-Sio track and to mop up stragglers. It departed on 1st November from Avin and on the 2nd reached Toocoomwah. "Village stinks with dead Japs in the area," reported the patrol leader. Later in the morning two Japanese armed with grenades were killed in a near-by garden. After lunch the patrol followed a track from the gardens down to a large creek. Crossing the creek the track was broken by landslides and was very difficult to negotiate. The four men climbed steeply up rocks and across loose earth, then through gardens and jungle until they reached a camp of the retreating enemy.

---

[9] Sgt A. F. Jackson, MM, VX109125; 24 Bn. Draughtsman; of Ashfield, NSW; b. Newcastle, NSW, 6 Mar 1909.

[1] Lt A. W. Brack, VX20952. 2/14 and 24 Bns. Guillotine operator; of West Brunswick, Vic; b. Morwell, Vic, 10 Oct 1916.

[2] Sgt D. C. Cowen, VX15198. 2/14 and 24 Bns. Railway porter; of Noble Park, Vic; b. Belfast, Ireland, 6 Dec 1918.

The site, which had originally held about 1,000 Japanese, was macabre. Many corpses were lying about. Apparently they had perished from cold or starvation, or both. Even weapons had been stripped of their wood to make fires. There was no food in this cold wilderness or beyond. After climbing a hill with a grade of 1 in 1 the patrol reached a grassy spur where it established wireless contact with Baindoung. In intense cold the men camped on a hillside about 6,500 feet up.

Guided by a local luluai the patrol left along the Sio Track early on the 3rd, but a quarter of an hour later the track disappeared in a sheer impassable drop. According to natives the track followed the Sanem River Valley to its headwaters and thence over the range to Sambanga, but was broken in two more places before the head of the valley was reached. The Japanese could hardly have chosen a more pitiless route. As there was little point in attempting to negotiate the giant landslides the patrol returned to Avin. Thus the curtain came down on this chapter of the tale of the *51st Japanese Division*.

One last patrol, this time of three Papuan soldiers led by Sergeants Macilwain[3] and Duncan,[4] left the platoon base on 8th November on a ten days' patrol for Bungalumba and Mount Salawaket. The only information available about the track came from old natives who remembered the track as boys but said that it had not been used by the natives for at least twenty years. There were no bridges and no huts, leeches would prevent lengthy halts, and it would be difficult to light fires because of the perpetual damp. The luluai of one village stated that even hill natives would die of cold on top of the mountain and that the Madang natives who accompanied the enemy as carriers would certainly have died. In spite of all this, ten natives volunteered to cross the mountain with the patrol to act as guides and rebuild bridges, provided they were given shirts and trousers to keep out the cold. Nothing further was heard from the patrol to the cold mountain until a runner returned to Musom from near the top of Mount Salawaket. He reported that the patrol had climbed to approximately 10,000 feet and "found that a select party of Japs, well organised with food, etc., had crossed the range" on the way to Iloko and Sio.

For the remainder of the year the 5th Division supplied garrisons and working parties for the Lae base. The troops were constantly patrolling without much chance of meeting any Japanese. A description of three interesting patrols will serve to conclude the story of the 5th Division in Lae.

On 21st October the commander of the 24th Battalion instructed Captain Peck to fly to the newly-cleared Boana airstrip and look after the lines of communication to the forward company. Peck left Nadzab in a Piper Cub at 11.30 a.m. on 23rd October, but when it did not arrive at Boana during the next three hours, some anxiety was felt. Although

---

[3] Lt R. I. Macilwain, NGX146. 2/25 Bn, Angau, Papuan Inf Bn and BBCAU. Clerk; of Rabaul, TNG; b. Semaphore, SA, 14 Apr 1914.

[4] Lt C. J. Duncan, MM, NX29174; Papuan Inf Bn. Bush worker; b. Terrace Creek, Kyogle, NSW, 28 Dec 1918.

patrols searched along the probable route of the plane, nothing further was heard until the night of 28th October when the doctor boy of Dzenzain reported to the 24th Battalion's adjutant with a message handed to him by a native child. The message, signed by Peck, was:

> To 24 Aust Inf Bn. Badly burnt both legs, broken jaw, 2 bad eyes. Picked up by party of natives. Pilot killed and buried. Boy starting 4 day trip Sunday. Might make it.

The natives carrying Peck on a stretcher were met at Old Munkip by medical officers on 29th October. Although very weak he was able to tell his story of the devotion and compassion of the mountain natives. The plane, flying through heavy rain, had crashed into the mountain killing the pilot instantly and throwing Peck into a stream. He walked down the stream and slept in a hut during the night. On the morning of the 24th he could not walk and so began to crawl, but had gone only a few yards when natives found him.

Having found the crashed aircraft the natives had removed and washed the pilot's body, buried it, and placed his gear in a hut constructed over the grave. Thinking that there was too much gear for one man the natives began to look for another. They soon found Peck, washed him, tended his injuries and carried him to a village. In case he should die Peck gave his rescuers a letter so that searchers would not think the natives had killed him. On the 25th he wrote the message which was received at Boana three days later. At first the natives were frightened to send a runner or move Peck because they feared the Japanese were in the area. The appearance of two police boys on the 26th reassured them, however, and they carried Peck out from the wilderness of mountains, arriving at Badibo on the 28th.

Many other Allied servicemen in the island campaigns owed their lives to the natives who rescued them from the gloom of jungles and the horror of wounds. Doubtless many lost or wounded Japanese soldiers had been similarly treated. Reduced to fundamentals it was the kindliness of the native which often caused him to guide the lost and succour the wounded so tenderly.

An epilogue to the Peck story resulted from the Americans' determination to recover the bodies of their dead for re-burial in a cemetery before eventual removal to the United States. On 13th November a patrol from the 24th led by Corporal Knight[5] and including three men of the battalion, one police boy and 13 natives left Nadzab with a casket to recover the body of the pilot, Lieutenant Harry H. Dunham. On the third day the patrol met the tul tul of Souse who led them to the Erap River gleaming some 3,000 feet below. A hand and rail bridge had been built that morning by the tul tul. Knight commented:

> A first class job had been done, hand rail and all. Then we looked up at this sheer face of rock. . . . It was about 14 feet high, the natives had built ladders and placed them against the rock. A great job had been done so up we went. How

---

[5] Sgt J. A. C. Knight, GM, VX104461; 24 Bn. Bricklayer; of Burwood, Vic; b. Camberwell, Vic, 21 Apr 1921.

they got the casket up is beyond me. They had big pieces of vine which they took out in front with about 6 boys on it pulling all the way, with 6 or 7 boys behind pushing. It was marvellous. We never thought such a thing was possible.

After this crossing the patrol climbed 8,000 feet sometimes on hands and knees and sometimes using more ladders which the natives had prepared. When the exhausted Australians reached the village of Norwal on the top they found a new hut with beds built for them.

At Norwal the patrol met a native called Gartan who had found Peck. Knight had some difficulty in persuading natives to accompany him to the plane two hours and a half away as the track was so dangerous. The route led round a patch of rock running around the side of a mountain without any track. The patrol feared to slip into the river so far below, but when "Marys" ahead made footholds the rock was safely negotiated. Finally a sheer razor-back with a track only a foot wide led precipitously down to the Erap. Cutting its way through scrub, climbing over landslides and wading waist deep in water the patrol finally came to the pilot's lonely grave close to the river. Knight reported:

> They had planted flowers around the grave which was very decent of them. . . . The natives had put leaves over him to keep the dirt away. They think of the least little things.

The plane itself was still poised on a rock hanging on its left wing and one wheel 30 feet over the river. The natives did not like Private Gee[6] venturing into it as it might fall into the river below; Gee entered the plane along a limb, but when the tul tul pointed to the gathering storm and explained the danger of the Erap flooding between its cliffs which were 300 feet high, the patrol hastily gathered its possessions and the casket and body and began the terrible climb out of the river area.

On the 17th the patrol had labour set-backs after leaving Gartan's village. These natives could carry no farther. They had already carried out Peck. Knight later explained how this had been overcome:

> Things looked black for us. Then the doctor boy came up and said his baby was sick. A mosquito had got him so Private Gee said he would go and see what he could do so he took some atebrin with him but when he saw the baby was only a month or so old he knew it couldn't take an atebrin. The doctor boy seemed to think he could but they tried by different ways but all failed so Private Gee hit on a great idea. He told the doctor boy to tell his wife to take it then the baby would get the effect of it. Well he had to show the doctor boy what he meant so he got the baby, put it on the breast of its mother and then the doctor boy woke up. He was very pleased and gave us some boys for our trip after dinner.

The remainder of the patrol was uneventful.

During the advance of the 22nd Battalion round the coast from Lae to Finschhafen a force of Japanese had been bypassed and had taken to the hills. On 15th October the commander of the 4th Brigade, Brigadier Edgar, learnt from Milford's headquarters that on the previous day natives

---

[6] Pte K. E. Gee, V40761; 24 Bn. Storeman and motor driver; of Armadale, Vic; b. Armadale, 20 May 1911. Killed in action 11 May 1945.

had seen about 200 Japanese along the Mongi River between Kaming and Butala, apparently moving towards the coast. Edgar was ordered to send a force of not more than two companies to destroy or capture any enemy in the Mongi River area.

Edgar issued his orders on the 16th to Lieut-Colonel Cusworth[7] of the 29th/46th Battalion. Under the command of Major Tilley[8] two companies and two Papuan sections were detailed for the task. Tilley Force departed from Lae in L.C.V's on the morning of the 17th. A platoon landed on the beach south of Hopoi and, after collecting about fifty carriers, on the 18th began a trek along the coast from Hopoi to Bukasip where the remainder of Tilley Force had already landed. Despite native reports of a large Japanese force along the Mongi River down to the coast no contact was made by patrols operating east and west from Bukasip. On 19th October the force moved west to Butala and established a new beach-head nearer the Mongi's mouth. Here it was joined on the 20th by the coast patrol whose only excitement had been the sight of crocodiles and the crossing of the swiftly flowing Mongi in small Japanese boats with wire cables which had been found near the beach.

On the 20th also patrols began to penetrate inland when Captain Eames'[9] company and a Papuan section moved to the Buga area. Patrols scoured the area and the creeks and tracks round the Mongi but found no signs of Japanese. When the remainder of the force moved into the Buga area Eames went farther north. A patrol to Kaming was followed on the 24th and 25th by the arrival of the remainder of the company which for the next few days patrolled the steep tracks in the Kaming and Sambeang areas. By 27th October Tilley Force was camped on the Mongi where the men enjoyed the blessings of a clear mountain stream. On the same day one platoon arrived at Wamuki in the far north. By the 29th Tilley Force had completed its task without finding any Japanese. There had been an enemy force of about two companies of *II/80th Battalion* along the east bank of the Mongi down to the sea. Tracks found by the 9th Division south of the Mape River seemed to indicate that these companies had withdrawn to Sattelberg even before the fall of Finschhafen on 2nd October. On 3rd November Tilley Force arrived back at its beach-head and on the 8th it rejoined the battalion at Finschhafen.

As well as clearing out the remaining Japanese from the Lae-Nadzab area and building a huge base, troops of the 5th Division, here as at Milne Bay, had also set a standard of malaria control which achieved splendid results. The A.D.M.S. of the division, Colonel Lovell,[1] considered that the 24th Battalion in particular had achieved remarkable success and held up its record as an example. Throughout the Salamaua campaign

---

[7] Lt-Col K. S. Cusworth, ED, VX14046. 2/14 Bn; CO 29/46 Bn 1942-45. Commercial traveller; of Ormond, Vic; b. Ballarat, Vic, 25 Oct 1906.

[8] Lt-Col Q. A. Tilley, VX58. 2/6 and 29/46 Bns. Journalist; of Elwood, Vic; b. Toorak, Vic, 17 May 1915.

[9] Capt R. B. Eames, MC, VX117183; 29/46 Bn. Salesman; of Northcote, Vic; b. Melbourne, 10 Oct 1917.

[1] Col S. H. Lovell, ED, NX451. CO 2/4 Fd Amb 1940-42; ADMS 5 Div 1942-43; CO 103 AGH 1944. Surgeon; of Bellevue Hill, NSW; b. Sydney, 22 Sep 1906.

this battalion had been dispersed over a large area, rendering the control of malarial precautions a difficult task. Colonel Smith decided to institute a campaign of rigid anti-malarial discipline when over 50 cases of malaria occurred in three weeks in the Sunshine area. He made it imperative not only for platoon commanders or senior N.C.O's to supervise the actual swallowing of atebrin tablets by each of their men, the application of mosquito lotion and the wearing of gaiters and long sleeves, but to report the carrying out of these duties every night personally or by telephone. Each malaria patient admitted to hospital was interviewed and the evidence used against the soldier's immediate commander if necessary. Sleeping under nets was rigorously enforced by inspections at all times of the night.

The proof of Smith's methods was contained in a message to N.G.F. from Moriarty on 6th December:

> It will be noted that the strength of 24 Aust Inf Bn over a period of seven months during which time the battalion has mainly been operating as an independent force, has only decreased by all reasons from 766 all ranks to 615 all ranks. It is considered that the case of 24 Aust Inf Bn proves by a standard of supervision that the application of individual protection can control and reduce the malaria incidence within a unit or force.

Indeed, having beaten the Japanese in the largest operation yet undertaken by the army, the Australians here and elsewhere were also on the road to defeating the mosquito.

CHAPTER 15

FROM THE MARKHAM TO THE RAMU

WHEN the fall of Lae was imminent General Blamey's task was enlarged to include the seizure of areas suitable for airfields near Kaiapit in the Markham River Valley and Dumpu in the Ramu River Valley. This was in accordance with General MacArthur's instruction of June 1943 in which the task of the 7th Australian Division was to be the prevention of enemy penetration south into the Markham Valley, and the protection of Allied airfields in the Bena Bena and Garoka areas.

On the day that Lae fell—16th September—General Vasey flew to Port Moresby for a series of conferences with Australian Army commanders and American Air Force commanders. At the headquarters of the Fifth Air Force Brigadier-General Whitehead told Generals Herring and Vasey that fighters should be installed at Kaiapit by 1st November.

Although the movement of the 25th Brigade to Nadzab was incomplete by 61 aircraft-loads of troops and 205 loads of stores, and the 21st Brigade by 362 loads of troops and 178 of stores, Whitehead hoped that movement and maintenance of troops and stores would be kept to a minimum. All realised that every day saved in Army transport requirements meant a day earlier in establishing air bases in the Markham Valley for later operations. This could not be done, of course, until the aviation engineer battalions could be flown in. Once the Markham Valley Road from Lae to Nadzab was finished stores could be built up at Nadzab by the sea and land route; the Americans estimated that the road would take two months to build, however, and Vasey agreed, as his senior engineer had reached much the same conclusion two days previously. As the Finschhafen operation was to be launched as soon as possible Whitehead pointed out that he would be unable to give adequate air support to both the Kaiapit-Dumpu and Finschhafen operations at the same time.

General Herring said that he would reduce maintenance as much as possible and suggested that the Independent Companies in the 7th Division and Bena Force, aided by the Papuan Infantry Battalion, could take Kaiapit. Later in the day Generals Herring and Vasey conferred with General Blamey and the outline plan for operations up the Markham was decided upon. Herring was toying with a bold plan for capturing Dumpu first and then Kaiapit, but this did not commend itself to Blamey who feared the consequences if all air support had to be committed to the simultaneous Finschhafen operation. It was therefore decided that the 21st Brigade with the 2/6th Independent Company and supporting troops would be concentrated at Nadzab where maintenance would be reduced to a minimum. Vasey would send the 2/6th Independent Company and a company of the Papuan Battalion overland to capture Kaiapit as soon as possible. The 21st Brigade would follow, probably overland from Nadzab, except for the 2/27th Battalion which might be flown direct to Kaiapit from Port Moresby. For the time being the 25th Brigade would remain round Nadzab. For the capture of Dumpu the 25th Brigade, airborne from Nadzab, and the 18th Brigade, airborne from Port Moresby, would probably be used, preceded by the American parachute regiment.

On 17th September the 7th Division was very dispersed. The 25th Brigade with the 2/2nd Pioneer Battalion was returning from Lae to Nadzab. Of the 21st Brigade, the 2/14th Battalion was on the way to Boana on the trail of the Japanese retreating from Lae, the 2/16th Battalion was in the Yalu area trying to cut the Japanese escape route, and the 2/27th with the 18th Brigade at Port Moresby. When it was clear that the *51st Division* had escaped from Lae both Brigadier Dougherty's battalions in the area were recalled because of the probable role of the 21st Brigade in the Markham Valley.

Despite the many documents found in Lae the Australian command still had an incomplete picture of the Japanese dispositions in New Guinea. It was known that General Adachi's *XVIII Army* consisted of the *20th, 41st* and *51st Divisions*, but so far only the *51st* with a few elements from the others (battalions from the *80th* and *238th Regiments*) had been encountered. It was assumed that the *51st Division*, assisted by marines and a medley of other troops, had been responsible for the Salamaua-Lae-Finschhafen areas. Bena Force patrols had found evidence that part of the *20th Division* was in the Ramu Valley and in the Finisterre Ranges. It seemed likely that the *20th's* headquarters was in the Bogadjim-Madang area and that the Rai Coast was also its responsibility. Little was known about the detailed dispositions of the *41st Division*, thought to be in the Wewak-Hansa Bay area. Thus, an advance by the 7th Division from the Markham into the Ramu seemed likely to encounter heavy opposition.

For three days before the 17th the 2/6th Independent Company had moved to the marshalling yards in Port Moresby but flying was cancelled because of bad weather. "Getting a bit monotonous," commented the company's diarist. At 8 a.m. on the 17th, however, the company took off in thirteen Dakotas, and at 10.15 a.m. landed on an emergency landing ground west of the Leron River. This area had been chosen by the American airborne engineer, Lieutenant Frazier, who had landed there in his Cub a few days earlier. As the aircraft arrived the troops could see Captain Chalk's company of the Papuan Battalion on the track towards Sangan. Two aircraft were damaged in the landing and were left on the strip. Captain King,[2] the new commander of the 2/6th Independent Company, now in its second New Guinea campaign, sent patrols to the west and found that two of the Papuan platoons (one was with the 2/14th Battalion) had reached Sangan, where they came under King's command.

At 4.30 p.m. an aircraft dropped a message to Chalk and just after 5 p.m. a message was also dropped to King. These contained General Vasey's orders for the next day. "As far as is known," King read, "the

---

[2] Lt-Col G. G. King, DSO, NX71008. 2/6 Indep Coy, 2/6 Cdo Sqn (OC 1943-45). University student; of Gordon, NSW; b. Gordon, 22 Sep 1918.

enemy has very small forces in the Markham Valley. They are reported to be in Sangan and a small patrol is reputed at Kaiapit. It is possible that small parties escaping from Lae may move into Kaiapit from the hills to the north of the Markham Valley. Their morale is very low." King's task was to "occupy Kaiapit as quickly as possible and prepare a landing field 1,200 yards long, suitable for transport aircraft, as well as carry out limited patrols and destroy any enemy in the area". In the message dropped to Chalk it was stated that the Papuan company would be "for use recce forward".

The Markham and Ramu Valleys, in which the 7th Division was now to operate, were like a giant corridor some 115 miles long running from south-east to north-west and separating the Huon Peninsula from the rest of New Guinea. From end to end of the river corridor towering mountains rose on the north and south. The valley itself was flat and kunai-clad and most suitable for airfields. Apart from the main rivers—the Markham and Ramu—there were many tributaries which in rainy weather would impede progress, but movement up the Markham was relatively easy, except for the heat.

Vasey knew that the Japanese were pressing ahead with the Bogadjim Road. No. 4 Squadron R.A.A.F. kept a close watch on the road but Vasey needed also a report from the ground and this was immediately available because of a small but daring patrol from the 2/7th Independent Company to the road itself. On the last day of August, Lieutenant Dunshea, Corporal Wilson,[3] and Constable Kalamsie (of the Papuan Constabulary) crossed the river and headed into the Finisterres. They returned to Maululi on 5th September. Next day Dunshea signalled a brief report to Colonel MacAdie of Bena Force, stating that the road was getting near the headwaters of the Mindjim River and that the survey trail was farther south. Parties of 50 coolies or unarmed soldiers each with an armed overseer were working on sections about 200 yards long and sometimes 100 yards apart. Several strong Japanese patrols were seen in the vicinity of the roadhead and on the 15-foot wide track running west from Kesawai, which was probably occupied by about 100 Japanese. In Dunshea's opinion there was no practicable route to the roadhead for troops except through Kesawai. Along the north bank of the Ramu the Japanese had a screen of natives who would be difficult to avoid.

A patrol from the 2/7th Independent Company at Aiyura met a patrol from Tsili Tsili Force (57th/60th Battalion) at Arau on 6th September; thus met for the first time the two forces which had played such an important part in the events leading up to the assault on Lae and Nadzab. A few days later the linking process was carried a step further when patrols from Bundi and Maululi met at Kaireba on the south bank of the Ramu. During these early days of September the Onga observation post reported that the Japanese were still in Sagerak. The screen of natives reported by Dunshea was apparent on the 6th when a patrol from Maululi towards

---

[3] Cpl J. M. Wilson, NX95078. 2/7 Indep Coy, 2/7 Cdo Sqn. Student; of Cheltenham, NSW; b. Granville, NSW, 31 May 1921.

the mouth of the Evapia River dispersed two armed bands in the bed of the Ramu.

On the afternoon of 14th September a patrol reported that natives had said that the Japanese were in Kaiapit and had cut the grass on the old Kaiapit airfield. About 35 were later seen moving east towards the Leron. Next day the Onga observation post reported that more Japanese had arrived; between 60 and 100 were camped in or near Kaiapit. On the 16th a small Japanese force from Kaiapit moved off towards Sangan. There now seemed to be between 150 and 200 enemy in the area.

On the 18th Captain King remained behind on the Leron to meet General Vasey while his company moved towards Sangan. At the meeting Vasey elaborated his instructions in his typical style: "Go to Kaiapit quickly, clean up the Japs and inform Div." He added that the 21st Brigade would relieve the 2/6th Independent Company as soon as possible.

At Sangan King, Captain Chalk and Lieutenant Stuart (of the Papuan Battalion) found that the Japanese had been there recently and had dug foxholes and erected shelters, but had withdrawn when they heard of a Papuan patrol moving up. A report now came in from Lieutenant Talbot,[4] who was commanding a detachment of the 57th/60th Battalion stationed at Intoap, that enemy headquarters (about 40 strong) was at Kaiapit with patrols to Sangan and Intoap. Other detachments were at Narawapum and Narantap with the line of communication through Sagerak and Marawasa. In order to find out whether or not the Japanese were in Kaiapit, Lieutenant Maxwell's[5] section left Sangan at 3.20 p.m.; after reaching Marangits the section moved into the foothills where they bivouacked late at night.

King gave his orders early on the morning of the 19th. "We will move from here to Kaiapit 0830 hrs destroying any opposition and occupy Kaiapit this afternoon." One section of Papuans accompanied the Independent Company to make contact with the local natives and to begin work on the Kaiapit airstrip as soon as it was captured. At Sangan King left most of the Papuans, his engineer section and some signallers. These were to act as a message-relaying centre to division and to collect a carrier line for moving stores and ammunition from the Leron to Kaiapit on the 20th. Maxwell's section was to meet the main body just outside Kaiapit on the afternoon of the 19th. The distance to be covered by King's force of about 190 men was ten miles, and the route lay through open kunai country. The advance during the morning was rapid and gruelling and the oppressive heat of the kunai and stunted savanna country bore down on the men. They reached Ragitumkiap at 2.45 p.m. and here found that the 208 wireless set would not work back to Sangan. It was vital for Vasey to know what was happening so that he could arrange to send forward the 21st Brigade at the right time, but there was nothing that King could do about it at this stage. There was no

---

[4] Capt L. S. Talbot, VX14600. 57/60 Bn, and "Z" Special Unit. Clerk; of Melbourne; b. Carlton, Vic, 10 Nov 1914.

[5] Lt B. F. Maxwell, NX2333. 2/2 Bn, 2/6 Indep Coy, 2/6 and 2/10 Cdo Sqns. Linotype operator; of South Grafton, NSW; b. South Grafton, 13 Jan 1919.

sign of Maxwell, but firing was heard in the foothills about a mile to the north and an enemy patrol seen there, and King presumed, correctly, that the Japanese were in contact with Maxwell's patrol.

At 3.15 p.m. the company formed up in the flat kunai on the edge of a swamp about 1,200 yards from Kaiapit. King decided that, as it was essential to occupy Kaiapit on the 19th, he would have no time to send in reconnaissance patrols, which in any case would do away with surprise. Captain G. C. Blainey's platoon therefore advanced on a wide front with Lieutenant Westendorf's[6] section on the right, Lieutenant Hallion's[7] on the left and Lieutenant Southwood's[8] in reserve. Thirty-five minutes later the leading section was fired on from foxholes 150 yards from the first Kaiapit village.[9] The platoon went in hard and the first rush took the leading section into the village, which it cleared. Westendorf's section swung out to the right flank at 4.5 p.m. and, with the help of the other two, cleared the main foxholes behind the first village with the use of bayonets and grenades. Westendorf was killed leading a charge but his men killed 11 Japanese where he fell. Against these fierce attacks the enemy broke and fled to the north-west abandoning Kaiapit and leaving 30 dead and several weapons. The Independent Company had 2 killed and 7 wounded, including King who had been forward with Blainey's company. King carried on. During the mop-

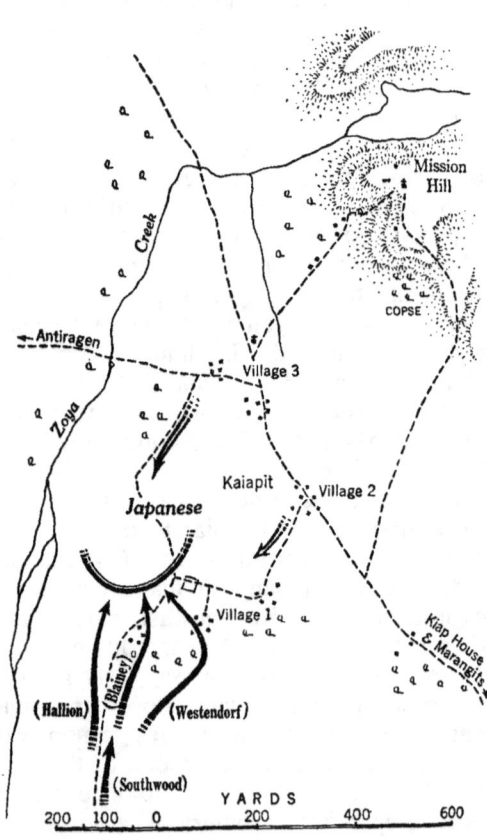

Kaiapit, 19th September

---

[6] Lt A. K. Westendorf, VX45889; 2/6 Indep Coy. Farmer; of Dimboola, Vic; b. Nhill, Vic, 24 Jun 1916. Killed in action 19 Sep 1943.

[7] Lt R. T. Hallion, VX56119; 2/6 Indep Coy. Cabinet maker; of Coburg, Vic; b. Brunswick, Vic, 20 Jun 1914. Killed in action 20 Sep 1943.

[8] Capt E. F. Southwood, WX17097. 2/6 Indep Coy, 2/6 Cdo Sqn. Bank officer; of Cottesloe, WA; b. Swanbourne, WA, 3 Jun 1917.

[9] As with many other villages in New Guinea there were several Kaiapits—Nos. 1, 2 and 3 as well as Kaiapit Mission.

ping up Corporal Graham,[1] who had played a leading part in the attack, was wounded in the face but he too carried on.

At 5 p.m. the company dug in on the captured ground which included the Japanese huts. The wounded were brought in and Captain Row's[2] regimental aid post was established near company headquarters inside the area. The commander of one of the Papuan platoons left in Sangan —Lieutenant Stuart—then arrived to find out what had happened since the wireless had failed. King gave him a message for Vasey that Kaiapit had been occupied and that he needed ammunition speedily, if possible by air, and gave orders that the Papuan company was to move to a point a mile short of Kaiapit at dawn on the 20th with a No. 11 set and reserve ammunition. Stuart left at once for Sangan.

At 7.30 p.m. a native approached the perimeter waving a paper. This was secured from him and when he tried to run away he was shot. The document was later translated: "We believe there are friendly troops in Kaiapit; if so how many and what units?" This was signed with a code name. During the night several Japanese, thinking the area was still in friendly hands, walked up to the Japanese huts with their rifles still slung over their shoulders. Six were killed.

The Independent Company had apparently done its job and King prepared for mopping up as well as securing, and if possible completing, the airstrip on the morrow. The determination and spirit of Blainey's men had forced the enemy from his foxholes. Had the advance been made with less dash the Japanese may well have stuck to their defensive positions and exacted heavy casualties as they had done so often before. Now, over half their garrison had been killed. It was puzzling that the native should have arrived with the paper, and that Japanese should walk into the Australian perimeter.

Meanwhile Maxwell's patrol had reached the high ground overlooking Kiap House on the 19th and had quietly observed for three hours. As only natives could be seen the patrol decided to visit the house. At 3 p.m. they hastily withdrew in face of an advance from the north-west by what Maxwell reported to be "two platoons hostile native troops". By some misunderstanding the patrol did not keep its rendezvous with the company and went straight back to Sangan. This was unfortunate as it had information that would have been valuable to King about the general layout of the airfield and three villages.

Before dawn on the 20th King gave his orders. He thought that there would now be only scattered resistance and ordered Lieutenant Watson's[3] platoon to leave the perimeter at 6.15 a.m. and move through the other two Kaiapit villages to the Mission and airstrip and back. A few minutes before it was due to move what appeared to be a powerful enemy force

---

[1] Cpl S. J. Graham, MM, SX15673. 2/6 Indep Coy, 2/6 Cdo Sqn. Wool sorter; of Broken Hill, NSW; b. Broken Hill, 3 Dec 1914.

[2] Capt R. Row, QX42691. RMO 2/6 Indep Coy and 2/6 Cdo Sqn. Medical practitioner; of Brisbane; b. Kilcoy, Qld, 14 Aug 1917.

[3] Capt W. D. Watson, VX20422. 1 Indep Coy, 2/6 Indep Coy, 2/6 and 2/8 Cdo Sqns. Bank officer; of Black Rock, Vic; b. Burnie, Tas, 17 Dec 1912.

attacked the section of the perimeter it held which covered the track entering Kaiapit from the west. The company's report says that there was "a hell of a lot of firing and shouting, but very little offensive spirit shown".

Captain King decided to counter-attack despite the fact that he had very little ammunition left. A quarter of an hour after the first enemy attack, Watson's platoon charged and drove the enemy back about 200 yards to the No. 3 village where heavy fire forced them to ground. They lost several men including one of the section commanders, Lieutenant Scott,[4] seriously wounded.

With Watson's platoon held up, King sent Blainey's platoon round on the right flank. The shortage of ammunition was becoming desperate and King saw that he might eventually have to withdraw for lack of it. The third platoon (Lieutenant G. A. Fielding), less one section, was therefore directed to form a firm base and cover the evacuation of the increasing number of wounded, who were later met a mile from Kaiapit by the Papuan company with a carrier line.

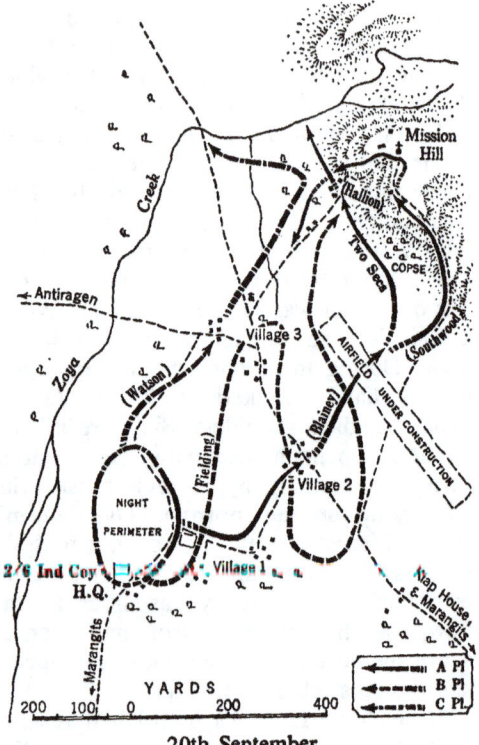

20th September

At 6.45 a.m. Blainey's platoon attacked to the right through No. 2 village and pursued some enemy bands into the kunai to the east, using the 2-inch mortar on a small copse surrounded by wire near the foot of Mission Hill. It then fanned out, Lieutenant Southwood's section making for Mission Hill and the other two moving on parallel lines towards some huts at the foot of this hill. Corporal Graham was now wounded twice more. In the intervening kunai several enemy were killed. By this time at least 100 Japanese had been killed and many of the others were showing signs of having had enough.

Soon after 7 a.m. a small carrying party of signallers and other men from headquarters carried forward to Watson's platoon some ammunition

[4] Lt R. T. Scott, WX11399. 2/6 Indep Coy, 2/6 Cdo Sqn. Stock agent; of Katanning, WA; b. Cottesloe, WA, 12 Oct 1916.

which they had been able to scrape together. It was a pitifully small amount but enough to encourage the platoon to rise to its feet and with fixed bayonets break out from the village. Lieutenant Balderstone[5] set a fine example by leading his section across 70 yards of open ground and wiping out three machine-gun posts with grenades. The Japanese, superior in number but not in valour, turned and fled into the kunai and pit-pit with the Australians hot on their trail.

By 7.30 Southwood's section had secured Mission Hill and remained there observing and directing the two platoons below it towards enemy bands and barracking as if at a football match. Lieutenant Hallion was killed when leading his section against an enemy machine-gun post. Corporal Wilson,[6] who had carried in two wounded men under heavy fire during the fighting on the previous day, now took command of Hallion's section. With bayonets and grenades the section captured the machine-gun and killed twelve Japanese where Hallion fell. This was the last organised resistance.

This decisive success had cost the enemy well over 100 lives and caused him a severe tactical defeat. The Japanese were thoroughly demoralised. Dumping their gear they tried to crawl away through the kunai. By 10 a.m. only the dead and dying were left. Small enemy parties occasionally raced through the kunai towards the Antiragen Track giving the men of the Independent Company flying shots. All were relieved when at 11.30 a carrier line arrived with ammunition. A quarter of an hour later Chalk's Papuan company of two platoons arrived. One platoon was based in the Kaiapit villages and another included in the tenuous perimeter on Mission Hill. Soon arrived that ubiquitous and enterprising American, Lieutenant Frazier, who landed on the strip in a light aircraft at 12.30 p.m. According to him the strip must be ready for transports by 11 a.m. on the 21st.

At 9.30 a.m. on the 20th a small patrol had left for Sangan with a message for the 7th Division. However, when Chalk arrived with his Papuans and a No. 11 set, King after some difficulties was able to let General Vasey know what was happening. During the afternoon the dead were buried, and packs were collected from where they had been dumped at the previous day's start-line. At 2 p.m. Japanese approached from the north-west but were driven away, three of them being killed and one Australian mortally wounded. Two hours later another Japanese patrol approached from the same direction. They were waved on by Sergeant McKittrick[7] but after advancing a little distance became suspicious and disappeared, leaving one killed.

Even before King got through to divisional headquarters by wireless his rear link at Sangan had received the message by runner from King asking them to signal through to Nadzab the information that Kaiapit had

---

[5] Lt R. T. Balderstone, MC, VX54281. 2/6 Indep Coy, 2/6 Cdo Sqn. Jackeroo; of Narrandera, NSW; b. Melbourne, 2 May 1921.

[6] Cpl J. A. Wilson, MM, SX1165. 2/3 Fd Regt, 2/33 Bn, 2/6 Indep Coy, 2/6 Cdo Sqn. Farm labourer; of Medindie, SA; b. Adelaide, 16 Oct 1917.

[7] Lt F. W. McKittrick, NX80699. 2/6 Indep Coy, 2/6 and 2/4 Cdo Sqns. Heating engineer-plumber; of King's Cross, NSW; b. Melbourne, 31 Mar 1914.

been taken and a request for ammunition, medical supplies and aircraft to evacuate the wounded. By wireless King added a request for reinforcement; his own effective force was now down to 139, but he was sure that the company's aggressive action and wide-moving patrols had confused the enemy as to the Australian strength, and they had therefore hesitated to counter-attack. The situation was, however, by no means secure. Division replied to King's request that they would try to bring in part of the 21st Brigade on the 21st if the strip was ready.

A splendid success had been won and the way was now open for a 50-mile aerial advance by the 7th Division. King's men counted 214 corpses and estimated that about 50 more bodies were lying concealed in the kunai. Blood-stained abandoned packs and equipment indicated that there must have been many wounded. At least 10 officers and 30 N.C.O's were among the killed. Equipment captured included 19 light and heavy machine-guns, 150 rifles, 6 grenade throwers, 12 swords, four W.T. sets and a large amount of ammunition, picks and shovels. Most important was the large number of documents, notebooks and diaries taken from the enemy dead. The 2/6th Independent Company had lost 14 killed or died of wounds and 23 wounded.

On the morning of the 20th, not yet knowing what had really happened at Kaiapit, Vasey had Dougherty and the 2/16th Battalion standing by at Nadzab for rapid movement west. At Moresby that day General Chamberlin rang General Berryman and asked what the Australians were doing about Kaiapit. Berryman replied that Vasey was in command on the spot and that General Blamey was content to leave it to him. Berryman that day noted down the subsequent conversation: "He said General MacArthur would not be satisfied with that. I told him General MacArthur should ring up my chief. Chamberlin said MacArthur was hot foot after him." When the Americans learnt what had happened their praise and their generosity knew no bounds. The Independent Company received General Kenney's thanks and an offer to fly in a plane-load of whatever the company wanted, and in due course a consignment mainly of soft drinks, sweets, cigarettes and reading matter arrived.

During the night at Kaiapit the Papuans killed five wandering Japanese. Spasmodic firing all night prevented any sleep for the tired and strained men of the Independent Company. From early in the morning of the 21st Australians, Papuans and natives worked hard to prepare the strip while patrols moved two miles north and west, killing one Japanese and capturing another. At 9 a.m., soon after an enemy patrol had been driven off to the north, Captain King received a message from the 7th Division that they would try to land part of 21st Brigade at Kaiapit that day.

At 10 a.m. on the 21st Brigadier Dougherty learnt that his Kaiapit command would consist initially of the 2/16th Battalion, the troops already in Kaiapit, medical, supply and engineer detachments, Major Duchatel of Angau, an interpreter from the American Army, and 600 natives. Vasey told him that his role would be to "secure" Kaiapit and occupy the Markham Valley as far as Arifagan Creek to cover the construction of landing fields west of Marawasa.

Tropical warfare was no new experience for Dougherty. He was an enthusiastic and unassuming soldier who had been a schoolmaster before the war. He had commanded the 2/4th Battalion in battle in Libya, Greece and Crete; and, then aged 35, the 21st Brigade in operations in Papua from November 1942 onwards.

Colonel Hutchison of the Second Air Task Force was with Vasey when Dougherty was there. No one yet knew whether the Kaiapit strip would be ready on the 21st; Hutchison said that a length of 4,000 feet would be needed as the aircraft had to land up wind and the hill made approach difficult.[9]

At 3.30 p.m. Hutchison, a splendid airman who had done this sort of thing before, made a test landing on the new airfield with a transport plane. He picked up King's wounded and returned to Nadzab with them. An hour later he returned to Kaiapit with a load of rations and ammunition. Dougherty and some of his headquarters went in the transport, which landed on the Kaiapit strip soon after Vasey had landed in a Piper Cub; Vasey ordered the wounded King back to Nadzab for treatment. By 6 p.m. six transports had arrived at Kaiapit ferrying up one company of the 2/16th Battalion. The 22nd was a good day for flying and the remainder of the 2/16th Battalion and brigade headquarters as well as a party of American engineers arrived at Kaiapit. During the morning Warrant-Officer Ryan of Angau questioned a Marawasa native about the route to Marawasa. The native said that there had been a landing strip just west of Sagerak as well as the one marked on the map at Atsunas; in pre-war days this strip could take Junkers transport aircraft. Dougherty decided that Sagerak and the country just beyond it would be a good early objective, for, if the brigade met opposition in the narrow part of the valley near Wankon it would have a landing ground on the other side of the Maniang and Umi Rivers, which themselves could be serious obstacles.

At 3 p.m. on the afternoon of the 22nd therefore Lieut-Colonel Sublet's 2/16th Battalion moved west towards the Maniang, intending to cross it that day and move on to the Umi next day. By dusk the battalion was across the many channels of the Maniang which spread over a breadth of about 2,000 yards.

Twenty minutes after the departure of the 2/16th Vasey's senior staff officer, Lieut-Colonel Robertson, flew to Kaiapit and told Dougherty that documents captured at Kaiapit showed that the Japanese force destroyed by the 2/6th Independent Company was not an isolated standing patrol but the vanguard of a Japanese force consisting of some 3,500 troops comprising the *78th Regiment* of the *20th Division* and a battalion of the *26th Field Artillery Regiment* with twelve 75-mm guns.

---

[9] The strip was a new one built below Mission Hill on the advice of Lieutenant Frazier; the old pre-war strip was abandoned.

The Japanese order had been signed by the commander of the infantry of the *20th Division*, Major-General Masutaro Nakai, on 8th September: "The force will coordinate movements with *51st Division* and advance to Kaiapit area in order to attack enemy coming north from Wau area." The advance-guard consisting of the *III/78th Battalion* under Major Yonekura would leave Saipa on 12th September, secure Kaiapit and prepare for an attack on Nadzab. Next day an engineer company would leave Saipa with the task of reopening the supply route to Kaiapit. Next would come a "key points capturing party", consisting of most of the other two infantry battalions and the *I/26th Artillery Battalion* under the artillery commander Lieut-Colonel Kagayama. This party would be ready to move at any time and would be followed on 17th September by the main body led by the *78th Regimental Commander*, Colonel Matsujiro Matsumoto. Nakai himself would be with his force headquarters at Yokopi by 11th September after which he would establish his battle headquarters at Marawasa by 25th September. A protection force on the right flank of the advance would be supplied by the provosts whose task would be also to "conciliate natives and with their cooperation make them work in the supply lines", to occupy Usini and to reconnoitre "enemy situation" in the Bundi area. The provosts would thus help the three infantry companies who were already on outposts directed against Bena Force. Ten days' rations would be carried by the advance-guard but all troops would be on half rations and would "dress lightly as possible". Supplies for Nakai's force would

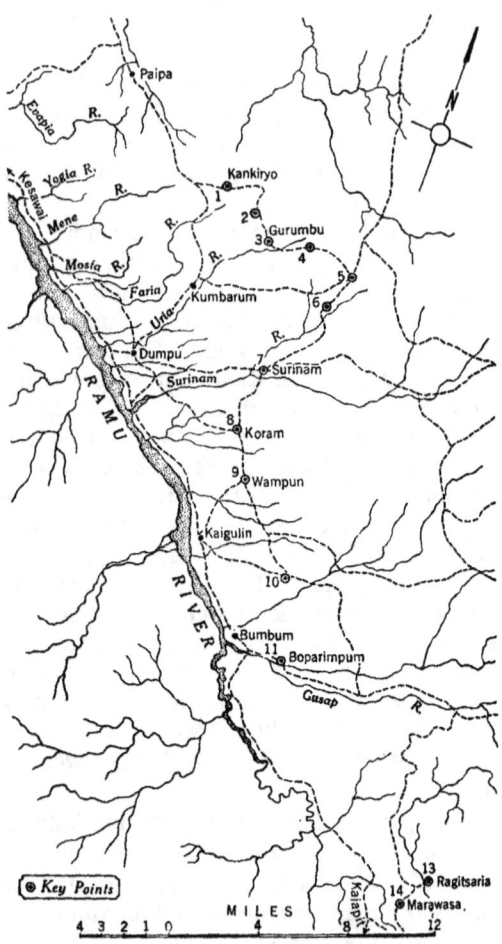

Key points and route as set out in *Nakai Force* operation order

depend on the work of the *Automobile Company* which would carry them forward from the coast to Yokopi; the *Independent Pack Transport Company* which would carry them forward from Yokopi to Kankiryo; and the natives recruited by the provosts who would carry on from there. The route for the advance would be from Paipa through Gurumbu, Surinam, Wampun, Boparimpum, Ragitsaria, Marawasa to Kaiapit; in other words along the line of the key points.

The establishment of the "key points" delayed the enemy and dissipated his strength so that Nakai lost the race for Kaiapit when his advance-guard of two infantry companies, a platoon of machine-guns, a platoon of engineers and a section of engineers arrived at Kaiapit on 20th September.

Before the assault on Lae General Adachi had intended to attack and capture the Bena Bena plateau with a force of about 6,000 men. He was also apprehensive about his strength in Finschhafen which he expected might be the scene of large-scale Allied landings and decided to reinforce it. In the Lae-Salamaua area before 4th September was a total of about 11,000 men. In the Finisterres was the *20th Division* less the *80th Regiment* and plus other troops. The task of this force of 20,000 men was to supervise the building of the Bogadjim Road and to advance down the Markham Valley. Most of the *80th Regiment* on 4th September was at about Saidor on its way along the Rai Coast to reinforce Finschhafen where there were about 4,000 men from shipping units, base troops and transit troops. Madang contained about 10,000 base troops including air force ground staff. Wewak was the biggest base and contained the headquarters of the *41st Division* less the *238th Regiment*—a total of 12,000 men—and about 20,000 men from shipping and air force units.

The loss of Lae caused Adachi to change his plans rapidly. He gave up the idea of an offensive to the Bena Bena plateau and instead decided to concentrate on the defence of Finschhafen. On 5th September he ordered the fresh *20th Division* less the *78th Regiment* to move to Finschhafen from its positions on the Rai Coast and in the Finisterres between Bogadjim and Kankiryo.

Nakai's role was thus a vital one. The Australian capture of Nadzab made it impossible for the *51st Division* to join the *78th Regiment* in the Markham Valley as originally intended, but a bold thrust down the Markham by Nakai would make the withdrawal of the *51st Division* easier and might possibly upset the Australian plans for an offensive up the Markham. Thus the Japanese anticipated attacks on both the Kaiapit area and Finschhafen. They were surprised, however, at the speed with which the Australian vanguard reached Kaiapit. The leisurely Nakai was outwitted by the quick-thinking and aggressive Vasey. Vasey in his turn was enabled to carry out his plan by the enterprise and efficiency of the American 54th Troop Carrier Wing. The prize of Kaiapit was in Australian hands. Nakai thought that he had half completed his object by "drawing" the Australian force from the trail of the *51st Division*. It would be much easier to resist the Australians in the rugged Finisterres, and Adachi had left it to Nakai to decide how far to go forward down the Markham.

The information given by Robertson did not greatly change Dougherty's ideas about the 21st Brigade's advance. The Australian commanders did not yet know that two regiments of the *20th Division* were on their way to Finschhafen, but thought that they must be prepared to meet the whole strength of the *20th Division* beyond Kaiapit. They knew, however, that the enemy's striking power would be limited by shortage of supplies even when the Bogadjim Road was in use. Robertson had also told Dougherty that Vasey hoped to secure Dumpu in the Ramu Valley by 4th October so that supplies and service detachments could be flown in before the period 10th-20th October when there would be no fighter cover for transports. Thus Dougherty was keen to push ahead when his other two battalions arrived. The 2/14th Battalion on the 22nd moved to Nadzab ready to fly on to Kaiapit, and Vasey asked that the forward move of the 2/27th Battalion from Port Moresby should be speeded up.

Writing to Herring on the 22nd Vasey had some interesting comments to make:

> The situation at Kaiapit is now, I am sure, well in hand as, by this evening, we will have the whole of the 2/16th and perhaps some of the 2/14th there also. There is, however, one object lesson in the action. It is that, in view of the opposition that appears to be likely to be met in the valley, it is quite wrong to send out a small unit like 2/6th Australian Indep Coy so far that they cannot be supported. May future plans take full account of this lesson.

Whatever the value of the lesson, a bold risk had been taken and a triumph won. It was fortunate that, before the Kaiapit action, no one knew of the advance of the *78th Regiment*. Had this fact been known an Independent Company and two platoons of Papuans would undoubtedly not have been sent to seize Kaiapit. There were no other troops available at the time so that Kaiapit would have been in Nakai's hands and the 7th Division would have been faced with a formidable and tiring advance up the Markham Valley. It is not often that it is well not to know the enemy's intentions, but Kaiapit was an example.

Vasey also gave Herring his views about the future:

> Yesterday I had all the talent of the Air Corps and the U.S. Engineers here. . . . The Air Corps seems to have trouble in determining whether they will establish their next permanent station at Kaiapit or Marawasa. Whitehead is very keen on Kaiapit, but some engineers say it is not suitable terrain.[1] However, as far as I am concerned I don't really mind where they go, for I am proceeding north-west along the valley by the bounds Kaiapit-Marawasa-Dumpu. The task of securing the Marawasa area has been given to 21 Bde.

Vasey was already planning his move beyond Dumpu. "I presume that, on arrival at Dumpu," he wrote to Herring, "my task will be to secure Bogadjim. This will involve construction of 14 miles of road to join up with the one the Japanese have built for us." Vasey would have been disappointed had he known that General Blamey's intention was that the 7th Division's task would be to carry out a holding operation in the hills north of Dumpu.

While Dougherty was gathering his forces at Kaiapit Angau representatives, Warrant-Officers Ashton[2] and Seale,[3] were recruiting as many local carriers as possible. Although many of these had been working for the Japanese they were ready to return to their old masters. There was some evidence that the Japanese had trained native troops in a school at Sagerak, and at this time Australian patrols from Bena Force into the Ramu Valley

---

[1] The decision about which airfields to develop is discussed in W. F. Craven and J. L. Cate, *The Pacific: Guadalcanal to Saipan, August 1942 to July 1944*, p. 190: "Before the end of the month the advance had progressed as far as the junction of the Gusap and Ramu Rivers. The valley in this area seemed so admirably suited to airfield construction that Colonel Murray C. Woodbury and Colonel Donald R. Hutchinson, both of the newly organized Third Air Task Force, decided to limit the establishment at the swampy and malaria-ridden Kaiapit location and build the base for the Third Air Task Force at a point which they chose to call Gusap."

[2] Lt S. L. A. Ashton, MM, NGX31. 2/9 Bn and Angau. Alluvial miner; of Ashgrove, Qld, and Wau, NG; b. Bowen, Qld, 22 Apr 1899.

[3] Lt H. P. Seale, NGX348. NGVR and Angau. Public servant; of Rabaul, TNG; b. Cheltenham, NSW, 17 Sep 1909.

encountered more armed natives than Japanese. Even these Japanese-trained natives were not averse, however, to changing sides, particularly because of the contrast between Australian and Japanese treatment. In one of the huts at Kaiapit were three dead natives who had had their

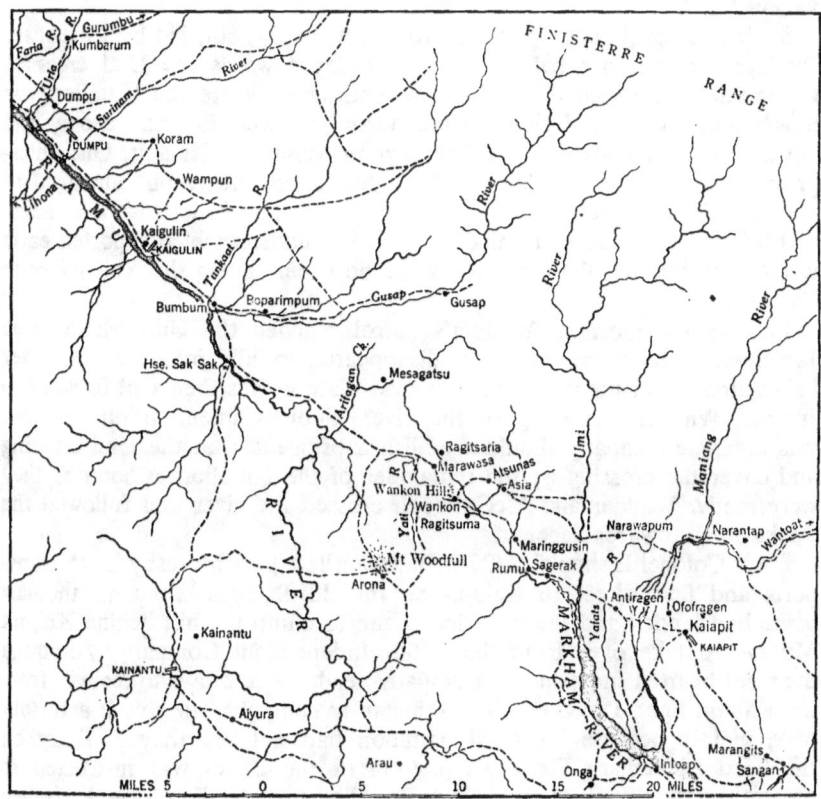

hands and feet tied and had been bayoneted by the Japanese. Such treatment did not endear the Greater East Asia Co-Prosperity Sphere to the natives.

In the Ramu Valley many of the natives were hostile to any intruders and in the Markham German Lutheran Missions, at such places as Kaiapit, were thought before the war not to have insisted on loyalty to the Australian administration among their converts. One of the senior Australian commanders in the area thought that the mission "had done much to sow the seeds of anti-British feeling".

Half an hour after midnight on the 22nd-23rd September Dougherty received orders from the division for "no further movement in strength until commander visits you earliest 23 Sep". At 2 a.m. on the 23rd a message was therefore sent to Sublet ordering him not to move to the

Umi until he had enough carriers, but to send out a platoon to reconnoitre the crossing. Dougherty did not believe that a battalion move to the Umi would constitute a forward movement "in strength". Later in the morning Vasey flew from Nadzab to Kaiapit to confer with Dougherty about plans to meet the Japanese presumably advancing down the river valleys.[4]

Swift and lightly equipped a patrol from the 2/16th, led by Lieutenant Wallder,[5] moved out before dawn that day towards the Umi crossing. Other patrols scoured the area from Antiragen, where the battalion was now based, and found signs to the north and west that the enemy had left the area after his defeat a few days previously at Kaiapit. One enterprising patrol along the Yafats River found no enemy but managed to return with sweet potatoes, bananas and corn. The belief that the enemy had left the area was confirmed by No. 4 Squadron which reported early in the morning that there seemed to be no enemy along the Yati River to Marawasa.

Late in the morning Wallder's patrol reached the Umi where three Japanese, seen across the river, disappeared rapidly into the hills after being fired at. Lieutenant McCullough's[6] platoon was then sent forward to support Wallder's crossing of the river. Sublet's intention on this day was that one company should establish a bridgehead at the Umi crossing and cover the crossing by the remainder of the battalion as soon as they were ready. Wallder and McCullough crossed the river and followed the tracks north towards Sagerak.

Lieut-Colonel Bishop's[7] 2/27th Battalion left Port Moresby in 45 transports and flew direct to Kaiapit on the 23rd. By 10.50 a.m. the last plane had landed and the battalion began to climb the hill behind Kaiapit Mission to take over from the 2/6th Independent Company. Although the stout-hearted Independent Company needed a few days to recover from the Kaiapit fight, Dougherty was reluctantly compelled to give it a further task, mainly because his third battalion had not yet arrived. Early on the 23rd Lieutenant Fielding's platoon of the 2/6th was instructed to protect the right flank of the 2/16th Battalion by patrolling from Antiragen north towards Narawapum.

Thus, on the evening of the 23rd, with the threat of the Japanese advance down the river valleys apparently looming, the 21st Brigade was spread out between Sagerak and Kaiapit. But Dougherty was confident that, once his 2/14th Battalion arrived, he could hold Kaiapit and

---

[4] Vasey informed Herring that he should have at least two light aircraft. "They are the equivalent of a car in normal operations," he wrote. "In addition to enabling me and my staff to keep in touch with the forward elements, they would also be valuable for the carrying of urgent medical or other supplies and evacuation of casualties before a strip fit for transports is available." Vasey's relations with the American Air Force were cordial and he usually managed to have the use of a small aircraft if one was available.

[5] Lt J. R. Wallder, WX7593; 2/16 Bn. Signwriter; of Nedlands, WA; b. Perth, 4 Jul 1920. Died 25 Apr 1944.

[6] Capt K. McCullough, WX4335; 2/16 Bn. Timber worker; of Jardee, WA; b. Kalgoorlie, WA, 3 Apr 1913.

[7] Maj-Gen J. A. Bishop, DSO, OBE, ED, VX35. 2/7 Bn 1939-41; BM 17 Bde 1941; CO 2/27 Bn 1943; GSO1 6 Div 1943-45 (Admin Comd 19 Bde Jun-Jul 1945). Department manager; of Box Hill and Hawthorn East, Vic; b. Malvern, Vic, 16 Jan 1908.

(*Australian War Memorial*)
Kaiapit village, scene of the fighting by 2/6th Independent Company on 19th-20th September 1943.

(*Australian War Memorial*)
Men of the 2/16th Battalion arrive at Kaiapit by plane on 21st September 1943 to begin their advance on foot along the Markham and Ramu Valleys.

The Markham-Ramu divide. It was impossible to pinpoint the divide on the ground. The only indication was that the rivers were flowing in opposite directions—the Ramu to the west (left of picture) and the Markham to the east (right of picture).

(as he said in his report) "crack the Jap if he attacked, and at the same time secure the Umi crossing, and, with vigorous patrolling, hit the Jap hard in the Sagerak area". He told Sublet to secure the high ground south of Sagerak on the 24th "leaving something to hold the crossing place with the view of later driving the enemy from Sagerak and preparing an airstrip in its vicinity".

The 24th was a busy day for the 2/16th Battalion and the 2/6th Independent Company. As they probed forward towards Sagerak Wallder's men were fired on by machine-guns and rifles. The patrol's 2-inch mortar fire, however, caused this enemy rearguard to withdraw. Meanwhile patrols from Fielding's platoon of the 2/6th were moving towards Narawapum and the 2/16th Battalion was advancing from the Yafats River towards the Umi. The Papuan company was patrolling the northern foothills trying to trace a possible route into the Australian area for the Japanese from the Boana-Wantoat areas.

Half an hour after midday two companies of the 2/16th were across the swollen Umi and moving forward to join the two platoons already on the high ground south of Sagerak. The Pioneer platoon manned the rope ferrying the stores across and rescued the washaways. The ease with which the natives "bounced" their way across the fast-flowing river was a source of wonder and envy to the heavily-burdened troops battling their way inch by inch along the rope.

During the afternoon there were two brushes with enemy patrols. In the Narawapum area a patrol from the 2/16th Battalion joined Lieutenant Maxwell's section of the 2/6th Independent Company and clashed with about 20 Japanese carrying full packs and equipment including at least three machine-guns. The enemy rapidly withdrew. Across the Umi Lieutenant W. J. Duncan's platoon of the 2/16th became the vanguard, and by 2.40 was overlooking Sagerak and getting ready to move towards it. At 5 p.m. the Australians skirmished with an enemy patrol and Duncan was wounded by a sniper. It was not until well after dark that the West Australians finished their arduous crossing of the swollen river.

During the day Dougherty visited the Umi crossing place. The main channel was about 50 yards wide and 4 feet 6 inches deep in its deepest part and fast flowing. He was convinced that at flood-time the river would spread to a width of up to 200 yards and would then be impossible to cross with existing equipment. After anxiously watching the crossing for two hours Dougherty returned to his headquarters at Kaiapit to find out what troops and supplies had arrived. No aircraft had arrived during the day so there was no 2/14th Battalion, and the only reserves of food and ammunition were those actually carried by the 2/16th and 2/27th. Native reports were arriving that the Japanese were holding the villages along the foothills and in the upper Umi area, and the Boomerangs reported that there were suspected Japanese positions on the upper Umi which might be held in strength. Dougherty began to consider concentrating his brigade in a more favourable position, and was not altogether sorry when, towards dusk, he received a signal from divisional headquarters that, as the enemy in the area was double the brigade's strength, Vasey was most concerned about a part of the brigade being separated from the rest by the Umi. Dougherty therefore decided to order the 2/16th back across the Umi at first light on the 25th, leaving a standing patrol south of Sagerak. This message reached the battalion at 8.30 p.m., half an hour after the dangerous crossing had finally been completed. "The order to withdraw was received without enthusiasm," wrote the battalion's historian. "The idea of falling back was repugnant and the prospect of crossing back over the Umi River was a dismal one; but orders had to be obeyed."[8] Sublet reluctantly withdrew his battalion across the Umi before dawn on the 25th, leaving a platoon (Lieutenant Crombie[9]) in the area overlooking Sagerak. Re-crossing the Umi in the dark presented special difficulties but was finished by 8 a.m. and the battalion moved back to an area between the Maniang and Yafats Rivers.

It was ironical that, after all the effort entailed in crossing and re-crossing the Umi River, Crombie's platoon should find Sagerak deserted that day. A party of about sixteen Japanese fled hurriedly on his approach, leaving documents, diaries, medical stores and other equipment. In fact the Japanese seemed to have departed so speedily that they were carrying only their rifles. Lieutenant Frazier walked north-west from Sagerak and pegged out a landing strip which required only four hours' labour to fit it for the landing of transport planes.

That morning (the 25th) Dougherty was about to climb into a Dauntless dive bomber for a reconnaissance flight to the Ramu when Vasey landed in his Cub. Vasey told Dougherty to go ahead and look at the country about the Umi; he said that if the Japanese decided to attack then the area between the Umi and Kaiapit was a good place to destroy them. Dougherty flew up the Markham and down the Ramu to beyond Dumpu looking particularly at the country through which the Japanese track was thought to go from the Gusap River to the upper Faria River. Carefully examining the country east of the Umi, he agreed that if the Japanese ventured on to the low country it would be to the Australians' advantage and a winning fight could be fought there. On Dougherty's return Vasey said that he thought that the enemy would attack Kaiapit because it was their custom blindly to persevere with a plan once formed. Dougherty, however, did not think that the Japanese would do this as they would have difficulty in maintaining a sufficient force so far forward. Vasey finally decided to bring the 25th Brigade to Kaiapit before he made any forward move; originally his idea had been to fly the 25th Brigade in farther forward after the 21st Brigade had secured a landing ground to the west. Thus Dougherty's activities were restricted to reconnoitring crossings over the Maniang River and patrolling. The 21st Brigade would create the impression of minimum strength in the hope that this would encourage the Japanese to attack.

---

[8] M. Uren, *A Thousand Men at War—The Story of the 2/16th Battalion, A.I.F.* (1959), p. 198.
[9] Lt R. G. Crombie, WX2742; 2/16 Bn. Clerk; of Cottesloe, WA; b. Cottesloe, 8 Jan 1916.

Back in Nadzab Brigadier Eather received instructions that the 25th Brigade was to be flown to Kaiapit, starting with the 2/31st Battalion next day. At last, on the 25th, the 2/14th Battalion, with part of a battery of the 2/4th Field Regiment, landed at Kaiapit. While patrols of Papuans searched the foothills, Dougherty instructed Captain Rose-Bray,[1] now commanding the 2/6th Independent Company, to reconnoitre Narawapum. That day the air force struck Marawasa, and "frightened six months' growth out of [the 2/6th Independent] Company by dropping auxiliary belly tanks within a hundred yards".

During these last nine days Lieut-Colonel MacAdie's Bena Force had been maintaining its watching brief over its vast area of mountains and valleys fronting the Ramu River. Patrols of Bena Force were trying out the crossing places over the Ramu in preparation for new operations. On the 20th a patrol from the 2/7th Independent Company reported that the Gusap and Ramu Rivers were in flood. One man, however, swam both rivers and reconnoitred Bumbum, naked and unarmed. Here he saw seven Japanese before he again swam the rivers. Two days later patrols from the most western platoon of the 2/2nd Independent Company reported that they were unable to cross the Ramu between Sepu and Yonapa.

"When I get to Marawasa," wrote General Vasey to General Herring on the 22nd, "will Bena Force come under my command? I think it should so that they may clear the hills north of Bena Bena and join me on the Ramu west of Dumpu." Herring agreed, and decided that Bena Force should be placed under Vasey's command before Marawasa was actually reached by the 7th Division. Gradually Bena Force began to press forward and even to cross the Ramu. In conformity with higher plans MacAdie had been holding his men on a leash for several months, but it now seemed obvious that Bena Force would have to clear the way ahead from Dumpu as far west as Kesawai at least.

On the 24th a patrol of the 2/7th reported that the enemy was occupying Dumpu and the mouth of the Uria River. There were now, however, no Japanese in Bumbum although there were signs that a small Japanese party had moved from there to Kaigulin recently. By dusk on the 24th another 2/7th patrol reported that there were about 100 Japanese in Arona on the upper slopes of Mount Woodfull and that there seemed to be a large number of Japanese at Marawasa.

The 2/2nd prepared to patrol the Kesawai and Evapia River areas directly opposite Maululi. Corporal J. F. Fowler led a routine patrol to Waimeriba on 23rd September and found unmistakable signs that the Japanese had set up an ambush at the Wei River crossing south of the Ramu and had waited there hopefully but without reward for about a day. At midnight on the 23rd-24th September Lieutenant Nagle[2] and two

---

[1] Capt A. E. B. Rose-Bray, NX6068. 2/6 Indep Coy, 2/6 Cdo Sqn. Bank officer; of Marrickville, NSW; b. Croydon, NSW, 12 May 1916.

[2] Lt V. F. Nagle, VX1042. 2/9 Fd Regt, 2/2 Indep Coy. Solicitor; of Albury, NSW; b. Albury, 15 Apr 1915. Killed in action 4 Oct 1943.

men crossed the Ramu and sneaked[3] as close as they could to Kesawai which they identified by smoke from fires, wood-chopping, voices, and stray shots probably from pig-hunting parties. When watching and listening in a dry watercourse the patrol was suddenly confronted by one of the pig hunters who was immediately shot. As the patrol rapidly withdrew another startled Japanese met them and "fell on his haunches in a cowering suppliant attitude". Farther east on the night of 23rd-24th September Lance-Corporal J. W. Poynton led a two-man patrol across the Ramu near its junction with the Evapia River. This was a difficult area for patrolling undetected because the natives seemed pro-Japanese and many were armed. Nevertheless the three men did manage to watch from a high observation post the activities of native carrying parties escorted by a few Japanese moving from the Evapia towards Kesawai. When the patrol was discovered by the native observation posts the three raced for the Ramu and escaped from a pursuing force of 9 Japanese and about 50 natives.

MacAdie had been expecting that the attack on Lae might precipitate an enemy attack in strength across the Ramu River to the Bena-Mount Hagen plateau. However, the Japanese had not crossed the river for some time, and it almost seemed that they might be thinking of withdrawing not only from the Markham Valley but also from the upper Ramu. If the Dumpu-Kesawai area could be cleared before the arrival of the spearhead of the 7th Division, Bena Force would indeed have fulfilled a useful task.

The enemy must have been in something of a quandary at this stage. The vanguard of the *78th Regiment* had been soundly thrashed at Kaiapit. If they crossed the Ramu they encountered resistance at various points along a front of 100 miles. Not only that, but the *XVIII Japanese Army* had met parties of Australians from Mosstroops, A.I.B. and F.E.L.O. in the remote west of the Sepik Valley on several occasions. The Japanese commander must have wondered how many Australians were in the area, for one of his patrols from Atemble had driven out one of MacAdie's patrols at Kumera far down the Ramu on 20th September. The loss of wireless equipment, maps and codes by this Australian patrol was perhaps balanced by the enemy's fear that the Australians were everywhere.[4] His reconnaissance aircraft had also seen the rapid construction of roads, bridges and buildings on the Bena plateau.

Determined to gain all possible information about the area between Dumpu and the 21st Brigade, MacAdie instructed Captain Lomas of the 2/7th Independent Company to send out two linking patrols on the 26th. Lieutenant Dunshea set out on a long patrol direct from Lihona in the upper Ramu Valley through the Dumpu area and down the Markham Valley to Kaiapit. Lieutenant Danne's patrol took a more indirect route from Kainantu, through Onga to Kaiapit. He arrived at dusk and reported

---

[3] They were actually wearing rubber "sneakers" (boots) which were on issue to Independent Companies but seldom used. Nagle found them a great help in silent movement although they were slippery on hills and inclined to "draw" the feet.

[4] An unusually detailed enemy account exists of this Japanese raid. Although Australian records reported that the attack was made by 60 Japanese apparently only 16 participated. The Japanese killed one man and took one prisoner.

that there were no signs of Japanese having been in the area for the past month.

Back at Kaiapit patrolling and building up of stores continued. Lieutenant Crombie found on the 26th that Rumu, forward from Sagerak, was unoccupied. With all this evidence of a non-aggressive enemy confronting him Dougherty was anxious to get moving. Vasey understood his feelings for, on the 26th, he sent him a message—

> I am terribly sorry about the delay in getting 25 Brigade up to your area but this b——y Air Force is too tiresome. I cannot guess when the move will be completed. In the meantime I would like you to get all possible information of the Jap, particularly in the foothills east of the Umi. I have a feeling that he will not now attack us at Kaiapit but has withdrawn *51 Div* to Marawasa area where we shall have to attack him.[5] If you can confirm this feeling for me it will save time when 25 Brigade does come up and I remove your leash. Will you consider the possibility of crossing the Umi at night so as to get a flying start for Marawasa at daylight on the day you do move? I don't know whether this is practicable.

Unfortunately the 25th Brigade did not begin arriving until the 27th. At a conference in Port Moresby the previous day between Generals Mackay, Herring, Berryman, Kenney, and Admiral Carpender, Kenney had pointed out that his air resources were so strained that he would be unable to move the 18th Brigade from Port Moresby unless the tactical situation demanded it. He had also urged that the construction of the Lae-Nadzab road was all important. Thus Vasey knew that once his two forward brigades were committed he would not be able to use his third brigade as a reserve except in an emergency.

Vasey protested to Herring that the delay was "giving the Jap adequate time to implement any plan he may have for controlling the upper reaches of the Markham and Ramu Valleys". He thought that, if the Japanese decided not to attack Kaiapit, "the most likely Japanese course now appears to be to hold the Valley in the Marawasa defile". He pointed out that, although the Fifth Air Force had two squadrons of transports available at Nadzab, the restriction on landing at Kaiapit between the hours of 9.30 a.m. and 3.30 p.m., imposed by the Americans on the 26th evidently because of shortage of forward-based fighters, reduced by more than 50 per cent the number of possible landings at Kaiapit.

"I am not in the position to know of the Air Force's problems," he wrote, "but I would stress that until the rate of movement can be increased considerably, the progress of this division towards Dumpu, or even Marawasa, will be materially delayed." Vasey was right—he was not in a position to know. The Air Force was fully committed and the reinforcement of Finschhafen took priority.

Only the advanced headquarters of the 25th Brigade arrived at Kaiapit on the 27th. The planes were now landing on the new airstrip which had

---

[5] From captured documents and prisoners captured during the Lae campaign it was now clear that the *51st Division* was in any case a shattered force and would be incapable of offering effective resistance in the Markham Valley even if it could have got into the Kaiapit-Marawasa area from Boana. A sketch map captured in Lae, however, showed plans for a pack-horse route from Lae through Ngafir, Wain and Boana to Wantoat.

been built mainly by "Marys", under the direction of Angau officers, as the native men had been recruited for the carrier trains.

As patrols from the 2/6th Independent Company and the Papuans reported on the 26th and 27th that Narawapum was deserted and that natives said that the Japanese had retreated across the Umi River, Vasey decided to wait no longer. Late on the 27th he signalled Dougherty that if he was convinced that there were no enemy east of the Umi he was to cross the river on the night of the 28th-29th September and move as quickly as possible to Marawasa.

Dougherty promptly ordered Sublet to send two of his companies across the Umi to hold the crossing. On this occasion the leading company crossed the river in eight minutes soon after midday and formed the bridgehead. The second company to cross occupied Sagerak and sent forward a patrol under Lieutenant Bremner[6] to clear and hold the Maringgusin area. By 5 p.m. Bremner reported that the area was clear and that the track from Sagerak to Maringgusin was suitable for jeeps. Half an hour later the rest of the battalion crossed the river in rubber boats and dug in at Sagerak. The 2/14th and 2/27th Battalions, relieved at Kaiapit by the arrival of the 2/31st and 2/33rd, followed across the river. When dawn broke on the 29th Dougherty was ready for a sprint to the west.

On 27th September two patrols from the 2/7th Independent Company were already crossing the areas between their Kainantu base and the vanguard of the 21st Brigade. "You will continue with your present role," said a message from 7th Division to MacAdie on the 27th. "G.O.C. will visit 28th September if possible." Encouraged by MacAdie, Major Laidlaw of the 2/2nd decided that the "present role" was a little too inactive. On the afternoon of the 27th therefore he signalled Captain Dexter at Maululi that further information was required about the enemy in the Kesawai area and that the platoon should "take advantage of all favourable chances to harass". Thus when Vasey was flown into Bena Bena on the 28th a strongly-armed patrol from Maululi had already set out to cross the Ramu two miles west of Waimeriba.

Leading a patrol which consisted of Lieutenant Fullarton's[7] section, a few men from platoon headquarters, two police boys and five lowland carriers, Dexter reached the crossing at 3.30 p.m. and took compass bearings on Kesawai. A route for the night advance on Kesawai and the all-important rendezvous were selected before darkness fell. Three Australians, a police boy and the carriers were left to cover the crossing. The patrol to cross the river was armed with 2 Brens, 9 Owens and 4 rifles besides a liberal supply of grenades and a grenade discharger.

In pitch darkness at 9.30 p.m. the patrol prepared to cross the Ramu which was here flowing in eight streams, the bed of the river being about

---

[6] Capt L. D. Bremner, WX3865; 2/16 Bn. Railway fireman; of North Perth; b. Kalgoorlie, WA, 19 Aug 1911.

[7] Lt D. R. Fullarton, WX8507. 2/2 Indep Coy, 2/2 Cdo Sqn. Tally clerk; of Victoria Park, WA; b. Cookernup, WA, 21 Jul 1912.

half a mile wide. The last stream was a very difficult one to cross but, as the strong swimmers had already taken a wire across the river, the patrol crossed safely and the Brens were kept dry. At 11 p.m. the patrol marched off on a bearing of 87 degrees through kunai, swamp, creek beds, pit-pit and bamboo until it reached the fringe of the rain forest in the foothills of the Finisterres about 1.30 a.m. on the 29th. Wet and weary and with many barked shins, the men lay down to get what rest they could, assailed by hordes of mosquitoes. At 6.30 a.m. the patrol had its breakfast of bully beef and biscuits, and half an hour later moved to a spot west of Kesawai where an ambush was set.

From previous reconnaissance it was thought impossible to find Kesawai because of the heavy timber in the surrounding country. Rather than stumble on unknown Japanese positions it was therefore decided to try and lure the Japanese towards the ambush. At 7.40 a.m. Lance-Corporal Poynton, Private Birch[8] and police boy Tokua advanced boldly for about a mile and a half east towards Kesawai. Just outside this Japanese base the patrol was sighted and fired on by the Japanese. Half an hour after setting out the patrol returned briskly.

All was quiet and tense after Poynton made his report and the men wondered whether the ruse would be successful. They were arrayed in a semi-circle on both sides of the track with their weapons pointing towards the bend about 100 yards away. At 9.50 a.m. there was some noise to the east and round the bend came two natives armed with bows and arrows followed by many Japanese in twos and threes, watching the tracks made by Poynton's men and talking and gesticulating. Over 60 had rounded the bend and the leaders were within 30 yards of the ambush when the Australians opened fire. The heavy volume of automatic fire was like a reaper's scythe among the Japanese. A few staggered back around the corner and some dived down the slight slope on the right flank where Private Campbell's[9] Bren raked the bushes. Fullarton's Bren firing straight down the road was responsible for many of the Japanese casualties.

A large Japanese force now moved rapidly west from Kesawai towards the ambush. Taking up positions around the bend in the road they returned the fire of the Australians who were now running short of ammunition. One man was killed and Dexter wounded. On a pre-arranged signal the action was broken off and the men disappeared silently and rapidly south of the road to the rendezvous, whence they raced for the Ramu and crossed it in broad daylight. The Japanese had misjudged the Australian line of withdrawal, and scoured the kunai-covered foothills of the Finisterres.

The Japanese had been hit hard at Kaiapit in the Markham Valley and now at Kesawai in the Ramu. It was little wonder therefore that Major-General Nakai decided that he could best draw the Australian force and

---

[8] Tpr A. J. Birch, NX46537. 2/2 Indep Coy, 2/2 Cdo Sqn. Labourer; of Bonalbo, NSW; b. Kyogle, NSW, 19 Dec 1918.
[9] Cpl P. W. Campbell, WX11299. 2/2 Indep Coy, 2/2 Cdo Sqn. Dairyfarm hand; of Brunswick Junction, WA; b. Pingelly, WA, 18 Jan 1921.

so facilitate the retreat of the *51st Division*, not in the river valleys, but at Kankiryo Saddle. Only delaying forces were left in the river valleys while the Japanese prepared their defences in the difficult Finisterre Ranges.

Vasey informed General Herring that he intended to move the 2/2nd and 2/7th Independent Companies into the Ramu Valley as the forward elements of the 7th Division moved to the north-west. As far as Vasey was concerned the Bena Bena-Mount Hagen plateau did not now need to be garrisoned. Besides the two Independent Companies there were about 38 specialist troops, 40 Angau men and 120 Americans, whose main task was to keep the new Garoka airstrip in operation as a forward or emergency airfield and to establish a radar station. The troops on the plateau would need some local protection, and Vasey recommended that one militia company be stationed there.

On 29th September the 21st Brigade had been moving more rapidly westward from Sagerak through the overpowering heat of the kunai-clad valley. Behind the advance some jeeps and light guns were dragged across the Umi but beyond Sagerak the track soon became impassable. The Sagerak strip was made ready during the day and transport aircraft landed bringing jeeps and trailers; and Vasey arrived in his Cub.

There was nothing to stop the advance; Lieutenant Dunshea's patrol from the 2/7th Independent Company arrived at brigade headquarters early in the morning from the Dumpu area, and reported that Marawasa (where Vasey had expected the enemy to make a stand) was deserted. The 2/16th Battalion had previously occupied Wankon Hill, a natural observation post about 300 feet above river level with observation far into the Ramu Valley beyond Marawasa, and patrols from the 2/16th had probed forward and confirmed that Marawasa was empty. The 2/14th Battalion pushed through to occupy it by 5 p.m. The 2/27th Battalion which had had some difficulty crossing the Umi occupied the Wankon villages. From Wankon Hill at night the 2/16th could see many fires on the north side of the Ramu among the foothills: these may have been native hunting fires or they may have been the fires of Japanese withdrawing before the 2/6th Independent Company to Atsunas along the right flank of the 21st Brigade.

The remainder of the 25th Brigade arrived at Kaiapit by dusk on the 29th, and late at night Brigadier Eather issued his orders for an advance to the Umi next day by two battalions, leaving the third, the 2/25th, to guard Kaiapit until it could be relieved by the 2/2nd Pioneers.

At Ragitsuma on the afternoon of the 29th Vasey and Dougherty discussed the future. Vasey's instructions were left with Dougherty in a document called "Development of Operations". "All our information points to the Jap withdrawing north-west to the Marawasa area," it began. "Whether he will attempt to hold the line of the Gusap River or will continue to fall back towards his M.T. road from Bogadjim is not yet clear." After saying that the enemy's main line of withdrawal seemed to be along the north-east side of the river valley, Vasey continued: "It is not my intention at present to follow the Jap along the north-east side of the valley but rather to move along the southern side and secure his crossings over the Gusap River wherever they may be." Vasey therefore decided that the 21st Brigade would move along the south part of the river valley to the Gusap and then eastwards along that river until the Japanese crossing place was found.

The advance of the 21st Brigade along the main valley and of the 2/6th Independent Company on the right flank—actually in pursuit of the *78th Regiment* along the north-eastern side of the valley—continued rapidly on the 30th. The 2/16th Battalion again took over the lead and had one of its most gruelling day's marching. The day's objective for the battalion was Arifagan Creek, but as this was an inhospitable and waterless area the battalion pushed on to the bank of the Ramu. In the battalion's report the crossing of the river divide between the Markham and Ramu was described as follows: "It was a complete surprise to most of the battalion to learn that during the day's march—actually just before reaching Arifagan Creek—they had crossed the divide between the Markham and Ramu River basins. The divide was impossible to pinpoint on the ground as the gradients were imperceptible. The only visible indication that a divide had been crossed was that rivers were now flowing in the opposite direction from the Markham drainage basin." The 2/27th followed the 2/16th across Arifagan Creek.

Since early on the 29th the 2/6th Independent Company, advancing on Atsunas by the northern track, had been out of wireless contact. Dougherty intended the company to follow and harass the enemy in the Ragitsaria area, but he decided not to move the 2/14th Battalion forward until he knew where the Independent Company was. It was not until late in the day, when Lieutenant Hall's newly-arrived Papuan platoon managed to make contact with Captain Rose-Bray, that Dougherty decided to send the 2/14th about a mile beyond Marawasa. The Independent Company had left Asia early on the 30th following native guides. All "information" from native rumours seemed to indicate that the Japanese had retired through this area a few days previously. The Atsunas natives said that about 80 Japanese had passed through there on the 26th carrying several wounded. Their footwear and clothing were in bad shape, their ammunition light and some were without weapons. It therefore seemed to Rose-Bray that the Japanese had retired up the track to the Gusap River. Soon after midday the company reached Marawasa where Rose-Bray reported to brigade headquarters and learned that Papuan patrols and aircraft had been out looking for him. Dougherty then ordered the company north to Ragitsaria to harass any Japanese there.

Late on the evening of the 30th Dougherty received an unpalatable message from divisional headquarters saying that the 25th Brigade would not cross the Umi until further orders. No reason was given, but this information affected Dougherty's decision about his moves for the next day. If the 25th Brigade was to follow he could advance to carry out the role as set out in the document which Vasey had left with him on the

29th. If, however, the 25th Brigade were not coming and Dougherty had to fight a battle alone, he would have to leave some of his brigade round the landing strip.

The main reason for this change in plan was that Vasey, on the 30th, received a message from General Herring that, because of commitments at Finschhafen, Generals Mackay and Herring did not wish to become heavily committed in the Markham and Ramu Valleys. The main efforts were now bent on reinforcing Finschhafen. Indeed it soon appeared that the main body of the *20th Japanese Division,* which Vasey had anticipated meeting near Marawasa, was, in fact, not advancing down the river valleys but round the Rai Coast, by barge and any other available means, and over the inland trails towards Finschhafen, and that the *78th Regiment* alone faced the 7th Division. This change in Japanese plans made Nakai's decision to hold at Kankiryo Saddle, and not in the Markham or Ramu Valleys, the only possible one. The Australians were not yet aware of the precise Japanese decisions but their general intentions were rapidly becoming apparent.

Herring now gave Vasey three tasks: first "to prevent Japanese penetration southward through the Ramu and Markham Valleys"; secondly, "to seize the Marawasa area with a view to further advances to Dumpu after 18th Australian Infantry Brigade has become available and the maintenance situation permits"—the 21st Brigade had in fact already seized the Marawasa area; and thirdly, "to ensure the protection of Allied Air Force installations in the Bena Bena-Garoka area". The force to be maintained in the Kaiapit area would not "be reduced below one infantry brigade without reference to this headquarters".

There was also the supply situation to consider. By the evening of the 30th the 2/16th Battalion spearheading the advance along the Ramu was well ahead of its supply columns and rations had to be dropped from aircraft that evening and next morning. Progress had been so rapid during the last few days that service troops and stores were left far behind, thus necessitating the dropping of stores from the air, a never-very-satisfactory procedure. The problem of supplying the Independent Companies, which were in remoter areas than the battalions, was more difficult. For instance, the heavier gear of the 2/6th Independent Company, dumped before the Kaiapit action, was only now catching up to the company and the men were at last receiving their bed rolls. On the Bena Bena plateau itself there was little difficulty in living off the land provided enough cowrie shells and salt were available for barter, but once the men crossed the Bismarck Range the supply problem became very acute.

On 1st October General Vasey reported: "Bena Force reports Japs withdrawn from positions held for some time. This, together with lack of contact by 21st Brigade, strongly indicates Japs withdrawn from Markham and upper Ramu Valleys." He therefore decided to bring an Independent Company from the plateau into the Ramu to make sure that the area ahead of the 21st Brigade was clear. On the same day he signalled MacAdie:

In view rapid advance 21st Brigade concur in your suggestion to concentrate 2/7th Independent Company Bumbum area where contact will be made with 21st Brigade.

Vasey flew to Lae for a conference with Generals Mackay, Herring, Milford, Wootten and also General Morshead who was preparing to take over in New Guinea at a later stage. The conference mainly concerned the Finschhafen situation, but the Ramu Valley operations were also discussed. Vasey said that, having achieved his original objective, he now required further orders and, as his maintenance was by air, an advance of a few miles would not affect his administrative plot. There was no objection to him pushing on to Dumpu but he was not permitted to remove the whole of the two Independent Companies from the Bena Bena plateau. Vasey thereupon ordered Dougherty to concentrate on the Gusap on the 2nd; Eather would arrive there on the 3rd.

On 2nd October the 7th Division made ready for its punch at Dumpu. By dusk the 25th Brigade was camped in the Marawasa area and it was here that reinforcements arrived to build the 2/33rd Battalion up to strength after the disaster at Port Moresby. The 2/14th and the 2/27th Battalions moved up to the junction of the Gusap and Ramu Rivers during the day and the 2/16th established a bridgehead across the Gusap.

Pushing on from the Gusap Captain G. W. Wright's company of the 2/16th picked up a message left on the track by Dunshea in which he said that the Japanese were not in Bumbum and Boparimpum on 28th September. Wright crossed the Tunkaat River on his way to Kaigulin, but heard firing from trees about 1,000 yards ahead. The 2/7th Independent Company was on its way into the Kaigulin-Bumbum area. Lomas reported to Dougherty at the junction of the Gusap and Ramu Rivers about the time when the 2/16th Battalion was starting to cross the Gusap. The firing heard by Wright's men came from a Japanese outpost in Kaigulin which contested the crossing of the Ramu by the forward troops of the 2/7th Independent Company. The Australian patrol withdrew to the south side of the Ramu.

About 4.30 p.m. a patrol from the 2/7th managed to cross the Ramu elsewhere and work round on the right flank. Wright's men then moved straight into the attack and, half an hour later, struck opposition from the enemy outpost. One Australian was killed but the enemy was driven out leaving six killed, including one who had been decapitated with a captured Japanese sword brandished by the leading platoon commander, Lieutenant R. D. Watts.

Elsewhere in Vasey's area extensive patrolling continued during the 2nd, mainly by the Independent Companies. The 2/6th found plenty of evidence in the foothills of the recent presence of the *78th Japanese Regiment*. At Mesagatsu they found signs of a Japanese headquarters—staging camp, foxholes, dugouts, shelters of all descriptions and even a two-storey hut. The Papuans were also patrolling the foothills from their base at House Sak Sak, and assisting in the construction of the airfields. Since the Kesawai ambush, patrols from Mauluti, now commanded by Captain D. K. Turton, were probing the tracks and foothills on both sides of Kesawai. On the far west flank the main difficulty encountered by Captain Nisbet's platoon was in crossing the flooded Ramu. One patrol tried to cross on the night 30th September-1st October. Placing all their gear on top of a raft the swimmers tried to propel the raft across, but swimmers and raft were swept downstream, collided with a snag which caused the raft to overturn, and all gear was lost. Major Laidlaw determined that in future a lifeline would be strung across the river to assist crossings. As a result of MacAdie's requests an aircraft on the 3rd dropped Mae Wests and cordage at Bundi.

On this western flank native police sent out by Angau reported that the enemy were now keeping a mere skeleton force at Sepu, Usini, Obsau and Glaligool while more substantial bodies of troops were at Urigina, Kulau, Egoi and other places in this general area south-west of Madang. The main body of troops formerly in this western area, however, had been recalled to meet the threat from the Markham Valley. A small patrol led by Corporal Harrison between 28th September and 4th October found that there were actually no enemy in New and Old Glaligool[2] or Sepu.[3]

The 3rd October was a Sunday and, while waiting for the 25th Brigade to move up to House Sak Sak, Dougherty restricted his brigade's activities to patrolling only, while his men enjoyed a swim in the Ramu and Gusap Rivers and "the administrative side of affairs was consolidated". After this spell the battalions were fresh and ready for the final advance on the 4th.

Early on the 4th the 21st Brigade set out towards its western objectives—the 2/14th on the right flank towards Wampun and the 2/16th on the left flank towards Dumpu. Farther down the Ramu the Japanese were again hit from Maululi when a patrol led by Lieutenant Nagle attacked an enemy outpost in the village of Koropa about 10 miles west of Kesawai. Nagle was killed and although only a few Japanese were accounted for, this further evidence of the Australian intention to strike the enemy all along the Ramu Valley undoubtedly helped to cause the Japanese commander to pull in his remaining outposts in the river valley.

By 2 p.m. Captain C. L. McInnes' company of the 2/14th found Wampun deserted, as expected. After a hot and tiring day's march the native porters, who carried no water, had nothing to drink or cook their rice in. Colonel Honner, therefore, sent McInnes' company towards Koram to find whether the area was clear and also to look for water. The company moved west and then climbed rising ground on the right where they

---

[2] Just as groups of villages in New Guinea were often called Nos. 1, 2, 3, etc., of a particular name (e.g. Kesawai 1, Kesawai 2, Kesawai 3), so they were called "Old" and "New" using the same village name, e.g. Old Glaligool and New Glaligool.

[3] Harrison had led the previous reconnaissance to Sepu in August when one of his men had fallen into a hole and he himself had listened at a fence across the track. He now found that the hole was only 20 yards from the Japanese sleeping quarters and that the fence was ten yards from the guard hut. The Japanese had left these extensive camps about two weeks before. Among other items of interest Harrison found an old observation post in a tree overlooking the Sepu crossing, a maze of kunda vines to which were attached tins to act as warnings, a dog kennel, and a canoe, which was used to cross the Ramu.

had a more secure position and a better view. A second company was sent to the east and a third to the south-west of Wampun.

Honner soon after 2 p.m. decided to follow the trail of McInnes' company towards Koram to find whether there was any water in this vicinity, so that he could quickly reach a decision whether to push on towards the next day's objective or ask for water to be sent up by jeep. Later he was joined by a water party consisting of Sergeant Pryor[4] and three others. After about a mile Honner's small party saw a banana plantation and noticed troops moving about breaking down banana leaves. As these ignored his approach Honner assumed they were from McInnes' company. The banana plantation was astride the main track and merged into a belt of vegetation stretching across the river valley. The track itself ran north-west towards the plantation through kunai grass, a patchy regrowth after fire, varying from two to four feet in height. The small patrol was about 130 yards from the plantation when a burst of machine-gun and rifle fire wounded both Honner and Pryor. Pryor, wounded in the chin and the chest, tried to drag his commanding officer back but Honner, wounded in the thigh, and only able to crawl with difficulty, ordered him to return to the nearest company with information about the strength

The 2/14th Battalion action, 4th October

and position of the enemy. On his way out Pryor met Private Bennett,[5] one of the other three. Bennett decided to stay with Honner, who had crawled, using hands or elbows and one leg, about 250 yards into tall kunai. The enemy now sent out patrols towards these two men. The Japanese fired into the kunai and hit Honner again, in the left hand. Bennett was preparing for a one-man charge when fortunately the patrols stopped short and returned to the banana plantation.

After crawling 500 yards Pryor reached a dry watercourse where he got up and bolted down the track towards the battalion position picking up the other two men on the way. On receiving Pryor's report, Captain O'Day[6] immediately sent out a lightly-armed platoon under Lieutenant

---

[4] Sgt T. G. Pryor, VX15226; 2/14 Bn. Railway fireman; of Benalla, Vic; b. Truro, England, 6 Oct 1918.

[5] Pte W. H. G. Bennett, QX27023; 2/14 Bn. Barman; of Townsville, Qld; b. Townsville, 14 Jun 1915.

[6] Maj G. O. O'Day, VX14097; 2/14 Bn. Costing clerk; of Hawthorn, Vic; b. Brighton, Vic, 8 Aug 1919.

A. R. Avery to move fast to Honner's rescue and then followed with another platoon with heavier weapons.

Leaving O'Day to move cautiously towards the scene of action the adjutant, Captain Bisset, branched off to try and trace McInnes' company. McInnes had already sent a patrol to find out what was happening when he heard the firing. Although this patrol located the direction of the firing they could see nothing of the action. Bisset then suggested that McInnes should secure the high ground stretching for a distance of about 1,500 yards on the right of the banana plantation.

At 4.30 p.m. Avery's patrol, under fire, found Honner and Bennett. Using Avery's wireless set the wounded battalion commander ordered Bisset to arrange that two companies be sent forward to make an attack and to ask brigade headquarters to send up water by jeep if none had yet been found. As McInnes' company was already moving to the high ground and could not be brought into position for an attack, Bisset, who had now returned, and the senior company commander, Captain Hamilton,[7] decided to send forward Hamilton's own company, commanded by Lieutenant Levett,[8] to support O'Day's. Honner, still in full control of his battalion, was told of these changes and also that a stretcher party was going forward for him. While there was so much firing Honner refused to allow the stretcher party to come forward from a dry watercourse 300 yards behind him for fear of unnecessarily endangering the men's lives.

At 5 p.m. O'Day reached Honner, who told him his plan of attack: by Levett on the right with O'Day swinging out to the left and attacking through the plantation from that side. At 5.30 p.m. O'Day collected his two platoons in the watercourse, led them round to the left and began his attack. As the enemy's fire was now concentrated on the attackers, the stretcher bearers came up to Honner and adjusted his field dressings and, crawling, dragged him on a stretcher for 150 yards through the grass before rising and carrying him back to the watercourse. Here Honner met Levett's newly-arrived company, rapidly gave them the necessary information, and sent them in through a scattered line of trees on the right.

It was now 6 p.m. and O'Day's two platoons were pushing their attack with speed and determination. The attackers sustained a few casualties but they killed a Japanese officer and 11 troops and drove the rest of them back in disorder where Levett's men, on the right flank, their approach unnoticed by the Japanese, had little difficulty in killing 11 more. Next morning two more of the runaways were killed. For the loss of 7 men wounded the 2/14th Battalion had killed 26 Japanese and taken one prisoner.

Meanwhile the 2/16th was moving on Dumpu. It started at 8.15 a.m. on the 4th from the Bumbum-Kaigulin area and by 3.30 p.m. it had

---

[7] Capt I. W. Hamilton, VX14032. 2/14 Bn, and Wau Fixed Defence Force 1943. Salesman; of Brunswick, Vic; b. Melbourne, 24 Nov 1913.

[8] Capt P. M. Levett, VX35782; 2/14 Bn. Sales representative; of Melbourne; b. Bridlington, England, 20 Oct 1916.

crossed the Surinam River without opposition. Lieutenant Scott's[9] platoon now set out for Dumpu, but at 4.40 p.m. he indicated, by sending a pre-arranged signal, that Dumpu was still occupied. Major Symington[1] then led forward the remainder of this company and soon after 5 p.m. it formed up to attack. No opposition was encountered and the enemy was seen withdrawing rapidly to the north. One straggler only was killed, but quantities of food, clothing and ammunition were captured. All along the river valleys troops were gathering evidence about the low morale and poor health of the *78th Japanese Regiment*. It was already known from documents that they were on half rations and neither the Finisterres nor the Ramu were good areas for living off the country. While Symington's company dug in for the night and enjoyed an evening meal from captured Japanese rice and tinned fish, the rest of the 2/16th camped at the Surinam. The 2/14th Battalion was at Wampun, the 2/27th Battalion at Kaigulin 1 and 2 and the Biwi River improving river crossings, the 2/6th Independent Company (to which Captain King returned this day) joined brigade headquarters at Kaigulin, the 2/7th Independent Company moved into the Kaigulin-Bumbum area and the 25th Brigade remained in the House Sak Sak area.

Despite many stops and starts, the 21st Brigade had achieved its object on the originally planned date. Thanks largely to the brilliant initial stroke of the 2/6th Independent Company the enemy's spearhead from the Ramu down the Markham had been not only blunted but broken. Having lost Finschhafen to the 9th Australian Division on 2nd October the *XVIII Army* had now lost Dumpu to the 7th Australian Division two days later. The *78th Japanese Regiment* had failed to relieve pressure on the retreating *51st Division*, and had now retreated into the Finisterres. The march of events had prevented the Japanese from capturing the Bena plateau behind the formidable barrier of the Bismarcks. Indeed, after the 2/6th Independent Company had prepared the way at Kaiapit, it was largely due to the patrolling of the 2/2nd and 2/7th Independent Companies of Bena Force that the 7th Division had enjoyed a relatively uninterrupted march to Dumpu.

The Bogadjim Road over the Finisterres on which the Japanese had laboured so long was originally intended as a great highway from the coast, down over the mountains, into the Ramu and Markham Valleys as far as Lae. Now it could be at best only a supply route to the enemy's forces as far forward as Kankiryo Saddle. All of General Adachi's major resources were now directed towards the east of the Huon Peninsula where a determined effort was to be made to snatch back the initiative from the 9th Australian Division. Both sides were sending reinforcements into that area, and it was not certain whether the Australians would hold it. Only the incomplete *78th Regiment* could be spared to confront the 7th Division, and so for the Japanese the campaign in the Ramu Valley and the Finisterre Ranges would be a grim holding operation.

---

[9] Lt J. Scott, MC, WX5607; 2/16 Bn. Farmer; of Katanning, WA; b. Cottesloe, WA, 25 Nov 1914.
[1] Maj W. G. Symington, WX1597; 2/16 Bn. Clerk; of Cottesloe, WA; b. Chatswood, NSW, 4 Feb 1916.

CHAPTER 16

SCARLET BEACH TO THE BUMI

GENERAL MacArthur's operation instruction issued on 13th June 1943 had given the general outline of the Allied offensive: "Forces of the S.W.P.A. supported by South Pacific Forces will seize the Lae-Salamaua-Finschhafen-Markham River Valley area and establish major elements of the A.F. therein to provide from the Markham Valley area general and direct air support of subsequent operations in northern New Guinea and western New Britain, and to control Vitiaz Strait and protect the north-western flank of subsequent operations in western New Britain."[1]

By 16th September Lae, Salamaua and the Markham Valley east from Nadzab were in Australian hands. The success of the attack on Lae from east and west and the speed with which this vital area had been captured caused a quick readjustment of plans. American misgivings about Australian planning, which for the time being was concentrated solely on the capture of Lae, have already been related. Under hard-headed battle-seasoned leaders the Australians' planning was of a more flexible and practical nature and they were more ready for emergencies and more able to profit by unexpected opportunities. Such an opportunity seemed now to have presented itself.

Because the Australians had produced no detailed plan for the capture of Finschhafen before Lae was assaulted, this did not of course preclude the staffs from having plans ready to exploit any sudden success. Indeed a broad plan had been produced at General Herring's I Corps headquarters on 24th August 1943 for the capture of Finschhafen by a brigade group of the 9th Division, after which the 9th Division would carry out shore-to-shore operations to Bogadjim and the 6th Division exploit to Madang. Herring decided that the landing should be made just south of the Song River.

> In the early stages of planning (wrote General Blamey later) the operation necessary for the capture of Finschhafen had been studied, but completed plans were not prepared since its capture would be dependent on the amount of enemy resistance encountered at Lae and the length of time necessary to reduce it. It was considered that, if the capture of Lae was effected quickly, a brigade group from 9 Aust Div could be used to carry out the operation against Finschhafen.[2]

As in the days before Lae, the American Navy and Air Force and the Australian Army were busy with cooperative planning for a landing in the Finschhafen area, even before Lae fell. At a conference with the Australians at his headquarters in Buna, Rear-Admiral Barbey, on 9th September, stated that craft for an attack on Finschhafen could not be made available until ten days after the capture of Lae. He had originally been planning for a four weeks' gap. On 16th September General Cham-

---
[1] GHQ Operation Instruction No. 34 of 13 June 1943.
[2] Commander Allied Land Forces, Report on New Guinea Operations, 4 September 1943 to 26 April 1944.

berlin telephoned General Berryman in Port Moresby, stating that General MacArthur desired the capture of Finschhafen as soon as possible. Next morning, the day after the fall of Lae, MacArthur called a conference at Port Moresby to discuss accelerating the assault on Finschhafen. He and Blamey agreed that a brigade group of the 9th Division should be sent to the Finschhafen area as soon as possible and that Herring should determine the date. Because of the uncertainty about enemy strength at Finschhafen, Blamey thought that more than one brigade would be necessary. He wrote later:

> I requested that an additional brigade group be moved to the Finschhafen area immediately after the assaulting force had made the landing. This was approved and Commander I Aust Corps was so informed and laid his plans accordingly.[3]

Towards midnight on the 17th Herring arrived at Lae by P.T. boat for discussions with General Wootten. Even before the Allied armada had left Milne Bay for the beaches east of Lae, Wootten had been warned by Blamey and Herring that he might be required to carry out an attack on Finschhafen at short notice, and Wootten had told Brigadier Windeyer to look at Finschhafen on the map because it might interest him later.[4] Before Herring's arrival at "G" Beach warning orders were already passing down the line. At 2.30 p.m. Lieut-Colonel R. J. Barham, Wootten's principal staff officer, rang Windeyer's headquarters and asked that Windeyer be informed immediately that a brigade would soon be required for an amphibious operation. Later that night, shortly before Herring landed, another message was received by Windeyer that a planning team from the 20th Brigade for "a future operation" was to attend a conference at divisional headquarters next morning. At 9 a.m. on 18th September Windeyer and his staff attended this conference at 9th Division headquarters on the Bunga River. The conference was attended also by the commanders and principal staff officers of I Corps and the 9th Division. Herring outlined a plan for the capture of the Finschhafen-Langemak Bay-Dreger Harbour area with a quick swoop which would help to gain control of the east coast of the Huon Peninsula and thereby of Vitiaz Strait.

Confidence and boldness marked the planning of this operation. It was unusual in three respects: Allied troops rarely undertook large infantry assaults through jungle at night, let alone after landing on a hostile shore; the notice for mounting the operation was so short as to be probably unique for an amphibious undertaking of such size, particularly when it is considered that the troops were a long day's march from their assembly areas; the information about the enemy available to the commander could hardly have been more nebulous. A New Guinea Force Intelligence summary of 15th September had put the strength of the enemy round Finschhafen at 2,100, but after the fall of Lae this was reduced to 350, which was the

---

[3] Report on New Guinea Operations, 4 September 1943 to 26 April 1944.
[4] Had Lae been defended stubbornly the 16th Brigade or the 7th Brigade would have been used for the Finschhafen attack. As late as 7th September plans were still being made by American and Australian staffs to transfer the 6th Division to New Guinea. It was only on 21st September that a signal was sent from NGF to II Corps deferring the movement of the division.

estimate of the G.H.Q. Intelligence staff. On 18th September the I Corps estimate was "between 1,800 and 350"; the 9th Division's, however, on 19th September was between 4,000 and 1,500. The divisional staff estimated the strength of units identified as probably being at Finschhafen at 2,070. Windeyer, however, had received only the Corps estimate when he made his outline plan and thus all he knew was that some people considered that the brigade would encounter only about 350 Japanese and some that it would encounter 1,800, and that no sizable fighting force would be round Finschhafen.

The reason why such confusing estimates were reaching the field formations was that the G.H.Q. Intelligence staff headed by General Willoughby and the L.H.Q. Intelligence staff headed by Brigadier Rogers,[5] each working on different principles, had, on this as on other occasions, reached very different answers. These could not be reconciled and as a result the field formations were given both figures.[6] As shown above, when the various estimates reached the fifth link in the chain—the 9th Division— it rejected the lowest figure, 350.

The 20th Brigade was selected for the landing as it already had the experience of carrying out the initial landings east of Lae and was also relatively fresh. Wootten felt that the task was too much for one brigade and wished to use the division less one brigade. Herring explained, however, that a brigade group was the maximum which MacArthur would allow, taking into account the opposition expected, the difficulty of maintaining a larger force, and the limitation of the available naval resources. The craft already allotted by Barbey for the landing—4 A.P.D's, 15 L.C.I's and 3 L.S.T's—(in addition to 8 L.C.M's from Colonel Brockett's boat battalion) were capable of lifting only a brigade group. To aid in supplying Windeyer's brigade a boat battalion and half a shore battalion from the 532nd Engineer Boat and Shore Regiment would be available.

Among Herring's reasons for selecting the beach south of the Song as the landing place were the facts that a landing south of the Mape River would involve the crossing of this major obstacle, and that from aerial reconnaissance and information derived from former residents the only suitable beach appeared to be the one chosen. The beach was called Scarlet Beach to avoid confusion with Red Beach—at this period the main landing beach was usually named "Red". A further reason for choosing a beach well north of Finschhafen was that most Japanese troops were thought to be facing south near Langemak Bay expecting a coastal advance, and thus a landing at Scarlet Beach would cut their line of supply and withdrawal. Although it was known that there were several enemy garrisons on the coast towards Madang, it was felt that air and P.T. boat attacks on Japanese coastal traffic would prevent a rapid build-up. "The operation was hurried forward to forestall such a move and was

---

[5] Brig J. D. Rogers, CBE, MC, ED, VX40124. (1st AIF: Pte to Capt 6 Bn.) GSO2 (Int) I Corps 1940-41; Director Mil Int LHQ 1942-45. Oil company executive; of Melbourne; b. Penguin, Tas, 29 Apr 1895.

[6] The differences between these two Intelligence staffs reached a climax a year later as recorded in the next volume of this series.

successful, though substantial movement of enemy troops was already taking place southward as was later discovered. By 22nd September the enemy strength in Finschhafen was approximately 5,000 all ranks."[7]

Lieut-Commander Adair, who represented the American Navy at the conference on the 18th, was anxious that the landing should take place soon after moonrise on D-day. On 22nd September moonrise would be at 25 minutes past midnight. The Americans were anxious to unload the craft and leave the beach before first light because of the danger of air attack. Windeyer did not favour landing in darkness because he doubted whether the navy could land them on the correct beach, and in this Wootten supported him. Adair was confident, however, that, because of the irregular and distinctive coastline, consisting, except for Scarlet Beach, of cliffs 15 to 20 feet high fringed by coral reefs, the navy could not fail to find the correct beach even if clouds obscured the moon. Because of the difficulty of resupplying Windeyer on this beach, it was decided that he would take with him supplies for twenty days.

It seemed inconceivable that Scarlet Beach would not be defended. Actually ten men, four of them natives and the remainder American "amphibian scouts" of the 532nd E.B.S.R., had been put ashore near Scarlet Beach during the night 11th-12th September in rubber boats launched from P.T. boats. Because of Japanese activity in the area, they were unable to obtain the desired hydrographic information and were withdrawn on the 14th. They saw no guns but thought there were machine-gun nests at the north end of the beach. Although the information gathered by this reconnaissance party was useful and, as far as it went, accurate, they were unable to establish definitely whether the beach was defended and may well have been observed themselves.

As a secondary and later objective, Windeyer was ordered to be ready to capture Sattelberg.[8] It was also decided that, concurrently with the landing at Scarlet Beach, a landing would be made on the Tami Islands, south-east of the Huon Peninsula, to establish a radar station. Windeyer also suggested that a battalion should move round the south coast of the Huon Peninsula from Lae to Finschhafen to deceive the Japanese as to the real direction of the threat. The suggestion was approved in principle, but it was agreed that the battalion would not begin its advance before the landing lest it prejudice surprise.

At 5 p.m. on the 18th Windeyer explained his outline plan to Wootten. Briefly, it amounted to an assault on the beach-head by two battalions, the 2/17th on the right and the 2/13th on the left. After the beach-head had been secured the 2/15th Battalion would advance south along the main road towards Finschhafen. If heavy resistance were met frontally on the coastal plain, troops would advance along the fringe of the hills to the west in order to outflank the Japanese. Both agreed that the time for landing desired by the Americans was not suitable.

---

[7] Report on Operations of 9 Aust Div in the Capture of Lae and Finschhafen—4 Sep-2 Oct 1943.
[8] German for "Saddle Mountain". At the time, because of an error in the map, Sattelberg was spelt "Satelberg". The correct spelling has been used in all quotations printed in this volume.

That evening a further conference was held between the commanders and staffs of corps, division and brigade. Windeyer asked that the operation be postponed a day as his troops were tired from constant marching and road work, and still had half a day's march ahead before reaching the concentration place at the mouth of the Burep. Windeyer wanted time to issue orders, give his troops some rest, instruct them fully in their tasks, and assemble the artillery and stores. Herring agreed that the expedition should leave "G" Beach on the evening of 21st September and land at Scarlet Beach on 22nd September.

Windeyer then asked that the landing should be made at first light—5.15 a.m. To the Australians this appeared to be the earliest time which would give the assaulting battalions some light for work in the jungle; and, more important, would ensure that the navy landed them on the correct beach. Adair stuck to his original arguments that the landing should be as soon as possible after moonrise. To overcome the American objection to the late unloading of the L.S.T's and the consequent danger of air attack, Herring decided to reduce the amount of supplies to be carried from 20 days' to 12 days' supply of ammunition and 15 days' supply of rations. The average load of each L.S.T. would thus be reduced to between 115 and 120 tons. Wootten then asked Adair to arrange for the first re-supply mission to take place five days after the landing.

While the staffs were completing the details of their plans, infantry commanders told the troops what their tasks would be. They were shown their objectives on sand models and the general plan was explained. The speed with which the operation was planned, organised and launched was evidence of the training, experience and discipline of the 20th Brigade.

There were many others, of course, with fingers in the planning pie. While the Lae conferences were taking place on the 18th, General Berryman and Colonel L. de L. Barham (brother of General Wootten's G.S.O.1) were conferring with Admiral Barbey and General Chamberlin aboard the *Conyngham* off Buna. D-day and H-hour were discussed, but no finality was reached because Herring was still at Lae. Barbey stated that while the Japanese were using the Cape Gloucester airfield it would not be possible to supply Finschhafen continuously. The main conference occurred on the 19th. Writing to Wootten on the same day, Herring reported the conference thus:

> Reached Buna safely about 6 a.m. and was taken straight to Admiral Barbey's destroyer where I found Berryman and Chamberlin waiting for me to hear how and when we planned to take Finschhafen. So I set in to tell them and when the tale was told the Admiral wanted 0200 hours as H-hour. I refused to budge, but when it became clear that my continued refusal to what had gradually become only one half hour's change, would involve a reference to G.H.Q. with any possible result, it seemed better to have immediate decision at the price of half an hour. The change of H-hour to 0445 from 0515 will not, I hope, involve any change in Windeyer's plan. I felt it should not to any real extent.

Replying two days later, Wootten wrote:

> The change of H-hour from 0515 to 0445 did not involve any change in plan. Windeyer was quite happy about it.

Opinions regarding another sudden development were exchanged in the same letters. Herring wrote:

> Since sitting down to write this, Hopkins[9] has turned up with a message which at first shook me to my foundations, but which on further thought may prove more of a help than a hindrance. It appears that a close examination of the photos just to hand shows that there is a sand bar on [the southern] half of the beach which will preclude the landing of L.S.T's on that half, but will not interfere with the landing of any other craft. Result is that three L.S.T's only can be beached at one time and so it is now planned that wave six at H plus 80 should comprise three L.S.T's only, while the other L.S.T's will arrive on the beach at 2300 hours on D-day. . . . The only problem will be the sorting of your vehicles so that those you need immediately go on the first 3 L.S.T's and the remainder will arrive when the beach is better able to receive them. I think really, on a frank reconsideration, this new plot that has been forced on the Navy is really better from your point of view. . . . You know that I hate mucking you about, but you are one who can be trusted to deal with difficulties as they arise.

After a very early morning conference with Windeyer to discuss this unforeseen event, Wootten replied:

> Provided the second 3 L.S.T's are unloaded on the night of D-day at the far shore, that change in previous arrangements will not matter. Roughly, it means that one bty 25-pdrs, one lt AA bty, about one-quarter engineer stores and the C.C.S. with vehicles will be on the second wave of L.S.T's.

Plans for air and naval support were simple. Blamey decided on 19th September that preliminary air attacks on the Finschhafen area and Scarlet Beach in particular would only serve to warn the enemy of the landing. This decision, of course, did not prevent the bombing, in the few days remaining, of the airfields, supply dumps and reinforcement routes between Wewak and Finschhafen. In particular, American Liberators set about rendering Cape Gloucester unserviceable, while R.A.A.F. Kittyhawks attacked Gasmata and Bostons and Mitchells prepared to attack the enemy in the Finschhafen area after the landing.

Barbey only just had time to move the landing craft and destroyers up from Milne Bay and Buna to load the troops at Lae. While the bombers pounded Japanese installations, the fighters covered the naval movement to Lae and the loading. Naval support for the landing would consist of a preliminary bombardment from destroyers. The task force itself would be protected by an air umbrella of American and Australian planes. These would protect the convoy during daylight to and from the beach and during loading and unloading, and would also blockade the Finschhafen area. North of Scarlet Beach the aggressive American P.T. boats would operate in Vitiaz Strait to give warning of any approaching naval threat.

The concern of Barbey and his chief, Admiral Carpender, to have adequate air cover and avoid such losses as occurred at Lae, was indeed understandable when air photographs on 20th September showed 23 naval ships including 9 destroyers in Rabaul Harbour. One submarine was thought to be north of Vitiaz Strait and two or three in the Solomon Sea,

---

[9] Brigadier R. N. L. Hopkins, an Australian, was on the staff of Seventh Amphibious Force.

while one was reported to be moving along the south coast of New Britain. Barbey therefore included seven sub-chasers in his task force. Despite the battering which it was receiving, the Japanese Air Force was still capable of hitting back. Nine bombers and ten fighters attacked Nadzab on 20th September and Japanese reconnaissance planes daily flew over the Allied supply route from Buna to Lae.

Windeyer's detailed orders were issued on the 20th. As laid down by I Corps, the objects of the landing were to deny the area to the enemy, gain a base from which future coastwise operations could be launched, provide a base for P.T. boats in Vitiaz Strait, and provide fighter strips. Windeyer stated his intention simply: "20 Bde will land on Scarlet Beach with a view to the capture of the area Finschhafen-Langemak Bay." With each of the three battalions would be a battery of the 2/12th Field Regiment, a platoon of the 2/3rd Field Company, and a light advanced dressing station from the 2/8th Field Ambulance. The 10th L.A.A. Battery and a company of the 2/2nd Machine Gun Battalion would be responsible for defence of the beach-head area, while two platoons of the Papuan Infantry Battalion would be used to patrol the coastal track to Bonga, the inland track to Sattelberg, and assist Angau to collect natives.

Watching the improvised arrangements at Red Beach, Windeyer had come to the conclusion that an experienced combatant officer with a staff officer and some signals communications should command all troops in the beach-head area. Major Broadbent, the second-in-command of the 2/17th Battalion, was chosen as this Military Landing Officer.[1]

With the object of unloading the L.S.T's in two hours and a half from the time of beaching, the 2/23rd Battalion, the 2/48th Battalion, the 2/2nd Machine Gun Battalion and the Left Out of Battle group of the 20th Brigade were ordered to provide sufficient men to supply two companies, each of about 100 men, to each of the six L.S.T's. After unloading at Scarlet Beach the men would travel in the L.S.T's back to Buna and would then load and accompany the first re-supply mission about five days later. The 22nd Battalion was detailed for the coastal move from Hopoi to Finschhafen.

The 21st was a day of great activity for the 20th Brigade. Unfortunately there were not enough good aerial photographs of the landing area, and during the morning, while the rain pelted down incessantly, a continuous stream of visitors called at brigade headquarters to inspect the few air photographs. The lack of proper photographs was due to the fact that only one aircraft fitted with equipment essential for beach photographs was available.[2]

Maps were also in short supply. References in orders were made from the Finschhafen photomap. Just before the brigade embarked a supply of Sattelberg 1:25,000 (1st Edition) sheets arrived. As it was too late to

---

[1] The arrangements made provided in embryo the main essentials of the beach group organisation developed later.

[2] It was this aircraft which had taken a colour photograph disclosing the shoal water off the southern side of Scarlet Beach and thus prevented disaster to the equipment carried by half the LST's.

pack them only twenty copies could be accepted and most of these were given to the artillery.[3] "Consequently," wrote the diarist of the 20th Brigade, "the remainder of the brigade group did not have the benefit of this excellent map in the early stages, which were fought off the photo-map."

In the afternoon of 21st September the smaller and slower craft—8 L.C.M's and 15 L.C.V's—left the Lae area for Scarlet Beach. At 3 p.m. loading of the L.S.T's began. Each L.S.T. loaded about 38 vehicles as well as the 200 unloading troops. By experience the 9th Division had proved that "bulk loading"—as far as possible in one-man loads—was more efficient than "vehicle loading". During the loading the fighter cover was much in evidence. When nine Japanese bombers, escorted by fighters, approached "G" Beach and the ships riding at anchor they were driven off by Allied fighters and an impressive anti-aircraft display from the various guns on the ships and on land. Aboard the *Reid* the fighter detector officer recalled a homeward air patrol which shot down several of the Japanese aircraft. The L.S.T's were loaded smoothly and ahead of time. Soon after dark three of the L.S.T's, with a strong escort, left for Scarlet Beach while the other three moved south to disperse in the Morobe area until needed later that night.

The troops had moved to the ship assembly areas on the jungle fringe of "G" Beach at 4.30 p.m. Two hours earlier the L.C.I's and A.P.D's, led by Barbey in his flagship, sailed from Buna, arriving at the embarkation beach at 7 p.m. The embarkation, which was arranged by the navy and Wootten's staff, proceeded according to plan except that one L.C.I. failed to arrive because of engine trouble. Lieut-Colonel Colvin, one of whose companies was to embark on the missing craft, was able to arrange for this company to be distributed on other craft.

Aboard the *Conyngham* Barbey was worried about a message from the coastwatchers that Japanese aircraft were coming over. For a while he wondered whether it would be better to "call it off" until next day. Supported by Hopkins, Windeyer urged that no change be made in the plan. The voyage proceeded. The convoy pulled out from Lae at 7.30 p.m. Soon after midnight Barbey overtook the earlier waves and the convoy steamed east and then north through the night to meet its destiny. Arrangements for the troops aboard the L.C.I's were more satisfactory than for the voyage preceding the Lae landings, while once again the arrangements for the troops aboard the A.P.D's were excellent and cemented still further the good relations existing between the men of the 20th Brigade and the crews of the A.P.D's. During the night enemy aircraft shadowed the convoy.

The target, Scarlet Beach, lay in a small indentation in the coast, making a well-defined bay with definite headlands. It was about 600 yards long and 30 to 40 feet wide with good firm sand which would take L.S.T's. At the northern end of the sandy beach was the mouth of the Song River

---

[3] There proved to be a serious survey error in this edition which necessitated making substantial corrections when shooting off it away from the coast.

and at the southern end a small headland and then a small cove into which Siki Creek flowed. South from Scarlet Beach to Finschhafen lay a narrow coastal strip varying from half a mile to 300 yards in width; to the west the mountainous and difficult country of the Kreutberg Range rose steeply. Creeks and rivers were fordable, but usually ran between deep banks and were not easy to cross, thus constituting good defensive positions for the enemy. Along the coast were coconut plantations overgrown with vegetation to a height between four and eight feet.

As the convoy headed north the troops in the A.P.D's prepared for the landing.[4] Reveille was at 2.45 a.m. Broadly, Windeyer's plan was that two companies of the 2/17th Battalion would land on the right of the beach and two from the 2/13th on the left. Each of these companies had therefore embarked in one of the four A.P.D's which had been instructed to land their barges at definite places. Windeyer intended that the right company of the 2/17th should land as near as possible to the northern end of Scarlet Beach to enable it to capture quickly a dominating feature called North Hill on the northern headland; and that the left company of the 2/13th should land in Siki Cove so that it could, as speedily as possible, capture Arndt Point, the southern headland.

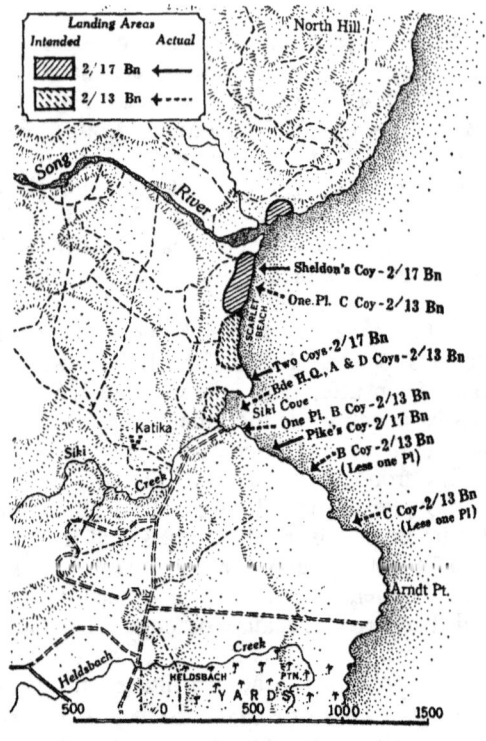

The landing at Scarlet Beach, 22nd September

This time, as the craft carried the invaders northward towards Scarlet Beach, the troops could not see the green jungle fringe or the beach. All that could be seen by the assaulting troops as H-hour approached were the dim outlines of funnels and barges about to be lowered from the davits.

---

[4] The landing plan was as follows:
    Wave 1—H-hour—16 barges from 4 APD's—2 companies each from 2/17 and 2/13 Bns.
    Wave 2—H+20—8 LCI's, 4 LCM's—40-mm guns on flanks. Balance 2/17 and 2/13 Bns. Advanced details of supporting arms, etc.
    Wave 3—H+35—7 LCI's—2/15 Bn, Brigade HQ, HQ supporting arms.
    Wave 4—H+40—6 LCM's, 4 LCV's } ESB
    Wave 5—H+60—11 LCV's }
    Wave 6—H+80—3 LST's—Equipment, stores, etc, personnel.
    Wave 7—10.30 p.m.—3 LST's—Equipment, stores, etc, personnel.

There was no comforting sight of neighbouring craft, nor was there any impression of the might of the invading force. There was a final burst of speed by the A.P.D's and when, according to *Conyngham's* radar, Scarlet Beach was abreast, the A.P.D's trembled to a stop. "Lower barges", "Get ready to land", "Away the landing force". This was by now a familiar routine for the men of the four assaulting companies—Captain Sheldon's[5] and Major Pike's[6] of the 2/17th and Captain Deschamps'[7] and Major Handley's[8] of the 2/13th.

For eleven minutes before the landing five destroyers bombarded the shoreline from 5,000 yards, the flashes of the explosions lighting up the blackness of the beach and giving the barges from the A.P.D's some idea of direction in the darkness. The destroyers were using red tracers which looked like giant fireflies. The bombardment probably had considerable effect on the Japanese, even though it did not cause many casualties. Under cover of it the barges sped for the shore. "It's on again," men muttered as the machine-guns on the barges raked the shore in reply to machine-gun fire from the shore. The enemy fire and the difficulty in the pre-dawn gloom of distinguishing between Scarlet Beach and Siki Cove caused some of the barges to veer to the left. "Generally," reported Windeyer later, "the whole wave beached much to the left of the appointed places. Most of the assault troops were thus landed in Siki Cove or further left on the southern headland of the bay at Arndt Point."[9] Nor did they land in order for the barges of both assaulting battalions became hopelessly mixed in the darkness.

The experience of one of the 2/13th's platoons, which should have landed near the centre of the line, illustrated the confusion. Number 4 barge was detailed to tow another which had broken down the night before and had defied the crew's efforts to get it into working order. The speed of the two barges was thus reduced and soon they dropped behind, and after some indecision became hopelessly lost. Everyone stood up, straining their eyes and ears for signs of the remainder of the wave. It was no use; blackness hemmed the barges in on all sides. Then the explosions of the naval shells began to light the shore. "Put her straight in! Make for those shell bursts! Get her to the shore somehow. Anywhere will do!" These were the sentiments of the platoon commander as he directed the American coxswain. The bombardment died away and once again the two barges were left with only a dark shoreline to steer a course by. It was then that some of the barges which were landing closer to their planned landing places began raking the shoreline with their machine-guns and once again the lost barges had a bearing.

---

[5] Capt T. C. Sheldon, NX28145; 2/17 Bn. Clerk; of Point Piper, NSW; b. Sydney, 25 Feb 1907.
[6] Lt-Col P. H. Pike, NX12220; 2/17 Bn. Bank officer; of Greenwich, NSW; b. Epping, NSW, 4 Oct 1916.
[7] Capt P. Deschamps, MC, NX12223; 2/13 Bn. Salesman; of West Ryde, NSW; b. Mullumbimby, NSW, 9 Sep 1915.
[8] Maj E. A. Handley, MC, NX12222; 2/13 Bn. Salesman; of Ingleburn, NSW; b. Kogarah, NSW, 8 Aug 1917.
[9] 20 Aust Inf Bde Report on Operations, 22 Sep 1943-21 Jan 1944.

Closing in on the shore the two barges were hailed by the wave leader, who drew alongside and ordered the leading barge to slip its tow rope. Thus released it raced to the shore while the men in the disabled barge were transferred to the wave leader's barge. On the leading barge someone suddenly shouted at the coxswain: "Look out! You'll get us run down. Put her hard to the left!" The black bulk of an L.C.I., seeming enormous in the gloom, towered above the barge which had become mixed with the second wave just coming in. The coxswain shot the barge to the left and then straightened for the shore. The platoon's troubles were not yet over for the keel bumped and scraped several times on a reef. The barge bounced off and then ended up with a splintering shudder off the rocky headland of Arndt Point, hundreds of yards south of the correct landing beach. The ramp was lowered gingerly lest the barge founder. Stumbling and swearing in the darkness the men clambered up the rocks. One or two fell into pot-holes and came up spluttering and swearing. Finally, the platoon made its way to the jungle fringe.

In their training the troops of the 9th Division had learnt what they were to do if landed on the wrong beach, as had been done at Gallipoli. They knew that wherever they landed their task was to wipe out the enemy posts in their vicinity, then reorganise and make for their correct objectives.

The four assaulting companies were landed not only on the wrong beaches but mixed with one another. Captain Sheldon's company of the 2/17th on the extreme right, together with the anti-tank platoon, appeared less disorganised than the other three because it had landed generally in the Scarlet Beach-Song River area and was soon under control. The next company to the south was Major Pike's of the 2/17th. Landing in the Siki Cove-Arndt Point area his troops became so badly mixed with those of the 2/13th that he decided that as he had no opposition the best course would be to move inland about 100 yards and wait for daylight. This sensible action enabled the two assaulting companies of the 2/13th on his left to get clear.

The right-hand company of the 2/13th Battalion (Captain Deschamps') landed from Siki Cove to Arndt Point. The barge carrying Deschamps' headquarters was first to land and for a considerable time he had no idea where his three platoons were. By good luck, however, these platoons, including the two which had been lost, landed more or less in the same place. The fourth company in the initial line-up (Major Handley's) landed all over the place. One platoon (Lieutenant Huggett's[1]) veered off to the right and landed near the mouth of the Song, while the others landed near Arndt Point.

Huggett's platoon was the only one to experience serious opposition after the landing. It drew fire from machine-gun posts near the mouth of the Song. Engaging the enemy with grenades and small arms fire, Huggett's men eventually silenced two enemy posts. They were aided by

---

[1] Capt C. Huggett, NX14681; 2/13 Bn. Salesman; of Leichhardt, NSW; b. Paddington, NSW, 29 Aug 1911.

Lieutenant Herman A. Koeln, an American amphibious scout who had been landed at the wrong spot and decided to remain and fight with Huggett. Another American amphibious scout, Lieutenant Edward K. Hammer, ran into a party of Japanese, shot a few and continued on. Both these scouts were handicapped by having to carry marking signs ten feet high—two long poles and a piece of red-painted canvas.[2] When the 2/17th Battalion began to become organised in this area Huggett moved his platoon south along the beach to rejoin his company. On the way he passed several bands of 2/17th Battalion men moving north.

By landing too far south most of the wooden barges from the A.P.D's escaped fire from enemy positions on Scarlet Beach. The mission of the assault wave, however, was the capture of Scarlet Beach and its immediate jungle fringe. This had not been captured when the second wave, consisting of L.C.I's and L.C.M's, headed for the shore. In this wave the men were ready behind the landing ramps, kneeling as though in prayer. Enemy fire, not neutralised by the assault waves, spat at the L.C.I's as they came in. This fire and the darkness caused them to veer to the left also and most of this wave beached in Siki Cove. One eye-witness in the second wave described his experiences thus:

> We were the second wave this time, and we expected that the first wave of Diggers would have "done over" the Japanese before we hit the sand. But the first wave missed Scarlet Beach entirely in the darkness and ran into Siki Cove and on to coral farther south. Our wave, also of six or eight L.C.I's, ran into the cove, but our boat hit coral with a jarring, creaking crash on a small headland between Scarlet Beach and Siki. One gang-plank was immediately out of action, and we began jumping off the other. Odd sniping shots snapped out from the shore. . . . To our left a machine-gun fired a stream of white tracers down on to the beach. . . . Ahead and above us, on top of the headland about 100 feet away, a Japanese machine-gun opened fire with tracers. Its first burst went high into the air, the second into the water beside the boat. The third burst crashed over my head and hit two men behind me; I heard them cry out as I jumped on to the coral and splashed through a pool or two to the beach.[3]

Because of a sand bar at Siki Cove some of the L.C.I's dropped their ramps in deep water. Most men from these craft were soaked as they struggled to the shore. Some lost their footing, and, loaded as they were, they would have drowned but for helping hands. Two L.C.I's, having struck the bar, retracted and came in closer. Among the casualties on the beach and in the surf the stretcher bearers and medical orderlies were busy at their work. Soon after the event an eye-witness[4] described the scene:

> Abruptly our Sig Sgt ordered us to ground and down we went to the sands awash with the surf. Dimly I was aware of sea water washing over my boots and swirling round my chest. Near by someone groaned, and, glancing quickly to my

---

[2] From the beginning of the landing the Australian and American "amphibious scouts" (mainly from the 532nd EBSR), whose task was to erect beach markers, had attempted to gather on Scarlet Beach from the various positions in which they had been landed by the first wave. The commander of these scouts, Lieut-Commander J. M. Band, RANVR, was mortally wounded while moving north from Siki Cove to the beach. Carrying his equipment to measure depths he floundered into the water, after being wounded, in a desperate attempt to carry out his task.

[3] J. A. Crawford (ex-Pte 2/17 Bn), "The Landing at Finschhafen", in *Stand-To*, December 1950.

[4] Signalman C. M. Tighe, 2/13 Battalion (of Granville, NSW).

right, I saw the inert figure of a man, face towards the still visible stars, a stained hand resting on his chest. A little farther down from him lay another man gently rocking back and forth to the rhythmic beat of the surf. "Poor devils," you think then "Thank God", as a crawling figure looms up out of the lifting veil of darkness. A stretcher bearer! You shudder a little as he merely glances at the gently rocking one, for already he is in hands far greater than any mere human's. Next moment he is by the side of one who is not beyond his aid.

To deal with the enemy fire from the beaches one of the L.C.I's poured heavy fire from its 20-mm into a machine-gun post. Although instructions had been given at Lae that the L.C.I's were not to fire, the sudden bursts from one seemed to release the fingers of the gunners of all the L.C.I's who were soon firing at the jungle fringe and behind the beach or at the tree tops. Although not in orders,[5] this heavy firing may have helped to cause the Japanese to leave the beach defences. But had the assaulting troops and the troops in the second wave actually landed at Scarlet Beach, casualties would have been heavy among the Australians.

All this confusion "meant that Wave 3 (L.C.I's) were the first craft to land any large number of troops on Scarlet Beach proper".[6] The troops of this wave (brigade headquarters, headquarters of supporting arms and the reserve battalion—2/15th Battalion) thus landed under enemy fire, some of which was neutralised by point-blank fire from the L.C.I's. In this disorganisation timings had not been adhered to. The first wave was seven minutes late in landing; by the time the third wave landed it was half an hour behind schedule. Moving in slowly the L.C.I. leader appeared hesitant when he heard the firing and when an enemy bomber flew over. Other L.C.I's which were taking their dressing from him began to lower their ramps well off shore. Some men jumped off into deep water and swam ashore. Once the guns of the third wave began to fire, however, determination revived and the third wave sped to the shore at the good speed necessary to beach an L.C.I. Even after most of the troops were ashore some of the L.C.I's continued firing and in futile anger some of the men bunched ashore beneath the fire yelled at the gunners to cease. Because of these delays the three L.S.T's were half an hour late in coming to the beach. Unfortunately Colonel Brockett's men were an hour late due to unexpected navigational difficulties.[7]

Although the early waves were landed in such confusion, it did not take long to clear the jungle fringing the beaches. The invaders' one idea had been to get their feet on dry land and "have a go at the Jap". Most of the Japanese did not stay to fight in the face of the fire from the L.C.I's and the thrust from the beach, which soon became congested as

---

[5] Windeyer's operation order stated specifically on this point: "In the event of enemy resistance from the north and south headlands, weapons of the flank L.C.I's will be prepared to engage during approach to the beach, but not after H plus 15 mins."

[6] 20th Brigade report.

[7] The American naval historian summed up the landing tersely: "Barbey suggested a midwatch landing under a bright quartering moon. The Australians demurred and a compromise resulted —H-hour to be in the darkness before dawn, ships to clear the beach before daylight air attacks could develop. The Australians proved to be right; 'Uncle Dan's' outfit was not prepared for a neat night landing. The usual snafu [situation normal all fouled up] developed." (S. E. Morison, *Breaking the Bismarcks Barrier, 22 July 1942-1 May 1944*, p. 270.)

various platoons in the light of dawn used it as the quickest route to their correct positions.

At this stage much of the battalion commanders' time was spent in finding just where their troops were and in directing platoons towards their companies. Colonel Simpson, sitting with bandaged head on a log near the edge of a kunai patch, warned his troops against snipers who were still exacting their toll.

By the time portions of brigade headquarters landed, in the third wave, there were about 300 to 400 troops near the south end of Scarlet Beach trying to find their units or to climb the cliff along a single track. When Windeyer and his brigade major, Wilson,[8] arrived on an assault barge from *Conyngham,* Broadbent, aided by other officers, had the troops cutting their own tracks and preparing lanes for the clearance of stores. Air raid alarms, however, proved the most effective means of clearing the beaches quickly.

By 6.30 a.m., with the beach and jungle fringe cleared of all but dead Japanese, Windeyer had established his headquarters and was in telephone communication with each of his battalion commanders. As brigade headquarters went forward round the edge of a kunai patch about 200 yards in from the beach a Japanese threw a grenade which mortally wounded Corporal Appel[9] and wounded Captain Maughan,[1] the brigade Intelligence officer. The Japanese was soon killed with an Owen burst.

By 6 a.m. the A.P.D's and L.C.I's were on their way back to Buna. Three hours and a half later the L.S.T's pulled out. Two were completely unloaded, but the unloading of the third was not quite finished. The men of the 2/23rd and 2/48th Battalions and 2/2nd Machine Gun Battalion unloaded with a will, clearing an average of 50 tons of stores and 20 vehicles an hour; according to Barbey's report, this was much faster than hitherto. From first light high and low fighter umbrellas were over the landing area and dealt effectively with enemy planes which bombed the beach soon after the L.S.T's pulled out, causing one casualty but no damage. Before the landing six P.T. boats from the Morobe base were stationed north of Fortification Point watching for surface and underwater craft, and during the landing four destroyers swept an area to the north.

On the right flank the 2/17th Battalion, after sorting itself out, proceeded towards its objectives. The first report which Simpson received, at 6.15 a.m., was from Lieutenant Gibb's[2] platoon from one of the reserve companies (Captain Dinning's)[3] which had landed in some sort of order on each side of the Siki headland and had advanced inland with one platoon on each side of the head. Gibb's platoon on the left had met a

[8] Lt-Col B. V. Wilson, MBE, NX328. 16 Bde 1940-41; 6 Div 1941-42; BM 20 Bde 1942-44; and various LHQ staff appointments. Salesman; of Wollongong, NSW; b. Wollongong, 9 Jun 1911.

[9] Cpl A. Appel, NX6758; 2/1 Guard Bn. Boilermaker; of Belmore, NSW; b. Leichhardt, NSW, 11 Nov 1903. Died of wounds 24 Sep 1943.

[1] Lt-Col D. W. B. Maughan, MC, NX21195. 2/13 Bn 1940-43; HQ 20 Bde 1943-44; South-East Asia Comd 1944-45. Barrister-at-law; of Sydney; b. Woollahra, NSW, 7 Oct 1912.

[2] Lt K. J. Gibb, NX14839; 2/17 Bn. Grazier; of Wallendbeen, NSW; b. Mosman, NSW, 13 Aug 1910.

[3] Maj J. H. Dinning, MC, NX14374; 2/17 Bn. Buyer; of Croydon, NSW; b. North Sydney, 9 Aug 1914.

machine-gun post which Private Spratt[4] knocked out before most of his platoon had left the L.C.I. and before he was mortally wounded. "Doing over MG post," reported Dinning. Half an hour later Simpson learnt that the right-hand platoon had killed seven Japanese withdrawing from the south end of Scarlet Beach. Dinning then immediately departed for his objective 400 yards up the Song River.

At this time Simpson, whose headquarters was established half way between Katika and the Song, had little idea where his other three companies were. He hoped that Sheldon's company, accompanied by the Papuan infantrymen, would be on North Hill. The second rear company —Lieutenant Main's[5]—also landed near the Siki headland at the same time as Dinning's. After killing two Japanese who waded into the water in a puny effort to attack the L.C.I., Main collected his company and advanced inland a short distance to a garden patch about 100 yards west of the coastal track. He then patrolled to the north and by 9 a.m. his company joined Dinning's on the Song River. Pike's company reported at 6.45 a.m. that it was about to pass west through Katika, controlling the outlet to Sattelberg, to the high ground beyond, having already made contact with troops from the other two battalions. Even though he did not know the whereabouts of Sheldon's company, Simpson felt confident enough to report at 6.50 a.m., "Progress satisfactory—little opposition."

By 7.30 a.m. Simpson received his first intimation that the Japanese had stayed to fight, when Pike reported opposition just outside Katika. A quarter of an hour later he heard from Sheldon: "Am across river—present strength 51—trying to locate 10 Pl who landed north of Song River—2 Pl [of 2/2nd Machine Gun Battalion] with us—moving to North Hill—PIB have passed on to Bonga." Thus, about two hours and a half after the landing, Simpson had a fair idea of the general location of his companies—one across the Song moving to North Hill, two on the Song or moving towards it, and one in the Katika area.

On the left flank Lieut-Colonel Colvin's experiences were similar to those of Simpson. When the second two companies of the 2/13th Battalion landed they were unable to find the first two. Colvin ordered the second companies—Captain Cooper's[6] and Captain Cribb's[7]—into the timber fringing the beach. A few remaining pill-boxes were cleared and a prisoner was captured. The two companies then advanced to the coastal track with battalion headquarters close behind. As efforts to contact Deschamps and Handley by walkie-talkie were unsuccessful, Colvin sent his Intelligence officer, Lieutenant Murray,[8] down the track to the south to look for

---

[4] Pte A. L. Spratt, NX18827; 2/17 Bn. Compositor and nurseryman; of Guildford, NSW; b. Werombi, NSW, 10 Nov 1903. Killed in action 22 Sep 1943.

[5] Capt H. H. Main, MC, NX14840; 2/17 Bn. Share grazier; of Illabo, NSW; b. Cootamundra, NSW, 25 Mar 1919.

[6] Maj H. H. Cooper, NX12383; 2/13 Bn. Clerk; of Hornsby, NSW; b. Armidale, NSW, 30 Apr 1914.

[7] Maj B. G. Cribb, NX12443; 2/13 Bn. Flooring manufacturer; of Hornsby, NSW; b. Eastwood, NSW, 3 May 1914.

[8] Maj J. Murray, MBE, NX20884; 2/13 Bn. MHR since 1958. Stationhand, miner and drover; of Sydney; b. Melbourne, 31 Dec 1915.

the forward companies. About 150 yards down the track he met Captain Snell's[9] company of the 2/15th, who informed him that elements of Deschamps' company had moved on towards Siki Creek, and warned that snipers were still in the area.

It was just on daylight (6.20) when Colvin got through to Deschamps on the walkie-talkie. Not knowing where his other two platoons were, Deschamps and one platoon (Lieutenant Appleton[1]) had headed north from his landing place and had crossed Siki Creek about 400 yards from its mouth. Passing through Snell's company he found the Katika Track and turned south to seek the junction of the track and the creek. After firing at some fleeing Japanese in the shadows Deschamps' company approached Siki Creek again. About 100 yards down the track two Japanese appeared and both were shot by the leading scout, Private O'Malley.[2] Another 50 yards farther on he shot one more. At the creek Appleton went forward to investigate a crossing. Two Japanese rushed out from under the creek bank and in the exchange of shots Appleton was fatally wounded. Seeing his platoon commander's predicament, Private Howlett[3] jumped into the creek and shot both Japanese with his rifle.

Deschamps then ordered the platoon, now under Sergeant Crawford's[4] command, to cross the creek. It did so and took up a position on the far side. At this stage Murray, guided by the noise of battle, found Deschamps, and, to the best of his ability, told him what the rest of the battalion was doing. Hearing movement on the left, Crawford's men were alert, but the noise materialised as Lieutenant Hall's[5] platoon came up along the south side of Siki Creek. Soon afterwards the third missing platoon—Lieutenant Angel's[6]—followed from the same area. The two platoon commanders, who had met no opposition, informed Deschamps and Colvin that Handley's missing company had landed to their south. Deschamps placed his two platoons on the north bank of Siki Creek, one on each side of the Katika Track. The company had thus reached its objective and there it stayed all day.

Apart from Huggett's platoon, the remainder of Handley's company had landed on the coral cliffs between Siki Cove and Arndt Point. With Lieutenant Thomson's[7] platoon, Handley's headquarters clambered up the cliffs and set off for the south. Handley reached Heldsbach Creek

---

[9] Maj L. Snell, MC, QX6226; 2/15 Bn. Clerk; of Bowen, Qld; b. Bowen, 4 Sep 1915.

[1] Lt F. C. Appleton, NX14765; 2/13 Bn. Commercial traveller; of Wollstonecraft, NSW; b. Ashfield, NSW, 18 Oct 1911. Killed in action 22 Sep 1943.

[2] Pte W. J. O'Malley, NX14524; 2/13 Bn. Labourer; of Woollahra, NSW; b. Sydney, 6 Nov 1913.

[3] Pte R. Howlett, NX23141; 2/13 Bn. Labourer; of Mungindi, NSW; b. Combara, NSW, 6 Aug 1905.

[4] Sgt G. R. Crawford, DCM, NX14899; 2/13 Bn. MLA NSW since 1950. Share farmer; of Rob Roy, NSW; b. Inverell, NSW, 16 Dec 1916.

[5] Lt K. J. Hall, MC, NX15009. 2/13 Bn; served with The Border Regt, British Army in India, 1945. Bank officer; of Armidale, NSW; b. Tamworth, NSW, 4 Nov 1921.

[6] Lt K. S. Angel, NX36373; 2/13 Bn. Bank officer; of Wagga Wagga, NSW; b. Wagga Wagga, 17 Aug 1918.

[7] Capt A. S. Thomson, NX14979; 2/13 Bn. Butcher; of Taree, NSW; b. Newcastle, NSW, 30 Sep 1918.

without opposition, but was unable to get through on the walkie-talkie to battalion or brigade until 11.30 a.m.

Lieutenant Mair's[8] platoon, which had landed south of Handley, ran into a Japanese gun position, where five Japanese huddled behind logs were killed by the platoon, which then led the march south. Mair arrived without further incident at Launch Jetty at 8.50 a.m. and, using his initiative, sent a section to the north end of the airstrip where no enemy were seen. About the same time Handley's second-in-command, Captain Fletcher,[9] with one man, advanced south looking for the rest of the battalion (Handley was still out of contact) and reconnoitred the Heldsbach Plantation ahead of the southward advance of Cooper's company.

Meanwhile at 6.30 a.m. Cribb's company on the northern flank of the 2/13th was ordered to capture Zag, where the track to Jivevaneng zigzagged. Cribb was informed that the stream on his right was Siki Creek, and decided to advance up the creek and across to Zag. The stream was not Siki Creek but another little one flowing from just north of Katika. About 150 yards after starting along the narrow track following the creek Lieutenant Birmingham's[1] platoon had three men killed, and three wounded, one mortally, when a Japanese threw a well-directed grenade. About 7 a.m., after advancing along the creek's left bank for 60 yards, the leading scouts were fired on and the company soon lost another two men killed and one wounded. Cribb was unable to attack immediately because some of Pike's men were on his left flank and close to the line of fire.

Two hours and a half after the landing, Colvin knew where three of his companies were—Cooper's advancing on Heldsbach, Deschamps' guarding the track where it crossed Siki Creek, and Cribb's under fire 200 yards north of Katika. The fourth company (Handley's) was missing, although Huggett's platoon had joined battalion headquarters.

The reserve battalion of the 20th Brigade—Lieut-Colonel Grace's 2/15th—landed in much the same sort of disorder as the other two battalions. Three hours after the landing, Grace was not sure of the whereabouts of two of his companies—Captain Christie's[2] and Captain Snell's. The other two companies—Captain Angus'[3] and Major Newcomb's—were with battalion headquarters, concentrated in the area between Katika and Scarlet Beach. Snell meanwhile pushed on to the Katika Track where he met Pike of the 2/17th preparing to attack Katika. Christie's company was also in the general area east of Katika.

Pike's men were the first to attack Katika. After reaching the main track, Pike saw some high ground to the west, and leaving the track he

---

[8] Lt D. C. Mair, NX14880; 2/13 Bn. Stock and station agent; of Moree, NSW; b. Narrandera, NSW, 16 Feb 1913.

[9] Capt A. C. Fletcher, NX20365. 20 A-Tk Coy and 2/13 Bn. Grazier; of Walcha, NSW; b. Walcha, 7 Apr 1917.

[1] Lt W. B. Birmingham, NX33688; 2/13 Bn. Clerk; of Randwick, NSW; b. Sydney, 4 Sep 1916.

[2] Capt E. McN. Christie, QX6230; 2/15 Bn. Storeman; of Ingham, Qld; b. Ingham, 5 Nov 1914. Killed in action 24 Sep 1943.

[3] Capt W. Angus, MC, QX6243; 2/15 Bn. Bank officer; of Warwick, Qld; b. Edinburgh, Scotland, 9 Oct 1917.

(Australian War Memorial)

Brigadier I. N. Dougherty, commander of the 21st Brigade, boarding a Dauntless dive bomber at Kaiapit on 25th September 1943 for a reconnaissance flight over the Markham and Ramu Valleys.

(Australian War Memorial)

Brigadier F. O. Chilton, of the 18th Brigade, outside his hut on the side of a steep slope in the foothills of the Finisterres, 8th February 1944.

(Australian War Memorial)

Lieut-General Sir Edmund Herring (G.O.C. I Corps), Lieut-Colonel J. A. Bishop (C.O. 2/27th Battalion), Major-General G. A. Vasey (G.O.C. 7th Division) and Lieut-General Sir Leslie Morshead (G.O.C. II Corps) at Gusap on 1st October 1943.

(*Australian War Memorial*)
Sappers of the 2/6th Field Company bridging the Gusap River on 3rd October 1943 while troops of the 2/14th Battalion pass over.

(*Australian War Memorial*)
Troops of the 7th Division in the Ramu Valley resting in a village after a 20-mile march through kunai grass in sweltering heat.

advanced for 200 yards. The leading scout came to a clearing ahead with two dilapidated huts. This was Katika, but at the time Pike's doubts as to what it was were shared by all those with him. Pike ordered the forward platoon—Lieutenant Waterhouse's[4]—to advance, skirting the

clearing. When it reached a deep re-entrant leading off from the clearing the company was stretched out in a half moon behind it round the clearing with Pike in communication with his platoon commanders by walkie-

---

[4] Lt S. G. J. Waterhouse, NX60388; 2/17 Bn. Articled clerk; of Moss Vale, NSW; b. Killara, NSW, 29 Nov 1913. Killed in action 22 Sep 1943.

talkie. Lieutenant McLeod,[5] whose platoon was following company headquarters, suddenly reported seeing movement in the clearing and sent out a section to investigate.

Firing simultaneously broke out from the direction of Waterhouse's position 50 yards ahead and from McLeod's section near the huts. After McLeod reported killing four and losing four wounded, Pike ordered him to attack the huts frontally and Waterhouse to reconnoitre a route round the enemy, who were apparently on the high ground immediately ahead. Before McLeod moved round the huts into the open Pike sent his third platoon—Lieutenant Craik's[6]—round to the left to pin the enemy with fire. As these two platoons were moving into position intense fire came from the enemy defences along a 100-yard front on the high ground immediately to the west. The Japanese then attempted to encircle Pike's left flank, but fire from Craik's men killed two of them and drove the remainder back. At this stage Snell, who had picked up the gist of what was happening by listening with his walkie-talkie to Pike's orders, called Pike and told him that he would watch the left flank. Snell moved into the positions occupied by McLeod's and Craik's platoons and farther left.

Waterhouse then reported that the ground which the enemy occupied was high and that the approach was through thick undergrowth interlaced with vines. Snipers were firing from the trees, but so far there were no casualties. Seeking a better line of approach, Waterhouse moved farther right and then led the attack up the slope. He reached within eight yards of the enemy position before he was mortally wounded. The platoon withdrew into a re-entrant and temporarily lost contact with the company commander because the walkie-talkie was still with Waterhouse. When the new platoon commander, Sergeant Cunningham,[7] regained contact with Pike he stated that Cribb's men were in the re-entrant to his right and were going to attack.

The three battalion commanders, each with a company in the Katika area, began to wonder what was happening. The signal from Pike to Simpson was laconic—"Struck opposition at 633682, extent unknown—dealing with it." At 10.53 a.m. Colvin signalled Simpson about the three companies in the area—"They seem to be in trouble," he concluded. The next signal from Pike came to Simpson soon after 11 a.m. "I am in Katika village. On east of Katika and slightly north. Cribb 2/13 Battalion west of Katika—Snell 2/15 north and east of village. Waterhouse's platoon west of village. Cribb took over and doing a show."

When the companies of the 2/17th and 2/13th, led by Pike and Cribb respectively, found themselves close against one another, Cribb asked Pike's leading section to pull back so that he could bombard the enemy position with grenades and 2-inch mortars. Cribb then decided to attack the strong enemy defences on the high ground. With Birmingham's platoon

---

[5] Capt K. T. McLeod, NX65452; 2/17 Bn. Fire insurance inspector; of Burwood, NSW; b. Melbourne, 15 May 1914.

[6] Lt A. P. Craik, NX70966; 2/17 Bn. Car salesman; of Roseville, NSW; b. Guyra, NSW, 6 Jan 1920.

[7] Lt P. B. Cunningham, NX20674; 2/17 Bn. Storeman; of Sydney; b. Auckland, NZ, 29 Nov 1920.

giving supporting fire from the left and Lieutenant MacDougal's[8] watching what Cribb called "the back door", Lieutenant Pope's[9] platoon prepared to attack. Before the attack fifteen mortar bombs were sent over and a Vickers gun was set up on the left flank.

At 10.55 a.m. Cribb's attack went in. Stumbling over thick secondary growth and pushing through kunai, Pope's men advanced on the Japanese positions. The firing was heavy from both sides, but the odds were not even. Although he advanced to within grenade-throwing range, Pope, who was now wounded but remaining on duty, found what many another commander had found, that it was usually futile to attack frontally against strong enemy defences. With two men killed and ten wounded, including himself, he "went to ground", but held on until called back by Cribb.

During the attack Private Dutton[1] carried out three of the wounded men on his back. Other casualties were sent back along the signal wire, but it was very difficult to remove all casualties under fire. Colvin told Cribb that he could have mortar support if he could give a reasonably accurate map reference. Under cover of fifteen 3-inch mortar bombs all the dead and wounded were removed, except for one dead man who was brought out later. Strangely, there was no fire from the enemy during this period. Cribb's company had suffered 28 casualties including 8 dead.

By midday Windeyer decided that no further advance would take place towards Finschhafen until the beach-head was stabilised. Battalions would mop up stragglers and snipers within their areas, and the 2/15th, which had concentrated as brigade reserve east of Katika, would capture that village and destroy the enemy as soon as possible.

The efforts of Pike's and Cribb's men, although unsuccessful in capturing the high ground west of Katika, were nevertheless sufficient to cause the enemy to doubt his ability to withstand another attack. Thus when Snell's and Christie's companies attacked at 3.15 p.m. after a bombardment by 3-inch mortars, they found the strong position deserted and eight corpses lying there. No more opposition was encountered on the day of the landing, and by last light the battalions had sorted themselves out and were on their objectives. On the northern flank a platoon of the Papuan Infantry reported Bonga deserted. The 2/17th Battalion was guarding the northern sector with Sheldon's company on North Hill, Pike's on the high ground south of the Song, and the remainder of the battalion half way between Scarlet Beach and this high ground. In the southern sector the 2/13th Battalion had driven rapidly south after the clearing of Katika; Cooper's company having taken the wrong turning was at Tareko, Handley's at Launch Jetty with a patrol on the Quoja River, and the remainder of the battalion in the Heldsbach area. Brigade headquarters was in a hollow just west of Scarlet Beach.

---

[8] Lt L. R. MacDougal, NX21577; 2/13 Bn. Bank officer; of Mosman, NSW; b. Cremorne, NSW, 10 Jan 1916.
[9] Maj H. W. Pope, MC, NX59154; 2/13 Bn. Served Malaya 1957. Law student; of Vaucluse, NSW; b. Sydney, 19 Mar 1920.
[1] Cpl R. C. Dutton, NX57305. 20 A-Tk Coy and 2/13 Bn. Auctioneer; of Walcha, NSW; b. Quirindi, NSW, 3 Sep 1910.

The Papuan company's tasks were to get platoons astride the Bonga and Sattelberg Tracks, report movement, harass the enemy and assist Angau to collect natives. The two Papuan platoons available (Numbers 9 and 10)—101 men—had shared in the confusion of the landing. Landing on the right 10 Platoon pushed inland behind the enemy posts on the beach in an attempt to bring down cross-fire on the defenders. In doing so the Papuans were the first troops to get behind the enemy, but they came under fire from both the enemy and the Allies and suffered seven casualties. The other platoon and company headquarters were on an L.C.I. in the third wave. When the gangway jammed and broke Captain Luetchford[2] led his troops over the side and jumped into deep water. Badly wounded, Luetchford was helped ashore but on arrival at the medical dressing station he was dead. By dusk the two platoons had done valuable reconnaissance work. No. 10 Platoon, after reporting Bonga deserted, camped with Sheldon's company on North Hill and 9 Platoon was with Cooper's company at Tareko.

Two batteries of the 2/12th Field Regiment landed from the L.S.T's in the morning and were shelling Finschhafen by last light. The third battery arrived when the other three L.S.T's came to Scarlet Beach half an hour before midnight on the 22nd. The whole regiment (735 men) was then ashore. Major Pagan's[3] 2/4th Light Anti-Aircraft Regiment (less one battery)—489 men—had Bofors guns in action by 7 a.m. and all its guns in position by 9.30 a.m. At 10 a.m. a gun of the 10th L.A.A. Battery was bombed at the north end of the beach and five men were wounded, one fatally.

Judging from previous experience the sappers would have one of the hardest tasks in making roads and bridges and clearing obstacles. Specifically, the 270 men of Major Moulds'[4] 2/3rd Field Company and the detachment of the 2/1st Mechanical Equipment Company were to make a crossing over the Song, a bridge over the Mape, and "trs and brs in sp of the op [tracks and bridges in support of the operation] and the maintenance thereof". Moulds also had for support Major Siekmann's[5] company of the 2/3rd Pioneer Battalion. Part of the headquarters of the 2/3rd Field Company had an exciting period when they found themselves ahead of the leading infantry. This small party, led by Captain Eastick,[6] shot a Japanese in the foot and captured him. After sorting themselves out sappers and pioneers began work on beach exits, tracks and dumps.

On the beach itself, Major Broadbent's task was to coordinate the defence of the beach, the movement of stores, the development of the beach-head, the requirements of small craft, and the control of traffic.

---

[2] Capt A. B. Luetchford, QX38410; Papuan Inf Bn. Contractor; of Brisbane; b. Clayfield, Qld, 8 Mar 1919. Died of wounds 22 Sep 1943.

[3] Brig J. E. Pagan, MBE, NX12402. 2/1 LAA Regt, OC 2/3 LAA Bty, 2/4 LAA Regt (Admin Comd 1943). Salesman; of Hay, NSW; b. Killara, NSW, 13 May 1914.

[4] Maj W. J. Moulds, MBE, QX6233. 2/3 Fd Coy (OC 1943). Architect; of Brisbane; b. Oakey, Qld, 14 Jul 1909.

[5] Lt-Col P. E. Siekmann, ED, SX9038; 2/3 Pnr Bn. Manager; of Port Noarlunga, SA; b. North Norwood, SA, 18 Oct 1909.

[6] Maj R. F. Eastick, MBE, VX39192. 2/3 Fd Coy (OC 1943-45). Civil engineer; of Mildura, Vic; b. Nhill, Vic, 8 Feb 1913.

Broadbent, quick, energetic and full of initiative, proved an excellent choice, and in the succeeding days the force owed much to his drive and flair for improvisation. Broadbent carried out his tasks in conjunction with Pagan of the 2/4th Light Anti-Aircraft Regiment, Brockett of the 532nd Engineer Boat and Shore Regiment, and Captain Nicholas,[7] whose company of the 2/2nd Machine Gun Battalion provided 12 Vickers guns for beach defence.

The positions occupied at last light by all the units and sub-units of the 20th Brigade group were those actually planned by Windeyer, except that Cooper's company of the 2/13th should have been astride the Sattelberg Road near Zag instead of at Tareko. The fact that these troops had reached their first day's objectives despite the confusion of the landing said much for their training, determination and leadership.

By midday Windeyer had been forced to ground the bulldozers which were severing the telephone lines to his forward troops at a time when he was trying hard to follow the fight. Despite this temporary lull in their major activities, the sappers by dusk had bridged Siki Creek and constructed a road from the south end of Scarlet Beach to link with the coastal road in Heldsbach Plantation. By 11 a.m. on the 22nd Windeyer's adviser on native affairs, Lieut-Colonel Allan,[8] appreciating the labour difficulties, brought in the luluai of Tareko and sent out messages through him to tell the "kanakas" to come in and work. In Allan the brigade commander had the support of an officer not only widely known and respected throughout New Guinea but one who had served with the brigade in its Middle East campaigns both as a regimental officer and as its brigade major.

At 10.30 a.m. on the 22nd a grave administrative deficiency was discovered: very little 9-mm ammunition for the brigade's main close-quarter weapon—the Owen gun—had been landed. About five-sixths of the 9-mm ammunition loaded at Lae had apparently remained on the third L.S.T. which had not been fully unloaded that morning, though Admiral Barbey's report stated buoyantly that the unloading was "virtually complete". The battalions were immediately warned to conserve their Owen gun ammunition—a difficult task for the companies preparing to assault Katika. At the same time Windeyer authorised an "emergency ops" signal to the 9th Division repeated to I Corps asking for an air dropping of 9-mm ammunition.

This signal bearing as it did the highest franking produced speedy results. Dropping was arranged for after dark on the 22nd. The dropping area was a kunai patch near brigade headquarters and instructions were to illuminate the area. As they had no other means of illuminating it, the brigade staff asked all who possibly could to lend their torches. At 7.15 p.m. the men of brigade headquarters stood in a circle round the kunai

---

[7] Maj W. P. Nicholas, NX34664; 2/2 MG Bn. Veterinary surgeon and jackeroo; of Sydney; b. Sydney, 17 Mar 1915.

[8] Col H. T. Allan, OBE, MC, ED, NX12229. (1st AIF: Capt 17 Bn.) 2/17 Bn; BM 20 Bde 1941; Base and Sub-Area Comds 1943-45. Gold miner; of Wau, NG; b. Hunter's Hill, NSW, 5 Jan 1895.

patch shining their torches, while 115,000 rounds of 9-mm ammunition were dropped; 112,000 rounds were recovered and the situation was saved. It was a fine achievement on the part of the R.A.A.F. Boomerang crews and Captain Garnsey,[9] the Air Liaison officer.

While the capture of Scarlet Beach was being consolidated on 22nd September, Barbey's convoy was steering south from the landing beach. About noon the destroyer *Reid*, again acting as fighter controller, began to chart the approach of a formidable air force from New Britain and within about 70 miles of the convoy. Surprised by the landing at Scarlet Beach, the Japanese only now sent 20 to 30 bombers and 30 to 40 fighters from Rabaul. Off Finschhafen they swerved south-east to attack the retiring convoy. But three American fighter squadrons were then patrolling the Lae-Finschhafen area as an air umbrella and were due soon for relief by other squadrons which were now warming up. The result was that five squadrons were ready above the convoy when the Japanese flew into the trap.

The American fighters claimed they shot down 10 bombers and 29 fighters for the loss of three Lightnings. Anti-aircraft fire from the destroyers, the landing craft and a tug also "splashed" nine out of ten torpedo planes which swept in too low for the radar to detect them. There were no losses among the ships. "Actually this little action helped to dispel an old South-West Pacific bugaboo, the fear of land-based air attack which had long kept ships out of the Solomon and Bismarck Seas."[1]

The three L.S.T's which had been unable to participate in the morning landing because of the discovery of a sand bar in Scarlet Beach, sailed from Morobe at 6 p.m. with the remainder of the 20th Brigade's units and stores and the unloading parties. They began unloading at 11.30, and by 4 a.m. on the 23rd were empty and steering south. While patrolling off Scarlet Beach about midnight the destroyers guarding the L.S.T's sank three barges full of Japanese sailing north. American naval records state that on 22nd September Barbey's force landed on Scarlet Beach: 5,300 troops, 180 vehicles, 32 guns and 850 tons of stores comprising 15 days' rations and 12 days' ammunition.

Except that a lone Japanese walked into Sergeant Crawford's platoon of the 2/13th on the south bank of Siki Creek and was promptly shot, the night was uneventful. Windeyer's orders for the next day were: "20 Bde will continue advance on Finschhafen." The 2/15th Battalion would lead the advance to the Bumi River; the 2/13th would assemble in the Heldsbach Plantation-Launch Jetty area, ready to move at 30 minutes' notice. Thus the brigade was geared for an advance to the south, but Windeyer could not neglect possible threats from the north or west, and his orders were to be ready for Sattelberg after Finschhafen. General Wootten had told him before he left Lae that he should get at least a company on to Sattelberg as soon as possible. At the time neither realised

---

[9] Maj R. C. Garnsey, MC, NX51115. 2/17 Bn; and Air Liaison appointments with 9 Div and Adv LHQ. Regular soldier; of Lindfield, NSW; b. Tuggerah, NSW, 4 Jan 1919. Died 24 Feb 1946.

[1] Morison, p. 270.

how inaccessible Sattelberg was and both thought of its occupation merely as a method of guarding the open right flank of the advance.

From prisoners and documents, captured on the first day, Windeyer learnt that an enemy force of 300 to 400 had been holding the Scarlet Beach-Katika area at the landing. These Japanese defenders had killed 20 Australians, including 3 officers, and wounded 65; 9 were missing. The Japanese defenders were companies from the *80th* and *238th Regiments*. The survivors had withdrawn along the Katika Track towards Sattelberg.

A captured map showed troops of the *80th Regiment* east of the Mongi River. Soon after the Australian landing east of Lae the Japanese had sent this force of about three companies together with two 75-mm guns to the mouth of the Mongi to resist an anticipated drive by the Australians from Hopoi to Finschhafen. Towards them was moving Lieut-Colonel O'Connor's[2] 22nd Battalion which had departed from Blue Beach near Hopoi at 6 a.m. on 22nd September, and by last light reached Wideru without opposition after a rough and slippery march.

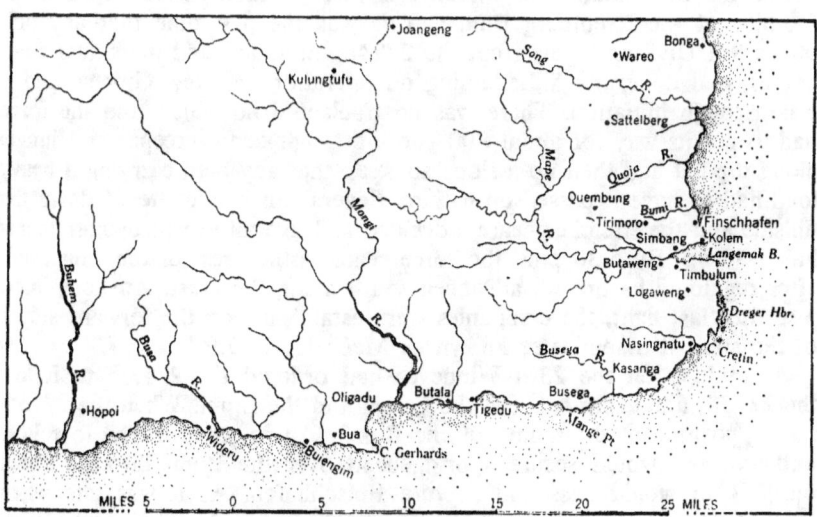

Hopoi to Scarlet Beach coastline

At 8 a.m. on the 23rd, the 2/15th began its advance along the coastal track, with Major Newcomb's company in the lead. Three hours and a half later the leading platoon approached the Bumi near its mouth. The river appeared easily fordable. As the leading scout neared Kamloa at 12.40 p.m., however, he saw two Japanese sitting under a hibiscus. He fired but missed, whereupon the two Japanese fired their rifles into the air, obviously as signals, and disappeared. Soon after 1 p.m. the leading

---

[2] Col J. C. W. O'Connor, NX102552. CO 22 Bn; and various staff and training appointments. Regular soldier; b. Perth, 17 Feb 1907.

section under Corporal Tart[3] advanced through the undergrowth to the cover near the river bank. Walking on to the bank to survey the crossing, Tart was shot dead. Heavy fire came from the south bank, where the Japanese had strongly fortified and wired positions, as Corporal Cousens'[4] section covered the extrication of Tart's men. When bringing in one of the wounded men, Cousens himself was wounded.

Colonel Grace was moving with the forward company. He had a quick word with Windeyer by telephone, and promptly put into operation an alternative plan. Windeyer had previously agreed with Grace that, if heavy opposition were met along the flat, a detached column should swing off the coastal track and continue the advance along the ridges to the west. Thus Grace left two companies at the north bank of the Bumi near Kamloa while Major Suthers[5] led Christie's and Snell's companies with some Pioneers, stretcher bearers and mortar men into the hills. Lieutenant Shrapnel[6] brought up six 3-inch mortars in support of the companies at the Bumi crossing, established an observation post overlooking Salankaua Plantation and, using his mortars as a battery, pounded the plantation area.

Leaving the battalion at 4 p.m. this force hacked its way up into the foothills of the Kreutberg Range. This was the first time that any unit of the 9th Division, apart from the 2/24th Battalion and individual companies, had done any hill-climbing on operations in New Guinea, and it was a tough initiation. There was no track and no water, and the force had to cut its way for about 800 yards through dense creeper and jungle along the flat and then up a slope so steep that any man carrying a heavy load had to have it passed up to him. Several tin hats clattered down the hillside and the stretcher bearers decided to leave all except two stretchers half way up. By 5.30 p.m. the force reached the crest of the ridge and, after regaining its breath, advanced south along the crest. An hour later, just after last light, the companies were established on the forward slopes of the spur at a spot later known as McKeddie's O.P.[7]

At midday on the 23rd Windeyer had ordered the 2/13th to follow the 2/15th and camp between the Quoja and the Bumi. When the 2/15th met opposition at the mouth of the Bumi, Colvin was ordered to follow Suthers, who would secure a bridgehead over the Bumi through which the 2/13th would pass and capture Finschhafen. As it was late when these orders were received and one company was protecting the guns and brigade headquarters at Launch Jetty, Colvin asked for permission to delay until early next morning and Windeyer agreed.

While the 23rd Battery was moving to the Finschhafen airstrip area there was some intermittent enemy shelling from 70-mm guns in Finsch-

---

[3] Cpl R. Tart, QX16765; 2/15 Bn. Farm hand; of Tannymorel, Qld; b. Featherstone, Yorks, England, 28 Dec 1919. Killed in action 23 Sep 1943.
[4] Cpl H. M. Cousens, MM, QX11364; 2/15 Bn. Farmer; of Ingham, Qld; b. Charters Towers, Qld, 15 Sep 1914.
[5] Lt-Col R. A. Suthers, QX6221. 2/15 Bn; BM 18 Bde 1945. Solicitor; of Townsville, Qld; b. Kingaroy, Qld, 10 Mar 1916.
[6] Maj G. S. Shrapnel, QX842; 2/15 Bn. Bank officer; of Taringa, Qld; b. Brisbane, 14 Sep 1920. (He is a descendant of the inventor of shrapnel.)
[7] Named after Lieutenant J. E. McKeddie of the 2/12th Field Regiment.

hafen. In the late afternoon enemy aircraft bombed Scarlet Beach and destroyed 500 cases of ammunition belonging to the Engineer Boat and Shore Regiment. During the night it rained heavily and the Australians on the coast heard much barge movement off Finschhafen. Harassing fire by the Australian artillery soon caused the noises to cease.

At first light on the 23rd the 22nd Battalion had resumed its advance along the coast from Wideru. By 8 a.m. the first signs of Japanese occupation, all old, were seen. Soon afterwards the leading company saw smoke ahead, and natives reported that the Japanese had slept on the previous night at Buiengim. At 1.35 p.m. Captain Martin's[8] company approached Bua where the leading troops had a sharp skirmish with a Japanese outpost which withdrew. By 4 p.m. a section of Australians seized a steep rise where the track passed through a deep cutting approximately 250 yards east of Bua. Just after dark this section was fired on and several shells from a mountain gun were fired over the main Australian positions.

Reveille for the 2/13th Battalion on the 24th was at 4.15 a.m. and an hour later the battalion was slipping and staggering up the foothills in the wake of the 2/15th, following its signal wire. At 7.30 a.m. Colvin tapped the wire and informed Suthers of his progress. Now that the 2/13th was close behind, the 2/15th moved off for the river. Progress was still slow and by 8.15 a.m. when the men of the 2/13th lay panting on the top of the ridge Suthers was still about 350 yards from the Bumi. At 10 a.m. the leading company reached the river and found an unoccupied enemy position on the south bank of the river which was 15 to 20 yards wide. Barbed wire on the opposite side of the river, however, was an ominous sign. Half an hour later Lieutenant Rogers'[9] platoon fired on two Japanese seen on the south side. Deciding that it would be foolish to attempt a crossing at that particular spot, Suthers with Captain Christie, Lieutenant Harpham,[1] and one platoon, went upstream about 150 yards and found a more suitable place. Christie went forward to reconnoitre this crossing and was hit by a Japanese sniper firing from the north bank. The sniper was actually seen for an instant recrossing the creek. Harpham went forward to see if Christie was dead—he was—and, while in the open, was sniped and himself killed.

Suthers now ordered Captain Snell to cross the river and seize a bridgehead on the opposite bank. The artillery shelled the kunai patch on the south bank overlooking the river about 12.30 p.m. As the company formed up for the crossing enemy fire inflicted three casualties. A slight delay ensued while a section of machine-guns got into position. They were ready at 1.15 p.m. and a quarter of an hour later Snell's men advanced again. The stream was up to the men's waists, but only one man was killed

---

[8] Capt G. E. Martin, VX108143; 22 Bn. Plumber; of Leongatha, Vic; b. Hawthorn, Vic, 25 Feb 1910.
[9] Lt W. E. Rogers, DX48. HQ 9 Div and 2/15 Bn. Stockman and truck driver; of Darwin, NT; b. Coonabarabran, NSW, 30 Nov 1912.
[1] Lt N. L. Harpham, QX6647; 2/15 Bn. University student; of Dalby, Qld; b. Brisbane, 8 Sep 1919. Killed in action 24 Sep 1943.

during the crossing; most of the enemy's strength appeared to be farther downstream.

Although stray bullets were flying, one going through the seat of Snell's pants, the company scrambled up a very steep hill without serious opposition to a track junction on the left and stopped there. The bridgehead was thus established, and with the other company, now led by Captain Stuart,[2] guarding the crossing from the south bank, the task of the 2/13th was to cross and continue the advance. Major Handley's company had little difficulty in crossing the river at the bridgehead, despite harassing fire from snipers and machine-guns concealed in the undergrowth farther downstream, and by last light had linked with Snell's company higher up.

As there had been no enemy activity in the Scarlet Beach sector, two companies of the 2/17th were moved south along the coast as brigade reserve. This left in the Scarlet Beach area only two companies of the 2/17th along the Katika and Sattelberg Tracks, one company of the 2/3rd Pioneer Battalion, the 10th L.A.A. Battery with six guns, one company of the 2/2nd Machine Gun Battalion, and engineers and others. Brigadier Windeyer knew well that, with such a thin scattering of troops, Scarlet Beach was vulnerable. As yet, however, there was no sign of any threat from north or west, and, as his objective was Finschhafen, Windeyer felt it imperative to have a reserve within close call. That there was no immediate cause for anxiety about his exposed right flank seemed evident when a signal from Lieutenant Main of the 2/17th Battalion on the 24th stated. "Coy less one pl now approx 3 miles along main track and proceeding to Sattelberg. Patrol P.I.B. moving ahead of coy."

Just before Handley's company crossed the Bumi, Colvin suggested that, as evacuation and resupply would be very difficult along the route traversed by the 2/13th and 2/15th, some attempt should be made to cut a track around the foothills to the bridgehead positions. The difficulty was underlined when the rain began and men floundered and slipped carrying supplies and ammunition up and stretchers down. Windeyer therefore directed that a jeep track should be cut through the jungle from the coastal track just north of Kamloa to the bridgehead. A platoon from the 2/3rd Pioneers and men from the 2/17th and the reserve companies of the 2/13th and 2/15th were employed for carrying along the rough and arduous route while the track was being cut.

Japanese aircraft were over the Scarlet Beach area from early in the morning while Allied planes were attacking airfields on New Britain. At 12.30 p.m. on the 24th the Japanese air force enjoyed unusual success when 12 bombers and over 20 escorting fighters attacked the Australian gun positions at the north end of the airstrip; the guns had been shelling enemy positions in the Kakakog and Salankaua Plantation areas. Although the 60-odd bombs which were dropped did not damage the guns, 18 casualties (including Captain Nelligan[3] killed and one man who later

---

[2] Maj M. R. Stuart, QX6224; 2/15 Bn. Clerk; of Longreach, Qld; b. Longreach, 13 Jun 1919.
[3] Capt P. W. Nelligan, MC, WX1581. 2/7 and 2/12 Fd Regts. Public servant; of Leederville, WA; b. Subiaco, WA, 25 Jul 1910. Killed in action 24 Sep 1943.

died of wounds) were inflicted on the gunners, and the 2/3rd Field Company lost 14 killed and 19 wounded. The air liaison party from the Fifth Air Force lost all its equipment and its commander, Captain Ferrel, was killed. For once the Japanese radio reports about the damage and casualties inflicted by their air force were only too true.

Looking at the photo-map of the Finschhafen area, Windeyer estimated that his forward troops were on the high ground about a quarter of a mile west of the M.T. ford, while the enemy were entrenched in the Salankaua Plantation and the foothills to the west. For the 25th he ordered the securing of the Kreutberg Range with the 2/13th passing through the 2/15th's bridgehead and establishing itself, with two days' rations and ammunition, overlooking the main enemy positions. The companies of the 2/15th at Kamloa would stage a mock attack.

Along the south coast of the Huon Peninsula the advance of the 22nd Battalion continued on the 24th. North of Bua a large deserted Japanese camp containing equipment and documents was found and a large dump of ammunition, petrol and tools. By 11.15 a.m. the forward troops arrived at Tamigudu near Cape Gerhards where they saw signs that a gun had been dragged along. At noon an abandoned ammunition dump for a 75-mm gun was found near Oligadu. At 1.40 p.m. the battalion reached the Mongi, thus achieving its original objective, and dug in along the river and on its islands. During this process one Japanese was killed.

A patrol led across the river by Sergeant Hogan[4] was overdue at nightfall when heavy fire came from the direction taken by the patrol. At the same time the enemy suddenly opened fire from the east bank of the river. Rifles, sub-machine-guns, machine-guns and mortars mingled with about 70 rounds from a 75-mm gun. It was as though the Japanese, realising the hopelessness of their position, were determined to fire off as much ammunition as possible before it fell into Australian hands. During this half-hour bombardment one man was killed and one wounded.

The enemy air force was again active on 25th September. Between 4.45 a.m. and 7.30 a.m. there were three raids and again the Allies suffered relatively heavy casualties—8 killed and 40 wounded—mainly anti-aircraft and administrative troops. There was a further raid at 5.15 p.m. which was more in accordance with the usual pattern—no casualties or damage. The Allied air force, which had been concentrating mainly on near-by Japanese airfields in New Guinea and New Britain, retaliated at 9.35 a.m. when about 20 Bostons and Vultees bombed and dive-bombed Japanese positions in the Finschhafen area.

Some of the hardest worked troops in Windeyer's force at this time were the men of Lieut-Colonel Outridge's[5] 2/8th Field Ambulance. When the three L.S.T's of Wave 7 departed from Scarlet Beach in the early hours of 23rd September only the walking wounded were able to get aboard in time. The more seriously wounded from the first day as well

---

[4] Sgt D. G. Hogan, VX82966; 22 Bn. Rigger; of Parkville, Vic; b. Morwell, Vic, 3 Jun 1916.
[5] Lt-Col L. MacD. Outridge, QX6475. CO 2/12 Fd Amb 1942-43, 2/8 Fd Amb 1943-44, 2/2 CCS 1944-45. Medical practitioner; of Gympie, Qld; b. Brisbane, 1 Nov 1900.

as those wounded subsequently by enemy land and air operations were unable to receive any attention other than that provided by the 2/8th Field Ambulance and Major Gayton's[6] section of the 2/3rd Casualty Clearing Station. As there was no re-supply mission for ten days the wounded could not be evacuated and normal medical installations became holding centres. The recovery of fracture cases was seriously prejudiced by the lack of proper facilities for treatment. The third L.S.T., which had not completed unloading on the morning of the landing, sailed with the lighting plant for the M.D.S. and C.C.S. operating theatres still on board, and not enough stretchers had been landed. It was no part of the brigade or divisional commander's job to clear this M.D.S. It was the responsibility of the higher headquarters to provide the necessary ships. Within the brigade, medical arrangements were as good as could be expected under the circumstances, but the higher planning was proving faulty in this respect.

In addition, as a result of the speed with which the operation had been undertaken, there were few canteen goods, canned heat, razor blades and hospital comforts. The main shortages were in tobacco, cigarettes, matches and chocolate. Only three ounces of tobacco a man were available during the battle for Finschhafen and other canteen issues were limited. One of the most serious deficiencies was canned heat. This had been developed so that men in forward areas, where the lighting of fires would disclose their positions to the enemy, could still have a cup of tea. Only 1,152 tins were landed and some men in the areas where fires could not be lit went for three days without a hot drink.

In the Bumi sector the 25th was spent in patrolling, consolidating the bridgehead, bringing up supplies and completing the jeep track. A patrol led by Lieutenant Mair of the 2/13th Battalion was sent out soon after first light to deal with a troublesome enemy mortar to the east. At 8.45 a.m., after following an old and indefinite track down into a very rough gully, Mair found a Japanese strongpost 20 feet above him. He lost two killed and four wounded, and with great difficulty extricated his wounded. It seemed that this enemy position, containing bunkers and foxholes and barbed wire from the river up, was the left flank of enemy defences opposing the crossing at the ford. It had also inflicted most of the casualties during the crossing.

Snell's and Handley's companies found themselves on a razor-backed ridge running in a south-west direction towards the main Kreutberg Range. On top the ridge was bamboo clad and varied in width between 5 and 15 yards. On each side steep slopes fell into thick gullies. In case the Japanese should push up from the east, Handley, on orders from Colvin, sent Angel's platoon west along the south bank to reconnoitre for another battalion crossing. As the country consisted of a series of steep razor-backs running down to the river there seemed little point in establishing another

---

[6] Maj W. R. Gayton, VX61253. 6 AGH, 2/3 CCS, 116 and 2/8 AGH's. Medical practitioner; of Richmond, Vic; b. Melbourne, 8 Feb 1912.

crossing, particularly as Suthers reported in the late morning that men could now cross the river without opposition.

During the day the 2/3rd Field Company and the Pioneers of the 2/15th finished cutting the jeep track through dense secondary growth from the main track to the crossing, and the task of those carrying supplies and evacuating wounded became easier. After visiting the area, Windeyer directed that there should be no further advance south of the Bumi until two days' supplies were near the river crossing.

It was on the 25th that Windeyer received his first indication that there might be some danger from his right flank. Main's company of the 2/17th was advancing along the Sattelberg Road with orders to occupy Sattelberg, reported by the Papuan infantrymen to be unoccupied. Leaving one platoon to watch the Zag area, Main advanced with his other two platoons and 9 Platoon of the Papuans. After passing Jivevaneng the Papuans realised that they had originally mistaken Jivevaneng for Sattelberg. Some 800 yards beyond Jivevaneng it became clear that the Sattelberg area was anything but unoccupied: a strong Japanese position was astride the track.

While one platoon tried unsuccessfully to get round the right flank, Japanese patrols infiltrated with considerable success and cut the Australian telephone line in two places. Main's mortars and grenades did little damage to the Japanese position. By this time it was apparent that it would take one company all its time to capture the Japanese position immediately ahead, let alone Sattelberg. When he received Main's report, Windeyer decided that his meagre resources did not permit of further operations against Sattelberg until the primary objective—Finschhafen—had been captured. Main was therefore ordered to hold the road and not dissipate his strength by attacking. When he recommended a withdrawal to Jivevaneng, where there was a cleared field of fire controlling the junction of the Sattelberg Road and Tareko Track, Windeyer agreed.

Along the Bumi and on the Sattelberg Road there were ominous portents. During the night 25th-26th September the Japanese could be heard digging in higher up the spur from Snell and Handley. About a dozen Japanese blundered into Main's perimeter at Jivevaneng. Three were killed and the rest ran. "Tac R" (reconnaissance aircraft) reported that the Salankaua Plantation was heavily defended. At sea the enemy was active. A submarine was reported moving south from Scarlet Beach at 7.40 p.m. Twenty minutes later a sentry reported that some sort of craft was sneaking into Launch Jetty cove. Although it appeared to withdraw when fired at, Windeyer was not convinced that a raiding party of Japanese had not landed to spike the guns. In pitch blackness a company of the 2/17th was hurriedly sent back to protect the artillery. There was no sign of any raiding party, but the fitful sleep of the defenders was disturbed by the noise of enemy barges.

On the 25th the 22nd Battalion on the south coast realised that the enemy opposing them were clearing out. Sergeant Hogan's patrol returned from the east bank of the Mongi at first light after having been pinned down during the previous night's bombardment. Lieutenant Prendergast's[7] platoon left at the same time to cross the river and reconnoitre the coast beyond Butala and Tigedu. The platoon returned just on dusk with an interesting tale. There was no sign of the enemy for about five miles beyond the Mongi, but there were plenty of signs of a hasty retreat. Just beyond the Mongi the platoon found two 75-mm guns destroyed. Near by were the bodies of six natives bound and shot. They had apparently been used to haul the guns and had then been destroyed with the guns. Another abandoned gun was found near Oligadu.

The 26th was a day of bitter fighting all round Windeyer's front. He left early in the morning to visit each of his battalions. After discussion with Colvin and Grace at Suthers' headquarters, he gave orders for an operation designed to enlarge the bridgehead and to get the whole of the 2/13th on the Kreutberg Range. In this operation the 2/15th would capture the high ground south-east from the crossing place, while the 2/13th, moving south-west, would occupy a spur controlling the track coming from Tirimoro. Before his conference with Brigadier Windeyer, Colvin had informed him that he would try to get Handley to the top of the ridge as soon as possible and send the remainder of his battalion across. By 9 a.m. Cribb's company was across the Bumi to support Handley. During the day Cooper's company followed and guarded the south side of the crossing while Deschamps' company moved down to the river. At 2 p.m. Colonel Grace sent Stuart's company across to help Snell. Angus meanwhile reconnoitred the Bumi from Kamloa to the crossing and prepared to send a platoon from Kamloa to prevent enemy penetration up the river as the assaulting troops advanced.

Opposition was expected by both the 2/13th and 2/15th. Ahead of Handley's forward positions, Lieutenant Webb's[8] platoon of the 2/13th heard enemy voices and digging about 400 yards up the shell-pitted western track where it widened out as the spur neared the main feature. The enemy position was in thick bamboo, but Webb's patrol was unobserved and the artillery F.O.O., Lieutenant Stewart,[9] was able to call for fire on the general position, although he could not obtain good observation.

Soon after Windeyer's visit both commanders of the assaulting battalions issued their orders. Colvin told Handley to attack at 3.30 p.m. and capture the Japanese position encountered by Webb. "We must get through to the top today. The enemy must not hold us up," urged Colvin. "[Major] Handley said there will be no doubt about it," recorded the battalion diarist.

Grace ordered Suthers to secure the bridgehead firmly by widening it downstream so that the 2/13th could pass through. Grace then left the detailed plan to Suthers who went forward to Snell's position accompanied

---

[7] Lt N. F. Prendergast, VX108161; 22 Bn. Schoolteacher; of Newlyn, Vic; b. Newlyn, 25 Jul 1911.
[8] Capt D. S. Webb, NX34169; 2/13 Bn. Farm hand; of Dubbo, NSW; b. Dubbo, 1 May 1918.
[9] Lt-Col G. Stewart, MC, VX14442; 2/12 Fd Regt. Library assistant; of Malvern, Vic; b. Armadale, Vic, 30 Dec 1915.

by Stuart. While Grace arranged a ten minutes' shoot by two troops of artillery and four 3-inch mortars from 3.15 p.m., Suthers prepared to attack the kunai-topped hill south-east of the crossing with two companies (Snell's and Stuart's), each with two platoons forward.

Stuart's men forded the river at 2 p.m., and at 3.25 the two companies, with Snell's on the right, crossed their start-line—a bamboo clump on the ridge near Handley's position. Five minutes later Handley crossed his start-line while Cribb's company prepared to follow and pass through when the objective was captured.

The men of the 2/15th's two assaulting companies literally fell for the first 150 yards from their start-line. Tumbling over vines, crashing through bamboo and heavy timber, the men stumbled to the bottom of the valley. About 450 yards from the start they came to a precipitous slope. Pulling themselves up hand over hand for about 200 feet, their training and stamina came to their aid so that near the summit the formation was maintained and the companies advanced upwards on a front of about 150 yards.

On top of the hill was a company of what were regarded as Japan's *corps d'élite*—the marines. Faced with the Australians' unfaltering advance upwards, the marines began to shower them with grenades which fortunately were largely ineffective. Had they been good grenades, the attacking companies would have suffered heavy losses. Corporal Norris,[1] leading the first section of Snell's company, was blown down the hill by a grenade landing a foot away. He picked himself up and climbed back to lead the assault. Apparently the Japanese explosive was not quick enough and the metal was too light. The marines now opened up with all their weapons, but most of the fire passed over the Queenslanders as their relentless advance continued. In order to keep down the defenders' heads the attackers replied with fire as they advanced, although they could not yet use grenades which would have rolled back on them.

The marines, who should have been able to hold the position against a battalion, at first wavered and then panicked. Cold steel flashed as the Australians came to the summit and charged with their bayonets. Most of the Japanese, who were much taller than the average, turned and fled. On the right flank Snell sent Sergeant Fink[2] round a kunai patch to come in behind the remaining enemy, clearing machine-gun posts on the way. It was during this sweep that most of the ten Australian casualties were suffered. Fink's men drew the fire of the defenders, thus relieving the pressure on the remainder of the attackers. Although wounded, Fink caught the marines fleeing towards Kakakog and he and his men killed 30.

On the left flank of the assault, Stuart's men were equally successful. Two yards from the foremost Japanese post Lance-Sergeant Guilfoyle,[3] who had been leading his section's assault, was wounded, but he remained

---

[1] Cpl R. C. Norris, MM, QX5802; 2/15 Bn. Overseer; of Dalby, Qld; b. Dalby, 2 Mar 1918.

[2] Lt F. J. Fink, MM, QX8529. 2/15 and 2/17 Bns. Farm hand; of Yandina, Qld; b. Brisbane, 18 Dec 1915.

[3] Capt C. C. Guilfoyle, MM, QX14730. 2/15 Bn, 1 Parachute Bn and SEAC. Clerk; of Windsor, Qld; b. Cooktown, Qld, 10 Oct 1921.

in the open shouting his section on. On the left flank, Lieutenant Nesbitt's[4] platoon swung left while Lieutenant Starmer's[5] followed by Lieutenant Rogers' went into the kunai patch. Here they ran into two 13-mm machine-guns, one of which was hit in the magazine and caught fire. Overrunning the enemy's posts, Starmer's platoon charged through the open kunai. The Japanese then panicked and 40 or 50 of them ran back towards their observation post.

Joining with Lieutenant Douglas'[6] platoon from Snell's company, Stuart's three platoons advanced in what he termed "extended line—desert formation, not in file according to orthodox jungle tactics". The booty captured included three 13-mm guns, seven L.M.G's, many mortars and rifles. Fifty-two marines were buried and several others who died in the surrounding scrub made their presence known in the next few days. Probably about 100 casualties were inflicted by the 2/15th, who in return lost 2 killed, one died of wounds and 7 wounded. The 3 who died were all "old originals".

During the advance to the newly captured kunai-capped hill, subsequently known as Snell's Hill, each company had used 550 yards of line. Most of the requests for mortar and artillery support and most of the information passed back by telephone were routed through Corporal Giltrow,[7] a signaller, who sat placidly on the near side of the river doing his vital job with only one telephone.

A triumph such as that gained by the 2/15th was not often achieved in an attack on a fixed position. "The position was a strong one," wrote Windeyer, "held by about 100 to 150 Japanese marines. They broke and fled as our assault came upon them. . . . The result of the operations was that the whole of the enemy defences in Salankaua Plantation and Kakakog were dominated by our forces."[8]

On the right flank Handley (of the 2/13th) advanced to attack the Japanese position ahead and to cut the Tirimoro Track five minutes after Snell and Stuart moved into the gully below. He planned to attack with two platoons forward—Thomson's on the west slope of the spur on the right of the track and Webb's along the track. At 4.25 p.m. Colvin heard sounds of heavy fire coming from the direction taken by Handley. Although it had seemed to Webb earlier in the day that two platoons might be able to advance abreast to the attack, Thomson now found that his men could not crawl along the slope which narrowed steeply towards the enemy position, and were forced to join the platoons on the track. As the spur narrowed the company clambered up, sometimes on hands and knees through thick bamboo. Progress was slow and noisy until the leading men

---

[4] Lt A. W. Nesbitt, QX12842; 2/15 Bn. Sales agent; of Alderley, Qld; b. Aldershot, England, 27 Mar 1909.
[5] Lt A. C. Starmer, MC, QX8001; 2/15 Bn. Shop assistant; of Gladstone, Qld; b. Hughenden, Qld, 5 Mar 1920.
[6] Capt H. M. Douglas, QX1720; 2/15 Bn. Clerk; of Townsville, Qld; b. Townsville, 27 Nov 1920.
[7] Cpl J. Giltrow, QX5624; 2/15 Bn. Farm labourer; of Goondiwindi, Qld; b. Goondiwindi, 5 Apr 1913.
[8] 20th Brigade report.

suddenly broke through bamboo at the foot of a very steep rise and came under enemy fire from positions on the top. The two leading platoons took what cover they could, but any attempt to move forward brought down a storm of fire.

Handley now decided to attack from the left flank with Mair's platoon, but as it was forming up the enemy fired with an L.M.G. from a position down the next spur. The Australian formation was broken and Colvin at 5.15 ordered the company to pull back about 150 yards for the night and make another attempt in the morning. During this unsuccessful attack the Australians had lost nine men including Thomson wounded.

While this fierce fighting was taking place, Windeyer was faced with a grave problem. Enemy activity flared up along the Sattelberg Road and on the approaches to Scarlet Beach. He was in something of a quandary about how to guard his lengthening flank and at the same time press on to Finschhafen. Two companies of the 2/17th Battalion were available behind Kamloa in reserve, and two companies were guarding the approaches to Scarlet Beach along the Katika and Sattelberg Tracks. The actual beach-head itself was guarded from the Song to the Siki by a platoon of the 2/17th Battalion, the company of the 2/2nd Machine Gun Battalion and members of the American shore company of the 2nd E.S.B. Inside the beach-head the 60-odd men of the L.O.B. groups from the three battalions were unloading the American barges, loading motor transport, digging graves and serving as the main blood donors for the wounded.

Early on the 26th Major Pike, whose company of the 2/17th was guarding the approaches to Scarlet Beach from Katika, sent out a small patrol to go as far as Garabow if possible. About 2,500 yards to the west, after passing about sixty foxholes on a knoll, the patrol met a strong enemy position and withdrew towards Katika. About midday some thirty Japanese attacked Lieutenant McLeod's positions in the kunai west of Katika. Two Japanese were killed including an officer who was carrying a marked map and document which looked like an operation order.

In the south Windeyer was informed of these patrol clashes and ordered Pike to send out a strong patrol to attack the enemy position along the track or to bring down artillery fire upon it. A platoon set out in the afternoon towards the track laying line as it went. After about 2,000 yards the platoon tried to bring down artillery fire, but it was difficult to see whether the actual enemy position was shelled.

The difficulties of jungle warfare now became apparent to the platoon. As it moved forward an unseen enemy fired on it. Sergeant Brightwell,[9] commanding the leading section, was wounded when rounding a bend. Undaunted by the chatter of the machine-gun which had wounded his section leader, Private Moore[1] dashed forward and picked him up.

---

[9] Sgt T. P. Brightwell, NX23056; 2/17 Bn. Carpenter; of Artarmon, NSW; b. Brookvale, NSW, 15 Dec 1920. Died of wounds 27 Sep 1943.

[1] Cpl B. B. Moore, MM, NX19113; 2/17 Bn. Carpenter; of East Maitland, NSW; b. Kempsey, NSW, 25 Jul 1919.

Another bullet hit Brightwell in the foot and, with its hammer-like force, knocked both men over. Moore picked up Brightwell, but the sergeant was again hit, this time fatally. After finally carrying Brightwell out, Moore organised the withdrawal of the section. The platoon then pulled back to Katika where the company of the 2/3rd Pioneers relieved Pike's company.

At Jivevaneng, Lieutenant Main's company was busy. During the night 25th-26th September about a dozen Japanese crept up to the Australian perimeter. Three were shot and the rest ran. On the 26th patrols found that the telephone line was again cut. It seemed that the Japanese had dug in strongly about 600 yards south-west of Jivevaneng. The artillery observer gamely climbed a tree and directed fire on Sisi and the Sattelberg Road.

Along the south coast of the Huon Peninsula the 22nd Battalion spent the day patrolling, preparing new beach-heads, searching for a missing airman and establishing a small boat and steel cable ferry across the deep east arm of the Mongi. At 4.20 p.m. a liaison officer from brigade arrived at O'Connor's headquarters near the Mongi with orders to continue the advance the next day to seize Mange Point.

From documents and prisoners the Australian commanders were now gathering a clearer idea of the strength and order of battle of the enemy opposing them. The enemy force which had fled before the onslaught of Snell and Stuart, but which had held its ground before Handley, consisted largely of naval men of the *85th Garrison Unit*. Before the landing at Scarlet Beach this force had consisted of about 1,000 men. The 400 enemy actually opposing the landing had been identified on the first day as a company of the *80th Regiment* and a company of the *238th Regiment*. On the south coast documents captured at Bua by the 22nd Battalion had identified the *II/80th Battalion*. Apparently this battalion had arrived from the north in the Finschhafen area about the time of the Australian landing east of Lae. While a small portion of the battalion had disembarked at Scarlet Beach, one of the few practical landing places in the area, most of the battalion had continued in barges to the mouth of the Mongi to forestall any Australian advance east. Apprehensive of a drive from Hopoi to Finschhafen, this force was augmented by the addition of two 75-mm guns. After the landing at Scarlet Beach, the enemy, who had concentrated most of his force south of Langemak Bay in the Logaweng area to face an overland advance, was forced to make a hurried readjustment. He decided to abandon his positions south of Langemak Bay and concentrate on annihilating the invader north of the Mape River. Thus the *II/80th Battalion* had fired off most of its ammunition in one grand Guy Fawkes' night and had then withdrawn across the Mape through Quembung towards Sattelberg.

As documents began to accumulate, and were translated by the tireless American Nisei Japanese assisting Captain Maughan, it became increasingly clear that the Australian landing had taken place while the enemy were in the process of reinforcing the area. They had been caught off balance and the majority of their reinforcements had not yet arrived. By 26th September Windeyer was convinced that there were elements of at least three enemy battalions threatening his flank from the Sattelberg area. That day came definite indications that the enemy was determined, not merely to defend, but to attack. The order so obligingly carried by Captain

Saranuma, a company commander of the *80th Regiment*, who was slain before McLeod's position, turned out to be an order by Lieut-Colonel Takagi for an attack mainly by elements of the *III/80th Battalion*, with companies from the *238th Regiment* attached. The attack was to be made down the Katika and Sattelberg Tracks "from daybreak of 26 Sep . . . and [will] cut off the enemy . . . at the north-east side of Heldsbach and will annihilate them". Unfortunately for Japanese plans the two companies of the 2/17th Battalion, by aggressive patrolling along these tracks, turned the threatened attack into a succession of patrol skirmishes.

The threat to his flank was now obvious to Windeyer, and urgent reinforcement was required if Finschhafen was to be captured. On the 27th, therefore, he signalled Wootten asking for the dispatch of an additional battalion to guard the beach-head and enable him to concentrate the 20th Brigade for the capture of Finschhafen. He also asked for a squadron of tanks, hoping to use them against enemy defences in Salankaua Plantation. Between Lae, Dobodura, Milne Bay, Port Moresby and Brisbane, many signals had already been exchanged about the reinforcement of the 20th Brigade.

CHAPTER 17

THE BATTLE FOR FINSCHHAFEN

BEFORE he left Port Moresby for Brisbane on the day of the Scarlet Beach landing, General Blamey had directed General Herring to reinforce Finschhafen with the headquarters of the 9th Division and one additional brigade. Herring signalled General Wootten on the same day warning him to be ready for the move and to hand over the Lae area to General Milford as soon as possible. "Further details after conf Adm Barbey 23 Sep," signalled Herring.

On 23rd September General Chamberlin visited New Guinea Force and discussed the Finschhafen situation with General Berryman. An operation instruction from MacArthur's headquarters had been issued the previous day, stating that the Finschhafen operation was "to be so conducted as to avoid commitment of amphibious means beyond those allotted"; that is, a boat battalion was to pass to Australian command at Finschhafen on 3rd October for operations north of Finschhafen. According to the instruction, "obligations for over-water supply and air force support will be kept to a minimum". When Berryman informed Chamberlin of Blamey's intention to reinforce Windeyer immediately, the American was unable to state what craft of the amphibious force would be available. Thus it was difficult to plan reinforcement and maintenance.

While Berryman and Chamberlin were discussing the problem in Port Moresby, Herring met Barbey aboard soon after *Conyngham's* return from the landing beaches. He informed Barbey of Blamey's order and asked him to move the extra brigade forward. Describing the outcome later, Herring wrote:

> Under G.H.Q. directions, Amphforce was bound to move troops to such places as Commander Phosphorus [Blamey] might direct. Commander Amphforce, however, having information that a new order was to be issued by G.H.Q. refused, and said that he would not move an extra brigade without reference to G.H.Q. At this stage also the question of re-supply of 20 Bde at Finschhafen was considered. Before the initial landing, there had been no suggestion that there would be any trouble in this regard. The contrary was rather the case, the Commander Amphforce's representative assuring G.O.C. I Aust Corps that re-supply would take place after 3 or 4 days had elapsed from the initial landing. The position was further complicated at this stage by the departure of the Commander Amphforce from Buna to Milne Bay and the fact that no officer was left behind within reach of HQ I Aust Corps to represent him with any real authority.[1]

Barbey declined to transport the extra troops to Finschhafen on the grounds that it was against G.H.Q's orders. The new operation instruction placing a restriction on the commitment of amphibious means was read by Barbey and Herring, but Herring was not shown Annex 3 (logistics). He was surprised and upset when he later received his own copy and read Annex 3, which stated that the Allied naval force

---
[1] Report on Operations of NG Force and I Aust Corps in New Guinea from 22 Jan 43 to 8 Oct 43.

will continue to provide over-water transportation of personnel, organisation, equipment materials and supplies to Binocular [Lae] and Diminish [Finschhafen] as required by the Commander Phosphorous.

These orders were clear enough. Soon afterwards, in a letter to Blamey, Berryman wrote:

> After you left some difficulty was experienced in getting approval to move more troops into Finschhafen. It appears that a staff officer from G.H.Q. visited Admiral Barbey on 23 September and informed him that G.H.Q. did not wish the Navy to move more troops into Finschhafen. Consequently, Admiral Barbey refused requests from General Herring to move more troops. Relations, according to Comd A.N.F. [Carpender] became somewhat cool and Admiral Barbey sailed from Buna to Milne Bay.[2]

To Blamey the decisions of the conference of 17th September were clear and he could see little point in waiting until hostile strength had grown beyond that capable of being tackled by the 20th Brigade. But MacArthur's staff continued to submit that the opposition facing Windeyer was small and that, before any reinforcements were undertaken with the valuable landing craft, "information should be supplied which would indicate the strength of the hostile forces opposing 20 Aust Inf Bde".[3]

Having received contradictory instructions it was only natural that Herring and Barbey could not agree on a common course of action. After the departure of MacArthur's advanced headquarters for Brisbane two days after Blamey's had left, there was no authority left in New Guinea with power to decide the question. In a report to Blamey, on 20th October, General Mackay, the commander of N.G.F., wrote:

> It was necessary to send signals to L.H.Q. and G.H.Q. with attendant delay. Commander N.G. Force was given a definite mission, but he was not informed specifically of the transportation means that would be available, with the result that it was not practicable to make and implement a plan. It is considered that G.H.Q. should state definitely the numbers and types of craft that will be available so that the commander charged with the mission will be able to make definite plans.

Blamey himself put his finger on the spot where the trouble began when he wrote to Mackay:

> Berryman has told you, of course, that I brought up specifically, at the conference on 17th September at G.H.Q., Port Moresby, the question of transferring the second brigade of the 9th Division to Finschhafen, and it was agreed that this should be done. Apparently no preparation was made to do so. In conversation with General Herring . . . I informed him that this had been agreed to, and naturally he planned on that basis. It appears, however, that this has not been carried out, and of course our difficulties arise largely from this.

Herring informed Mackay on 24th September that he was unable to comply with Blamey's orders for lack of necessary transport. Early on the 25th Berryman signalled Chamberlin that the troublesome G.H.Q. operation instruction had only allotted a boat battalion to N.G.F. and

---

[2] Later in the war at Hollandia when talking over previous campaigns Barbey told Berryman that his only regret in the war was about Finschhafen, where he made the mistake of refusing to carry the additional troops.

[3] Commander Allied Land Forces, Report on New Guinea Operations, 4 September 1943 to 26 April 1944.

not a shore battalion, which would be required for landings "wherever boat battalion used". He asked for the complete 532nd Engineer Boat and Shore Regiment, stating that Barbey was agreeable as he felt that the 542nd E.B.S.R. would satisfy his needs for the future operations in New Britain.

With Herring, who had flown in from Dobodura, Mackay, Berryman and Admiral Carpender then went to General Kenney's headquarters for a conference. After examining G.H.Q's instruction Carpender and Kenney apparently agreed that Allied naval forces were responsible for the operational movements and necessary air cover required by Herring. The Australians then asked Carpender to provide the transport for headquarters of the 9th Division and one brigade to Scarlet Beach. On the understanding that this transport would be provided, Herring flew back to Dobodura and issued a warning order to Wootten.

On the evening of the 25th Berryman amazed Herring by informing him that Carpender had not yet made any arrangements to reinforce Windeyer, and did not propose to do so until the matter had been referred to G.H.Q. on the grounds that, at the conference with Barbey on 23rd September, Herring had agreed to such a reference. Herring was angry. "I made no such agreement," he wrote to Mackay, "but made it clear that as Admiral Barbey would not do as I asked so as to enable me to carry out my orders, I would have to refer the matter to higher authority and, if necessary, to G.H.Q. as my orders were definite."

Carpender's reply to Mackay's request, received on the 26th, stated that "transportation of additional troops to Finschhafen will be undertaken in increments by small craft staging out of Lae when Finschhafen area cleared and when my representatives, who will make reconnaissance, determine Finschhafen and Langemak harbours are usable".

Windeyer's urgent need was for more troops immediately, not when Finschhafen had fallen. Therefore, as an impasse had developed, Mackay and Berryman, late on the 26th, sent an urgent "most secret" signal to Blamey and repeated it to MacArthur. In Herring's view this long struggle to obtain shipping should have been made by New Guinea Force, not by him, and this signal should have been sent much earlier.

> After six days hard fighting (said the signal) 20 Inf Bde is on a front of 9 miles with a depth of 6 miles. Although successfully launched the operation is far from completed and enemy is resisting in numerous bunker strongholds. Frequent enemy air attacks have made the operations more difficult besides causing casualties. To carry out the mission of capturing Finschhafen and exploiting to Sio at least 60 miles along the coast, HQ 9 Aust Div and second inf bde are required. This was foreseen and ordered by you, and both commanders NGF and I Aust Corps consider it essential this be done earliest possible. . . . The question of reinfts and re-supply is now becoming acute and early action to move above forces is urgently required.

The reasons for this discreditable situation were not hard to find. Both the senior commanders, MacArthur and Blamey, had left New Guinea at the time of the Scarlet Beach landing and both liked to keep control in their own hands. There was no one on the spot to solve the problem quickly, and MacArthur's planners felt that Finschhafen would be a "pushover" and that the operation could be considered as finished. They could now settle down to working out the "logistics" of future campaigns which would use the landing craft of the naval task force.

Watching the developments in the Finschhafen area with anxiety, and those to the rear with impatience, Wootten on 27th September signalled Herring:

> Windeyer again asks for immediate reinforcement strength one bn to protect his beach-head and communications. In view situation last two days recommend div troops and bde group be sent Finschhafen immediately. If not possible then recommend one bn at once.

The reply from Corps was not very hopeful—"GHQ does not approve reinforcement Finschhafen with bde group and div tps." The reply did state, however, that Carpender had authorised Barbey "to act regarding reinforcement of one bn". It also stated that Herring would fly to meet Barbey at Milne Bay on the 28th, and that it had been suggested to Barbey that one battalion should embark from Lae on the night of 28th-29th in either one L.S.T. or two destroyers.

Along the battlefront on the east coast of the Huon Peninsula the infantry knew nothing of the strife which the question of their reinforcement was causing. On 27th September they were still engaged against stubborn resistance across the Bumi and along the Sattelberg Road. Even though their plans for the 26th had been dislocated by the aggressive action of Main's and Pike's companies of the 2/17th, the enemy was again active. Telephone lines to Jivevaneng and Zag were cut, and one of Main's patrols made contact with a Japanese patrol between Jivevaneng and Sattelberg. With a troop of artillery at his disposal, Main arranged for harassing fire on Sattelberg and along the track. Soon after dusk a platoon of screaming Japanese, blowing whistles and shouting "Tojo", rushed at the Jivevaneng defences. Six of them were killed, one on the defenders' parapets.

In the main battle area Brigadier Windeyer had the choice of pressing on where Major Handley of the 2/13th was held up or attacking through the area gained by the 2/15th. He decided on the latter course and issued orders accordingly: the 2/13th Battalion was to pass through Captain Snell's and Captain Stuart's companies and to capture the Kakakog area. At the same time as Colonel Colvin gathered his forces for the attack, Captain Angus' company (one of the two companies of the 2/15th still at Kamloa) moved up to guard the Bumi crossing, thus releasing all the 2/13th for the main attack. Handley's company would be responsible for right flank protection. From about 9.30 a.m. on the 27th the remainder of the 2/13th Battalion moved across through the 2/15th's position with Cooper's company leading and getting ready to reconnoitre Kakakog.

An hour earlier Sergeant Chowne,[4] the mortar sergeant, led a patrol which penetrated as far as Handley's company had reached in its attack

---
[4] Lt A. Chowne, VC, MM, NX24405. 2/13 and 2/2 Bns. Shirt cutter; of Willoughby, NSW; b. Sydney, 19 Jul 1920. Killed in action 25 Mar 1945.

the previous afternoon. With telephone line trailing behind him, Chowne crawled ahead to the edge of the bamboo where he could observe the Japanese position twenty yards ahead. Although he was so close to the enemy, he then directed 3-inch mortar fire on to them; he had only 15 bombs and had to be very economical. Seeing no enemy movement, Chowne returned and informed Handley that it would be possible for a platoon to attack the position.

Guided by Chowne, one platoon, led by Sergeant McVey,[5] advanced to the edge of the bamboo. Here Chowne lined them up ready to charge through the 20 yards of more open jungle. The other platoons followed at 50 yard intervals. Suddenly, and with a shout, McVey's men charged up the slope, completely surprising the enemy, some of whom could be seen sitting on top of their defences. The Japanese fled. Although seven had been seen just before the attack started, they may have been a rearguard preparing to withdraw as no discarded weapons were found. The position, shaped like a new moon, had been dug for a company to meet attack from the west, and was on a commanding feature controlling the tracks to the north and north-east down the spurs and the track to Tirimoro.

Handley's company occupied this position which soon became known as Starvation Hill. Here the company remained for seven days guarding the right flank. It took a largish party of men to carry out a stretcher, and the whole company spent one-third of each day (each man took three hours) carrying up food, water and stores from the Bumi. Everywhere there was mud and the troops attempted to cut steps in the glassy black ooze. Bully and biscuits were the fare for the seven days, and fires could not be lit for cooking.

Documents captured during the advance of the 22nd Battalion along the south coast of the Huon Peninsula raised some doubt in the minds of those who translated them as to whether all the Japanese (about 500), who had come to the Mongi about 6th September, had withdrawn or whether about 200 were still in the area. All the indications from the 22nd Battalion itself were that the entire Japanese force had withdrawn. This fact was emphasised when, after a 10-hour advance on the 27th, the battalion found deserted Japanese positions at Mange Point.[6]

By the 28th reports from the Papuans of enemy movement from Finschhafen on inland tracks to Sattelberg, observed enemy movement in Salankaua Plantation, and the noise of barge traffic each night, suggested that the Japanese might be gradually withdrawing from Finschhafen. Any exposed movement by the 2/13th and 2/15th, however, was fired at, and captured documents showed clearly that the enemy naval troops had been exhorted to stand firm and hold Finschhafen. Air reconnaissance also disclosed extensive defences in the Salankaua Plantation. Bearing

---

[5] Lt J. McVey, NX15279; 2/13 Bn. Storeman; of Northbridge, NSW; b. Newcastle on Tyne, England, 22 Nov 1920.

[6] As mentioned, Tilley Force from the 29th/46th Battalion was later sent to deal with this supposed force of 200 Japanese.

all these factors in mind, Windeyer decided that, in order to gain control of Finschhafen, Kakakog must first be captured as command of this area would make the enemy's positions in the Salankaua Plantation untenable. His orders for the 28th stated that the 2/13th Battalion would capture the Kakakog Ridge area, the 2/15th Battalion would continue probing

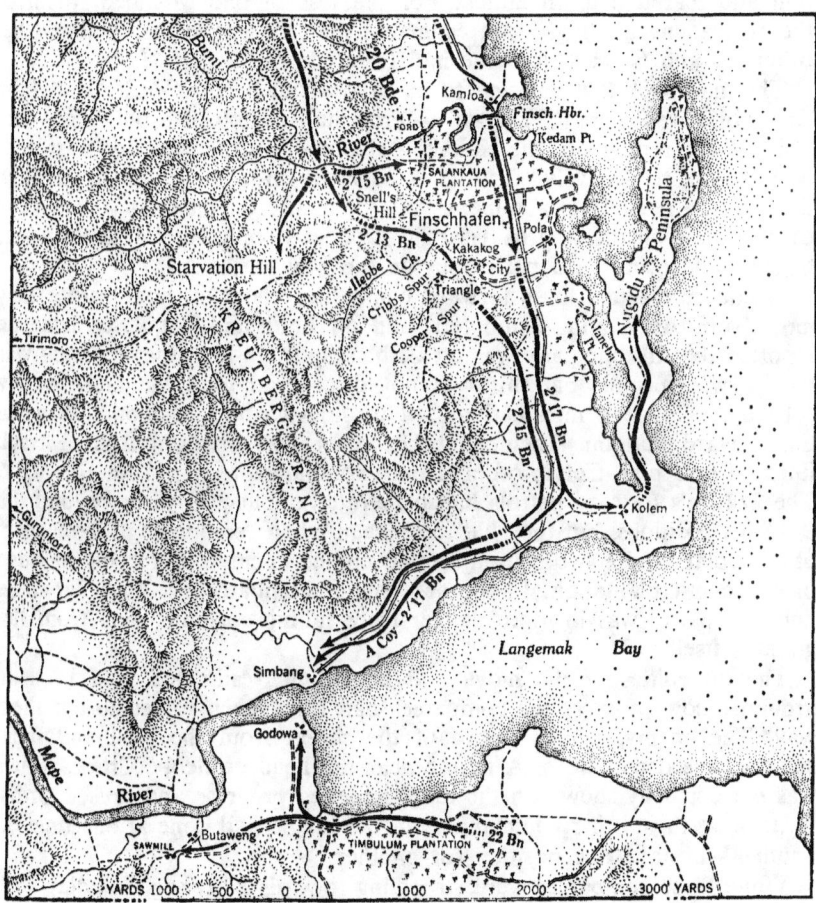

From the Bumi to Finschhafen

enemy defences, the 2/17th Battalion would remain brigade reserve, and "Sattelforce" (principally Main's and Pike's companies) under Major Maclarn[7] would control the Sattelberg Road and tracks leading to the beach-head, as well as the brigade's lines of communications.

Maclarn concentrated part of Sattelforce at Tareko where four Japanese stalking the position were killed. Between 3 p.m. and 8 p.m. about a

---

[7] Maj L. C. Maclarn, MC, NX12228; 2/17 Bn. Chain store manager; of Sydney; b. Wellington, NZ, 5 Jul 1911.

company of Japanese made three attacks on Main's isolated position at Jivevaneng. All attacks came from the same place, to the front and left. As they came in the Japanese shouted and cheered, although by the end of the fighting they had little for their cheer leaders to be pleased about. By the end of the last attack, Main's company was low in ammunition and feared a dawn attack. For the loss of one wounded so far in the Jivevaneng fighting, Main estimated that the enemy had suffered between 50 and 60 casualties; he had counted 20.

The main task that day was to be carried out by the 2/13th Battalion. The objectives were "Triangle"—three half-demolished buildings—and "City"—the remains of the Kakakog Hospital, on the west and east ends of Kakakog respectively. Cribb was to move his "D" Company through the position reached by Cooper's "A" Company on the 27th and occupy Cribb's Spur on the way to Triangle. Cooper's company would then pass through and occupy Cooper's Spur on the way to City.

Windeyer reached these forward companies about an hour before they moved off. At 2 p.m. Cribb left, and an hour and a quarter later he reported that his company was on Cribb's Spur. In fact, the company was on the wrong spur, but this was not discovered until the morrow. By 4.10 p.m. Cooper's men had passed through Cribb's position, but when the forward platoon (Lieutenant Green's[8]) was fired on from a track junction at 5 p.m. Colvin ordered both companies to dig in for the night. The 2/13th's forward patrols had penetrated about 300 yards beyond the 2/15th's positions, but they had been seen when "scrounging" three pairs of binoculars and a sword from an unoccupied enemy position on the edge of a coconut plantation. In the subsequent bombardment by a Japanese gun, the patrol was in more danger from falling coconuts than from the gunnery itself.

The difficulties of the move had been under-estimated, and in their arduous, slow progress the companies had often been forced to cut their way. The enemy seemed aware of the threat from the west and their snipers caused casualties. A ravine near the head of Ilebbe Creek, which was not correctly shown on the map, impeded progress and caused Cribb to do what most other commanders in the jungle had done at one time or another—mistake one position for another.

While these companies were struggling towards Kakakog, Handley sent out Lieutenant Webb's platoon from Starvation Hill to patrol north-east towards battalion headquarters. After about 150 yards the platoon ran into heavy fire. The leading men of Lance-Sergeant Arnott's[9] section were within ten yards of the enemy position when the Japanese opened up. Private Thorpe[1] was wounded in the leg. Arnott, although wounded himself, applied a field dressing to Thorpe's wound before crawling out

---

[8] Lt D. H. Green, NX58329; 2/13 Bn. Grazier; of Nyngan, NSW; b. Dubbo, NSW, 1 May 1919.
[9] L-Sgt M. R. Arnott, NX21679; 2/13 Bn. Farm manager; of Wallendbeen, NSW; b. Strathfield, NSW, 9 Jan 1911.
[1] Pte R. Thorpe, NX24421; 2/13 Bn. Labourer; of Marrickville, NSW; b. Nottingham, England, 16 Jun 1904. Killed in action 28 Sep 1943.

through the bamboo. A stretcher bearer, Sergeant Shambler,[2] then tried to reach Thorpe, but he was hit five yards from Thorpe and died later. Handley then decided to mortar the Japanese position. Thorpe was killed by Japanese bullets while he lay there. An accurate mortar bombardment enabled the Australians to extricate their three dead and six wounded, all from Arnott's section. Colvin now ordered Handley to "sit tight" and not to worry about attacking the enemy post between the company and the battalion. In the following days, however, the company did harass the Japanese position which seemed to be occupied by about a company, and Chowne again brought down mortar fire on it.

Back in high places the struggle about reinforcement continued. MacArthur's headquarters replied on 27th September to Mackay's signal of the previous day by stating that "before definite decisions are reached further information is requested as to the size of the hostile forces which have been encountered". On the same day Mackay sent another signal to Blamey asking for the immediate dispatch of one battalion to Finschhafen. Another conference was held on the 27th between Carpender, Mackay and Berryman. When the Australians stressed the urgency of reinforcing Windeyer, Carpender stated that Barbey should be able to begin moving troops into Finschhafen in three to five days, starting with about 800 men on the first night and continuing with a similar number every second or third night until all were moved. Writing to Herring on the same day, Mackay said:

> I consider that the move of troops as above will meet your requirements. . . . My own feeling is that our representations will result in a distinct improvement although we may not get everything we ask for.

On the 28th General Herring, Brigadier Sutherland and Brigadier Bierwirth[3] entered a plane at Dobodura, intending to fly to Milne Bay to see Barbey and try to hasten the shipping of men and supplies to Finschhafen. When taking off the aircraft crashed and Sutherland, in whom Herring had placed great trust, was killed. It began to seem on the 28th that a battalion would soon sail to join Windeyer. Carpender himself flew to Milne Bay to give effect to his promise of the previous day. In reply to G.H.Q's request for information about enemy strength, Mackay replied late on the 28th:

> 20 Bde is operating with expedition over considerable area and difficult country and has to guard its dumps and beach-head. Object is to destroy enemy and not allow him to evacuate. Windeyer has captured Japanese order instructing bn combat team attack Australians from direction Sattelberg on 26 Sep, but attack not yet developed and Windeyer has requested reinforcement one bn as soon as possible. On capture Finschhafen intend exploit to Sio with small craft and consider one inf bde after a period of hard fighting not sufficient to accomplish mission with expedition. Huon

---

[2] Sgt L. E. R. Shambler, NX16855; 2/13 Bn. Clerk; of Newcastle, NSW; b. Mosman, NSW, 29 Sep 1910. Died of wounds 28 Sep 1943.

[3] Lt-Gen R. Bierwirth, CBE, VX289. Comd 25 Bde 1940-41; AA & QMG 6 Div 1941-42; DAQMG III Corps 1943, I Corps and NGF 1943-44, First Army 1944-45. Regular soldier; of Melbourne; b. Adelaide, 30 Jan 1899.

Peninsula is defensive flank and vital for [New Britain] operation. The reasons against increasing the force at Finschhafen were both fully understood and considered before requesting movement of additional inf bde, but to date we have been prevented from making good our casualties which to 26 Sep exceed 320. Troops required for Finschhafen are already at Lae so there is no increase in the number being maintained from Buna. Japanese strength estimated maximum 1,800 minimum 500. . . .[4]

Meanwhile at 11 a.m. on the 28th Blamey had signalled MacArthur reminding him of the agreement of 17th September that an additional brigade and Wootten's headquarters should be sent in if necessary; Blamey considered it most desirable that Wootten should personally direct the movement to Sio to establish radar there. The possibility of a Japanese counter movement should not be entirely ruled out. He would be glad if MacArthur would "concur in dispatching additional requirement". MacArthur's reply, sent at 6.15 p.m. that day, said that to accelerate the movement of additional brigades and 9th Division Headquarters "would cause disarrangement of amended program upon which we are engaged. If tactical necessity require it will of course be done at once. I am sure, however, that this is not the case and that Finschhafen within a reasonable time will be in our hands without serious loss."

On the 29th G.H.Q. informed Mackay that Carpender was being directed to move an additional battalion to Finschhafen at the earliest possible date. Carpender, however, had taken the quickest means to end the unfortunate controversy and had already determined that some reinforcement was necessary. On the day before G.H.Q's final authorisation he had sent Commander Adair to Herring's headquarters with full authority to act for Barbey and arrange for the dispatch of reinforcements.

Wootten, impatient to have the matter solved quickly and sensibly, learnt of the decisions of those above him in this manner. At 4 p.m. on the 28th he was advised that two A.P.D's would arrive that night. At 6 p.m. he was informed that no naval craft were available. He then decided to send the headquarters of the 24th Brigade and one battalion by small craft to join the 22nd Battalion at Mange Point and advance on Finschhafen from the south. Finally, at 8 p.m. he was told that the first L.S.T. to finish unloading at Lae that night would be sent to "G" Beach to load troops, who would then be taken to Buna for transfer to A.P.D's and movement to Finschhafen. Soon after 2.30 a.m. on the 29th, when torrential rain was falling over the battle area, the L.S.T. pulled in and by 3.20 a.m. the 2/43rd Battalion and a platoon of the 2/13th Field Company were on board and ready to depart for Buna. Colonel Joshua was warned by Wootten that his probable role would be "to take over protection of beach maintenance area including seizing and holding Sattelberg".

During the 29th torrential rain continued in the battle area. This increased the difficulty of carrying supplies forward and wounded out, particularly as the sappers had been unable to rig up a flying-fox over the

---

[4] These estimates were in fact far too low.

Bumi. The difficulties applied mainly to Handley's men who had suffered nine casualties on the previous day. Haggard men juggled stretchers down treacherous and slippery tracks to the Bumi, while others crawled up with bully and biscuits and ammunition. Both the 2/13th and 2/15th Battalions sent out several probing patrols on the 29th, but by the afternoon it was obvious that surprise had been lost and that the enemy was aware of the Australian intentions. Cooper's patrols, during the morning and early afternoon, met nothing but trouble as they attempted to find their way towards Kakakog spur and Triangle. Enemy artillery inflicted some casualties, and patrols were unable to make headway. Worried about the outflanking movements, Colvin at 4 p.m. ordered Cooper to withdraw to Cribb's position.

Patrols from the 2/15th met with better luck. Two from Stuart's company penetrated east to Ilebbe Creek without meeting any Japanese. The forward section of Lieutenant Nesbitt's platoon went about 50 yards into Salankaua Plantation and about 20 yards from a bridge. Nesbitt then patrolled about 100 yards above the bridge and met a patrol from Angus' company which had found a deserted but well-built enemy position 50 yards below the crossing—obviously the one which had opposed the original crossing. Further movement by the 2/15th was stopped by enfilading fire from Kakakog.

Windeyer's main headache at this time was caused by the supply problem. Engineers, pioneers and infantry were all carrying supplies and ammunition to the forward troops along the precipitous slippery slope and were carrying the wounded down to the jeep road. The water problem was acute and Windeyer was particularly worried because few water containers were available. In spite of all the difficulties, however, he was now becoming a trifle impatient as his forward troops were not keeping ahead of the supply situation. No real progress was being made although the rations, carried up at the expense of so much sweat and labour, were being consumed. Windeyer therefore decided that the plan of outflanking Kakakog from the west should be abandoned.

During these frustrating days the Salvation Army and Y.M.C.A. were, as ever, up with the troops. Of all the admirable religious and welfare organisations that looked after the troops' physical and spiritual comfort, few could rival the "Salvos". There are few Australian ex-soldiers who will not put a coin in the Salvos' box when it is passed round on the street corner or in the pub, for it brings back memories of help during bitter fighting and tough going. One soldier who took part in the fighting across the Bumi wrote soon afterwards:

> Another army came down to the Bumi—its weapons a coffee urn, its captain a Good Samaritan. Proudly he hoisted his unit's flag.[5] . . . He came not to reproach us for past sins or preach of the men we might have been. It is ideal, practical Christianity; he succoured the wounded and sick, revived the tired and weary; his was a happy little half-way tavern for those that passed.

---

[5] Its emblem was a Red Shield. Equally well known was the accompanying notice—a leaping kangaroo and the words, "Hop in, you're welcome."

Windeyer was now becoming more concerned about his right flank. A Papuan Infantry patrol made contact with a large enemy force moving east along the tracks in the Kumawa and Sisi areas, while Papuan headquarters saw four Japanese officers and 50 men moving east towards Sattelberg. Reports from natives were also beginning to reach Windeyer through Colonel Allan, who had been collecting native carriers and sending out native observers since the landing. By the 29th Allan was able to attach the first substantial line of carriers to the troops on the Sattelberg Road. Allan's hard work and the confidence which his return inspired among the local natives were now paying dividends. Native reports on the 29th supplemented those of the Papuan soldiers to the effect that large numbers of Japanese were withdrawing from the Finschhafen, Langemak Bay and Logaweng areas and were passing through Tirimoro, Gurunkor and Kumawa towards Sattelberg. Although this news possibly meant that the task of gaining Finschhafen would be easier, it also caused concern for the security of the maintenance area at Scarlet Beach. The news that the 2/43rd Battalion was on the way was therefore very welcome.

After leaving "G" Beach at 3.30 a.m. on the 29th the 2/43rd Battalion reached Buna fourteen hours later, and left for the battle area in three A.P.D's soon after dusk. The ships arrived off Scarlet Beach at 2 o'clock next morning, and by dawn the battalion had been guided to its assembly area. A tank reconnaissance party landed with the 2/43rd, but lack of shipping made it impossible for Wootten to send the tanks Windeyer wanted. The A.P.D's, after landing 838 troops, took away 134 walking wounded. Although this relieved the harassed and overworked medical authorities to some extent, the A.P.D's were unable to stay long enough to take off the more serious cases, some of whom had been held at the M.D.S. and C.C.S. for over a week. Hearing that maintenance of Finschhafen was now to be his responsibility, Wootten wasted no time and ordered six L.C.M's belonging to the Engineer Special Brigade to return from Finschhafen for resupply missions.

When Joshua landed, Broadbent handed him an instruction from Windeyer. "You will," said the instruction, "relieve the troops known as Sattelforce. . . . This relief to be completed as speedily as possible to enable 2/17th Bn to concentrate for operations against Finschhafen." Upon the completion of the relief, Joshua would control all routes leading into the Scarlet Beach and Heldsbach areas and would prepare to capture Sisi and Sattelberg. This instruction was elaborated when, at 9 a.m. on the 30th, Windeyer and Joshua conferred. By the end of the day Captain Siekmann's company of the 2/43rd had relieved Pike's company in the Katika area, Captain Grant's company relieved Main's company at Jivevaneng, while the other two companies were at the mouth of the Song and at Zag. During the morning Main's men were again attacked by about a platoon, but the enemy soon retired, leaving three dead. When Main handed over, leaving six of his men there as guides, his company had had three men wounded and had counted 30 dead Japanese. The company had maintained a magnificent defence in its isolated position, often short of ammunition and food. Water was obtained, from a spring about 200 yards from the perimeter.

In the afternoon Angus' and Stuart's companies of the 2/15th advanced towards Ilebbe Creek and by dusk both were dug in on a knoll facing what appeared to be a strong Japanese defensive position on a ridge east of the creek. This advance, by confining the enemy to the east side of the creek, made it possible to use the motor transport ford and bring the jeephead south of the river. With the whole of the 2/17th Battalion now available as a reserve Captain Sheldon's company of the 2/17th relieved Major Newcomb's company of the 2/15th at Kamloa, thus enabling the 2/15th, apart from its two forward companies, to concentrate near the ford.

At 6.20 a.m. on the 30th Colvin visited the two forward companies of the 2/13th. When he returned to his headquarters he telephoned Windeyer that the companies were not far enough south and not high enough to attack City or Triangle from their present positions, and he was dubious about an attack from the west as it would take Cooper's men a long time to move around to higher ground. Windeyer, then at Scarlet Beach conferring with Joshua, felt that he must again see the area for himself.

While Windeyer was on his way south, Colvin's patrols were active. One under Lieutenant Angel set out at 9.40 a.m. to reconnoitre a route south towards Triangle, and returned at 1.20 p.m. having reached the bottom of the spur leading up to Triangle without seeing any signs of the enemy. A few minutes later Windeyer arrived, and at 1.30 p.m. he and Colvin surveyed the ground towards City and Triangle from the 2/13th's observation post. They decided that an attack from the north-west would be feasible, using Angel's approach as the forming-up place.

The plan for an attack at midday next day soon took shape. The 2/13th would attack with Cribb on the right towards Triangle and Deschamps on the left towards City, with Cooper's company in reserve in the initial stages of the attack. The 2/15th Battalion would concentrate round Snell's Hill as brigade reserve; while the 2/17th would have two companies ready to exploit into Salankaua Plantation.

In the afternoon Angel's platoon moved cautiously out to cover the forming-up place already discovered by him behind a small knoll. By dusk the platoon, with a telephone, was in position, and reported that the route which the two companies would follow towards the forming-up place next morning was mostly covered from view. About the same time, however, a more ominous report was received from Cooper to the effect that the Japanese could be heard digging in on the next spur about 100 yards away.

Now that the 2/13th Battalion had a clearer idea of where it was, and had better land communications since the occupation of the M.T. ford, Windeyer felt that the battalions were at last grouped for what he believed would be a series of decisive battalion actions. It was felt within the brigade that 1st October would be a decisive day.

Just before first light Deschamps sent Lieutenant Hall's platoon to a small kunai knoll to the south-east on the east bank of Ilebbe Creek to secure the ground ahead of the forming-up place, after which the platoon would join its company during the advance. At 7.30 a.m. the companies began to move. As Deschamps left, Cribb moved in, while Cooper took Cribb's place.

The assaulting companies were warned that an air-strike on enemy positions by Bostons and Vengeances would take place between 11 a.m. and midday. Twenty guns would fire a concentration of 30 rounds a gun immediately after the air strike, which would be signalled by pyrotechnics from the aircraft. At the same time Handley would mortar the enemy who had been attempting during the night to get round his positions. The companies were warned to be in position by 10.45 a.m.

Ten minutes before that time all were awaiting the attack, glad that something decisive was likely to happen after trying days of uncertainty. From Hall's platoon, about 300 yards ahead of the forming-up place on the reverse slope of a kunai knoll at the end of a spur running up to City about 250 yards away, some grenade or mortar fire could be heard from 10 a.m. At 10.45 a.m. Hall reported that he had two casualties and that every time he made any forward move towards the top of the kunai knoll enemy machine-guns from City sent the platoon to earth. At the same time, Hall informed Deschamps that he could see an enemy position on the east bank of Ilebbe Creek near the Salankaua Road; the enemy was moving round in the position, which was screened by heavy timber.

In his planning for the attack, Windeyer had requested air support not before 11 a.m. and not after midday. This would be followed by artillery concentrations on the targets as the companies attacked. For some reason, inexplicable to Windeyer and his men, the air attack began at 10.35 a.m., about half an hour before the scheduled time. Ten Vultee Vengeances and eight Bostons dive-bombed and strafed the Salankaua Plantation and Kakakog areas. Apparently they did no damage, but they did at least keep the Japanese heads down while Cribb and Deschamps were getting into position. It had been so often stressed in the lessons from jungle warfare that the air force must, as far as possible in any set attack, abide by the attacking infantry's timetable; this failure to do so, after all the experience round Salamaua and Lae, was regrettable. Fortunately the infantry were already on the forming-up place so that when the aircraft disappeared at 11 a.m. the artillery and supporting arms opened up their clamour as a background to the advance of the two companies at 11.15.

Deschamps received Hall's report about the enemy on his left flank about a quarter of an hour before zero. Fearing an attack on his exposed flank if he advanced straight south towards City, Deschamps changed his plan at the last minute. To his request that the company should take this position first, Colvin replied that the position could be included in the company's left flank, but that the battalion's attack must go in on City and Triangle as arranged.

Deciding that the position must be captured, Deschamps committed the whole of his company, except for Hall's platoon, forward on Hall's Spur. Thus, while Cribb's men advanced south as planned, Deschamps' switched direction and advanced due east. Angel's platoon reached Ilebbe Creek without interference. Sergeant Crawford's platoon followed, but came under heavy fire from enemy positions to the north and north-east and suffered a few casualties before dispersing behind whatever cover they could find in the bed of the creek. Deschamps, following with his headquarters, quickly withdrew Crawford's rear section and moved back with the object of rejoining his two platoons from another direction. Unable to do this, he tried to join Hall's platoon but took the wrong spur and ran into an enemy pocket well up towards Triangle.

The covering fire for the attack on Kakakog was now in full throat with the artillery firing concentrations on Kakakog and the Vickers sweeping the Salankaua Plantation. The enemy was retaliating from many points east of Ilebbe Creek and from Kakakog Ridge with heavy small arms fire. Soon the harsh coughing of the Japanese machine-guns was intermingled with the crash of bombs as they began to mortar the two beleaguered platoons in Ilebbe Creek.

Meanwhile Cribb's company was having a torrid time. After the finish of the air attack the company advanced south towards Triangle with two platoons forward (Lieutenant MacDougal's and Lieutenant Birmingham's) and the third (Lieutenant Pope's) following 75 yards behind. Expecting that the other company would be advancing on the left, Cribb suddenly realised that all was not well when, as his leading men drew level with Hall's platoon, fire from the direction of Hall's Spur was poured into his company's flank. Sliding down a 12-foot slope the men reached a narrow track. After advancing 25 yards beyond the creek, MacDougal's platoon was halted by snipers, while Birmingham's was pinned down by fire from Triangle. Pope's men had the misfortune to be hit by their own artillery and three were killed.

With both companies pinned down and out of communication there was little Colvin could do except to send Cooper's company to the forming-up place to be ready for anything as soon as some information became available. When Lieutenant Murray, the Intelligence officer, told his battalion commander what was happening, Colvin ordered Cooper to send one platoon round the left and engage the enemy, thus allowing the two platoons in the creek to attack. By 12.10 p.m. telephone communication was established by Cribb, who asked that the artillery fire should be lifted about 100 yards to the right. A quarter of an hour later Corporal Kennedy[6] came up from the creek and reported that Crawford was organising an attack as the two platoons could not remain much longer in the creek because of the steady drain of casualties. Colvin told Kennedy to return and inform Crawford and Angel that Lieutenant Ryan's[7] platoon would

---

[6] Sgt R. J. Kennedy, NX16361; 2/13 Bn. Salesman-storeman; of Manly, NSW; b. West Maitland, NSW, 12 Aug 1915.
[7] Lt J. W. Ryan, NX14881; 2/13 Bn. Motor mechanic; of Inverell, NSW; b. Inverell, 4 Mar 1919.

be supporting them from the left. At 12.30 p.m. Ryan moved north-east from the hill on to the flat and formed up ready to attack.

Always when a situation seemed desperate the Australian Army appeared to have the knack of producing a leader of the necessary character. This time it was Crawford. With Angel's aid he organised the five sections

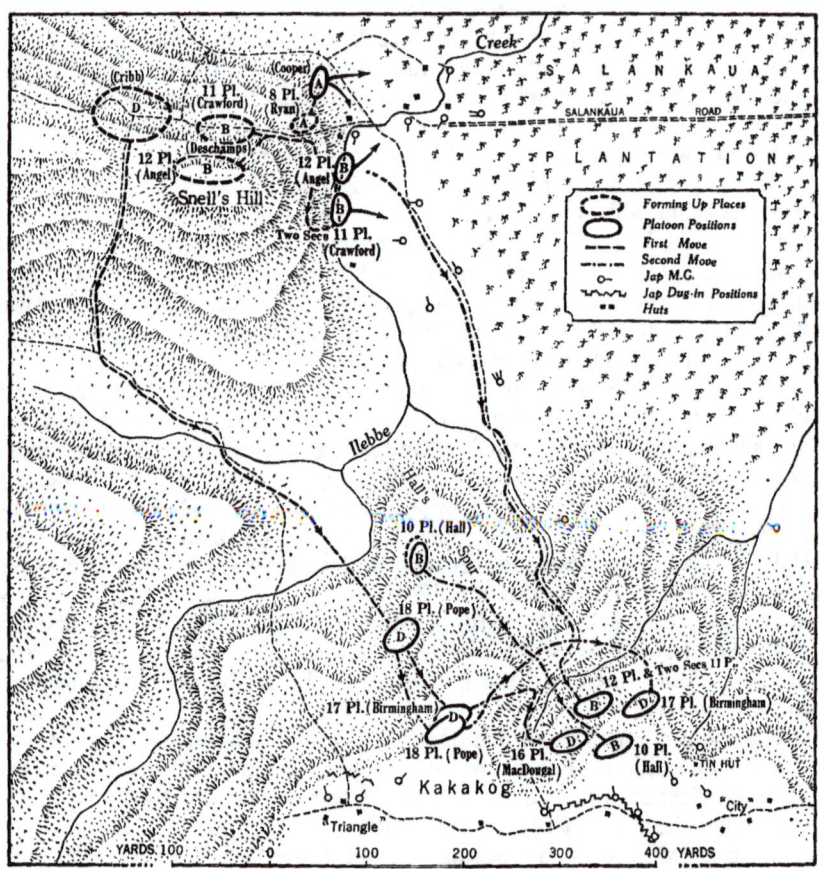

The 2/13th Battalion's attack on Kakakog to 3 p.m. 1st October

for a direct attack. Feeling that they could not wait much longer, Crawford arranged that when he threw a grenade over the top the two platoons would come out of the creek and, with fixed bayonets, rush the enemy post. Suddenly Private Rolfe[8] stood up on the bank of the creek and, firing his Bren from the hip, silenced one of the most troublesome posts. At the same time, Ryan's men left their forming-up place and immediately came under heavy fire which hit three men. One section

[8] L-Cpl A. J. Rolfe, DCM, NX86223; 2/13 Bn. Wool classer; of Goulburn, NSW; b. Nowra, NSW, 6 Nov 1921.

dashed to the right into the creek, hoping to cross and attack, while the other forward section got into a small re-entrant on the left from which it was able to fire on the enemy position which was holding up the remainder of the platoon. Enemy snipers were also inflicting casualties from the tree tops. Crawford divided his platoon and himself took command of the left flank, adjoining Angel, while Corporal Clothier,[9] who carried on although wounded, led on the right.

Crawford's grenade exploded. The men scrambled out of the creek, their bayonets gleaming. Charging across the open ground towards the main enemy position near a hut on the bend of the creek, they came under heavy enemy fire, but the 40 yards' charge could not be stopped. Some Japanese fled, dodging among the coconut palms. After putting his platoon in position facing Kakakog, Crawford went back to see how the wounded had fared. At the hut was the Japanese post which had been bypassed, and was still in action. While this post was being engaged Crawford was wounded. Angel also was wounded, but he and Crawford carried on until the action was over. Rolfe silenced another enemy post with his Bren, but was wounded when advancing on another. Despite the casualties the spirit of the Australian charge carried all before it. With bayonets and small arms fire the Japanese defenders were killed. In the close fighting the wounded Angel actually came to grips with a Japanese against a wall of the hut, but the Japanese was quickly bayoneted by one of Angel's men.

Swinging to the right and still under fire from enemy positions farther out in the plantation, this gallant band of men, under its wounded but inspired leaders, rapidly covered the 30 yards to the second enemy post and destroyed the enemy there. As tree snipers were still proving troublesome, Colvin ordered Cooper to fire a Bren from the hillside and sweep the tree tops. This silenced the snipers. There was still one enemy post farther north on the east bank of Ilebbe Creek which continued to fire on Crawford's and Angel's men. Twelve bombs from a 2-inch mortar helped to keep this post quieter while a section from Ryan's platoon, under cover of the bombs, moved round on the left towards the post. The Japanese did not wait, and, like a few who got away from the fury of Crawford's attack, they fled east into the plantation. About 50 Japanese were killed in the main attack. The two platoons lost 4 killed and 17 wounded, while Ryan's platoon had 2 killed and 4 wounded.

At this substantial cost of 27 men the battalion's left flank was cleared. More extensive reconnaissance on the preceding days might have disclosed these enemy positions. Colvin had asked for air photographs of the plantation area, but only one set was available in the brigade and these were brought forward by Windeyer on the day of the attack. Many other battle commanders, confronted with Deschamps' problem at the last moment, would have reacted similarly. Although experience has proved the danger of changing a plan or a direction of attack at the last moment,

---

[9] Sgt L. A. Clothier, NX21765; 2/13 Bn. Fitter and turner; of Leichhardt, NSW; b. Sydney, 8 Mar 1919.

it may well have been that there was no alternative. Deschamps believed it would have been fatal to advance on the original objective leaving his left flank open, and he was the only man who could really decide.

By 12.55 p.m. the position across Ilebbe Creek was mopped up. As the platoon commanders were both wounded, Lieutenant Murray, who was on the spot, sent the remnants of Crawford's platoon followed by Angel's to join Hall's platoon. Ryan watched the captured ground with sections on both sides of the creek. At 1 p.m. Deschamps set out from battalion headquarters to join Hall. As he arrived, just before his other two platoons, Japanese tracer bullets set fire to the grass round Hall's position. The Japanese laughed as the men leapt out of their holes to beat out the fire.

While the fight across Ilebbe Creek was raging Cribb's company continued to meet strong opposition and found progress difficult. The enemy posts at Triangle were on top of a cliff-face hidden by thick undergrowth. Having failed to find a feasible approach to Triangle, and held up by fire from City and a tin shed as well at Triangle, Cribb reorganised his men and moved south-east towards City. At 1 p.m. six Japanese were observed crawling up to attack company headquarters which, in its movement south-east, had now reached a position south of Hall's position. Sergeant Morris,[10] standing and firing his Bren from his shoulder, killed four and the other two were killed by rifle fire. Five of these Japanese had been acting as magazine carriers for the first one who had a machine-gun.

Colvin was anxious to push on, but he considered that because the country was so thick it would be useless to attempt to operate on more than a two-company front. As it was, his leading companies had become disorganised and, instead of advancing in line, one was now behind the other. At 1.25 p.m. Colvin told Windeyer what was happening and asked whether he could have a company from the 2/15th to take over the Ilebbe Creek area as he intended to hold Cooper's company ready to push through the other two. Windeyer agreed and Snell's company of the 2/15th was sent forward to take over from Cooper's.

By 2.30 p.m., with artillery, for which Lieutenant McKeddie[1] of the 2/12th Field Regiment was a fearless observer, bombarding Triangle and City, Cribb was on the move again towards City. Lieutenant Ash's[2] platoon relieved Hall's, thus enabling Deschamps' battered but reunited company to move forward on the left of Cribb. While MacDougal's platoon held the present company position, Pope's moved to high ground on the right of City and Birmingham's to some high ground on the left to support Deschamps' advance. Throughout the afternoon the Australians continued to lose men. The task of evacuating the wounded was a heavy one.

---

[10] Lt F. W. Morris, NX18256. 2/13 and 2/6 Bns. Grazier-horsebreaker; of Denman, NSW; b. Muswellbrook, NSW, 22 Dec 1913. Killed in action 9 Mar 1945.

[1] Capt J. E. McKeddie, MC, VX17668; 2/12 Fd Regt. Clerk; of East Malvern, Vic; b. Meeniyan, Vic, 25 Nov 1902.

[2] Capt W. P. Ash, NX66507. 2/13 Bn; Legal Officer 7 Bde 1944-45. Barrister-at-law; of Turramurra, NSW; b. Neutral Bay, NSW, 19 Sep 1915.

Engineers and pioneers, whose arduous task it was to bring up supplies and ammunition, cheerfully volunteered to carry the wounded men up the hill to the 2/15th's area and then down to the jeephead south of the M.T. ford.

By 3 p.m. when Snell's company had taken over Cooper's area including the Ilebbe Creek positions, Colvin exhorted his two company commanders to push on as fast as possible, if necessary by attacking from the lower slopes. Both companies, however, found it difficult to move forward because of the heavy fire from positions on Kakakog Ridge and because the country over which they were advancing was a series of spurs and gullies with each spur covered by enemy fire.

Reconnoitring for the best line of advance, Deschamps climbed a hill to the east of his troops and saw enemy troops near a tin hut on a spur running in to City. From his position the hut was only 25 yards away, but fire from it and from City prevented any advance. Trying to reconnoitre the tin hut area from the flat to the north, he met another enemy post. He decided, therefore, to attack the tin hut by advancing along the ridge through Cribb's positions under cover of concentrated fire of all his Brens.

The Brens were being collected when the alert enemy mortared the gathering place and inflicted some casualties. Finally, however, the Brens were installed on the ridge where they began their vicious clatter, and Hall's men began to advance. Soon after the start the Japanese fired heavily with mortars and machine-guns and stopped the move. For an hour and a half Deschamps tried all routes to the ridge, but could not advance. Finally, at 5 p.m. he recalled Hall and telephoned Colvin. Windeyer, who was with Colvin, then decided that it was useless to go on battering at the stubborn Kakakog Ridge with the same troops and Deschamps was ordered to hold his ground. During this afternoon of frustrating search for lines of advance the company had suffered more casualties, including Deschamps wounded. Of the officers in the company only Hall was left unscathed and he had had his batman and platoon sergeant wounded beside him. Windeyer warned the 2/15th to be ready to carry out the attack next day but not until he had made a reconnaissance and given further orders.

Cribb's men had no more success than Deschamps' during the long afternoon. By 3 p.m. the forward platoons were again pinned down. At this stage of the action the companies were intermingled—Pope's platoon was on the right of the line, then MacDougal's, then Deschamps' three platoons with Hall's platoon in the lead, and finally Birmingham's on the left of the line. For two hours Cribb's company sought means of advancing, but on each occasion heavy fire from the excellently sited enemy positions on Kakakog Ridge stopped the advance after a few yards. A steady drain of casualties was having its effect. By sheer slugging, however, the company had made some little progress when the order came for the two forward companies, plus Cooper's company which had now come up, to hold the ground gained. When the forward platoons came back a short distance, crawling on hands and knees, to join the three-company perimeter, there were further casualties. A Japanese with a machine-gun sneaked on to the east end of the spur which the forward platoons were leaving and, firing along the track, wounded Pope and a few others as they stood up. While Morris carried Pope to dead ground the firing, including grenades, continued and one of the medical orderlies was wounded. Pope was unfortunate enough to be badly wounded by a Japanese counter-attack on a position which he could doubtless have safely held had he not been pulled back. For the loss of 10 killed and 70 wounded, the 2/13th Battalion had killed between 80 and 100 Japanese during the fight for Kakakog on 1st October.

While the depleted forward companies were digging in for the night the wounded were on the way back. By 6.30 p.m. all the walking wounded had reached battalion headquarters and the last of the stretcher cases had been collected. Throughout the day the stretcher bearers had carried out with traditional calm their task of attending to the wounded and carrying them back under fire to where weary sappers and pioneers took them out to the jeephead. Darkness had fallen before all the wounded were brought out. All day long Sergeant Halcroft[3] had been tending the wounded. At one stage he had been stunned by the blast of a mortar bomb but after recovering, he continued his work during darkness. Finding one man so badly wounded that he could not be moved, Halcroft stayed with him throughout the night trying to save his life even though he knew the Japanese had the wounded covered.

The results of the fighting on 1st October appeared inconclusive. The 2/13th Battalion had not gained its objective, although it was close to it. The threat to Kakakog, however, had the effect of causing the Japanese to abandon some positions in Salankaua Plantation. Towards last light, when they were seen moving towards Pola, patrols from the 2/17th Battalion crossed Ilebbe Creek and found abandoned positions in the plantation, although the Japanese were still resisting at the mouth of the Bumi. The night was quiet except for harassing fire from the Australian artillery.

Evidence of Japanese evacuation of the Finschhafen area was seen by the 22nd Battalion during its rapid advance on 1st October. At 6 a.m. the battalion began to advance from Kasanga, which it had reached the previous day, and two hours later the head of the column reached Nasingnatu. One company then patrolled northwards towards Logaweng, and another led the advance towards Dreger Harbour. By midday the two companies were north of Dreger Harbour and were ordered to patrol towards Timbulum, where natives reported large numbers of Japanese, and to make contact with the 20th Brigade. In the afternoon patrols returned from Timbulum and from 1,000 yards north of Logaweng without making any contact with the Japanese or the Australians. By the late afternoon Colonel O'Connor was able to report, in reply to a question from Brigadier Edgar, that Dreger Harbour was secured, but that facilities for barges appeared limited because of the narrowness of the channels.

---

[3] Sgt J. R. Halcroft, MM, NX16075; 2/13 Bn. Grocer; of Stanmore, NSW; b. Sydney, 19 Oct 1917.

Early on 2nd October the 2/17th Battalion found signs that there would be no opposition. The mouth of the Bumi was unoccupied and by 9.15 a.m. a company of the 2/17th had formed a bridgehead across the river with one platoon at Kedam Point. Two companies then passed through, and soon after 9.30 a.m. they were approaching Pola, having met no opposition in the Salankaua Plantation.

At this time the 2/13th Battalion was still in the same position, although patrols had scoured the base of Kakakog Ridge. No chances were taken, however, as it was thought that the enemy might be holding fire until the Australians were descending the exposed slope towards Kakakog. A few rounds of artillery were therefore fired on to the Japanese positions of yesterday. As there were no reactions the 2/13th Battalion was ordered to occupy Kakakog and to mop up and patrol on the Kreutberg Range. The 2/15th Battalion was ordered to move to Simbang, and the 2/17th Battalion to continue its advance along the main Finschhafen Road to Kolem, mopping up as it went.

By 11.25 a.m. Cooper's company of the 2/13th reported that it was moving up the track into Kakakog and that it was in touch with the 2/17th Battalion moving south on the left. At midday Ash's platoon entered City where a lone Japanese defender, wounded, was found sitting dejectedly on the steps of a battered hut. A patrol sent to Triangle found hurried signs of evacuation as well as dead Japanese and much equipment. "Imperial Marines and the spirit of Samurai had taken advantage of the night and fled," wrote one of the men first into Kakakog. In the Australian Army it was universally believed that the marines were Japan's crack troops. The 20th Brigade felt, justifiably, that in overcoming such a formidable adversary the seal had been fixed to its reputation for fighting efficiency gained against Germans and Italians.

While the 2/13th Battalion was occupying Kakakog, the 2/15th was bypassing Kakakog and the forward elements of the 2/17th were entering Finschhafen and Maneba Point. Windeyer did not think it desirable to report the capture of Finschhafen until Maneba Point was reached. The diarist of the 2/13th Battalion wrote that at 12.15 p.m. the "Brig" said that "Finsch" could be regarded as having "fallen", although it was extremely hard to know just where "Finsch" was. By 2 p.m. the 2/17th was at Kolem. While Main's company patrolled the Nugidu Peninsula, Sheldon's moved along the north shore of Langemak Bay to Simbang which was also reached by the 2/15th at 5.15 p.m. During these mopping-up operations the 2/17th captured two prisoners and killed three stragglers.

From early morning on the 2nd the 22nd Battalion was on the move. One patrol from the Timbulum area failed to reach its objective at Butaweng sawmill after meeting a small Japanese rearguard south of Godowa. A platoon then set out for the sawmill and returned at 5 p.m. with the report that no Japanese were in the area, but that the men had spoken to a company of the 2/17th across the Mape River at 4.30 p.m. Throughout its advance the 22nd Battalion had been entirely maintained by craft of the 532nd E.B.S.R. operating from Lae and by native porters carrying the stores forward from the beaches.

Although it appeared that the 20th Brigade would soon have another fight on its hands to the west and north, the men were able to relax for the first time since the landing. The troops were soon "scrounging" for souvenirs, one section finding an eight-day clock which was hung up to facilitate its guard duty. "Came evening," wrote one participant, "and we went down to Finschhafen by the sea; here lay peace, and primitive civilisation, native pads avenued by hibiscus in bloom, stately palms almost regal in their look, flowering frangipani, island fruit in abundance. . . . All were happy, we had done our job, once more the 20th had got through."

Eleven days after the landing at Scarlet Beach the 20th Brigade had reached its objective. It had killed a large number of Japanese and captured a vital area from which future offensives could be launched and which contained excellent facilities for air and naval support. The cost in casualties was 20 officers and 338 men, of whom 8 officers and 65 men had been killed. As well, 6 officers and 295 men were evacuated from their units sick but some of these were back by 2nd October.[4] The 532nd E.B.S.R. had 50 casualties including 8 killed.

The fighting for Finschhafen had been bitter. At the beginning of October it was becoming clearly apparent that, though the Japanese had yielded the coastal strip, they were assembling to the west where the 3,400-foot peak of Sattelberg dominated the surrounding country. Already one attack from that direction had been beaten back by the 2/17th Battalion, but for the past 48 hours the 2/43rd had been trying to fight through to rescue one of its companies at Jivevaneng. Thus, although Finschhafen itself was captured, it was by no means secure. And evidence was now coming in from the Papuan Infantry and the local natives that more enemy troops were entering the Wareo-Sattelberg area from the north.

---

[4]

	Strength of inf bns on embarkation, 21 Sep 1943		Strength of inf bns on 3 Oct 1943	
	Offrs	OR's	Offrs	OR's
2/13 Bn	33	660	26	485
2/15 Bn	29	680	25	569
2/17 Bn	29	626	26	546

CHAPTER 18

EASY STREET AND THE SATTELBERG ROAD

FINSCHHAFEN had been captured on 2nd October, but Brigadier Windeyer realised that "to secure the gains it would be necessary to continue the offensive and to get possession of Sattelberg as soon as possible".[1] Even before 30th September, when the company of the 2/17th Battalion had been relieved at Jivevaneng by Captain Grant's company of the 2/43rd, it had become obvious that one company could just hold its own there, and by dusk on 30th September only two of Grant's platoons had reached Jivevaneng. Grant had no time to work out a fire plan before the enemy were heard moving in the undergrowth. At this time it was Colonel Joshua's intention that Grant's third platoon and a second company should reinforce Jivevaneng next morning.

The enemy closing round Jivevaneng were from Lieut-Colonel Takagi's *III/80th Battalion*, which had attacked unsuccessfully down the Sattelberg Road on 26th September. Four days later Colonel Sadahiko Miyake, the commander of the *80th Regiment*, noted that "it seems the enemy attacking our regiment on the Finschhafen naval front turned towards Heldsbach at about noon on the 27th". He then attached some of his troops to the Finschhafen naval force and ordered the *III/80th Battalion* to "continue its present duties", which accounted for the pressure on Jivevaneng.

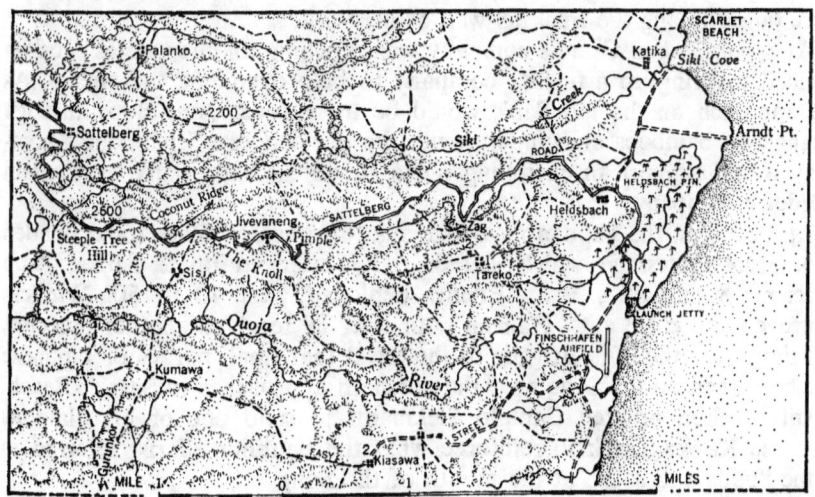

At 6.15 a.m. on 1st October the enemy cut the telephone line between Joshua and his forward company, and much firing was heard from the direction of Jivevaneng. Grant's men were alert when the first attack came, from the north-east, and, despite the yells of the Japanese "cheer-leader", the attack was driven off. The Australians retaliated with 2-inch and 3-inch

---

[1] 20 Aust Inf Bde Report on Operations, 22 Sep 43-21 Jan 44.

mortar bombs, while the relieving force was advancing cautiously up the Sattelberg Road. At 9.20 a.m. when about a quarter of a mile from its objective the leading platoon was fired on and its commander (Lieutenant Dost[2]) killed. Lieutenant Richardson[3] from the next platoon went forward to investigate and was wounded. By this time Grant's men had beaten off two more attacks, both from the same direction. With no communications between the beleaguered company and the relieving force, neither knew what the other was doing, although each knew, from the noise of Owens and Brens, that the other was in action. For the remainder of the morning the South Australians and Japanese exchanged desultory fire, and enemy mortars inflicted casualties on the defenders of Jivevaneng.

One of Grant's problems was that a platoon of Papuans was cut off with his own two platoons. The Papuans, perhaps unrivalled at scouting and patrolling, were not fitted for a grim defence, as was well known. At 11.25 a.m. Grant wrote in his log: "Two PIB went bush"; at 6 p.m., "6 PIB go through." Soon after midday Grant sent two Papuans to sneak out with a coded message for Joshua, and distributed the remainder "with our chaps to keep their courage up".

During the late morning Joshua tried again to clear the enemy position east of Jivevaneng. While one platoon (Lieutenant Williams'[4]) "fixed" the enemy position from the left of the track, another fired on the position to support an encircling move by the remainder of Captain Richmond's[5] company round the right flank; but this effort failed because the Japanese were dug in along the track as well as across it.

At 3 p.m., when Grant's company was repelling another attack, Joshua decided to bring up a further company to help overcome the enemy. As the approach on the left flank would be up a precipitous slope through a tangle of bamboos and undergrowth, he decided that Richmond's company would support an encircling move round the right flank by Captain Gordon's company.

At 3.30 p.m. the Papuan messengers got through to Joshua and handed him Grant's message which stated: "HQ attacked on 2 flanks. Amn deficient. 8 casualties. . . . Enemy deployed west 40 to 50. Wireless destroyed and cable cut." Half an hour later he received another message, this time from the 20th Brigade to the effect that small parties of Japanese had been seen on the Song near the northern approaches to Scarlet Beach. Hastily Joshua ordered Captain Siekmann to send one of his platoons from the Katika Track to reinforce what the battalion diarist referred to as the "odds and sods" at the mouth of the Song.

The two-company effort fared no better than the earlier one. By 5.20 p.m. two of Gordon's platoons were deployed 100 yards on the right of Richmond's positions, but when the right-hand platoon (Lieutenant

---

[2] Lt L. H. Dost, SX8765; 2/43 Bn. Secretary-manager; of Croydon, SA; b. Croydon, 13 Dec 1905. Killed in action 1 Oct 1943.
[3] Lt K. E. Richardson, SX6239; 2/43 Bn. Clerk; of Henley Beach, SA; b. Mile End, SA, 4 Jun 1921.
[4] Lt R. G. Williams, WX6571; 2/43 Bn. Clerk; of St Peters, SA; b. Melbourne, 11 Jan 1919.
[5] Capt C. R. Richmond, SX5250; 2/43 Bn. Clerk; of Westbourne Park, SA; b. Gawler, SA, 4 Mar 1918.

Coen's[6]) tried to move forward it was fired on from a steep feature ahead. As no advance seemed possible the companies dug in for the night.

In and around Jivevaneng Grant and his platoon commanders (Lieutenants Foley[7] and Clifford[8]) were now very worried about the shortage of ammunition, and the men were warned to fire only at movement or observed targets. By last light Grant had suffered 12 casualties including two killed. There was no chance of sending out patrols to find the encircling enemy as the perimeter would have been too depleted. The only possible course was to defend, and to go on defending, even though the men were well aware that by this time the enemy should know nearly every one of their foxholes. Once when Grant told a man to be quiet he replied: "It's all right, Skipper, they know we are here."

Most of these enemy attacks on Jivevaneng came from the direction of what would normally be regarded as the platoon's rear. The fifth attack was beaten off at 5 p.m. mainly by the 3-inch mortar, fired at 200 yards. Two hours later a bugle call sounded, followed by yells, as the Japanese prepared to attack. Two more 3-inch mortar bombs into the same northeastern area from the same range changed the yells to screams. Another bugle call sounded and then silence. Later a dog prowled barking, and sounds of digging were heard until midnight.

On the morning of 2nd October the policy of firing only at definite targets was resulting in a large number of casualties being inflicted on the enemy, but the small force in Jivevaneng was also losing men under the steady enemy bombardment. At 11.30 a.m. it began to rain and soon the weapon-pits were full of water. Two hours later the Japanese opened up with many weapons, but so heavy was the downpour that it was difficult to tell the noises apart. The din ceased at 2 p.m. and the men began to bail out their dismal weapon-pits. Two more attacks during the afternoon were beaten off; almost invariably the Japanese attacked from the same position.

At 1.15 p.m. in heavy rain Richmond's company, supported by fire from Gordon's on the right, advanced. Lack of precise knowledge of the enemy positions doomed the attack to failure, and despite the courage of the men they were forced back after having pushed ahead for 80 yards. On the extreme right flank Private Ronan[9] crawled to within 20 yards of a Japanese position and shot 6 Japanese with his rifle. The Australian casualties were heavy—7 missing and 12 wounded.

It seemed to Windeyer as he hurried north from the Bumi on 2nd October that Finschhafen had fallen just in time. He knew that he had taken a risk in concentrating his force to the south, but Finschhafen was his objective and his bold plan had succeeded. What was the situation now confronting him? After a bitter fight the Japanese had retreated, and

---

[6] Maj J. C. Coen, TX2694; 2/43 Bn. Student; of Hobart; b. Sydney, 13 Jan 1918.
[7] Lt W. G. Foley, VX35360; 2/43 Bn. Miner; of Long Gully, Vic; b. Long Gully, 22 Dec 1916.
[8] Lt A. V. Clifford, WX7591; 2/43 Bn. Accountant; of Perth; b. Bunbury, WA, 26 Mar 1914. Killed in action 18 Oct 1943.
[9] Pte R. J. Ronan, MM, SX13399; 2/43 Bn. Mason's labourer; of Gawler, SA; b. Gawler, 16 Oct 1921.

the coastline from Lae to just south of Bonga was in Australian hands; but round Finschhafen the captured territory was held by only a thin red line; and, if the Japanese had inland bases and the strength and determination to attack, they could choose where to do so. Indeed the initiative might soon pass to the enemy unless reinforcements arrived quickly.

The three battalions of the 20th Brigade were now in the southern area; the 22nd, now under Windeyer's command, was in the area south of Langemak Bay and the Mape River. Three companies of the 2/43rd Battalion were fighting along the Sattelberg Road and a fourth was along the Katika Track. A mixed group of machine-gunners, Pioneers and Papuans was guarding the area from the Song to North Hill.

Windeyer had to hold the area from Bonga to Dreger Harbour and capture Sattelberg. He regarded this as a large order. To attempt to force a way to Sattelberg via Jivevaneng where the enemy had dug in, however, would not be "propitious", as Windeyer termed it. He decided, therefore, to press on and capture the Kumawa area with the 2/17th Battalion in order first to disorganise the enemy's retreat from Finschhafen by cutting the track through Gurunkor-Kumawa-Sisi-Sattelberg, and then to bring pressure on Sisi in order to secure the road junction there and assist an advance up the Sattelberg Road. Thus at 7 p.m. on the 2nd, Colonel Simpson received orders to move early next morning to an assembly area near the airstrip where the battalion would probably move west towards Kumawa.

In his planning Windeyer had also to take account of a signal received from General Wootten on the 2nd, that the 2/43rd Battalion should not be used operationally if possible, but should be kept in reserve ready to join the 24th Brigade which was soon due to arrive. As the 2/43rd had already suffered casualties along the Sattelberg Road, Windeyer decided that it should be withdrawn after the 2/17th had captured Kumawa and Sisi, thus severing the enemy's lines of communication to Jivevaneng. In the meantime the 2/43rd would close the gap of about 400 yards between it and its isolated company, preferably by advancing, but, if necessary, Grant should fight his way back to the main body.

The 22nd Battalion was made responsible for searching, mopping up and holding the area south of Langemak Bay with detachments at Logaweng and Dreger Harbour. The 2/15th Battalion would hold Simbang and patrol to Tirimoro; while the 2/13th would be in reserve at Kakakog and would also patrol to Tirimoro.[1]

---

[1] On 1st October an operation instruction was issued showing clearly the organisation and command of Allied Land Forces in New Guinea.

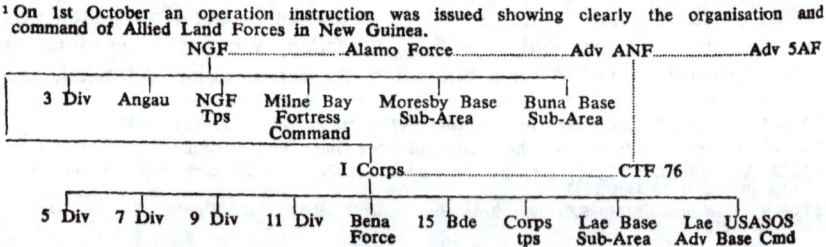

By this time the senior commanders had before them an operation instruction from N.G.F. issued on 29th September stating that on 10th October General Kenney's main bomber force with necessary fighter escort would be diverted to assist operations in the South Pacific; on 1st November Admiral Carpender's naval forces would be relieved of responsibility for sea transportation to Lae and on 15th November to Finschhafen; and towards the end of November both air and naval forces would again be diverted to support operations against western New Britain. Allied air and naval forces, however, would "support I Aust Corps operations as far as practicable without interference with missions assigned in support of [New Britain] operation".

On 30th September General Herring had flown to Lae for a conference with Generals Wootten and Milford. Anticipating the fall of Finschhafen, Herring gave verbal orders for Wootten to defend Finschhafen, develop it as a base sub-area, and gain control of the east coast of the Huon Peninsula up to and including Sio. Wootten was to move the balance of the 9th Division, less one brigade, to Finschhafen "at his discretion". He was told what he had already guessed: that the only craft available would be the boat battalion of the 532nd E.B.S.R. and a boat company from the 542nd E.B.S.R. The operations for the capture of Sio, which entailed the clearing of the flank at Sattelberg, should begin as soon as possible. An immediate task would be the capture of the Tami Islands. Wootten immediately warned Brigadier Evans to have a reconnaissance party from his brigade headquarters and from one of his battalions (2/28th) ready to join in a divisional party leaving soon for the Dreger Harbour area.

It was now evident that there was much Japanese barge movement along the east coast of the Huon Peninsula. More by luck than by good management the American P.T. boats so far had not sunk any barges and other craft belonging to Task Force 76 or to the 2nd Engineer Special Brigade. On several occasions, however, lack of close cooperation between land and naval forces had nearly resulted in a catastrophe.[2]

To prevent such possibilities in future, Admiral Carpender on 30th September discussed with General Berryman and the commander of the P.T. boats the question of producing a workable system of cooperation so that P.T. boats could give more effective support to the land forces. It was clear that coordination could not be effected from 200 miles away. The only satisfactory system would be one of direct personal contact in

---

[2] The most recent example was during the move of the 2/43rd Battalion to Scarlet Beach. Corps headquarters had asked the commander of the PT boats for direct support of the Finschhafen operations. He had agreed, provided the movement of American barges was restricted in that area and provided the Australian artillery did not fire seawards. Barge hunts from Gagidu to Arndt Point were arranged for the night of 28th-29th September and the following night between 6 p.m. and 5 a.m. On the morning of the 28th the commander of the PT boats heard that APD's might be going to Finschhafen, and, therefore, on his own initiative, he switched the mission to north of Fortification Point. Later that day I Corps advised him that six LCM's would be leaving Scarlet Beach for Lae soon after midnight on the night 28th-29th September and asked for an assurance that they would not be attacked by the PT boats. As the PT boats had already sailed from Morobe, and as it was doubtful whether they would receive a wireless message, the LCM's may well have been sunk but for the commonsense and initiative of the commander of the PT boats.

the actual area of operations between the P.T. boat command and the local army command.

On 1st October General Mackay, accompanied by General Morshead who had arrived in Port Moresby on 29th September, flew to Lae for a conference with Generals Herring, Milford, Vasey and Wootten. It had been arranged that for the supply of Finschhafen half the shore battalion of the 532nd E.B.S.R. would come under command of the American advanced base at Lae immediately, and on 3rd October the rest of the 532nd E.B.S.R. would come under I Corps' command at Finschhafen. The remainder of the 2nd E.S.B. would stay under Carpender's command except for a boat company of the 542nd E.B.S.R., which would be reinforced by twenty L.C.M's and would be employed to support the U.S.A.S.O.S. base at Lae and for supply along the coast to Finschhafen. The support to be expected being known, the role of I Australian Corps could now be more clearly defined. The main tasks of the 9th Division had already been outlined by Herring to Wootten on the previous day. In addition, the corps commander would be responsible for establishing in the Finschhafen area by 1st December an air base for staging one group of fighters and two light bomber squadrons, and a naval base from which light naval vessels could operate in Vitiaz Strait; he would need to keep in mind the later development of Finschhafen as a major army, navy and air base. Operations and construction activities must be so conducted as to require minimum air support after 9th October. The consolidation of the Huon Peninsula would be effected by infiltration up the coast by operations so conducted as to avoid commitment of amphibious forces beyond those of the boat battalion under command; exploitation beyond Sio should not be undertaken without reference to New Guinea Force.

The instruction gave the 7th Division a similar role: protection of newly-constructed airfields, and limited its operations beyond Dumpu to patrolling only. Finally, after the capture of Sio and Dumpu, "the role of I Aust Corps will probably be restricted to active patrolling and vigorous infiltration and defence of the I Aust Corps area".[3]

---

[3] On 6th October General Mackay withdrew this "Operation Instruction 96" on receipt of a signal from General Blamey stating that General MacArthur had directed attention to a breach of security, in that the instruction had used place names instead of code names for future operations. The instruction was reissued on 8th October using code names.

Writing to Blamey on 8th October, Berryman stated: "In future we shall take care to use place code names when referring to future operations originated by GHQ. In our own instructions it is not altogether practicable because so many places have not been allotted code names, and unlike GHQ we do not use names of places in code and in clear in the one instruction or give away the code names in the distribution list; e.g., Binocular USASOS Adv Base in the instruction and Lae USASOS Adv Base in the distribution list. General Morshead and some of our senior officers have drawn my attention to breaches of security in the GHQ communiqués and have stated our men comment about it. We have educated our troops to a reasonable standard, but it will become increasingly difficult to maintain that standard unless more attention is paid to this question in GHQ communiqués."

Mackay wrote to Blamey on 20th October stating that "the present system of security including the use of code names for places does not adequately guard the security of future operations" because the GHQ operation instructions contained enough information to break code names for places, particularly the practice of stating place names in code and in clear in the one instruction. Mackay then gave an exhaustive list of GHQ operation instructions where place names were shown in clear as well as in code. Mackay contended that the use of codes for place names had proved unsatisfactory in the Middle East and had been abolished by GHQ ME.

He then drew Blamey's attention to an article in American Time of 12th July 1943, which indicated the direction of the next attacks through New Britain. "It states," he wrote, "that

At the conference on the 1st Herring spoke mainly of his supply difficulties and stated that the development of the airfields areas was entirely dependent on the navy. He pointed out that some of the landing craft which took five hours to load at Buna only stayed two hours at Lae, thus discharging only portion of their cargoes. Wootten stated that when he got the boats due on the 3rd he could "clean up Finschhafen and go on to Saidor".

General Blamey had already decided that the time had come to give Herring a rest and bring in a new corps commander and staff. Since the return of the 9th Division, General Morshead had been promoted to command and train II Corps (the A.I.F.) on the Atherton Tableland. He then suffered the not-unexpected experience of having the 7th and 9th Divisions sent to New Guinea while he remained in Australia, a corps commander without a corps. On 23rd September Morshead lunched with Blamey and learned that he was at last to have an active command against the Japanese, as his corps headquarters would soon relieve Herring's in New Guinea. As previously narrated, he arrived in Port Moresby on 29th September and attended the conference at Lae on 1st October. Blamey meanwhile signalled Mackay to arrange the changeover whenever he wished. It was decided that the relief should take place on 7th October. Morshead arrived at Dobodura at 11.15 a.m. on the 7th and half an hour later Herring left for Port Moresby and Australia.

With his departure from New Guinea, General Herring's period of active service was over—although this was not known at the time. He had given able service in a high appointment through the vicissitudes of a year's fierce campaigning, starting with the anxious Papuan battles, and needed a rest. When he left New Guinea it seemed certain that in due course he would relieve Morshead, but in February 1944 he became Chief Justice of the Supreme Court of Victoria.

Now that the general outline of the plans for supplying Finschhafen were known the commanders could proceed with greater confidence. In order to find out exactly how many landing craft were actually at his disposal, Wootten sent Colonel Barham, his G.S.O.1, to Dobodura, where he ascertained that the craft available from the 532nd E.B.S.R. would be 63 L.C.V's and 10 L.C.M's, while those from the company of the 542nd E.B.S.R. would be 54 L.C.V's and 19 L.C.M's.

At this time the subsidiary operation was taking place against the Tami Islands. As mentioned, when the planning for Finschhafen was being

---

Rabaul is the objective and that our offensive has two parts, one aimed at Salamaua-Lae, the other at Munda. As this has been proved correct in practice it can only be assumed that greater attention would be paid to that part of the article dealing with further operations. The map shows arrows leading from the coast of the Huon Peninsula to western New Britain, thence to Rabaul. . . . In view of the general trend of operations and in view of the article in *Time*, it would be surprising if the enemy was not already expecting our next attack to be directed against western New Britain. The steady increase in enemy strength in this area is a definite indication."

Berryman wrote to Chamberlin on 18th October: "I was very pleased to hear you had been made a major-general and offer you my heartiest congratulations. . . . With reference to our Operation Instruction No. 96, I shall try in future to satisfy your requirements, although I do not share your apprehension, nor do I see any consistency in the matter. . . . If you want a digest of our future operations read *Time*, July 12, 1943, pages 11 and 12."

rushed ahead, Herring ordered Wootten to establish a radar station on the Tami Islands which were well placed to give warning of the approach of hostile aircraft from New Britain towards Lae and Buna. A company was deemed sufficient to capture the islands and guard the radar station, and Wootten gave the task to Brigadier Edgar of the 4th Brigade, who detailed a company of the 29th/46th Battalion for the task. It was to land at the same time as the 20th Brigade's landing on Scarlet Beach. The operation was postponed, however, when Wootten was informed that Barbey considered that navigational difficulties made it desirable to wait until he could provide suitable naval escort. On 25th September two barges were reported to be moving from the Tami Islands towards Langemak Bay; on the 27th Mackay informed Herring that the navy and air force were anxious that radar equipment should be installed on the islands.

It was now decided that the expedition should be made by a company of the 24th Brigade and Evans gave the task to the 2/32nd Battalion. Major Mollard, administering command of the battalion in place of Lieut-Colonel Scott who was ill, chose Lieutenant Denness' company. As well as the company, "Denness Force" would consist of a radar detachment, pioneers, mortars, signals and a section of six .50-calibre machine-guns from the 532nd E.B.S.R. which also provided the landing craft (2 L.C.M's and 14 L.C.V's). This expedition left the loading beaches at Lae at 11.15 p.m. on the 2nd. After encountering very rough weather, high seas and continual rain, the convoy arrived off Wonam Island, which seemed to have the best beach. The six rear boats reduced speed while the command craft moved in for a reconnaissance. When the craft was about 30 yards from the beach four natives came out of the jungle fringe waving their arms in a friendly manner. The interpreter then learnt that there were no Japanese on the islands. The natives swam and paddled canoes to the craft and were taken aboard as guides through the channel into

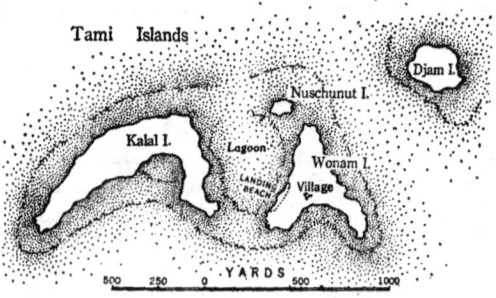

the lagoon between Kalal and Wonam. As Kalal was the highest island Denness landed on the south-east corner at 8 a.m. and rapidly decided on the location for the radar station. All the assault craft unloaded and one was sent back to guide the supply and equipment craft from Kasanga. By 2 p.m. unloading was finished and all the landing craft, except the two to remain with Denness Force, returned to Lae.

One of Denness' first tasks was to round up the natives—74 in all. They were short of food, and, because of their terror of bombers and strafers, they had been living in dank, low-roofed and foul-smelling caves

(Australian War Memorial)
Chimbu and Bena Bena carriers arriving at the 2/7th Independent Company's headquarters on 3rd October 1943.

(Australian War Memorial)
Men of "A" Company, 2/16th Battalion on Johns' Knoll, 17th October 1943.

(Australian War Memorial)

An L.S.T. landing troops of the 9th Division at Scarlet Beach, near Finschhafen, on 22nd September 1943.

(Australian War Memorial)

General Morshead at 24th Brigade headquarters on 25th October 1943 during a visit to units under his command in the Finschhafen area. *Left to right*: Colonel A. R. Garrett (B.G.S. I Corps), Major-General G. F. Wootten (G.O.C. 9th Division), Brigadier B. Evans (commanding 24th Brigade) and General Morshead.

A jeep negotiating mud and slush near 9th Division headquarters in the Finschhafen area, 7th November 1943.

Men of the 2/24th Battalion accompanied by scouts of the Papuan Battalion setting out on patrol in the Sattelberg area, 15th November 1943.

(*Australian War Memorial*)
Men of the 2/48th Battalion, supported by Matilda tanks, making their way forward to attack Coconut Ridge on the Sattelberg Road on 17th November 1943.

(*Australian War Memorial*)
The attack on Coconut Ridge, 17th November 1943.

dug out of the coral. All were set to work and treated well. In his report Denness wrote:

> Information gained from them [the natives] is that about last Easter a force of over 100 enemy were encamped on the islands, but left after about a month. Returning with a stronger force of approx. 200 about two months ago, they set up a wireless station, and a complete defence system on the islands. The evidence of this defence system still exists. They were strongly entrenched around the whole of the islands, in large, heavily-reinforced bunkers and air-raid shelters dug in the side of the coral cliffs. Allied bombers and strafing planes made several attacks, the success of which is very evident. Later many barges came in one night and the whole enemy force was withdrawn. The distress of the natives was brought about by the shortage of food, as all pigs, chickens and vegetables were commandeered by the enemy.[4]

Meanwhile, elements of Windeyer's five infantry battalions were moving to their new positions. From 8 a.m. on 3rd October the 2/17th Battalion was being ferried in three-tonners north from Kolem to a track junction near the airstrip. From here the battalion was to be led by native guides along a track negotiable by jeeps to Kiasawa 1 and thence by a native pad through Kiasawa 2 to Kumawa. This very difficult route was ironically named Easy Street.[5]

Grant's company of the 2/43rd Battalion was still at Jivevaneng, where, on the 3rd, no attacks were made by the Japanese. Four hundred yards east were two other companies of the 2/43rd. A patrol from Captain Gordon's company in the morning reported that the Japanese who had halted the Australian attack on the previous day were still in position. At 11.30 a.m. Colonel Joshua sent another message to Grant by a small Papuan patrol led by Sergeant Scott-Holland,[6] ordering him to withdraw to Zag via the Tareko Track. Half an hour earlier, however, Grant had already decided on a plan to evacuate, and because of the ensuing bombardment of Japanese positions the Papuan patrol was unable to get through that day.

From midday till 1 p.m. the artillery fired 100 shells on the Japanese about Jivevaneng. Some of the shells fell among the defenders, but no casualties were suffered as all were below ground. Under cover of this bombardment and 152 mortar bombs another patrol of platoon strength from Gordon's company tried without success to get through to Jivevaneng. At 3.40 p.m. Windeyer went to the 2/43rd's headquarters, informed Joshua of his plan that the 2/17th should capture Kumawa and ordered the 2/43rd to attack in the Jivevaneng area with the double object of supporting the 2/17th and relieving Grant.

After fifteen minutes of artillery and mortar fire, Lieutenant Combe[7] led a company into the attack at 5.45 p.m. to the left of the track. Fierce

---
[4] On 11th October the 9th Division Carrier Company was organised into a force of about 40 to relieve the company of the 2/32nd. The relief was completed on 19th October.
[5] It was so steep and muddy that, on one occasion, two tractors were attached to one jeep but all were bogged.
[6] WO2 T. H. Scott-Holland, MM, QX32170. Papuan Inf Bn, 1 NG Inf Bn, 36 Bn. Engine driver; of St Lucia, Qld; b. Maleny, Qld, 24 Jan 1922.
[7] Capt G. D. Combe, MC, SX6977; 2/43 Bn. Parliamentary officer; of Adelaide; b. Gumeracha, SA, 12 Jun 1917.

fighting ensued as the attackers tried desperately to do what had so often been proved costly in jungle warfare: attack well-dug enemy defences by a route well known to the enemy. Soon the company was pinned down. In a leading section Private Dabner[8] manned the Bren when one of the gunners was wounded. Running out of ammunition he then silenced two enemy posts with grenades, and, when his platoon commander was killed, he took charge of the platoon. The two forward platoons were both pinned down when Combe, wounded and with his Owen shot out of his hands, led his reserve platoon forward. After half an hour's severe fighting he sent back a message: "Held up by frontal and enfilade fire, unable to proceed further." Having suffered 17 casualties including 6 killed, Combe withdrew.

Since its arrival the 2/43rd Battalion had lost 47 including 14 killed and 5 missing. Late at night Windeyer ordered Joshua to attack on the 4th if Grant were not extricated by then.

Windeyer had also to contend with a sudden threat from the north. The track north from the Song to Bonga had been regularly patrolled since the landing, and a patrol skirmish had occurred along the track on the previous day. At 7.15 a.m. on the 3rd one Japanese was seen approaching the position of the 2/43rd's anti-tank platoon (Lieutenant McKee[9]) 450 yards north of the Song on the coastal track. The scout was shot, but during the next four hours three attacks were made on the platoon's position, each time by 30 to 40 Japanese advancing at a jog trot. The platoon repulsed all attacks, and the Japanese withdrew about 1,000 yards and dug in.

These Japanese now appearing on the northern front were from Lieut-Colonel Shobu's *II/80th Battalion* which had recently been on the Mongi River. On 28th September Colonel Miyake of the *80th Regiment* had ordered that "the Shobu battalion is to seek out and attack the enemy who is advancing in our direction from the Song River". After a circuitous march, probably through Wareo and Gusika, this battalion was now ready to attack.

Major Broadbent, worried by the proximity of the Japanese threat to Scarlet Beach, immediately sent Major P. E. Siekmann's company of the 2/3rd Pioneers hurrying north to reinforce Captain Nicholas' company of the 2/2nd Machine Gun Battalion and the elements of the 2/43rd west of the mouth of the Song. Later in the day Lieutenant Blackburn's[1] platoon from the Pioneers counter-attacked the Japanese positions along the track, but came under heavy fire from a small knoll. Two men were wounded before the platoon made a flank attack. Leading his section, Corporal Moreau[2] stood up and threw grenades at the Japanese, and drove them off.

---

[8] Cpl H. J. Dabner, MM, TX5534; 2/43 Bn. Lorry driver; of Launceston, Tas; b. Avoca, Tas, 3 May 1921.

[9] Capt R. R. McKee, WX8972; 2/43 Bn. Senior clerk; of Nedlands, WA; b. Fremantle, WA, 1 Jul 1909.

[1] Lt N. G. Blackburn, NX59688; 2/3 Pnr Bn. Woolclasser; of Woollahra, NSW; b. Dubbo, NSW, 26 Aug 1917. Killed in action 4 Oct 1943.

[2] Cpl M. H. Moreau, MM, NX27000; 2/3 Pnr Bn. Farmer; of Asquith, NSW; b. North Sydney, 15 Dec 1908. Died in road accident 22 Apr 1944.

By the time the 2/17th Battalion reached the Easy Street junction, Windeyer knew about the attack north of the Song and decided that Broadbent's small force must be reinforced immediately. The 2/13th Battalion was too far away in the Kakakog area to be an effective reserve for Scarlet Beach; Windeyer wished to proceed with his plan of sending the 2/17th to Kumawa, as this seemed the most likely place in which to regain contact with the enemy who had retreated from Finschhafen; it seemed best, therefore, as an *ad hoc* solution, to divide the 2/17th Battalion into two groups. Two companies—Major Pike's and Captain Sheldon's—were detached and organised with a separate headquarters under Major Maclarn, the commander of Headquarters' Company. By last light Maclarn's detachment had joined Broadbent near Scarlet Beach, while Colonel Simpson led the remainder of the battalion to Kiasawa 1.

On the 4th pressure suddenly eased on both the trouble fronts. Grant received Joshua's message to evacuate at 7.30 a.m. when Scott-Holland, with two Papuans, finally got through. On the previous afternoon the three men had worked through the jungle at the head of the Quoja River, avoiding several parties of Japanese. When the Australian mortars had opened up the patrol was 150 yards south of the village. After retiring, the patrol lay in the jungle all night and finally reached Grant's positions at dawn.

At 9.15 a.m., after Grant had given his orders to withdraw, Boomerangs of No. 4 Squadron dropped ammunition and supplies and a message instructing Grant to fight his way out. Soon after midday a reconnaissance aircraft reported that the supplies had been dropped in Jivevaneng, but there were no signs of anyone coming to collect them. Led by Scott-Holland's patrol, Grant's Australians and Papuans, carrying their wounded, had already left Jivevaneng. At 1 p.m., strangely unmolested, they met a patrol which had been sent out by Joshua to reach Jivevaneng by the left flank. The defenders had suffered 12 casualties including two killed, but Grant estimated that at least 50 enemy had been killed. By 3 p.m. the weary men reached battalion headquarters and were sent down the track towards Zag to protect the lines of communication.

To the north Windeyer at 8.30 a.m. instructed Maclarn to find a position north of the Song whence his detachment could attack the Japanese force. During the morning two platoons of Siekmann's Pioneer company moved forward with the 2/43rd's anti-tank platoon on the left flank. Skirmishes, during one of which Blackburn was mortally wounded, forced the enemy to withdraw, although they continued intermittently to fire on the Australians from farther north. At 11.30 a.m. an officer in an L.C.V. reconnoitred the Japanese positions from the sea. About 900 yards north of the Song he drew fire, but from no farther north. Thus the general whereabouts of the enemy was established, and Maclarn was instructed to attack.

By 2.15 p.m. a platoon of the 2/43rd re-established contact with the Japanese north of the Song; and soon afterwards Maclarn's men reached the Song. At 5 p.m. he was ready to send Pike's company into the attack, his plan being to push east to the coastal track, hold it with one platoon and attack south towards the platoon of the 2/43rd. An hour later, after an artillery bombardment, Pike's company moved forward in single file across the kunai to the edge of the timber where the ground dropped sharply for about 50 feet. After walking through kunai for most of the day it was like going into an air-conditioned picture show to walk into the jungle. Heavy fire from the edge of the jungle wounded three men in the leading platoon. Because of failing light and the amount of fire coming from the gloom, Maclarn decided to wait until next day to press the attack. By last light a Papuan patrol reported that the Japanese had withdrawn from their positions round Jivevaneng, apparently about the same time as Grant, probably because of casualties suffered in attacking Jivevaneng and in withstanding the 2/43rd's attacks. Two companies of the 2/43rd occupied Grant's former position.

On the 5th Maclarn moved farther up North Hill in a deeper encircling move before launching a two-company attack at 4.50 p.m. He met no opposition and joined the platoon of the 2/43rd to the south after passing through Japanese positions which showed signs of hurried evacuation. By last light it was arranged that a company of the 2/43rd would take over the North Hill area from the 2/3rd Pioneers and Maclarn's force at dawn.

Along the track to Kumawa on the 5th a Papuan patrol made contact with an enemy post in the village. The patrol returned and informed Captain Dinning, whose company was in the lead, that natives in the enemy's camp had spotted the patrol. By 12.30 p.m., after a sharp encounter in which six casualties were inflicted on the enemy, Kumawa was captured by Dinning's company. By last light Simpson's headquarters was in the village and Main's company near by. That night the artillery shelled Sisi.[3]

On the 6th Captain D. C. Siekmann's company of the 2/43rd relieved Major P. E. Siekmann's company of the 2/3rd Pioneers—they were brothers. The Pioneers took up a position about 800 yards west of Katika. As patrols found no sign of the enemy up to Bonga, Maclarn's detachment of the 2/17th was withdrawn to the mouth of the Song. During the morning a Papuan patrol from Jivevaneng found the enemy in position on a feature known as "the Knoll" about 500 yards west of the village.

It was in the Kumawa area that the enemy now appeared most active. Early on the 6th a platoon of the 2/17th accompanied by a Papuan section, patrolled the track north to Sisi with the hope of occupying it, but the Papuan scouts soon reported an enemy position on the rising ground to the west of the track about 700 yards north of Kumawa near the Quoja River. Simpson then sent Dinning's company forward up the track to keep contact.

---

[3] Lieut-Colonel Houston (of the 2/12th Field Regiment) on 5th October sent Windeyer a report from the 3rd Survey Battery regarding the Sattelberg and Langemak Bay 1:25000 sheets from which the war was now being fought: "The apparent errors in these sheets were first discovered by variations in range and line found by shooting from the map [from] line and range found in subsequent registrations by air on the same targets. . . . The maps are wrong in themselves and worse when the join is made."

During the day there were several skirmishes with the enemy to the west. One Japanese soldier of the *III/80th Battalion* wrote in his diary that day: "I went on an officer patrol to Kumawa village. Saw for the first time enemy soldiers at a distance of 30-40 metres wearing green uniforms."

In particular, a platoon left at the track junction near Kumawa had to deal with several bands of Japanese still escaping from Finschhafen, and Simpson became anxious about his lines of communication. It was obvious too that, if the 2/17th were to vacate Kumawa as originally intended and advance through Sisi to the Sattelberg Road, the Kumawa area and Gurunkor Track junction might be occupied by the enemy. Kumawa was too valuable to lose; it controlled the main route to Sattelberg from the south (although tracks existed through Moreng and Mararuo); it gave observation and access to the Sattelberg Road and Sattelberg itself. But at least one company must remain to protect Kumawa from north, south and west, thus depleting the force available for a push to the north-east.

While adhering to his original intention of eventually concentrating the 2/17th on the Sattelberg Road, Windeyer considered that, for the present, Simpson must remain about Kumawa. At the same time he decided to bring Maclarn's detachment to Jivevaneng to relieve the companies of the 2/43rd, and thin out his southern flank by bringing the 2/15th to Kumawa. He hoped that, once the 2/15th was at Kumawa, the offensive could be continued with one battalion advancing up the Sattelberg Road and one moving round through Mararuo.

The engineers were beginning to convert Easy Street into a jeep track, a difficult task, for the slope was extremely steep. Heavy rain fell throughout the night, filling the foxholes and trenches and turning the tracks into small streams.

North of the Song, Siekmann's company of the 2/43rd Battalion moved to a position near Bonga on the 7th. This was in accordance with a message which Windeyer had received from Wootten that the junction of the Gusika-Wareo track should be seized. A patrol forward to Bonga found it unoccupied. Early on the 7th Maclarn's column of the 2/17th Battalion was on the move again, and relieved one company of the 2/43rd just east of Jivevaneng. During the afternoon two patrols from the 2/17th, led by Lieutenants Bennie[4] and McDonald,[5] found the positions of the enemy's left and right flanks respectively, a useful task to have accomplished so soon after arrival.

From very early on the 7th the Japanese were pressing on Simpson's half-battalion at Kumawa from the north-east, west and south. As his positions were so thinly held, and as the platoon at the track junction appeared to be in danger of encirclement, Simpson withdrew Dinning's company to thicken his line and preserve his communications. Often

---

[4] Lt R. J. Bennie, MC, NX34299; 2/17 Bn. Dairy farmer; of Nowra, NSW; b. Nowra, 18 Aug 1919.
[5] Lt N. E. McDonald, NX59131; 2/17 Bn. Schoolteacher; of Dulwich Hill, NSW; b. Albury, NSW, 15 Nov 1914.

during the day fire was exchanged with infiltrating bands of the enemy, upon whom several casualties were inflicted. Ammunition and one day's rations were carried forward to the track junction by natives during this miserable day when it rained so hard that the slit trenches were again filled and the area was turned into a quagmire. From the track junction the stores were carried forward by the troops themselves so that the native carriers would not be unduly exposed to fire.

It was obvious that the enemy was very alarmed at the loss of Kumawa and would do all in his power to regain it. There was little Simpson could do except hold on to his positions and hope that the 2/15th would soon arrive. Taken in trucks to the track junction near the airfield, the 2/15th Battalion, less two companies which were returning across the Mape River, reached Kiasawa by last light. The remaining two companies bivouacked near the Easy Street junction. Further heavy rain during the night gave the troops in the forward areas a most uncomfortable night, made it impossible to use jeeps on Easy Street, and swept away the engineers' bridge over the Song.

On the 8th the men learnt that headquarters of II Corps had relieved headquarters of I Corps. The diarist of one 9th Division battalion expressed the affection and esteem in which General Morshead was held by the men whom he had led in the Middle East:

> We learnt tonight that 9 Aust Div is again a part of 2 Aust Corps. As it is commanded by Lt-Gen Sir Leslie Morshead, this re-allocation is welcomed by us.

At 8 a.m. on the 8th Dinning reported seeing a large force of Japanese moving north along a ridge about 200 yards west of the track. On this excellent target the concentrated fire of the company inflicted heavy casualties. An hour and a half later all lines from battalion headquarters to Dinning's company and to brigade headquarters were cut by a Japanese party which crossed the track between Kumawa and Dinning's position. During the next three hours the Japanese made several attacks on the two platoons in Kumawa. This was no new experience to Main's men, who threw back all the attacks. By 1 p.m. a patrol from Kumawa reopened the track to Dinning's company and a telephone line was quickly relaid.

The vanguard of the 2/15th Battalion now reached the Kumawa area, and by 4 p.m. the two rear companies arrived and the battalion dug in between Kumawa and the track junction while Dinning's company moved to Kumawa. The heavy rain had made it impossible for jeeps to use the track from Kiasawa. Along the long and difficult supply route native and Australian porters had to carry the supplies. Since the 5th Simpson's men had only had nine scanty meals and by last light on the 8th there were no rations left at all. "This problem of supplies," commented the battalion's diarist, "prevented us from being able to take further offensive action towards Sisi."

To the south the 2/13th Battalion was now in position, from Simbang to Tirimoro, to protect Finschhafen. South of the Mape the 22nd Battalion watched the approaches to Finschhafen in the Butaweng-Logaweng area. Colvin had already sent a patrol to Logaweng to get in touch with the luluai and tell him to bring in native carriers.

In Jivevaneng on the 9th Maclarn decided to capture the Knoll in order to improve his tactical positions. At 9.30 a.m. Sheldon's company set out to encircle the Japanese round their left flank positions which had been discovered the previous day. An hour later Sheldon reported that his company was in position undetected about 50 yards from the Japanese positions north of the track. Artillery then bombarded the Knoll for a quarter of an hour. Led by Papuan scouts, Bennie's platoon sneaked to within ten yards of the Japanese. Lieutenant Williams'[6] platoon followed closely, with McDonald's in the rear. The approach up which Bennie was about to attack was a steep and heavily wooded slope rising from a ravine. The approach from the south was similar, while that from the east was along the road, where the turns, first to the right and then to the left, were guarded by machine-guns.

Suddenly, at 11.10 a.m., Bennie's men opened up on the enemy posts ahead. There was no stopping the dash of the attack and the 75 yards to the road were covered quickly and several Japanese posts wrecked. Three posts and their occupants were destroyed by Private Brooks[7] firing his Bren from the hip. In the final assault on the Knoll itself only one Japanese was encountered and he ran. Nine Japanese had been killed for the loss of four wounded. By 1 p.m. Sheldon's company was digging in on the Knoll where there were about 60 Japanese holes.

Half an hour later Lieutenant McLeod's platoon moved up to reinforce Sheldon. After mortar fire, the Japanese counter-attacked from the low ground north of the road where they had been driven. Preceded by a bugle call and encouraged by the usual cheers, the Japanese attacked viciously and some got to within five yards of the defences before they were beaten back. Grenades were rolled down among them and the automatics of the defenders ran hot repulsing the counter-attack. When Sheldon was wounded by mortar fire Bennie took charge of the defence and handed over his platoon to Sergeant Wood.[8] At 6.45 p.m. a second counter-attack, this time of company strength and in grim silence without the bugle and cheers, was also repulsed. Most of the attacks were being made against Wood's platoon. When one of his Bren gunners was wounded Wood dashed forward to the weapon-pit and manned the Bren. For the loss of 13 casualties, including 4 killed, Maclarn's detachment had captured a vital feature.

The supply difficulty was such that Windeyer felt that, before the 2/17th and 2/15th could advance, reserves of ammunition and general supplies must be built up. The 2/17th Battalion diarist, describing the day for Simpson's column, wrote: "The enemy caused us no trouble . . . but our stomachs did." Maintenance of the 2/15th was becoming pre-

---

[6] Capt S. M. Williams, NX52495; 2/17 Bn. Clerk; of Glenbrook, NSW; b. Manly, NSW, 11 Sep 1915.

[7] Cpl R. C. Brooks, MM, NX27607; 2/17 Bn. Of Penshurst, NSW; b. Sydney, 2 Dec 1919.

[8] Lt J. N. Wood, MM, NX4541. 2/4 and 2/17 Bns. Farm manager; of Bundanoon, NSW; b. Mosman, NSW, 26 Oct 1917.

carious because of the very bad state of the wet track and the risk of the enemy cutting it, but Colonel Grace turned down an offer by Windeyer to arrange an air drop because he believed that the Japanese did not yet know of his men's presence in Kumawa, where he had a chance of intercepting any belated parties moving towards Sattelberg along the track from Tirimoro. At present the toiling engineers had pushed the jeephead to Kiasawa 2. The few native porters available were used on the Easy Street supply line, together with a company of the 2/15th and another of the 2/3rd Pioneer Battalion.

All round the Australian front on the 10th there was evidence that the Japanese intended to contest the Australian gains. A patrol of the 2/43rd Battalion found signs of considerable enemy movement along the tracks in the Bonga and Gusika areas, indicating that large numbers of reinforcements were arriving from the north. As he now had two of his companies north of the Song (the others being still on the Sattelberg Road), Colonel Joshua moved his headquarters 200 yards north of the river. To the south Lieut-Colonel Gallasch's[9] 2/3rd Pioneer Battalion, all of which had now arrived, was made responsible for close defence of Scarlet Beach. That the enemy was patrolling extensively became clear when a patrol from the 2/43rd encountered a Japanese patrol between Zag and the main coastal track, and killed four of them.

At 1.30 p.m., an Australian and Papuan patrol led by Lieutenant Graham[1] of the 2/17th arrived at Jivevaneng after finding a feasible route from Kumawa across the Quoja River. Graham had left Kumawa at 8 a.m., and after going about 1,000 yards east of Kumawa had moved directly north to Jivevaneng. At 2.45 p.m. an enemy 70-mm mountain gun began firing rapidly on the Knoll. Within five minutes 53 shells were fired, and two men were killed and two wounded. Then the Japanese attacked with what appeared to be two companies, one on each flank. The attack, which was the fiercest yet, was repulsed, and three more counter-attacks during the afternoon were also driven back. During each thrust the Japanese were encouraged by the blowing of bugles, and as they charged upwards they shouted what appeared to be "Ya". After the first attack the defenders replied with "Ya's" and "Ho, Ho's".

West of Finschhafen the 2/13th Battalion also met Japanese stragglers and rearguards for the first time since the capture of Finschhafen. A patrol from Simbang, moving west along the north bank of the Mape, saw a lone Japanese sitting on the track. He escaped as did six others 50 yards farther along. At the junction of the river and Tirimoro tracks the patrol was fired on. As Colvin's orders, received the previous day, were to patrol to Quembung and Tirimoro, but not to become involved in a serious fight, Captain Cooper was instructed to hold the position. Two light attacks were repulsed, and at 8.30 p.m. Japanese bombers dropped three bombs on the position, destroying a Bren gun and some equipment.

---

[9] Col A. V. Gallasch, MC, NX35132. (1st AIF: Capt 27 Bn.) 2/3 Pnr Bn (CO 1941-43); Area Comd Nadzab 1943-44. Bank officer; of Sydney; b. Gladstone, SA, 7 Jun 1893.

[1] Lt W. A. Graham, NX50991; 2/17 Bn. Station overseer; of Cooma, NSW; b. Hamilton, NZ, 6 Nov 1917. Died of wounds 3 Nov 1943.

All was in readiness for the move of the headquarters of the 9th Division and the 24th Brigade to Finschhafen. At midday and again at 2.15 p.m. on the 10th landing craft departed from Lae for Finschhafen carrying the two headquarters. The first group had an uneventful voyage, but the second, of four L.C.V's, carrying Brigadier Evans and part of his headquarters, was bombed by two enemy aircraft near Finschhafen at 8.15 p.m., without much effect; these were possibly the same aircraft that had bombed Cooper's position. Evans' group disembarked at 11 p.m. at Finschhafen Harbour; Wootten landed at Finschhafen half an hour after midnight.

The area in which the 9th Division was now to operate was a formidable one. It lay between Sattelberg and Sio and the Mongi River Valley. The Cromwell Mountains, to the north of the Mongi, were a continuation of the high Saruwaged Range which terminated at its south-east end at Mount Salawaket (13,400 feet), where the range divided to form the Mongi Valley. The Cromwells dropped fairly rapidly from Mount Salawaket to an area about ten miles to the east where there were extensive areas of grass and swamp at between 5,000 and 7,000 feet. They continued at this elevation for almost all the remainder of their length, and fell away towards Sattelberg to a little over 3,000 feet. As the Cromwells were used for hunting by the natives there were innumerable tracks running towards the coast. Except for the track from the Hube district to Sattelberg, however, all were foot tracks only.

To the north of the range was the Kwama River Valley system containing the well-populated Selepe and Komba districts. A good track ran up the main valley of the Kwama to Iloko where the top of the Saruwageds could be reached in one day. It was along this track that some of the *51st Japanese Division* had escaped. Another track ran from Iloko to Geroun, thence over the Cromwells to the Hube district. The northern and eastern slopes of the Cromwell Range were a series of coral terraces rising to between 1,500 and 2,000 feet. At the lower levels they were grass-covered, but south from Bonga into the Finschhafen area they were covered in jungle. Movement along the terraces resolved itself into a series of steep ups and downs in unpleasantly warm surroundings, and it was quicker, particularly in the Kalasa district, to go down to the coast, follow the coastal track and return inland at the required spot.

At that time it was estimated that about 47,000 natives lived in the Huon Peninsula, half of them on the Finschhafen-Sio fall of the ranges where the 9th Division would be operating. About 5,000 were coast natives of good physique, while the remainder were short, stocky mountain people. As with the folk of the Bena plateau, these mountain natives were poor labourers, and prone to malaria and tropical ulcers if employed on the coast. Unlike the wilder people of the Bismarck Ranges, however, they would seldom attack isolated men. It was these natives that Colonel Allan had been recruiting since the landing at Scarlet Beach. He found that the former administrative system of using luluais and tul tuls had been retained by the natives and could be immediately used.

Wootten decided that the vital ground was the Sattelberg mountain feature and the long narrow ridge running west from the coast at Gusika to Wareo. Patrols from the 2/43rd and from the Papuan Infantry had already established that the enemy was using the Gusika-Wareo track to carry supplies from the barges into the Wareo-Sattelberg area. Possession of this ridge would not only cut the enemy's main supply route from the coast, but would prevent him observing the Australian activities along the coast as far south as Dreger Harbour. Wareo, at the western end of the ridge, was on a 2,600-foot plateau which dominated the Song River Valley and the country from Scarlet Beach to Sattelberg. It was also a junction of several important tracks—the Japanese inland track from Kalasa; the track from Kulungtufu in the rich Hube district; tracks down to the coast at Gusika, Kiligia and Lakona; and tracks to Sattelberg, Palanko and Nongora. All these tracks through Wareo were supply routes for the enemy based on Sattelberg, and routes which the enemy could use should he wish to contest the Australian possession of the coast.

"The capture of the Gusika-Wareo line would therefore both secure the Finschhafen area and provide the ground from which an offensive could be launched to drive the Japs from the east coast of Huon Peninsula and capture Sio, which were the two operational tasks given to the Div."[2] Unless Sattelberg were first captured, however, an attack on the Gusika-Wareo line could be endangered by an enemy attack on the left flank. Wootten therefore decided on two preliminary operations: first, the capture of Sattelberg, and second, the control of track junctions in the Bonga area with the object of cutting the enemy supply line from the coast and attacking Wareo from the east along the spur which joined it with Gusika.

He issued his first operation order in the new area on 11th October: "9 Div will reorganise and continue offensive ops to gain control of approaches to Wareo and Sattelberg with view to capture that area." He divided the area into three sectors of responsibility. North of the Sattelberg Road and a line from Heldsbach Plantation to Arndt Point, the 24th Brigade, consisting at present only of the 2/43rd Battalion and the 2/3rd Pioneers, would protect the Scarlet Beach area in depth against any attack from west or north-west, and gain control of the Bonga Track junctions. The 20th Brigade would be responsible for the central sector between the Sattelberg Road and the Mape River, both boundaries being inclusive, and would "continue pressure towards Sattelberg with a view to its capture". In the southern sector the 22nd Battalion would protect the area south from the Mape River and defend Dreger Harbour.

From the date of the Scarlet Beach landing the staff of the division had done all in their power to maintain the 20th Brigade by sending up supplies in the craft of the 532nd E.B.S.R. As the units themselves had also to be carried to Finschhafen in these small craft, the maintenance position was complicated: for example, it was impossible, with the craft available, to guarantee to replace an expenditure of more than 600 rounds of artillery ammunition each day, and at one stage only two days'

---

[2] 9 Aust Div Report on Operations 2 Oct 43-15 Jan 44.

balanced rations were held at Finschhafen. Difficulties were increased by the irregularity with which supplies were brought to Lae from Buna. Lack of suitable craft resulted in a shortage of vehicles and workshop facilities and this remained acute throughout the campaign.[3]

For three weeks Windeyer had led his force in a fierce campaign to capture Finschhafen and then to hold it against an enemy whose strength had been under-estimated; Wootten thoroughly approved the dispositions as he found them. The courage and tenacity of the men of the 20th Brigade from 22nd September had been matched by the skill and determination of their leader. The brigade had lost 82 officers and men killed or missing and 276 wounded.

The main activity in the forward areas on the 11th was the move of Simpson's column from Kumawa via Graham's route to Jivevaneng. The Kumawa area was handed over to Grace at 9 a.m.; Simpson's two companies departed half an hour later and arrived at Jivevaneng after a seven hours' march. After Simpson's arrival the 2/17th took up positions in depth along the Sattelberg Road from the Knoll 500 yards west of Jivevaneng to the feature known as "the Pimple" 400 yards east of the village.

Action on the 12th was mainly confined to patrolling. That day Joshua wrote to Evans that "patrolling has revealed the use by enemy of certain tracks on the high ground inland from Bonga some 1,500 yards. . . . The enemy may be withdrawing by this route, or may be supplying and reinforcing Sattelberg area from a point on the coast further north."

At Jivevaneng, Pike's company, which was now on the Knoll with Bennie's, prepared to occupy a small knoll forward from the main one. Captain Rudkin's[4] platoon was given the task of capturing this feature. The platoon managed to go only about 40 yards forward when it was fired on and pinned down; the forward scout was killed and four men including two section leaders were wounded. Sergeant Cunningham's platoon then advanced along the south side of the road under cover of a ledge and reached unoccupied Japanese holes about 100 yards forward and level with the knoll. They could see the enemy level with and behind them, but because of the strong defences and the rugged terrain, the platoon was withdrawn and the enemy position mortared. The battalion decided to leave any further move forward until later, and to neutralise the enemy position by artillery and mortar fire.

On the 12th Wootten informed Captain Gore, who had arrived to command "C" Company of the Papuan Battalion, that he would have complete control of his company which would come under divisional and not brigade command. Experience had shown in the recent New Guinea campaigns that it would be difficult to keep the Papuans under one command as all front-line units were constantly asking for a few Papuans as scouts. Wootten stated that the Papuan company's main task would be

---

[3] In January 1944 a number of the 9th Division's vehicles were still awaiting transport to Finschhafen from Lae.

[4] Maj R. S. Rudkin, MC, NX14875; 2/17 Bn. Bank officer; of Sydney; b. Nyngan, NSW, 4 Jul 1919. His unit did not know that he had been promoted to Captain in September.

to obtain information about the country and the enemy by deep patrols; first, into the Bonga-Wareo area, and second in the Wareo-Sattelberg-Mararuo area. No Australians were to accompany the Papuans outside the areas held by the 20th and 24th Brigades.

At 9 a.m. on 13th October Captain Angus' company of the 2/15th attacked the enemy positions west of Kumawa; the company was fired on by enemy machine-guns sited about 150 yards from its start-line. Fierce fighting then began and raged for a quarter of an hour as the men attacked one Japanese post after another, sited in a line. Despite heavy casualties, Sergeant Else[5] kept urging his platoon forward, and thus prevented the attack from becoming pinned down. Private Woods,[6] commanding the leading section, from a distance of 30 yards immediately charged the first enemy machine-gun to open fire. Two of his men were killed and 4 wounded, leaving only himself and another man unhit, but Woods continued to advance, firing his Owen gun and throwing grenades, and silenced the post. Woods then engaged a medium machine-gun 20 yards away which had been causing casualties in another section. This enabled the rest of Else's platoon to storm the remaining two posts. During his undaunted fight, Woods used 12 grenades and about 15 Owen gun magazines. A rifleman himself, he had discarded his rifle for an Owen and gathered the ten extra grenades from his fallen comrades. As with the attacks on Snell's Hill, the east bank of Ilebbe Creek and the Knoll west of Jivevaneng—positions which seemed impregnable—the enemy company was unable to withstand so spirited and determined a challenge. Having lost 39 killed, the defenders fled; the attacking company suffered 30 casualties including 5 killed; in Else's platoon 15 of the 26 men were hit.

The loss of this position west of Kumawa affected the Japanese of the *III/80th Battalion* keenly. A soldier wrote: "Enemy is now closing on our position. With tears in our eyes we had to withdraw. . . . Muddy roads, steep mountain trails. . . . The trench, which is the safest place, is filled with water."

Japanese security regarding documents, maps, prisoners, marks of identification and diaries, was still extremely poor. Vital operation orders and marked maps were still being carried in the front line by Japanese officers. Japanese headquarters still refused to believe that soldiers of Japan could be taken prisoners, and consequently the soldiers were given no instructions as to their behaviour when captured. Their only instructions were that they should save their last grenade to blow themselves up, and thus avoid disgracing Japan, and incidentally falling into the hands of the brutal Australians and Americans who would probably eat them or torture them.

Sullen at first, and fatalistically expecting the worst, Japanese prisoners seemed surprised at the fair treatment accorded to them, and soon were keen to give information. Often they would ask to see the interpreter again and tell him everything. Their motive probably was that, having disgraced themselves in their country's eyes by becoming prisoners, they sought to regain self-esteem by raising their stature in the eyes of their captors.

It was from diaries that the Allies were learning most about their enemies. Most Japanese soldiers carried diaries, in which they wrote down their reactions to

---

[5] S-Sgt A. Else, MM, QX5495; 2/15 Bn. Farmer; of Pullenvale, Qld; b. Brisbane, 20 Aug 1916.
[6] Cpl W. A. Woods, DCM, QX8178; 2/15 Bn. Stockman; of Nambour, Qld; b. Bangalow, NSW, 15 Oct 1910.

events. Diaries captured at this time were usually compounded of frustration at the failure and limitations of Japanese arms, despair at their own situation, optimism at the slightest hint of a change for the better, vitriolic hatred of their enemies, propaganda slogans, and some doubts about ultimate victory.

Around the remainder of the divisional front on 13th October activity was confined largely to patrolling. Captain Cribb's company of the 2/13th occupied Tirimoro while Captain Cooper's found the enemy position at the track junction deserted, and patrolled along the Quembung Track where marks of a field gun were seen.

The 14th was a quiet day on most fronts. In the northern sector Lieut-Colonel Norman and half his 2/28th Battalion arrived at 2.30 a.m. in craft from Lae, after being harmlessly bombed off Finschhafen. Only along the Katika Track was there any evidence of aggressive intentions by the Japanese. From his position about a mile and a half west of Katika, Captain Fisher[7] of the 2/3rd Pioneers patrolled forward along the track at 2 p.m. with two warrant-officers—Bernard[8] and Hughes[9]—and Privates Brown[1] and Page.[2]

About 450 yards forward of the company position Brown and a Japanese saw one another on the track and the Japanese was shot dead. Bernard, attempting to find the enemy flank, was killed. Covered by Brown, who fired eight Owen magazines during the action, the other men attempted to reach Bernard. Page was killed and Fisher wounded, but under cover of Brown's grenades and Hughes' rifle fire, Fisher managed to escape. Brown's aggressive action was mainly responsible for the three men withdrawing safely, and probably for preventing the enemy from making a direct attack to the east. At 5 p.m. the signal wire was tugged from the direction of the enemy. As Captain Knott's[3] company of the 2/3rd Pioneers was about half a mile farther along the Katika Track where it took a bend to the south, it appeared that the enemy had infiltrated between the two companies.

On 5th October documents captured north of the Song by Maclarn's detachment had indicated clearly that the enemy was not in full retreat, but apparently intended some offensive action. At night on the 11th Wootten's newly-arrived headquarters had warned the two brigade commanders that an intercepted enemy wireless message sent between Sattelberg and Sisi stated that "the crisis is at hand". The probability of a counter-attack was indicated also by aerial and naval reconnaissance. During the night 12th-13th October P.T. boats patrolling as far north

---

[7] Capt H. W. Fisher, SX9041; 2/3 Pnr Bn. Clerk; of Medindie Gardens, SA; b. Adelaide, 30 Jan 1917.

[8] WO2 P. McL. Bernard, NX54748; 2/3 Pnr Bn. Accountant; of Five Dock, NSW; b. Marrickville, NSW, 7 Jun 1917. Killed in action 14 Oct 1943.

[9] Lt B. H. Hughes, NX30961; 2/3 Pnr Bn. Stockman; of Copmanhurst, NSW; b. Grafton, NSW, 21 Apr 1919.

[1] Cpl J. H. Brown, MM, NX88806; 2/3 Pnr Bn. Paper ruler; of Bondi Junction, NSW; b. Ultimo, NSW, 24 Jul 1910.

[2] Pte D. K. Page, NX18218; 2/3 Pnr Bn. Garage assistant; of Muswellbrook, NSW; b. Muswellbrook, 18 Jun 1919. Killed in action 14 Oct 1943.

[3] Maj C. C. Knott, MBE, WX432; 2/3 Pnr Bn. Draftsman; of Nedlands, WA; b. Wagin, WA, 1 Mar 1919.

as Umboi Island, sank an enemy ketch and damaged another off Tuam Island, strafed the beaches at Gizarum, and damaged about eight barges. Another important barge hide-out on Long Island had also been found. The heavy damage inflicted on barge traffic first by air attack and later by P.T. boats as well, caused the Japanese to pay careful attention to camouflage of their barge hide-outs and adjacent bivouac areas, and to use the barges only at night. Again, in the early morning of the 15th, P.T. boats sank four Japanese barges laden with troops heading southeast from Sio. By this time aerial reconnaissance and special patrols had indicated that the following were the most likely barge-staging areas between Madang and Gusika: Marakum, Mindiri, Biliau, Fangger, Gali, Kiari and Sio-Nambariwa.

The Allies' difficulty in supplying Finschhafen was as nothing compared with the difficulties which the Japanese staff was experiencing in supplying Sattelberg. On 13th, 14th and 15th October submarines were seen moving from Rabaul to New Guinea, but it seemed unlikely that regular and substantial supplies could be carried by them. Barge traffic along the north coasts of New Guinea and New Britain, starting just before dusk, carried most supplies. Mostly the barges unloaded troops at Sio and Sialum Island, whence they moved by tracks to Kalasa for overland movement to Sattelberg, but occasionally the barges ran south as far as Gusika. They would be more likely to take this risk with stores than with troops. From Sio and Sialum there were two main routes to Wareo and Sattelberg: the coastal route from Sio to Gusika taking about five days, and the inland route from Kalasa to Sattelberg taking about four. To supplement their rations the Japanese were forced to gather produce from native gardens, and as their methods usually included pillage and arson, they incurred the hostility of the natives.

"Tac R" reports between 13th and 15th October underlined the probability that the enemy was reinforcing the area. No. 4 Squadron's report for the 13th and 14th stated that the coastal track was well used and that "it is not considered that inter-village movement would produce such a well defined track". The report for the 15th stated that "the coastal track north of Lakona to Fortification Point appears to have been used extensively overnight. Black soil well churned up with footprints."

Warnings of a Japanese attack now began to reach Wootten also from higher formations. At 7.15 p.m. on the 14th he received from Morshead a message which had in turn come from Mackay, to the effect that an intercepted message showed that a Japanese divisional commander had been ordered to attack, at dusk on 16th October, positions from Arndt Point to Langemak Bay. On the morning of the 15th Wootten learnt from Morshead that the principal objectives would be the airfield and P.T. boats near the mouth of the Mape.

Like Windeyer during the Finschhafen campaign, Wootten was finding the shortage of infantry a constant handicap "not only to offensive and counter-offensive operations, but also to the creation of an adequate div reserve".[4] By the 15th, however, the remainder of the 2/28th Battalion had arrived at Scarlet Beach. Thus, by 15th October, Wootten had two-thirds of his division in the area; and a signal from Morshead informed him that G.H.Q. had ordered C.T.F. 76 to prepare to move the 26th Brigade from Lae to Finschhafen at 30 hours' notice. This was indeed heartening news, and contrasted strongly with the protracted negotiations which had been necessary to send the 2/43rd Battalion to Scarlet Beach at the end of September. It was indicative of the gravity of the situation, and of the fact that the various commanders had learned their lesson. Relations between the American air and naval commanders on the one hand, and the senior Australians on the other, were now excellent, and there was little difficulty in securing sympathetic cooperation. The enemy, however, had been given a chance to seize the initiative. Writing to Blamey on 20th October, Mackay stated:

> Through not being able to reinforce quickly the enemy has been given time to recover and we have not been able to exploit our original success. Through the piecemeal arrival of reinforcements the momentum of the attack has not been maintained. As was proved in the Lae operations the provision of adequate forces at the right place and time is both the quickest and most economical course.

To the north of the Song two patrols, important in their results, had been made on the 15th. Along the river's north bank Lieutenant Cavanagh[5] led one from the 2/28th Battalion about 3,000 yards west. On the way back at 3.20 p.m. it captured a slightly-wounded Japanese who was carrying a white flag. He later stated that he was a corporal from the *I/238th Battalion* of the *41st Division*. His battalion had moved from Wewak to Lae and Salamaua in August, except for 100 men, of whom he was one, who had arrived in Finschhafen in September, when it was too late to send them on. Forward of Gusika a Japanese officer's satchel was found after a patrol clash. It contained a copy of an operation order issued on Sattelberg on 12th October by Lieut-General Shigeru Katagiri, the commander of the *20th Japanese Division*.

Most Allied Intelligence reports before the landing on Scarlet Beach made a point of emphasising that the loss of Lae and Salamaua destroyed the principal usefulness of Finschhafen to the enemy. In point of fact the loss of Lae and Salamaua made the enemy more determined than ever to hold Finschhafen.

When the Allies began to close in on Salamaua from late July, General Adachi began to send reinforcements to the Huon Peninsula. Under the command of Major-General Eizo Yamada, Colonel Miyake's *80th Regiment* (less its *I Battalion* which was in the Salamaua fighting), the *III/26th Field Artillery Battalion*, the *7th Naval Base Force* and other sub-units—a grand total of about 3,200 troops—left Madang on 23rd August and arrived at Finschhafen on 15th September, one day before the fall of Lae. The *80th Regiment* remained at Finschhafen to reinforce the 1,000 troops from assorted units there. Later they were joined by about 1,000 more troops who had been on their way overland from Finschhafen to Lae when Lae fell. Thus

---

[4] 9th Division report.
[5] Capt C. O. Cavanagh, WX7221; 2/28 Bn. Farmer; of South Kumminin, WA; b. Midland Junction, WA, 19 Sep 1905.

a force of over 5,000 Japanese troops was in the general Finschhafen-Mongi River area when the 20th Brigade landed behind them at Scarlet Beach. Parts of all three Japanese divisions of the *XVIII Army* were in the Finschhafen area on 22nd September. As well as the *80th Regiment* of the *20th Division*, there were portions of the *238th Regiment* of the *41st Division*, which, like the *I/80th Battalion*, had been sent to Salamaua, and even the battered company of the *102nd Regiment* of the *51st Division* which had first met the Allies at Nassau Bay.

"With the cooperation of the Navy," stated General Imamura's order from Rabaul on 20th September, "the essential places of the Dampier Strait and Bougainville Island will be held. The Army, Navy and Air Forces will combine their strength to eliminate the enemy on land and sea." In order to carry out this intention it was necessary to send more troops to Finschhafen. Little could be expected from the broken *51st Division*, the remnants of the *I/80th Battalion*, and the main portion of the *238th Regiment* now retreating over the Saruwaged Range to the north coast. Thus, the main body of Katagiri's *20th Division* departed from Madang by land and sea on 15th September. The *79th Regiment*, 3,196 troops, comprised the majority. As the task of opposing the 7th Australian Division was being undertaken by the *78th Regiment*, Katagiri would have in the Finschhafen area his *79th* and *80th Regiments* and the equivalent of another regiment from the various sub-units and reinforcements in the area. The equivalent of a division of Japanese would soon be in the Finschhafen area.[6]

It can thus be seen how narrow was the margin between victory and defeat in the battle for Finschhafen. The *20th Japanese Division* was already on the way to Finschhafen when the 20th Australian Brigade, one-third its size, landed ahead of it, and secured a foothold on the east coast of the Huon Peninsula. Bold planning, determined fighting, skilful generalship and luck had combined to give the Australians at Finschhafen a good chance of weathering the storm which they now knew was gathering at Sattelberg.

When Adachi learnt of the landing at Scarlet Beach he ordered the *80th Regiment* to occupy the Sattelberg feature until the arrival of the rest of the *20th Division* when an attack would be launched on Finschhafen. When the attempt was made on 26th September by Lieut-Colonel Takagi's *III/80th Battalion* to attack east along the Sattelberg and Katika Tracks but was beaten back, Colonel Miyake, of the *80th Regiment*, decided to wait until more of his force arrived from the Logaweng area before renewing the attack at the end of September. When this attack, in its turn, made no real progress the Japanese decided to wait for the larger number of reinforcements from the north.

Hearing of the Australian landing at Scarlet Beach General Katagiri hastened his advance. It had been intended that all of this force would arrive by 25th October, but now they pressed ahead as fast as their physical condition and the difficult terrain would permit. By the 10th, Katagiri and part of his force had arrived in the Sattelberg area. The main body, including most of the *79th Regiment*, came to Sio and Sialum by barge and then marched to Kalasa and Sattelberg along

---

[6] The Japanese order of battle on the mainland of Australian New Guinea was now known to the Allies in some detail. The main formations were:

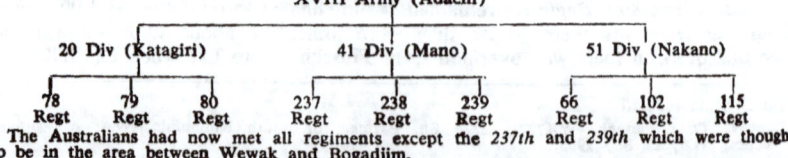

The Australians had now met all regiments except the *237th* and *239th* which were thought to be in the area between Wewak and Bogadjim.

the inland track. Other units and sub-units, including the headquarters of the *26th Field Artillery Regiment* and the *II/26th Field Artillery Battalion*, marched with the *79th Regiment*. The *5th Shipping Engineer Regiment*, from 23rd September onwards, aided the *9th Shipping Engineer Regiment*, which was already carrying stores along the coast. Because of the transport difficulties the artillery were able to take with them only six mountain guns.

Along the overland route from the north coast members of the *79th Regiment* had seen survivors of the *51st Division* from Lae and Salamaua struggling north in small groups. They were starving and in pitiful condition, but the *79th Regiment* either would not or could not give their miserable comrades any rations. During October what was left of the *51st Division* arrived at Kiari, and, after recuperating and reorganising, took up defensive positions there to strengthen the rear of the *20th Division*.

Thus the Australian and Japanese divisional commanders arrived in the Finschhafen area at the same time. General Wootten's orders for a resumption of the offensive were issued on 11th October, and General Katagiri's orders for a counter-attack on the following day.

"After dusk on X Oct," stated Katagiri's order, "the main strength of *79th Infantry Regiment* will attack the enemy in Arndt Point area from the north side. The assault boat Butai will penetrate through the north coast of Arndt Point on the night of X-day."

The order continued that the commander of the *II/26th Artillery Battalion*, with two companies of the *I/79th Battalion*, would destroy the enemy in the northern sector by occupying the Bonga area by the evening of 14th October.

Katagiri's attack was to be three-pronged. First, there would be a diversion from the north by the *II/26th Artillery Battalion* and portion of the *I/79th Battalion*. Secondly, a seaborne attack by *10 Company* of the *79th Regiment* which had been left behind at Nambariwa, supported by a detachment of the *20th Engineer Regiment* with explosives and demolition charges, would take place "on the night of X-day". Instructions to this "Boat Penetration Tai" were that "ammunition dumps, artillery positions, tanks, enemy H.Q., moored boats, barracks, etc. should be selected as objectives". Thirdly, the main attack from the west would be made by the *80th Regiment* astride the Sattelberg Road towards Heldsbach and the artillery positions, and the *79th Regiment* to the north with the object of destroying the enemy north of Arndt Point.

"X-day," stated Katagiri's order, "will be decided on X-minus-1-day at 2200 hrs and a fire will be seen for 20 minutes on the Sattelberg heights. When the fire is seen answer back at a suitable spot (by fires)."

The information which General Wootten had received from higher formations about signs of an impending attack had given no clear indication as to the probable nature or direction of the attack. Even before the capture of General Katagiri's order on the afternoon of 15th October, however, he had changed his plans in order to fight a defensive battle. After a conference with senior commanders on the morning of the 15th he issued an operation order stating that "indications are that the enemy may counter-attack towards either or both Finschhafen airfield and Langemak Bay" by sea or land or a combination of both. It can thus be seen that on the 15th the Australians were not clear as to where the main Japanese attack would occur, except that they thought it would be in the southern sector. Windeyer was ordered to coordinate the defence of Langemak Bay and "hold important ground at all costs", defend in depth, maintain a mobile reserve, and organise coastwatching stations and beach defences. Wootten ordered that the ground to be held should include the track junctions in the Bonga area, North Hill, the high ground about two miles west of Scarlet Beach between the Song and Jivevaneng, Kumawa, Tirimoro, Butaweng, Logaweng and the 532nd E.B.S.R. base at Dreger Harbour.

Two companies of the 2/2nd Machine Gun Battalion were placed under Windeyer's command and one under Evans'. Light anti-aircraft guns were given an extra role of beach defence, extra guns were sited to protect the beaches, infantry 2-pounder guns were sited along the coast, and coastwatching stations were established. When the 2/32nd Battalion arrived on 15th October, it and the 2/2nd Machine Gun Battalion less three companies became the divisional reserve.

Then came news of the translated document—an even more important document than the Japanese evacuation order captured by the 7th Division four days before the capture of Lae. Thereupon, at 3.35 p.m., Wootten instructed Evans to "site and hold at all costs a post north of River Song on direct track running through 620700 to Wareo, which track possible axis of enemy land attack". This was the only redisposition considered necessary by Wootten as a result of the capture of the plan of attack.

As rain fell and the mists came down, anxious Australian eyes were turned to the western mountains where Sattelberg heights faded into the dusk. Wootten's instructions were clear: "All units whose location permits will establish lookouts to report immediately . . . the lighting of any fires at night on Sattelberg heights and any answering fires."

CHAPTER 19

THE JAPANESE COUNTER-ATTACK

EVEN before General Wootten had informed his subordinates of General Katagiri's intention to attack with the *20th Division*, fierce fighting had occurred along the Sattelberg Road. Before dawn on 16th October the 2/17th Battalion at Jivevaneng was heavily attacked. By the time the Japanese order of 12th October had been translated it was obvious that this thrust was part of the main plan.

At 4.45 a.m. on the 16th the Papuan platoon (Lieutenant Macfarlane[1]) with the 2/17th heard movement and was fired on as it withdrew into the 2/17th's positions. By this time the enemy had crept to within 20 yards of battalion headquarters on the eastern edge of Jivevaneng and now launched a series of fierce attacks. Most of them were beaten back by components of Major Maclarn's Headquarters Company as well as battalion headquarters. For two hours after 7.30 a.m. the main track and positions occupied by a platoon of machine-gunners and one of mortars were subjected to severe shelling from a 70-mm and a 75-mm gun. Throughout the day four more attacks were made on the battalion's positions but all were repulsed. At 3.15 p.m. battalion headquarters was heavily mortared and, indeed, a hail of mortar bombs and grenades from cup dischargers descended upon the battalion's positions during the day; it suffered 19 casualties including 5 killed or died of wounds. Judging from the squeals and groans many casualties were inflicted on the enemy although only six bodies were left in the area.

Colonel Simpson estimated that the attacking force was probably larger than a company. Paybooks were taken from the Japanese corpses and it was not long before it was known that the *80th Regiment* was opposing the 2/17th.

There was no other heavy fighting on the 16th, but there were indications of the approach of the counter-attacking division. North-east from the 2/17th three companies of the 2/3rd Pioneer Battalion were holding the high ground south of the Song and the Katika-Palanko track about 1,500 to 2,000 yards west of Katika. On three occasions a forward platoon exchanged shots with parties of Japanese, apparently heading east, and a patrol skirmished with an enemy force moving east during the afternoon. Elsewhere the divisional front from Gusika to Dreger Harbour was quiet.[2]

---

[1] Lt G. D. Macfarlane, NX86595. 2/1 Pnr Bn and Papuan Inf Bn. Insurance inspector; of Rose Bay, NSW; b. Townsville, Qld, 6 Feb 1916.

[2] An incident occurred late in the day which kept the troops occupied. At 7.45 p.m. four Kittyhawks, nearly out of petrol, asked for lights to be shown on the airfield. Before this could be done the four pilots baled out. Fifteen minutes after one crash Colonel Gallasch's headquarters heard whistling. It was raining and pitch dark but Warrant-Officer G. A. Curby dashed straight through a booby-trapped area and about 20 minutes later returned carrying across his shoulders 2nd-Lieutenant D. J. La Nore, 8 Fighter Squadron, 49 Fighter Group. La Nore remained with the battalion until the next afternoon and proved himself a worthy rifleman. The remaining three pilots were found on the 17th.

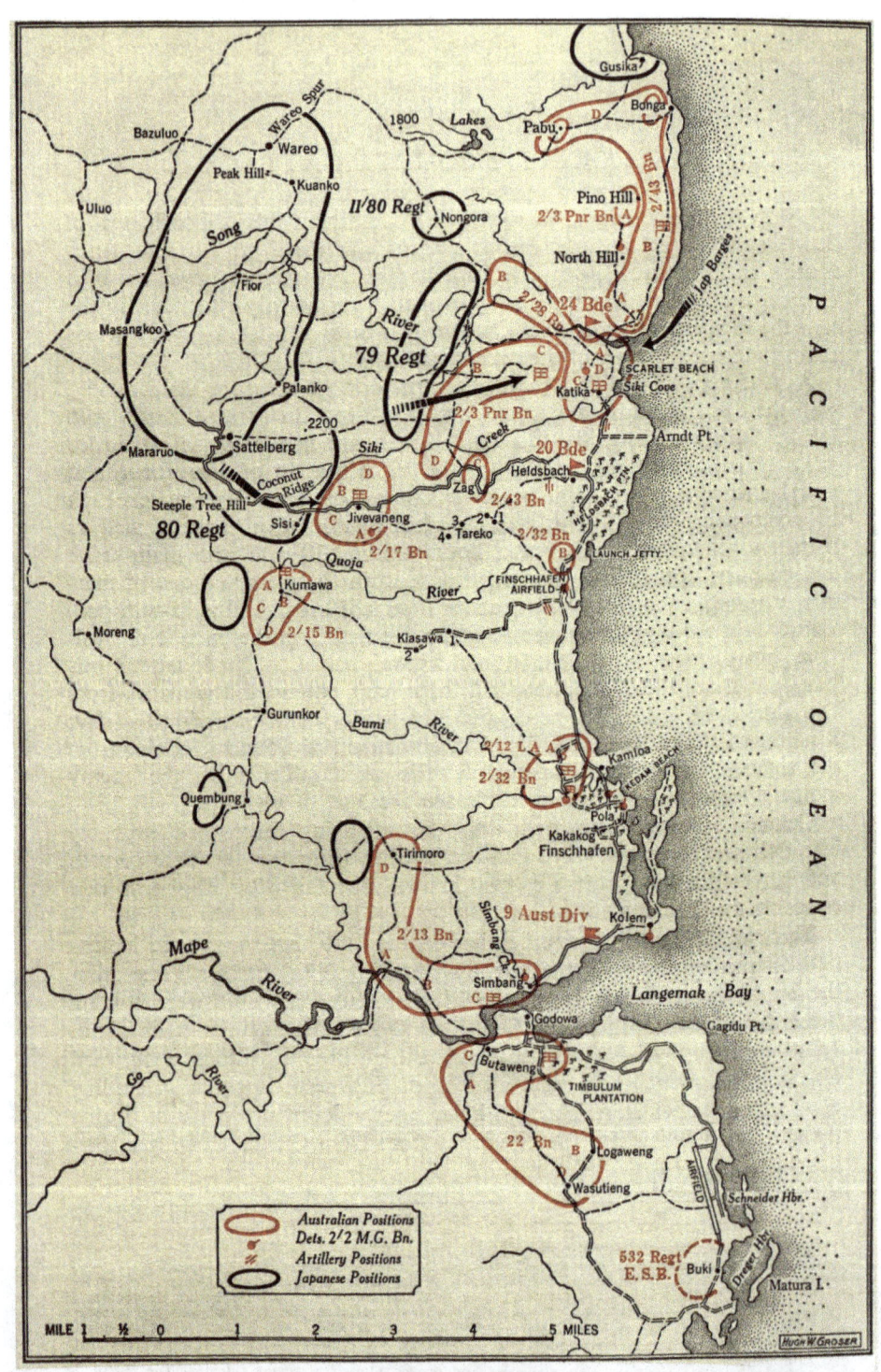

Australian and enemy dispositions, Finschhafen area, 16th-17th October

It now seemed that a Japanese force might have infiltrated between the widely dispersed companies of the 2/3rd Pioneer Battalion and that the expected counter-attack was imminent. "[You] must patrol vigorously," Brigadier Evans ordered Colonel Gallasch of the Pioneers, "to prevent enemy getting in close in force." Actually the full strength of the *79th Regiment* had been infiltrating through the Pioneers and Colonel Hayashida was preparing to attack to the east.

General Wootten believed that 16th October must be the "X-1-day" referred to in General Katagiri's order, even though there was no sign yet of the "diversion" from the north. Worried by the lack of an adequate reserve he yet felt that his two brigades were disposed as efficiently as possible to meet the threat. During darkness on the 16th, when rain was pelting down, all the Australians were watching Sattelberg for the signal fire. It seemed impossible that a fire could be lit in the steady downpour, but at 8.30 p.m. a company of the 22nd Battalion at Logaweng reported observing a large fire on Sattelberg's dominating crest, and, according to its war diary, reported it "to Division". For some reason, however, no report of this fire reached divisional headquarters. Indeed the divisional Intelligence summary stated categorically against 17th October that "none of the pre-arranged signs for D-day were observed by our troops".

All along the coast occupied by the Australians, and particularly at Scarlet Beach, eyes and ears were strained seawards waiting for the threatened seaborne attack. The night was quiet until 3.15 when a heavy Japanese bombing raid began on the Finschhafen area and lasted for about two hours. Although 66 bombs were dropped there was little damage and few casualties. This heralded the seaborne attack, however, for at 3.55 a.m. on 17th October the lookout of Captain D. C. Siekmann's coast-watching patrol at Gusika reported four Japanese barges heading south. Brigadier Evans was immediately informed and the 2/43rd stood to. A quarter of an hour later three barges almost hidden in the rain and darkness and with muffled motors were seen approaching Scarlet Beach from the north.

As planned, the Japanese in the three barges were the remnants of the *10th Company* of the *79th Regiment* and picked platoons from the *20th Engineer Regiment* and the *5th Shipping Engineer Regiment*. General Adachi himself has left the best description of what the Japanese raiders intended to do:

"The above units, having received orders to prepare to attack the enemy's rear by boat in connection with the division's operations to annihilate the force which has landed north of Finschhafen, undertook intensive training for about 20 days under command of company commander 1st-Lieutenant Sugino at Nambariwa base. The men all awaited the appointed day firm in their belief of certain victory. On 16th October 1943 at the time of the attack by the division's main strength to annihilate the enemy north of Katika, the unit received orders to penetrate the shore south of the mouth of the Song River. After drinking the sake graciously presented to the divisional commander by the Emperor, the unit vowed anew its determination to do or die and departed from the base boldly at dusk on the same day. Repulsing the interference of enemy P.T. boats on the way, the unit arrived at the designated point at 0230 hours on the 17th."

It is probable that the "interference of enemy P.T. boats" dismissed so lightly by Adachi cost Sugino more than half his force. It will be recalled that P.T. boats in the early morning of 15th October reported having sunk four barges laden with troops heading south-east from Sio. It seems that Sugino's force had originally embarked on seven barges and that three or four of these were sunk on the 15th or 16th. Thanks to the Japanese habit of carrying operation orders to the front line, the Allies were ready for the seaward attack. Wootten's staff were right in their deduction that it would take place between 6 p.m. on the 16th and 8 a.m. on the 17th. Between these times American small craft had been forbidden to move in the area and all craft moving along the coast were to be treated as hostile.

On Scarlet Beach were two companies of the 2/28th Battalion, Captain Coppock's[3] on the north and Major Stenhouse's[4] on the south; a detachment of Captain Harris'[5] 10th Light Anti-Aircraft Battery (a Bofors gun); detachments of the 2/28th's anti-tank platoon with two-pounder anti-tank guns, and of the machine-gun platoon; and a detachment of the 532nd E.B.S.R. manning two 37-mm and two Browning .50 calibre machine-guns.

At 4.10 a.m. the spotter for the light anti-aircraft detachment saw three barges coming round the north point. He immediately called, "Take post, barges" and the detachment manned the gun. At the same time Sergeant John Fuina, in charge of the American beach detachment, manned his 37-mm gun 40 yards south from the Bofors. The Americans tumbled out of their hammocks and into their weapon-pits.

It was very dark and the barges were moving quickly and quietly towards the north end of Scarlet Beach. When they were about 50 yards from the shore the 37-mm and the Bofors opened fire simultaneously, firing three and five rounds respectively. The Bofors commander saw that his rounds were high of the target, and, as he could not depress his gun, he ordered his men into their weapon-pits.

Two of the barges had now beached and were being attacked by the 37-mm, a Bren manned by two men of the 2/28th Battalion, and small arms fire from the anti-aircraft detachment. About fifteen yards from where the barges landed was a .50 Browning, manned by Private Nathan Van Noy, Junior, and his loader Corporal Stephen Popa. While the other guns of the beach defenders were firing, Van Noy held his fire until the Japanese, led by a bugler and two flame-throwers, were almost under the nose of his camouflaged gun as they leapt from the ramps of the first two barges to the shore. As they charged the Japanese threw grenades ahead and one lucky toss landed in Van Noy's gun emplacement, shattering one of Van Noy's legs and wounding Popa. At that moment Van Noy pressed the trigger and stopped the Japanese charge. The Browning caused great slaughter and pinned down the enemy at the beach's shelving edge.

---

[3] Maj H. T. Coppock, WX3404; 2/28 Bn. Salesman; of Mount Hawthorn, WA; b. Perth, 30 Aug 1908.

[4] Maj T. R. Stenhouse, WX3406; 2/28 Bn. Clerk; of Leederville, WA; b. Perth, 27 Jul 1915.

[5] Lt-Col T. J. Harris, MC, ED, VX14643; 2/4 LAA Regt. Salesman; of Caulfield, Vic; b. Windsor, Vic, 12 Jan 1915.

Here the Japanese could be seen only when they moved. Grenades were now hurled by both sides, and, naturally, most damage was inflicted upon the raiders as they were exposed.

Soon after the first two barges landed the anti-tank guns farther south joined in and holed each barge, rendering them completely unserviceable. The third barge, under concentrated fire from all the defending weapons along the north shore of Scarlet Beach, made off with a number of 2-pounder shells in it.[6]

The enemy on the beach kept throwing grenades despite the casualties which were being inflicted on them. Van Noy put a second magazine on his gun which "traced patterns among [the Japanese] forms as they tried to crawl forward".[7] Another grenade landed in the pit, but still the gun which had done so much damage to the raiders continued to fire, although one of Van Noy's legs was

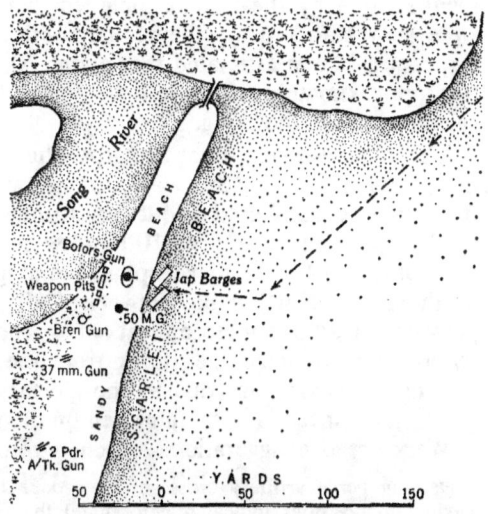

Japanese seaborne attack on Scarlet Beach, 17th October

almost blown off and the other badly damaged. A third grenade landed in the pit and the gun went silent. With his finger still on the trigger the gallant American youth was dead.[8] The wounded Popa managed to grab a rifle and fire a bullet into the head of a Japanese coming at him with a bayonet. When found he was alive but unconscious with the body of the dead Japanese sprawled across him.

With the light improving the Japanese were in a precarious position. Sergeant Sitlington,[9] commanding the section of Bofors anti-aircraft guns, who was in the best position to see what was happening on the northern end of the beach, had already telephoned to Captain Harris and asked if more troops could be sent up as there were about 60 Japanese on the beach. He also stated that the Japanese now seemed to be trying to cross

---

[6] The report of the 2/28th Battalion stated: "The third [barge], hit by 2-pounder AP was in full flight north with Japanese wounded bawling loudly. From the number of bodies washed ashore north of the Song mouth it may be presumed sunk." The Papuan Battalion's listening post near Bonga also heard a barge full of groaning Japanese heading north.

[7] *History of Second Engineer Special Brigade*, p. 53.

[8] For this action Private Van Noy was posthumously awarded his country's highest decoration—the Congressional Medal of Honour. He was the first American engineer in the war of 1941-45 to win the award. A year later when the Army had developed a new type of port repair ship, a seagoing vessel of 2,500 tons, the first to be launched was christened *Junior Van Noy*.

[9] WO2 K. G. Sitlington, VX47207. 2/3 and 2/4 LAA Regts. Accountant; of Caulfield, Vic; b. Ararat, Vic, 31 Jul 1908.

to the north bank of the Song. Harris immediately went to Captain Coppock of the 2/28th, who was in charge of the beach defences, and Coppock sent a detachment northward. At first light Lieutenant Cavanagh led his platoon of the 2/28th Battalion north along the beach. In the two wrecked barges and just above the water line were 39 dead Japanese. The Allied defenders had lost one killed and four wounded. The armament carried by the raiders included flame-throwers (but their operators were shot before using them), demolition charges, mines and bangalore torpedoes. It was estimated that about 70 Japanese had landed and therefore approximately 30 must have succeeded in crawling north along the spit and across the Song.

The Japanese who escaped across the Song were seen by a coastwatching patrol of the 2/43rd stationed at the mouth of the river; they said the Japanese numbered about 30. Joshua spoke to Evans who said that the Japanese might number 100 and were to be hunted down by the company of the 2/43rd, under Captain Fleming,[1] stationed on the coastal track north-east of North Hill. Between 1.30 and 2.15 p.m. Fleming's company killed 24 Japanese and about 4 were known to have escaped. Bad security had doomed the attack from the start. The defeat of the actual landing, however, was due to the alertness and courage of a handful of gunners, engineers and infantrymen on the northern shore of Scarlet Beach.

Wars breed exaggeration. Adachi wrote in his report:

> Defying fierce artillery crossfire, the troops landed from the boats immediately. Taking up positions indicated beforehand the three platoons advanced in columns in different directions. The infantry and engineers advanced as one body creeping through the jungle. They annihilated the panic-stricken enemy everywhere, and achieved glorious and distinguished success. They killed more than 430 of the enemy, destroyed seven AA guns, five machine-cannons and MG's and five ammunition and supply dumps. Moreover they blew up the enemy headquarters and bivouac tents, thus destroying the centre of command [these were in fact the tents of the casualty clearing station]. Raiding the area at will and with raging fury, they surprised and overwhelmed the enemy. By disrupting his command organisation they established the foundation for the victory of the division's main strength. With the company commander as the nucleus, the entire group put forth a united effort and demonstrated the unique and peerless spiritual superiority of the Imperial Army. . . . All those who fell severely wounded committed suicide by using hand grenades, and, of the total of 186 men, all except 58 became guardian spirits of their country.

To the west of Scarlet Beach the headquarters and scattered companies of the 2/3rd Pioneers heard the noise of battle from Scarlet Beach, but Colonel Gallasch had little time to wonder about it because soon after first light Japanese began to appear around his headquarters.

Unknown to the Pioneers, Colonel Kaneki Hayashida's *79th Regiment* was now assembled in strength about one mile west of Katika. The Pioneers' skirmishes of the preceding day had really been with the advance and flank guards of this large Japanese force. Except for his companies of the *I/79th Battalion* detached for the diversion in the north Hayashida had the whole of his relatively fresh regiment as well as part of the *III/26th Artillery Battalion*. He divided his regiment

---
[1] Maj J. A. Fleming, SX9459; 2/43 Bn. Clerk; of Adelaide; b. Mount Gambier, SA, 18 Sep 1919.

into two—the Song attacking force consisting of Major Takehama's *II/79th Battalion* and the Katika attacking force consisting of Major Uchida's *III/79th Battalion*. Hayashida's intention was "to charge in and attack and annihilate the enemy located north of Arndt Point". The general plan was for the Song force, followed by the Katika force, to penetrate "an enemy gap in the Katika-Song sector". While Katika force held the gap Song force would attack along the right bank of the Song and then swing south. "Depending upon the progress of the Song attacking force," stated the order, "Katika attacking force will attack and surprise the enemy in Katika from the rear and annihilate them." Hayashida would then link up with the raiders from the sea and take them under command. Song force would attack at 4 p.m. on the 16th.

By the early morning of the 17th Hayashida's plan had met with some success and some failure. His Song force had penetrated the gap on the preceding afternoon, a relatively easy task because of the distance between the Pioneer companies; but the landing force had been almost wiped out.

During the 17th the men of the 2/3rd Pioneer headquarters were called upon to face the *79th Regiment*. The Japanese were behind the three Pioneer companies, and, if they only knew it, there was little to stop a bold and immediate attack reaching Scarlet Beach. The battalion's armourer sergeant, Glasgow,[2] and six men constituted the first patrol from battalion headquarters against a band of Japanese who were seen near a creek early in the morning. Glasgow was killed and the patrol withdrew, heavily outnumbered. A section patrol came across a strong party of Japanese decorating themselves with leaves for camouflage. In an exchange of fire the section leader was wounded and the patrol withdrew. A platoon set out for this party of Japanese who were near the battalion's isolated "C" Company. The Japanese were found forming up for an attack on battalion headquarters. After a heavy exchange of fire the opposition proved too strong and the patrol withdrew.

At 11 a.m. the Pioneers' headquarters on the high ground west of Katika was heavily attacked by at least one enemy company. Some of the attackers reached as close as ten yards from one platoon's position but all attacks were repulsed. Forward of this position, which was on a hill, Warrant-Officer Curby[3] watched a party of Japanese climbing upwards, and when they were about ten feet from the top, rolled grenades among them, killing at least three.

The firing then slackened and patrols scoured the area within 100 yards of headquarters in accordance with an order from Evans to "ensure vigorous patrolling to find out position of infiltration with object of bringing down artillery fire". Soon after midday another heavy attack developed on battalion headquarters and lasted for an hour. As the impetus of the attack began to peter out Curby led 15 men armed with extra grenades round to the rear of the Japanese. Unfortunately this patrol walked into some booby-traps. After returning to headquarters with the casualties, the patrol set out again and got behind about 20 Japanese whom they showered

---

[2] Sgt K. L. S. Glasgow, NX58001; 2/3 Pnr Bn. Grazier; of Julia Creek, Qld; b. Narrandera, NSW, 13 Aug 1908. Killed in action 17 Oct 1943.
[3] Lt G. A. Curby, NX52067. 2/3 Pnr and 42 Bns. Shunter; of Cronulla, NSW; b. Hornsby, NSW, 19 Feb 1913.

with grenades. The Japanese replied with heavy fire, then scattered and fled.

During the day Gallasch's headquarters had lost 9 including 3 killed. The telephone line to his three forward companies had been cut. Gallasch needed all possible support for the Pioneers but had few automatic weapons and no mortars. His headquarters positions were slightly divided with elements of one platoon only on the steep hill overlooking the whole position. Soon after last light, at 7.20 p.m., about a company of Japanese launched what the battalion diarist described as "a furious attack" on this hill. Very heavy fire continued for ten minutes when three badly wounded men were sent down from the hill for medical attention. Another man whose own rifle had been smashed by enemy fire was also sent down with an urgent request for more ammunition and another rifle. While he was waiting for the ammunition the remainder of the platoon came down from the hill because they were short of ammunition and thus felt unable to hold on.

Whenever soldiers withdraw forlornly from a position which has previously defied enemy attempts to capture it, and which might have been held a little longer, a certain amount of consternation is bound to follow. This is particularly so if rumours accompany withdrawals to the effect that the enemy is following closely. So it was in this case and, when the Japanese appeared cheering and yelling on top of the newly-captured hill, the headquarters of the Pioneers, laden with the bulk of the reserve ammunition and rations, withdrew to Katika "to strengthen 2/28th Battalion positions". The three forward companies were thus left on the high ground farther west without telephone communication and without a secure supply route.

During daylight battalion headquarters and part of Headquarters Company of the 2/3rd Pioneers had withstood the Japanese attack and had gained some respite for Brigadier Evans to redispose his forces. By 9 p.m. they were passing through the forward positions of Captain Newbery's company of the 2/28th Battalion. Colonel Norman ordered Newbery to place in position all men of the Pioneers whom he wished, including those with automatic weapons, and to send the remainder to his headquarters.

In this crisis General Wootten's divisional reserve was very slender—only part of the 2/32nd Battalion. It would certainly be beyond the capacity of the small craft of the 532nd E.B.S.R. to move his third brigade from Lae and maintain the entire division at Finschhafen. Back in Dobodura General Morshead had read General Katagiri's captured order and had followed the early fighting as well as he could from "sitreps". On 17th October he waited no longer and sent a message to Admiral Barbey which he repeated to Generals Mackay and Wootten.

> Strong enemy attack developing Finschhafen. Desire move 26 Aust Inf Bde and one Field Ambulance from Lae to Finschhafen earliest possible. Require 14 L.C.I's to load personnel "G" Beach. . . . Require also 6 L.S.T's load Buna ammunition and supplies urgently needed Finschhafen.

Without further ado Morshead warned Generals Milford and Wootten that the 26th Brigade would immediately revert to Wootten's command and prepare for an urgent move to Finschhafen. In Port Moresby Mackay received Morshead's signal and also Wootten's latest report saying that the enemy was within 3,000 yards of the beach-head. He immediately repeated the request and the information to Generals MacArthur and Blamey and to Admiral Carpender. At 9.30 p.m. on the 17th, when the Pioneers were withdrawing through the 2/28th's positions, Morshead's senior staff officer, Brigadier Wells, rang through to General Berryman in Port Moresby and asked for the latest information about the move of the 26th Brigade. Just before midnight Berryman learnt that Barbey's Task Force 76 would provide the 14 L.C.I's and 6 L.S.T's and would leave Buna for Lae at 2.30 p.m. on the 18th to transport the 26th Brigade to Finschhafen.

The initiative and cooperation of the senior Allied commanders in New Guinea had ensured that there would be no nonsense about reinforcement this time. Indeed, MacArthur's signal authorising and ordering the use of Task Force 76 was received some time after arrangements had been made by the local commander. In his order to Admiral Carpender and Generals Kenney and Mackay, MacArthur stated that at the "earliest practicable date" the reinforcement would take place; the navy would transport and protect, and the air force would support "irrespective of present commitments".

Opposite Katika and Jivevaneng the night of 17th-18th October was quiet. Indeed the 2/17th Battalion had enjoyed a relatively peaceful day—"a quiet day judging by yesterday's standard" was the comment of the battalion diarist. During the mid-afternoon 9 Mitchells and 9 Bostons accurately bombed and strafed the Sattelberg area. Soon after dusk several units reported a large fire on Sattelberg, but the signal, if such it was, had now lost its point.

As he contemplated the battle situation in his northern area Brigadier Evans was worried by the dispersal of his troops. His companies were thinly spread from the Bonga-Gusika area in the north to the Katika area in the south; there was little depth from east to west; and moreover three of his companies were out of contact. He decided, therefore, to use part of his brigade reserve—two companies of the 2/28th Battalion— early on the 18th to clear up the situation west of Katika and to re-establish communications with the isolated companies. Thus at 10.45 p.m. on the 17th Evans ordered Norman to recapture the Pioneer headquarters position recently lost to the Japanese.

In order to keep some reserve Evans also decided to withdraw his forces from the Gusika, Bonga and Pino Hill areas, and to hold at least two companies ready to move south of the Song if required. It will be recalled that Wootten had described the area of the Bonga Track junctions as "vital ground to be held at all costs". By 9 p.m. Joshua received orders to move his two northern companies to the mouth of the Song.

During darkness the northern companies moved south. It was hard for any commander to give up so much important and hardly-won ground, but Evans believed that he must shorten his lines and present a continuous front to the enemy. The beach-head itself between the Song and Katika was very thinly held. The five miles' journey of the northern companies in darkness and in rain along a track ankle-deep in mud was extremely difficult and tiring, but by first light on the 18th the two companies had reached the mouth of the Song.

Because the night of the 17th-18th was quiet and because the enemy's main attacks west of Katika and Jivevaneng appeared to have been stopped, Wootten decided to regain the initiative. At 8.15 a.m. on the 18th his operation order stated "9 Aust Div will resume the offensive immediately". The 24th Brigade would "regain effective control of area held by it on 16th October and any posts vacated will be re-established in strength", and would also take the first steps to capture the high ground north of the Song in the Nongora area, ready for an advance on Wareo. The 20th Brigade would "exert pressure with 2/15th and 2/17th Battalions along previous lines of advance and gain ground wherever possible".

At 7.30 on the morning of the 18th Norman of the 2/28th gave his orders—Stenhouse's company to lead, followed by Newbery's, and Coppock's company to move from the beach into Stenhouse's old position on the right of Katika to protect the flank. The start time of 8.45 a.m. was delayed for 45 minutes because Coppock's company was unable to relieve Stenhouse's in time. At 9.15 a.m. as the companies were forming up for their counter-attack Newbery's company on the left fired on two Japanese scouts moving down the Katika Track. A quarter of an hour later a party of Japanese was reported on the left of the track and Lieutenant Vanpraag's[4] platoon was sent out to counter any attempt at left flank encirclement. By 9.45 a.m. it was quite obvious that the West Australians would have to postpone any idea of an advance because the enemy savagely attacked Stenhouse's company on the right. The attack was repulsed but Norman informed Evans that the attack was being made by at least two, if not three, enemy companies.

Intermittent fighting continued in the Katika-Siki Creek area. The first intimation that the enemy were thrusting south of Siki Creek was supplied by Captain Kimpton's[5] troop of anti-aircraft gunners protecting the field gun area south of Siki Creek when at 10.5 a.m. they reported that about 20 Japanese were attacking troop headquarters and one of the Bofors guns. Firing over open sights the isolated anti-aircraft and field gunners repulsed the enemy thrust. Typical of the determination of the gunners not to budge despite their lack of infantry support was Lance-Bombardier Kirwan,[6] a Bofors gunner, who not only remained on the job though wounded but later went forward to reconnoitre enemy positions.

---

[4] Capt J. B. Vanpraag, WX6886; 2/28 Bn. University student; of Perth; b. Perth, 24 Dec 1919.
[5] Capt S. MacD. Kimpton, VX38174; 2/4 LAA Regt. Manager; of Melbourne; b. Melbourne, 5 Mar 1914.
[6] Sgt P. J. Kirwan, MM, NX48590. 2/1 Fd Regt, 2/4 LAA Regt. Lithographer; of Strathfield, NSW; b. Merrylands, NSW, 10 Sep 1919.

In an attempt to forestall further attacks Norman ordered Stenhouse to send out a platoon (Lieutenant Wedgwood's[7]) at 10.30 a.m. to move north to a creek, west for about 500 yards, and attack the enemy on the north side of the Katika Track. While the platoon was moving forward another determined enemy attack, this time on the left flank, was beaten back.

With the Japanese attack gathering momentum Evans hastened to strengthen Scarlet Beach by arranging a semi-circle of infantry companies between the Song and Siki Creek. By the time Wedgwood's patrol was on its way Coppock's company together with 15 men from the machine-gun platoon had reached a position north of the Katika creek, thus closing the immediate right flank of the other companies. At the same time Fleming's company of the 2/43rd Battalion crossed the Song and took up a position west of brigade headquarters. Although very weary, Gordon's company of the 2/43rd which had hurried the previous night all the way from the junction of the Gusika and Wareo Tracks, known as Exchange,[8] was ordered at 10.45 a.m. to close the gap south of the Song between Fleming and Coppock. Just as Gordon's company was beginning to fill the gap the Japanese attacked. As the battalion diarist expressed it: "As 'D' Company were moving into their positions just west of the old M.D.S. position they were fired on, they went to ground and fought where they stood." The attack was beaten off but the Japanese now seemed to be aware of the 70 yards gap between the two companies of the 2/43rd. There was also a large gap between Gordon of the 2/43rd and Coppock of the 2/28th which the latter company was ordered to fill by patrolling.

The tide of battle was summed up in the late morning by brief messages from the 2/28th Battalion to the 24th Brigade; at 11.5 a.m. "attack still going on and still determined"; at 11.50 a.m. "attack repulsed C.O. estimates more Japanese than own strength, he thinks they are coming in again". Most of these attacks were made with great determination down the Katika Track but all were repulsed with very heavy casualties by the steady, controlled fire of the 2/28th Battalion whose own losses were remarkably light.

By 11.55 a.m. Wedgwood's platoon reported being astride the track after an outflanking move in which it had killed 33 Japanese but had suffered 11 casualties. During the advance Padre Holt[9] had acted as a tireless stretcher bearer. Thinking that the ground gained was hardly worth the cost Norman ordered Wedgwood to withdraw, but the platoon commander asked leave to remain as he was dominating the track from a good position. It was undoubtedly the presence of Wedgwood's little band astride the track, together with the resolute defence of the other West

---

[7] Lt V. C. Wedgwood, MC, WX5477; 2/28 Bn. Mining engineer; of Perth; b. Moora, WA, 24 Apr 1915.

[8] The 2/43rd Battalion named many places in this area after the hotels of its native capital—Adelaide. Thus "Oriental" was a spot half way between Bonga and "Exchange". Other features were named "Imperial" and "Norfolk".

[9] Chaplain Rev W. E. Holt, VX67089; 2/28 Bn. Church of England clergyman; of Bendigo, Vic; b. Gillingham, Kent, England, 12 May 1909. Died of wounds 22 Jun 1945.

Australians and Pioneers farther west, which caused the Japanese to pause. Soon after midday there was a lull in the fierce fighting and the thrust of Hayashida's attacking Katika force was slowed down.

His Song force which was really to lead the attack had not yet come up against such stubborn opposition. Light anti-aircraft guns of the 10th Battery were disposed in the kunai south of the Song for the protection of Scarlet Beach and also south of Siki Creek covering the position of the 24th Battery. One troop had two guns on the beach and two in the kunai about 300 yards west of it. The other troop had four guns in the kunai south of Siki Creek and two at Launch Jetty. This latter troop had already beaten back one enemy attack, firing 60 rounds over open sights.

While the attacks on the 2/28th Battalion were growing in intensity 10th Battery Headquarters and several of its guns, unscreened by infantry, were twice heavily attacked in the kunai west of Scarlet Beach. Here again the gunners fired over open sights and the attackers were halted, but not before one Bofors was abandoned and the others withdrawn under a heavy mortar bombardment. Some time afterwards Captain Harris led a party to the abandoned gun and, under fire from the Japanese 100 yards away, rendered it unserviceable. In the afternoon this Bofors was recovered undamaged and withdrawn to Scarlet Beach. Two other Bofors from the same area which had been ordered south, took the wrong turning and arrived at Scarlet Beach, making a total of eight Bofors in the beach-head area.

The guns of the 2/12th Regiment had played a big part in the battle. For two days they had been in continuous action, and had created havoc among the Japanese, particularly when shelling the massed attacks on the 2/28th Battalion. Harassing fire at night had also upset the Japanese. Katagiri had no effective counter as he had been able to bring only a few mountain guns in his trek from the north. The raiders from the sea would have done a great service to the Japanese cause had they been able to disable the Australian guns.

After two hours and a quarter of almost continuous fighting the two forward companies of the 2/28th Battalion were glad when the lull came, particularly as they were short of ammunition. At 12.35 p.m. Norman informed them that he was unable to get ammunition up from the beach apparently because of enemy infiltration down Siki Creek. Lieutenant Giles[1] was therefore sent east with a patrol and at 1.50 p.m. reported the track to the coast clear. During his absence the enemy again attacked down the track towards Katika but not as heavily as before. Ten minutes before Giles' return Wedgwood reported the track clear back from his position to the forward companies. His platoon had also taken a prisoner. It seemed that the enemy might have drawn back or that they might be trying some other plan.

---

[1] Lt L. H. Giles, WX10671; 2/28 Bn. Woolclasser and woolbuyer; of Perth; b. Tarcoola, SA, 9 Sep 1913.

Evans was anxious to plug the gaps. The fog of war was very thick over Scarlet Beach that day. Communications with the forward companies were difficult and flanking patrols from the forward ring of companies were unsure whether they would encounter friend or foe. In addition three companies of the 2/3rd Pioneers and one company of the 2/28th Battalion were isolated well behind the Japanese forward troops. The noise of near-by battle, the stray shots flicking over Scarlet Beach and rumours such as those of the beach signallers who reported hearing a grenade and machine-gun fire on the beach at 1 p.m., all helped to create uncertainty.

The Main Dressing Station established by Colonel Outridge's 2/8th Field Ambulance about 300 yards west of Scarlet Beach and about 200 yards south of the Song had been under intermittent fire and on the 18th Outridge thought it best to move it. On the afternoon of this day, when the 2/43rd had dug in to the west, mortar bombs and machine-gun fire really began to trouble the M.D.S., where about 80 battle casualties were being held. One mortar bomb landed beside the dispensary and another between trenches where patients were sheltering. On his own initiative Outridge moved to the south end of the beach, his men carrying stretchers and patients, but being unable to move technical and personal gear. Evans' staff meanwhile arranged for L.C.M's bringing up ammunition to take the patients to the 2/3rd Casualty Clearing Station at Langemak Bay. The beach Advanced Dressing Station and the surgical team were also sent south to assist, leaving the bulk of the M.D.S. and one A.D.S. (a total of eight medical officers) on the beach and one M.D.S. on North Hill. After returning to their original position with some of the equipment next day, Outridge's men set up the M.D.S. below the beach embankment. Here it remained for a week treating wounded and sending some out by barge.

At 2.50 p.m. on the 18th Evans received a signal from division that the 24th Brigade must hold Scarlet Beach and as much of North Hill as would control the beach. "If any withdrawal must be to Scarlet Beach," stated the order.

At 3.30 p.m. a report came in from the Papuan Infantry that the Japanese were 1,000 yards up the Song. Ten minutes later when attacks on both the north and south sectors of the front between the rivers had been repulsed Evans asked Joshua whether he could both hold North Hill and supply more troops for the defence of the beach-head. When Joshua replied that he could supply troops but in that case could not be responsible for holding North Hill, Evans left the forces north of the river intact, even though he was fairly certain that attacks there were of a diversionary nature.

During the late afternoon fighting was sporadic, as though the Japanese had given up trying to break through the semi-circle of the West and South Australian companies. It was soon evident, however, that they had succeeded in outflanking the 2/28th Battalion by moving to its south down Siki Creek and reaching the sea at Siki Cove. The enemy had suffered heavy casualties—202 dead had been counted by the 24th Brigade on 17th and 18th October—but they had reached the sea and, if they could exploit this success, the 9th Division would be in danger of disorganisation. In fact the Japanese forces, who had attacked like a bull at a gate, were now mostly bruised and bewildered, but the Australians did not yet know the extent to which their sturdy defence had disorganised the attackers.

When the Japanese reached Siki Cove Wootten signalled to Evans to "hold at all costs area inclusive North Hill and Scarlet Beach to inclusive Siki Creek". Evans informed Wootten, however, that because of the threat to Scarlet Beach itself from west and south, he would be unable to include Katika in his defences. At 3 p.m. he sent a message to Norman saying that Scarlet Beach must be held at all costs, if necessary by a withdrawal from Katika and a strengthening of the beach perimeter extending from North Hill southwards with a depth of only 400 to 500 yards west from Scarlet Beach and having its southern flank resting on the small promontory just north of Siki Cove.

Thus at 3.30 p.m. Wedgwood's gallant platoon was withdrawn after a long period in which it not only deflected the attack on to what was for the enemy the worst approach but commanded the track and gave warning of further attacks. At 4.45 p.m. the 2/28th began to withdraw. It must indeed have been distasteful for the men of the 2/28th to give up, without a fight,[2] such a dearly held and dominating position as Katika for the sake of sitting in a tight perimeter round the beach. Uncounted piles of Japanese dead lay before the battalion's Katika position. It was the brigadier's belief, however, that withdrawal was necessary to prevent infiltration of the supply route, and he had the courage of his own convictions, even to the extent of not carrying out the suggestions of his divisional commander.

By last light the battalion anti-tank platoon had closed the gap between the two companies of the 2/43rd Battalion. The defensive semi-circle then ran from the Song in the north to the headland north of Siki Cove. By 8 p.m. Lieutenant Head's[3] company of the 2/28th reported in from its uneventful task north of the Song and became Evans' slender brigade reserve. Division, brigade and battalion staffs were all busy pushing ammunition, supplies and particularly communication equipment up to the front line. By 7 p.m. the telephone line had been cut and Evans was out of communication with the rest of the division. Wireless, not always reliable, remained the only means of communication, apart from the small craft of the 532nd E.B.S.R. which continued to run to Scarlet Beach throughout the battle.

Unaware of the withdrawal from Katika, Hayashida issued an order to his *79th Regiment* at 6.30 p.m.:

---

[2] Ammunition used at Katika by the 2/28th Battalion before withdrawal consisted of 12,280 rounds of .303 carton, 3,600 rounds of .303 bandolier, 14,560 rounds of 9-mm, 36 x 36-M rifle grenades, 432 x 36-M hand grenades, 18 x 69 grenades. These latter were "useless".

[3] Capt J. M. Head, WX7644; 2/28 Bn. Regular soldier and farmer; of Wandin, Vic; b. Melbourne, 29 Dec 1917.

"1. The enemy north of Arndt Point [24th Brigade] is retreating to Finschhafen. The enemy in front of *II Battalion* [2/28th Battalion at Katika] is stubborn.
2. Main strength of the regiment will advance to the area south of Katika and demolish the retreating enemy."

This was exactly what Wootten feared. Evans was now confident of being able to hold the enemy and prevent any penetration to Scarlet Beach but, as far as Wootten was concerned, by dusk a wedge was driven between the 24th and 20th Brigades. "They're screwing the scrum," he said to Windeyer. There were three routes into the beach-head area—the Sattelberg Road, the back track through Katika, and the line of Siki Creek—and the Japanese were now obviously advancing down the Siki. The greatest danger now, Wootten believed, was that the enemy would swing south from Katika and south-east from Siki Cove and attack through the gun and headquarters area at Heldsbach towards the supply area at Launch Jetty. This move, if successful, would isolate Windeyer's battalions along the Sattelberg Road. In this case, the precariousness of supply and difficulty of control, added to the onslaught by the *80th Regiment* might produce a grave situation.

At 10.30 a.m. on the 18th while two of his companies were patrolling towards Gurunkor and Quembung respectively, Colonel Colvin received a warning order that his headquarters and half the 2/13th Battalion should be ready in an hour to move to Heldsbach Plantation. By midday, when the diarist of the 20th Brigade commented, "There are now no troops between brigade headquarters and the enemy to the north", two companies of the 2/13th were approaching Kedam Beach. Here they embarked on L.C.M's, and at 2.30 p.m. disembarked at Launch Jetty and marched to Heldsbach where the company commanders—Captains Deschamps and Fletcher—reported to Windeyer. He directed Deschamps to block the main road to the north and to protect the guns in the kunai south of Siki Creek; and Fletcher to occupy the area from the Katika Track south of Siki Creek to the coast. Windeyer also placed Captain Walker's[4] company of the 2/32nd Battalion under Colvin's command as a reserve.

Wootten now phoned Windeyer that the loss of Katika was the most serious threat yet. Wishing to contain this threat at the bottleneck where the main road crossed the Siki, Wootten instructed Windeyer to move the three companies under Colvin to the south bank of the Siki. When Windeyer pointed out that he would then have no reserve to keep open the main track back to division, Wootten said he would make troops available if the necessity arose. Walker's company was therefore sent forward to support the other two companies.

At 5.45 p.m. Deschamps reported that his men were in position south of the Siki. Soon afterwards Fletcher, with four platoons, was in position astride the track from Katika and thence eastward to the coast. Later in the night Fletcher reported firing from the direction of the coast but was unable to give any further information as the telephone line to his

---

[4] Capt J. E. Walker, VX3604; 2/32 Bn. Labourer; of West Footscray, Vic; b. Geelong, Vic, 16 Jan 1916. Killed in action 22 Nov 1943.

right platoon had been cut. Firing was also heard across the cove from the 2/28th's positions.

It was during this night—at 11 p.m.—that Hayashida, having found Katika vacated, issued another order to the *79th Regiment*.

1. The night attack on the Katika position was successful with great fighting of the front line units, who captured it at 2000 hours.
2. *79th Infantry Regiment* will mop up the Song and Arndt Point area as already planned. A portion will secure firmly Arndt Point and Katika against the enemies in the direction of Heldsbach. The main strength will be concentrated one kilo N.W. and make preparations for the future attacks.

Hayashida's main strength was to be assembled and reorganised north-west of Katika for an assault on Heldsbach and then Finschhafen. When Fletcher re-established contact with his right platoon (Lieutenant Suters[5]) early on the 19th, Suters reported that he had repulsed two attacks from Siki Creek during the night. These proved to be the last attempts by the enemy to strike south. But for Wootten's skilful generalship and the rapid advance north by half the 2/13th Battalion the Japanese might have been able to seize important ground south of the creek that night.

The enemy was also active on the other side of the creek and cove. Half an hour before midnight a platoon of the 2/28th in an outpost position forward of the left flank—Lieutenant Vanpraag's—reported hearing Japanese voices. Just after midnight fresh movement was heard and at 1.30 a.m. an enemy force of about 50 began to attack Vanpraag's positions. The attacks consisted of a series of short hard thrusts and continued for two hours. When the platoon's listening post was overrun and one man killed, Norman ordered Vanpraag to withdraw to the high ground on the right flank of a detachment of the 532nd E.B.S.R. overlooking the cove.

Meanwhile the attacks by the *80th Regiment* against the 2/17th Battalion at Jivevaneng had met with little success, although, as the battalion's diarist noted on the 18th, "this morning revealed that the enemy had cut the main Sattelberg Road to our east and was sitting astride the track". A patrol early in the morning estimated that about a platoon of Japanese was on the track east of Jivevaneng; at 1.15 p.m. another patrol reported that the position was stronger than that. The area was shelled and small skirmishes took place west, north and east of Jivevaneng. Japanese snipers, mortar bombs and grenades from cup dischargers made things unpleasant for the defenders. As the main route was cut, there was some anxiety about a supply route for the 2/17th Battalion.

At Kumawa all was quiet and the 2/15th Battalion was ordered to patrol aggressively towards the Siki and the Sattelberg Road. Patrols scoured the area on the 18th but only one saw any Japanese. Although the 2/15th's part in the battle on this and succeeding days was not a spectacular one, the threat to its rear caused the *80th Regiment* to detach a considerable proportion of its strength to watch the southern flank

---

[5] Lt T. W. Suters, NX68275; 2/13 Bn. Bank officer; of Smithfield, NSW; b. Wauchope, NSW, 10 Aug 1919.

with a resultant decrease in the force available for use against the 2/17th. About this time a route into the 2/17th's positions from Kumawa was found and thereafter a 2/15th platoon escorted a native carrying party to the 2/17th each day until the Sattelberg Road was opened.

The Japanese of the *80th Regiment* in this more static fight along the Sattelberg Road and Kumawa Track had more time for contemplation and therefore for diary writing than did their more hard-pressed comrades of the *79th Regiment* to the north. "I eat potatoes and live in a hole," wrote one infantryman, "and cannot speak in a loud voice. I live the life of a mud rat or some similar creature." "What shall I eat to live?" wrote another. "What has happened to the general attack . . . the enemy patrol is always wandering around day and night." A third was more sanguine: "Heard that [*79th Regiment*] has forced the enemy in the sector of Arndt Point to retreat. This is the first good news I have heard since I left for the front."

To the south two companies of the 22nd Battalion came under command of the 2/2nd Machine Gun Battalion on arrival at Kakakog, thus giving Wootten a slightly larger but still inadequate divisional reserve. Two companies of the 2/13th Battalion were watching the Mape River track junctions and Tirimoro and were now part of "Kelforce"—under the command of Major Kelly[6] at Simbang.

The three missing companies of the 2/3rd Pioneers had been seen by Tac R planes waving to the aircraft, still in the positions they had been ordered to hold, and apparently not in difficulties. As they had three days supply of rations and ample ammunition, there was little cause for anxiety on this score, although there was a scarcity of water. Wootten decided, however, that as they were no longer in a position to affect the course of the battle they should be withdrawn. At 4.30 p.m. he ordered Windeyer, whose headquarters could make contact with one of the companies, to arrange for them to move south to the Sattelberg Road, where they would come under his command.

Actually, the three Pioneer companies had carried out the tasks allotted to them. It was not their fault that the *79th Regiment* had been able to infiltrate to the east. Rather was it due to the extensive gaps covered by thick country between the companies, and to skilful Japanese fieldcraft All day long on the 18th the companies had heard the noise of battle behind them seeming to get nearer to Scarlet Beach. The northern company—Major P. E. Siekmann's less one platoon on standing patrol 2,000 yards away on the Song—had been out of communication since last light on the 17th. At 7 o'clock next morning the company opened fire on five Japanese approaching from the east. Two of them were killed, one proving to be Major Takehama, commander of the *II/79th Battalion*. As usual, detailed operation orders for the landing and thrust towards the beach were found on the dead officer.[7] When the Pioneers approached to

---

[6] Lt-Col J. L. A. Kelly, DSO, NX12214. 2/13 Bn; CO 31/51 Bn 1944-45. Regular soldier; of Bondi, NSW; b. Cowra, NSW, 10 Mar 1907.

[7] This constant security weakness of the Japanese contrasted with the usually reliable security of the Australians. For instance, when he found no Australian troops between his headquarters and the Japanese on Siki Creek on the morning of 18th October, Windeyer sent back to the 9th Division all the brigade's secret documents. On the previous evening the Pioneer battalion's Intelligence officer had torn up and buried the battalion's secret documents before withdrawing to the 2/28th Battalion.

examine the body they found a Japanese watching over it. He promptly killed himself by exploding a grenade in his face. At midday the Japanese, doubtless surprised at finding a strong Australian position astride the line of advance of their Song force, attacked but were repulsed. The Australians, now on only two meals per day, stood to throughout the night.

Captain Knott's company—farthest west along the Katika-Palanko track—spent the day patrolling to find the company to the east and to pinpoint the Japanese attacking the 2/43rd Battalion. As the company was out of communication with all 24th Brigade formations, Knott signalled Windeyer late in the afternoon outlining his situation. The third isolated company (Lieutenant Dunn's[8]) was out of communication with all other units and sub-units.

Thus, by 19th October, the *20th Japanese Division* had succeeded in splitting the 9th Division into two groups divided by Siki Creek. But the Japanese, depleted and disorganised by the defenders, for the next three days failed to follow up their success. For their plan to succeed it was essential that the thrust to the coast should be vigorously exploited before the Australians, with their more secure lines of supply and reinforcement, could reorganise and regain the initiative. Wootten now fixed the brigade boundary as Siki Creek, the creek being inclusive to 24th Brigade, and ordered Evans to re-establish contact with the 20th Brigade and drive the enemy from the Siki Cove-Katika area.

While Evans at 6.30 a.m. on the 19th was instructing Norman by telephone to patrol to the Siki, the enemy in the creek made several more sharp attacks on Newbery's positions to the north. All were repulsed, and then the battalion's mortars bombarded the general area of the enemy positions near Siki Cove. After this action had died down, Evans ordered a vigorous patrolling policy to gain information for the attacks ordered by divisional headquarters. Patrols were to leave Coppock's and Stenhouse's companies of the 2/28th and reconnoitre to the west for between 1,000 and 1,500 yards, while another patrol from Head's company was to try to make contact with the 2/13th Battalion across the creek. The patrols were to depart at 10 a.m. and return with information about 3 p.m., and none was to become involved in heavy action. Just before they moved out Evans informed Norman that he expected that the main enemy force had withdrawn to the west, because of the high casualties suffered on the 18th, and because of the effectiveness of the artillery fire.

The patrol from Coppock's company returned within an hour after a skirmish with about twenty Japanese 350 yards to the west. A patrol led by Sergeant Stark[9] returned at 12.15 p.m. after penetrating a considerable distance to the west without making any contact with the enemy. Norman then asked permission to attack Katika. He believed that the enemy had suffered about 50 per cent casualties and considered that if

---

[8] Capt R. L. Dunn, NX46688; 2/3 Pnr Bn. Business manager; of Newcastle, NSW; b. Richmond, Vic, 17 Jun 1915.

[9] Lt J. A. Stark, WX8095. 2/28 and 2/16 Bns. Clerk; of Rottnest Island, WA; b. Perth, 26 Oct 1919.

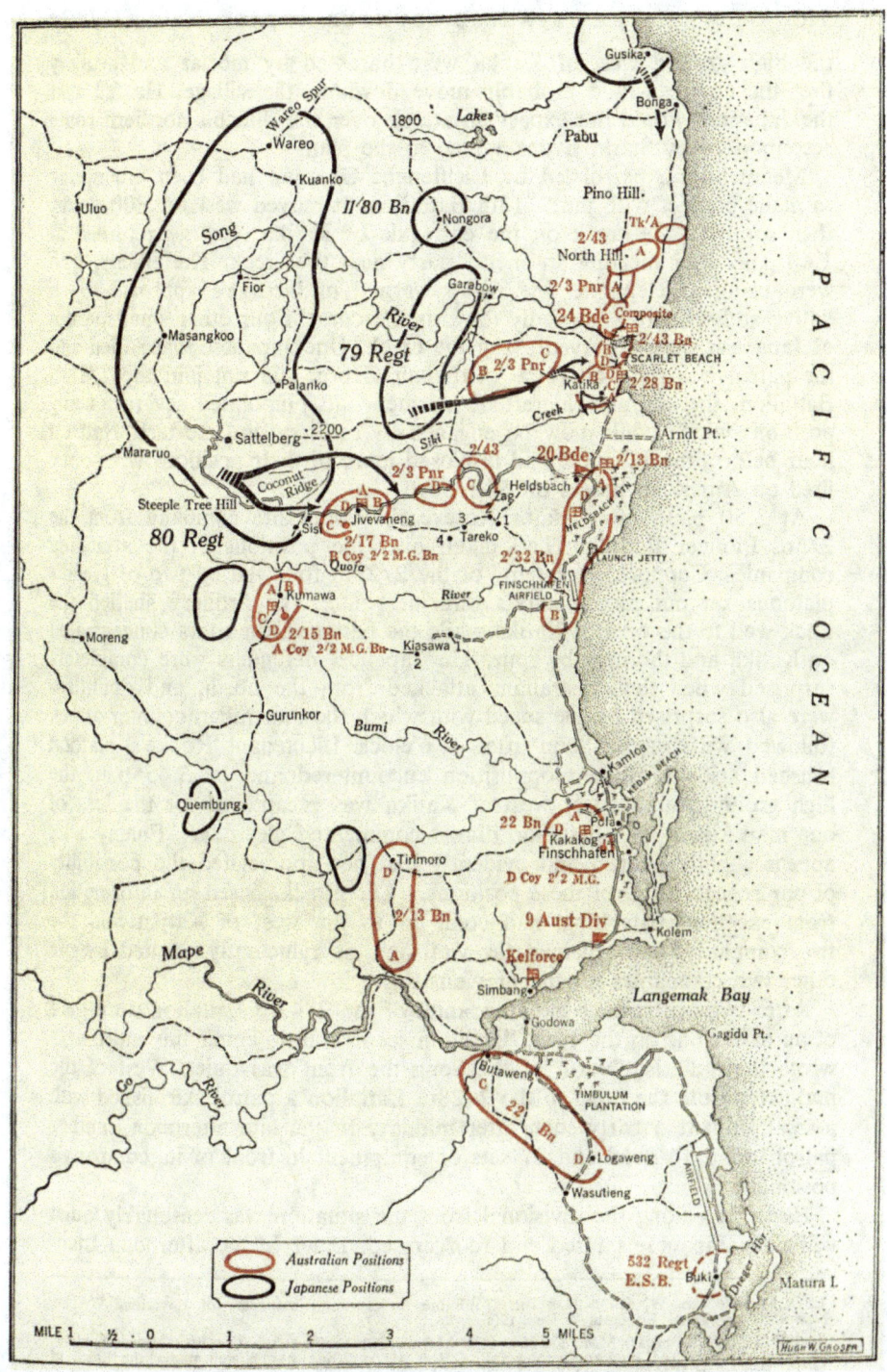

Australian and Japanese redispositions, last light 18th October

the high ground west of Katika were harassed by mortar and artillery fire, the enemy would probably move down to the village. He felt that the Japanese would not expect an attack over the difficult northern route reconnoitred by Stark. Evans agreed to the plan.

Meanwhile, a patrol led by Lieutenant George,[1] had been attempting to make contact with the 2/13th Battalion. It moved west for 200 yards, then south to the creek on the east side of Katika. George returned at 1.40 p.m. after meeting an enemy party near the creek. The enemy, who were using a telephone line, were warned of George's approach by a native and withdrew hurriedly towards the coast. Four other small parties of Japanese were observed along the creek. One Japanese was killed and the patrol was fired on twice. Although George did not join the 2/13th Battalion, the skilful fieldcraft of his men had pinpointed several enemy positions which could now be engaged by artillery and mortars. Half an hour before, the Japanese had disclosed more of their positions when they fired on American barges off Siki Cove.

At 3.50 p.m., after Major Rosevear's[2] composite company from the 2/3rd Pioneer Battalion had taken over the positions of the attacking companies, Coppock's company of the 2/28th followed by two of Head's platoons set out along Stark's difficult route. The artillery shelled the track well to the west of Katika while the battalion's mortars concentrated on Katika and the near-by spur. The Japanese defenders were completely surprised when the Australians attacked from the north, and doubtless were also surprised by the speed with which the Australian counter-attack followed withdrawal. Soon after 4 o'clock Lieutenant Rooke's platoon brushed aside the slight opposition encountered and by 5.45 p.m. the high ground immediately west of Katika was recaptured for the loss of one man killed. The battalion diarist commented gleefully: "Enemy . . . appear slightly peeved and evidently had not appreciated the possibility of our reoccupation of these positions." The attack, based on information from excellent patrolling, had come in to the west of Katika and the two companies had regained the vital area so reluctantly vacated by the other two companies on the previous day.

After two hectic days the companies of the 2/43rd Battalion were glad of an easier one on the 19th. "Position seems a little better this morning," wrote their diarist. North of the Song the front was quiet. West of the perimeter from the Song to the 2/28th Battalion a patrol skirmished with a small Japanese party soon after midday. In the late afternoon another patrol found 14 dead and 27 sets of equipment in front of its company's positions.

Elsewhere along the divisional front the situation was reasonably quiet while the Japanese paused and reorganised. Later in the afternoon Lieu-

---

[1] Lt A. E. George, WX6243; 2/28 Bn. Goldmine underground manager; of Laverton, WA; b. Newcastle on Tyne, England, 4 Dec 1906.
[2] Maj H. G. M. Rosevear, MM, SX8264. (1st AIF: L-Cpl 12 Bn.) 2/3 Pnr Bn. Cost accountant; of Black Forest, SA; b. Launceston, Tas, 6 Jun 1900. When he enlisted under the name of H. G. Brown in 1916 Rosevear gave his year of birth as 1895.

tenant Suters of the 2/13th took a patrol to the mouth of the creek but was fired on from the north bank. Returning to his platoon overlooking the Japanese track to the Siki, he was able to report by 5.30 p.m. that his men had sniped twelve Japanese moving west from the creek towards Katika. Brave though they were the Japanese often displayed incredible stupidity. In this case they followed the same track each time and crossed the open ground stopping to look at their dead comrades. Thus they were easy targets.

On the southern front the commander of the Japanese *80th Regiment* must have been feeling very frustrated at this stage, for the 2/17th Battalion simply refused to budge. By this time it was no new experience for the battalion to be surrounded by Japanese, or at least to have its main supply route severed. The battalion was annoyed, rather than alarmed, that the Japanese had established a strong post to the east between Captain Rudkin's company of the 2/17th and Captain Richmond's company of the 2/43rd. At midday artillery shelled the troublesome Japanese pocket but the Japanese moved closer to Rudkin's company during the shelling and afterwards hopped back into their holes. The 2/17th's worry about supply was reduced when at 4 p.m. Sergeant Allman[3] of the Papuans guided a patrol across country from Tareko 2 to Jivevaneng. In the patrol was Major Broadbent, now released from his duties at the beach. By this route stretcher cases and walking wounded were evacuated to Tareko 2 by last light despite a Japanese patrol which chased them for half the way.

During these days of uncertainty Captain Gore's Papuan company had been playing a notable role. His third platoon—Lieutenant Bruce's—had rejoined the company after harassing the stragglers of the *51st Division* in the ranges north of Lae, and was now helping to patrol the Heldsbach area. Lieutenant Macfarlane's platoon was patrolling mainly for the 2/17th Battalion, while Lieutenant Rice's had been reconnoitring the Fior-Wareo area for three days. It reported on 18th October that there were heavy Japanese troop concentrations near Palanko, that strong positions were dug east of Sattelberg and along Siki Creek, and that the enemy was heading for Katika. On the 19th this platoon reported the coast track clear as far north as Bonga, although it saw two Japanese patrols in that area.

Meanwhile the isolated companies of the 2/3rd Pioneers, who had not yet received Wootten's order to move south, had been playing their parts in forcing the Japanese to pause. Richmond's company of the 2/43rd Battalion on the track to the east of the 2/17th was keeping contact with the Pioneers. At 12.45 p.m. on the 19th a combined patrol from Richmond's company and Knott's company of the Pioneers attempted to destroy the enemy blocking the track to the 2/17th, but were forced back under fire from eight machine-guns. In the afternoon Knott's company moved south and took up a position near Richmond's.

---

[3] Sgt B. B. Allman, NX23946. 2/1 Pnr Bn and Papuan Inf Bn. Textile mechanic; of Forest Lodge, NSW; b. Orange, NSW, 24 Jan 1920.

With the other two Pioneer companies, however, there was no communication. At first light a booby-trap set in front of Lieutenant Dunn's company on the Katika Track exploded and heralded an attack. After a pause during which the Japanese held what the battalion diarist termed a "corroboree" the company was heavily attacked. It held its fire until the Japanese were close and then opened up, killing at least 20 and causing the attackers to withdraw to a gully on the right. Grenades hurled by the defenders into the gully caused more casualties and another withdrawal. At 10 a.m., when Dunn was about to send back a patrol to make contact with his battalion headquarters, which he imagined to be in its original position, the Japanese came charging again up the steep slope of the gully, yelling. They were again easily repulsed, mainly with grenades. On the high ground to the north Major Siekmann's company repulsed an attack in the morning, largely by mortaring the enemy's forming-up place south of the Song. Documents and maps were later taken from dead Japanese, and swords, which were later given to pilots of the supporting Boomerangs.

The night 19th-20th October and the 20th were quiet and there was no interference with the 26th Brigade which loaded into Admiral Barbey's landing craft at 6 p.m. on the 19th and arrived in Langemak Bay from Lae just on midnight. Japanese bombers came over a little later, but they did no damage. South of Langemak Bay the landing craft were fired on from an enemy submarine but it did not come close enough to do much damage.

Accompanying the 13 L.C.I's of Brigadier Whitehead's brigade were 3 L.S.T's, one carrying a squadron of the 1st Tank Battalion.[4] Major Ford[5] of this battalion had investigated the Finschhafen area on 9th October and reported that "tanks could have operated in small numbers", and that "infantry enthusiastic and require tanks to deal with strong points". Referring to the coastal crossing of the Bumi he reported: "Six tanks would have dealt successfully with strong enemy bunker positions, would have reduced infantry casualties and speeded up advance." Early in October, however, there was no indication that the tank squadrons would be used. Normal training continued. Then events best described by the battalion's diarist began to occur:

> The event of the month has been the departure of "C" Squadron group to Finschhafen. On the 18th, the squadron was put on six hours' notice to move and they left by L.S.T. the next day at 3 o'clock. Nine officers and 136 O.R's embarked. The orders strictly limited the number of vehicles to be taken to 18 tanks, 5 jeeps and trailers, 1 slave carrier[6] and 1 fitter's carrier. Ten days supply of rations, ammunition and P.O.L. had been taken on at Buna and the loading of vehicles and personnel was completed in fifty minutes.

---

[4] Later named 1st Australian Armoured Regiment.
[5] Maj J. T. Ford, SX9610. 2/9 Cav Regt, 2/9 Armd Regt, 1 Tk Bn, 1 Armd Regt. Storekeeper; of Orroroo, SA; b. Orroroo, 6 May 1909.
[6] Carrier adapted to carry stores.

An L.S.T. with Major S. Hordern's "C" Squadron aboard sailed in convoy at 3.30 p.m. on the 19th and at 3.30 next morning with steady rain falling the ship began to unload at Langemak Bay.[7]

An unloading party met the ship (said the battalion's report) but appeared to have little or no organisation and showed a desire to watch the tanks rather than unload, and squadron personnel unloaded the greater bulk of the stores which were packed in the tank deck, and some confusion was caused by unloading both tanks and stores together. The narrow strip of beach and the track from the beach was soft and muddy. Operations were done under blackout conditions as enemy aircraft were attacking shipping farther out in the bay. The ship's commander had expressed his intention of leaving in one hour irrespective of whether all stores were off. Stores were being dumped at the unloading point causing much congestion. A number of tanks got off, then one bogged on the track just clear of the beach, and the remainder had to be diverted and a detour made through thick secondary growth necessitating a sharp turn on the soft beach. Despite these difficulties all vehicles were unloaded and moved off the beach. . . . At 0430 the L.S.T. commenced to move away with large quantities of P.O.L., ammunition and rations still on board. Men were still throwing ammunition off, and jumping into the water themselves with the ramp half up.

Evans was now mainly concerned to strengthen his positions at Katika and to eliminate the Japanese pocket in Siki Cove and north-east of Jivevaneng. In support of the infantry the artillery pounded the Japanese positions. About midday the men of the 2/28th's forward companies watched the shells falling among the Japanese again massing west of Katika. Late on the 19th Norman issued orders to Stenhouse's company to mop up the enemy positions between the battalion's forward localities and Siki Creek next morning. The idea was that this company should advance south-east across the track joining the beach and Katika and reach the cove, where it would reorganise and advance south-west.

At 8.38 a.m. on the 20th, with two platoons forward, Stenhouse moved out to attack the Japanese position on the razor-back ridge south of Newbery's company overlooking the cove. By 9.26 Lieutenant Giles' platoon was heavily engaged with the enemy on the ridge and was pinned down by machine-gun fire. Lieutenant Wedgwood's platoon then attempted a left encirclement, but was stopped too. Despite the example set by leaders such as Lance-Corporal Nankiville,[8] who was seriously wounded but continued to lead the point section, all further attempts to dislodge the enemy were unsuccessful. Losses mounted and by the time that Stenhouse had only 42 men left, Norman decided to withdraw the battered company.

Although the attack was unsuccessful the enemy machine-guns had been located and they were now subjected to a merciless bombardment. At 2.30 p.m. the Vickers were placed forward to harass the cove. "This caused considerable retaliation by the enemy," wrote the 2/28th's diarist, "and terrific fire-fight ensued causing mild panic amongst beach defence

---

[7] LST's (as their name indicated) were designed to carry tanks but this was the first occasion on which they had carried them into the battle area for the Australian Army.
[8] L-Cpl H. E. Nankiville, DCM, WX13372; 2/28 Bn. Labourer; of Kalgoorlie, WA; b. Kalgoorlie, 6 Jul 1917.

personnel who thought enemy were breaking through." Eventually the Japanese machine-guns were silenced, mainly by 3-inch mortar fire. Across the cove Captain Fletcher's company of the 2/13th heard the fight and at times could see Stenhouse's men. The 2/13th had located machine-guns on each side of the main track on the north bank of Siki Creek and let the 2/28th know by the only means possible at this time—wireless.

As the two battalions—2/28th and 2/13th—were now so close it became more imperative to re-establish telephone communication. Back in his headquarters at Langemak Bay Wootten had been unable to follow the battle for Scarlet Beach as clearly as he would have wished since the severing of the telephone line to the 24th Brigade. At 3.30 p.m. Lieutenant Cavanagh led a patrol from Coppock's company of the 2/28th in an attempt to make contact with the 2/13th. While the patrol was away the battalion ration party, returning from the forward companies to battalion headquarters, was ambushed at a spot described by the brigade diarist as a "nasty position"; it was indeed nasty as this small Japanese party "controls water of 'A' and 'B' ". An hour and a half after leaving Katika, Cavanagh arrived without incident at Lieutenant Hall's position south of Siki Creek. He was taken to see Colonel Colvin who suggested that Cavanagh should return to Katika laying line behind him, and that Stenhouse should push down the coast to the mouth of Siki Creek and join his own company there. Cavanagh explained that Stenhouse had been trying to do just that. At 6.15 p.m. Cavanagh returned to Katika laying the line behind him and thus re-establishing contact between the 20th and 24th Brigades. Evans promptly asked Wootten for his third battalion—the 2/32nd—then divisional reserve in the Heldsbach area.

Around the remainder of the front the pressure of the past few days was not so fierce on the 20th. The Japanese pocket east of Jivevaneng was attacked by Knott's Pioneer company after supporting mortar fire had missed the pocket and landed in the 2/17th's positions. Starting at 2.30 p.m. it took the two forward platoons an hour and a half to bash their way 100 yards through the thick jungle. Forward scouts were just below the Japanese position before they were pinned down. There Private Minter[9] stood up and fired two magazines at the Japanese, thus allowing his comrade to escape. The company then withdrew after the wounded Minter had pinpointed the enemy positions on the track. At 7.40 the enemy attacked Knott's company, but were repulsed.

Five minutes later the Japanese attacked the two companies of the 2/28th in the Katika area. At 9.10 Coppock's company reported that the enemy had dug in all round the Australian positions and that an attack was expected during the night.[1]

---

[9] Cpl H. A. Minter, MM, NX43950; 2/3 Pnr Bn. Storeman; of North Parramatta, NSW; b. Marrickville, NSW, 26 Jan 1915.

[1] L-Cpl J. C. Buckley (of Dulwich Hill, NSW), wounded during the Japanese attacks on the 2/28th, was attended to by medical orderlies operating by torchlight on telephone instructions from the battalion's medical officer, Captain K. R. Barder (of Darling Point, NSW), but just as the stretcher bearers arrived in the morning Buckley died.

Meanwhile, what of the two lost companies of the 2/3rd Pioneer Battalion? Lieutenant Dunn's company was still in position along the Katika Track. It had given no ground and had repulsed all attacks. By the 20th the men were on quarter rations. At 11.45 a.m. a Boomerang dropped a message which stated: "Stragglers instructed to come in moving south to road Sattelberg to Heldsbach or direct to Scarlet Beach. Destroy weapons abandoned. Carry all possible." Resentful at the unfortunate term "stragglers",[2] the company marched out at 1.30 p.m. with all its weapons. On the way to the beach it met several Japanese parties and killed four men. At nightfall it bivouacked on the side of a valley just off the Katika Track.

Major Siekmann's two platoons had also maintained their positions without wavering, and, judging by the odour of death wafting in from the south side of their position, they had caused many casualties. At first light on the 20th the company was subjected to Australian artillery fire. Siekmann therefore made a huge sign with bandages and blankets: "A.I.F., S.O.S." At 11.15 a.m. a Boomerang spotted the sign and dropped cigarettes and tobacco. Half an hour later the Boomerang dropped an identical message to "stragglers". Siekmann and his men were riled by this message, and decided to stay where they were as they did not regard themselves as stragglers. A new sign was displayed: "C.140 (the company serial number) here awaiting orders." Though the company was shelled again by its own artillery it refused to move, and at 4.45 p.m. its message was seen by an aircraft.

These two resolute companies of Pioneers had given an admirable example of what Wootten was constantly drilling into his infantry battalions, namely, that in holding defended localities the Japanese might be behind the Australians but the Australians were also behind the Japanese. The Pioneers had not borne the brunt of the main attack, but their very presence in the rear caused concern and uncertainty to the enemy. In some quarters it became fashionable to blame the Pioneers for letting the *79th Regiment* through without notice, but it was too much of a tall order to expect the three companies, situated as they were, to cover the whole area between the Song and the Siki.

The Japanese counter-attack had been halted, and Wootten now had his third brigade on hand. He believed therefore that he had a chance to regain the initiative and issued orders aimed at achieving this. One battalion from the 26th Brigade (2/23rd Battalion) would become divisional reserve near the Quoja. In accordance with Evans' request, the 2/32nd Battalion would move by sea to Scarlet Beach to rejoin the 24th Brigade. All elements of the 2/3rd Pioneer Battalion would be sent to Finschhafen. As soon as the Pioneers reached Finschhafen the two companies of the 2/13th Battalion at Kakakog would rejoin the remainder of the battalion, which, in its turn, would be relieved by the 26th Brigade, and would move up the Sattelberg Road to support the 2/17th. The

---

[2] It may have been used for security reasons, since the message might have fallen into enemy hands.

26th Brigade, less one battalion, would take over the sector from south of Siki Cove to the bend on the Sattelberg Road north of Heldsbach. Evans and Whitehead would then cooperate in driving the enemy from the Katika-Siki Cove area and advance west of the main coast road. Two troops of the tank squadron were allotted a defensive role in Timbulum Plantation south of Langemak Bay and the third was moved in L.C.M's to Kedam Beach and thence to near Pola.

By first light on the 21st the attacks expected by Norman on his two forward companies had not taken place. At 7.30 a.m. Lieutenant Hindley led his platoon from Newbery's company to "clean up" the Japanese ambush position astride the supply route to the two companies overlooking Katika. A quarter of an hour later Newbery's men fired on a party of 15 Japanese heading west from Siki Cove and killed 6. At 7 a.m. Captain Davidson's[3] company of the 2/32nd Battalion left for Scarlet Beach aboard an L.C.V. and arrived about three hours later. Evans told Norman that if Hindley's patrol got through Davidson's company would be placed in "three platoon localities" between Katika and the beach.

At 11.45 a.m. Coppock reported that Dunn's company of the 2/3rd Pioneers had come in. Moving out at 7 a.m. the Pioneers had skirted a Japanese position and then advanced through an area pock-marked by Australian shells. Here they killed two Japanese and then bashed a track through the jungle until they again came to the main Katika Track at their old battalion headquarters position. Several enemy and one Australian dead were lying there. Pushing farther east they came to the battalion's former "B" Echelon area and were chagrined to see abandoned mail strewn about.

Just west of Katika they were challenged by the 2/28th Battalion. They replied with a password several days old. It was not immediately accepted, but all doubts were removed when one of the 2/28th whistled "Waltzing Matilda", and the Pioneers replied and thankfully entered the positions. Having been without rations for the past day the men were affected by strain, hunger and thirst. They were made as comfortable as possible by the West Australians who at this time were short of rations themselves because of the enemy ambush position astride the supply route. The outcome of Hindley's patrol was therefore awaited with interest.

At 12.35 p.m. Hindley reached Coppock's company of the 2/28th without opposition and was ordered to return immediately escorting a ration party. Two hours later a formidable patrol left for Katika—Davidson's company of the 2/32nd escorting the 2/28th's ration party. By 5.10 p.m. the rations arrived in the forward area. Davidson's company now occupied the gap between Norman's two forward companies and Stenhouse's company.

Siekmann's missing company of the 2/3rd Pioneers reported in to Evans' outposts at 6.25 p.m. At 9.15 a.m. a Boomerang had dropped another message: "You will rejoin main body North Hill, Scarlet Beach

---

[3] Maj J. J. G. Davidson, QX6092; 2/32 Bn. Regular soldier; of Red Hill, Qld; b. Murwillumbah, NSW, 14 May 1913.

or Zag. Suggest route crossing Song River moving along it to North Hill." A quarter of an hour later a plane dropped three canisters of ammunition. Siekmann already had plenty of ammunition and was hoping for some rations. The company—80 men strong with one 3-inch mortar and two Vickers guns besides the usual weapons of two infantry platoons —then buried the surplus ammunition and marched out to the north in single file after a meal of hot stew and with only one tin of bully beef a man left. Since the mortar was too heavy its firing pin and sights were removed and it was buried. To facilitate carrying, the Vickers belts were cut in halves; 400 grenades were carried. Through the kunai and jungle the company marched to the Song River, which was reached at 3 p.m., when it was bombarded by a mortar of the 2/43rd Battalion. A shout of "Ho, ho, ho, ho" caused the mortarmen to cease fire. Because the area was strewn with booby-traps the company moved down the centre of the Song to brigade headquarters, where the men were well fed and the two Vickers used to thicken the defences.

In Windeyer's sector south of Siki Creek preparations were made for Brigadier Whitehead's two battalions to relieve the 2/13th Battalion. At 9 a.m. the company commanders of Colonel Ainslie's 2/48th Battalion left to reconnoitre the positions occupied by Colvin's companies. Colonel Gillespie's 2/24th reconnoitred the Heldsbach area and the 2/23rd, now commanded by Lieut-Colonel Tucker,[4] remained in divisional reserve. By 1.30 p.m. the 2/48th began relieving the 2/13th, and the 2/24th took over in Heldsbach.

The 21st was a fairly quiet day for the 2/17th and 2/15th at Jivevaneng and Kumawa respectively. The Japanese force astride the Sattelberg Road east of the 2/17th Battalion was well entrenched and had been reinforced. As Simpson was unable to deal with this enemy pocket to the east as well as counter the main enemy attack from the west, Windeyer decided to send the 2/13th Battalion up to open the Sattelberg Road to Jivevaneng.

By last light on the 21st the tide of battle seemed to have turned in the Australians' favour. Had the enemy not allowed three days to pass without making a major move the tale might have been different. On most fronts during the night the enemy were heard digging in; fires and flares, probably signals, were seen from the direction of Sattelberg. It seemed possible that the enemy might make another attack on the 22nd, but the Australians, reorganised and redisposed, would be ready for him. Already the 24th Brigade estimated that about 500 Japanese had been killed by it since 15th October. Round the valiant 2/28th there were literally piles of dead.

As expected there was much activity on the Katika front on the 22nd. From early morning the 2/28th was alert. At 8.50 a.m. forward companies reported enemy movement to the west. As all reports seemed to indicate a Japanese withdrawal, Norman prepared to push his defences farther west. At 10.10 a.m. Dunn's company of the 2/3rd Pioneers was sent

---

[4] Lt-Col F. A. G. Tucker, DSO, ED, SX10310. 2/48 Bn; CO 2/23 Bn 1943-46. Schoolmaster; of Fullarton, SA; b. Fullarton, 2 Nov 1911.

to establish a firm base on the track and creek junction. By 11.45 a.m. a patrol from Newbery's company reported that the area of the cove and the creek was clear and that they had met the 2/48th Battalion across the creek. The patrol found that the area previously attacked by Stenhouse's company had been occupied by at least 200 Japanese!

By 12.30 p.m. Brigadier Evans ordered the 2/28th to move about 500 yards to the west. Coppock's and Head's companies were hardly settled into their new areas when at 7.45 p.m. the Japanese made a determined charge straight down the track from the west. Although under cover of machine-guns mounted about 150 yards forward of the Australian positions, and urged on by a bugle call, the Japanese were driven back with heavy casualties. The brunt of the attack was borne by Lieutenant Rooke's platoon astride the track. Ably assisted by his section commanders, Corporal Isle[5] and Lance-Corporal Broun,[6], Rooke and his platoon heavily defeated the enemy attack.[7] A similar attack but less bold was beaten off 20 minutes later. Five minutes before midnight they attacked again but were easily repulsed. The 2/28th Battalion had played a key role at a crucial time in the defence of Scarlet Beach.

The moving of the 2/28th Battalion 500 yards west had dislocated the Japanese plans for an attack on positions near Scarlet Beach by the *II/79th Battalion*. An operation order issued after the 2/28th Battalion's move stated that at dusk "*II Battalion* will attack the enemy [2/28th Battalion] in front of *8 Company* before attacking the enemy boat landing point". As already described the three attacks made on the 2/28th Battalion were all easily repulsed.

Elsewhere in the 24th Brigade's area the day was reasonably quiet. An Australian and Papuan patrol from Captain Grant's company of the 2/43rd Battalion on North Hill reached Bonga and Oriental and found them deserted and undistributed stores abandoned. The remainder of the 2/32nd Battalion arrived at Scarlet Beach and at 1.30 p.m. Lieutenant Denness' company left for Katika, where at dusk it dug in.

At last light on the 22nd General Katagiri changed his tone somewhat, and brought two companies of the *I/79th Battalion* into the battle to support the battered *II* and *III Battalions*.

> "1. The enemy is gradually increasing his strength in Arndt Point area. The enemy has increased his strength in R. Song area. They have their eyes towards Wareo. A portion of the enemy in Kumawa area is advancing towards Sisi-Sattelberg heights. . . .
> 2. The [*79th Regiment*] will attack the enemy in the east of Katika at daybreak of the 23rd and secure the line firmly. From 1000 hrs execute an attack on the enemy [2/32nd Battalion] constructing the position. Direct the main strength to the right flank and attack.
> 3. Other units will continue their present duty."

---

[5] L-Sgt J. F. Isle, WX6066; 2/28 Bn. Clerk; of Shenton Park, WA; b. Geraldton, WA, 17 Sep 1917.

[6] L-Cpl W. O. T. Broun, MM, WX19033; 2/28 Bn. Farmer; of Beverley, WA; b. Beverley, 8 Sep 1906.

[7] When Rooke was sent back to the area after relief he counted 47 dead Japanese forward from his platoon's position. There were also signs of others having been dragged back.

With enemy confidence and morale waning the stage was set on 23rd October—the anniversary of El Alamein, as various diarists noted—for a further reorganisation of the Australians in preparation for a resumption of the offensive. The 20th Brigade was now compact in the Kumawa and Jivevaneng areas; the 26th also had a specific task in the area from the Siki to Heldsbach. In the 24th Brigade it was imperative to sort out the battalions whose locations and tasks had become mixed during the Japanese attack. Thus orders were issued for the 2/43rd Battalion to hold the area on the right from the coast through North Hill to the Song; the 2/28th, aided by a mixed force of Pioneers under Major Rosevear, to hold the centre from the Song for 1,000 yards south; and the 2/32nd thence to the Katika and Siki areas where it would link with the 26th Brigade.

The two leading companies of the 2/32nd were hardly in position on an excellent feature 300 yards west of Katika when the Japanese arrived hoping also to occupy it. Indeed, just before arriving in one position, the point section, led by Corporal Scott,[8] routed an enemy patrol of fifteen. At 3.15 p.m. the Japanese attacked. This attack and several others which came intermittently during the late afternoon, were repulsed. Soon after dusk at 6.20 a heavy attack developed along the track, but as the enemy made no change in his tactics or in his line of approach this also was driven back. The enemy's only fire support was from machine-guns while the Australians had mortars and machine-guns, and the artillery had registered the area. All this meant more casualties for the Japanese round Katika; before its departure the 2/28th had counted 308 corpses on the north side of the track alone. The enemy continued his attacks during the night, but none had the slightest success.

On this day, 23rd October, General Morshead visited General Wootten at Finschhafen. They decided that before the 9th Division could resume the offensive a further brigade (probably the 4th) was needed. Wootten said that he would have to attack Sattelberg and Wareo before advancing to Sio, and would like to attack them simultaneously. He would probably be able to do so if the extra brigade were available, but if not, he would have to attack the two strongholds in succession. Morshead then signalled Mackay in Port Moresby: "At present am wholly disposed along northern sector. Langemak Bay area inadequately held against possible seaborne attack. Present average strength battalion 600. To enable resumption of offensive at first opportunity and to provide effective defence Langemak area consider another brigade required." Mackay quickly decided that it would be best to send the remainder of the 4th Brigade, and he also decided to send General Berryman forward to investigate.

Wootten's staff on the 23rd was uncertain about the next intention of the enemy. "Although enemy appears to be withdrawing west from vicinity Katika," stated a divisional order to all units, "and to have most of his forces to the N.N.W. or N.W. of our position he may possibly be pre-

---

[8] Cpl A. F. Scott, MM, WX11405; 2/32 Bn. Millhand; of Busselton, WA; b. Byford, WA, 7 Aug 1918.

paring to attack 20th Brigade area or to move round our left flank between Sattelberg-Mararuo and R. Mape." Accordingly the 20th Brigade and 22nd Battalion were warned to prepare for an attack, which was, however, hardly likely to eventuate in view of the battering the enemy had taken and was still taking round Katika.

Despite Wootten's assurance to Captain Gore on 12th October that Gore would have "complete control" of his company the 9th Division was now using the Papuans piecemeal as other divisions had done. Thus the divisional order on 23rd October stated that "C Company P.I.B. will support both 20th Brigade and 22nd Battalion in addition to giving support in 24th and 26th Brigade sectors". This was a large order for any one company, but experience had shown that even a section of the Papuan Battalion in every area was invaluable to the local infantry commander for scouting, patrolling and gathering information.

An indication of the growing confidence of those in high places was that on the 23rd the first American base unit—the 808th Engineer Battalion—landed at Langemak Bay. From this date a constant stream of American units, vehicles and stores poured into Dreger Harbour to make airfields for one group of fighters, and a staging area for another group of fighters and a group of medium bombers. As mentioned this work was to be ready by 1st December, the main object being to provide continuous fighter cover over Vitiaz Strait for the invasion of western New Britain. The acceleration in the airfield building program was caused largely by General MacArthur's signal of 20th October to Mackay, Carpender and Kenney: "The immediate development of an airfield at [Finschhafen] is an urgent necessity. The movement of engineers and materials for this development should be given high priority."

The *20th Division* was losing heart. The *80th Regiment* was unable to make headway against the 2/17th Battalion, now supported by the 2/13th, and was worried by the aggressive patrolling of the 2/15th Battalion on its right flank. To the north the *79th Regiment* had failed and its orders lacked the fire of previous ones. "Battalion [*II/79th*] will do its utmost to try and take these positions [Katika]," stated a battalion order of the 24th.

Patrols from the 24th Brigade were active on the 24th. From the right flank of the 2/32nd's position a 75-mm enemy gun was fired as though in a last defiant bid to knock out the Australians. At 1 p.m. an anti-tank gun from the 2/28th scored eight hits on the enemy gun position, but an hour later had to repeat the performance as the enemy gun was still firing.

The enemy was still lingering west of Katika. When Walker's and Davidson's companies on the right of the 2/32nd's line sought to fill the gap between them, they met bitter resistance. Patrols of the 2/28th on the other hand penetrated west for 1,000 yards without meeting opposition, while the only indication of Japanese activity north of the Song was a report from the Papuans that they were using the track from Bonga to Exchange. Several patrols from the 2/48th Battalion made contact with the enemy between the Katika area and the south bank of the Siki. One patrol of four men met trouble along the Siki and all were wounded except Private Scanlan,[9] who remained on guard over the wounded for several hours, despite the proximity of the enemy.

Many Australians reported seeing 14 parachutes dropped from two Japanese aircraft on the north-east slopes of Sattelberg early on the 24th. These were obviously supplies for the harassed division whose supply lines by land and sea were so vulnerable. The mainland supply line from Bonga and Gusika to Wareo could be cut as had been demonstrated by the 2/43rd Battalion before the Japanese counter-attack. The sea line was being constantly interrupted by Allied planes and P.T. boats. A Japanese submarine had been attacked south-east of the Tami Islands by light surface craft and hit on the conning tower. It was a forlorn hope for the enemy to expect to maintain regular supply by air, particularly when the Allies had air supremacy and Japanese planes seldom approached except in the early hours of the morning. In one such raid before dawn on the 25th divisional headquarters was hit, and among the killed was Brigadier Goodwin commanding the artillery of the division.[1]

During the 24th Morshead and Wootten visited the 20th Brigade. In describing Morshead's visit the brigade diarist expressed the affection in which he was held.

> Wherever General Morshead went the troops made it evident that they were glad to see him. News of his visit rapidly spread amongst all troops and produced a general feeling of confidence which was most noticeable.

Later in the day, at 2.50 p.m., the generals arrived at Evans' headquarters. Evans was sure that he had done the right thing in pulling back to a perimeter round Scarlet Beach, but the others felt that he had sacrificed vital ground unnecessarily. This, they maintained, should have been occupied in a series of defended localities and enemy penetration should have been accepted as normal in jungle warfare. They also thought that by concentrating on a continuous line, which did not include Katika, Evans had neglected to keep an adequate reserve, which could have been used to punch any Japanese force breaking through round Scarlet Beach. On the other hand, whatever Evans' methods, there was no doubt that the Japanese counter-attack had been defeated. The question whether Katika and the area north of North Hill could have been held, without danger of losing Scarlet Beach, can never be determined. Wootten now believed, however, that the 24th Brigade should have a new commander, and in this he was supported by Morshead, and next day by Berryman.

It can be argued on the side of Wootten and his seniors that it was Wootten's prerogative as divisional commander to determine the tactical objectives and Evans' duty to conform. In fact Evans at times used his own judgment. It can be maintained on Evans' side that he was on the spot, that he won the battle, and that tactics which succeed are correct tactics. The difficult situation with which he had to cope was a result of

---

[9] Cpl M. D. Scanlan, MM, WX10148; 2/48 Bn. Labourer; of Guildford, WA; b. Kalgoorlie, WA, 4 Jul 1913.
[1] He was succeeded by Brigadier W. N. Tinsley.

the failure of higher headquarters to appreciate the strength of the Japanese round Finschhafen and to reinforce promptly. General Vasey had summed up shrewdly in the course of a letter to General Morshead on 20th October.

> I have been following the sitreps of 9 Div with great interest. Undoubtedly George has had his hands fairly full. If, from this distance, I may draw a lesson, it is that the original plan sent a boy on a man's errand. I am convinced that when operating in this country, where there are no secure flanks, it is essential that one has adequate numbers either to attack the Jap on the flank or, if necessary, provide protection for your own flanks. It is for this reason that I have no desire to get myself committed into these hills until I am convinced of our relative strengths.

It is evident that Evans' brigade did not lose confidence in him and was very sorry to see him go, when, on 1st November, he was replaced temporarily by Lieut-Colonel Simpson. And since Evans' difference of opinion with the divisional commander concerned tactical doctrines and problems it is indicative of Blamey's continued confidence that he appointed him to the Beenleigh Tactical School (near Brisbane) which he commanded until the end of the war.

In a letter to Blamey on 24th October Mackay described the situation as it appeared to him in Port Moresby:

> For the time being at least the Nips have almost wrested the initiative from 9th Division. Had 24th Brigade followed 20th Brigade immediately to Finschhafen, I agree with you that the result may well have been very different and Sattelberg could have been seized early whereas now it will probably mean a very stiff fight to take it. With all due respect to our friends I think this incident shows the weakness of trying to fight battles from a distance with fixed assumptions that the enemy is bent on withdrawal and that he is incapable of increasing the number of his forces. In point of fact, far from withdrawing, his intention seems to be just the opposite.[2]

On the 25th General Morshead left for Lae and the Ramu. Before leaving, Morshead signalled General Milford warning him of the likely forward movement of the 4th Brigade. Writing to Blamey on 25th October, Mackay said: "Morshead seems to fear the possibility of an attempted enemy landing at Langemak Bay and asks for another brigade to reinforce 9th

---

[2] A sequel to the differences of opinion about reinforcing Finschhafen, now happily ended, was a severe censorship at MacArthur's headquarters of reports from Australian correspondents with the 9th Division, with a view to making it appear that the Japanese resistance was less severe than it actually was. At this stage the correspondents' reports were censored in the field by the Australian army censor and censored again at GHQ by an American censor and by the Australian publicity censor from the Department of Information. When, for example, reports written by one correspondent (Geoffrey Hutton) reached GHQ, having already been censored at 9th Division headquarters, about 600 words out of about 1,500 were cut. They included such statements as:

"The vastly increased weight behind the second Japanese counter-attack is clear proof that they have brought in strong reinforcements."
"Night after night the Japanese have sown the area with bombs sometimes using single planes for their nuisance value and sometimes sending over 30 to 40 planes in relay."
"They (the aircraft) are usually unopposed from the air or the ground."

An Australian liaison officer at GHQ reported that the censorship was "on lines personally indicated by General MacArthur" and was intended partly to prevent conflict between the newspaper reports and MacArthur's communiqués, the one issued on 25th October, for example, having contained the following words:

"The enemy's efforts to break through to the coast north of Finschhafen apparently for the purpose of escape, evacuation or of sea supply have terminated. . . . His forces are weak in numbers and of little significance."

The liaison officer reported also that MacArthur did not accept the estimates of Japanese strength made by either New Guinea Force or his own Intelligence staff and that his own estimate was said to be 3,000.

Division. . . . Berryman will be at Finsch (25/10) and I shall reserve my decision until he returns." Berryman agreed with Morshead.

Only on the 2/32nd's front was there severe fighting on the 25th. On the main Katika front the Japanese tried to infiltrate between the forward companies but on all occasions were repulsed. Against Katika they had tried everything they knew and had attacked persistently and irrespective of casualties. Sometimes they attacked silently and sometimes heralded by a bugle-call. Once they called out, "We'll be back Aussie," and they were.

During the next three days the 24th and 26th Brigades pushed their "FDL's" (forward defended localities) west to ground well-sited for defence, giving a depth of over 1,200 yards inland from Scarlet Beach and Katika. Whitehead was instructed to include the Katika Track in his dispositions, thus giving the 24th Brigade more opportunity to build up a reserve. Divisional orders emphasised the importance of defence "in depth". Lanes of visibility and fire were cut, head cover was added to well-dug positions, trip wires and booby-traps were laid, and standing patrols were sent out on all likely approaches. Strong fighting patrols scoured the area on the 26th, 27th and 28th, locating and harrying the retreating enemy. Artillery and mortars, with fire directed by observers with the fighting patrols, helped to compel the enemy to go on withdrawing. There were numerous skirmishes in these three days between the Australians and groups of retreating enemy.

On the Sattelberg Road and Kumawa Track, however, the situation remained very much the same with each side exerting pressure but unable to shift the other. The 20th Brigade's main task during this period was to get rid of the obstinate pocket of Japanese between the 2/17th and 2/13th. Patrols could not do much against such a position because of the steep ground and the thickness of the surrounding bamboo which gave away any movement. The Japanese were under heavy bombardment, however, though it was difficult for the artillery observer with the 2/13th to direct fire accurately because of the small gap between the two Australian battalions. "2/17th cannot observe our firing," wrote the 2/13th diarist, "they can only let us know when it gets too close to them."

On 26th October a strong fighting patrol from the 2/43rd and the Papuan Battalion led by Sergeant Joy[3] found Pino Hill, Exchange and Oriental unoccupied. Near by a few Japanese who were foraging in a native garden were attacked, but the patrol itself was attacked from the rear by a band of Japanese. Next day a patrol about three miles up the Song found a newly-occupied Japanese position. Four Papuans dressed as local natives reached a position overlooking Bonga and hid in the jungle. When they returned late on the 27th they reported that there were no Japanese in Bonga but 37 were dug in along the line of a creek 100 yards north of the village.

---

[3] Lt F. N. Joy, MM, SX5093; 2/43 Bn. Labourer; of Poochera, SA; b. Streaky Bay, SA, 26 Jan 1913.

There were few encounters on the 28th, by which time the enemy was becoming more difficult to find. The *79th Regiment* on which the bulk of the casualties had fallen was in full retreat to the Sattelberg-Wareo fortress. Only in the Jivevaneng area did the enemy hold an equal initiative.

The counter-attack by the *20th Division* had resulted in heavy losses to the Japanese: 679 enemy dead had been counted by the Australians, and many more had been killed by artillery and mortar fire, or dragged away at night and buried. Many more must have perished in unknown places in the jungle and kunai. Wootten's staff believed that a conservative estimate of Japanese casualties was 1,500. The victory had been won mainly by the determination and valour of the individual units which had stubbornly held on when the fog of war was thickest and when disaster seemed imminent. As a result of this dogged resistance the enemy was forced to pause in his furious assault, thus allowing the Australians time to reorganise. When the assault was resumed it was stopped in its tracks and finally turned into a retreat. "It appeared at one stage," stated General Adachi after the war, "that the attack was on the verge of success, but it ended in a complete failure." To the Australians the cost of this key battle was 228 casualties, including 49 killed.

CHAPTER 20

IN THE RAMU VALLEY

WHILE the 9th Division was locked in fierce and decisive conflict with the main striking force of the *20th Japanese Division*, the 7th Australian Division had been fighting its own smaller campaign far to the west in the Ramu Valley and the foothills of the Finisterres. Both opposing commanders in New Guinea, General Mackay in Port Moresby and General Adachi in Wewak, had been watching the outcome of the Finschhafen operations with grave anxiety. While it was going on, the subordinate commanders in the Ramu Valley, Major-General Vasey and Major-General Nakai, were each instructed to hold what they had, to patrol extensively and attempt no big advances.

These orders were conveyed to Vasey in a Corps instruction the day Dumpu fell—4th October. They confirmed verbal instructions given to him by General Herring at Lae on the 1st. The 7th Division would now concentrate in the Dumpu-Marawasa area, but would make no advance "in strength" beyond Dumpu without reference to Corps headquarters. One battalion would be left for the protection of the Kaiapit airfield area and "adequate" troops would remain on the Bena Bena-Garoka plateau to guard the American air installations and radar equipment. Responsibility for the protection of Nadzab and control of the 15th Brigade passed to Major-General Milford of the 5th Division on 3rd October.

Late on the 4th, after a company of the 2/16th Battalion had secured Dumpu, Brigadier Dougherty of the 21st Brigade received an order from Vasey to "prepare to move in strength to Key Point 3". This was a point shown on captured Japanese maps and seemed to be on the line of communications along which the Australians thought the enemy was withdrawing. From the little information available Dougherty believed that Key Point 3 was where the Japanese track crossed the Uria River but, because the maps of this area were very sketchy, he could not be sure. Actually, what the Japanese called "Key Points" were really staging points and supply dumps.

On 5th October there was a general move forward—the 21st Brigade into the Dumpu area and into the foothills and the 25th Brigade into the Kaigulin area. By midday the 2/16th Battalion in Dumpu was digging a defensive position. Among the equipment captured at Dumpu was a crate of silk lap laps; later in the day one company paraded in the coloured lap laps while their newly-washed jungle-greens were drying. A patrol moved out with Major Duchatel of Angau who reported a suitable area for a landing strip about 2,000 yards long which could be made ready by the morning of the 6th. Other patrols moving out from Dumpu in all directions met no Japanese. One returned laden with zebu steaks but, said the battalion's report, "the spirit in which the steak was tackled was willing enough but on this occasion the flesh was far too strong".

Dumpu was about 3,000 yards from the Ramu River and south of the Uria. To the newly-arrived battalion it seemed an ideal spot for an air supply point.

Dumpu was destined to be of major tactical importance in the later stages of the campaign (said its report). The primary object of the current operations had been to clear the enemy from the valley and establish (and protect) a fighter strip as

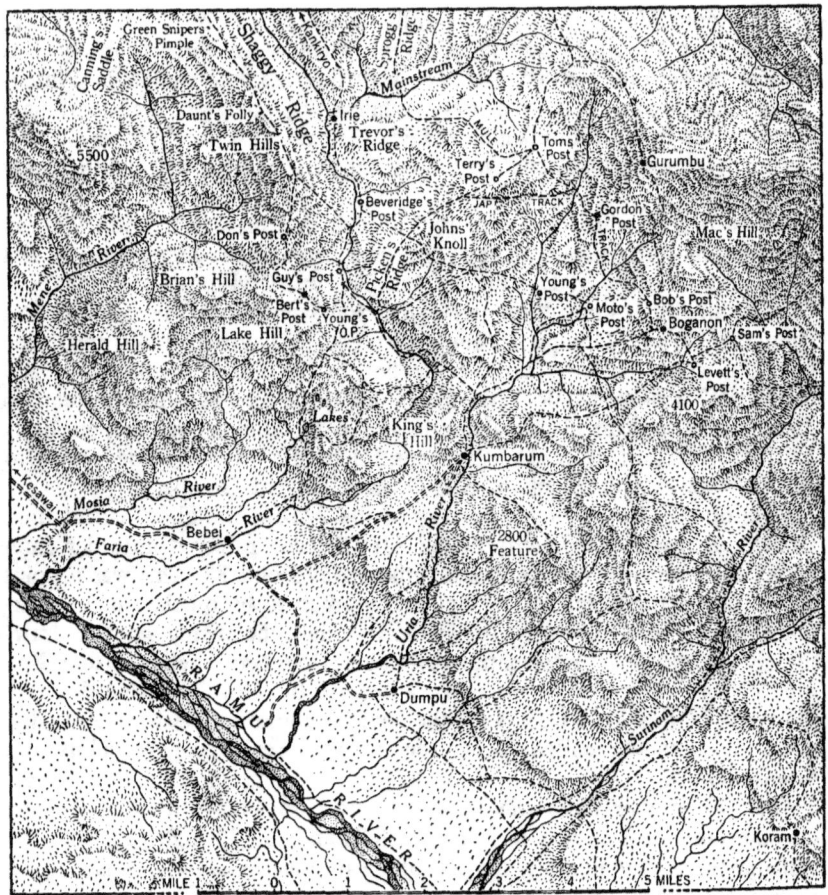

a base for air operations against Bogadjim and Madang on the north coast of New Guinea. This fighter strip was already in process of development at Gusap and the role of 21 Brigade now was to assist in its protection. This would entail taking up defensive positions north of Gusap and in the Finisterres. To maintain these protective forces an air supply point was vital—and even more so if later attempts were to be made against the Jap roadhead at Daumoina about fourteen miles away.

Dougherty planned that Lieut-Colonel Bishop's 2/27th Battalion would lead the advance into the Finisterre foothills. Before doing so, however, it had to be relieved from its task of making a road from Kaigulin to the Surinam River. The 2/14th Battalion was therefore recalled from the Wampun area, scene of its stiff fight on the previous day, and relieved the 2/27th Battalion on the 5th. The 2/6th Independent Company relieved the 2/14th in the Wampun area, and in the afternoon its patrols skirmished with an enemy force between Koram and the valley of the Surinam. As the enemy held the favourable ground the Independent Company withdrew for the night to the west bank of the Surinam. Dougherty's other reconnaissance unit, "B" Company of the Papuan Battalion, moved during the day to a position 600 yards west of Dumpu. Dougherty recommended on the 5th that the Papuans should have a complete rest as the native soldiers were suffering from foot trouble. Officers and N.C.O's were also feeling the strain: the company had marched from Bulldog and fought through the Salamaua campaign and onward to Dumpu.

Dougherty hoped that the 2/27th would reach Kumbarum in the Finisterre foothills on the 5th. By 3.20 p.m. the battalion reached the timber on the bank of the Uria River and began to advance north along the difficult valley of the Uria. By 4.30 p.m., led by Major Johnson's[1] company on the left, and Captain C. A. W. Sims' on the right, it was ready to attack the area which seemed from the map to be Kumbarum. In a heavy storm the infantrymen advanced steadily, and by 5.30 p.m. the Kumbarum area was overrun without opposition.

Bishop had advanced up the river valley fully deployed, with picquets on the surrounding foothills. These were able to see that the enemy was occupying the key feature guarding the exits of the Faria and Uria Rivers from the mountains north-west of Kumbarum. Under cover of the continuing rain Lieutenant King[2] and eight men scrambled up this feature (subsequently known as King's Hill); the enemy panicked and fled thus abandoning an important tactical position and observation post.

Because of the heavy rain on the previous day Duchatel's landing strip was not ready on the morning of the 6th. The activities of the 21st Brigade that day were therefore confined to patrolling, for the 2/27th Battalion could not move forward until more supplies had been flown in. Patrols from the 2/16th Battalion and the 2/14th, now led by Major Landale,[3] went as far west as the Mosia River without seeing any enemy.

The artillery was now beginning to play its part. Headquarters of the 2/4th Field Regiment and the 8th Battery had moved to Nadzab on the 4th and the 54th Battery to Kaiapit. A light section under Lieutenant Pearson, who had led the paratroop gunners over Nadzab, was forward with the infantry at Dumpu, and in the advance to Kumbarum Bishop had used Pearson's No. 511 wireless set, which proved to be light, easily handled and very efficient. "It is noticeable," wrote the battalion's diarist,

---

[1] Maj R. L. Johnson, DSO, SX2925; 2/27 Bn. Solicitor; of Prospect, SA; b. Adelaide, 15 Mar 1916.
[2] Maj G. A. King, SX2668; 2/27 Bn. Salesman; b. Penola, SA, 28 Mar 1915.
[3] Maj W. G. A. Landale, VX14682; 2/14 Bn. Clerk; of Deniliquin, NSW, and Toorak, Vic; b. Melbourne, 17 Feb 1914.

"the number of favourable comments made by our troops re this U.S. paratroop wireless set model." This praise was in striking contrast to the universal condemnation handed out by battalion diarists to the No. 208 set.

At 11.30 a.m. on the 6th Lieutenant King reported seeing 20 Japanese moving north-west along the Faria River Valley and Bishop asked for artillery support. Pearson directed 35 rounds on to a Japanese-occupied village near the position subsequently known as Guy's Post[4] in the Faria Valley. Later King's men killed two Japanese moving down the Faria; their papers showed that they had been members of the *78th Regiment*.

On the 6th the 25th Brigade had patrols out in all directions to the north of the Ramu Valley. Captain Milford's[5] patrol from the 2/25th into the Boparimpum area was out for three days and found many signs of the enemy once having occupied the area. Captain Cox's[6] patrol from the 2/33rd into the area north of Koram had similar experiences. Only Captain Rylands' patrol from the 2/31st made any contact. In the hills north of Koram Rylands encountered what he believed was an enemy company in well-dug positions with numerous outposts on high ground from which snipers were active. While guides went back to the battalion to bring up reinforcements, Rylands worked slowly round to the north-east to capture an enemy outpost. A small patrol forced the enemy to keep their heads down while the company continued to the north-east. Next morning it was found that the enemy had disappeared during the night. This was probably one of the last Japanese outposts in the foothills east of the valley of the Surinam and was the position encountered on the previous day by the 2/6th Independent Company.

While the 7th Division was consolidating in the Dumpu area, Major Laidlaw's 2/2nd Independent Company was patrolling its vast area from the Sepu to the Waimeriba crossings of the Ramu, and was proving that the enemy was either evacuating the valley or else thinking of doing so. Captain Nisbet's platoon from bases forward of Bundi had several patrols across the swirling Ramu early in October.

One small patrol which crossed on the night of the 4th-5th met a small enemy patrol on the track between Saus and Usini and killed two Japanese. A second patrol crossed the Ramu at Yonapa on the 5th and went east along the main Ramu Valley track to Kesawai; it found indications that the Japanese had used this area extensively but had recently evacuated it. Another patrol found that the area between Saus and Urigina had recently been deserted by substantial enemy forces.

Captain Turton's patrols meanwhile were searching for the enemy across the Ramu from the Maululi area and were on their way to join the 21st Brigade in the Dumpu area. On the night of the 4th-5th October

---

[4] After Captain Guy Fawcett of the 2/27th Battalion.

[5] Maj C. F. Milford, QX14477; 2/25 Bn. Solicitor's clerk; of Rockhampton, Qld; b. Rockhampton, 7 Jul 1912.

[6] Capt R. W. Cox, NX12554; 2/33 Bn. Jackeroo; of Mudgee, NSW; b. Mudgee, 24 Dec 1920.

Turton led a section across the river and early next morning entered Kesawai, once an important Japanese position but now abandoned. While Turton examined the Kesawai base, and tunnels containing a large amount of supplies, ammunition and equipment, Lieutenant Fullarton led five men towards Dumpu. After marching all day along the hot valley, the men slept that night in the kunai and at first light continued their journey. One of the men later reported the junction with the 21st Brigade on the 6th as follows:

> When we were nearing Dumpu we stopped to have a pawpaw and while we were eating we heard rifle fire. We could then see Aussie soldiers so waved our hats to show we were Australians. We were able to tell them the Ramu Valley was clear of Japs as far as Kesawai. We were looked after very well by the 7th Div and had eggs, butter, bread and jam, the first of that diet we had had for weeks, as our ration was bully beef and biscuits, dehydrated potatoes and margarine, and not a lot of any of it.

These linking patrols proved conclusively that the Japanese had left the actual valley of the Ramu and had retreated into the foothills. As far as Bena Force was concerned the days of the enemy raids across the Ramu were over, and fighting would henceforward be confined to the mountains north of the valley.

It was on 6th October that Generals Vasey and Wootten received a signal that the 2/2nd, 2/4th, 2/6th and 2/7th Independent Companies "will be re-designated forthwith" 2/2nd, 2/4th, 2/6th and 2/7th Australian Cavalry (Commando) Squadrons. Since the beginning of the year the term "commando" had been increasingly used to describe a member of an Independent Company. The term was an alien one for the Australian Army, and the tasks undertaken by the Independent Companies since the beginning of the war against the Japanese had little in common with the tasks carried out by the British commandos, although on some occasions there were some striking similarities with those of the original Boer commandos. In the short space of two years the Independent Companies had built up a proud tradition. The men regarded the term "Independent Company" as a much better description of what they did than the terms "cavalry" and "commando", and they resented the change of title. There was little they could do about it, however, except to record their displeasure in their war diaries and to call themselves in their private correspondence cavalry squadrons, leaving out the term commandos. The report of the 2/6th probably summed up best what everyone felt.

> It is submitted that the name "commando" as applied to these units is unfortunate. British "commandos" are the flower of the British Army; our personnel are, at the moment, merely a cross-section of the Australian Army. In common usage in Australia a "commando" has come to mean a blatant, dirty, unshaven, loudmouthed fellow covered with knives and knuckle-dusters. The fact that the men in this unit bitterly resent the commando part of their unit name speaks highly for their *esprit de corps*. It is obvious, however, from the attitude of many of the

reinforcements received that the blatant glamour of the name is being used to attract personnel into volunteering for these units. Personnel acquired in this manner are always undesirable.[8]

By 7th October documents captured by the 2/27th at Kumbarum were translated. They were orders for delaying actions in the foothills round the valley of the Surinam and for the blocking of the Uria River Valley by the *1/78th Battalion*. This was further evidence that General Adachi intended to fight delaying or holding actions in the Finisterres while he tried to win a decisive battle at Finschhafen. From their bitter experiences on the Papuan coast Vasey and Dougherty knew just how difficult it was to root out an entrenched and determined enemy. Despite their superiority in numbers, fire power and air support, therefore, the Australian leaders expected no easy successes.

All identifications found by the 7th Division confirmed that the *78th Regiment* was opposing the advance of the 21st Brigade. The *III/78th Battalion*, battered at Kaiapit, had withdrawn towards Yokopi near the head of the Bogadjim Road and Kankiryo Saddle. The *1/78th Battalion* had clashed with the 2/14th Battalion in the Wampun area and was now east of the Uria River ready to contest any Australian move there. The *II/78th Battalion* was either still in reserve as suggested by one prisoner or was carrying supplies forward to the *1/78th Battalion*. Except for the *1/78th Battalion* the *78th Regiment* had therefore withdrawn early in October to the rugged area south of the Bogadjim roadhead.

The supply problem would also limit the Australian advance, for the 7th Division was supplied from the air and the Fifth Air Force had many commitments. Thinking about these limitations and the order given to him to move "in strength" to Key Point 3 when the "administrative situation" permitted, Dougherty found it difficult to decide what "in strength" meant. Key Point 3 was more than a day's carry each way from the jeephead and with his available native carriers he could maintain only one

---

[8] At this stage of the war there were seven Independent Companies in the AIF. The 2/2nd, 2/6th and 2/7th were with the 7th Division in the Ramu Valley and the 2/4th was with the 9th Division on the Huon Peninsula. The 2/3rd and 2/5th were on the Atherton Tableland. The 2/8th alone had not yet seen action and was still vegetating in the Northern Territory. The 2/1st Independent Company had never been re-formed since the time when many of that unit were captured in New Ireland.

The 7th Division's Cavalry Regiment (2/7th Aust Cav Regt) had suffered heavily in the fighting in Papua and as there seemed little place for mechanised cavalry in jungle warfare against the Japanese it was decided not to re-form it. At the same time it was thought desirable to have an administrative headquarters for the seven Independent Companies when they were in Australia. Consequently on 4th April 1943 Vasey received instructions to disband the 2/7th Aust Cav Regiment and to raise the 2/7th Aust Cav (Commando) Regiment.

Apparently it was originally intended to brigade the Independent Companies in groups of three. In the war diary of LHQ for 30th July 1943 it was stated that the organisation of the 2/7th Aust Cav (Commando) Regiment "is being changed from Regimental Headquarters and three Independent Companies to Regimental Headquarters, Headquarters Squadron and three Squadrons". Despite this decision, however, the seven Independent Companies were henceforth noted as sub-units of the 2/7th Aust Cav (Commando) Regiment on LHQ Location statements.

Confusion grew worse confounded, until the LHQ diary on 1st September noted: "Instructions have been issued clarifying the position in regard to the 2/7th [Aust Cav (Commando) Regt]. The H.Q. of this unit has no operational role and will administer the squadrons under command as well as carrying out certain administrative functions for other squadrons or Independent Companies. Should the H.Q. be required operationally the necessary administrative personnel could be detached from the regiment and allotted to the Training Squadron." Here it will be seen that LHQ was referring to the units as squadrons a month before the change in title. The next step, changing the Independent Companies into squadrons, the platoons into troops, and the privates into troopers was inevitable and came early in October.

In January 1944 the 2/6th and 2/9th Cavalry Regiments were also remodelled and four commando squadrons were formed from them, making the total eleven. Nine of these squadrons (all but the 2/2nd and 2/8th Squadrons)—now called Commando, not Cavalry (Commando) Squadrons—were brigaded in the 2/6th, 2/7th and 2/9th Aust Cav (Commando) Regiments.

battalion a day out from the jeephead. He therefore decided that his move "in strength" would be limited to sending one battalion a day's carry away whence the battalion would send a company patrol to find Key Point 3 and harass the Japanese there. On the afternoon of the 6th Vasey drove through the fast-flowing Surinam in his jeep and told Dougherty his plan would suit admirably.

On the 7th, when Australian and American Army and Air Force commanders were deciding in Port Moresby to build airfield groups in the Nadzab and Gusap areas, patrols from the 7th Division were active all along the Ramu Valley. To achieve extra security on the western flank Dougherty sent Lieut-Colonel Sublet's 2/16th Battalion to occupy a defensive position at Bebei. Here the battalion dug in, sent out patrols north and east, and provided large working parties to assist on the Dumpu strip.

On the 7th Captain Christopherson's[9] company of the 2/14th was sent to Kumbarum, where "B" Echelon of the 2/27th was established, and was instructed to patrol along a track running east towards the Surinam River. On this occasion the Australians were accompanied by a small American patrol with trained dogs.[1] Christopherson's task was also to provide escorts for the native carrying parties moving forward to the 2/27th Battalion.

The 2/27th Battalion was now cautiously investigating the upper reaches of the Uria and Faria River Valleys. As Dougherty thought that "administrative arrangements could be made sound enough" by 8th October for the 2/27th to move on that day, Colonel Bishop sent Captain Fawcett's[2] company to reconnoitre the route up the Faria River Valley so that the rest of the battalion could follow on the 8th. Twenty-six native carriers were allotted to the company but even so the Australians were each carrying up to 80 pounds. After bivouacking for the night on a shelf above the Uria River, Fawcett moved forward at 8 a.m. on the 7th following the Faria River with the high ground on his east side. Soon after 1 p.m. his rear section in the narrow area between the two rivers suddenly met a party of eight Japanese also on the move and killed three of them with no casualties themselves.

Fawcett pushed on during the afternoon past the saddle between the Uria and Faria River Valleys where he found many Japanese camp sites

---

[9] Maj F. A. Christopherson, VX14038; 2/14 Bn. Bank officer; of Ballarat, Vic; b. Port Augusta, SA, 4 Feb 1915.

[1] Lieutenant R. Jonson of the American Army, with five sergeants and four dogs—one messenger dog and three scout dogs—had arrived at Dougherty's headquarters on 27th September. The dogs had been trained in the United States and had been brought to New Guinea as an experiment to find out how they would work under tropical conditions. They had originally been trained for use in Alaska, in snow country, and three of the sergeants were actually ski troops. If considered satisfactory the dogs would be taken over by the battalions and the American party would return to the United States and submit their reports. The 2/27th Battalion reported thus on the use of the dogs: "This venture with this type of trained dog has great possibilities as the first day they were used with our unit they were very efficient and performed any task asked of them. Scout dogs smelt out positions Japs had occupied—messenger dog carried messages between Comd and Rear BHQ in excellent time. Extreme heat and height of kunai were against the dogs." Speaking for the 2/14th Battalion, W. B. Russell, in *The Second Fourteenth Battalion* (1948), p. 231, wrote: "At Dumpu four American dogs . . . showed a high degree of training, but failed to stand up to fire and were therefore of no use." Although regarded affectionately by the Australian soldiers the dogs were not really of much use and henceforward were not used by the 21st Brigade.

[2] Lt-Col G. H. Fawcett, OBE, SX6219. 2/27 Bn; training and staff appointments. Regular soldier; of Hurstville, NSW; b. Oakey, Qld, 5 Nov 1911.

with the fires still warm in some of them. The Japanese had obviously just left, and had made no attempt to prevent the Australians from moving up the Faria towards a plateau on the east bank opposite a spot where a stream flowed into the Faria from the west. The company camped for the night on this plateau with a picquet opposite the spot known later as Guy's Post. About 5 p.m. the Australians noticed some enemy positions just opposite on the east bank, on a small feature later named Buff's Knoll.[3] When they attacked the Japanese again withdrew.

That afternoon Dougherty was with the 2/27th Battalion. On King's Hill Dougherty told Bishop that he should move into the mountains and occupy an area selected by him as a base about a day's carry away. His route would be along the Faria River Valley to somewhere beyond Guy's Post and then he would take the line of a suitable spur running north-east towards Key Point 3. From this base he would patrol to, and harass, the enemy at Key Point 3. Above all, Bishop was to regard the 2/27th as a battalion fighting patrol; he need not necessarily regard his base as a fixed place that he must hold. The 2/6th Commando Squadron would occupy King's Hill when the 2/27th Battalion moved on, and the 2/14th Battalion would provide escorts for Bishop's carriers.

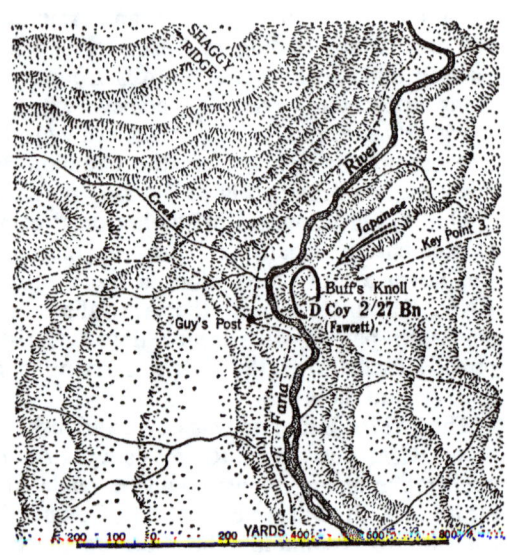

7th-8th October

Meanwhile, the Japanese commander south of the saddle at Kankiryo must have been perturbed at the ease with which Fawcett's men had captured such an important feature as Buff's Knoll. It was a dark rainy night but the position must be regained. An hour after midnight a strong Japanese attack, probably of platoon strength, was suddenly launched on the knoll. The first attack lasted for about half an hour before petering out, and in the dark the section on the knoll slipped down into the river bed, almost a precipice. Fawcett decided that it would be necessary to concentrate his company on Guy's Post and this was done about dawn, after a slide down to the Faria and a climb on hands and knees up the other side.

---

[3] After Corporal B. S. ("Buff") Deering, 2/27th Battalion.

On 7th October there had been a change in high command when, as mentioned, General Morshead's II Corps relieved General Herring's I Corps. Next day the corps role was re-defined by New Guinea Force. The first stated task given to the 7th Division was something of an anachronism; "as soon as practicable after seizure of [Kaiapit] area the [Dumpu] area will be secured".[4] The second task was a more topical one and outlined the role to which the 7th Division would actually be committed throughout.

> After the capture of [Dumpu] operations north of [Dumpu] will be so conducted as to avoid a logistic commitment outside resources of I [II] Aust Corps. Operations against the village on coast (Bogadjim) 17 miles SSW of [Madang] will be restricted to patrol activities until other orders are given by [N.G.F.].

Other parts of the 7th Division's role included establishment and guarding of air installations, radar and air-warning stations in the Ramu Valley and on the Bena plateau, the construction of a road from Nadzab to Dumpu and the supply of the division from Lae and Nadzab rather than from Port Moresby and Dobodura. The "priority of establishment of airfield facilities" would be first—Lae and Nadzab; secondly—Finschhafen; thirdly—Kaiapit; fourthly—Dumpu.[5]

There was much improvement all along the Ramu Valley on the 8th. In the main battle area Bishop did not know what had happened to Fawcett's company until communication was re-established. As a result of his discussion with Dougherty, however, Bishop and the 2/27th were already moving forward early on the morning of the 8th. At 2 p.m. they arrived at Guy's Post but, surveying the rugged country before him, Bishop decided that he would need to picquet the hills on each side of the Faria before advancing farther and that it would take the afternoon for the picquets to get into position.

On the previous night a patrol under Lieutenant R. D. Johns, advancing up the Uria and laying signal wire, had come to a creek junction and camped for the night about 700 yards up the western creek. Just after dusk the telephone line was cut, and at 8.30 a.m. on the 8th one of the sections, moving to investigate this break, was fired on from high ground above the creek junction. Failing to find any sign of the enemy's lines of communication up the creek Johns then moved north-west to some high ground whence he could see enemy positions and shelters at the top of the kunai ridge about half a mile up the eastern branch of the creek. Continuing on a semi-circular route, the patrol reached the Uria River again 500 yards below the creek junction about 4.40 p.m. just as firing began from there.

Meanwhile, in accordance with Dougherty's instructions, the 2/6th Commando Squadron had moved to King's Hill. At 2 p.m. on the 8th

---

[4] Dumpu had been secured 4 days previously but such details had not been watched when the order of 27th September, mentioned earlier, was re-issued on 8th October.

[5] Here again more attention might have been paid to details before this important instruction was re-issued. The Gusap airfield was far more important than the Kaiapit and Dumpu airfields and the decision to accord it a higher priority was already being carried out.

Lieutenant Graham's[6] platoon from the commando squadron, believing Johns' patrol to be in position ahead of them, advanced up the river from Kumbarum following Johns' signal wire. At 4.40 p.m. a fierce burst of firing was heard but no information was available about the cause of it until, at 5.55, a trooper arrived almost exhausted and reported that Graham's patrol had been ambushed. It was only later when the remnants of Graham's patrol and Johns' patrol arrived back that it was possible to report what had actually happened.

At 4.40 p.m. Graham's leading scout, Trooper Mudford,[7] saw a Japanese squatting on the track ahead near the creek junction cutting telephone lines. As Mudford fired at him the Japanese jumped for cover. Graham then sent Corporal Brammer[8] and three men up the steep jungle bank on his right to cover the patrol and himself stood up directing the remainder to close up and move on. From positions some 70 yards away and about 40 feet above the patrol on a kunai spur, there was a sudden heavy burst of fire. In this first burst Graham was killed instantly and Mudford was wounded. Trooper Eddy,[9] trying to cross the creek for a better shot at the enemy, was also killed, while the rest of the troops, sheltering under the creek bank, returned fire as best they could.

Brammer then scrambled back to rejoin the patrol and ordered the men to withdraw while he himself, assisted by two of his men, covered the withdrawal with a machine-gun. Then he went forward and found that Graham and Eddy were already dead. Although under heavy fire, he secured their papers and personal effects and withdrew his covering party. During its withdrawal Trooper Tyter[1] suffered a compound fracture of the leg but, assisted by Trooper Little,[2] Brammer carried Tyter for a little while and then floated him downstream for about 400 yards where his leg was dressed and splinted. Johns' patrol had now arrived to see what all the firing was about.

It seemed fairly certain that the Japanese who had ambushed Graham's patrol were those who had fired on Johns' patrol earlier in the morning. It was also evident that this ambush party of about 20 Japanese were an outpost for a stronger body located on the spur seen by Johns' patrol farther up the left arm of the creek, probably to protect a key point on the enemy's lines of communication reported by reconnaissance aircraft as passing through this area. Despite the 2/27th's spearhead being thrust into their main position north of Guy's Post, the Japanese had by no means yet retreated wholly from the area east of the Uria River Valley.

---

[6] Lt J. H. Graham, VX54840. 2/24 Bn, 2/6 Indep Coy, 2/6 Cdo Sqn. Bank officer; of Elsternwick, Vic; b. Elsternwick, 20 Sep 1920. Killed in action 8 Oct 1943.

[7] Tpr G. J. Mudford, NX83469. 2/6 Indep Coy, 2/6 Cdo Sqn. Farm hand; of Stewart's River, NSW; b. Tinonee, NSW, 27 Oct 1922.

[8] L-Sgt J. McA. Brammer, DCM, NX152731. 2/6 Indep Coy, 2/6 Cdo Sqn. Student; of Mona Vale, NSW; b. Griffith, NSW, 26 Feb 1923.

[9] Tpr C. E. Eddy, WX15415. 2/6 Indep Coy, 2/6 Cdo Sqn. Miner; of West Leederville, WA; b. Northam, WA, 21 Apr 1917. Killed in action 8 Oct 1943.

[1] Tpr C. F. Tyter, NX90569. 2/6 Indep Coy, 2/6 Cdo Sqn. Station hand; of Quirindi, NSW; b. Dubbo, NSW, 5 Nov 1922.

[2] S-Sgt B. J. F. Little, VX64251. 2/6 Indep Coy, 2/6 Cdo Sqn. Timber worker; of Naradhan, NSW; b. Sydney, 10 Jun 1920.

The fact that they were still in this eastern area was confirmed by a company patrol led by Captain Power of the 2/33rd Battalion on the 8th and 9th October. Power set out at dawn on the 8th to patrol the area from Koram to the Surinam River and north as far as possible. He bypassed Koram and went towards the Surinam passing through many old Japanese positions which had been deserted within the last few weeks. In the afternoon the patrol came across three bridges which had been blown up by the retreating enemy, and a small patrol to the north-east found an extensive well-dug position where there had recently been about 200 Japanese. Next morning Power pushed on along a well-graded, three foot wide track running along the west bank of the Surinam up into the foothills. At midday his men captured a prisoner and saw immediately ahead a well-dug position on a razor-edged spur occupied by about a company. As this position would have been too costly to attack Power withdrew for the night. The enemy was occupying a dominating feature shown on the map as being 4,100 feet high, about one mile south-east of where Boganon was thought to be and about four miles east of Kumbarum.

On the 9th Bishop began to move his battalion forward to try to get astride the main Japanese route from the east towards Kankiryo Saddle. Fawcett's company moved off from Guy's Post at 8 a.m., the remainder of the battalion following about an hour later. At 8.30 the leading platoon commander, Lieutenant Trenerry,[3] reported that three Japanese were coming towards him along the track. Two of these were killed and one wounded and, about 100 yards forward, the patrol saw about 20 Japanese scattering in all directions. Trenerry waited in ambush for about an hour and was then recalled. This area, about a mile along the river north from Guy's Post, was subsequently known as Beveridge's Post, after Private Beveridge[4] who was wounded there.

When Trenerry first struck the enemy Fawcett sent a section to the high ground to the right to get flanking fire on the enemy. Bishop came forward and told Fawcett to send a platoon out to this section with instructions to get as high as possible and Lieutenant Macdonald's[5] platoon climbed up the ridge on the right subsequently known as Trevor's Ridge.[6]

The Japanese were on the high ground ahead of the battalion up the Faria and Bishop decided that the valley was too much of a defile, where a platoon of Japanese could hold up the advance of the battalion. He therefore decided to take his battalion round on the high ground to the east side of the river. At the same time Bishop consulted Lieutenant Snook (as mentioned earlier, he was an engineer with experience in New Guinea before the war), now attached to the battalion. Snook knew the

---

[3] Capt A. R. Trenerry, MC, SX2795; 2/27 Bn. Clerk; of Unley, SA; b. Broken Hill, NSW, 27 Jan 1913.

[4] Sgt G. A. Beveridge, NX127061; 2/27 Bn. Plaster fixer; of Wallsend, NSW; b. Wallsend, 2 Sep 1920.

[5] Capt G. G. Macdonald, SX3238; 2/27 Bn. Jackeroo; of North Walkerville, SA; b. Adelaide, 8 Apr 1919.

[6] After Lieutenant E. T. (Trevor) Martin killed in action there on 9th October 1943.

area well and he had with him a houseboy who also knew it and who had been forced into service by the Japanese but had run away. It seemed clear to Bishop that his battalion was very near the Japanese lines of communication. Before the 2/27th actually started to move to the high ground on the right Bishop beckoned to some men, on a point to which he had sent a picquet, to come down and follow the battalion. The men did not come and later proved to be a Japanese force which had beaten the Australian picquet to the point by half an hour. Behind the advance, platoons were left at Guy's Post and at Beveridge's Post.

The 2/27th was ready to move off soon after 10.30 a.m. east from the rugged slopes of the Faria River Valley. By midday the men were clambering up towards the crest of the ridge where Macdonald's platoon and another were now in position. Captain Toms[7] had now taken over the lead from Fawcett's company. On the other side of the ridge could be seen a well-defined track, obviously much used by the enemy. Lieutenant Snook and Corporal Lundie,[8] manning an observation post watching this Japanese track, heard a rustling on both sides of the hillside below them. As one section of Australians climbed up one side of the ridge a soldier was heard panting as he climbed up on the opposite side. The soldier turned out to be a Japanese who panicked when he saw the Australians and jumped over a steep cliff about 100 feet high. Toms came forward to the observation post and saw 14 Japanese moving along the track in the gully below. The track seemed to run from the Faria River north-east across a saddle about 400 yards away and separating Trevor's Ridge from a knoll to the south-east.

Bishop, who was with the leading company, now sent Macdonald's platoon forward to move on to the saddle and find the track, at the same time setting an ambush. As they approached the saddle at about 3 p.m. through pit-pit cane the Australians "heard a lot of noise such as tins rattling and a lot of talking going on in the centre of the track". Fifteen Japanese were already on the saddle but they were quite unaware of the Australians' approach and were preparing their meal. Without pause Macdonald attacked and killed eight of the Japanese while the remainder escaped; the Japanese each carried seven days' rations. It was now about 3.30 p.m. but as the Australians began to withdraw their wounded a further party of 14 Japanese were seen approaching up the track. One section held the saddle while two sections, led by Corporal Sullivan,[9] went to intercept the Japanese force. Although wounded Sullivan led his small force with such determination that a possible Japanese counterattack was beaten off. For 5 men wounded in these two actions Macdonald's platoon killed 11 Japanese and captured 20 rifles, 3 machineguns, 3 mortars, as well as maps and papers. Bishop believed that his battalion was now right in the centre of Japanese territory. He was astride

---

[7] Lt-Col S. J. Toms, SX2924; 2/27 Bn. Clerk; of Gilberton, SA; b. Adelaide, 11 Apr 1916.
[8] Cpl F. J. P. Lundie, SX4083; 2/27 Bn. Labourer; of Renmark, SA; b. Alberton, SA, 21 Sep 1903.
[9] L-Sgt J. A. Sullivan, MM, SX3913; 2/27 Bn. Farm hand; of Bordertown, SA; b. Balaklava, SA, 27 Feb 1919.

a well-used track, and he had gained a good base position. The battalion therefore dug in along Trevor's Ridge leading up to the saddle, on the saddle itself and on the small knoll later known as Johns' Knoll, on the other side of the track.

Just after dawn on the 10th a small enemy force, after yelling for about four minutes, attacked straight along the track towards the company on Trevor's Ridge. The attack was beaten back. Describing this fight the battalion's diarist wrote:

> Tojo startled the early morning air with his usual heathen chorus, known to so many as a prelude to an attack; however, 13 Platoon showed him the error of his ways by killing two and wounding one of the six noisy intruders.

In the morning the Australians fired at some enemy seen climbing a steep ridge on the west side of the river about 600 yards from Beveridge's Post. One of the Japanese was seen to throw up his arms and disappear over the eastern side of what later was known as Shaggy Ridge.

During the afternoon of the 10th Lieutenant Macpherson's[1] platoon from Beveridge's Post patrolled north along the Faria seeking the body of a man killed the previous day about 300 yards north. The covering party moved off within 20 minutes of the burial party, but was ambushed when examining Japanese dead. One man was killed and another wounded. The casualties would have been heavier but for Private Simmons,[2] a member of the ambushed party, who worked his way under fire up the steep bank of the river and found a position across a ravine facing the enemy. He shot two Japanese and quietened the rest, thus enabling the remainder of his party to escape. Simmons then returned to Beveridge's Post and guided a small band to his firing position, whence several more Japanese were killed.

In the afternoon also two Japanese guns opened fire on the battalion from the Faria River area at very close range. The first shell passed close to the top of Trevor's Ridge, causing the native carriers to disperse, and exploded some thousands of yards farther on. By 2 p.m. Bombardier Leggo,[3] acting as F.O.O., noticed the gun flash and brought down counter-battery fire from the force's one short 25-pounder at a range of about 8,000 yards. He was successful in silencing the mountain guns for a while. When the Japanese guns fired again later in the afternoon at almost point-blank range, the shells began to land in the battalion's area and caused eight casualties, but Leggo again silenced them.

On the morning of the 10th Brigadier Dougherty sent the 2/14th Battalion from Dumpu to the Kumbarum-King's Hill area to relieve the 2/6th Commando Squadron. The 2/14th was already providing escorts for the 2/27th's carrier line, and by moving the whole battalion to the Kumbarum

---

[1] Lt W. N. Macpherson, SX2775; 2/27 Bn. Clerk; of Westbourne Park, SA; b. Adelaide, 9 Jun 1915.
[2] L-Cpl J. J. Simmons, MM, NX127185; 2/27 Bn. Farm hand; of Macksville, NSW; b. Port Macquarie, NSW, 13 Feb 1922.
[3] Bdr E. W. Leggo, VX18495; 2/4 Fd Regt. Laboratory assistant; of Elsternwick, Vic; b. Bendigo, Vic, 19 Apr 1918.

area Dougherty believed that more effective support could be given to the 2/27th in case of need.

The 2/16th was on the flat ground to the west of Bebei where malaria was taking its toll much to the concern of the commanders. The Ramu Valley was very malarious for hosts of anopheles mosquitoes bred in the swampy low-lying country. Although occupying a defensive position the West Australians were patrolling vigorously into the hills on the western flank of the 2/27th Battalion's advance. A patrol led by Warrant-Officer Young[4] had established a valuable observation post two days previously. From this position, known as Young's O.P., a report arrived on the 9th that an unidentified patrol had been seen on a feature about 1,200 yards north of the position. Lieutenant McCullough's platoon immediately set out from Bebei to investigate. Looking ahead from Young's O.P. over the rugged and precipitous country of the Finisterres McCullough estimated that it would take his patrol at least four days to reach the objective. Nevertheless, they set out, for the country was seldom as bad as it looked, and there was usually a way, however rough. The patrol camped for the night near a large Japanese defensive position vacated about four days before. Progress was slow on the 10th for the terrain was so steep that much of the climbing had to be done on hands and knees. McCullough's men were seen by the enemy who fired on them from a position subsequently known as Don's Post (after Lieutenant Don McRae[5]). McCullough wished to attack the position but he was instructed to withdraw. The patrol occupied Bert's Post (after Lieutenant Bert Sutton[6]) about 500 yards north-west of Young's O.P. This patrol was typical of several others carried out by the 2/16th Battalion in the mountains north of Bebei.

Meanwhile to the east the 25th Brigade was entering the fight. Brigadier Eather instructed Colonel Cotton of the 2/33rd Battalion to clean out the Japanese who opposed Captain Power's company patrol. The 2/33rd left the Ramu Valley soon after dawn on the 10th and followed the track of Power's company into the hills. By 1.30 p.m. the battalion reached the leading company which was below the 4100 Feature overlooking the track. Cotton immediately placed his battalion in position for the attack and at 4 p.m. Major MacDougal's[7] company led the ascent up the south end of the high feature, while Captain Mitchell's[8] company climbed the high ground on the left flank to give protection and covering fire for MacDougal's advance. The pace was slow and the amount of ground covered in the first hour was small because of the precipitous nature

---

[4] WO2 J. S. Young, WX4332; 2/16 Bn. Salesman; of Northam, WA; b. Preston, England, 30 Jun 1913.

[5] Lt D. C. McRae, NX127106; 2/27 Bn. Dairy farmer; of Barrington, NSW; b. Barrington, 10 Sep 1912.

[6] Lt A. J. Sutton, SX3121; 2/27 Bn. Labourer; of Tailem Bend, SA; b. Murray Bridge, SA, 1 Aug 1915.

[7] Lt-Col D. C. MacDougal, NX12539. CO Aust Contingent, Mission 204 (China) 1942; 2/33 Bn. Trust officer; of Mosman, NSW; b. Sydney, 19 Jun 1918.

[8] Capt D. A. Mitchell, NX12925; 2/33 Bn. Regular soldier; of Sydney; b. Liverpool, England, 17 Jun 1911.

of the feature. For the next three-quarters of an hour, from 5 p.m., Kittyhawks strafed the top of the Japanese-held ridge. A Boomerang flew off to drop a message on Eather's headquarters—that the Japanese were in foxholes and trenches immediately overlooking the 2/33rd. During the air attack the enemy replied to the planes with machine-gun and rifle fire and also fired on Power's company. The Japanese apparently did not see the approach of MacDougal's company, perhaps because the planes were keeping them busy.

At 7 p.m., three hours after the start, MacDougal was still pushing steadily towards the top. "Country terrific—very hard going," reported the diarist. The slope towards the top of the feature was almost sheer but Eather and Cotton were determined that, although a night attack was unusual in jungle fighting, the 4100 Feature must be captured before the morning. Under cover of darkness MacDougal's men reached the top of the ridge at 9.30 p.m. and moved straight towards the highest point to try their luck against whatever opposition was there. The Japanese defenders were surprised, probably because they did not expect the Australians to attack by night. As the Australians loomed out of the darkness on the flank the Japanese first panicked and fled, then tried to stop and fight, and were finally driven from the feature.

On the 10th General Vasey's three commando squadrons were also patrolling extensively or moving to new areas. While the 2/6th moved back to Dumpu from Kumbarum, the 2/7th was on its way from the Kaigulin-Bumbum area, where it had been resting, towards the Mosia River on the left flank of the 21st Brigade. Two days previously Vasey had warned Captain Lomas of the 2/7th that his squadron would eventually take over the Kesawai area. The 2/2nd would then be able to concentrate in the Faita area to the west, at the same time watching the air and radar installations on the Bena-Garoka plateau.

In these early days of October there were several savage fights for supremacy in which the Australians strove to secure dominating positions in the foothills of the Finisterres. The 11th was no exception. Early in the morning Lieutenant Robilliard's[9] platoon of the 2/27th patrolled from Trevor's Ridge towards the Faria River to seek out the enemy protecting the guns north of Beveridge's Post, and also to cover a renewed attempt to bring in the body of the man killed there on the 10th. Under cover of three mortar bombs on the enemy who were still strongly entrenched the dead man was carried in, but, because of the rugged nature of the country and the limited time, Robilliard was unable to reach the spot where the guns were thought to be.

At 1.15 p.m. the Japanese guns opened fire again, this time from a more distant range. Their second shell unfortunately put out of action Leggo's wireless set. By 2.30 p.m. a short 25-pounder had been sent as far north as possible and was ready to fire. Leggo remained in his observation post and shouted his orders about 30 yards to the battalion's Intelli-

---

[9] Lt G. H. G. Robilliard, NX112073; 2/27 Bn. Articled law clerk; of Parramatta, NSW; b. Parramatta, 2 Aug 1918.

gence officer, Lieutenant Reddin,[1] who told them to Colonel Bishop, who sent them on through his No. 11 wireless set—hit but not put out of action by the shelling—to Dougherty's headquarters whence they were passed by telephone to the guns. Throughout the afternoon Leggo stayed in the forward area observing the enemy gun flashes, and although the enemy guns stopped firing at 4 p.m., it could hardly have been the Australian short 25-pounders which forced them to do so, for their range was about 2,000 yards short.

As mentioned, Bishop's task was to establish a forward base and patrol to find Key Point 3. The base was now established and Captain Toms' company was sent out to complete the allotted task. At 3 p.m. on the 11th Toms moved off towards the high ground on the right flank. He also had to seek a suitable position in which to locate a counter-attacking force based outside the battalion's position; and to discover whether it would be possible to move round this high ground to the Kankiryo Saddle—the divide between the south-flowing Faria and the north-flowing Mindjim. After a five-hour climb, in which two miles were covered against slight opposition, Bishop instructed Toms not to move farther except on small reconnaissance patrols.

At this stage it was becoming obvious that it would be difficult to maintain and supply a sizeable Australian force in the mountains where the Japanese had a far easier supply route along the Bogadjim Road. The supply position was worrying Bishop for he had received little since leaving Kumbarum. Late in the afternoon of the 11th he received a report from Lieutenant Clampett,[2] whose platoons were at Johns' Knoll, Beveridge's Post and Guy's Post, that the stretcher party which had left Guy's Post for Kumbarum early in the morning had returned after being ambushed north of King's Hill. Also there was no news from Lieutenant Crocker's[3] platoon which was escorting forward a supply train of about 300 natives.

The 2/27th had actually been in peril of being cut off on the 11th. Lieutenant Pallier's[4] platoon of the 2/14th Battalion had occupied King's Hill the previous day. Soon after first light on the 11th Lieutenant Avery's standing patrol in the hills to the north-east reported seeing figures digging in on a high feature west across the Uria from the Three Pimples feature and north from King's Hill. When Crocker's escort and carrying party for the 2/27th was fired on by these Japanese near the Faria, the natives dumped the supplies and "went bush". It was thus established that about 30 Japanese had moved there during the night and were now digging in, not only on the high feature subsequently known as Pallier's Hill, but also astride the ridge over which the 2/27th's line of communication

---

[1] Capt J. W. Reddin, SX9362; 2/27 Bn. Sheep stud farm manager; of Gawler River, SA; b. Port Wakefield, SA, 11 Oct 1917.
[2] Capt R. W. Clampett, SX3169; 2/27 Bn. Clerk; of Glen Osmond, SA; b. Adelaide, 27 Jun 1920.
[3] Lt K. F. Crocker, SX2194; 2/27 Bn. Clerk; of Peterborough, SA; b. Peterborough, 13 Feb 1918.
[4] Lt N. W. T. Pallier, NX142877; 2/14 Bn. Plumber; of Woonona, NSW; b. Woonona, 9 Apr 1919.

ran to the north. Pallier's Hill had been occupied by the 2/27th but was not occupied by the 2/14th when it relieved the 2/27th.

Soon after the startling discovery of the enemy's determination to block the supply route to the 2/27th, the 2/14th's adjutant, Captain Bisset, climbed the rugged Three Pimples feature on the right, found a position between 700 and 1,200 yards from the enemy on Pallier's Hill, and by wireless sent back accurate information about their positions.

Learning of the Japanese threat, Dougherty sent forward his brigade major, Owens, carrying orders for prompt action by the 2/14th to clear the 2/27th's lines of communication. Major Landale of the 2/14th realised that there was only one way to attack Pallier's Hill—from King's Hill. He sent Captain O'Day with two platoons to take command on King's Hill, and decided not to attack until mortars and machine-guns could be dragged up into the very difficult country near the Three Pimples on the right whence they could give supporting fire. This was done in the late morning. Dougherty was chafing at the delay and sent Major A. J. Lee[5] across from the 2/16th Battalion to take command of the 2/14th.

On the Three Pimples feature a nine-man mortar detachment was already in position overlooking the enemy on Pallier's Hill when Bisset arrived back, and suggested that the only possible course was for Pallier's platoon to attack from King's Hill supported by fire from the Three Pimples —as Landale had planned. During the late morning a section with Vickers guns, a mortar control party and one infantry platoon climbed the Three Pimples so that covering fire could be brought to bear at right angles to any advance from King's Hill. While two other platoons were climbing King's Hill to relieve Pallier's platoon for the attack, Vickers machine-gun fire from the low-lying Kumba-

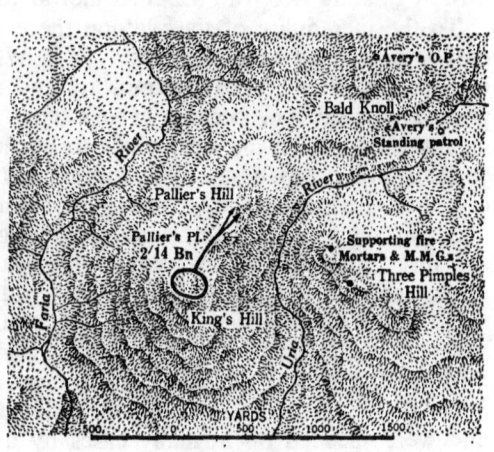

11th October

rum area and artillery fire from the Ramu Valley harassed the enemy on Pallier's Hill.

All was in readiness for the attack to begin at 4.50 p.m. "From the point of view of supporting fire it was an ideal text-book attack"[6] because the medium machine-guns from Three Pimples were firing at right angles

---

[5] Major Lee had now served in all three battalions of the 21st Brigade. Formerly a company commander in the 2/27th Battalion, he was second-in-command of the 2/16th before administering command of the 2/14th. He later commanded the 2/9th.
[6] W. B. Russell, *The Second Fourteenth Battalion*, p. 233.

to the line of advance of the assaulting troops and were able to fire within a few yards of them. The mortars and artillery also had excellent observation. The situation confronting the attacking platoon, however, was not encouraging. King's Hill and Pallier's Hill were about 1,000 yards apart and connected by a knife-edged ridge with a small pimple about half way between the two hills. Sloping down slightly to this pimple the ridge then sloped up to the summit of Pallier's Hill. On the right side the ridge was very steep and fell almost sheer to a swift stream hundreds of feet below. Apart from kunai grass which had been burnt in patches along the ridge, the only vegetation was a small patch of jungle near the pimple. It did indeed look a difficult, if not impossible, task and the men prepared for battle realising that there must be heavy casualties.

Pallier's plan was to advance with one section on the right and one on the left and the third section in reserve to give covering fire. The ridge was so narrow and the sides so steep, however, that it was difficult for the advance to be other than in single file, with some scrambling along the sides. At 4.50 p.m. the platoon left the protection of King's Hill and formed up as the Australian artillery, mortars and machine-guns stepped up their bombardment; this was so effective that the platoon reached the pimple without opposition. Here one man was stationed with a Bren gun and two with a 2-inch mortar to give close supporting fire.

To the incredulity of the platoon there was still no opposition as they moved rapidly up towards Pallier's Hill. When they were near the summit the artillery stopped, leaving mortars and machine-guns as the only support. The ridge now became even steeper and one false step could have meant sliding down the steep slope to hurtle into the creek below. Twenty yards from the Japanese on the summit the last of the covering fire ceased and then the expected opposition came with a vengeance. The Japanese, about a company of them, fired everything they had. They killed two of the three men left at the pimple, but not before the small band had given valuable supporting fire in the vital stages. The critical moment came when the Japanese raised their heads from their weapon-pits and rolled grenades down on the Australians some 20 feet below—Corporal Silver's[7] section on the right and Corporal Whitechurch's[8] on the left. Some of the grenades landed above the men, rolled down among them and were speeded on in many cases by a hearty push or kick. Most of them rolled too far down and did not do much damage. Hurling their own grenades up into the Japanese positions, the men began to scramble up the last few yards. Fortunately the artillery fire had loosened the soil enabling them to gain a foothold.

Most of the enemy fire was concentrated on the right-hand section where the platoon sergeant, L. A. Bear, was with Corporal Silver. Several casualties were suffered here as Bear and Silver led their men in a spirited

---

[7] Cpl E. P. Silver, MM, VX26258; 2/14 Bn. Timber worker; of Launching Place, Vic; b. Lilydale, Vic, 22 Feb 1912.
[8] Sgt J. H. Whitechurch, MM, VX23671; 2/14 Bn. Labourer; of Mangalore West, Vic; b. Nagambie, Vic, 6 Jun 1920.

and almost perpendicular charge straight up into the enemy position. Reaching the top Bear fired his rifle among the Japanese defenders and, as he and Silver scrambled over the ledge, they saw a Japanese in a foxhole at the same instant as he saw them coming above the ledge. The Japanese tried to fire at each of the Australians in turn and they at him point-blank but nothing happened for all three had emptied their magazines. "Bear heaved himself straight up over the ledge, lunging with the bayonet in the same movement. He hurled the Japanese like a sheaf-tosser, then he sprang clear to meet the next foe."[1] As the rest of the section followed Bear and Silver up, the left-hand section, led by Whitechurch firing his Owen gun from the hip, came charging in. Whitechurch reported later:

> We could see them now and opened fire on their heads as they bobbed up above their foxholes. Their fire began to slacken off. One of our chaps gave a shrill blood-curdling yell that startled even us, and was partly responsible for some of the Japs running headlong down the hill in panic. Unable to stop at the edge of the cliff, they plunged to their doom hundreds of feet below.[2]

The covering fire of the third section had helped the others during their advance and when they were scrambling up to the crest.

The valour of this platoon had carried all before it and a Japanese company, entrenched in a seemingly impregnable position, had been routed. Despite the heavy bombardment from the Australian supporting arms, the Japanese should have been able to hold their natural fortress. For the loss of 3 men killed and 5 wounded, including Pallier and Bear, the platoon had killed about 30 Japanese and captured the vital ground astride the lines of communication to the 2/27th. The capture of Pallier's Hill was a great relief to Dougherty who was watching the fight. Had it been held much longer by the Japanese, the 2/27th, with little ammunition and few rations, would have found it almost impossible to hold their positions in the fight looming ahead.

The Japanese were really nettled on 11th October and were fighting vigorously for their mountain trails. East of the valleys of the Faria and Uria Rivers the 2/33rd Battalion was patrolling forward from the 4100 Feature captured the previous night. While MacDougal's company guarded the feature, the battalion set out with Power's company leading to join the forward standing patrol established on the previous day by Lieutenant Haigh.[3] At 11.30 a.m. Power's company was ambushed. The enemy position was on a narrow kunai-clad spur about a mile long. By 1.20 p.m. the battalion's mortars were on high ground and opened fire on the enemy seen moving along the forward ridge. The Japanese replied with a mountain gun which did no damage, but Power's company had now lost several men and could show no other results. Colonel Cotton, who considered he was on the outskirts of Boganon, estimated that it would take about a day to encircle the high feature by the right flank. Towards dusk he

---

[1] Russell, p. 238.
[2] Quoted in Russell, p. 236.
[3] Lt D. R. Haigh, NX10090. 2/1 A-Tk Regt and 2/33 Bn. Regular soldier and farmer; of Gilgandra, NSW; b. Gilgandra, 7 Sep 1917.

was ordered by Brigadier Eather to continue seeking a line of attack. By 9 p.m. the battalion, again during darkness, managed to take up more favourable positions so that its mortars and machine-guns could worry the enemy.

That day General Morshead flew from Lae to Dumpu for a conference with Vasey. They visited Dougherty, whom Vasey told that the 25th Brigade would look after any enemy east of the Uria River and the 21st Brigade need concern itself only with operations west of it. From the conversations of the three leaders it was again clear that, because of "administrative limitations", there would be no question of a farther advance into the mountains for the time being.

During the night of the 11th-12th the Japanese were again on the move. Two hours after midnight they tried what they had already tried unsuccessfully to do at Sanananda and Salamaua—raid the guns. Six Japanese armed with 15 pounds of gun cotton, 50 feet of detonating fuse, small arms and grenades, crawled into the gun area 1,000 yards south of Kumbarum where two guns were protected by the gunners and a section from the 2/14th Battalion. Shots and grenades were exchanged between the Australians and Japanese before the raiding party dropped their bundles and fled.

At dawn on 12th October two incomplete companies of the 2/27th were stationed in the Trevor's Ridge area, with battalion headquarters and portions of Headquarters Company. Because of damage caused by the Japanese mountain gun, Bishop considered moving his battalion to a wooded ridge which adjoined the saddle on Trevor's Ridge. At 10.30 a.m. he sent a small patrol which immediately encountered about 18 Japanese moving astride the track from this ridge. After firing at the Japanese the patrol returned and at 10.45 a.m. the enemy attacked in strength. The attack was supported by five Woodpeckers; two mountain guns, mortars and light machine-guns also joined in the attack. The enemy plastered the ridge and the knoll with grenades from grenade-throwers and under very heavy supporting fire they attacked Johns' position with bayonets. They gained the lower easterly part of the ridge proper where the defenders were all wounded, but this lower slope could be brought under heavy fire from a section on the crest above, and was untenable by the enemy.

Immediately after the first attack Major Johnson sent across a section from Trevor's Ridge to reinforce Johns, and Bishop sent forward also Lieutenant Macdonald's platoon. About 11 a.m. Macdonald's men reached the knoll and raced through heavy enemy fire to fill the pits vacated by Johns' casualties. Macdonald arrived just after the second attack had been beaten back. "This arrival," reported Johns, "improved the situation considerably and claims to ownership of the ridge swung in our favour."

By this time Bishop was becoming very worried at the depletion of his ammunition, for there was no sign of the expected supply train. He had in this forward area only two Vickers guns and one 3-inch mortar. The Vickers were used to counter the fire from an enemy machine-gun on the plateau across the Faria River, which was really firing into the backs of the defenders, and the mortar, for which there were only 18 bombs, was placed in support of Johns' Knoll. When the enemy had reached within 20 yards of the Australian positions in the first assault, Sergeant Eddy[4] went forward and directed 12 mortar bombs at the enemy 20 yards in front of the Australians. The bombs caused havoc among the enemy and Bishop kept 6 as a last reserve. The two enemy mountain guns seemed to have been moved closer than on the previous day and Bombardier Leggo, late in the afternoon, managed to bring his own gunfire down near the enemy guns.

There were two more Japanese attacks on Johns' Knoll but both were thrown back with heavy casualties. By 3 p.m. four separate attacks had been defeated. Although there were many enemy dead before Johns'

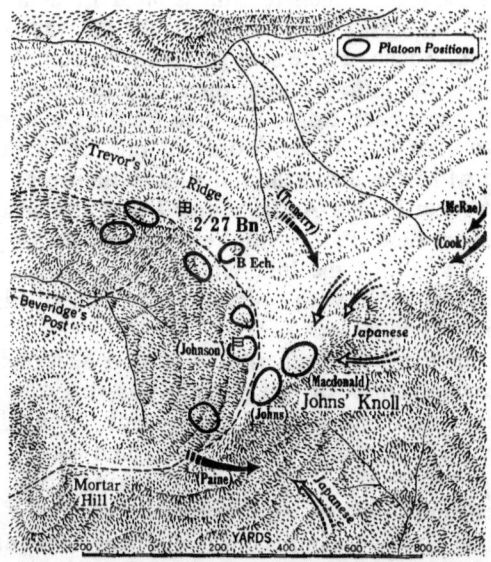

Defence of Trevor's Ridge and Johns' Knoll by 2/27th Battalion, 12th October

Knoll the position was dangerous, and the dogged infantrymen realised that they would have to pull out if no ammunition arrived. Teams were collecting ammunition from headquarters and even from the platoon on Trevor's Ridge and racing it forward to the two beleaguered platoons. On the knoll itself were many examples of gallantry. Although wounded Private Fisher[5] remained on duty and set a good example by making many trips under heavy fire to supply his section with such ammunition as he could obtain. Private Barnes[6] raced out under heavy fire to retrieve a Bren gun and ammunition from a dead gunner.

When, at 3 p.m., Bishop informed Dougherty by wireless that the ammunition situation was critical, Dougherty replied that if the ammunition actually ran out Bishop should leave Toms' company to fight its way back by a circuitous route to Guy's Post where the battalion would concentrate. Bishop did not like leaving the company "out in the blue" and hoped that Toms would attack downhill in the enemy's rear. An hour earlier he had ordered Johnson to launch a counter-attack to relieve the pressure on Johns' Knoll. Johnson promptly sent out two platoons, one

---

[4] Sgt G. Eddy, SX9986; 2/27 Bn. Barman; of Crystal Brook, SA; b. Kadina, SA, 2 Jul 1914.
[5] Pte C. R. Fisher, SX17771; 2/27 Bn. Painter; of Solomontown, SA; b. Port Pirie, SA, 12 Jan 1923.
[6] Pte R. K. Barnes, SX31562; 2/27 Bn. Warehouseman; of Southwark, SA; b. Medindie, SA, 18 Jun 1922.

to attack the enemy's right flank and one to attack his left. Lieutenant Paine's[7] platoon from a position astride the track was sent round the right to attack the Japanese left flank and Lieutenant Trenerry's from the company on Trevor's Ridge round the left. After giving his orders quickly and instructing his men to stuff a meal in their pockets, Paine set out about 1.45 p.m. and the platoon fought its way to a knoll on the right of the track. Thence Paine sent two sections round the right of the knoll and one round the left. Working their way up to about 20 yards from the top of the razor-back ridge, the men fired at a number of targets as they came into view but, in the words of one of them, "things got a bit sticky so we withdrew down the hill a little then made our way back to the end of the razor-back". As he thought that his orders were to stay out for only a short time, Paine withdrew to his own original positions, keeping close to the side of the hill. He arrived back at about 3.30 p.m. only to be sent out again with orders to stay out all night if necessary as the situation was so serious.

On the left, Trenerry, with two sections, set out soon after 2 p.m. Moving cautiously the platoon was ready by 4 p.m. to take advantage of heavy rain and raced for the track about 150 yards to the rear of the Japanese forward troops. The men could see six or seven groups of Japanese near by who were attacking Johns' Knoll. Suddenly Trenerry's men threw sixteen hand grenades into these groups. Many Japanese were killed and, in confusion and terror, the others dispersed very quickly running mainly into the Australians' fire. With five men Trenerry cleared the track to Johns' Knoll while five men cleared the track in the opposite direction and the remainder took up covering positions just below the crest of the ridge. "Both groups clearing the track ran backwards and forwards shooting at opportune targets," reported Trenerry. Private Blacker,[8] firing his Bren from the hip, killed five Japanese who tried to withdraw along the track. Private May[9] killed four Japanese before being hit himself and most of the other men killed at least two Japanese each. By the time Trenerry's men joined Johns they knew that they had killed at least 24 Japanese with small arms fire apart from those originally killed in the grenade bombardment. This successful counter-attacking patrol ran out of Japanese just before it ran out of ammunition.

It was raining heavily at 3.50 p.m. as Paine's weary men—literally taking a dim view of things—retraced their steps up the ridge. After killing a sniper, the platoon worked its way up the razor-back to the enemy positions attacked earlier. As there was still heavy firing along the razor-back they moved through the kunai grass just below the top, and attacked straight up the hill towards the Japanese positions, but were greeted with so much fire and so many grenades rolled down on them

---

[7] Lt R. Paine, SX3086; 2/27 Bn. Clerk; of St Peters, SA; b. Kadina, SA, 16 Jan 1918. Died of wounds 13 Oct 1943.

[8] Sgt D. R. Blacker, SX17410; 2/27 Bn. Wheat buyer; of Cummins, SA; b. Tumby Bay, SA, 26 Mar 1915.

[9] Pte F. W. May, SX17002; 2/27 Bn. Gardener; of Kingscote, Kangaroo Island; b. Cygnet River, Kangaroo Island, 13 Feb 1913. Killed in action 12 Oct 1943.

that they withdrew down the hill for a little while behind some cover, and waited. Here nearly every man had successful shots at Japanese moving along the razor-back. Just as dusk was gathering, Privates Green[1] and Searle,[2] with the wounded Corporal Box[3] who "said he would carry on as there weren't many in his section", moved back to the track along the razor-back and reconnoitred it towards Johns' Knoll.

The two counter-attacking platoons had relieved much of the pressure on Johns' Knoll, and Bishop now thought that if the battalion could only hold out until nightfall he would be able to find his missing company and defeat the enemy, provided the ammunition train reached the battalion during the night. Dougherty told Bishop that Lieutenant Crocker's platoon should rejoin him during the night with the ammunition, and that a company from the 2/14th would move to Guy's Post to be at Bishop's immediate call: Christopherson's company arrived at Guy's Post one hour before midnight.

On the knoll Johns' and Macdonald's depleted platoons could hear firing all around them during the late afternoon both from the enemy and from the counter-attacking platoons. Soon after 5.30 p.m. more firing was heard from the high ground east of the ridge; all hoped that this was from the missing company, and so indeed it turned out to be.

Toms first had an inkling that something was wrong when his telephone line was cut; then in the mid-morning firing started below him. He immediately sent Lieutenant McRae's platoon to find and repair the break in the telephone line but when McRae reached the foot of the hill on which the company was camped, he discovered that the ridge joining the feature with battalion headquarters was occupied by Japanese. McRae telephoned this news to Toms who sent out the Pioneer platoon under Lieutenant Cook[4] to clear the Japanese from the ridge. A few days later Cook wrote:

I met Mac and he gave me all he knew so I pushed forward to contact the enemy. I handed 5 Platoon over to Sergeant Underwood,[5] commonly known as "Underpants". The Japs were expecting us for they opened up with their Woodpecker and did they whistle but the boys kept pushing on. I sent Sergeant Yandell[6] round on the right flank while a section from B Company and Corporal Fitzgerald's[7] went around on the left; well, Lum's [Yandell's] section on the right did a wonderful job and made it possible to wipe out the Woodpecker. The boys must have killed 20 or more Japs on the first knoll and by the way they bawled you would think they were killing a hundred of them. We continued on along the ridge for another 100 yards when 3 LMG's opened up on us and inflicted our first casualties, 2 killed, 4 wounded. One of the killed was Dean[8] who had done a fine job killing several

---

[1] Pte E. J. Green, NX86289; 2/27 Bn. Labourer; of Richmond, NSW; b. Richmond, 15 Jan 1923.
[2] Sgt H. H. Searle, NX97885; 2/27 Bn. Labourer; of Taree, NSW; b. Kempsey, NSW, 9 Jun 1918.
[3] WO1 R. A. Box, SX4733; 2/27 Bn. Farm worker; of Denial Bay, SA; b. Denial Bay, 16 Oct 1917.
[4] Lt F. T. Cook, SX12503; 2/27 Bn. Dairyman; of Winkie, SA; b. Southsea, England, 9 Sep 1913.
[5] Sgt R. V. Underwood, SX4262; 2/27 Bn. Carpenter; of Bowden, SA; b. Adelaide, 27 Feb 1909.
[6] Sgt T. L. Yandell, SX4405; 2/27 Bn. Metal worker; of Mile End, SA; b. Islington, SA, 13 Jan 1908.
[7] Cpl P. E. J. Fitzgerald, SX3333; 2/27 Bn. Sawyer; of Adelaide; b. Tumby Bay, SA, 27 Apr 1912. Died 11 Feb 1956.
[8] Pte R. J. Dean, NX130090; 2/27 Bn. Labourer; of Forbes, NSW; b. Forbes, 6 Dec 1921. Killed in action 12 Oct 1943.

Japs while firing his Bren from the hip as he advanced. At about this time I found [a young soldier] of B Company alongside me so asked him what would win the Goodwood whereupon he told me not to be so bloody silly, it was no time to talk about races. Well, we had to shift these gunners so Lum kept moving his section forward on the right flank and two of the gunners got out while the other covered them. Then Lum volunteered to go over the top after the remaining one himself so I slipped up behind him to give him covering fire, but as Lum went over the top the Japs cleared off into the kunai.

The Japanese had almost had enough. At 5.25 p.m. Crocker's supply train had arrived at Guy's Post and went forward full speed ahead. About 6 p.m. Paine, on the razor-back to the right, sang out to Johns to ask if he could move up to his position. When Johns gave a cheery O.K., Paine moved up and found that the Japanese had disappeared from the area between his platoon and the men on the knoll. Paine reported that the area south and south-west of the knoll was clear of live Japanese and Trenerry, who moved back to his company area about this time, through Johns' men, reported that the saddle east of the knoll was also clear. The two patrols—Paine's and Trenerry's—actually met along the razor-back on their way back to their respective companies. All along the ridge were many small holes dug by the Japanese.

By nightfall the enemy attack had ceased and the battalion had not yielded one inch of ground. Just before dusk Bishop sent two men to try and find a way round the Japanese lines to Toms and tell him to remain on the ridge for the night and counter-attack in the morning. Later, under cover of darkness, Lieutenant Cook sent three volunteers—Sergeant Yandell, Sergeant O'Connor[9] and Private Napier[1]—to try to reach the battalion with the news that the company had two men killed and four stretcher cases. At 7.40 p.m. they reported in to Johns' Knoll having found the area in between clear of all except dead Japanese. The three men went on to battalion headquarters and were also given the message for Toms. A medical orderly accompanied them carrying morphia for the wounded. McRae mended the wire and passed on the message from battalion headquarters to Toms who immediately began to move straight down to Cook's platoon, arriving there at 5.30 a.m. on the 13th.

Two hours after midnight on the 12th-13th the native supply train arrived with the supplies, including the much-needed ammunition. The wounded were carried out by the returning native train, and the tired but triumphant unit waited confidently through a long wet night.

By its decision to sit tight and hope for the best the 2/27th Battalion had won a notable success. The battalion had lost 7 men killed and 28 wounded and had killed about 200 Japanese. The enemy's attack on the knoll coupled with his bold occupation of Pallier's Hill and vigorous defence against the 2/33rd Battalion farther east seemed to be all part of a move to push the Australians from the vantage points they had won.

---

[9] Sgt D. E. O'Connor, SX9657; 2/27 Bn. Woolclasser's assistant; of Adelaide; b. Swansea, Wales, 10 Jun 1919.

[1] Pte J. M. Napier, NX136959; 2/27 Bn. Farm hand; of Quandialla, NSW; b. Grenfell, NSW, 29 Jun 1922. Killed in action 13 Oct 1943.

The counter-attack had failed, not because the Japanese were in the minority nor because they were less adequately armed and supplied, but because they had no counter for the spirit of Pallier's attack and Bishop's defence. Just before the supply train arrived the 2/27th had enough ammunition for about another quarter-of-an-hour's fighting, but when the ammunition had been distributed rapidly, in darkness, Bishop felt secure and informed Dougherty that he would not withdraw.

Dougherty was now confident but, as an extra measure of security, ordered Christopherson's company of the 2/14th to move from Guy's Post up the spur leading to the high ground south of the 2/27th. There is little doubt that the 2/27th Battalion was now astride the main Japanese carrier route although, farther north, there was another well-used track which was bench-cut around the hills and had a good grade. Originally it was probably intended to continue the motor road from Bogadjim along this route. As far as they could ascertain the 2/27th were at Key Point 3 and east of them were the remnants of two battalions of the *78th Japanese Regiment*.

Prisoners and documents confirmed that the assault on the 2/27th Battalion had been made by the *II* and *III Battalions* of the *78th Regiment* which had moved down from the north for this purpose. Because of sickness and casualties the battalions were below strength; prisoners estimated that the *78th Regiment* was less than half strength. Defending the hills north of the Surinam against the 25th Brigade was the *I/78th Battalion*. Pressure by the 25th Brigade and the Japanese decision to withdraw farther was probably responsible for the fight at Pallier's Hill where a company of the *I/78th Battalion* withdrawing from the east found itself in the midst of Australian positions.

At first light on the 13th Lieutenant Cook of the 2/27th led a fighting patrol through to battalion headquarters from the east to clear the track of any remaining Japanese, but all were gone. At 6.45 a.m. a Woodpecker opened up from a new position just above the plateau across the Faria and Cook was sent to reinforce the company now facing that area. At 8 a.m. Johnson discovered that six Japanese were dug in about 200 yards to the south-east of his company—probably covering a burial party. Bishop decided to leave them there for the time being and save his battalion the task of burying the many enemy dead.

The Japanese artillery continued to fire from the plateau across the river and was occasionally aided by long distance fire from Woodpeckers. "The lads treat this Japanese action with great respect and are feeling the strain after yesterday's hard fighting," commented the battalion's diarist. One difficulty was that the native carriers disappeared each time the enemy guns opened up, giving the quartermaster, Captain J. D. Lee, a hard job rounding them up again. The spirits of the natives rose, however, when, at 2.20 p.m., Airacobras were led in by Boomerangs to attack known Japanese positions in the Faria River Valley.

On the morning of the 13th Vasey visited Dougherty and told him that he could move the 2/16th Battalion from the river flats; the 2/2nd Pioneer Battalion would be brought in to take its place. Dougherty decided to relieve the 2/27th Battalion with the 2/16th and to move his own headquarters to Kumbarum. The 2/6th Commando Squadron reverted to divisional command and was ordered by Vasey to maintain two troops in the Bebei area and probe the surrounding country.

By 5 p.m. on the 13th Christopherson (of the 2/14th) was on top of a wooded knoll and could see Johns' Knoll about 100 yards away on a bearing of 50 degrees. Bishop instructed him to continue his encircling move along that bearing and wipe out the Japanese pocket reported earlier in the day before joining the 2/27th. At 5.45 p.m. the company reached the 2/27th but had missed the Japanese pocket. Half an hour later Lieutenant Paine was sent out with two sections, found the Japanese position, and grenaded it. Unfortunately a grenade rebounded from a tree and killed Paine, an original member of the battalion. The patrol withdrew, but the Japanese had also had enough, and next morning had disappeared.

Meanwhile the 2/33rd Battalion, trying to move north from the 4100 Feature, had a frustrating and costly day. In the morning Boomerang aircraft reported that whenever the planes were overhead the Japanese left their foxholes rapidly and retired into the timber. The Boomerangs could give almost a ball to ball description of the movements of Japanese in threes and fours on the spur. After directing mortar fire to the ridge the aircraft strafed it while Captain Connor's[2] company moved forward to attack along the open ridge. Progress was slow and the attack costly because the enemy, on the steep ridge above, could throw down grenades on the attackers. During the morning Colonel Robson of the 2/31st Battalion arrived and carried with him a report from the 2/33rd's company on the 4100 Feature that the enemy could be seen on a ridge approximately north-west of Major MacDougal's company. To MacDougal there appeared to be about a company dug in on this ridge—and a company could hold up a battalion in this precipitous country.

By midday Colonel Cotton realised that his attack was unsuccessful. His leading company had lost 3 men killed and 21 wounded including 2 officers. As soon as he received news of the 2/33rd's unsuccessful attack Eather informed Vasey that any further attempt to capture this enemy feature without artillery support would be very costly. Vasey agreed and at 5.30 p.m. signalled Eather to "maintain contact" but not to become heavily engaged until he received artillery support. Late at night the 2/31st relieved the 2/33rd which prepared to return to Kaigulin.

Farther down the Ramu Major Laidlaw's 2/2nd Commando Squadron —now the only remaining operational unit of Bena Force—was patrolling the Ramu Valley and the foothills with two troops from Kesawai on the right to the Sepu area on the left. The third troop (Captain McKenzie's) had arrived in the Guiebi area on the extreme left flank on 6th October, leaving one section at Chimbu to continue patrolling the Mount Hagen plateau.[3] McKenzie was ordered by Laidlaw to patrol across the Ramu,

---

[2] Maj G. B. Connor, NX34870; 2/33 Bn. Student; of Roseville, NSW; b. Lugarno, NSW, 8 Nov 1919.

[3] During this period the towering, snow-capped Mount Wilhelm was climbed by the squadron's medical officer, Captain J. C. McInerney, one of the very few men to have climbed it.

to harass and raid the Japanese, and, if possible, to establish a position north of the Ramu. McKenzie sent two sections across the river under Lieutenant Rodd[4] to remain there as a standing patrol and to prepare extensive diggings on the high ground in front of the Sepu crossing overlooking Glaligool.[5] Laidlaw's three troops soon found that the enemy had left all his positions from Kesawai to Usini and Glaligool, although there was a clash with a Japanese patrol on a razor-back ridge two miles west of Egoi on the 13th.

The changeover between the 2/27th and the 2/16th Battalions was a smooth affair. By 2 p.m. on the 14th the 2/16th reached the Johns' Knoll area. Half an hour later Bishop sent Lieutenant Clampett's company to occupy Shaggy Ridge, so named after Clampett's nickname. This rugged feature dominating Guy's Post had not previously been occupied but Bishop thought that Guy's Post would be insecure unless he had at least a company on Shaggy Ridge. Soon after Clampett's departure Bishop set out with the company which had had the task of finding and burying the enemy dead. The final estimate of enemy killed on the 12th was about 190. The battalion's return journey was made in heavy rain and the Faria River was in flood, necessitating the formation of a human chain for the crossing. Even so, one of the signallers was swept away and drowned in the raging torrent.

East and west of the main Australian thrust—if such it could be called —there was evidence on the 14th that the Japanese intended to play a more passive role. There was minor contact only in the main area. To the east the 2/31st Battalion found that the enemy had left the powerful two-company position which had been holding up the 2/33rd and they occupied it. To the west a patrol of the 2/2nd Commando Squadron, led by Captain Turton, fought a spirited action with the Japanese four miles north-east of Kesawai. Having failed in their major thrust on 12th October the *78th Japanese Regiment* seemed now content to pull farther back into the hills leaving outposts against the forward Australian positions.

After the vigorous fighting and anxious moments of the preceding days the 15th set the tempo for the succeeding days. Only on the eastern flank where Captain Jackson's company of the 2/31st Battalion were following the trail of the retreating Japanese was there any contact. The trail led towards the Gurumbu area where three Japanese stragglers were killed during the day.

From Guy's Post, which Vasey visited on the 16th, Clampett's company was reconnoitring Shaggy Ridge. A patrol found a Japanese outpost wired with four strands of barbed wire to which were attached tins which would undoubtedly rattle as a warning on Green Pinnacle about 1,500

---

[4] Capt C. J. Rodd, VX46494. 2/2 Indep Coy, 2/2 Cdo Sqn. Research chemist; of East Camberwell, Vic; b. Melbourne, 30 Jul 1920.

[5] Later McKenzie said:
"Bull [Laidlaw] and I had a mighty blue over this. I interpreted his order to establish a base over the river—he nearly sacked me for, as he said, 'bogging down two sections out in no-man's land'. A Jap lieutenant's diary later proved how great had been the deception—they thought we were over the river in great strength holding a bridgehead and they believed we were outflanking Bogadjim Road en route to Madang via Bagasin Road. Consequently they smartly pulled in a number of screening outposts which had previously held us up and caused casualties"

yards up the ridge. Later another patrol heard movement behind the wire.

In the daily situation reports from now on appeared brief accounts of the work of the innumerable patrols sent out by the division. Sometimes "contact" was made and sometimes not. Clashes with the enemy were numerous, sudden and often bloody. If no enemy were encountered patrols were able to add to the division's topographical knowledge by pointing out that such and such a track did not exist or such and such a mountain

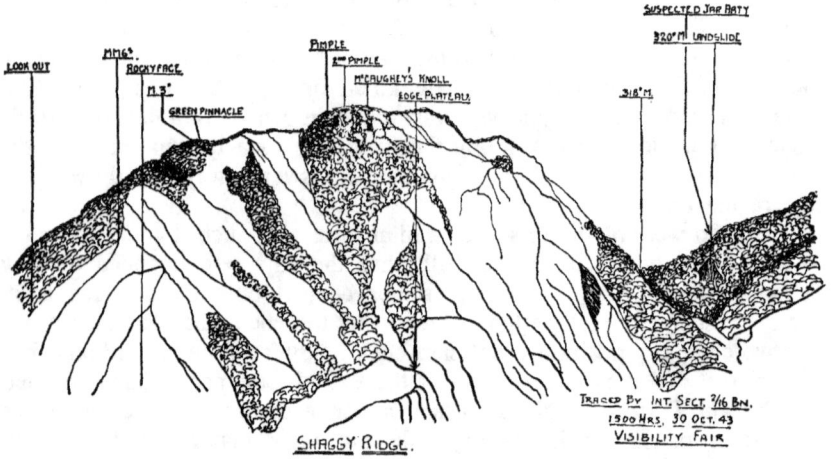

Reproduction of sketch in war diary of 2/16th Battalion for October 1943

was in the wrong place. The "front", such as it was, was now becoming more or less stabilised; the Japanese were clinging to Shaggy Ridge, Kankiryo Saddle and the area of the upper Faria River with several outposts in a wide semi-circle among the foothills protecting approaches from the west to Madang and Bogadjim. It was understandable that both sides wished to stabilise the position in the Ramu Valley for the full might of the Japanese counter-attack round Scarlet Beach was now being met.

The period was also one of administrative consolidation. Lieut-Colonel Tompson, the C.R.E., pressed on with the construction program in the Dumpu area, using the 2/5th and 2/6th Field Companies to build airstrips, roads, bridges, culverts and buildings. Tactical reconnaissance by aircraft, particularly along the Bogadjim Road, supplemented the topographical reports of patrols and helped the staff to prepare the basis for better maps. Realising the danger from malaria a determined effort was made to increase anti-malarial precautions.

Two patrols from the 2/31st Battalion on 17th October attempted to contact the 21st Brigade to their west. A small lightly-equipped patrol led by Major Hall[6] set out from the battalion's position at 8.30 a.m. north to a track junction three miles ahead. For three hours it followed this track which was about four to five feet wide, graded, well-used and with mud up to about a foot deep in patches. Generally it followed the contours round the headwaters of the Uria River and there were many signs of recent use by the Japanese. Some saddlery and a horse were found. Uphill and down and over several streams the patrol continued until, near Young's Post, it met a patrol from the 2/14th under Lieutenant N. H. Young which had moved about three miles east along the Japanese track. Thus contact was at length made between the two brigades in the rugged country separating them and it was proved that along this track at least there were now no Japanese.

The other patrol—Captain McKenzie's company—set out at 7.30 a.m. to try to contact the 2/16th. Along the track were signs of very recent use by the Japanese: bivouac positions, discarded gear, supply dumps, bridges destroyed within the last 48 hours and areas fouled by human excreta. After camping for the night the company made further attempts on the 18th to reach the 2/16th, but, although they must have been very close, they were unable to do so before they were due to return.[7]

Now that Vasey was sure that there was no substantial body of Japanese to the east of the 21st Brigade, he instructed Eather to bring the 2/31st out of the mountains to Dumpu. He intended eventually to move the 25th Brigade to the western flank but, because of supply difficulties, he told Eather that the brigade would stay in its present position for a time. To watch the immediate western flank Vasey sent two commando squadrons into the Kesawai area on the 18th—the 2/7th to Kesawai 1 and the 2/6th to Kesawai 2. The area was not suitable for landing strips. It would therefore be necessary to supply these western squadrons, either by pushing the jeep track through to the Kesawai area or by using native carriers.

It was imperative for the enemy to hold Shaggy Ridge which led directly to Kankiryo Saddle, the gateway to the Bogadjim Road. In accordance with Vasey's suggestion Dougherty prepared for a limited advance and on the 17th reconnoitred the area in a Wirraway. That day Bishop also reconnoitred Green Pinnacle and prepared to attack this southernmost peak of Shaggy Ridge on the 20th with Clampett's company, supported by Toms'. Bishop's main concern was to discover whether the Japanese strongpost on the Pinnacle, deeply entrenched and wired, could be encircled. For three days from the 17th his patrols crept as near as they could, and early on the 20th, Captain Whyte,[8] the F.O.O. of the 54th Battery, directed the fire of his guns on to the Japanese position. Before the attack Clampett

---

[6] Maj K. S. Hall, DSO, SX4855; 2/31 Bn. Farmer; of Willunga, SA; b. Willunga, 19 Jun 1917.
[7] The only sign of the enemy met by either patrol was one lone Japanese facing McKenzie's advance; he was covering the track from a foxhole with a bag of grenades and a rifle.
[8] Maj W. A. S. Whyte, MC, DX149. 2/3 and 2/4 Fd Regts. Regular soldier; of Kerang, Vic; b. Ballindrait, Co Donegal, Eire, 26 Aug 1918.

was actually on the southern extremity of Shaggy Ridge and Toms was on the saddle between Bert's Post and Shaggy Ridge.[9]

At midday Clampett reported that his men were within five yards of a four-strand barbed-wire fence; the Japanese position on the kunai-covered Pinnacle was about 30 yards away and overlooked his own troops. Between the enemy position and his men, there was a steep gully about 100 feet deep with precipitous slopes on both flanks. The Japanese had cut fire lanes through the kunai and were dug in and heavily bunkered from the cliff face on Clampett's right flank round to his left. The original plan was for Clampett's men to rush the position with artillery support. At this stage Lieutenant Crocker's platoon was sitting quietly within 20 yards of the Japanese wire on the steep left slope of Shaggy Ridge. As the position was astride a narrow razor-back with almost sheer sides, an attack would probably have been suicidal. Bishop therefore decided to pause and to send a company round to the north-west to see whether the Japanese position could be outflanked. The artillery would, meanwhile, bombard the Pinnacle with the object of tricking the enemy into retiring temporarily to gain shelter. The artillery fire program for the night of the 21st-22nd, the 22nd, and the night of the 22nd-23rd was varied so that the rate of fire was never the same and the fire never at the same hours. However, it continued for an hour after first light to enable the platoon to get into position near the wire. If the platoon commander saw that the enemy had taken shelter north along the ridge he was to cut the wire and get on to the Pinnacle as quickly and quietly as possible.

This now became the pattern for operations on Shaggy Ridge. Lieutenant Robilliard's patrol on the 22nd crept so close to the wire that some men noticed where the warning tins were hanging on the barbed wire, and could see some of the Japanese with machetes cutting down bamboos, others observing the track, others digging positions, others splitting cane and others standing together and talking. A large amount of bamboo had been stacked behind the barbed wire fence so that it would crackle when trodden on. Lieutenant Garnock's[1] platoon occupied this strong enemy position next day. Creeping under the wire the platoon noticed that no sentry was watching, and when Sergeant Lord[2] crawled forward, he found that the enemy foxholes and trenches were empty. By 5 p.m. Garnock had occupied the position which consisted of 32 foxholes. It had been taken, by guile, without a casualty.

Extensive and continuous patrolling was now carried out by the 2/16th Battalion in the area of Johns' Knoll and Trevor's Ridge, and towards the Mainstream area but patrols from the battalion's base were forced to move

---

[9] A seven days' patrol was now being made by Lieutenant Stuart's Papuan platoon from Mount Prothero, which was in the battle area, to the headwaters of the Mindjim which could be reached by bypassing Shaggy Ridge. Prothero was named after Sergeant R. R. Protheroe of the Papuan Infantry Battalion who was drowned in the Watut River on 4th July 1943.

[1] Lt J. C. Garnock, NX123471; 2/27 Bn. Grazier; of South Bukalong, Bombala, NSW; b. Bombala, 1 Jun 1913.

[2] WO2 R. S. Lord, QX36468. 2/27 Bn and 2 NG Inf Bn. Jackeroo; of Nelia, Qld; b. Burketown, Qld, 18 Dec 1916.

out towards the right flank because the almost precipitous lower slopes of Shaggy Ridge to the left, commanded by well-placed Japanese pill-boxes, made any attempt at out-flanking useless. It was decided on 25th October to attempt to deal with Japanese across from Mainstream near the island in the river and on the wooded north bank. At midday Mitchell bombers attacked the Japanese positions. Covered by two sections, under Lieutenant

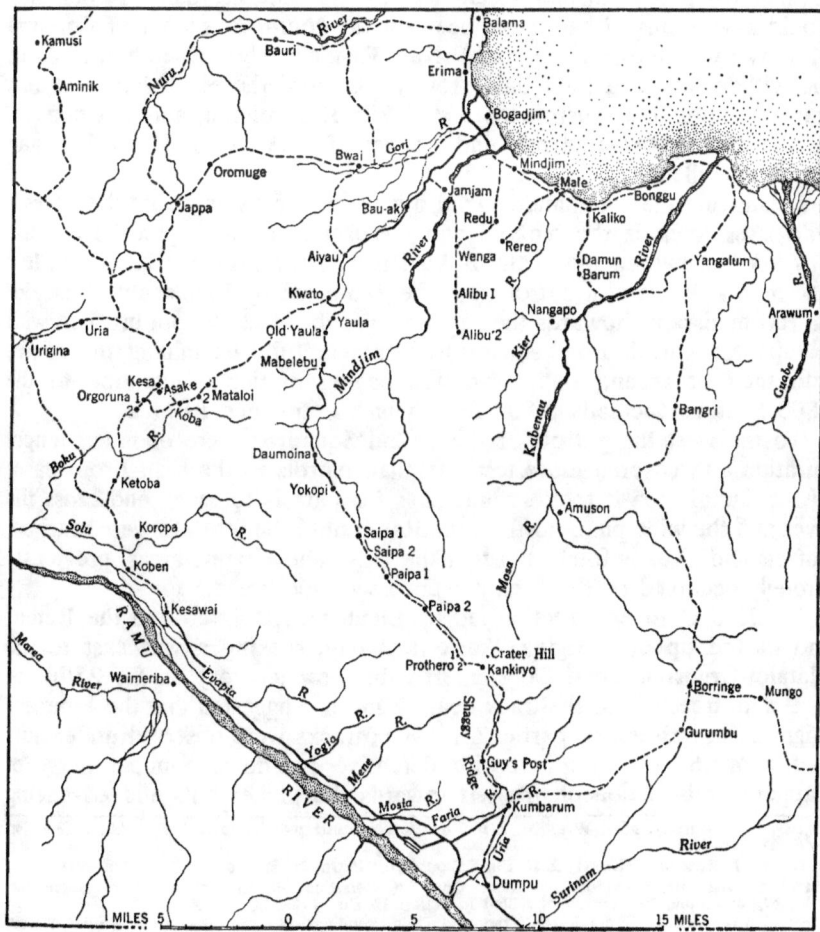

Dumpu-Bogadjim area

Watts, Sergeant Johnston[3] led two other sections across the river. As mortars and machine-guns were now firing on the enemy position Johnston hoped that if there were any Japanese left they would still be in so dazed a condition that there would be little opposition. As they crossed the river, however, they were fired on heavily from previously concealed Japanese

---

[3] Sgt D. Johnston, WX2744; 2/16 Bn. Clerk; of South Perth; b. Adelaide, 26 Oct 1918. Killed in action 25 Oct 1943.

positions on the high ground overlooking the Faria. Despite casualties the advance continued across the island and to the north bank where the Australians reached what appeared to be a large pill-box in a natural stone wall 8 to 10 feet high. Because of the very heavy grenade and machine-gun fire from this natural fortress, Johnston ordered a withdrawal, but was himself killed while crossing the river, and seven others were missing when the patrol reassembled on the opposite bank. Fewer men would have returned had it not been for the courageous work of Corporal Murphy,[4] who took charge, and Private Rendell[5] who helped him to cover the withdrawal to a high bank 150 yards from the south bank. In this spirited action the Australians lost 2 killed, 3 missing and 8 wounded. Of the missing two returned under cover of darkness but the other man had been killed.

Meanwhile the commando squadrons were skirmishing from their Kesawai bases towards the Yokopi and Orgoruna areas. A patrol from the 2/7th killed two enemy at the Boku River crossing on the 22nd and lost one man killed, and a patrol from the 2/6th led by Lieutenant Teasdale[6] on reconnaissance towards the Japanese roadhead at Yokopi brushed with a Japanese patrol. Both squadrons were carefully examining the routes into their areas and the 2/6th was paying particular attention to the 5800 Feature (actually 3,800 feet) which dominated its area.

To the west the patrols of the 2/2nd Squadron were of much longer duration and covered more territory than patrols to the east. From bases in the Bundi area it took several days for patrols to reach and cross the river and the wide plain north of the Ramu until the foothills were reached. Patrols had already found out that the Usini and Urigina areas, previously strongly occupied by the enemy, were now unoccupied.

On 23rd October a section led by Lieutenant Doig crossed the Ramu[7] and moved up the Urigina Track next day, seeking a way east to the Mataloi-Orgoruna area. Doig entered this new territory on the 25th and by 9 a.m. trees across the track near Orgoruna suggested that the Japanese might be in possession, particularly when tracks were observed under huts —one of the enemy's favourite defensive positions. Sending Sergeant Tapper's[8] sub-section on the left towards the higher huts and advancing

---

[4] Sgt G. B. J. Murphy, MM, WX3006; 2/16 Bn. Clothing cutter; of Victoria Park, WA; b. Boulder, WA, 18 Feb 1919.

[5] L-Cpl H. J. Rendell, WX4931; 2/16 Bn. Labourer; of Perth; b. Subiaco, WA, 24 Jun 1918.

[6] Lt C. K. Teasdale, QX31506. 2/6 Indep Coy, 2/6 Cdo Sqn. Forestry employee; of Barcaldine, Qld; b. Barcaldine, 19 May 1918. Killed in action 12 Dec 1943.

[7] "Patrol proceeded to Ramu River," reported Doig, "and crossed same by use of native dug-out canoe and by swimming. The stream was in full flood and flowing at about ten knots per hour. The method of crossing used was to pole dug-out up the bankside of stream which was more or less dead water for about a mile, switch over into the stream and paddle madly across current until the opposite side was reached. This process occupied most of the mile which had previously been made upstream. The swimmers adopted similar tactics to this and allowed themselves to be carried forward by the current at the same time striking across the current and eventually gaining sanctuary on the opposite bank. This usually took about one mile of river. The crossing occupied approximately two to three hours. [Later patrols always crossed the Ramu in the Faita-Sepu areas by using the dug-out canoes only. These were manned by natives who knew rivers—usually the Sepiks.] Next stage was to move in a north-easterly direction and cross a tributary of the Ramu about two miles away. This crossing was effected in a dug-out canoe which was pulled over the river hand over hand on an overhead kunda rope. This stage was effected quite rapidly although only five men at a time could be carried in the canoe. The crossing of these two streams occupied most of the day."

[8] Sgt D. L. Tapper, WX10512. 2/2 Indep Coy, 2/2 Cdo Sqn. Clerk; of North Perth; b. Williams, WA, 26 Dec 1919.

with the other towards the lower huts, Doig came to a barbed-wire fence. Suddenly "everything including the kitchen sink flew through the air", and Doig was "forced to withdraw rapidly (and how)". Tapper's men, however, were in a better position where they could fire on the enemy. Trooper Craig[9] killed about six Japanese with his sniper's rifle. After inflicting about 12 casualties and having 2 men missing believed killed and 2 wounded, Tapper decided to withdraw. The section rendezvoused and crossed the Ramu two days later. In Doig's opinion it would require at least a company to dislodge the enemy.

The three commando squadrons were encountering supply problems. It was a hard enough task for the air transports to keep the 7th Division supplied by landings at Dumpu. The 2/6th and 2/7th Squadrons had to be supplied either by native carriers, who were few and were needed for the main supply trail into the Finisterres, or by biscuit bombing. On 22nd October an air supply drop was arranged for the squadrons in the Kesawai area. Although this was a flat area the difficulty of finding canisters and supplies dropped into the kunai was sometimes greater than finding them in mountainous positions covered with jungle. A certain loss was always expected but generally the air force was now fairly experienced and the losses could be borne. The supply drop to the 2/7th was reasonably accurate and they recovered five days' rations. The 2/6th, however, lost all the fruit juice, half the biscuits, one bag of flour, two bags of rice, a quarter of all the tinned meat, and all the canned vegetables and fish.

For the forward troops of the 2/2nd Commando Squadron supplies were flown into Garoka at fairly irregular intervals, depending on the mood of the weather and the availability of aircraft, and were then sent over the long, winding tracks, through the plateau and over the mountain passes to the Bundi area, whence they were sent out again to the several sections. This supply line was so tenuous that shortages often restricted patrolling because there was not enough bully beef and biscuits to enable patrols to stay out for the required time. On 22nd October divisional headquarters signalled MacAdie: "Please investigate possibility transport strip Bundi-Faita area . . . and construct Cub strip 400 yards by 30 yards." MacAdie replied on the same day: "Airfield site Faita area already selected." The Faita area comprised about 25 square miles of flat country east of the Sepu crossing and it was believed that it was not affected by rains or floods. MacAdie instructed Major Laidlaw to begin constructing a Cub strip, and soon Laidlaw reported that one would be ready by the 26th, and that if a strip was required for transport aircraft it could be completed within five days.

There were many who wondered why the 7th Division should halt and not drive the Japanese right out of the Ramu Valley and the Finisterre mountains. The 2/6th Squadron's diarist wrote: "Obviously it is part of some large-scale plan but troops are restless, and officers, who share the

---

[9] Tpr K. Craig, NX130057; 2/2 Cdo Sqn. Farm hand; of Gilgandra, NSW; b. Trangie, NSW, 14 Jan 1921.

feeling but cannot show it, are wondering what it is all about." Vasey was no less dissatisfied than his men. In a letter, written about this time, he said: "Role very passive. [The 9th Division] having all the excitement and finding difficulty in the difference between desert and jungle warfare." On 25th October Morshead flew to Dumpu. Morshead was, of course, primarily concerned with building up Allied strength at Finschhafen. He told Vasey that there was no change in the role allotted to the 7th Division.

Vasey took the opportunity to dispose of some administrative matters. He told Morshead that if he were relieved of protection of the Bena plateau he would require only one commando squadron instead of three. Leading on from this, Morshead said that he intended to obtain a definite statement of air force policy on radar stations, which, he believed, should be established only in conformity with the operations and dispositions of the ground troops. At present he considered that they were a considerable strain, requiring small detachments for their protection which had to be maintained under difficult conditions and required too high a proportion of other arms and services. Vasey then pointed out that the airfields at Gusap for whose protection he was responsible were twenty miles behind his present divisional area at Dumpu and that there were no road communications. Morshead said that the 6th Machine Gun Battalion would be flown from Port Moresby to Gusap and, under Vasey's command, made responsible for the immediate protection of the airfields in that area.

As a result of their corps commander's tour, the three divisional commanders—Wootten, Milford and Vasey—received an operation order from corps headquarters dated 29th October. The 7th Division's role was to consolidate positions now held in the Markham and Ramu Valleys. Unless the situation warranted otherwise, the force disposed for the immediate protection of the approaches to the river valleys should not exceed one infantry brigade group and infantry brigades should be rested and refitted in turn. The 2/7th Commando Squadron which had been on operations in New Guinea since October 1942 would be withdrawn for leave as soon as possible.[1] The boundary between the 5th and 7th Divisions would be the Erap River. Finally the order outlined the locations of radar installations, which for the 7th Division would be at Bena Bena, Garoka, Dumpu, Guruf and Bundi.[2] So the 7th Division settled down to a long period of patrol activity—its role merely that of a stopper preventing Japanese penetration south.

Thus the army's task had been redefined more clearly by the time General Blamey flew into Port Moresby on 30th October. Vasey flew south over the mountains on the same day and next day Morshead arrived from Dobodura. After some discussion with his commanders, Blamey announced on 2nd November that General Mackay (now aged 61) would go to New Delhi as first Australian High Commissioner to India. In his

---
[1] This unit had probably been on active operations against the Japanese for a longer period than any other unit except the 2/2nd Commando Squadron, which noted in its diary on 7th December, when the war with the Japanese was two years old, that it had been on active service overseas for 18 months of that time.

[2] Other radar stations operating at this time were at the Tami Islands, Finschhafen, Nadzab, Hopoi and Salamaua.

place General Morshead would be appointed as "G.O.C. Second Aust Army and Adm Comd N.G. Force". General Berryman would succeed Morshead as commander of the II Corps. General Milford became M.G.G.S. New Guinea Force. Brigadier Ramsay,[3] the C.R.A. of II Corps, replaced Milford in command of the 5th Division.

It is evident that in Blamey's mind the choice of a new corps commander to replace Morshead lay between Berryman, his chief of staff in the field, and Vasey. So far as seniority went there was little to separate them: Vasey had succeeded Berryman as G.S.O.1, 6th Division, in Libya in 1941; Berryman had succeeded Vasey as D.C.G.S. in Australia in 1942; in their present temporary rank Vasey was the senior. Vasey's experience as a field commander was more extensive than Berryman's, and their staff experience, until 1942, had run closely parallel. Since late in 1942, however, Berryman had been at Blamey's right hand in New Guinea and had known his mind, and this factor may have tipped the scales. Blamey decided to detach Vasey's division from the corps and place it directly under Morshead's command.

On 28th October, Colonel Blyth's headquarters of the 2/4th Field Regiment moved to Dumpu; next day the 8th Battery began to support the 21st Brigade and the 54th Battery moved into a position to support the 25th Brigade. On the 28th also the 2/2nd Pioneer Battalion moved to Kumbarum and came under command of the 21st Brigade to patrol and watch the rugged area on Dougherty's right flank. The leading company immediately set out for Levett's Post[4] where there was a Japanese inscription copied by the 2/14th Battalion and translated as "Mule Track to Kankiryo".[5] The 2/14th, now commanded by Lieut-Colonel P. E. Rhoden, was relieved by the 2/2nd Pioneers from the long-range patrols which it had been sending out to guard this flank of its two sister battalions.

The divisional Intelligence staff believed from captured documents and the few prisoners that the Japanese force which had opposed the 25th Brigade along the track from Wampun to Gurumbu had possibly withdrawn along the track leading from Boganon to Borringe and thence north to the coast.

A typical long-range patrol took place between 25th and 31st October when Captain Haydon's company of the 2/25th Battalion tried to reach the Japanese track between Paipa and Kankiryo. After moving up the Evapia River and then through rugged unmapped country for four days the patrol leader was forced to return as he realised that it would be impossible for him to reach his objective without further rations and

---

[3] Maj-Gen A. H. Ramsay, CB, CBE, DSO, ED, VX27. (1st AIF: Gnr to Lt in 22 and 4 AFA Bdes.) CO 2/2 Fd Regt 1939-40; Comd Med Arty I Corps 1940; CRA 9 Div 1940-43; CRA II Corps 1943-44; GOC 5 Div 1944-45. Schoolteacher and university lecturer; of Essendon, Vic; b. Windsor, Vic, 12 Mar 1895.

[4] Named after Lieutenant P. M. Levett of 2/14th Battalion.

[5] From information available at this time it was fairly certain that there were two main Japanese tracks passing through this eastern area. First was the L of C for which the Japanese had fought bitterly early in October. The Mule Track branched north from Boganon to Toms' Post, and thence north-west across Mainstream to Kankiryo where it again joined the main L of C.

without making further wide detours to cross the headwaters of the Evapia River. Such results were not unusual and underlined the difficulties confronting patrols in this unknown country.

Although much time and effort were being expended on producing topographical information, both by the reconnaissance aircraft and by the ground patrols, the maps of the Finisterres were still hazy and sketchy. After one particularly frustrating experience a patrol commander wrote:

> Maps of the area were found to be very approximate with regard to watercourses and main features. Form lines were in most cases very inaccurate and tended to minimise the steepness of slopes, even when showing these slopes with any accuracy as regards shape. Upper reaches of river are a series of deep gorges with sides from 300-400 feet high and width at base rarely exceeding 50 yards. From the surrounding ridge tops these gorges cannot be detected.[6]

On the 29th four other patrols were on the preliminary stages of long journeys. From the 2/7th Commando Squadron an engineer, Captain Gossip (of the 2/6th Field Company), and two others left to reconnoitre the possibility of making a road from the Ramu Valley across the Finisterre Ranges towards the Japanese road. This patrol returned on 1st November reporting that there was no possibility of making a road from the Kesawai area towards the Japanese roadhead. Lieutenant Maxwell of the 2/6th Commando Squadron, on a three-day reconnaissance towards Yokopi, walked right into an enemy defensive position on the first day out, saw five Japanese looking at him from about 20 yards away, and retired before they could fire at him. Sergeant Berrell[7] of the Papuan Battalion led his section, three men from the 21st Brigade, and 50 native carriers on a 13 days' patrol into the ranges to reconnoitre enemy movement in the Kankiryo area. He returned on 11th November without having found a worthwhile observation post near Kankiryo.[8]

The fourth patrol was ordered by divisional headquarters on 20th October when MacAdie was instructed to send a patrol from the 2/2nd Squadron to Josephstaal to find out whether the Japanese were there, and whether a strip could be constructed. The task was given to the 2/2nd's engineer officer, Lieutenant Green;[9] but MacAdie considered that Josephstaal would almost certainly be occupied in view of recent enemy moves from Atemble to Annanberg.

Accompanied by Sergeant-Major England of Angau, Green's small patrol

---

[6] With the aid of battalion Intelligence Sections, the Survey Corps and the Allied Geographical Section, the topographical information gained was soon added to the existing maps. This static period enabled the mapping to catch up with operations so that by the time the Australians were ready to assault Shaggy Ridge and Kankiryo Saddle the maps were more reasonably accurate. On 10th November there was a new issue of 1:25,000 maps for Dumpu, Kumbarum, Paipa, Amuba, Amuson. All map references in future were to be given from these new editions, but of course they were not consistently given, a fact which renders an historian's task in trying to trace the movements of particular units almost impossible at times.

[7] WO2 E. J. Berrell, NX4496. 2/3 Bn, Papuan Inf Bn. Labourer; of Goulburn, NSW; b. Goulburn, 19 Sep 1915.

[8] Throughout the period 18th October onwards the 2/6th Squadron, although limited by supply difficulties, had cleared the 5800 Feature and controlled the upper reaches of the Solu River, thus protecting the 2/7th Squadron's right flank. By the 25th an outpost was established three hours forward of the 5800 Feature as a base for patrols into the Japanese defences in the Yokopi area. This base was in fact only two hours from the enemy outpost positions round Yokopi. By 29th October the squadron controlled all the country forward of the enemy outposts on the Yokopi feature.

[9] Lt G. I. Green, WX12145. 2/2 Indep Coy, 2/2 Cdo Sqn. Linesman; of East Perth; b. Melbourne, 31 May 1916.

of five troopers, 32 native carriers and five police boys left for Sepu where it remained until setting out on the main journey on 3rd November. Some idea of the Australian soldier on long-range patrol may be gained by the equipment carried by Green's men. From the experience of trial and error, patrols now travelled as lightly as possible and carried only the essentials with them. The rations carried by the natives consisted of 8 days' field operation rations, 8 days' emergency rations, 100 pounds of chocolate and a bag of rice. Extra stores comprised one axe and 32 bush knives. The patrol was armed with four Owen guns, one Bren gun and two rifles. The men themselves wore their jungle green shirts and trousers, underpants and perhaps singlets, boots, socks, gaiters, berets, and identification discs round their necks. In their webbing equipment they carried a grenade, one emergency ration, pencil and paper. On their backs they carried their packs which held five days' field operation rations, a ground sheet, a gas cape, a mosquito helmet, mosquito repellent, soap, toothbrush, toothpaste, shaving gear, a towel, a dixie, a spoon and two spare pairs of socks. As a fault had developed in the radio transmitter at Sepu the wireless operators were left behind and intercommunication between Green's patrol and squadron headquarters would have to be by native runner.

Josephstaal was about half way between Atemble on the Ramu and Hansa Bay. The route chosen by Green and England did not follow the known native tracks as the Australians wished to avoid any contact with Japanese patrols. Thus the journey took nine days. Naturally Atemble, where the Japanese were known to be in some strength, was bypassed and, although there were tracks of Japanese horsemen at Sambanga and reports from natives that the Japanese did occasionally patrol the area between Atemble and Josephstaal and Madang, there were no encounters. On 13th November Green arrived at Josephstaal, which was not occupied and which had only been visited occasionally by small enemy patrols in recent months. While Green reconnoitred for an airstrip and made his report on it, England collected as much information as possible from the local natives. There was evidence to suggest to the patrol that they were unlikely to be disturbed at Josephstaal. Green estimated that, with a small party of engineers and local native labour, an airstrip could be prepared in about three days. The patrol returned to base on 26th November.

Early in November two further long-range patrols tried to investigate the enemy's lines of communication in the Kankiryo area. On the 2nd a patrol of 42 from the 2/33rd Battalion led by Lieutenant Scott[1] set out, urged on by Eather's hope that it would be able to blaze a track into the heart of the Japanese defences at Kankiryo from the west and get a prisoner. Moving up the Mene River Valley and across the 5500 Feature, Scott established a base on a steep ridge. Next day—the 4th—he moved down a spur to some native huts where the dense jungle was replaced by kunai. Seeking a covered approach along the timber line Scott found a

---
[1] Lt T. H. Scott, NX40512; 2/33 Bn. Station hand; of Boggabilla, NSW; b. Moree, NSW, 15 Jun 1921.

connecting spur crossed by a native track. Waiting until the clouds came down and keeping five yards between each man, the patrol rapidly crossed the spur to the timber on the other side. In the afternoon the men cautiously climbed the spur leading to the crest of the objective and a few hours later the leading scout saw the imprint of a Japanese rubber boot. Pushing on, they reached the crest of the spur and discovered a well and recently-used Japanese track. "As enemy appeared to be in possession of the high ground," reported Scott, "and the terrain did not favour an attack we withdrew to defensive perimeter."

Scott was instructed to remain in observation of the enemy road and to send back guides to the 5500 Feature to lead the remaining two platoons of Major MacDougal's company forward.[2] By 8 a.m. on the 8th MacDougal reported that his company was assembled at Scott's forward position and that, with the number of men available, it was "absolutely out of the question to attack". He was ordered to return to the battalion with the minimum of delay, and by the 9th the company was back in the battalion area.

Meanwhile a patrol from the 2/2nd Pioneer Battalion was attempting to observe the Kankiryo Saddle area from the east. On the 7th Lieutenant White[3] led out eight Pioneers, two Angau warrant-officers and 20 natives from Bob's Post following the Japanese Mule Track north to Toms' Post. There were numerous foxholes and other diggings less than a week old, and the natives said that the enemy had been using the track a lot in the past few days. Next day the patrol moved on along this well-surveyed track, and, about 1,500 yards beyond Toms' Post, saw a strong enemy position ahead on a high feature astride the track. On the 9th and the morning of the 10th White tried to work round to the north of the enemy position to carry out his original task, but dwindling rations, heavy rain, and rugged country forced his return to the track. Accompanied by two men White then advanced along the track but after 20 minutes he came under heavy fire. The three men ran back down the hill which they had been climbing but White was hit by machine-gun fire and fell. Neither of these patrols to the Kankiryo Saddle area had achieved its objective. A combination of factors were responsible—terrain, a stubborn enemy, and under-estimation of the time and therefore the rations required. The patrols, however, had discovered that the enemy was as sensitive to any jabs at his flanks as he was to thrusts on the main front.

Seldom during these last days of October and early days of November did patrols achieve spectacular results. The divisional summary of operations described the period as "patrolling activity" with "minor clashes with

---

[2] Late on the 5th Scott was informed that, as soon as possible after 10 a.m. next morning, red and green Very lights would be fired from the forward positions of the 2/16th and 2/27th Battalions to enable him to pinpoint his position more accurately. As so often happened in New Guinea fighting, these Very lights could not be seen by Scott because of low cloud; nor could mortar smoke, fired from the 2/27th's mortars on to the north end of Shaggy Ridge be observed later on the 6th for the same reason. A third attempt at location was made when Scott asked that the 2/27th should fire one round of high explosive and one round of smoke from their mortars. Although the results were not good, he was able to estimate that his position was about 3,000 yards from the 2/27th.

[3] Lt R. B. White, NX69757; 2/2 Pnr Bn. Bank officer; of Lavender Bay, NSW; b. Hamilton, Vic, 2 Oct 1913. Presumed killed in action 10 Nov 1943.

the enemy". Some of the longer patrols have been described and it can readily be seen how much effort was put into producing sometimes disappointing and frustrating results. However, the longer patrols and the daily fighting, standing and reconnaissance patrols were all playing their role in finding out what the country was like and where the Japanese were. It was known now that the Japanese defences and outposts lay in a large semi-circle round Kankiryo Saddle and Shaggy Ridge.

Vasey now decided to give each of his two brigades a period in the forward area. On 2nd November he told Dougherty and Eather that the 25th Brigade would relieve the 21st and that the relief was to be completed by 9th November. The 2/6th Commando Squadron would be relieved by the Papuan company in the Kesawai 2 area and would move farther west to take over the Kesawai 1-Isariba area from the 2/7th. Bena Force would be disbanded and the 2/2nd Commando Squadron would come under direct command of the 7th Division and be based on the Faita airstrip, to provide protection for radar installations there and in the Bena-Garoka areas. Besides this static role the squadron would also patrol the huge area west of a line from Inomba and Yonapa to Jappa.

On the 7th Lieut-Colonel L. G. Canet of the divisional staff arrived at Garoka in a Wirraway and went by jeep to MacAdie's headquarters at Sigoiya. Here he made administrative arrangements with MacAdie for the closing down of Bena Force at 6 a.m. on 10th November. Early in the afternoon four Japanese fighters strafed Bena, Sigoiya and Garoka in steep dives, coming down to 100 feet above the ground. A Fairchild Cub was destroyed and Canet's Wirraway was damaged. Later in the afternoon Canet and the Wirraway pilot flew back to Dumpu in a transport aircraft.[4]

MacAdie signalled Laidlaw on the 8th that Bena Force would close on the 10th. Thus, almost ten months after Lieutenant Rooke and his platoon of the 2/7th Battalion had arrived on the rough and crude Bena airstrip on the 23rd January 1943, Bena Force ceased to exist.[5] For the

---

[4] The amount of flying carried out in New Guinea by senior force and corps commanders such as Generals Herring and Morshead, has already been noted. General Vasey's bold flights in Cub aircraft over the battle area have also been described. With one of his brigades still in Port Moresby, he often flew back there over the mountains to see it. Staff officers such as Canet and isolated commanders such as MacAdie also necessarily did much flying. The accident to Canet's aircraft underlined how a key man in the divisional organisation could become isolated through enemy air action. MacAdie himself and one of his liaison officers on Bena Force headquarters, Lieutenant Dunshea, had both crashed in aircraft while taking off for conferences at divisional headquarters on the 25th and 30th October respectively.

[5] The composition of Bena Force for the main period of its operation was as follows:

	Officers	OR's
HQ	4	19
2/2 Cdo Sqn	18	270
2/7 Cdo Sqn	19	280
MG Section 2/7 Bn	—	9
Detachment 2/2 Fd Amb	1	11
Detachment 2/115 Gen Transport Coy	1	11
Detachment 3 Aust Fd Survey Section	1	11
Detachment 2/2 Special Dental Unit	1	1
Detachment Army Postal Service	—	1
NG Cypher	—	2
Angau	10	33
Royal Papuan Constabulary	1	234
NGAWW Sigs	1	42
Bty "C" 210 Coast Arty AA (US)	1	28
Other American detachments under operational command	7	150
	65	1,102

loss of 12 men killed, 16 wounded and 5 missing it had killed about 230 of the enemy. It had built the Garoka airfield for fighters and bombers; it had constructed 78 miles of motor transport road between Bena and Garoka, Sigoiya, Asaloka and Kainantu; and it had produced maps of a vast and hitherto unknown area.

In his final report MacAdie wrote:

> The force fulfilled its task. Every enemy patrol which crossed the Ramu River was driven back with casualties, and very determined enemy attacks were repulsed with heavy casualties. In addition the enemy lost many men in ambushes on tracks north of the Ramu River. . . . There is no doubt that the enemy regarded this force as a menace to his flank, and little doubt that the size of the force was grossly overestimated. This is borne out by the constant heavy air attacks in June and July, and by the A.T.I.S. translation of the operation order for the enemy attack on Bena scheduled for the end of September. This over-estimation of the force is not unnatural, since the Jap encountered resistance at several points on a frontage of 140 miles, and was well aware of construction activities with roads, bridges and buildings from his Tac R reports. Furthermore, there were 23 WT stations (mainly No. 11 sets and 3 B's) operating in the area, and four large-sized, plainly-marked hospitals. It seems therefore likely that the threat to his L. of C. from this quarter must have contributed largely to his decision to withdraw from the Markham and upper Ramu Valleys.

The 7th Division with the 21st Brigade as spearhead, 25th Brigade in reserve, and the commando squadrons, Papuans and Pioneers on the flanks, had performed the exceedingly difficult and gruelling task of driving the enemy back from the Ramu Valley into the Finisterres. Other than the determined and successful fights for Pallier's Hill and Johns' Knoll, the period had largely been one of routine patrols. Vasey was convinced that he could push on to Bogadjim if only given the support. "Eather gave me an unconscious compliment today," he wrote about this time in a letter, "said I was a commander who stood on the toes of my brigadiers —one of the reasons my brigadiers turn out to be good ones." Dougherty, "no jeephead brigadier" as one of his battalion commanders described him, wrote later of this period: "From my point of view there were no 'might have beens' in this campaign. All ranks of the brigade played their parts admirably. This applies, too, to the personnel of non-brigade units who were under command of, in support of, or working in cooperation with, 21 Brigade." The success of the 7th Division, however unspectacular it now appeared, had been won by fine leadership, stirring fighting qualities of the men and close cooperation of all arms.

The *78th Regiment* was part of *Nakai Force* which had originally been formed, as will be recalled, to advance overland from Madang down the Markham to Lae. Towards the end of October *Nakai Force* had a ration strength of 12,167 men. General Nakai's headquarters of about 200 men was at Kwato. The *II/78th Battalion* plus two companies of the *III/78th*—about 990 men—was at Kankiryo Saddle. The *I/78th*, less one company and attached troops at Saipa 2 (about 340) and one company in the Huon Peninsula fighting (about 138), was in the Yokopi area with about 514 men. The main body of the *III/78th Battalion* was at Yaula with about 450 men, and one company of the *80th Regiment* (about 123) was at Yokopi. The *239th Regiment* (about 2,300 men) was in the Madang-Erima-Rai Coast area with outposts in the area patrolled by the 2/2nd Commando Squadron. About

2,000 reinforcements of various arms of the Services were available to Nakai. Of the 866 gunners of the *26th Artillery Regiment,* a battery of 115 men was at Kankiryo, another of 154 men at Yaula and the remainder in the Bogadjim-Erima area (most of this artillery regiment were in the Huon Peninsula fighting). Six hundred engineers of the *37th Independent Engineer Regiment* were at Kankiryo and Saipa 2 and there were about 3,520 headquarters, signallers and lines of communication troops.

Thus Nakai had a considerable force nominally under his command but it was thinly spread and actually his only available troops for holding the Australian advance were the depleted battalions of the *78th Regiment.* He could expect no more reinforcement, for the mounting Allied air and sea offensives were hitting General Adachi's supply lines hard; Nakai might even be obliged to send some of his present force to bolster up portions of the sagging *XVIII Japanese Army* elsewhere. It was fortunate for the Japanese that Allied strategy and supply problems in this period had necessitated holding the 7th Division on a leash.

CHAPTER 21

ROUND SATTELBERG AND PABU

BY the end of October the counter-offensive by the *20th Japanese Division* had been defeated. Only enemy stragglers now remained in the whole area held by the 9th Division before the counter-attack began, except for the determined company from the *80th Regiment* astride the Sattelberg Road in the rear of the 2/17th Battalion. Thus it was possible for the Australian commanders again to plan an offensive. On 5th October, in General Herring's last operational order, the 9th Division had been instructed to defend Finschhafen, develop it as a base, and gain control of the east coast of the Huon Peninsula up to and including Sio. Many dramatic events had occurred since then, and now it seemed opportune for the new corps commander, General Morshead, to re-state the objective. This he did on 29th October when General Wootten was instructed, as before, to protect Finschhafen, including the Dreger Harbour airstrip, clear the remaining enemy from the general Finschhafen area, and gain the coast as far as Sio.

There was now more chance of carrying out the last part of the order because further troops were available. On 20th October General Mackay passed on to Morshead General MacArthur's signal that two batteries of the 2/6th Field Regiment at Lae would be moved to Finschhafen. The 11th Anti-Tank Battery and 2/4th Commando Squadron were also warned to prepare for movement to Finschhafen. The most important addition to Wootten's strength, however, was the 4th Brigade. On 27th October Mackay gave Morshead permission to move it to Finschhafen except for part of one battalion which would remain at Lae. Next day Morshead ordered the brigade, less the 22nd Battalion, already there, and one company of the 29th/46th Battalion, to move to Finschhafen. An additional field company of engineers—the 2/7th—would also move from Lae to Finschhafen as craft became available. The Mongi River would be the boundary between the 9th and 5th Divisions.

On 28th October Mackay received a message from MacArthur's headquarters giving details of a delay of fifteen days in the launching of the projected operation by Alamo Force against western New Britain. As a result Admiral Carpender's naval forces would continue to support the II Corps until about 20th November.

Since his conference with Morshead on 25th October Wootten had already decided that the next step must be to secure his flank before advancing north along the coast. This would entail the capture of Sattelberg, followed by an advance to the Gusika-Wareo line. Even with the extra brigade at his disposal he had discarded the idea of attacking Wareo and Sattelberg at the same time. It was obvious that, before there could be any advance up the Sattelberg Road, the stubborn enemy position east of Jivevaneng must be destroyed. This would be a difficult task because the Japanese were elaborately entrenched and were favoured by the steepness of the ridge along which the road ran, as well as by the thick bamboo which betrayed any movement. To the north of the enemy position was a steep ravine on the far side of which was a dominant ridge topped with a coconut grove. On 29th October Lieutenant Rackham[1] of the 2/13th Battalion occupied this coconut area and a patrol from the 2/17th set up a post at Cemetery Corner where the Sattelberg Road could be controlled by fire for another 50 yards to the north-east. "We are now regaining the initiative in this area," wrote the 2/17th's diarist on the 29th, "and hope to be able to deal offensively with the enemy in the very near future and again open the road as a main supply route." Evidence of this determination was contained in Brigadier Windeyer's operation order received by his three battalion commanders late that night: the 2/13th would attack west from Coconut Grove and guard the Tareko supply route; the 2/17th would engage the enemy from Cemetery Corner and attempt to ambush the suspected Japanese supply route.

As there were now only 35 men in Captain Deschamps' company of the 2/13th Colonel Colvin sent two more platoons to join him at Coconut Grove. At the same time Major Handley's company, reinforced by a platoon, began squeezing the Japanese pocket in conjunction with a platoon of the 2/17th at Cemetery Corner. First, Lieutenant Simmons'[2] men in small groups, each with a Bren, leap-frogged up each side of the road until they reached four strands of wire across it. With eight men Lieutenant Birmingham then moved on in an attempt to locate the actual enemy positions. Skirting the right of the road Birmingham's small band penetrated thicker bamboo and reached a position near a dead tree and fallen log on the edge of a clearing of smashed down bamboo. Here they saw some Japanese about 15 yards away in their foxholes, and noted that the position extended west for about 60 yards and north for another 100. After watching for some time the patrol threw grenades into the holes and opened up with the Bren and Owens before withdrawing. After Birmingham returned at 12.30 p.m. Simmons was ordered to occupy the log position, which he did without interference, although the nearest enemy position was but 12 yards away. Just after midday Deschamps sent Rackham's platoon south-west along the track from Coconut Grove. A patrol from the 2/17th was already in its ambush position to support the 2/13th's advance. Rackham met the Japanese 250 yards from the grove and inflicted some casualties. Lieutenant Suters' platoon now took over the advance and cleaned out this Japanese position. He then attacked a machine-gun post 25 yards farther on, killed its occupants and caused the surviving Japanese to flee.

Suters' platoon then dug in while Lieutenant Hall's platoon moved up to a position in the 400 yards' gap between company headquarters and the forward platoon. In the afternoon the Japanese attacked Suters' rear,

---

[1] Lt A. J. Rackham, NX36162; 2/13 Bn. Bank officer; of Reservoir, Vic; b. Auckland, NZ, 26 Jul 1907.
[2] Lt N. W. Simmons, NX26744; 2/13 Bn. Storekeeper; of Kiama, NSW; b. Kiama, 25 Dec 1917.

but a patrol led by Rackham cleared the track and stayed forward until dusk. The track was clear at last light but, during the night, the enemy were heard digging in between the two forward platoons. Two of these Japanese diggers lost their way and blundered into the forward platoon's position. One was shot a few yards from the perimeter but as the other had actually entered the defences and, as it would be dangerous to fire inside, he was left there and shot in the morning.

The squeeze continued on the 31st. An added incentive was that all knew they were soon to be relieved by the 26th Brigade and they wished to clear the road before then. While the 2/17th patrolled towards the Japanese positions on both sides of Jivevaneng Deschamps' company of the 2/13th prepared to move south-west from Coconut Grove. At 8 a.m. Hall's men rose from their holes in the ground, hastily dug the previous night, and moved off along the track to join Suters. The platoon was fired on 100 yards ahead from a Japanese position established during the night, but with dash and determination and with hardly a pause the band of 19 men attacked the enemy post on the left and cleaned it out, then formed up again and destroyed the right-hand post. Again the platoon attacked and this time destroyed the enemy machine-gun post straight ahead. The track was now clear and Hall joined Suters and learnt of another Japanese position 100 yards to the north. Nothing daunted, the gallant platoon attacked again and its spirit carried all before it. Several Japanese were killed and the remainder fled.

It was bad luck that Hall's spirited series of actions could not be capitalised, but the commanders felt that this thrust through an area which probably included the vital enemy supply line would need a stronger shaft than was available to support the spearhead. Thus Deschamps' company gathered again in the area around and forward of Coconut Grove while two other companies of the 2/13th blocked up on the right and left of the road towards the enemy position. During the afternoon Colvin called all his company commanders together and said that they would exert pressure now and keep it up. He pointed out that in such a close fight captured ground must not be given up as it would only have to be fought for again. At 7 p.m. Simpson rang Colvin and told him that the 2/17th would attack the Japanese positions on the Sattelberg Road; he asked Colvin to indicate his forward posts by firing a Very light at 8.30 a.m. Sickness and sniping had depleted the ranks of the 2/17th, living conditions were most unpleasant, and the supply line was precarious. The battalion diarist at the end of October wrote:

> The battalion at present is rather uncomfortable owing to the almost incessant rain over the past 48 hours. This afternoon mist obscured the whole area and seriously hampered vision. Everyone presents rather sorry spectacle as we are now reduced to one set of clothing. A relief will be welcome when it arrives. The main Sattelberg Road has been cut now for 13 days but it is hoped that this situation will be rectified in the very near future.[3]

---

[3] About this time the brigade asked for flame-throwers and tanks but flame-throwers were not available and the tanks were being held for the later advance on Sattelberg.

As might have been expected, damp prevented the Very lights being fired on 1st November but, as requested by Simpson, Lieutenant Simmons' platoon at the log was ready to advance and occupy the positions captured by the 2/17th. Simpson himself was not present as he had received orders to report immediately to brigade headquarters. He left Major Broadbent in command of the 2/17th.

At 11.30 a.m. the companies of the 2/13th Battalion on the road kept their heads down as the 2/17th attacked the Japanese position on the north of the road east of Cemetery Corner. Lieutenant McLeod's platoon led the attack along the north side of the road. The thickness of the bamboo and the rugged nature of the country forced the men to advance in single file. After 20 yards they were fired on and suffered two casualties. As such an advance could only result in further casualties Broadbent called it off. He then rang Colvin and stated that he would attack on both sides of the track on the 2nd and would the 2/13th please create a diversion.

The Japanese pocket was now in an unenviable position. Deschamps on the north, the 2/15th to the south, and two battalions surrounding it in the centre were all exerting pressure on the position itself or on its supply line, but the Japanese were still very much in occupation next morning, when at 8.45 a.m. a company of the 2/17th under Major Maclarn moved off from the east side of Jivevaneng to take over where McLeod had left off on the previous day. A quarter of an hour later pandemonium broke out from the 2/13th as all its weapons were fired for 15 minutes in a grand diversionary demonstration. Birmingham's platoon which had relieved Simmons' at the log on the previous evening added to the racket by yelling. Broadbent on the previous day had been asked by the 2/13th to lower the range of his mortars which were falling near the log. Now it was his turn to ask his enthusiastic sister battalion to fire farther to the right and not into his advancing troops. At 9.30 a.m. Birmingham's men smartly lay low in their holes as the mortar bombs of the 2/17th once again began to fall near the log.

By 10 a.m. Maclarn was ready to attack. Despite the determination of the attackers progress could be measured only in yards and the advance almost came to a standstill. About 6,000 rounds fired from Maclarn's Vickers forced the Japanese—and the 2/13th—to keep their heads down. It also served the useful purpose of clearing much of the bamboo cane and tangled growth surrounding and covering the Japanese position. Grenades were now out of the question because of the fragmentation danger to both battalions. Despite this constant pressure the Japanese did not falter and any careless movement from either of the battalions drew immediate fire.

By midday Maclarn's men had inched forward to a position north of the road, where they could be seen from a 2/13th Battalion observation post. Only about 150 yards separated the forward troops of both battalions but the enemy was still firmly wedged in between them in the tangle of broken bamboo. Colvin and Broadbent arranged to call out and try to estimate the distance between both battalions. "What shall we yell out?" said Colvin. "Tally ho—the Red Fox [Simpson's nickname]," replied Broadbent.[4] Birmingham's men at the log shouted the well-known cry but there was no answer.

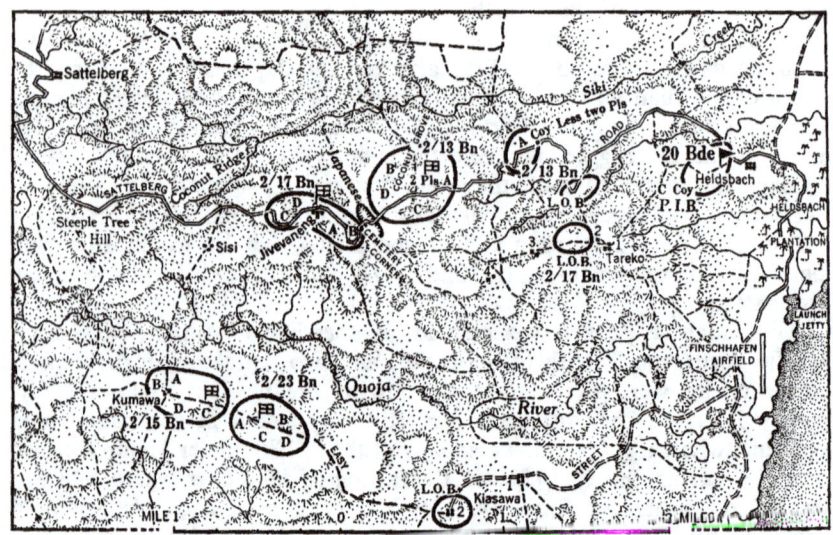

Clearing the track to Jivevaneng, 2nd November

While this fighting was going on, Wootten was holding a conference at Windeyer's headquarters. He outlined the future role of the 20th and 26th Brigades and stated that the relief of the 20th Brigade by the 26th could not await the opening of the Sattelberg Road. Windeyer replied that he expected the road would be opened in time for the relief. This conference met after lunch; at 2.15 p.m. his battalions received an order from Windeyer that they must try to link up; at 4 p.m. they received another stating that the road must be opened "today". The 2/17th therefore battered into the Japanese position. At 4.30 the leading men of both battalions waved to one another from both sides of the clearing. A Japanese in the centre waved to both. Three-quarters of an hour later Birmingham found that the Japanese had evacuated the near-by defences which he had been intending to grenade. It now seemed that the Japanese had left the south side of the road but the gathering darkness prevented further investigation. The fierce squeeze by the two battalions on 2nd November had its effect. At 6.30 a.m. on the 3rd Lieutenant Mair of the 2/13th led his company forward along the road and found all the enemy positions abandoned. Telephone line was immediately laid and the road was opened a few hours before the advanced guard of the 26th Brigade

---

[4] Some said the nickname had been given because Simpson was red-haired and crafty. In the Western Desert he had agreed to having a red fox painted on his Bren carrier and at El Alamein his battalion had gone into action shouting the cry now being used.

came up the road. The 20th Brigade had done its job and the Sattelberg Road was open for the next phase of operations.

Meanwhile, to the north, patrols had been active. Lieutenant Buckley,[5] of the 2/48th, led a patrol about 1,000 yards west from Katika on the 30th. He was attacked by about 35 Japanese but before withdrawing killed 14 of them including an officer. A patrol of 13 led by Lieutenant Harvey[6] of the 2/43rd and Lieutenant Rice of the Papuan Battalion left North Hill on 29th October to investigate Japanese activity north and west of Bonga, and particularly round Imperial. Next morning the patrol found that the position occupied by the 2/43rd's anti-tank platoon before the Japanese counter-attack had not been touched, and then moved west to a good position where the main track could be clearly watched. At 10.25 a.m. three Japanese came down the track towards the coast; one was armed but sick and the others were wounded and unarmed. Half an hour later three more Japanese came down carrying heavy packs; only one was armed. At 12.10 p.m. one Japanese went hurriedly to the west along the 1,000 yards stretch of visible track. Later two more small parties of unarmed Japanese were seen moving with heavy loads towards the coast. It was apparent that the Japanese were using this track as an evacuation route and as a supply route also.

On the 1st the diarist of one of the battalions of the 24th Brigade noted "we learnt with regret" that Brigadier Evans was leaving the brigade. As mentioned, Colonel Simpson was appointed to administer command of the brigade. With only the briefest of warnings, Simpson entered a jeep and sped north to take over. Evans was waiting. "You'll find the brigade in good heart," he said as he entered his own jeep and left for the south.

That night, Simpson outlined his coastal patrol policy to Colonel Joshua of the 2/43rd: the aim was eventually to reoccupy Pino Hill and ambush the Japanese using the coastal track. Simpson's other two battalions were actively patrolling west in the area between the Song and the Siki but could seldom find any Japanese. On the 2nd Lieutenant Harvey led a patrol of four men from the 2/43rd Battalion and ten Papuans north on a patrol destined to play an important part in later planning. Harvey's subsequent report was illuminating.

Reached OP 1500 hrs NMS—last 200 yards crawled through kunai. At 1650 hrs 2 Japs moved down track with rifles slung moving in a confident manner, no hats. 0200 hrs till dawn movement was heard but unable to distinguish cause. Considerable troop movement both ways along track. 0635 hrs 27 Japs moved up track. These troops appeared fresh and were armed with LMG's and rifles. Full heavy packs. Some had caps camouflaged with steel helmets on packs. These packs appeared larger than normal packs—blanket roll on pack. 3 were carrying what appeared to be large map cases and 4 carrying bags in excess of packs (in one group). 0712 hrs 2 Japs with rifles and very heavy packs one with cap and one without— both with steel helmets on packs moved up track. 0745 hrs 1 lone Jap with full pack and rifle (complete pack camouflaged with net and in net grass and small

---

[5] Lt J. A. R. Buckley, MC, SX7985; 2/48 Bn. Insurance clerk; of Glandore, SA; b. Prospect, SA, 14 Jan 1911.

[6] Maj B. L. Harvey, WX7395; 2/43 Bn. Salesman; of Mount Lawley, WA; b. Claremont, WA, 6 Sep 1914.

branches) very nervous, small dixie in hand. 0945—2 more Japs up track (heavy packs and rifles). At same time party of 4 Japs seen travelling down carrying small haversacks on back. 1 armed with what appeared SMG—remainder unarmed. No further movement until relieved. . . . Throughout night into early morning barge movement heard. . . . Highly probable troops moving up track had just been landed from barges heard. Their equipment and physical condition were not of troops brought back for rest. Our OP was within 50 yards of track and enemy is unaware of his being watched. During night consider unwise to post sentries closer to track as earlier recce disclosed that enemy were in the habit of resting on track in area of OP. Should a fighting [patrol] be required strongly recommend a company job owing to nature of ground. 1 platoon could inflict casualties but could not fully cover enemy dispersion. No water in OP area. . . . All troops moving on track appeared confident and not anticipating trouble.

From these invaluable reports came the germ of a big idea destined to have a profound effect on the campaign.

On 1st November Wootten sent his plans to the three brigadiers and next day two conferences took place, first at divisional headquarters and then at Windeyer's headquarters. At the Heldsbach conference were Wootten and his senior staff officers, the commanders and staffs of the 20th and 26th Brigades, the commanders of the tank squadron, divisional artillery and divisional engineers. Wootten's general intention was to resume the offensive, now that the enemy's counter-attack had failed and additional Australian troops had arrived. "The immediate object," stated the divisional report, "was to be the capture of the high ground Sattelberg-Palanko by the 26th Brigade, supported by all available divisional resources, with a view to a subsequent advance to the Gusika-Wareo line." Brigadier Whitehead was instructed to reconnoitre the area "at once" and to make his detailed plan. As tanks could probably be used on the Sattelberg Road, the 26th Brigade and the tank squadron (18 tanks) would immediately begin training together to work out the best tactics, and methods of cooperation and control.[7] Wootten also stressed that the arrival of the tanks must be concealed from the enemy; they were to be covered from air observation, and were to move forward only with infantry protection. Whitehead estimated that he would probably need about nine tanks.

Wootten ordered the 20th Brigade to take over the central sector. The role of both 20th and 24th Brigades would then be to continue vigorous patrolling in order to drive the enemy farther back and distract his attention from the 26th Brigade's preparations. Finally the 24th Brigade would prepare to send a battalion north, possibly as a diversionary operation, to occupy a position astride the Gusika-Wareo track, and thus cut the enemy supply line and threaten Wareo from the east.

In such rugged country there was need for careful administrative planning to prepare roads and supply dumps before an offensive could be

---

[7] In the few days that the brigade and the tank squadron were together at Milne Bay Whitehead had arranged for a sand-model exercise covering possible employment of tanks round Lae, and for communication exercises. These contacts were renewed soon after the squadron arrived at Finschhafen. Already Lieutenant J. G. Emmott of the tank battalion with a patrol from the 2/48th Battalion had been credited with the squadron's first kill in an affair in which seven Japanese were killed; and Lieutenant H. C. Curtayne (of Randwick, NSW) had reconnoitred the Kumawa area for the possible use of tanks.

successfully launched against the Sattelberg citadel. The roads were very cut up because of the rains in the last three days of October and it became necessary to restrict the movement of vehicles other than jeeps. It was imperative to build up large forward supply dumps, so that wet weather would not slow up an offensive. By jeep and trailer and by native carrier reserve dumps were built up at Kumawa (20 days for 500) and at Jivevaneng (20 days for 2,000) by 14th November.[8] As water might be scarce all available two-gallon containers were filled and stored at Jivevaneng.

As usual, maintenance of the Finschhafen area proved a difficult task. MacArthur's decision to delay the opening of the New Britain operation helped, however, and more troops and supplies were poured into Finschhafen. For instance, on 1st November there were only 12,000 rounds of 25-pounder ammunition in the area, but stocks were now increased by two L.C.M. loads a day. As the daily average expenditure during this period of preparation was only 500 rounds, a satisfactory reserve was available when the Sattelberg offensive began. A large number of American troops, equipment and stores were coming in during this period to establish the base for the Fifth Air Force and a base for P.T. boats at Dreger Harbour. In the 9th Division's report the period was described thus:

> All construction units, AA units, and administrative detachments, with their personnel, vehicles, equipment and stores, were landed on Godowa Beach, from LST's. The beach became chaotically overcrowded because of insufficient means to clear it, and heavy rain for several days turned Timbulum Plantation behind the beach into a quagmire. Vehicles had to be dragged off the beach by bulldozers and left in the mud behind. Gradually, however, roads were built to Dreger and the congestion slowly abated.

In preparation for the attack on Sattelberg the enemy supply lines were increasingly attacked by Allied aircraft and P.T. boats. From aerial reconnaissance, patrol information, native reports, captured documents and prisoners, the staffs now had a fairly clear picture of the enemy's rearward supply and reinforcement system. Nambariwa, near Sio, was known to be his main forward supply distribution base, where barges from Madang and submarines from Rabaul discharged their cargoes. Supplies and troops thence moved down the coast in barges to staging points at Sialum Island, Kanomi, Walingai, Wandokai and Lakona, or overland along the track recently taken by the *79th Regiment* from Kalasa to Wareo. This area of sea and land was vigorously strafed and bombed. For instance on 2nd November 12 Vultees and 15 Thunderbolts dive-bombed and strafed suspected dumps and bivouac areas at Nambariwa and the track south.

By November the Japanese had a healthy horror of the P.T. boats which had many accomplishments to their credit. For instance, on the

---

[8] Despite the efforts of Colonel Allan and officers of Angau and the Papuan Battalion the number of native carriers in the area was very limited, only 250 being available for the 26th Brigade. N.G.F., however, arranged to fly 1,000 natives down the Markham Valley to Lae, whence they were dispatched to Finschhafen in craft of the 2 ESB at the rate of about 200 each two days. Eventually 600 were allotted to 26th Brigade—enough to carry for the whole brigade on a one-day turn around.

night of 1st-2nd November they sank two empty Japanese barges heading south from Walingai; next night two more empty barges were sunk heading south-east three miles off Blucher Point; next night off Kelanoa five were sunk loaded with stores and heading south-east. The tempo of barge hunting was increasing; in the period 3rd September to 22nd October 15 Japanese barges, 6 of which were carrying troops and the remainder stores, were sunk and 7 damaged; now in three nights 9 were sunk.

The *20th Japanese Division's* supply difficulties, already acute, were thus accentuated. Further evidence of its plight was furnished when on 31st October 285 native men, women and children came in through the 2/28th and 2/32nd Battalion lines from the Fior and Palanko areas, and said that the Japanese were short of food, and were raiding native gardens. Reinforcements were coming in mostly in small groups along the Gusika-Wareo track and many wounded had left the area along the same track in the past few days. This confirmed the information from the patrols of the Papuan Battalion and the 2/43rd.

The 2/23rd took over from the 2/15th on 3rd November after having slithered and cursed its way up Easy Street. The battalion's task was now to hold Kumawa at all costs and patrol to find enemy strength, and routes round enemy positions. The 2/24th was next to move when, on the 3rd, half the battalion set out up the track. There still remained an enemy pocket near the road north of Jivevaneng, and Windeyer hoped to clear it before the final relief. That afternoon Captain Dinning's company of the 2/17th began an attack on the position. The plan was that the company should drive the enemy off the ledge close to the road and force him into a re-entrant. From Dinning's start-line near the road to his objective would be a mere 75 yards. Without any opening fire support, the company attacked with two platoons forward. After advancing only about 20 to 30 yards the leading platoons came under heavy fire from enemy positions concealed in bamboo; one of the leading platoon commanders—Lieutenant Graham—was fatally wounded, four men were killed outright and 8 wounded. Though only 15 yards from the Japanese the leading section commander, Lance-Sergeant Dawes,[9] dragged in the wounded.

The Australian advance was stopped and the Japanese confidently left their holes to attack the leading section of the right-hand platoon. Dawes held his fire while about 25 Japanese charged in a bunch. At a distance of 10 yards his men opened up with small arms and grenades. The entire enemy force disappeared, killed or fleeing. A Vickers machine-gun was then placed on the left of the line to harass the Japanese position and a 3-inch mortar bombarded his rear. The Vickers bullets landed among the 2/13th Battalion until the range was dropped. Just before dusk the enemy retaliated with 40 bombs from an 81-mm mortar on the 2600 Feature. Five casualties were inflicted by the enemy mortar bringing Dinning's total for the day to 19 including 8 killed.

---

[9] Sgt B. G. Dawes, DCM, NX15984; 2/17 Bn. Bread carter; of Queanbeyan, NSW; b. Queanbeyan, 28 Dec 1912.

Then the rain came—a real deluge. Weapon-pits were flooded, troops soaked and equipment damaged. The area was soon a quagmire. Throughout the 4th both sides exchanged harassing fire and grenades. The Australians could now see the Japanese pill-boxes better, for the bamboo had been cut down by machine-gun fire. As the Coconut Grove position was no longer valuable, Windeyer agreed that Deschamps (2/13th) should be withdrawn. While two of Broadbent's companies of the 2/17th remained, the other two were relieved by the two companies of the 2/24th. There was no movement during the night and, early on the 5th, a patrol found that the Japanese had vacated the whole area.

> It was a scene of desolation with bodies and equipment everywhere (wrote the diarist of the 2/17th). The distance between enemy positions and those of C Company varied from 3 yards near 14 Platoon to 20 yards forward of 13 Platoon. This gives some indication of the severity of the task which C Company undertook and how well they stuck to their job. . . . We were now in the pleasant position of being able to hand over the area to 2/24th Battalion clear of enemy. The work of the battalion had been of great tactical importance as the area could now be used as a base for further offensive operations against the enemy in the Sattelberg area.

The magnificent defence by the 2/17th at Jivevaneng was over. At dusk the last two companies rejoined the remainder of the battalion in the Heldsbach area. The men looked thin and drawn yet fit and full of spirit. They were wearing the same green shirts and trousers issued to them in Cairns and they had hardly had the opportunity of washing them since Milne Bay. The clothes were heavy with grease and mud and many of the men had not taken them off for the past eight days. In the New Guinea jungles in wartime dry clothes were the exception rather than the rule among the forward troops. The men were carrying very little beyond their weapons and equipment; for bedding they carried a groundsheet and blanket—and Jivevaneng had been two-blanket country.

The men joked and grinned at the sight of the Y.M.C.A. "bloke" and his urn of tea and, as usual, they thought it was fine of him to have it ready. They wanted to know the "news" but actually they were well informed and had heard the latest sitreps. The 2/17th Battalion had suffered fairly heavy losses and had been living in wretched conditions of weariness, danger, wet and dirt but, no less than the men of their sister battalions who had not been under constant pressure for such a long time, their spirit of cheerfulness and patience was exemplary. "You'll have to get us some new mates," one private said to the brigadier who wandered among the men as they were throwing off their packs and drinking their tea, "there's only eleven left in our platoon."

In the northern sector of the divisional front interesting information was being collected at the observation post overlooking the Gusika-Wareo track, and now manned continuously by small patrols from the 2/43rd and the Papuan Battalion. From first light on the 5th the group had a full-time job recording the movement along the Japanese vital supply route. The procession started when one unarmed Japanese was seen travelling east and 13 with weapons hidden by capes travelling west. For the next hour enemy were seen travelling east and west; the wounded moving towards the coast, reinforcements towards Wareo, and some appearing to be moving to the east and then returning west with stores. At 7.40 a.m. came the highlight for the unseen observers—29 Japanese pulling to the west a gun camouflaged with bush, probably a 75-mm. The Japanese shortage of artillery in the general area was well known to the Australians, and this piece of observation was of great interest: perhaps the advent of this and other guns might presage a further Japanese attempt to regain the initiative. When this patrol was relieved at 11.40 a.m. it had observed 115 Japanese travelling west and 44 travelling east. The troops heading west had carried many heavy stores such as boxes of ammunition, tarpaulins, stretchers, an extra gun barrel, and other items.

By last light on the 6th the observers had established that most of the movement on these days was to the east by wounded—about 300 of them. As this coincided with barge traffic heard at night it seemed obvious that wounded were being concentrated for evacuation. These large numbers of unarmed Japanese presented tempting ambush targets but Colonel Simpson had decided that, although there was no harm in the artillery registering the area, an ambush, or even an attempt to capture a prisoner, might compromise the observation post.

Despite his severe losses in the counter-offensive,[1] which had reduced several fighting units to below half strength, and despite his lack of air and artillery support and supply difficulties, the enemy had not abandoned his object of recapturing the Finschhafen area. General Adachi visited the divisional commander, General Katagiri, at Sattelberg at the end of October. On 3rd November, Katagiri issued another order.

> "1. The enemy in the Finschhafen area, approximately the size of a division and a half, appears to consist mainly of 9th Australian Division. They have secured Finschhafen, Langemak Bay, and also Heldsbach airfield. It appears as if they are planning to control the Dampier Strait. Their front line runs along both sides of River Song. It is certain that they have secured Jivevaneng, Kumawa and Butaweng. The enemy at present is supplying its position and at the same time is trying to remove the strong pressure of [*79th Regiment*] north of Jivevaneng.
> 2. 20th Division, with the object of capturing Finschhafen, will attack locally and gradually annihilate the enemy. In order to accomplish this, a powerful force (*80th Infantry Regiment*) must occupy Sattelberg height quickly and make it secure. Distribute units in vital points in the rear to meet enemy landings and endeavour to protect the supply simultaneously. Main body (*79th Infantry Regiment*, Div HQ, Div Troops) will assemble at Nongora."

In a preliminary plan for the capture of Sattelberg Brigadier Whitehead's brigade major, Mackay,[2] outlined on 4th November the information available to the 26th Brigade. According to this the enemy had constructed positions west of Jivevaneng in the Sisi area, and probably had sufficient strength to fight a series of delaying actions along the Sattelberg Road.

---

[1] The Australians estimated that Katagiri's fighting strength at this time was between 4,000 and 7,000 men although his total force was about 12,500.
[2] Col K. Mackay, MBE, NX12365. 2/8 Fd Regt 1940-41; BM 26 Bde 1942-44; and various staff appointments. Regular soldier; of Sydney; b. Sydney, 17 Feb 1917.

The plan continued that "Tac R and reports received from other sources indicate that the main enemy strength may be to the north of Sattelberg in the Wareo-Bonga area where he may be preparing for an attack or more likely is expecting an attack by us". The accuracy and soundness of these forecasts were equalled by the care and attention to detail in the plan itself. It was another example of the highly intelligent and efficient planning carried out by experienced units before going into battle. The men themselves would be loath to move without knowing what it was all about; and officers and N.C.O's passed on the necessary information under the headings set out in *Field Service Regulations*: Information (enemy and our troops), Intention, Method, Administration, Intercommunication. As many of the officers in the fighting units had risen from the ranks themselves they knew what was required by the men, and from the mutual respect and admiration between men and officers of these units arose the vital cooperation and reliance on one another so essential to success.

On 6th and 7th November patrols from all three battalions of the 26th Brigade moved forward closer to the Japanese. From Kumawa Lieutenant Barrand's[3] patrol of the 2/23rd came to a derelict native garden where one Japanese was sitting near a fence. The patrol surrounded him stealthily until the patrol commander seized him and bound and gagged him. Unfortunately the prisoner managed to loosen the gag and shouted for help after the patrol had gone 70 yards on the homeward journey. When answering cries were heard near by to the north and movement to the east the patrol withdrew minus its prisoner.

It remained for the tanks to move forward to Jivevaneng. Five were moved by L.C.M's from Kedam Beach to Launch Jetty during the afternoon of 8th November, and, half an hour before midnight, began to move up the Sattelberg Road towards Jivevaneng in bright moonlight. The going was hard as the road was steep and the surface glassy, causing the tanks to slip, and great difficulty was experienced in rounding the two really sharp bends on the road. Two of the tanks bogged and the other three were towed to within about half a mile of Jivevaneng. On the night of 9th-10th November all nine tanks had negotiated the difficult road and were hidden in bamboo thickets east of Jivevaneng. The 26th Brigade found that from many points along the road Sattelberg could be seen, now only about 3,000 yards from the 2/48th's forward positions. The forward slopes of Sattelberg were pitted with bomb craters, but the plateau looked a formidable fortress with its walls rising steeply from the surrounding mountains for 600 yards to the flat open tableland about 3,200 feet above sea level.

For the next few days the fresh battalions patrolled vigorously while the bulldozers improved the road behind. On the 8th Lieutenant Gregory[4]

---

[3] Lt R. S. Barrand, VX25125; 2/23 Bn. Commercial traveller; of Albert Park, Vic; b. Colac, Vic, 2 Feb 1914.
[4] Lt J. T. M. Gregory, NX50508; 2/48 Bn. Shop assistant; of Killara, NSW; b. Ashfield, NSW, 14 Jul 1920.

of the 2/48th led a patrol forward to White Rock where they killed 9 Japanese. Next day the White Rock position was occupied by Captain Hill's[5] company.

A company of the 2/24th moved to the high ground north of Jivevaneng where a patrol base was established to find the flanks and estimate the numbers of the Japanese in the northern sector. By last light Captain Mackenzie's company dug in 100 yards from a Japanese position to the north. To the south the 2/23rd Battalion was also patrolling. On the 8th and 9th a patrol under Lieutenant Gilmour[6] watched Japanese activity on the Sattelberg Road; early on the 9th it had an interesting few moments thus described in Gilmour's report:

Approximately 9 Japanese moving east down road halted and prepared their breakfast within 15-20 yards of our patrol positions. Although our patrol was not expecting to see Japanese so soon, they remained unobserved. An Owen gun was accidentally fired into the ground, but the Japanese, after interrupting their conversation for a few moments, carried out no investigation. This party of Japanese remained for approximately 35 minutes; meanwhile other small parties of Japanese moved up and down the road. . . . No picquet was placed by the Japanese while halted and one man moved to within 5 yards of our patrol to gather bamboo for his fire. He was unarmed.

Brigadier Whitehead called a conference at Jivevaneng on 9th November of all his unit and sub-unit commanders. These knew that west from Jivevaneng an enemy post had been located covering the road from the north side on the nearest high ground, and behind that the enemy had a strong patrol base at Steeple Tree Hill (2600 Feature).[7] Whitehead's intention was that the brigade would open the Sattelberg Road west to the Sisi Track junction. The 2/24th Battalion would be on the right along a general line from Jivevaneng to Palanko with the object of covering or overcoming the enemy at the 2200 Feature; the 2/48th in the centre along the Sattelberg Road supported by tanks and sappers; and the 2/23rd Battalion from Kumawa and Sisi on the 2/48th's left.

For the next few days patrols from the 26th Brigade were very active against an alert enemy. On the 12th, for example, a patrol from the 2/48th penetrated as far west as Green Ridge, at the junction of the Sisi Track and the Sattelberg Road, and reported it occupied. On Melbourne Cup Day (the 13th) an American officer demonstrated the firing of the American rocket gun "Bazooka". That day Whitehead learnt that the 2/4th Commando Squadron would be placed under his command to relieve the 2/23rd Battalion for the attack to the west. By 14th November he felt that his preparations were complete.

Meanwhile, patrols from the 24th Brigade were pushing west without contact. To the north the Japanese were found round Bonga and on Pino

---

[5] Capt D. P. Hill, SX10307; 2/48 Bn. Salesman; of Glenelg, SA; b. Adelaide, 1 Dec 1919.

[6] Capt N. B. Gilmour, MC, VX8944; 2/23 Bn. Clerk; of Pascoe Vale, Vic; b. Glen Alvie, Vic, 1 Dec 1918.

[7] The accurate description of operations round the 2600 Feature, and the 2200 Feature mentioned later, was made difficult by the fact that on the map in use at the time of the action in mid-November the former feature was marked "2400" and the latter "2600". These heights were corrected in a second edition of the map and later references to the two features (in the divisional report, for example) give the corrected heights.

Hill, a mile north of North Hill. The men of the 2/43rd Battalion believed that their Papuan comrades could veritably smell out the Japanese, so expert were they at detecting their presence. Between 9th and 11th November five native soldiers dressed as villagers penetrated north of Bonga. From an observation post they observed 340 Japanese, whose arms included 35 machine-guns, moving south to Bonga. Thirty-two armed with rifles were seen moving north to Lakona. The natives reached within 300 yards of the 2/28th's old position but when Japanese sentries saw them and sounded an alarm they hurriedly withdrew. The men of the Papuan Battalion were now patrolling from Bonga and the Wareo Track in the north, through the Palanko and Sattelberg areas, to Mararuo, Tirimoro and Simbang. Native porters and guides attached to the battalions were also doing a vital job. After the fall of Lae one native called Pabu, whom Major Mollard had employed in Lae before the war, became Mollard's personal boy and journeyed wherever the 2/32nd went. On 11th November Pabu led into the 2/32nd about 90 natives from the Bonga area. He and two Angau natives had just returned from a reconnaissance to the Sowi and Masaweng Rivers where they reported there were large numbers of Japanese carrying supplies south, sometimes in handcarts.

On 11th November the new corps commander, General Berryman, set out in a P.T. boat from Buna for Finschhafen. He was accompanied by Brigadier S. H. W. C. Porter, newly appointed to command the 24th Brigade. The new brigade commander was an impressive figure who looked the part of an infantry brigadier and had a way with troops. He had had wide experience as a battalion and brigade commander: command, briefly, of the 2/6th Battalion in Cyrenaica; command of the 2/31st during arduous operations in Syria; of the 30th Brigade which he had vigorously re-trained round Moresby in 1942 and led, in retreat and in advance, in the Papuan operations. Since the disbanding of that brigade in September 1943 he had been chief instructor at the Tactical School. Porter took over the 24th Brigade on 12th November; Simpson returned to the 2/17th Battalion next day, but on the 14th assumed command of the 20th Brigade because Windeyer was ill.

Porter found his brigade rather smarting under the implication that the battle for Scarlet Beach could have been handled better. The men were depressed and felt that the brigade had been slighted. He immediately set about his task of lifting their spirits. Both Simpson and Porter saw some weaknesses in the brigade's administration and communications, and these Porter set out to eradicate. It did not take long for the brigade to recapture its fine spirit; its valour it had never lost.

Final arrangements for the assault on Sattelberg were now discussed by Berryman and Wootten. When Berryman asked for five days' warning in order to coordinate the air plan with the ground attack Wootten stated that his preparations were complete. D-day was therefore fixed as 18th November but was changed on the 14th to 17th November. Berryman agreed to move the third battery of the 2/6th Field Regiment on highest priority to Finschhafen. "M" Heavy Battery and a section of the 2nd

Mountain Battery (75-mm) would also move by the fastest means to Finschhafen.

The final plan was issued by Whitehead at his headquarters on 15th November. It called for action on D-1 day when the 2/48th Battalion would capture Green Ridge, the 2/4th Commando Squadron would occupy Kumawa, and a company of the 2/2nd Machine Gun Battalion would support the rear of the 2/48th from White Rock. On D-day there would be a simultaneous advance by all three battalions. The first intermediate objectives were the dominating 2600 Feature—Steeple Tree Hill—and the junction of the Sattelberg Road with the north-west track from Kumawa. From these positions Whitehead would decide the best route for the final assault after reconnaissance. The 2/48th Battalion would advance west along the Sattelberg Road supported initially by four tanks; the 2/23rd would advance north from Kumawa along both the north-east and north-west tracks and link with the 2/48th on the Sattelberg Road; the 2/24th would advance north-west from Jivevaneng across the Siki, capture the 2200 Feature and exploit west across the saddle and up the spur to Sattelberg.

Along the *20th Division's* supply route the P.T. boats were enjoying good hunting, helped by the reports from the Australian observation posts about nightly barge traffic in the vicinity of Bonga and Gusika. Two Japanese barges were probably sunk off the mouth of the Tewae River on the night of the 7th; four, laden with stores, were sunk moving south off Walingai two nights later; three more heading south laden with stores were destroyed on the following night off Ago. On the night of the 11th-12th two barges were sunk heading north with troops off Cape King William. On the 13th-14th five store-laden barges heading south were sunk at different spots—Hardenberg Point, Cape King William and Reiss Point. Off Kelanoa Point, however, four guns fired at the P.T. boats. Again on the night 15th-16th the P.T. boats were driven off by heavy fire from Cape King William after sinking two barges. On the night before D-day the P.T. boat commanders reported seeing much movement south along the coastal track between Sialum Island and Walingai.

Except for one battery there were now two complete artillery regiments in the area. The 2/12th Regiment less one battery would support the 26th Brigade, the 24th Battery of the 2/12th would support the 24th Brigade, and the 11th and 12th Batteries of the 2/6th Field Regiment would support the 20th and 4th Brigades respectively; if required the 24th and 11th Batteries would join in the support of the 26th Brigade.

At 8.20 on the morning of the 16th two batteries and the company of the 2/2nd Machine Gun Battalion opened up on the near portion of Green Ridge-Near Feature. Under cover of this bombardment Captain Isaksson's[8] company of the 2/48th moved up to the start-line and took over from a patrol. The advance began at 8.30 and five minutes later the bombardment ceased except for one battery which lifted to Far Feature. The attacking company now found what many another attacking com-

---
[8] Lt-Col O. H. Isaksson, MC, SX9461; 2/48 Bn. Salesman; of Adelaide; b. Exeter, SA, 29 Jun 1917.

pany had discovered in similar circumstances: they were unable to keep up to schedule and therefore take advantage of the artillery fire. Despite the fact that an elaborate sand-table model had been closely studied, the ridge seemed so narrow and the bamboos so thick that the men could advance at only a very slow rate and on a narrow front. Both Near and Far Features were not strongly held, however, the former falling at 10 a.m. and the latter at 12.45 p.m. The capture of Far Feature was aided considerably by the machine-gunners who used 26,000 rounds to keep down enemy heads and to silence some troublesome enemy machine-guns.

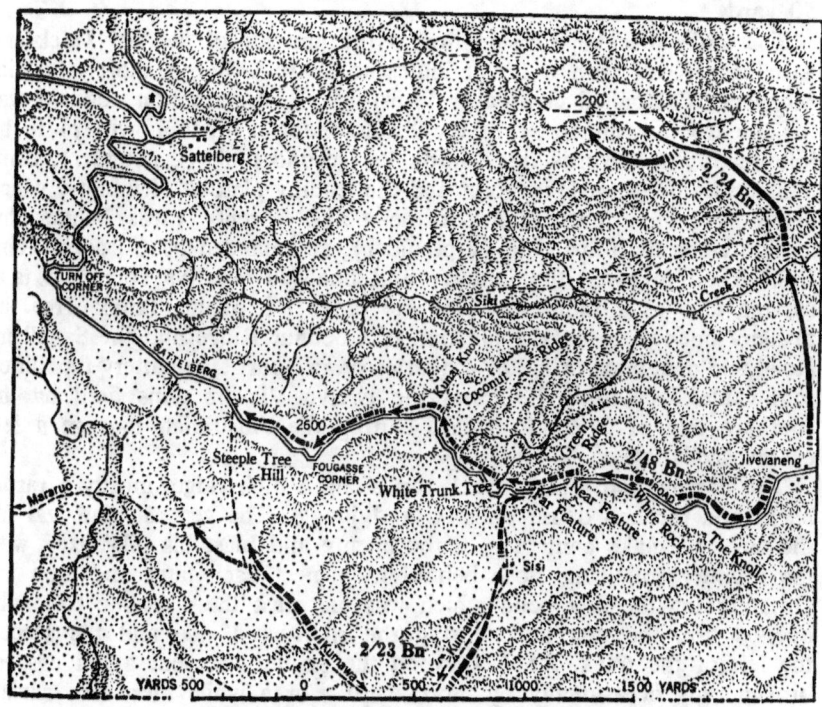

26th Brigade offensive, 17th-21st November

While Captain Brocksopp's[9] company guarded Green Ridge Isaksson's captured White Trunk Tree at the junction of the Sattelberg Road and Sisi Track by 1.40 p.m. For the loss of 5 wounded, 3 of whom died, the 2/48th Battalion had opened the attack auspiciously by killing 18 Japanese on Green Ridge, and capturing 4 machine-guns and a mortar.

That day Whitehead's other units prepared for the morrow. The two leading companies of the 2/24th Battalion were ready for the advance on the 2200 Feature. At Kumawa the 2/4th Commando Squadron relieved the 2/23rd Battalion. The tanks were ready for the second and third phases—the attacks on Coconut Ridge and on Steeple Tree Hill.

[9] Maj A. E. Brocksopp, SX175; 2/48 Bn. Commercial artist; of Burnside, SA; b. Surrey Hills, Vic, 20 Mar 1913.

At first light on D-day the engines of the three tanks of Lieutenant O'Donnell's[1] troop, which were to support the 2/48th, and Major Hordern's headquarters tank began to hum, and from 6.30 a.m. the Matildas began to rumble up to the start-line. Here Captain Morphett's[2] company was ready to lead the advance followed by Captain Hill's. The noise of the tanks moving up was covered partly by an American rocket barrage of 35 fragmentation rocket-propelled bombs, fired from 6.30 a.m. until zero—7 a.m. Several of the rockets were duds, but those which did explode had a very lethal effect, sometimes killing within a radius of 50 yards.[3]

The tanks reached the start-line at the junction of the Sisi Track and Sattelberg Road with a few minutes to spare. After a short talk with Morphett, O'Donnell crossed the start-line. The formation adopted was for the troop commander in the leading tank (3-inch howitzer) to be followed at a 10-yards interval by the second tank (2-pounder), commanded by Sergeant Dudgeon,[4] and the leading platoon of infantry which acted as ground protection for the tanks. Twenty yards behind this section came the third tank (2-pounder), commanded by Corporal Tomlins.[5] Then followed the infantry and finally Hordern's command tank serving also as a radio link. As the tanks left White Trunk Tree the artillery opened up on the junction of Coconut Ridge and the Sattelberg Road and continued firing for a quarter of an hour. One battery then lifted to Steeple Tree until 7.30 and the twelve Vickers guns fired on the southern end of Coconut Ridge. During the Australian barrage a few enemy shells fell on Green Ridge.

The narrow and muddy track ran along a high ridge, mostly a razorback, and through dense bamboo and jungle. The general plan was for the tanks to make contact with the enemy and blast his pill-boxes, with the infantry following close behind to protect each tank and mop up. On rounding the first bend which was just past the start-line the tanks opened fire, the first tank hosing the right-hand side and the second the left of the track. At 7.30 when the artillery ceased, a lull ensued, broken only occasionally by mortar fire. For a while there was silence except for the noise of the tanks. At the same time Captain Cudlipp's company of the 2/23rd found Sisi unoccupied, moved north towards the Sattelberg Road and took over the defence of Green Ridge, thus freeing the 2/48th of this responsibility.

---

[1] Lt J. L. O'Donnell, NX101469. 1 Tk Bn, 1 Armd Regt. Clerk; of Wahroonga, NSW; b. Sydney, 10 Aug 1920.

[2] Maj H. C. Morphett, MC, SX9990; 2/48 Bn. Oil company representative; of Burra, SA; b. Corowa, NSW, 31 Mar 1906.

[3] This rocket projector comprised a frame holding 12 rocket guides and could be fired from a landing craft, a jeep, or from the ground. The bombs weighed 30 pounds and the maximum range was about 1,200 yards. The 9th Division decided that the projector was unsuitable as a close support weapon in the jungle because it was cumbersome, hard to conceal and had so short a range. "Better sighting, greater range and accuracy would permit of its wider useful employment," concluded a divisional report on the projector.

[4] Sgt R. J. Dudgeon, NX114535. 1 Tk Bn, 1 Armd Regt. Cattle breeder; of Camden, NSW; b. Jamberoo, NSW, 30 Nov 1919.

[5] Cpl M. C. Tomlins, NX114518. 1 Tk Bn, 1 Armd Regt. Farmer; of Gerringong, NSW; b. Gerringong, 28 Jan 1919.

Knowing that his southern flank was secure Colonel Ainslie continued the advance. The lull did not last long, for about 50 yards up the track on the right-hand side the first opposition was encountered—a heavy machine-gun post. The first tank was unable to see it because of the upgrade and the dense jungle, but after some of the jungle had been blown away by 3-inch howitzers and 2-pounders, the third tank put the gun out of action. Actually most of the tanks' firing was more or less blind. The infantry platoon commander supporting the tanks would give the order, "Rake with Besa area between [this tree and that]." The attack continued in a series of short bounds with the tanks firing rapidly on both sides of the road at enemy defences, mainly pill-boxes and foxholes all with strong overhead cover and sited in depth along the track. Despite his surprise, and his fear of the steel monsters, the enemy held his ground tenaciously and replied with machine-guns, mortars and grenades until literally blown out by the fire of the tanks. In the excitement of going into action after nearly two years of waiting the tank crews spent their ammunition very liberally and by 8.20 a.m., about half way to Coconut Ridge, had almost run out of ammunition for their Besa guns. The Besas had been firing in bursts of about 50 rounds when bursts of 10 would probably have done as well. Three jeeps were loaded with ammunition at Jivevaneng and sent forward. The tanks backed with great difficulty for about 60 yards to refill and the infantry went forward to protect them. Morphett's company, which had trained with the tanks in the Salankaua Plantation, knew the tank crews and was keeping in close touch with them by using the walkie-talkies of which all the sets in the division had been allotted to the brigade.

During this delay in the centre both the 2/24th and 2/23rd Battalions continued to advance. At 7.45 a.m. Captain Harty's[6] company of the 2/24th with Captain Mackenzie's following set out from their start-line near Siki Creek to assault the 2200 Feature. An hour later the leading platoon, after a stiff climb, cut the track leading east from the summit. The second platoon then set out at 9.20 a.m. to find the enemy's main defences and to test his strength on the summit. Two hours later it reported finding the enemy strongly entrenched and wired in dense bamboo and jungle. South of the Sattelberg Road Major Brown's[7] company of the 2/23rd, advancing along the north-west track from Kumawa towards Steeple Tree, met no opposition until half way to its objective where it found an enemy outpost at the southern foot of the spur leading up to Steeple Tree. So stubborn was the opposition that Colonel Tucker sent a second company from Kumawa to help, and the two began a long and arduous attempt to encircle the enemy.

At 10.20 a.m., with the clouds sitting close on Sattelberg, the tanks and the 2/48th Battalion were ready to continue. "Company with tanks going well and mopping up," signalled the 2/48th to brigade; "12 Japanese

---
[6] Capt E. P. Harty, VX46436; 2/24 Bn. Chartered accountant; of Double Bay, NSW; b. East Melbourne, 6 Apr 1914.

[7] Maj W. F. Brown, VX48589; 2/23 Bn. Grocer's assistant; of Numurkah, Vic; b. Wangaratta, Vic, 9 Jun 1916.

just seen to leave foxholes on side of road and run up track. Were machine-gunned by tanks." The weather was too thick for the bombers, however, and the air strike was cancelled except for a dive-bombing attack at 10.30 on Masangkoo. The advance continued steadily with the tanks eliminating one pocket of resistance after another. At 11.35 the 2/48th reported, "Progress very slow." To those watching and listening behind there would be periods of silence followed by bursts of firing. Just on midday there was a fierce 15 minutes' burst of firing by the tanks. "They're getting some curry with their rice today," commented one observer. The tanks and infantry were now on the forward slopes of Kunai Knoll at the southern end of Coconut Ridge.

Soon afterwards the Besa in the second tank failed with a broken piston. The third tank then moved into second position. The advance continued for about 100 yards to a kunai ridge whence the first objective—Coconut Ridge—could be seen. The tanks engaged likely enemy positions. The infantry then moved forward but found the reverse slopes still occupied. After conferring together Ainslie and Hordern decided that the tanks should advance up the track over Coconut Ridge and attack the enemy from the rear. Unfortunately, as O'Donnell's tank reached the crest and rounded a narrow bend it struck what was at first thought to be a mine or a mortar bomb but later proved to be an unexploded 25-pounder shell. The tank's track was blown off, thus preventing any farther advance by the others as the road was too narrow for passing. Being disabled just round the bend the first tank could not be towed out by the second. As O'Donnell's wireless aerial had been blown away Tomlins moved his tank closer to relay messages. Taking advantage of this impasse the enemy poured in such heavy machine-gun fire that the infantry was unable to advance. One bold enemy party crept up to the two tanks attempting to grenade them. Before the gunners could depress their guns sufficiently to deal with these Japanese, one threw some explosive on to the front of Tomlins' tank, blowing the Besa back into the turret, slightly wounding Tomlins and another member of the crew and putting the Besa and wireless out of action.

Ainslie then decided that he would press forward without the tanks. Morphett sent his reserve platoon, commanded by Lieutenant Gregory, to deal with the Japanese on the reverse slopes of Kunai Knoll. The leading section commander, Corporal Leary,[8] was wounded and had his rifle smashed by enemy fire soon after the start. Despite this he crawled forward alone without weapons to within a few feet of the enemy positions and relayed back valuable information. By 4 p.m. Gregory's men cleared the position, but the enemy was still stubbornly resisting from the northern slopes of Coconut Ridge across the Sattelberg Road.

The reserve company commander, Captain Hill, now sent Lieutenant Norton's[9] platoon round on the right flank to attack the position, but it

---

[8] Cpl R. Leary, MM, WX10241; 2/48 Bn. Labourer; of Kalgoorlie, WA; b. Kalgoorlie, 27 Sep 1918.

[9] Lt F. A. Norton, VX81080; 2/48 Bn. Electric welder; of Carnegie, Vic; b. Wonthaggi, Vic, 4 Jul 1920. Killed in action 17 Nov 1943.

was unable to make any headway in the face of heavy fire and, after Norton was killed, the platoon withdrew. Hordern and Lieutenant Emmott[1] then reconnoitred the area, but informed Ainslie that the rugged nature of the country would prevent the tanks moving off the road on to the northern slopes of Coconut Ridge. As the enemy position was too close to be mortared Ainslie decided that the position should be assaulted by two platoons from Hill's company in the late afternoon.

Supported by fire from Morphett's company and from the leading disabled tank, Lieutenant Buckley's platoon followed by Lieutenant Robinson's[2] charged down the northern slopes of Kunai Knoll. Despite the impetus of the charge Buckley's men were pinned down under heavy fire about 15 yards north of the road and Robinson's farther back. Corporal Radbone's[3] section on the left, however, succeeded in reaching its objective and killed 19 Japanese. Notwithstanding this fine effort, Buckley sent back a runner reporting that the position was too strong for two platoons, and that it was hopeless to continue the attack along the narrow razor-back ridge littered with boughs of trees torn off by the artillery. The platoons were therefore withdrawn and the battalion reorganised for the night with two companies on Kunai Knoll and a third back along the track towards White Trunk Tree, where the fourth company was stationed.

As the 2/24th and 2/23rd Battalions had been unable to advance beyond the positions reached in the morning, both formed perimeters at nightfall—the 2/24th Battalion east of the 2200 Feature and the 2/23rd Battalion half way along the track from Kumawa. It seemed evident that there would be plenty of fierce fighting before Sattelberg could be reached; the Japanese had defended resolutely all day and had not panicked when the tanks suddenly rumbled upon them.

A perimeter was formed around O'Donnell's scarred and disabled tank. He and his crew had been closed inside for about eight hours before being able to get out through the driver's hatch. They took with them the breech-blocks of the 3-inch howitzer, the Besa and their Bren and Owen guns. During the day the tanks had fired 120 rounds of 3-inch howitzer shells, 11,700 rounds of Besa and 234 rounds of 2-pounder ammunition.

Just before last light an enemy gun shelled White Rock from Steeple Tree. The 30 shells fired caused some casualties. In the early days of the Jivevaneng fighting White Rock had been covered with bananas and secondary growth, but now, because it had received such a bombardment from both sides, it was bare grey earth with many doovers[4] built in the reverse slopes. Fortunately the men at the machine-gunners' observation

---

[1] Lt J. G. Emmott, NX123452. 1 Tk Bn, 1 Armd Regt. Farmer; of Bodalla, NSW; b. Moruya, NSW, 20 Mar 1913.

[2] Capt M. Robinson, SX7047; 2/48 Bn. Shipping clerk; of Glenelg, SA; b. Adelaide, 19 Dec 1909.

[3] Sgt G. G. Radbone, SX7139; 2/48 Bn. Gardener; of Bridgewater, SA; b. Burnside, SA, 6 May 1918.

[4] A slang term for a thingumbob, specifically applied in this instance to soldiers' shelters or humpies.

post spotted the enemy gun. Such a bombardment was then directed at this area by the 62nd Battery that the gun did not fire again that day.

At 7.10 a.m. on the 18th a patrol edged forward from the disabled tanks and reported no signs of the enemy on Coconut Ridge. Since progress by the tanks was still barred by the one with the broken track, Morphett decided to send Gregory's platoon into the attack without tanks. At 8.30 the platoon advanced the 200 yards towards where the enemy position had been seen and, as anticipated, found the area abandoned. All efforts were now bent towards getting the Matildas ready. Hordern ordered forward two 2-pounder tanks and one 3-inch howitzer tank to aid the tanks already committed. Two tanks clambered on to Coconut Ridge to help the infantry with the mopping up. Soon after midday the two disabled tanks had been repaired.

In front of the two companies of the 2/23rd on the track from Kumawa to Steeple Tree there had been no withdrawal by the enemy during the night. Tucker sent Lieutenant Gray's[5] company in an encircling movement round the left flank and by 10.55 it reached one of the tracks leading west to Mararuo, and, by thus threatening the enemy's rear, forced a small withdrawal. Major Brown's men then advanced, but progress was slow and tedious as the Japanese continually withdrew to positions slightly higher up the spur, which fell away sharply on either side. At 12.25 p.m., when the leading men of the 2/23rd thought that they were about 400 yards from the Sattelberg Road, Tucker was warned that the 2/48th would resume the advance in 25 minutes.

At 1 p.m. O'Donnell's troop of tanks and Isaksson's company of the 2/48th moved off. Thirty-five minutes later they met the first opposition for the day from an entrenched and camouflaged enemy position on a high feature north of the track. After engineers had cut away part of the steep bank one Matilda succeeded in reaching the top, and, against desperate opposition, cleared the ground immediately ahead. By 2 p.m. the battalion had advanced about 250 yards after striking opposition on both sides of the road. A small feature some 30 yards ahead of the first obstacle, however, could not be taken. Despite the blasting of the tanks which had already knocked out two 37-mm guns, the Australians could not dislodge the Japanese from this feature. At 2.50 p.m. an enemy 75-mm gun began shelling Green Ridge again, and mortally wounded Captain Cudlipp before an intense Australian bombardment caused the Japanese gun to cease fire.

During the fighting enemy tree snipers were active, but towards last light the sun shone behind the trees in which they were concealed. The Australians then had pleasure in picking them off and six were shot down before darkness. The forward troops were withdrawn slightly for the night and the seven tanks leaguered at Coconut Ridge.

Colonel Tucker concluded that the enemy opposing the advance of the 2/23rd were part of the same defensive system that was holding up the

---

[5] Capt H. Gray, VX50364; 2/23 Bn. Theatre operator; of Caulfield, Vic; b. North Shields, England, 25 Apr 1915.

2/48th. He therefore sent Gray's company in a second wide encircling movement, this time to cut the main Sattelberg Road, and at 5.30 p.m., after moving 600 yards to the north-west, Gray reported cutting the main road west of Steeple Tree. Actually he had only reached another better-defined track to Mararuo, but this was not then known. The fog of war descended when his telephone line was cut, and a patrol from Brown's company ran into a force of about 40 Japanese "rallying between the two companies".

To those in command it appeared that if Gray's company of the 2/23rd Battalion had in fact cut the Sattelberg Road, there would be a distinct possibility of squeezing out the Japanese at Steeple Tree. Indeed, in the two hours before midnight on 18th November the signal lines were humming with orders for the 19th. In Whitehead's original operation order the task of the 2/24th Battalion was to hold a firm base covering the route to be used for the advance of two companies to secure contour 2200. After studying the latest sitreps at night on the 18th, General Wootten, soon after 10 p.m., ordered Whitehead to "drive to Sattelberg via 2200". Thus, the attack on Sattelberg would now be double-pronged. Just before midnight Mackay told Tucker of the "change in plot" and warned him that his reserve companies at Kumawa and Green Ridge might be needed on the 19th to "exploit success of the 2/24th Battalion and possibly pass through to Sattelberg".

During the night 18th-19th November, the 2/48th and the Japanese, about 30 yards apart, engaged in grenade and small arms duels. By 8 a.m. on the 19th new crews were in the forward tanks and the advance recommenced with two tanks on the high ground just north of the main road and a third moving along the road. Isaksson's company was again leading. Forty minutes later the small knoll ahead was cleared without much opposition. Leaving the dead Japanese where they lay, the tanks rumbled on with the green-clad infantrymen following. The speed with which the Japanese were organising anti-tank measures was impressive. About 100 yards from the start-line the advance was halted by an anti-tank ditch six feet wide and four feet deep. With the aid of Major Moodie's[6] engineers of the 2/13th Field Company the tanks were soon able to bypass the ditch, beyond which was a 37-mm gun knocked out by the Australian artillery. Beside the derelict gun lay three dead Japanese. A little farther along the road the tanks overran an 81-mm mortar position, and farther still they knocked out a Woodpecker and two light machine-guns. A second anti-tank ditch was encountered another 150 yards along the road soon after 10 a.m. Here there was some delay while the sappers filled and corduroyed the ditch. With progress so slow Wootten now became a little restive. At 11.10 a.m. Whitehead passed on to Ainslie that Wootten considered that "tanks might be holding battalion up and suggests that if this is so they be taken away".

---

[6] Maj R. O. K. T. Moodie, QX6522. 2/13 Fd Coy (OC 1942-44); SORE 2 VIII British Corps 1944-45; OC 2/11 Fd Coy 1945. Mining engineer; of Sydney; b. Sydney, 1 Sep 1916.

Lieutenant Farquhar's[7] platoon was sent past the tanks and met an enemy position solidly dug in on the slope of a large feature at the bend in the Sattelberg Road just before Steeple Tree. Heavy fire pinned down Farquhar's men who were glad to see the tanks coming forward again. No sooner had they joined up, however, than another anti-tank ditch was found astride the road and the infantry again moved forward alone, only to be pinned down once more. While patrols from the two leading companies tried to move around the left and right flanks, the engineers studied the ditch and its immediate environment. Ahead of the ditch were some suspicious-looking mounds which were soon found to contain mines. Prepared charges with strings attached for pulling them under the tanks were found in dug-outs on both sides of the road and three mines were deloused.[8]

Soon after midday divisional headquarters sent a few questions to Whitehead: When was contact with the enemy lost by the 2/48th Battalion? Has the 2/48th moved forward since then and if so how far? If they have not pushed on, why? Are the infantry waiting for the tanks? Whitehead's reply was short and laconic. "Contact was never lost," he replied to the first question; "Yes, 300 yards," to the second; and "No" to the fourth. When the questions reached Ainslie in the thick of battle, his remarks to Whitehead were in the same vein: "Cost would have been very large if tanks were not there. Division do not understand nature of terrain." One other battalion commander considered that in these operations the general staff officers of the division should have seen the ground more often despite the long time it took to get there and back.

Every attempt made by Isaksson's and Brocksopp's companies to outflank the enemy failed because of the enemy's skilful placing of machine-guns on the flanks. By 1 p.m. the hard work of the 2/13th Field Company enabled two tanks to cross the ditch, move forward, and "clean up" another 37-mm gun. One of the tanks was hit by this gun but the damage was soon repaired. In their advance, however, the two tanks broke away the side of the road and were in danger of slipping down the steep left-hand side of the hill. Quickly using hand tools the sappers prevented such a disaster.[9] There was now some delay while jeeps replenished the 2/48th's ammunition and the engineers cut another track higher up the hillside for the tanks to outflank the objective. As the afternoon went on, however, it became apparent that the tanks would not be able to reach the top

---

[7] Maj M. F. Farquhar, SX6786; 2/48 Bn. Clerk; of Broken Hill, NSW; b. Broken Hill, 7 Jul 1918.

[8] At the beginning of the Sattelberg offensive New Guinea Force requested GHQ to withhold news of the use of the tanks as it was considered that the enemy would use anti-tank equipment against them. On 19th November, however, the NGF diarist commented: "It had been found that the news of the arrival of tanks at Finschhafen had been announced approximately fourteen days previous to their operational use." Morshead and Wootten were incensed when they learnt that news that the American Navy had landed tanks at Finschhafen had been proudly broadcast in the United States and rebroadcast in Australia. Yet General Adachi stated after the war that his first inkling of the use of tanks against the *20th Division* was when they suddenly appeared on 17th November. If this was indeed so, it was another example of the ineffectiveness of the Japanese Intelligence work.

[9] If the Australian sappers had had the task of stopping the tanks they would have blown the road at the narrow bends, thus leaving a cliff on one side and a precipice on the other.

of the feature. Lieutenant Spry[1] of the 2/13th Field Company was now instructed to prepare two fougasses. Filling two 4-gallon drums with petrol and dieseline Spry hoped that the fougasse would burn for about five minutes.

At 5.45 p.m. Spry fired electrically the first fougasse used in New Guinea. The drums burst and a large pall of smoke and flame shot forward about 20 feet high over the enemy position 30 yards away. Unfortunately the flame lasted but an instant, so that by the time the infantry arrived at the spot whence they had withdrawn the smoke had disappeared.

The enemy was obviously shaken, however, and this enabled Lieutenant Barry's[2] platoon to do the only practical thing in the circumstances—charge up the hill. Many times in this campaign it had been proved that courage and determination could do what armour and bombardment had failed to do. So it was now. According to the diarist of the 2/48th "the men advanced across the ground shoulder to shoulder, with Bren and Owen guns blazing from the hip and the riflemen hurling grenades". "We ran in with a Ho, Ho, Ho" said one participant later. Lieutenant McKinnon's[3] platoon moved forward on the right flank. Stunned by the suddenness of the fougasse and the power of Barry's attack the enemy wavered. The Australians reached the top and in hand-to-hand fighting drove the enemy out. During this brave and successful advance all available men not in the actual fight, including the ubiquitous sappers, were busy filling Bren and Owen magazines and priming grenades. Just on last light the Japanese counter-attacked, but a position captured with such spirit was not likely to be yielded easily. Nevertheless, the fire from a tank as well as from engineers and headquarters was needed to drive the counter-attack back down the steep slope of Fougasse Corner up which it had surged. During the day the 2/48th suffered 20 casualties, including 4 killed, and killed 46 Japanese as well as capturing 7 machine-guns and 5 mortars.

Just to the south the 2/23rd was also meeting vigorous opposition. Gray's company spent an uncomfortable, isolated night on the 18th-19th with the enemy on three sides. Gray still believed he was on the main road, but because he had few stores and was out of communication, he decided to withdraw, and after a rugged four-hours journey, rejoined the supporting company.

To the north also little progress had been made by the 2/24th Battalion on the 19th. After artillery bombardment Lieutenant Caple's[4] platoon was able, unopposed, to occupy a knoll near the summit of the 2200 Feature. Another platoon then began an encircling movement to the west but withdrew after heavy enemy fire and bamboo—rendered an im-

---

[1] Capt A. F. Spry, QX983. 9 Div Engrs; 2/13 Fd Coy. Master printer; of Eagle Junction, Qld; b. Brisbane, 14 Dec 1905.

[2] Lt J. H. Barry, MC, VX41687; 2/48 Bn. Stock and station manager; of Kyneton, Vic; b. Kyneton, 28 May 1915.

[3] Lt N. K. McKinnon, SX6740. 2/43 and 2/48 Bns; Angau. Public servant; of Adelaide; b. Mount Gambier, SA, 28 Nov 1919.

[4] Lt J. H. Caple, VX33860; 2/24 Bn. Farmer; of Warracknabeal, Vic; b. Warracknabeal, 19 Dec 1918.

penetrable tangled mass by the artillery—prevented any progress. Skirmishing continued until 2.30 p.m. when the remainder of the company joined Caple's platoon on the knoll. When the battalion's own 2-inch mortars dropped short on the knoll the battalion lost one man killed and 10 wounded, to add to an identical number of other casualties suffered during the day.

Resting from its labours the 20th Brigade played no part in the Sattelberg campaign except for routine patrolling and for one patrol in particular. On 16th November Colonel Grace informed Major Newcomb of the 2/15th that "in conjunction with the opening of the attack towards Sattelberg . . . you are to command a diversionary force" in order to "broaden the apparent front of the attack on Sattelberg by simulating a new threat towards Wareo". Newcomb was not, however, to move beyond Garabow or become embroiled in a serious fight. He set out early on the 17th and camped in the kunai near the Song. On the 18th the company reached Garabow which had been accurately bombed, although there were no signs of recent occupation. Next day, while the 26th Brigade was inching forward against dogged resistance in the south, Lieutenant Roberts[5] led a patrol to the 1800 Feature north-west of Garabow, where he saw and heard Japanese.

From the detailed reports of the 2/43rd's observation post it seemed clear to Brigadier Porter that the enemy was sending out large parties to the coast, presumably to carry in supplies. If a strong position could be seized astride the track, the enemy's main supply line could be cut and his grip loosened on Sattelberg and Wareo. On 15th November Porter was called to divisional headquarters by Wootten to discuss future operations.

> General Wootten indicated that we were to advance from North Hill to the Lakes as a first stage; and suggested that we should take a direct route (wrote Porter later). Subsequently, we were to advance to Wareo. I had been studying the terrain astride the Bonga-Wareo track, using air photos and stereoscope. I was keen to seize the feature which was subsequently named Pabu, and to clear an L of C between it and our present positions before venturing through the defile at the Lakes. The terrain which lay along a direct line from the mouth of the Song to the Lakes was very rough, and not really suitable for an L of C. I favoured the capture of Pino, and an extension of our L of C through North Hill. This appealed to me for tactical as well as engineering reasons.
>
> At first the General was inclined to favour bypassing all features north of North Hill, and making straight for the Lakes. He compromised, however, and agreed with my plan for seizing Pabu before pressing westward.
>
> I was aware that the enemy would react violently to our occupation of Pabu; and plans were made to ring the area with artillery defensive fire tasks.

On the 16th Porter, accompanied by his brigade major, White,[6] and Major Mollard (administering command of the 2/32nd), reconnoitred his northern area from North Hill. It was obvious that the 24th Brigade's task when the time came would be against the Wareo-Gusika ridge. Porter

---

[5] Lt D. W. Roberts, QX20740; 2/15 Bn. Advertising copywriter; of Ashgrove, Qld; b. St George, Qld, 11 Oct 1913.

[6] Maj P. F. B. White, VX19444. HQ 9 Div; BM 24 Bde 1943-44. Grazier; of Beaufort, Vic; b. Melbourne, 18 Feb 1914. (Younger son of General Sir Brudenell White.)

and his staff had already noted from aerial photographs a dominating feature on this ridge near the observation post of the 2/43rd Battalion and the Papuan Battalion. "What shall we call it?" said the brigadier to his companions. Several names were suggested and all were turned down. "What's your name?" said the brigadier then to Mollard's personal boy. "Pabu," he replied, and so Porter named the feature Pabu Hill—usually shortened to Pabu.

In wartime remote features, nameless in peacetime, sometimes had names bestowed upon them by the troops who fought there. Often unknown beforehand and unregarded afterwards, these distant spots, for a fierce moment of time, were the scenes of some of the nation's grandest military exploits. Porter gazed at the aerial photographs of the Gusika-Wareo ridge. Along the track were large kunai patches and these, outlined against the jungle on all sides, looked something like the gangling horse created by Walt Disney. Hence the kunai area, where Porter rightly deduced there would be much fighting, became known as Horace the Horse.

On 18th November Porter was warned that, in addition to holding North Hill, Scarlet Beach and the high ground west of Katika, his brigade would capture with one battalion the high ground at Pabu and control all tracks in the area as far west as the Lakes. The newly-arrived 2/7th Field Company would construct a jeep track to follow the battalion (the 2/32nd was chosen). Until the completion of the track, 150 native carriers were allotted for maintenance. The 2/32nd Battalion (less a company) set out for Pabu on the afternoon of the 19th. As the men were carrying very heavy loads of up to 80 pounds each, Mollard had decided to stage for the night at a creek crossing about a mile from Pabu.

Early on the morning of 20th November reconnaissance patrols from the 2/48th were probing the track ahead of Fougasse Corner. By 9 a.m., when Captain Hill's company was ready to resume the advance, a patrol had heard the Japanese digging about 140 yards ahead. "Country opens out here," signalled battalion to brigade, "so tanks should have a good time later." "Thank God it's keeping dry," said one soldier, "if it rains it'll stop the tanks." Unfortunately Hill's advance had to begin without the tanks as the two leading Matildas half slipped off the narrow road cut into the cliff at Fougasse Corner. The sappers of the 2/13th Field Company now had the task of digging out the tanks and building up the road at the corner, a task which was not finished until 5.30 p.m. Under the track of one of these tanks Sergeant Mellor[7] disarmed a charge which fortunately had not exploded when the tank slipped. Typical of the spirit of the 2/13th Field Company was Sapper Daniell[8] who had been wounded when acting as a runner on the previous day but who had requested to stay on the job. On the 20th he was killed in action.

---

[7] S-Sgt J. Mellor, QX3004; 2/13 Fd Coy. Plumber; of Hawthorne, Qld; b. Halifax, England, 30 Mar 1908. Died 18 May 1947.
[8] Spr R. E. Daniell, QX579. 2/9 Bn, 2/13 Fd Coy. Labourer; of Yeronga, Qld; b. Greenslopes, Qld, 21 Sep 1916. Killed in action 20 Nov 1943.

Hill's men, leaving the tanks, advanced through very difficult country. The diarist of the 2/48th Battalion wrote that

> some idea of the difficult nature of the country can be gained from the fact that it had taken B Company one hour fifty minutes to traverse 250 yards. Except for the narrow track the area was a mass of thick bamboo, impossible to penetrate except by crawling on hands and knees.

By 9.30 a.m. other tanks managed to bypass the stranded two and caught up with Hill's men. To the south the two companies of the 2/23rd were still trying to drive out the enemy from the southern approaches to Steeple Tree Hill. Colonel Tucker was now mainly concerned with establishing just where his two forward companies were, and he arranged for smoke signals. A patrol from the 2/23rd moved east and then north to join the 2/48th.

"Go ahead as fast as possible," Whitehead ordered Ainslie just on 10 a.m. Fifty minutes later Hill's men skirmished with the first enemy positions. Here the ground was slightly clearer, and impatient higher formations were informed that "contact drill" was being applied. The enemy held very strong positions right up to the 2,600-foot Steeple Tree Hill. His system of defence was to site positions at every possible line of approach to the almost impenetrable bamboo but not to fire until the forward troops were only a few yards away. Although the enemy was not holding any one position in great strength it would have required a major operation for the infantry to drive him out without the aid of the tanks.

"Pushing ahead very slowly. Gaining a little ground," reported the 2/48th at 3 p.m. Half an hour later its report stated: "Getting along up ridge, tanks on ridge. Good progress." So the slugging battle proceeded, usually with one platoon supporting the attacking tanks and another going round the flank. The enemy then invariably withdrew unless he was overrun first. The progress was still not rapid because when the tanks moved off the road into the thick bamboo they were blind and had to be guided every yard of the way.

At 4.40 p.m. the battalion reported: "Now almost at the top of Steeple Tree. Making rather slow progress. Very heavy going. They are having to cut their way all the time, but are still going." It was not until 6.35 p.m. that the 2/48th was able to report the capture of Steeple Tree. Once again the battalion dug in in semi-darkness. Ainslie was informed that he was responsible for the protection of Hordern's tanks, then outside the perimeter.

For most of the day the 2/23rd had been awaiting the result of the patrol sent to make contact with the 2/48th. By 2.25 p.m. Tucker reported that the patrol had met Morphett's company of the 2/48th. At 4 p.m. a mortar bombardment preceded an attack by Brown's men up the slope towards Steeple Hill from the south. The Japanese defended stubbornly but were gradually forced back. An hour later Tucker reported that Brown's company was approximately 300 yards away from the 2/48th, but the 2/23rd could not dislodge the small party of Japanese between it and the 2/48th before night. On the 20th the 2/48th lost 2 killed and 15 wounded.

The 2/24th Battalion was unable to make any progress on the 20th. This was a disappointment for it had seemed at one stage that an attack on Sattelberg through the 2200 Feature would be more profitable than along the road itself. Strong Japanese defences, thick bamboo and precipitous slopes were largely responsible for this lack of progress. In an attempt to force the pace Wootten decided to commit another troop of tanks to assist the 2/24th, but it would be some time before the Matildas could climb the 2200 Feature.

By first light on the 21st patrols from the 2/48th and 2/23rd were probing forward. On a small knoll ahead of Steeple Tree was a small Japanese party which could not be mortared because of the nearness of the 2/23rd. A fighting patrol from the 2/48th was about to move out to deal with this position, when a number of "Ho, Ho's" were heard and the leading sections of the 2/23rd appeared south of the road. Guided by the patrol which made contact with the 2/48th Battalion on the 20th, Brown's men had advanced about 900 yards without opposition.

Led by Captain Isaksson's company the 2/48th Battalion then continued the advance while the 2/23rd prepared to send patrols west to investigate the tracks towards Mararuo in the hope of bypassing the next enemy positions on the Sattelberg Road. Brown's company met no opposition in this task and was able to advance 1,500 yards. Similarly the 2/48th Battalion met little opposition.

> At first fully completed defensive positions were found, that is, dug positions camouflaged and with head cover (wrote the battalion diarist); then positions with head cover cut but not placed in position; then positions dug with no head cover; then positions only partly dug. As, however, the whole of the ridge except the track was covered with dense bamboo, all these positions had to be investigated and it was not until 1300 hours that contact was made approximately 700 yards from the [2600] Feature. The Japanese, however, on this occasion showed no inclination to stand and fight as on previous days.

This party of about 15 Japanese fled leaving their equipment soon after the leading platoon attacked. Near by a hospital area was discovered. Large numbers of wounded had apparently passed through recently and there were large multiple graves.

After the constant tension of the past five days when the enemy had fought hard for every tactical feature on the road, it was a relief for the 2/48th to find no opposition ahead. It seemed that Whitehead's assumption that Steeple Tree Hill was the main Japanese defensive position before Sattelberg was correct. Now that this line was broken Ainslie sent Brocksopp's company through Isaksson's in single file straight up the road without making any attempt to clear the ground on either side. This bold policy enabled the battalion to advance rapidly, leaving the tanks behind.

Brocksopp's company had almost reached the first hairpin bend at 4.35 p.m. when enemy machine-guns opened up at point-blank range. Mortar and tank support was immediately requested and three tanks lumbered up and pounded the enemy positions. At 7.20 p.m. Lieutenant Lewin's platoon assaulted the position and captured it. For the fifth successive night the 2/48th then reorganised in darkness, but the practical planning of the battalion staff, led by Major Batten[9] the second-in-command, ensured that water, ammunition and rations were rapidly carried forward. With contact established between the 2/48th and 2/23rd Battalions Tucker moved his headquarters and reserve company up the Sisi Track to the road and thence along the road to Steeple Tree.

Again on the 21st there was little progress in the difficult and frustrating area confronting the 2/24th Battalion. The Japanese remained in position despite an arduous left flanking move by Captain Bieri's[1] company. At 9.20 a.m. Colonel Gillespie reported to brigade, "Party in contact, some firing but he is very hard to get at." This enemy opposition was a patrol and was brushed aside by Bieri's men who continued their laborious trek until, by the late afternoon, they were almost on the saddle connecting the 2200 Feature with Sattelberg.

Meanwhile, what of the 2/32nd Battalion which had reached the creek south of Pabu on the night of the 19th? "We were destined to be unbelievably fortunate," wrote Mollard later, "as we not only avoided all Japanese forces on the approach march, but after a short artillery concentration, were able to take possession of Pabu Hill with no casualties to ourselves."

Part of the battalion's success in advancing so far without detection or arousing the enemy's suspicion had been due to two natives whose remarkable eyesight helped the Australian scouts to move with certainty and reasonable speed. Soon after 2 p.m. on the 20th the battalion had advanced on the heels of an artillery bombardment, directed by Captain Mollison,[2] and without opposition the two forward companies occupied Pabu. An almost identical feature 300 yards away turned out to be heavily guarded. In its advance to Pabu the 2/32nd had passed under the very noses of the Japanese there.

Captain Walker's company was now on the northern and eastern sides of Pabu, Captain Davidson's on the west and Captain Davies' on the south. Mollard also had a section of 3-inch mortars and a section of Vickers guns on the feature. The battalion set fire to the surrounding kunai with tracer fire because it might afford cover to the enemy and large areas were still burning fiercely when the native carrier party arrived with water, ammunition and rations. The smoke screened the carriers and subsequently the defenders had a good view over the ground leading to their defences. Already it was evident to Mollard that water would be a main problem as there was no water on Pabu. Each man had started out with only a water-bottle full, plus a two-gallon tin for every seven men as a reserve. The men were exhausted and dehydrated after their hard day

---

[9] Maj R. L. Batten, SX8894; 2/48 Bn. Department manager; of Prospect, SA; b. Prospect, 5 Jun 1904. Died of wounds 23 Nov 1943.

[1] Maj K. J. T. Bieri, VX14596; 2/24 Bn. Clerk; of Brighton, Vic; b. Toorak, Vic, 27 Feb 1917.

[2] Capt C. D. Mollison, VX912; 2/12 Fd Regt. Clerk; of South Yarra, Vic; b. Melbourne, 22 Nov 1904. Killed in aircraft accident 19 Dec 1943.

and the doctor recommended that some of the precious supply be used. Just before dusk the Vickers guns accounted for 12 Japanese walking down the track towards the coast. As night fell and the grass fire burnt itself out the battalion was left in occupation of a "jungle island surrounded by open spaces somewhat like the old familiar desert".

Next morning two patrols were sent out from Davies' company. Lieutenant Bell's[3] platoon patrolled towards Exchange and observed considerable enemy movement there. More important, however, they found good water in a creek and the battalion replenished its supply. Lieutenant Keley's[4] platoon to the west, keeping mainly to the jungle on the right side of the track, found large numbers of Japanese about 500 yards west, and inflicted three casualties before withdrawing.

On the 22nd Davies' company, temporarily under the command of Lieutenant Keley as Davies was sick, was sent by Mollard to investigate the prominent feature overlooking Pabu from the west and to harass any enemy there.

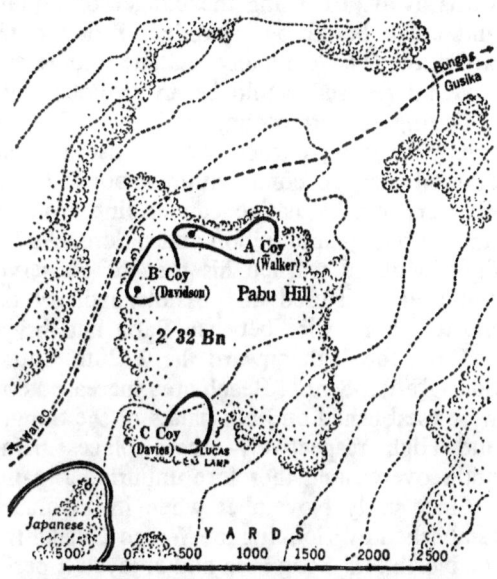

The 2/32nd Battalion on Pabu, 20th November

The men (about 60) moved off at 8.30 a.m. led by two native guides. They marched south into the jungle and from there worked their tedious way over rugged spurs intersected by deep ravines. About noon they came upon a well-defined track running north and south. As the guides seemed to sense Japanese in the area Keley paused and presently "three sons of Nippon armed with rifles sauntered down the track from the north and were unceremoniously dispatched to their forefathers". Keley pushed on and at 4 p.m. emerged from the jungle into an extensive kunai patch—Horace's Hoof. Fifteen minutes later the company moved into the foreleg and with the main east-west track only 200 yards distant "it seemed guineas to gooseberries (said the company's report) that the game would soon be on for us".

About 5.30 p.m. two Japanese signallers were seen on the main track running out wire towards Wareo. They were allowed to pass, as Keley scented bigger game. Ten minutes later about a company of Japanese

---
[3] Lt C. F. Bell, TX5989; 2/43 Bn. Clerk; of Burnie, Tas; b. Sandringham, Vic, 20 Aug 1920. Bell was attached to the 2/32nd Battalion at this time.
[4] Capt M. J. Keley, MC, WX9926; 2/32 Bn. Farm hand; of Katanning, WA; b. Port Germein, SA, 12 Jan 1914.

appeared. Just as the Australians were about to open fire the Japanese saw them and dived for cover into a tongue of jungle on Keley's left whence they returned the fire. Keley lost no time in calling for mortar support and very soon bombs were landing among the Japanese. A Japanese mortar, replying from the Wareo area, also landed its bombs among the Japanese.

It was now last light and the Japanese were digging in about 100 yards away. Realising the danger of remaining in this exposed position, and encumbered by wounded, Keley obtained Mollard's permission to withdraw. The company snatched some fitful rest before setting out on what all realised would be an arduous and testing withdrawal.

During the afternoon, while Keley's patrol was on the move, several enemy carrying parties tried to use the main track past Pabu. Mollard allowed them to come within about 250 yards before opening fire; about 40 were hit. A native carrier line from the south also arrived at this time bringing ammunition and rations. As he anticipated a long and savage fight, Mollard warned his men to conserve their ammunition. That day Mollison registered all possible artillery targets in the area. At 9 p.m. the telephone wire between Pabu and brigade was cut.

From the 19th onward the 2/28th Battalion's patrol activity from the Song-Katika-Scarlet Beach area increased considerably and standing patrols were established on both banks of the Song, at Stinker, Pong, Smell, Whiff and High respectively—these places being so named because of the undiscovered and therefore unburied Japanese dead.

Since early November when its invaluable observation post had been established overlooking the Wareo-Gusika track, the 2/43rd Battalion from the North Hill-Song area had enjoyed a period of relative calm and routine patrolling against little opposition, but its activity also increased after 19th November when a patrol heard Japanese calling out to one another near Bonga and soon after saw 30 of them on the main track. Next day Lieutenant Wright[5] led a larger patrol north along the coastal track. About half a mile south of Bonga the Papuan scouts with the South Australians were fired on. Whistles and noises of Japanese running and calling out were heard on all sides as the patrol withdrew. After Wright had gone some distance south to report to Colonel Joshua on the telephone, a Papuan scout pointed out about 100 Japanese moving south. While on the phone Wright saw his men dive for cover and immediately rushed back to take charge. The patrol then withdrew rapidly into dead ground on the south side of Pino Hill. On the 21st the Japanese were even more aggressive on the 2/43rd's front. Three of Joshua's companies were situated from North Hill to the Song; the fourth—Captain Gordon's—was guarding the coastal track approximately level with the most southern of the other three companies. In the late afternoon there were several clashes in Gordon's area.

---

[5] Lt H. J. Wright, VX42063; 2/43 Bn. Radio mechanic; of Essendon, Vic; b. Essendon, 21 Oct 1921.

On the evening of 21st November Wootten surveyed the situation with mixed feelings. On his main battle front, along the Sattelberg Road, the preliminary line of Japanese resistance had been broken at Steeple Tree, and Whitehead was issuing his orders for the next phase—Sattelberg itself. To the north the sudden thrust of the 2/32nd Battalion to Pabu looked like being even more of a master stroke than when it had been originally conceived primarily to disrupt the enemy's main supply route to Wareo and Sattelberg. The Japanese had not yet presented the Australians with their operation order, but it was clear from evidence gained in the past two days that General Katagiri was about to launch another counter-attack.

CHAPTER 22

TORPY SITS ON SAT.

WHEN it came, the Japanese counter-attack on 22nd November was no surprise to the Australians. It will be recalled that on 3rd November General Katagiri had issued orders for the *80th Regiment* to concentrate in the Sattelberg area and the *79th Regiment* in the Nongora area with *20th Division Headquarters*. General Wootten knew the general dispositions of these units and also that the *II/238th Battalion* (of the *41st Division*) had recently arrived in the Gusika area. The *80th Regiment*, withstanding the assault of the 26th Brigade, was incapable of launching a counter-attack. The *79th Regiment*, however, was in a different situation and the battalion from the *238th Regiment* was relatively fresh. The Australians estimated, fairly correctly, that there were about 6,200 Japanese front-line soldiers in the area: 2,400 from *79th Regiment*, 2,000 from *80th Regiment*, 800 from *II* and *III Battalions*, *26th Artillery Regiment*, 1,000 from the *238th Regiment*.

Documents captured by the 2/32nd Battalion soon confirmed Wootten's deduction that attacks could be expected from the north, north-west and west. The Japanese encountered along the coast by patrols on the preceding days were the vanguard of the *II/238th Battalion* preparing to attack south "to annihilate the enemy north of the Song River". A second and heavier attack by the main portion of the *79th Regiment* was being launched over difficult country from the north-west. The third and smallest prong of the enemy attack, also consisting of elements of the *79th Regiment*, crossed the Song near Stinker and was preparing to attack Scarlet Beach, once again from the west. The counter-attack would thus again fall on the 24th Brigade.

At Pabu small parties of Japanese continued to use the main track on the 22nd and were killed by the machine-gunners. Towards dusk, Japanese mortars and a 75-mm gun from Pino Hill began to shell Pabu, and in a few minutes 19 casualties were sustained by "A" Company whose commander, Captain Walker, was mortally wounded; while dressing his wounds, two stretcher bearers—Corporal Ridley[1] and Private Langford[2]—were killed. Two others, including a platoon commander, Lieutenant Lewis,[3] were badly wounded and died later. As fast as possible the wounded were carried back to Major Dorney's[4] medical post, but when it became too dark to move the last three men Captain Kaye,[5] the battalion

---

[1] Cpl V. R. Ridley, WX17364; 2/32 Bn. Labourer; of Cue, WA; b. Northampton, WA, 11 Oct 1907. Killed in action 22 Nov 1943.

[2] Pte T. Langford, MM, WX12098; 2/32 Bn. Labourer; of Gosnells, WA; b. England, 9 Dec 1915. Killed in action 22 Nov 1943.

[3] Lt R. R. Lewis, WX13115; 2/32 Bn. Fibrolite moulder; of Victoria Park, WA; b. Perth, 19 Feb 1917. Died of wounds 24 Nov 1943.

[4] Lt-Col K. J. J. Dorney, DSO, VX327. 2/2 Fd Amb; RMO 2/2 MG Bn; CO 2/3 Fd Amb 1944-45. Medical practitioner; of Beaumaris, Vic; b. Ascot Vale, Vic, 9 Jan 1912.

[5] Maj P. Kaye, VX59291. 2/8 Fd Amb; RMO 2/32 Bn; DADMS First Army 1944-45. Medical practitioner; of Kew, Vic; b. Melbourne, 4 Jun 1915.

medical officer, came down the rough and slippery track and did what he could in pitch blackness to alleviate the suffering of the wounded, crawling round with a morphia syringe guided only by the sounds of the wounded.

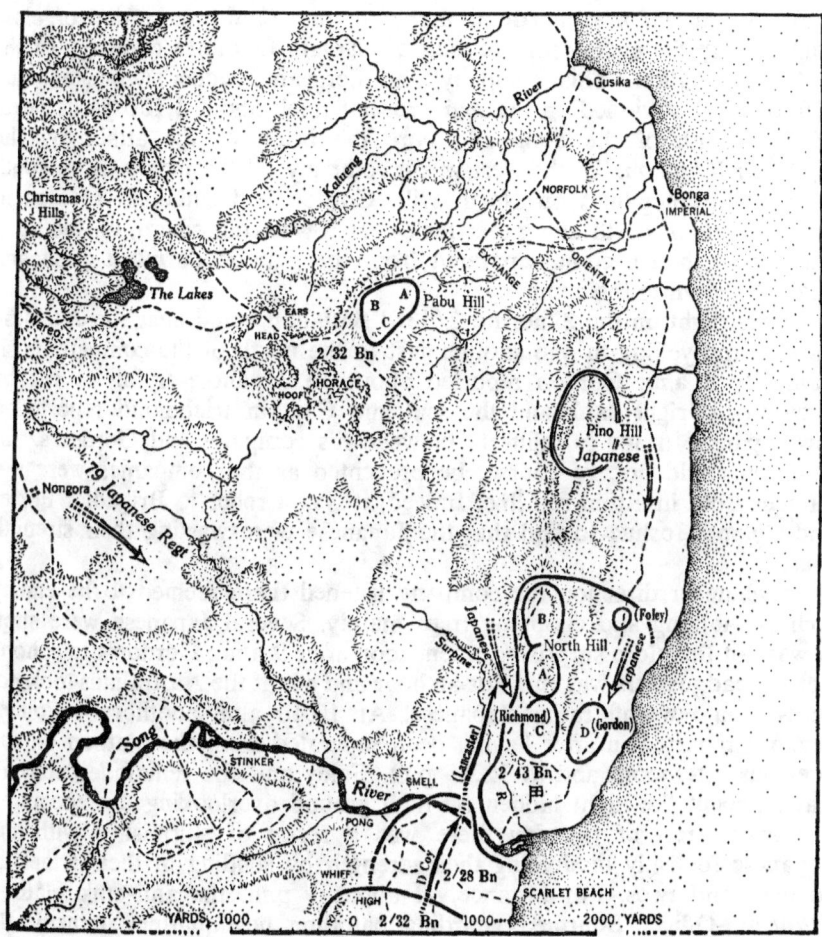

The Japanese counter-attack on the 24th Brigade, 22nd-23rd November

"We were now an Australian island in a Japanese sea," wrote one participant later.[6]

The presence of the 2/32nd Battalion on Pabu was a piercing thorn in the side of the enemy counter-attack. The continuous toll of casualties inflicted on his carrying parties, the damage done by the artillery, and the enemy's surprise at finding Keley's company so far west must undoubtedly have disconcerted him and upset his time-table. Mollard's tele-

---

[6] Pte J. Ritchie, 2/32nd Battalion, "Epic Siege of Pabu Was Ten Days of Hell", in *Red Platypus —A Record of the Achievements of the 24th Australian Infantry Brigade 1940-45*, p. 69.

phone line had been cut, repaired and cut again several times. The repair team which went out on the 22nd to find the break was astounded to find what looked like a Japanese battalion staging in the exact area where the 2/32nd Battalion had been on the 17th.

In the coastal area north of the Song the 22nd was a day of close contact with the enemy for the men of Captain Gordon's company of the 2/43rd Battalion. This company and Sergeant Pedder's[7] machine-gun platoon were stationed on the main coastal track about 1,100 yards north of the mouth of the Song and bore the brunt of the attack by the *II/238th Battalion*. To the west was a company on the jungle fringe south of the two companies on North Hill. Gordon had stationed Lieutenant Foley's platoon north along the track near a waterfall where, on the 21st, one section had become separated from the platoon during a clash and had withdrawn to the company.

At first light on the 22nd the 2/43rd Battalion could hear the Japanese moving and yelling to one another just to the north of the company positions. By 8 a.m. Gordon reported about 15 Japanese trying to get by between his right flank and the sea, and Captain Richmond reported a few Japanese trying to infiltrate between his company and Gordon's. Infiltration could not, of course, be prevented as the companies were not stretched out in a thin red line. Indeed, it was a relief to Brigadier Porter and Colonel Joshua to find that the Japanese were wasting their strength thus.

In whatever direction the company listened there seemed to be enemy sounds—talking and chopping trees mainly. Several Japanese were shot. It was not therefore surprising when, soon after 9 a.m., Gordon's telephone line to headquarters was cut. For an hour and a half the Australians took pot shots at a few infiltrating Japanese. At 10.40 a.m. another of Foley's sections reported in after having been separated from the platoon on the previous afternoon; and at 12.15 p.m. Foley and the remainder arrived, having spent the night hidden on high ground overlooking the enemy.

For the rest of the day there was a series of skirmishes with the Japanese foolishly dissipating their strength by sending in their attackers in ones and twos. For instance, at about 1 p.m. the anti-tank platoon (Warrant-Officer Bourne[8]) guarding battalion headquarters immediately north of the Song, saw a few Japanese on the right flank; a line party from the 2/28th Battalion killed four Japanese south of Gordon's position; at 2 p.m. three Japanese were killed in a creek west of battalion headquarters; an hour later a prisoner was captured behind Gordon's company.

This prisoner, from the *II/238th Battalion*, stated that the attack by two companies of his battalion was to be coordinated with artillery fire from Pino Hill. Actually a small Australian and Papuan patrol led by Lieutenant Cawthorne[9] had been observing Pino Hill on the 21st and

---

[7] Sgt B. W. Pedder, SX5664; 2/43 Bn. Waterman; of Magill, SA; b. Forest Range, SA, 12 Oct 1911.

[8] WO2 C. E. Bourne, SX6623; 2/43 Bn. Wood machinist; of Marryatville, SA; b. Adelaide, 14 Jun 1912.

[9] Lt C. H. Cawthorne, MM, SX5399; 2/43 Bn. Physiotherapist; of Adelaide; b. Lydd, Kent, England, 7 Dec 1907.

22nd. At first light on the 22nd, as the patrol was about to move off, the Japanese artillery opened up and Cawthorne's men were able to pinpoint roughly the positions of two guns, a machine-gun, and a mortar.

All day small bands of Japanese were seen on all sides and most were cut down by the defenders' fire. By 5 p.m., when there seemed only a few odd Japanese in the area, Gordon decided to regain the initiative, and sent out patrols. One of these under Lieutenant Glover[1] found about 10 Japanese slain by the Vickers. While the Australians searched the bodies two more Japanese leapt to their feet firing. Both were shot. When his patrols returned Gordon reported that there were no Japanese within 100 yards of his position to the front and to the right, although there were still a few on the left.

While the Japanese coastal attack was being shattered by the resolute defence of Gordon's company the *79th Regiment* was approaching the Australian positions from the Nongora area to the north-west. The Japanese did not use the main trail, which was being watched by the 20th Brigade, but advanced over country extremely difficult not only for movement but for control and coordination. Nevertheless, a Japanese attack coming from that direction, if powerful and determined enough, could break the Australian defences from North Hill to the Song. The 2/32nd Battalion had now been out of communication for 24 hours, and Brigadier Porter was arranging for it to be resupplied by air.

Porter was not happy about the plan for the defence of Scarlet Beach as he found it. It was based on a chain of section posts with little depth to the forward companies, and the defenders by cutting fields of fire had made it easy for the enemy to pinpoint the Australian positions. Porter could not do much, in the time and in the circumstances, to reorganise the defences, but he made some small adjustments, posted standing patrols forward of the perimeter, and had provided himself with a reserve of two companies, one from the 2/28th and one from the 2/32nd.

From dawn sporadic artillery fire falling over a large area came from the Pino Hill area; about 10 enemy planes bombed and strafed in midmorning, but wounded only one man. At 10.30 a.m. a listening post north of the Song exchanged shots with seven Japanese and then withdrew. As Stinker had been out of communication for over 24 hours Lieutenant Browning[2] led out a patrol from the 2/28th to lay an alternative telephone line.

Porter decided that, as the 2/32nd needed reinforcing on Pabu, he could no longer afford the luxury of a two-company reserve. He therefore ordered the company of the 2/32nd in reserve forward from the Katika area to Pabu. Thus by 10.30 a.m. when the first Japanese were seen by the 2/28th's listening post, Browning was on his way north-west

---

[1] Capt M. H. E. C. Glover, MC, TX2910; 2/43 Bn. Schoolmaster; of Moonah, Tas; b. Melbourne, 14 Apr 1910.

[2] Lt J. F. Browning, NX5897. 2/4 and 2/28 Bns. Clerk; of Batlow, NSW; b. Caxton, England, 25 Jan 1909.

towards Stinker, Captain Lancaster's[3] company of the 2/32nd was across the Song and moving north towards the jeephead, and Hayashida's spearhead was approaching the Australian positions from the north-west. Later in the morning both Browning and Lancaster skirmished with Japanese patrols. By 1 p.m. it began to appear that Lancaster's company and the Japanese vanguard had crossed one another's tracks, an easy thing to do in this wild country. Captain Coppock's company of the 2/28th on the Song drove back a few Japanese, but the enemy managed to force the anti-tank platoon of the 2/43rd to the east of Coppock to withdraw slightly. This platoon had been under heavy fire during the day. On several occasions the enemy tried to break through but was driven back. In a weapon-pit on the right of the platoon's position three men were doggedly defending an area where the enemy was persistently attempting infiltration when a mortar bomb fell into the pit. With the supreme courage which an emergency breeds, Private Grayson[4] who was between his two companions placed his foot on the lethal bomb. He was grievously wounded, but the other two were able to continue the defence.

It was at this point that the movement of Lancaster's company like the movement of Keley's earlier, helped to disorganise the Japanese. At 1 p.m. Lancaster had just resumed his progress when, directly west of North Hill, the leading platoon (Lieutenant Smith[5]) saw the enemy in force near some huts. Artillery fire was brought down on them. The other two platoons were then passing through the 2/43rd's anti-tank platoon. Lancaster sent Lieutenant North's[6] platoon to the left and Sergeant McCallum's to the right to help the anti-tank platoon. As the Japanese advanced they were confined more and more towards the creek bed by pressure from both flanks. The R.Q.M.S. of the 2/43rd Battalion, Crellin,[7] from his pit on the bank of the creek killed four Japanese who stepped into the shallow water. McCallum's men crept to within eight yards of the enemy's position and killed five. Heavy enemy fire prevented any further advance but the platoon dug in and inflicted heavy casualties on the enemy as he tried to reconnoitre. Lieutenant North's platoon on the left also inflicted casualties but, despite two fierce attacks, was unable to dislodge the now strongly entrenched Japanese. The Japanese had used captured anti-tank mines as booby-traps, and one man was killed and four others, including North, were wounded, by them.

Lancaster then recalled Smith's platoon which rejoined the company at 3 p.m. Joshua ordered that 200 2-inch mortar bombs be directed at the enemy now bottled up in the Surpine Valley. At 5.40 p.m. Smith's platoon attacked and captured the whole area. Here the company dug in for the night, having blunted the main Japanese counter-attack. The

---

[3] Capt C. G. Lancaster, WX477; 2/32 Bn. Baker; b. Coolgardie, WA, 25 Sep 1906.

[4] Pte A. J. Grayson, DCM, SX18206; 2/43 Bn. French polisher; of Adelaide; b. Adelaide, 24 Jan 1916. (His real name was Gray.)

[5] Lt E. A. G. Smith, WX2110. 2/11 and 2/32 Bns. Goldminer; b. Dwellingup, WA, 19 Nov 1916.

[6] Major S. F. North, WX10752. 2/28 and 2/32 Bns. Departmental manager; of Mount Barker, WA; b. Bunbury, WA, 3 Dec 1909.

[7] WO1 H. Crellin, VX6918; 2/43 Bn. Tobacco grower; of Nathalia, Vic; b. Camberwell, Vic, 22 Jul 1905.

enemy withdrew in the night from his uncomfortable position in the Surpine Valley leaving 43 dead. Lancaster's arrival could not have been more fortunately timed.

It was fairly obvious to Wootten and Porter at the end of the 22nd that the Japanese counter-attack could be held and that it might already have been defeated. This counter-attack had nothing like the ferocity of the October one and seemed perhaps to be General Katagiri's last attempt to turn the tide of battle. Like General Nakano he had contributed to his own defeat by the piecemeal nature of his attacks. Infiltration could never

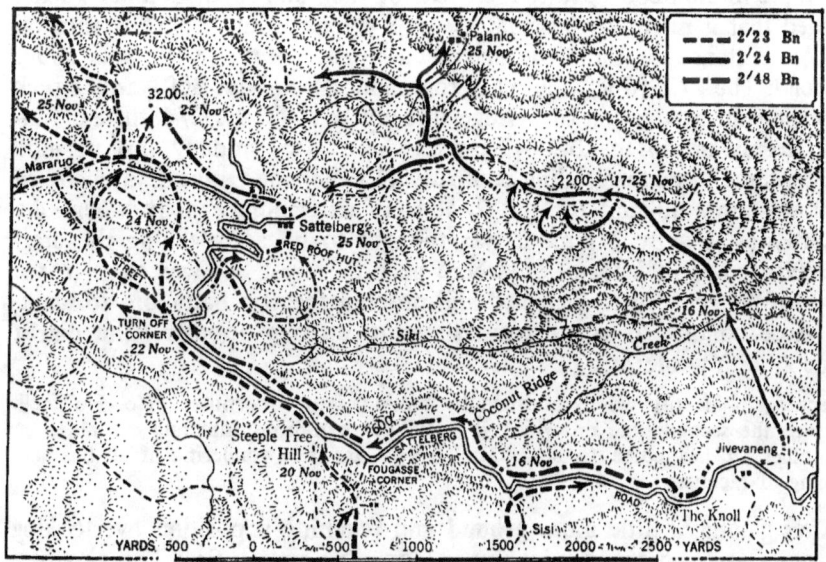

The capture of Sattelberg, 16th-25th November

win a battle against the tactics employed by the Australians in the last year or more. This day 89 Japanese had been killed but the Australians lost only one killed and a few wounded.

Meanwhile, the advance had been resumed in the main battle area along the Sattelberg Road. Having captured Steeple Tree Hill, his immediate objective, Brigadier Whitehead, late on the 21st, issued orders for the capture of Sattelberg itself. The 2/48th Battalion accompanied by a troop of tanks would continue along the road; the 2/23rd would advance west along the road to the position subsequently known as Turn Off Corner and then north to the 3200 Feature, north-west of Sattelberg; the 2/24th would continue to advance from the 2200 Feature via the saddle towards Sattelberg.

The road to Sattelberg now became steeper, cutting into the side of the hill with high ground to left or right. With Captain Hill's company leading, the 2/48th on the 22nd advanced north from Turn Off Corner without opposition. The 2/23rd then moved past the corner to the west. After about 150 yards the leading men of the 2/48th came to what was at first thought to be the ford across Siki Creek but was later found to be another crossing farther south. Although the Japanese could be heard in the general area there was no opposition as the men carefully pushed forward for about another 100 yards to the real ford. At 3.25 p.m. they came to a landslide and four mines laid by the Japanese. Colonel Ainslie reported that it would be impossible to use the tanks further because of the landslide and the honeycomb of shell holes.

The 2/23rd Battalion had studied aerial photographs to determine the best route to the 3200 Feature after leaving the main road. Colonel Tucker decided that it might be possible to use a bypass route from the turn off a short distance to the west and then north parallel with and above the road. The 2/23rd left the main road and after about 300 yards struck the enemy in occupation of a ridge directly west of the 2/48th and running steeply up to the 3200 Feature. Soon after midday this position was captured after the leading company (Lieutenant Gray) had encircled it. It was now difficult for the 2/48th to determine exactly where the 2/23rd was, but by 2 p.m. it was thought to be approaching the crest of 3200. It was in fact not anywhere near the crest but was close to the 2/48th. Whitehead was disturbed and ordered the two battalions to maintain close contact so as to avoid shooting up one another. The diarist of the 2/48th wrote:

Once again identity was established by the officially-condemned "Ho, Ho" call. This was the second time on which it saved the battalions inflicting casualties on each other. It has come to stay. The troops are all wondering if it has any meaning in Japanese.

After gaining a little more ground and reaching a position overlooking the ford Gray's company was pinned down by enemy fire. The two battalions withdrew slightly for the night to more favourable ground. The country ahead was New Guinea jungle at its worst. The battalion commanders considered that, unless some means of outflanking the Japanese defences could be found, a full-scale attack supported by artillery and tanks would be necessary.

In the late afternoon the Japanese artillery, in the course of its regular evening bombardment of headquarters areas, enjoyed a success similar to that on Pabu when several officers of the 2/32nd had been put out of action. Shells falling on the 2/48th Battalion headquarters inflicted 7 casualties, including 3 mortally wounded (the second-in-command, Major Batten, the adjutant, Captain Treloar,[8] and the Pioneer officer, Lieutenant Butler[9]), and four wounded, including the medical officer, Captain Yeatman.[1]

---

[8] Capt H. F. Treloar, SX9064; 2/48 Bn. Wool appraiser; of Adelaide; b. Adelaide, 22 Feb 1917. Died of wounds 22 Nov 1943.

[9] Lt G. J. Butler, SX12499; 2/48 Bn. Financier and money lender; of Perth; b. Perth, 19 Aug 1910. Died of wounds 23 Nov 1943.

[1] Capt J. C. Yeatman, SX15351. 2/3 Fd Amb; RMO 2/48 Bn. Medical practitioner; of Adelaide; b. Adelaide, 6 Jul 1914.

The 2/24th Battalion continued its slow progress over very tough country on the 22nd. Colonel Gillespie sent Captain Harty's company in an outflanking movement to the north and Captain McNamara's to join Captain Bieri's at the saddle connecting the 2200 Feature to Sattelberg. That morning Bieri was attacked from three sides. Gillespie's plan was for Harty's company to attack from the north while Bieri's or McNamara's companies cut the main track on the east and west sides of the saddle respectively. After the attack McNamara's company would press on towards Sattelberg. At this stage Whitehead ordered Gillespie to make a more concerted attack and send both McNamara and Bieri towards the re-entrant on the west to block the track. Both companies worked round the ridge towards the track, and by 5.30 were in position near the track with a Japanese encampment in front on the high ground and another below in a gully. Further progress to the west was barred by a gorge.

By this time Harty was in position north of the Japanese originally encountered by Bieri. Harty attacked at 5.50 p.m. but the leading platoon was pinned down and so was the second which attempted an encirclement. Thus, by nightfall three companies of the 2/24th Battalion were more or less on the saddle and the Japanese on the 2200 Feature were in danger of being cut off. If only the promised tanks could arrive the progress of the 2/24th Battalion might be more spectacular.

Up the Sattelberg Road from the east day after day a procession of jeeps carried forward rations, water, ammunition and men. Down the road empty jeeps, or jeeps loaded with men hitch-hiking back trundled busily along. Now and then a jeep would come along the road at little more than walking pace carrying a bandaged and blanketed wounded man lying on a stretcher, or with a less seriously wounded man sitting in the seat beside the driver, grinning bravely, cigarette in mouth. Along the track on many days climbed parties of sweating reinforcements, loaded like packhorses. "Chuck it away, you'll never carry all that up there," advised the old hands.

Graders were at work on the road which, despite the fine weather since the opening of the Sattelberg campaign, still needed corduroying with tree trunks in the lower stretches where there was sticky black soil. Higher up where the coral was nearer the surface and the grey soil a mixture of black topsoil and coral, the road was firm and dry except where hidden springs soaked across it.

Up the road too from Jivevaneng went another lifeline—the native carriers, moving at a slow easy pace which made the gait of the soldiers look stiff and awkward. One native could carry three 3-inch mortar bombs or a case of rations. Cheerful but grave, expressionless but watchful, they had already proved many times over how vital was their role. A few would say "Good day" to the soldiers they passed, and receive a "Good day, George" in return.

Early on the 23rd Ainslie visited Tucker's headquarters. Both went forward to Gray's position whence Sattelberg could be seen. After studying the rugged jungle-clad ground towards Sattelberg they agreed that the

2/23rd should try to find a way round on the left flank and the 2/48th on the right. While the patrols were out mortars and machine-guns harassed the Japanese defences, and for the fifth successive day Allied aircraft attacked the general area—this time Sattelberg itself. A few Japanese planes also attacked between Kumawa and the Sattelberg Road causing the diarist of the 26th Brigade to comment on the "strange spectacle" offered to the men on the ground when Allied and enemy bombers and fighters, Allied supply planes for the 2/32nd Battalion, and two Boomerangs for artillery reconnaissance all appeared over the target area within ten minutes of each other. The artillery, increased since 20th November by the 2nd Mountain Battery, also kept up an intermittent bombardment.

There seemed little hope of finding a satisfactory route through the wild country on the right, and it was therefore a pleasant surprise when a patrol of the 2/48th penetrated to the hairpin bend without opposition although the enemy was heard digging in to the west. From here it seemed that the enemy might have neglected the precipitous country on the right on the grounds that it was too rugged for operations. It might just be possible therefore for a company or even the whole battalion to attack Sattelberg from the direction of Red Roof Hut spur. Wootten had suggested to Whitehead earlier in the day that the assault "seems like a two-company show for each battalion". He visited Whitehead later that day to discuss the latest reports. The last hour of daylight was spent by the leading company commander, Captain Hill, in poring over aerial photographs and issuing the necessary warning orders for an advance and possible attack on the right.

The engineers of the 2/13th Field Company were given the task of preparing a track for tanks, to the left, known later as Spry Street (despite an instruction from New Guinea Force forbidding the bestowal of such names "without reference to G.S. Branch, N.G.F.").[2] Believing that the 2200 Feature might be the site of an enemy base for a push to the east, particularly as large Japanese patrols and carrying parties had been seen moving thence from Sattelberg, Wootten decided that 2200 must be "absolutely freed", and ordered the making of a track to carry tanks towards the feature. At the same time Whitehead ordered the withdrawal of Bieri's and McNamara's companies to enable the artillery and mortars to pound the Japanese positions without danger to their own men. At 12.15 p.m. Major Hordern, with a bulldozer, arrived at 2/24th Battalion headquarters, and arrangements were promptly made to bulldoze a route for tanks from Katika forward.

While the 26th Brigade was inching closer to Sattelberg the Japanese counter-attack against the 24th Brigade was finally shattered on the 23rd. On the coastal track Gordon's company of the 2/43rd was fired on from

---

[2] The order which N.G.F. felt it necessary to issue on 23rd November was addressed to all troops in New Guinea and stated: "Names will not be used for new places or areas, in connection with works projects, without reference to G.S. Branch, N.G.F. . . . Should it be necessary for construction purposes to refer to a locality by temporary name it is not to be a personal name. Such names tend to be ephemeral and also to create invidious distinctions unless soundly based and properly controlled." The order can be criticised as being ambiguous, pompous and unlikely to be obeyed.

high ground about 250 yards to the north-west. Further attempts to infiltrate round the company's left flank were broken up and the retreating Japanese were harassed with mortar fire. From the northern company of the 2/43rd Corporal Redman[3] led a small patrol of Australians and Papuans early in the day to reconnoitre Pino Hill. In the mid-afternoon they came "hot-footing" back to the company lines reporting that the Japanese were in strength on Pino.

The 24th Brigade was still expecting a main enemy attack from the north-west as it had now, as usual, captured the Japanese operation orders. It soon became apparent, however, that the *79th Regiment* was a spent force as far as this counter-attack was concerned. The Japanese had obviously become disorganised and disheartened by the Pabu surprise, the resolute Australian defence of the previous day, the vigorous Australian patrolling leading, as it did, to a constant hammering by artillery and mortars, and the supply difficulties created by the foul nature of the country.

Over 1,000 hastily dug foxholes were found in the areas near the company of the 2/43rd on the coast and the company of the 2/28th on the Song. Before the latter company there were 60 enemy dead, 112 rifles, 2 machine-guns, 2 mortars, one flame-thrower, bombs and ammunition. Japanese patrols were still in the area, however, for Papuans reported seeing about 40 of them 1,000 yards north of the 2/28th.

On Pabu the 2/32nd Battalion now had only two companies; but Lieutenant Keley's, which had withdrawn to the jungle fringe after its sharp encounter on the evening of the 22nd, set out for Pabu at first light next morning. The respite of the night enabled Keley to bury the dead and construct two bush stretchers. The journey back to Pabu by an indirect and tortuous route took the company a day and a quarter; the two Papuans on the previous evening took three quarters of an hour. About 2 p.m. on the 23rd some 15 Japanese, who may have been tracking the company, approached from the rear but were quickly dispersed. The company was within 500 yards of Pabu when night fell and once more camped in the jungle.

The two companies on Pabu—Captain Thornton's[4] and Captain Davidson's—and particularly the machine-gunners, went on killing Japanese carrying parties and reinforcements who continued to use the same track regardless of the fate of their comrades—further evidence of the primitive nature of Japanese communications and staff work. By the end of this day 82 had been killed round Pabu. As serious casualties had been inflicted on the Australians by enemy gunfire the previous night Mollard instructed his men to build log roofs over their slit trenches. Although the telephone line to this isolated position had been cut in several places and could

---

[3] Cpl A. V. Redman, SX10883; 2/43 Bn. Labourer; of Croydon, SA; b. Denial Bay, SA, 15 Apr 1912.

[4] Capt J. J. Thornton, VX35129; 2/32 Bn. Farmer; of Numurkah, Vic; b. Numurkah, 31 Jul 1916. He had taken over command of "A" Company after Captain Walker was killed on the 22nd.

not at present be repaired, Mollard's two wireless sets continued to work, and Captain Mollison was able to call for artillery support in an attempt to silence the three enemy field guns on Pino Hill. One opened up again at 8.55 a.m., but it soon seemed to be silenced by counter-battery fire. Actually the Japanese guns, which here as elsewhere would fire only about 20 shells in one bombardment, were cunningly hidden at the bottom of natural cliffs when not firing, and were almost impossible to hit except during their short bursts of activity.

On the 23rd Major Dorney became anxious about his wounded and stressed the importance of evacuating them. Porter ordered the 2/43rd to repair the line to Pabu from North Hill and guard the lines of communication, but realised that any such re-establishment of communication would be purely temporary while the Japanese occupied Pino Hill. After the 2/43rd Battalion re-established the telephone line at 6 p.m., Porter came on the line and told Mollard that an effort would soon be made to capture Pino. Early that day five Mitchells dropped supplies by parachute, but scattered them over a wide area including that occupied by the Japanese. Eighteen capsules were recovered, 14 of them from no-man's land. Unfortunately none contained rations and the battalion was now very hungry. Worse still, the Japanese were found near the place whence the battalion had been drawing its water.

There was always a lighter side, however. Mortar bombs were dropped. The fuses were not in the bombs but were delivered in pieces ready for assembly, with a roneoed document directing the recipients to ensure that the fuses were not assembled except under the supervision of an ordnance officer. Only the shortage of batteries for the wireless sets prevented the adjutant from sending a signal requesting that an ordnance officer also be dropped. Sergeant Anderson[5] assembled the fuses and tested the first bomb successfully with the aid of a forked stick and a long string. Using these bombs the mortarmen scored direct hits on a machine-gun post and an artillery observation post which had been overlooking Pabu. (After its relief the 2/32nd found that all the occupants of these two enemy posts had been killed.)

Round Sattelberg, meanwhile, Brigadier Whitehead's three battalions were closing in. All knew that the kill would not be easy. If the Japanese defenders were alert the Australian attackers would have little chance of capturing the rugged and towering fortress without a protracted siege and much bombardment. As a result of splendid reconnaissance patrolling on 23rd November, however, it was decided that the 2/48th Battalion might be able to sneak a force across the headwaters of Siki Creek and attack Sattelberg up the escarpment from the south-east.

At first light on the 24th Hill's company moved down into the deep ravine formed by Siki Creek on the east of the road. Brocksopp's company was ready to follow in case Hill struck opposition. As everything

---

[5] WO2 N. C. Anderson, WX1746. 2/3 Fd Regt, 2/32 Bn. Farmer; of Claremont, WA; b. Claremont, 5 Mar 1906.

depended on surprise and silence, however, Hill's men began their journey towards Sattelberg unsupported. "It was appreciated," wrote the 2/48th's diarist, "that if resistance was anything but light the almost impassable nature of the country would prevent the company taking the feature and that if the noise of the company advance was heard from Sattelberg itself, a handful of enemy could make it impossible for the company to climb the precipitous slopes."

While Ainslie went back to discuss the day's plan with Whitehead, Hill's company advanced slowly and cautiously down to the Siki and up again on the other side trying to avoid the breaking of a branch or the dislodgment of a stone. The plan and subsequent activity of the 2/23rd Battalion out on the left flank was well summarised in a signal from brigade to the 2/48th:

> Gray ["C" Company] is going to put on a Chinese attack [much noise] to confine the Nip. Lyne[6] ["B" Company] is moving around the left flank and Tietyens[7] ["D" Company] will be prepared to move along behind should the necessity arise.

To the north, along the bulldozer's new track from Katika to the 2/24th Battalion on the 2200 Feature, a troop of tanks rumbled forward over the most difficult country they had yet encountered. With all this concentration of effort towards the one dominating objective it was not surprising that Whitehead, having been visited by the divisional commander yesterday, was visited by the corps commander today. General Berryman's understanding of the historic moment and his instinct for being in at the kill were remarkable.

Despite all this power blocking up behind, the battle was yet dependent on the ears and eyes of Hill's forward scout. Slowly the tortuous advance continued. The 26th Brigade began to send irritable signals to the 2/24th Battalion such as: "Perturbed at no information. Enemy are only 100 yards in front and a patrol has been out for 3 hours." The truth was that the departure of the patrol had been delayed for a mortar shoot, and, as the 2/24th replied tersely, "although enemy only 100 yards ahead patrol had to go a long way round, otherwise it was suicide". By 10.20 a.m. Colonel Gillespie reported that his first patrol thought that the enemy had "pulled out" from the top of 2200.

At the same time, on the left flank, Lieutenant Lyne's company of the 2/23rd, carrying only essential gear but the largest possible amount of ammunition, crept as quietly as they could through rugged jungle to get behind the Japanese holding up Gray's progress. At 11.10 a.m. Tucker signalled to brigade: "Lyne has got round on top of Gray—enemy between the two—going to deal with them now."

Hill now began the stealthy climb up towards Sattelberg: Brocksopp's and Isaksson's companies then moved along the road to the hairpin bend and Brocksopp's continued to the Siki. Out on the left the 2/48th Bat-

---

[6] Capt A. Lyne, VX41643; 2/23 Bn. Clerk-accountant; of Malvern, Vic; b. Ararat, Vic, 31 Jul 1915.
[7] Maj F. W. Tietyens, VX19432; 2/23 Bn. Solicitor; of Albury, NSW; b. Albury, 13 Sep 1910.

talion heard a sudden storm of fire. This began as Gray's support fire for Lyne's attack. It rapidly developed into something else, however, when Lyne at the end of his left flank encirclement ran into Japanese defences higher up the ridge. A hail of machine-gun fire from these positions and then from others to the west forced the company to withdraw. At 11.10 a.m., just as Tucker received Lyne's signal saying that he was ready to attack, the telephone line was cut and a pandemonium of firing broke out from up the slopes of the 3200 Feature.

The fight was one of steps and stairs. Highest up the ridge were Japanese of the *80th Regiment,* then came Lyne's company, then more Japanese of the *80th Regiment,* and finally Gray's company. The noise of battle was only equalled by the depth of the confusion on the slopes of the 3200 Feature. That the position was baffling to all concerned was apparent from Tucker's signal to brigade at 5 p.m.:

> Japanese counter-attacked the company which moved in after Lyne moved out. Then Lyne moved in again. Position confused. Tietyens on good high ground on razor-back but has Nips in front of him and perhaps behind. Flanks secure.

Tietyens' company had occupied a deserted Japanese position on the spur during the morning and thereafter he had steadily pushed forward. Lyne's men were forced to return in small groups with 22 casualties. Soon after Lyne's return the Japanese sharply attacked from higher up the ridge but the two companies drove them back.

This fight was over by the time Hill's men approached their objective—the edge of the Sattelberg plateau. The ground from the Siki rose at an angle of never less than 45 degrees and, over the last stages, of about 60 degrees. So steep was the slope at the end that the men could not even crawl up unaided, but moved in single file and dragged one another up. It was not until a few minutes after 4 p.m. that the enemy became aware of the approach of the Australians. To those behind, anxiously awaiting news, the situation was obscure for the telephone line was severed one minute before the first Japanese were encountered.

Towards the top of the spur on which Red Roof Hut was situated were about 20 Japanese deeply entrenched in two-man pits with head cover of logs and earth and weapons firing through slits. This force was considered sufficient by the Japanese commander to guard against so unlikely a move as an attack from the south-east. As soon as these Japanese heard movement to the east they began firing in that general direction.

Hill now sought ways up the spur. Sergeant Daniels[8] tried to move up the western slopes but failed because the Japanese rolled down grenades and fired machine-guns at short range. Another attempt was made from the south but failed for the same reason. Hill then ordered his third platoon commander, Sergeant Derrick,[9] already a famous leader, to try from farther

---

[8] Sgt R. G. Daniels, MM, SX7863; 2/48 Bn. Fibrous plasterer; of Rosewater Gardens, SA; b. Exeter, SA, 7 Mar 1918.

[9] Lt T. C. Derrick, VC, DCM, SX7964; 2/48 Bn. Orchardist; of Berri, SA; b. Medindie, SA, 20 Mar 1914. Died of wounds 24 May 1945.

round on the right flank. Derrick's platoon met the same precipitous country and was also held up by machine-gun fire and grenades. Soon after the firing started from this quarter a runner came back from Derrick and gave Hill a message: "I can't get forward and the slopes are so steep I can't hold the position for more than five minutes."

Hill was by now convinced that he could not reach the objective or even hold his position. The company was spread around three sides of the feature and the enemy was able to prevent practically any movement. If the enemy ran out of grenades Hill believed they could use rocks effectively. " 'B' Company has struck M.G's and grenades on 3 sides 50 yards from the top," signalled Ainslie to Whitehead at 5.50 p.m. "Will probably have to come back." Whitehead replied ten minutes later: "Plan for tomorrow. 2/48 with tanks to go through Lyne's company. 2/23 to hold firm." With hope abandoned for an assault up Red Hut spur, Ainslie ordered Hill to withdraw. Within three minutes of the receipt of this order the left-hand platoon came back. Hill then ordered Derrick to withdraw under covering fire from the remaining platoon on the left. It was then 6.18 p.m.

Derrick climbed down towards Hill who clambered up to meet him. Derrick said: "I think we can get forward, we've done over about 5 posts." Hill hesitated and explained his orders, but agreed when Derrick said, "Tell the C.O. I'm pinned down and can't get out—give me another 20 minutes."

Derrick had decided that the only possible way of approach was through an open kunai patch situated directly beneath the top of the cliff. During the advance from Jivevaneng this kunai patch, a third of the way down the steep face, and two big bomb scars near the bare summit, had ingrained themselves into the minds of the attackers. When his platoon was held

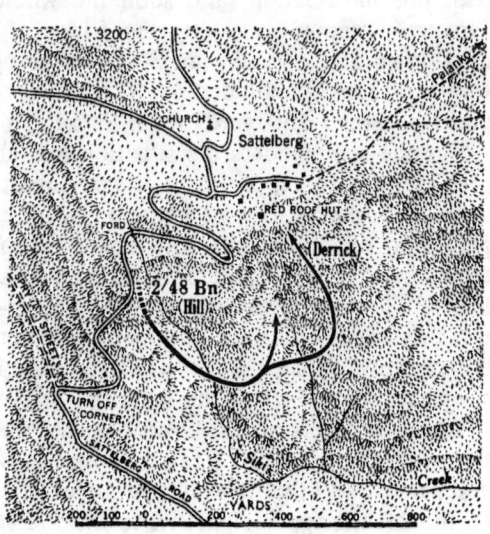

Sattelberg, 24th November

up Derrick had clambered forward and with grenades had knocked out the post holding up the leading section (Corporal Everett's[1]). He then led forward the second section (Lance-Corporal Connelly's[2]) to attack

---

[1] L-Sgt W. A. Everett, SX7261; 2/48 Bn. Labourer; of Adelaide; b. Essex, England, 5 Jun 1915.
[2] L-Cpl F. K. Connelly, WX9821; 2/48 Bn. Labourer; of East Fremantle, WA; b. Fremantle, 4 Jun 1910.

on the right and when it was halted by fire he scrambled ahead to within six yards of the enemy and threw grenade after grenade at the weapon-pits above him.

Now fortified by Hill's agreement, Derrick led his platoon up the slope with the three sections following one another. It was about 6.45 p.m. Derrick and his men soon took two more posts. The platoon fired with Brens and Owens into the openings of these covered posts at 10 or 12 yards' range and then one man—Derrick in one instance, Private "Slogger" Sutherland[3] in the other—rushed forward and dropped a grenade in the slit of a post. The Japanese then ran from several other posts; two were shot scrambling down the slope to the right and the others—about eight—made off towards Sattelberg. Two of them threw grenades at their pursuers and wounded three men. Then Private Washbrook[4] moved forward firing his Bren from the hip and killed both Japanese. Fifteen had been killed since the attack opened.

Derrick was now in the bush at the edge of the grass-covered plateau. In front of him the Japanese were in strength round some buildings 140 yards away and were firing with three machine-guns. Darkness was setting in. The platoon was only 18 strong. Derrick sent a runner back to Hill with this information, and soon the whole company was in position in Japanese weapon-pits along the fringe of the kunai. The Japanese fire died down about 7.15 p.m. Soon Brocksopp's company which had been waiting at the Siki climbed up. The two companies spent the night in these positions about 150 yards from Sattelberg itself.[5]

For the commanders the situation had changed dramatically. One main problem was to supply the two companies clinging to the side of Sattelberg. In darkness men of battalion headquarters and Headquarters Company and others set out with water, ammunition and rations. Although they travelled only some 500 yards, the round journey took about eight hours. The new tank track—Spry Street—was ready; a third company was preparing to support the two forward companies in the final assault on the morrow. "There were very few men in the battalion who had any sleep that night," wrote the battalion diarist.

After last light on the 24th the 2/24th reported that the position on the crest of the 2200 Feature seemed to have been "knocked out or evacuated", and that it would be attacked early the next day. At first light on the 25th, brigade signalled to the 2/24th, "Important and urgent that tanks should get to 2/24th immediately. . . . Necessary to put the pressure on from your side as early as possible."

The morning was overcast. Registration by the artillery assisted by mortar smoke began at first light, but the close nature of the country neces-

---

[3] Pte D. Sutherland, SX7195. 2/48 Bn, 2/8 Fd Amb. Fireman; of Richmond, SA; b. Keswick, SA, 27 Nov 1914.
[4] Cpl W. L. Washbrook, VX72722; 2/48 Bn. Farm hand; of Swan Hill, Vic; b. Swan Hill, 22 Nov 1919. (Served also as F. W. Francis.)
[5] Derrick was awarded the Victoria Cross for this action.

sitated the separate registration of each gun.[6] This took some time, and it was not till 8.25 a.m. that patrols from Hill's company of the 2/48th could push forward to see if the enemy were still in the positions which they occupied at last light. Forty minutes later the patrols reported that these positions were unoccupied. At 9.15 a.m. the leading men of Hill's company entered the abandoned shell of Sattelberg which had at one time been a health resort for the Finschhafen and other Lutheran Missions in New Guinea. Because of previous experience the withdrawal of the Japanese during the night was not altogether unexpected. At 10 a.m. the Australian flag, hoisted on to a tree by Derrick, was flying over Sattelberg. The battalion's diarist commented:

> It was rather an inglorious end to the days of hard fighting where the difficult terrain made it possible for a very small force of the enemy to hold up a complete battalion. The advance of "B" Company had been made over heavily timbered country rising almost vertically at times and at no time less than 45 degrees. The Japanese might well be excused if he considered that line of approach impossible.

On the right the bulldozer and the troop of tanks crawled up towards the 2200 Feature, which the 2/24th Battalion at 10.30 a.m. found unoccupied; a patrol from the 2/24th during the afternoon found Palanko empty. On the left a company of the 2/48th occupied the 3200 Feature without opposition. Farther to the left patrols from the 2/23rd Battalion and the 2/4th Commando Squadron found Mararuo deserted and evidence (from wheel marks) that the Japanese had dragged a 75-mm gun towards Wareo. Another commando patrol found Moreng empty.

There was evidence that the Japanese were eating ferns and the core of bamboo. The state of their corpses and the many documents and diaries captured all stressed the Japanese supply difficulties. The prisoner captured by the 2/43rd on 22nd November said that even the main barge point of Nambariwa was supplied only by fishing boat, air dropping and submarine, as barges were too vulnerable to the air and naval attacks. The supply of Sattelberg from such bases as Nambariwa had recently become a nightmare for the Japanese commanders. The supplies which the Australians had seen dropping from aircraft over Sattelberg were insignificant.

"Every day just living on potatoes," wrote a diarist of the *79th Regiment*. Later he wrote: "Divided the section into two groups, one group for fighting and the other to obtain potatoes. Unfortunately none were available. On the way back

---

[6] The 25-pounders of Lieut-Colonel G. D. Houston's 2/12 Field Regiment remained on the flat coastal strip because they could cover the whole area from there, although it had originally been planned that they should be hauled up the Sattelberg Road. The 75-mm guns of the Mountain Battery, however, came up the road. Towards the end the ranges of the 25-pounders were well over 7,000 yards. During and after the war Japanese prisoners, high and low, claimed that the jungle artillery of the Australians was one of the most potent factors in their defeat, and bitterly compared its power with the comparatively ineffectual efforts of their own few artillery pieces which they hardly dared to use because of the Australian counter-battery fire and air support.

The artillery could not have been so effective without the excellent cooperation of the Boomerangs of No. 4 (Army Cooperation) Squadron of the RAAF which spotted for them. The audacious crews of these aircraft were very highly regarded by the men of the 9th Division, the artillery no less than the infantry. Communication between airman and gunner was conducted in a very conversational way. For example:

The gunner: "Is there a machine-gun post at ——?"
The airman: "I'll have a look at the bastard"; and then, "The last shot was 100 yards over and 200 yards left—good shot though—I can see pots and pans flying all over the place."

sighted a horse, killed it and roasted a portion of it. . . . At present, our only wish is just to be able to see even a grain of rice." One diarist of the *80th Regiment* jubilantly wrote in mid-November: "Received rice ration for three days. . . . It was like a gift from Heaven and everybody rejoiced. At night heard loud voices of the enemy. They are probably drinking whisky because they are a rich country and their trucks are able to bring up such desirable things—I certainly envy them."[7]

Many Japanese dead were found—59 in front of the 2/24th Battalion alone. Two 75-mm guns were captured bringing the total of captured weapons during the Sattelberg campaign to two 75-mm guns, three 37-mm guns, 18 Woodpeckers and large numbers of light machine-guns, mortars, and rifles. The Australian casualties had not been excessive during the period 17th to 25th November—49 killed and 118 wounded—considering the rugged nature of the country between Jivevaneng and Sattelberg. The *80th Regiment* retreating towards Wareo was a broken force.

The Sattelberg campaign was the first continuous and fierce action against the Japanese by the 26th Brigade and its reactions as listed by one of the battalion diarists were interesting. "Many of the lads consider it to have been harder and more nerve-racking than any 10 days at Tobruk or El Alamein," wrote this diarist. "Whether that is so or not is doubtful." He then listed the main difficulties; the precipitous country and bamboo, the close contact, the lack of hot meals, the scarcity of water, the fitfulness of sleep, the necessity to carry everything on one's back, and the enervating climate. "Against these matters," he concluded, "must be weighed the comparative lack of enemy shelling or mortaring; the absence of the khamsin, etc. But whatever the answer one almost invariably gets the reply, 'It's not as bad as we were told'."

The 26th Brigade knew how much of its triumph was due to the work of the 24th Brigade in the north. The courage and determination to advance displayed by the 26th was equalled by the courage and stubborn defence of the 24th. This brigade had repelled a fierce counter-attack during the critical days of the 26th Brigade's advance, and by the sudden thrust to Pabu it had not only disorganised this counter-attack but had cut the enemy supply line to Wareo and Sattelberg and thus weakened the Japanese resistance there.

The Japanese counter-attack on the northern front had been broken by the 24th Brigade in one day—the 22nd—but the Japanese were still in evidence throughout the 24th Brigade's area two days later and the men were anxiously expecting attack from any direction. From Pabu several large parties of Japanese were attacked along the main track. Unlike those

---

[7] These Australians were, of course, not drinking anything stronger than tea, but their rations, although not particularly appetising, were infinitely superior to those of the Japanese. From a study of captured documents it seemed that under favourable circumstances—which now seldom obtained—the following daily ration was issued to each Japanese soldier in New Guinea:

rice (polished)	870 gms.
tinned beef	90 "
dehydrated vegetables	120 "
soy sauce	15 "
powdered bean paste	15 "
sugar	15 "
salt	15 "
Total per man per day	1140 " = 2.5 lb.

encountered inland by the 2/4th Commando Squadron these Japanese had plenty of rice and tinned rations. Again the 2/32nd's machine-gunners mowed them down. Mollard himself has left the best description of the Japanese reaction to the fate of their comrades:

> During all this fighting Japanese soldiers kept walking up and down the Bonga-Wareo track. They were supply parties, either carrying food and ammunition to Wareo, or returning for a new load. The most astounding thing was their complete lack of protective measures. They walked along the track as though they were strolling in a park back at home, despite the fact that corpses of their comrades were piled along on either side. Our Vickers gunners were almost hysterical with joy as these successive parties kept offering the machine-gunner's dream target—a line of men one behind the other who could be fired on at ranges of less than 400 yards. As for ourselves, we were speechless with astonishment and kept thinking that each successive party must be the last. Why the Japanese infantry who were attacking us so relentlessly did not warn their comrades of the danger is something that none of us can answer.

One of Mollard's most pressing problems was how to evacuate the wounded. The sight of so many wounded and dying in the centre of the perimeter had a depressing effect on the men, and it now became imperative that something should be done. Boomerangs had already dropped morphia and bandages right into the centre of the area and bush stretchers were ready. Now that there were three companies on Pabu, Porter decided that a risk should be taken and the wounded evacuated in the care of one of the companies. Thus Davidson's company, guided by the line party from the 2/43rd Battalion, set out at 12.30 p.m. with twelve stretcher cases and the walking wounded. In an hour it travelled only about 400 yards as the jungle ahead had to be cleared for the stretchers. A platoon from the 2/43rd went out to meet the newcomers and helped them into their area, whence the wounded were rushed south in jeeps.

Meanwhile the 2/43rd was patrolling in search of Japanese. North of Gordon's company patrols found hundreds of foxholes and about 40 dead Japanese, many wearing Australian steel helmets and carrying Australian grenades. In the afternoon of the 24th Papuan and Australian patrols encountered Japanese rearguards about 800 yards north. To the left patrols from the 2/28th and 2/15th Battalions met, with mutual surprise, near Stinker.

Four tanks arrived in the brigade area on the 24th when Porter and Colonel Scott, of the 2/32nd, who had now returned from hospital, reconnoitred Pino Hill from the North Hill area. As mentioned, Porter's plan was to secure the supply line to Pabu by occupying Pino Hill. He decided to use the two companies of the 2/32nd Battalion not on Pabu, but, because of the fatigue of Davidson's company, postponed the attack until the 26th.

Guided by a patrol of two Australians and six Papuans, two platoons of the 2/43rd set out towards Pabu at 9 a.m. on the 24th guarding the carrier line. The journey was a long and difficult one and late in the afternoon of the 25th the telephone line to the 2/32nd was found severed again. Sergeant O'Riordan[8] of the Papuan Battalion, two signallers (McMahon[9] and Farrelly[10]) and two Papuans went forward to repair it. They were half way across a kunai patch when several light machine-guns and a Woodpecker opened up from about the 700 feet contour line. All were killed except one of the Papuans who managed to get back.[1] The two platoons probed the area but because the Japanese were in some strength they withdrew after cutting the telephone lines of the Japanese who in turn cut theirs.

On Pabu itself on the 25th the 2/32nd experienced a quiet day for a change. A Boomerang at 10.20 a.m. dropped parcels containing batteries, and later four Mitchells dropped much-needed rations. Twenty-four parachutes were recovered this time. In the afternoon communication by Lucas lamp was established between Pabu and North Hill whence the 2/43rd Battalion signalled that the carrier train could not get through. At last light a 75-mm gun and mortars bombarded the 2/32nd Battalion for about twenty minutes. The tide was running strongly in the Australians' favour, however, causing the diarist of the 2/32nd Battalion to rejoice: "Our spirits were given a lift when we heard that 2/48th Battalion had occupied Sattelberg." The signal to the 2/32nd was, "Torpy sits on Sat."[2]

Since 11th November the Australians had counted 553 more enemy dead, making a total of 1,848 since the Scarlet Beach landing. The Japanese loss of Sattelberg was a serious blow to their chances of holding the vital straits area between New Guinea and New Britain.

A Japanese N.C.O. left the following message at Sattelberg addressed to "Australian soldiers":

> We were not successful in our attack against enemy north of Song River due to heavy enemy fire power and subsequently had to withdraw. Our fire power is not strong enough. The Japanese army is really strong but at present we have no fire power and therefore have lost this battle. Just wait and see. Hundreds and thousands of Japanese soldier comrades have died and we will avenge them. We will definitely recapture Finschhafen and Lae. You Australian soldiers have been fooled by Roosevelt. Think it over. New Guinea is a stepping stone to Australia for Japan in the South Seas.

Despite this fine spirit which had been drilled into the Japanese soldiers, their commanders knew that the writing was indeed on the wall. General Adachi said later that after the loss of Sattelberg he realised that the Finschhafen area was lost. He said:

---

[8] Sgt J. M. O'Riordan, NX113095; Papuan Inf Bn. Clerk; of Randwick, NSW; b. Coogee, NSW, 26 Jun 1921. Killed in action 25 Nov 1943.

[9] Sig P. C. McMahon, NX38850; 24 Bde Sigs. Grazier; of Burren Junction, NSW; b. Wee Waa, NSW, 8 Mar 1918. Killed in action 25 Nov 1943.

[10] Sig M. A. Farrelly, VX37133; 24 Bde Sigs. Postman; of Preston, Vic; b. North Fitzroy, Vic, 25 May 1911. Killed in action 25 Nov 1943.

[1] Porter was alarmed at the security risk when he learnt that his "Q" staff had mistakenly and thoughtlessly handed the two signallers, for delivery to Pabu, ration papers showing unit strength. When the bodies of the two signallers were recovered on 9th December Porter anxiously enquired whether there was any sign of the vital papers. There were no papers but near the bodies was a pile of ash, as though the last act of two brave and mortally wounded men had been to burn the papers.

[2] Brigadier Whitehead was known as "Torpy" after the Whitehead Torpedo. He had been one of the CO's of the 2/32nd Battalion. Where signals might be intercepted by the enemy they were sometimes disguised by use of slang.

Horace the Horse. The bare areas are kunai grass.

(R.A.A.F.)

(*Australian War Memorial*)

The last steep pinch of the Sattelberg Road, just before reaching the summit, on 27th November 1943. The white coral formation shown here was typical of this area.

However, local resistance in small pockets continued in order to keep the Australian troops in action and prevent the 9th Division from being free to make an attack on Cape Gloucester and Marcus Point (east of Gasmata) should resistance cease altogether. While delaying action was being fought at Finschhafen the *17th Division* was being moved by land and sea from Rabaul to Cape Gloucester to resist the anticipated attack in that area.

Thus the capture of Sattelberg was a turning point in the New Guinea campaign. Until then the Japanese still hoped to stem the advance by the green-clad Australians, but now they began to look to the rear. And of all the causes of the Japanese defeat at Sattelberg and subsequent Japanese despondency, perhaps Pabu was one of the prime ones. General Adachi himself later described the effect of the loss of Pabu:

> The most advantageous position for the launching of a successful counter-attack was given up; also Pabu provided excellent observation for artillery fire, and after its capture the position of the Japanese forces was precarious. Even after the failure of the attack on Scarlet Beach we still retained some hopes of recapturing Finschhafen, but at this point the idea was abandoned.

In November, Admiral Halsey's forces in the Solomons and Admiral Nimitz's in the Central Pacific had made further advances. In the Solomons the next objective was Bougainville, the largest island in the group and, politically, part of Australian New Guinea. On it were some 65,000 Japanese, one-third of them being naval men; but the Allied estimate was lower than this. The Japanese had been there since March and April 1942 and had established airfields and naval stations. They were deployed in four principal areas: Buka, Kieta, Buin and Mawaraka. Their *XVII Army Headquarters* was in the Buin area and the fighting formations included the *6th Division, 38th Independent Brigade* and two naval landing forces each with a strength somewhere between that of a battalion and a brigade group. Few aircraft were now on the island, and in October the Japanese ceased sending surface ships to Bougainville.

Admiral Halsey decided to land on the northern shore of Empress Augusta Bay near Cape Torokina using the 3rd Marine Division. As a preliminary operation the 8th New Zealand Brigade group (Brigadier Row[3]) was given the task of taking the Treasury Islands south of Bougainville. It landed on 27th October with little opposition (there were fewer than 300 Japanese in these islands). Organised resistance ceased on the 2nd-3rd November; a total of 223 Japanese had been killed and 8 captured.

The Japanese expected a landing on Bougainville but the choice of Torokina surprised them, and only a company, with one field gun, was deployed in the area on 1st November. The gun sank four landing craft but, in spite of two air attacks, one of them by about 100 carrier aircraft, about 14,000 men were ashore and firmly established by the end of the day. A Japanese cruiser squadron was at Rabaul and, when news arrived that the American convoy was moving north, it was sent out to intercept but missed the American force and returned. On 1st November it was

---

[3] Brig R. A. Row, DSO. Comd 8 Bde NZEF 1942-43. Regular soldier; of Upper Hutt, NZ; b. Christchurch, NZ, 30 Jul 1888.

sent out again, escorting 1,000 troops in destroyers. When aircraft were seen the troops were sent back but the escort continued and, on the night of the 2nd-3rd, the 4 Japanese cruisers and 6 destroyers were intercepted in Empress Augusta Bay by an American force of 4 cruisers and 8 destroyers. In the ensuing battle the Japanese lost a light cruiser and a destroyer; no American ship was sunk.

By 5th November the marines had established a beach-head extending inland about a mile, having lost only 78 killed and 104 wounded. By the 14th 33,000 men, including the 37th Division, were ashore. The Americans extended their perimeter, in the face of ineffective enemy attacks, until it was about 15 miles long and reached about five miles inland at its deepest point. On 15th December command was taken over by Major-General Griswold of XIV Corps and in December and January the Americal Division replaced the 3rd Marine.

The offensive in the Gilbert Islands proved a tougher one. It was the first of a series of large-scale amphibious operations that were to carry the Allied forces almost to Japan itself. The plan was to assault Makin and Tarawa with the V Marine Corps, one regimental team of the raw 27th Division landing on Makin and the 2nd Marine Division on Tarawa. Early in November a convoy carrying 35,000 troops escorted by a huge naval force began to converge on the Gilberts from Pearl Harbour and the New Hebrides. Makin was defended by only about 500 men mostly engineers and air force. On 20th November the attackers landed 6,400 men supported by battleships and carrier aircraft. At the first landing place the troops met only friendly natives but at the second there was some opposition. The attackers made slow progress but, by 23rd November, the little atoll had been secured. The Americans lost 64 killed, and, in enemy air and submarine attacks on the escorting fleet, lost an escort carrier, with 644 of its crew, and many aircraft.

Tarawa is an atoll with a radius of about 18 miles. The first American objective in the area was Betio, an island of about 290 acres where an airstrip was defended by about 3,500 Japanese including the *7th Sasebo Naval Landing Force* who had built very strong defences and had many guns, ranging from 8-inch to 37-mm. On 20th November after a heavy naval and air bombardment, in which the naval ships shot 3,000 tons of projectiles, the first waves of Americans advanced towards the island in amphibious tractors designed to clamber over coral reefs or beaches. The bombardment had not been effective—far heavier ones were employed in later operations—and tractors and men were under severe fire during the landing. By midday the attackers had lost heavily and the situation was dangerous.

> Most of the amphtracs had been knocked out; and owing to the tide's refusal to rise no landing craft could float over the reef. Everything was stalled; reinforcements could not land and some 1,500 Marines were pinned down on the narrow beach under the coconut-log and coral-block wall, unable to advance or retreat . . . the beach-head was almost nonexistent.[4]

---

[4] S. E. Morison, *Aleutians, Gilberts and Marshalls, June 1942-April 1944* (English edition 1952), p. 165, a volume in the series *History of United States Naval Operations in World War II*.

By the end of the day about 5,000 men were ashore but 1,500 of them had been killed or wounded. A reinforcing battalion landed next day, came under heavy fire on the beach and soon had lost as many men as the two battalions already ashore had lost on the first day. About midday, however, the marines advanced, and captured three guns which had commanded the beach; reinforcements were landed. On the 22nd the marines held most of the island. By the afternoon of the 23rd the 3,500 defenders had been wiped out. In the four days 980 marines and 29 sailors were killed and 2,101 wounded.

CHAPTER 23

THE WAREO-GUSIKA ADVANCE

ON the 25th General Berryman discussed with General Wootten the possibility that the Japanese might withdraw from the Gusika-Wareo spur, and urged him to begin the drive north along the coast as soon as possible in order to cut the Japanese lines of withdrawal. Wootten understood the anxiety of the higher commanders that the east coast of New Guinea should be cleared before the American assault on New Britain. Nevertheless his operation order, issued on 26th November, contained no reference to a coastal advance. Twice since the landing at Scarlet Beach the 9th Division, when spread out along the coast, had been vigorously counter-attacked by an enemy pushing eastward from an inland base, and on the first occasion disaster had been very close. Although he knew that the *20th Division* was doomed Wootten had had enough experience of the fighting powers of the Japanese at bay to know that, even during retreat, they might damage an Australian coastal advance by attacking towards the sea behind the point reached by the Australians, and thus isolating them. He therefore decided to clear the Wareo-Gusika ridge, or at least control most of it, before setting off along the coast. Berryman grumbled that this "desire to over insure may take some of the dash out of his [Wootten's] drive". He was a good enough commander himself, though, to respect Wootten's experience and judgment and not to interfere unduly with the man on the job.

Thus, on 26th November, Wootten ordered that the 24th Brigade would capture the area from Gusika to the Lakes, the 20th Brigade would seize Nongora and Christmas Hills and exploit to Wareo, and the 26th Brigade would exploit north from Sattelberg to Wareo. The 4th Brigade would guard the Scarlet Beach and Heldsbach area. Berryman had already made plans to send native labour forward from Lae to release working parties from the 4th Brigade which would then be available for a coastal advance.

It will be recalled that Brigadier Porter had decided to open a shorter line of communication to the two isolated companies of the 2/32nd Battalion on Pabu, and that the simplest route would be via Pino Hill which was occupied by the enemy. In any case the enemy must be cleared from Pino Hill before the attack on the Gusika-Wareo line could be launched. Colonel Scott of the 2/32nd was ordered to capture this feature. His striking force would be his other two companies and four tanks under Lieutenant Watson.[1] The attack was to open at 8.30 a.m. on the 26th. Scott planned that Captain Lancaster's company on the right would capture Pino Hill itself and Captain Davidson's, on the left, occupy the jungle fringe. Two tanks would assist each company.

Three hours before this force set out from North Hill the other two companies of the 2/32nd faced the fiercest enemy assault since the occupa-

[1] Lt C. J. Watson, NX123602. 1 Tk Bn, 1 Armd Regt. Shipping timekeeper; of Muswellbrook, NSW; b. Tamworth, NSW, 21 Nov 1921.

tion of Pabu. At 6 a.m. two Japanese 75-mm guns, firing from less than 1,000 yards, and mortars bombarded Pabu. Constant losses caused by shelling and bombing had been perhaps the most serious problem confronting Mollard and the two medical officers in the area. The men were well dug in with overhead cover but would not remain cramped in these shelters, particularly if a wounded comrade called. Sergeant Robino[2] in charge of the stretcher bearers was just such a man. Throughout the Pabu campaign he had gone to the assistance of the wounded wherever they were lying. On this day he dressed the wounds of one man in full view of the enemy. While his comrades shouted to him to jump into a slit trench, and while shells and mortar bombs were exploding in the trees above him, he calmly splinted a compound fracture of a leg and carried the patient to cover. With such men within the Pabu perimeter it was no wonder that the vital position was held against such odds.

Under cover of the shelling the enemy attempted to infiltrate from north-west and south-west into the area held by Lieutenant Keley's company on Pabu. The enemy fire cut to pieces a large tree on the battalion's observation post on a rocky outcrop about 6 feet high. Private Saaby,[3] although wounded, remained at his post in a weapon-pit in an exposed position at the observation post whence he could see the advancing Japanese. Removing the pins from grenades, he waited for two seconds and then dropped them among the enemy who had crawled up and were sheltering below him.

The 2/12th Field Regiment rapidly ringed Pabu with shells. Documents captured later proved that the desperate enemy had planned an assault on Pabu by companies of the *I* and *III Battalions* of the *79th Regiment* from three directions in an attempt to reopen the Gusika-Wareo track. The Australian shelling broke up the attack from the east and disorganised the one from the south. The attacks lasted for about two hours and a half. Well-dug positions enabled Keley's company to repulse them all, even though some of the Japanese pressed near enough to be killed in hand-to-hand fighting. The company suffered 20 casualties including 3 killed. Lieutenant Bell, whose platoon withstood most of the enemy assaults, and Keley himself were both wounded.

Help was at hand for the beleaguered companies. Scott's start time was delayed half an hour until 9 a.m., by which time the enemy had been bombarded with 2,360 shells. Pino Hill was jungle clad and the approaches to it lay up a steep slope covered mainly in short kunai interspersed with clumps of jungle. Assisted by a platoon of the 2/7th Field Company, the four Matildas advanced in pairs through the kunai covered by the infantry companies and Papuan patrols moving along the jungle fringes. By 9.25 a.m. the tanks were on Pino Hill and half an hour later it was occupied, the enemy having abandoned his extensive positions before the arrival

---

[2] Sgt P. Robino, DCM, QX3703. 2/12 Bn, 2/3 Fd Amb. Cane farm worker; of Babinda, Qld; b. Cairns, Qld, 18 Apr 1918.

[3] Pte J. E. Saaby, MM, QX3164. 2/9 and 2/32 Bns. Labourer; of Proston, Qld; b. Carrington, NSW, 19 Mar 1907.

of the tanks. Four snipers and one python were destroyed by the American rocket machine and two machine-gun posts by the tanks.

At 10.30 a.m. Captain Richmond's company of the 2/43rd Battalion was ordered to move to Pino Hill to relieve Lancaster's, which would then march to Pabu and relieve Keley's battered company. At 11.45 a.m., and again at 1 p.m. when the two companies were changing over on Pino Hill, Japanese guns shelled the feature causing 25 casualties including 3 killed. Lancaster and one of his platoon commanders, Lieutenant E. A. G. Smith, were wounded. Despite this misfortune the company set out at 2.15 p.m. across open kunai country to Pabu. To speed the advance two Matildas carried out a diversion on the left flank, and in doing so destroyed two machine-gun nests. The company arrived at Pabu at 4 p.m. and, half an hour later, Keley's departed for Pino Hill escorting 6 stretcher cases and 19 walking wounded and sick. Jeeps drove into the kunai as far as they could to meet the cavalcade. By 7.30 p.m. it reached Pino; at the same time the telephone line to Pabu was cut again.

By 27th November Wootten's plan for a three-brigade attack on the Gusika-Wareo ridge was ready to begin. On this day, however, Berryman, Wootten and Whitehead visited Sattelberg and the 3200 Feature. Looking at the rugged country towards Wareo through which ran the precipitous valley of the Song, and thinking of the effort which would be needed to supply the 26th Brigade alone, Berryman considered that it would be unwise to commit the 20th Brigade in the centre, and another outline plan was decided upon for a two-pronged attack by the 26th and 24th Brigades on Wareo and the Gusika-Wareo ridge respectively. Whereas hitherto the general opinion had been that the enemy had important inland supply routes in addition to the coastal route, a special staff created at corps headquarters to study the enemy's supply system had now reached the conclusion that he really depended on the coastal route. For this reason the 20th Brigade was re-allotted to support the coastal thrust.

For some time natives had reported that the Japanese were in the rich and populous Kulungtufu district, and later reports suggested that these were convalescents from the Sattelberg-Wareo area and not fugitives from Lae as originally thought. They were collecting vegetables from native gardens for transport twice a week by a native carrier line to Wareo. Kulungtufu and its supply routes now became important targets for bombing and strafing. For instance, Kulungtufu was attacked on two successive days—19th and 20th November—by 27 and 32 planes respectively.

Aircraft and P.T. boats had continued their ravages during and since the Sattelberg operation. Besides giving close support to the army and bombing enemy airfields, Allied aircraft had bombed barges between Cape Gloucester and Rein Bay on 19th November and on most other days barge hunts and strafing attacks on suspected hideouts and the coastal track had been organised. In the ten nights from the opening of the Sattelberg campaign the P.T. boats had destroyed a barge near Sialum on the 16th-17th, and attacked three others off Hardenberg Point on the next night. Four nights later six heavily laden barges southward bound were sunk—three off Sio and three off Blucher Point. Two more were sunk on the 23rd-24th off Hardenberg Point, two on the 24th-25th near Sialum, and four off Annen Point on the 26th-27th. All these barges were going south laden with stores or troops. The Japanese attempted to drive off the P.T. boats by setting up guns along the coast, and by mid-November 13 guns had been identified between Vincke Point and Bonga, but only once had they been able to protect the barges successfully. This constant gnawing at the Japanese vitals had its effects. The Japanese still fought savagely against the 9th Division but the end seemed now only a matter of time. Although not yet starving they were very hungry.

The Japanese force in the coastal area comprised the *II/238th Battalion*, part of the *II/79th Battalion* and part of the *26th Field Artillery Regiment*. To the west, from the Pabu area to the Lakes and Nongora area, was the remainder of the *79th Regiment* and the *26th Field Artillery Regiment*. Attached to the *79th Regiment* was a company of the *II/78th Battalion*—a company which had been previously in the Finisterres and had then been sent round the coast to reinforce the *20th Division*. Despite all its marching this company had not fought; two-thirds of the men were ill with malaria; and most of the time of the fit men was spent searching for food. Defending the Wareo area against the 26th Brigade were the *II* and *III Battalions* of the *80th Regiment*. There was evidence that the *I/80th Battalion* had been re-formed after its near destruction in the Salamaua-Lae fighting and was now in the Kanomi area.

By 27th November the 24th Brigade's task was enlarged to include the clearing of the area south of the Kalueng River between Gusika and the Lakes. An obvious first move was to secure the coastal flank of the Gusika-Wareo ridge. The 2/28th Battalion had already been detailed for this task and Major Brown,[4] now commanding the battalion because of Colonel Norman's illness, called the company commanders together early on the 27th for orders. The battalion was to capture Imperial, Oriental, Norfolk and Exchange—the area from Bonga west to the junction of the Bonga-Wareo track with the Gusika-Wareo track. Captain Coppock's company was to move to Pabu and come under Mollard's command; next day it would clear the area from Pabu towards Exchange. Meanwhile Lieutenant Hannah's company supported by a troop of tanks would advance up the coastal track.

Actually, the move of Coppock's company to Pabu would solve more than one problem. Mollard's two companies of the 2/32nd had suffered further casualties and he now told Porter that unless a diversion could be staged towards the two Japanese bases on either side—Exchange to the north-east and a feature near Horace's Rump to the south-west—he would urgently need reinforcement if he was to hold Pabu. Coppock's company, escorting a native carrier line, arrived at Pabu at 5.30 p.m.

Soon after 1 p.m. Hannah's company, followed by the tanks, passed through the 2/43rd, advanced up the coast without opposition, and at 4.40 p.m. dug in for the night north of the waterfall. The advance continued at 9 a.m. on the 28th. Hannah's company led, with the tanks and

[4] Maj C. C. Brown, NX12354. 2/2 MG and 2/28 Bns. Quantity surveyor; of Mosman, NSW; b. Edinburgh, Scotland, 7 Sep 1908. Died 30 Jun 1957.

a detachment of the 2/7th Field Company behind, and then the remainder of the battalion (less one company). The artillery observer moved with the command group just behind the tanks. Then came a bulldozer which improved the track so that jeeps could rapidly bring up supplies. The coastal strip was flat, marshy and covered with dense jungle, and the tanks could not leave the track, but the country was unsuitable for pro-

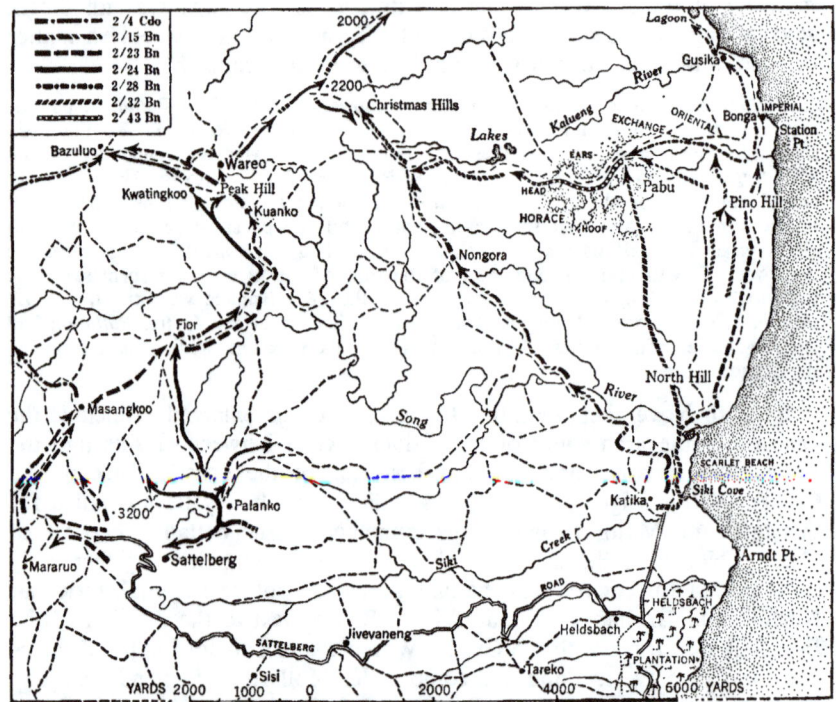

Capture of Wareo-Gusika position, 27th November-15th December

longed defence. The plan was for the tanks to follow the leading company and come to the front only when opposition was encountered. The Japanese sawed through some of the bridges, thus delaying the advance; most of the creeks in the area were also obstacles for the tanks, because crossings had to be made either by bridges or by breaking down the banks to provide fords.

Slowly but surely the battalion advanced. At 2.25 p.m. the forward scouts reported opposition from the north bank of a creek about 500 yards south of Bonga. The tanks initially could not join the company because a small stream farther back had to be bridged. Hannah sent a platoon to encircle the enemy position round the left flank, but it found the country too difficult and withdrew with two wounded. Porter and Brown came forward to see what was happening. The tanks crossed the newly-made bridge and bombarded the Japanese positions from a range of 100 yards. This was too much for the defenders who rapidly withdrew. About the same time a platoon from Coppock's company at Pabu found the high wooded ground at Exchange deserted. Here the men found a gun position for a 75-mm gun which had obviously been firing on Pabu. By dusk the rest of the company joined the platoon, and the track east from Pabu was clear as far as Exchange.

Porter thought that the 2/32nd Battalion had had about enough for the time being. He therefore ordered the 2/43rd to relieve it and prepare to advance west. At 3.35 p.m. Captain Grant's company of the 2/43rd arrived at Pabu escorting a native carrier train. It was now the turn of Captain Thornton's men, who had been on Pabu throughout, to have a spell; they escorted the natives and stretcher cases back to North Hill.

At first light on the 29th the 2/28th Battalion resumed the advance north and at 11.10 Bonga was occupied without opposition. A patrol from Hannah's company probed to the north and at 12.15 p.m. found Gusika unoccupied. Half an hour later Head's company occupied Oriental without opposition. The battalion had gained its objectives without loss and the division's right flank was secure.

Early on the 29th Porter had been so sure that the 2/28th would have no difficulty in reaching Gusika that he ordered Colonel Joshua to start the thrust west from Pabu to the Lakes the same day. Joshua arrived on Pabu with two companies at 12.20 p.m. and at 3 p.m. Mollard with the remainder of his men left the battle-scarred hill which had been their home for ten perilous but decisive days. For the loss of 25 dead and 51 wounded the men of the 2/32nd had counted 195 dead Japanese and captured 10 machine-guns and 2 mortars; many other Japanese dead had been buried by their comrades.

As Mollard left for the south Grant moved cautiously west towards Horace's Head. The leading scout reached Horace's Ears about 400 yards west of Pabu when he noticed four Japanese walking down the track. An ambush was quickly set but the Japanese jumped into pits. The leading section promptly attacked. Private Bamess,[5] the Bren gunner, took command when the section commander was killed and led the men forward until they were stopped by fire from two machine-guns sited in depth. Bamess went forward alone and destroyed the first machine-gun and then the second. His men then killed the Japanese in six weapon-pits before being stopped by fire from the right flank. Another section then attacked on the left flank and destroyed two more machine-gun posts before it, too, was pinned down by fire from a Japanese position behind a rock straight ahead.

Grant sent Sergeant Bonner's[6] platoon round on the right flank. It crept up the steep rise as close as possible to the enemy position, which was in a narrow kunai patch 15 yards wide between bamboo and thick

---

[5] L-Cpl B. A. Bamess, DCM, WX10180; 2/43 Bn. Bogger; of Nyabing, WA; b. Busselton, WA, 16 Oct 1914.

[6] Sgt R. J. Bonner, MM, SX5279; 2/43 Bn. Truck driver; of North Adelaide; b. Prospect, SA, 18 Apr 1918.

jungle, and thence Bonner led it into the attack until heavy fire from the right flank forced the men to take cover. Like Bamess before, Bonner moved forward under heavy fire and threw grenades at the Japanese machine-gun positions. He destroyed two and then returned to lead his platoon forward in a fierce assault. The Japanese retaliated with grenades but the attack was too determined to be withstood, and the defenders were overwhelmed, some being shot in their slit trenches. "Come this way", and "Don't shoot, they are ours", shouted three Japanese who ran from the holes. Two were shot. The ground cleared was steep and covered with rocks and roots under which the Japanese had burrowed. It was doubtless valuable ground, but Joshua felt that the company should withdraw to a more favourable position. It was unfortunate that this ground, dearly won by skilful stalking and fierce fighting, had to be sacrificed.

Meanwhile, the 26th Brigade was probing north towards the Song River. Patrolling along the main track towards Fior on the 27th Lieutenant Gray's company of the 2/23rd found an enemy position 700 yards before Fior. Patrols unsuccessfully searched the area to the north-west to find suitable crossings over the Song which loomed as the brigade's main obstacle. The 2/24th patrolled north from Palanko. One platoon reached the 1800 Feature but could find no suitable tracks towards the Song. After some skirmishing two platoons pushed on towards Fior but were stopped by a strongly entrenched enemy position in bamboo and dug in for the night.

Next day the 2/23rd and 2/24th found that the Japanese had abandoned their positions during the night. The 2/23rd descended some 2,300 feet and passed through many small streams where the troops enjoyed their first baths for some time. Fior was empty. When they neared the Song the Australians and Papuans found that the suspension bridge had been destroyed and was lying in the stream. Gray's company moved to within 150 yards of this main crossing place and drew heavy fire. Patrols found another possible crossing place where they waded through the river to the north side. By nightfall Lieutenant Lyne's company of the 2/23rd was across the river and the bridgehead was secure.

On the 29th Wootten sent a warning to Brigadier Edgar of the 4th Brigade: "On a date to be notified 4 Inf Bde will advance by coast route to first objective—area about mouth of Masaweng River. . . . Advance will be by bounds from and to beach maintenance areas only two of which will be used concurrently and which until relinquished will be protected by 4th Brigade." Wootten planned that the brigade would concentrate in the Bonga area by 2nd December.

Like Wootten, Dougherty and Chilton, Edgar, whose brigade was now to enter the fight, had come from the 2/2nd Battalion, which he had commanded in the Owen Stanley campaign. Most of his long service in the militia between 1922 and 1939 had been in artillery. Thus this experienced and genial leader was well fitted for the task ahead; he knew the jungle and the Japanese, and would be keen to use artillery to overcome opposition. Lieut-Colonels Cusworth of the 29th/46th Battalion and

Rowan[7] of the 37th/52nd had commanded companies in the Middle East. Lieut-Colonel O'Connor of the 22nd was a regular officer until recently on the staff of New Guinea Force.

By the 30th, the 9th Division was poised for what all hoped would be a knockout blow. As well as his 12 infantry battalions Wootten had a tank squadron, a machine-gun battalion, a Pioneer battalion and a commando squadron; in the area a powerful array of artillery and engineers was now available.[8]

The 2/28th led off on the morning of the 30th when a patrol crossed the Kalueng River on its way to the Lagoon area. A quarter of a mile north of the river it was halted by Japanese entrenched at the jungle fringe, and called for artillery and mortar support. From Pabu two companies of the 2/43rd, led by Captains Grant and Fleming, set out at 4 p.m. on the 30th to capture Horace's Ears. Supported by two tanks, they advanced along a track running along a high spur with many ravines on each side. When the leading Australians were fired on from the eastern Ear the tanks came forward and blasted the position with such effect that by 7.15 p.m. the infantrymen captured the Ears against slight opposition.

On 1st December Lieutenant Rooke led a patrol from the 2/28th across the Kalueng towards the Lagoon after an artillery shoot on the positions occupied by the Japanese the previous day. Rooke's men patrolled almost to the Lagoon. Late in the afternoon he decided to return but, after pushing south about 600 yards, his scouts heard sounds of digging and chopping ahead. After killing one Japanese and wounding another, Rooke moved west and then south to avoid the enemy position. Towards dusk he met a strong Japanese patrol to the south-west of the original position and had three men wounded. Moving north-east to avoid the enemy, the patrol dug in for the night, while Rooke climbed a tree and saw Japanese to the north-west and north-east. He then sent two volunteers—Privates Hutton[9] and Wade[1]—to try to slip through to battalion headquarters and summon aid. Both were killed.[2] At 8 p.m. the patrol sneaked out under cover of rain and darkness and dug in for the night near the Kalueng. It arrived back at 9 a.m. on the 2nd.

Captain Fleming's company of the 2/43rd was forming up with the tanks to advance to the Lakes early on the 1st when it was fired on from

---

[7] Lt-Col J. G. Rowan, MC, ED, VX157. 2/6 Bn; CO 37/52 Bn 1942-45. Farmer; of Colac, Vic; b. Colac, 26 Oct 1905.

[8] Artillery:
2/12 Fd Regt (23, 24, 62 Btys)
2/6 Fd Regt (11, 12, 56 Btys)
2/4 Lt AA Regt (10, 12 Btys)
2/3 Lt AA Bty (Airborne)
11 Bty 2/3 A-Tk Regt
"M" Hvy Bty
2 Mtn Bty (less sec)
1 Fd Sec 2/3 Survey Bty

Engineers:
2/3 Fd Coy
2/7 Fd Coy
2/13 Fd Coy
2/24 Fd Pk Coy
2/29 Camouflage Unit
Detachment 2/1 Mech Eqpt Coy
18 Fd Coy

[9] Pte H. G. Sutton, SX13447; 2/28 Bn. Labourer; of Sanderston, SA; b. Mount Pleasant, SA, 9 Jan 1917. Killed in action 1 Dec 1943.

[1] Pte C. J. A. Wade, VX91902; 2/28 Bn. Salesman; of North Fitzroy, Vic; b. Brunswick, Vic, 20 Apr 1917. Killed in action 1 Dec 1943.

[2] They had left with 4 grenades and about 40 rounds of ammunition each. When their bodies were found it could be seen that one man had been killed soon after encountering the Japanese. The other, although wounded, had continued the fight and had used all his grenades and almost all his rifle ammunition before he died.

the direction of Horace's western Ear. The tanks soon blasted this opposition aside also, thus enabling Fleming to occupy Horace's Jaws and later dig in on the Nose and the western Ear. Late in the afternoon a small patrol under Corporal Squibb[3] set out to destroy an enemy position between the two companies. Throwing grenades and firing from the hip, the men overwhelmed these Japanese. One of the Japanese had a Bren, another a rifle and most were wearing Australian clothing and carrying Australian rations, probably obtained from inaccurate air drops on Pabu.

Captain Richmond's company of the 2/43rd took over the advance towards the Lakes from the two companies which had now captured all of Horace. Richmond left Pabu at 8 a.m. on 2nd December with one tank in support, reached the edge of the kunai immediately east of the Lakes against slight opposition, and advanced another 250 yards, but withdrew slightly when his line of communication was attacked. Joshua decided to add punch to the attack by sending Fleming's company and another tank round the right flank, and by 3.30 p.m. it reached the southern edge of the bigger lake. There a tank crawled up past Fleming's company and fought a duel with two Japanese guns—a 75-mm and a 37-mm—firing from high ground north of the lake at 200 yards' range. The tank was perhaps over venturesome and as it was in an exposed position on top of a rise it was eventually damaged after taking 50 hits. No shells penetrated the armour but tracks and track-adjusting mechanism were damaged; the crew eventually backed the tank out.

Wootten had finally satisfied himself that it would not be necessary to use the whole of the 20th Brigade in the central sector; only the 2/15th Battalion (now under Major Suthers' command) with a platoon of Papuans would be needed to capture Nongora and send fighting patrols towards Christmas Hills. Thus on the 30th Captain Stuart's company had advanced across rugged country to the Song, which was crossed about a quarter of a mile upstream from the ford. About 200 yards north-west of the crossing one man was killed and three wounded by machine-gun fire. The company then guarded the crossing while Captain Jenkinson's[4] company and Major Newcomb's passed through and advanced towards Nongora, going round the Japanese position ahead of Stuart. At 2.30 p.m. a patrol from the reserve company south of the crossing found the enemy position deserted and occupied it; the leading companies dug in about a quarter of a mile from Nongora.

Early on 1st December these companies faced Japanese on a high ridge running north and south to the east of the village. At 2.30 p.m. Jenkinson's company attacked the Japanese positions on the south end of the ridge. The attack was fierce but unsuccessful, the Australians suffering 13 casualties. That night, however, the Japanese withdrew, and about midday on the 2nd Newcomb's company entered a deserted Nongora, once the head-

---

[3] WO2 A. C. Squibb, MM, TX5553; 2/43 Bn. Orchard labourer; of Devonport, Tas; b. Isle of Wight, England, 25 Nov 1918.

[4] Lt-Col R. G. Jenkinson, QX6274; 2/15 Bn. Regular soldier; of Mackay, Qld; b. Adelaide, 17 Aug 1916.

quarters of the *20th Japanese Division*. Colonel Simpson instructed Major Strange,[5] now commanding the leading companies, to patrol towards Christmas Hills and east towards the Lakes to assist the 24th Brigade.

During this three-day period the 26th Brigade had also been pushing forward over very difficult country. At first light on the 30th Captain Tietyens' company of the 2/23rd crossed the Song at Lieutenant Lyne's crossing place. The plan was now for both companies to cut the main Kuanko Track; Lyne would then advance north and Tietyens would move south and destroy the Japanese opposition at the regular crossing place. The companies scrambled up the steep slope to the track and, after a short rest, set out in their respective directions. After 200 yards Tietyens met strong resistance. In two sharp fights his men destroyed what must have been the rear positions of the enemy garrison defending the crossing. In a third attack Lieutenant Lazer's[6] platoon, with fixed bayonets, overwhelmed the remaining Japanese. About 30 casualties were inflicted on the enemy in this spirited assault. Soon the whole battalion had crossed the Song. When Lyne's company met opposition about 900 yards from the river a battalion perimeter was formed for the night.

Throughout the Sattelberg campaign the weather had fortunately remained dry. It rained on the day Sattelberg fell and now late on the 30th it rained again, making the steep track from the Song to the 2/23rd even more difficult. Even without the rain it would have been impossible to use the tanks on the wretched tracks across the valley of the Song. Whitehead was finding it difficult to supply his brigade, even though only one of his battalions was in action. Despite the work of the engineers and a company of the 2/3rd Pioneer Battalion, the jeephead, at the end of November, had only reached Palanko. In wet weather the whole route almost as far back as Katika became impassable for jeeps which had to be towed by tractors. To supply the 2/23rd Battalion from Palanko a three-day turn around over steep country was necessary. Because such native carriers as could be spared for the 26th Brigade were insufficient, the whole of the 2/24th Battalion had to carry for the 2/23rd.

An attack by the 2/23rd cleared Kuanko on 1st December; dumping their non-essential gear to lighten and quicken their task of climbing the steep slope Lieutenant Gilmour's company destroyed several small pockets of Japanese defenders along the track. At 12.15 p.m. the company smashed the last opposition south of Kuanko and entered the remains of the village. The Japanese still clung doggedly to the ridge beyond, however, as Lieutenant Gray's company found at 2.30 p.m. when it advanced 300 yards north-west. Colonel Tucker signalled Whitehead that the opposition was "pretty solid", adding, "think they may have to stick there for some time". Supply difficulties now increased. The track was wet and slippery as heavy rain had fallen; this solved the water problem but made the task of the

---

[5] Maj B. D. Strange, DSO, QX6222; 2/15 Bn. Departmental manager; of Townsville, Qld; b. Brisbane, 5 Apr 1913. Accidentally killed 20 Sep 1944.

[6] Lt B. L. B. Lazer, VX33517; 2/23 Bn. Professional golfer; of Oakleigh, Vic; b. Windsor, Vic, 24 Dec 1919.

2/24th Battalion even more unpleasant as the men struggled forward with supplies to a dump near Kuanko. The 2/24th, which had not had quite the same recent successes as its sister battalions, did not relish its task but stuck to it loyally.

At first light on 2nd December patrols from the 2/23rd north of Kuanko found the Japanese in strength along the ridge towards Peak Hill. Because of the thick bamboo the patrols could only crawl. At 8.30 a.m. the Japanese sprayed the whole Kuanko area with machine-gun fire. Thereupon artillery and mortars bombarded the Japanese position, and machine-guns increased the din of battle. At dusk the Japanese suddenly attacked Lyne's company. They used bombs made of gelignite which had a frightening blast effect but did little damage. The company was caught on the wrong foot, some of the men withdrew, and some equipment was lost. The worst feature of the Japanese attack was the loss of the commanding ground north of Kuanko. So serious was the situation that Tucker sent Gilmour's company into a night attack—the battalion's first in New Guinea. The leading platoon lost several men including the platoon commander. Corporal Lay[7] took charge and under heavy fire he and his men clung to the little ground gained until he was ordered to return. During this action Lieutenant McKeddie of the 2/12th Field Regiment was forward and for an hour and a half directed artillery fire which was mainly responsible for smashing the enemy attacks. Despite this the battalion was forced into what its diarist described as a "somewhat congested perimeter".[8]

While the infantry were battling for Kuanko, the 2/4th Commando Squadron was scouting and patrolling. On 2nd December, when a company of the 2/48th Battalion took over Mararuo, Major Garvey moved to the Masangkoo area. Whitehead now ordered Garvey to arrange two patrols—one to find crossing places over the Song north from Masangkoo and the other into the Kulungtufu area. For this latter patrol a platoon of the Papuan Infantry joined the 2/4th. Captain Gore's company of the Papuan Battalion had now been in action for three months and corps headquarters believed that it needed a rest, particularly as it had been subjected on occasions to artillery fire. General Morshead therefore decided that "A" Company of the Papuan Battalion, which had fought throughout the Salamaua campaign, should move forward from Lae and relieve Gore's "C" Company which would rest in the pleasant Kulungtufu-Hube area and use its influence to enlist the local natives for Angau. It remained to be seen, of course, whether the Japanese were still in Kulungtufu.

For a brief two days, training teams from the "resting" battalions of the three A.I.F. brigades were attached to Brigadier Edgar's three battalions to pass on their recent experience in jungle fighting. Wootten

---

[7] Cpl R. E. Lay, MM, VX57290; 2/23 Bn. Storeman; of Carlton, Vic; b. Ulverstone, Tas, 4 Jan 1917.

[8] Writing to Colonel Houston later Tucker commended "the work of the gun team of No. 2 Gun of F Troop, which on the night of 2nd-3rd December 1943 fired a total of 210 rounds in an hour into a very close target within 100 yards of our own forward troops".

then decided to attach "experienced A.I.F. personnel" from his brigades to Edgar's three battalions as "advisers" during the 4th Brigade's forthcoming operations. Thus the 20th, 24th and 26th Brigades would each supply to the 29th/46th, 37th/52nd and 22nd Battalions respectively a team consisting of 3 officers, 9 N.C.O's, 9 privates capable of leading sections, one private experienced in "Q" work, and one 3-inch mortarman capable of commanding a mortar detachment. The 2/2nd Machine Gun Battalion would also attach an N.C.O. and a private capable of commanding a machine-gun section to each battalion of the 4th Brigade. When these attachments were made the training teams returned to their brigades.

All was ready for a new phase of the Australian offensive. On 2nd December Wootten's new operation order stated that the division would advance along the coast to an "ultimate objective to be notified". The first phase would be the completion of the capture of the Gusika-Wareo-Sattelberg area and the capture of Fortification Point. The 26th and 24th Brigades would continue the thrust towards Wareo and Christmas Hills while the 4th would advance to Fortification Point.[9] Edgar's first brigade operation order, issued also on the 2nd, stated that the advance to Fortification Point would be by bounds, the first two to the area west of Kamlagidu Point and north of the Lagoon, and the third to Kiligia. On these bounds the 29th/46th Battalion would lead, with a company of the 37th/52nd Battalion assisted by the Papuan platoon as flank protection in the foothills to the west. Wootten decided that supply by sea would be quicker and more efficient than by land. Successive beach-heads must therefore be captured and protected until the next beach-head up the coast was opened. At the most, even for a two-brigade advance, only two beach-heads would be in use concurrently.

Lieut-Colonel Searl[1] wished to use the small Gusika beach at the mouth of the Kalueng River as the first beach-head, but the engineers had first to remove underwater and hardwood obstacles and build a bridge over the steep-banked Kalueng for the tanks and jeeps to cross. Consequently Edgar ordered the 22nd Battalion to cross the river on the 3rd and capture a bridgehead.

At first light on the 3rd Colonel O'Connor moved forward to Gusika to reconnoitre the crossing; at 9 a.m. he gave his orders—capture the high ground north and west of Gusika and secure the Gusika beach-head. Captain Dodd's[2] company at 10.15 a.m. moved to cover the Kalueng

---

[9] Under Edgar's command, in addition to his three battalions, were:
"A" Coy 2/2 MG Bn   Lt Sec 2/8 Fd Amb
"C" Sqn 1 Tk Bn less 11 tanks (7 tanks)   Det 9 Div ASC
9 Pl Papuan Battalion   Det Angau
4 Fd Amb (less 1 Coy)   Det 532 EBSR
In support were: 2/6 Fd Regt, 2/7 Fd Coy.
Air support and artillery air reconnaissance would be by request and there would be a daily Tac R sortie along the coastal strip and tracks leading to the coast from inland.

[1] Col B. R. W. Searl, OBE, NX492. (1st AIF: Pte 4 Bn.) HQ 20 Bde 1940-41; DAQMG 7 Div 1941-42; AA & QMG 9 Div 1943-44; AQMG LHQ 1944-45, DQMG 1945. Company manager; of Newcastle, NSW; b. Mudgee, NSW, 23 May 1899.

[2] Capt H. H. Dodd, VX108148; 22 Bn. Retail drapery buyer and sub-manager; of Leongatha, Vic; b. Flemington, Vic, 9 Dec 1915.

ford. Half an hour later three companies—Captain McFadden's,[3] Captain Guild's[4] and Captain Martin's—crossed. After McFadden's men on the coastal track had scrambled up a 30-foot bluff overlooking the Kalueng, the leading platoon advanced about 100 yards before being stopped by machine-gun and mortar fire from the track ahead. McFadden called for artillery support but there was a delay of an hour because of faulty communications. When the artillery bombardment ceased at 12.45 p.m. the company attacked, but without success. A quarter of an hour later Guild's company reached unmolested a knoll about a mile north-west of Gusika, while Martin's company was fired on about half way between the other two companies. Unable to encircle the Japanese position because of a cliff to the left, Martin withdrew south and west and then took up a position just north of the Kalueng.

After more artillery fire McFadden's company attacked again, this time assisted by a section of machine-gunners who fired north along the timber edge and then switched to the tree tops to deal with snipers. By 5 p.m. the company had driven out the enemy. Thus the 22nd Battalion established the bridgehead and reached a position about 500 yards south of the Lagoon.

The 22nd Battalion fought hard on the 4th to clear the enemy south of the Lagoon, but without success. Patrols discovered the enemy dug in near the creek half way from the Kalueng to the Lagoon. At 11.55 a.m. one of McFadden's platoons which had attacked the Japanese position was forced to withdraw because of strong enemy fire; it reported that the track was mined against tanks. McFadden now tried to arrange an artillery shoot on the Japanese position but, for the third time in three days, the artillery signal lines failed, so that it was not possible to begin the shelling until 2.15 p.m.

The attack, this time by two platoons, began when the shelling finished at 2.45 p.m. Lieutenant Holdsworth's[5] platoon on the right reached a garden area before turning left and cutting the track. The left-hand platoon did not arrive in time to support the right-hand one. When Holdsworth opened fire the Japanese replied from west and south of the garden and also from the creek. Holdsworth and others were wounded in the first burst and the platoon became disorganised. Even at this early stage the company had not enough leaders; there were no N.C.O's in the platoon, and it was because of the initiative and coolness of Private Lindhe[6] that it did not panic. He was commanding the right-hand section in the northern end of the garden when he found his left flank unprotected because the other two sections had withdrawn. Leaving his own section, he rallied the other two, recovered the wounded, and led the platoon out of a difficult situation towards the coast and then to the south. The left-

---
[3] Capt R. J. McFadden, VX108144; 22 Bn. Store manager; of Toora, Vic; b. Kilrea, N Ireland, 15 May 1912.
[4] Capt W. S. Guild, VX108145; 22 Bn. Public servant; of Toorak, Vic; b. Arbroath, Scotland, 3 Jul 1905.
[5] Capt H. Holdsworth, VX108156; 22 Bn. Dairy farmer; of Toora, Vic; b. Rawalpindi, India, 10 Feb 1911.
[6] Sgt N. Lindhe, VX13582; 22 Bn. Clerk; of Bendigo, Vic; b. Swan Hill, Vic, 28 Apr 1923.

hand platoon was too late to join in the fighting and was fired on before it too withdrew. It seemed that there was at least a company of Japanese well dug in between the creek and the coast.

During this action a platoon from Martin's company, led by Lieutenant Prendergast, reached the upper sections of the creek. It was fired on at 3.45 p.m. from enemy positions lower down, and later from the north bank of the creek. A runner reached Martin's headquarters at 5 p.m. and immediately set out again to guide the company to the beleaguered platoon. The wounded were recovered before the reunited company withdrew in the face of strong enemy pressure.

To 13 casualties suffered on the first day were now added 17 on the 4th. During the day the sappers finished the bridge over the Kalueng and the tanks were ready to cross. The bridgehead had been established for the loss of 30 men—a high loss which would undoubtedly be avoided in similar conditions after more experience. The other two battalions were ready for their part on the 4th; the diarist of the 37th/52nd Battalion noted the "air of expectancy" within his battalion.

The Japanese opposing the 22nd Battalion were probably from a mixed force of infantry (*II/238th Battalion,* and a company from *78th Regiment*), engineers and artillery under Major Tashiro, the commander of the *II/238th Battalion.* The force order stated that "the force, while avoiding any decisive engagement, will carry out successive resistance to try to delay enemy advance".

On the Wareo Track Brigadier Porter was worried by the physical condition of the 2/43rd Battalion. "It was apparent," he wrote, "that they were not equal to the task of attacking beyond the Lakes area." When, on 3rd December, he ordered the 24th Brigade to capture Christmas Hills he decided that he must pep up or relieve the 2/43rd. He hoped to use the 2/28th Battalion but, as all senior officers of that battalion were sick and it was commanded by the adjutant, Captain Freedman[7] (although himself ill), Porter decided that the most rested portions of the 2/32nd Battalion must be used. The 2/32nd had expected a real spell and the men were relaxing and swimming and enjoying canteen supplies. "It is a great tonic," wrote the battalion's diarist, "to wear fresh clean clothes again." But at 9.30 a.m. on the 3rd Colonel Scott with two companies left the Pino Hill-North Hill area to help the 2/43rd.

When Scott's force arrived at the Lakes—Bacon and Egg as they were named—he found Captain Richmond's company of the 2/43rd in a fierce fight with the Japanese; it was covering the tanks, now bogged and disabled, and attempting to dislodge the Japanese 50 yards ahead. By midday the enemy could withstand the pressure no longer and withdrew 100 yards. Scott now took command in the Lakes area with two companies of the 2/43rd under command. He planned to use Gordon's company to cut the main track half way between the Lakes and Christmas Hills after a wide flanking movement to the south; Fleming's would next clear the track from there back to the 2/32nd which would then resume the advance to Christmas Hills.

---

[7] Maj H. J. Freedman, WX3393; 2/28 Bn. Salesman; of North Perth; b. Perth, 4 Aug 1908.

Early on the 3rd a patrol from the 2/15th led by Lieutenant Richardson[8] probed forward from Nongora towards Christmas Hills (1800 Feature). About 900 yards south of Christmas Hills the patrol met the Japanese and Richardson, going forward to investigate, was killed. Strange issued his orders for the capture of Christmas Hills—the 2/32nd's objective. The 2/15th were warned to keep in close touch with Scott.

Scott's composite force which began the attack on the 4th was tired; his own two companies still needed a long rest after Pabu and the companies from the 2/43rd Battalion were only capable of carrying on when they were "culled of semi-sick personnel and supplemented by HQ company personnel".[9] Battle casualties, sickness and the strain of three months of jungle fighting were having their effects. Malarial casualties were heavy. All battalions were well below strength, and it was just as well that the end appeared to be in sight.[1]

From 7 a.m. on the 4th the 24th Battery bombarded the Japanese positions along the track. An hour later the 3-inch mortars took up the plastering. Gordon's company of the 2/43rd at the same time travelled south from the main track and to the west parallel with it. The route was very rough and led along razor-backs. As they moved west the men could hear the Japanese talking and moving about on the main track to the north. After moving silently in a wide semi-circle, the company, by good navigation, reached the track at the spot intended, about 800 yards behind the Japanese. Fleming's company also reached the track and by 2 p.m. both companies were digging their positions along the track. Although the Japanese were at each end of the length of track occupied by the two companies, both company commanders told Scott that the position was quite tenable.

To save the 2/32nd for the final phase, Scott ordered Fleming's company to attack east and clear the track. Fleming set off at 3.30 p.m. but half an hour later the company was stopped by Japanese firing from a saddle. The 2/43rd's frame of mind was evident from the comment in its diary that "B" Company had been instructed "to move 800 yards down track to clear out enemy pocket that frightened 2/32nd Battalion"—not the normal sort of remark by one illustrious battalion about another.

By this time the 2/15th Battalion had also found that its expectations could not be fulfilled. Captain Stuart's company left confidently at 2.45 p.m., keeping to the east of the main track. The company reached to within a quarter of a mile of the main Wareo-Gusika track south of Christmas Hills, where further progress was stopped by a steep gorge. It then returned and Captain Snell's company prepared for another attempt, this time to the north-west. Late on the 4th Wootten instructed Simpson that the 2/15th would cease to take an active part in the fight towards

---

[8] Lt F. Richardson, WX1790. 2/3 Fd Regt, and 2/33, 2/11 and 2/15 Bns. Farmer; of Broomehill, WA; b. Katanning, WA, 17 Jan 1922. Killed in action 3 Dec 1943.

[9] Lessons on Operations 24 Aust Inf Bde from 12 Nov to 8 Dec 43 by Brig S. H. Porter.

[1] On 4th December, for instance, the total strength of the 24th Brigade was 35 officers and 842 men: 2/28 Bn, 12 officers and 314 men; 2/32 Bn, 10 and 272; 2/43 Bn, 13 and 256. The normal establishment of an infantry battalion was then 33 officers and 773 other ranks, including attached personnel.

Christmas Hills, but would hold Nongora until the jeephead arrived there. He intended to save the 20th Brigade for the coastal advance.

In the Kuanko area on 3rd December the 2/23rd Battalion was clinging grimly to the unfavourable position to which it had been pushed by the enemy on the previous evening. The brigade "sitrep" early in the morning stated: "Enemy in strong positions overlooking our positions and seems determined to hold the ground." Despite the efforts of the 2/24th Battalion, the 2/23rd Battalion still had too few supplies. Tucker's second-in-command, Major Spier,[2] had a hard task organising and leading supplies forward from the Song to Kuanko. At first light on the 3rd Tucker was better able to estimate the damage done by the loss of the high ground. A patrol discovered that the battalion's supply route where it curled and entered Kuanko from due north-east was under Japanese fire, and that the Japanese had dug in within 20 yards of the sharp bend. A new supply route was rapidly cut and the porters from the 2/24th were not molested during their stiff climb to Kuanko.

Enemy snipers were troubling the 2/23rd, but the battalion more than held its own in the sniping and firing duel. After midday the Japanese fired from both sides "but", wrote the battalion's diarist, "such attention from the enemy became merely an uncomfortable portion of the daily routine, without causing undue inconvenience". Late in the day Captain Dennys'[3] company of the 2/24th moved up the Kuanko Track and dug in 900 yards south of the 2/23rd.

Next morning both the 2/23rd and 2/24th Battalions prepared to deal with the Japanese. It was not long, however, before Tucker found that the Japanese had moved round to his rear in the night and seemed certain to cut his communications. Five minutes after receiving this news, Whitehead at 8.25 a.m. ordered Colonel Gillespie to have Dennys' company of the 2/24th "squeeze" the portion of the track occupied by the Japanese and join the 2/23rd. An hour later Dennys advanced north towards the 2/23rd's position without seeing any Japanese. At 11 a.m. Dennys was fired on by Japanese to the east of the main track when he had reached a track junction about 75 yards south of the 2/23rd. He dug in and sent out patrols which found that the enemy was occupying the track between Kuanko and the company's position. "Leaving Japanese where he is for moment," wrote the brigade diarist, "as we know where he is." While the enemy was being left where he was Lieutenant Shattock[4] of the 2/24th led a patrol to cut the Wareo-Kuanko track at Peak Hill. At 3.30 p.m. the patrol joined the 2/23rd Battalion to discuss routes to Peak Hill.

In the mid-afternoon Gillespie suggested using the artillery more than it had been recently used. Brigade agreed and asked for targets. It was a pity that the brigade at this stage did not have the support of the 2nd

---

[2] Maj P. E. Spier, ED, VX48398; 2/23 Bn. Architect; of Heidelberg, Vic; b. Charters Towers, Qld, 2 Feb 1909.

[3] Capt G. E. Dennys, NX4731. 9 Div Sigs and 2/24 Bn. Radioman and salesman; of North Sydney; b. Muswellbrook, NSW, 4 Mar 1917.

[4] Capt E. J. Shattock, VX32828; 2/24 Bn. Commercial artist; of Essendon, Vic; b. Essendon, 28 Jun 1913.

Mountain Battery. Whitehead had several times asked for it, but Division had other plans, plans which came to nothing. On 29th November Whitehead informed Lieutenant Cunningham,[5] who was reconnoitring the Sattelberg area for new gun positions, that he wanted the guns to cover the advance on Wareo. On 1st December the battery commander reported to 26th Brigade headquarters, where he was told that the brigade expected to occupy Wareo by 2 p.m. and that the guns would probably not be needed in the next move along the Lakona Track to the coast. "No job at all for us . . ." exploded the battery's diarist next day. "It is hard to see why we were brought here in the first place. . . . Under present conditions no orders at all forthcoming from R.A.A. who will not allot us in support of a brigade or give us a defensive role or zone or tell us that there is nothing to do. The only orders are to 'wait'."[6]

On the left flank the 2/4th Commando Squadron and a platoon of the Papuan Infantry assisted by some Angau men were patrolling. On the 4th a patrol to the west reached Joangeng where the natives reported that 44 Japanese had recently been in the area. The gardens were good and native foods were plentiful. Brigade now decided to establish a dump of stores at Joangeng; about 100 natives with signal equipment and rations for 30 men for 8 days were warned to move west. Information from the patrols confirmed native rumours that Japanese convalescents from the *20th Division* in the Joangeng-Kulungtufu area had been moving north-east towards Zagahemi.

There was still some tough fighting and wretched country ahead before Wareo could be taken, but the end could not be long delayed. Poorly administered, indifferently led, and badly supplied, the Japanese of the *20th Division* had only their courage and determination left to withstand the Australians' relentless pressure towards Wareo. The Australians were very tired but the Japanese were desperately so.

Between the Lakes and Christmas Hills Scott's force pushed west on 5th December. The companies of the 2/43rd Battalion early found that the enemy between their positions and the 2/32nd had disappeared during the night, leaving dead men of the *79th* and *80th Regiments,* equipment, rifles and, near an anti-tank ditch, a gun position and a dump of 81-mm mortar bombs. Thornton's company of the 2/32nd Battalion now led the advance and dug in about 250 yards farther west and within striking distance of Christmas Hills. When Davidson's company took over these positions Thornton tried to outflank Japanese 50 yards farther on. After moving south and parallel to the track for 200 yards he found the Japanese between his company and the track. Trying to break through, the Australians found the Japanese well dug in on another ridge nearer the track.

---

[5] Lt D. M. Cunningham, VX1057. 2/2 Fd Regt, 2 Mtn Bty. Traveller; of Brighton, Vic; b. Brighton, England, 30 Sep 1909.

[6] It would be hard to find a more useful task for the mountain guns (75-mm) than the support of 26th Brigade over the rugged country to Wareo. It was in similar country in the Salamaua campaign that the 1st Mountain Battery had made such a name for itself. The 2nd Mountain Battery had joined in the fight for Sattelberg only on 22nd November.

Six Japanese were killed but the company lost seven men, including a platoon commander, Corporal Bemrose,[7] killed. Private Curley[8] was given command of this platoon, which covered the extrication of the wounded. The company then withdrew to the lower slopes of Christmas Hills.

Early on the 6th the 24th Battery bombarded Christmas Hills with 500 shells in 40 minutes. Davidson's company, followed by Thornton's, then tried to approach Christmas Hills from the north-east but were halted by heavy fire. For the remainder of the day 25-pounders and 3-inch mortars shelled the Japanese. The day ended with the 2/32nd Battalion dug in on the eastern slope near the top of Christmas Hills, and the Japanese about 100 yards away on the western slope.

True to form the Japanese abandoned these last positions in the night. The end came none too soon, for the companies of the 2/32nd Battalion were down to about 30 tired men each. Scott later wrote:

> It is admitted that our advance was slow. . . . Our advance due to terrain was made principally along the track except for the cutting of the track 800 yards behind the enemy's F.D.L's in the first phase of the attack and even then the "going" was so difficult that our wounded could not be evacuated along our outward track and had to wait till the following day when the enemy between our forces were eradicated. The enemy successively took up positions on commanding ground— our attack was made on continually rising ground right to the top of Christmas Hills —and each time we attempted an outflanking movement our progress was frustrated by unscaleable cliffs on the top of which sat the Jap. It was impossible to use tanks. Our companies were little more than platoons in strength. . . . The only feasible plan under the circumstances was to pin-point the enemy defences and then "bash" him with mortars and artillery; this method proved really effective causing many casualties and forcing him to evacuate his positions leaving his wounded, equipment, ammunition and some weapons behind. Admittedly we could have possibly captured the positions quicker by a "death or glory" assault on the enemy defences. However, our casualties would have been heavy and we could ill afford to risk such a venture at this stage due to our sadly depleted strengths, and further our troops were almost exhausted mentally and physically—actually in this operation our casualties were light—one killed and nine wounded.

The 26th Brigade's experience was similar as it strove to advance the short distance from Kuanko to Wareo. On the 5th heavy rain prevented the jeeps getting far with the supplies. By the strenuous efforts of the natives, the 2/24th, and part of brigade headquarters, enough supplies were carried forward to enable Whitehead to use the 2/24th for fighting again. It was now obvious to him that an enemy company on the high ground north and north-east of Kuanko could hold up a battalion. This is exactly what was happening. Patrols from the 2/23rd towards the north-east were unable to penetrate far because of the rugged country. Captain Bieri's company of the 2/24th was now ordered to follow Shattock's platoon which continued its out-flanking move on the 5th and dug in west of the track between Kuanko and Peak Hill. Gillespie's head-

---

[7] Cpl R. Bemrose, QX3019; 2/32 Bn. Timber worker; of Goomari, Qld; b. Napier, NZ, 7 Mar 1916. Killed in action 5 Dec 1943.

[8] Cpl W. S. Curley, WX15063; 2/32 Bn. Farm hand; of Goomalling, WA; b. Goomalling, 9 Jan 1920.

quarters moved up during the day to about 500 yards south of the 2/23rd and both commanding officers discussed plans.

Early on the 6th three companies of the 2/24th were following Shattock's platoon. At 8.40 a.m. Tucker discovered that the Japanese had left their positions to his north-east. Here extensive diggings for about 50 men were found. By 10 a.m. Shattock reached a position just south of Peak Hill while the three companies crawled up behind over the rugged and exhausting country. The 2/23rd Battalion an hour later saw movement along the ridge running north-east of Wareo. While the artillery shelled the Wareo area the men speculated whether the Japanese were withdrawing and hoped that it might be so.

At 3.20 p.m. Shattock cut the Kuanko-Kwatingkoo track, and 20 minutes later found the Kuanko-Wareo track. Without wasting any time Gillespie gave his orders: Bieri's company would occupy the Kuanko-Kwatingkoo track at Shattock's position and then attack east to Peak Hill; Captain McNamara's company would follow to Peak Hill and then advance north along the Kuanko-Wareo track; Lieutenant Greatorex's[9] company would follow and then advance west to cut the Kwatingkoo-Peak Hill-Wareo track. The brigade major, Mackay, passed on this information to Tucker at 3.50 p.m. and asked him to try a deception when the 2/24th attacked. Tucker replied that his battalion would arrange a "synchronised hate session" when the 2/24th attacked and would fire a flare when Bieri was seen coming over the opposite slope.

At 4.48 p.m. Gillespie told brigade and the 2/23rd that Bieri expected to reach the track junction five minutes after the start time (5 p.m.). At 4.56 watches were checked; three minutes later the 2/24th was ready to begin the advance and the 2/23rd was "lined up" to start firing in a minute. At 5 p.m. the 2/23rd's "hate session" began with a shattering roar in which the 25-pounders joined the battalion's mortars, machine-guns and small arms.

Meanwhile Bieri's company advanced east towards Peak Hill and the other two companies prepared to follow to their destinations. At 5.50 Bieri reported that a spur on the north side of a track running down the hill towards the 2/23rd Battalion was heavily defended. Gillespie ordered him to outflank this position to the north, a difficult task as any route other than the track lay through the inevitable dense bamboo. By 6.45 the company was ordered to dig in on the western slopes of Peak Hill. After dark at 8.5 a band of Japanese apparently trying to withdraw from Kuanko ran into Bieri's position and six were killed.

By last light both the following companies reached their objectives—Greatorex's near Kwatingkoo and McNamara's with Bieri's. Judged on past performances it seemed reasonable to expect that the Japanese would have left the Kuanko-Peak Hill area by the following morning. Whitehead now planned that the two battalions would clear the track between them;

---

[9] Capt A. G. W. Greatorex, MC, WX11512; 2/24 Bn. Farmer; of Pinjarra, WA; b. London, 4 Feb 1905.

the 2/24th would then pinpoint the Japanese on the Wareo Track, and the 2/23rd would pass through and capture Wareo.

Early on the 7th, Lieutenant Stevens led a patrol of the 2/24th to the north of Kwatingkoo and it killed 12 Japanese. There was no answering fire when, at first light, the 2/23rd fired on the enemy positions north of Kuanko. As expected the enemy had gone in the night. At 9.25 the 2/23rd reported to brigade that Bieri's leading platoon had just joined the 2/23rd after an unopposed advance south of about 600 yards. Peak Hill and Kuanko were thus in Australian hands.

At this stage the pilot of the daily Tac R plane dropped a message to the 2/23rd giving the positions of enemy diggings along the track to Wareo. By 11 a.m. Gray's company of the 2/23rd Battalion had passed through the 2/24th and met the Japanese 600 yards from Wareo. Bieri was on Peak Hill and McNamara and Greatorex on a hill north of Kwatingkoo. Whitehead now ordered Gillespie to "stand fast" until Tucker could come forward and decide by which route he would advance to Wareo. While Tucker was reconnoitring the area patrols from the 2/24th discovered that Kwatingkoo was still held strongly by the enemy. To the west McNamara's company began to encircle Kwatingkoo at 4.30 p.m. In the village the Japanese seemed to have at least four machine-guns and a mortar, and a platoon patrol to the south and east reported that the slopes towards the village from these directions were steep and well covered by enemy weapons.

While the tired battalions were thus stalled before Wareo, divisional headquarters began to think that brigade headquarters should urge the battalions on. This thought process seemed to be inevitable whenever the cutting edge was unable, for a variety of reasons, to cut in accordance with the planners' schedule. Colonel Barham, during the afternoon, discussed the possibility of switching over to an advance through Nongora, and informed Whitehead that divisional headquarters felt that his headquarters should be farther forward than Sattelberg. Whitehead pointed out that Wareo was the "limit of exploitation" from the supply viewpoint. Until more supplies were available "we would do what was humanly possible, but this may prove dangerous and foolish". He mentioned also that two battalions had been used for carrying and road making "which was worse than fighting". It was strange that anyone should seriously think of advancing through Nongora at this stage.

At 7.45 a.m. on the 8th McNamara's company of the 2/24th occupied Kwatingkoo without opposition. Tietyens' company of the 2/23rd followed by Gilmour's was now leading on the road to Wareo. By 9.15 Tietyens was very close to the Wareo ridge, which was as silent as the track from Peak Hill had been. A quarter of an hour later both companies were on the ridge. Gilmour's men hoisted the Australian flag on the highest point. "Wareo has been captured," signalled Tucker to Whitehead.

The *20th Division* had had enough and General Adachi had decided to cut his losses. When General Katagiri lost Sattelberg, Pabu and Gusika, the early fall of

Wareo was inevitable. Early in December, therefore, Katagiri received orders to withdraw. By 5th December the *80th Regiment,* still holding Kuanko, and the *79th Regiment,* still defending the Lakes, had orders to withdraw north.

Divisional headquarters and the *79th Regiment* would retire by inland tracks to Kalasa and Sio, while the *80th Regiment* would move north-east to Lakona and then retire to the north along the coast after the withdrawal of the *79th Regiment.* In the fighting of October and November the *79th Regiment* had suffered heavier casualties than the *80th.* To help the speedy movement of divisional headquarters and the *79th Regiment* to Kalasa, divisional engineers and the *79th's* regimental labour company would build a new and better track branching north from the Wareo-Lakona track. It would be the task of Major Tashiro of the *II/238th Battalion* to delay the Australian coastal advance until the two Japanese regiments had passed safely by.

While the 2/23rd Battalion occupied the ruins of Wareo the 2/24th prepared to pursue the enemy east and west. Bieri's and Greatorex's companies on the 8th set out north-east to occupy the track junction half way between Wareo and Christmas Hills. From the opposite direction Scott assembled as many fit men from battalion headquarters and the Headquarters Company of the 2/32nd as he could and sent them under Lieutenant Worner[1] north-west along the track from Christmas Hills to await the 2/24th at the track junction, which Bieri reached at 3 p.m. Here the two companies were stopped by heavy enemy fire from a strong position on the 2200 Feature covering the track junction. This feature was actually the objective, and the companies now dug in and tried unsuccessfully to find a route round the feature through the precipitous country to the north. After dark at 8 p.m. the enemy attacked Bieri's right flank but were driven off with casualties.

West of Wareo the 2/24th met more serious opposition. After occupying Kwatingkoo early in the morning McNamara was ordered to cut the Wareo-Bazuluo track and then occupy Bazuluo. At 1.50 p.m. the company, advancing rapidly west, was ambushed from an ideal ambush position just east of Bazuluo and 4 men were wounded and 8, including McNamara, were missing.

Lieutenant Halliday[2] took command, and within an hour the depleted company brought in the 4 wounded and found 2 of the missing men dead. "B" Company of the 2/23rd Battalion now commanded by Captain McMaster[3] moved rapidly west to help Halliday. Soon after 4.35 p.m. when the two companies joined forces McMaster sent out two patrols. The first tried to cut the track north from Bazuluo to prevent the escape of the Japanese, but dusk came before it could get into position. A second patrol found the bodies of the men still missing. In the brigade's hour of triumph the loss of 8 men killed, including McNamara, had a dampening effect. The death of McNamara, who had become a legend in the battalion and the brigade, cast a cloud over the closing stages of the

---

[1] Capt J. F. Worner, WX213; 2/32 Bn. Bank officer; of Dalkeith, WA; b. Leederville, WA, 1 Sep 1914.

[2] Lt-Col I. C. Halliday, VX29028. 26 A-Tk Coy and 2/24 Bn. Clerk; of Dandenong, Vic; b. Ararat, Vic, 10 Apr 1916.

[3] Capt N. E. McMaster, VX40314; 2/23 Bn. Hardware salesman; of Toorak, Vic; b. Melbourne, 30 Jun 1919.

campaign. He was typical of the superb young leaders who flourished in the Australian Army at this time. Their natural courage, leadership and vigour, tempered now with experience and skill, played no small part in making Australia's jungle army such a formidable fighting organisation. Like others of his kind, McNamara was a born leader, and a man of kindness, courage and riotous good humour who inspired his men to attempt seemingly impossible tasks by his own personal example. When his body was brought in it was found that most of his equipment and his huge boots had been removed by the Japanese. This worried his company as "Big Mac" had always ordered that he was to be buried in his boots, and an unofficial patrol set out to recover them. At dawn the patrol returned and placed the boots in the grave with their company commander.

There were still some Japanese to drive from the rugged country between Wareo and Christmas Hills. On the 9th Worner's platoon from the 2/32nd advanced about 1,800 yards to the north-west when the leading scout's hat was knocked off by machine-gun fire from a strong Japanese position on a razor-back overlooking the track. Worner withdrew 100 yards and listened to the two companies of the 2/24th west of the razor-back exchanging fire with the enemy. Shattock's platoon of the 2/24th spent the afternoon moving round the south flank towards the 2/32nd Battalion where, at Worner's request, Bieri threw two grenades at 30 seconds' intervals for identification. Later this signal was changed to three rifle shots at half-minute intervals. When Worner replied with the same signal Bieri estimated that something between 500 and 1,000 yards separated the two brigades. Towards last light the distance between seemed more like 300 yards.

In the Bazuluo area McMaster sent a platoon of the 2/23rd on the 9th to cut the track to the north. The two companies entered a deserted Bazuluo about midday and found there a 200-bed Japanese hospital. Most Japanese had now gone but Halliday's patrols of the 2/24th met a small Japanese force about 200 yards west of Bazuluo soon after 3 p.m. About that time a 2/4th Commando patrol probing towards Bazuluo met a small Japanese rearguard which withdrew to the north. Two hours later Halliday encountered stronger opposition on a track leading north but not marked on the map. At 5.20 p.m. brigade signalled Garvey: "Could you send party forward to contact Nips?" Garvey sent off a patrol within ten minutes, found the Japanese by 6.15 p.m. and attacked. At 7.5 p.m. he reported that his patrol had driven away the Japanese but it was too late to go on to Bazuluo.

On the 10th the 24th and 26th Brigades were linked at last when at 10.15 a.m. Shattock's platoon from the 2/24th reached Worner's of the 2/32nd. The two platoons then moved west along the track, but were held up by the enemy clinging defiantly if despairingly to the high ground north of the track junction. On the western flank the commando patrol passed through the Japanese position captured the previous evening and 400 yards from Bazuluo met Halliday's men. Thus was junction made across the whole battlefront. For several of the weary battalions rest, hot meals and regular washing were now possible.

With all hope gone the Japanese on the 11th were still holding grimly the 2200 Feature at the track junction. At 2.25 p.m. Bieri, supported by Greatorex and Halliday, began an encircling move. Reaching the high ground above the track at 5.30 p.m. Bieri's forward troops met some scattered opposition which was quickly overcome, but because of the difficult country and the fast approaching night Bieri was unable to silence the enemy positions covering the track junction, and he dug in at last light.

The Japanese rearguard was still on the 2200 Feature on 12th December. From before first light the enemy replied to Bieri's fire. By 9.50 a.m. an ammunition party from Wareo reached the company and Shattock from the east also joined Bieri. It now seemed that only about 250 yards of track remained to be opened. Bieri's company searched for a route to the west and north trying to come in behind the enemy. The Japanese meanwhile were still facing Greatorex. At 11.45 Bieri's men were in position and began to drive south-west along the 2200 Feature to clear the enemy from the track junction. Two platoons (Lieutenants Nolan[4] and Stretch[5]) came under heavy machine-gun fire from 20 yards' range; two men were killed and Nolan wounded. Shattock's platoon continued the advance, Private Ball[6] being killed on top of the first machine-gun post after a brave advance firing his Owen gun. Corporal Boully[7] was killed and Shattock wounded at the same time. Private Legg,[8] a Bren gunner, then advanced 20 yards alone firing from the hip at the first machine-gun. Single handed he killed the three Japanese manning the gun and captured it. He then advanced unconcerned through heavy fire towards the second machine-gun and again killed all the Japanese manning it. Inspired by Legg's heroism the rest of the company steadily pressed forward hoping for this last Japanese defence to crack. They were rewarded when, by 3.30 p.m., those Japanese who were not among the 27 killed, fled. Greatorex's company then prepared to move through and pursue the enemy along the Lakona Track towards the 2000 Feature. At 3.55 brigade signalled division: "After heavy fighting today last enemy positions 2200 Feature captured 1530 hours. Bonga-Wareo track now open."

For the next five days patrols from the two brigades sometimes met Japanese stragglers but mostly went deep into the areas forward from their sectors without meeting any. All that now remained to complete the rout of the *20th Japanese Division* from this area was attended to by

---

[4] Lt J. C. Nolan, NX123827; 2/24 Bn. Stock salesman; of Young, NSW; b. Warialda, NSW, 23 Jun 1917.

[5] Lt W. G. Stretch, MC, WX9506. 2/11 and 2/24 Bns. Farm worker; of Bridgetown, WA; b. Bridgetown, 15 Aug 1919.

[6] Pte T. L. Ball, VX52296; 2/24 Bn. Station hand; of Hamilton, Vic; b. Eaglehawk, Vic, 4 Feb 1900. Killed in action 12 Dec 1943.

[7] Cpl H. E. Boully, SX11126; 2/24 Bn. Clerk; of Port Augusta, SA; b. Port Augusta, 22 Sep 1920. Killed in action 12 Dec 1943.

[8] Pte L. R. Legg, DCM, VX47870; 2/24 Bn. Timber cutter; of Emerald, Vic; b. St Kilda, Vic, 27 Dec 1921.

Greatorex's company. On the 13th they began to climb the razor-back to which the Japanese were still clinging and dug in for the night half way up. Next day at 3.15 p.m. Greatorex sent two platoons to attack the crest of the razor-back. By 4.40 p.m. they reached the upper slopes where they met the Japanese. They found it impossible to get to the top round the left flank, and sought a better route round the right. The third platoon now joined the other two near the top. Two gave covering fire while Lieutenant Hewitt's[9] attacked frontally along the east side of the razor-back. An hour later it drove out the Japanese who left four dead when fleeing into the cane on the west side.

On the 15th Halliday's company continued the advance. When descending into a gully at the base of the 2000 Feature the company was fired at by at least two machine-guns on a small ridge across the gully. For the rest of the day patrols tried to get round both flanks, an almost impossible task because of the steep slopes. The Japanese ahead disappeared during the night but so steep was the country that it took the company most of the day to establish this fact. Early in the morning Halliday found that the Japanese were not in position across the gully; he then advanced cautiously up the slope of the 2000 Feature.

Brigade headquarters was becoming impatient and "annoyed at loss of time this morning", according to its signal to the 2/24th. The advance was slow, unavoidably, but it was also sure. By 11.20 Halliday was climbing up the 2000 Feature. At 5 p.m. Captain Mackenzie's company passed through and at last light reached huts near the summit. Next day at 9 a.m. this company occupied the crest of the 2000 Feature unopposed. Both companies then scoured the area which had been a Japanese headquarters. A track to the north with a signpost was obviously the Japanese escape route.

This was the end of the 26th Brigade's exploitation. In many parts of the Gusika-Wareo area, captured by the 24th and 26th Brigades, were abandoned Japanese headquarters and equipment. This was not surprising as General Katagiri had set up his headquarters in the Nongora area early in November. All that remained of the *20th Division* in this area consisted of abandoned foxholes, entrenchments, ammunition and ration dumps, equipment, weapons, camps, medical aid posts and graves. Over all this the relentless jungle was crawling, and the rain was helping to obliterate all traces of the once-proud conqueror. The valour, stamina, rugged determination and resources of the 9th Australian Division had proved too much for the *20th Japanese Division*. Like the *51st Division* in September, most of the remnants of Katagiri's battered division were retreating by inland trails to Lakona and Sio. His rearguard was now being smashed by the 4th Australian Brigade between Gusika and Fortification Point.

---

[9] Lt E. J. Hewitt, MM, VX33872; 2/24 Bn. Farmer; of Werrigar East, Vic; b. Warracknabeal, Vic, 16 Apr 1920.

CHAPTER 24

TOEHOLD ON SHAGGY RIDGE

BEHIND its screen of patrols, late in October and November, the 7th Division's task remained the same: to prevent enemy penetration into the Ramu and Markham Valleys and protect the Gusap airfield and the various radar installations. The 25th Brigade was now forward. On the right was the 2/25th Battalion on Johns' Knoll, Trevor's Ridge and Beveridge's Post, one company being forward at Mainstream on the east bank of the Faria River with the huge mass of Shaggy Ridge rising sheer on the west. On the left was the 2/33rd Battalion based on Guy's Post, with one company forward on the southern slopes of Shaggy Ridge and another on the saddle to the left at Don's Post. On clear days the men could sometimes see barges and ships off the coast. On the right the 2/2nd Pioneer Battalion was based on the Moto's Post area with two companies to the south-east at Levett's Post. The 2/31st was in reserve.

After its relief the 21st Brigade moved to the Mene River area. The 2/14th Battalion occupied an area near the Yogia (Ioge) River with patrols forward to the vicinity of the Evapia River, and the 2/16th and 2/27th Battalions occupied an area east of the Mene River and on the high ground north of the road. "B" Company of the Papuan Battalion was forward of the Evapia River with patrols on the 5800 Feature. Patrols from the 2/6th Commando Squadron, under divisional command, now began to penetrate the Isariba-Orgoruna country to the north-west from the squadron base at Kesawai. Farther west the 2/2nd Squadron was operating with two troops from the new Faita airstrip while one troop rested and guarded Garoka.

In these new positions the division settled down to a month of solid and arduous patrolling. As usual in New Guinea fighting, the Japanese were content to sit in their defences while the Australians patrolled and dominated the rugged no-man's land. This policy would prove disastrous to the Japanese in the end although, at the time, it seemed to the sweating and swearing Australian patrols that the Japanese idea of sitting in their defences was a good one. The Japanese had established themselves strongly in natural defensive positions on Shaggy Ridge and in flanking positions on both sides of it. From the Pimple—a rocky peak rising steeply about half way along the crest of Shaggy Ridge—the Japanese found it relatively easy to resist any advance. Patrols from the 2/27th Battalion had already found that the Pimple could be approached only along the top of the spur, for the slopes were too steep to move along, and the top of the spur was wide enough for only one man at a time. Often the Pimple was a blurred shape capped by mist and hidden by rain clouds.

First blood was shed by the 25th Brigade in its new positions on 11th November when a patrol from the 2/25th, moving in the Mainstream-kunda bridge area, clashed with a small Japanese patrol and inflicted a few casualties for the loss of two men wounded, including the patrol commander, Lieutenant Wells.[1] Patrols from the commando squadrons also clashed with enemy patrols on the 11th—Corporal Busk's[2] patrol of the 2/6th while moving down the rugged slopes of the Haile River, and a 2/2nd patrol moving towards Bagasin met the enemy in the Aminik area. The 2/6th were worried about their new position for the Papuans were not in the old positions of the 2/6th but in a more concentrated area with only standing patrols out, thus allowing the Japanese greater freedom in the upper Solu River area. The native soldiers of the Papuan Battalion at this stage were weary and footsore and there was a high rate of sickness among their Australian officers and N.C.O's. The Papuans, however, were still regularly called upon by the infantry to assist in scouting, and on the 12th one of their standing patrols repulsed a Japanese patrol of 20 men.

Throughout all areas supplies were built up and strenuous attempts made to improve the health of the division. Malaria in this valley of death (as the Ramu was known to the natives) was still the cause of the greatest number of casualties. Despite more rigorous precautions there were many new cases and recurrences daily.[3]

Topographical information improved and ahead of the forward posts the Allied airmen made a thorough study of the Bogadjim Road and did their best to destroy its bridges. The engineers of the 2/5th and 2/6th Field Companies kept the airstrips inland in perfect condition and pushed their roads forward into the hills to the Lakes and as far west as Kesawai. The diarist of the 2/5th Field Company described activities during November thus:

> Work generally was road construction and maintenance. . . . This work was divided into sections and each section was a platoon task. The work included crossings of Faria River, Mosia, Mene and Ioge [Yogia] Rivers, which entailed in most parts timber beam bridge constructions . . .; gaps were generally between 70 feet and 80 feet and entailed two trestles, each usually 10-14 feet high. In the early part of the month no precast type culvert sections were available. To overcome this difficulty pipe culverts were constructed from 25-pdr shell and cartridge cases, apple drums, 44-gallon drums. These culverts proved quite satisfactory if 1 foot 6 inches-2 feet of cover was provided.

By the end of the month the engineers had finished building two landing strips at Dumpu, which were now taking traffic in all weather.[4]

---

[1] Lt G. R. Wells, QX14417; 2/25 Bn. Chemist; of Tweed Heads, NSW; b. Childers, Qld, 20 Feb 1912.

[2] Cpl P. N. Busk, VX75791. 2/6 Indep Coy, 2/6 Cdo Sqn, 2/6 Fd Coy. Fisherman; of San Remo, Vic; b. Welshpool, Vic, 19 Apr 1920.

[3] In the first ten weeks of fighting in the Markham and Ramu Valleys 90 per cent of the total sickness casualties in the 7th Division were caused by malaria. In the 9th Division the casualties caused by malaria were 60 per cent. For further details see A. S. Walker, *Clinical Problems of War* (1952), a volume in the Medical series of this history.

[4] It was during this static period that a new method of expressing time was devised. New Guinea Force headquarters instructed that from the 15th November a new method for the designation of time in orders, instructions, reports and messages, would commence. "Time of origin," said the instruction, "will be expressed in six figures followed by a zone letter. The first two digits of the figure group will denote the date, the second pair the hour and the third pair the minutes. The first nine days of the month are expressed as 01, 02, etc. For example, the time of origin of a message originated in the Eastern States at midday on the 16th day of the month will be shown as "161200K" (when daylight saving is operating "161200L") instead of "1200K/16" (or "1200L/16") as previously."

For the first time the troops were permitted to mention in letters home that they were in the Ramu Valley, although no place names or references to operations could be made. One unit diarist, commenting on this order, wrote, "Radio and newspapers have made it clear for some weeks just where we are."[5]

During November the artillery pounded the Japanese positions. Observers from the 2/4th Field Regiment were forward with most units in the main area and directed the fire of the 10 guns, including the two light 25-pounders. Even the most daring of forward observation officers, however, could not direct the fire with much accuracy on certain targets because of the rugged nature of the country. If the Pimple could be captured it would make an excellent artillery observation post, when not hidden by cloud, and would enable artillery fire to be guided more accurately.

A system of cooperation with the Wirraway and Boomerang aircraft of No. 4 Squadron became highly developed during the month. This army cooperation squadron, which had trained with the army on the Atherton Tableland, was highly regarded by all troops who had anything to do with it, particularly those in isolated areas. The November war diaries of several units mention that the squadron dropped packets of cigarettes, tobacco, newspapers, and copies of *Guinea Gold,* the army newspaper.

The Australian gunners could not entirely silence the Japanese 75-mm guns, although they did manage to dissuade them from firing for long periods. On 15th November the 54th Battery set a trap for a Japanese gun which was apparently defending a headquarters—a tender spot which invariably brought retaliation when shelled by the Australian guns. While one troop fired on the suspected Japanese headquarters, another laid on the Japanese gun when it began to fire. A Tac R aircraft which suddenly appeared over the Japanese position reported that they thought that the Japanese gun was run back into a cave after firing and so needed to be lured out. However, on this occasion "the Japanese did not arise to bait".

An astute plan was decided upon for the 18th. Mortars from the 2/25th Battalion would bombard the Japanese Shaggy Ridge position at 11 a.m. when the planes would come over as usual, make wireless contact with brigade headquarters, and then appear to fly off; in reality they would fly low in the valley obscured from the Japanese positions. It was expected that, about three or four minutes after the Australian mortars began firing, the Japanese would wheel their gun out and open up on the mortars; the planes would then immediately try to pinpoint it and direct the artillery on to it. Everything went according to plan except that low cloud prevented the aircraft from observing; otherwise the Japanese did exactly what was expected of them. The same plan was followed at a different hour on

---

[5] In "Report on Japanese Operations in New Guinea—Ramu Valley Campaign Sep 43-Apr 44", compiled under the instructions of Brigadier Irving, commanding the 8th Military District and dated 8th August 1946, is the following statement based on one of a series of questions written by the Official War Historian and answered by General Adachi, the Commander of *XVIII Army*, and one of his staff: "The Japanese commander did not know until after the surrender that the force engaged in the Ramu Valley operation was the 7th Division, but he knew from the Australian Broadcasting Commission that the 9th Division had landed at Buso River soon after the landings." This statement says a lot for the front line security of the 7th Division soldier.

the 19th when there were no clouds to obscure the aircraft's vision. Even so the Japanese withdrew the gun before the aircraft could fly from the valley where they were hiding. The airmen did, however, see a levelled portion of ground north-east of Kankiryo Saddle with an eight-foot wide track from here to the back of the ridge. A similar position was seen farther east near the headwaters of the Mosa River where a platform was cut out of the side of the ridge and a wide and well-used track ran back behind the ridge. On the 20th the planes reported a new position in the same general area where a gun platform with a track to a hideout behind the feature had been definitely constructed in the last 24 hours, and wheel tracks were seen along the route. The Australian artillery was now concentrating upon these gun platforms but although shells were in the target area, the platforms were not hit. On the 26th, when the Japanese artillery was particularly aggressive, the Boomerangs, although prompt to answer the call, were unable to find any traces of Japanese guns. So the hide-and-seek artillery duel went on throughout November. In such rugged country it would be very good shooting if the Australians secured a direct hit on the Japanese guns; the Japanese gun did not have enough range to shell the Australian artillery.[6]

The speed, accuracy and efficiency with which the Wirraway and Boomerang pilots found their targets in the tangled mass of the Finisterre mountains was accepted by all as part of the daily routine. It was only when an accident occurred, as on the 26th November, that the high quality of the work of these Jacks-of-all-trades was realised. On this day eight Kittyhawks returning from a mission to the north-west strafed a hut on the edge of the Faita airstrip where the 2/2nd Commando Squadron was based and then strafed the 2/6th Commando Squadron in the Kesawai area. Nobody there had taken shelter, for the aircraft had been identified as friendly and, after 20 minutes, they had done considerable damage and had killed one man and wounded two others. One native had also been killed and the remainder had gone bush. This strafing had been inadvertently carried out by American pilots new to the area. Four days later the commander of the American squadron called on the 2/6th Commando Squadron to express his regrets.

Nobody liked a static period much and Brigadier Eather, like his divisional commander, was restless. A company commander describing an incident which occurred while the 25th Brigade was in reserve gave a glimpse of the brigadier's character:

> Bde HQ is just down the river from us. Two days ago a small war started there —rifles and L.M.G's firing everywhere. We heard later that the Brig got a bit restless at the inaction of the past week. He spotted a couple of blokes shooting ducks over a river—against regs of course—so called for a Bren and 2 mags. In the best Section Leader style he got an estimate of the range . . . and then

---

[6] The Japanese "mountain guns" encountered in New Guinea were usually either the 75-mm "infantry gun" (range 7,800 yards) or the 75-mm "mountain gun" (range 8,750 yards). Normally an infantry regiment had six 70-mm guns and four 75-mm guns; and the divisional artillery had 36 75-mm guns. The British gun had a far longer range and fired a 25-lb shell against the Japanese 13-lb.

let a few bursts go into the water near the sportsmen. The effect was amazing. A lot of ducks flew up, men appeared everywhere in the grass and opened up on the ducks with rifles. Eventually the Brig had to send a patrol across the river to arrest the sportsmen and found that they were two of his M.P's.

On the 11th November New Guinea Force received a report that a patrol moving north from Gusap had returned because of native reports that a strong enemy force was at Wamunti. It took a report such as this to accelerate the movement from Port Moresby to Gusap of the 6th

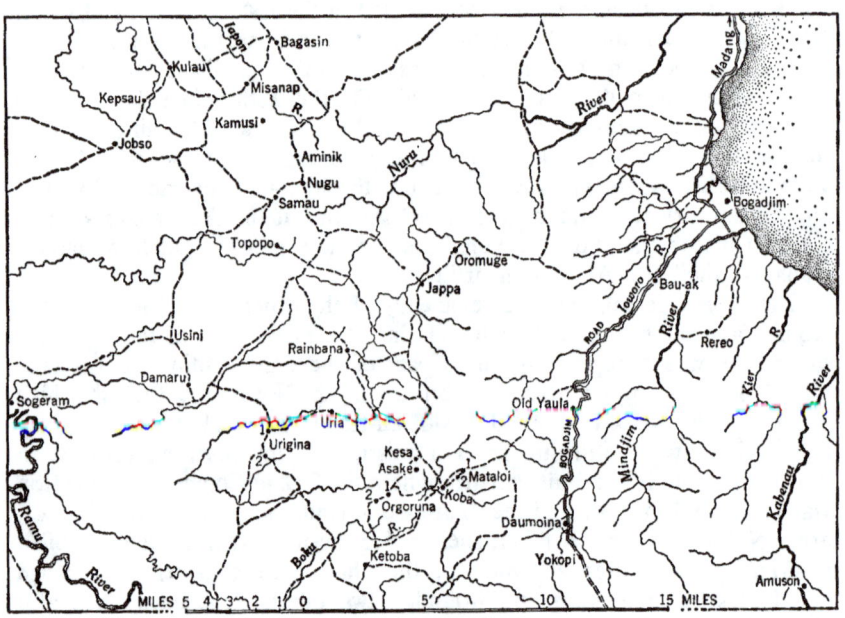

Western patrol area

Machine Gun Battalion. The Fifth Air Force flew them in on the 11th and 12th November and agreed to ration them as part of the growing Gusap fighter air base. The battalion employed one company patrolling to the north, and on 19th November a patrol reached Wamunti and found no signs of the enemy or of recent occupation.

The most extensive patrolling was taking place on the left flank where the 2/2nd Commando Squadron was entering new areas with patrols sometimes lasting more than a week. The Sepu, Usini and Urigina areas which the Japanese had previously occupied, were all now deserted and the Japanese had pulled well back into the hills, so far indeed that venturesome Australian patrols on this left flank were now nearer to Bogadjim than was the main striking force of the 7th Division to the south. Towards the end of October and in early November patrols began to move north-east from Urigina towards Uria, north-east from Usini towards Samau, north-east from Damaru towards Topopo and north from Usini towards Jobso

Shaggy Ridge, looking south-west to the Ramu Valley.

(R.A.A.F.)

(Australian War Memorial)

21st Brigade troops marching down a winding jeep track in the foothills of the Finisterres on 9th November 1943, after their relief by the 25th Brigade.

(Australian War Memorial)

Natives carrying food and ammunition through the Mosa gorge to Australian troops at advanced positions in the Finisterres.

and Kepsau. Farther afield were the enemy's most important bases in the hills west of Madang and Bogadjim—Bagasin and Kulau, where the natives said there were "plenty too much" Japanese. Angau representatives often accompanied patrols or went into the areas to which the patrols had been with the object of winning back the natives.

A typical patrol was that led by Lieutenant Adams[7] which arrived at Samau on 9th November from its base south of the Ramu River with the task of reconnoitring the Bagasin area. Accompanied by five of his men, two police boys and two cargo boys, Adams set off from Samau on the 10th along the track leading to Nugu, Aminik, Kamusi and Bagasin. The patrol had difficulty in following the map because "the Bagasin sheet is all astray here as Aminik is not on top of a peak but is down in a valley and is close to a river".[8] As the patrol was crossing a saddle about half way between Aminik and Kamusi, the leading scouts heard voices round a corner. One of the police boys went round the corner and saw a native and two Japanese. He spoke to them and asked if they were alone and was it safe for him to come. It was too much for him when he was asked to carry cargo for the Japanese and he ran back round the corner followed by the small Japanese patrol, three of whom were killed by the Australians. When increasing fire came from more Japanese the Australians withdrew to Samau.

Adams was determined to reach Bagasin but unfortunately one of his police boys and two cargo boys fled when the firing commenced, having "diced all our cargo in the scrub". This loss left him with only two days' rations for the patrol, so with two of his own men and two natives he set out on the 11th to try to recover some of the stores. Passing through Aminik he came to the scene of the previous day's action and found some of the rations. With these he believed that six men would be able to operate for at least four days forward from Samau and also make the long return journey to their base south of the Ramu. The rest of the men he sent back and prepared to move along a direct track from Samau towards Bagasin which itself was visible from a ridge not far away. The six men moved north on the 12th and camped off the track that night. The natives encountered along the track were for the most part friendly and keen to give him information about where the Japanese were and where they were not. Adams learnt what he had already suspected, that the Japanese used natives to observe movements of Australian patrols and to call out when they were coming. The natives insisted that Bagasin, Kulau and Kamusi were all occupied strongly by the enemy. After passing through Misanap on the 13th, the patrol split into two parties of three when it reached the Iapon River—one under Sergeant Davies to break bush to the left of the track and observe Bagasin, and one to the right

---

[7] Capt T. B. Adams, QX1011. 2/11 Fd Regt, 2/2 Indep Coy, 2/2 Cdo Sqn. Bank officer; of Jandowae, Qld; b. Glen Innes, NSW, 18 Sep 1918.

[8] In his report Adams wrote: "It appeared to us that the Strat Series was most accurate as to direction of tracks, etc., but some of the place names are out of date. The direct route from Samau to Misanap is not shown on either map. It is practically impossible to reconcile the positions of villages shown on the Provisional Series map with their correct positions on the ground."

under Adams to observe Bagasin from that side as well as Kamusi and to watch the track.

For the next two days and on the morning of the 16th Adams observed the area and concluded that Bagasin was occupied. Despite the fact that natives encountered along the route said that Kamusi was occupied, Adams and his two companions advanced boldly towards it. Although all the evidence was that the Japanese would be in the village the three men went in and found that they were not there. Adams reached Samau that night and his base the next day—the 18th. Davies had meanwhile been less successful in trying to approach Bagasin from the west, where the country was very rough, and no suitable observation post could be found before it was time to go back to base.

This patrol has been described at some length, not because its results were so important—although it secured identifications of the *239th Regiment* in the Aminik area and opened the way for further patrols towards Bagasin and Kulau—but because it was typical of the work of these long-range western patrols and the difficulties which they met and overcame.

So November continued with the 25th Brigade keeping a close watch on the Japanese positions on Shaggy Ridge and the 21st Brigade in reserve to the south-west. The Ramu Valley continued to be a favourite battle area for visiting generals. One of the most welcome was Major-General Lethbridge[9] who, with his party, visited the 7th Division between 19th and 22nd November.

Towards the end of November there were indications that the Japanese might become a little more aggressive. On the 21st observation posts of the 2/6th Commando Squadron at Ketoba and overlooking Kesa reported hearing much firing from the Kesa area. The men in the Kesa observation posts were diverted by the spectacle of three Japanese sections training between Kesa and Asake—practising patrolling, skirmishing and ambushing. They were also seen to be building strong defences there. On the same day a Papuan Infantry patrol heard enemy movement about 300 yards down a hill from a village north of the 5800 Feature. On the night of the 23rd-24th November the Japanese fronting the 25th Brigade began

---

[9] Maj-Gen J. S. Lethbridge, CB, CBE, MC. Comd 220 Military Mission 1943-44; Chief of Staff Fourteenth Army 1944-45. Regular soldier; b. Barrackpore, India, 11 Dec 1897.

On 26th June 1943 General Blamey was informed from London that the United Kingdom Chiefs of Staff were sending a military mission to the Pacific and Indian theatres to study at first hand the organisation and equipment of the forces there in preparation for the time when the Allies would be able to concentrate against Japan. The mission would be led by Major-General Lethbridge and would include nine colonels representing technical directorates. The object of the Lethbridge Mission was to investigate at first hand in the Pacific and Indian theatres
    (*a*) the technique
    (*b*) the types and scale of equipment
    (*c*) the organisation of units and formations required for the most effective and economical prosecution of all-out war against Japan, and to make recommendations upon which planning, production and development will be based.

It comprised 27 officers, including three from the RN, two from the RAF, two from the Canadian Army, one from the Canadian Air Force and four American officers. The mission arrived in Australia in October 1943, spent about six weeks in Australia and New Guinea and then went on to India. New Guinea Force compiled for them a statement, long enough to fill a small book, on administration and organisation, and another detailed report containing answers to the mission's questions about tactics, equipment and other topics. Necessarily these notes were based largely on the experiences gained in Papua and round Lae but in November the members of the mission went to New Guinea and saw for themselves.

firing flares but, for every flare fired by the Japanese, the Australians replied with flares of similar colour—an old dodge to confuse an enemy's signals.

Against the enemy on the southern tip of Shaggy Ridge there was little that the 2/33rd Battalion could do except to keep a tag on Japanese positions and intentions. To the right, however, the 2/25th Battalion had a little more scope for its patrols. For instance, on 24th November, a patrol from the 2/25th moved across the Faria and advanced for about 600 yards until it encountered a Japanese platoon, very strongly entrenched. The scouts calmly and silently cut the wire, and watched the weapon-pits and two Japanese looking at American Mitchell bombers trying to strafe the Japanese mountain gun position. These two Japanese and another were killed with a grenade before the patrol was forced to withdraw rapidly with four wounded under the concentrated fire from the weapon-pits.

Meanwhile, on 22nd November, Vasey had warned his two brigades that the 21st would relieve the 25th by 1st December. The next relief after this would be completed by the 22nd December "if situation permits". The 2/27th Battalion relieved the 2/2nd Pioneers on the Kankiryo mule track, and by early December was established with its headquarters first at Bob's Post and later at Gordon's Post with a forward locality at Toms' Post. The 2/14th Battalion, with headquarters and four companies on Johns' Knoll and Picken's Ridge and forward elements (five platoons) on the general line of Mainstream, had relieved the 2/25th and was responsible for controlling the area to the Faria River. Artillery observation posts were maintained at Terry's Post[1] and Toms' Post. The 2/16th was occupying part of Shaggy Ridge and Lake Hill with patrols on Brian's Hill, and was responsible for the area as far east as the Faria River. The 25th Brigade, with the Papuan company under command, moved to the foothills and river valley where the 21st Brigade had been, and the 2/6th Commando Squadron remained as they were.[2]

There were several changes in senior staff and command appointments in this first week of December. On the 1st Lieut-Colonel Canet, Vasey's senior administrative officer, left to join the staff of New Guinea Force and was succeeded by Lieut-Colonel Lahey.[3] On the same day Colonel Sublet left the 2/16th Battalion to attend the Tactical School and Major Symington took command of the battalion. Lieut-Colonel Picken had now arrived from the 2/7th Battalion to take command of the 2/27th in place of Lieut-Colonel Bishop who had been appointed G.S.O.1 of the 6th Division.[4]

---

[1] After Lieutenant Terry Feely, 2/4th Field Regiment, who was killed later in the campaign.

[2] On 1st December American air transport completed at one swoop an inter-troop relief of the 2/2nd—flying "A" Troop over the Bismarcks from Garoka to Faita and returning "B" Troop to Garoka.

[3] Lt-Col K. C. C. Lahey, OBE, QX6343. 2/2 A-Tk Regt 1940-42; DAQMG First Army 1942-43; AA & QMG 7 Div 1943-45. Chain store manager; of Brisbane; b. Brisbane, 13 Sep 1907.

[4] It was indicative of the way in which citizen soldiers, after regimental and staff experience in the field and training at the staff schools, were being promoted to senior staff posts that the GSO1's of both the 6th and 7th Divisions were now in this category.

In accordance with a suggestion by General Vasey, Brigadier Dougherty decided to send a patrol into the mountainous country on the right of the 2/27th Battalion to see whether any Japanese were concentrated there. On the 4th Vasey received a report from the Air Warning Wireless Station at Wantoat that natives reported Japanese to the north of the station. This, coupled with an Angau report that a strong Japanese party was moving overland from Finschhafen, prompted Dougherty to send out a strong patrol from the 2/2nd Pioneers under Lieutenant Coles. Coles' instructions were to depart on the 4th and find out whether the activity reported in the upper Surinam Valley as far as Mungo was "in the nature of isolated parties who were cut off in our advance or whether it is patrol activity with a view to future ops". The patrol would be out for twelve days and was to try to capture a prisoner.[5]

The main enemy positions on Shaggy Ridge fronting the 2/16th Battalion were described thus by the battalion's historian:

> Shaggy Ridge was a narrow razor-back with an altitude of 5,000 feet. A thick rain forest covered the crest of the ridge. Heavy mists frequently obscured the position for days at a time. Then observation was limited to less than 100 yards. Such was the vantage point of the eminence that on clear days observation was possible as far as the sea near Madang. The ridge was at no part wider than a few yards narrowing at the foremost section position. The most forward position, a foxhole, was occupied by a lone Bren gunner. For the first time in its history the battalion held ground with a one-man front. Ahead of him was the enemy who had had weeks to prepare his defences.[6]

Daily patrols from the 2/16th were probing Shaggy Ridge, both on the right and the left flank. A typical patrol towards the Japanese positions on Shaggy Ridge was that led by Lance-Corporal Coad[7] on 2nd December. With four companions he started out early in the morning, in single file with one scout forward, moving along the ridge very slowly because of the difficult country, fallen bamboo and low undergrowth. Going was so difficult that, for the most part, the patrol had to move on hands and knees. Stationing one rifleman to watch for enemy movements to the right, Coad led the patrol through country shattered by artillery fire until the forward scout was within four yards of the enemy position on the crest forward of the Pimple, where voices were heard. Coad's men then heard an enemy party moving to their rear about 40 yards down the ridge on the left, and rapidly began to withdraw, but, while attempting to do so, were fired on by the Japanese positions just ahead. The scout opened up with his Owen gun and that enabled the patrol to withdraw.

Again on the 3rd the 2/16th tried several approaches towards the Pimple and a patrol moving on the west side of Shaggy Ridge reached almost to the Pimple before being fired on. It then tried several approaches

---

[5] In fact, Coles' patrol remained out for a shorter period and the task was continued by Lieutenant D. O. Smith and three others.
[6] M. Uren, *A Thousand Men at War—The Story of the 2/16th Battalion, A.I.F.*, p. 212.
[7] Cpl V. V. Coad, WX5594; 2/16 Bn. Farm hand; of Narrogin, WA; b. Wagin, WA, 21 May 1917.

but was stopped by overhanging cliffs on each flank. Lieutenant Hill,[8] leading a patrol east of Shaggy Ridge with the object of scaling the ridge behind the enemy's front, found that the ridge grew steeper near the top until it passed the vertical position. When Hill was wounded, and other patrols failed to make any headway in climbing the rock face on the right or the steep shattered country on the left, it seemed that the only approach towards the Pimple was along the ridge, under observation.

Vasey wished to provide a diversion to attract the enemy's attention from other operations pending in New Guinea and New Britain. On the 6th he visited Dougherty and discussed with him the possibility of a raid on Kankiryo, and also the native carrier problem. Dougherty was particularly anxious to have a jeep road pushed through to the Guy's Post area to save the natives for other tasks. It was to work on this road that three companies of the 2/2nd Pioneer Battalion had been dispatched to the Lakes area.

As already indicated, there were signs that the enemy might have something up his sleeve and might attempt to throw into confusion the Australian force in the Ramu Valley and the Finisterres. On 1st December, for instance, the Bogadjim Road showed signs of recent heavy use by motor traffic. Tac R on the 3rd reported that the tracks from Orgoruna, Koba and Mataloi towards the Bogadjim Road at Old Yaula showed signs of heavy use. Patrols from the two commando squadrons proved again on the 6th and 7th December that the enemy was active in the western area.

With headquarters and one troop in the Kesawai area the 2/6th had one reinforced troop at Isariba, one day's journey north-west of Kesawai, with a forward section at Ketoba, an hour north from Isariba. The third troop was responsible for the wide gap between the 5800 Feature and Isariba. A patrol base was occupied at the junction of the Haile and Solu Rivers with the task of patrolling towards the Japanese road running from Daumoina to Yokopi and also for protection of the squadron's lines of communication to Isariba in case the enemy should attempt to infiltrate down the Haile or Solu Rivers. Since changing over with the Papuan company the 2/6th Squadron had felt that its right flank was vulnerable to enemy infiltration into the valley west of the 5800 Feature. One commando section was established as a standing patrol at a village about half way between the feature and Kesawai, but this section could obviously do very little to protect the wide gap between the 5800 Feature and the Solu River. With the threat which this gap entailed ever present, the 2/6th found it "a very nerve-racking period for all ranks". On 7th December the Japanese were also prowling round the Papuan Infantry's area near the 5800 Feature. All this activity by the Japanese on the west, so different from the main front where they were content to sit in their diggings, was unusual.

---

[8] Lt V. A. Hill, NX9675. 2/4 and 2/16 Bns. Farm worker; of Leeton, NSW; b. Brome, England, 8 Feb 1918.

A quarter of an hour after midnight on the 7th-8th booby-traps guarding the forward Papuan platoon on a spur north of the 5800 Feature exploded. The enemy were led by hostile natives and seemed to know the position well. When the Japanese did move out, their field craft was good and often they were able to creep right up to heavily defended positions before being detected. By 3 a.m. Captain Chalk knew only that all the booby-traps of his forward platoon had exploded, but at 11 a.m. on the 8th Lance-Corporal Apauka arrived back and said that large numbers of Japanese had attacked and driven back the forward platoon. Later a sergeant and 10 native soldiers arrived and reported that the forward positions had been attacked by what seemed to be two companies of Japanese led by "kanakas". As soon as the Papuans' positions were occupied the Japanese sent up a flare which brought up a carrier line consisting mainly of Japanese. By this time Eather had ordered Chalk to withdraw to the Evapia River. At that time the forward platoon commander, Lieutenant C. E. Bishop, two Australian sergeants, 42 native soldiers and three carriers were missing.

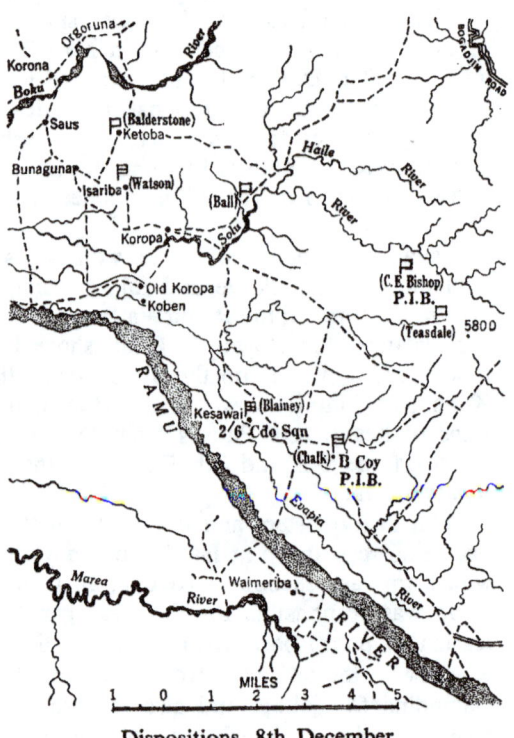

Dispositions, 8th December

Lieutenant Teasdale's section of the 2/6th Commando Squadron (with which was Lieutenant M. A. Bishop[9]) watching the wide gap between the 5800 Feature and the Kesawai-Isariba area, had been interested but unscathed observers of the Japanese activities. Soon after the first explosion at C. E. Bishop's position Teasdale's signallers found that their line was dead and the wireless could make no contact either with squadron headquarters or with the Papuans. About 6 a.m. Captain Blainey, now commanding the 2/6th[1] (Major King being in hospital), could see about 15

[9] Maj M. A. Bishop, MM, QX21559. 2/5 Indep Coy, 2/6 Cdo Sqn. Commercial traveller; of Brisbane; b. Moore, Qld, 29 Apr 1921.
[1] Major King was evacuated with scrub typhus on 30th November. Captain A. S. Palmer (ex 1 Independent Company as was also Lieutenant W. D. Watson) arrived as squadron second-in-command soon afterwards. Because Palmer was "in the dark" he left Blainey in command while this fight was on.

figures moving down kunai spurs from the top of the ridge north of Kesawai. About 7 a.m. Teasdale managed to tell Blainey by wireless that these were Japanese, but after getting this important message through the wireless could make no further contact. During the morning the Japanese were digging in north of Kesawai, whence they could dominate the track from Kesawai to the 2/6th's outlying troop at Isariba.

At 10 a.m. Teasdale's men could hear movement in a garden on the south side of their camp, and five minutes later a booby-trap in the form of a daisy chain of eight grenades on the east side of their camp went off. It transpired that one Japanese had been killed by the booby-trap; another was shot by one of Teasdale's men who went forward to investigate. Teasdale's section remained in position until 4 p.m. hearing enemy movement on all sides. When it started to rain heavily Teasdale withdrew in the general direction of squadron headquarters, and after midnight bivouacked high up on a ridge.

Between 1 p.m. and 2.30 p.m. on the 8th Boomerangs manned by Flying Officers Masson[2] and Carter[3] saw about 80 weapon-pits dug along both sides of the ridge overlooking Kesawai. Some big diggings were obviously for medical posts or headquarters. The airmen estimated that they had seen at least 200 Japanese, the main body being on the highest or eastern portion of the ridge. To the north-east the airmen observed Australian troops on a ridge. "They were in the prone firing position," reported the pilot.

It now seemed that the Japanese thrust was a double-headed one—about 200 moving from the main Bogadjim Road south-west over the 5800 Feature towards Kesawai and others from the Orgoruna-Mataloi area south-east towards the Ramu Valley. Half an hour after midnight on the 6th-7th December a booby-trap before the 2/6th Squadron's section outpost, under Lieutenant Balderstone, at Ketoba exploded. After dawn a patrol found bloodstains and abandoned equipment at the scene of the explosion and Japanese footmarks leading to the Boku River. At the same time as communications ceased between Teasdale and squadron headquarters the telephone line to Lieutenant Watson's troop in the Isariba-Ketoba area became silent. The gap which the 2/6th had feared since their change-over with the Papuans was now ominously wide and open: it soon seemed that the Japanese were trying to outflank the outlying troops, perhaps by coming down the valley of the Solu River. At 11.30 a.m. on the 8th a patrol to Ketoba from Isariba, approaching the Australian observation post there, found two Japanese with the body of a third. Both were killed and the papers and gear were sent back to troop headquarters. About the same time Lieutenant Ball's[4] section withdrew from the junction of the Solu and Haile Rivers towards Isariba because

---

[2] F-Lt F. Masson, DFC, 408693. 5 and 4 Sqns. Plumber; of Footscray, Vic; b. Mansfield, Vic, 25 Sep 1913.

[3] F-Lt S. R. Carter, DFC, 405375. 5, 4 and 7 Sqns. Mining geologist; of Mount Isa, Qld; b. Harrow, England, 11 May 1914.

[4] Lt C. H. Ball, MC, QX17719. 2/3 Indep Coy, 2/6 Cdo Sqn. Farm hand; of Lismore, NSW; b. Lismore, 13 May 1920.

the Japanese had obviously already bypassed his position. By 3.15 p.m. small enemy parties were seen on the ridge overlooking Ketoba.

For the 2/6th Squadron the situation became more serious as the afternoon dragged on. Eather was informed of their plight but decided not to send any troops forward until he had further information. Blainey's headquarters was in a dangerous position as there was no friendly force between them and the rapidly increasing enemy on the ridge above the valley. At 4 p.m. between 120 and 150 Japanese moved down from the main spur through rain forest to the kunai round the headquarters camp. There were many gullies to give them covered approaches. Blainey still had no news of his troop in the Isariba area. By 6 p.m. this strong Japanese force reached a position within 400 yards of squadron headquarters. An hour later Vasey placed the squadron under Eather's command so that the 25th Brigade now controlled both reconnaissance units on its immediate left. At 7.10 a small party, setting booby-traps to delay the Japanese advance into the Ramu Valley, was fired on and two men were killed. Ten minutes later two natives wearing red lap laps entered the perimeter making far more noise than usual, and asked if this was the area of the commando squadron, stating that they were members of the Papuan Battalion. They were immediately suspect and were shot.

When Captain Chalk reported that he was withdrawing to the Evapia River, Blainey decided to do likewise as his position was equally untenable. After dark the enemy began encircling his camp and, just before 8 p.m., Blainey rang brigade headquarters to report the situation before withdrawing. Squadron headquarters pulled back at 8.45 p.m., just before the enemy made a series of heavy attacks on the vacated position. By 11 p.m. squadron headquarters and the troop with it dug in close to their old position near the Evapia. The position could be serious, for the Japanese had cut off large elements of the commando squadron and Papuans. To Eather that night it appeared that the Japanese were making a concerted drive to push the Australians from the hills into the Ramu Valley, and he warned Colonel Marson that two companies of the 2/25th Battalion would move forward to the Evapia River next morning to establish a base and patrol forward. Eather asked for another section of 25-pounders to support his brigade as his only section would move forward in support of the 2/25th.

At this stage no one had much idea of what was happening in the Isariba-Ketoba areas, but Major Laidlaw at Faita had been warned to expect that parties from the 2/6th Squadron might move to Faita. Vasey and his senior staff officer, Robertson, were busy that night with signals. An hour before midnight on the 8th they signalled Laidlaw: "Owing necessity withdrawal 2/6 Cav Sqn your main task now protection radar station and patrolling should be confined to local patrols to give adequate warning of any Jap movement your direction." Laidlaw had several patrols out, but these were rapidly recalled.

On the same night Vasey sent an "emergency ops" signal to Morshead in Port Moresby asking that the 18th Brigade be sent forward. To amplify this signal he sent Morshead a note entitled "Review of Situation—Ramu Valley". He began: "The increased activity of the Japs in the high ground east of Kesawai 1, together with other factors, warrants a reconsideration of the position of this division." He then said that the Japanese in this area (believed not less than 200) might be the "foremost elements" of a larger Japanese force striking towards the Ramu Valley. "The area which he has now occupied is . . . where the valley is narrowest," he wrote. A further advance by the Japanese would cut across the valley and prevent maintenance of the 2/6th Squadron by natives from the Dumpu area. As the area of operations was about ten miles from the Dumpu strip, and as there were so few native carriers, he would be unable to maintain any force permanently in that area for the support of the 2/6th Squadron. "Consequently if the Jap should advance in strength in this area I shall be unable to prevent, though I will delay, his advance into the valley itself." He went on to outline other factors: the rapid repair by the Japanese of any air damage on the Bogadjim Road, the increase in anti-aircraft protection along the Bogadjim Road, the fact that the Gusap air base must form an attractive objective for the Japanese, and reports by the A.W.W. station at Wantoat of Japanese activity in that general area.

It is hard to believe that Vasey did actually fear for the safety of his positions; rather did he seem to be seizing the opportunity to scrape together reasons why his force should be augmented. He repeated the request that the 18th Brigade be moved to Dumpu, and asked that the battalions in the Ramu Valley should immediately be brought to full strength, that 1,000 more native carriers be made available, that another commando squadron be placed at his disposal to patrol into the Finisterres from the Marawasa and Kaiapit areas, and that continuous heavy air strikes should be made on the Bogadjim Road. These requests for reinforcements were not granted. "N.G.F. has just forgotten me," Vasey wrote in a private letter a few days later, "not even moral support from rear . . . left alone and don't understand it." The official reply to his signal came early on the morning of the 9th December before dawn. "No action being taken to move 18 Brigade Group at present. Other commitments preclude air strikes Bogadjim Road today."

Late on the afternoon of 9th December Vasey sent a signal to Morshead that "rifle tabs obtained from enemy killed night 6/7 December at Ketoba identified *239 Jap Inf Regiment*". About three-quarters of an hour later, at 7.30 p.m., he sent another personal signal for Morshead: "Believe I could clean up *239 Regiment* if I had 18 Brigade and natives and maul them with 18 Brigade only." Morshead replied just before midnight, "Much as I would like to do so sorry not practicable meet your request." By the 9th Vasey's Intelligence staff was beginning to think that two Japanese regiments, probably depleted, were opposing the division.

From 6.40 a.m. until 8.30 a.m. on the 9th a Boomerang aircraft examined the Japanese area from a low altitude. At the conclusion of the flight the pilot, Flying Officer Staley,[5] dropped messages reporting that the two ridges north-east and east of Kesawai were now "thoroughly studded with foxholes", most of them well-camouflaged, but discernible from the air because of the tracks leading to them. Staley, whose aircraft was fired on from several positions, estimated that there were at least 300 Japanese in this area.

Soon after 11.45 a.m. when Blainey reached the Evapia River, he linked in on the main telephone line and reported his position to brigade headquarters. As two companies of the 2/25th Battalion under Major Robertson were on their way forward to the Evapia, Blainey was instructed to withdraw to the Mene River. He knew little of the whereabouts of his other two troops except that Lieutenant Teasdale was withdrawing. Brigade said that they would try to make signal contact with the isolated troops.

In the Isariba-Ketoba areas with Watson's troop was a party of 14 artillerymen led by Captain Longworth,[6] who had been reconnoitring the tracks from Kesawai to Koropa and Isariba during the past two days to see whether guns could be moved there; they were at Isariba when the attack occurred. Late on the afternoon of the 8th Vasey had ordered the withdrawal of these troops, but the order had not gone beyond 25th Brigade headquarters. Thus, the troops in the Ketoba and Isariba areas were unaware on the 9th that they should withdraw, and were determined to hold what they had. At 2.30 a.m. Lieutenant Balderstone's forward section at Ketoba was heavily attacked by Japanese coming from the Orgoruna area, and was forced to withdraw towards Isariba.

At 7.15 a.m. the enemy began a series of attacks on Isariba. The attacks lasted an hour and a half but were unsuccessful because of the stubborn defence and because the Vickers and grenade dischargers rendered untenable the only ground available for the enemy's supporting arms. Half way through this attack Lieutenant Ball's section, withdrawing from the junction of the Haile and Solu Rivers, approached Isariba from the east, but was unable to get through and made for the Ramu. Soon after this first attack the defenders of Isariba were diverted by the spectacle of 20 Kittyhawks led in by Boomerangs bombing and strafing the Japanese-held ridges above Kesawai. The attack seemed very successful and 17 bombs apparently landed directly on the target. Another successful attack was made by 16 Kittyhawks in the early afternoon.

Earlier, at 10 a.m., Watson had withstood his second attack, this one lasting 45 minutes. At 11.15 a.m. the Japanese resorted to a bayonet charge on Isariba but they were wiped out, mainly by fire from the machine-guns. This fight for Isariba was still going on when Blainey linked by telephone with brigade headquarters. As a result the brigade tried to make signal contact with Isariba and succeeded at 3.30 p.m., half an hour after the Japanese had launched another unsuccessful attack. Watson gave an account of the happenings and asked for instructions and more

---

[5] F-Lt E. R. Staley, 401679. 5 and 4 Sqns. Farmer; of Natya, Vic; b. Bristol, England, 14 Aug 1911. Killed in action 31 Dec 1943.

[6] Lt-Col L. E. Longworth, OBE, ED, VX14109; 2/4 Fd Regt. Bank officer; of Brighton, Vic; b. Warrnambool, Vic, 30 Mar 1912.

ammunition. The signal message from brigade, however, ran: "Blainey back on Mene. You come to rejoin him." Watson was warned that when returning he should avoid previous squadron and Papuan positions but that "Evapia O.K." After defeating another half-hearted Japanese attack, Watson's troop at 4.15 p.m. withdrew undaunted south towards the Ramu and then up the river valley towards the Mene.

By dusk on the 9th the two companies of the 2/25th Battalion had dug in east of the Evapia River but had seen no Japanese. The Papuans (3 officers, 9 Australian N.C.O's, 79 native soldiers and 27 carriers, of whom one officer, 4 Australian N.C.O's, 30 natives and 3 carriers were still missing) were in the area of the foothills between the Mosia and Faria Rivers. The 2/6th Commando Squadron, less two troops, was in the Mene River area and would move first thing on the 10th farther up the valley of the Mene to higher ground. The two missing troops were presumably withdrawing to rejoin the squadron. For the morning of the 10th Brigadier Eather instructed the two companies of the 2/25th to patrol across the Evapia, the Papuans to patrol along both banks of the Ramu River, and the 2/6th Squadron to patrol the high ground in the Mene Valley. With this screen of patrols Eather hoped to find out just where the Japanese were and what they intended.

Action on the 10th started early when, just before dawn, a Japanese aircraft dropped about five bombs on a dump near brigade headquarters. At midday Lieutenant Searles'[7] platoon of the 2/25th ambushed a Japanese patrol of about 40 at a creek crossing about half way between the Evapia and Kesawai, killing 6 Japanese.

During the day more missing men from the commando squadron and the Papuan Infantry came back. In the morning Tac R aircraft saw about 50 Australians in the Koben area. The men were Balderstone's and a message was dropped instructing them to return to the Mene area via the south bank of the Ramu. Still missing at the end of the day were Teasdale's party of 2 officers and 15 men, Ball's party of one officer and 27 men and Watson with a small reconnaissance party. Native soldiers from the Papuan Infantry were still trickling in, and by the end of the day one officer, 4 Australian N.C.O's and 12 native soldiers were still missing, and it was known that 10 native soldiers had been wounded.

The ease with which the Japanese force had entered the Kesawai area, often moving by night along difficult mountain trails, was evidence that they had had help from native guides. On 10th December divisional headquarters signalled all units under command: "Three suspect natives killed to date all wearing red lap laps. Angau have been ordered to ensure none of our natives wear red lap laps." The alacrity with which the natives serving the Australians dispensed with any red lap laps was remarkable.

Because of the enemy activity west of the Evapia River, Vasey decided not to carry out the proposed relief of the two brigades about 21st December. It seemed to Vasey at this stage that the main enemy thrust

---

[7] Lt M. G. Searles, QX36518; 2/25 Bn. Motor mechanic; of Longreach, Qld; b. Longreach, 31 Jan 1921.

might be into the 25th Brigade's area and he hoped that when the 21st Brigade was relieved it would not have to fight from the reserve position but have a rest.

After the capture of Wareo and the defeat of the *20th Japanese Division* on the east of the Huon Peninsula, an examination was carried out by New Guinea Force to see how far it was necessary to exploit up the coast of the Huon Peninsula in order to complete the mission assigned to Allied Land Forces in this area. It will be recalled that General MacArthur, in May, had given Allied Land Forces the role of exploiting to Madang. Later instructions made the neutralisation of Madang a task for Alamo Force, New Guinea Force's role in the area being confined to operations in the Ramu Valley and/or northwards up the coast of the Huon Peninsula to assist Alamo Force. When General Krueger visited New Guinea Force headquarters at Port Moresby on 6th December, he was asked what help he required from New Guinea Force in carrying out his mission, but replied that, because of other operations which he was undertaking, plans for the neutralisation of Madang had not yet been finalised. At this stage Krueger was preparing for the invasion of New Britain and there was also a possibility that an American force would be detached to occupy Saidor on the north coast of New Guinea astride the line of withdrawal of the *20th* and *51st Japanese Divisions* from the Huon Peninsula. The lack of any American plan to deal with Madang may have reminded the Australian commanders of the fuss created at MacArthur's headquarters at the end of August when the Australians had not prepared any detailed plan for the capture of Madang at a time when the invasion of Lae was taking place. It now seemed that the capture of Madang might well be a job for New Guinea Force, but for the time being there was no change in the roles of the two Australian divisions. This was the situation when General Blamey arrived at Port Moresby (on 11th December) and stayed in New Guinea while General Morshead had some leave in Australia. On the 12th General MacArthur's Advanced G.H.Q. also opened in Port Moresby. There was now a wealth of senior headquarters in New Guinea. Clustered in Port Moresby with Advanced G.H.Q. and L.H.Q. was the headquarters of New Guinea Force. Across the Owen Stanleys at Dobodura was General Berryman's II Australian Corps headquarters. General Krueger's headquarters of Alamo Force was at Morobe.

In the Ramu Valley both sides were watchful on the 11th. During the day there were more reports of the missing men of the 2/6th Commando Squadron and the Papuan Infantry. One officer, two N.C.O's and a wounded native reported in to the forward company of the 2/25th. Ball's party finally reported in. Watson's small four-man party and Teasdale's party of 18 were still missing, but during the day Corporal Pickering[8] and two men from Teasdale's party arrived with news that they had been ambushed and Teasdale wounded.

---

[8] Cpl R. G. Pickering, VX76641. 2/6 Indep Coy, 2/6 Cdo Sqn. Labourer; of Dromana, Vic; b. Portarlington, Vic, 16 Jun 1915.

Since losing contact with his headquarters on the 8th, Teasdale's men had been steadily making their way through the tangled hills towards the Ramu Valley. On the 9th the section had moved off at dawn and continued all through the day until almost midnight. Next day they started at daylight and reached the top of a mountain where they tried their wireless again but without result. By 4 p.m. they reached the bank of the Solu River, very hungry, for all their food had been consumed the previous night. They crossed the Solu and moved down until they reached the track which had been the line of communication to Isariba. Along this track there were many Japanese bootmarks, so Teasdale decided to cross it and move through a swamp towards the Ramu. The men cut into the swamp, but it became so deep that they decided to move along the main track towards the east. It was almost dark when the track was reached and the section advanced about 200 yards when three shots rang out and Teasdale was wounded. Lieutenant M. A. Bishop now took charge and guarded Teasdale while he was bandaged and given a shot of morphia. Putting the wounded man on a bush stretcher the patrol moved back into the swamp for about 100 yards. All through the night it rained and at daylight Bishop sent Pickering and two men to reach base if possible and get help. A standing patrol saw 120 Japanese moving along the track. Deciding that they would have much trouble if they advanced along the track, the patrol set off on a south-west bearing through the swamp with the four natives carrying Teasdale. They reached three native huts where they found a bag of corn; one cob per man was issued and two cobs to each of the four devoted natives. On the 12th they reached the Ramu and moved along it until opposite the old squadron headquarters. Bishop sent two men and a native to find out whether it was still occupied by Australians, but when they were fired on he continued to move up the Ramu. Late in the afternoon Teasdale died. Struggling on, the patrol camped for the night in the kunai. They plodded on next morning and at 10.30 a.m. the 17 Australians and 4 natives, sick and exhausted, came to an artillery position. Here they were given food and were sent to hospital by jeep.

Meanwhile, on the 11th General Vasey was tightening his defences. As well as making their thrust into the Kesawai area the Japanese had, the previous night, delivered a small bayonet attack on the forward Australian section on Shaggy Ridge. On the right flank there were fragmentary reports of Japanese being in the upper Surinam Valley and in the Wantoat area, while on the left flank a patrol led by Captain McKenzie of the 2/2nd Commando Squadron had found that Kulau was strongly held by about 100 Japanese.

While the 2/25th Battalion was patrolling west from the Evapia River on the 11th, Vasey and Eather went forward and discussed operations with Marson. The 2/2nd Pioneer Battalion was in the Lakes area ready to prevent any Japanese infiltration between the two brigades, and to continue work on the jeep track. On the 12th a patrol from the 2/6th Commando Squadron (now commanded by Captain A. S. Palmer) prepared to occupy the 5500 Feature, and on the left the 2/2nd Squadron, less McKenzie's patrol was concentrated at Faita with standing patrols at all likely crossing places and patrols across the Ramu as far as Usini only. Although the Japanese thus seemed a little more active than usual throughout the whole area of operations, and although they had driven a deep wedge into the Australian positions in the Kesawai-Isariba area, the position seemed to be stabilising itself once more.

Facing the Japanese positions to the west in the Kesawai area were the two companies of the 2/25th Battalion. They were forward half a day's march from the main battalion position with the role of giving a firm base for extensive patrolling. On the right was Captain Cox's, dug in on a bald knife-edged hill with positions extending over 500 yards and dominating the track and jungle below. To the south was Major Robertson's, dug in in a jungle clearing on the flat ground at the deserted village of Kesawai astride the main track. The force was under Robertson's command, and by nightfall on the 12th his own company had been in position for four days and Cox's company for two days and a half. During this time patrolling by day and setting of ambush positions by night had given the men little rest. Lieutenant Feely,[9] the artillery officer with Robertson, was engaging opportunity targets.

Robertson sent out four patrols on the 12th, three of platoon strength and one of section strength. There were patrol clashes on the 12th between the men of Robertson's own company and the enemy, but Cox's company, although patrolling extensively, did not make contact. An hour after midnight, however, the men of Cox's company were suddenly alert for there were sounds of much movement ahead. In the moonlight sentries were soon able to see a large force and the company quietly stood to. The attack was coming in mainly towards Cox's northern platoon—Lieutenant Cameron's[1]—which fortunately was supported by a Vickers, under Corporal Johnston.[2] From a distance of 50 yards the platoon suddenly poured fire from three Bren guns and the Vickers into the enemy. The fire was soon returned, not only by rifles and grenades but from about six light machine-guns and two heavy machine-guns or Woodpeckers sited farther behind. This first enemy thrust was smashed before it started.

To the south the men of the other company were also standing to, and a quarter of an hour after the initial assault opened fire on about 30 Japanese moving down the track across the company's front. Robertson reported later that "grenades were thrown into the party which dispersed with considerable shouting, squealing and apparent confusion". The main grenadier was Corporal O'Brien[3] who threw dozens. "Our fire was im-

---

[9] Lt T. J. Feely, VX16298; 2/4 Fd Regt. Grazier; of Briagolong, Vic; b. Briagolong, 6 Dec 1918. Killed in action 13 Dec 1943.

[1] Lt A. A. Cameron, QX2605. 2/9 and 2/25 Bns. Farm worker; of Sarina, Qld; b. Mackay, Qld, 17 Jun 1916.

[2] WO1 H. W. Johnston, MM, QX13860; 2/25 Bn. Engine driver; of Wellington, NSW; b. Wellington, 11 Sep 1913.

[3] Cpl J. J. O'Brien, MM, QX3478; 2/25 Bn. Labourer; of Childers, Qld; b. Toowoomba, Qld, 24 Jun 1917.

mediately returned and large numbers of grenades were thrown into our perimeter." On the right flank, according to Cox, "the work of Corporal Johnston in keeping his gun firing was one of the outstanding factors in holding the Japanese attack". Johnston's feat was the more remarkable because three of his crew of six were wounded and the fusee spring of the gun was shot away. In this first hour most of the attacks fell on Cox's company where the enemy made a series of very strong assaults. Machine-gun fire repelled them when they attempted to climb the steep approaches on the flanks and the Queenslanders rolled grenades down on them. Towards the end of the hour the enemy's fire died down but the attack of the Japanese force which seemed to number at least 400 was by no means spent. On finding the approach to Cox's positions difficult, the enemy began crawling forward with much chattering and clicking of rifle bolts, apparently bent on drawing machine-gun fire so that the Woodpeckers and light machine-guns on the knoll 400 yards away "could get on to our positions before he got up and rushed us". The men held their fire until

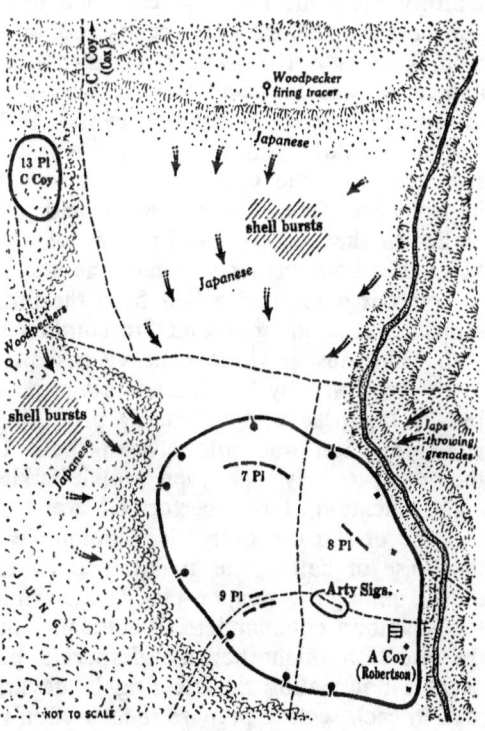

Night 12th-13th December

the enemy got up and charged. Machine-gun fire again broke up this attack. The enemy outnumbered the Australians, however, and Cox was worried, for the enemy was on three sides of his position and the attack on the other company almost completed the encirclement.

During the lull in the firing Robertson's men heard movement across the whole company front and it seemed that the Japanese were trying to get between the two companies. Robertson could also hear the enemy digging in a semi-circle round his front and fired with all weapons including his grenade-dischargers. In return for this bombardment the enemy returned "a terrific volume of fire", using at least five Woodpeckers dominating Kesawai village, and some mortars. At 2 a.m. another 100 men moved up to reinforce the Japanese stalled before Cox's company.

Robertson's line to battalion headquarters was cut at this time, but not before he had outlined the general situation to Marson. The artillery line was still intact and Robertson asked Feely to bring defensive fire on the immediate front. While giving his fire order Feely was mortally wounded but Robertson took over the telephone and brought the fire down to within 100 yards of his front. He then switched the fire to the strong enemy position facing the southern end of Cox's company, and, as far as he was able, on to the other positions facing the northern company. Unfortunately the artillery telephone line was cut at 2.45 a.m. and the guns ceased shelling the enemy positions for fear of hitting their own men. Robertson tried to make contact with a No. 511 wireless set but again and again was unsuccessful. At 3 a.m., however, Lieutenant Marsden,[4] in charge of the troop of guns beyond the Yogia River, decided to take the risk and brought down fire on the last recorded target, and thereafter switched from the positions ahead of Robertson's company to what he hoped were defensive fire tasks and which had been used effectively earlier in the battle. This fire was of the greatest assistance to the two beleaguered companies and gave the men heart.

For four hours and a half from the initial assault intermittent Japanese attacks and almost constant fire continued. All attacks were thrown back with what must have been heavy casualties. Ammunition had necessarily to be conserved by the defenders and so was expended less lavishly than by the Japanese who habitually fired off far too much. When telephone communication was cut between the two companies, about 3.30 a.m., they had to rely on seven walkie-talkie wireless sets used for inter-communication; these performed well but they were mostly inaudible because of the din of battle. Communication, rendered thus difficult by the noise of battle, was maintained by the commanders who constantly moved among the weapon-pits. It was while doing this that one of Robertson's platoon commanders, Lieutenant Saunders,[5] was killed. Aware that the situation might become desperate because of the Japanese Woodpeckers dominating the clearing in daylight Robertson had some of the men in each section prepare their section's gear for a possible withdrawal. By 4 a.m. the enemy were in a position below Cox's company and round his right flank and were bringing fire from a Woodpecker directly on to Robertson's area. With his right flank vulnerable Robertson thought that his position would be untenable in daylight and so attempted a gradual movement into the jungle fringe on his western perimeter. He managed to move part of his force there but found that his men were now within 20 feet of the Japanese in the jungle. Lieutenant Searles actually trod on a Japanese when moving round his area and when the Japanese complained he was shot. Half an hour later a Japanese shouted out insults about "white dingoes over there. Honourable Japanese gentlemen over here." A burst of Bren gun fire and a shriek followed this call and a Japanese officer was later found dead there.

---

[4] Capt E. C. H. Marsden, VX39363; 2/4 Fd Regt. Bank officer; of Brighton, Vic; b. Huntingdon, England, 9 Mar 1918.

[5] Lt R. E. Saunders, QX43779; 2/25 Bn. Clerk; of Longreach, Qld; b. Longreach, 26 Aug 1919. Killed in action 13 Dec 1943.

(*Australian War Memorial*)
Men of the 2/16th Battalion on the battle-torn Pimple (Shaggy Ridge) soon after its capture on 27th December 1943.

(*Australian War Memorial*)
A wounded member of the 2/16th Battalion being assisted to the R.A.P.

(*Australian War Memorial*)
"C" Company, 2/9th Battalion, dug in on a newly-occupied feature of Shaggy Ridge, 21st January 1944.

(*Australian War Memorial*)
Looking towards Madang from Shaggy Ridge with the Pimple in the foreground, 22nd January 1944.

(*Imperial War Museum*)

American marines boarding L.S.T's at Cape Sudest (Papua) in December 1943, bound for the Cape Gloucester landings.

(*Australian War Memorial*)

The landing of the 126th U.S. Regimental Combat Team at Saidor, 2nd January 1944.

(*Australian War Memorial*)
Men of the 2/2nd Commando Squadron crossing the Ramu River near Faita on 7th January 1944 after an eight-day patrol to Jappa, in Japanese territory.

(*Australian War Memorial*)
After a 5,000-foot climb into the mountains, the Australians found the mud just as deep as on the lower slopes.

On three sides of the Australian position the Japanese crept close under cover of darkness after the setting of the moon. At 5 a.m. Cox managed to tell Robertson on the walkie-talkie that his ammunition was getting low, he had five stretcher cases, and had recently seen at least another 100 Japanese walking round below him to join the 200 who were already attacking. As the forward platoon was now reduced to 16 men aided by three machine-gunners, a Japanese attack there might have some success and would undoubtedly render untenable the position not only of his company but also of Robertson's. Robertson estimated that there were about 150 Japanese in his immediate vicinity and agreed with Cox that the position would deteriorate in daylight, particularly as the Australians' supply of grenades was almost finished, and it would be impossible after dawn to get the stretcher cases out safely.

Withdrawal was a difficult and unpalatable course. The decision had to be made before the approaching dawn, however, so Robertson ordered Cox to begin withdrawing at 5.30 a.m. to a pre-arranged alternative area about a mile to the rear where both companies would take up another defensive position. Marson had approved this alternative position two days before. Robertson's own company would cover the withdrawal and hold as a rearguard until 5.45 a.m. Stretchers were made, the dead were buried, and the companies began thinning out to their assembly areas at the agreed times. Cox's company arrived at the rendezvous after dawn at 7.30 a.m. and was joined soon afterwards by Robertson's, which had withdrawn through thick jungle and pit-pit swamp, sometimes three feet deep in water. Lieutenant Burns, who had volunteered with a patrol to take up a supply of grenades at dawn from the battalion, followed the track almost into Kesawai before he saw a Japanese soldier with rifle at the slope on guard in the village. Burns had arrived with his precious cargo half an hour after the position was abandoned. The companies had retired with all their weapons intact. They had lost 5 killed, including 2 officers, and 14 wounded, but the company commanders estimated that they had killed at least 100 Japanese. As the two weary companies settled into their new area Robertson's second-in-command, Lieutenant H. W. Steel, tapped the line behind the break and arranged for the artillery to bring down intense fire on the area they had evacuated. About 170 rounds were fired. A patrol next day found the area completely abandoned by the Japanese. The intense battle and the artillery barrage had finally halted and turned the last Japanese thrust in this area.

Withdrawals are always unpopular, particularly with an army on the offensive, no matter how static or fluctuating a local situation may be. Marson who was moving forward early in the morning of the 13th to be with his two companies, had later to answer a detailed series of questions from Eather about types of weapon-pits, fields of fire, booby-traps, outposts, perimeters, and so on. The answers must have satisfied the brigadier and it is difficult, in any case, to see what other course was open to Robertson in those tense moments before dawn on 13th December.

One of the ever-ready aircraft of No. 4 Squadron, piloted by Flying-Officer Carter, took off early on the 13th. Carter and his observer picked out Robertson's companies below them waving to the aircraft and carrying stretchers. The timbered stretch from Kesawai to the area which the Japanese had captured showed signs of occupation, and the track from the Boku River through Ketoba, Isariba, Koropa and the Solu River was broad, well-worn and recently used. This and similar tactical reconnaissance seemed to indicate that the main Japanese thrust might have come from the Orgoruna-Mataloi area rather than from the Japanese roadhead. In the afternoon Flying Officers Miller-Randle[6] and Staley saw isolated parties of Japanese, well-used tracks and signs of occupation. Considering these and other reports, Eather thought that the Japanese might intend to outflank the 25th Brigade and come in between it and the 21st, thus threatening the Gusap airstrip, divisional headquarters and the main Australian lines of communication. He thought it inadvisable to extend his brigade's front or to weaken his rear by sending more troops forward, and decided therefore that Robertson's and Cox's companies would be withdrawn during the night to the east bank of the Evapia River, some two miles to the rear, where the remainder of the 2/25th was now concentrated. In the dark the two companies withdrew to the Evapia.

Documents captured during and since the Japanese attacks from 8th to 13th December proved that the attacking force was of three battalions. It seemed to Vasey's staff that the force in the Kesawai area was from the *78th Japanese Regiment*, while the force which attacked in the Ketoba-Isariba area was from the *239th Regiment*. The Japanese made no attempt to follow up their success. It seemed most probable therefore that the enemy's intention was, as the 7th Division put it later, "to carry out a rather large-scale raid with the object of clearing out our O.P's and patrol bases which had evidently been causing him some concern". Because the enemy had few reserves, he could not follow up his initial advantage even had he wished to do so.

As more documents were captured in succeeding operations it appeared that the *239th Regiment* had not taken nearly such an active role in the Kesawai and Isariba operations as was thought. The evidence, though scanty, indicated that the attacks on the 2/6th Squadron and the Papuans and then the 2/25th Battalion were made by the main body of the *I/78th Battalion* which came from the area between Yokopi and Yaula. Some members of the *239th Regiment* may have been in the attacks on Ketoba and Isariba but the main body of the regiment was undoubtedly still in the Madang area with an outpost at Kulau and patrols into the Aminik area.

Until the 12th Vasey had considered that the Japanese activities about Kesawai were "merely a defensive action" but on the 13th he wrote to Morshead that he then considered they were "the preliminary of something considerably bigger". If the advance continued he planned to hold it on the Yogia River. During the 14th Vasey visited both his brigade commanders. With Dougherty he discussed changes made desirable by the enemy's increased interest in the Ramu west of the Evapia. Afterwards Dougherty wrote:

---

[6] F-Lt A. Miller-Randle, DFC, 416170. 5 and 4 Sqns. Student; of Kensington, SA; b. North Adelaide, 19 Mar 1919.

It appeared that if there were a threat at all, then the main enemy threat appeared to be on our left. The General wanted me to swing my centre of gravity to the left in order to be in a better position to meet this threat, either by dealing with him on my own front or by moving to the support of 25th Brigade. In addition, the General wanted me to show signs of a push on our brigade front in order to make the Jap more careful in his moves towards the Ramu. With this in view, he asked me to consider an attack along the Shaggy Ridge feature by the 2/16th Battalion.

After Vasey had gone, Dougherty issued a warning order for the redisposition of his brigade. Together with its toehold on Shaggy Ridge the 2/16th Battalion would take over from the 2/14th in the Johns' Knoll-Faria River area leaving one company on Toms' Post to watch the right flank and fill the gap to the 2/27th Battalion on the right. The 2/14th would then move into reserve in the vicinity of the Lakes and the 2/2nd Pioneer would occupy Brian's Hill and Herald Hill to close the gap between the two brigades. These moves took place on 15th December when Dougherty also moved his headquarters from Kumbarum to the saddle above the Lakes.

Vasey discussed arrangements with Eather to link the two brigades to prevent any large-scale Japanese movement into the Ramu Valley from the north. He said that if the attack on Shaggy Ridge was successful, the Japanese would have to withdraw slightly along their main line of communication and would be deterred from attacking in strength on the 25th Brigade front. Meanwhile, the 25th Brigade would remain in its present position, and if any strong attack were made, the 2/25th Battalion would withdraw to the east bank of the Yogia River where the main strength of the brigade would be concentrated. It was soon apparent, however, that this withdrawal would not be necessary, for a patrol from the 2/25th found the scene of the battle of the 13th unoccupied.

The 15th was quiet. In the afternoon Lieutenant Burns led a patrol from the 2/25th across the Evapia River to this position, and found 11 dead Japanese. Burns also found 164 Japanese weapon-pits where the fight had raged on the 13th; and salvaged most of the gear—mainly small tents—which the companies had left behind.

By 16th December patrols and tactical reconnaissance had proved that Japanese activity round Kesawai was limited; Eather therefore decided that the area across the Evapia towards Kesawai and the 5800 Feature should be reconnoitred in strength. Captain B. G. C. Walker and 30 men of the 2/25th then set out on a two-day patrol and moved right through the scene of the Kesawai action and on to the Solu River without finding any Japanese. Eather then decided to send the 2/33rd Battalion, under cover of darkness, to the 5800 Feature to attack any Japanese there, and to move the Papuans across the Evapia to establish a patrol base for the Koben-Koropa-Solu River area.

With three of his companies Colonel Cotton of the 2/33rd moved off an hour and a half after midnight on the 18th-19th December towards the summit of the 5800 Feature, where he arrived just before dawn. At 2.10 p.m. a section made contact with the enemy about 700 yards south of the highest pinnacle on 5800. The patrol withdrew while the artillery fired 120 rounds. By 5 p.m. the enemy had had enough and withdrew enabling one company to occupy the pinnacle. Next day the battalion patrolled the whole area and found evidence of Japanese occupation and a hasty withdrawal.

Captain Milford led a patrol from the 2/25th Battalion at dusk on the 19th to follow the Japanese line of withdrawal north along the Solu and Haile Rivers and to try to observe the Japanese motor road. On the 20th it followed the Solu River, crossing and recrossing it several times until at 4 p.m. near the top of a steep wooded ridge four Japanese machine-guns fired on the leading section. The section withdrew and all got out except two. Milford considered the Japanese position "unassailable" because of the precipitous slopes on all sides and sent the patrol back to the Solu River while he and five others searched unsuccessfully for the missing men. The patrol returned to the 2/25th at 7 p.m. on the 21st and was joined half an hour later by one of the missing; he had escaped by rolling down a steep slope and following the course of the Solu. Thus by 21st December the western area of Kesawai and the 5800 Feature into which the Japanese had so suddenly thrust was deserted by them and they had pulled back, probably to a line from Orgoruna through the Solu ambush position to Shaggy Ridge.

Patrolling continued on the right of the divisional front where the 2/27th Battalion scoured the area. One patrol, led by Corporal Kemp[7] with four men, followed the track north from the forward company position just south of Mainstream and ran into Japanese machine-gun fire. Of the five men one was killed, one wounded and Kemp was missing, believed killed. The two unscathed men and the wounded man, after taking a wrong turning, ran into another Japanese position behind barbed wire defences and here the wounded man was killed. A land mine was electrically exploded by the enemy and stunned one of the two remaining men. After regaining consciousness this man stumbled east into a steep gully and then south, finally arriving at his company position on the 19th. The other man remained in position inside the Japanese wire for 33 hours during which period he was grenaded and fired on but not hit. He retaliated with his only grenade and the Japanese did not disturb him but improved their own positions by digging. About midday on the 19th he survived bombardment by the Australian artillery. Just before midnight on the 19th he crawled back through the Japanese wire and followed the route which his companion had taken, arriving back exhausted on the 20th.

Meanwhile on 17th December Dougherty sent instructions to Symington of the 2/16th to plan an attack on Shaggy Ridge. Next day, Dougherty having sprained his ankle, Symington went to brigade headquarters and discussed his proposed plan. Dougherty said that the attack would not take place before 26th December, as he wanted his troops to enjoy Christmas before assaulting Shaggy Ridge. Vasey instructed Dougherty

---

[7] Cpl D. W. C. Kemp, SX8157; 2/27 Bn. Labourer; of Prospect, SA; b. Hyde Park, SA, 2 Feb 1920. Missing believed killed in action 18 Dec 1943.

to be at the Dumpu airstrip on the morning of the 21st to fly to Port Moresby for medical examination and treatment.

Patrols from the 2/16th were active on the ridge searching for ways to attack the Pimple but, as previously stated, it was already obvious that this important feature could probably be taken only by frontal assault. With such close-range patrols it was necessary to restrict the activities of the artillery and on the 19th Major Gaunt[8] of the 2/4th Field Regiment arrived at Symington's headquarters to arrange artillery support.

On the 19th and 20th General Blamey visited the two brigades and discussed operations with Vasey and his brigadiers. So simple was the plan and so thoroughly had preparations been made, that the departure of the hobbling Dougherty on the 21st and the assumption of command of the brigade by Lieut-Colonel Rhoden—a battalion commander of only a few weeks' standing—just before the battle did not affect the arrangements.

On Christmas Day there was little activity. All fighting units enjoyed the best Christmas they had known in New Guinea. The diarist of the 2/16th Battalion outlined the menu for the day: "Breakfast—porridge, Burdekin ducks, buns and tea; Dinner—giblet soup, roast turkey and seasoning, green peas, mashed potatoes, shredded carrots, gravy, plum-pudding and sauce, tea and buns." A diarist noted, "It is worth while comparing this with Christmas Day at Gona last year." Church services were also held and in the 2/27th Battalion's lines, where the text of the sermon was "Peace on earth and good will towards men", it was given concurrently with harassing fire on Japanese positions.

From the evidence of his patrols and also from the number of machine-guns which had been fired at the 2/16th Battalion on Shaggy Ridge, Symington thought that the enemy confronting him comprised about three platoons spread from 300 to 400 yards along the razor-back ridge behind the Pimple. He ordered Captain Christian's[9] company to attack and capture the Pimple and exploit for about 400 yards along the ridge; Captain Anderson's[1] company would then move forward and consolidate the ground gained. Christian would have a detachment of 3-inch mortars and a section of Vickers machine-guns under his command, and in support a company of the 2/16th, a troop of the 8th Battery, a troop of the 54th Battery, the 41st Squadron (Fifth Air Force) and No. 4 Squadron R.A.A.F. Christian planned that the Pimple would be captured by his leading platoon with one section forward on the right, one on the left and the third section following closely with three machine-guns and the platoon's 2-inch mortar. The mortar ammunition would be carried by the supporting company and, on receiving the success signal from the leading platoon, Christian's second platoon would move through the objective for a distance of approximately 400 yards.

---

[8] Maj D. C. Gaunt, MC, VX14105; 2/4 Fd Regt. Audit clerk; of Regent, Vic; b. Footscray, Vic, 1 Oct 1911.

[9] Capt R. H. Christian, MC, WX3093; 2/16 Bn. Advertising clerk; of Hollywood, WA; b. Perth, 11 May 1918.

[1] Capt V. E. C. Anderson, QX6248. 7 Div Cav, 2/16 Bn. Grazier; of Goomeri, Qld; b. Brisbane, 17 Mar 1913.

The supporting fire plan for the assault on Shaggy Ridge was one of the most comprehensive and detailed yet arranged in New Guinea. The diarist of the 2/4th Field Regiment claimed that the artillery concentration was the "largest in the S.W.P.A. war".[2] The men carried the maximum of arms and ammunition and the minimum of other equipment.[3] Having had exasperating experience with the 208 wireless set, this was now discarded for the 536 set. Each of the two leading platoon commanders and the company commander had one of these sets and another one was available for use between the 3-inch mortar team and its observation post. Christian had a telephone line back to his battalion headquarters and to the Vickers machine-gun post. To assist the 2/16th, the 2/27th was to pretend to attack the main Japanese position in the Faria River and Mainstream area.

On the 26th no actual start time could be fixed for the attack: if the clouds were down, the aircraft would not be able to assault Shaggy Ridge. The decision about the weather would be Colonel Rhoden's responsibility, and if the attack were to take place the aircraft would be over the target 30 minutes after notification. As dawn broke on the 27th the Pimple was obscured by heavy mists, but they lifted before 8 a.m.

Breakfast for Christian's men was soon over, and the company moved forward to their start-line running east and west of the base of the Pimple. They were clad in jungle greens, boots and American pattern gaiters and were wearing khaki hats or tin helmets, whichever they wished. Besides their arms, ammunition and webbing equipment, each man car-

---

[2] Fire plan of aircraft and artillery supporting 2/16th Battalion's attack on Shaggy Ridge:
H—60 to H—40: 16 Kittyhawks (P-40's) led in by 2 Boomerangs dive-bomb the Pimple. Red Very light by Kittyhawks to indicate end of bombing attack.
H—40 to H—30: Artillery concentration on Pimple — 350 HE at rate 2 (in this and subsequent lifts 8 Bty fires 119 HE and 54 Bty 231 HE).
H—30 to H—15: 8 Kittyhawks strafe south and south-east slopes of Pimple and Ridge—time for two passes per plane. Last plane fires red Very light as it leaves area. Remaining 8 Kittyhawks stay in area until H+60.
H—15 to H—1: Artillery concentration on Pimple—350 HE at rate 4.
H to H+15: Artillery lifts 100 yards—350 HE at rates 3 and 5.
H+16 to H+20: Artillery lifts 50 yards—350 HE at rates 3 and 5.
H+21 to H+35: Artillery lifts 50 yards—350 HE at rates 4 and 3.
H+36 to H+41: Artillery lifts 100 yards (i.e. 300 yards forward of the Pimple) 350 HE at rate 5.
H+42 to H+50: Artillery lifts 100 yards—350 HE at rate 3.
H+51 to H+61: Artillery lifts 50 yards (i.e. 450 yards forward of the Pimple)—350 HE at rate 3.
Fire plan for 2/16th's own weapons as follows:
3-inch Mortars
H—10 to H—5: 5 bombs rapid fire on Pimple.
H+15 to H+30: 30 bombs normal fire on timbered area and then as ordered.
MMG's
H to H+20: 20 normal fire on to top of ridge and timbered area.
H+20 to H+40: 40 normal on timber at least 100 yards east of top of Ridge.

[3] The men in the two leading platoons would carry more than the normal battle scale of ammunition.
On man
  Bren—300 rounds
  Owen—300 rounds
  Rifle—100 rounds
  2-inch Mortar—27 HE
  EY Rifle—6 grenades (7 seconds) per section
  6 grenades (4 seconds) per rifleman
  MMG—10,000 rounds per gun
  3-inch Mortar—275 HE, 21 smoke
Reserve
  Bren—500 rounds per LMG—Total 4,500 (9 Brens)
  Owen—400 rounds per OSMG—Total 4,000
  Rifle—100 rounds per rifle—Total 6,000
  Grenade (4 seconds)—Total 100
  Grenade (7 seconds)—Total 100

ried only a haversack containing minimum necessities, a shovel for quick digging-in, and a field dressing carried in the right rear pocket of his trousers. The stretcher bearers moved with the first two platoons. Six minutes after 8 o'clock two Boomerangs strafed the Pimple with tracer bullets to indicate the target for the Kittyhawks. Dive bombing started three minutes later and the program of supporting fire then went on uninterrupted. Dive bombing, strafing and intense artillery concentrations were impressive sights and the valley and foothills reverberated with a roar which could be heard up and down the Ramu Valley, where many hills held spectators.

At 8.55 the Kittyhawks made their last run behind the Pimple from the east. One minute after 9 o'clock Lieutenant Geyton's[4] platoon moved over the start-line and left the cover of the rain forest to scale the rock face which led to the Pimple and which was now denuded of jungle growth by the bombardment. Those behind could see the men clambering up the steep incline to the Pimple slipping on shale and stones thrown up by the bombing and shelling. About a quarter of an hour after the start the leading platoon was about 50 yards from the top of the Pimple and had already used bamboo ladders which it had carried forward. The ladders were now discarded as too cumbersome and the platoon clambered forward with one section on the right, one on the left, and the third in reserve. On the left Sergeant W. T. McMahon's section was held up when the Japanese threw grenades down from a well-sited pill-box. In this shower of grenades, McMahon and Warrant-Officer G. E. Morris were wounded but Corporal Hall,[5] leading his section in from the right flank, dashed ahead and wiped out the pill-box single-handed. It was this action which allowed the platoon to get a footing on the ridge.

Hall's section gained this footing at 9.46 a.m. when, from watching posts to the south, the West Australians could be seen clambering on to the top of the Pimple. Lieutenant Pearson, the artillery observer, and his team were forward with the leading infantry and reported that all the artillery rounds were falling in the correct areas. Four minutes after the first section was on the Pimple, Christian set up his headquarters there. Geyton's platoon was now established along about 100 yards of Shaggy Ridge forward from the Pimple to another similar feature. A second platoon moved through to exploit beyond this second pimple. Three men charged a rock-made bunker but, despite heavy supporting fire, all three were wounded. Grenades failed to dislodge the Japanese and outflanking the position seemed impossible as the sides of the razor-back ridge guarded by the bunker were almost perpendicular. Christian therefore withdrew this platoon which dug in on a position just forward of the second pimple with the bunker immediately below them.

Just after 11 a.m., when Anderson's company finished relieving Christian's and began digging in with two platoons along the ridge and

---

[4] Lt C. A. Geyton, VX114946; 2/16 Bn. Physical culturist and masseur; of Caulfield, Vic; b. Walney I, England, 28 Jan 1920. Accidentally killed 9 Nov 1944.

[5] Sgt M. Hall, DCM, WX14757; 2/16 Bn. Labourer; of Cannington, WA; b. Claremont, WA, 15 May 1918.

one platoon in reserve just below the Pimple, a delayed tactical reconnaissance report by the Boomerangs indicated that large numbers of Japanese were streaming back towards the saddle. These were strafed by the Allied aircraft. At 11.40 a.m. the Japanese attacked the third pimple under the impression that it was occupied by the Australians. This pimple

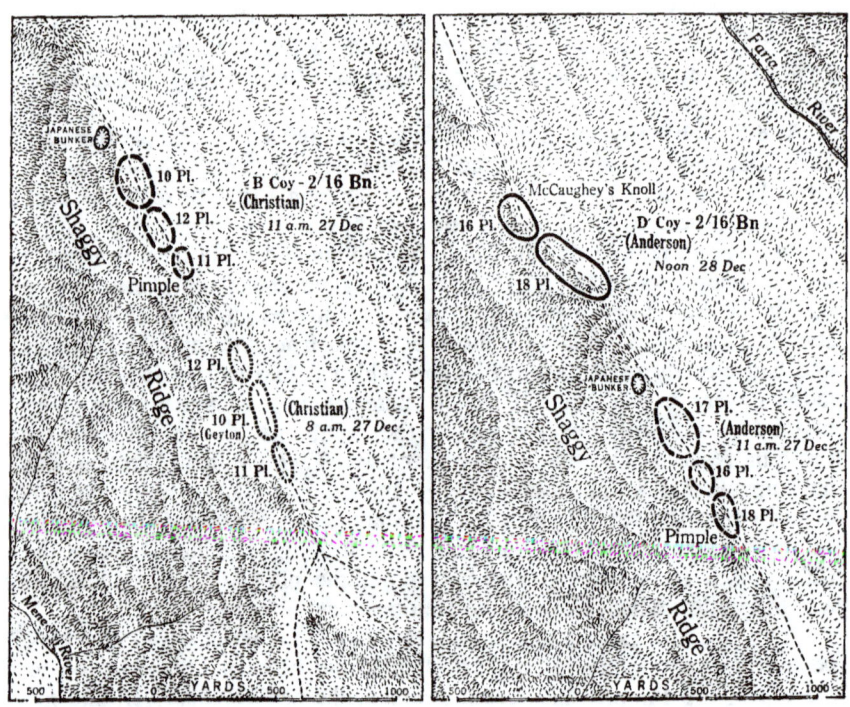

The 2/16th Battalion assault on Shaggy Ridge, 27th-28th December

was beyond the bunker which had held up the advance. The fire from the company's Brens prevented the Japanese from consolidating on the pimple and drove them back. A Japanese, who refused to surrender, covered the entrance to his pill-box with a groundsheet and for about two hours flicked away the grenades thrown at him before they could explode. Eventually he was blasted out when a grenade was tied to the end of a bamboo pole which was poked into the pit, the pin being pulled out by a length of string. More than 100 grenades were thrown during the day at the rock bunker in front of the second pimple.

With the two pimples in their hands the Australians could command a view of the north coast. Aircraft and artillery had played a notable part in helping to extend the area held on Shaggy Ridge. During the two-hour concentration the artillery fired 3,368 shells. "Guns were running hot and gunners received burns from either barrel or cradle," wrote the diarist of the 2/4th Field Regiment. Over the battle area, when the fight was hottest, flew a Piper Cub piloted by Flying Officer Staley and carrying General Vasey.

The forward troops of the 2/16th spent most of the night digging trenches around and from the second pimple so that they could approach the Japanese bunker from a more advantageous position. The Pioneers, protected from fire by the angle of the cliff, chiselled a track along the cliff face towards the bunker. Towards dawn the track was level with and just below the bunker. To deal with the bunker the engineers designed a special bomb which consisted of a grenade placed in a chemical and sealed in a field ration tin. At 8.30 a.m. on the 28th men on the newly-cut track and in the foremost positions pulled out the grenade pins and hurled the new bombs. The bunker was blasted away and inside its remains were found the bodies of a Japanese officer and a private who had held up the advance.

At the same time Lieutenant Scott's platoon was sent down the rugged and precipitous east slope of Shaggy Ridge to attempt a wide encircling movement of the third pimple. At 10.50 a.m. he reported being at the base of the third pimple and a quarter of an hour later the artillery and mortars began firing smoke to cover his advance on to this pimple. Scott reported the "going too tough" straight up the side of the pimple, decided on a different direction, and began climbing up through a belt of timber. Six minutes after midday, light and medium machine-guns opened up on the left flank to distract the enemy's attention and allow Scott to move in and attack from the right. Six minutes later those behind heard heavy firing from the direction of the third pimple and also saw figures climbing it.

At the foot of the objective Scott ordered his platoon sergeant, Longman,[6] to take a small party of Owen gunners up the third pimple. Under heavy enemy machine-gun fire Longman and three men charged an enemy machine-gun post near the top. Two of his men were wounded but Longman and the other continued to advance on the enemy post and eventually silenced it with Owen-gun fire. To reach the enemy post they had to pull themselves up a steep slope with one hand and fire their Owens with the other. Still under heavy fire from other enemy posts the two men covered the evacuation of the two wounded and neutralised the fire of another enemy post 40 yards away which was opposing the advance of the rest of the platoon, led by the wounded Scott, up the cliff face. The courage and dash of the West Australians had enabled them to gain a very difficult objective and consolidate their positions under continuous machine-gun and sniping fire. Nine minutes after Longman led the first assault, Scott was in possession of the third pimple and was covering the advance of Lieutenant McCaughey's[7] platoon to the fourth and highest pimple (later named McCaughey's Knoll), farther along the ridge. The two platoons then dug in on the newly-won ground.

---

[6] Sgt W. J. Longman, MM, WX4779; 2/16 Bn. Well sinker; of Trayning, WA; b. Perth, 27 Sep 1916.

[7] Lt S. M. McCaughey, NX165473; 2/16 Bn. Jackeroo; of Jerilderie, NSW; b. Melbourne, 2 Oct 1921. Killed in action 29 Dec 1943.

Early in the afternoon a Japanese gun began shelling the forward positions on Shaggy Ridge and was promptly answered by the Australian artillery. Soon after the gun opened fire about 80 Japanese were seen on the feature about 600 yards forward of the newly-captured ground. The artillery immediately shelled them. At 2.22 p.m. the Japanese, somewhat chastened by this shell fire, counter-attacked the forward positions of the 2/16th but were driven back by accurate fire. When Vasey visited the battalion later in the day he learned that the 2/16th's tally of Japanese dead was now 96.

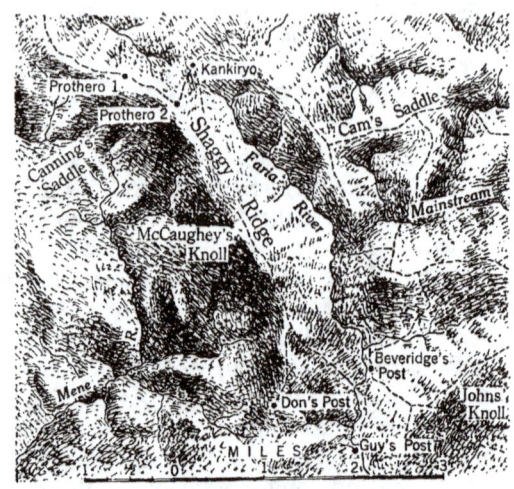

Shaggy Ridge area

The force which the 2/16th Battalion had attacked so successfully was a part of the *II/78th Battalion* whose task was to defend the Kankiryo Saddle-Shaggy Ridge-Faria Ridge area. As the result of the Australian assault the forward Japanese company was virtually annihilated. General Adachi and his staff officers, when questioned after the war, thought that the strength of the *II/78th Battalion* at this time was only about 400 but this figure seems too low.

An enemy gun was in action against the forward positions of the 2/16th on Shaggy Ridge at intervals during the period from the 29th to the 31st December, and on the 29th one of the leading platoon commanders, Lieutenant McCaughey, was killed by a tree burst which also wounded four others. Both the 2/16th Battalion on Shaggy Ridge and the 2/27th Battalion on the right were alert for any signs of Japanese withdrawal during these last days of December. At dawn on the 29th Lieutenant Lee[8] and Sergeant Holland[9] of the 2/16th crept forward a few yards and threw several grenades into a Japanese bunker.

Exchanges of artillery fire and small patrols in the forward area of the 21st Brigade continued until New Year's Eve when, at midnight "all guns fired a salvo as New Year's greeting", according to the diary of the 2/4th Field Regiment.

It will be recalled that, while the 21st Brigade was dealing with Shaggy Ridge, the 25th Brigade's task was to patrol deeply on the left flank. A company of the 2/31st Battalion, led by Lieutenant Oakhill,[1] left the area east of the Evapia River towards dusk on 26th December on a six-day

---

[8] Lt J. O. Lee, QX2887; 2/16 Bn. Clerk; of Clermont, Qld; b. Cooktown, Qld, 30 Nov 1916.
[9] Sgt E. S. Holland, WX4183; 2/16 Bn. Labourer; of Boulder, WA; b. Fremantle, WA, 19 Sep 1913.
[1] Capt R. S. Oakhill, QX16130; 2/31 Bn. Clerk; of Kalinga, Qld; b. Toogoolawah, Qld, 9 Jul 1918.

patrol. The route lay along the main track to the Solu River, then through Ketoba to the Boku River crossing and thence along the track to Orgoruna. Travelling mainly by night the patrol crossed the Solu after dark on the 27th and reached Koropa by dawn on the 28th. After a small skirmish with an enemy patrol the company moved into Isariba at 9.40 a.m. On the morning of the 29th a patrol of three was fired on as it approached Orgoruna by an enemy force of about a platoon dug in on the far side of the village. Lieutenant Robertson,[2] who was leading, killed a Japanese sentry. Oakhill then came up and engaged the Japanese. At 5 p.m. Boomerangs which had been scouting ahead of the company earlier in the day came over and strafed Orgoruna. Oakhill, having been told not to become heavily committed, withdrew and arrived back on the banks of the Evapia on the afternoon of 1st January.

There were other long patrols before the end of 1943. Major Laidlaw of the 2/2nd Commando Squadron accompanied Lieutenant Adams' section on a long-range patrol on the western flank. The patrol returned six days later, on 28th December, having penetrated farthest east yet along the Uria-Rainbana and Uria-Kesa tracks. It found that all enemy defences in these areas were abandoned and it now seemed that the enemy might be pulling back into a semi-circle of defences round Madang and Bogadjim. Another important patrol in the last days of December was from the 2/2nd Pioneer Battalion and can be best described in the words of the battalion's historian:

> Battalion activities ended for the year with an important patrol up the Mene River Valley. . . . Led by Captain McInnes,[3] the patrol carried stocks of rations to a cache near a low ridge named Canning's Saddle[4] and, using that area as a patrol base, a smaller party set out to scale the slopes of Shaggy Ridge. The patrol was skilfully manoeuvred inside a wired position on the crest and withdrawn just as adeptly. The enemy never suspected the presence of a patrol inside his defences and he was later to pay dearly for his lack of vigilance.[5]

On New Year's Eve occurred a loss which upset the fighting men of the 7th Division. One of the Boomerangs from No. 4 Squadron, piloted by Flying Officer Staley, was lost on reconnaissance near the 5800 Feature. These manoeuvrable tree-skimming aircraft, piloted by their valiant crews who seemed to know the tangled country so well, had appeared indestructible. The crashed plane and the body of the pilot were found by a patrol from the 2/6th Commando Squadron on 2nd January.

The year ended with Vasey's troops having gained a foothold on the dominating Shaggy Ridge leading to the main Japanese positions on Kankiryo Saddle. If the Americans landed at Saidor the Japanese in the Finisterres would undoubtedly be uneasy about their rear and might even have to detach troops from their mountain defences to take care of Saidor, thus facilitating an Australian advance across the Finisterres.

---
[2] Maj B. E. D. Robertson, MC, NX15540; 2/31 Bn. Schoolteacher; of Penshurst, NSW; b. Mortdale, NSW, 10 Oct 1916.
[3] Capt A. J. McInnes, NX56247. 2/1 and 2/2 Pnr Bns. Shop assistant; of Cooma, NSW; b. Kyogle, NSW, 23 Apr 1917.
[4] Named after Lieutenant B. L. Canning, 2/2nd Pioneer Battalion.
[5] B. F. Aitken, *The Story of the 2/2nd Australian Pioneer Battalion* (1953), p. 222.

Vasey flew to Port Moresby on the 29th (Morshead had returned on the 28th and saw Blamey off next day). On the 30th Vasey conferred with Morshead and Milford and later he visited G.H.Q. for a talk with MacArthur who had a soft spot for him. As a result of these conferences it was decided that the 18th and 15th Brigades would relieve the 21st and 25th. Brigadier Chilton received orders from Vasey that night at 7 p.m. that the 18th Brigade, using 36 aircraft a day, would relieve the 21st Brigade, starting from New Year's Day. On the last day of the year, when Vasey returned to the valley accompanied by Lieut-General Lumsden,[6] Mr Churchill's representative at MacArthur's headquarters, his two brigadiers—Dougherty and Eather—learnt that their brigades were to be relieved.

Before the Buna-Gona operations were over General Blamey had been impressed with the possibility of passing on to the British-Indian army in Burma the lessons that the Australians in New Guinea had so swiftly and successfully mastered. The Australians had established their tactical superiority over the Japanese in a long, exacting campaign fought under a variety of conditions; so far the army in Burma had not had such success.

Late in November 1942 General Wavell, then Commander-in-Chief in India, had sent a letter to Blamey by the hand of Major-General Dewing[7] who was on his way to Australia as a United Kingdom liaison officer. In it Wavell congratulated Blamey on the Australian successes and asked for as much detailed information as possible about the operations and about Japanese tactics and methods. It appears that Blamey did not receive the letter for some weeks. On 23rd January 1943 he replied that he understood that full information about Japanese tactics was sent continuously to India and suggested that Wavell should send him up to 50 of his officers. "They could learn all we have to teach them in about a month or so which would spread the methods we have found so successful more quickly through the Army. I think, however, the fundamental thing in dealing with the Japanese is to develop the psychology of the troops on a completely aggressive basis."

If this was to be done the sooner the better, in view of the distances involved; an alternative course, but one for Wavell rather than Blamey to suggest, was that a substantial group of Australian officers with New Guinea experience should go to India. It was 11th March, however, before Wavell wrote a reply to Blamey and 8th May before Blamey saw it. Wavell said that he was receiving valuable information from Australia; it would be difficult to spare so many officers; "we are getting a good deal of experience now ourselves in Arakan and north Burma, and with the

---

[6] Lt-Gen H. Lumsden, CB, DSO, MC. Comd 28 Armd Bde 1941-42; GOC X Corps 1942-43; Mr Churchill's personal representative on GHQ SWPA 1943-45. Regular soldier; b. 8 Apr 1897. Killed in USS *New Mexico* in Lingayen Gulf, 6 Jan 1945.

[7] Maj-Gen R. H. Dewing, CB, DSO, MC. Chief of Staff, Far East 1940-41; Senior UK Army Liaison Officer in Aust 1942, Head of UK Liaison Staff in Aust 1942-44; Head of SHAEF Mission to Denmark 1945. Regular soldier; b. Little Waltham, England, 15 Jan 1891.

material you are sending us I think this should be sufficient". He would like to visit Australia himself later.

Two Australian infantry majors—A. A. Buckley[8] and W. N. Parry-Okeden—instructed in India from May to November 1943.

In June 1943 General Auchinleck had replaced Field Marshal Wavell as Commander-in-Chief in India, Wavell becoming Viceroy. On 24th August Blamey made to Auchinleck by telegram a similar proposal to that which Wavell had rejected: he would be happy to accept up to, say, 50 regimental officers for regimental attachment during actual operations at the earliest opportunity and also to lend Brigadier J. E. Lloyd.[9] This produced a telegraphed reply on 1st September accepting both offers; and another telegram on the 16th suggesting that the Indian Army officers should go through the jungle warfare training centre at Canungra before attachment. The sending of other Australian officers to India in 1944 will be mentioned later.

On the 22nd General Vasey informed all his units that officers from the British Army in India and the Indian Army would be attached to the division for training in jungle warfare. Nineteen officers from India joined the 7th Division.

---

[8] Lt-Col A. A. Buckley, NX321. 2/2 Bn; CO 2/1 Pnr Bn 1944-45. Farmer; of Tamworth, NSW; b. Tamworth, 20 Jun 1916.

[9] He had commanded a brigade in the Kokoda-Buna operations and had served in the Indian Army from 1918 to 1922 after service in the First A.I.F.; at this time Lloyd was commanding the Tactical School.

CHAPTER 25

ON TO SIO

ON 5th December Lieut-Colonel Cusworth's 29th/46th Battalion, supported by a troop of tanks, two platoons of machine-gunners from the 2/2nd Machine Gun Battalion, the 56th Battery, and engineers from the 2/7th Field Company led the advance on the first stage along the coast from Gusika. For flank protection a company from the 37th/52nd Battalion assisted by a platoon of the ubiquitous Papuans moved along the foothills parallel with the main advance. The brigade's intention was to "clear coast to high ground area Fortification Point".

Before dawn on the 5th the 29th/46th moved to its assembly area near Gusika. The start-line was 300 yards north of the Kalueng River. Captain Eames' company was to advance from it along the coastal track, and Captain Fletcher's[1] to move parallel with Eames' round the western edge of the timber and take over from the 22nd Battalion on that flank. In the western foothills "Macforce", comprising Major Macfarlane's[2] company of the 37th/52nd Battalion and the Papuans prepared to advance level with the 29th/46th.

Just before reaching the start-line Eames' company was fired on. One minute later the supporting artillery began to fire. At ten-minute intervals the barrage lifted in bounds of 100 yards. Against sporadic Japanese fire the infantry, with three tanks, steadily advanced. By 8.45 a.m. they left the kunai for the jungle and reached the first creek. At 10 a.m. the leading tank ran over a land mine south of the creek and its tracks were blown off. This was a severe set-back, but worse was to come when the other two tanks were unable to cross the creek without the engineers' help, and the leading company had to advance alone. Several abandoned positions were passed before the company was held up by enemy fire and two men were wounded—the battalion's first casualties.

While Eames was advancing along the coastal track Fletcher's company was trying to keep parallel along the timber-edge to the west of the track. Its left platoon soon met opposition from well-concealed positions on the far side of the creek. To prevent any flanking move from this creek towards the battalion's main advance the platoon remained in this position until the early afternoon, and the other two moved to the right. Lieutenant Home[3] led a patrol up the north bank of the creek but was soon forced to return because of strong opposition. He was describing events to his company commander when he (Home) was killed by a sniper's bullet.

Both companies were thus held up by an enemy who was obviously trying to hold the line of the first creek where kunai merged into jungle.

---

[1] Maj S. E. Fletcher, VX4050. 2/7 and 29/46 Bns. Regular soldier; of Leongatha, Vic; b. Geraldton, WA, 10 Feb 1900.

[2] Maj C. W. Macfarlane, MC, VX5545. 2/7 and 37/52 Bns, 4 NG Inf Bn. Commercial traveller; of Glen Iris, Vic; b. Gardiner, Vic, 13 Jul 1914.

[3] Lt S. E. Home, QX45103; 29/46 Bn. Grocer; of Brisbane; b. Brisbane, 24 Jul 1915. Killed in action 5 Dec 1943.

The opposition confronting the right company, however, was brushed aside without the support of the tanks and by 1.30 the company was half way between the first creek and the Lagoon. The artillery could give little support to this advance because the observer could only guess at the whereabouts of the Australian spearhead in the dense scrub. Snipers' bullets were whistling among the men advancing in extended line. The opposition was too heavy and the leading platoon withdrew 100 yards and dug in with company headquarters.

By 2 p.m. Eames' company reached the northern edge of a neglected native garden among dense jungle south of the Lagoon. At the same time they heard firing from their south-west, where the two platoons of the flanking company, under Lieutenant Routley,[4] were attacking the Japanese position north of the creek. In the first burst of enemy firing Routley was wounded; Sergeant Herring[5] then took charge of the two platoons and led his troops towards the first enemy position which he rushed and wiped out with grenades. Under heavy fire the platoons continued up the terraces and drove the enemy from his forward positions, but found the fire too strong and withdrew 60 yards to a favourable position near the creek. Cusworth now ordered Eames to dig in for the night and the rest of the battalion to block up behind the forward company.

At first light on the 6th Captain Petersen's[6] company advanced along a track to the west of the main track; Eames moved parallel along the coastal track, and Major Tilley's company went to attack the enemy positions holding up the flanking company (now commanded by Captain Wilson[7] in place of Fletcher, who was ill), but found that the Japanese had left during the night. By 8.45 a.m. Eames was fired on from between the two tracks leading away to the north on the inland side of the Lagoon. The 29th/46th Battalion was now learning how frustrating it could be to be fired on by a hidden enemy in dense jungle. At 9.20, when Eames began an encircling movement round the general area where he thought the enemy were, bullets from a Woodpecker and light machine-guns caused casualties among the Australians. A section led by Corporal Deslandes[8] was cut off a few yards from an enemy gun. Although wounded, Deslandes bravely went forward to attack the gun; he was killed as he was pulling the pin from a grenade and all members of the section were either killed or wounded. Eames now sent two of his platoons into the attack, but found the enemy had hastily departed leaving six dead.

Along the axis of the left track Petersen's company in the thick jungle found progress slow and tiring, but drove out an enemy group that opposed

---

[4] Maj W. V. Routley, MBE, VX26713. 29/46 Bn, and training appointments. Transport driver; of Launceston, Tas; b. Launceston, 13 Mar 1914.

[5] WO2 H. H. Herring, MM, VX108987; 29/46 Bn. Farmer; of Korumburra South, Vic; b. Drouin, Vic, 23 Feb 1920.

[6] Capt N. H. G. Petersen, VX117182; 29/46 Bn. Salesman; of Korumburra, Vic; b. Korumburra, 21 Aug 1912. Killed in action 8 Dec 1943.

[7] Capt H. Wilson, VX104176; 29/46 Bn. Grocer; of Korumburra, Vic; b. Korumburra, 23 Dec 1913. Died 10 Aug 1957.

[8] Cpl R. C. A. Deslandes, VX105949; 29/46 Bn. Paint machinist; of Fitzroy, Vic; b. Fitzroy, 9 Dec 1920. Killed in action 6 Dec 1943.

them. Then Cusworth sent this company into the lead along the coastal track, and Tilley's company to clear the creek area on the west of the advance. For the next two hours the battalion steadily but slowly advanced against weakening opposition. At 2.40 p.m. Petersen was on Bald Hill level with the northern end of the Lagoon. On the flank Tilley reached the garden area west of the Lagoon early in the afternoon. Patrols then moved into the steep rugged country to the west of the garden and searched for Japanese in the many gullies. The leading platoon encountered a machine-gun post, but after ten minutes of artillery bombardment these Japanese hastily withdrew. As mentioned, the orders of the Japanese rearguard were "while avoiding any decisive engagement" to "carry out successive resistance to try to delay enemy advance".

During this two-day advance of the 29th/46th, "Macforce" of the 37th/52nd had been moving parallel along the foothills. On the 6th Papuan scouts saw an enemy patrol moving along a spur. Quickly setting an ambush Macfarlane's men killed eight Japanese including two officers, all from the *20th Engineer Regiment* of the *20th Division*.

On 7th December Wilson's company of the 29th/46th, leading the advance along the coastal track, was held up by heavy fire from an enemy position about half way between the Lagoon and the Tunom River. Unfortunately the tanks were still not up with the advance. A section of the 2/7th Field Company was searching for mines ahead of the tanks, but detectors were not available and probing was uncertain and dangerous. Even so this section on the first day lifted 14 mines from the track. On the second day detectors were sent forward but they proved unserviceable. While snigging logs a tractor broke a track when it ran over a mine. Worse misfortune followed on the 7th when a second tank blew a track, the remaining five were temporarily bogged, and then a third tank was permanently put out of action by mines. Since the first day of the offensive enemy mines had disabled three tanks, one bulldozer and one tractor—a great success for the Japanese rearguard. The engineers now cut another track which they rapidly corduroyed and the tanks set out to reduce the two-day gap between them and the leading infantry. This was the situation when at 12.55 p.m. on the 7th Wilson's company was ordered forward again. Supported by heavy artillery fire the company advanced a short distance against fierce enemy resistance, but the volume of supporting fire from the artillery and the machine-guns turned the tide.

Tilley's company now advanced from its high flanking position but after some distance the leading section was grenaded from well-concealed positions on the steep sides of the creek it was following and some men were wounded. A frontal attack by the leading section led to more Australian casualties. With four killed and four wounded the platoon was cut off from its company; moving east it joined the leading platoon of Petersen's company, which had taken over the advance only to be held up by sniper fire; Eames' company, which was trying to reach the mouth of the Tunom was also held up by fire from snipers. For the night the battalion dug in south of the last creek before the Tunom.

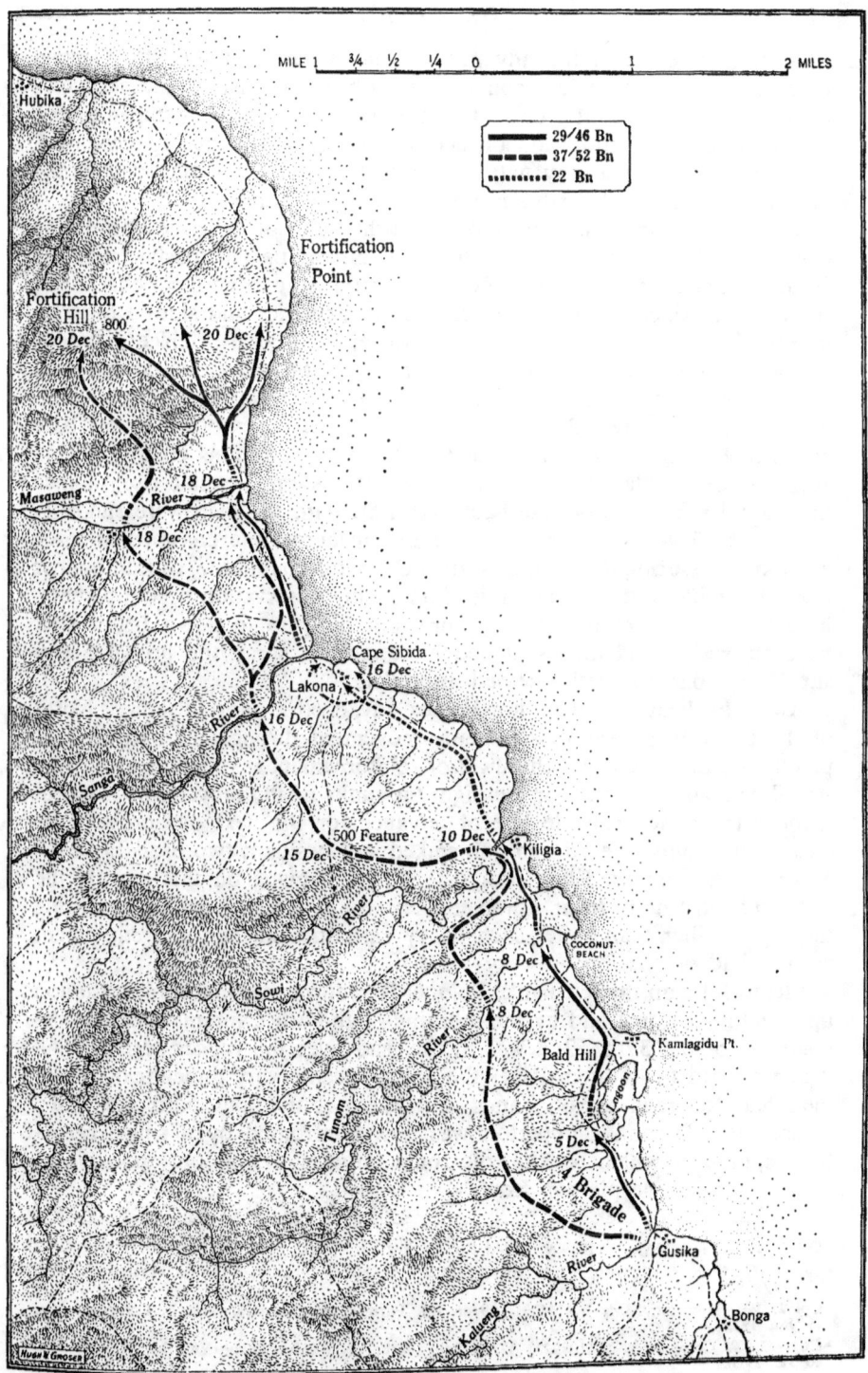

Advance to Fortification Point, 5th-20th December

After a quiet night the advance continued early on the 8th. Captain Petersen was killed while reconnoitring with a small patrol. Eames' company then took over the coastal thrust but both leading companies ran into stubborn opposition; it soon became apparent that the Japanese rearguard was clinging to any natural obstacles while the main body of the *20th Division* hurried north and north-east from Wareo.

Tilley's company gained no ground on the 8th, but its fierce skirmishing helped to relieve enemy pressure on the company on the coastal track. By 10 a.m. Eames was slowly advancing; fire from snipers across a chasm and from a well-concealed Woodpecker caused casualties and slowed progress in the dense jungle. At midday, however, Corporal McNee[9] charged forward, wiped out the gun crew with grenades and captured the gun. The company now pushed cautiously towards the creek where they encountered a chasm 30 feet deep and 20 feet wide at the bottom, almost bare and steeply walled. On the opposite side enemy positions could be seen. Sergeant Cole[1] placed one of his Bren teams on a small rise whence they could rake the opposite bank. At 1.50 p.m. the men were suddenly shelled at 75 yards' range by a 75-mm gun across the chasm, and three were killed. During the shelling Lance-Corporal Hamilton,[2] a Bren gunner from the right-hand platoon, noticed an enemy observation post apparently in the act of directing the gun's fire. Standing up to get a better shot he destroyed it and then switched his attack to spray the probable gun site. The Japanese gunfire ceased abruptly.

Aided by heavy artillery fire Eames advanced a short distance. North of the creek there was much enemy movement through a small coconut plantation, but whether withdrawal or reinforcement it was difficult to say. As all companies dug in for the night the tanks finally moved up. A patrol reconnoitring the probable line of advance for the next day crossed the chasm, and found the 75-mm gun spiked and beside it two dead Japanese and six fresh graves. Little progress had been made on this day. If the Japanese ran true to form, however, they would probably withdraw during the night rather than suffer such heavy casualties in men and equipment as they had on the 8th.

Meanwhile, on the left flank, Colonel Rowan moved his whole battalion up to join Macforce and by the morning of the 8th Captain Clapperton's[3] company of the 37th/52nd was in the lead over the rugged terraces. As it approached the Tunom River the going became very difficult; often the men had to crawl up on hands and knees; but about 5.30 p.m. they crossed the Tunom. Clapperton was now confronted by a single razorback spur over which lay the sole route forward. It was only possible to climb up on a one platoon front.

---

[9] Cpl L. J. McNee, MM, VX108999; 29/46 Bn. Packer; of Fitzroy, Vic; b. Fitzroy, 31 Aug 1920.
[1] Sgt F. O. Cole, VX105941; 29/46 Bn. Postman; of North Fitzroy, Vic; b. Fryerstown, Vic, 22 May 1910.
[2] Cpl J. W. Hamilton, MM, VX144391; 29/46 Bn. Farmer; of Cudgewa, Vic; b. Corryong, Vic, 15 Jan 1923.
[3] Capt G. T. Clapperton, VX108223; 37/52 Bn. Clerk; of Williamstown, Vic; b. Williamstown, 20 Jul 1918.

An hour after the crossing Lieutenant Innes'[4] platoon reached a false crest beyond which was a slight depression and from this the enemy opened fire. Caught on a narrow spur there was little the Australians could do as the sides were too steep to make encirclement feasible and any withdrawal could place the company in a hopeless position tactically if the Japanese counter-attacked. Innes tried an encircling movement round the left flank with one of his sections, but it withdrew after Innes and two of his men were killed.

The enemy immediately counter-attacked but once again the situation produced the man. Standing on the false crest Corporal Drew[5] fired his Bren from the hip into the advancing Japanese. The Japanese wavered and then made off while Clapperton rapidly brought up the rest of his company into a small area of dead ground just below the crest. Australians and Japanese now clung to their positions within about 30 yards of one another and consequently within grenade-throwing range.

By dusk on 8th December therefore Brigadier Edgar had two battalions forward along the line of the Tunom. His third battalion—the 22nd—had moved up to the Lagoon area. Wareo having fallen on this day it was likely that the Japanese would leave stubborn rearguards along the tracks from the coast to those leading north and north-east from Wareo. If the retreating *20th Division* was to be salvaged to fight again the rearguards must delay the Australian coastal advance as long as possible. Thus the Japanese were fighting as fiercely for the line of the Tunom against the 4th Brigade as they were for the tracks leading north-east from Wareo against the 24th and 26th Brigades. Clapperton was in fact warned that he might soon cross one of the main Japanese escape routes.

As so often happened, the Japanese had had enough and withdrew from the line of the creek. While the companies of the 29th/46th on the left searched for the Japanese who had opposed the crossing at the chasm and farther up the creek, Sergeant Cole's platoon led the advance towards the mouth of the Tunom and by 11.45 a.m. had reached it. By 1 p.m. when Eames reported that the Tunom beach would be suitable for barges and dumps, two companies of the 22nd Battalion were moving up to clear the last enemy pocket south of the creek.

The enemy defence had thus cracked near the coast but farther up the Tunom they refused to budge. Here, at first light on the 9th, the enemy opened up on Clapperton's company with Woodpeckers firing on fixed lines along both sides of the spur the company held. Realising that his only hope was to send a force back down the spur, along the Tunom, and up another spur well to the left, Clapperton sent Lieutenant Withington's[6] platoon to do this. At the same time Rowan sent Captain Kitney's[7]

---

[4] Lt R. W. Innes, WX3694. 2/16 and 37/52 Bns. Shop assistant; of Victoria Park, WA; b. Leederville, WA, 2 Jun 1915. Killed in action 8 Dec 1943.

[5] Cpl R. A. Drew, DCM, VX72101; 37/52 Bn. Labourer; of Glenhuntly, Vic; b. Maryborough, Vic, 20 Jun 1921.

[6] Capt E. A. Withington, VX101971; 37/52 Bn. Regular soldier; of Deepdene, Vic; b. Brunswick, Vic, 11 Sep 1916.

[7] Capt M. W. W. Kitney, VX108254; 37/52 Bn. Clerk; b. Kent, England, 7 Jan 1907.

company to capture a garden area closer on Clapperton's left flank and by 8.30 a.m. it had inflicted eight casualties on a Japanese force near the garden.

Meanwhile, Withington's platoon had reached the river where it saw 46 Japanese moving north-east along the south bank. As he had a task to do Withington pressed on ignoring these Japanese. By grasping vines and rocks the men climbed the left-hand spur and from the top opened up on the Japanese. The platoon was immediately fired on by other Japanese farther left, and withdrew. It seemed fairly obvious that the 37th/52nd Battalion was trying to intrude into an area which was vital to the Japanese escape plans.

Soon Kitney reported heavy opposition in precipitous country near the garden, and Rowan ordered Clapperton to withdraw. A skilful and hazardous withdrawal in the face of an aggressive enemy was successful mainly because of the determination of Corporal Lean's[8] rearguard section which gave the rest of the company 20 minutes' start and then raced the Japanese to the crossing by a few minutes. Quickly setting up two Woodpeckers the Japanese aimed them at a kunai patch through which lay the withdrawal route; two men were killed and two wounded during the withdrawal.

After this setback, which cost the 37th/52nd 10 killed, the positions of the leading battalions were reversed; the 29th/46th was now north of the Tunom and the 37th/52nd south of it. Edgar decided to use his three battalions on the 10th: 29th/46th on the right, 22nd in the centre, and 37th/52nd on the left. Accompanied by tanks the 29th/46th had an unopposed advance and by 1.40 p.m. was on the Sowi. With heavy supporting fire the battalion advanced at 3 p.m. and found Kiligia recently abandoned. This was a propitious moment for the arrival in this forward area of Generals Berryman and Wootten. The other two battalions also had a quiet day. The 22nd Battalion found the Japanese still occupying the troublesome position at the creek junction but after a mortar bombardment the only Japanese still there were seven dead. Farther west the 37th/52nd found little opposition.

The Japanese did not contest the crossing of the Sowi—a shallow stream in a wide rocky bed—and by last light on the 11th a company of the 22nd, now in the lead, crossed the river and dug in for the night. Colonel O'Connor's orders were to capture the area from Lakona to the high ground to the west. On the 12th the 22nd Battalion, supported by the tanks and two platoons of machine-gunners had a successful day; the enemy rearguard fired on the approaching infantry but disappeared when the tanks arrived. In the afternoon, however, there was opposition at two points, and at each a platoon commander—first Lieutenant Burleigh,[9] and then Lieutenant Grainger[1]—was killed.

---

[8] Cpl B. M. Lean, V41809; 37/52 Bn. French polisher; b. Auburn, Vic, 1 May 1917.

[9] Lt A. W. Burleigh, VX108134; 22 Bn. Schoolteacher; of Essendon, Vic; b. Chewton, Vic, 10 Jun 1912. Killed in action 12 Dec 1943.

[1] Lt C. H. Grainger, VX52901; 22 Bn. Schoolteacher; of Fish Creek, Vic; b. Northcote, Vic, 6 Aug 1912. Killed in action 12 Dec 1943.

The 4th Brigade was fighting with a determination which evoked the admiration of the combat teams from the 9th Division with each battalion. Its performance gladdened the A.I.F. brigades and helped to dispel the impression that there was any real difference between the men of the A.I.F. and the "militia". At this stage the newcomers' attitude was one of keenness to "be in it"; the A.I.F's was expressed by the frequent question—how could the new battalions be expected to be good if they were not given a chance?

As there was now little fighting elsewhere powerful artillery support was available for the 4th Brigade. With the brigade moved Engineer Special Brigade amphibious scouts who rapidly reconnoitred captured beaches from the landward side and called up reconnaissance craft from the 532nd E.B.S.R. Thus in the Kiligia area, as in others later, a beach-head group, consisting of A.A.S.C., medical and E.S.B. detachments, was rapidly brought in by craft to set up a detailed issue depot. The engineers managed to keep the jeep track up with the leading infantry on the coast, but the troops moving on the high ground to the west were supplied by native carriers.

Soon after dawn on the 13th O'Connor sent his leading companies forward. There was little opposition on the right and the advance reached a fourth creek before meeting opposition, mainly from snipers. On the left, however, Captain Martin's company was fired on but immediately attacked and overran the enemy position killing eight. Private Brilliant,[2] leading one of the forward sections, was severely wounded but continued to lead his section into the assault until the second platoon came forward and mopped up. It was now 2.40 p.m. and the two leading companies on the right were approaching a fifth creek, where they soon disposed of an enemy post opposing the crossing. By the night of the 13th the battalion had made substantial progress against isolated rearguards, and dug in near the fifth creek.

Two companies of the 37th/52nd spent the day in a wide left-flank movement. The march up kunai-clad terraces was difficult and hot but no opposition was met until 6.15 p.m. when Captain Wicks'[3] company was fired on. It dug in but four hours later was attacked by an enemy force firing grenades, mortars, machine-guns and rifles. For four hours the attack continued fiercely. Private Cameron,[4] manning a Bren gun in the forward section, was the sole survivor from his section, but continued to man the post alone throughout the night, thus helping to blunt and finally defeat the Japanese attack.[5]

---

[2] Cpl J. Brilliant, VX107913; 22 Bn. Farmer; of Melbourne; b. Mildura, Vic, 12 May 1923.

[3] Major S. W. Wicks, VX108221; 37/52 Bn. Schoolteacher; of Melbourne; b. Fitzroy, Vic, 31 May 1909.

[4] Pte G. R. A. Cameron, MM, VX75720; 37/52 Bn. Station hand; of Orford, Vic; b. Hawkesdale, Vic, 15 Apr 1912. Died of illness 11 Jan 1944.

[5] At this time two changes were made among the supporting troops. "A" Squadron of the Tank Battalion began to relieve "C" Squadron. General Morshead had agreed with General Berryman's suggestion, and "C" Company of the Papuan Battalion which had been continuously in action for three months and often under artillery fire, was relieved by "A" Company from the Lae area, commanded by Lieutenant E. C. Vickery (of Goulburn, NSW).

The hotch-potch of Japanese units which had been contesting the 4th Brigade's advance now joined in Lakona units of the *80th Regiment*, particularly the *I/80th Battalion*. The *II/79th Battalion* had been in the area between Lakona and Hubika earlier but it now probably joined the rest of the *79th Regiment* making for Kalasa.

Late on the 13th Edgar ordered O'Connor to secure a bridgehead over the Sanga River next day. After overcoming some resistance, the 22nd Battalion forced the Japanese back from the river, and at dusk the leading company was overlooking Lakona and dug in on the southern fringe of a coconut plantation south of the village.

Out on the left flank the 37th/52nd met stiff resistance on the 14th from Japanese dug in 40 yards ahead. It was impossible to circle round in the precipitous country on the left flank but patrols were moving round the right and the battalion's mortar platoon came forward to bombard the enemy. With support from artillery, mortars and machine-guns the leading company drove out the battered enemy rearguard in the early afternoon.

The 15th looked like being a decisive day. At 8 a.m. two companies of the 22nd began to move through the coconuts and one company down the creek towards Lakona. This was the acid test for the Japanese; Lakona must be held a little longer as it was the key point along the route of the *20th Division's* retreat. Captain McFadden's company on the right met the first opposition. About 8.45 a.m. it was pinned down by machine-gun fire. McFadden estimated that between 60 and 70 Japanese were holding up his advance. A platoon of the left company (Captain Baldwin[6]) advanced about 150 yards north along the west edge of the plantation, but by 9.18 a.m. it too was held up after beginning to move east across the plantation. Another platoon then bypassed the plantation by going farther to the west and reached the western edge of the village of Lakona at 11 a.m. The third company (Major Howieson's[7]), moving north along both sides of the creek towards Lakona, linked with Baldwin's at 1.30 p.m., and then advanced to the mouth of the creek to block the enemy's escape. There was thus a ring of companies around Lakona and indeed inside Lakona, and the supporting arms—artillery, mortars, and machine-guns—combined to keep down Japanese heads.

Howieson's company reached the mouth of the creek at 3.45 p.m. Some Japanese attempting to withdraw along the base of the cliffs were grenaded by this company. Towards dusk McFadden's company reached the cliff edge. The descent from the cliff was steep and as it would have been foolhardy to go down in darkness the company dug in 50 yards from the edge.

The engineers tried all day to fix a tank crossing but by last light it was still not ready. A torrential downpour scoured the roads, flooded the rivers, washed away some of the sappers' bridges, and made a quag-

---

[6] Lt-Col A. O. Baldwin, MC, DX850; 22 Bn. Regular soldier; of Petrie, Qld; b. Petrie, 14 Feb 1914.

[7] Maj T. F. Howieson, ED, NX71021. II Corps, I Corps and NGF, 22 Bn. Accountant; of Northbridge, NSW; b. Stanmore, NSW, 19 Dec 1909.

mire of the ravine. The leading tank bogged near the creek and, as it could not be extricated by the combined efforts of three others and the bulldozer, it was locked and guarded by the infantry for the night. Captain Watson,[8] now in command of the tanks, called back the other tanks into harbours guarded by the infantry. In preparing the crossing the sappers of the 2/7th Field Company were confronted on the far side by a hard coral bank which did not yield to pick and shovel work. They tried to get a compressor forward but it was marooned by the flood. Lieutenant Wyche[9] then decided to blast the far bank in a novel way. He asked the tanks to fire solid shot into the coral bank and then used blast bombs in the holes made by the shot.

For the 37th/52nd the 15th was a day of more substantial progress. Against some sporadic rearguard opposition it advanced to the top of the 500 Feature, and patrolled along the Lakona Track without opposition. The rain was welcomed by this battalion as there was no water on the features which it was tactically necessary for them to capture. Just as an exhausted water party returned from the Sowi the rain came. Gas capes, groundsheets and steel helmets were immediately laid out to catch the rain, and it was suggested to the water party by their comrades that they should return to the Sowi and tip the water back as the battalion now had enough.

The enemy was still clinging to the fringe of Cape Sibida at last light. They were surrounded and doomed when the 16th dawned, but intended to fight to the last man. From early in the morning the 22nd Battalion began steadily to exert pressure. Baldwin sent Sergeant-Major Ryan's[1] platoon forward at 9 a.m. to attack from the north end of the plantation. The platoon moved from the plantation in extended line towards the Japanese clinging precariously to the cliff edge. Under heavy fire from about 50 Japanese on his left Ryan was eventually forced to withdraw about midday. So close were the advancing Australians to the Japanese that two men on the left were wounded by Japanese grenades. The compressor so urgently needed by the sappers arrived early on the 16th. By 5.15 p.m. the crossing could be tried. The bulldozer pushed a tank across the ravine and four others were pulled across. At 5.30 p.m. the five tanks lined up ahead of Baldwin's company with their guns pointing at the doomed Japanese whose backs were now so literally to the sea. From 150 yards the deadly fire crashed into the Japanese positions. Eight minutes after the start the tanks reached the cliff and the infantry mopped up a Japanese pocket near the creek. Many Japanese were killed and others were thought to have leapt from the cliffs of Cape Sibida to the rocks below.

Next day several stragglers were shot, including some trying to swim the Sanga. Forty-seven dead Japanese were counted by the end of the

---

[8] Capt R. B. Watson, NX34919. 7 Div Cav Regt, 1 Tk Bn, 1 Armd Regt. Master process engraver; of Sydney; b. Sydney, 20 Dec 1912.
[9] Capt P. Wyche, QX21401. 9 Div Engrs, 2/7 and 2/3 Fd Coys. Civil engineer; of Brisbane; b. Malanda, Qld, 22 Mar 1919.
[1] WO2 V. J. Ryan, MM, VX144096; 22 Bn. Road contractor and bridge builder; of Fish Creek, Vic; b. Wonthaggi, Vic, 1 Jan 1911.

17th. There had probably been about 70 in the pocket. Among the captured equipment were one heavy machine-gun, 12 L.M.G's, one 81-mm mortar, six light mortars and 40 rifles. Fourteen more Japanese were killed on the 17th by men of the 2/2nd Machine Gun Battalion who found these miserable men sheltering in caves below Cape Sibida. They may have been the ones thought to have flung themselves over the cliff. The 16th was thus a decisive day. The Japanese, despite a fanatical fight, had lost Lakona, the pivot of their escape route, but they had probably held it long enough to give the *80th* and *79th Regiments* a useful start.

Late on the 16th Edgar issued his orders for the next day. The 29th/46th would again take over the advance on the coast; with tanks and machine-gunners it would pass through the 22nd Battalion and seize a bridgehead across the Masaweng River. The 37th/52nd would hold the high ground on both sides of the Sanga and exploit north-west to the huts on the south bank of the Masaweng.

From 8 a.m. on the 17th the artillery fired 2,000 shells into the area through which the 29th/46th would advance. At 9 a.m. "A" Company, since Petersen's death commanded by Lieutenant Purbrick,[2] crossed the shallow lime-clouded channel of the Sanga near its mouth, and then Eames' company crossed 300 yards up the river and advanced on a parallel line. On the right deserted positions and equipment were found and there was only half-hearted resistance during the morning. The battalion's historian described it thus:

> The general attitude and lack of initiative by the few enemy so far met with in the advance suggested that the terrific pounding had left them dazed and "bomb happy". The punishment imposed by the supporting arms seemed to have caused general demoralisation of the harassed rearguard.[3]

Both leading companies, with the tanks following, were near the creek about half way between the Sanga and the Masaweng soon after midday and saw Japanese ahead. After a bombardment the companies attacked. Purbrick's leading platoon was stopped in front of a 30-foot drop. A Japanese counter-attack developing from the left was broken up, but the company lost 3 killed and 3 wounded before pulling back and digging in 300 yards south of the creek. Eames, a quarter of a mile up the creek, made no better progress and he withdrew slightly to dig in. The stand by the Japanese at the creek was their last serious opposition to the advance of the 4th Brigade. In the afternoon of the 18th the 29th/46th reached the Masaweng and found two abandoned flame-throwers, three 75-mm guns, one 37-mm gun, one 4-inch mortar, one Woodpecker and many boxes of ammunition and detonators. The leading company crossed the river, which was about thigh-deep and 50 yards wide, and dug in along the strip of low jungle fringing the narrow beach.

To the west the leading companies of the 37th/52nd Battalion by last light on the 18th were just short of the Masaweng. This day General

---

[2] Lt W. I. Purbrick, VX51284; 29/46 Bn. Storeman and buyer; of Toorak, Vic; b. Camperdown, Vic, 6 Apr 1911.

[3] R. Charlott (editor), *The Unofficial History of the 29/46th Australian Infantry Battalion (A.I.F.)* (1952), p. 72.

Wootten moved his headquarters to Kiligia. The 4th Brigade's next objective was Fortification Point, an imposing landmark. All that could be seen of it at this stage was a cliff running out of sight to the north. It was heavily skirted with dense timber up to about 300 feet where rocky grasslands stretched westwards and ended in a partly timbered peak. Edgar gave the 29th/46th Battalion the task of securing Fortification Point while the 37th/52nd Battalion cleared the left flank.

The leading companies of the 29th/46th set out at 8 a.m. on the 19th expecting opposition in the jungle, particularly as the high rocky ground dominated the only possible line of advance along the track, but only a few mortar bombs disturbed the advance during the morning. At 1.20 p.m. the first opposition was encountered. In accordance with instructions both companies withdrew slightly while the supporting arms prepared to "soften" the enemy position. In half an hour the 25-pounders fired 750 rounds; then Tilley's company advanced, with four tanks. By 3.30 p.m. the company was in ground which strongly favoured the enemy; to the left was a steep slope of coral terraces mostly covered with jungle, and to the right was a cliff dropping sheer to the sea. Here the company again came under fire but the tanks crawled forward and, in line ahead on a narrowing track, their Besas and howitzers blasted the enemy positions. At 5.25 the leading tank was fired on by a 37-mm gun from close range. Walking beside the tank were Captain Watson and his reconnaissance officer, Lieutenant Hall;[4] both were among the wounded. Four direct hits were made on the forward tank but failed to damage it. While Sergeant Pile[5] rescued Hall, whose ankle was shattered, the tank destroyed the Japanese gunners with fire from its howitzer. Eighteen Japanese were killed in this area, but little further progress could be made before the tanks were held up by a steep ravine, and the company dug in.

Farther to the left most of the 37th/52nd crossed the Masaweng during the day and were on the southern slopes of Fortification Hill by nightfall. The Japanese resistance was now finally broken and they were nowhere to be found on the 20th. Triumphant, the 29th/46th and 37th/52nd Battalions occupied Fortification Hill, and gazed beyond to where the coral terraces stood out in bare kunai and the space between the track and the sea widened out into flat, heavily-grassed and sometimes swampy land.[6] To the north heavily-laden Japanese were hurrying, some carrying stretchers. These were speeded on their way by shell, mortar and machine-gun fire.

The 20th Brigade prepared to move through and take up what must now become a rapid pursuit. Supplies carried by the 532nd E.B.S.R. began to pour in to Masaweng—the fourth beach-head used in the 4th Brigade's

---

[4] Lt H. P. Hall, NX131844. 1 Tk Bn, 1 Armd Regt. Bank officer; of Beecroft, NSW; b. Parramatta, NSW, 13 Jul 1920.
[5] Sgt R. A. Pile, NX114545. 1 Tk Bn, 1 Armd Regt. Farmer; of The Entrance, NSW; b. Arncliffe, NSW, 6 Oct 1919.
[6] The casualties suffered by the 4th Brigade during the period 5th-20th December were 65 killed and 136 wounded.

advance.[7] On the 20th Wootten issued his orders to the 20th Brigade to advance on the 21st towards a line from the coast near Wandokai to the 1,000-foot feature dominating the coast there. In the next few days further reorganisation took place to allow this coastal advance to continue with two brigades (20th and 26th). The 24th Brigade took over the Gusika-Wareo-Sattelberg area with responsibility for the area south to Langemak Bay, and the 4th held the Fortification Point-Masaweng

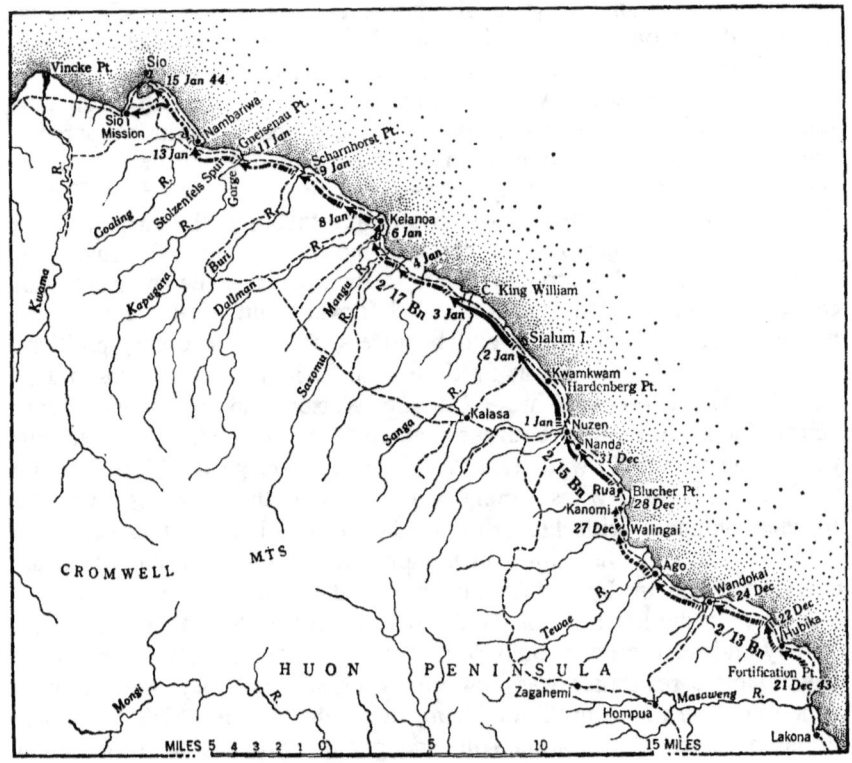

The 20th Brigade pursuit to Sio, 21st December 1943 to 15th January 1944

River area. The 26th moved down to the coast and was gradually ferried to the Masaweng's mouth in the faithful American craft.

From Fortification Point to Kapugara Gorge the coastal track ran along a flat kunai ledge, some hundreds of yards wide, between the sea on one side and sharply rising coral terraces on the other. There was very little cover along the line of the advance, the scanty timber occurring mainly along the line of the numerous rivers and creeks. Few natives inhabited the area, and these in a few villages marked by the inevitable

---

[7] Beaches used by the 4th Brigade were successively Coconut, Kiligia, Lakona, Masaweng.

coconut trees. This terrain offered more opportunity than previously for rapid and sustained movement, although the high ground to the left could be defended by a stubborn enemy.

Behind the 20th Brigade the 26th Brigade would follow closely to watch the leading brigade's rear, including the beach-heads, and protect its left flank by patrols to the main inland track from Zagahemi to Kalasa. The Papuans would patrol deep to the west; the 4th Brigade would cover the left rear of the advance by patrolling the inland area north of the Masaweng and linking at Hompua with patrols from Wareo, where the 2/4th Commando Squadron was now under command of the 24th Brigade which was responsible for patrolling south of the Masaweng.

The men of the 20th Brigade were not in the best physical condition when they began the pursuit. The brigade was weary, and hard hit by malaria. Colonel Simpson anticipated that, even if the enemy was reluctant to defend the heights, he would need to ensure the safety of his left flank by having one or two companies travelling parallel with the main coastal advance. This flank going would be difficult and Simpson prepared for fairly quick reliefs. It was rightly thought that there would be little water along the coast and that the heat in the long kunai would prove very trying. Bounds were therefore planned so that, as far as possible, the troops would reach flowing water each day.

For Wootten the rate of advance would be regulated by two main factors. The first was maintenance of the force and Wootten required that at least seven days' supplies should be within reach of the forward troops who might sometimes be isolated from the rear beach-heads by rough weather. The second factor was the necessity for providing continuous artillery support. Blamey, Berryman and Wootten visited Simpson's headquarters on 21st December and directed that the brigade should avoid unnecessary casualties by using artillery and tanks.

In addition, the 20th Brigade would continue to have air and P.T. boat support. Bostons, Mitchells, Marauders, Airacobras or Thunderbolts helped to cause material damage and moral confusion among the enemy by bombing and strafing supply and retreat trails and barge hideouts. No less disastrous for the enemy were the raids of the intrepid P.T. boats. For instance, from the 9th to the 13th the boats sank 23 barges along the coast, mostly south from Sio, and damaged many more.

Simpson's advance began at 8 a.m. on 21st December when the 2/13th Battalion followed by the 2/15th crossed the Masaweng. For the first time in the battalion's experience in New Guinea the walkie-talkies worked satisfactorily, probably because of the more open country. The troops advanced fast despite the heat of the kunai plain and the rugged going in the coral terraces. By 4 p.m. the leading company of the 2/13th entered Hubika. There was no opposition except when men advancing to the creek beyond Hubika were fired on by a rifle. Clearly visible on the terraces to the left were the other two companies. The battalion diarist wrote thus of the gravity of the Japanese plight:

Hubika Creek was an indescribable scene. Naked enemy dead everywhere. Evidently used as a dressing station. 40 dead in one small cave. None had been buried. The area was foul and nauseating.

"Japan soldier he go Wandokai," said a wounded Japanese captured in the kunai near Hubika. During the morning Wandokai, Walingai and Ago were bombed and strafed by eleven Bostons. On the 21st the jeep road reached Hubika. The engineers found that a gorge just beyond Hubika would prevent any progress by the tanks, now commanded by Captain Hardcastle.[8] There was no alternative route so the sappers set to work to cut and fill in the gorge. The outlook was not hopeful for tank support as the sappers estimated that this work would take several days. Without the tanks but preceded by a strike of 12 Bostons and 8 Marauders on targets between Hubika and Wandokai, the 2/13th Battalion advanced about 3,000 yards without opposition on 22nd December. The infantry were now beyond the range of effective artillery support. Groups of Japanese could be seen ahead.

The enemy had intended to defend the Wandokai area particularly as defences had been built in the area for some time by Colonel Michitoshi Iba, the commander of the *20th Transport Regiment* who was responsible for beach defence from Kanomi to Wandokai. The enemy had a long-standing fear of the Australians landing between the Song and Sio, however, and as the retreat was orderly the Japanese commander decided not to fight for Wandokai but to continue with his task of reaching Sio by 7th January. Thus Captain Yoshikawa, commanding the rearguard, issued orders to withdraw from Wandokai on the night 23rd-24th December: "Prepare to move towards Ago vicinity on the coast road." This was actually the fourth echelon in the coastal withdrawal. Ahead was the third—Lieut-Colonel Shobu's *II/80th Battalion*. The second comprised regimental headquarters and the *III/80th Battalion*. The leading echelon of the withdrawal was Colonel Joshiro Saeki's *26th Field Artillery Regiment*. Major Tashiro's mixed force was apparently ahead of this.

By nightfall the leading company of the 2/13th was 1,500 yards beyond Wandokai. At 6 p.m. Captain Yoshikawa from Ago mortared the leading company and about two hours later two 75-mm guns from the Walingai area opened up and fired 83 shells causing four casualties. Simpson was not surprised when Colonel Barham rang at 10 p.m. to say that there would be no forward movement on the 25th, and none on the 26th unless artillery and tank support were available. Another reason for a pause was that, as on Shaggy Ridge, all commanders wished Christmas Day to be treated as a rest day if possible. In any event the advance could not be resumed until stores caught up. Strenuous efforts were made by all headquarters on Christmas Day to see that the men enjoyed as happy a Christmas as possible. For the 26th, 24th and 4th Brigades this task was not difficult, and in most units ham, turkey, roast potatoes and Christmas puddings replaced the usual fare. Parcels from the Comforts Fund also arrived in time and supplemented free issues of canteen goods.

---

[8] Lt-Col G. H. Hardcastle, VX101918. 1 Tk Bn, 1 Armd Regt; ALO 10 Fleet Air Wing USN Philippines 1945. Regular soldier; of Sydney; b. Buenos Aires, Argentina, 9 Oct 1921.

Some unit diarists commented unhappily, "No beer", and the fine Christmas dinner was washed down with fruit drinks. A Piper Cub from No. 4 Squadron dropped Christmas fare to Captain Gore's Papuan company far to the west at Kulungtufu. In most units Christmas services were held. Late in the afternoon the 9th Division saw a thrilling sight, a huge convoy of landing craft and warships sailing steadily north. This was the American invasion force for Cape Gloucester. It was not so long ago that the 9th Division itself had presented to the watchers in the hills round Salamaua a similar display of might as it sailed to the hostile shore near Lae.

On Christmas afternoon the 28th was tentatively agreed upon as the date for resuming the advance. Simpson told division he had insufficient artillery, and on Boxing Day the 62nd Battery arrived in Wandokai and the 2/12th Field Regiment began to relieve the 2/6th which had earned a rest after the rigours of the Salamaua and Huon Peninsula campaign. The 26th was a day of achievement for the 2/3rd Field Company which finished crossings over the four obstacles which had held them up beyond Hubika.

The Americans landed at Cape Gloucester on 26th December and were undoubtedly profiting from the Australians' victory on the Huon Peninsula and from the consequent inability of the Japanese to help New Britain from New Guinea. As intended in the original planning Vitiaz Strait was now dominated by the Allies. The role of II Australian Corps would be "active patrolling and vigorous infiltration" in defence of the Corps area. The exploitation along the coast would continue but major forces would not be committed. With the American right hook now at length following the Australian straight left, the planners could look ahead. Berryman was warned that, depending on the speed and success of the Cape Gloucester operation, a detachment from Alamo Force might be able to hop across soon to Saidor. Such an operation could render hopeless the situation of the Japanese *20th* and *51st Divisions*. On the 27th divisional headquarters moved to Wandokai and next day corps headquarters moved to Heldsbach.

At 9 a.m. on the 27th, 18 Mitchells and 12 Bostons bombed and strafed the Walingai and Kanomi areas, and the 2/13th, which Simpson had decided to send ahead a day earlier than planned, advanced unopposed; first Ago and then Walingai were occupied. By last light the battalion was holding from Walingai forward to the Tewae River. The speed of the Australian advance was now beginning to tell. The enemy was finding it increasingly difficult to extricate himself, and his four echelons retreating along the coast began to get mixed up with one another.

At 11.15 a.m. on the 28th the forward patrol of the 2/13th was fired on from the last creek before Kanomi, and 14 Japanese were seen retreating north round Blucher Point. Half an hour later the two leading companies opened up with their Vickers and mortars on more Japanese moving round the point. By 6 p.m. the enemy was in full retreat and

70 were seen moving down the spur on the left towards Rua. As ready re-supply for the forward troops could not be guaranteed, Wootten halted the advance for two days.

Early on the 31st the 2/15th, accompanied by the tanks, moved through the 2/13th at Kanomi and resumed the advance with one company forward along the coastal track and another attempting to keep pace through the difficult country on the left. A few bands of Japanese hurrying north were seen during the day and were chased by artillery fire. At 5.30 p.m. the leading troops were fired on by about 40 Japanese in Nanda. Colonel Grace decided to avoid unnecessary casualties and halted at the last creek before Nanda. Grace and Major Thwaites, who was controlling the guns supporting the advance, suspected that there was a Japanese headquarters in Nanda and that harassing fire from artillery and mortars might ensure the flight of the Japanese before morning.

On 1st January 1944 Brigadier Windeyer returned to command 20th Brigade after a long period of hospital treatment and convalescence (Simpson resumed command of the 2/17th Battalion two days later). As expected there were no Japanese in Nanda and the advance continued throughout New Year's Day. The 2/15th Battalion dug in north of Nuzen and a patrol reached half way to Kwamkwam.

> The two days' spell by the 20th Brigade had given the Japanese a chance to get ahead. "Division will advance (*sic*) to Sio," ordered the *80th Regiment* on 30th December. "For this purpose a portion will firmly occupy Scharnhorst and Kalasa vicinity." A handwritten copy of an operation order dated 29th December said that "Divisional main force has not arrived at Kalasa yet". This probably referred to the *79th Regiment (20th Division)*. By this time the remnants of the *238th Regiment (41st Division)*, which had contested the advance of the 4th Brigade, and the battered *102nd Regiment (51st Division)* were in the Sio-Nambariwa area and were probably responsible for its defence.

The 2/15th kept up the momentum on 2nd January: it passed Kwamkwam early in the afternoon and at 4 p.m. reached Sialum Island. The capture of Sialum, about half way between Fortification Point and Sio, was an important event. It had a sheltered beach and all-weather anchorage, and there a big supply dump could be built up. This was an auspicious start for the year. The Japanese were in flight round the coast of the Huon Peninsula. Relentlessly pursued by the 9th Division they were hammered almost nightly at sea by the P.T. boats and often were attacked during the day by American and Australian aircraft. The landing of the Americans across their escape route at Saidor on 2nd January created another hazard for them.

On 17th December General Krueger, the commander of the Sixth American Army, had been ordered by General MacArthur to seize the Saidor area on the Rai Coast of New Guinea on or before 2nd January 1944. This landing was planned as an exploitation, and was contingent on quick success at Long Island,[9] Arawe and particularly Cape Gloucester. On 22nd December Krueger established the Saidor Task Force consisting mainly of the 126th Regiment from the 32nd Division. Brigadier-General Clarence A. Martin was to command this force, whose job would be to capture the Saidor area, control such adjacent areas "as would be required to ensure uninterrupted operation of our air and light naval forces", and help to establish air and naval facilities. By the 28th Martin was informed that the Cape Gloucester operation was proceeding better than expected and the Saidor operation would probably proceed as planned.

The task force arrived off Saidor unmolested on the morning of the 2nd. Because of low-hanging clouds, drizzling rain and darkness of the wooded beaches H-hour was postponed 35 minutes to 7.25 a.m. A naval bombardment covered the landing which was unopposed. By the end of the day about 8,000 troops were ashore. Among the troops were an Australian officer, an Angau detachment and 11 native police boys. By 3rd January the I/126th Battalion was patrolling the tracks to the south, the II Battalion was dug in along the Biding River and the III Battalion was dug in on Yaimas Ridge.

There were several skirmishes with the Japanese in the next few days. A patrol from the II/126th Battalion reached Sel on the 5th and established an outpost there. On the western flank a patrol from the III/126th skirmished with enemy parties at Teterei and Biliau. Patrols were also moving to the south but generally the Americans were content to remain in their areas. It was a pity that Brigadier-General Martin's orders did not provide for a vigorous

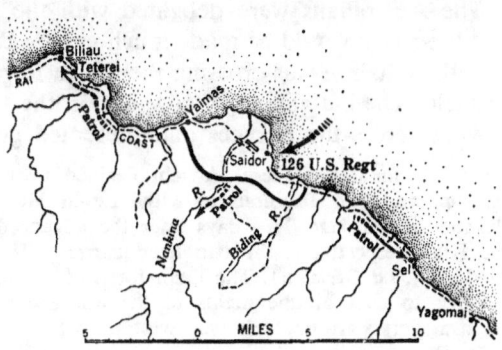

attempt to prevent the escape of the Japanese who were now beginning to hurry from Sio in the face of the steady Australian advance. It was

---

[9] On the night of 26th December a company from the boat battalion of the 592nd EBSR with an Australian radar detachment landed on Long Island, 105 miles north of Finschhafen and at the head of Vitiaz Strait—an excellent place for a radar and lookout station. The group of about 200 officers and men under the command of Major Leonard Kaplan went to Long Island on PT boats, arriving there soon after midnight on the 26th-27th. The men went ashore in rubber boats.

Three days before Major Kaplan and two scouts had reconnoitred the island and found no trace of enemy occupation. Although the Japanese had never garrisoned Long Island it had been used as a staging point for Japanese barges from Rabaul to Wewak. Seizure of Long Island stopped this traffic.

Since the island was some distance from the mainland resupply was difficult. Several LCM convoys carrying rations and supplies came through rough seas to Long Island in the next few weeks and PT boats frequently left supplies, but mostly the detachment was left entirely alone. "The men did not mind this a bit, for although life was somewhat boring, the natives were friendly, the island with its twin mountain peaks and large volcanic lake was beautiful, fishing was good—and there were no Japs. The detachment remained on Long Island almost two months during which time they set up the radar station and constructed a cub airstrip."—*History of the Second Engineer Special Brigade*, p. 65.

not that the Americans did not have enough troops, for the 128th Regiment arrived at Saidor on 19th January to reinforce the 126th. Martin apparently realised what could be done for he wrote in his report:

> It was apparent that an advance to the E and an attack on the enemy withdrawing westward towards Gali, coupled with a defense of the W, would, in addition to defending the Saidor area on the E flank, provide an opportunity to destroy the Japanese before they could reorganise for an attack on the Saidor position from the E. . . . On 21 Jan a letter from the Commanding General, Alamo Force, dated 18 Jan, was received. . . . It contained information relative to the possibility of attacks on both flanks and to the despatch of additional units to the Saidor area. This letter stated that the mission of the Task Force remained unchanged. The troops referred to in this letter had already reached the area when the letter was received.

Krueger put it this way in his report:

> The threat of enemy counter-attacks which had been further magnified by native reports, had already delayed the transition from the defensive to the offensive and the incessant torrential rains, which rendered all tracks and rivers impassable, caused great difficulty in the movement of troops and supplies to outlying sectors. Japanese units, brought from Madang, blocked access to the main escape routes, and although the task force pushed its attacks and patrolled vigorously, efforts to prevent the escape of the Japs retiring before the Australians were not completely successful.

The Australians were delighted with the Saidor landing and expected that their task would be made much easier. By midday on 3rd January the 2/15th Battalion was crossing the Sanga River which proved to be a tank obstacle. The battalion was now hot on the trail. Parties of Japanese were moving across the terraces and presented good targets.

> On 4th January General Adachi decided to give up the struggle and ordered his *20th* and *51st Divisions* to withdraw to Madang under command of General Nakano of the *51st*. Two days later the advanced units of both divisions left Sio and Kiari respectively; the two headquarters left on the 8th (*20th Division*) and the 11th (*51st Division*). The main force of the divisions followed, barges carrying the sick to Gali on the nights of the 8th and the 10th. By the 12th all except the stragglers were on their way west from Sio.

The 2/17th now took over the advance from the 2/15th, the 26th Brigade began to close up to the Sanga, and to the south other changes affecting the future of the 9th Division were ordered. For instance, the 24th Brigade was ordered to concentrate in the Scarlet Beach-North Hill area and prepare for embarkation to Australia. The 8th Brigade was moving to Finschhafen from Australia in ships which would backload the 24th Brigade.

The 2/17th Battalion reached its objective—the Sazomu River—without opposition on the morning of the 4th. A patrol then went forward to the Mangu River where there was some sporadic opposition. Eight Japanese were killed during the day, four dead were counted and three sick prisoners were taken. There was no opposition again on the 6th during the 2/17th's advance to the Dallman River.

The Japanese were now being shot at from all quarters. For the past three days Mitchells, Marauders, Kittyhawks and Thunderbolts had been attacking the enemy's hideouts and supply routes along the coast, Nambariwa being the main target. The Japanese commanders knew that their line of retreat had been effectively cut at Saidor. The plight of the numerous bands of enemy encountered inland by the Papuan and Australian patrols was pitiable; sick, hungry and often without weapons, they had no chance.[1]

The coastal belt west of the Dallman mouth, although not heavily timbered, offered more cover to the enemy than previously. No doubt realising that few opportunities remained to offer effective resistance, the Japanese now made their most determined stand since the 20th Brigade began its advance. Before pushing on again Windeyer decided to reconnoitre the area ahead carefully in order to avoid unnecessary casualties. At 8 a.m. on the 8th the 2/17th advanced; half an hour later the leading company was held up by fire from a track junction. There seemed to be about 40 determined Japanese with four machine-guns holding the area. Eight of them were killed and the Australians had one killed and two wounded. As the company could make no headway without further casualties Simpson withdrew it to a kunai patch south-east of the track junction so that artillery mortars and machine-guns could hit the Japanese.

By 9.30 a.m. next day the battalion passed through the position which had held them up the day before; it consisted of two pill-boxes and 12 foxholes, and several dead were lying around. Later in the morning a band of about 30 heavily armed and determined Japanese again held up the advance about 1,500 yards from the Buri River. Artillery, mortars and machine-guns bombarded the Japanese position and at 4 p.m. when the tanks arrived the enemy fled. The battalion reached the Buri River by nightfall.

Windeyer believed that the Japanese, with the difficult Stolzenfels Spur to cross, would not linger east of the Kapugara Gorge for fear of being cut off. This proved correct and the 2/17th Battalion reached the Kapugara River without opposition at 2.40 p.m. on the 11th. On the way the leading tank ran over a cluster of mines and had a track blown off; it was fixed in three hours, but the nature of the country ahead prevented further use of the tanks which returned and leaguered on the south side of the Buri. Fourteen dead Japanese were counted along the way and two prisoners were taken near the gorge. A patrol crossed the Kapugara on the sandbar at its mouth at 4 p.m. to investigate a track leading along the cliff face. Further progress round Gneisenau Point was barred when the patrol came to a sheer cliff face 20 feet high. The remains of rope and wooden ladders showed how the Japanese had negotiated this very difficult track.

It was obvious from the landward and seaward defences and the equipment lying around that the Japanese had attached great importance to this area. Round the river mouth had been a staging camp and the whole

---

[1] On 7th January Berryman instructed that, to save fatigue, deep inland patrolling would cease.

place was disgustingly filthy. The Australians were now becoming used to the sight of unburied dead lining the track. At the mouth of the Kapugara there was evidence of the destruction caused by the P.T. boats when two wrecked barges, an armed patrol boat and a submersible barge were found.

During the past few nights the P.T. boats had been particularly aggressive. On the 7th-8th five 70-foot barges were attacked a few miles north of Pommern Bay on a south-east course, two food rafts were sunk off Nambariwa and a submarine was attacked a few miles from there. In this submarine was General Adachi who had been trying for some days

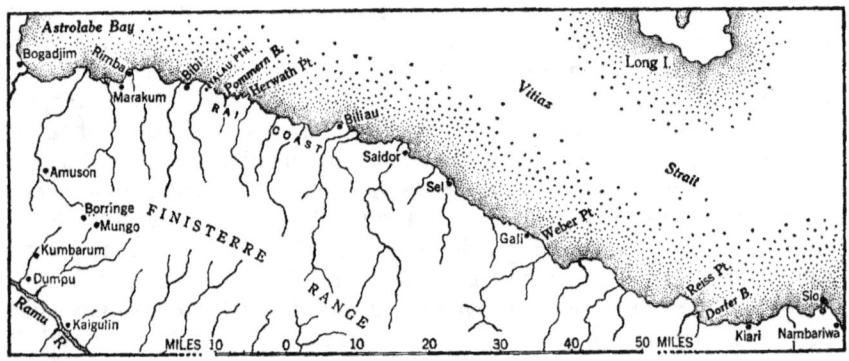

Sio to Bogadjim

to reach Sio from Madang in order to superintend the retreat. The submarine survived and entered Sio on the 8th. Next night the P.T. boats destroyed an enemy barge and engaged enemy troops on the Nambariwa beach, sank three barges—one loaded with about 100 troops—near Herwath Point, sank three loaded barges off Rimba, and destroyed three barges on the beach at Marakum. This was excellent hunting, but it was better still on the night 9th-10th January when the P.T. boats attacked six barges laden with troops off Dorfer Bay. The Japanese barges were armed with 13-mm guns and put up a stiff fight, but one was sunk and the others damaged. That night two out of 8 barges laden with troops going north-west were sunk off Weber Point and the remaining six damaged. Six more barges were destroyed on the beach at Bibi. On the 10th-11th three P.T. boats prowling north of Reiss Point sank three enemy barges each containing about 30 troops and took one prisoner. North of Sio two barges and a large lifeboat were destroyed.

The health of the 9th Division was steadily deteriorating. In the coastal area dengue was now causing heavy evacuations.[2] Of the 2/17th Bat-

---

[2] Writing to General Blamey early in the New Year Berryman said: "Our battle casualties have been kept very low. . . . Unfortunately a wave of dengue has swept through us. . . . All units not moving are holding the majority of their cases but the 26th Aust Inf Bde being on the move found it necessary to evacuate several hundred. Coming from the hills down to the coast the dengue hit them more severely than other units. Fortunately we have had two cool nights with a strong sea breeze and there has been a marked drop in the number of new cases. I am hoping that we have passed the peak."

talion's total casualties of 298 in December, 291 were evacuated sick. Of the 2/23rd Battalion's total casualties of 199 in December, 109 were sick; this battalion had been on comparatively high ground throughout the month and had therefore not suffered so much from newly-caught fevers. In the three months from its arrival at Scarlet Beach at the end of September the 2/43rd Battalion had a complete changeover in strength; 706 men landed and 130 were received as reinforcements; 742 casualties were suffered, including 600 evacuated sick, of whom 396 returned.

On the surface it seemed that the 9th Division's anti-mosquito discipline might not be strict enough, even though operational conditions had been difficult and many of those evacuated were recurrent cases. The diarist of one experienced unit thought that his unit was not "repellent conscious" and wrote that men were being returned from hospital without the mosquito nets which they took there. Those in authority were finding that it was not sufficient to instruct men to take atebrin, apply anti-mosquito repellent, roll down sleeves and trousers, wear gaiters and sleep under nets; such instructions must be enforced in the same way in which a child is made to take medicine. A sidelight on this anti-mosquito discipline was that the men had a horror of scrub typhus and never needed supervision when applying repellent in an area containing ticks.

The problem of getting the 2/17th Battalion over the Stolzenfels Spur was a very difficult one and for a while Windeyer thought of landing by sea at Nambariwa but shortage of craft ruled out this proposition. During the morning of 12th January a platoon succeeded in replacing a rope ladder, and after climbing two wooden ladders the men pushed along a well-worn track to an area which was very recently a Japanese headquarters. The platoon then returned and climbed the 550-foot feature at the tip of the Stolzenfels Spur and established a standing patrol which could see Sio and Nambariwa.

At 8 a.m. on the 13th, a company of the 2/17th crossed the Kapugara River and, accompanied by the Papuans, began the hazardous climb. Three hours later the men were moving forward along the coastal track, having successfully climbed the cliff face with rope ladders. Meanwhile, the sappers of the 2/13th Field Company improved the rope ladders for the infantry, who climbed up hand over hand, and rigged ropes for raising the infantry's packs and equipment. Lieutenant Spry found another route which was rapidly put into use with ladders so that both approaches could be used. The battalion crossed the Goaling River using small boats left behind by the Japanese and then entered the deserted shambles of Nambariwa. One prisoner was taken, six Japanese were shot, and nine more were found dead. On the 15th the 2/17th Battalion occupied Sio.

The Sio-Nambariwa area contained large dumps of all kinds which the enemy had made no systematic attempt to destroy. It was found that Nambariwa was the principal enemy supply base for the Finschhafen area. Both banks of the river had been used to provide barge off-loading points, barge hideouts, or dump areas. A huge fuel dump, a barge workshop, and an engineer stores dump were found. In the Goaling's upper reaches there were large bivouac and hospital areas. The various arms of the river had been used for hiding and off-loading barges and there were large dumps of various kinds. All principal dumps had suffered from aerial bombardment and six sunken barges were visible in one deep river.

The 9th Division had now completed its task. On 13th January Berryman ordered the commander of the 5th Division to take over the forward area as soon as Brigadier Cameron's[3] 8th Brigade could relieve the 20th. Cameron arrived in Nambariwa on 15th January.

Mopping up continued for the next six days. Patrols from Sio Mission killed 8 Japanese and counted 16 bodies on the 16th. Nine Japanese were killed on the 17th and a sergeant-major was taken prisoner. Patrols up the Goaling found further huge dumps of equipment and weapons. In the afternoon Captain Pursehouse, the devoted Angau officer whose local knowledge had been most valuable, was killed by a lone sniper south of Sio lagoon after interrogating about 350 natives collected by the 2/17th Battalion.

On the 21st the 4th Battalion, 8th Brigade and 5th Division took over the area from the 2/17th Battalion, 20th Brigade and 9th Division respectively.[4]

During the advance from Fortification Point to the Sio-Nambariwa area the 20th Brigade covered more than 50 miles in 24 days of which 16 were marching days. Up to the time of its relief by the 8th Brigade, 303 enemy had been killed or found dead and 22 prisoners had been taken. The 20th Brigade's casualties for the same period were 16 including three killed, but the evacuations for sickness numbered 31 officers and 927 men!

Besides a great quantity of equipment and stores of all kinds the 20th Brigade captured or destroyed six 75-mm guns, three 37-mm guns, three 20-mm guns, one heavy and six light machine-guns, three 81-mm mortars, five 90-mm mortars, four light mortars, four flame-throwers, one anti-aircraft gun, one 50-mm grenade discharger and 500 new rifles.

In the four months' campaign from 22nd September 1943 until 21st January 1944 the 9th Division had severely defeated the Japanese *20th Division*. At one stage 12,600 Japanese were forward of Sio. Out of this total 3,099 were counted dead, 38 were captured and the estimate for wounded at the rate of three wounded to two killed was 4,644; making a casualty total of 7,781.[5] This estimate by the 9th Division's Intelligence staff was substantiated by captured documents and prisoners. From prisoners and captured unit strength states it seemed that about 4,300 survived to withdraw from Sio towards Saidor. A large proportion

---

[3] Brig C. E. Cameron, MC, ED, NX110380. (1st AIF: Lt 20 Bn.) Comd 8 Bde 1940-44, 2 Bde 1944. Accountant; of Turramurra, NSW; b. Balmain, NSW, 13 Sep 1894.

[4] The 24th Brigade was first to return to Australia; the 2/28th Battalion embarked on 19th January, the 2/43rd on 23rd January, the 2/32nd on 31st January. The 26th Brigade was second to go; the 2/48th Battalion embarked on 7th February, the 2/23rd on 10th February and the 2/24th on 25th February. The 20th Brigade was last to go; the 2/13th Battalion embarked on 28th February and the 2/15th and 2/17th on 2nd March.

[5] When asked after the war about casualties for this campaign General Adachi said that they numbered about 7,000, but that he was then unable to give accurate casualty figures of the various phases.

of this miserable remnant was ineffective because of wounds, sickness or exhaustion. Between Sio and Saidor the 8th Brigade later counted about 1,200 dead. In gaining this victory the 9th Division had suffered 1,028 casualties during the period 2nd October 1943 to 15th January 1944; 283 of these, including 16 officers, were killed, 744 including 50 officers were wounded and one man was missing. By its devotion and fighting ability the 9th had turned aside the last Japanese attempts to regain the initiative in this part of New Guinea, and had thereafter remorselessly attacked, pursued and destroyed the enemy.

While they were doing this the Americans had been building up a big base in the southern part of the area which the 9th Division had seized. As the 2/13th Battalion was on its way to embark for home in a transport that was lying in Langemak Bay

everyone was amazed at the development that had taken place since its capture some five months previously. Where there had been foot-tracks, or at the best jeep tracks, there were now wide coral roads, Langemak Bay had been bridged, there were wharves and Liberty ships, an airstrip and seemingly endless dumps of all types of equipment. The base had been needed for future operations in the S.W.P.A. and the Yanks who moved in soon after its capture had developed it at a great rate.[6]

---

[6] G. H. Fearnside (Editor), *Bayonets Abroad—A History of the 2/13th Battalion A.I.F. in the Second World War* (1953), pp. 354-5.

CHAPTER 26

KANKIRYO SADDLE

BETWEEN New Year's Day and 3rd January 1944 Brigadier Chilton's 18th Brigade was flown to Dumpu in aircraft which back-loaded the 25th Brigade. By the 4th the relief of the 21st Brigade in the main sector was completed, the 2/2nd Pioneer Battalion remaining under Chilton's command. The veteran 18th Brigade, which had served in England and fought in North Africa at Giarabub and Tobruk, was now beginning its second campaign in New Guinea. Behind it were the battle for Milne Bay and the long and costly fighting round Buna. Now reinforced and fresh, the brigade had long been anxious to join the rest of the 7th Division in the fighting area.

The men of the 15th Brigade on the other hand were surprised at being called forward again so soon—less than four months after their withdrawal from action in the Salamaua campaign. Brigadier Hammer had been told in November that, as far as could be forecast, it was unlikely that his brigade would be required for operations before the end of January. When orders for movement came, the units were not fully equipped, and such important administrative items as emplaning tables did not exist. Hurried issues of equipment were made, orders for movement issued and the first unit moved within five days of receipt of the warning order. Such surprises were to be expected in war, however. In this brigade the 24th and 58th/59th Battalions had gained much in experience and confidence during the Salamaua campaign, but the 57th/60th, which had provided the garrison for Tsili Tsili, had not yet been in action.

At this time the American landing at Saidor placed them not only on the line of withdrawal of the *20th* and *51st Japanese Divisions* from the east of the Huon Peninsula, but endangered the rear of the *78th Regiment* and other units of *Nakai Force* that were opposing the 7th Division. To assist the Saidor operation New Guinea Force had instructed on 27th December that the 7th Division would "contain hostile forces in the Bogadjim-Ramu area by vigorous action of fighting patrols against enemy posts; major forces will not be committed".

General Vasey had instructed both his incoming brigade commanders about their new roles when he had been at Port Moresby late in the old year. On 4th January his senior staff officer, Lieut-Colonel Robertson, began a new operation instruction to the two brigades: "Owing to the threat of our repeated progressive landings along the north coast of the Huon Peninsula it is considered likely that the enemy may attempt to withdraw his main forces from the 7 Aust Div front, leaving only covering troops." To the division's role of preventing enemy penetration into the Ramu-Markham valley from Madang and protecting the Gusap airfield and the various radar installations the instruction added that the division would "create the impression of offensive operations against Bogadjim

Road by vigorous local minor offensive action". This was to be done by holding in strength with two brigades a "line of localities" from Toms' Post on the right to the Mene River on the left, the boundary between the 18th on the right and the 15th on the left being a line from Bebei through Herald Hill to Kankiryo Saddle. In addition the 18th Brigade would "by raids and harassing tactics ensure that no major Jap withdrawal takes place undetected" and, finally would "occupy the Mindjim-Faria divide and the high ground to the north and south of it as the administrative position permits". The 15th Brigade would hold the Yogia-Mene River area, delay any enemy advance up the Ramu from the Evapia River, patrol to the Solu River, and deny the 5800 and 5500 Features to the enemy.

It is interesting to note that although there had been no change in instructions from Port Moresby, Vasey had yet managed to include in his instructions to the incoming brigades a hint of more aggressive action forward from Shaggy Ridge. The occupation of the Mindjim-Faria divide (Kankiryo Saddle) would place the 7th Division in a good position for any further advance towards the north coast of New Guinea.

On the far left flank the 2/2nd Commando Squadron, based on the Faita strip, would continue to protect the radar installations at Faita and in the Bena-Garoka area, and would patrol into the Orgoruna-Uria area "with the object of providing adequate warning of Jap movement in the area or crossing to the south bank of Ramu River from incl Sepu to incl Inomba". At long last the Papuan company was to be relieved. On 3rd January these men, who had played so notable a part in operations from Salamaua to the Ramu, were flown out and rejoined their battalion headquarters at Bisiatabu near Port Moresby.

By the 3rd the entire 18th Brigade was in position with the 2/9th forward on Shaggy Ridge, the 2/10th on the right from Johns' Knoll to Mainstream, the 2/2nd Pioneers on the left and the 2/12th in reserve.[1] On the left flank were the 24th Battalion of the 15th Brigade and the 2/14th Battalion of the 21st Brigade. Back in Port Moresby the 57th/60th Battalion had time to win the final of the Australian Rules Football Competition, beating the 15th Field Ambulance by 12 goals 12 behinds to 8 goals 16 behinds, and so winning the Hammer Cup, before it was flown into Dumpu on 6th January. The inter-brigade relief was finished on the 7th when the 58th/59th Battalion flew in from Port Moresby to take over from the 2/14th. The smooth and efficient manner in which two brigades were flown in and two flown out over the towering New Guinea ranges was indicative not only of the ability of the American airmen but of the efficiency of the New Guinea Force staff headed by Major-General Milford.

From the beginning of the year the main interest of Vasey and his commanders was in preparing for the assault on Kankiryo Saddle. Planning for this operation began on 2nd January, the day after Chilton's arrival and two days before the distribution of Vasey's written operation

---
[1] The forward company commander later wrote: 'My own company position was the oddest I have ever known, three platoons echeloned one behind the other along a knife-edged ridge; in fact the position was only one weapon-pit wide."

instruction. Chilton outlined his tentative plan to his staff and commanders on the 4th: the brigade would improve its tactical position, worry the Japanese, divert their reserves from the coast, and provide battle experience for the inexperienced members of the brigade. In the war diary of the 18th Brigade on 4th January it was written: "Essentially the operation . . . was to be an attack on Mount Prothero from the south preceded by a diversionary local attack in the direction of Cam's Saddle[2] designed to draw his reserve from Kankiryo area and to deceive him as to ultimate direction of the main attack." Chilton and his staff, led by his brigade major, Jackson,[3] and his staff captain, Seddon, realised that the chief problem would be supply and that a period of some weeks must be anticipated for detailed reconnaissance and planning. He was happy in the knowledge that he would have good air support, subject to the weather being favourable, strong artillery support and probably enough native carriers. One surprising feature at this stage was the lack of good aerial photographs. Although good obliques of the east side of Shaggy Ridge were subsequently produced no adequate vertical coverage was yet available.

The problem confronting the 18th Brigade was described as follows in its report:

> The enemy was holding strong natural positions at the junc of Faria R and Mainstream, along the main spur east of the Faria R and on Shaggy Ridge. . . . He had had ample time to dig in, and his positions on Faria [Ridge] were known to be wired. On the enemy's left flank the only practicable approach appeared to be via Cam's Saddle, although little infm was available, and existing maps were known to be unreliable. On the enemy's right flank only two possible routes up the precipitous slopes of Shaggy Ridge had been found, namely up the steep, narrow spurs leading to Prothero 1 and McCaughey's Knoll respectively.[4]

Chilton, whose task it would be to launch the assault on Kankiryo Saddle, was well qualified for the task. Modest and self-effacing but with a keen sense of duty, Chilton had already proved himself a resolute leader and careful planner. Now 38, he had originally been commissioned between the wars in the Sydney University Regiment which had produced a number of notable A.I.F. leaders. On the outbreak of war in 1939, Chilton, then a solicitor in Sydney, was appointed as a major in the 2/2nd Battalion. In Libya and in Greece he had commanded that battalion. After Greece, he was for a while a staff officer in I Australian Corps with which he returned to Australia in 1942. He was then promoted to G.S.O.1 at New Guinea Force headquarters and was General Clowes' senior staff officer during the Milne Bay fight. In March 1943 he succeeded his former commanding officer, General Wootten, in command of the 18th Brigade.

From the beginning of his new task on Shaggy Ridge, Chilton realised that frontal attacks along Shaggy Ridge or Faria Ridge or both, while

---
[2] Named after Major A. C. ("Cam") Robertson, 2/25th Battalion.
[3] Col O. D. Jackson, OBE, NX12242. 2/25 Bn; BM 18 Bde 1943-44; Instructor, Staff College, Kingston, Canada, 1944-45. Regular soldier; of Sydney; b. London, 24 Nov 1919.
[4] 18 Aust Inf Bde, Report on Operation "Cutthroat".

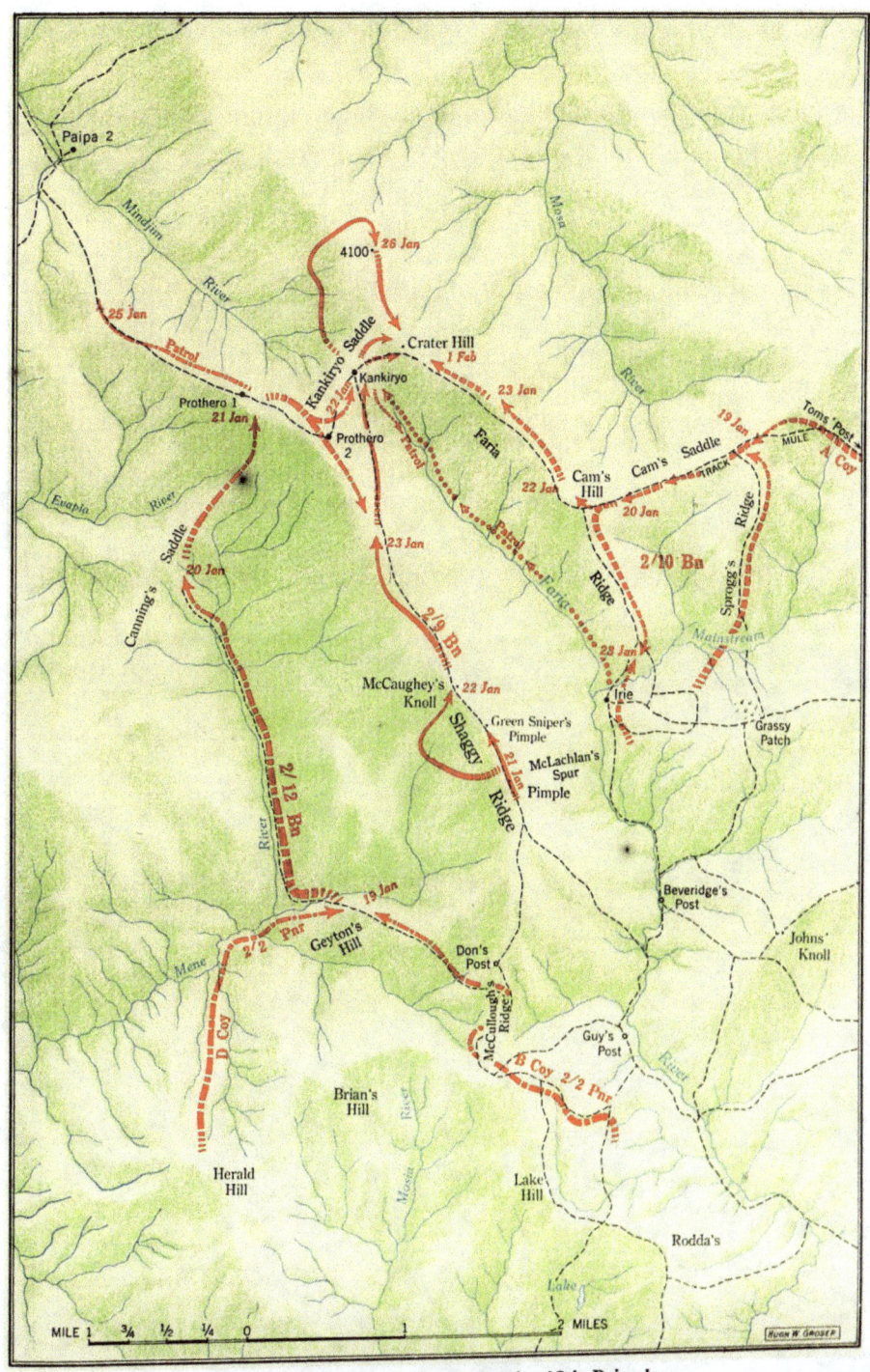

Capture of Kankiryo Saddle by the 18th Brigade,
19th January-1st February 1944

presenting no serious administrative problems, would not achieve surprise, and would probably encounter a series of strongly-defended positions back along the ridges. Even if these ridges could be cleared, the enemy would undoubtedly fall back to his natural fortress at Kankiryo Saddle and strongly reinforce it. Perhaps a flank attack by way of Cam's Saddle might divide the enemy force on Faria Ridge, but the Australians would then still have to fight their way up the remainder of the ridge to Kankiryo Saddle and their supply route would be most vulnerable. "The third alternative was to attempt a wide encircling movement on our left flank via Mene R and Canning's Saddle, and direct the main attack on the Prothero feature which appeared to dominate Kankiryo Saddle and the NW end of Shaggy Ridge. If practicable it was considered that this course was most likely to achieve quick and decisive results."[5]

This third course was the one which most commended itself to Chilton and he set out to prove whether, in fact, it would be physically possible to move his troops to Prothero 1; whether he could concentrate a battalion in the Canning's Saddle area without enemy observation; and, most important, whether it would be administratively possible, with the available native carrier resources, to maintain this isolated force of, say, a battalion in the Canning's Saddle area until a supply route along Shaggy Ridge could be cleared. Assuming the Prothero attack were possible Chilton thought that "appropriately timed subsidiary and diversionary attacks might be launched across Cam's Saddle on the enemy's left flank, and along Shaggy Ridge. In other words a three-pronged attack on the Kankiryo feature."

The possibility of occupying Prothero from Canning's Saddle had been suggested to Chilton by Lieut-Colonel Lang of the 2/2nd Pioneers as the result of Captain McInnes' patrol, which, it will be recalled, had succeeded in finding an approach along a steep, razor-backed spur to within a short distance of the summit of Prothero where Japanese were heard. While patrols from the 2/2nd Pioneers and the 2/12th Battalion were being used to obtain additional information about this area the 2/9th Battalion found a possible track from McCullough's Ridge via Geyton's Hill to the Mene River, thence up the river bed to Canning's Saddle. Two companies of the 2/12th subsequently spent some days constructing this track west to the Mene River. Special precautions were taken to prevent the enemy suspecting an attack on Prothero from Canning's Saddle. Reconnaissance patrols were carefully regulated and were instructed to avoid any contact with the enemy on Prothero. The guns of the 2/4th Field Regiment were dragged up to the Lakes area to give more effective support, but Chilton ordered Lieut-Colonel Blyth to ensure that there should be no obvious artillery registrations. The jeep track was hurriedly pushed to Guy's Post, existing tracks were improved and shorter and better tracks constructed to improve the supply routes to Shaggy Ridge and Mainstream; reserves of supplies in forward areas were built up, thus enabling a concentration of as many natives as possible to carry for the attacking bat-

---
[5] 18th Brigade report.

talion on the left, and arrangements were made for a limited air dropping at Canning's Saddle at an appropriate time.

The patrols carried out by the 2/2nd Pioneer Battalion while the 18th Brigade was settling in were of great importance. On 2nd January Captain Connolly[6] of the brigade staff followed up McInnes' work by leading eight men out on a reconnaissance of the area from Canning's Saddle to Prothero. Other patrols from the Pioneers were looking for the best routes to the Mene River whose bed was to be so important a supply line. On the night of 5th-6th January Connolly reconnoitred Prothero and observed enemy positions. Next day he had another look round Canning's Saddle and linked up there with a patrol from the 24th Battalion under Captain Duell—the first important patrol by the 15th Brigade in their new area.

During these early days of January the 15th Brigade, under Hammer's energetic direction, was engaged in "active defence with offensive patrolling". On the left flank even more extensive patrols were being carried out by the 2/2nd Commando Squadron. On New Year's Day Captain Dexter and Lieutenant K. S. Curran's section left on the longest patrol yet from Faita through Topopo to Jappa, where no patrols had yet ventured, and back. The patrol reached Topopo on the 3rd, Jappa next day, and returned to Topopo on the 5th. During the night of the 5th-6th a Japanese force, perhaps led by natives who had been seen in the area, surrounded the Australians who were on a slight knoll at Topopo commanding all approaches. At dawn when the patrol was about to stand to the Japanese opened heavy fire from a distance of about ten yards. As usual, their shooting did not measure up to the standard of their field craft. All the encircled men escaped with their weapons by doing a "back-flip" over the side of the ledge, through the Japanese and into surrounding jungle, where several fired on the Japanese from vantage points. Sergeant Cash,[7] who had been in charge of the native carriers on a knoll farther back along the main track, fired his Bren gun into the Japanese. The Australians then rendezvoused at Damaru, except for five who were missing for some days.[8] The Japanese had achieved complete surprise, point-blank range and overwhelming fire power, yet they had mortally wounded only one man and slightly wounded four others. The patrol reported: "The distance we had to travel to Jappa and the fact that we had to use the same track coming back enabled the kanakas to inform the Japs who sweated on us." This patrol which opened new territory showed that the enemy was still extremely sensitive to any deep probing on his vulnerable western flank.

---

[6] Maj P. D. Connolly, QX9500. 2/12 Bn and HQ 18 Bde. MLA Qld 1957-60. Student; of Brisbane; b. Sydney, 29 Sep 1920.

[7] Sgt M. C. Cash, WX12135. 2/2 Indep Coy, 2/2 Cdo Sqn. Clerk; of Mount Lawley, WA; b. Perth, 2 Jun 1919.

[8] Three of these missing men, including one wounded, were found on 10th January after they had been wandering through the bush for several days. The fate of the last two men was cleared up two days later when a rescue patrol, which entered a deserted Topopo, found Trooper A. E. Harper who had wandered lost in the scrub for several days while caring for the badly wounded Trooper R. L. Beardman. After Beardman's death, Harper decided that it would be worth the risk of moving on a main track in order to find some food and stop going round in circles. Although in enemy territory, he was befriended by the natives, who sent him on towards Topopo which they knew an Australian patrol was approaching.

The 18th Brigade spent the early part of January finding out more about each known enemy position for there were no new positions for them to discover in their various areas. The 2/9th patrolled as much as possible and slightly widened its "front" by occupying McLachlan's Spur[9] which gave good observation of Green Sniper's Pimple, McCaughey's Knoll, and the ridge running back through Prothero to Kankiryo Saddle. Both sides, however, knew one another's positions so well that there was little point in losing men by exposing them to fire from enemy strongpoints. Warfare here was static and in the forward Shaggy Ridge positions where there was not more than 80 to 100 yards between the forward dug-in posts, the Australians were using periscopes.

Particular attention was being paid to security. As the enemy were known to be using native spies any native on whom the slightest suspicion fell was held for questioning by Angau and those wearing red lap-laps were arrested. All units were warned to make every attempt to capture prisoners. In the war diary of the 2/10th Battalion on the 9th it was stated, "£5 reward is offered for the first enemy P.W. captured alive." On the 10th Chilton conferred with his brigade staff who had been round the area, and with Lieut-Colonel Bourne[1] of the 2/12th, to discuss the progress of the planning. Details decided on this day were that the artillery support for the 2/12th (making the left-flank attack) would consist initially of a "creeping concentration" up the spur running north-east on to Prothero; the attack would be silent until contact was made, the battalion would be built up to a full scale with wireless sets; and the water problem should be investigated as it was unlikely that there would be any on top of the ridge.

Work was started on a better line of communication for the 2/12th Battalion from McCullough's Ridge to Canning's Saddle via Geyton's Hill along a route reconnoitred by Lieutenant Hart's[2] patrol of the 2/9th Battalion. This route was essential to the plan to concentrate the 2/12th as close as possible to Prothero unseen. As a result of further reconnaissances and the arrival at last of a vertical air photograph, it was decided on the 12th that the peak previously known as Prothero would now be called Prothero 1 and that the high ground about 100 feet lower than Prothero 1, and 1,000 yards to the south-east, forming the south shoulder of Kankiryo Saddle, would be known as Prothero 2.

On the 13th Vasey and Chilton went forward on the right flank and, after discussion with Lieut-Colonel C. J. Geard of the 2/10th, decided to include in the operation a full-scale attack by the 2/10th from the direction of Cam's Saddle (the high north-eastern feature). This attack would be a diversionary one until the capture of Prothero 1 by the 2/12th when the 2/10th would exploit north to Kankiryo and south to the Mainstream area. On the 14th Chilton issued an operation instruction

---
[9] Named after Lieutenant O. C. McLachlan, 2/9th Battalion.
[1] Brig C. C. F. Bourne, DSO, ED, QX6008. (Midshipman RAN 1929.) 2/9 Bn; CO 2/12 Bn 1943-45. Public servant; of Gatton, Qld; b. Cunnamulla, Qld, 29 Dec 1911.
[2] Capt J. Hart, QX18224; 2/9 Bn. Cadet, Dept of Agriculture; of Boodua, Qld; b. Oakey, Qld, 11 Sep 1920.

for the attack. The information available was that one enemy battalion was holding Kankiryo Saddle and forward from there along Shaggy Ridge, that there were believed to be three enemy guns in the area, and that it was considered unlikely that he would reinforce his forward positions; the intention was to capture Kankiryo Saddle. The operation was to be carried out in five phases, but these would be discussed on the eve of the operation; the order merely gave the units a background from which to prepare their detailed plans. D-day was not to be before 20th January.

The 4,000-yard track to Geyton's was completed on the 18th. Thence it followed the bed of the Mene. On the 16th the 2/4th Field Company reported that the jeep track to Guy's Post was almost finished and they could get 16 jeep and trailer loads forward daily.

On the 18th while Mitchell bombers were using cannon against enemy positions at the junction of Mainstream and the Faria and on Shaggy Ridge, the 18th Brigade was regrouping for the coming operation. D-day was definitely fixed for the 20th and the leading elements of the 2/10th on the right and the 2/12th on the left moved off. One company of the 2/10th moved to Grassy Patch and, on the left, an advance party of the 2/12th, under the battalion's second-in-command, Major Fraser,[3] moved ahead to prepare the way for the coming of the battalion.

Preliminary moves were completed on the 19th when Captain Gunn's[4] company of the 2/10th moved out from Toms' Post for Sprogg's Ridge via the Japanese mule track and was followed later by Captain Kumnick's[5] company. On the left the 2/12th Battalion, with a company of the 2/2nd Pioneers attached, moved out along the new line of communication to Geyton's.

Chilton held a last coordinating conference on the 19th and gave his final instructions. The first of his five phases—the occupation of Sprogg's Ridge by the 2/10th Battalion—had already taken place on the 19th. The second phase would be the capture on 20th January by the 2/10th of Cam's Saddle, with subsequent exploitation to Faria Ridge and thence south to the junction of Mainstream and the Faria River. The third phase, on 21st January, would be the attack by the 2/12th on Prothero 1 with exploitation south-east along Shaggy Ridge and north across Kankiryo Saddle. Then the fourth phase would begin—an attack by the 2/9th Battalion north-west along Shaggy Ridge to join with the 2/12th Battalion. The fifth and final phase would entail the capture of the feature commanding the northern side of Kankiryo Saddle, but no firm timing could be set for this phase as it was dependent on the progress of the initial phases. Nine long and two short 25-pounders of the 2/4th Field Regiment were in support and about 7,000 shells were available. The guns had been dragged forward and were now concentrated in the Lakes-Guy's

---

[3] Col C. A. E. Fraser, MBE, QX6073. 2/12 Bn, and staff appointments (including GSO2 War Office 1944-45, as exchange officer). Regular soldier; of Adelaide; b. Nairobi, Kenya, 25 Sep 1918.

[4] Capt W. K. Gunn, QX36934; 2/10 Bn. Grazier; of Goondiwindi, Qld; b. Goondiwindi, 14 Jul 1915.

[5] Capt P. A. Kumnick, SX1158; 2/10 Bn. Storeman; of Balaklava, SA; b. Lameroo, SA, 18 Aug 1916.

Post area. Colonel Blyth established his artillery command post beside Chilton's headquarters, and a battery or troop commander was attached to each battalion commander as an adviser and to control the F.O.O's attached to forward sub-units. A detailed schedule of air strikes by medium and dive bombers was drawn up.

Meanwhile the 15th Brigade was patrolling deeper into enemy territory. By 7th January one company of the 24th Battalion was on the 5800 Feature and had linked up with the 2/2nd Pioneers. On the 10th a patrol from the 24th Battalion led by Captain Cameron[6] was ambushed at a position later known as Cameron's Knoll, north-east of the 5800 Feature. The two forward scouts, Privates Geraghty[7] and Filcock,[8] had just turned a corner of the track and had moved about 40 yards into the clearing on the crest when Geraghty saw a Japanese standing by a bush. Geraghty called out to Filcock who dived back to cover when the Japanese opened fire with their machine-guns. Both Geraghty and Filcock fired their Owen guns into the machine-gun nest, but they were forced to withdraw under heavy fire. It was this patrol which gave Hammer the idea for a diversionary attack at the time of the 18th Brigade's main operation.

On the same day aircraft of No. 4 Squadron were flying over Orgoruna and could see no enemy movement. On the 11th Lieutenant Anderson[9] of the 24th Battalion led out a small patrol from the Koropa area to see if Orgoruna was occupied. The forward scout was allowed to reach some barbed wire before the enemy opened fire. Under heavy fire the patrol extricated itself. It now occurred to Hammer that a raid on Orgoruna would be a good way of giving the 57th/60th Battalion experience, and his staff, led by his brigade major, Travers, and his staff captain, Molomby,[1] therefore set about building up a reserve of supplies in the Koropa and Kesawai areas.

Hammer's operation instruction of 12th January claimed that there were 3,000 enemy in the Kankiryo-Shaggy Ridge area and 1,000 in the Orgoruna-Mataloi area. This was an over-estimation and was possibly deliberate. From captured documents the Australians knew that Japanese units were less than half strength. They also now thought that only one battalion (the *II/78th*) was facing them because the other two battalions of the *78th Regiment* had been withdrawn to meet the Americans' threat at Saidor. (Actually only five companies of the *78th* were withdrawn.) Hammer allotted the "outpost locality" to the 24th Battalion, the Yogia feature position to the 58th/59th, and the Mene Hill area to the 57th/60th Battalion and the 2/6th Commando Squadron. By the 16th the 57th/60th

---

[6] Capt R. A. Cameron, VX104149; 24 Bn. Joiner; of Caulfield, Vic; b. Albert Park, Vic. 30 Aug 1905.

[7] Pte H. Geraghty, VX135511; 24 Bn. Timber worker; of Powelltown, Vic; b. Blackburn, Vic, 26 May 1917.

[8] L-Cpl J. Filcock, VX115545; 24 Bn. Labourer; of Dandenong, Vic; b. Bendigo, Vic, 21 Jul 1920.

[9] Capt N. D. Anderson, VX104065; 24 Bn. Clerk; of Caulfield, Vic; b. Beechworth, Vic, 21 Dec 1916.

[1] Maj T. A. Molomby, MBE, VX104157. 24 Bn, and staff appointments. Solicitor; of Hawthorn, Vic; b. Hawthorn, 7 Jun 1918.

Battalion had established an observation post overlooking Ketoba and Hammer obtained permission for the two attacks.

Farther west a patrol of the 2/2nd Commando, led by Lieutenant Denman,[2] set out on 8th January to try to capture a prisoner in the strong Japanese area of Kulau. The patrol (six in all) reached the area surrounding the Kulau ridge on the 10th. They had been there before and knew the positions of huts and most defences. They hoped to be able to sneak in, grab a prisoner without creating an uproar, and drag him away. Under cover of darkness they stealthily climbed the ridge and lay low until midnight on the 10th-11th January. Seeing and hearing no movement, with muffled boots and blackened faces, they advanced towards the main buildings north along the ridge, which was no more than 30 yards wide. They reached almost the centre of Kulau before they heard a number of thumps, which turned out to be not the beating of their hearts but probably the Japanese jumping into their weapon-pits, for suddenly the Japanese attacked with grenades, heavy and light machine-guns and rifles, and mortared the ridge behind. Denman's men fought back in the dim moonlight and fired about 10 Owen gun magazines and about 30 rifle rounds in the direction of the flashes from enemy weapons. Trooper Ramshaw[3] was wounded and as Denman dragged him towards the side of the large hut Lance-Corporal Carey[4] dashed over to help; under heavy fire the two men carried their companion down the slope of the ridge into the scrub where he died. Fire from the other men, Lance-Corporal Moloney[5] and Troopers Wilson[6] and McKinley[7] had assisted Denman and Carey during their arduous task, but when the patrol re-assembled at their rendezvous—a near-by re-entrant—Moloney was missing.

Vasey had been urging all his units to do their utmost to capture a prisoner, but the period had been a particularly sterile one, not only for prisoners but for documents, mainly because the Japanese security measures were at length improving. All units had tried their hardest to capture a prisoner but without success. It is doubtful whether there had been a more gallant attempt than this effort by six men who, after a four-day march, crawled into the very midst of a strong Japanese base.

D-day for CUTTHROAT as the 18th Brigade's attack was named—the 20th January—had arrived. The 2/10th Battalion was the first to move, when, at 8.45 a.m., Captain Gunn's company moved from Sprogg's Ridge to attack Cam's Saddle. Half an hour later Captain Kumnick's company followed. At 9.30 a group of Mitchells attacked the Protheros and Kan-

---

[2] Lt J. R. Denman, MC, WX12123. 2/2 Indep Coy, 2/2 Cdo Sqn. Clerk; of Kalgoorlie, WA; b. Kanowna, WA, 14 Nov 1915.

[3] Tpr D. McK. Ramshaw, WX29710. 2/2 Indep Coy, 2/2 Cdo Sqn. Farmer; of Geraldton, WA; b. Geraldton, 2 Feb 1923. Killed in action 10 Jan 1944.

[4] L-Cpl J. W. Carey, WX12423. 2/2 Indep Coy, 2/2 Cdo Sqn. Clerk; of Fremantle, WA; b. Fremantle, 19 Feb 1922.

[5] L-Cpl L. H. Moloney, VX135930. 2/2 Indep Coy, 2/2 Cdo Sqn. Stableman; of Leongatha, Vic; b. Geelong West, Vic, 17 Jun 1921. Killed in action on or after 10 Jan 1944.

[6] Tpr K. G. Wilson, NX77745. 14 Fd Regt, 2/2 Cdo Sqn. Shop assistant; of Stanmore, NSW; b. Glebe, NSW, 16 May 1921.

[7] Tpr S. A. McKinley, WX29880. 2/2 Indep Coy, 2/2 Cdo Sqn. Shop assistant; of Perth; b. Subiaco, WA, 19 Apr 1922.

kiryo Saddle with 1,000-lb bombs while another group of Mitchells strafed the area and a squadron of Vultee Vengeances dive-bombed Shaggy Ridge and the Protheros. By 11 a.m. Gunn was 300 yards from an enemy position on Cam's Saddle. The artillery shelled this position and at 12.30 p.m. the Australians found that the enemy had withdrawn. Farther on the company was pinned down by fire from a Japanese position at the western end of the Saddle. At the same time a Japanese patrol ambushed the signal line party 500 yards behind. After trying to outflank the enemy position Gunn withdrew 200 yards and dug in for the night astride the mule track which zig-zagged up the feature held by the enemy.

The 2/12th Battalion had reached the bank of the Mene River at nightfall on 19th January. It was then raining heavily and Colonel Bourne had noted with some dismay that the river, along whose bed he must advance next day, was rising. It was still raining early on the 20th when the 2/12th set out from Geyton's Hill but after seven hours of hard going the battalion reached Canning's Saddle at 3.30 p.m. For the night Major Cameron's[8] company, which was to lead the assault next day, was just below the Saddle with the rest of the battalion behind.

At 8.30 a.m. on the 21st the 2/12th moved forward to the start-line which was at the false crest below Prothero 1. The approach was so steep that ladders had to be used to enable the men to cross the start-line by 9.20 a.m. The plan provided for a silent attack, with one company forward, along the steep razor-back ridge which was the only possible way to Prothero 1. A second company would then pass through and secure the saddle between Prothero 1 and Prothero 2 while a third secured the northern slopes of Prothero 1. Two companies of the 2/2nd Pioneer Battalion were to protect the 2/12th's left flank by securing the western slopes of Prothero 1 and holding Canning's Saddle. Artillery concentrations would be fired only if surprise was lost. The advance up the steep and rugged ridge was very quiet and surprise was almost achieved. About 100 yards below the summit of Prothero 1 the leading men met a small enemy party who had prepared a large demolition charge on the razor-back approach; the Japanese had no time to blow the charge but were able to warn others on the summit. Cameron's men, however, raced towards Prothero 1 and captured it at 1.20 p.m. After reaching the summit the companies fanned out and prepared to attack towards Prothero 2. At 3 p.m. a Japanese 75-mm gun which had been shelling the 2/9th Battalion switched to the 2/12th from less than 100 yards, inflicting serious casualties, including Bourne badly wounded. Major Fraser now took command and called up a platoon under Lieutenant Braithwaite[9] from one of the reserve companies to destroy the gun.

It was 4 p.m. when Braithwaite set out. Twenty minutes later the guns of the 2/4th Regiment, directed by Captain Stirling,[1] shelled the Japanese

---

[8] Maj I. B. Cameron, NX106996; 2/12 Bn. Grazier; of East Gresford, NSW; b. Dungog, NSW, 2 Apr 1909.

[9] Lt E. C. Braithwaite, QX34578; 2/12 Bn. Farmer; of Murgon, Qld; b. Murgon, 12 Jul 1920.

[1] Maj C. H. Stirling, MC, VX1058. 2/4 and 2/2 Fd Regts. Accountant; of Caulfield, Vic; b. St Kilda, Vic, 4 Feb 1918.

gun area on Prothero 1. At the same time Braithwaite reported that he was within grenade-throwing range of the gun, but that heavy machine-gun fire from supporting positions prevented any nearer approach. The platoon was forced back and at 4.40 p.m. the artillery again hammered the area. Stirling was with the forward troops during the fierce exchanges of artillery fire. His success in directing his own guns on to such a small target was to a great extent due to the efforts of Signalman Green[2] who laid the telephone line under fire, three times went forward to repair breaks and stuck to his tasks although wounded. The enemy shells, bursting among the tree tops, scattered shrapnel over a wide area and the casualties mounted as Braithwaite, now reinforced by a second platoon, approached the gun position on a narrow, two-man front. With frontal assault impossible, the enemy gun position was gradually surrounded although an almost sheer ridge had to be scaled to do so.

At 5.30 p.m. Braithwaite rushed the gun. Foremost in the rush was Private Lugge,[3] a Bren-gunner. Leaping from an embankment overlooking the gun and falling flat on his stomach within six feet of the entrance, Lugge opened fire on the enemy gunners. Then, rolling on his side, he fired at a Japanese pill-box where a Woodpecker on the flank was giving supporting fire to the gun. The occupants of the pill-box were killed and wounded and the cessation of their covering fire enabled the rest of Braithwaite's men to rush up and finish off the Japanese gun crew with grenades. The gun crew of 16 men fired defiantly until the end when they were all killed. The gun was captured intact and with it, in an excellently constructed gun-pit, were about 50 rounds of ammunition.

This spirited action completed the capture of Prothero 1, and the 2/12th Battalion dug in round it for the night. Fraser expected the Japanese to the south of him, or to the north, to counter-attack because Prothero 1 was such vital ground. For the loss of 11 killed and 44 wounded, including 5 officers, the 2/12th had captured the key point in the Japanese defences of Shaggy Ridge. During the night there was much firing and the Japanese attacked Captain Thomas'[4] company south-east of Prothero 1, but were repulsed leaving 9 killed.

The dominating feature confronting the 2/9th on Shaggy Ridge was McCaughey's Knoll. The battalion's objective on the 21st was Green Sniper's Pimple, a small but commanding eminence on the south-east end of the knoll only about 80 yards from the forward posts of the 2/9th. Lieut-Colonel C. J. Cummings' plan was to attack the knoll from his left up the very steep but wooded slopes, using one company. He planned a frontal diversion to distract the enemy's attention from the flank and drown the noise.

---

[2] L-Cpl W. O. Green, MM, VX36233. 7 Div Sigs, 2/4 Fd Regt. Printer; of West Footscray, Vic; b. Ballarat, Vic, 10 Nov 1918.

[3] Pte R. A. Lugge, MM, QX33421; 2/12 Bn. Drover; of Murgon, Qld; b. Charters Towers, Qld, 30 Jun 1920.

[4] Maj K. B. Thomas, OBE, MC, TX885; 2/12 Bn. 2 Bn RAR Korea 1953. Regular soldier; of Ulverstone, Tas; b. Launceston, Tas, 5 Jul 1914.

(*Australian War Memorial*)

Australian troops, on the way towards Japanese-held Bogadjim, rest after a hard climb in the Finisterres.

(*Australian War Memorial*)

A weary soldier rests for a few moments on the side of a muddy track in the Finisterres.

The road from Bogadjim to Yaula, built by the Japanese.

About 10.30 a.m. the forward platoon was led out by Sergeant McDowell[5] who had already taken part in three night patrols to Green Sniper's Pimple. The leading section got right among the Japanese pits before the Japanese had recovered from the air strike preceding the attack. As soon as the Australians were established on the pimple about 2 p.m., the Japanese began firing into them with a field gun and mortars, and a counter-attack began to develop. Major Loxton[6] made his way forward under this heavy fire and, by walkie-talkie, ordered McDowell to hold the position at any cost. While speaking from a very exposed position Loxton was killed by a shell. The Australians held on, and when the gun ceased fire a second platoon joined McDowell's. The only satisfactory mortar observation post for the 2/9th was in an exposed position under heavy fire from the enemy. Despite this, Sergeant Henricksen[7] remained there for five hours directing his mortar fire on to the Japanese. Soon after midday he was knocked unconscious by the explosion of a shell but he recovered five minutes later and continued to direct his mortars. About 2 p.m. a shell hit Henricksen's observation post burying his companion. Henricksen continued with his vital job but managed to dig out his companion.

Lieutenant Stephenson[8] was sent to take command of the forward company, and Captain J. A. Cumber, one of the officers from India, was delighted when he found himself with a job as Stephenson's second-in-command. During the night the enemy worried the two forward platoons with grenades and mortars but there were no casualties. For the loss of 7 men killed, including the company commander, and 17 wounded, the company had captured a vital position; it had advanced only 100 yards, but possession of the pimple gave the Australians a toehold on McCaughey's Knoll, the position commanding the whole of the Shaggy Ridge area.

On the right flank the artillery had fired a heavy concentration early on the 21st on the position which had held up the 2/10th Battalion on the previous evening. In the morning patrols investigated this position and one returned at 2.30 p.m. to report that there had been no reply when they had thrown two grenades. Gunn moved his company through the enemy position and went north along Faria Ridge until just on dusk he saw the enemy digging in ahead. The 2/10th then dug in for the night.

By the end of 21st January the main enemy force on Shaggy Ridge was between the 2/9th on the south and the 2/12th on the north. The Japanese still held two miles of Shaggy Ridge between the Australians on Green Sniper's Pimple to the south and Prothero 1 to the north, but they were in a serious position and could not overlook the threat on the east where

---

[5] WO2 R. A. McDowell, QX13779. 7 Div Cav, 2/9 Bn. Car salesman; of Brisbane; b. Moonee Ponds, Vic, 8 Feb 1914.

[6] Maj F. E. C. Loxton, QX6030; 2/9 Bn. Barrister-at-law; of Ascot, Qld; b. Cairns, Qld, 28 Apr 1912. Killed in action 21 Jan 1944.

[7] WO2 H. G. V. Henricksen, MM, QX5547; 2/9 Bn. Labourer; of Warwick, Qld; b. Warwick, 26 Oct 1917.

[8] Capt E. V. Stephenson, MC, NX102513. Norfolk Island Detachment, 2/9 Bn. Civil servant; of Norfolk I; b. Norfolk I, 23 Apr 1915.

the 2/10th was now established about a mile from the main Japanese defences on Kankiryo Saddle.

On the 22nd Captain Thomas' company of the 2/12th set off at 8.30 a.m. to capture Prothero 2. An hour later, after a watchful advance against snipers in trees, the company occupied the saddle between Prothero 1 and Prothero 2. At 10.40 the artillery shelled Prothero 2 and at 11.15 a.m. Thomas' forward platoon advanced but was held up by sniper and machine-gun fire. A Bren gunner, Private Bugg,[9] immediately dashed forward and fired on the Japanese positions from a distance of 30 yards. Bugg's Bren gun magazines were set on fire by enemy bullets but he threw off the webbing and kept on firing. Sending his section round to a flank under his covering fire, he killed the Japanese machine-gun crew, and his section then rushed Prothero 2 and captured it. Captain Geason's[1] company now passed through Thomas' and continued south along Shaggy Ridge until, at 3.30 p.m., after an advance of about three-quarters of a mile, they were held up by machine-gun fire. From this position Geason reported that he could see the 2/9th Battalion through binoculars. Both battalions were then ordered to remain where they were in readiness for the 2/9th to attack with artillery support next day. Meanwhile another patrol from the 2/12th had penetrated 1,000 yards north-west from Prothero 1 without seeing any enemy. Later in the afternoon Lieutenant Coles led a small patrol from the 2/2nd Pioneer Battalion along the track from Prothero 1 to Kankiryo, brushed aside light opposition from an enemy patrol, and established himself almost on Kankiryo Saddle.

The 2/12th counted 40 dead Japanese on the way from Prothero 1 to Prothero 2. Despite the fact that the Japanese were being attacked from both sides, they were still fighting doggedly and on the 22nd inflicted 21 casualties on the 2/12th Battalion.

A reconnaissance patrol from the 2/9th at dawn on the 22nd found pill-boxes 20 yards ahead occupied by the enemy with several machine-guns. At 10.45 a.m., when the artillery was bombarding Prothero 2 for the attacks from the north by the 2/12th, Captain R. Taylor's company of the 2/9th was standing by ready for the attack on the battalion's next objective—McCaughey's Knoll. At 1.15 p.m. Cummings received a report from Fraser: "Prothero 2 captured, battalion pushing along Shaggy." During the afternoon Taylor's company moved to a forming-up place down the precipitous western side of Shaggy Ridge, ready to try a flanking attack on McCaughey's Knoll. Zero hour was set for 6 p.m., and for half an hour before that time artillery and mortars pounded the knoll. Taylor's company was only about 40 yards from the top of McCaughey's Knoll at 6.25 when the enemy discovered them. Despite a heavy and sudden storm of fire the Queenslanders assaulted and captured McCaughey's Knoll, cleaning up one pill-box after the other. The battalion's diarist noted on this day: "This flanking move by 'D' up heavily timbered and pre-

[9] Cpl L. F. Bugg, DCM, TX1394; 2/12 Bn. Labourer; of Cooee, Tas; b. Wynyard, Tas, 11 May 1918.
[1] Capt U. J. Geason, TX2019; 2/12 Bn. Mental nurse; of New Norfolk, Tas; b. Woollahra, NSW, 12 Jan 1914.

cipitous western slopes must have been a complete surprise to the enemy who had begun to withdraw in panic." Once again the enemy had been deceived by the Australians' ability to clamber up almost perpendicular slopes which the defenders regarded as unscaleable. After advancing to a position about 600 yards from Green Sniper's Pimple the advance of the 2/9th was held up by two enemy machine-guns about 30 yards ahead.

For the loss of 8 men wounded, the 2/9th Battalion had played its part in smashing the last hold of the Japanese on Shaggy Ridge. More than 100 enemy dead had been counted in the Prothero-Shaggy Ridge area and documents captured this day by the 2/9th showed that a platoon of the *78th Regiment* had held Green Sniper's Pimple. By dark the forward elements of the 2/9th and 2/12th Battalions were only about 900 yards apart, both being held up by sporadic machine-gun and artillery fire from the area ahead of the 2/10th Battalion.

During this successful push by its two sister battalions the 2/10th had made advances on the right flank both north and south from the spot where Cam's Saddle joined Faria Ridge. All day on the 22nd Gunn kept up the pressure on the enemy position to the north of his foothold on Faria Ridge and, by late in the afternoon, the enemy had had enough and left the position known as Cam's Hill, which was occupied by the 2/10th at 5.20 p.m.

As well as pushing north Colonel Geard decided to wipe out the troublesome enemy position on the southern tip of Faria Ridge opposite the Australian positions at Mainstream, thus opening a direct line of communication from the Faria River-Mainstream junction. The task of clearing this position on the 22nd was given to Captain Bray's[2] company. From the junction of the two spurs the company pushed south passing through several deserted enemy positions and approached the southern tip of Faria Ridge. The approach to the enemy position was down a ridge so narrow that the men had to move in single file. Bray planned that one platoon would attack down the ridge, covered on the left flank by supporting fire from a second platoon with all Brens from both platoons. When the artillery finished firing Bray's machine-guns opened up to cover the advance, but the leading section was pinned down within 25 yards of the enemy position under heavy fire, apparently from two Woodpeckers and three light machine-guns. Bray then tried unsuccessfully to send sections round on either flank and finally committed his entire company. When it too was stopped by heavy fire Bray decided to withdraw; the Japanese defences seemed to extend for at least another 100 yards. Enemy casualties were probably not severe; Bray lost 5 killed and 7 wounded. The evacuation of the wounded in darkness up the steep spur was an extremely difficult task and was not completed until midnight. One of the runners, Private Baggaley,[3] had crawled forward to help a wounded man before the withdrawal. As it was impossible to get the man out before

---

[2] Maj A. C. Bray, SX650; 2/10 Bn. Orchardist and regular soldier; of Adelaide; b. Campbelltown, SA, 8 Dec 1907.

[3] L-Cpl R. O. Baggaley, MM, QX35938; 2/10 Bn. Farm hand; of Bootawa, NSW; b. Casino, NSW, 6 Nov 1922.

dark, Baggaley remained with him (although his steel helmet was shot off his head), tended his wounds and, after dark, assisted him to safety.

During the night and early in the morning of the 23rd two mild counter-attacks were repulsed by the 2/12th. Early on the 23rd also patrols from the 2/12th and the 2/9th were converging. There was only slight opposition and after midday the forward patrols of both battalions joined up. The whole of Shaggy Ridge was thus in Australian hands and the way was open to Kankiryo Saddle.

About this time Captain Haupt's[4] company of the 2/12th moved down the track from Prothero 2 to Kankiryo Saddle. By 6 p.m. the company was at the Saddle near the foot of Crater Hill. They found a gun position containing 150 rounds of 75-mm ammunition and half an hour later they met opposition from enemy positions on the slopes of Crater Hill. As it was late the company withdrew to Kankiryo Saddle for the night.

While finally capturing Shaggy Ridge and gaining a foothold on Kankiryo Saddle the 18th Brigade had killed over 100 Japanese and captured many weapons and documents; the guns firing on the Australians from the Shaggy Ridge area had been a 75-mm, a 70-mm and a 37-mm.

Facing the Japanese positions at the southern tip of Faria Ridge, Bray's men on the 23rd were tired, for they had worked most of the previous night cutting steps into the feature to evacuate their wounded. At midday they found the position unoccupied. It extended for about 120 yards along a sharp ridge, was surrounded by barbed wire, and as usual was extremely well dug with some shelters up to 15 feet deep and connected by communication trenches. It could accommodate about 40 men.

While the fact that the Japanese had abandoned the position opposite Mainstream was being established, Captain Kumnick's company was advancing north-west along Faria Ridge from Cam's Hill. After about 1,500 yards, it encountered a strongly entrenched enemy position about half way to Kankiryo Saddle. An artillery bombardment, however, caused the Japanese to leave it hurriedly and to dig in on the reverse slope. The company attacked again about 6.20 p.m. but the enemy was prepared, and the leading platoon commander and his sergeant were wounded. Private Bloffwitch,[5] in charge of the leading section, now took command of the platoon and, although under heavy fire, managed to withdraw it and remove his casualties.

All that now remained of the Japanese forces south of Kankiryo Saddle was the rearguard opposing the advance of the 2/10th along Faria Ridge. As the Australians had occupied Kankiryo, the Japanese on this spur were threatened with the same fate as those who had been on Shaggy Ridge. Kumnick's company probed the enemy position all day on the 24th and late in the afternoon it was found to have been abandoned; the 2/10th established itself in a position about 1,200 yards south-east of Crater Hill whose crest was about 800 yards north-east of Kankiryo.

---

[4] Maj F. K. Haupt, TX882; 2/12 Bn. Regular soldier; of Launceston, Tas; b. Hamley Bridge, SA, 14 Jun 1913.

[5] Cpl H. W. Bloffwitch, MM, SX1071; 2/10 Bn. Labourer; of Bowden, SA; b. Prospect, SA, 3 Apr 1916.

Already, from captured documents, Chilton knew that Crater Hill had been Japanese regimental headquarters and that it was supposed to be occupied by an enemy company. Although small patrols from the 2/12th reached almost to the top of Crater Hill on the 24th, strong enemy positions were found on the southern slopes. Despite artillery bombardments no progress was made against these by either the 2/10th or the 2/12th. Actually the Japanese had re-occupied some of the positions which they had abandoned the previous evening in the face of Haupt's advance.

Despite the enemy's loss of Kankiryo Saddle and Shaggy Ridge, it seemed obvious by the 25th that he intended to put up a last ditch fight for Crater Hill. On the 25th the 2/10th and 2/12th probed the enemy defences on all sides of Crater Hill seeking the most suitable way for attack. There were several skirmishes in which both sides suffered casualties, and during the day linking patrols joined the two battalions, now stalled on the southern slopes of the feature. A patrol led by Lieutenant Coles of the 2/2nd Pioneers, reconnoitring the Paipa mule track along the valley of the Mindjim, fired on small bands of retreating Japanese and saw numerous empty buildings and ammunition dumps which had been deserted.

Chilton determined that the pause would be no longer than necessary and, when he learnt that the main thrust was held up on the southern slopes of Crater Hill, decided again to try encirclement. While the 2/10th and 2/12th held the enemy on the southern slopes and tried to push their way forward or round the flanks, the 2/9th was to assault the feature by sending two companies in a wide outflanking movement to the north across the tip of the Mindjim Valley and round the enemy's right flank.

Captain A. Marshall's company led off at 10.35 a.m. on the 26th, passing from Shaggy Ridge through Kankiryo Saddle and then to the north, with Captain Taylor's company following to provide flank protection. By midday Marshall reported that he had advanced some 600 yards and passed through several old positions although he had seen no enemy. Cautiously but steadily he pushed on; at 5 p.m. he reached the summit of 4100. The main enemy position was now to the south between Marshall and the 2/10th and 2/12th Battalions. Leaving Taylor to occupy the summit of 4100 Marshall moved south towards Crater Hill in an attempt to surprise the enemy from the rear. He met them about 300 yards south-east from the summit just on dusk. The leading platoon attacked along the usual razor-back but withdrew because of heavy machine-gun fire. At 7 p.m. Marshall sent Lieutenant White's[6] platoon round the right flank but approach from this flank was also very difficult and White was killed.

As had been the case with their comrades on Shaggy Ridge and Faria Ridge, the Japanese on Crater Hill were now surrounded. However, they evidently intended to fight it out; possibly they did not know that they were surrounded and, indeed, the Australians themselves did not know exactly where they were. Chilton reported later:

---
[6] Lt E. K. White, QX34589; 2/9 Bn. Storekeeper; of Gympie, Qld; b. Pittsworth, Qld, 9 Mar 1914. Killed in action 26 Jan 1944.

It was apparent at this stage that the existing 1/25,000 map was very inaccurate, and considerable difficulty was experienced in determining the relative positions of the fwd elements of the three bns and the nature of the ground. In particular, great difficulty was experienced in controlling the arty; when an F.O.O. attempted to register targets to his immediate front, fire would be stopped by FOO's with other bns. It became obvious therefore that we had closed in on the enemy along three very narrow ridges, which all met at a "pimple" . . . called Crater Hill. The relative positions of our tps were later established by Contact R, fwd tps firing 2-inch mortar flares. The enemy was holding along these three ridges radiating from the pimple. The sides of each ridge were extremely steep.[7]

Chilton was convinced that, although his battalions were now occupying the three ridges leading towards Crater Hill and although they had really captured their objective—the vital ground of the Mindjim-Faria divide—the Japanese would try to hold on to Crater Hill. The ground was very difficult and the defences were exceedingly well prepared with a large number of automatic weapons deployed. Chilton decided to use siege tactics. His brigade would sit close round the Japanese, harass them and make sure that they did not withdraw undetected. By means of heavy artillery bombardments, mortar fire and dive-bombing, Chilton hoped to destroy the Japanese defences, inflict crippling casualties and "generally soften up the position for a final assault".

The siege of Crater Hill continued until the end of January. During the first two days—the 27th and 28th—Chilton redisposed his brigade so that the 2/9th Battalion took responsibility for the southern slopes of 4100 as well as for the feature itself and for Kankiryo Saddle, while the 2/12th held the Protheros and Shaggy Ridge, and the 2/10th maintained pressure on the south-eastern slopes of Crater Hill. On the 27th and 28th there were minor skirmishes but the main activity was the artillery bombardment. Captain Whyte of the 2/4th Field Regiment used 2,000 shells in the bombardment, shattering the trees. Unfortunately the mass of fallen timber added yet another obstacle to the approach.

At 9.30 a.m. on the 29th 19 Kittyhawks dive-bombed Crater Hill. The bombs seemed to be in the target area and were followed by ten minutes of artillery fire. At 1.30 p.m. the artillery laid down a barrage and machine-gun fire covered an assault on Crater Hill from the west by Captain Daunt's[8] company of the 2/9th. The leading platoon attempted to rush the enemy position up a very steep and open slope but the Japanese, entrenched on a razor-back, were too strong and drove back the platoon. The Australians also had the bad luck to be shelled by their own artillery—an increasingly rare accident. Among the 14 casualties suffered in this attack and from the shelling were two of the officers from India, Captains D. A. Wright and A. J. Stanton, the latter being mortally wounded.

There was no change on the 18th Brigade's front on the 30th January when the 15th Brigade raided Orgoruna successfully. It was raining heavily

---

[7] 18th Brigade report.

[8] Lt-Col W. W. D. Daunt, QX6016. 2/9 Bn; staff and training appointments. Schoolmaster; of Brisbane; b. Kobe, Japan, 19 Oct 1909.

in the Kankiryo area and the weather was cold and misty so that the intended air strike had to be cancelled. In a message to his troops Colonel Cummings said: "It is the intention to reorganise in the next few days, using aircraft and arty to soften up before our next move. Patrolling must be very active and all possible information gained of the enemy positions."

Continually harassed by patrols and hammered by aircraft, artillery and mortars, the Japanese on Crater Hill were coming to the end of their endurance. Just after dawn on 31st January a patrol from Marshall's company of the 2/9th found four bunkers unoccupied on the slope of the 4100 Feature forward from the company's position on Kankiryo Saddle. The defensive fire from the enemy positions seemed much weaker than usual and there had been reports during the last few days from Australian patrols that bands of the enemy were retreating from the battle area towards Paipa. In an advance of 600 yards Marshall occupied the empty Japanese positions. About 10.30 a.m. the Japanese held any further advance for a while by hurling down grenades from a high ledge. A Bren gunner, Corporal Berrell,[1] managed to move into a position whence he could silence the enemy post. The Japanese then withdrew, leaving behind at least 16 dead, while the Australians followed for about another 100 yards. Confronted by heavy enemy fire the company would have been in danger of counter-attack but for the accurate fire from the wounded Berrell's gun. The ground was held and his successful attack placed the company forward at the base of a steep rock face within 100 yards of the summit of Crater Hill.

Both to the north and to the south-east the country was exceedingly rough and difficult and the advance of the troops was handicapped by the timber felled by the artillery bombardment. While Marshall's company pulled back to Kankiryo Saddle, Taylor's took over the forward area and managed to kill another 12 Japanese.

For four days Gunn's company of the 2/10th pressed towards Crater Hill from the south-east. On 31st January Lieutenant Meldrum's[2] platoon reached a position about 40 yards from the crest. Gunn went forward to observe the enemy's positions and was wounded by a grenade. Lieutenant Mallyon[3] took command.

The siege of Crater Hill ended on 1st February when Mallyon's company of the 2/10th and Taylor's of the 2/9th closed in and found it unoccupied.[4] By 10.20 a.m. the whole ridge from Crater Hill to the 4100 summit was in Australian possession. Crater Hill was a ghastly mess. At least 14 dead were found and evidence of many burials; a 75-mm and a 70-mm gun, a grenade discharger, and the usual quantity of diaries, documents and equipment lay around. The diggings were

---

[1] Sgt M. M. Berrell, MM, NX113332; 2/9 Bn. Mill operator; of Braidwood, NSW; b. Cootamundra, NSW, 19 Dec 1921.

[2] Lt E. C. S. Meldrum, SX12030; 2/10 Bn. Police instructor; of Adelaide; b. Adelaide, 23 Jun 1915.

[3] Lt A. R. St V. Mallyon, SX461; 2/10 Bn. Sales manager; of Port Pirie, SA; b. Port Pirie, 15 Apr 1913.

[4] As Mallyon and his leading platoon arrived on Crater Hill they were amazed to see two perspiring Salvation Army officers, laden with comforts, approaching from the other edge. They explained that they had been told that the hill had been captured the previous day.

connected by a maze of communication trenches, all built with infinite care. The area had been devastated by air and artillery bombardment. The defended position itself was about 500 yards long by 60 yards wide with about 40 pill-boxes and foxholes on Crater Hill and 110 on the razor-back leading to it.

After the occupation of Crater Hill on the 1st, Chilton signalled Vasey: "Task completed. Awaiting further instructions." All that now remained was to mop up in the general area of Kankiryo Saddle, Shaggy Ridge, Faria Ridge and Crater Hill. Between the 1st and 6th February the battalions took up new positions in preparation for another period of static warfare. The 2/10th was on the right in the area from the 4100 Feature to Crater Hill, including Kankiryo Saddle; the 2/9th on the left holding from the north-west of Shaggy Ridge to the two Protheros; and the 2/12th holding the line from McCullough's Ridge to Lake Hill.[5]

The mopping up was done mainly by patrols down the Mindjim Valley and to the rugged areas on the flanks of the brigade position where there were still a few stray Japanese, who were killed in the succeeding days. On the 1st the 2/12th's observation post on the Paipa Track had seen several parties of Japanese moving north along the Mindjim Valley and probably escaping from Crater Hill. Kumnick's company of the 2/10th was sent down the valley of the Mindjim to catch them. Patrols from the other battalions moved along the ridges north and south of the Mindjim Valley to guard the advance of the larger patrol from the 2/10th. Kumnick reached Paipa 2 on the 2nd. When approaching Paipa 1 on the morning of the 3rd, the leading platoon came under sporadic fire. After keeping up the pressure all day and after a bombardment by the 4th Field Regiment (which was relieving the 2/4th) the patrol occupied the position, which was found to be in a village 200 yards south-east of Paipa 1. Next morning a patrol found Paipa 1 clear. Another patrol reached Amuson on the 6th and found it unoccupied; a native said there were many Japanese farther along the Mosa River.

Thus by 6th February the 18th Brigade was firmly astride the Mindjim-Faria divide. Between 19th January and 6th February the brigade had lost 46 killed, including 3 officers, and 147 wounded, including 9 officers. It had buried 244 dead Japanese and had found several mass graves containing many bodies which could not be counted. Chilton concluded that, of an enemy force of about 790 holding the area on 19th January, at least 500 had been either killed or wounded. The brigade had captured three 75-mm guns, one 70-mm, one 37-mm and one 20-mm.

It will be recalled that Brigadier Hammer on 19th January had got permission for a company of the 24th Battalion to create a diversion by

---

[5] According to the historian of the 2/10th Battalion, when word was received that General Vasey would visit the area on the 2nd a signal was sent to all companies: "Other ranks will cease calling officers by their Christian names and will cease wearing pork-pie hats." The historian adds that "although not lacking anything in discipline or morale, many of the troops had taken on the guise of bushrangers, and as such must have struck terror into the hearts of their enemies". F. Allchin, *Purple and Blue—The History of the 2/10th Battalion, A.I.F. (The Adelaide Rifles) 1939-1945* (1958), p. 349.

attacking Cameron's Knoll and for the 57th/60th to raid the Orgoruna-Mataloi area. Colonel Smith of the 24th Battalion gave the task of capturing Cameron's Knoll to Captain Kennedy's company. The Pioneer platoons of the three battalions made a jeep track from the Evapia to Kesawai to shorten the long supply line. This made it possible also to have artillery support; previously the guns could not be dragged into this western area. Vasey allotted Hammer two guns and 1,000 rounds of ammunition for the attack. After nine days of preparation, in which 527 boy-loads of ammunition, rations, heavy weapons, medical and signal stores were carried forward, the 24th was ready to launch the attack.

West of Cameron's Knoll was a spur—later known as Spendlove—where also the enemy was thought to be in position. To divert the enemy's attention during the main attack of the 18th Brigade, Kennedy, on 21st January, led a feint attack on Spendlove Spur. The enemy replied with heavy fire and in so doing disclosed previously unsuspected positions. For the next two days patrols probed the area.

Kennedy planned that one platoon would move round the left flank and attack up Spendlove Spur, with another giving covering fire along the main track and the third in reserve. At 6.30 a.m. on 24th January the company was ready. Directed by Lieutenant Agar,[6] the two guns opened up at 9.25 a.m. and, in an hour, fired 150 shells into the Japanese position. As Lieutenant Laughlin's[7] platoon moved round to the left flank to get ready for the attack, the leading men could see that the artillery fire was to the right of the target but, because of a breakdown

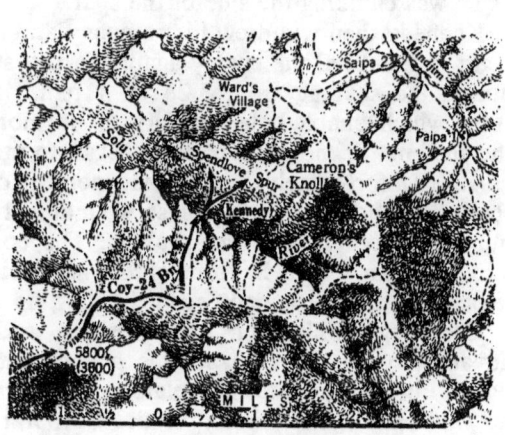

24th January

of communications, they were unable to tell the artillery observer. At 11.10 a.m. the attacking platoon, with Corporal Warner's[8] section in the van, was just below Spendlove Spur. Five men had actually clambered on to the spur when Warner saw a Japanese standing up on the track about ten yards away. He killed the Japanese, but heavy enemy fire and a grenade rolled down the slope wounded two of Warner's men and caused Laughlin to withdraw.

---

[6] Lt S. L. Agar, VX14399; 2/4 Fd Regt. Salesman; of East Malvern, Vic; b. Armadale, Vic, 21 Mar 1914.

[7] Lt J. Laughlin, VX54060; 24 Bn. Clerk; of Camberwell, Vic; b. Oakland, California, USA. 12 Apr 1919.

[8] Cpl N. A. Warner, VX104534; 24 Bn. Butcher; of Kew, Vic; b. Malvern, Vic, 20 Oct 1918. Died 9 Dec 1947.

Soon after the start of Laughlin's attack, Sergeant Spendlove's[9] platoon moved into thinner timber along the steep track about 50 feet below the Japanese-held spur. The platoon poured in a heavy volume of fire but it was answered just as heavily and, for interest, the Japanese rolled down grenades. Kennedy decided not to batter away at the enemy position without further artillery fire, but first he wished to know the whereabouts of Laughlin's platoon which had been out of communication since its abortive attack. Corporal Goodwin[1] volunteered to find the missing platoon but nothing further was heard from him and his body was found two days later 25 yards from the top of the enemy position—he had fired off a magazine from his Owen gun. When Goodwin did not return, Sergeant McLennan[2] moved out also to search for the missing platoon but, like Goodwin, he must have stumbled into the enemy camp and his body was found next day. A third attempt was made by the commander of the mortar detachment, Corporal Carney,[3] who set out with a telephone and trailing line behind him. About 10 minutes after Carney left, however, Warner reported in from the missing platoon and said it was back on the main track. A runner went forward rapidly and managed to find Carney as he was climbing the side of the spur.

Kennedy then withdrew his company and arrangements were made with Agar to bombard the enemy again. Carney stayed forward with his phone during the shelling from 3.25 to 4 p.m. and passed back messages to Agar which enabled the artillery to be more accurate. Near the end of the shelling, Spendlove's platoon began to move forward to make a direct assault. Unfortunately, just at that moment one of the last of the artillery shells fell shorter than the rest wounding two of his men and giving a number of others a severe shaking. The company's 2-inch mortars then laid a smoke screen in front of the advancing troops but the wind blew it back on the men, once again holding up the advance.

Encouraging his men and brushing aside these mishaps, Spendlove advanced yet again and put his platoon into a position behind a small bank. For five minutes the platoon fired on the Japanese but there was no answering fire. With Lance-Corporal Metcalf,[4] Spendlove then cautiously moved forward. They were five yards from the top of the spur when the enemy opened up. Metcalf was killed but Spendlove managed to get back and report to Kennedy, suggesting that another platoon should be sent to try from the right flank.

Lieutenant Mason's[5] platoon was then sent up a spur on the right. Under covering fire from the rest of the company, it advanced up a

---

[9] Lt N. J. Spendlove, DCM, VX106341; 24 Bn. Warehouse assistant; of Glenferrie, Vic; b. Geelong, Vic, 16 Jul 1920.

[1] Cpl F. E. Goodwin, VX136014; 24 Bn. Farmer; of The Basin, Vic; b. Mallala, SA, 10 Feb 1917. Killed in action 24 Jan 1944.

[2] Sgt T. A. L. McLennan, VX15497. 2/14 and 24 Bns. Labourer; of Heidelberg, Vic; b. Sea Lake, Vic, 21 Nov 1918. Killed in action 24 Jan 1944.

[3] Sgt J. P. Carney, MM, VX120994; 24 Bn. Student; of West Brunswick, Vic; b. Brunswick, Vic, 30 Jan 1917.

[4] L-Cpl O. G. Metcalf, VX70579; 24 Bn. Farmer; of Tolmie, Vic; b. Shepparton, Vic, 13 Oct 1913. Killed in action 24 Jan 1944.

[5] Lt H. M. Mason, VX104472; 24 Bn. Bank officer; of Lilydale, Vic; b. Lilydale, 18 Mar 1920. Killed in action 24 Jan 1944.

steep slope and four men, scaling a final steep rock face, actually reached the top of the main spur and were in the midst of the enemy position. Here the Japanese opened up from a range of about five yards with at least three machine-guns and many rifles. The Australians in supporting positions answered but the four men were in an untenable position. Three of them were killed and the fourth jumped over the edge; Mason also was killed during this fighting.

The enemy's position seemed impregnable, but it had several times been proved in New Guinea warfare that a pounding by artillery allied with dogged and persistent attacks would eventually force the enemy to leave dominating positions which he should have been able to hold. It was so on this occasion. The Australians had tried thrice and each time had been driven back. Towards dusk there was no reply to the company's small arms fire. Spendlove's platoon therefore advanced straight up the main precipitous track and without opposition reached the top of the spur named after the gallant platoon commander. The company then occupied the spur and rapidly dug in expecting a counter-attack, but the enemy had had enough.

On the 26th a patrol moved out along the track up the spur in an easterly direction about 1,000 yards east of Spendlove Spur and found a recently-vacated Japanese position. It had about 50 slit trenches with underground sleeping quarters and, from an observation post in a 40-foot tree, a perfect view of all approaches to the position could be obtained. Practically all the Australians' movements during the attack on Spendlove Spur could have been observed from this tree. As this position — Cameron's Knoll—was more suitable for defence the company occupied it.

Meanwhile Colonel Marston of the 57th/60th was concentrating his battalion in the Ketoba area

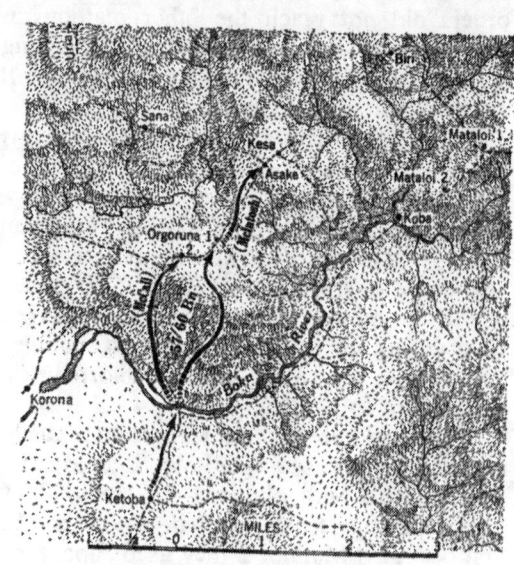

The 57th/60th Battalion in the Orgoruna-Kesa area, 30th January

ready to attack Orgoruna 1 and 2 and raid Kesa and Koba. The battalion started off at 12.30 p.m. on the 30th. Major McCall's[6] company found

---

[6] Maj W. McCall, ED, VX81103; 57/60 Bn. Public servant; of North Fitzroy, Vic; b. Wangaratta, Vic, 25 Jul 1910.

Orgoruna 2 unoccupied, and by 7 p.m. Captain McIntosh's[7] company had found Orgoruna 1 and Kesa unoccupied, although in Kesa there were extensive defences. All indications pointed to a hasty Japanese withdrawal during this day. From the Asake-Kesa area on 31st January McIntosh patrolled to Sana and Biri but found no signs of the enemy.

Marston then ordered Major Barker's[8] company to Kesa whence a patrol entered Koba on 1st February and pushed on towards Mataloi 2. There were signs of very recent occupation and, 200 yards along the track, the patrol was ambushed. Barker brought heavy fire down on the Japanese ambush position and occupied Koba that night.

On the morning of the 3rd, about 400 yards east of Koba, Barker again struck a Japanese ambush position which was, however, outflanked, the enemy withdrawing through Mataloi 2 towards Mataloi 1. By the time Mataloi 2 was occupied at 6.30 p.m., there was not enough time to exploit to Mataloi 1 nor to allow adequate consolidation in Mataloi 2 before dark. At 9.30 p.m. the Japanese counter-attacked from the direction of Mataloi 1, preceding the attack with a heavy mortar bombardment. As Mataloi 2 could be commanded from three sides, Barker decided that he could hold the area best from high ground to the south which would also be out of range of the enemy mortars. Accordingly he ordered a withdrawal and departed with his headquarters and one platoon. Apparently the orders did not reach the other platoons who were encircled while the remainder of the company was withdrawing to Koba. Long-range enemy machine-gun fire was directed at Kesa at the same time as the counter-attack developed at Mataloi 2.

By the 4th there was no news of the two missing platoons although much heavy firing had been heard from the Mataloi 2 area. The depleted company was withdrawn and McIntosh's was sent to the Koba area to patrol vigorously towards Mataloi 2 and make contact with the missing platoons. The patrols neither found the missing men nor discovered what was happening in Mataloi 2. At 7.30 p.m. on the 4th the commander of one of the missing platoons reported in. He had been stunned by a mortar blast during the counter-attack and, unable to find his platoon, had wandered back. It was not until the morning of the 5th that the two platoons reported in to Ketoba.

What had already been suspected was then confirmed—they had not received the order to withdraw. Soon after 9.30 p.m. on the 3rd Lieutenant Jacobs[9] with both platoons—29 men—had been encircled by an enemy force attacking from the right and from the front. When the Australians first occupied Mataloi 2 they used Japanese defensive positions near which the Japanese had fixed sticks with pieces of white paper attached. Later

---

[7] Capt R. H. McIntosh, VX81077; 57/60 Bn. Insurance officer; of Pascoe Vale, Vic; b. Melbourne, 19 May 1910.

[8] Maj W. F. Barker, VX48332. 2/23 and 57/60 Bns. Bank officer; of Balwyn, Vic; b. Melbourne, 6 Jul 1908.

[9] Lt H. J. Jacobs, VX1921. 6 Div AASC, 23/21 and 58/59 Bns. Motor driver; of Melbourne; b. North Fitzroy, Vic, 21 Dec 1913. (Jacobs, with three other officers of the 23rd/21st Battalion, was attached for duty with the 57th/60th from 19th January 1944. He transferred to the 58th/59th Battalion on 26th February 1944.)

the Australians dug new positions well away from the Japanese ones. Expecting them to use the old Japanese pits, the enemy directed most of his fire at them. The Japanese firing was wild and ineffective and caused no casualties. At very close range Jacobs gave the order to fire and estimated that about 30 of the enemy were hit. The attack lasted for 40 minutes before being beaten off and although there was further sporadic firing up to 2 a.m. on the 4th the Japanese did not counter-attack heavily again and spent the night dragging out their killed and wounded.

Jacobs was still holding his position at 9 a.m. on 4th February but he was out of communication with the battalion. He knew that the battalion's advance into this area was in the nature of a raid, and therefore decided to withdraw and try to regain touch with the remainder of the company or return to battalion headquarters at Ketoba. A previous patrol up the Boku on the 1st had found a practicable though difficult route to Koba. Without casualties and carrying all their weapons, except one 2-inch mortar which had been lost in the Boku during the night, Jacobs' two platoons rejoined the battalion at Ketoba on the morning of the 5th.

The withdrawal of the 57th/60th then continued according to plan. By the evening of the 6th all troops were east of the Boku River and by the 10th the battalion was back in the Mene Hill area. The raid had given some experience to the 57th/60th Battalion. It probably also caused some consternation to the enemy when he found that so large a striking force of Australians could occupy his important flank positions with such apparent ease.

Vasey was troubled during this period by a large number of high-ranking visitors. Visits such as those from the commander and staff of New Guinea Force, from commanders of units training in Australia who had not yet had experience in such an area, from American and Australian pilots who were acting in cooperation with the 7th Division, and from British Commonwealth colleagues, were of course understandable, welcomed and necessary. On the other hand there were others whose visits could not be termed strictly necessary.[1] Vasey himself exploded when writing of the matter on the day when CUTTHROAT began: "These visitors are a curse! We've had 280 of them—16 Generals and 1 Admiral—cheap tour of the world—a lot of them being able to say they've been to the war."

The Japanese force which had opposed the 18th Brigade in the fight for Kankiryo Saddle comprised a battalion group—Captain Yano's *II/78th Battalion*. A captured ration statement dated 2nd January showed that there were then 787 Japanese in the battle area under Yano's command. Captured documents referred to the movement of the other two battalions of the *78th Regiment* to the coast to counter the American landing at Saidor. A company group from the *III/78th Battalion* was identified, however, in the Orgoruna area at the end of January and another company possibly from the *I/78th Battalion* was in the area from Cameron's Knoll to the Bogadjim Road. This emphasised once again the piecemeal methods of the Japanese commanders. It also emphasised the lack of reserves. "Not one soldier

---

[1] One company commander on the southern slopes of Shaggy Ridge before CUTTHROAT had signs erected, reading, "Is your journey really necessary?", and "Starvation Corner, no lunch provided."

in the rear," lamented a diarist who was a participant in the fight for Kankiryo Saddle.

Questioned after the war General Adachi and his staff said that the *II/78th Battalion* which defended Shaggy Ridge in December and Kankiryo Saddle in January consisted of only about 400 men. Five companies of the *78th Regiment* had left for the coast before the Kankiryo Saddle fight in order to support the *III/239th Battalion* against the Americans at Saidor.[2] In other interviews Adachi and his staff were quoted as saying:

> "As the result shows, one division of the Australian forces was nailed down by only three battalions of Japanese forces, and during the period Jan-Feb 1944, when the 7th Division was actively committed to the offensive at Kankiryo, there were only 7 Japanese companies in this area, the other 5 companies being employed at Saidor to hold off the American landings. From the point of view of supply, it cost a great number of jeeps and transport planes to keep in action such a big force as the division in the Ramu Valley where it could not be as effective as it could have been in other areas. In other words, it would have been much more advisable for the Australian forces to have employed about a brigade strength in the Ramu Valley, as a threat only to Madang, and use the bulk of the forces for the operations along the coastline. In New Guinea operations it is taboo for the raiding party to engage in inland actions. The operations should have been carried out along the coast. This is the doctrine to which the Japanese have always adhered rigidly."[3]

These views and claims of the Japanese leaders are interesting but wide of the mark. With the capture of Kankiryo Saddle by the 7th Division, as with the capture of Sio by the 9th Division, a phase ended. In the four months since the great offensive began at Lae and Nadzab the enemy had been pushed back from areas necessary to the Allies for the building of bases to support the onward thrust against Japan. From early in 1943 when the enemy had been deluded into pouring troops into the Salamaua area against the 3rd and 5th Australian Divisions, he had been caught on the wrong foot. Sending units here and there piecemeal to plug the front line had availed General Adachi nothing either against the rugged fighting of the 3rd and 5th Divisions or against the veteran 7th and 9th. The *51st* and *20th Japanese Divisions* had been defeated and partly annihilated, and units of the third Japanese division in Australian New Guinea—the *41st*—had shared in the defeat. Now the remnants of the *20th* and *51st* were fleeing in despair along the Rai Coast from the Australians and were apparently trapped by the American landing at Saidor; while the garrison in the Finisterres—the *78th Regiment*—had lost the vital position astride the divide at Kankiryo Saddle to the 7th Australian Division, and was casting backward eyes and sending troops against the actual threat at Saidor and the potential threat at Madang. It was only a year since the Japanese had set out confidently from Salamaua to capture Wau.

---

[2] Information from document compiled by Lieutenant W. N. Prior of 5 Military History Field Team in Rabaul after the war.

[3] Commander Eighth Military District, Report on Japanese Operations in New Guinea—Ramu Valley Campaign, Sep 43-Apr 44.

CHAPTER 27

THE PURSUIT TO MADANG

THE Australian operations along the Rai Coast and in the Finisterre Mountains in the early part of 1944 were being undertaken as a result of a policy directive for the summer of 1943-1944 issued by General Blamey on 23rd December. Blamey had warned that "the operational role of the Australian Military Forces engaged in forward operations in New Guinea will be taken over by U.S.A. forces in accordance with plans now being prepared. Aggressive operations will be continued and reliefs necessary to maintain the initiative will be made by G.O.C. New Guinea Force until Commander, U.S.A. Forces, takes over responsibility." The reliefs would be effected gradually, first on the Huon Peninsula and second in the Ramu Valley. "As relieved, and subject to operational or emergency requirements," the 6th, 7th and 9th Divisions would be allocated to I Australian Corps and would return to the mainland for training and rehabilitation. Three militia divisions—3rd, 5th and 11th—would be allocated to II Australian Corps for garrison duties, training and rehabilitation in New Guinea and on the mainland. The already depleted III Australian Corps in Western Australia would be further reduced by one infantry brigade which would be transferred to the 3rd Division at Atherton. Blamey instructed that movement of units to the mainland should begin immediately "in accordance with the principle of earliest relief for longest service in New Guinea", and that "the force remaining at the conclusion of the relief will be an Army Corps of approximately two full jungle divisions plus base troops required for maintenance".

Thus the role of the Australian Army in 1944 would be small in comparison with the one it had played in the previous two years when it had carried the main burden of the fight against the Japanese in the South-West Pacific.

At this stage, on 22nd January 1944, the War Cabinet decided to present to General MacArthur a revised statement of the combat forces to be assigned to him—the first such statement since the original one of 18th April 1942. The new statement set out the forces assigned in greater detail than hitherto, specifying individual brigades; as far as the army was concerned, it again gave control of all mobile operational formations to MacArthur, but provided that future assignments should be specifically made by the Government. Thus, if a new brigade or division was formed it would be necessary to assign it individually to MacArthur.

In New Guinea the main body of the retreating Japanese divisions was marching westward along the coastal route, and a smaller column consisting principally of the *III/238th Battalion* was using an exhausting inland route from Nambariwa to Nokopo. From Gali 2 the route would lead round the American beach-head at Saidor through Nokopo and

Tarikngan. Here, as mentioned, was a covering force of about 2,000 men under Major-General Nakai, comprising the *III/239th Battalion* and five companies of the *78th Regiment*.

For the Rai Coast advance Major-General Ramsay of the 5th Division would have in the forward area only the 8th Brigade (4th, 30th and 35th Battalions); the 4th and 29th Brigades were to remain in rear areas. The commander of the 8th Brigade, Brigadier Cameron, was the only officer now commanding a brigade who had not served in the Middle East. He had returned from the war of 1914-18 as an infantry lieutenant, and had led the 8th Brigade since May 1940.

Ramsay's intention was to "advance to make contact with the U.S. forces at Saidor". He estimated that an enemy force of not more than 3,000 troops was in the area between Sio and Saidor, that their morale and health were low, and that organised resistance was unlikely. Behind his statement that "U.S. forces have established a bridgehead at Saidor extending approx five miles in the direction of Sio, but are not expected to extend further in this direction", there may have been a suggestion that the 32nd American Division was losing a golden opportunity by letting the retreating *20th* and *51st Japanese Divisions* bypass them. And on 17th February General Morshead wrote in a letter to Blamey that the Saidor force appeared not to have made "any appreciable effort" to cut off the retreating Japanese.

Besides the 8th Brigade the main units taking part in the advance were the veteran company of Papuans, the 23rd Battery (short 25-pounders) from the 2/12th Field Regiment, the 2/13th and 8th Field Companies, and a detachment of the 2/8th Field Ambulance. Because of the difficulties of supply not more than one battalion group would be used forward of Kelanoa and the remainder of the brigade would occupy "healthy areas" at Kelanoa. The maximum use would be made of the Papuans to precede the forward battalion, and, as subsequent maintenance of the striking force would depend on the selection of suitable beaches, land reconnaissance parties from the American 2nd Engineer Special Brigade would accompany it.

On 19th January Cameron's headquarters and the 4th Battalion (Lieut-Colonel Crosky[1]) began to arrive at Sio and Nambariwa. In the 4th, as in many more-experienced units before it, there was a certain amount of nervousness known colloquially as "itchy finger" on the first few nights. On the night of the 21st-22nd January the forward platoon imagined that they saw some Japanese and opened fire. The "Japanese" were their own men, two of whom were killed and two wounded. The raw 8th Brigade, however, had the benefit of the skill and experience of the Papuan company. The Papuans were in their element as hunters and were busy looking for scattered bands of Japanese. They would have been disappointed had they been recalled (as was intended at one stage) and, as events turned out, two companies of Papuans could probably have

---

[1] Lt-Col P. W. Crosky, ED, NX112661. CO 4 Bn 1942-44. Managing law clerk; of Arncliffe, NSW; b. Rozelle, NSW, 29 Jun 1908. Died 7 Jan 1957.

advanced to Saidor quicker and with less effort than any brigade of Australians.

On the 22nd a native reported that there were about seven Japanese in the hills south-west of Sio Mission. A small patrol of Papuans, under Corporal Bengari, whose reputation was similar to that of the best of Gurkhas, immediately set out and arrived on the outskirts of the village of Lembangando on the night of the 24th. He sent forward a local native who said on his return that another 22 Japanese had now arrived. Next morning Bengari and his five companions ambushed the enemy force and killed every one without the Japanese firing a shot. Another Papuan patrol to Vincke Point found 20 dead Japanese on the track and killed one other on their return journey to Sio. Thus, even before the advance began, the Papuans had cleared the way as far as the end of the first bound planned by Cameron; he had ordered that the 4th Battalion, preceded by the Papuans, would begin on 25th January a series of daily bounds, designed to take them to the Timbe River in six days. It was planned that the 4th Battalion would advance to Malasanga, the 30th thence to Gali, and the 35th would then take over and link with the Americans in Saidor. General Berryman signalled to Ramsay on the 25th: "Consider brigade rather over cautious but do not propose to push them yet."[2]

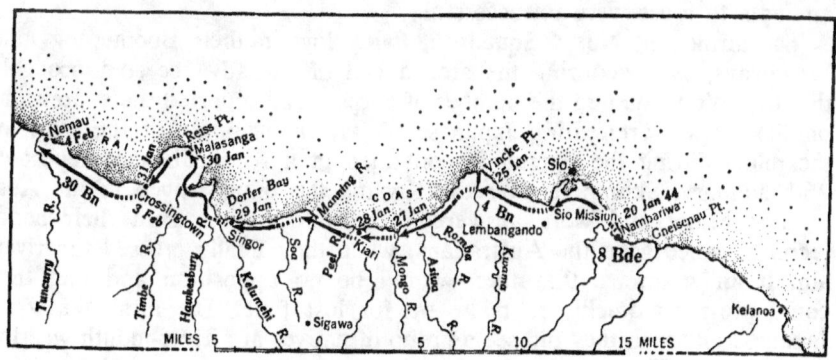

The 8th Brigade's pursuit along the Rai Coast

It would be difficult to find sheltered beach-heads because the north-west monsoon would blow until the middle of February, causing sudden flooding of the rivers and rough seas which would limit barge landing points to areas protected from the north-west. The terrain of the Rai Coast

---

[2] The following table shows the planned daily progress of the advance between Sio and Saidor:

Bound		Day	Date	Bound		Day	Date
1	Kwama River	1	25 Jan	8	Putubutu	9	2 Feb
2	Romba River	2	26 Jan	9	Roinji 2	10	3 Feb
3	Peel River	3	27 Jan	10	Weber Point	11	4 Feb
4	Soa River	4	28 Jan	11	Malalamai	12	5 Feb
5	Hawkesbury River	5	29 Jan	12	Yagomai	13	6 Feb
6	Crossingtown	6	30 Jan	13	Seure	14	7 Feb
7	Nemau	8	1 Feb	14	Sel	15	8 Feb

consisted of a coastal belt whose width varied from about a mile to almost nothing, cut by many rivers and swamps. The whole operation would obviously be governed by supplies moved by sea. The Australians would thus, once again, depend upon their well-tried friends, the American boatmen of the 532nd E.B.S.R., of whom only one company remained with them.

Because of the terrain the advance could be at most on a company front, probably mainly on a platoon front with Papuans scouting ahead. Behind these forward troops was an imposing array of headquarters: behind the one leading battalion a brigade commander, behind him a divisional commander, behind him a corps commander, and behind him a force commander. Two of these might well have been removed from the chain of command and the task allotted to a brigade group directly under the command of New Guinea Force—an arrangement that was, in effect, adopted later with regard to this very brigade.

The advance began on the 25th when the Papuans in the van arrived at the Kwama River soon after midday. Near a possible ford was the heap of dead bodies previously discovered. As they tried to cross the river a Japanese hiding among these bodies began to fire at them and was dealt with. When the battalion arrived the river was neck-deep and running at about 10 knots, and although one platoon crossed on an improvised bridge the river then washed the bridge away and further attempts to cross were unsuccessful.

The airmen of No. 4 Squadron, flying low in their Boomerangs and Wirraways, were scouring the area ahead of the advance so thoroughly that they often counted the number of corpses and reported the expressions on the faces of retreating Japanese. A typical example of the work of the pilots during the pursuit is contained in a reconnaissance report of 26th January. Skimming over the Kwama the pilots waved to the Australians below and were answered. The information from their aerial reconnaissance gave the Australians, when they finally crossed the river, almost an assurance that there would be no opposition and that they could press on quickly to make up for lost time. The airmen saw no Japanese although they did see a group of natives at a river-mouth wearing red lap-laps. They reported empty villages, five parachutes hanging in trees—an indication that the Japanese may have tried, in desperation, to supply their retreating army from the air—"very slight recent usage" along the main tracks, possibly because of the heavy rain, several clearings where Japanese might have been about to set up camp and then decided otherwise, and caves in the area from Kiari to Sigawa where the defeated *51st Japanese Division* had come to rest after escaping from Lae and Salamaua.

The battalion crossed the falling Kwama on the afternoon of the 26th. Next day it moved rapidly to the Asiwa River, and reached the Kiari area on the 28th, and on the 29th Singor. Each day at this stage the Papuans were killing 12 to 15 Japanese, and finding similar numbers of corpses. Supply difficulties caused delay, and the advance was slowed because of corps and divisional instructions that artillery support was to be immediately available. This necessitated the permanent allotment of barges to the artillery and so far there were not enough barges to supply even the infantry. The engineers were having difficulty in making river crossings, partly because it was so hard to move forward the engineering equipment required. For instance, when the Kwama's bridge was washed away the troops beyond the river, but well behind the leading barge point, found supplies very short and there were other difficulties along the supply route: the increasing length of signal communications, the uncertainty of wireless communications, and the marshy country west of Kiari which prevented the use of motor transport and placed an additional strain on the barges.

The fifth bound—Malasanga—was reached in the afternoon of the 30th, and on the 31st the Papuans and Australians advanced to Crossingtown. The men were now on three-quarter rations. More troops were concentrating in the Singor area on the 31st, thus increasing the ration shortage. Among the arrivals were the 30th Battalion, a section of the 2/4th Light Anti-Aircraft Regiment and the 64th Battery of the 2/14th Field Regiment (Lieut-Colonel Hone[3]), with its regimental headquarters,[4] which arrived to relieve the 23rd Battery of the 2/12th Field Regiment.

After a confused start the 4th Battalion had reached its objective only one day behind schedule without, however, being able to catch the retreating enemy. The advance obviously could not be continued until rations became available, and early on 1st February Cameron cancelled the advance for that day. Along the coast behind the forward troops floods had washed away bridges over the Mongo, Asiwa and Romba Rivers. Jeeps and bulldozers were therefore isolated and their crews, like the forward troops, were almost without rations. The Papuans, having been without proper food for the last three days, camped and waited. Rough seas, flooded rivers, broken bridges and lack of supplies continued to delay the advance until 3rd February when Lieut-Colonel Parry-Okeden's 30th Battalion set off from Singor to take over from the 4th Battalion at Crossingtown. Meanwhile the Papuans reached Nemau. Supplies were dropped from the air on the 4th and the recovery was 82 per cent.

The 30th Battalion on the 4th reached Nemau and on the 5th Butubutu, where the next supply beach was established. Increasing numbers of dead were now being found along the route and the inland trails— 52 on the 4th. On the 5th came orders that all commanders must make every endeavour to capture prisoners, and with this in view Cameron called off the Papuans from leading the advance and sent the leading Papuan platoon to reconnoitre the inland trails while the infantry led the advance on the right. Final arrangements were made on the 5th for

---
[3] Lt-Col R. B. Hone, ED, VX38996. CO 2/14 Fd Regt 1942-46 (CRA 5 Div Feb-May 1945). Manager; of Adelaide; b. Morphett Vale, SA, 3 Jul 1899.
[4] The 2/14th Field Regiment was the last fighting unit of the four infantry divisions of the AIF to go into action. It had been at Darwin while other parts of the 8th Division were in action in Malaya and the Indies, and thereafter it had suffered a degree of frustration comparable with that endured by certain units of the 1st Armoured Division.

linking the Americans and Australians. Major Watch of Ramsay's staff, with a section from the 30th Battalion, was to move to Saidor by barge, go to the American outpost at Yagomai, cross the Yaut River on the 10th, and meet the 30th Battalion advancing west. Communications between Watch's section and the forward elements of the 30th Battalion would be maintained by wireless or alternatively by Very lights. No. 4 Squadron would report the positions of the advancing Australians.

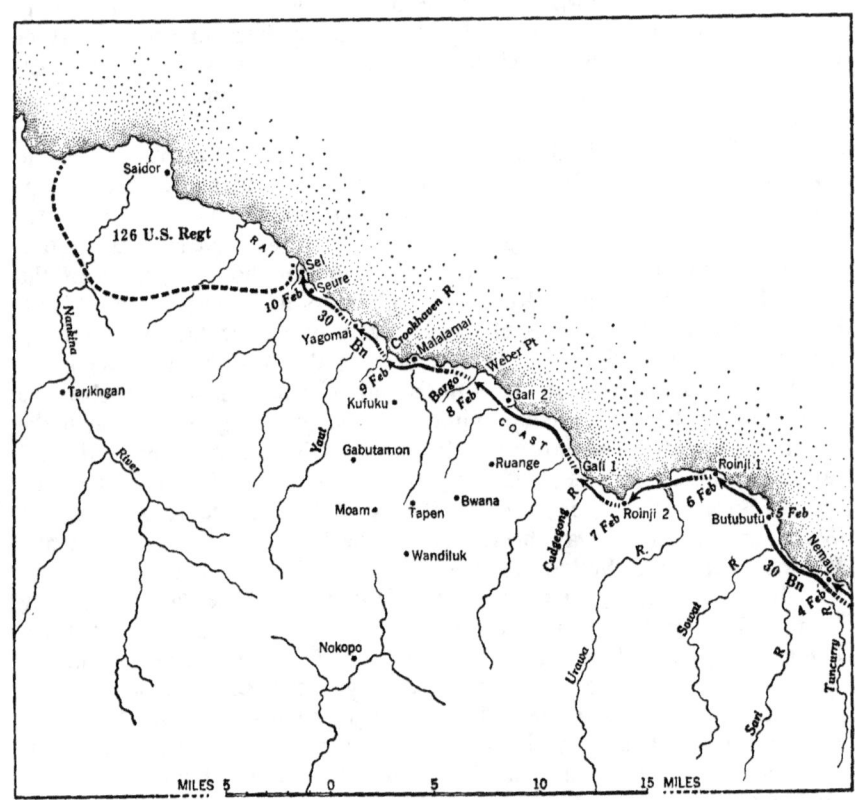

The 8th Brigade's advance to Saidor

The beginning of the next bound on 6th February was temporarily held up because of the difficulty of moving the artillery forward. Finally Ramsay agreed that the advance should continue without it, and the 30th Battalion marched along a very muddy track and reached Roinji 1. There was no contact with the fleeing enemy who were then estimated to be between 24 and 48 hours ahead. The pursuers began to catch up on the 7th when the 30th Battalion advanced to Roinji 2 along a track littered with 60 enemy dead. In the afternoon the Papuans, now carrying two days' rations, resumed the lead and reached Gali 1. Twenty-four Japanese were killed that day by the 30th Battalion and the Papuans, and three prisoners were taken.

Watch, on the 6th, signalled Ramsay about the locations of the forward American posts and also that an American patrol to Yagomai had captured two prisoners on the east bank of the Yaut River on that day. Late on the 7th he signalled that one of the prisoners taken on the Yaut River said that there were no Japanese between Gali and Yagomai.

On 8th February, the first opposition from the Japanese rearguard was met near Weber Point. For the first time in the advance therefore the leading platoon put on a formal attack, killing five Japanese and having two men wounded. During this day 53 Japanese were killed in a running fight and four were taken prisoner. By nightfall on the 9th the leading company was 2,000 yards west of Malalamai and 3,500 yards from the American outpost at Yagomai. Sixty-one Japanese were killed and 9 prisoners taken in the day.

At 10.30 a.m. on 10th February the leading platoon met the section from the 30th Battalion which had been sent into the Saidor area and which had been joined by two Americans at Yagomai. Soon after this junction Cameron and his brigade major, Gregory,[5] arrived at Yagomai by gunboat and awaited the arrival of the remainder of the 30th. By the end of the day one company of the 30th was at Seure with patrols already among the Americans in the Sel area.[6]

Cameron was now instructed to mop up Japanese forces south-east of the Yaut River. It was decided that the 5th Division would not operate west of the Yaut, which would be the boundary with the Saidor force, but would clear first the Tapen area and then the Nokopo area. The task of patrolling these areas was given to Lieut-Colonel Rae's[7] 35th Battalion which would be meeting the enemy for the first time. The country over which the 35th Battalion was to operate was extremely rugged and little was known of it. The battalion arrived in barges which back-loaded the 30th Battalion to Kelanoa. The advance began on the 14th when Captain Farmer's[8] company, accompanied by a section of Papuans, moved off from Gali 2 towards Ruange. It was deserted but patrols looking for water killed three Japanese, and between Bwana and Ruange next day the Papuans killed 31. A column under Major Delbridge[9] which set off on the 15th towards Kufuku found 11 dead Japanese and the Papuans killed 9. Next day Delbridge reached Kufuku, counting 30 dead on the way.

---

[5] Maj E. W. Gregory, NX112720. BM 8 Bde 1942-44. Chartered accountant; of Woolwich, NSW; b. Hunter's Hill, NSW, 28 Jan 1904.

[6] On 10th February an Angau officer and an officer from India had, with the aid of police boys, captured four Japanese in the area south of Sio. From these prisoners and from native sources it was estimated that there were about 100 Japanese living in various villages in the ranges south of Sio, about four days' march away for patrols. Natives were therefore sent out with pamphlets ordering the Japanese to surrender and it may be that some of the surrenders in the succeeding days were a result of these pamphlets. The surrender pamphlet said in Japanese: "Gentlemen. The Japanese forces in New Guinea have been defeated and have fled from this region. You cannot escape. If you surrender now these natives will lead you to us. When you surrender do not carry any arms. You will receive good treatment. You will be sent to Australia where you will be able to meet hundreds of your comrades."

[7] Lt-Col D. F. Rae, MC, NX116990. BM 8 Bde 1940-41; CO 35 Bn 1942-44. Woolbroker; of Pymble, NSW; b. Sydney, 21 Oct 1894.

[8] Capt F. C. S. Farmer, NX125301; 35 Bn. Asst foreman; of Petersham, NSW; b. St Gallen, Switzerland, 21 Aug 1918.

[9] Maj E. K. Delbridge, NX125284; 35 Bn. Woolbuyer; of Inverell, NSW; b. Inverell, 9 Mar 1910.

In this way the advance continued along both the main tracks. On the outskirts of Gabutamon, on the 18th, the leading platoon found that it was occupied and immediately attacked, killing 40 Japanese and finding at least as many dead in the village. Sneaking up to the outskirts of Tapen in the early afternoon of the 18th Farmer discovered that the enemy had a force of at least 100 there. He decided to gain full advantage of surprise and concentrated fire by sending in first those of his men who had automatic weapons, followed by riflemen, while the Papuans moved round the flanks to mop up in the gardens. With a savage burst of automatic fire the Australians charged Tapen. For the first time the 35th Battalion came under fire. One section was pinned down at first by this enemy fire but, for the loss of one man wounded, Farmer's men killed 52 Japanese. The Papuans on the flanks killed another 51 Japanese, Corporal Bengari and two other Papuans accounting for 43 of them. There were still Japanese round the Tapen area on the 19th when the Papuans killed 39 more, mainly escapers from the previous day's engagement.[1]

A patrol sent out from Gabutamon on the 20th to investigate the track towards Moam and Tapen, was often forced to crawl on hands and knees along the muddy, slippery tracks winding along the ridges. About 1,500 yards south of Gabutamon the patrol reached the bottom of a 100-foot chasm along which the track wound for a short distance before going straight up the slope. Broken rope ladders, swinging from the top of the cliff, showed how the Japanese had climbed out of the chasm—or tried to. In a macabre heap beneath the swaying ropes were the decomposing and smashed bodies of about 80 Japanese who had apparently been so weak that they could not haul themselves up.

By the 21st Farmer had a fair indication that Wandiluk would be occupied and was ordered to attack it. The track was now the worst encountered. The mud and water were frequently waist-deep, and the track was very narrow. Farmer considered that his estimate of 80 dead along the track was conservative. Most of these had probably died of sickness, exhaustion or starvation, but cold may have killed some for, in these mountains, the nights were intensely cold and there were heavy frosts. In Wandiluk 40 Japanese were killed, not counting 7 wounded who staggered away and jumped to their death into a steep gorge at the lower end of the village, and in the surrounding gardens 10 more were killed.

From the 22nd the pursuit was largely carried on by the Papuans. Other than patrolling by the Papuans farther south into the pitiless mountains towards Nokopo, the 8th Brigade had now really completed its task. From 20th January until the end of February, the brigade had killed 734 Japanese, had found 1,793 dead and taken 48 prisoners; the Australians and Papuans had lost 3 killed and 5 wounded. Such casualties, added to those inflicted on the *51st Division* in the Salamaua and Lae

---

[1] At Tapen, which was in a filthy condition, the Australians and Papuans found human flesh cooking in a billy. Two corpses had flesh cut from them. There was further evidence of cannibalism at Wandiluk.

campaigns and in its subsequent retreat over the mountains, and on the *20th Division* in the Huon Peninsula campaign, gave a fair indication of the plight of the *XVIII Japanese Army,* which now had only two unscathed regiments of its original nine.

In a letter to Blamey on 21st March Berryman wrote: "About 8,000 semi-starved, ill equipped and dispirited Japanese bypassed Saidor. It was disappointing that the fruits of victory were not fully reaped, and that once again the remnants of *51st Division* escaped our clutches." By 26th February American observers overlooking Tarikngan, south of Saidor, reported that they had counted 3,469 Japanese passing through there in small disorganised groups. The number which actually did pass through must have been far greater.

The chase was almost over when Berryman and Ramsay visited Cameron on 26th February. The 532nd E.B.S.R. was to concentrate in the Finschhafen area by 1st March for other operations with the Americans and only a few American barges would be available to the 8th Brigade thereafter. The plan was now to withdraw to the Kelanoa area in preparation for a move farther south to Kiligia, to concentrate the Papuans at Weber Point, and send forward a small patrol to Nokopo. The men of the 8th Brigade and the Papuan Battalion could not leave the wretched area quickly enough. At the beginning of March the brigade began to concentrate round Kiligia, and early in March the Papuans were withdrawn to a camp north of the Song River except for small detachments which patrolled the Rai Coast at intervals.

On 18th January Vasey had received a note from Morshead's headquarters in Port Moresby giving notice of the forthcoming relief of the 7th Division's headquarters by the 11th Division's. Vasey flew to Port Moresby on the 26th to discuss the relief. He had already decided to change over his two brigades and give the 15th the task of patrolling forward from Kankiryo Saddle, but sickness prevented him from supervising the change-over.

From the 9th to 21st February the relief took place. The 58th/59th Battalion relieved the 2/10th in the right-hand sector from 4100 through Crater Hill and Kankiryo Saddle to Cam's Hill, with the task of patrolling the area east of Cam's Hill, the headwaters of the Mosa River, and forward along the upper Mindjim River Valley to Paipa 2. The 57th/60th relieved the 2/9th on the left with positions on the 4100 Feature, the Protheros and Shaggy Ridge, and the task of patrolling forward from Canning's Saddle along the high ground west of the Mindjim. The 24th Battalion relieved the 2/12th in reserve.

The country facing the Australians beyond Kankiryo Saddle was formidable. The jagged Finisterre mountains tumbled away towards the sea, about 20 miles away as the crow flies but treble that distance as the soldier plods, and through the mountains the Japanese motor road was reported to follow the valley of the Mindjim down to the coast at Bogadjim. "The country in the Finisterre Ranges is rugged, steep, precipitous and covered with dense rain forest. It rains heavily almost every day thus making living conditions uncomfortable. By day it is hot, by night three blankets are necessary. There is, therefore, a constant battle with mud, slush, rain and cold. To allow freedom of movement over this mud it was necessary to corduroy every track in the area."[2] The actual Kankiryo Saddle was an ideal holding position as approaches from the north, east and west were precipitous. It formed a link between the high ground of Crater Hill and the 4100 Feature on the right or east, and the Protheros on the left or west; the whole massive feature was shaped like an H with Kankiryo Saddle the crosspiece.

On the right flank Lieutenant Brewster[3] with a small patrol from the 58th/59th investigated the valley of the Mosa River as far as Amuson, and returned after four days, on 20th February, to report the area clear. In the central area a patrol from the 57th/60th on the 23rd brushed with an enemy patrol near Saipa 2, which the guns of the 4th Field Regiment then bombarded. On the 28th a patrol from the 57th/60th, led by Lieutenant Besier,[4] attacked Saipa 2 three times with supporting artillery fire, but all attempts to enter the village were repulsed.

When there seemed to be no sign of movement on the right flank in the Kabenau Valley, Brigadier Hammer on 26th February instructed Major Newman, temporarily in command of the 58th/59th, to establish a company patrol base at Amuson and send out a "platoon recce patrol" to the coast in the Mindjim-Melamu area. Besides gathering information about the enemy and the country the patrol was to establish observation posts overlooking Astrolabe Bay; these would operate from a forward base at Nangapo. Captain Cuthbertson[5] was given the task of establishing these bases which he did early in March. Hammer also secured permission to send the whole of the 57th/60th into the Paipa area in preparation for an attack on Saipa 2.

While this was going on two battalions of the 32nd American Division from Saidor landed on 5th March at Yalau Plantation between Saidor and Bogadjim. It was a full-scale landing with 54 craft unloading 1,348 troops in the first nine waves, but there was very little opposition and the landing was made without incident. Patrolling east and west from Yalau the Americans killed a few Japanese and found many dead. By the 9th they reached the Bau Plantation where they brushed with a small party of Japanese. Attempts to cross the Kambara River during the next few days were unsuccessful because of the opposition of a band of about 40 Japanese. On the 11th Hammer was instructed to send a patrol to Yangalum four days later to join an American patrol believed to be moving forward from the Bau Plantation. To reach Yangalum the Americans would have to cross two large rivers, the Kambara and the Guabe.

---

[2] 15th Australian Infantry Brigade—Report on Operations in Ramu Valley, Mindjim Valley, Kabenau River, Bogadjim, Madang Area, 1 Jan 44 to 30 Apr 44.
[3] Capt D. J. Brewster, MC, NX113231. 3 and 58/59 Bns. Hardware merchant; of Bowral, NSW; b. Lithgow, NSW, 12 Oct 1916.
[4] Lt J. C. Besier, TX4719; 57/60 Bn. Clerk; of Hobart; b. Hobart, 12 Nov 1910.
[5] Capt C. C. Cuthbertson, VX102648; 58/59 Bn. Grazier; of Bylands, Vic; b. Elsternwick, Vic, 8 Jul 1914.

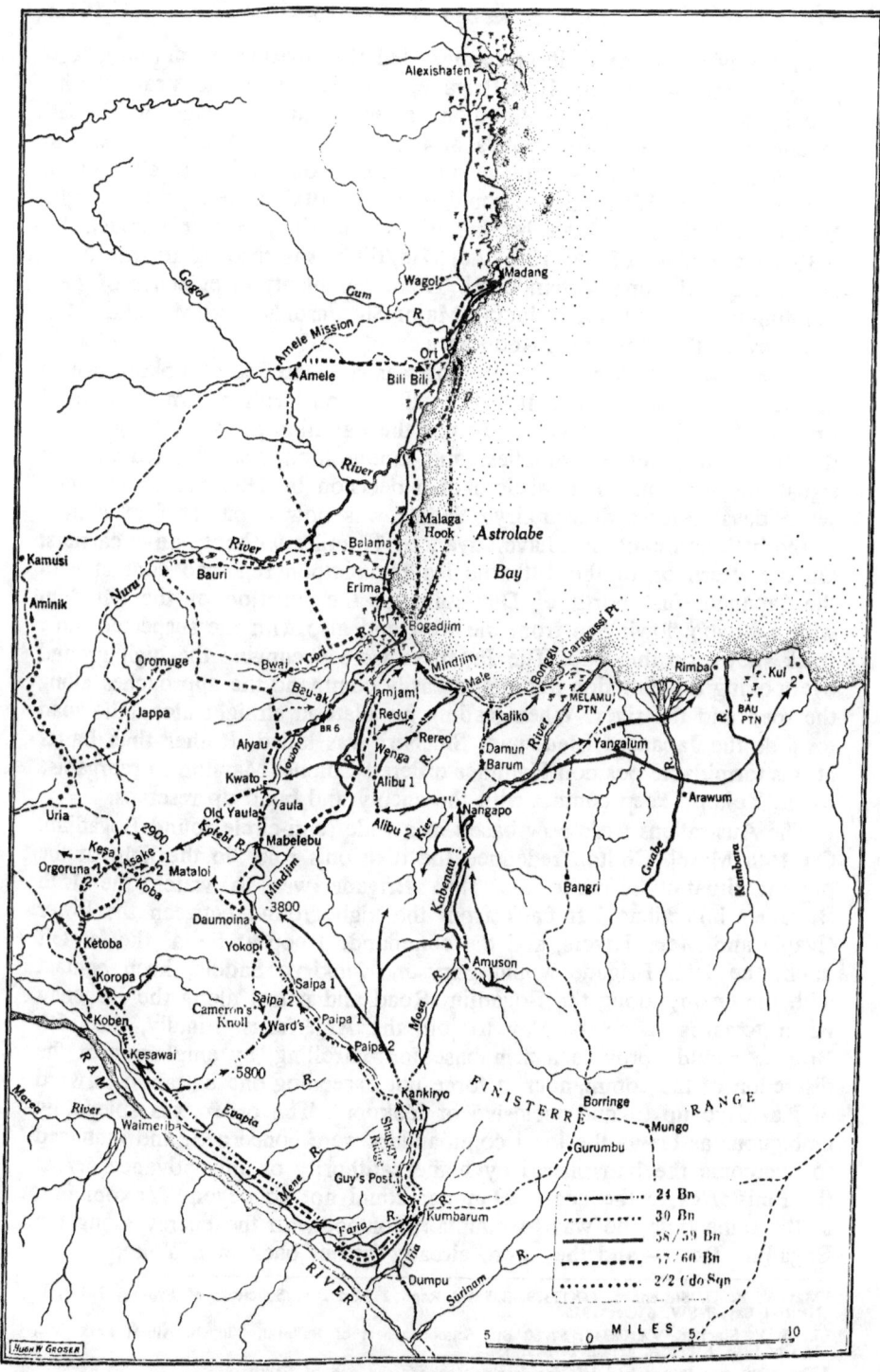

Across the Finisterres to Madang

In Vasey's absence Chilton commanded the division. Cummings, temporarily commanding the 18th Brigade, now determined to straighten his line by having the 2/12th Battalion capture Ward's Village on the left to coincide with the 57th/60th's attack on Saipa 2. When the 2/12th Battalion found Ward's Village unoccupied on 12th March Chilton decided that the 15th Brigade could move a battalion along the Mindjim Valley to Yokopi without becoming involved in a major conflict. By 9.30 on the night of the 12th the 57th/60th was moving forward, and next day found Saipa 2 abandoned. There was plenty of evidence of good shooting by the artillery, including Major Stevenson's[6] 2nd Mountain Battery, now in the Cameron's Knoll area.

By the 14th the 57th/60th Battalion was concentrated at Yokopi, where the Japanese road began. It was well formed, with a firm red-gravel surface. To achieve this swift advance the battalion moved by night and, during the day, stores, supplies, and ammunition were carried up and signal line was laid. The wisdom of a decision by Hammer to maintain seven days' reserve at Kankiryo Saddle was now apparent for, without it, the battalion could not have advanced 17 miles without native carriers. On the afternoon of the 14th the leading platoon regained contact with the Japanese just north of Daumoina at the junction of the Mindjim with a stream flowing in from the west and also with the suspected mule track shown on the map. The Japanese were occupying the high ground overlooking this junction and could easily command the approaches along the road and the river. When leading his platoon straight along the road towards the Japanese Lieutenant Sinclair[7] was killed. Rather than batter at this formidable position Hammer ordered Colonel Marston to reorganise round Yokopi, keep contact with the enemy and build up reserves.

The Australians were now based in a wide semi-circle round Bogadjim. On 16th March Chilton redefined the division's role "in the light of the present situation". While the 18th Brigade was to watch the 15th Brigade's immediate left flank from the high ground between the lower Evapia and Mene Rivers, and the commando troop at Faita[8] the far left flank, the 15th Brigade would garrison Kankiryo Saddle, keep contact with the enemy along the Bogadjim Road and patrol along the Kabenau River towards Astrolabe Bay to join the Americans. Finally, the 15th Brigade would "provide a firm base for patrolling, by employing at the discretion of the commander, a force not exceeding one battalion forward of Kankiryo up to and inclusive of Yokopi". The order was splendidly ambiguous as far as the local commanders were concerned, and managed to overcome the ban placed by higher authority on any advance across the Finisterres to the coast: Hammer could not go beyond Yokopi but, at the same time, he was to maintain contact with the enemy along the Bogadjim Road—and they were already farther back than Yokopi.

---

[6] Maj W. R. D. Stevenson, NX12379. 2/5 Fd Regt, 2 Mtn Bty. Solicitor; of Pymble, NSW; b. Neutral Bay, NSW, 6 Oct 1915.

[7] Lt S. V. Sinclair, VX108342; 57/60 Bn. Schoolteacher; of Ballarat, Vic; b. Albert Park, Vic, 14 Oct 1918. Killed in action 14 Mar 1944.

[8] The other two troops had left for Isariba towards the end of February.

The country between the leading company of the 57th/60th and the Japanese rearguard at the mule track junction was very rough and heavily timbered. About 170 of the 500 native carriers available had been allotted to the 58th/59th Battalion in the Nangapo area near the coast, and as the remainder were required to maintain the lines of communication to Kankiryo Saddle, it was necessary for the men of the 57th/60th, other than those in the leading company who were patrolling, to help the 24th Battalion to carry supplies forward. Hammer now decided that, before he could resume the advance, the supply route from the Saddle to the 57th/60th Battalion must be developed. Thus the sappers of the 15th Field Company were given the task of building Saipa, Yokopi and Daumoina into staging areas. They corduroyed the track forward from the Saddle to Saipa 2 and began another jeep track from Guy's Post to Mainstream designed to shorten the native carry to the Saddle and thus enable the natives to carry along the route twice daily instead of once.

For almost a fortnight the patrols of the 57th/60th made little impression on the Japanese rearguard. The 3800 Feature, which overlooked the Australian positions at Yokopi and Daumoina, seemed to be the main Japanese position and here they hung on. Hammer anticipated, however, that the constant patrolling and bombardment would have its effect, and, on the 27th, ordered the 57th/60th to patrol vigorously "as it is thought that the enemy has now withdrawn". He was right; when patrols reached the mule track junction on the 28th they found that the enemy had gone. It began to seem that the enemy might now be about to withdraw from the Finisterres after their long and determined stand. The two broken Japanese divisions were now no longer in immediate danger of being caught along the Rai Coast or trapped by an advance across the Finisterres.

Hammer now ordered Marston to clap on all possible speed and chase the enemy. He believed that the next line of resistance would be at Yaula and he wished to get there before the Japanese could dig in. The advance was resumed and by 4 p.m. on the 30th contact was regained when the leading troops came under fire from a bridge (No. 22) over the Kofebi and from points on the road where it wound steeply up from the river towards Yaula, four hours march away. Major Connell,[9] commanding the leading company, decided to cross the Kofebi, bypassing the next two bridges (Nos. 22 and 21A), attack the Japanese from the rear and then press on to Yaula. A small party under Lieutenant Maddison[1] was left to protect the native carriers. The bypassing was successful and Lieutenant Berman's[2] platoon continued towards Yaula while the remainder of the company proceeded to clear the road behind. At the nearest bridge (21A), however, these came under heavy fire and four men were hit. Maddison's group then came under fire from the Kofebi bridge and from a gun in

---

[9] Maj J. W. D. Connell, VX81067; 57/60 Bn. Architect; of Preston, Vic; b. Brunswick, Vic, 22 Oct 1913.

[1] Capt A. Maddison, VX101817; 57/60 Bn. Regular soldier; b. Seghill, Northumberland, England, 4 May 1911.

[2] Lt M. E. Berman, MC, NX76217; 57/60 Bn Regular soldier; of Fairfield, NSW; b. Aberdeen, Scotland, 30 Dec 1913.

Yaula, with the result that the carriers went bush. One gun of the 2nd Mountain Battery, which had been dragged forward to Daumoina, fired back into Yaula and Kwato. It was now dark. At 7.45 the line between company and battalion was cut. The Japanese, pinched between Connell and Maddison, began to make off to Yaula into which the solitary Australian mountain gun fired all night.

At dusk Berman's platoon had been within 600 yards of Yaula with Lieutenant Passlow's[3] 400 yards behind and the third platoon and company headquarters a corresponding distance farther back. After dark Berman's platoon was strongly counter-attacked. His communications severed, Berman nevertheless hung on although he knew nothing of what was happening in the rear. Passlow, however, moved his platoon up to within 200 yards of the forward platoon and himself crept forward to discuss the attack with Berman. While he was there another party of Japanese attacked his platoon. Throughout the night the Japanese continued their attacks but were driven back with probably about 40 casualties. With communications severed and with no rations, Berman and Passlow decided to withdraw intact to Mabelebu, which they did before the night was over. It later appeared that the Japanese had not planned a counter-attack but had merely been withdrawing from the flanks of the advance. Having reached the road where it was occupied by the two leading platoons, they had decided to fight their way out and had done so, with heavy casualties to themselves.

On 1st April the leading company took up a defensive position in the Mabelebu area. Marston, whose headquarters were also at Mabelebu, brought a second company forward. Patrols probed forward during the next few days.

Meanwhile patrols from the 2/2nd Commando Squadron had been harrying the Japanese from the left flank. Captain Nisbet led out the largest patrol (a troop plus a section) yet sent out by the squadron in over nine months of continuous patrolling. By 17th March a patrol base was established at Jappa, and next day about eight Japanese coming from the north-east towards Jappa walked into one of Nisbet's booby-traps and several were hit. On the 19th and again on the 22nd the patrol met opposition from enemy parties along the track towards Oromuge.[4] Farther west Lieutenant Doig's patrols from Faita were scouring the western area round Topopo and Aminik and skirmishing with enemy outposts. Lieutenant Adams' patrol through Kesa on the 22nd found the general Mataloi area abandoned, but discovered a strongly held position on the 2900 Feature behind Mataloi 1. After making half a dozen attempts in the next few days to get into this position the patrol withdrew. The enemy could be found nowhere else in this area. On 30th March 12 Bostons bombed and strafed the position and, after the raid, a patrol reported that Mataloi 1 was empty.

---

[3] Maj V. Passlow, MC, NX76326; 57/60 Bn. Mercer; of Wagga Wagga, NSW; b. Wagga Wagga, 11 Jan 1919.

[4] Corporal A. Stewart (of Manjimup, WA), an original member of the squadron, was killed during patrolling on the 19th.

The 2/2nd Squadron exploited this situation rapidly. The 57th/60th Battalion was on its way north, towards Yaula, when a squadron patrol led by Lieutenant Fox[5] set out north-east from Mataloi 1 towards the same objective. On the morning of 4th April, Fox's patrol entered Yaula, and soon the vanguard of the 57th/60th joined him.

Thus the evacuation of Yaula by the Japanese was hurried not only by the pressure of the 57th/60th Battalion along the main road, but by the patrolling of the 2/2nd Squadron on the left flank (the 2/6th had now left for home). Yaula was occupied by the 57th/60th and one company immediately took over the advance, reaching Kwato late that night.

Along the Bogadjim Road, which wound its way over the range, often forming a ledge with a drop of 300 feet or so on one side, were signs of a hasty Japanese withdrawal. Thirty-seven 3-ton trucks, one 10-horsepower sedan, 14 jungle carts, one rotary engine, one 75-mm mountain gun, 3 heavy machine-guns, 4 light machine-guns, 3 mortars, 3 flamethrowers and much miscellaneous engineer and ordnance stores were captured in the rapid advance of the battalion. The Yaula area had undoubtedly been an important Japanese stores depot for it was honeycombed with tracks showing evidence of heavy use. On the 5th the leading company reached Aiyau and patrols set out towards the Bogadjim Plantation.

On the right flank the 58th/59th in the valley of the Kabenau had been patrolling from Nangapo. Major Newman was now mainly interested in linking up with the American forces from Saidor who were presumably patrolling west towards the valley of the Kabenau. The rendezvous was fixed at Arawum but a patrol under Lieutenant Brewster waited there from the 16th to the 18th March without seeing any signs of the Americans. He was therefore ordered, two days later, to take sufficient rations and patrol from Yangalum to Kul 2 where the Americans were believed to be.

An accidental meeting had already taken place between the patrols of the two Allies. An American reconnaissance patrol was being towed in a rubber boat by a P.T. boat with the object of landing at Male and seeing if the Japanese were at Bogadjim. Off Garagassi Point the tow rope broke and the Americans rowed to shore in their rubber boat which they deflated and hid in the bush near Melamu. Moving inland for about a mile they turned west and nearing the Kaliko Track met Lieutenant Norrie's[6] patrol of the 58th/59th Battalion and accompanied the Australians to Barum, where the Americans were given supplies and a guide; moving via Wenga, they reached Jamjam on the 18th and found no signs of the enemy. On this day at noon about 30 Japanese with three machineguns and a mortar attacked Norrie's position at Barum. The situation would have been serious had it not been for Sergeant Matheson[7] and

---

[5] Capt J. Fox, SX25427. 2/2 Indep Coy, 2/2 Cdo Sqn. Regular soldier; of Mount Schank, SA; b. Mount Gambier, SA, 20 Nov 1912.

[6] Lt F. J. Norrie, MC, NX114337; 58/59 Bn. Retail store manager; of Cheltenham, NSW; b. Plymouth, England, 15 Nov 1912.

[7] Sgt J. A. Matheson, MM, VX140461; 58/59 Bn. Carpenter; of Trentham, Vic; b. Trentham, 28 Dec 1920.

his two men who had remained behind at Kaliko and managed to bear the first brunt of the attack and warn those at Barum. The Australians were forced to withdraw to a feature just north of Nangapo where natives came to them and told them that four of the attacking enemy had been killed and there were some stretcher cases. On the 19th Boomerangs strafed Barum and reported that it was empty, a fact which was confirmed at 2 p.m. by a small patrol from Nangapo.

The Americans moved on the 20th to Yangalum and next day set out for Kul 2, along almost exactly the same route as that taken by Brewster, who had departed on 20th March. Brewster reached Kul 2 on 21st March where he joined the Americans from Saidor and remained with them until the 26th. In this period he went to Saidor where he met Major-General William H. Gill, the commander of the 32nd American Division, gave him information about the area east of the Kabenau River and learnt of the American intentions and dispositions. Brewster then returned to Yangalum having carried out an important and lengthy linking patrol—35 miles each way.

As patrolling in the valley of the Kabenau forward from Nangapo was so strenuous, Lieutenant Fraser's[8] company took over from Cuthbertson's on 22nd March.

> Now began a game of hide and seek which lasted from 22 Mar until 11 Apr 44 (wrote Hammer in his report). It became apparent that the Jap force in the Melamu-Bonggu area was a flank protection to his main delaying force in the Mindjim Valley. Thus, when 58/59 Aust Inf Bn appeared in strength patrolling in that area, the Jap was not sure of our intention. He therefore patrolled vigorously and widely to discover our intentions. 58/59 Aust Inf Bn on the other hand avoided contact as their task was purely reconnaissance.

Several patrols just missed one another in the Wenga, Barum, Damun, Rereo and Redu areas. There were also several clashes. For instance, on 26th March, reports from local natives and police boys indicated that the Japanese were again approaching Barum, which had become the main trouble area, from the direction of Damun just to the north. Both sides engaged one another with fire, particularly mortar bombs, but the brush was a cursory one with neither side gaining any advantage. Exchange of fire and a few sporadic attacks by the Japanese continued for about five hours from 5 p.m. While Corporal Tremellen,[9] in the leading section, was moving among his weapon-pits, with a Bren gun in his left hand and two magazines in his right, he was attacked but, not being able to bring his Bren into action, he bashed the Japanese over the head with the Bren magazines. This Japanese thus had the distinction of probably being the only one to be killed by the Bren magazine rather than what was inside it.

For the remainder of the month Fraser patrolled towards the coast and the Mindjim Valley. In the Barum area there were almost daily skirmishes

---

[8] Capt R. J. W. Fraser, VX102652; 58/59 Bn. Clerk; of Seymour, Vic; b. Leongatha, Vic. 1 Jul 1910.

[9] Sgt H. A. Tremellen, MM, VX141681; 58/59 Bn. Share farmer; of Bunbartha, Vic; b. Shepparton, Vic, 18 Nov 1916.

but by the end of the month the Japanese withdrew north. On 1st April the luluai of Male sent a native to Barum to report that, in the valley of the Kier River, he had met a Japanese patrol which asked to be shown the track to Barum. The luluai had replied that the only track to Barum was from Kaliko on the coast. The Japanese had therefore returned north along the river. At 2 p.m. Lieutenant Forster[1] led out a patrol from Barum towards Kaliko but, three-quarters of an hour along the track, they ran into an ambush in which Forster and three men were killed, three were wounded and several weapons were lost.

Patrols by the 58th/59th Battalion on the right flank as well as the 2/2nd Commando Squadron on the left undoubtedly worried the enemy and helped to speed his withdrawal before the 57th/60th Battalion along the Bogadjim Road. By 4th April when Yaula was occupied the Australians were pointing like an arrow-head at Bogadjim; the point was the 57th/60th and the sides the 58th/59th Battalion and the 2/2nd Commando Squadron.

General Morshead had decided that it was time to rest the 7th Divisional Headquarters. Major-General A. J. Boase and his 11th Divisional Headquarters therefore on 8th April assumed responsibility for all units in the Ramu Valley and the Finisterres.[2]

Morshead was now sure that there was no need to maintain more than one brigade in the area, and suggested on 9th April that it would be possible to withdraw the 18th Brigade, yet not bring the 6th Brigade forward to relieve it as he had intended in February. On the same day he wrote to Brisbane seeking further definition of his responsibility in regard to the Bogadjim area. Blamey had already in February reminded Morshead that the 7th Division's tasks remained as defined in the New Guinea Force instruction of 3rd November 1943, and on 3rd April 1944 L.H.Q. had signalled that these "still appear applicable". In his letter on the 9th Morshead gave the present disposition of the two forward battalions of the 15th Brigade and continued:

GHQ Operational Instruction No. 46 of 28 Mar [for the Hollandia operation] . . . states New Guinea Force will "continue pressure against the Japanese in the Bogadjim area". G.H.Q. communiqué No. 723 of 2 Apr stated, "our ground forces advancing towards Bogadjim are nearing Yaula 11 miles to the south-west", and A.B.C. news reports (presumably emanating from and passed by G.H.Q.) indicate that the objective of Australian troops in the area is Bogadjim, though undue regard need not necessarily be given to these reports. But they do accord with the role specified in G.H.Q. Operation Instruction No. 46.

Morshead went on to say that it was planned to establish a strong base at Yaula and push forward from there. "Apart from tactical considerations," he wrote, "the breaking of contact would lower the present

---

[1] Lt J. Forster, VX101386; 58/59 Bn. Railway clerk; of Surrey Hills, Vic; b. Footscray, Vic, 11 Jan 1922. Killed in action 1 Apr 1944.

Boase, a regular, was now commanding in operations for the first time in this war. He had commanded the 16th Brigade in the last part of 1941 and the Australian force in Ceylon in 1942, and for a year until September 1943 had been senior staff officer of the First Army.

high morale of 11 Aust Div units and would deprive them of an opportunity to gain valuable experience in jungle warfare."

Blamey embarked for the United States and England with the Prime Minister on 5th April and did not return to Australia until 27th June. There is no record of any reply to Morshead's request for this redefinition. There was probably no need for one. The 15th Brigade was now close to Bogadjim. Indeed, there was a Nelson touch about the Australians' advance over the Finisterres, for it had been made despite orders that no such advance should be made.

While I Corps was at Atherton Lieut-General Herring had retired and, on 10th February, Major-General Savige had been appointed to command I Corps, Major-General Robertson succeeding him in command of the 3rd Division. When recommending Savige's appointment Blamey had written to the Minister for the Army:

> Two officers have been considered for this vacancy—Major-General S. G. Savige and Major-General G. A. Vasey. Both have been very successful in command in New Guinea operations, and I have some difficulty in determining the recommendations to be submitted, since each is capable and very worthy of advancement to higher responsibilities. Having regard to their respective careers, however, I recommend that Major-General S. G. Savige be appointed.

The significance of Blamey's final sentence is a matter for speculation. It could hardly refer to past careers since Vasey's experience in command was wider than that of Berryman, a contemporary who had recently become a corps commander, and no less than Savige's.[3]

The L.H.Q. signal of 3rd April warning of the changeover of corps headquarters was occasioned, as usual, by the Commander-in-Chief's desire to give as much experience as possible to all his main headquarters, and also to prevent any of them becoming stale because of too prolonged a spell in the tropics. In accordance with his directive of 23rd December 1943, moreover, I Corps was to consist of the A.I.F. divisions now in Australia, and II Corps of the 3rd, 5th, and 11th Divisions. Blamey decided that the personnel of I Corps should relieve that of II Corps. Thus Berryman and his staff returned to Atherton and Savige and his staff took over in New Guinea; but the corps at Atherton was still called I and the corps in New Guinea II.

There were other changes in the senior commands in the early months of 1944. From 1st March Lieut-General Lavarack became Head of the Military Mission at Washington and Lieut-General V. A. H. Sturdee, who had been in Washington since September 1942, replaced him as commander of the First Army. Lieut-General Bennett, commanding the dwindling III Corps in Western Australia, asked Blamey whether he was

---

[3] It was widely believed that Vasey declined the promotion, preferring to remain with his division in the field than to go to a corps in an inactive role. Blamey wrote later that this was not so, but that he had discussed the matter with Vasey who "expressed himself as perfectly contented with my decision". (Letter, Blamey to Forde, 28th February 1945.)
Vasey, however, expressed himself forcibly in a private letter on 3rd February when he wrote of the "wild scramble now to get into his [Herring's] boots. Presume I'm in the running. I can assure you I'm doing nothing to help myself in any way. I personally see no use for Corps Headquarters in our war here and when one gets to that giddy height you are too far removed from the troops. I would only object to not getting up if I were superseded."

(Australian War Memorial)

Brigadier C. E. Cameron (commander of the 8th Brigade), Lieut-General S. G. Savige (G.O.C. II Corps) and Major-General A. H. Ramsay (G.O.C. 5th Division) at Alexishafen, 5th May 1944.

(Australian War Memorial)

An aerial picture of Finschhafen Harbour, taken six months after its capture in October 1943. The harbour and airfield were rapidly developed, and Finschhafen became a major base for future operations.

(R.A.A.F.)

Hollandia, April 1944. Allied aircraft systematically attacked airfields at Hollandia before the invasion in April.

The Allied invasion convoy in Humboldt Bay, April 1944.

to be given a command in the field and, having been informed by Blamey that he would not, applied for return to civil life. The request was granted, and a few months later Bennett published a book about the campaign in Malaya.

A visitor to Port Moresby in April was Major-General Dewing of the United Kingdom Army liaison mission. He had just returned from a tour of certain areas in New Guinea believed to be suitable for training and acclimatising British divisions to jungle warfare.[4]

In addition the British Army in India was showing increased interest in learning from the experiences of the Australians. On 25th June 1944 General Auchinleck wrote to General Blamey thanking him for having the officers from India mentioned earlier and forecasting that

we shall soon be asking you for a large number of officers for duty with the Fourteenth Army and in India, if you can spare them. We need them badly— I believe the number is over 600.

As mentioned, a few Australian officers had been sent to India in 1943 to pass on the lessons of the experiences in New Guinea, among them being Brigadier Lloyd. Lieut-Colonel Ford,[5] a leading malariologist, went to India in June 1944, four engineer officers had gone in January 1944, one instructor for a jungle warfare school in April 1944. But it was not until October 1944 that a substantial group of regimental officers of the sort who should have gone early in 1943 arrived in India.[6]

The plan to send "a large number" of junior officers to the Fourteenth Army in Burma encountered a hitch when on 24th January 1944 Blamey found that his Staff Duties Branch had agreed that no guarantee would

---

[4] Plans for employing British troops in the Pacific after the defeat of Germany will be described in the next volume.
The United Kingdom liaison and other groups in Australia included (in July 1944): Lieut-General Lumsden, Mr Churchill's representative at GHQ; the U.K. Army Liaison Staff led by Major-General Dewing and including nine other officers; 17 officers of the Services Reconnaissance Department, the senior being Colonel J. Chapman-Walker; the Indian Ordnance Mission (three officers); the British members of the Joint Planning Staff (ten officers) not including 13 naval and 4 air force officers. In addition 25 other officers were serving with the Australian Army or attending Australian Army schools. Dewing and his staff had been in Australia since January 1943, Lumsden since November 1943. Looking at the other side of the ledger, in July 1944 there were 75 Australian Army officers serving in Britain and Europe, and 28 in other theatres.

[5] Col Sir Edward Ford, OBE, NX445. CO 1 Mobile Bacteriological Laboratory 1940-42; Asst Dir of Pathology I Corps 1942-43; Senior Malariologist LHQ 1943-44; Dir of Hygiene, Pathology and Entomology LHQ 1945. Professor of Preventive Medicine and Director, School of Public Health and Tropical Medicine, Sydney University since 1947; Director of Army Health since 1950. University lecturer; of Sydney; b. Bethanga, Vic, 15 Apr 1902.

[6] They were:
Armoured: Capt C. F. G. McKenzie, 2/2 Commando Sqn
　　　　　Maj K. F. Tye, 2/6 Armd Regt
Artillery: Maj M. P. O'Hare, 1 Aust Mtn Bty
　　　　　Capt N. Tinkler, 2/5 Fd Regt
Engineers: Maj S. B. Cann
Signals: Maj N. S. Smith
　　　　Capt N. C. McDonald
Infantry: Maj A. C. Robertson, 2/25 Bn
　　　　 Maj R. L. Johnson, 2/27 bn
　　　　 Maj A. L. Vincent, 2/1 MG Bn
　　　　 Maj C. W. Hyndman, 2/31 Bn
　　　　 Maj D. N. Fairbrother, 2/2 Bn
　　　　 Capt D. E. Williams, 2/3 Bn
　　　　 Capt P. Deschamps, 2/13 Bn
　　　　 Capt R. G. Jenkinson, 2/15 Bn
Intelligence: Capt K. Pilcher, 2/6 Armd Regt
AASC: Capt C. M. Macartney
AAMC: Maj D. W. Macpherson
AAOC: Maj W. M. Tolson
AEME: Maj C. M. Dimond

be given that an officer arriving in India would be accepted and that two Indian Army lieut-colonels were in Australia as a selection board. He wired Auchinleck that the proposal that Australian officers should be subject to selection by a non-Australian authority was "obnoxious and unacceptable" and the selection board could not function. Auchinleck agreed, employment of officers selected by an Australian board was guaranteed, and one Indian Army colonel was attached to the board as adviser. Before these officers, 168 in all, had been selected, Blamey received news that the army in Burma would welcome a far larger contingent. Air Vice-Marshal Cole[7] who was attached to the Air Command, South-East Asia, from the R.A.A.F., wrote that he had met the commander of the Fourteenth Army, General Slim,[8] who had said that he required urgently about 400 young Australian officers as company and platoon commanders. Also the head of the Airborne Operations Division had asked for trained airborne troops from Australia. Blamey replied that the number of officers already being sent to India had been fixed by the Government and was the ultimate that could be spared "having regard to our commitments and the manpower situation generally". As for the airborne troops, all Australian forces had been assigned to the South-West Pacific Area.

Meanwhile, in New Guinea, the 15th Brigade had been pressing on towards Bogadjim. Marston of the 57th/60th sent his leading company forward from Yaula on 4th April, and on the 6th contact was regained when the Japanese, entrenched near Bridge 6 on the Bogadjim Road, dispersed several Australian patrols. On 8th April—the day the 11th Division took command[9]—Marston ordered Major McCall, the leading company commander, to clear the enemy from Bridge 6 and occupy the high ground beyond at Bau-ak. About the same time Marston ordered deep patrols on the right flank into the Bogadjim Plantation and on the left to Bwai on the Gori River.

As Hammer was certain that the Japanese were on the run along the main Bogadjim Road, he found it difficult to understand why they were still maintaining a force of more than a company between the Mindjim and Kabenau Rivers. To be on the safe side therefore he ordered the 57th/60th and 58th/59th Battalions to "make contact" at Alibu 1 in order to guard against the unlikely threat of a Japanese thrust up the Mindjim while the main attack on Bridge 6 went in.

---

[7] AVM A. T. Cole, CBE, DSO, MC, DFC. (1916-18: 1 and 2 Sqns AFC.) Comd Southern and Central Areas 1939-41, 235 Wing RAF 1941-42; fwd air controller Dieppe Raid 1942; AOC RAF N Ireland 1942-43, North-western Area 1943-44. Regular air force officer; of Malvern, Vic; b. Glen Iris, Vic, 19 Jun 1895.

[8] Field Marshal Rt Hon Viscount Slim of Yarralumla, KG, GCB, GCMG, GCVO, GBE, DSO, MC. Comd 10 Indian Inf Bde 1939-41; GOC 10 Indian Div 1941-42; Comd XV Indian Corps 1942-43, Fourteenth Army 1943-45; C-in-C Allied Land Forces SE Asia 1945-46. Chief of Imperial General Staff 1948-52. Governor-General of Australia 1953-60. Regular soldier; b. Bristol, England, 6 Aug 1891.

[9] The war diarist of 15th Brigade noted: "In 13 months this brigade has changed command nine times. This constant chopping and changing makes continuity in administration difficult as the methods of the formation under whose command we are have to be adopted. It seems that as soon as we are settled in one system, we are moved to a new formation." Before this campaign finished the brigade was to have its tenth change, and in 1945 its eleventh.

On the 9th Lieutenant Brookes[1] returned from a five-day patrol down the Mindjim Valley through Jamjam into the Bogadjim Plantation. He had stayed there on the night of the 7th-8th April and found no signs of the Japanese. The Bogadjim natives, who were not particularly friendly, told Brookes that there were no Japanese in the general area. While at Bogadjim Brookes' patrol was fired on by what he was convinced was American artillery and strafed by an American aircraft.

The attack on the 10th on the enemy position at Bridge 6—two steep heavily-timbered spurs running down from each side of the Ioworo River and making a defile—was described by Hammer as "a textbook operation and in actual fact it developed perfectly". One platoon advanced down the road to "fix" the enemy positions while the remainder of the company encircled the enemy position to come in from the high ground to the north. In the first encounter the leading platoon lost two men killed and two wounded. While it engaged the enemy with fire the rest of the company with Lieutenant Jackson's[2] platoon in the lead clambered into position and, later in the day, clashed with the enemy in a garden

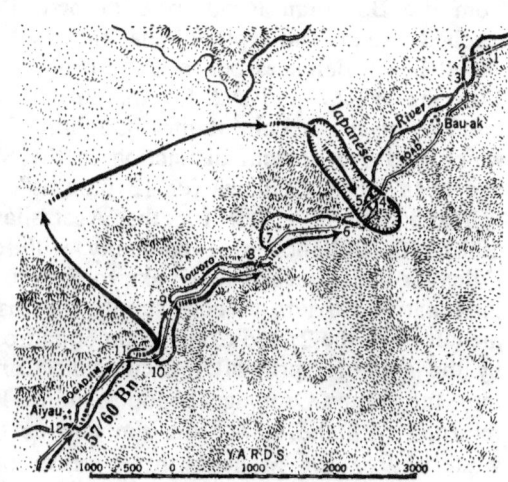

10th-11th April

area on one of the spurs. For a while the Japanese held on, but the pressure of the Australians and the accurate fire from Private Hillberg's[3] Bren in an exposed position in the enemy's rear forced them to withdraw. Towards dusk an Australian patrol moved down a track towards the road where a small Japanese band was found to be still resisting with machine-gun fire. The Australians did not attack for they were sure that the enemy would disappear during the night. As expected there were no signs of the Japanese next morning at Bridge 6—only bloody bandages and bloodstains on the tracks to remind the Australians of yesterday's fight. McCall occupied the area and sent patrols forward to Bau-ak, the last high ground overlooking Bogadjim.

On the 12th two patrols from the 57th/60th led by Captain Fox[4] and Lieutenant Atkinson[5] set out for the Erima and Bogadjim areas

---
[1] Capt J. D. Brookes, MC, VX81068; 57/60 Bn. Science student; of Woodend, Vic; b. Melbourne, 29 Jun 1921.
[2] Lt R. S. Jackson, MC, VX56025; 57/60 Bn. Clerk; of Corowa, NSW; b. Corowa, 12 May 1920.
[3] Pte M. Hillberg, MM, V190340; 57/60 Bn. Herd tester; of Poowong South, Vic; b. Melbourne, 15 Mar 1922.
[4] Capt R. E. Fox, VX81076; 57/60 Bn. Farmer; of Berrigan, NSW; b. Berrigan, 14 Jun 1918.
[5] Lt G. H. Atkinson, MC, VX81112; 57/60 Bn. Grazier; of Finley, NSW; b. Berrigan, NSW, 21 Dec 1914.

respectively. At 1 p.m. on the 13th Atkinson entered a deserted Bogadjim and reconnoitred the tracks on both sides of it to the Gori and Mindjim Rivers. There was much evidence that Bogadjim had been an important base, for many trucks, an engineer dump and a signals centre were found there. The Angau representative with Atkinson immediately set about his task of resuming relations with the local natives, many of whom were dressed in Japanese clothes. On the 15th an American patrol of six men from the east joined forces with Atkinson in Bogadjim.

From Bogadjim Marston's patrols then investigated the line of the Nuru River from Bauri east to Balama; and the three tracks leading north from the Bogadjim Road were probed. By the 15th Fox's patrol had reached Erima, and reported that there were about 1,000 yards of abandoned beach defences between there and the mouth of the Gori. On the 17th the B.B.C. and A.B.C. announced that "Bogadjim has been captured by an Australian infantry battalion of an Australian infantry brigade which had fought with distinction in the Salamaua campaign and which had been in New Guinea for 13 months".[6]

There was little left for the Australian flanking units to do. The 58th/59th Battalion was gradually withdrawn from the valley of the Kabenau and returned to Kankiryo Saddle by 28th April, thus releasing their native carriers to help supply the distant 57th/60th Battalion. On the left flank the 2/2nd Commando Squadron returned to the Kesawai area by the end of April, after Lieutenant Curran had led a ten-day patrol into the Jappa-Oromuge Topopo-Amimik-Kamusi area, from which he returned with the news from the natives that the Japanese had left the western area for Madang three weeks previously. During this period also the first battalion of the 18th Brigade—the 2/10th—was flown to Lae ready to return to Australia.

Far behind the spearhead of the 15th Brigade, and as though to emphasise the lost cause of the *XVIII Japanese Army,* there was a flurry northeast of Kaiapit. As a result of an Angau report that there were some enemy in the Wantoat area, a platoon from the 11th Division Carrier Company (which had relieved the 6th Machine Gun Battalion at Gusap), accompanied by the company commander, Major Armstrong,[7] was flown

---

[6] Acknowledgment of their deeds over the air or in the Press was always valued by Australian soldiers despite the fact that the deeds were often over-glamorised. In the case of the 15th Brigade, the headlines for their occupation of Bogadjim which had for so long seemed an invulnerable Japanese base, were doubly welcome. Two battalions of this brigade had seen much action in the Salamaua campaign and might have expected home leave after it; instead they and the third battalion had now completed another hard campaign. Rumours, particularly among reinforcements, to the effect that the brigade was being "punished" had been so rife that Hammer had written to Lieut-Colonel H. M. Hoare of the 1st Advanced Reinforcement Depot near Moresby on 25th March: "Recent reinforcements from the A.R.D. have brought with them some ridiculous rumours which, whilst being of no consequence in themselves, may possibly have a bad influence on the future of the Bde. The general terms of the rumours are that both 24 Aust Inf Bn and 58/59 Aust Inf Bn are serving long terms of field punishment for varying reasons, such as running away at Salamaua and refusing to go into action. Of course I realise that these rumours are just idle chatter, but I would appreciate it if you would pass on to your staff the record of service of the two units concerned, and if the staff there, on hearing these rumours, would tell the reinforcements the true facts." The record of service of the two units, as listed by Hammer, was impressive. The units had indeed had their teething troubles, but it is more likely that they were chosen for the task in the Finisterres because of their experience.

[7] Maj A. A. Armstrong, MC, VX111035. 11 Div Carrier Coy, 19 Bn. Grazier and company director; of Deniliquin, NSW; b. East Melbourne, 1 Jul 1906.

to Kaiapit on the 15th and ferried thence by Cub to Wantoat. Advancing along the Ikwap Track the platoon learnt that the Japanese were in Tabut. Surrounding the village the Australians attacked at dusk. Four Japanese were killed and two escaped. Next day one of the stragglers was speared by a native and on the 16th Armstrong led a patrol to the upper reaches of the Wantoat River where four Japanese were seen with about 20 natives, squatting in the river bed. Warrant-Officer Seale of Angau sent his police boys to mingle with these natives and at a pre-arranged signal the police boys grabbed the Japanese and overpowered them. Thus Armstrong returned with four times as many prisoners as the 7th Division had been able to capture in several months. Two of the prisoners were from the *20th Division's* engineers and two from the *238th Regiment*.

Other offensives were now imminent and for one of these the 32nd American Division at Saidor was required. On 13th April MacArthur's headquarters instructed that a brigade group of the 5th Australian Division would relieve the Americans at Saidor as soon as possible. General Ramsay then warned the 8th Brigade to prepare to move to Saidor whence it would maintain contact with the Japanese withdrawing to Hansa Bay and Wewak. The 15th Brigade would move across from the Ramu and come under Ramsay's command. On the 17th Savige was instructed that the 5th Division should occupy Madang but that the 15th Brigade should be used operationally only in an emergency. On the 22nd the headquarters of the 8th Brigade, portions of the 30th Battalion and "A" Company of the Papuan Battalion were flown to Saidor. Next day the 32nd American Division made available 12 L.C.M's which carried these 300-odd troops to Bogadjim. The remainder of the 30th Battalion and part of the 35th arrived at Saidor by air on the 23rd.

Although Madang might well be empty, like Salamaua and Lae before it, Hammer was anxious to get there first. While the order for the relief at Saidor and the subsequent advance to the west was passing down the line from MacArthur's G.H.Q., General Boase, Brigadier Hammer, Colonels Smith and Marston and Major Travers, with Lieutenant Leahy[8] as guide, were marching over the Finisterres to the north coast. When the party reached Bridge 6 on the 20th, Boase, who astonished the younger men by the fast pace he maintained, received a signal that the 5th Division would take charge of the Madang operations. The plan was that the 30th Battalion would occupy Madang. Hammer immediately secured Boase's permission to dispatch patrols to Amele and Madang. On the 21st Boase met Lieut-Colonel Kyngdon,[9] of Ramsay's staff, at Bogadjim and discussed Ramsay's tentative plan whereby the 15th Brigade would march over the Finisterres to the north coast. The administrative

---

[8] Capt J. L. Leahy, NGX308. NGVR and Angau. Goldminer; of Watut, NG; b. Toowoomba, Qld, 24 Jan 1909.

[9] Col C. W. T. Kyngdon, VX20318. AASC 7 Div 1940-41; GSO1 1 Armd Div 1942-43; AA & QMG 5 Div 1944; and various staff and training appointments. Regular soldier; of Melbourne; b. Bowral, NSW, 8 Mar 1910.

difficulties of such a move were pointed out and it was also suggested that it might be preferable to wait until the 57th/60th crossed the Gogol River and fully reconnoitred the area south of Madang for suitable areas where the 8th Brigade could land.

Already on the 20th the 57th/60th was probing north along the coast towards the Gogol River and north-west towards Amele Mission. Dumps of ammunition and all manner of stores and equipment were found in the swampy Bogadjim area and to the north. A patrol to Balama found 16 trucks damaged by air strafing, and on the 21st a patrol to Malaga Hook found six 6-wheeled vehicles. A patrol led by Captain Fox reached Amele without incident on the 24th and returned through Bili Bili on the coast.

Meanwhile a patrol led by Lieutenant Atkinson was instructed to find out if Madang and its airfield were occupied. With 13 men he boarded an American P.T. boat at 10.45 a.m. on the 22nd. There were several officers and batmen from various headquarters hoping to be there for the kill, and these accompanied the 14 Australians and 14 Americans to Malaga Hook where a landing was made soon after noon. Atkinson found the Gogol a major obstacle. He therefore signalled with a Very pistol to the boat standing off shore. After discussion it was decided that the Americans and a small party from the 8th Brigade which had moved along the coast would rejoin the boat, which would return at noon next day with crossing equipment.

As the boat did not arrive by noon on the 23rd, and as wireless communications had failed Atkinson led half his patrol south and met the signallers laying telephone line near Erima. Information was passed back to his headquarters and he returned to rendezvous with the boat. On the way back a despondent and sick straggler from the *79th Regiment* was captured. He also had been unable to cross the Gogol which he had reached five days before and was looking for food when he saw Atkinson's men. He said that his companions had left the area about a month ago. Returning to the Gogol Atkinson found that the other half of his patrol had unsuccessfully attempted to wade across the river. On returning to the south bank Sergeant Dick[1] shot two crocodiles between 12 and 15 feet long. The P.T. boat arrived at 5 p.m., landed a small party of Americans, took off the prisoner and gave Atkinson a message that over 100 troops would be landing at Bili Bili next day. A dinghy was left for the crossing of the Gogol, which was now urgent.

At dawn on the 24th the patrol tried to cross but the current was too strong. Twenty minutes later when two P.T. boats were seen near the mouth of the Gogol Atkinson sent out a message in the dinghy asking to be ferried to Bili Bili. By 8.45 a.m. his patrol was aboard. Just at this time four L.C.M's and a tender on the way north from Bogadjim passed the two boats. The L.C.M's contained Lieut-Colonel Parry-Okeden's headquarters and one company of the 30th Battalion, together with the brigade

---
[1] Lt L. S. Dick, MM, VX122339; 57/60 Bn. Motor driver; of Croxton, Vic; b. Heidelberg, Vic, 23 Mar 1917.

major, Nicholls,[2] who was to reconnoitre the Madang area for 8th Brigade headquarters. Atkinson's patrol was transferred to an L.C.M. and at 9.20 a.m. landed with the 30th Battalion at Ort just south of the Gum River.

Parry-Okeden had no objection to Atkinson attaching his patrol to the 30th Battalion. Indeed it was appropriate that representatives of both the brigades which had finally cleared the Japanese from the Huon Peninsula should be together for the last triumph. At 12.30 p.m. the junction of the Madang and Alexishafen Roads was reached. While a platoon from the 30th Battalion moved along the road towards the airfield a second platoon accompanied Atkinson in a cautious advance towards Madang. During the advance a mountain gun fired a dozen shells, and there was a sudden burst of machine-gun fire and a couple of grenade explosions from somewhere in the Wagol area. The machine-gun fire did not appear to be directed at the Australians and the shells from the gun landed out to sea. In all probability this was the final defiant gesture by the rearguard of the *XVIII Army* as it left its great base of Madang which had been in Japanese hands since 1942. As the Australians continued along the Madang Road they saw about ten figures at a distance of about 1,000 yards running north-west. After investigating all the side tracks the patrol from the 57th/60th Battalion and a platoon of the 30th entered a deserted Madang at 4.20 p.m. on 24th April. At 5.30 eight L.C.M's nosed into the harbour to land Brigadier Cameron and the vanguard of the 8th Brigade.

Madang had been heavily hit by Allied air attacks and possibly some demolitions had been carried out by the retreating Japanese. The airfield was cratered and temporarily unserviceable; the harbour was littered with wrecks, but although the two wharves were damaged they could be repaired and Liberty ships could enter the harbour.

The occupation of Madang rang down the curtain on the Huon Peninsula and Ramu Valley campaigns. Quickened planning for the future and further changes in command were pending, ready to meet the changed circumstances in which for six months only a small part of the Australian Army would be in contact with the enemy.

Before his journey to England General Blamey had already decided to return to the old organisation whereby New Guinea Force and Corps Headquarters in New Guinea were amalgamated. On 25th February he had written to Berryman:

> I have not been able to obtain a final decision in relation to commands, etc., necessitated by your campaign recently terminated, although the recommendations were made to the Government prior to the beginning of the campaign. This has been influenced to some extent by the pressure of politicians such as Foll, Page, and particularly Cameron.

He informed Morshead on 3rd March, however, that Morshead himself would return to the Second Army, personnel of New Guinea Force Head-

---
[2] Col N. A. M. Nicholls, NX334. 2/4 Pn, BM 8 Bde and staff and training appointments. Regular soldier; b. Wallaroo, SA, 12 Aug 1917.

quarters would be sent to other appointments, and II Corps Headquarters would become N.G.F. Headquarters. Thus, on 6th May Savige's II Corps Headquarters, which had moved from Finschhafen to Lae in preparation for the change, was designated "Headquarters, New Guinea Force" and he became responsible for all Australian activities in New Guinea. In July Morshead was transferred from Second Army to command of the A.I.F. Corps—actually a far more important task—and Berryman became "Chief of Staff, Advanced Land Headquarters".

The build up of the 5th Division (4th, 8th and 15th Brigades) in the Madang-Bogadjim area continued as fast as limited shipping and air facilities permitted. While the Papuans patrolled to the west from Madang, detachments from the 30th Battalion landed on small islands off the coast and two companies advanced towards Alexishafen. The enemy had sown many land mines, and before the Pioneers started delousing them the 30th Battalion lost 5 killed and 3 wounded from mine explosions. The battalion entered a deserted Alexishafen on 26th April. On the 27th Savige informed Ramsay that only one battalion would be needed at Saidor, and that apart from patrols no major units in the Alexishafen area would move north of the Murnass River. Ramsay was warned that his planning should take into account New Guinea Force's decision to establish a Base Sub-Area at Madang capable of meeting the requirements of a force of 35,000. Next day Ramsay issued orders that the 8th Brigade would be forward in the Alexishafen area, the 4th and 15th Brigades (less the 24th Battalion destined for Saidor) in reserve about Madang.

In March and April there had been sweeping changes in the organisation and policy of the Japanese forces along their southern front. The headquarters of the Japanese *Second Area Army* under General Korechika Anami had arrived in Davao, Mindanao, from Manchuria in late November 1943. Anami controlled Lieut-General Fusataro Teshima's newly-arrived *II Army* based at Manokwari and Lieut-General Kenzo Kitano's *XIX Army* based at Ambon. The *Second Area Army* was responsible for the area from 140 degrees east longitude west to Macassar Strait and south from 5 degrees north latitude. Thus Hollandia and Australian New Guinea remained the responsibility of General Imamura's *Eighth Area Army*. The Admiralties campaign (described in the next chapter) caused a sweeping change in command, for the *Eighth Area Army* and *XVII Army* were then cut off. On 14th March General Imamura was ordered to hold out as best he could, and the *XVIII Army* and *IV Air Army* were transferred to the *Second Area Army*, whose boundary was moved east to 147 degrees east longitude.

The Japanese forces facing the Allies in the South-West Pacific Area had been augmented in recent months. Thus in April Count Terauchi's *Southern Army Headquarters*, then in Manila, controlled the *Second Area Army* (150,000 men), the *XIV Army* in the Philippines (45,000 troops), the *XXXI Army* in the Pacific islands (50,000 troops), and the *14th Division* and other troops in the Palaus (30,000) now based on Menado. Under the *Second Area Army* were the *II Army* in western New Guinea and the Halmaheras (*32nd, 35th,* and *36th Divisions*, about 50,000 men), the *XIX Army* in the rest of the Netherlands East Indies (*5th, 46th, 48th Divisions*, about 50,000 men) and the *XVIII Army* (*20th, 41st, 51st Divisions*, 50,000 to 55,000 men). The isolated *Eighth Area Army* (140,000 including naval troops) was now directly under *Imperial General Headquarters* and controlled the *XVII Army* (*6th Division* and other troops) and the *17th* and *38th Divisions*.

At this time the *XVIII Army* was reorganising at Madang and beyond, and General Adachi was hoping to hold the area between Madang and Hansa Bay. He was ordered instead to pull back west as quickly as possible to Wewak, Aitape and Hollandia, which was to be developed into a major base. The withdrawal as far as Wewak was already under way in March when rearguard companies of the *78th* and *239th Regiments* were still delaying the American advance west from Saidor and the Australian advance north over the Finisterres. The general picture during March was that the *51st Division* was concentrating in the Wewak area, the *20th Division* in the Hansa Bay-Aitape area and the *41st Division* the Madang-Bogadjim area. The *41st Division* was deployed with the *237th Regiment* north from Madang, the *238th Regiment* between the Gum and Gogol Rivers and the *239th Regiment*, assisted by elements of the *78th*, responsible for the defence of the southern approaches.

As the Australians pressed closer to Bogadjim and Madang in April, the *XVIII Army* began a slow withdrawal. When, on 25th March, General Adachi received the orders to withdraw and concentrate at Hollandia, he instructed the *41st Division* to hold Madang by rearguard action until the end of April. At the same time he sent the main body of the division to Hansa Bay to relieve the *20th Division*, which would then move on to Wewak and Aitape, allowing the *51st* to advance to Hollandia in July or August.

The next chapter will explain how the 8th Australian Brigade, advancing from Madang to the Sepik, met only the stragglers of the trapped army. Even with better and more alert planning by Adachi's staff, however, it is doubtful whether the *XVIII Army* could have reached Hollandia before the invasion of that base. In April there were still 30,000 men east of the Sepik, and only 770 were being ferried across that river each day. The obstacles to its march were the marshes of the Ramu and Sepik River basins, the mud, the swarms of mosquitoes, the fast river currents and the attacks of Allied planes and naval craft.[3] At Lae and at Salamaua the elements had aided the Japanese retreat; thereafter they were pitiless.

---

[3] On 25th April General Katagiri, the commander of the *20th Division*, was killed when a landing barge in which he was travelling from Hansa Bay to Wewak was attacked by an American torpedo boat. He was succeeded by General Nakai.

CHAPTER 28

TO MOROTAI AND THE PALAUS

WHILE the Australian offensive was in progress the planning of future Allied operations in the Pacific had gone far ahead—as far as the Philippines and the Marianas. In August 1943 at Quebec Mr Churchill, President Roosevelt and their staffs had held their first conference since the one at Washington in May. The Chiefs of Staff arrived on the 12th, Churchill and Roosevelt on the 17th. On the 15th Marshal Badoglio, the Italian commander, opened negotiations to surrender and join the Allies; and recently the Russian Army had opened an offensive which was making spectacular progress. Once again the Pacific area was in the background of a conference at which crucial decisions were made about other theatres. The target date for the invasion of western Europe (1st May 1944) was confirmed; it was decided to establish an Allied South-East Asia Command with Lord Louis Mountbatten in command; certain specific operations in the Pacific in 1943-44 were approved in principle.

In the discussion of future operations in the Pacific the British representatives asked whether operations in New Guinea should not be curtailed and the main effort made in the Central Pacific. Admiral King would have preferred this, but the Americans presented a solid front and insisted on continuing a dual advance.[1]

Finally the conference approved the American program. In the Central Pacific this included the seizure of the Gilberts, the Marshalls, Ponape and Truk, and either the Palaus or Marianas or both. MacArthur's plans to take Rabaul were not approved. His task for the next 16 months was to gain control of the Bismarck Archipelago, neutralise Rabaul, capture Kavieng, the Admiralties and Wewak, and advance to the Vogelkop in a series of "step by step airborne-waterborne operations".

MacArthur was not happy about some aspects of the Quebec decisions. The failure to define any role for his forces after the Vogelkop had been reached would, he argued, have an adverse effect on his own staff and might lead to a let-down of the Australian war effort. General Marshall thereupon asked MacArthur to plan also for a move into the Philippines.

Consequently on 20th October MacArthur's staff produced a new outline plan RENO III. As before, the general object was to advance the bomber line northwards to the Philippines by the occupation of widely spaced bases along the north coast of New Guinea. In the first phase Hansa Bay would be occupied on 1st February, and then Kavieng (by South Pacific forces) and the Admiralty Islands (by South-West Pacific forces) on 1st March. These operations would provide air bases from which the neutralisation of Rabaul could be completed. In the second phase advances would be made along the New Guinea coast to the

---

[1] The discussions at Quebec and the subsequent planning are described in detail in L. Morton, *Strategy and Command: Turning the Tide, 1941-1943*, a volume in the official series *United States Army in World War II*.

Hollandia area and in the islands of the Arafura Sea south-west of New Guinea. The aim of the advance into the Arafura was to protect later movements to the Vogelkop Peninsula. By moving to Hollandia MacArthur would bypass the strong Japanese forces at Wewak but his own forces were to infiltrate eastward towards Wewak from Aitape. In the third phase MacArthur's forces would advance to Geelvink Bay and the Vogelkop, beginning on 15th August 1944. In the fourth phase airfield sites would be captured in the Halmaheras or Celebes. If necessary for flank protection Ambon to the south and the Palaus to the north would also be taken. These operations were to start on 1st December 1944. On 1st February 1945 the final phase, the invasion of Mindanao, would open.

A decision whether Admiral Nimitz's advance should turn northwards through the Marianas and Bonins towards Japan depended on two main considerations. One was that an operation against Truk seemed likely to precipitate a decisive fleet action and, from the middle of 1944 onwards, the Pacific Fleet was so strong that it would welcome such an action. It was decided that strong carrier attacks should be undertaken to test the strength of Truk, the final decision whether to attempt to capture it or not to depend on the result. The other consideration was how to employ the big B-29 bombers (Superfortresses) now being produced in large numbers. At first it had been planned to use B-29's to bomb Japan from airfields in China but General Arnold was not confident that the Chinese could hold these airfields. On the other hand, Saipan and Tinian in the Marianas were closer to Tokyo than were the airfields in China. Admiral King also favoured the plan to advance by way of the Marianas.

In November and December 1943 the British and American leaders and staffs met twice at Cairo, where the Combined Chiefs reaffirmed the principle established by the American Joint Chiefs that where conflicts of timing and requirements existed between the Central and South-West Pacific areas the claims of the Central Pacific should take precedence. This was the culmination of the discussion concerning the respective advantages of the South-West Pacific and the Central Pacific routes to Tokyo. The Joint Chiefs believed that the Central Pacific route was "strategically, logistically, and tactically better than the South-West Pacific route", but, as mentioned, decided that they should continue to advance along both axes. It would be wasteful to transfer all their forces to the Central route and the use of both routes would prevent the enemy from knowing where the next blow would fall. Thus, in the next phase, there would be a main offensive in the Central Pacific, carried out chiefly by the American Navy and Marines, and a secondary offensive in the South-West Pacific, carried out by Allied army forces with such naval support as was appropriate.

As an outcome of these deliberations and decisions Nimitz's staff on 13th January completed a new time-table. His forces would move into the eastern Marshalls about 31st January; the carrier attack on Truk would be made late in March; in May his forces would advance into the western Marshalls; and on 1st August would be ready either to invade

Truk or to bypass it and move directly to the Palaus. The first landings in the Marianas would take place about 1st November.

At the same time MacArthur's staff elaborated their plans. The operations against Manus in the Admiralties and Kavieng, hitherto scheduled for 1st March, were moved on to 1st April, partly as a result of the inability of the Pacific Fleet to provide support on the earlier date.

On 27th and 28th January officers of the South-West Pacific, the South Pacific and the Central Pacific Commands conferred at Pearl Harbour to coordinate details for the forthcoming operations. It was agreed that Truk could be bypassed, but that the Palaus should be taken by the Central Pacific forces to protect the right flank of the South-West Pacific advance along the New Guinea coast. Nimitz now put forward a revised time-table: the invasion of the eastern and central Marshalls on 1st February and the western Marshalls on 15th April; and if the proposed carrier attack on Truk drove the Japanese carrier fleet westward it might be possible to bypass Truk, take the Marianas about 15th June and invade the Palaus early in October.

The Japanese leaders had also made plans for the next phase in the Pacific. They decided to concentrate on a defensive front through Timor, the Aru Islands, the Wakde-Sarmi area 125 miles north-west of Hollandia, the Palaus and the Marianas. Thus not only the *Eighth Area Army* round Rabaul but the *XVIII Army* falling back on Wewak and the forces at the base at Hollandia were now forward of the main front. The Japanese plan was not, however, purely defensive. On 8th March orders were given that when the American Fleet entered the Philippine Sea the Japanese Fleet would attack and annihilate it. It had always been the Japanese leaders' intention to seek a decisive naval engagement. They had done so at Midway, but had not been able to make a second attempt sooner because of heavy losses of carrier-borne aircraft pilots there and in the Solomons. By April 1944, however, they would have a first-line strength of about 500 well-manned carrier aircraft.

Before the long-range Allied plans could be carried out, however, there was work to be done round New Guinea. With the Huon Peninsula firmly in Australian hands, the divisions of the *XVIII Army* in retreat towards Wewak, and an American air base established at Torokina on Bougainville, the time had come to complete the isolation of Rabaul. This was to be achieved in four moves: first, seizure of western New Britain thus gaining control of the straits between that island and the mainland of New Guinea; second, seizure of the Green Islands; third, seizure of the Admiralty Islands where naval and air bases would be established well to the rear of the *Eighth Area Army's* actual "front" which ran more or less from Wewak, through the Madang area and New Britain to Bougainville; fourth, seizure of Kavieng in New Ireland.

Since October a concentrated air offensive against Rabaul had been in progress. General MacArthur's plan was to occupy the western part of New Britain along a general line Gasmata-Talasea. Command of this operation was given to General Krueger of the Sixth American Army. While the New Britain operation was being planned a group of coast-watchers was at work in the Cape Orford area. These included Lieutenant

Wright[3] (R.A.N.V.R.), Captain P. E. Figgis and Lieutenant Williams.[4] In September, well in advance of the invasion, it was decided to establish a more elaborate organisation to give warning against possible air attacks from Rabaul: the Cape Orford post was to be retained and others set up near Gasmata and on Open Bay, on Wide Bay, and near Cape Hoskins. On 28th September 16 Europeans and 27 natives were landed by a submarine which was signalled in by Wright. Wright led the Cape Hoskins party, Captain J. J. Murphy the Gasmata party, and Captain Skinner[5] the one to Open Bay. Each had a line of native carriers. Murphy's party

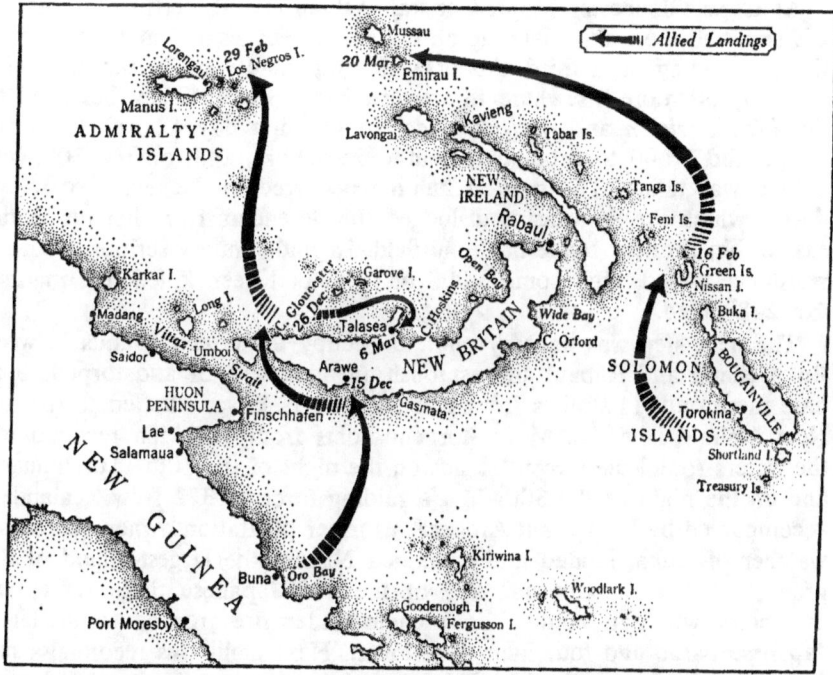

American operations in the South-West Pacific, December 1943-March 1944

met disaster. A native led a Japanese patrol to them and in the ensuing fight two Australians were killed and Murphy captured. The other parties reached their positions and reported air and barge movements during the subsequent operations.[6]

---

[3] Lt-Cdr M. H. Wright, DSC; RANVR. Coastwatcher, AIB. Patrol officer; of Toowoomba, Qld; b. Bendigo, Vic, 21 Dec 1913.

[4] Capt H. L. Williams, MC, VX62790. "Z" and "M" Special Units. Patrol officer; of Essendon, Vic; b. Melbourne, 24 Apr 1916.

[5] Maj R. I. Skinner, MC, VX48785. 2/4 Lt AA Regt, and "M" Special Unit. Patrol officer; of Grafton, NSW; b. Delungra, NSW, 7 Oct 1914.

[6] The experiences of these parties in this period and later are described in E. Feldt, *The Coast Watchers*, pp. 341-63. The American force landed at Arawe was accompanied by Lieutenant G. R. Archer, and the one at Cape Gloucester by Captain L. E. Ashton, both experienced coastwatchers.

After much discussion and some changes of plan MacArthur ordered, late in November, that a landing be made at Arawe on the south-west coast on 15th December and that the main attack, on Cape Gloucester, be made on the 26th. The Arawe landing was made by the 112th Cavalry Regiment (Colonel Alexander M. Miller). At a subsidiary landing place the Japanese were ready and opened fire on rubber boats carrying a covering party of 152 troopers, sinking 12 out of 15 boats and preventing any landing. The main landing, in amphibious tractors, was carried out in some confusion but the enemy were weak and the objectives were taken with few losses.

At Cape Gloucester Major-General William H. Rupertus' 1st Marine Division had the task of landing on two main beaches and making a diversionary landing on a third. About 1,000 Japanese were in the area with about 9,000 more elsewhere in western New Britain. They belonged to the *17th Division* and *65th Brigade.* In the first day 12,500 American troops and 7,600 tons of equipment were ashore, and, on the 30th, the airfield was taken. The hardest fighting occurred in the next two weeks during which the Americans dislodged the defenders from heights to the east within artillery range of the airfield. In mid-January serious Japanese resistance ended, after some 3,000 of them had been killed; the marines lost 248 killed.[7]

The next step was an easy one: to occupy the Green Islands between Buka Island and Rabaul and establish an advanced air and torpedo-boat base there only 117 miles from Rabaul. The task was allotted to the 3rd New Zealand Division. Motor torpedo-boats from Torokina reconnoitred the waters round the Green Islands on the night of the 10th-11th January, and on the night of the 30th-31st a raiding force of 322 New Zealanders accompanied by Lieutenant Archer,[8] a former plantation owner and coastwatcher of Buka, landed and examined Nissan, the largest island of the group, without encountering any of the 100 Japanese there, except at one point where a landing craft came under fire from a camouflaged Japanese barge and four men were killed. Next night this reconnaissance force was withdrawn. On 15th February Major-General Barrowclough with divisional troops and the 14th New Zealand Brigade landed on Nissan where they found no Japanese that day. On the third day a company group was landed on a near-by island, where natives reported that Japanese had taken refuge, and in a sharp engagement killed all 21 of them. The few Japanese on Nissan proper were found on the 20th and destroyed that day. The final clash took place on an adjoining island on

---

[7] S. E. Morison, the historian of the United States Navy, considers that the New Britain operations were in fact a waste of effort because the Japanese had nothing in western New Britain to prevent an advance to the Admiralties and Hollandia. No important base was developed on New Britain.

On the other hand, as we have seen, Blamey had urged in August that western New Britain be occupied before the advance to Madang on the ground that "the Land Forces might anticipate much more vigorous assistance from the Naval Forces if we control Vitiaz Strait from both sides", and events at Finschhafen in September justified his advice.

[8] Lt F. P. Archer, P514. (1st AIF: AFC 1917-19.) British Solomon Is Defence Force; Angau. Plantation owner; of Jame I, Buka Passage, TNG; b. East Melbourne, 17 Dec 1890.

the 23rd. When it was over 120 Japanese had been killed for a loss of 10 New Zealanders and three Americans.[9]

This was the last major task of the 3rd New Zealand Division, which had proved itself an excellently trained amphibious division. It was impossible for New Zealand, with a population of only 1,600,000, to maintain two divisions in action in addition to an air force which in December 1943 numbered 38,000. In 1944 the 3rd Division was disbanded, many of its members going to Italy to reinforce the 2nd New Zealand Division there.

A reconnaissance aircraft, after flying low over the Admiralties on 23rd February, reported that no signs of Japanese occupation could be seen, although the Intelligence estimate was that there were 4,600 Japanese in the group. This greatly interested General Kenney, who proposed to General MacArthur that he should make a reconnaissance in force as soon as possible. MacArthur agreed, and on the 24th instructed General Krueger to land a strong reconnaissance force of not more than about 1,000 men of the 1st Cavalry Division in the vicinity of Momote airstrip on Los Negros Island, not later than 29th February. The force was to be withdrawn if the resistance was too heavy.

On 27th February, two days before the proposed landing, Krueger sent six scouts on to Los Negros to test the accuracy of the air report. Early that morning they were landed in a rubber boat from a Catalina, and that afternoon sent out a message that the island was "lousy with Japs"; next day the party was taken off. Thus MacArthur's change of plan had been based on evidence that was slender at the outset (merely that no Japanese activity had been visible when aircraft flew overhead) and had now been proved to be inaccurate. However, the operation was not delayed.

Admiral Barbey of the Seventh Amphibious Force was in command of the landing operation. The naval attack group consisted of 8 destroyers and 3 A.P.D's carrying a force under Brigadier-General William C. Chase, about 1,000 strong including the 2nd Squadron of the 5th Cavalry Regiment, with artillery and other supporting detachments. The 1st Cavalry Division (Major-General Innis P. Swift), the only formation of its kind in the United States Army, was originally a Regular formation and, although in the rapid expansion of the army in 1941 it had taken in raw recruits until they totalled 70 per cent of its strength, it was probably the most capable division of the American Army which had yet been in action in the South-West Pacific.[1]

The attacking force arrived off Hyane Harbour before dawn on the 29th, escorted by cruisers and destroyers. There was little opposition on the beach. In fact the Japanese defences were pointing the wrong way,

---

[9] This operation is described in detail in O. A. Gillespie, *The Pacific*, pp. 168-88.

[1] In the American cavalry the terms "brigade", "regiment" and "squadron" were used in different senses to those employed in Australia. The 1st Cavalry Division included two brigades, each of two regiments, each of two squadrons, each of three troops. But the squadron normally had a strength of 20 officers and 465 men, and thus was comparable with an Australian cavalry regiment. In Australian terms the American division possessed eight dismounted cavalry regiments.

having been deployed to meet a landing in the spacious Seeadler Harbour on the west side of Los Negros. By 9.50 the cavalrymen had occupied an arc about 4,000 yards in extent enclosing Momote airstrip. At 2 p.m. MacArthur came ashore and ordered Chase to maintain his hold on the island. In the evening Chase decided to pull his troops back to a shorter line of about 1,500 yards enclosing the neck of the peninsula at the southern end of the harbour and there await the probable counter-attack.

A detachment of 25 Angau officers and men and 12 native police of the Royal Papuan Constabulary were with the attacking force. Of these the commanding officer, Major J. K. McCarthy, Lieutenant Hoggard,[2] Warrant-Officers A. L. Robinson and Booker[3] with four Papuan constables landed with the 2nd Squadron on the morning of the 29th. The task of the Angau party in the early stages

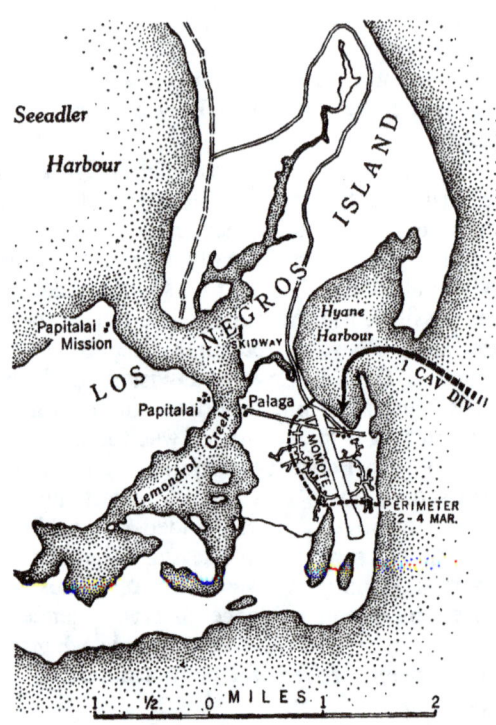

The attack on Los Negros, 29th February to 4th March

was to collect information and guide patrols, in the later stages to administer the natives. On the first day Booker, an outstanding scout, led a patrol including 10 American troops and one Papuan through the Japanese lines and penetrated a mile and a half to the south, finding dumps, trenches and pill-boxes, capturing many documents and destroying weapons. Robinson, in the first few days, patrolled through the enemy's lines with two men of the Royal Papuan Constabulary on four occasions and each time brought back valuable information.

Colonel Yoshio Ezaki, the Japanese commander, ordered his troops on Manus to annihilate the invaders. That night they made a poorly-coordinated attack, but infiltrated dangerously into the American lines. The attack was resumed next day, and on the night of the 1st-2nd March reached its greatest intensity, but heavy and steady American fire halted

---

[2] Capt I. Hoggard, N393286; Angau. Public servant; b. Wellington, NZ, 22 Sep 1906.
[3] Lt R. J. Booker, DCM, NX191699; Angau. Plantation manager; of East Melbourne; b. England, 6 Jul 1913.

the Japanese with calamitous losses. McCarthy counted 75 dead Japanese in a single revetment next morning, and considered that this night attack was "the last serious attempt by the enemy at organised resistance".

American reinforcements arrived on the 2nd, and by 4 p.m. were dug in on the western edge of the strip. Booker with one Papuan patrolled the Skidway, a narrow causeway leading north towards Seeadler Harbour, penetrated the enemy's lines and reached the Japanese beach-head at Salami Plantation on Seeadler Harbour.

The Japanese attacked on the night of the 2nd-3rd and again lost heavily. Next day the Americans again enlarged their perimeter a little and that night the Japanese attacked once more; a total of 750 of their dead had now been buried. The Japanese on Los Negros had exhausted their strength whereas the American force was regularly being reinforced. On the 6th the cavalrymen, following the route of Booker's patrol of the 2nd, reached the shores of Seeadler Harbour. Mopping-up continued. On the 7th a Mitchell bomber was landed on Momote strip, and on the 9th Wing Commander Steege[4] of No. 73 Wing R.A.A.F., with 12 Kittyhawks of No. 76 Squadron, landed on Momote; 12 more Kittyhawks landed next day.

The task remained of capturing the airstrip at Lorengau on Manus. It was decided to cover a landing there with guns sited on two islands off Lorengau, one of which—Hauwei—was occupied. There 26 men, including Warrant-Officer Robinson and a local native, landed from a barge but soon were under heavy fire. The landing craft was sunk while trying to re-embark the patrol, but the 18 survivors swam until they were picked up by a P.T. boat—except the native, Kiahu, who swam from island to island, and reached Seeadler Harbour that afternoon. Robinson swam for five hours supporting a wounded American before they were picked up. Next day a whole squadron landed covered by naval gunfire, field guns and Kittyhawks and captured Hauwei.

On 15th March the 8th Cavalry made a shore-to-shore landing near Lorengau. The cavalrymen pushed eastward slowly and secured the airstrip on the 17th and Lorengau village on the 18th. By the 16th some 900 Australians of the ground staff of No. 73 Wing and its attached units had landed at Momote and a well-provided forward air base in the Admiralties was in being. By 18th May 3,317 Japanese had been buried. The American force lost 330 killed and 1,189 wounded.[5]

---

[4] Gp Capt G. H. Steege, DSO, DFC, 213. 11 and 3 Sqns; Comd 450 Sqn 1941-42, 73 and 81 Wings 1943-44; SASO Eastern Area 1945. Comd 77 Sqn Korea 1951. Regular air force officer; of North Sydney; b. Chatswood, NSW, 31 Oct 1917.

After the operations in New Guinea, New Britain and the Admiralties the G.H.Q. Intelligence Section, headed by General Willoughby, MacArthur's devoted admirer, produced a summing-up. It is interesting as illustrating the satisfaction felt in Brisbane at the successful outcome, the atmosphere of flattery which surrounded MacArthur, and the tall talk indulged in at G.H.Q.

"Although the General's current consolidation of the Huon Gulf Army was momentarily exposed to air attack on both flanks, from Wewak and Rabaul, the subtle advantage of this position lay in its poised offer of opportunity for a classic operation on interior lines, laying open the strategically important Admiralties as the ultimate breakthrough objective. He drove between the two immediately opposing enemy masses at Finschhafen and on New Britain, which were geographically prevented from significantly reinforcing each other. Turning first to his left flank, he took Finschhafen by direct frontal amphibious assault and set jungle-wise Australian troops to rolling up the battered Jap *XVIII Army* elements along the coast northwest toward Saidor. That flank secured, the General immediately wheeled to

At the time of the attack on the Admiralties the plan was that on 1st April the South Pacific forces would attack Kavieng. Admiral Halsey, however, convinced that the effective air onslaughts on Rabaul had made the capture of Kavieng unnecessary, wished instead to take Emirau Island, conveniently situated between Kavieng and Manus.

The acceleration of the advances by both Nimitz's and MacArthur's forces made revision of the Joint Chiefs' directives urgently necessary. Early in February MacArthur had sent General Sutherland to Washington to advocate his plan to concentrate all Pacific forces along the New Guinea axis, bypassing both Truk and the Marianas. Later Nimitz and some of his staff arrived to discuss the future. Nimitz presented a revised schedule which provided for landings in the Marianas on 15th June, the capture on 15th July of Woleai in the Carolines (to protect his lines of communication), the seizure of the Palaus from 1st October, and of Ulithi Atoll (which he needed for a fleet base in substitution for Truk) as soon as possible thereafter.

Meanwhile Sutherland also presented a revised plan which provided that in the first phase Hansa Bay should be bypassed and two divisions supported by carriers of the Pacific Fleet should land in the Hollandia area on 15th April. Subsequent advances would be supported from Hollandia or from other air bases which MacArthur's forces would occupy as they moved forward. The Geelvink Bay area would be occupied on 1st June. In the second phase, beginning on 15th July, three divisions would seize the Arafura Sea islands whence air forces would cover the advances to the Vogelkop and Halmaheras and attack targets in the Indies. In the third phase operations against the Vogelkop and Halmaheras would open on 15th September. Mindanao would be invaded on 15th November and Luzon in March 1945. The joint planners at Washington disagreed in part with both Nimitz's and MacArthur's proposals.

At length, on 12th March, the Joint Chiefs issued a new directive.

Reaffirming their belief that Allied strength in the Pacific was sufficient to carry on two drives across the Pacific, the Joint Chiefs' directive was, in effect, a reconciliation among conflicting strategic and tactical concepts. The Joint Chiefs took into consideration the Army Air Forces' desire to begin B-29 operations against Japan from the Marianas as soon as possible; Admiral King's belief that the Marianas operation was a key undertaking which might well precipitate a fleet

---

the opposite shore of vital Vitiaz Strait and established beach-heads at Arawe and Cape Gloucester on New Britain. After further swift widening of the breach by amphibious envelopment of Talasea and Gasmata the approach to the Admiralties lay miraculously open, with a Japanese Army on each flank rendered powerless to hinder the projected breakthrough.

"In this context, 'miraculous' is a superficial word. To immobilize with a relatively small force the Japanese *Eighth Army* on the Rabaul flank represents a professional utilization not only of astute staff intelligence but of time and space factors cannily converted into tactical advantage. It was correctly anticipated that not only would the projected Arawe landing immobilize enemy New Britain reserves in fear of further coastal assaults threatening Rabaul, but that the bulk of enemy opposition to be met at Arawe would be reinforcements caught belatedly en route to Lae. . . . And through these seemingly scattered actions, there runs a red thread of design, the operative 'leitmotif', the flexible, inexorable advance on the Philippines—somewhere—somehow—some time!"—Quoted in C. A. Willoughby and J. Chamberlain, *MacArthur: 1941-1951*, pp. 139-40.

The summary is illustrated with a map comparing the New Guinea operations with Waterloo, with MacArthur in Napoleon's role, not the victor's, the implication evidently being that he had succeeded where Napoleon had failed.

showdown; the knowledge concerning the weakness of Truk gained during the February carrier attacks; the proposals offered by various planners concerning the feasibility of bypassing Truk; Admiral Nimitz's belief that the occupation of the Palaus and Ulithi was necessary to assure the neutralization of Truk and to provide the Pacific Fleet with a base in the western Pacific; and, finally, General MacArthur's plans to return to the Philippines as early as possible via the New Guinea-Mindanao axis of advance.

The Joint Chiefs instructed General MacArthur to cancel the Kavieng operation, to complete the neutralization of Rabaul and Kavieng with minimum forces, and to speed the development of an air and naval base in the Admiralties. The Southwest Pacific's forces were to jump from eastern New Guinea to Hollandia on 15 April, bypassing Wewak and Hansa Bay. The Joint Chiefs stated that the principal purpose of seizing Hollandia was to develop there an air center from which heavy bombers could start striking the Palaus and Japanese air bases in western New Guinea and Halmahera. After the occupation and development of the Hollandia area, General MacArthur was to conduct operations northwest along the northern New Guinea coast and "such other operations as may be feasible" with available forces in preparation for the invasion of the Palaus and Mindanao. The target date for the Southwest Pacific's landing in the Philippines was set for 15 November.[6]

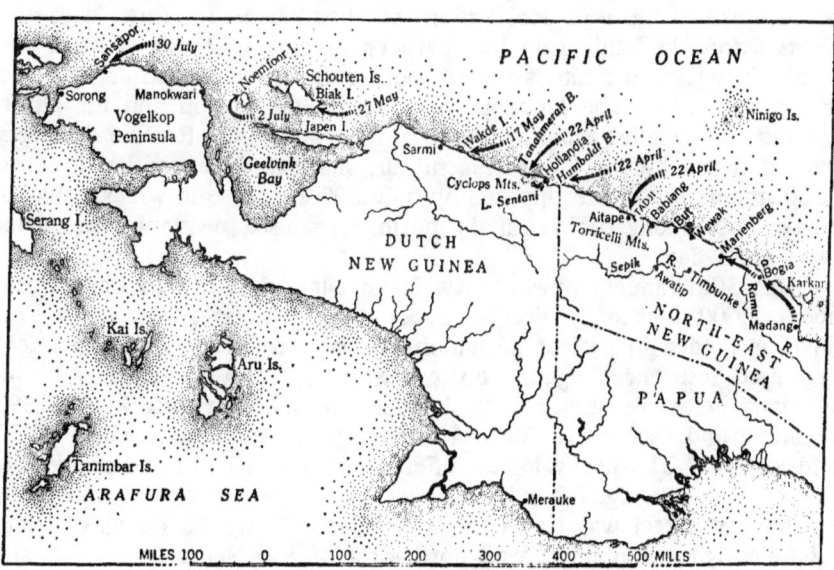

Operations along the north coast of New Guinea

Nimitz's forces would occupy the Marianas from 15th June (as he had proposed) and the Palaus from 15th September. The proposal to occupy Emirau was accepted in Washington and on 20th March four battleships, accompanied by two small aircraft carriers and fifteen destroyers, bombarded Kavieng as though in preparation for a landing, while the 4th Marine Regiment landed instead on Emirau, without opposition. Emirau was rapidly developed as a torpedo-boat base and airstrips were constructed.

---

[6] R. R. Smith, *The Approach to the Philippines* (1953), pp. 11-12, a volume in the official series *United States Army in World War II*.

Meanwhile the advance of Admiral Nimitz's Central Pacific forces into the Marshall Islands had begun. An immensely strong naval force was assembled to support the operations. It included three fast carrier groups each of three carriers and three battleships and 297 other warships and transports. The troops numbered 54,000 and included the 4th Marine Division and 7th (Army) Division. The plan was to occupy first an undefended atoll, Majuro, to provide an anchorage for supply vessels, and next day to attack the big Kwajalein Atoll; Eniwetok was to be attacked soon afterwards; other defended atolls in the Marshalls were to be bypassed. Kwajalein is an elongated coral atoll enclosing an area of 839 square miles, but only three islands or pairs of islands in the long chain were big enough to house a large military base. The plan was simultaneously to attack two of these—Roi-Namur in the north (with the 4th Marine) and Kwajalein in the south (with the 7th). About 3,700 Japanese defended Roi-Namur, about 4,500 Kwajalein Island.

Majuro was occupied on 31st January—the first Japanese territory to be occupied in the war. Roi-Namur was bombarded for three days and nights before the landing on 1st February, about 6,000 tons of shells and bombs being thrown into an area about a mile and a quarter long and half a mile wide. The landing ships entered the lagoon and the attack was launched against the inner shore of Roi-Namur. On Roi the defenders seemed dazed by the bombardment; the marines were on the objective in 20 minutes and were opposed by only 300 Japanese in wrecked blockhouses and among rubble on the north. Organised resistance ceased on the second day.

From 30th January onwards Kwajalein Island was heavily bombarded, about 5,600 tons of projectiles being used. On 1st February the 7th Division landed in perfect formation and secured the beach-head before organised resistance began. This was strong, however, and it was 4th February before resistance was subdued. This southern force killed 4,398 Japanese and lost 177 of its own men; the northern force killed 3,472 and lost 195. The heavy losses suffered at Tarawa had been avoided by intense and prolonged bombardment.

The next target was Eniwetok, a circular atoll with a radius of about 12 miles lying 326 miles west-north-west of Roi-Namur. On 16th and 17th February the Americans occupied several islets on the north side of the ring of coral islands and on the 19th a regiment of the 27th Division was launched against Eniwetok Island proper. There were some 800 Japanese there, but they had concealed themselves and it was not until the last moment that the attackers knew that Eniwetok was defended, and consequently the preliminary bombardment had not been heavy. The infantrymen got ashore successfully but made slow progress and a battalion of marines was sent in. Such intimate cooperation between American marines and army units was difficult because of their different tactical doctrines, and the situation on Eniwetok caused the historian of the United States Navy to offer the following comment, specially interesting from an Australian point of view because Australian troops had found that their doctrines differed from those of the American Army in very much the same way.

> The marines consider that an objective should be overrun as quickly as possible; they follow up their assault troops with mop-up squads which take care of any individuals or strong points.[7]

Resistance ended on Eniwetok on the 21st. Then the 22nd Marine Regiment landed on Parry Island, which was garrisoned by about 1,300 Japanese. Parry had been subjected to a thorough bombardment, and after a day of bitter fighting the Japanese resistance ceased. In the whole Eniwetok operation the Americans lost 195 killed and 2,677 Japanese died; only 64 became prisoners.

Thus by the end of March the Japanese armies in New Britain and the Solomons had been isolated, the American Central Pacific forces from the east had established themselves on Japanese island territory at Kwajalein and Eniwetok, and in New Guinea the *XVIII Japanese Army* was in retreat to Wewak. Nearly all the six Japanese divisions deployed on the South-West Pacific front had suffered heavily and were now practically cut off from any supplies except what submarines might bring them. Meanwhile, however, between December 1943 and April 1944 the Japanese had brought fresh troops forward to the new defensive line mentioned earlier: in the Carolines and Marianas the *XXXI Army* now included the *14th, 29th, 43rd* and *52nd Divisions*; in western New Guinea, as mentioned, the *II Army* had the *32nd, 35th* and *36th Divisions*. In the whole area east of Java there had been, in November 1943, nine Japanese divisions (and other smaller formations). There were now 17, five of the new divisions having been drawn from Manchuria and North China and three from Japan.[8]

The isolated Japanese forces to the south did not intend, however, to remain inactive if they could avoid it. As mentioned earlier, within the 14-mile perimeter round Torokina on Bougainville was General Griswold's XIV Corps (37th and Americal Divisions). Outside it was a Japanese force of some 45,000 troops and 20,000 naval men. General Hyakutake of the *XVII Army* decided to drive the Americans into the sea. The offensive was launched on 9th March by 15,000 men supported by 10,000 employed in rear echelons, and particularly in carrying supplies. It made little progress, and later attacks from 12th to 24th March met no better success. The American force lost 263 killed and the Japanese perhaps 7,000-8,000. It was a severe defeat, but nevertheless the Japanese force continued to detain an American corps of two divisions defending the Torokina perimeter, not counting a third division garrisoning the outlying islands.

The next Allied step—the seizure of Aitape and Hollandia—would be the most ambitious amphibious operation yet undertaken in the South-West Pacific. Not only was the force to be employed—some 80,000 men

---

[7] S. E. Morison, *Aleutians, Gilberts and Marshalls, June 1942-April 1944*, p. 298.

[8] At this time in the area from Java westward there were: 6 Japanese divisions in Burma, 2 in Sumatra and one in Malaya. There was one in the Philippines and one in Thailand.

including two divisions—the largest yet carried forward in an assault phase, but the objective was 425 miles beyond the forward positions, round Bogadjim, and part of the force was embarked 1,000 miles from the objective. In one move a longer advance would be achieved than that which had been made on the New Guinea mainland in the previous 18 months of foot-slogging and coastwise movements.

In the Hollandia area MacArthur's first objective was Humboldt Bay, the only first-class harbour on the north coast. Above it the Cyclops Mountains rose steeply, and, six miles west of the bay and near the foot of the range, lay Lake Sentani, about 15 miles in length, near which the Japanese had made three airfields. A track led to this area from Tanahmerah Bay 25 miles west of Humboldt Bay.

Since the supporting aircraft carriers could remain for only a limited time and Hollandia was 500 miles from the nearest big air base, at Gusap, it was decided to capture a Japanese airfield at Tadji near Aitape, 125 miles to the east in Australian New Guinea. Possession of Aitape should also enable the invading force to prevent the Japanese *XVIII Army* at Wewak from moving westward. MacArthur decided, therefore, to land forces at Tanahmerah and Humboldt Bays and Aitape simultaneously on 22nd April.[9]

The advance into Dutch New Guinea would carry MacArthur's forces into country less developed than Australian New Guinea and less well known by Europeans. In the Australian territories before the war there were some 6,200 Europeans (hundreds of whom were now in Angau, the "cloak and dagger" forces, and the native battalions) and about 50,000 indentured labourers were employed; in Dutch New Guinea the European population was only about 200 in approximately the same area. Dutch New Guinea, the Dutch administrative officers used to say, was "a colony of a colony", and its great natural resources had hardly begun to be exploited. It would be difficult to find Netherlanders with knowledge of the areas now to be attacked.

Hollandia was in territory known to few Australians, but it was decided that a party of veteran Australian scouts should reconnoitre the area. Captain G. C. Harris, who had served behind the Japanese lines for about a year on the Rai Coast and in New Britain and had reconnoitred Finschhafen before the invasion, was chosen as leader. There were six Australians, four New Guinea soldiers and an Indonesian interpreter. They were to be landed at Tanahmerah Bay by submarine, make a deep patrol and be picked up again by submarine 14 days later. An American submarine landed the party on the night of 23rd March.

---

[9] Except where otherwise noted these brief accounts of American operations in 1944 are based on R. R. Smith, *The Approach to the Philippines*; S. E. Morison, *New Guinea and the Marianas, March 1944-August 1944* (English edition, 1953), a volume in the series *History of United States Naval Operations in World War II*; notes on amphibious operations, written at the time by Brigadier R. N. L. Hopkins, who was detached from Australian headquarters to report on these operations; the following volumes prepared by the Historical Section of the United States Marine Corps: J. N. Rentz, *Bougainville and the Northern Solomons* (1948), F. O. Hough and J. A. Crown, *The Campaign on New Britain* (1952), C. W. Hoffman, *The Seizure of Tinian* (1951), F. O. Hough, *The Assault on Peleliu* (1950); and American divisional histories.

The rubber boat carrying a reconnaissance party of five was swamped and their walkie-talkie was ruined. They found they had come ashore near a native hut whose four occupants seemed untrustworthy. Harris flashed a signal to the submarine not to send the remaining men ashore, but it was misunderstood, and they landed, their boats being overturned as the other had been. In the morning Harris' party set off inland. It was learnt later that the natives informed the Japanese as soon as they left the beach. Next morning a strong party of Japanese armed with machine-guns and mortars caught up with them. The Japanese opened fire and the Australians fired back. Harris who was wounded waved to Able Seaman McNicol[1] to escape to the south. At length all the Australian party had withdrawn except Harris and Privates Bunning[2] and Shortis[3] who kept up an accurate fire against the Japanese and drew the whole enemy force to them. "The three kept up the action for four hours, until Bunning and Shortis lay dead and Harris, alone, wounded in three places, faced the enemy with an empty pistol. Then they rushed him."[4] The Japanese propped Harris against a tree and questioned him. He was silent. At length they bayoneted him. The Indonesian escaped, was helped by a friendly native and remained in the area until American troops landed. Lieutenant Webber[5] and Private Jeune[6] walked east and south for five days then decided to remain where they were and try to survive until the landing. After three weeks with very little food they heard the bombardment and began to make their way to the beach. The two men, almost too weak to walk, encountered a Japanese whom they killed in a hand-to-hand struggle. That afternoon they limped on until they met some American soldiers. McNicol and a native sergeant, Mas, lived in the bush for 32 days, almost starving, until the landing. The sergeant was too weak to move. The emaciated McNicol reached the Americans but a patrol sent out to rescue Mas could not find him. Sergeants Yali and Buka set out to walk east to join the nearest friendly troops. As far as they knew these were at Saidor, 400 miles away. Buka became too ill to walk and Yali, having left him while he reconnoitred, and having met Japanese troops and run some distance to escape from them, could not find him again, though he searched for two days. At length Yali reached Aitape, 120 miles from his starting point. Eight months later the last of the five survivors, Private Mariba, who had been captured, escaped and made his way to Allied lines.

---

[1] AB J. B. McNicol, DSM; RANVR. Coastwatcher, AIB. Plantation manager; of Brina Plantation, New Britain, TNG; b. Rabaul, TNG, 22 May 1907.
[2] Pte J. I. Bunning, VX105183; "M" Special Unit. Shipping clerk; of North Brighton, Vic; b. Brixton, England, 27 Aug 1911. Killed in action 25 Mar 1944.
[3] Pte G. Shortis, NX69784. 1 and 2/3 Indep Coys, "M" Special Unit. Clerical officer; of Dulwich Hill, NSW; b. Marrickville, NSW, 29 Jan 1917. Killed in action 25 Mar 1944.
[4] Feldt, p. 369. All these details are from Feldt's account, which is based partly on captured Japanese reports.
[5] Lt R. B. Webber, NX69755. 1 Indep Coy, 2/10 Cdo Sqn, "M" Special Unit. Woolbuyer; of Cremorne, NSW; b. Sydney, 18 Aug 1915.
[6] Cpl P. C. Jeune, NGX255. NGVR, 2/8 Indep Coy, "M" Special Unit. Alluvial miner; of Morobe, NG; b. Gisborne, NZ, 31 Mar 1901.

The landing at Aitape was made on 22nd April by the 163rd Regimental Combat Team, which had fought at Sanananda in 1943. The Japanese strength, estimated to be 2,000 was in fact about 1,000, of whom only 240 were fighting men, and there was little opposition. The Americans lost only 2 killed and 13 wounded. Within 48 hours No. 62 Works Wing, R.A.A.F., had the Tadji airfield ready for the Kittyhawks of No. 78 Wing R.A.A.F. On 23rd April the 127th Regiment (of the 32nd Division) landed, and during May the remainder of the division arrived, relieving the 163rd Regiment for another task.

The Hollandia operation was commanded by General Eichelberger of I American Corps, which included the 24th Division and the 41st, less one regiment. The Japanese strength was estimated at from 9,000 to 12,000. The 24th Division landed at two points in Tanahmerah Bay on the 22nd and immediately the lack of knowledge of Dutch New Guinea became evident. The main landing beach proved to be skirted by impassable swamps, the secondary one to be fringed by coral which made it impossible to beach the craft except at high tide. Troops were transferred from the main to the secondary beach; fortunately the landings were not opposed; and by nightfall patrols had been eight miles inland. Next day Eichelberger and Barbey decided to transfer the main effort to Humboldt Bay.

There on the 22nd the 41st Division had landed on two beaches. The defenders fled and by 26th April the airfields had been occupied. The subsequent mopping-up lasted until 6th June. To that time the Hollandia operation had cost the Americans 159 killed; some 3,300 Japanese were killed and 611 surrendered—a surprising happening never repeated on the same scale in 1944, and probably due to the fact that the 11,000 Japanese in the area were practically all base troops. Indeed, General Adachi had expected the attacks to fall at Hansa Bay and Wewak, and, when the landings took place, the *41st Japanese Division* was round Madang, facing the 5th Australian Division, and the *20th* and *51st* moving towards Wewak and But, one regiment of the *20th* being under orders to move to Aitape. Thus in a few days at a cost of 161 Allied troops killed the *XVIII Japanese Army* was isolated and the main Japanese base east of the Vogelkop occupied. It was a classic illustration of the advantages of possessing command of the sea, and the air above it.

The Hollandia area was swiftly converted into an immense military and air base.

> Road construction had proceeded simultaneously [with building runways], and this was a gigantic task. Sides of mountains were carved away, bridges and culverts were thrown across rivers and creeks, gravel and stone "fill" was poured into sago swamps to make highways as tall as Mississippi levees. . . . Hollandia became one of the great bases of the war. In the deep waters of Humboldt Bay a complete fleet could lie at anchor. Tremendous docks were constructed, and 135 miles of pipeline were led over the hills to feed gasoline to the airfields. Where once I had seen only a few native villages and an expanse of primeval forest, a city of 140,000 men took occupancy.[7]

---

[7] R. L. Eichelberger, *Our Jungle Road to Tokyo* (1950), pp. 113-14.

On 10th April MacArthur had issued a warning order for the capture of the airfields on Wakde, a small island off the New Guinea coast about 120 miles west of Hollandia, and near Sarmi on the mainland to the west. The area was defended by the *36th Japanese Division*, less one regiment which was on Biak Island, and a force of about two battalions advancing east against Hollandia.[8] The American forces were again directed by General Krueger, who allotted the task to the 41st Division.

Wakde itself, an island only 3,000 yards by 1,200, was garrisoned by a reinforced company of infantry about 280 strong, 150 naval men and about 350 other troops. On 17th May, as a preliminary move, a regiment landed on the mainland with no opposition; and a force landed on a very small unoccupied island near Wakde whence mortars and machine-guns fired on Wakde itself. After an intense bombardment from land, sea and air, a battalion was landed and after three days of severe fighting in which 40 Americans and 759 Japanese were killed the island was handed over to the air force.

Krueger now set about clearing the Japanese from the Sarmi area. This led to a long and bitter struggle. In the second week of June the 6th American Division was brought in and by 25th June the Japanese force had been defeated and dispersed, having lost about 3,800 killed in the Wakde-Sarmi area; about 400 Americans were killed in the whole operation.

Biak, the next objective, 315 miles west of Hollandia, is a coral-fringed island consisting mainly of tangled, jungle-clad hills but possessing in the south-west a narrow coastal plain large enough to house several airstrips. Allied Intelligence estimated the garrison at some 2,000; actually there were about 11,000 Japanese on the island. Against this force was to be launched the 41st Division (less one regiment), which was to land on 27th May east of the airstrip area on a narrow coral shore dominated by a high cliff. The craft drifted westward and reached the shore, which was veiled by haze from the bombardment, 3,000 yards west of the intended places, but the landing was virtually unopposed and by nightfall the beach-head seemed secure. On the 28th and 29th, however, the Japanese attacked, and cut the road behind the 162nd Regiment which was advancing along the coastal shelf to the airstrips and hemmed it in. It was re-embarked and brought back to the beach-head. The third regiment of the division arrived on 31st May. The division advanced slowly westward and on the 7th June captured the easternmost airstrip, but it was still under fire from Japanese in the hills.

Progress was very slow and on 13th June a regiment of the 24th Division from Hollandia was ordered to Biak. It was a hard task to clear the Japanese from deep caves above the airfields, a strongly-defended pocket to the east, and from the jungle-clad northern part of the island,

---

[8] The *II Japanese Army* which now lay ahead of the advancing Allied forces in Dutch New Guinea had suffered very severely as a result of American submarine attacks before the land battle was joined. Four transports in a convoy carrying the *32nd* and *35th Divisions* were sunk and about five battalions of infantry were almost wiped out.

and it was 22nd July before it could be said that effective Japanese resistance had ceased. About 400 Americans and 6,000 Japanese were killed.

While the long struggle for Biak continued the next task on the timetable—the capture of Noemfoor Island, midway between Biak and Manokwari, headquarters of the *II Army*—was carried out. Noemfoor contained airfields from which fighters could patrol the Vogelkop Peninsula and also was a base from which Japanese barges might run to Biak. The island was believed to be garrisoned by about 3,000 troops, the main fighting unit being a battalion of the *35th Division*; there were in fact fewer than 2,000 Japanese but about 1,000 Formosan and Javanese labourers.

Krueger allotted Noemfoor to the 158th Regimental Group, reinforced for this operation to a strength of 8,000. The landing on 2nd July was unopposed and, by the end of the first day there, had met no organised resistance. On the early morning of the 6th, however, the Japanese made a desperate counter-attack in which they lost 200 killed; mopping-up was virtually complete on 31st August. The Americans had lost 70 killed, the Japanese about 1,900.

The 6th American Division landed in the Sansapor area on the Vogelkop west of Manokwari on 30th July. There was no opposition. The *II Japanese Army Headquarters* had moved to the narrow neck of the Vogelkop and most of the *35th Division* to Sorong.

Meanwhile, 730 miles to the rear, the isolated but resolute *XVIII Japanese Army* had made a determined counter-attack, just as the *XVII Army* had done on Bougainville. In May the 32nd American Division had been concentrated at Aitape where it formed a perimeter about 9 miles wide by two deep round the Tadji airfield. Patrols moved east as far as Babiang, 25 miles from Aitape, and in that area from 7th May onwards there were clashes with strong parties of Japanese. The divisional commander, Major-General Gill, decided to maintain a forward position on the Dandriwad River, but the Japanese pressed on and forced a withdrawal to the Driniumor, about 12 miles from the perimeter.[9]

Radio messages intercepted in June suggested that the *XVIII Japanese Army* would attack the Aitape perimeter in the first ten days of July using 20,000 men and with 11,000 in reserve. Thereupon the 112th Cavalry Regiment was sent to Aitape and XI American Corps headquarters (Major-General Charles P. Hall) took command. The 43rd Division and the 124th Regiment were also ordered to Aitape to help meet the coming attack.

---

[9] Two parties of Australians of Angau moved into the Torricelli Mountains south of Aitape to discover whether Japanese forces from Wewak were trying to bypass Aitape along the inland route, and two parties from the Allied Intelligence Bureau moved into the Sepik River area to learn whether the Japanese were using it as an escape route.

On 31st March Lieutenant G. A. V. Stanley, who had been in the Sepik Valley from March to October 1943 with Corporal J. M. Conboy and 50 natives, was flown in to the Sepik about 200 miles by air from the mouth. There the party established an Intelligence network.

On 20th May 1944 Lieutenant B. W. G. Hall and two others were landed at Timbunke; and, a week later, Captain H. A. J. Fryer with 8 Australians and 25 natives, was landed on a lagoon near Awatip, 20 miles west of Hall. Natives told them there were Japanese posts up and down stream and a canoe mail service. Fryer intercepted the latest mail and sent it out to be translated, then travelled to the head of the Screw River. The parties continued to operate during the period with which this volume deals.

By 10th July the Japanese had three regiments on the Driniumor and early next morning they attacked and broke through the American line. The defenders withdrew about four miles. Counter-attacks carried the Americans forward again to the Driniumor, and by 18th July they held the river line from Afua to the coast. By the end of July the Japanese pressure was easing. The enemy troops were ill-fed and many were sick. Nevertheless General Adachi decided to make one more attack. This was repulsed and almost simultaneously the Americans attacked and were soon thrusting the *XVIII Army* eastward to the Dandriwad where a Japanese rearguard halted them. The defenders had lost 450 killed and estimated that 8,800 Japanese had been killed from 22nd April to 25th August.[1]

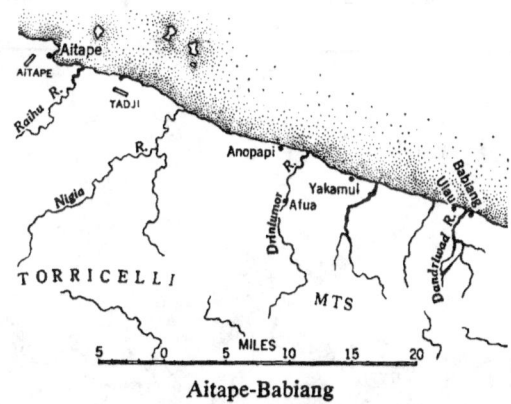

Aitape-Babiang

In this period there had been little contact between the *XVIII Army* and the Australians to the east. In the early days of May the 5th Division carried out only local patrols from Madang and Alexishafen. All trails leading into the two towns were patrolled and a few Japanese were mopped up. When General Savige issued his first instruction as G.O.C. New Guinea Force on 8th May he reiterated the tasks already given to General Ramsay, but there was a more positive call to action in one sentence which said, "Maintain pressure on the enemy northward of Alexishafen by patrol activity." Savige suggested that an infantry company with a Papuan platoon should move to Mugil Harbour whence patrols could operate and where a base could perhaps be established for a battalion and a Papuan company which could be "used for patrols into the back country". Any movement would, of course, be limited by the ability of the company of the Engineer Special Brigade to support it and that company also had to carry out maintenance of the Madang-Alexishafen area.

The 35th Battalion moved to Megiar Harbour on 10th May and gradually the patrols stretched out along the coast. Ahead of their advance H.M.A.S. *Stawell* bombarded Karkar and Manam Islands on 12th May, drawing light fire from Manam. Four days later an Australian frigate accompanied by two corvettes shelled Hansa Bay, Bogia and Uligan Harbour.

---

[1] The losses suffered by each side in the advance of the 6th Australian Division from Aitape to Wewak in 1945 were somewhat similar to these. The Australians lost 451 killed and the Japanese 7,200.

At the beginning of June the 35th Battalion reached Kronprinz Harbour without opposition. Patrols reached Suara Bay five miles west from Dugumur Bay on 9th June. Here the 35th Battalion was relieved by the 4th, which resumed the advance towards Hansa Bay accompanied by the Papuan troops. Patrols reached Bogia on 13th June and were told by a solitary Chinese that the Japanese had departed before the end of

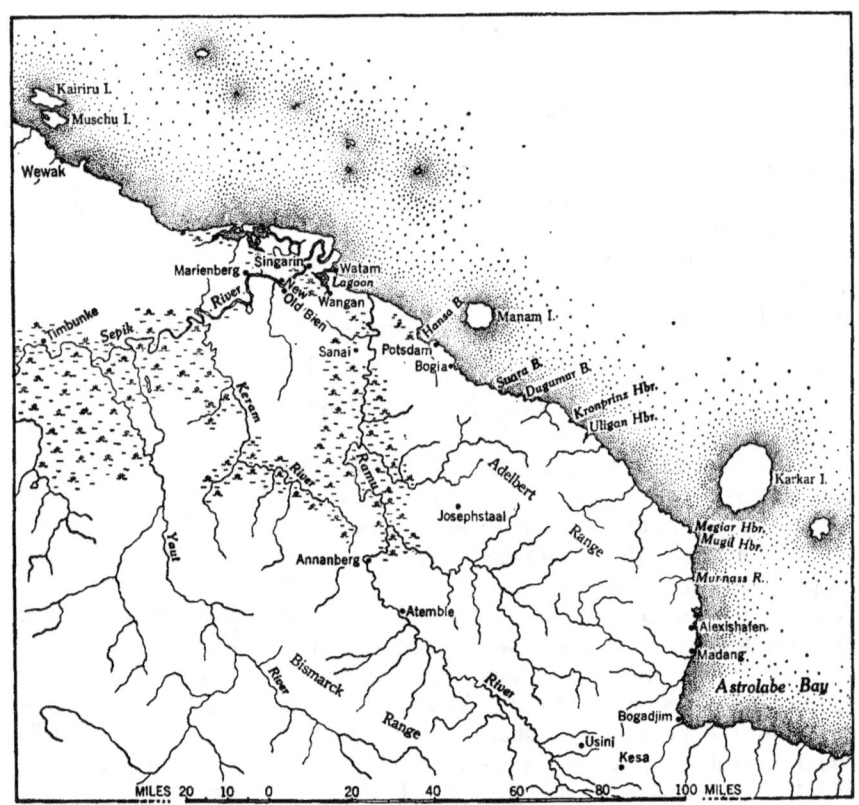

Madang-Wewak

April. By the 14th patrols passed through Potsdam, deserted except for about 90 emaciated Chinese, and during the next few days the 4th Battalion explored a deserted Hansa Bay, reaching the northern tip of the harbour on 17th June. The Australians learnt from the Chinese that there were no Japanese anywhere in the area and that the withdrawal of thousands of them had taken place by day and night weeks ago.

Meanwhile, on 19th May, an American fighter pilot, flying low over the area between the Sepik and Ramu Rivers searching for a pilot who had crashed, saw a party of dark-skinned troops in green who tried to attract his attention. On 1st June Lieutenant Barnes, an American pilot flying a Cub, flew low over a village west of the Ramu and saw three soldiers about 4 miles north-east of the village. They had a ground signal displayed and a message suspended between two poles. The Cub picked up the message and from it Barnes learnt that the troops below were Sikhs of the Indian Army who had been captured at Singapore, and who had escaped on 6th May during the Japanese withdrawal from Hansa Bay to Wewak. A subadar-major of the 1/14th Punjab Regiment was in charge. His message gave a detailed map and full report of the Japanese evacuation routes. After reading the message Barnes dropped instructions to guide the Indians to the emergency strip he had used to rescue the American pilot mentioned above. In the afternoon he returned from Saidor and dropped rations and medical stores to the Indians.

The Indians were apparently in very poor health, and a medical sergeant, Gregory[2] of the 24th Battalion, volunteered to land at Sanai by parachute so that he could attend to the Indians until arrangements could be made for their rescue. He left Saidor on 4th June and was landed by Staff-Sergeant J. L. Henkle on the emergency strip. Gregory found the Indians—now 29 in number—after two days' searching and led them back to the strip where a Flying Fortress from Nadzab guided by Barnes had dropped three tons of rations, clothing, equipment, arms, ammunition and medical stores. The Indians were in a pitiable condition, suffering from malaria, dysentery and starvation, and Gregory, assisted by Henkle, did his best to nurse them back to health. By 17th June all had been evacuated to Dugumur Bay whence some were flown to Saidor and some sent by barge to Madang.

The Indians brought with them first-hand knowledge of the plight and intentions of the *XVIII Army*. They themselves had escaped from a party of 547 Indian prisoners who left Hansa Bay for Wewak on 21st April as part of the general retreat. The Japanese had begun to evacuate Hansa Bay in March and had finished in May. The evacuation was at the rate of about 1,000 a day. Only one in ten was armed and the remainder carried packs and rice only. Hundreds were said to have died between Hansa Bay and the Sepik. The Japanese went by foot to the mouth of the Ramu which was crossed at night in boats, by foot to Wangan, by barge up the Sepik to Marienberg, and finally by foot to Wewak. Craft used were three big barges each carrying 70 men, three or four small launches, holding 20 to 30 each, and native craft.

There was no material change in troop dispositions late in June and early in July. The 4th Battalion continued to patrol the Hansa Bay-Bogia area while the Papuans went farther afield and probed the area between the mouths of the Ramu and the Sepik. The Papuans found the Sepik natives seemingly friendly but unable to understand the bombing and strafing of their villages long after the departure of the enemy. Another Papuan patrol down Watam Lagoon to Wangan on 6th July found that the Japanese had excavated a passage linking the lagoon with the Sepik, thus enabling launches to negotiate the passage through to Singarin. The

---

[2] Sgt R. H. Gregory, MM, VX104443; 24 Bn. Woodcutter; of Carlton, Vic; b. Carlton, 21 Apr 1908.

natives showed that they were on the Japanese side. When a Papuan patrol reached Wangan on 4th July natives told them that there were about 100 Japanese at Singarin. The patrol cut across the swamp country and three days later reached Old Bien on the Sepik. Here they waited while local natives went to bring canoes. The natives fetched the Japanese instead, and before dawn on the 9th the patrol was attacked by a mixed band of about 50 Japanese and natives and was forced to disperse, losing much equipment and many weapons. The patrol arrived back at Wangan on the 11th, footsore after clambering through the sac sac swamp. The Japanese apparently had forces at Singarin, New Bien and Marienberg, and the Sepik was probably an outpost defence line.

There were few other developments before the story of the great New Guinea offensive dwindled to a close. The only fighting unit left in the Ramu Valley was Captain Chalk's company of the Papuan Battalion, which returned there in June from Port Moresby and was based at Dumpu and Faita with an air-sea rescue party far down the river at Annanberg which the Japanese had left two months earlier. On 13th July the 30th Battalion relieved the 4th Battalion at Hansa Bay and continued patrolling towards the Ramu while the Papuans set up bases at Watam and Wangan and patrolled to the Sepik. August opened with a Papuan patrol near the mouth of the Sepik watching the Japanese on the other side through field glasses.

Throughout 1943 and 1944, while large-scale fighting was taking place along the northern littoral of New Guinea, only a few skirmishes and some desultory air action occurred along the south coast. The Japanese evidently decided in 1942 that an advance along the south coast of Dutch New Guinea offered few prospects of paying military dividends. The country was inhospitable, with vast areas of swamp, and the island-studded Torres Strait presented an awkward barrier between the Arafura and the Coral Seas. At the beginning of 1943 the foremost Japanese post of any size was at Kokenau, on the coast 325 miles north-west of Merauke. A sprinkling of Dutch and Indonesian officials and missionaries remained in the area east of Kokenau. Merauke had been bombed by the Japanese and the population had dispersed. At Tanahmerah, a penal settlement on the Digoel River, were some hundreds of political exiles from Java—a possible embarrassment if military operations began in the area—and they were soon removed to Australia. At the Wissel Lakes, in the mountains north of Kokenau, was a Dutch outpost with a radio set. It seemed likely that, if the Japanese advanced in southern Dutch New Guinea, Wissel Lakes, on which flying-boats could alight, Tanahmerah, where an airfield could be built, and finally Merauke would be among their main objectives. At intervals during 1943 there were fears—unfounded, it transpired—that such an advance might be undertaken.

After the reinforcement of Merauke from December 1942 to February 1943, mentioned earlier, "Merauke Force" included an American anti-aircraft battery and port detachment, the 62nd Australian Battalion, and a company of N.E.I. troops. An air force radio station had been at Merauke since 1942. The tasks of the force were to deny the Merauke airstrip and docks to the enemy. This little force, situated more than 200 miles from Thursday Island, and on the edge of a sea in which Japanese naval control was unlikely to be seriously disputed, would not

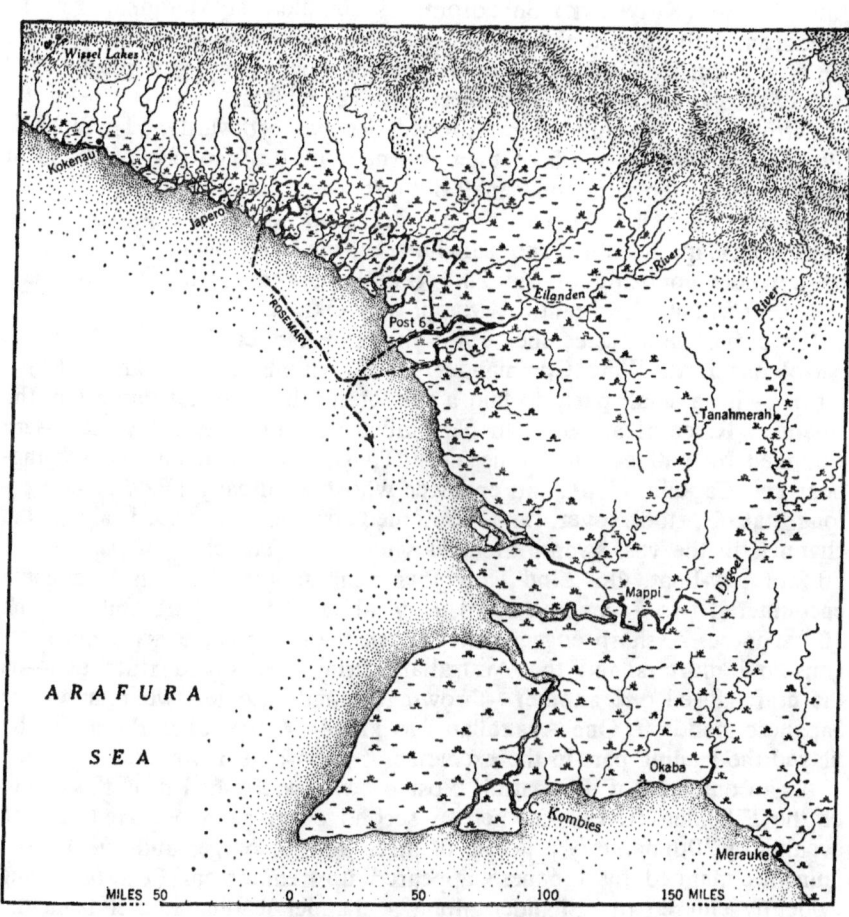

Area of Merauke Force operations

have been able to hold Merauke against a strong attack by the Japanese, who then had two divisions—the *5th* and *48th*—in the Timor-Ambon-Aru Islands area.

In mid-March 1943 Intelligence concerning a possible Japanese offensive against northern Australia reached G.H.Q. and MacArthur, in April, ordered a general strengthening of the Torres Strait area. As a result the headquarters of the 11th Brigade and one more infantry battalion—the 31st/51st—were ordered to Merauke, with a strong force of engineers. In May a company of the 26th Battalion arrived. Brigadier J. R. Stevenson of the 11th Brigade became commander of the force, whose tasks now included construction of airfields, roads, wharves and other requirements of a substantial base. The air base, when completed, was to be occupied by No. 72 Wing, with one fighter and one dive bomber squadron. The first aircraft landed on the airfield on 30th June, and by 3rd July No. 86 (Kittyhawk) Squadron was complete at Merauke. No. 12 Squadron, with dive bombers, came later. Merauke was under intermittent air attack during 1943. On 9th September, for example, it received its twenty-second raid—by 16 bombers and 12 fighters.

Patrols from Merauke Force probed deeply northward and westward, often making all or parts of their journeys in the network of rivers in small craft. At the same time small outposts were thrust farther and farther westward. Thus, by August, there were outposts with R.A.A.F. radar stations at Cape Kombies and Tanahmerah, the latter being now protected by a whole company of the 26th Battalion, and small outposts, each under an infantry sergeant, at Mappi and Okaba.

It was not until December 1943 that the first clash with a Japanese patrol occurred. Wing Commander D. F. Thomson, an anthropologist, set out with a small party to find a suitable position for an outpost in the Eilanden River area. On 24th November he and two of his men were wounded by natives with stone axes. They were taken out by a flying-boat and Captain Wolfe,[3] an engineer who had already made some very long patrols, took over, and continued probing westward along the channels in the vast swamp area, moving in the launch *Rosemary* and a 20-foot tow-boat. On 22nd December near Japero the patrol suddenly encountered two Japanese barges, each about 40 feet long and carrying 10 Japanese. A sharp engagement followed, the Japanese firing machine-guns and mortars and the Australians firing Brens and rifles and—as the craft closed one another—throwing grenades. After two minutes the Japanese made off. One Australian was killed—Corporal Barbouttis[4] who played the leading part in the exchange of fire—and 6 wounded.

As an outcome of this patrol "Post 6" was established near the mouth of the Eilanden River, and here a second clash soon occurred. In the evening of 30th January a flotilla of three 30-foot barges and five 15-foot launches manned by Japanese appeared upstream from Post 6, having evidently entered the Eilanden along a channel leading into it from the west in search of the Australian post. The Australians under Lieutenant Roodakoff[5] held their fire until the three leading craft were only 150 yards away, poured fire into them for a few minutes, killing about 60 (they estimated) and then pulled back from the river bank. The Japanese fired towards both banks of the river for 20 minutes, without effect, and, after dark, sailed downstream and out to sea. Next day aircraft from

---

[3] Maj C. C. Wolfe, NX35106. 2/4 and 16 Fd Coys; attached SEAC 1945. Agricultural engineer; of Bellevue Hill, NSW; b. Bolton, England, 8 Jul 1906.

[4] Cpl A. Barbouttis, QX37339; 31/51 Bn. Cafe assistant; of Townsville, Qld; b. Darwin, NT, 6 Aug 1920. Killed in action 22 Dec 1943.

[5] Lt A. Roodakoff, QX40798; 31/51 Bn. Clerk; of Tully, Qld; b. Russia, 3 Feb 1920. (Later changed his name to Ross.)

Merauke strafed four barges in the vicinity. After this Post 6 was reinforced, and eventually a company was stationed there.

The 62nd Battalion was replaced by the 20th Motor Regiment in February 1944. In August the 11th Brigade was withdrawn to prepare for other more active tasks, leaving the 20th Motor Regiment as the main infantry component of the garrison. Merauke Force succeeded in establishing a well-developed base, patrolling a very large area of difficult country and advancing fairly strong outposts more than 200 miles north and north-west, eventually extending its military control to most of that part of Dutch New Guinea that lies south of the central range.

During the advance along the coasts of Dutch New Guinea General MacArthur's staff had been considering the need for air bases in the islands between the Vogelkop and Mindanao. At length on 15th June 1944 a revised plan (RENO V) was completed which provided for an advance into the Halmaheras area on 15th September—the date tentatively fixed for Admiral Nimitz's invasion of the Palaus. It will be recalled that MacArthur's staff still considered that it would be necessary to seize islands in the Arafura Sea from which to give land-based air cover to the operations farther north. It was now decided that these islands would be occupied only if land-based aircraft from Darwin and the New Guinea bases could not secure the left flank from attack by Japanese aircraft based on Ambon, Ceram and Celebes. The landing on Mindanao was scheduled for 25th October. It was believed that the Japanese had some 30,000 troops in the main islands of the Halmaheras whereas Morotai, some 50 miles to the north, was lightly defended. Consequently on 19th July an outline plan for the occupation of Morotai was completed.

Meanwhile, in June, the offensive against the Marianas Islands had been mounted by Admiral Nimitz's forces. In some respects this expedition was on an unprecedented scale. Over the last 1,000 miles a fleet of 535 fighting ships and transports would carry 127,000 troops. They included the V Marine Corps (2nd and 4th Marine Divisions) aimed at Saipan and Tinian, the III Marine Corps (3rd Marine Division and 1st Marine Brigade) aimed at Guam, and as a floating reserve the 27th Division; the 77th Division was in general reserve. D-day for Saipan was 15th June, but the dates of Guam and Tinian were not to be decided until the outcome at Saipan was known. It was impressive evidence of the immense volume of shipping now available to the Allies that, while this seaborne Pacific operation was making ready, the invasion of Europe began.

There were some 32,000 Japanese on Saipan including the *43rd Division* and *47th Independent Mixed Brigade* and 6,700 naval men; there were 71,000 Americans in the V Corps. From 11th to 13th June the aircraft of fifteen carriers struck at the objectives, and on the 13th, 14th and 15th June battleships and smaller vessels bombarded them. At 7 a.m. on the 15th the landing craft carrying the V Corps set off from a line 4,000 yards from the shore and on a front of almost four miles. The

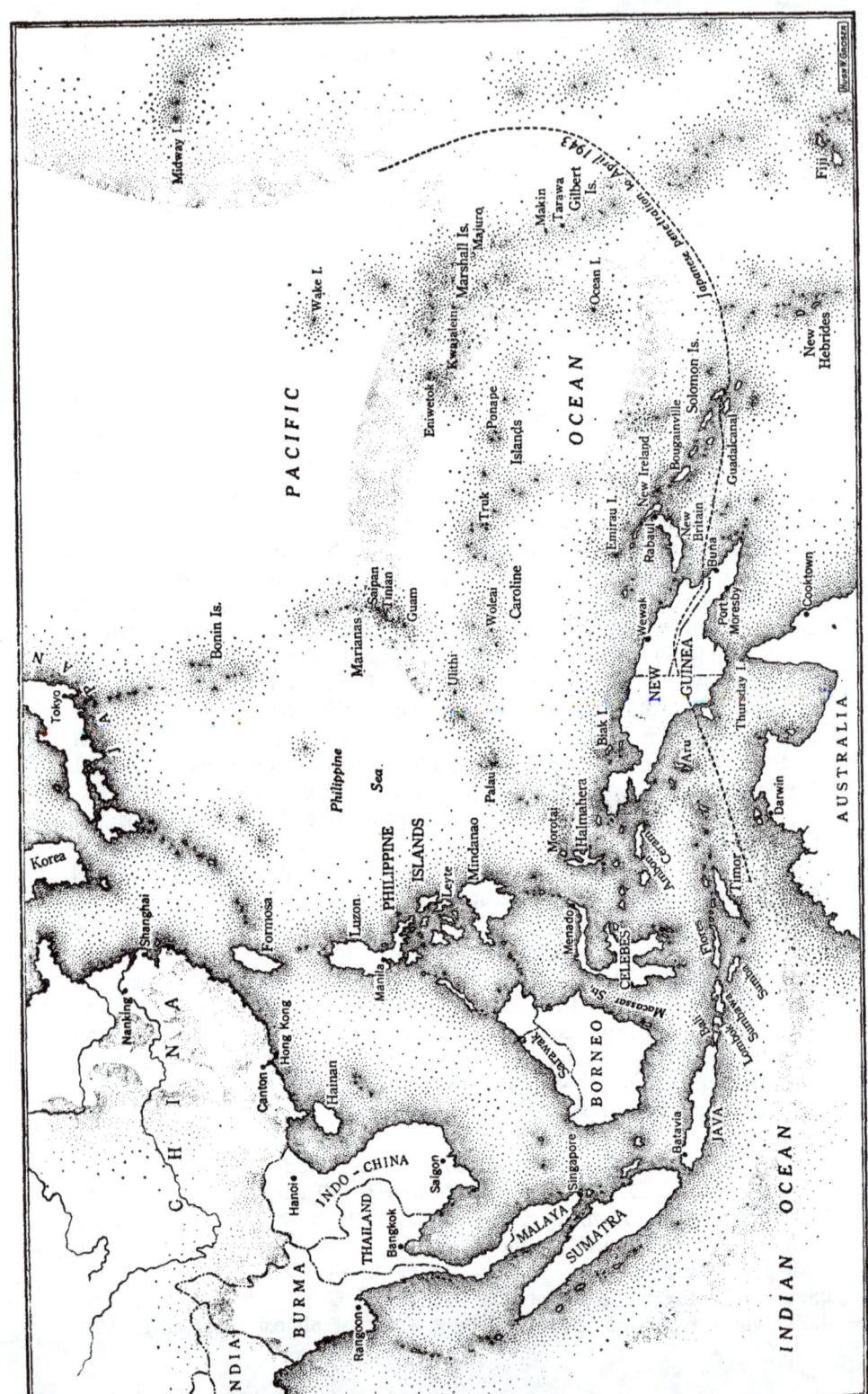

The Allied offensive in the Pacific, April 1943 to September 1944

troops were met by intense fire and at the end of the first day were far short of the objective and clinging to narrow beach-heads. They broke up Japanese counter-attacks, however, but the position seemed perilous on the 16th. It was decided to send the 27th Division ashore and it began landing at dusk. By the 17th the beach-head seemed secure but a long battle lay ahead. By 21st June the Americans had secured the southern one-third of the island, by the 27th the southern half, and by 6th July had confined the defenders into a pocket about four miles long. The last resistance ended on the 9th.

There were perhaps 20,000 Japanese civilians on Saipan. Hundreds of these fled to the northern end of the island, where they refused to surrender and, eventually, on 11th and 12th July

believing that the end had come, embarked on a ghastly exhibition of self-destruction. Casting their children ahead of them, or embracing them in death, parents flung themselves from the cliffs onto the jagged rocks below. Some waded into the surf to drown or employed other gruesome means of destroying themselves. How many civilians died in this orgy of mass hysteria is not known.[6]

The Americans lost 3,426 killed. Only 971 Japanese troops were taken prisoner.

While the fight for Saipan was in progress the Japanese sought to carry out their intention to engage in a decisive naval battle. On 15th June the Japanese *"Mobile Fleet"*, including 9 carriers and 5 battleships, sallied out into the Philippine Sea against the American Fifth Fleet, which had 15 carriers and 7 battleships. In the ensuing clashes on the 19th and 20th the Japanese lost 3 carriers, two sunk by submarines, the Americans none, although a number of their ships were damaged.

Lessons learnt at Saipan were applied at Tinian which was taken by the 2nd and 4th Marine Divisions. The landing took place on 24th July and the whole island was in American hands by 1st August, with a loss of 389 killed; more than 5,000 Japanese were buried.

On Guam (the first American territory to be regained) were 19,000 Japanese including the *29th Division*. The attacking force was the III Marine Corps including the 3rd Marine Division, 1st Brigade and 77th Division, an army formation not previously in action. The two marine formations landed at separate beaches each side of the harbour on 21st July, threw back the counter-attacks and, with the 77th, gained control of the island by 10th August, although thousands of Japanese were then still at large in the jungle. The Americans lost 1,435 killed, all but 213 being marines. Japanese casualties included about 10,600 killed and 1,250 taken prisoner.

MacArthur gave the task of taking Morotai to General Hall's XI Corps, with the 31st Division and a regiment of the ubiquitous 32nd under command. Two of the attacking regiments were embarked at Aitape, 920 miles from the objective. There was no opposition on the beaches, which was fortunate since coral boulders and mud made landing extremely

---

[6] C. W. Hoffman, *Saipan: the Beginning of the End* (1950), a volume in the series prepared by the Historical Section of the U.S. Marine Corps.

difficult and there was some confusion. The objective—an area 7,000 yards by 5,000 round the airfield—was reached on the second day (16th September) and thereafter there were only patrol actions against Japanese groups at large in the bush to the north. The perimeter was later extended.

The Palaus operation was a far larger affair, carried out by the III Marine Corps which included the veteran 1st Marine Division and the 81st Division, an unblooded army formation, the first to take Peleliu and the second Angaur. The 77th Division and the 5th Marine Division were in reserve.

There was little opposition as the troops came ashore at Peleliu on 15th September, but resistance increased as they pressed inland, and by nightfall the perimeter was only 400 to 700 yards deep except at one point where the marines had pushed across the narrow atoll. In the next six days the marines pressed on but had 4,000 casualties. A regiment of the 81st Division was landed, but it was not until 30th September that only mopping-up of resolute parties remained. The Japanese dead were estimated at 11,000; and pockets of Japanese still remained which were not defeated until 27th November. It had been a costly operation, the 1st Marine Division losing about 1,250 killed and the 81st Division 278.

The 81st Division was landed on Angaur on 17th September and by the morning of the 20th it had killed 850 Japanese and reported that the island was secure. It was 21st October, however, before the last pockets of Japanese resistance had been cleared. By that time 1,300 Japanese had been killed and 45 captured. The Americans lost 264 men killed and their total casualties, including 244 cases of "battle fatigue", were 2,559 (nearly twice the strength of the enemy garrison).

Between January and September 1944 the American amphibious forces had advanced from a line through the Huon Peninsula, Torokina and the Gilbert Islands to one through Morotai, the Palaus and Saipan. They were half way to Tokyo. Thirteen Japanese divisions, apart from smaller formations, had been destroyed or isolated. In the process the American forces had gained greatly in experience and skill. Although the Pacific war was two years old when this drive began, the only divisions of the American Army that had fought against the Japanese were four (the Americal, 25th, 37th and 43rd) in the Solomons, two (the 32nd and 41st) under MacArthur, and two (the 7th and 27th) in the Central and North Pacific; three marine divisions had been in action. Now 16 army divisions and four divisions of marines had been in action, some of them several times.[7]

In the third quarter of 1944 fewer Australian troops were in contact with the enemy than at any time since the few weeks that elapsed between the relief of the siege of Tobruk and the opening of the war against Japan. Most of the divisions of the Australian Army were re-training for

---

[7] The Army divisions were: 6th, 7th, 24th, 25th, 27th, 31st, 32nd, 33rd, 37th, 40th, 41st, 43rd, 77th, 81st, Americal, 1st Cavalry.

the final effort in 1945 in which every division would be involved. They needed rest, and some reorganisation, for the offensive of 1943-1944 had brought the nation near the limit of its resources. At the end of July 1944, 697,000 men and women—nearly one in ten of the Australian population—were still serving in the armed Services.[8] In their long, hard fight in 1943 and 1944 the Australians had defeated a brave and tenacious foe. Old traditions had been worthily upheld. Courage, determination, self-sacrifice, team work, initiative, endurance—and humour—had enabled them to triumph over a fanatical enemy, and over the rugged and pitiless terrain and the rigours of a tropical climate. Throughout this period they had been uplifted by the knowledge that they were the spearhead in the land battle against the Japanese, and they had developed a confident and masterful efficiency in jungle warfare. Australian Army battle casualties to 26th August 1944 totalled 57,046, including 12,161 deaths, 15,726 wounded, 3,548 missing and 25,611 prisoners. In the operations described in this volume 1,231 Australian soldiers were killed and 2,867 wounded.

After the war General Kane Yoshiwara, of General Adachi's staff, gave the maximum strength of the *XVIII Japanese Army* as 105,000, including those lost at sea—about 3,500.[9] By March 1944 its strength, he writes, was 54,000. About 13,000 Japanese had died in Papua by January 1943. Therefore about 35,000 must have died during the fighting and the retreat described in this volume.

In April 1943 Australia, according to her Prime Minister, had still been under the shadow of Japanese invasion. One seasoned brigade of Australian troops and two Independent Companies were holding the Japanese in the forbidding ranges between Wau and Salamaua—the only place in the Pacific theatre where there was then any fighting. The onrush of the Japanese invaders through New Guinea had already been stopped in the fierce Papuan campaigns, and in the South Pacific the Americans had held Guadalcanal. Months of fighting, patrolling and planning were followed by the triumphant Australian offensive which shattered the *XVIII Japanese Army*, drove it back beyond the Sepik, and paved the way for the spectacular American advance towards the Philippines. In 16 months of war the Japanese had passed from the exhilarating heights of victory to the grim verge of defeat.

---

[8] In August 1943 the strength of the three Services had been 732,000, from a population of 7,270,000. In 1944 the strength of the American armed Services was about 11,700,000, from a population of 135,000,000.

[9] In *Southern Cross, An Account of the Eastern New Guinea Campaign* (1955).

APPENDIX

ABBREVIATIONS

A—*Acting, Assistant.*
AA—*Anti-aircraft.*
AAG—*Assistant Adjutant-General.*
AAMC—*Australian Army Medical Corps.*
AAMWS—*Australian Army Medical Women's Service.*
AANS—*Australian Army Nursing Service.*
AAOC—*Australian Army Ordnance Corps.*
AA&QMG—*Assistant Adjutant and Quartermaster-General.*
ADC—*Aide-de-Camp.*
Admin—*Administration, Administrative.*
ADMS—*Assistant Director Medical Services.*
ADOS—*Assistant Director Ordnance Services.*
Adv—*Advanced.*
AEME—*Australian Electrical and Mechanical Engineers.*
AGH—*Australian General Hospital.*
AIB—*Allied Intelligence Bureau.*
AIF—*Australian Imperial Force.*
Angau—*Australian New Guinea Administrative Unit.*
APD—*Destroyer-transport.*
Armd—*Armoured.*
Arty—*Artillery.*
Asst—*Assistant.*
A-Tk—*Anti-Tank.*
AVM—*Air Vice-Marshal.*
AWAS—*Australian Women's Army Service.*

BBCAU—*British Borneo Civil Affairs Unit.*
Bde—*Brigade.*
Bdr—*Bombardier.*
BGS—*Brigadier, General Staff.*
BM—*Brigade Major.*
Bn—*Battalion.*
Brig—*Brigadier.*
Bty—*Battery.*

CA(AA)—*Coast Artillery (Anti-aircraft).*
Capt—*Captain.*
CASC—*Commander, Army Service Corps.*
Cav—*Cavalry.*

CCRA—*Commander, Corps Royal Artillery.*
CCS—*Casualty Clearing Station.*
Cdo—*Commando.*
Cdr—*Commander.*
CE—*Chief Engineer.*
CGS—*Chief of the General Staff.*
C-in-C—*Commander-in-Chief.*
CO—*Commanding Officer.*
Col—*Colonel.*
Col GS—*Colonel, General Staff.*
Comd—*Command, Commander, Commanded.*
Coy—*Company.*
Cpl—*Corporal.*
CRA—*Commander, Royal Artillery (of a division).*
CRE—*Commander, Royal Engineers (of a division).*
CSO—*Chief Signals Officer.*
CTF—*Commander, Task Force.*

DAPM—*Deputy Assistant Provost Marshal.*
DAQMG—*Deputy Assistant Quartermaster-General.*
DDME—*Deputy Director Mechanical Engineering.*
DDMT—*Deputy Director Military Training.*
DDST—*Deputy Director Supply and Transport.*
DGMS—*Director-General of Medical Services.*
Div—*Division.*

EBSR—*Engineer Boat and Shore Regiment.*
Engrs—*Engineers.*
Eqpt—*Equipment.*
ESB—*Engineer Special Brigade.*

FA—*Field Artillery.*
Fd—*Field.*
FDL—*Forward Defended Locality.*
FELO—*Far Eastern Liaison Office.*
F-Lt—*Flight Lieutenant.*
FOO—*Forward Observation Officer.*

Gen—*General.*
GHQ—*General Headquarters.*
Gnr—*Gunner.*

ABBREVIATIONS

GOC—*General Officer commanding.*
Gp—*Group.*
GSO1—*General Staff Officer, Grade 1.*

HE—*High Explosive.*
HQ—*Headquarters.*

i/c—*in command.*
Indep—*Independent.*
Inf—*Infantry.*
Instr—*Instructor.*
Int—*Intelligence.*

LAA—*Light Anti-aircraft.*
LCI—*Landing Craft, Infantry.*
LCM—*Landing Craft, Mechanised.*
L-Cpl—*Lance-Corporal.*
LCT—*Landing Craft, Tank.*
LCV—*Landing Craft, Vehicle.*
LCVP—*Landing Craft, Vehicle, Personnel.*
LHQ—*Allied Land Forces Headquarters.*
LO—*Liaison Officer.*
L of C—*Lines of Communication.*
LSO—*Legal Staff Officer.*
LST—*Landing Ship, Tank.*
Lt—*Lieutenant, light.*
Lt-Cdr—*Lieut-Commander.*

Maj—*Major.*
ME—*Middle East.*
MG—*Machine-gun.*
MGRA—*Major-General, Royal Artillery.*
MHR—*Member of the House of Representatives.*
Mil—*Military.*
MLC—*Member of the Legislative Council.*
MMG—*Medium machine-gun.*
Mtn—*Mountain.*

NEFIS—*Netherlands East Indies Forces Intelligence Service.*
NG—*New Guinea.*
NGAWW Sigs—*New Guinea Air Wireless Warning Signals.*
NGF—*New Guinea Force.*
NGIB—*New Guinea Infantry Battalion.*
NGVR—*New Guinea Volunteer Rifles.*
NT—*Northern Territory.*

OC—*Officer Commanding.*
OP—*Observation Post.*

Ops—*Operations.*
OSMG—*Owen sub-machine-gun.*

PIB—*Papuan Infantry Battalion.*
Pk—*Park.*
Pnr—*Pioneer.*
PT—*Patrol torpedo (boat).*
Pte—*Private.*

RAA—*Royal Australian Artillery.*
RAAF—*Royal Australian Air Force.*
RAE—*Royal Australian Engineers.*
RAN—*Royal Australian Navy.*
RANVR—*Royal Australian Naval Volunteer Reserve.*
RAR—*Royal Australian Regiment.*
Regt—*Regiment.*
RFA—*Royal Field Artillery.*
RMO—*Regimental Medical Officer.*
RSM—*Regimental Sergeant-Major.*

Sec—*Section, Secretary.*
Sgt—*Sergeant.*
SHAEF—*Supreme Headquarters, Allied Expeditionary Force.*
Sig—*Signalman.*
Sigs—*Signals.*
SNLF—*Special Naval Landing Force (Japanese).*
SOPAC—*South Pacific (Command).*
SORE—*Staff Officer, Royal Engineers.*
Spr—*Sapper.*
Sqn—*Squadron.*
S-Sgt—*Staff-Sergeant.*
SWPA—*South-West Pacific Area.*

Tk—*Tank.*
TNG—*Territory of New Guinea.*
Tpr—*Trooper.*
Tps—*Troops.*
TSMG—*Thompson sub-machine-gun.*

UK—*United Kingdom.*
US—*United States.*
USAFFE—*United States Army Forces in the Far East.*
USASOS—*United States Army Services of Supply.*

WO1—*Warrant-Officer, Class 1.*

INDEX

ABRAU (Sketch p. 262), 263
ADACHI, Lt-Gen Hatazo, 46, 82, 158, 201, 231, 395, 415, 443, 530, 561, 566, 601, 612, 624n, 675-6, 682n, 710, 734, 807, 817; commands XVIII Army, 11; on Salamaua operations, 57, 325; fears Allied landing Lae-Salamaua, 135; plans operations in Bena plateau, 251-2; reinforces Finschhafen area, 425, 523-4; on Japanese counter-attack at Finschhafen, 524-5, 529, 532, 560; on loss of Sattelberg, 652-3; orders withdrawal to Madang, 732; estimates Japanese casualties in Huon Peninsula, 736n; on Kankiryo Saddle operations, 762; withdraws to Hollandia, 789, 804
ADAIR, Lt-Cdr, 447-8, 488
ADAMS, Capt T. B., 685-6, 711, 776
ADELAIDE (Sketch p. 15), 16, 537n
ADMIRALTY ISLANDS (Map p. 28; Sketches pp. 793, 796), 232, 788, 790, 792, 794n, 798-9; American landings on, 795-7
AFUA (Sketch p. 807), 807
AGAR, Lt S. L., 757-8
AGO (Sketch p. 726), 616, 728-9
AINSLIE, Brig R. I., 380, 553, 619-21, 623-4, 628-9, 640-1, 645, 647; commands 2/48 Bn, 368
AIRCRAFT, in Fifth Air Force, 12; production of, 13. Types: *Airacobra*, 585, 727; *Anson*, 236; *Beaufighter*, 52, 66, 71, 81, 99, 387; *Boomerang*, 387, 429, 466, 511, 548, 551-2, 575, 585-6, 642, 649n, 651-2, 682-3, 691, 693-4, 706n, 707-8, 711, 729, 766, 778; *Boston*, 28, 30, 34, 52, 119, 128, 344, 387, 449, 471, 492, 535, 727-8, 776; *Catalina*, 259, 261-3, 795; *Dauntless*, 430; *Douglas*, 20, 71, 234, 255, 276, 343-4, 357, 415; *Fairfield Cub*, 599; *Fortress*, 119, 190, 344-5, 387, 809; *Junkers*, 423; *Kittyhawk*, 449, 527n, 575, 683, 694, 706n, 707, 733, 754, 797, 804; *Liberator*, 119, 185, 189-90, 344, 358, 449; *Lightning*, 242-3, 259, 334, 387, 466; *Marauder*, 727-8, 733; *Mitchell*, 87, 119, 121, 141, 185, 234, 277, 344, 376, 387, 449, 535, 591, 644, 652, 687, 727, 729, 733, 744, 746-7, 797; *Piper Cub*, 160, 256, 357, 409, 415, 423, 430, 436, 709, 729, 785, 808-9; *Superfortress*, 275, 791, 798; *Thunderbolt*, 609, 727, 733; *Tiger Moth*, 256; *Vultee Vengeance*, 471, 492, 609, 747; *Wirraway*, 97, 589, 599, 682-3, 766; *Zero*, 46
AIRFIELDS, 20; in Markham Valley, 55-6, 268; on Bena plateau, 234, 236, 239-40, 243; Allied development in New Guinea, 402n, 426n, 507, 556, 569, 593; protection of, 594. *Japanese*, at Munda, 7; Allied plans for seizure of, 220; on Bougainville, 653; Allied attacks on, 658
AIR RECONNAISSANCE, Bogadjim Road, 588; in Finisterres, 589
AIR SUPPLY, 742, 809; in Burma, 6; Salamaua area, 86-7, 132, 166; early developments in New Guinea, 233-4; in Sepik River area, 262; in Markham-Ramu Valleys, 341, 438; of ammunition at Finschhafen, 465-6; by Japanese, 557, 649
AIR SUPPORT, in Salamaua campaign, 31, 38, 81, 92, 105, 109, 112, 119-21, 128, 129n, 161, 185, 189-90; for 1943 New Guinea offensive, 231, 506; in Nadzab-Lae operations, 269, 366, 381, 387; in Finschhafen operation, 449, 451, 492; in Finisterres, 586, 745; in advance to Fortification Point, 667n
AIR TRANSPORT, 119; of 7 Div to Nadzab, 414; in Ramu Valley, 433
AITAPE (Map p. 28; Sketches pp. 799, 807), 260, 789, 791, 803, 815; Japanese strength and development, 20, 232; U.S. attack on, 801-2, 804; Japanese counter-attack, 806-7
AITKEN, Lt-Col E. F., 711n
AIYAU (Map p. 773), 777
AIYURA (Sketches pp. 235, 427), 236, 238-40, 416
AKYAB (Sketch p. 218), 5, 217
ALANBROOKE, Field Marshal Viscount, 1n, 2n, 218-19
ALEUTIAN ISLANDS (Sketch p. 5), 1, 4; Americans plan seizure of, 3-4, 220; attack on, 226-7
ALEXANDER, Field Marshal Earl, 264, 283
ALEXISHAFEN (Map p. 773; Sketch p. 808), 807; entered by 30 Bn, 788
ALEXISHAFEN ROAD (Map p. 773), 787
ALIBU (Map p. 773), 782
ALLAN, Col H. T., 465, 490, 517, 609n

ALLAWAY, Lt-Col A. G., 267n
ALLCHIN, Lt-Col E. F., 756n
ALLEN, Maj-Gen A. S., 280n; commands NT Force, 16
ALLEN, Cpl L. C., 162, 166
ALLEN, Capt P. H., 45, 203, 289, 298
ALLEN, Sgt W., 42
ALLIED AIR FORCES, 20, 242, 259, 263, 334, 341, 451, 484, 508-9, 557, 652, 681, 787, 789, 795; strength in South and South-West Pacific areas, 11; in Bismarck Sea Battle, 26; in Salamaua campaign, 33-4, 70-1, 87, 92, 112, 119-21, 221, 253, 278; attack Wewak airfields, 232; bomb Lae and Cape Gloucester, 278-9; in Nadzab-Lae operations, 282, 343-5, 381, 387, 389-90; and Bena Force, 438; role in NG offensive, 444, 505, 733; attack airfields on New Britain, 470; in Finschhafen campaign, 471, 492, 535, 641; attack barge traffic, 522, 658-9; in Finisterres, 744, 746-7, 754, 776
ALLIED GEOGRAPHICAL SECTION, 596n
ALLIED INTELLIGENCE BUREAU, 432; operations of coastwatchers and special units in 1943, 257-60; NEFIS, 261; Mosstroops, 261-3, 432; Services Reconnaissance Detachment, 781n; Sepik River area, 806n
ALLIED LAND FORCES HEADQUARTERS (L.H.Q.), 12, 16, 56, 197n, 261, 279, 320, 338n, 780; predicts Japanese strategy, 10n; Intelligence estimates, 11n, 446; role restricted by General MacArthur, 221-2; plans NG offensive, 230; seeks information about Sepik area, 260; composition of reserves, 280n; relations with US planning staffs, 281-4; reinforcement of Finschhafen, 481; organisation and command in New Guinea, 504n; redesignates Indep Coys, 566n; plans neutralisation of Madang, 696; on tasks of 7 Div, 779
ALLIED NAVAL FORCES, 284, 307, 362, 504n, 505, 507-8, 557, 789; strength, 11-12; in Salamaua-Lae operations, 221, 266, 278-9, 282, 363; reinforcement of Finschhafen, 480-1, 482
ALLIED TRANSLATOR AND INTERPRETER SECTION, 600
ALLIES, THE, 259, 523, 686n, 729; strategy of, 4-10
ALLMAN, Sgt B. B., 547
ALUKI (Map p. 327), 333-4, 336-7, 348
ALUKI TRACK (Map p. 327), 349
AMAMI (Sketch p. 235), airstrip at, 256
AMBON ISLAND (Map p. 814; Sketch p. 15), 11, 788 791, 811, 813
AMBUSHES, *Australian*, 315; in Salamaua area, 28, 31, 67-8, 115, 202-3; at Buang River, 128, 135; at Kesawai, 435; in Finisterres, 572. *Japanese*, in Salamaua area, 88-9, 115-16, 124, 130, 212-13
AMBUSH KNOLL (Map p. 27; Sketches pp. 116, 196), 115-17, 131-2, 151, 153, 165-6, 188, 193n, 208, 311; action at, 152-5
AMELE (Map p. 773), 785-6
AMERICA, UNITED STATES OF, 14-15, 84, 219, 272; envisages withdrawal from European theatre, 3; Service rivalry in, 12; and China, 217; strength of population in Armed Services, 817n
AMERICAN AIR FORCE, 20, 177, 230, 254, 426, 428n, 567, 609, 739, 783, 798, 808; strength and deployment, 2, 9, 16, 57, 227n; bombs Wewak, 204; in Finschhafen operations, 444, 466, 471, 506; attacks retreating Japanese, 727-30; attacks Cape Gloucester, 449; relations with Australians, 523; in Finisterres, 585, 591, 683; radar policy, 594; losses in Gilberts, 654
—FORCES: *Second Air Task*, 210, 255, 423; *Third Air Task*, 426n; *Fifth*, 8, 12, 34n, 57, 87, 234, 239, 255n, 402n, 414, 504n; in Salamaua operations, 58-9, 105, 121, 129n; in Lae operations, 182, 231, 273-6, 338, 359, 388-9, 433; in Finschhafen operations, 535, 609; in Ramu Valley, 566, 684; *Eleventh*, 227; *Thirteenth*, 11; *Fourteenth*, 220n
—GROUPS: *49th Fighter*, 527n
—WINGS: *54th Troop Carrier*, 338, 425
—SQUADRONS: *41st*, 705-8; *67th Fighter*, 223
AMERICAN ARMY, 1, 59-60, 65, 273, 422, 567, 763, 786, 817; strength and deployment, 2, 16-17, 57, 227n; relations with navy, 3n, 12; compared with Japanese, 11n; Australian cooperation with, 105, 138-41, 145, 159-61, 180-2, 280n, 281-4; casualties, in New Georgia and Aleutians, 226, in Admiralties,

AMERICAN ARMY—continued
797, in Marshalls, 800-1, on Bougainville, 801, in Wakde-Sarmi operations, 805, on Biak, 806, on Noemfoor, 806; on Bena plateau, 243; staff appointments, 266n; training and outlook compared to Australian, 321n, 444; Nisei translators, 478; uses dogs in Ramu, 567n; and Lethbridge Mission, 686n; develops Finschhafen base, 737; dismounted cavalry compared with Australian organisation, 795n; tactics, 800-1; develops experience and skill, 816
—UNITED STATES ARMY FORCES IN FAR EAST, Reconstituted, 221, 402n
—UNITED STATES ARMY SERVICES OF SUPPLY, 282, 401-2, 504n, 506
—ARMIES: *Third*, 222. *Sixth*, 792; composition and role, 220-1, 280n, 730-1; arrives Australia, 221; staff, 222; establishes HQ near Brisbane, 402n. *Seventh*, 283
—CORPS, compared with Japanese, 11n; I, 280n, at Rockhampton, 17, composition, 220, at Hollandia, 804. XI, 806, 815. XIV, 225, 654, 801
—DIVISIONS, strength and deployment, 219; number with experience against Japanese, 816; Americal, 2n, 11, 224, 816; in Solomons, 220, 354, 801; 1st Cavalry, 220; composition of, 280n; lands on Los Negros and Manus Islands, 795-7; 6th Infantry, 805-6, 816n; 7th Infantry, 227, 800, 816; 24th Infantry, 2n, 816n; composition of 280n; at Hollandia, 804; on Biak, 805-6; 25th Infantry, 2n, 11, 816; in Solomons, 220, 226, 27th Infantry, 2n, 816; lands Makin Island, 654; in Marshalls, 800-1; in Marianas, 813, 815; 31st Infantry, 815, 816n; 32nd Infantry, 2n, 12, 17, 220, 816; condition of, composition of, 280n; at Saidor, 731-2, 764-5, 769, 771-2, 785; links with Australians, 777-8; patrols to Bogadjim, 784; at Aitape, 804; counter-attacked, 806-7; at Morotai, 815; 33rd Infantry, 816n; 37th Infantry, 2n, 11, 816; in Solomons, 220, 224-6, 654, 801; on New Georgia, 225-6; on Bougainville, 801; 40th Infantry, 2n, 816n; 41st Infantry, 2n, 12, 17, 57, 84n, 102, 105, 220, 321n, 816; in Salamaua campaign, 58, 60, 138, 182, 185, 200; at Nassau Bay, 95, 139-40; composition, 280n; at Hollandia, 804; lands Wakde and Biak Islands, 805-6; 43rd Infantry, 2n, 11, 816; in Solomons, 220, 224-6; reinforces Aitape, 806; 77th Infantry, in Marianas attack, 813, 815; in Palaus operation, 816; 81st Infantry, attacks Angaur, 816
—FORCES: *Alamo*, 504n, 602, 696, 729, 732; creation of, 221-2. *Coane*, 139-40, 182n; composition and strength, 138n, 160-1; in Salamaua campaign, 141-5, 158-9, 168, 179. *MacKechnie*, 84, 109, 138-40, 142n, 158; in Salamaua campaign, 90-1, 94-106; strength, 103. *Saidor Task, see 126th Regt*
—ARTILLERY, 321n, 783; *Anti-aircraft*, 119, 810; 162 Lt AA Bty, 192n; 209 Coast Bn, 109n; 210 Coast Bn, 559n. *Field*: 205 Bn, 142, 158, 192n; 218 Bn, 103, 124, 138n, 142, 147, 158, 192, 212
—ENGINEERS, 103, 106, 276, 423, 426; at Marilinan and Tsili Tsili, 255-6; in Lae operations, 332, 400-2, 414. 2 ESB, 84, 265, 477; establishment, 85; at Nassau Bay, 95-6, 102n; in Lae operations, 230, 266-7, 275, 332, 354, 363, 366, 401; trains with 9 Div, 266; in Finschhafen operations, 490, 505-6, 609n, 721, 726, 764; Madang-Alexishafen, 807. 3 ESB, 85; 4 ESB, 85. 532 EBSR, 265, 272, 534, 667n; at Nassau Bay, 91; in Lae operations, 329, 331-2, 334, 368n; in Finschhafen operations, 446-7, 455-6, 464, 469, 481-2, 500, 505-7, 518, 526, 530-1, 540, 542, 721, 725, 771; at Tami Islands, 508; in advance to Saidor, 766. 542 EBSR, 482, 505-7; 592 EBSR, 731n. 871 Airborne Bn, 357; 808 Bn, 556.
—CAVALRY, INFANTRY AND PARACHUTE REGIMENTS: *Cavalry*, 5th, 28n; lands Admiralties, 795-7; 7th, 280n; 8th, 280n; 12th, 280n; 112th, 280n; lands Woodlark, 223; lands Arawe, 794; reinforces Aitape, 806. *Infantry*, 19th, 280n; 21st, 280n; 34th, 280n; 35th, 226; 124th, 806; 126th, 17, 280n; lands Saidor, 731-2; 127th, 17, 280n; at Aitape, 804; 128th, 17, 280n; reinforces Saidor, 732; 145th, 225; 148th, 224; on New Georgia, 225-6; 158th, 14, 17, 280n; lands Kiriwina Island, 223; lands Noemfoor Island, 806; 162nd, 17, 84, 199, 280n; in Salamaua campaign, 86, 133, 137-9, 182-3, 185, 187, 192, 201-2, 285, 291-4, 304, 308-9, 316, 318, 321; returns

AMERICAN ARMY—continued
to Australia, 321n; lands Biak, 805; 163rd, 17, 84, 280n; at Aitape, 804; 169th, 225; 172nd, 225-6; 186th, 17, 280n. *Parachute*, 503rd, 268, 277, 280n, 415; in Nadzab operation, 270, 338-9, 343-6
—INFANTRY AND PARACHUTE BATTALIONS: *Infantry*: I/126 Bn, 731; III/126 Bn, 731; I/162 Bn, 85; at Nassau Bay, 71-3, 84, 90-1, 96-100, 102-4, 135, 144, 182n, 215; in Salamaua operations, 107, 136, 310; in Mubo operations, 122-4, 126-8; at Lake Salus, 141, 213-15; Komiatum-Mt Tambu, 145-7, 149, 160, 163, 165-8, 189, 199-200; Roosevelt-Scout Ridges, 185, 187, 292, 295, 308-9; returns to regimental command, 201-2; Bitoi Ridge, 210; Charlie Hill, 297; casualties, 324n; II/162 Bn, 138n; Lababia Island, 142; Tambu Bay, 143, 159; Roosevelt Ridge, 159, 183-5; Nassau Bay, 180; Scout Ridge, 292, 308-9; at Salamaua, 321n; casualties, 324n; III/162 Bn, 84, 159, 309, 321n; at Nassau Bay, 138-40; at Tambu Bay, 142-5; Roosevelt and Scout Ridges, 180, 183-5, 201, 292, 308; casualties, 324n. *Parachute*: I/503 Bn, 339; II/503 Bn, 339; III/503 Bn, 339; in Nadzab-Lae operations, 378, 385, 397-8
AMERICAN GOVERNMENT
—COMBINED INTELLIGENCE COMMITTEE, 10n
—JOINT CHIEFS OF STAFF, 1n, 791; at Casablanca, 2-4; plans and directives, 3, 7-9, 55, 217-18, 220, 798-9
—NAVY DEPARTMENT, 3n
—WAR DEPARTMENT, 3n
AMERICAN NAVY, 283, 624n, 789n; strength in Pacific, 2, 218; relations with US Army, 3n, 12; in Solomons campaign, 7, 273, 654; role in Pacific, 8, 56, 217-19, 278; in Finschhafen operations, 444, 447-9, 451-7, 480-3, 602; relations with Australians, 523, 535; in Gilberts, 654; at Cape Gloucester, 729; at Saidor, 731; in Central Pacific, 791, 800-1, 813; bombards Kavieng, 799; tactics, 800-1
—FLEETS: *Pacific*, 9, 792, 798-9; *Fifth*, 815; *Seventh*, 12, 449n, 466, 795; in Lae operations, 330, 378-9; reinforcement of Finschhafen, 480, 488, 523
—FORCES: *Task Force 76*, 182, 266-7, 272-4, 354, 504n, 505; in Lae operations, 330, 332; reinforcement of Finschhafen, 535
—MARINE CORPS, 802n; strength in Pacific, 2; on Guadalcanal, 3n; New Georgia, 224; role in Central Pacific, 791; casualties, 801; extent of experience against Japanese, 816. III Corps, in Marianas, 813, 815; attacks Palaus, 816; V Corps, 654-5; in Marianas, 813; at Saipan, 813
—MARINE CORPS DIVISIONS: 1st, 7, 12, 220, 228; on Guadalcanal, 273; lands Cape Gloucester, 279, 794; attacks Peleliu, 816; 2nd, 11, 220; lands Tarawa, 654-5; in Marianas, 813, 815; 3rd, 11, 220; on Bougainville, 653-4; in Marianas, 813, 815; 4th, in Marshalls, 800; in Marianas, 813, 815; 5th, 816
—MARINE CORPS BRIGADES AND REGIMENTS: 1st Bde, 813, 815; 4th Regt, 799; 22nd Regt, 801
—SUBMARINE OPERATIONS, 3, 227
—PT BOATS, 85, 318; in Salamaua-Lae operations, 58-9, 90-1, 95-6, 102, 328, 505; in Finschhafen area, 616
AMIES, Brig J. L., 304, 306-8, 316, 395; commands 15 Bn, 285
AMINIK (Map p. 773; Sketch p. 684), 680, 685-6, 702, 776, 784
AMMON, Cpl C., 353n
AMMUNITION, 489; *Australian*, lack of forward dumps in Salamaua campaign, 31; at Lababia, 75, 79; shortages at Mubo, 123n, in Lae operations, 349, at Scarlet Beach, 465-6, at Katika, 534; expenditure at Katika, 540n; shortages in 2/27 Bn, 580-5. *Japanese*, capture of, 565, 786
AMOS, Spr L. C. B., 355-6
AMPHIBIOUS OPERATIONS, first American in SWPA, 222
AMUBA, 596n
AMUSON (Map p. 773; Sketches pp. 591, 684), 596n, 756, 772
ANAMI, General Korechika, 788
ANDAMAN ISLANDS (Sketches pp. 5, 218), 218
ANDERSON, Sgt A. R., 110-11, 170
ANDERSON, Lt H. K., 174, 176
ANDERSON, Lt J. R., 390

INDEX 823

ANDERSON, WO2 N. C., 644
ANDERSON, Capt N. D., 745
ANDERSON, Capt V. E. C., 705, 707
ANGAUR ISLAND, 816
ANGEL, Lt K. S., 459, 472, 491, 493-6
ANGUS, Capt W., 460, 474, 483, 489, 520, 591
ANNANBERG (Sketches pp. 258, 808), 242, 596, 810
ANNEN POINT (Map p. 28), 659
ANTIRAGEN (Sketch p. 427), 428
ANTIRAGEN TRACK (Sketches pp. 418, 420), 421
APAUKA, L-Cpl, 690
APO (Map p. 327), 336, 348
APO FISHING VILLAGE (Map p. 327), 336, 348-9
APOWEN (Sketch p. 258), 258
APPEL, Cpl A., 457
APPLETON, Lt F. C., 459
APRIL RIVER (Sketch p. 258), 261-2
ARAFURA SEA (Sketch p. 799), 11, 14, 791, 798, 810, 813
ARAI, Capt, 216
ARAKAN, 5, 18, 712
ARAKI, Colonel Katsutoshi, 82-3, 99, 113-15, 117, 119, 125, 168, 181; commands 66 Regt, 54
ARAU (Sketch p. 427), 416
ARAWE (Map p. 28; Sketch p. 793), 731, 793, 798n
ARAWUM (Map p. 773), 777
ARCHER, Lt F. P., 794
ARCHER, Capt G. R., 793n
ARCHWAY, 72
ARIFAGAN CREEK (Sketch p. 427), 423, 437
ARMITAGE, Pte H. L. W., 372
ARMSTRONG, Maj A. A., 784-5
ARNDT POINT (Map p. 528; Sketches pp. 452, 461), 452-4, 459, 505n, 518, 522, 533, 541-3, 554; Japanese plan counter-attack at, 525
ARNOLD, Capt E., 207, 287-8, 300-1, 303, 314n
ARNOLD, General of the Army H. H., 1n, 2n, 4, 7, 220n, 791
ARNOLD'S CREST (Sketches pp. 290, 302), 286-7, 300-4, 314-17, 321
ARNOTT, Pte K. G., 52
ARNOTT, L-Sgt M. R., 486-7
ARONA (Sketch p. 235), 244, 251, 431
ARTHUR, Brig A. E., 24n
ARTIE FADDEN (Sketch p. 290), 316
ARTILLERY, 185, 203, 305, 309, 312-13, 315, 366, 683; equipment of Australian Army, 24n; support allotted for Pimple-Green Hill attack, 30-1, in Old Vickers attack, 129, 170, at Komiatum, 192-3; effectiveness of mountain guns, 81, 149n; importance in Mubo attack, 123, 127; Bofors employed against pill-boxes, 185; Japanese raids on, 210-16; in Charlie Hill attack, 296-7; in Lae operations, 351-2, 364, 387, 389-90; in Ramu Valley, 692; at Shaggy Ridge, 706-7, 757; in advance to Fortification Point, 721, 727; in Saidor advance, 767. American, 321n; at Tambu Bay, 142-4, 161. Japanese, 683, 728, 747; Australian use of, 173, 191n; in Lae operations, 368; in Finschhafen operations, 489; at Kankiryo, 752
ARU ISLANDS (Map p. 814), 792, 811
ARUNDEL ISLAND (Sketch p. 224), 226
ASAKE (Sketches pp. 684, 759), 686, 760
ASALOKA (Sketch p. 235), 238-40, 243, 251, 600
ASH, Capt W. P., 496, 499
ASHKANASY, Lt-Col M., 279n
ASHTON, Maj L. E., 259, 793n
ASHTON, Lt S. L. A., 426
ASIA (Sketch p. 427), 437
ASIWA RIVER (Sketch p. 765), 766-7
ASSAI RIVER (Sketch p. 258), 259
ASSAM (Sketch p. 218), 5-6, 217
ASTROLABE BAY (Map p. 773), 772, 774
ATEMBLE (Sketch p. 258), 258-9, 432, 596-7
ATHERTON, Qld, 280-1, 763, 780
ATHERTON TABLELAND, 14, 133, 228, 242, 264, 268, 507, 566n, 682
ATKINSON, Lt G. H., 783-4, 786-7
ATKINSON, Lt J. W. H., 347
ATLANTIC OCEAN, 2, 4, 7, 217-18
ATSUNAS (Sketch p. 427), 423, 436-7
ATTU ISLAND (Sketch p. 5), 3, 227
ATZERA RANGE (Map p. 327; Sketch p. 388), 275, 377, 398, 407
AUCHINLECK, Field Marshal Sir Claude, 713, 781, 782
AURE RIVER (Map p. 28), 236

AUSTRALIA (Sketch p. 15), 2-3, 6, 10n, 17, 55, 84, 391, 652, 686n, 810; manpower problems, 12-13; General Blamey's views on defence of, 13-14; strength of Australian Services, 15, 817; US Army strength in, 16; possible invasion of, 18, 811
Australia, Australian cruiser, 12
AUSTRALIAN AIR FORCE, 261, 263, 279, 281, 567, 782; strength and deployment, 12, 15, 57, 227n; rescue and communication flight, 235; in Lae operations, 274, 390; attacks Gasmata, 449; in Finschhafen operations, 466, 548, 551; in Finisterres, 585, 695; in advance to Saidor, 730; at Merauke, 811-12
—WINGS: No. 62 Works, 804; No. 72, 812; No. 73, 797; No. 78, 804
—SQUADRONS: No. 4, 522, 651, 691, 709, 729; recces Bogadjim Road, 416; in Ramu Valley-Finisterres operations, 428-9, 682-3, 693-4, 702, 705-8, 711, 745, 778; in Finschhafen operations, 511, 649n; in advance to Saidor, 766, 768; No. 12, 812; No. 76, 797; No. 79, 223; No. 86, 812
AUSTRALIAN ARMY, 131, 223, 329-30, 407, 494, 499, 543n, 549n, 565, 567, 677, 731; Intelligence estimates, 10, 11n, 20; strength and deployment, 12-13, 14-17, 55, 220, 227n, 280n, 817; ratio of AIF to militia brigades in NG, 17; problems of jungle warfare, 21; establishes rest camps, 22; clothing and equipment, 51; relations with Americans, 138-41, 145, 159-61, 180-2, 281-4, 451, 523; role of, 221, 227-8, 763; not represented on GHQ, 222; training of, 228-9; air cooperation with USAAF, 231; relations with NG natives, 244, 246; organisation and command, 279-81, 787-8; transfer of militia battalions to AIF, 295n, performance in battle, 721; tactics compared with American, 321n; casualties in Salamaua campaign, 324, at Scarlet Beach, 467, in Sattelberg operations, 650, in New Guinea, 817; quality of staff planning, 444; and censorship, 558n; attachment of British officers to, 712-13, 781n; passes on experience to army in Burma, 781-2; strength, casualties and achievements 816-17
—ARMY HEADQUARTERS, 18
—MILITARY DISTRICTS: 8th, 682n, 762n
—ARMIES: First, 13, 779n, 780; composition, 16, 280; Second, 13, 18, 57, 279n, 280, 595, 787; composition, 16
—CORPS: I, 57, 279-81, 401, 465, 504n, 740; staff, 279n, relieves II Corps, 780; composition, 280n, 763; role, 282, 506; in Finschhafen operation, 444-6, 450, 480-3, 488; Allied naval and air support allotted, 505; relieved by II Corps, 514, 569; defines role of 7 Div in Ramu Valley, 561. II, 242, 264, 268, 281, 445n, 595, 696. 729; composition, 16, 280, 763, 780; relieves I Corps, 507, 514; role, 569. 729; defines roles of 5 and 7 Divs, 594; naval support of, 602; becomes NG Force, 788. III, 763, 780; composition, 16, 280n
—DIVISIONS: compared with Japanese, 11n; number of, 220. 1st Armoured, 17, 767n; strength and composition, 13, 16, 227, 280n; training, 18; disbandment, 227n; 2nd Motor, 13, 227; 3rd Armoured, 17; strength and composition, 13, 16, 227, 280n. 1st Infantry, 227; composition, 16, 280n; 2nd Infantry, 227; composition, 16, 280n; 3rd Infantry, 18, 91n, 123n, 227, 238, 271n, 279, 504n, 762-3, 780; composition, 16, 60-1, 280n; establishes HQ at Bulolo, 17, at Guadagasal, 168-9; in Salamaua campaign, 21, 23, 26, 34-5, 50-2, 54, 58-60, 133-4, 136, 285, role, 137, 166, 182, 210, 230, 391, casualties, 54, 324n; staff of, 26n; air support policy, 34n; problems of, 37-8; cooperation with 41 US Div, 60, 105. 138-41, 160; supply of, 65-6, 70-1, 137-8, 269; relations with Fifth Air Force, 129n; strength of infantry battalions in, 161n; artillery units under command, 192; relief of, 199, 289; achievements, 216; casualties inflicted on Japanese, 324; 4th Infantry, 227; composition, 16, 280n; reinforces Torres Strait-Merauke, 228; 5th Infantry, 227, 279, 304n, 359, 504n, 594-5, 602, 762-3. 780; organised as jungle division, 13; composition, 16, 60, 280n, 561; at Milne Bay, 17, 57, 290; relieves 3 Div, 199, 216, 289; in Salamaua campaign, 291, 321, 323, 325, 346, 391, 393, 400, casualties, 324n; supply of, 292; at Lae, 401, 404, 407-9, 411, 420; standard of malaria control in, 412; relieves 9 Div, 736; in advance to Madang, 764, 769, 785, 788, 804, 807; 6th Infantry, 7n, 18, 55, 131, 227, 234, 264-5, 687,

824 INDEX

AUSTRALIAN ARMY—continued
763; organised as jungle division, 13; composition, 16, 280; absorbs disbanded militia units, 17; proposed role at Finschhafen, 444, 445n; casualties Aitape-Wewak, 807n; 7th Infantry, 55, 227-8, 264-5, 274, 279, 282n, 289, 337-8, 395, 416-17, 421-2, 426-7, 429, 431-2, 504n, 507, 526, 596; condition of, 7; organised as jungle division, 13; composition, 16, 280n; role in Lae operations, 166, 182, 230, 268, 273, 276; supply of, 269, 271, 403, 414, 438, 566-7, 601; staff of, 269n; in Nadzab-Lae operations, 346, 359, 377-8, 381, 385-7, 389-91, 397, 400-1, casualties, 392; ration scales, 355; at Tsili Tsili, 358; in Ramu Valley and Finisterres, 415, 437-9, 443, 506, 524, 561, 564-6, 569, 593-5, 598-9, 682, 684, 164-5, 170-3, 702, 738-9, 774, 785; takes Bena Force under command, 434; achievements of, 600; malaria rate, 681n; air cooperation, 711; attachment of officers from India to, 713; plagued by visitors, 761; General Adachi on operations against, 762; relief of, 763, 771, 779; 8th Infantry, 767n; 9th Infantry, 55, 227, 268, 271, 276, 278-9, 282n, 289, 322, 325, 338n, 468, 504n, 507, 529, 543n, 566n, 594, 649n, 653, 659, 672, 721, 762; returns from Middle East, 7, 18, 264-5; organised as jungle division, 13; composition, 16, 280n; role in Lae operations, 166, 230, 266-7; training of, 265; relations with 2 ESB, 266; staff, 267n; in Lae operations, 273-5, 328-32, 336, 344, 346, 350n, 359, 378, 381, 385-8, 391-2, 395-6, 400, 682n, casualties, 392; ration scales, 355; supply of, 362, 403, 519n; in Finschhafen operations, 412, 443-6, 451, 454, 465, 480-2, 488, 505-6, 517-18, 522-3, 535-6, 540, 544, 555-6, 558-602, 608-9, 612, 624, 626, 656, 675, 679, 725, bombing of, 557; holds General Morshead in high regard, 514; censorship of correspondents' despatches, 558n; tests American rocket projector, 618n; in coastal advance, 663, 729-30, 732; malaria casualties, 681n; sickness rates, 734-5; relief of, 736, 763; casualties received and inflicted, 736-7; 11th Infantry, 17, 57, 227, 279, 504n, 780, 782; organised as jungle division, 13; composition, 16, 280n; relieves 7 Div, 771, 779; 12th Infantry, 227; composition, 16, 280n
—FORCES: Bena, 57, 60, 263, 279, 414-16, 424, 426-7, 438-9, 504n, 586; composition, 25, 599n; formed, 234-5; operations, 236-52, 431-5, 565; achievements, 443, 599-600; casualties received and inflicted, 600; Denness, 508; Home, 18; Hunt, 396; Kanga, 18-19, 23, 26, 28, 31, 235; Kelforce, 543; Laver, at Komiatum, 192-3, 195-6, 198; Macforce, 714, 716, 718; Merauke, 14, 231, 810-13; New Guinea, 18, 46, 100, 123n, 142n, 174n, 240, 242, 247, 261, 266, 269. 271n, 276, 279, 341, 359n, 401, 403, 413, 445n, 488, 504n, 505-6, 595, 609n, 624n, 663, 681n, 684, 686n, 687, 693, 739-40, 761, 763, 766, 779, 787-8, 807; composition and strength, 16-17, 57, 210, 280n; plans NG offensive, 55-6; Salamaua operations, 58-60, 73, 87, 104, 137-8, 164, 276; relations with Fifth Air Force, 129n; with US Army, 139-41, 281-3; in Lae offensive, 182, 221, 230, 273, 378; and Bena Force, 234, 236, 238, 599n; Mosstroops, 263; Finschhafen operations, 445-6, 480-3, 558n; redefines role of II Corps, 569; place naming, 642; plans neutralisation of Madang, 696; Ramu Valley-Finisterres, 738; Northern Territory, 16, 280n; Picken, 287, 298; Sattelforce, 490; Tilley, 412; Torres Strait, 14, 16-17, 280n; Tsili Tsili, 210, 279, 404, 416; Wampit, 210, 279, 341, 360, 404; Warfe, 287, 297-8
—ARMOUR AND CAVALRY: 1st Armd Bde, 16, 227n, 280n; 2nd Armd Bde, 16, 280n; 3rd Army Tk Bde, 13, 16-17; 4th Armd Bde, 13, 16-17, 227n, 280n; 1st Motor Bde, 16, 268; 3rd Motor Bde, 16, 227n, 280n; 1st Tk Bn, 227n, 667n; moves to Finschhafen, 548-9; in Finschhafen operations, 552, 608, 613, 656-61, 663-4, at Sattelberg, 616-25, 627-30, 639, 642, 645, advance to Fortification Point, 668-9, 714-16, 720-5, to Sio, 728, 733; becomes 1st Armd Regt, 548n; 2/4th Armd Regt, 227n; 2/5th Armd Regt, 227n; 2/6th Armd Regt, 227n, 781n; 2/9th Armd Regt, 227n; 2/10th Armd Regt, 227n; 2/6 Cav (Cdo) Regt, 556n; 7 Cav Regt, 566n; becomes 2/7 Cav (Cdo) Regt, 242; 2/7 Cav (Cdo) Regt, 242, 280n, 566n; 2/9 Cav (Cdo) Regt, 566n; 9 Div Carrier Coy, 509n; 11 Div Carrier Coy, 784-5
—ARTILLERY, equipment, 24n; in Salamaua operations, 324n; in Lae operations, 328, 331, 369;

AUSTRALIAN ARMY—continued
in Finschhafen operations, 469, 478, 492-3, 498-9, 509, 515, 549, 551, 559, 616; Japanese praise of, 649n; in advance to Saidor, 768; in Finisterres, 774. RAA 9 Div, 389-90, 557, 672. Anti-aircraft: 2/4 LAA Regt, 663n, 767; at Finschhafen, 464-5, 530-2, 536, 538; 2/3 LAA Bty, 663n; 10 LAA Bty, 450, at Finschhafen, 470, 530, 538. Anti-tank, 2/3rd, 602, 663n. Field: 2/1st, 18n, 74; 2/2nd, 24n; 2/4th, 276; Nadzab, 338-9, 340, 343-5; advance to Lae, 365, 373, 376-7, 384, 389, at Kaiapit, 431, 563; Ramu-Finisterres, 573, 575-8, 589, 595, 682-3, 687, 694, 698-701, 704-10, 741, 744-5, 747-52, 754-8; 2/5th, 781n; 2/6th, 138n, 663n, 667n; in Salamaua campaign, 142-4, 158, 164-5, 170-3, 189-90, 192, 213-15, 308, 315, 319; in Lae operations, 364; in Finschhafen operations, 602, 615-16; in advance to Sio, 668, 714-16, 718, 722, 725, 728-30; 2/7th, 724; 2/12th, 468n, 663n, 764, 767; in Lae operations, 352n, 364; in Finschhafen operations, 450, 464, 468-71, 474, 496, 512, 538, 616, 618, 622, 630, 632, 644, 648-9, 657, 666, 670-1, 673-4, 729; 2/14th, 767; 4th, 756, 772, 14th, 364; 1 Mtn Bty, 672n, 781n; in Salamaua campaign, 18n, 24, 30, 34, 40, 42, 75, 81, 120, 123, 127, 147, 149, 158, 161, 192, 649n; equipment, 24n; 2 Mtn Bty, 663n; in Finschhafen operations, 615-16, 642, 671-2, in Finisterres, 774, 776; "M" Hvy Bty, 615-16, 663n
—ENGINEERS, 811; build Wau-Bulldog Road, 20; in Salamaua campaign, 106, casualties, 324n; in Watut Valley, 119; in Lae operations, 328, 331-2, 337, 400-2; in Finschhafen operations, 489, 497-8, 513-14, 516, 665; in Finisterres, 709. Field Coys: 2/3rd, 450, 464, 471, 473, 663n, 728-9; 2/4th. 744; 2/5th, 339, 588, 681; 2/6th, 270-1, 276, 337-41, 344-6, 357, 588, 596, 681; 2/7th, 355-6, 361-2, 367-9, 602, 627, 657, 660, 663n, 667, 714, 716, 721-3; 2/13th, 488, 623-5, 627, 642, 663n, 735, 764; 8th, 764; 11th, 292; 15th, 775; 18th, 663n. Field Park Coys: 2/24th, 663; 59th, 401. 2/1st Mechanical Eqpt Coy, 464, 663n; 2/29th Camouflage Unit, 663n
—INDEPENDENT COMPANIES AND COMMANDO SQUADRONS: 414, 432n, 600; tasks in New Guinea, 17; training of, 228-9; headquarters unit created, 242; supply of, 438, 593; redesignated, 565-6. 1 Indep Coy, 566n, 690n. 2/2 Indep Coy, at Canungra, 229; reinforces Bena Force, 242-3; on Bena plateau, 243, 244n, 245-51; in Ramu Valley, 431, 434-6, 440, 443, 564-5; redesignated 2/2 Cdo Sqn, 565-6; in Ramu Valley area, 575, 586-7, 592-3, 596-7, 599-600, 680-1, 683, 687n, 692, 697-8, 711, 739, 742, 746, 774, 784; length of operational service, 594n; in Finisterres, 684-6, 776-7, Bogadjim area, 779. 2/3 Indep Coy, 18n, 32; in Salamaua campaign, 23-6, 28, 33, 35-6, 44-50, 61-2, 66-8,88, 107-8, 111-13, 115-17, 120, 124, 131-5, 150-6, 169, 171-2, 176, 187, 189, 191, 203-5, 207-8, 287, 289, 298, 300, 315, 317, 320, 323, 817; strength and casualties, 177, 324; redesignated 2/3 Cdo Sqn, 566n. 2/4 Indep Coy, 242; at Canungra, 229n; in Lae operations, 335, 349-50, 355, 361, 366-7, 369, 379, 386, 396-7, 404-6; redesignated 2/4 Cdo Sqn, 565-6; in Finschhafen operations, 602, 614, 616-17, 649, 651, 663, 666, 672, 677, 727. 2/5 Indep Coy, 18n, 24, 25n; redesignated, 566n. 2/6 Indep Coy, 242, 258-9, 414-15, 423; at Canungra, 229n; at Wesa, 246; at Kaiapit, 417-22, 426, 428; in Ramu Valley, 429, 431, 434, 436-9, 443, 563-4; redesignated 2/6 Cdo Sqn, 565-6; in Ramu Valley and Finisterres, 568-70, 573, 575, 586, 589, 592-4, 596, 599, 680-1, 683, 686-7, 689-93, 694-8, 702, 711; returns to Australia, 777. 2/7 Indep Coy, 18n, 24, 257, 817; on Bena plateau, 60, 238-47, 251; recces Bogadjim Road, 416; in Ramu Valley, 431-2, 434, 436, 439, 443; redesignated 2/7 Cdo Sqn, 565-6; on Sepik, 263; in Ramu Valley, 575, 589, 592-3, 596; relieved 594, 599. 2/8 Indep Coy, 566n
—INFANTRY: Brigades 1st, 16, 280n; 2nd, 16, 280n; 3rd, 16, 280n; 4th, 16-17, 60, 280n, 279, 401, 411-12, 508, 764; at Milne Bay, 57; at Lae, 357, 361; reinforces Finschhafen, 555, 558, 602; at Finschhafen, 616, 656, 662; AIF teams attached to, 666-7; in coastal advance, 667, 679, 714-30; casualties, 725n; at Madang, 788; 5th, 16, 280n; 6th, 16, 280n, 779; 7th, 16-17, 57, 280n, 445n; 8th, 16, 280n, 789; reinforces Finschhafen, 732, 736; in coastal advance, 737, 764, 769, 771, 785-8; casualties, 770; 9th, 16,

INDEX 825

AUSTRALIAN ARMY—continued
280n; 10th, 60-1; 11th, 16, 280n, 811-13; 12th, 16, 280n; 13th, 16, 280n; 14th, 16-17, 280n; 15th, 16-17, 24, 57, 401, 504n, 561; moves to Wau, 51, 60; origin and composition, 60-1; in Salamaua operations, 59, 66, 68, 71, 84, 87-8, 106-17, 128, 133-4, 137, 144, 150, 152-4, 156, 158, 163, 169, 176-7, 179, 183, 186-8, 192, 203, 206-7, 280n, 286-91, 300, 303, 309, 314-16, 318, 320, 322-3; casualties, 176, 324; Lae-Markham Valley, 403, 406; Ramu Valley-Finisterres, 712, 738-9, 742, 745, 754, 771, 774, 779; in advance to Bogadjim, 780, 782, 784; at Madang, 785-8; 16th, 16, 228, 280n, 445n, 779n; 17th, 16-19, 280n, 817; in Salamaua operations, 24, 26, 31, 42-3, 47, 59-60, 62-3, 66, 75n, 82, 84, 86, 88, 104-5, 107, 114, 119-29, 134n, 137, 144-6, 149, 153-5, 158-9, 168-9, 179, 183, 185, 188-9, 192, 197, 201, casualties, 324n; and Independent Companies, 46; relations with Americans, 139-40; returns to Australia, 285; 18th, 16, 264, 268, 280n, 340, 403, 415, 433, 438, 784; arrives Port Moresby, 269; reinforces 7 Div, 692-3, 712, 738; in Finisterres, 739-57, 761, 774, 779; 19th, 16, 280n; 20th, 16, 267, 271-2, 280n, 330, 670; trains with 2 ESB, 266; in Lae operations, 275, 326, 334, 503; chosen for Scarlet Beach attack, 445-8, 450-1; at Scarlet Beach, 454-60, 463, 465-6, 508; in Finschhafen operations, 466, 476, 479-83, 487, 491, 498-500, 502, 504, 518, 520, 524, 536, 541, 544, 550, 555-9, 606-8, 615-16, 626, 637, 656, 658, 664, casualties, 500, 519; attaches experienced team to 29/46 Bn, 667; in coastal advance, 725-6, 727, 730, 733, casualties, 736; 21st, 16, 268, 280n, 417, 434, 577n, 680; arrives Port Moresby, 269, 271; in Nadzab-Lae operation, 276, 378, 385, 398, 414-15; arrives Kaiapit, 422-3, 425; advance to Dumpu, 428-30, 432, 436-40, 443, 561-6, 567n, 575, 580; in Finisterres, 586, 589, 595-6, 599-600, 686-7, 695-6, 702-4, 710, 712; relieved, 738-40; 23rd, 16, 280n; 24th, 16, 267, 271, 280n, 505, 508; trains with 2 ESB, 266; in Lae operations, 337, 348-9, 363, 366, 368, 370, 379-80, 386, 390n; in Finschhafen operations, 488, 517-18, 520, 535-7, 539-41, 544, 550-1, 553-9, 607-8, 614-16, 626-7, 634, 642-3, 650-1, 656, 658-9, 665, 667, 669-70, 672-3, 677-9, 719, 726, 728-9, 732; returns to Australia, 736n; 25th, 16, 280n, 350n, 358, 390n, 414; arrives Port Moresby, 269; in Nadzab-Lae operations, 276-7, 339, 359, 364-5, 377, 387-9; advance to Dumpu, 415, 430-1, 433, 436-40, 443, 561, 564, 574, 580; in Finisterres, 585, 589, 595, 599-600, 680, 683-4, 686-7; in Ramu Valley, 692, 694-6, 702-3, 710; relieved, 712, 738; 26th, 16, 266-7, 271-2, 280n, 609n; in Lae operations, 275, 326, 328, 334, 337, 347-9, 351, 355n, 361, 366-9, 379, 386-7, 406; in Finschhafen operations, 523, 534-5, 548, 551-2, 555-6, 559, 604, 606, 662; in Sattelberg operations, 608, 612-14, 616, 619-21, 627-8, 630, 634, 642, 645, 648, 650; Gusika-Wareo, 656, 658-9, 665, 667, 671-3, 675, 677-9, 719; coastal advance, 726-9, 732, 734n; returns to Australia, 736n; 28th, 16, 280n; 29th, 16-17, 280n, 401, 764; at Milne Bay, 57; composition, 168; in Salamaua campaign, 179-81, 211, 215-16, 285, 289-91, 297, 309, 316, 318, 321, 323, casualties, 324n; in Markham Valley, 403; 30th, 16, 17, 615.
Battalions, 489; establishment, 46, 161n. 2/2nd, 662, 740, 781n. 2/3rd, 781n. 2/4th, 423. 2/5th, 18n, 215n, 297, 304; in Salamaua campaign, 24, 43, 60-1, 72, 78, 80, 107, 119-27, 134, 145-50, 161-7, 179, 181, 187, 189, 192, 195-200, 286; strength, 161n; casualties, 324n. 2/6th, 18n, 37, 306, 615; in Markham area, 24; in Salamaua campaign, 26, 43, 47, 51-3, 60-6, 74-83, 106-7, 119-27, 147, 154-5, 163-9, 169, 179, 186, 189, 191-6, 198, 200, 208; at Nassau Bay, 71-3, 86, 91-102; strength, 161n, 187n; casualties, 324n. 2/7th, 18n, 687; in] Salamaua campaign, 24-5, 28-31, 33-5, 37-43, 47, 50-2, 60-1, 82, 156, 163, 167, 171, 173-6, 189-91, 203-8, 242-3, 287-9, 298-301, 303, 314-15, 320-1; in Bena Force, 25n, 234, 599; returns to Australia, 323; casualties, 324, 2/9th, 577n; Shaggy Ridge, 739, 741, 743-4; Kankiryo Saddle, 747-52; attacks Crater Hill, 753-6; relieved, 771. 2/10th, Johns' Knoll area, 739; Kankiryo Saddle, 743-4, 746-7, 749-52; Crater Hill, 753-6; relieved, 771, 784. 2/12th, 739, 741; Kankiryo Saddle, 743-4, 747-51; Crater Hill, 753-4; McCullough's Ridge-Lake Hill area, 756; relief of,

AUSTRALIAN ARMY—continued
771; occupies Ward's Village, 774. 2/13th, 781n; in Lae operations, 275, 326, 328, 330-1, 333, 336, 347; in Finschhafen operations, 447, 451-6, 458-60, 462-3, 465-6, 468-78, 483-7, 489, 491-9, 504, 511, 514-16, 521, 541-4, 546-7, 550-1, 553, 556, 559, 603-6, 610-11, 737; casualties, 500n; in coastal advance, 727-30; returns to Australia, 736n. 2/14th, in Nadzab-Lae operations, 385, 399-400, 405, 415, 428-9; moves to Kaiapit, 425-6, 431; in Ramu Valley-Finisterres, 434, 436-7, 439-43, 563, 566-8, 573-4, 576-80, 583, 585-6, 589, 595, 680, 687, 703; relieved, 739. 2/15th, 781n; in Lae operations, 326, 331, 333, 380; in Finschhafen operations, 447, 456, 459-60, 462-3, 466-76, 478, 483-6, 489, 491, 496-7, 499, 504, 513-16, 519-20, 536, 542-3, 553, 556, 605, 610, 626, 651, 664-5, 670-1; casualties, 500n; advance to Sio, 727, 730, 732; returns to Australia, 736n. 2/16th, 350n; in Nadzab-Lae operations, 385, 398-9, 415; moves to Kaiapit, 422-3, 426; advance to Dumpu, 429-30, 434, 436-40, 442-3, 561-3; in Ramu Valley-Finisterres, 567, 574, 577, 585-7, 589-92, 598n, 680, 687-8, 703-10. 2/17th, 450; in Lae operations, 326, 331, 333-4, 336, 344, 347, 361-2, 371, 380, 447; in Finschhafen operations, 452-8, 460-4, 470, 473, 477-9, 483, 485, 490-1, 498-501, 504, 509, 511-16, 519, 527, 535-6, 542-3, 547, 550-1, 553, 556, 559, 602-6, 610-11, 615, 730; casualties, 500n, 734-5; advance to Sio, 732-6. 2/23rd, in Lae operations, 326, 328, 332, 334, 336-7, 347-50, 355, 362-3, 368, 370, 379-80, 386-7, 390; in Finschhafen operations, 450, 457, 551, 553, 610, 613-14, 616-19, 621-3, 625, 628-30, 639-42, 645-7, 649, 662, 665-6, 671, 673-6, 677; casualties, 735; returns to Australia, 736n. 2/24th, 468; in Lae operations, 326, 334, 336, 349-50, 379-80, 386, 396-7, 404-6; at Busu River, 354, 355-6, 361-2, 367-70; in Finschhafen operations, 553, 610-11, 614, 617, 619, 621, 623, 625-6, 629-30, 639, 641-2, 645, 648-50, 662, 665-6, 671, 673-9; returns to Australia, 736n. 2/25th, 740, 781n; Nadzab-Lae operations, 270, 339, 359-60, 364-5, 372-7, 385, 387-90; at Tsili Tsili, 358; at Kaiapit, 436; Ramu Valley-Finisterres, 564, 595, 680-2, 687, 692, 694-704. 2/27th, 414-15, 426, 781n; at Kaiapit, 428-9; Ramu Valley-Finisterres, 434, 436-7, 439, 443, 562-3, 566-77, 579-90, 598n, 680, 687-8, 703-6, 710. 2/28th, in Lae operations, 348-9, 356-7, 363, 368, 372, 380-1; at Busu River, 350-4; in Finschhafen operations, 505, 521, 523, 530-2, 534-42, 543n, 544-6, 549-50, 552-6, 610, 615, 632, 636-8, 643, 651, 659-61, 663, 669, 679; returns to Australia, 736n. 2/31st, 350n, 359, 615, 781n; in Lae-Nadzab operations, 339, 365, 373, 381-5, 387, 389-90; moves to Kaiapit, 431, 434; in Ramu Valley-Finisterres, 564, 586-7, 589, 680, 710-11. 2/32nd, 271, 347, 351, 615; in Lae operations, 348, 354, 363, 371-2, 380, 386-7, 389-90; at Tami Islands, 508; in Finschhafen operations, 526, 534, 541, 550-2, 554-6, 559, 610, 638-9, 669-70, 672-3, 676-7; at Pabu, 626-7, 630-8, 640 642-4, 651-2, 656-7, 659, 661; returns to Australia, 736n. 2/33rd, 350n, 392n, 434, 439; in Nadzab-Lae operations, 270, 339, 359, 372-3, 375-7, 381-5, 387, 389; Liberator disaster at Port Moresby, 358; in Ramu Valley-Finisterres, 564, 571, 574-5, 579-80, 584, 586-7, 597-8, 680, 687, 703-4. 2/43rd, 523; in Lae operations, 348, 352, 354, 363-4, 368, 370-1, 380, 387; in Finschhafen operations, 488, 490, 500-5, 509-13, 516, 518. 529, 532, 535-7, 539-40, 544, 546-7, 553-5, 557, 559, 607, 610-12, 615, 626-7, 632, 636-8, 642-4, 649, 651-2, 658-9, 661-4, 669-70, 672; casualties, 735; returns to Australia, 736n. 2/48th, 330, in Lae operations, 326, 328, 348, 355, 368, 370, 380, 386; in Finschhafen operations, 450, 457, 553-4, 556-7, 607, 608n, 666; in Sattelberg attack, 613-14, 616-25, 627-30, 639-40, 642, 644-9, 652; returns to Australia, 736n. 3rd, 17. 4th, in Rai Coast advance, 736, 764-7; advance to Sepik, 808-10. 9th, 17. 15th, 168; strength, 161n, 324; in Salamaua campaign, 180-1, 189, 211, 215, 285, 291, 294-5, 304-8, 316, 318-20, 323, 393, 395-6; casualties, 324n; see also Hunt Force. 22nd, 357, 663; coastal advance to Finschhafen, 411, 450, 467, 469, 471, 473-4, 478, 484, 488, 498-500; at Finschhafen, 504, 514, 518, 529, 543, 556, 602, 667; in advance to Sio, 667-9, 714, 719-24. 23rd/21st, 760n. 24th, 24, 26, 37, 60-1, 137, 271n, 738-9, 784n, 788; Markham-

826 INDEX

AUSTRALIAN ARMY—continued
Lae area, 25n, 52-4, 59, 69-70, 88-90, 117-18, 177, 209-210, 277, 341, 364-6, 377, 390, 395, 404-5, 409-11; Salamaua operations, 47-50, 288, 291, 315-17, 322-3; on Hote-Malolo track, 68, 88, 107, 113, 133, 208, 303; on Buang River, 118-19, 135, 156-8, 177-8, 393-4; strength, 161n; in Watut Valley, 253-4; becomes AIF, 295n, 406n; casualties, 324; on Boana Track, 406-9; malaria control in, 412-13; in Finisterres, 742, 745, 756-9, 771, 775; recovers Indian prisoners, 809. 25th, 17. 26th, 811-12. 29th/46th, 357, 412, 484n, 508, 662; reinforces Finschhafen, 602; in coastal advance, 667, 714-20, 724-5. 30th, in Rai Coast advance, 764-5, 767-9, 785; advance to Madang and Alexishafen, 785-8; advance to Sepik, 810. 31st/51st, 811-13. 35th, in Rai Coast advance, 764-5, 769-70, 785; Madang-Sepik area, 807-8. 36th, 17. 37th/52nd, 357, 667; in advance on Lae, 380; in advance to Fortification Point, 667, 669, 714, 716, 718-20, 721-5. 39th, 17. 42nd, 168, 291, 323; in Salamaua campaign, 179-81, 185, 187, 189, 192, 194-5, 198-203, 215, 285-6, 294-7, 309-12, 316, 318-22; casualties, 324n; Lae operations, 406, 408. 47th, 10, 168, 323; strength, 161n, 324; in Salamaua campaign, 211-15, 285, 297-9, 310, 312-13, 316, 320; casualties, 324n. 49th, 17. 55th/53rd, 17. 57th/60th, 57, 60, 137, 348, 738, 757; in Watut Valley, 70, 117, 119, 210, 255-7, 263, 404; strength, 161n; in Markham and Ramu Valleys, 416-17, 739; in Finisterres, 745-6, 759-61, 771-2, 774-6; advance to Bogadjim, 777, 779, 782-4; advance to Madang, 786-7. 58th, 60-1. 59th, 60-1. 58th/59th, 51, 53, 57, 60-1, 174, 738, 760n; in Salamaua campaign, 66, 68, 87-8, 107-16, 128-31, 134, 150-2, 155, 169-73, 176, 187-8, 203, 207-8, 287-9, 298, 300-3, 314-15, 317, 320, 322; strength, 161n, 177n; casualties, 177, 206, 324; moves to Dumpu, 739; in Finisterres, 745, 771-2, 775, 784; in Kabenau Valley, 777-9; in advance to Bogadjim, 782. 61st, 17. 62nd, at Merauke, 17, 810; relieved, 813. NGVR, 22n, 25n, 246, 324. Papuan Infantry, 57, 256, 412, 739; in Salamaua campaign, 72, 84, 91, 95, 99-102, 117-18, 134, 138n, 141-5, 158-9, 183, 211, 214-15, 294; casualties, 324n; in Watut Valley, 70, 119; in Markham-Lae operations, 86, 90, 177, 209-10, 227, 340, 344, 346, 349, 355, 371, 378-9, 385, 396-7, 403-6, 429, 431, 434; establishment, 86n; patrols to Mt Salawaket, 409; at Kaiapit, 414-17, 419-22, 426; in Ramu Valley-Finisterres, 437, 439, 563, 590n, 596, 599-600, 680-1, 686-7, 689-92, 695-6, 702-3, 810; in Finschhafen operations, 450, 458, 463-4, 470, 473, 484, 490, 500, 502, 504, 509, 511-12, 515-16, 518-20, 527, 531n, 539, 547, 554, 556, 559, 607, 609n, 610-12, 615, 627, 632, 636, 643, 651-2, 657, 662, 664, 666-7, 672, 729, 771; in advance to Saidor, 714, 716, 721n, 727, 733, 735, 764-70; at Bogadjim, 785; Madang-Sepik area, 788, 807-10. 20th Motor Regiment, 813. Sydney University Regiment, 330, 740

—MACHINE-GUN BATTALIONS: 2/1st, 781n; 2/2nd, 347; in Lae operations, 335, 380; in Finschhafen operations, 450, 457-8, 465, 470, 477, 510, 526, 543, 616, 667; in advance to Fortification Point, 714, 720, 722, 724; 6th, 594, 684, 784

—PIONEER BATTALIONS: 2/2nd, 382, 436; in Nadzab-Lae operations, 270-1, 276, 337-41, 344-6, 364-5, 375-7, 384-5, 403-5, 415; in Ramu Valley-Finisterres, 585, 595, 598, 600, 680, 687-9, 697, 703, 709, 711, 738-9, 741-2, 744-5, 747, 750, 753; 2/3rd, 380n; in Finschhafen operations, 464, 470, 478, 489, 497-8, 504, 510-12, 516, 518, 521, 527-9, 532-5, 538-9, 543-4, 546-8, 550-5, 663, 665

—AUSTRALIAN NEW GUINEA ADMINISTRATIVE UNIT, 70, 234, 236, 253, 256, 279, 504n, 599n, 666, 667n; in Salamaua campaign, 37n, 42, 54, 66, 75, 119; Markham-Lae area, 25n, 89-90, 118, 275, 341, 385, 398, 405-6; relations with natives, 90; on Bena plateau, 235, 237-9, 241, 243, 246, 436; and coast-watchers, 257; in Ramu Valley, 258, 440, 561, 596; on Sepik River, 261-3; at Kaiapit, 422-3, 426, 434; Finschhafen area, 450, 464, 609n, 615, 672, 688; in Finisterres, 598, 685, 743; at Saidor, 731; on Rai Coast, 736, 769n; at Bogadjim, 784; in Admiralties, 796-7; in Dutch New Guinea, 802-3, 806n

—BASE SUB-AREA AND FORTRESS COMMANDS: Lae Fortress Comd, 401; Milne Bay Fortress Comd,

AUSTRALIAN ARMY—continued
504n; Buna Base Sub-Area, 504n; Lae Base Sub-Area, 402-3, 504n; Madang Base Sub-Area, 788; Moresby Base Sub-Area, 504n
—MEDICAL AND DENTAL UNITS: 2/3 CCS, 472, 539; 2/2 Fd Amb, 559n; 2/8 Fd Amb, 450, 471-2, 539, 667n, 764; 4 Fd Amb, 667n; 15 Fd Amb, 71, 314, 739; 2/2 Special Dental Unit, 599n
—5TH MILITARY HISTORY FIELD TEAM, 762n
—POSTAL SERVICE, 599n
—1ST ADVANCED REINFORCEMENT DEPOT, 784n
—SCHOOLS: Canungra, 228-9, 242, 713; OCTU, 229; Beenleigh Tactical, 558, 615, 687, 713n
—SERVICE CORPS, 721; 9 Div ASC, 667n; 2/115 AGT Coy, 599n; 158 AGT Coy, 358
—SIGNALS, 3 Div Sigs, 213; NG Air Warning Wireless Unit, 25n, 234, 237, 599n, 688, 693
—SURVEY CORPS, 596n, 599n; 3 Bty, 512n, 663n
—VOLUNTEER DEFENCE CORPS, 14
—WOMEN'S SERVICES, AANS, 15n; AAMWS, 15n; AWAS, 15n
AUSTRALIAN BROADCASTING COMMISSION, 682n, 779, 784
AUSTRALIAN COMFORTS FUND, 728
AUSTRALIAN GOVERNMENT, 14, 782, 787; and Beat Hitler First policy, 6; passes Militia Bill, 16
—DEFENCE DEPARTMENT, 14
—INFORMATION DEPARTMENT, 558n
—MILITARY MISSION, WASHINGTON, 197, 780
—WAR CABINET, 14; manpower problems, 13; halts Australian tank manufacture, 17n; on strength of Australian Army, 227; assigns forces to General MacArthur, 763
—WAR COMMITMENTS COMMITTEE, 13
AUSTRALIAN NAVY, 223, 257, 267, 281, 793; strength, 15, 227n; at Scarlet Beach, 455n; supports Sepik advance, 807
AVERY, Lt A. R., 442, 576
AVIN (Sketch p. 394), 407-9
AWATIP (Sketch p. 799), 806n
AYRE, Sgt G. R. C., 111

BABER, Lt E. C., 88, 342, 360
BABIANG (Sketch p. 807), 806
BABWUF (Map p. 327), 270, 277, 340
BACON AND EGG 669; see also LAKES (Christmas Hills)
BADEN BAY (Sketch p. 85), 58
BADIBO (Sketch p. 394), 410
BADOGLIO, Marshal Pietro, 790
BAGASIN (Sketch p. 684), 680, 685-6
BAGASIN ROAD, 587n
BAGGALEY, L-Cpl R. O., 751-2
BAINDOUNG (Sketch p. 394), 406-7, 409
BAIRD, Capt V. C., 34, 40-1, 203-7, 288, 301
BAIROKO (Sketch p. 224), 225-6
BALAMA (Map p. 773), 784, 786
BALDERSTONE, Lt R. T., 421, 691, 694-5
BALD HILL (Finschhafen area; Map p. 717), 716
BALD HILL (Salamaua area; Map p. 293), 294
BALDWIN, Lt-Col A. O., 722-3
BALL, Lt C. H., 691, 694-6
BALL, Pte T. L., 678
BALLALE ISLAND (Sketch p. 224), 224
BAMBOK (Sketch p. 394), 399
BAMBOO KNOLL (Sketch p. 290), 203, 285, 295-6
BAMBOOS (Map p. 293), 304-8
BAMESS, L-Cpl B. A., 661-2
BANANA (Map p. 32), 78
BAND, Lt-Cdr J. M., 455n
BANDA SEA (Sketch p. 15), 15, 232
BANGDAP (Sketch p. 394), 408
BANGETA, Mount (Sketch p. 394), 378
BANGKOK (Sketch p. 218), 218
BARAULU ISLAND (Sketch p. 224), 225
BARBEY, Vice-Adm Daniel E., 271-2, 275, 278, 281, 282n, 329, 332-3, 335, 354, 357, 378, 444, 448-51, 456n, 457, 465-6, 508, 534-5, 548, 795, 804; commands Seventh Amphibious Fleet, 12, 56; plans landings on Kiriwina and Woodlark Islands, 222-3; in planning for Lae operations, 267, 269, 273, 279, 337n; allots landing craft for Finschhafen, 446; and reinforcement of Finschhafen, 480-3, 487-8
BARBOUTTIS, Cpl A., 812
BARDER, Capt K. R., 550n
BARHAM, Maj-Gen L. de L., 448
BARHAM, Brig R. J., 267, 445, 507, 675, 728

INDEX

BARKER, Maj W. F., 760
BARLING, Maj D. R., 208, 317, 408
BARNES, Lieutenant, 808-9
BARNES, Pte R. K., 581
BARNETT, Lt L. A., 299
BARR, Capt F. A., 34, 43, 47, 52, 189-90
BARRACLUFF, Lt J. T., 261-2
BARRAND, Lt R. S., 613
BARRINE (Sketch p. 15), 16, 280*n*
BARROWCLOUGH, Maj-Gen Rt Hon Sir Harold, 794; commands 3 NZ Div, 226
BARRY, Lt E. J., 45, 115-16, 152, 205
BARRY, Capt H. W. K., 109, 111
BARRY, Lt J. H., 625
BARTLEY, Sgt G. T., 53-4, 118, 342
BARUM (Map p. 773), 777-9
BARWISE, Pte H. C., 98
BASES 1 and 2, 23*n*
BASE 3 (Map p. 27), 23, 115, 134
BASE 4 (Map p. 27; Sketch p. 131), 67, 88, 117, 124, 132, 134, 146, 150, 167
BASSIS (Sketch p. 92) 52, 94, 99-100, 102, 117
BATAAN, 3
BATTEN, Maj R. L., 630, 640
BATTERU ISLAND (Sketch p. 85), 90
BAU-AK (Map p. 773; Sketch p. 783), 782-3
BAU PLANTATION (Map p. 773), 772
BAURI (Map p. 773), 784
BAWAN (Sketch p. 394), 406
BAYLISS, Pte W. A., 298
BAYONETS, use of, 343*n*, 395
BAZULUO (Sketch p. 660), 676-7
BEAR, Lt L. A., 578-9
BEARDMAN, Tpr R. L., 742
BEARE, Col F. H., 269*n*
BEAT HITLER FIRST POLICY, 1, 6, 7
BEAUMONT, Cpl A. G. W., 113
BEAVEN, Sgt B. V., 99
BEBEI (Sketch p. 562), 567, 574, 586, 739
BECK, Lt A. J., 255
BELL, Brig A. T. J., 403
BELL, Lt C. F., 631, 657
BELL, Sgt H. J., 371-2
BELL, Lt L. J., 257
BEMROSE, Cpl R., 673
BEN (Map p. 32), 53
BENA BENA (Sketch p. 235), 57, 60, 235-6, 243, 244*n*, 257-8, 402*n*, 414, 425, 431-2, 434, 436, 438-9, 443, 517, 561, 569, 575, 594, 599, 600, 739; airfields, 231, 234, 239-40, 247, 256, 599; plateau described 233; Australian operations and patrols, 236-49; Japanese air attacks, 238, 245; Japanese plan capture, 251-2
BENA BENA VALLEY, 235
BENCH CUT TRACK (Sketches pp. 109, 204), 31, 35, 108-9, 111-13, 128-30, 150-2, 155, 165, 171-2, 203, 207, 300
BENGARI, Sergeant, 86, 765, 770
BENNETT, Maj A. C., 134, 146, 149, 167, 197-200
BENNETT, Lt-Gen H. Gordon, 280*n*; commands III Corps, 16; returns to civil life, 780-1
BENNETT, Pte W. H. G., 441-2
BENNIE, Lt R. J., 513, 515, 519
BENSON, S. E., 180*n*, 296*n*
BERGER, Lt-Col Armin E., 294; commands II/162 Bn, 292
BERGER HILL (Map p. 293), 292, 309
BERMAN, Lt M. E., 775-6
BERNARD, WO2 P. McL., 521
BERRELL, WO2 E. J., 596
BERRELL, Sgt M. M., 755
BERRY, Cpl C. S., 191, 236
BERRYMAN, Lt-Gen Sir Frank (Plate p. 13), 71-3, 116*n*, 216, 230, 359, 378, 422, 433, 445, 448, 505, 506*n*, 535, 555, 557, 559, 615-16, 645, 656, 658, 696, 721*n*, 727, 729, 733*n*, 734*n*, 736, 765, 771, 780, 787; visits General Savige at 17 Bde HQ, 197-200; appointed MGGS, NGF, 280; on relations with American planning staffs, 281; reinforcement of Finschhafen, 480-2, 487; commands II Corps, 595; becomes Chief of Staff, Adv LHQ, 788
BERT'S POST (Sketch p. 562), 574, 590
BESIER, Lt J. C., 772
BEST, Lt L. D., 305, 308
BETHUNE, Capt J. F., 115, 287, 289, 301-3
BETIO ISLAND, 654-5
BEVERIDGE, Lt A. R., 247, 249-50

BEVERIDGE, Sgt G. A., 571
BEVERIDGE'S POST (Sketch p. 562), 571-3, 575-6, 680
BEWANI MOUNTAINS (Sketch p. 258), 260
BHAMO (Sketch p. 5), 6
BIAK ISLAND (Sketch p. 799), American landing on 805-6
BIBI (Sketch p. 734), 734
BICEP (Sketch p. 319), 318, 320-1
BICKLE, Pte J. H., 374
BIDING RIVER (Sketch p. 731), 731
BIEN (Sketch p. 808), 810
BIERI, Maj K. J. T., 630, 641-2, 673-8
BIERWIRTH, Lt-Gen R., 65*n*, 279*n*, 487
"BIG ROAD", 69
BILIAU (Sketch p. 731), 522, 731
BILI BILI (Map p. 773), 786
BILIMANG (Sketch p. 394), 404
BIRCH, Tpr A. J., 435
BIRCH, Lt F. D., 310-12
BIRD, WO1 N. M., 385, 405
BIRI (Sketch p. 759), 760
BIRIN (Sketch p. 262), 263
BIRMINGHAM, Lt W. B., 460, 462, 493, 496-7, 603, 605-6
BISHOP, Lt C. E., 99, 134, 690
BISHOP, Maj-Gen J. A. (Plate p. 460), 562-4, 567, 569, 571-3, 576, 580-1, 583-7, 589-90, 687; commands 2/27 Bn, 428
BISHOP, Maj M. A., 690, 697
BISIATABU, 739
BISMARCK ARCHIPELAGO (Map p. 28), 9, 220, 790
BISMARCK RANGE (Sketch p. 235), 233, 237, 240-1, 245, 251, 438, 443, 517, 687*n*
BISMARCK SEA (Map p. 28), 466
BISMARCK SEA, BATTLE OF, 10, 26, 54, 257
BISSET, Capt S. Y., 399, 442, 577
BITOI RIDGE (Sketches pp. 25, 212), 22, 26, 65, 72-4, 84*n*, 86, 104, 106-7, 122, 124, 127, 187, 211
BITOI RIVER (Sketches pp. 25, 62), 22-4, 26, 34, 37, 43, 59, 62-5, 72, 74-5, 86, 90-1, 97-103, 118, 121-2, 124, 126-7, 134, 147, 180, 211
BITOI TRACK, 91, 101, 103
BITTER LAKE, 265
BIWI RIVER (Sketch p. 441), 443
BIZERTA, 1
BLACK, Capt G. B., 263
BLACK, Lt-Col J. R., 234-5, 240-1
BLACKBURN, Lt N. G., 510-11
BLACK CAT TRACK (Map p. 32), 31
BLACKER, Sgt D. R., 582
BLACKSHAW, Capt J. R., 206
BLAINEY, Capt G. C., 418-20, 690-2, 694-5
BLAMEY, Field Marshal Sir Thomas (Plates pp. 13, 348), 24*n*, 46, 58, 200*n*, 242, 278, 359*n*, 391, 422, 523, 535, 558, 686*n*, 705, 727, 734*n*, 764, 794*n*; commands Allied Land Forces, SWPA, 12; reorganises Australian Army, 13-14, 279-81; plans offensive in New Guinea, 23, 55-7, 73, 216, 230, 231; visits New Guinea, 197, 696; orders relief of 3 Div, 199; relations with General MacArthur, 221-2, 281-4; on strength and training of Australian Army, 227-8, 264; and Mosstroops, 260, 263; seeks larger transports for move of 9 Div to Lae, 266-7; on role of 7 Div, 268-9, 426, 779; issues Operation Instruction for Lae-Nadzab, 273; and Japanese withdrawal from Lae, 378, 771; returns to Australia, 401; role enlarged to include seizures Kaiapit and Dumpu, 414; in Finschhafen planning, 444-5, 449, 480-3, 487-8; on use of code names, 506*n*; reallots senior commands, 507, 594-5, 780-1, 787-8; exchange of Australian and Indian Army officers, 712-13, 781-2; relief of Australian Army in New Guinea, 763; visits USA and UK, 780
BLOFFWITCH, Cpl H. W., 752
BLOOD, Capt N. B. N., 261-2
BLOW, Sgt M. W. G., 311
BLOXHAM, Maj A. A., 236
BLUCHER POINT (Sketch p. 726), 610, 659, 729
BLUE BEACH, 467
BLUNDELL, Lt H. N., 342-3
BLYTH, Lt-Col A. J., 338-9, 595, 741, 745; commands 2/4 Fd Regt, 276
BLYTHE, Sgt S. G., 301
BOANA (Map p. 327), 89, 241, 378-9, 385-6, 396-400, 403-5, 408, 410, 415, 429, 433*n*; airstrip at, 406, 409
BOANA TRACK, 397, 405
BOASE, Lt-Gen A. J., 785; commands 11 Div, 779

INDEX

BOBADU (Map p. 32), 23, 50
BOBDUBI (Maps pp. 27, 32; Sketches pp. 109, 194), 35, 45-6, 52, 108, 111-13, 115, 117, 136, 140, 150-2, 169, 188-91, 203-4, 207, 300; Japanese strength, 57; Japanese estimate of Allied strength, 118*n*
BOBDUBI RIDGE (Map p. 27; Sketch p. 194), 22, 28, 32-3, 35, 43-6, 50, 61, 88, 90, 107-8, 112, 115, 128, 134*n*, 136-7, 151, 153, 169, 171, 177-8, 186*n*, 188, 191, 204, 207, 216, 300; described, 23; plans for capture, 59, 68, 73, 84, 87; 15 Bde operations against, 108-17, 150-3; Japanese strength on, 71; Japanese account of operations, 173-4
BOBDUBI RIDGE TRACK, 112
BOBDUBI TRACK (Sketch p. 204), 108, 115, 191, 203
BOB'S POST (Sketch p. 562), 598, 687
BOGADJIM (Map p. 773; Sketch p. 235), 237, 241, 325, 415, 425-6, 444, 524*n*, 562, 566, 569, 588, 600-1, 684-5, 711, 738, 771-2, 774, 777, 785, 788-9, 802; Japanese strength at, 238; 15 Bde advance to, 782-4; General Morshead seeks definition of responsibility in area, 779-80; entered, 784; Japanese equipment at, 786
BOGADJIM PLANTATION (Map p. 773), 777, 782-3
BOGADJIM ROAD (Sketch p. 235), 236-8, 244, 247, 251, 416, 425, 436, 566, 576, 585, 587*n*, 588-9, 681, 689, 691, 693, 738-9, 761, 774, 777, 779, 782, 784; usefulness to Japanese reduced, 642
BOGANON (Sketch p. 562), 571, 579, 595
BOGIA (Sketch p. 808), 20, 807-9
BOIKIN, 232
BOISEN, Capt F. N., 261-2
BOISI (Sketch p. 141), 72, 143-4, 159, 181, 183-4, 187, 189, 202, 213, 311; Japanese strength, 142
BOKU RIVER (Sketch p. 759), 592, 691, 702, 711, 761
BONGA (Map p. 528; Sketch p. 660), 450, 458, 464, 504, 510, 512-13, 516-20, 525-6, 531*n*, 535, 537*n*, 547, 554, 556-7, 559, 607, 613-16, 626, 632, 651, 659-60, 662, 678; occupied, 661
BONGA TRACK, 464, 518, 535
BONGGU (Map p. 773), 778
BONIN ISLANDS (Map p. 814), 791
BONNER, Sgt R. J., 661-2
BOOBY-TRAPS, *Australian*, 40, 44, 47-8, 50-1, 77, 157, 690-1; *Japanese*, 67, 208, 317, 553
BOOKER, Lt R. J., 796-7
BOPARIMPUM (Sketch p. 424) 424, 439, 564
BOROAI (Sketch p. 235), 244, 247
BORRINGE (Map p. 773), 595
BOUGAINVILLE (Map p. 28; Sketch p. 224), 36*n*, 224, 226, 524, 792, 801, 806; Allied plans for assault on, 8, 9, 220-1; Americans land on, 653
BOULLY, Cpl H. E., 678
BOURNE, Brig C. C. F., 747; commands 2/12 Bn, 743
BOURNE, WO2 C. E., 636
BOWAMU (Sketch p. 394), 396
BOWEN, WO2 L., 41
BOWERS, Lt F. 315
BOX, WO1 R.A., 583
BOYLE, Lt L. C., 342
BRACK, Lt A. W., 408
BRAIMBRIDGE, Lt F., 356, 370
BRAITHWAITE, Lt E. C., 747-8
BRAMMER, L-Sgt J. McA., 570
BRAY, Maj A. C., 751-2
BREHENY, Maj D. J., 26*n*
BREMNER, Capt L. D., 434
BREWSTER, Capt D. J., 772, 777-8
BRIAN'S HILL (Sketch p. 562), 687, 703
"B" RIDGE (Map p. 293; Sketch p. 290), 201, 285, 292, 294
BRIDGE 6 (Map p. 773; Sketch p. 783), 782-3, 785
BRIDGE 21A, 775
BRIDGE 22, 775
BRIDGEFORD, Lt-Gen Sir William, commands 3 Armd Div, 17
BRIGGS, Cpl H. G., 175-6
BRIGHTWELL, Sgt T. P., 477-8
BRILLIANT, Cpl J., 721
BRISBANE (Map p. 15), 9-10, 56, 220, 223, 228, 230, 238, 401, 479-81, 779, 797*n*; US Army at, 16-17
BRITAIN, GREAT, 2, 15; American Army strength in, 2*n*, 4, 219; designs landing craft, 272
BRITISH AIR FORCE, 686*n*, 782
BRITISH ARMY, 310, 565, 782; in Burma-India theatre, 5, 18; officers to train with Australian Army, 712-13, 781; Dieppe and North African landings, 273; liaison missions in Australia, 781

BRITISH ARMY—*continued*
—ARMIES: First, 1; Eighth, 1, 264, 283; Fourteenth, 781-2
—INDEPENDENT COMPANIES: 272-3
BRITISH BROADCASTING CORPORATION, 784
BRITISH GOVERNMENT,
—CHIEFS OF STAFFS, 218; at Casablanca conference, 1-4; and Lethbridge mission, 686*n*
—JOINT INTELLIGENCE COMMITTEE, 10*n*
—WAR CABINET, 3*n*
BRITISH NAVY, 283, 686*n*
BRITISH SOLOMON ISLANDS PROTECTORATE DEFENCE FORCE, 225
BRITTEN, Major, 339
BROADBENT, Brig J. R., 333, 336, 450, 457, 464-5, 490, 510-11, 547, 605-6, 611
BROCKETT, Col E. D., 446, 456, 464; commands Shore Bn, 532 EBSR, 329
BROCKHURST, Sgt H. E., 360
BROCKSOPP, Maj A. E., 617, 624, 629, 644-5, 648
BROOKE, General Sir Alan, *see* ALANBROOKE, Field Marshal Viscount
BROOKES, Capt J. D., 783
BROOKS, Lt J. W., 356-7
BROOKS, Cpl R. C., 515
BROUN, L-Cpl W. O. T., 554
BROWN, Pte A. C., 286
BROWN, Maj C. C., 659-60
BROWN, Cpl J. H., 521
BROWN, Maj W. F., 619, 622-3, 628-9
BROWNING, Lt J. F., 637-8
BROWNING, Rear-Adm Miles R. 8
BRUCE, Lt T. A., 379, 397, 547
BRYAN, J., 10*n*, 225*n*
BRYANT, Sir Arthur, 3*n*, 218*n*, 219*n*
BRYANT, Lt J. R., 214
BUA (Sketch p. 467), 469, 471, 478
BUANG RIVER (Map p. 32; Sketch p. 156), 53-4, 59, 163, 177-8, 209-10, 281; 24 Bn at, 118-19, 135, 157-8, 322-3, 393-4
BUANG TRACK, 135
BUANG VALLEY, 158, 177-8, 209
BUARU (Map p. 327), 336
BUCKLEY, Lt-Col A. A., 713
BUCKLEY, Lt J. A. R., 607, 621
BUCKLEY, L-Cpl J. C., 550*n*
BUCKLEY, Lt W. M., 386
BUFF'S KNOLL (Sketch p. 568), 568
BUGA (Sketch p. 394), 412
BUGASU (Sketch p. 48), 47
BUGG, Cpl L. F., 750
BUHEM RIVER (Map p. 327), 347
BUI ALANG CREEK (Map p. 108), 107, 123, 127, 134 145-6
BUIAMBUM (Sketch p. 141), 142
BUIAPAL CREEK (Map p. 108), 29, 74, 119, 125
BUIBAINING (Map p. 32), 24
BUIEM RIVER (Map p. 327; Sketch p. 348), 334, 336, 347
BUIENGIM (Sketch p. 467), 469
BUI EO CREEK (Map p. 108), 147, 150, 169, 179, 199-200
BUIGAP CREEK (Map p. 108; Sketch p. 25), 22, 28, 34, 38, 65, 71-2, 107, 119, 122-8, 132, 134, 145, 147, 165, 169
BUIGAP VALLEY, 210
BUI KUMBUL CREEK (Map p. 108), 107, 123-5, 127, 133, 311
BUIN (Map p. 28; Sketch p. 224), 220, 226, 653
BUIRALI CREEK (Map p. 27), 22, 23*n*, 28, 31, 153-4, 165-7, 186, 207-8, 287, 289
BUIRIS CREEK (Map p. 27), 134, 152, 163, 207-8, 300, 303
BUISAVAL RIDGE (Map p. 32), 87
BUI SAVELLA CREEK (Map p. 108), 72, 107, 120-7
BUI TALAI CREEK (Map p. 108), 127
BUITWARFE CREEK (Map p. 27), 22, 181, 208
BUKA, Sergeant, 803
BUKA ISLAND (Sketches pp. 224, 793), 224, 653, 794
BUKA PASSAGE (Sketch p. 224), 220
BUKASIP (Sketch p. 394), 412
BUKUAP (Sketch p. 291), 107, 119, 315-16, 393
BULLDOG (Map p. 28), 20, 87*n*, 563
BULLDOG ROAD, 236, 269, 270*n*
BULOLO (Map p. 32), 17, 19-20, 23, 31, 42, 58, 60, 71, 156, 160, 164, 253, 270; airfield at, 26

INDEX   829

BULOLO VALLEY (Map p. 32), 23-4, 26, 61, 68, 156, 178, 210, 268-70, 281, 292, 314
BULU PLANTATION (Sketch p. 333), 275, 333
BULU RIVER (Sketch p. 333), 333
BULWA (Map p. 32), 66; airfield at, 20, 26, 61
BUMBUM (Sketch p 427), 244, 431, 439, 442-3, 575
BUMBU RIVER (Map p. 327; Sketch p. 388), 275, 378-9, 381, 385-90, 397-8, 401-3
BUMBU VALLEY, 398
BUMI RIVER (Map p. 528; Sketch p. 461), 466-70, 472-4, 483-4, 489, 498-9, 503, 548
BUNA (Map p. 28), 12, 14, 55, 57, 84, 142, 144, 168, 226, 227*n*, 231, 253, 264, 271, 280*n*, 328-9, 337, 357, 359, 401, 403, 444, 448-51, 457, 480-1, 488, 490, 507-8, 519, 534-5, 548, 615, 712, 713*n*, 738; port developed, 230, 267
BUNBOK RIVER (Sketch p. 394), 399, 400
BUNBURY, Maj C. R., 365, 395, 408
BUNDI (Sketch p. 235), 237-8, 242-6, 258, 416, 424, 440, 564, 592-4
BUNDI-CRAI (Sketch p. 235), 245
BUNGALUMBA (Sketch p. 394), 378, 404, 409
BUNGA RIVER (Sketch p. 350), 348, 445
BUNNING, Pte J. I., 803
BUNSELL, Maj A. W. C., 254
BUREP RIVER (Map p. 327; Sketch p. 350), 275, 336, 349, 350*n*, 352, 354, 361-4, 367, 369, 389, 448; described, 355
BURING, Capt O. G., 352, 354
BURI RIVER (Sketch p. 726), 733
BURKE, Capt D. B., 62-5, 72-3, 86, 91-4, 95*n*, 100
BURLEIGH, Lt A. W., 720
BURMA (Sketch p. 5), 1, 6, 11, 18, 220, 712; future operations discussed at Casablanca Conference, 2-5; Japanese strength, 11*n*; Allied plans, 217-18
BURMA ROAD, 2, 217
BURNET, Lt J. W., 246
BURNS, Pte G. A., 377, 384
BURNS, Capt R. T. C., 373-4, 701, 703
BURWOOD, NSW, 280*n*
BUSAMA (Map p. 32), 107, 119, 315-16, 393
BUSAN (Sketch p. 394), 395
BUSBY, Capt H., 148
BUSIP RIVER (Sketch p. 394), 399
BUSK, Cpl P. N., 681
BUSO (Sketch p. 85), 72, 86, 91, 95, 99
BUSO RIVER (Map p. 327; Sketch p. 333), 333-4, 336-7, 682*n*
BUSUNGO (Sketch p. 394), 404
BUSU RIVER (Map p. 327; Sketch p. 369), 275, 334, 336-7, 349, 359, 363, 365, 378-80, 386, 389, 391, 396-8, 404, 407; crossing of, 350-6, 361-2, 366-70; flooding helps Japanese to escape, 392
BUT (Map p. 28), 232
BUTALA (Sketch p. 467), 412, 474
BUTAWENG (Sketch p. 485), 499, 514, 526, 612
BUTIBUM (Sketch p. 369), 386-7, 401
BUTIBUM RIVER, see BUMBU RIVER
BUTLER, Lt G. J., 640
BUTLER, Maj W. G., 373-4, 387-9
BUTUBUTU (Sketch p. 768), 765*n*, 767
BUYAWIM RIVER (Map p. 32; Sketch p. 141), 23-4, 43
BWAI (Map p. 773), 782
BWANA (Sketch p. 768), 769
BWARIP (Map p. 327), 209
BWUSSI (Map p. 32), 54
BWUSSI RIVER (Map p. 32), 54
BYRNE, Capt E. F., 240-2, 244-6
BYRNE, Lt-Col J. H., 384
BYRNE, Capt L. W., 306-7
BYRNE'S O.P. (Map p. 293), 307

CABOOLTURE, Qld, 60
CAFFIN, Lt M. L., 149*n*
CAFFIN'S TRACK (Map p. 27), 149, 161-2
CAIRNS (Sketch p. 15), 266, 271, 611
CAIRO, 791
CALABASH MOUNTAIN, see ARNOLD'S CREST
CAMBRIDGE, Capt R. C., 257*n*
CAMEL RIDGE (Sketch p. 290), 286, 300-1, 303
CAMERON, Lt A. A., 698
CAMERON, Hon A. G., 787
CAMERON, Brig C. E. (Plate p. 780), 764-5, 767, 769, 771, 787; commands 8 Bde, 736
CAMERON, Pte G. R. A., 721
CAMERON, Maj I. B., 747
CAMERON, Capt L. A., 125-6, 146-9, 161-2, 165-6, 181
CAMERON, Capt R. A., 745
CAMERON, Lt S. A., 202
CAMERON, Maj W. J., 78-9, 86, 126
CAMERON'S KNOLL (Map p. 773; Sketch p. 757), 745, 761, 774; attack on, 757-9
CAMERON'S TRACK (Sketch p. 146), 147, 149
CAMPBELL, Lt-Col A. J., 267*n*
CAMPBELL, Pte P. W., 435
CAMPBELL, Col R. W. C., 279*n*
CAMPBELL, Gp Capt S. A. C., 233*n*
CAMP CABLE, Qld, 280*n*
CAMP COLUMBIA, Qld, 280*n*
CAMP DIDDY (Map p. 327), 385, 400, 403-5
CAM'S HILL (Map p. 740), 751-2, 771
CAM'S SADDLE (Map p. 740), 740-1, 743, 751; attack on, 744, 746-7
CANADIAN AIR FORCE, 686*n*
CANADIAN ARMY, 686*n*; 13 Bde lands on Kiska Island, 227; in Dieppe landing, 273
Canberra, Australian ship, 269
CANE KNOLL (Sketch p. 174), 174
CANET, Maj-Gen L. G., 269*n*, 599, 687
CANN, Maj S. B., 781*n*
CANNIBALISM, 770*n*
CANNING, Lt B. L., 711*n*
CANNING'S SADDLE (Map p. 740; Sketch p. 710), 711, 741-3, 747, 771
CANUNGRA (Sketch p. 15), 242, 713; becomes army training centre, 228-9
CAPE COD, 84
CAPE YORK PENINSULA (Map p. 28), 228
CAPLE, Lt J. H., 625-6
CARDEW, Maj R. H. C., 262
CAREY, L-Cpl J. W., 746
CAREY, Cpl V. F., 162
CARNEY, Sgt J. P., 758
CAROLINE ISLANDS (Map p. 814; Sketch p. 5), 2-3, 220, 798, 801
CARPENDER, Admiral Arthur S., 267, 278, 433, 449, 505-6, 535, 556, 602; and plans for landings on Kiriwina and Woodlark Islands, 222; controls water transportation system north of Buna, 231; and reinforcement of Finschhafen, 481-3, 487-8
CARR, Lt J. W., 32, 45
CARRIERS, NATIVE, 37, 130, 150, 346, 514-15, 576, 585, 741, 793; in Salamaua operations, 65-6, 75, 89-90, 115-16, 291, 310-11; with Bena Force, 234, 236, 240, 244; in Markham and Ramu Valleys, 341, 407, 409, 422, 426-7, 434, 693; in Finisterres, 566-7, 593, 689, 775-6; in Finschhafen operations, 590, 609, 641
CARROLL, Capt C., 376
CARTER, Capt Jesse H., 278
CARTER, F-Lt S. R., 691, 702
CASABLANCA CONFERENCE, 1-4, 6-7, 12, 217
CASEY, Maj-Gen Hugh J., 402*n*
CASH, Sgt M. C., 742
CASINO, NSW, 60
CASUALTIES, *American*: in New Georgia and Aleutians, 226-7; at Tarawa, 655; at Cape Gloucester, 794; in Admiralty Islands, 797; in Marshall Islands, 800; on Bougainville, 801; at Hollandia, 804; at Aitape, 807; at Saipan, Tinian and Guam, 815; at Peleliu and Angaur, 816. *Australian*: in Salamaua operations, 54, 324; in Liberator crash at Pt Moresby, 358; in Lae operations, 392; in Finschhafen operations, 467, 500, 519, 560; in Sattelberg operations, 650; in coastal advance, 725*n*, 736; in 9 Div, 734-5, 737; in 7 Div, 756; in Aitape-Wewak campaign, 807*n*; to August 1944, 817. *Japanese*: in Bismarck Sea Battle, 26-8; in Lae-Salamaua operations, 54, 324, 392; in New Georgia and Aleutians, 226-7; in Finschhafen operations, 560; in coastal retreat, 736-7, 770-1; in the Finisterres, 756; at Cape Gloucester, 794; in Admiralty Islands, 797; in Marshall Islands, 800; on Bougainville, 801; at Hollandia, 804; at Aitape, 807; at Saipan, Tinian and Guam, 815; at Peleliu and Angaur Islands, 816; in Papua and New Guinea operations, 817
CATCHLOVE, Maj W. E. L., 363-4
CATE, J. L., see CRAVEN, W. F.
CATERSON, Lt R. D. W., 40*n*
CAVALIERI, Lt C., 237
CAVANAGH, Capt C. O., 523, 532, 550
CAVENAGH, Capt T. J. D., 306-7
CAWTHORNE, Lt C. H., 636-7

830 INDEX

CELEBES (Sketch p. 15), 791, 813
CEMETERY CORNER (Sketch p. 606), 603, 605
CENSORSHIP, by GHQ, 558n
CENTRAL AMBUSH, 360
CENTRAL PACIFIC AREA (Sketch p. 5), 653, 800-1, 816; US strength in, 2n; role of forces, 7; Allied strategy in, 8, 790-2
CERAM (Sketch p. 15), 11, 813
CEYLON (Sketch p. 5), 5
CHALK, Capt J. A., 90, 118-19, 177, 209-10, 277, 340, 344, 346, 415-17, 421, 690, 692, 810
CHAMBERLAIN, J., 221n, 798n
CHAMBERLIN, Lt-Gen Stephen J., 8, 263, 422, 444-5, 448, 480, 507n; relations with Australian planning staffs, 281-2; and reinforcement of Finschhafen, 481
CHAMBERS, Capt D. G. N., 257n
CHAMPION, Lt I. F., 233
CHAPMAN-WALKER, Col J., 781n
CHARLIE HILL (Map p. 293; Sketches pp. 194, 290), 201, 203, 208, 286-7, 291, 294, 300, 304, 313, 316, 325; attacks on, 295-7, 309-12
CHARLOTT, R., 724n
CHARTERS TOWERS, Qld, 228
CHASE, Maj-Gen William C., 795-6
CHENNAULT, Lt-Gen Claire L., commands US Fourteenth Air Force, 220
CHILDS, Capt F. H., 341-3, 360
CHILTON, Brig F. O. (Plate p. 460), 662, 712, 738, 745, 753, 756; commands 18 Bde, 340; plans attack on Kankiryo Saddle, 739-41, 743-4; estimate of, 740; redisposes brigade in attack on Crater Hill, 754; commands 7 Div, 774
CHIMBU (Sketch p. 235), 237, 239, 241-2, 251, 586; pre-war patrols into area, 233; airstrip, 243
CHIMBUS, The, 234, 236, 240-1, 245
CHINA (Sketch p. 5), 2, 220, 272, 801; US interest in, 3, 217-18; strength of Japanese forces, 6, 11n; airfields in, 791
CHINATOWN (Sketches pp. 319, 388), 25n, 318, 381, 386-7, 390; occupied, 321
CHINDITS, 18; see also INDIAN ARMY
CHINDWIN RIVER (Sketch p. 5), 6
CHINESE, in New Guinea, 61, 386, 396, 808
CHINESE ARMY, 6, 18
CHINNER, Lt-Col J. H., 267n
CHIVASINO (Map p. 32; Sketch p. 252), 70, 89-90, 118, 209-10, 256, 346
CHOWNE, Lt A., VC, 483-4, 487
CHRISTENSEN, WO2 G. H., 90
CHRISTIAN, Capt R. H., 705-7
CHRISTIE, Capt E. McN., 460, 463, 468-9
CHRISTMAS HILLS (Sketches pp. 635, 660), 656, 664-5, 667, 669, 676-7; attacks on, 670-3; see also FEATURE 1800
CHRISTOPHERSON, Maj F. A., 567, 583, 585-6
CHURCHILL, Rt Hon Sir Winston, 2n, 712, 781n; at Casablanca Conference, 1, 3; on US interest in Burma-China theatres, 217; at Washington Conference, May 1943, 218-19; at Quebec Conference, Aug 1943, 790
CISSEMBOB (Sketch p. 48), 47-50, 58, 68, 133
CITY (Sketch p. 485), 487, 491-2, 496-7, 499
CLAMPETT, Capt R. W., 576, 587, 589-90
CLAPPERTON, Capt G. T., 718-20
CLARK, Pte L., 383
CLARKE, Sgt J. T., 110
CLAYTON, Lt A. C., 339
CLEMENS, Maj M., 225
CLIFFORD, Lt A. V., 503
CLOTHIER, Sgt L. A., 495
CLOWES, Lt-Gen C. A., 70, 740; commands 11 Div, 17, 57
CLUES, Sgt W. J., 205
COAD, Cpl V. V., 688
COANE, Brig-Gen Ralph W., 140, 142-4, 158, 163, 168, 179-80; commands "Coane Force" in Nassau Bay operations, 138; to become CRA 3 Aust Div, 141; relations with General Savige, 159-61, 180-1; relieved of command, 182
COASTWATCHERS, 224-5, 451; on Woodlark Island, 223; operations in 1943, 257-8; on New Britain, 792-3
COCHRAN, Lt-Col G. P., 212n
COCHRAN BEACH (Sketch p. 212), 212-14
COCHRANE, Lt M., 123, 149
COCONUT BEACH (Map p. 717), 726n
COCONUT GROVE (Sketch p. 606), 603-4, 611

COCONUT RIDGE (Bobdubi area; Sketches pp. 190, 204), 47, 170, 189-91, 204
COCONUT RIDGE (Sattelberg Road area; Sketch p. 617), 617-22
COCONUTS (Bobdubi area; Map p. 27; Sketches pp. 109, 190), 35-6, 44-5, 87, 109, 112, 114, 116, 152, 170-2, 186n, 188, 207, 300; attacks on, 173, 189-91
COCONUTS (Komiatum area; Sketch p. 196), 186, 193, 196, 198
CODE NAMES, and breaches of security, 506n
COEN, Maj J. C., 503
COLE, AVM A. T., 782
COLE, Sgt F. O., 718-19
COLE, Maj R. B., 195, 202-3, 285, 309
COLEBATCH, Lt-Col G. T., 292
COLEMAN, Col E. A., 279n
COLES, Lt S. A., 376, 688, 750, 753
COLLESS, Capt J. M., 30
COLLINS, Cpl R. F., 150-1
COLVERT, Captain, 142, 159, 184, 309
COLVIN, Lt-Col G. E., 347, 451, 458-60, 462-3, 468-70, 472, 474, 476-7, 483, 486-7, 489, 491-3, 495-7, 515-16, 541, 550, 553, 603-6; commands 2/13 Bn, 333
COMBE, Capt G. D., 509-10
COMBINED CHIEFS OF STAFFS, at Casablanca Conference, 1-4; Pacific strategy, 4, 10n, 219; and capture of Rabaul, 7; give claims of Central Pacific precedence over SWPA, 791
COMMANDOS, 565-6
COMMUNIQUES, GHQ, 390-1, 624n
CONBOY, Cpl J. M., 806n
CONNELL, Maj J. W. D., 775-6
CONNELLY, L-Cpl F. K., 647
CONNOLLY, Maj P. D., 742
CONNOR, Lt E. M., 368
CONNOR, Maj G. B., 586
CONROY, Lt-Col T. M., 134, 148, 161, 163, 165, 198, 200; commands 2/5 Bn, 78
Conyngham, American destroyer, 329, 334, 448, 451, 453, 457, 480
COOK, Lt F. T., 583-5
COOPER, Maj H. H., 458, 460, 463-5, 474, 483, 486, 489, 491-3, 495-7, 499, 516-17, 521
COOPER, Col M. C., 274
COOPER'S SPUR (Sketch p. 485), 486
COPPOCK, Maj H. T., 530, 532, 536-7, 544, 546, 550, 552, 554, 638, 659, 661
CORAL SEA (Sketch p. 15), 810
CORRIGAN, F-Lt J. A., 225
CORY, Lt George L., 335
COSTELLOE, Maj J. A., 241
COTTON, Lt-Col T. R. W. (Plate p. 348), 350n, 359, 376-7, 382, 389, 574-5, 579-80, 586, 703; commands 2/33 Bn, 339
COUGHLIN, Captain, 159, 184
COUSENS, Cpl H. M., 468
COUSIN, Lt-Col A. E., 279n
COVENTRY, Sqn Ldr G. W., 262
COWEN, Sgt D. C., 408
COWRIE SHELLS, 438
COX, Major, 254-5
COX, Capt D. L., 270, 271n, 698-702
COX, Capt R. W., 564
COX, Capt W. M., 355, 361
COX ROAD CAMP (Sketch p. 383), 385-6
CRAIG, Tpr K., 593
CRAIK, Lt A. P., 462
CRAMP, Capt S. M., 173-5, 207, 287, 289, 298
CRATER HILL (Map p. 740; Sketch p. 591), 752-4, 771-2; captured, 755-6
CRAVEN, W. F. and CATE, J. L., 219n, 255n, 426n
CRAWFORD, Capt A. W., 32-3
CRAWFORD, Sgt G. R., 459, 466, 493-6
CRAWFORD, Pte J. A., 455n
CRELLIN, WO1 H., 638
CREMOR, Brig W. E., 26n
CRETE, 268, 270
CRIBB, Maj B. G., 458, 460, 462-3, 474-5, 486, 489, 491-3, 496-7, 521
CRIBB's SPUR (Sketch p. 485), 486
"C" RIDGE (Map p. 293), 292, 294
CRIMMINS, Cpl B. L., 109-10
CRIMMINS, Cpl K. J., 109n
CROCKER, Lt K. F., 576, 583-4, 590
CROMBIE, Lt R. G., 430, 433
CROMWELL MOUNTAINS (Map p. 396), 517

INDEX 831

CROSKY, Lt-Col P. W., 764
CROSSINGTOWN (Sketch p. 765), 765n, 767
CROSSLEY, Tpr A. E. G., 49
CROSSWELL, Maj C. N., 202, 295-7, 309
CROUCHLEY, Sgt J., 354
CROWN, J. A., 802n
CRUTCHLEY, Admiral Sir Victor, VC, 12
CUDLIPP, Capt J., 349, 618, 622
CULLEN, Maj H. D., 377, 382
CUMBER, Capt J. A., 749
CUMMINGS, Col C. J., 750, 755; commands 2/9 Bn, 748; commands 18 Bde, 774
CUNNINGHAM, Lt D. M., 672
CUNNINGHAM, Lt P. B., 462, 519
CURBY, Lt G. A., 527n, 533
CURLEY, Cpl W. S., 673
CURRAN, Lt K. S., 742, 784
CURRAN-SMITH, Pte J. W., 258-9
CURTAYNE, Lt H. C., 608n
CURTIN, Rt Hon John, 7, 391, 780, 817; on Casablanca Conference, 6; announces enlistment figures, 15n
CUSWORTH, Lt-Col K. S., 662-3, 714-16; commands 29/46 Bn, 412
CUTHBERTSON, Capt C. C., 772, 778
CUTTHROAT OPERATION, 740n, 746, 761
CYCLOPS MOUNTAINS (Sketch p. 799), 802

DABNER, Cpl H. J., 510
DAHO (Sketch p. 48), 48, 68
DALI (Map p. 32), 50
DALLMAN RIVER (Sketch p. 726), 732-3
DALY, Maj-Gen T. J., 197, 294, 297, 304, 318
DALZIEL, WO2 G. A., 371
DAMARU (Sketch p. 684), 742
DAMPIER STRAIT (Map p. 28), 524, 612
DAMUN (Map p. 773), 778
DANDARAGAN, WA, 280n
DANDRIWAD RIVER (Sketch p. 807), 806-7
DANIEL, Sgt J. H., 65, 74
DANIELL, Spr R. E., 627
DANIELS, Sgt R. G., 646
DANNE, Lt R. V., 246, 432
DARWIN (Sketch p. 15), 10n, 14, 16, 280n, 390n, 767n, 813
DAUMOINA (Map p. 773), 247, 562, 689, 774-6
DAUNT, Lt-Col W. W. D., 754
DAVAO, 788
DAVIDSON, Lt-Col Hon C. W., 168n, 181, 195, 200-3, 285, 286, 295-7, 309-12, 316; commands 42 Bn, 180
DAVIDSON, Maj J. J. G., 552, 556, 630, 643, 651, 656, 672-3
DAVIDSON RIDGE (Sketches pp. 194, 290), 168, 179, 181, 187, 189, 195, 198, 201-2, 215-16, 285-6, 295
DAVIES, Capt H. G., 371, 380, 630-1
DAVIES, Capt J. F., 362
DAVIES, Sgt R. M., 251-2, 685-6
DAVIS, Maj S. E., 242
DAWES, A., 326n
DAWES, Sgt B. G., 610
DAWSON, Lt-Col B. F., 361-2, 368
DAWSON, Capt P. R., 118n, 135, 156-8, 177
DAWSON, Capt R. H., 144, 171, 173, 191n, 192, 315
DAWSON, Pte W. H., 171
DAY, Lt D. P., 371
"D" BEACH, 362, 366, 368
DEADMAN'S GULLY, Qld, 266
DEAL, L-Sgt F. S., 285
DEAN, Pte R. J., 583
DEEP CREEK (Map p. 327; Sketch p. 342), 37, 118, 177, 341-2
DEERING, Cpl B. S., 568n
Defence (Citizen Military Forces) Act 1943, 16
DEHNE, Pte A. E., 306
DELBRIDGE, Maj E. K., 769
DENGARAGU (Sketch p. 235), 242-3, 245
DENGONDO (Sketch p. 394), 404
DENGLIE, 734
DENMAN, Lt J. R., 746
DENNESS, Maj A. P., 371, 386, 508-9, 554
DENNYS, Capt G. E., 671
DERRICK, Lt T. C., VC, 646-9
DESCHAMPS, Capt P., 453-4, 458-60, 474, 491-3, 495-7, 541, 603-5, 611, 781n
DESLANDES, Cpl R. C. A., 715
DEWING, Maj-Gen R. H., 712, 781
DEXTER, Maj D. St A., 243, 245-6, 434-5, 742

DEXTER, Lt-Col W. R., 43, 47, 61-2, 64-5, 73, 75, 77-80, 86, 91, 92, 97, 99-101, 121-3, 125
DHU, L-Cpl R. C., 251n
DHU RIVER (Sketch p. 248), 251
DIARIES, carried by Japanese, 520-1
DICK, Lt L. S., 786
DICK'S CREEK, Qld, 280n
DIDDYMAN'S PLANTATION (Sketch p. 388), 388
DIEPPE, 273
DIERKE'S O.P. (Map p. 27; Sketch p. 116), 32, 115-16, 152, 188
DIERKE'S TRACK (Map p. 27), 156
DIGOEL RIVER (Sketch p. 811), 810
DILL, Field Marshal Sir John, 1n, 4
DILLARD, Lt Rowland W., 335
DIMOND, Maj C. M., 781n
DINGA, CAPE (Map p. 32; Sketches pp. 62, 92), 37, 60, 86, 90-1, 99-103, 135
DINNING, Maj J. H., 457-8, 512-14, 610
DINSMORE, Lt B. M., 28-30, 33-4
DINSMORE, Lt W. B., see DINSMORE, Lt B. M.
DIXON, Maj R. F., 29
DOBODURA (Map p. 28), 87, 230, 270n 279, 280n, 281, 344, 479, 482, 487, 507, 534, 569, 594, 696
DODD, Capt H. M., 667
DOGS, 567
DOIG, Capt C. D., 246, 592-3, 776
DOMIN, Pte R. J., 299
DON'S POST (Sketch p. 562), 574, 680
DOOVERS, 621
DORFER BAY (Sketch p. 734), 734
DORNEY, Lt-Col K. J. J., 634, 644
DOST, Lt L. H., 502
DOT INLET (Map p. 293; Sketch p. 141), 101, 134, 141-2, 201, 292, 295, 306
DOT ISLAND (Map p. 293; Sketch p. 141), 142
DOUBLE MOUNTAIN (Map p. 32), 53, 109
DOUGHERTY, Maj-Gen I. N. (Plate p. 460), 270, 378, 385, 398-400, 415, 425-30, 433-4, 436-40, 561-3, 566-9, 573-4, 576-7, 579, 581, 583, 585-6, 589, 595, 599, 600, 662, 688-9, 702-5, 712; commands 21 Bde, 268; role at Kaiapit, 422; estimate and experience of, 423
DOUGLAS, CAPT H. M., 476
DOVERS, Cpl R., 50
DOVERS' JUNCTION (Sketch p. 48), 48, 50
DRAKE, Lt L. R., 167n
DRAKE'S O.P. (Sketch p. 196), 167, 186
DREGER HARBOUR (Map p. 528; Sketch p. 467), 498, 504-5, 518, 526-7, 609; plans for capture, 445; airstrip at, 556, 602
DREW, Capt F. A., 111-12
DREW, Cpl R. A., 719
"D" RIDGE (Map p. 293), 294, 304-5
DRINIUMOR RIVER (Sketch p. 807), 806-7
DUCHATEL, Maj C. F., 398, 422, 561, 563
DUCKHAM, L-Sgt J., 374, 376
DUDGEON, Sgt R. J., 618
DUDLEY, Maj J., 337, 347-8
DUELL, Maj A. R., 118, 341-4, 742
DUGUMUR BAY (Sketch p. 808), 808-9
DUMPU (Map p. 396; Sketches pp. 235, 424), 235, 241, 247, 251, 425, 430-3, 506, 561, 563-5, 569, 573, 575, 580, 589, 593-5, 596n, 599, 693, 704, 738-9, 810; Allies plan seizure of, 414-15; Australian advance to, 426, 436-43; destined to become important air base, 562; airfield at, 567, 681; construction program at, 588
DUNCAN, Lt C. J., 409
DUNCAN, Lt W. J., 429
DUNCANSON, Cpl R. G., 110
DUNGATUNG (Sketch p. 254), 253
DUNHAM, Lt Harry H., 410-11
DUNKLEY, Lt-Col H. L. E., 207, 287-8, 299, 300, 320-1
DUNN, Col B. J., 279n
DUNN, Capt R. L., 544, 548, 551-3
DUNPHY, Maj W. J., 276, 337, 340, 344
DUNSHEA, Capt C. J. P., 251, 416, 432, 436, 439, 599n
DUNTROON, ACT, 290
Duntroon, Australian troopship, 269
DURAND'S AIRFIELD, 358
DUTCH, THE, 12, 802, 810
DUTCH ARMY, 260, 802, 803, 810, 811
DUTCH NAVY, 259

832 INDEX

DUTTON, Cpl R. C., 463
DWYER, Cpl T. W., 311, 312
DYBING, Cpl R. A., 209
DZENZAIN (Sketch p. 394), 410

EAMES, Capt R. B., 412, 714-16, 718-19, 724
EAST CAPE, 328
EASTICK, Maj R. F., 464
EASTICK, Brig T. C., 269n
EAST POST (Sketch p. 262), 263
EASY STREET (Sketches pp. 461, 501), 509, 511, 513-14, 516, 610
EATHER, Maj-Gen K. W. (Plate p. 348), 277, 359, 365, 372, 375-8, 381-2, 384-5, 387, 389-90, 431, 436, 439, 574-5, 580, 586, 589, 597, 599, 600, 683-4, 690, 692, 695, 697, 701-3, 712; commands 25 Bde, 276; issues orders for advance on Lae, 339
EATON, Lt N. E., 69
EDDLESTONE, Pte G. H., 195
EDDY, Tpr C. E., 570
EDDY, Sgt G., 581
EDGAR, Maj A. G. S., 191, 198
EDGAR, Brig C. R. V., 411-12, 498, 508, 666-7, 719-20, 722, 724-5; commands 4 Bde, 357; service and experience, 662
EDIE CREEK (Map p. 32), 22, 26, 253
EDWARDS, Lt E. C., 318, 395
EDWARDS, Lt N., 313
EDWARDS, Maj O. L., 300, 314n
EDWARDS' HOUSE, 382
EDWARDS' PLANTATION (Sketch p. 383), 375-7, 381-2, 384, 387
EDWARDS' SPUR (Sketch p. 301), 300, 303, 314n, 321
EGAN, Maj C. J., 288
EGAN, Lt H. L., 36, 44, 132, 151, 153-4
EGAN, Cpl P. K., 376
EGG KNOLL (Map p. 293), 295-6, 309, 311-12
EGOI (Sketch p. 235), 238, 440, 587
EICHELBERGER, Lt-Gen Robert L., 280n, 804; commands I US Corps, 17
EILANDEN RIVER (Sketch p. 811), 812
EISENHOWER, General of the Army Dwight D., 219, 222n
EISENMENGER, Sgt W. L., 312
EL ALAMEIN, 1, 264-5, 330, 347, 349
ELKTON III OPERATION, 220, 225
ELLEN, Sgt L. G., 52, 62-3, 92-4, 122-3
ELSE, S-Sgt A., 520
EMERY'S PLANTATION (Sketch p. 388), 379, 387, 388n, 389-90
EMIRAU ISLAND (Sketch p. 793), 798-9
EMMOTT, Lt J. G., 608n, 621
EMPRESS AUGUSTA BAY (Map p. 28), 653-4
ENGLAND, Lt P. R. N., 258, 596-7
ENIWETOK ATOLL (Map p. 814), 800-1
ENIWETOK ISLAND (Map p. 814), 800-1
ENOGAI (Sketch p. 224), 225
EQUIPMENT, Allied, in Lae operations. 332. Australian, damaged at wharves, 271; of 2/16 Bn in attack on Shaggy Ridge, 706-7. American, for engineers in Lae operations, 276; at Finschhafen, 737. Japanese, captured in Lae operations, 376, in Sattelberg operations, 650, in advance to Sio, 724, 736, in Yaula area, 777
ERAP RIVER (Map p. 327; Sketch p. 394), 277, 346, 403-4, 410-11, 594
ERICSON, Sgt A. H., 50
ERIMA (Map p. 773), 600-1, 783-4, 786
ERSKINE, Lt D. D., 35-6, 44, 88, 108n
ERSKINE CREEK (Sketch p. 109), 108-13, 128-30, 151-2, 169, 172, 183, 188, 199, 203, 206, 208, 216; area occupied, 207
ERSKINE CREEK TRACK (Sketch p. 109), 208
ESKELL, Brig S. L. M., 62, 199
EUROPE, 3, 7, 18; Allied plans for invasion, 218-19, 790
EVANS, Lt A. D., 338-9
EVANS, Brig B. (Plate p. 508), 351, 354, 371, 505, 508, 517, 519, 526, 529, 532-7 539-41, 544, 546, 549-52, 554; commands 24 Bde, 337; estimate of, 348-9; clashes with General Wootten, 363; tactics examined, 557-8; relief of, 607
EVANS, Lt J., 170-1
EVAPIA RIVER (Map p. 773; Sketches pp. 591, 690), 417, 431-2, 595-6, 680, 690, 692, 694-5, 697, 702-3, 710-11, 739, 757, 774
EVERETT, L-Sgt W. A., 647

EXCHANGE (Sketch p. 635), 537, 556, 559, 631, 659, 661
EXTON, Maj E. G., 75, 78-80, 165
EXTON'S KNOLL (Sketch p. 196), 167, 206
EZAKI, Colonel Yoshio, 796

FAIRBROTHER, Maj D. N., 781n
FAIRFAX-ROSS, Maj B., 257
FAIRLIE, Cpl D. J., 336, 347
FAISI (Map p. 28), 220
FAITA (Sketch p. 235), 251, 575, 592n, 593, 687n, 692 698, 739, 742, 774, 776, 810; airstrip at, 599, 680 683
FANGGER (Map p. 396), 522
FAR EAST, 4, 218
FAR EASTERN LIAISON OFFICE, 261, 432
FAR FEATURE (Sketch p. 617), 616-17
FARGHER, Lt-Col L. W., 26n
FARIA RIDGE (Map p. 740), 710, 740-1, 744, 749, 751-3, 756
FARIA RIVER (Map p. 740; Sketches pp. 562, 568) 430, 563-4, 567-9, 571-3, 575-6, 579-80, 585, 587-8, 592, 680-1, 687, 695, 703, 706, 739-40, 744, 751, 754, 756
FARIA VALLEY (Map p. 740), 564, 567-8, 572, 585
FARLEY, Capt A. W., 307, 316, 395
FARLOW, Maj R. M., 262-3; commands "Mosstroops", 261
FARMER, Capt F. C. S., 769-70
FARQUHAR, Maj M. F., 624
FARRELLY, Sig M. A., 652
FARRELLY, Lt R. P., 171
FAULKNER, Capt F. A., 338, 345
FAWCETT, Lt-Col G. H., 564n, 567-9, 571-2
FEARNSIDE, Lt G. H., 737n
FEATURE 500 (Map p. 717) 723
FEATURE 800 (Sketch p. 394), 397, 404-5
FEATURE 1800 (Maps pp. 528, 545), 626, 670; see also CHRISTMAS HILLS
FEATURE 1800 (Palanko), 662
FEATURE 2000 (Sketch p. 660), 678; occupied, 679
FEATURE 2200 (Sattelberg area; Sketches pp. 617, 639), 614, 616-17, 619, 621, 623, 625, 629-30, 639, 641-2, 645, 648; captured, 649
FEATURE 2200 (Christmas Hills area; Sketch p. 660), 676; captured, 678
FEATURE 2500 (Sketch p. 394), 405
FEATURE 2600 (Sketch p. 617), 610, 614, 616, 629; see also STEEPLE TREE HILL
FEATURE 2900 (Map p. 773), 776
FEATURE 3200 (Sketch p. 639), 639-40, 646, 658; occupied, 649
FEATURE 3800 (Map p. 773), 775
FEATURE 4100 (Levett's Post area; Sketch p. 562), 571, 579, 586; captured 574-5
FEATURE 4100 (Kankiryo Saddle; Map p. 740), 753-6, 771-2
FEATURE 5500 (Sketch p. 562), 597-8, 698, 739
FEATURE 5800 (Sketches pp. 690, 757), 592, 596n, 680, 686, 689-91, 711, 739, 745; captured 703-4
FEELY, Lt T. J., 687n, 698, 700
FELDT, Cdr E. A., 257n, 793n, 803n
FERGUSON, Capt J. B., 358
FERREL, Captain, 471
FERTIG, Colonel Charles A., 158
FIELDING, Capt G. A., 420, 428-9
Field Service Regulations, 613
FIENBERG, Capt D. M., 263
FIETZ, Lt W. H., 52, 190-1, 207
FIGGIS, Maj P. E., 793
FIJI, 11, 224
FILCOCK, L-Cpl J., 745
FINISTERRE RANGE (Map p. 396; Sketch p. 235), 234, 236-8, 241-2, 260, 325, 415-16, 435-6, 561-3, 566, 574-5, 593, 596, 600, 659, 683, 689, 693, 711, 762-3, 774-5, 779-80, 784n, 785, 789; strength of Japanese forces in, 425, 443; described, 771-2
FINK, Lt F. J., 475
FINLAY, Capt J. T., 370
FINN, Cpl B. D., 175, 298
FINSCHHAFEN (Maps pp. 396, 528; Sketches pp. 461, 485), 8-9, 54, 82, 89, 145, 231, 242, 257, 260, 265n, 279, 281-2, 321n, 334, 395, 397, 411-12, 414-15, 433, 438-9, 443, 452, 463-4, 501, 503-6, 511, 513-14, 516-17, 521-3, 548, 551-2, 555, 558, 561, 566, 594, 608n, 615, 624n, 649, 688, 731n, 732, 735, 771, 788 794n, 797n, 802; Japanese strength at, 20, 425

INDEX

FINSCHHAFEN—continued
445-7, 523; plans for capture, 55-6, 282, 444-51; attacked by Allied air and naval forces, 278; Japanese reinforcement of, 425, 523-4; Australians advance on, 466-79, 484-9, 491-8; Australian reinforcement of, 480-3, 487-8, 534-5, 558-9, 602, 615-16; Japanese withdraw from, 490, 498-9; captured, 499-500; supply problem, 507, 519, 609; Japanese plan counter-attack, 524-5, 540-42, 612; airfield at, 525, 556, 569; bombed by Japanese Air Force, 529; Australian artillery, 616; General Adachi on operations, 652-3
FINSCHHAFEN ROAD (Map p. 528; Sketch p. 501), 499
FIOR (Map p. 545; Sketch p. 660), 547, 610, 662
FISHER, Pte C. R., 581
FISHER, Capt H. W., 521
FISHER, Sgt J. C., 64
FISHER, Pte J. R., 288n
FISHER, Sgt M., 302
FISHER'S KNOLL (Sketch p. 302), 302
FITZGERALD, Cpl P. E. J., 583
FLEAY, Lt-Col N. L., 323, 341
FLEIGEN ISLAND (Sketch p. 85), 90
FLEMING, Maj J. A., 532, 537, 663-4, 669, 670
FLEMING, Lt W. A., 206
FLETCHER, Capt A. C., 460, 541-2, 550
FLETCHER, Maj S., 714-15
FLY RIVER (Map p. 28), 233
FOLEY, Lt W. G., 503, 636
FOLL, Hon H. S., 787
FORD, Colonel Sir Edward, 781
FORD, Maj J. T., 548
FORDE, Rt Hon F. M., 780
FORST, Pte H. C., 174
FORSTER, Maj A. E., 279n
FORSTER, Lt J., 779
FORTIFICATION HILL (Map p. 717), 725
FORTIFICATION POINT (Maps pp. 396, 717), 457 505n, 522, 726, 730, 736; Australian advance to, 667-9, 714-25
FOSTER, Lt T. A., 248-50
FOUGASSE, 625
FOUGASSE CORNER (Sketch p. 617), 625, 627
FOWLER, Cpl J. F., 431
FOX, Capt J., 777
FOX, Capt R. E., 783-4, 786
FOX, L-Sgt W. P., 209
FRAINEY, Maj J. F., 311-12
FRANCE, 4, 18, 272
FRANCIS, Cpl M. J., 373
FRANCISCO RIVER (Maps pp. 27, 32; Sketch p. 194), 22-3, 28, 31, 33, 35-6, 45-6, 58-9, 71-3, 88, 109, 115, 133, 137, 152, 166, 188, 191, 207, 286-9, 291, 295, 297, 299-301, 316-18, 320-21, 325
FRANKLIN, Maj L., 114-15, 169-71, 173
FRASER, Col C. A. E., 744, 747-8, 750
FRASER, Capt R. J. W., 778
FRAWLEY, L-Cpl T. I., 321
FRAZIER, Capt Everette E., 254, 256, 415, 421, 423n, 430
FREEDMAN, Maj H. J., 669
FRENCH ARMY, 283
FREW, Lt S. L., 345-6
FRIEND, Capt G. C., 285-6
FRIEND, Sgt P. J. C., 148-9
FRYER, Capt H. A. J., 259-61, 263
FUINA, Sgt John, 530
FULLARTON, Lt D. R., 434-5, 565
FULLER, Maj-Gen Horace H., 97, 142n, 160, 182; commands 41 US Div, 58; relations with Australians, 60, 102-5, 138-40

GABENSIS (Map p. 327), 341
GABMATZUNG (Map p. 32; Sketches pp. 68, 69), 69-70, 89, 339, 359
GABRIEL, Cpl, 209 10
GABSONKEK (Map p. 32; Sketches pp. 68, 69), 69-70, 339
GABUTAMON (Sketch p. 768), 769-70
GAGIDU POINT (Map p. 528), 505n
GALI (Sketches pp. 734, 768), 522, 732, 763, 765, 768-9
GALLASCH, Col A. V., 380n, 527n, 529, 532, 534; commands 2/3 Pnr Bn, 516
GALLIPOLI, 329
GAMBLE, Lt I. E., 213-15
GAMON, Capt R., 24n

GANTER, Capt A. G., 312, 318-20
GARABOW (Map p. 545; Sketch p. 461), 477, 626
GARAGASSI POINT (Map p. 773), 777
GARAMBAMPON CREEK (Sketch p. 252), 277
GARLAND, Lt B. J., 297
GARLAND, Maj R. S., 153, 298, 315
GARNOCK, Lt J. C., 590
GARNSEY, Lt K. A., 372
GARNSEY, Maj R. C., 466
GAROKA (Map p. 396; Sketch p. 235), 233, 238, 242, 244n, 414, 438, 561, 575, 593-4, 599, 680, 687n, 739; airfield at, 239-40, 243, 247, 436, 600
GARRARD, Maj N. F., 345, 376-7, 384
GARRETT, Lt-Gen Sir Ragnar (Plate p. 508), 279n
GARRISON HILL (Sketch p. 25), 25, 127
GARTAN, New Guinea native, 411
GARVEY, Maj K. B., 369, 379, 666, 677; commands 2/4 Indep Coy, 349
GAS CAPES, 181n
GASMATA (Map p. 28; Sketch p. 793) 221, 449, 652, 792-3, 798n
GATWARD, Capt G. McG., 386
GAUNT, Maj D. C., 705
GAWAN (Sketch p. 369), 379, 397, 403-4
GAYTON, Maj W. R., 472
"G" BEACH (Sketch p. 350), 352n, 355n, 362, 364, 366-7, 445, 448, 451, 488, 490, 534
GEARD, Lt-Col C. J., 751; commands 2/10 Bn, 743
GEASON, Capt U. J., 750
GEE, Pte K. E., 411
GEELVINK BAY (Sketch p. 799), 791, 798
GEHRING, Captain, 142-3
GENERAL HEADQUARTERS, SWPA, 58, 138, 221, 260, 266, 402n, 712, 781n, 785, 792, 811; and formation of "Mosstroops", 260-1; relations with Australian planning staffs, 281-4; operation instructions, 444, 779, 813; in planning Finschhafen operation, 445, 448; estimates Japanese strength at Finschhafen, 446, 558n; and reinforcement of Finschhafen, 480-3, 487-8; on use of code names, 506n; relations with Australian commanders, 523; censors Australian correspondents' reports, 558n; releases news of arrival of tanks at Finschhafen, 624n; opens at Port Moresby, 696; plans advance to Philippines, 790-1; on General MacArthur's conduct of operations, 797n
GEORGE, New Guinea native, 49, 107-8
GEORGE, Captain, 96-8, 100, 121, 123-4, 126-7, 200, 294-6, 308
GEORGE, Lt A. E., 546
GEORGE, Gnr F. S., 214
GERAGHTY, Pte H., 745
GERHARDS, CAPE (Sketch p. 467), 471
GERMAN ARMY, 268, 270
—SIXTH ARMY, 1
GERMANY, 10n, 219, 272, 499; Allied strategy against, 1-2, 4, 218
GEROUN (Sketch p. 394), 517
GEYTON, Lt C. A., 707
GEYTON'S HILL (Map p. 740), 741, 743-4, 747
GIBB, Lt K. J., 457
GIBBONS, Cpl C. F., 303
GIBBONS, Lt E. N., 64-5, 73, 91, 92
GIBLETT, Cpl A. R., 88-9
GIBSON, Pte J. D., 49
GIBSON, Sgt J. S., 65, 74, 122
GIBSON, Cpl R. B., 110
GILBERT ISLANDS (Map p. 814), 3, 816; Allies plan capture, 4, 790; American landings on, 654-5
GILES, Lt L. H., 538, 549
GILES, Cpl T. B., 250
GILL, G. H., 257n
GILL, Pte R. A., 307
GILL, Maj-Gen William H., 806; commands 32 US Div, 778
GILLESPIE, Lt-Col A. B., 349-50, 361, 404, 406, 553, 630, 641, 645, 671, 673-5; commands 2/24 Bn, 336
GILLESPIE, O. A., 16n, 795n
Gilmer, American destroyer-transport, 328
GILMOUR, Capt N. B., 614, 665-6, 675
GILTROW, Cpl J., 476
GIZARUM (Map p. 396), 522
GLALIGOOL (Sketch p. 235), 238, 243, 440, 587
GLALIGOOL TRACK (Sketch p. 235), 251
GLASGOW, Sgt K. L. S., 533
GLIDERS, 270

834   INDEX

GLOUCESTER, CAPE (Map p. 28; Sketch p. 793), 54, 278, 652, 658, 731, 793n, 798n; air attacks on, 449; American landing at, 729, 794; airfield, 794
GLOVER, Capt M. H. E. C., 637
GNEISENAU POINT (Sketch p. 726), 733
GOALING RIVER (Sketch p. 726), 735-6
GOBLE, Lt-Col N. L., 149
GODOWA (Map p. 528; Sketch p. 485), 499
GODOWA BEACH, 609
GOGOL RIVER (Map p. 773), 786, 789
GOLDEN, Sgt J. A., 246
GOLDEN STAIRS (Sketch p. 342), 342, 360
GONA, 17, 226, 705, 712
GOOD, Sgt R. R. S., 32
GOODENOUGH ISLAND (Map p. 28), 10, 14, 57, 402n
GOODVIEW JUNCTION (Maps pp. 27, 32; Sketch p. 131), 56, 67-8, 88, 115, 117, 119, 124, 131-4, 145-6, 149-50, 153, 161, 163, 165-9, 181, 183, 189, 193n, 196, 206; described, 22; captured, 198
GOODVIEW SPUR, 162, 198
GOODWIN, Cpl F. E., 758
GOODWIN, Brig S. T. W., 267n, 364, 557
GORARI, 55
GORDON, Lt-Col J. D., 363, 502-3, 509, 537, 632, 636-7, 642, 651, 669-70
GORDON'S POST (Sketch p. 562), 687
GORDONVALE, Qld, 268
GORE, Capt R. St G., 117, 211, 215, 519, 547, 556, 666, 729
GORI RIVER (Map p. 773), 782, 784
GOSSIP, Capt R. D., 346, 596
GOVERNMENT BENCH CUT TRACK, see BENCH CUT TRACK
GOW, Maj G. A. T., 365, 373-6, 389
GRACE, Col C. H., 460, 468, 474-5, 516, 519, 626, 730; commands 2/15 Bn, 333
GRAHAM, Lt J. H., 570
GRAHAM, Cpl S. J., 419-20
GRAHAM, Lt W. A., 516, 519, 610
GRAINGER, Lt C. H., 720
GRANT, Maj E. C., 370, 490, 501-4, 509-12, 554, 661, 663
GRASS MOUNTAIN, see CHARLIE HILL
GRASSY KNOLL (Sketch p. 174), 174-5
GRASSY PATCH (Map p. 740), 744
GRASSY SPUR (Map p. 293), 308
GRAVEYARD (Map p. 27; Sketch p. 109), 44, 109-10, 128, 150-2, 169, 203, 206, 208
GRAY, Pte A. J., see GRAYSON, Pte A. J.
GRAY, Col C. M., 279n
GRAY, Capt H., 622-3, 625, 640-41, 645-6, 662, 665, 675
GRAY, Cpl H. D., 37, 342-3
GRAYSON, Pte A. J., 638
GREATER EAST ASIA CO-PROSPERITY SPHERE, 427
GREATHEAD, Maj G., 257-9
GREATOREX, Capt A. G. W., 674-6, 678-9
GREECE, 18-19
GREEN, Lt D. H., 486
GREEN, Cpl D. K., 382
GREEN, Pte E. J., 583
GREEN, Lt G. I., 596-7
GREEN, Lt H. R., 211, 214
GREEN, L-Cpl W. O., 748
GREENE, Pte D. M., 49
GREENE, Pte J. H., 195
GREEN HILL (Sketches pp. 25, 39), 25-6, 28-31, 33-4, 66, 71-2, 123-4, 126-8, 147 161; origin of name, 22
GREEN ISLANDS (Sketch p. 793), 792; NZ landing on, 794-5
GREEN PINNACLE (Drawing p. 588), 587, 589-90
GREEN RIDGE (Sketch p. 617), 614, 616-18, 622-3
GREEN SNIPER'S PIMPLE (Map p. 740), 743, 748-9, 751
GREER, Capt F. R. M., 194, 201, 309-12
GREGORY, Maj E. W., 769
GREGORY, Lt J. T. M., 613-14, 620, 622
GREGORY, Sgt R. H., 809
GRENADES, American, 308n. Australian, 540n, 698-9, 708; effectiveness in jungle warfare, 77. Japanese, 475, 578, 699
GRIFF, Lt-Col E. M., 110-15, 128-30, 151-2, 172-4, 176, 315, 320
GRIFFIN, Col E. A., 26n, 65, 71, 132, 164
GRIFF'S TRACK, 176
GRIMSON, Capt J. E., 262

GRISWOLD, Lt-Gen Oscar W., 226, 654, 801; commands XIV US Corps, 225
GROUNDWATER, Cpl R. J., 383
GROVE, Lt L. B., 213-14
GUABE RIVER (Map p. 773), 772
GUADAGASAL (Map p. 32), 22, 24, 26, 34, 37-8, 60, 71, 75, 82-3, 86-7, 168n, 169, 179
GUADAGASAL RIDGE, 66, 120
GUADALCANAL (Map p. 28; Sketches pp. 15, 224), 1, 3n, 7, 10-11, 18, 220, 224, 226, 228, 273, 817
GUAM ISLAND (Map p. 814), 4, 813; capture of, 815
GUDE, Capt P. T., 314n
GUIEBI (Sketch p. 235), 237, 242, 244n, 245, 586
GUILD, Capt W. S., 668
GUILFOYLE, Capt C. C., 475-6
Guinea Gold, 682
GUINN, Col H. G., 25, 29-31, 33-4, 38-43, 47, 50-1, 108, 111-14, 148, 175, 290; commands 2/7 Bn, 24; temporarily commands 15 Bde, 87-8
GULLETT, Maj H. B. S., 119-23
GUMBUK (Sketch p. 394), 399, 405
GUM RIVER (Map p. 773), 787, 789
GUNJI, Lieutenant, 46
GUNN, Capt W. K., 744, 746-7, 749, 751, 755
GURUF (Sketch p. 252), 594
GURUMBU (Sketch p. 424), 424, 587, 595
GURUNKOR (Map p. 545; Sketch p. 461), 490, 504, 541
GURUNKOR TRACK, 513
GUSAP (Map p. 396), 684, 693, 784, 802; airfield at, 402, 426n, 562, 567, 569n, 594, 680, 702, 738
GUSAP RIVER (Sketch p. 235), 247, 426n, 430-1, 436-7, 439-40
GUSIKA (Map p. 528; Sketches pp. 635, 660), 510, 513, 516, 518, 522-3, 527, 529, 535, 557, 602, 608, 610-11, 616, 626-7, 632, 634, 656-9, 667-8, 670, 675, 679, 714, 726; occupied, 661
GUSIKA-WAREO TRACK, 537, 657, 659; observation post established on, 611-12
GUY'S POST (Sketches pp. 562, 568), 564, 568-72, 576, 581, 583-5, 587, 680, 689, 741, 744-5, 775
GWAIBOLOM (Map p. 27; Sketch p. 109), 44-5, 88, 108-13, 130, 145, 151-3, 155, 165, 169, 176; origin of name, 35

HAGEN, MOUNT (Map p. 28), 57, 234, 239, 252, 259, 261, 432, 436, 586; Japanese interest in, 231; prewar and wartime patrols into area, 233; airstrip at, 247, 258
HAIGH, Lt D. R., 579
HAILE RIVER (Sketch p. 690), 689, 691, 694, 704
HALCROFT, Sgt J. R., 498
HALL, Lt A. J., 385, 437
HALL, Lt B. W. G., 257, 806n
HALL, Lt-Gen Charles P., 815; commands XI US Corps, 806
HALL, Lt H. P., 725
HALL, Lt K. I., 459, 492-3, 496-7, 550, 603-4
HALL, Maj K. S., 589
HALL, Sgt M., 707
HALLIDAY, Lt-Col I. C., 676-9
HALLION, Lt R. T., 418, 421
HALL'S SPUR (Sketch p. 494), 493
HALMAHERA ISLANDS (Sketch p. 15), 11, 788, 791, 798-9
HALSEY, Fleet Admiral William F., 9, 12, 221, 225-6, 653, 798; commands South Pacific area, 7-8; relations with General MacArthur, 9-10, 223; forces under command, 11, 220
HALSTEAD, Lt T. T., 192
HALY, L-Cpl A. R., 366-7
HAMANA, Private, 198
HAMER, Lt-Col R. J., 267n
HAMILTON, Lt H. I., 382-3
HAMILTON, Capt I. W., 442
HAMILTON, Maj J. McK., 259
HAMILTON, Cpl J. W., 718
HAMMER, Lt Edward K., 455
HAMMER, Maj-Gen H. H. (Plate p. 157), 115, 131, 137, 145, 151-2, 155, 158, 163-4, 168n, 172, 177, 199, 203, 207-8, 286-7, 288, 291, 299, 301, 303, 314-17, 322, 406-7, 738, 742, 745-6, 756-7, 772, 774-5, 782-3, 784n, 785; commands 15 Bde, 114; plans operations in Salamaua area, 116-17, 132-4, 150, 153-4, 176, 188-9, 300, 309; on 58/59 Bn, 128-9, 169; on Japanese tactics, 778
HAMMOND, S-Sgt V. W., 170
HAMPEL, Pte E. C., see HEMPHILL, Pte E. C.
HAMPTON, Lieutenant, 234

INDEX 835

HANCOCK, Maj R. N., 35n, 36, 45, 67, 88, 132-3, 203-4, 288n, 289, 298, 315
HAND (Sketches pp. 290, 319), 288n, 300, 303, 320-1
HANDLEY, Maj E. A., 453-4, 458-60, 463, 470, 472-8, 483-4, 486-7, 489, 492, 603
HANEY, Col H., 84n
HANNAH, Capt J. F., 352-3, 356, 372, 659-61
HANOBMAIN (Sketch p. 394), 407
HANSA BAY (Sketch p. 808), 232, 260, 415, 597, 785, 789-90, 798-9, 804, 807-10
HANSEN, Rev Father, 259, 262
HANSON, Col B. S., 267n
HARDCASTLE, Lt-Col G. H., 728
HARDENBERG POINT (Sketch p. 726), 616, 658-9
HARE, Cpl L. D., 288
HARPER, Tpr A. E., 742n
HARPHAM, Lt N. L., 469
HARRIS, Capt G. C., 802-3
HARRIS, Lt-Col T. J., 530-2, 538
HARRISON, Lt F. B., 151
HARRISON, L-Sgt P. J., 251, 440
HARRISON, WO1 W. J. C., 198
HART, Capt G. C., 355, 361, 366-7, 396-7, 404-5
HART, Capt J., 743
HARTY, Capt E. P., 619, 641
HARVEY, Maj B. L., 607-8
HARVEY, Lt C. N., 311
HAUPT, Lt-Col A. G. K., 17
HAUPT, Maj F. K., 752-3
HAUWEI ISLAND, 797
HAWKER, Lt W. E., 247, 249-51
HAWKESBURY RIVER (Sketch p. 765), 765n
HAYASHIDA, Colonel Kaneki, 529, 538, 540-2, 638; commands 79 Regt, 532-3
HAYDON, Maj F. B., 360, 364-5, 595
HAYES, Maj H. F., 382-3, 385, 387
HEAD, Capt J. M., 540, 544, 546, 554, 661
HEATH'S PLANTATION (Map p. 327; Sketches pp. 68, 375), 70, 133, 135, 339, 344, 359-60, 372-3, 375-6
HEATH'S TRACK, 365, 376
HEAVEY, Brig-Gen William F., commands 2 ESB, 265
HEDDERMAN, Lt J. W., 65, 75, 77-9, 122, 167, 186
Heiyo Maru, Japanese ship, 99
HELDSBACH (Map p. 528; Sketches pp. 461, 501), 460, 463, 479, 490, 501, 525, 541, 547, 550-3, 555, 608, 611, 656, 729; Japanese plan attack on, 542; airfield at, 612
HELDSBACH CREEK, 459
HELDSBACH PLANTATION (Map p. 528; Sketches pp. 461, 501), 460, 465-6, 518, 541
HELWIG, MOUNT (Sketch p. 235), 237, 245-6
HEMPHILL, Pte E. C., 88
HENKLE, S-Sgt James L., 809
HENRICKSEN, WO2 H. G. V., 749
HENRY, Capt R. L., 338n, 345n, 373n, 384n, 389n
HENTY, Capt W. M., 368
HERAKLION, 268
HERALD HILL (Sketch p. 562), 703, 739
HERRING, Lt-Gen Hon Sir Edmund (Plate p. 460), 16n, 70, 82, 105, 121, 143, 154, 156, 160, 177, 180, 182, 197, 210, 255, 257n, 260, 270, 271n, 276-7, 292, 318, 323, 337, 338n, 357, 360, 366, 399, 414, 426, 428n, 431, 433, 436, 439, 445, 488, 508, 561, 569, 599n, 602; commands New Guinea Force and I Corps, 55, 57, 279; confers with General Blamey, 56-7, 73, 230, 280-1, 282n; plans for Salamaua operations, 58-60, 71-2, 137, 145, 179-80, 324-5; on supply problems, 87, 507; relations with Americans, 104, 129n, 138-41; relations with General Savige, 163-4, 215-16; in Lae operations, 166, 266-7, 273-4, 378, 381, 400-2, 438; and Bena Force, 238, 240, 242, 244-5; in Finschhafen operations, 444, 446, 448-9, 480-3, 487, 505-6; becomes Chief Justice of Victoria, 507, 780
HERRING, WO2 H. H., 715
HERROD, Lt J. E. I., 300, 314n
HERTZOG RANGE (Map p. 32), 25n, 37
HERWATH POINT (Sketch p. 734), 734
HETHERINGTON, Pte O. T., 49-50
HEWARD, Maj H. M., 109-11, 116, 128, 130
HEWITT, Lt E. J., 679
HEWITT, AVM J. E., 274
HIGH (Sketch p. 635), 632
HILBERT, Capt H. H., 111n, 114, 128
HILBERTS (Sketch p. 109), 111, 203-4, 206-7
HILL, Sgt B. S., 374

HILL, Capt D. P., 370n, 614, 618, 620-1, 628, 639, 642, 644-5, 646-9
HILL, Lt V. A., 689
HILL 7 (Map p. 108), 123n
HILLBERG, Pte M., 783
HILLBRICK, Cpl R. G., 53, 157-8
HIMALAYAS, 6
HINDENBURG RANGE (Map p. 28), 233
HINDLEY, Lt R. G., 372, 552
HIPSLEY, Capt J. W., 362
HIRONDA, 280n
HITCHCOCK, Capt E. P., 72, 84, 86, 90-1, 95, 100, 102, 117-18, 134, 141-2, 158, 211, 214, 294
HITLER, Adolf, 6, 219
HOARE, Lt-Col H. M., 784n
Hobart, Australian cruiser, 12
HODGE, Capt B., 167
HODGE'S KNOLL (Sketch p. 196), 167, 197
HODGMAN, Lt-Col S. T., 180
HODSON, Capt C. P., 213
HOFFMAN, C. W., 802n, 815n
HOFFMAN, Lt W. N., 211-14
HOGAN, Lt D. A., 69-70, 89
HOGAN, Sgt D. G., 471, 473
HOGAN, Sgt P. E., 295
HOGGARD, Capt I., 796
"HO, HO" CRY, of 9 Div, 265, 625, 629, 640
HOLDSWORTH, Capt H., 668
HOLLAND, Sgt E. S., 710
HOLLANDIA (Map p. 28; Sketch p. 799), 231, 259-60, 481n, 779, 788-9, 791-2, 794n, 798-9, 805; capture and development of, 801-2, 804
HOLLEY, Maj V. H., 399
HOLT, Chaplain Rev W. E., 537
HOME, Lt S. E., 714
HOMPUA (Sketch p. 726), 727
HONE, Lt-Col R. B., 767
HONG KONG (Sketch p. 218), 217
HONNER, Lt-Col R., 399, 440-2; commands 2/14 Bn, 385
HOPKINS, Harry L., 1n, 4, 217-18
HOPKINS, Maj-Gen R. N. L., 235, 449, 451, 802n
HOPOI (Map p. 327; Sketch p. 394), 390, 404, 412, 450, 467, 478, 594n; airfield at, 347
HORACE (Sketches pp. 635, 660), 627; captured, 664
HORACE'S EARS (Sketch p. 635), 661, 663-4
HORACE'S HEAD (Sketch p. 635), 661
HORACE'S HOOF (Sketch p. 635), 631
HORACE'S JAWS, 664
HORACE'S NOSE, 664
HORACE'S RUMP, 659
HORDERN, Maj S., 549, 618, 620-2, 628, 642
HORONIU (Sketch p. 224), 226
HOSKING, Brig F., 66, 87; commands 15 Bde, 61
HOSKINS, CAPE (Sketch p. 793), 793
HOTE (Map p. 32; Sketch p. 48), 23, 33, 46-8, 50, 68, 87, 107, 118n, 133-4, 163, 208, 303
HOTE TRACK (Map p. 32), 48, 107
HOUGH, F. O., and CROWN, J. A., 802n
HOUGH, Lt R. W., 130
HOUSE SAK SAK (Sketch p. 427), 439-40, 443
HOUSTON, Lt-Col G. D., 649n, 666n; commands 2/12 Fd Regt, 512n
HOUSTON, Lt W. F., 109, 111
HOWES, Capt J. F., 373-4
HOWIE, Capt T. M., 374
HOWIESON, Maj T. F., 722
HOWLETT, Capt L. F., 70, 89
HOWLETT, Pte R., 459
HUBBLE, Sgt C. E., 40
HUBE DISTRICT (Sketch p. 394), 517-18, 666
HUBIKA (Map p. 717; Sketch p. 726), 722, 727-9
HUBIKA CREEK, 728
HUCKER, L-Sgt S. J., 377
HUGGETT, Capt C., 454-5, 459-60
HUGHES, Lt B. H., 521
HUGHES, Col R. L., 100, 104, 140
HULSE, Lt T., 364, 375-6
HUMBOLDT BAY (Sketch p. 799), 802, 804
HUNGO, Colonel, 113n, 117
HUNT, Pte H. H., 258
HUON GULF (Maps pp. 28, 32), 25n, 59, 278, 378, 797n
HUON PENINSULA (Maps pp. 28, 396), 234, 260, 278, 282, 329, 404, 416, 443, 445, 447, 471, 478, 483-4, 487-8, 507n, 518, 566n, 600-2, 696, 729-30, 738, 763, 771, 787, 792, 816; Allied plans for operations

HUON PENINSULA—*continued*
on, 8, 221, 223, 505-6; native population of, 517; Japanese reinforce, 523-4
HURN, Pte E. G., 74
HUTCHINSON, Colonel Donald R., 426*n*
HUTCHISON, Brig-Gen David W., 255, 423
HUTTON, Geoffrey, 558*n*
HUTTON, Pte H. G., 663
HUTTON, Capt J. W., 364*n*
HYAKUTAKE, Lt-Gen Haruyoshi, 801; commands *XVII Army*, 11
HYANE HARBOUR (Sketch p. 796), 795
HYNDMAN, Maj C. W., 781*n*

IAPON RIVER (Sketch p. 684), 685
IBA, Colonel Michitoshi, 728
IKEDA, Colonel, 184
IKWAP TRACK, 785
ILEBBE CREEK (Sketch p. 485), 486, 489, 491-3, 495-8, 520
ILOKO (Sketch p. 394), 378, 404, 406, 409, 517
IMAMURA, General Hitoshi, 231, 252, 334, 524, 788; commands *Eighth Area Army*, 11
IMPERIAL (Sketch p. 660), 537*n*, 607, 659
IMPHAL (Sketch p. 5), 6
INDIA (Sketch p. 5), 5-6, 10*n*, 220, 686*n*, 712; British plans in, 218; Australian officers sent to, 713, 781-2
INDIAN ARMY, 18, 712-13; exchange of officers with Australian Army, 713, 749, 754, 769*n*, 782; ordnance mission to Australia, 781*n*
—77 INDIAN BRIGADE, 5-6
—1/14 PUNJAB REGT, 809
INDIAN OCEAN (Sketch p. 5), 218
INKSTER, Lt J. J., 370
INNES, Lt R. W., 719
INOMBA (Sketch p. 235), 599, 739
INTELLIGENCE, *Allied*, 325, 523, 805, 811; of strength of Japanese Army, Apr 43, 10-11. *American*, of Japanese strength at Finschhafen compared with Australian, 445-6. *Australian*, of Japanese strength and dispositions in New Guinea, 10-11, 20, 57, 415, 445-6; of Japanese intentions after Lae, 404. *Japanese*, 32, 95*n*, 101, 161*n*, 624*n*
INTOAP (Sketches pp. 252, 427), 256*n*, 417
INYWA (Sketch p. 5), 6
IOGE RIVER; *see* YOGIA RIVER
IOWORO RIVER (Map p. 773; Sketch p. 783), 783
IRRAWADDY RIVER (Sketch p. 5), 6
IRVING, Brig R. G. H., 682*n*
ISAKSSON, Lt-Col O. H., 616, 622-4, 629, 645
ISARIBA (Sketch p. 690), 599, 680, 689-92, 694, 697-8, 702, 711, 774*n*
ISHIJIMA, Private, 106
ISLE, L-Sgt J. F., 554
ITALY, 1, 219, 391

JACKSON, Capt A. C., 151-2, 171-2
JACKSON, Sgt A. F., 408
JACKSON, Maj J. G., 382, 384, 587
JACKSON, L-Cpl J. J., 148
JACKSON, Col O. D., 740
JACKSON, Lt R. S., 783
JACKSON, Brig-Gen William D., 141, 160, 179, 182, 192-3, 210; commands Allied artillery, Salamaua, 158
JACKSON'S AIRFIELD, 276, 358
JACOB, Lt-Gen Sir Ian, 3*n*
JACOBS, Lt H. J., 760-1
JACOBSEN'S PLANTATION (Sketch p. 388), 379, 381, 387, 389
JAGGAR, Maj B. K., 367
JAGO, Capt E. O., 110-12, 114, 128, 289, 317, 320
JAMJAM (Map p. 773), 777, 783
JAPAN (Sketch p. 5), 13, 18, 272, 652, 762, 798, 801, 815; Allied strategy against, 1-11, 217-20; shipping losses, 3; proposed bombing of, 791
—IMPERIAL GENERAL HEADQUARTERS, 11, 231, 788
JAPAN, EMPEROR OF, 135, 529
JAPANESE AIR FORCES, 135, 256, 451, 524, 548, 654; strength in New Guinea and Solomons, 11, 57, 653; losses, 14, 278, at Wewak, 204, 232; in Salamaua area, 46, 75, 87; at Nassau Bay, 102; bomb Woodlark Island, 223; attack Bena area, 238-40, 245, 252, 599; in Sepik area, 263; bomb Allied bases in New Guinea, 278-9; in Lae operations, 331-2, 334-5, 349, 363; attack Nadzab, 450; at Finsch-

JAPANESE AIR FORCES—*continued*
hafen, 457, 466, 469-71, 516-17, 529, 557; in Ramu Valley, 695; attack Merauke, 812
—FORMATIONS: *Fourth Air Army*, 232, 788; *XI Air Fleet*, 231; *6th Air Division*, 232; *7th Air Division*, 232
JAPANESE ARMY, 13, 55, 128, 129*n*, 251, 798*n*; in Burma, 6; Allied Intelligence, 10-11, 20, 24, 32, 57, 119, 300, 375, 377-8, 478, 484, 520-1, 543*n*, 566, 702; in Salamaua operations, 23, 31-2, 37-43, 46, 54, 57, 71, 75, 82, 90, 117, 118*n*, 131, 149, 162, 176, 198, 276, 278, 314-16, 321*n*, 322-5, 391-4; Markham-Lae operations, 70, 89, 268, 274-7, 295, 377-8, 392, 395*n*, 396-400, 404-9; in New Georgia and Aleutians, 226; strength and deployment, 238, 260, 415, 425, 445-6, 524*n*, 788-9, 801; relations with natives, 244; hygiene arrangements, 312, 386, 390; in Finschhafen operations, 447, 467, 471, 478, 488, 521-4, 548, 558*n*, 609, 612*n*, 634, 651-2; on Tami Islands, 509; supply problems, 649-50; in withdrawal to Madang, 733, 736, 763-4, 769, 770*n*, 777-8, 784; in Finisterres, 752, 755-6; at Cape Gloucester, 794; on Green Island, 795; in Admiralties, 797; in Marshalls, 800-1; at Aitape and Hollandia, 804; Wakde-Biak-Noemfoor, 805-6; at Merauke, 812; on Saipan, 813, 815
—AREA ARMIES: *Burma*, 5; *China Expeditionary*, 6, 11*n*; *Japan Defence*, 11*n*; *Kwantung*, 6, 11*n*; *Southern*, 11, 232, 788; *Second*, 788; *Eighth*, 11, 181, 232, 334, 788, 792, 798*n*
—ARMIES: II, 788, 801, 805, 866; XIV, 11, 788; XVI, 11; XVII, 11, in Bougainville, 231, 653, 788, 801, 806; XVIII, 11, 193, 392, 432, 443, 524, 601, 682*n*, 784, 792, 797*n*, 809; reinforces NG bases, 231; composition, 415; plight, 770-1; withdraws to Hollandia-Wewak, 787-9, 801-2; isolated by Hollandia landing, 804; attacks Aitape perimeter, 806-7; casualties and strength, 807, 817; XIX, 11, 231-2, 788; XXXI, 788, 801
—DIVISIONS, destroyed or isolated in 1944 US offensive, 816; 5th, 788, 811; 6th, 231, 653, 788; 14th, 788, 801; 17th, 231, 653, 788, 794; 20th, 11, 101, 182, 415, 527, 624*n*, 656, 659, 771, 788; reinforces Wewak, 231; proposed role Bena plateau, 251-2; leaves Salamaua, 325; at Kaiapit, 423-4; in Finschhafen operations, 425, 438, 523-6, 544, 556, 560-1, 602, 612, 634, 665, 672, 675-6, 678-9; supply of, 610, 616; withdraws from Huon Peninsula, 696, 716, 718-19, 722, 729-30, 732, 738, 762, 764; casualties, 736-7; Aitape-Wewak area, 789, 804; 29th, 801, 815; 32nd, 788, 801; 35th, 788, 801, 806; 36th, 788, 801, 805; 38th, 231, 788; 41st, 11, 181-2, 198, 415, 523-4, 634, 730, 762, 788; at Wewak, 231, 425; withdraws from Salamaua and Lae, 325, 407; Madang-Bogadjim area, 789, 804; 43rd, 801, 813; 46th, 788; 48th, 788, 811; 51st, 11, 47, 82, 113*n*, 135, 346, 524, 547, 679, 770, 788, 801; on jungle conditions, 21-2; losses in Bismarck Sea, 26, 28; reorganised, 47; strength Lae-Salamaua area, 54, 392; at Salamaua, 97, 145, 148, 182, 198, 216, 231, 285, 325; in Lae operations, 391-2, 396, 407, 409, 415, 424-5, 433, 436, 443, 517, 525; withdraws from Huon Peninsula, 696, 729-30, 732, 738, 762, 764, 766, 771; in Wewak area, 789, 804; 52nd, 801
—ARTILLERY, 144, 637, 640, 649*n*, 669, 683*n*, 747, 752; *14 Fd Regt*, 26, 28, 54, 101, 325; *26 Fd Regt*, 423-4, 523, 525, 532, 601, 634, 659, 728
—ENGINEERS, 341, 654, 669, 785; *5 Engr Shipping Regt*, 525, 529-32; *9 Engr Shipping Regt*, 525; *20 Engr Regt*, 525, 529-32, 716; *37 Indep Engr Regt*, 601; *51 Engr Regt*, 54, 391
—FORCES: *Mubo Defence*, 47, 135; *Nakai*, 600, 738; *Nassau Defence*, 47, 135, 142; *Salamaua Defence*, 47; *South-Eastern Detachment*, 232
—INFANTRY BRIGADES AND REGIMENTS: *38th Indep Bde*, 653; *47th Indep Mixed Bde*, 813; *65th Bde*, 794; *66th Regt*, 68, 524*n*; in Salamaua operations, 82-3, 99, 113-14, 168, 181, 187; strength, 392; *78th Regt*, 425, 601, 649; at Kaiapit, 423-4, 426, 432; in Ramu-Finisterres, 437-9, 443, 524, 564, 566, 585, 587, 702, 738, 751; strength and composition, 600; Saidor area, 745, 761-2, 764, 789; *79th Regt*, in Finschhafen operations, 524-5, 529-33, 538, 540-3, 551, 554, 559-60, 609, 612, 634, 637-8, 643, 649-50, 659, 672; withdraws, 676, 722, 724, 730; Madang area, 786; *80th Regt*, 415; strength, 392; in Finschhafen operations, 425, 467, 478-9,

INDEX

JAPANESE ARMY—*continued*
501, 510, 523-5, 527, 541-3, 547, 556, 600, 602, 612, 634, 646, 650, 672; withdraws, 676, 722, 724, 730; 102nd Regt, 82, 99, 133, 524*n*; in Salamaua operations, 46, 54, 71, 97, 158, 214; strength, 392; in Finschhafen operations, 524; in Sio area, 730; 115th Regt, 21, 42, 54, 112, 524*n*; losses in Bismarck Sea, 26, 28; in Salamaua operations, 46, 133, 135, 145, 158, 169, 187, 199, 325; strength, 392; 237th Regt, 524*n*, 789; 238th Regt, 251, 415, 425, 785; at Lae, 391; strength, 392; in Finschhafen operations, 467, 478-9, 524, 634; Sio area, 730; Madang area, 789; 239th Regt, 524*n*; on Rai Coast, 600, 789; in Finisterres, 686, 693, 702; at Madang, 702
—INFANTRY BATTALIONS: I/66 Bn, 54, 101, 112, 114, 117, 133, 152, 181; II/66 Bn, 54, 114-15, 117, 119, 125, 133, 151-2, 311-12; III/66 Bn, 97, 99, 135, 145, 181; I/78 Bn, 566, 585, 600, 702, 761; II/78 Bn, 566, 585, 600, 659, 710, 745, 761-2; III/78 Bn, 424, 566, 585, 600, 761; I/79 Bn, 525, 532, 554, 657; II/79 Bn, 533, 541, 543, 554, 559, 659, 722; III/79 Bn, 533, 554, 657; I/80 Bn, 101, 112, 114, 117, 131, 136, 152, 173-4, 182, 187, 523-4, 659, 722; II/80 Bn, 412, 478, 510, 659, 728; III/80 Bn, 479, 501, 513, 520, 524, 659, 728; I/102 Bn, 26, 42; II/102 Bn, 26, 42, 67-8; III/102 Bn, 26, 43, 64-5, 96, 99, 102, 106, 135, 145, 216, 391; I/115 Bn, 135; III/115 Bn, 50, 391; I/238 Bn, 523; II/238 Bn, 395, 634, 636, 659, 669, 676; III/238 Bn, 181, 407, 763; III/239 Bn, 762, 764
—SENTRY GROUPS: No. 1, 300; No. 2, 300
—SERVICE CORPS: *Automobile Company*, 424; *Independent Pack Transport Company*, 424; *Provisions Transportation Unit*, 32; *20th Transport Regt*, 728
JAPANESE NAVY, 12-13, 46, 294, 391, 466, 524; strength and deployment, 11, 449-50, 813; losses, 14, 26, 815; in Solomons, 653-4; plans destruction US Fleet in Philippine Sea, 792
—FLEETS: *Eighth*, 231; *Mobile*, 815; *South-Eastern*, 231
—GARRISON AND BASE UNITS: *7th Base Force*, 26, 523; *82nd Garrison Unit*, 392; *85th Garrison Unit*, 478
—MARINES, 415, 475-6, 499; *7th Combined SNLF*, 232; *8th Combined SNLF*, 232; *6th Kure SNLF*, 232; *2nd Maizeru*, 392; *5th Sasebo*, 306-7, 309, 321*n*, 325, 392; *7th Sasebo*, 654-5; *5th Yokosuka*, 392; *7th Yokosuka*, 232
—SUBMARINES, 278, 522, 609
JAPERO (Sketch p. 811), 812
JAPPA (Map p. 773; Sketch p. 591), 599, 742, 776, 784
JAP TRACK (Sketch p. 39), 29, 31, 38-9, 41, 47, 61, 74-81
JARI (Map p. 32), 50
JAVA (Map p. 814), 810; British plans in, 218; Japanese dispositions, 801
JEFFERY, Lt S G., 23*n*, 44, 205-6, 288*n*
JEFFERY'S O.P. (Map p. 27), 23
JENKINSON, Lt-Col R. G., 664, 781*n*
JENKS, Capt A. E., 286, 295-7, 309, 311
JENSEN'S PLANTATION (Map p. 327), 360, 364
JENYNS, Maj J. R. T., 393
JENYNS' PLANTATION (Map p. 327), 360, 364-5
JENYNS' TRACK, 364-5
JEUNE, Cpl P. C., 803
JINNO, Colonel, 114, 117, 131, 152, 173-4
JIVEVANENG (Map p. 528; Sketches pp. 461, 617), 460, 473, 478, 483, 486, 490, 500-4, 509, 511-13, 515-16, 519-20, 526-7, 535-6, 542, 547, 549-50, 553, 555, 560, 602, 604-5, 609-14, 616, 619, 621, 641, 647, 650
JOANGENG (Sketch p. 394), 672
JOBSO (Sketch p. 684), 684
JOHNS, Lt R. D., 569-70, 580, 582-4
JOHNS' KNOLL (Sketch p. 562), 573, 576, 586-7, 590, 600, 680, 687, 703, 739; Japanese attack on, 581-4
JOHNSON, Lt A. T., 308
JOHNSON, Gnr H. W. J., 214
JOHNSON, Capt L. C., 65, 74, 122, 167, 186, 193, 195
JOHNSON, Maj R. L., 563, 580-2, 585, 781*n*
JOHNSON'S KNOLL (Sketch p. 196), 193, 195, 198
JOHNSTON, Sgt D., 591-2
JOHNSTON, Capt H. R., 377
JOHNSTON, WO1 H. W., 698-9
JONES, Sgt F. P., 373

JONES, Lt-Col George M., 338-9, 385*n*
JONSON, Lt R., 567*n*
JOSEPHSTAAL (Sketch p. 258), 258-9, 596-7
JOSHUA, Lt-Col R., 488, 490-1, 501-2, 509-11, 516, 519, 532, 535, 539, 607, 632, 636, 638, 661-2, 664; commands 2/43 Bn, 370
JOY, Lt F. N., 559
JUNGLE TRAINING CENTRE, 228-9
Junior Van Noy, American ship, 531*n*

KABENAU RIVER (Map p. 773; Sketch p. 591), 774, 777-8, 782, 784
KABENAU VALLEY, 772
KAGAYAMA, Lieut-Colonel, 424
KAIAPIT (Map p. 396; Sketches pp. 235, 418, 420), 89, 237-8, 241, 256, 427-8, 430-2, 434-6, 438, 443, 563, 566, 569, 693, 784-5; operations against, 414-21; airfield at, 417, 419, 421-3, 433, 561; Japanese account, 424-5; lessons of, 426
KAIAPIT MISSION (Sketches pp. 418, 420), 418*n*, 419, 428
KAIGULIN (Map p. 396; Sketch p. 427), 238, 244, 431, 439, 442-3, 561-2, 575, 586
KAINANTU (Map p. 396; Sketch p. 235), 233, 236, 238-9, 240*n*, 242, 246, 251-2, 256, 432, 434, 600
KAIREBA (Sketch p. 235), 251, 416
KAIRI, Qld, 264
KAKAKOG (Map p. 528; Sketches pp. 485, 494), 470, 475-6, 483, 489, 504, 511, 543, 551; attacks on, 485-7, 491-9
KAKARI POINT, 329
KALAL ISLAND (Sketch p. 508), 508
KALAMSIE. Constable, 416
KALASA (Sketch p. 726), 517-18, 522, 524, 609, 676, 722, 727, 730
KALIKO (Map p. 773), 777-9
KALUENG RIVER (Sketch p. 660), 659, 663, 667-9, 714
KAMBARA RIVER (Map p. 773), 772
KAMING (Sketch p. 394), 412
KAMKAMUN (Sketches pp. 369, 388), 366, 379-80, 386-7
KAMLAGIDU POINT (Map p. 717), 667
KAMLOA (Map p. 528; Sketch p. 461), 467-8, 470-1, 474, 477, 483, 491
KAMUSI (Sketch p. 684), 685-6, 784
KANE, Pte F., 306
KANKIRYO (Maps pp. 740, 773), 424-5, 568, 595-7, 601, 687, 689, 740, 743, 745, 750, 752, 755, 762, 774
KANKIRYO SADDLE (Map p. 740), 436, 443, 566, 571, 576, 588-9, 596*n*, 599, 683, 710-11, 753-6, 761-2, 771-2, 774-5, 784; Australian patrols to, 598; Japanese strength at, 600, 745; assault on, 739-41, 743-52
KANOMI (Sketch p. 726), 609, 728-30
KAPLAN, Lt-Col Leonard, 731*n*
KAPUGARA RIVER (Sketch p. 726), 726, 733-5
KARIUS, C. H., 233
KARKAR ISLAND (Sketch p. 808), 807
KASANGA (Sketch p. 467), 498, 508
KATAGIRI, Lt-Gen Shigeru, 524, 527, 529, 534, 538, 633-4, 639, 679, 789*n*; commands *20 Div*, 523; in Finschhafen counter-attack, 525, 554, 612; ordered to withdraw to north, 675-6
KATIKA (Map p. 528; Sketch p. 461), 458, 465, 467, 490, 512, 527, 529, 534-6, 552-3, 557, 607, 627, 632, 637, 642, 645, 665; operations at, 460-3, 477-8, 521, 532-3, 537-8, 540-2, 544-50, 554-6
KATIKA TRACK (Map p. 528; Sketch p. 461), 459-60, 467, 470, 477, 479, 502, 504, 521, 524, 536-7, 541, 548, 551-2, 559
Katoomba, Australian transport, 269
KAVIENG (Map p. 28; Sketch p. 793), 8, 790, 792, 798-9
KAYE, Maj P., 634-5
KEDAM BEACH (Maps pp. 528, 545), 541, 552, 613
KEDAM POINT (Sketch p. 485), 499
KELA (Map p. 32; Sketch p. 319), 46, 88, 119, 316-19
KELA HILL, 45, 59, 84, 107-8, 112, 145, 291
"KELA KITTY", 45
KELANOA (Sketch p. 765), 610, 764, 769, 771
KELANOA POINT (Sketch p. 726), 616
KELA POINT (Sketch p. 319), 322
KELA RIDGE, 316-17
KELEY, Capt M. J., 631-2, 635, 638, 643, 657-8
KELLIHER, Pte R., VC, 374
KELLY, Lt-Col J. L. A., 543
KELLY, Lt J. T., 384

KEMEN (Sketch p. 394), 399, 405-6
KEMP, Cpl D. W. C., 704
KENDRICK, Cpl K. J., 372
KENNEDY, Maj D. G., 224
KENNEDY, Maj E. M., 53, 757-8
KENNEDY, Sgt R. J., 493
KENNEDY'S CROSSING (Sketch p. 319), 207, 316
KENNEY, General George C., 12, 20, 57, 222, 239-40, 242, 253, 255n, 256, 278-9, 281, 344, 359n, 403, 422, 433, 505, 535, 556, 795; commands Fifth Air Force, 8; relations with Australians, 129n; reinforcement of Finschhafen, 482
KENT, Maj W. R., 267n
KEPSAU (Sketch p. 684), 685
KERAM RIVER (Sketch p. 808), 241
KERMODE, Capt R. G., 367
KESA (Sketches pp. 684, 759), 686, 711, 759-60, 776
KESAWAI (Map p. 396; Sketches pp. 235, 591), 235, 238, 247, 251, 416, 431-2, 440, 564, 575, 586-7, 589, 596, 599, 680-1, 683, 689-91, 693-5, 697, 702-4, 745, 757, 784; Independent Company ambush at, 434-5; occupied, 565; commando operations based on 592-3; Japanese attack on, 698-701
KESIKENA, 236
KETOBA (Map p. 396; Sketch p. 759), 686, 689, 691-4, 702, 711, 746, 759-61
KEYFABEGA, MOUNT (Sketch p. 235), 251
KEY POINT 3 (Sketch p. 424), 561, 566-8, 576, 585
KIAHU, native, 797
KIAP HOUSE (Sketch p. 418), 419
KIARI (Sketches pp. 394, 765), 378, 407, 522, 732, 766-7; Japanese withdraw to, 325, 525; Japanese strength at, 392
KIASAWA (Map p. 528; Sketch p. 461), 509, 511, 514, 516
KIDD, Maj K. B., 271, 277, 337
KIDNEY (Sketch p. 290), 288, 300, 317
KIER RIVER (Map p. 773), 779
KIETA (Map p. 28), 220, 653
KILIGIA (Map p. 717), 518, 667, 721, 725, 726n, 771
KIMPTON, Capt S. MacD., 536
KIMURA, Major, 99, 145, 168, 181
KINDT, Captain, 142-3, 159
KING, Captain, 254-5
KING, Fleet Admiral Ernest J., 220n, 790-1, 798; at Casablanca Conference, 1n, 2-4, 7; at Washington Conferences, 8, 219; creates American Seventh Fleet, 12
KING, Maj G. A., 563-4
KING, Lt-Col G. G., 417-19, 421-3, 443, 690; commands 2/6 Indep Coy, 415-16
KING, Lt R. S., 370
KING'S HILL (Sketch p. 562), 568-9, 573, 576-8; captured, 563
KING WILLIAM, CAPE (Sketch p. 726), 616
KINSLER, Colonel Kenneth H., 270, 277, 338-9, 345-6; commands 503 Parachute Regt, 268
KIRIWINA ISLAND (Map p. 28), 9, 56, 230, 280n, 402n; airfield on, 58; American landings on, 221-3, 273
KIRKLAND'S DUMP (Map p. 327; Sketch p. 68), 89, 270-1, 277, 337, 340-1, 344-5
KIRWAN, Pte D., 147
KIRWAN, Sgt P. J., 536
KISKA ISLAND (Sketch p. 5), 3, 227
KITANO, Lt-Gen Kenzo, 788
KITCHEN, Capt Robert E., 122, 124, 127
KITCHEN CREEK (Sketch p. 39), 29, 38, 50, 71-2, 75, 119-23, 125-6
KITNEY, Capt M. W. W., 719-20
KLEINITZ, Cpl J., 157
KNIGHT, Sgt J. A. C., 410-11
KNOLL (Jivevaneng area; Sketch p. 501), 512, 515-16, 519-20
KNOLL (Lokanu Ridge area; Map p. 293), 307-8
KNOTT, Maj C. C., 521, 544, 547, 550
KNOX, Pte D. R., 314n
KNUDSEN, Cpl G. V., 320n
KOBA (Sketches pp. 684, 759), 689, 759-61
KOBAYASHI, Sergeant, 169
KOBEN (Sketch p. 591), 695, 703
KOCHIABU (Sketch p. 262), 263
KOELN, Lt Herman A., 455
KOFEBI RIVER (Map p. 773), 775
KOIKE, Private, 64-5
KOKENAU (Sketch p. 811), 810
KOKODA (Map p. 28), 713n
KOKODA TRAIL, 17

KOLEM (Sketch p. 485), 499, 509
KOLOMBANGARA ISLAND (Sketch p. 224), 224-6
KOMAKI, Major, 47, 112
KOMBA DISTRICT, 517
KOMBIES, CAPE (Sketch p. 811), 812
KOMIATUM (Maps pp. 27, 32; Sketches pp. 196, 290), 22, 23n, 26, 28, 32-3, 35, 38, 43, 45, 59, 61-2, 65-8, 72, 75, 82, 86, 113-17, 124-5, 132-4, 137, 140, 142, 145-6, 150, 152, 158, 164, 166, 168, 172, 179, 181, 183, 185-6, 188-90, 193n, 201, 206-7, 210, 216, 285-6, 298, 300, 325
KOMIATUM RIDGE (Map p. 27; Sketch p. 196), 28, 32, 44, 73, 154, 167-8, 178-9, 181, 185-7, 198-9, 200n, 201-2, 207, 216; described, 22; air attack on, 161; operations at, 189, 191-7
KOMIATUM SPUR, 167-8, 197
KOMIATUM TRACK (Map p. 27; Sketches pp. 131, 196), 26, 28, 31-2, 33n, 35-6, 42, 44, 61, 67, 74-5, 108, 111-13, 115, 124, 127-9, 131-3, 145-6, 150-3, 155, 162, 165, 167-8, 172, 183, 186, 188, 193, 197-200, 203, 205-8, 287, 289, 291, 297
KOMINIWAN, Constable, 244
KORAM (Sketch p. 562), 440-1, 563-4, 571
KORI, Lance-Corporal, 210
KOROPA (Map p. 396; Sketch p. 591), 237, 440, 694, 702-3, 711, 745
KORTUNI (Sketch p. 235), 243, 251
KRA ISTHMUS (Sketch p. 218), 218
KRAKEMBACK (Sketch p. 235), 245
KREUTBERG RANGE (Sketch p. 485), 452, 468, 471-2, 474, 499
KRONPRINZ HARBOUR (Sketch p. 808), 808
KRUEGER, General Walter, 280n, 696, 792, 795, 805-6; commands Sixth Army, 220; comments on creation of Alamo Force, 221-2; estimate of, 222; in Saidor operations, 730-2
KUANKO (Sketch p. 660) 665-6, 670, 673-4, 676; captured, 675
KUANKO TRACK (Sketch p. 660), 665, 671
KUFUKU (Sketch p. 768), 769
KUL (Map p. 773), 777-8
KULA GULF (Sketch p. 224), 226
KULAU (Sketch p. 684), 440, 685-6, 697, 702, 746
KULUNGTUFU (Sketch p. 467), 518, 658, 666, 672, 729
KUMAWA (Map p. 528; Sketch p. 461), 490, 504, 509, 511, 513-14, 516, 519-20, 526, 542-3, 553-5, 608n, 609-10, 612-14, 616-17, 619, 621-3, 642; captured, 512
KUMAWA TRACK (Map p. 528), 543, 559
KUMBARUM (Sketches pp. 562, 591), 566-7, 570-1, 573, 575-7, 580, 586, 595, 596n, 703; captured, 563
KUMERA, 432
KUMNICK, Capt P. A., 744, 746, 752, 756
KUNAI KNOLL (Sketch p. 617), 620-1
KUNAI SPUR (Map p. 293; Sketch p. 290), 188, 286-7, 289, 299, 304, 309; attacks on, 298, 312-13; see also LEWIS KNOLL
KUPER RANGE (Map p. 32), 23
KURDISTAN, 18
KUSAKA, Vice-Admiral Jinichi, 231
KUVANMAS, LAKE (Sketch p. 258), 260-2
KWAJALEIN ATOLL (Map p. 814), 800-1
KWAMA RIVER (Sketch p. 765), 765n, 766-7
KWAMA VALLEY, 517
KWAMBELANG (Sketch p. 394), 404
KWAMKWAM (Sketch p. 726), 730
KWATINGKOO (Sketch p. 660), 674-6
KWATO (Map p. 773), 600, 776-7
KWATOMANE (Map p. 32), 50
KWUPSANEK (Sketch p. 32), 397
KYNGDON, Col C. W. T., 785
KYNGDON, Maj L. G. R., 70, 118

LABABIA CAMP (Sketch p. 39), 40, 42
LABABIA ISLAND (Map p. 32; Sketch p. 62), 47, 63, 103, 142
LABABIA O.P. (Sketches pp. 39, 76), 64, 74-7, 80
LABABIA RIDGE (Map p. 108; Sketches pp. 25, 76), 22-6, 30, 34, 43, 52, 61, 63, 65, 74, 84, 86, 91, 101, 119, 121, 125, 147-8; defence by 2/6 Bn, 75-83
LABABIA TRACK (Sketches pp. 25, 76), 29, 42, 61-2, 75, 78-81
LABU (Map p. 327; Sketch p. 394), 25n, 118, 157, 177, 394-5
LABU ISLAND (Sketch p. 342), 68, 177, 209
LACK, Maj H. H., 393

INDEX

LAE (Maps pp. 28, 327; Sketches pp. 369, 388), 11, 25n, 26, 28 46, 53, 69-70, 73, 75, 82, 87, 89, 118, 133, 137, 163, 177-8, 204, 209, 233, 236-8, 242, 247, 251-3, 263, 271, 277, 281, 286, 289, 291, 294-5, 307, 315, 318, 322, 325, 344, 346, 348, 391, 393, 395, 414-16, 432-3, 439, 443-51, 456, 465-6, 478-83, 488, 492, 500, 504-8, 517, 519, 521, 523, 525-6, 534-5, 547-8, 558, 561, 569, 580, 600, 602, 608n, 615, 652, 656, 658, 666, 686n, 696, 721n, 729, 762, 766, 770, 784-5, 788-9, 798n; Allied plans for capture, 3, 8-9, 23, 55-7, 166, 182, 220-1, 230-1, 266-9, 273, 277, 281-2, 326; Japanese strength and deployment at, 20, 54, 57, 135-6, 231-2, 274-6, 392, 425; area of 9 Div advance, 275; attacked by Allied air and naval forces, 278-9; Japanese from Salamaua withdraw to, 323; 9 Div advance on, 333-4, 336-7, 343-4, 347-57, 361-4, 366-72, 378-81, 385-7, 389; 7 Div advance on, 359-60, 364-6, 372-8, 381-5, 387-8; airfield at, 364, 389, 401-2; Japanese withdraw from, 377-9, 391, 394-400, 403-9; entered, 389-90; developed as Allied base, 400-3; Australian patrols from, 409-12; see also NADZAB, RED BEACH, YELLOW BEACH
LAE O.P. (Map p. 32), 25
LAGOON (Map p. 717; Sketch p. 660), 663, 667-8, 715-16, 719
LAHEY, Lt-Col K. C. C., 687
LAIDLAW, Maj G. G., 243, 245, 434, 440, 564, 586-7, 593, 599, 692, 711; commands 2/2 Indep Coy, 242
LAKE HILL (Map p. 740; Sketch p. 562), 687, 756
LAKEKAMU RIVER (Map p. 28), 20
LAKES (Christmas Hills area; Map p. 528; Sketch p. 635), 626-7, 656, 659, 661, 664-5, 669, 672, 676
LAKES (Ramu Valley area; Sketch p. 562), 681, 689, 697, 703, 741, 744
LAKONA (Map p. 717; Sketch p. 726), 518, 522, 609, 615, 676, 679, 720, 722, 726n; captured, 724
LAKONA TRACK, 672, 678, 723
LALOKI RIVER, 276
LAMB, Cpl B. A., 32, 67
LANCASTER, Capt C. G., 638-9, 656, 658
LANDALE, Maj W. G. A., 563, 577
LANDING CRAFT: Allied, 85, 230; in Nassau Bay operations, 91, 94-7, 99; in Lae operations, 266, 326-32, 452-3; development of, 272-3; in Finschhafen operations, 446, 451; Japanese, 394
LANE, Lt G. R., 157, 320
LANE'S PLANTATION (Sketch p. 375), 376
LANG, Lt A. B., 122-3
LANG, Lt-Col J. T., 337-8, 340, 344-6, 365, 376, 385, 741; commands 2/2 Pnr Bn, 270
LANGEMAK BAY (Map p. 528; Sketch p. 485), 445-6, 450, 478, 482, 499, 504, 508, 512n, 522, 525, 539, 548-50, 552, 555-6, 558, 612, 726; Japanese withdraw from, 490; developed by Americans, 737
LANGFORD, Cpl D. A., 178, 253, 408
LANGFORD, Col H. R., commands Torres Strait Force, 17
LANGFORD, Pte T., 634
LA NORE, 2nd-Lt D. J., 527n
LASANGA ISLAND (Sketch p. 85), 58, 85, 90, 94
LASHIO (Sketch p. 5), 6
LAUGHLIN, Lt J., 757-8
LAUNCH JETTY (Sketch p. 461), 460, 463, 466, 468, 473, 538, 541, 613
LAUPUI POINT (Sketch p. 319), 316; see also MACKECHNIE, CAPE
LAVARACK, Lt-Gen Sir John; commands First Australian Army, 16, 280; heads Military Mission to Washington, 780
LAVER, Maj H. L. (Plate p. 204), 167, 186, 191, 193, 195-6, 198, 200
LAVER'S KNOLL (Sketch p. 196), 187, 191-4, 196-8, 200
LAWRENCE, Cpl C. P., 320n
LAWRIE, Lt D. C., 336-7, 348
LAWS, Lt D. A., 257n
LAWS' TRACK (Sketch p. 25), 29, 30, 38
LAY, Cpl R. E., 666
LAZER, Lt B. L. B., 665
LCI-339, 332
LCI-341, 332
LEACH, Maj I. A., 299, 312
LEAHY, Capt J. L., 785
LEAHY, Fleet Admiral William D., 1n, 2n, 217-18
LEAN, Cpl B. M., 720

LEARY, Cpl R., 620
LEE, Lt-Col A. J., 577
LEE, Capt J. D., 585
LEE, Lt J. O., 710
LEGA (Map p. 32; Sketch p. 156), 53, 118-19, 157-8, 177
LEGA TRACK (Sketch p. 156), 157
LEGG, Pte L. R., 678
LEGGO, Bdr E. W., 573, 575-6, 581
LEMBANGANDO (Sketch p. 765), 765
LEONARD, Lt B. I., 162
LEONARD, Pte J. E., 357
LERON RIVER (Maps pp. 327, 396; Sketch p. 235), 247, 277, 281, 378, 415, 417
LERON VALLEY, 402n
LESLIE, Capt J. B., 303
LETHBRIDGE, Maj-Gen J. S., 686
LETHBRIDGE MISSION, 686n
LEU, Capt R. S., 180, 307
LEVETT, Capt P. M., 442, 595n
LEVETT'S POST (Sketch p. 562), 595, 680
LEVISTON, Lt G. W., 36, 45
LEWIN, Capt J. E. (Plate p. 173), 107-8, 116, 153, 171-2, 189, 191, 203-6, 311, 317, 320
LEWIN, Capt R. W., 386, 630
LEWIS, Capt E. A., 312-13, 320
LEWIS, Lt-Col R. R., 11n
LEWIS, Lt R. T., 634
LEWIS KNOLL (Map p. 293), 313, 316; see also KUNAI SPUR
LIAISON, AIR, dependence of Australian commanders on, 599n
LIDGERWOOD, Gnr W. J., 345
LIHONA (Sketch p. 235), 237-8, 243-4, 251, 432
LILLIE, Lt J. C., 35
LIMBIEN (Sketch p. 235), 243n, 244n
LIND, Lt W. A. T., 167
LINDHE, Sgt N., 668
LINEA CREEK (Map p. 32), 177-8
LINEHAM, Capt D. J. F., 289, 298
LITTLE, S-Sgt B. J. F., 570
LITTLER, L-Cpl J. W., 360
LLOYD, Brig J. E., 713, 781
LOCKYER, Maj N. W., 267n
LOGAWENG (Sketch p. 467), 478, 490, 498, 504, 514-15, 524, 526, 529
LOGUI (Sketch p. 319), 137, 316, 318-19, 321
LOKANU (Maps pp. 32, 293; Sketches pp. 141, 194), 37, 59, 71-2, 94, 137, 140, 142, 146, 159, 173, 213, 285, 306-9
LOKANU RIDGE (Map p. 293; Sketches pp. 141, 290), 142, 294, 304, 306-8, 316
LOMAS, Maj F. J., 240, 432, 439, 575
LONG ISLAND (Maps pp. 28, 396), 522, 731
LONGMAN, Sgt W. J., 709
LONGMORE, Sgt J. R., 126
LONGWORTH, Lt-Col L. E., 694
LOOKER, Lt L. W. A., 47-50, 303, 316, 322
LOOKER'S RIDGE (Sketch p. 291), 303, 315
LORD, Capt C. R., 144, 192
LORD, WO2 R. S., 590
LORENGAU (Sketch p. 793), 797
LOS NEGROS ISLAND (Sketch p. 796), 795-7
LOVELL, Capt F. K., 355
LOVELL, Col S. H., 412
LOWE, Lt-Col Arthur L., 183; commands II/162 US Bn, 159
LOWEN, Brig I. H., 269n
LOXTON, Maj F. E. C., 749
LST-452, 335
LST-458, 335
LST-471, 335
LST-473, 334-5
LUETCHFORD, Capt A. B., 464
LUGGE, Pte R. A., 748
LUMB, WO2 H., 253
LUMBAIP (Sketch p. 394), 378, 399, 404-6
LUMI (Sketch p. 258), 259
LUMSDEN, Lt-Gen H., 712, 781n
LUNAMAN, MOUNT (Sketch p. 388), 25n, 389-90
LUNDIE, Cpl F. J. P., 572
LUTHERAN MISSIONS, 649
LUZON ISLAND (Map p. 814), 798
LYNE, Capt A., 645-7, 662, 665-6
LYON, Maj H. McM., 66
LYON, Maj L. H., 351-3, 372

840 INDEX

MABELEBU (Map p. 773; Sketch p. 235), 244, 776
MACADIE, Brig T. F. B., 239-47, 251, 256, 416, 431-2, 434, 438, 440, 593, 596, 599-600; commands Bena Force, 238
MACARTHUR, General of the Army Douglas, 58, 104, 182, 200n, 260, 263, 265, 268-9, 278, 344, 414, 422, 556, 602, 609, 696, 712, 730, 785, 791, 794-6, 798-9, 802, 805, 813, 815-16; complains of inadequate forces, 7; plans offensives, 8-9, 55-6, 218, 221, 230-1, 444; directives, 9, 220, 790; estimate of, 9-10, 797n; strength of forces under command, 12-14, 16, 227, 763; confers with General Herring, 138; relations with General Blamey, 221-2, 281-4; confers with Admiral Halsey, 223; reinforces Torres Strait, 227-8, 811; and planning for Lae operations, 266, 390-1; on Finschhafen operations, 445-6, and reinforcement of area, 480-3, 487-8, 535; on use of code names, 506n; communiqués and censorship, 390-1, 558n; plans occupation of New Britain, 792
MACARTHUR-ONSLOW, Lt-Col E., commands 2/2 MG Bn, 380n
MACARTNEY, Maj C. M., 781n
MACASSAR STRAIT (Map p. 814), 788
MCBRIDE, Capt D. A., 59, 84, 94-5, 100, 104, 106
MCBRIDE, Maj I. H., 62
MCCAFFREY, Maj R. K., 26n
MCCALL, Maj W., 759, 782-3
MCCALLUM, Sgt C. R., 371, 638
MCCALLUM, WO2 W. H., 356
MCCARTHY, Lt-Col J. K., 796-7
MCCARTNEY, Lt William F., 84n, 95n, 166n, 185n, 200n, 321n
MCCAUGHEY, Lt S. M., 709-10
MCCAUGHEY'S KNOLL (Map p. 740; Sketches pp. 708, 710), 709, 740, 743; attacks on, 748-50
MCCOLL, Lt K. H., 257
MCCORMACK, Sgt F. J., 147
MCCOY, Lt K. J. P., 146
MCCULLOUGH, Capt J. B., 396
MCCULLOUGH, Capt K., 428, 574
MCCULLOUGH'S RIDGE (Map p. 740), 741, 743, 756
MACDONALD, Col. A. B., 229
MACDONALD, Capt G. G., 571-2, 580, 583
MCDONALD, Capt N. C., 781n
MCDONALD, Lt N. E., 513, 515
MCDONALD, Lt R. L., 176
MACDOUGAL, Lt-Col D. C., 574-5, 579, 586, 598
MACDOUGAL, Lt L. R., 463, 493, 496-7
MCDOUGALL, Pte W. J., 67
MCDOWELL, WO2 R. A., 749
MCELGUNN, Sgt J. T., 52, 65, 91, 102
MCELROY, Capt J. L., 192, 319
MCEVOY, Cpl K. A., 150-1
MCFADDEN, Capt R. J., 668, 722
MACFARLANE, Maj C. W., 714, 716
MACFARLANE, Lt G. D., 527, 547
MCFARLANE, Cpl L. M., 289
MCGRATH, Pte L. R., 74, 78
MACGREGOR, Sgt A. C., 356
MACHINE-GUNS, 79n; Owen preferred to Tommy, 51n; shortage of ammunition for, 123
MACILWAIN, Lt R. I., 409
MCINERNEY, Capt J. C., 244n, 586n
MCINNES, Capt A. J., 711, 741-2
MCINNES, Maj C. L., 440-2
MCINNES, L-Cpl L. M., 69, 90
MCINTOSH, Capt R. H., 760
MCKAY, Lt-Col C. S., 269n
MACKAY, Lt-Gen Sir Iven (Plate p. 13), 59, 61, 280, 433, 438-9, 507-8, 522, 534-5, 556, 561, 602; commands Second Army, 16, 57, New Guinea Force, 16, 279, 359n, 401; estimate of and career, 18; reinforces 3 Div, 20; instructions to General Savige, 20-1, 37-8; condemns slouch hat, 51n; and reinforcement of Finschhafen, 480-2, 487-8, 523, 555, 558-9; role of I Corps, 506; on use of code names, 506n; appointed High Commissioner to India, 594
MACKAY, Col K., 612, 623, 674
MACKECHNIE, Colonel Archibald R., 84, 90, 95n, 96-101, 105-6, 117, 134, 141-2, 159, 179-80, 184, 192, 199, 201-2, 292, 296, 316, 318, 321; commands 162 US Regt and Nassau Bay landing force, 71-3, 85, 102-4; relations with Australians, 138-40, 185; relieved of command, 138, 158, returns to command, 182

MACKECHNIE, CAPE (Sketch p. 319), 316, 321; see also LAUPUI POINT
MCKEDDIE, Capt J. E., 468n, 496, 666
MCKEDDIE'S O.P., 468
MCKEE, Capt R. R., 510
MCKENZIE, Maj C. F. G., 243, 586-7, 697-8, 781n
MACKENZIE, Capt I. S., 397, 614, 619, 679
MCKENZIE, Maj N. B., 242, 251, 263
MCKENZIE, Capt S. J., 382, 589
MACKIE, Lt J. W. S., 52
MCKINLEY, Tpr S. A., 746
MACKINNON, Maj A. S., 269n, 398
MCKINNON, Lt N. K., 625
MCKITTRICK, Lt F. W., 421
MCLACHLAN, Lt O. C., 743n
MCLACHLAN'S SPUR (Map p. 740), 743
MACLARN, Maj L. C., 485, 511-13, 515, 521, 527, 605
MACLEAN, Col F. W., 26n
MCLENNAN, Cpl R. H., 257n
MCLENNAN, Sgt T. A. L., 758
MCLEOD, Capt K. T., 462, 477, 479, 515, 605
MCMAHON, Sig P. C., 652
MCMAHON, WO2 W. T., 707
MCMASTER, Capt N. E., 676-7
MCNAMARA, Capt D. W., 261-2
MCNAMARA, Capt J. F., 370, 641-2, 674-7
MCNEE, Cpl L. J., 718
MCNICOL, AB J. B., 803
MACPHERSON, Maj D. W., 781n
MCPHERSON, Capt Henderson E., 363
MACPHERSON, Lt W. N. 573
MCPHERSON RANGE, 228-9
MCRAE, Lt D. C., 574, 583-4
MACRAE, Lt D. G., 374-5
MCRAE, Lt-Col E. H., 337, 347-8, 362; commands 2/23 Bn, 336
MCRAE, Cpl K., 32-3
MAC'S CAMP (Sketch p. 394), 398
MCVEY, Lt J., 484
MCWATTERS, Capt A. W., 10n, 299
MADANG (Maps pp. 396, 773; Sketch p. 808), 112, 173, 236-7, 244, 246, 253, 268, 277, 279, 281, 284, 328, 386, 395-6, 406-7, 409, 415, 440, 444, 446, 522-4, 562, 569, 587n, 588, 597, 600, 609, 685, 688, 711, 734, 738, 762, 784, 789, 792, 794n, 804, 807, 809; Allied plans for attack on, 8-9, 55-6, 220-1, 696, 785-6; Japanese strength and dispositions at, 20, 231, 235, 238, 425; attacked by Allied air and naval forces, 278; Japanese withdraw to, 732; captured, 787; airfield, 787; base sub-area to be established at, 788
MADANG ROAD (Map p. 773), 787
MADDISON, Capt A., 775-6
MAGERI POINT (Sketch p. 85), 85, 90-1, 95, 138
MAIBANG, 257
MAIN, Capt H. H., 458, 470, 473, 478, 483, 485-6, 490-1, 499, 512, 514
MAINSTREAM (Map p. 740; Sketch p. 562), 590-1, 595n, 680, 687, 704, 706, 739-41, 743-4, 751-2, 775
MAIR, Lt D. C., 460, 472, 477, 606
MAISON, Brig-Gen Harold G., 180, 182-3, 185
MAITLAND, Brig G. B. G., 279n
MAJURO ATOLL (Map p. 814), 800
MAKEME (Sketch p. 262), 263
MAKIN, Sgt F., 144
MAKIN ISLAND (Map p. 814), Americans land on, 654
MALAGA HOOK (Map p. 773), 786
MALAHANG (Maps pp. 32, 327; Sketch p. 394), 364, 366, 379-81, 401, 403
MALAHANG ANCHORAGE (Sketch p. 369), 363, 366, 368, 371-2, 379-80
MALAHANG MISSION (Sketches pp. 369, 388), 366, 379-80, 386, 389
MALALAMAI (Sketch p. 768), 765n, 769
MALARIA, 268, 517, 670; in Salamaua campaign, 39, 314; among native carriers, 234; in Lae operations, 362; control achieved by 5 Div, 412-13; in Ramu Valley, 574, 588, 681; in Japanese Army, 659; in 9 Div, 727, 735
MALASANGA (Sketch p. 765), 765, 767
MALAYA, 781
MALE (Map p. 773), 777, 779
MALEY (Sketches pp. 235, 248), 245, 247
MALEY, Cpl J. L., 245n, 249-50
MALLYON, Lt A. R. St V., 755
MALOLO (Map p. 32; Sketch p. 291), 23, 36, 48, 59, 68, 84, 88, 107, 133, 137, 208, 303

INDEX

841

MALOLO TRACK (Sketch p. 291), 113, 315, 317, 322
MALONE'S JUNCTION (Sketch p. 109), 208
MALONEY, Capt V. N., 155
MAMBARE RIVER (Map p. 28), 99
MANAM ISLAND (Sketch p. 808), 807
MANCHUKUO, 11n
MANDALAY (Sketch p. 5), 6
MANDER-JONES, Col E., 279n
MANEBA POINT (Sketch p. 485), 499
MANGE POINT (Sketch p. 467), 478, 484, 488
MANGU RIVER (Sketch p. 726), 732
MANIANG RIVER (Sketch p. 427), 423, 430
MANILA (Map p. 814; Sketch p. 5), 788
MANN, Sgt W., 79
MANNION, Tpr F., 369
MANO, Lt-Gen Goro, 524n
MANOKWARI (Sketch p. 799), 788, 806
MANPOWER, in Australia, 12-13
MANUS ISLAND (Sketch p. 793), 792, 796-8
MAPE RIVER (Map p. 528; Sketch p. 485), 412, 446, 464, 478, 499, 504, 514, 516, 518, 522, 543, 556
MAPOS (Map p. 32), 53-4, 118, 323
MAPPI (Sketch p. 811), 812
MAPS, 239, 685; Salamaua campaign, 129; inaccuracies in, 158, 203, 300; captured from Japanese, 311-12, 314, 375; Finschhafen operation, 450; inaccuracies in Sattelberg maps, 512n, 614n; in Finisterres, 596
MARAKUM (Sketch p. 734), 522, 734
MARANGITS (Sketch p. 427), 417
MARARUO (Map p. 528; Sketch p. 660), 513, 520, 556, 615, 622-3, 629, 649, 666
MARAWASA (Sketch p. 235), 243, 251, 277, 417, 423-4, 426, 428, 431, 433-4, 436-9, 561, 693
MARCUS POINT, 652
MAREA RIVER (Sketch p. 248), 251
MARIANAS (Map p. 814; Sketch p. 5), 798-9, 801; Allies plan advance to, 2, 4, 790-2; operations against, 813-15
MARIBA, Private, 803
MARIENBERG (Sketch p. 808), 809-10
MARILINAN (Map p. 327; Sketch p. 254), 89, 119, 257, 270, 344; airfield at, 70, 253-6
MARINGGUSIN (Sketch p. 427), 434
MARKHAM POINT (Maps pp. 32, 327; Sketch p. 342), 46, 53, 59, 61, 88, 90, 118, 135, 177, 209, 323, 344, 360, 364-5, 377, 390-1, 394-6; patrols to, 37, 68-9; attacks on, 277, 341-3
MARKHAM-RAMU DIVIDE, 437
MARKHAM RIVER (Maps pp. 32, 396; Sketches pp. 68, 252), 23-4, 26, 37, 43, 55, 61, 88, 117-18, 156, 177, 233, 247, 253, 256n, 257, 266, 268-71, 275-6, 281, 323, 337-8, 340-1, 343-4, 360, 364-5, 375, 385, 393, 395-6, 401, 404, 416, 430, 437, 443; crossed by Colonel Lang's force, 345-6
MARKHAM VALLEY (Map p. 327; Sketch p. 68), 73, 231, 234, 251-2, 281, 325, 338, 375, 391, 398-400, 402-3, 414-15, 423, 425-7, 432-3, 435, 438, 440, 443-4, 594, 600, 609n, 680; plans and operations, 8, 55-6, 182, 221, 268-9, 273, 282, 355, 359, 738; Australian patrols in, 53, 68-70, 209-10; native population of, 89-90; Japanese defence of, 135; air bases to be established in, 220, 230, 268-9; described, 277, 416; and malaria, 681n
MARKHAM VALLEY ROAD (Sketches pp. 375, 388), 210, 339, 360, 364, 373-7, 381-2, 387, 389, 402, 414
MARSDEN, Capt E. C. H., 700
MARSDEN, Capt H. McL., 186
MARSH, Lt-Col R. R., 26n
MARSHALL, Cpl A., 247-8
MARSHALL, Maj A., 753, 755
MARSHALL, General of the Army George C., 218, 220n; at Casablanca Conference, 1n, 2-4, 7; at Washington Conference, 8-9, 219; plans advance to Philippines, 790
MARSHALL ISLANDS (Map p. 814; Sketch p. 5), Allies plan capture, 2-4, 220, 790-2; American operations in, 800-1
MARSON, Col R. H., 359, 365, 373-4, 388n, 389, 692, 697, 699, 701; commands 2/25 Bn, 339
MARSTON, Lt-Col R. R., 119, 210, 256, 759-60, 774-6, 782, 784-5; commands 57/60 Bn, 70, Tsili Tsili Force, 255
MARTIN, Brig-Gen Clarence A., 731-2
MARTIN, Lt E. T., 571n
MARTIN, Cpl G., 79, 126
MARTIN, Capt G. E., 469, 668-9, 721

MARTIN, Lt H. H., 148, 162
MARUI (Sketch p. 258), 259
MARUOKA, Lieut-Colonel, 47
MAS, Sergeant, 803
MASANGKOO (Map p. 528; Sketch p.660), 620, 666
MASAWENG RIVER (Map p. 717; Sketch p. 726), 615, 662, 724-7
MASON, Lt H. M., 758-9
MASSON, F-Lt F., 691
MATAHAUSA (Sketches pp. 235, 248), 237-8, 241-2, 245-7, 251
MATALOI (Map p. 773; Sketch p. 684), 592, 689, 691, 702, 745, 757, 760, 776-7
MATHESON, Sgt J. A., 777-8
MATHEWS, Pte N. L., 208
MATHEWS, Capt R. L., 129n, 208, 289
MATLOFF, M., and SNELL, E. M., 2n
MAT MAT (Sketch p. 25), 24, 26, 29, 34, 43, 61, 74-5, 78, 81-2, 121, 123n, 125-7
MATSUDA, Lieutenant, 173
MATSUI, Lieut-Colonel, 112, 114, 117, 133, 181; commands I/66 Bn, 83, 101
MATSUMOTO, Colonel Matsujiro, 424
MATTHEW, Lt D. H., 215n, 304-6
MATTHEW, Lt G. N., 215, 306
MAUGHAN, Lt-Col D. W. B., 457, 478
MAULULI (Sketches pp. 235, 248), 245, 247-8, 250-1, 416, 431, 434, 440, 564
MAUND, Rear-Admiral L. E. H., 272n
MAWARAKA, 653
MAXWELL, Lt E. F., 417-19, 429, 596
MAY, Pte F. W., 582
MAY, Tpr H. F. C. (Plate p. 156), 49
MAY, S-Sgt N., 353
MAYMYO (Sketch p. 5), 6
MEARES, Capt W. A., 23n, 33, 35-6, 45, 115-17, 132, 150-1, 153, 172
MEARES' CAMP (Map p. 32), 23, 46
MEARES' CREEK, 88, 108, 132
MEDICAL ARRANGEMENTS, Scarlet Beach area, 472, 490, 539
MEDITERRANEAN THEATRE, Allied plans and strategy in, 3-4, 219
MEGIAR HARBOUR (Sketch p. 808), 807
MELAMBI RIVER (Sketch p. 394), 404, 406
MELAMU (Map p. 773), 772, 777-8
MELANPIPI (Sketch p. 394), 404, 406
MELBOURNE (Sketch p. 5), 228
MELDRUM, Lt E. C. S., 755
MELLOR, S-Sgt J., 627
MELVIN, Lt Howard L., 192
MENADO (Map p. 814), 788
MENE HILL, 745, 761
MENE RIVER (Map p. 773; Sketch p. 591), 680-1, 694-5, 739, 741-2, 744, 747, 774
MENE VALLEY, 597, 695, 711
MENZIES, Capt J. R., 28, 31-3, 66-7
MERAUKE (Map p. 28; Sketch p. 811), 280n, 810-13; Australian garrison at, 14, 17, 227-8; Japanese air attacks on, 812
MERCHANT SHIPPING, see SHIPPING
MERGUI (Sketch p. 218), 218
MERIRE, Corporal, 244, 247
MERLE-SMITH, Colonel Van S., 260
MERRY, Maj E. O., 271
MESAGATSU (Sketch p. 427), 439
MESSEC, Lieutenant, 187, 210-11, 213-15
METCALF, L-Cpl O. G., 758
MIDDLE EAST, 7, 18, 229, 280
MIDDLE SPUR (Sketch p. 204), 203-4, 207
MIDWAY ISLAND (Sketch p. 5), 4, 792
MILES, Lt C. H., 125-6, 148
MILFORD, Maj C. F., 564, 704
MILFORD, Maj-Gen E. J., 296, 304, 308, 317-18, 322, 324, 393, 404, 411, 439 480, 505-6, 535, 558, 561, 594, 712, 739; commands 5 Div, 17, 57; in Salamaua operations, 199, 216, 290-2, 294, 316; service and experience, 289-90; plans to pursue Japanese to Lae, 323, 395; supervises development of Lae-Nadzab, 400-1, 403; appointed MGGS, NGF, 595
MILILUGA (Sketch p. 394), 397
MILITIA BILL (Map p. 15), area of, 16
MILLER, Colonel Alexander M., 794
MILLER, Cpl D. A., 201
MILLER, J., Jnr, 3n, 84n, 223n
MILLER-RANDLE, F-Lt A., 702
MILLIGAN, Maj J. S., 262

MILLIKAN, Maj H. R., 108, 314
MILNE, Cpl R. A., 53
MILNE BAY (Map p. 28), 9, 14, 17, 168, 222, 231, 264, 267, 274, 279, 280n, 290, 323, 326, 328, 355, 357, 412, 445, 449, 479-81, 483, 487, 608n, 611, 738, 740; garrisoned by 5 Div, 57
MINDANAO ISLAND (Map p. 814), 788, 798-9, 813; Allies plan invasion, 791
MINDIRI (Map p. 396), 522
MINDJIM (Map p. 773), 772
MINDJIM RIVER (Map p. 773; Sketch p. 235), 247, 416, 576, 590n, 739, 753-4, 756, 782, 784
MINDJIM VALLEY, 753, 756, 771, 774, 778, 783
MINGENEW, WA, 280n
MINTER, Cpl H. A., 550
MISANAP (Sketch p. 684), 685
MISSIM (Map p. 32), 20, 23-4, 26, 28, 33, 35, 44, 48, 53, 61, 66-8, 87-8, 107-8, 114, 116, 132-3, 163
MISSIONARIES, 236; in Mount Hagen area, 233; on Bena plateau, 240; in Ramu and Markham Valleys, 427; in Merauke area, 810
MISSION HILL (Sketches pp. 418, 420), 420-1, 423n
MISSION POINT (Map p. 32; Sketch p. 319), 36, 318, 322
MITCHELL, Capt D. A., 574
MITCHELL, Sgt F. P., 257n
MITCHELL, Sig R., 370
MIYAKE, Colonel Sadahiko, 510, 523-4; commands 80 Regt, 501
MOAM (Sketch p. 768), 770
MOLLARD, Maj K. F., 351-2, 390n, 508, 615, 627, 630-2, 635, 643-4, 651, 657, 659, 661; commands 2/32 Bn, 626
MOLLISON, Capt C. D., 630, 632, 644
MOLLISON, Lt P. J., 223
MOLLOY, Brig A. D., 279n
MOLLOY, Cpl J. W., 93
MOLOMBY, Maj T. A., 745
MOLONEY, L-Cpl L. H., 746
MOMOTE (Sketch p. 796), 795-7
MONAGHAN, Brig R. F., 211-12, 215-16, 285, 289, 291, 295-7, 299, 309-12, 316, 318, 320n, 321, 323; commands 29 Bde, 168
MONEY, Capt W. A., 275
MONGI RIVER (Map p. 394), 403, 412, 467, 471, 473-4, 478, 484, 510, 524, 602
MONGI VALLEY (Map p. 394), 517
MONGO RIVER (Sketch p. 765), 767
MONK, L-Sgt K. J., 247-8
MONOTTI, Capt F. R., 404-5
MONSEN, Sgt A., 244n
MONTGOMERY, Field Marshal Viscount, 283
MONTGOMERY, Lt-Col K. H., 299, 312-13, 316; commands 47 Bn, 215
MOODIE, Maj R. O. K. T., 623
MOONYOONOOKA, WA, 280n
MOORA, WA, 280n
MOORE, Cpl B. N., 477-8
MOORE, Lt-Col Malcolm A., 255-6
MOORE. Pte R. T., 320n
MOORHOUSE, Capt D., 346
MORALE, *American*, in Salamaua operations, 201-2; *Australian*, at Finschhafen, 611, 615; *Japanese*, in Salamaua operations, 187-8, 198
MOREAU, Cpl M. H., 510
MORENO (Map p. 528), 513, 649
MORIARTY, Brig G. V., 403, 413
MORISON, Rear-Admiral S. E., 11n, 12n, 223n, 226n, 278n, 328n, 456n, 466n, 654n, 794n, 801n, 802n
MOROBE (Map p. 32; Sketch p. 85), 58, 72, 84, 91, 96-7, 99, 135, 138, 180, 211, 230, 267, 275, 278-9, 328, 333-5, 337, 352n, 451, 457, 466, 505n, 696
MOROTAI ISLAND (Map p. 814; Sketch p. 5), 11, 813; Americans capture, 815-16
MORPHETT, Maj H. C., 618-22, 628
MORRIS, Lt F. W., 496, 498
MORRIS, WO1 G. E., 707
MORRIS, Maj Jack E., 183, 292, 294
MORSE, Maj S. L., 119-24, 134, 146, 149, 162
MORSHEAD, Lt-Gen Sir Leslie (Plates pp. 460, 508), 265, 283, 439, 506, 522-3, 557-9, 569, 580, 599n, 624n, 666, 696, 702, 712, 721n, 764, 771; commands II Corps, 16, 264; and command arrangements in NG, 280-1; relieves General Herring's I Corps, 507; troops' estimate of, 514; and reinforcement of Finschhafen, 534-5, 555; and role of 7 Div, 594, 692-3; appointed GOC, Second Army and com-

MORSHEAD, Lt-Gen Sir Leslie—*continued*
mands NGF, 595, 787; defines role of 9 Div, 602; seeks definition of responsibility in Bogadjim area, 779-80; commands I Corps, 788
MORTAR KNOLL, 188
MORTON, L., 790n
MOSAPA (Sketch p. 258), 258
MOSA RIVER (Sketch p. 591), 683, 756, 771-2
MOSIA RIVER (Sketches pp. 562, 591), 563, 575, 681, 695
MOSS, Sgt R. K., 121-2
MOTEN, Brig M. J. (Plates pp. 13, 204), 22, 25, 30, 34, 40, 51, 81, 92-3, 99-100, 105-6, 119-21, 124, 126-7, 133, 138, 142, 146, 149, 154, 158, 161, 164, 168n, 169, 177-81, 185-8, 193, 195, 197-202, 208, 285; commands 17 Bde and Kanga Force, 18; in Salamaua operations, 23-4, 26, 31, 39, 42-3, 59-62, 74-5, 78, 82, 87, 107, 128, 137, 145, 150, 165-7, 189; in Nassau Bay operations, 62-4, 71-3, 86, 97, relations with Americans, 101-4, 139-40
MOTO'S POST (Sketch p. 562), 680
MOULDS, Maj W. J., 464
MOUNTBATTEN, Admiral of the Fleet Rt Hon Earl, 272; at Casablanca Conference, 1n; commands South-East Asia Command, 790
MOUNT FAIRFAX, WA, 280n
MOUNT LAWLEY, WA, 16, 280n
MOUNT MARTHA, Vic, 228
MOUNT TAMBU TRACK (Map p. 27), 168, 199-200
MUBO (Maps pp. 32, 108; Sketch p. 39), 18, 20, 24-6, 28, 31, 33, 35, 37, 44, 47, 50, 52, 56, 58, 60, 66-8, 72, 74, 83, 99, 103-4, 106, 108, 112-15, 117, 128, 132-8, 145-6, 153-4, 163, 165, 168, 178, 234, 311, 314; area described, 22; Japanese withdraw to, 23, strength and dispositions at, 43, 54, 57, 82, aircraft bomb Australian positions, 75, estimate of Allied strength, 118n, account of operations, 125, withdraw from, 129; Australian operations, 34-5, 38-42, 59, 61-5, 71-3, 84, 107, 119-28; airfield, 127
MUBO TRACK (Map p. 32), 28
MUBO VALLEY, 22, 25, 72, 75, 120
MUDFORD, Tpr G. J., 570
MUGIL HARBOUR (Sketch p. 808), 807
MUGUNSIF (Sketch p. 258), 258
MUIR, L-Sgt A. S., 35-6, 172
MULE TRACK (Sketch p. 131), 132, 167, 186, 192, 197, 200, 595, 598
MULLER, Lt-Col D. O., 267n
MUNDA (Sketch p. 224), 7, 224-6, 507n
MUNGO (Sketch p. 591), 688
MUNKRES, Lieutenant, 294
MUNUM (Maps pp. 32, 327), 135, 359
MUNUM WATERS, 398
MURDOCH, Maj-Gen I. T., 279n
MURGON, Qld, 280n
MURNASS RIVER (Sketch p. 808), 788
MUROYA, Maj-Gen Chuichi, 97, 112, 114, 133, 135
MURPHY, Lt B. N., 176
MURPHY, Capt C. D., 386
MURPHY, Sgt G. B. J., 592
MURPHY, Cpl J. H., 157
MURPHY, Capt J. J., 793
MURRAY, Maj J., 458-9, 493, 496
MUSAK (Sketch p. 235), 237
MUSOM (Map p. 327; Sketch p. 369), 334, 355, 361, 367, 378-9, 397, 403-4, 406, 409
MUSTON, Capt P. C., 313, 320
MYITKYINA (Sketch p. 5), 6

NADZAB (Maps pp. 327, 396; Sketches pp. 69, 339), 55, 135, 182, 252-3, 358-9, 372, 378, 390, 398-401, 403-5, 409-10, 412, 414-16, 421-5, 428, 431, 433, 444, 450, 561, 563, 569, 594n, 762, 809; airfield at, 61, 70, 255, 269, 357, 364-5, 385, 402, 567; Australian patrols to, 69-70; Allied plans for capture, 269-70, 273 275-7, 281, 337; seizure of, 338-9, 344-6
NAGLE, Lt V. F., 431, 440
NAISMITH, Sgt A. K., 50, 174-5
NAKAI, Lt-Gen Masutaro, 425-6, 435, 438, 561, 600-1, 764; commands infantry *20 Div*, 424; commands *20 Div*, 789n
NAKANO, Lt-Gen Hidemitsu, 32, 42, 46-7, 50, 54, 82, 97, 106, 117, 145, 158, 168, 173, 184, 325, 346, 391, 407, 524n, 639, 732; commands *51 Div*, 26; plans defence Lae-Salamaua area, 135-6
NAKA RIVER, *see* BITOI RIVER

INDEX 843

NAMBARIWA (Sketches pp. 726, 765), 522, 525, 529, 609, 649, 730, 733-4, 736, 763-4; captured, 735
NAMLING (Map p. 27; Sketch p. 109), 23, 28, 31, 33, 35, 44-6, 110, 115-16, 134, 150-5, 164, 169, 176
NAMLING RIDGE, 150, 152-3, 155
NAMUR ISLAND, 800
NANDA (Sketch p. 726), 730
NANGAPO (Map p. 773), 772, 775, 777-8
NANKIVILLE, L-Cpl H. E., 549
NANTUCKET SOUND, 84
NAPIER (Map p. 27; Sketches pp. 62, 141), 23-4, 37, 43, 47, 52, 60-5, 72-6, 81, 86, 91, 97, 99-103, 106, 122, 124, 138, 182n
NAPIER, Pte J. M., 584
NARAGOOMA (Map p. 327), 53, 270
NARAKAPOR (Sketch p. 68), 69, 135, 209, 364
NARANTAP (Sketch p. 427), 417
NARAWAPUM (Sketch p. 427), 417, 428-9, 431, 434
NARINSERA WATERS (Sketch p. 375), 365
NASH, Maj J. W., 269n
NASINGNATU (Sketch p. 467), 498
NASSAU BAY (Map p. 32; Sketches pp. 85, 92), 23-4, 26, 37, 43, 52, 58, 84, 86, 92, 97, 99, 102-3, 107, 109, 113, 115, 117, 118n, 119, 134-5, 142, 144-5, 160, 168, 171, 178, 180, 182n, 211, 213-14, 216, 223-4, 230, 266, 285, 391, 401, 524; Allied plans for capture, 56, 59-60, 71-3; Japanese strength at, 57, 71; 2/6 Bn patrols to, 62-4; US landing at, 90-7, 106, 273; confusion of command at, 138-41
NEAR FEATURE (Sketch p. 617), 616-17
NELLIGAN, Capt P. W., 470
NELSON, Lieutenant, 192
NELSON, Lt-Col D. J. A., 269n
NELSON, Maj St E. D., 24, 29-30
NEMAU (Sketches pp. 765, 768), 765n, 767
NESBITT, Lt A. W., 476, 489
NETHERLANDS EAST INDIES (Sketch p. 5), 1, 4, 11, 232, 788, 798; estimated Japanese strength in, 11n
NETHERLANDS EAST INDIES ARMY, 17
NEW ASINI TRACK, 113
NEWBERY, Brig J. C., 356, 372, 534, 536, 544, 549, 552, 554
NEW BRITAIN (Map p. 28; Sketch p. 5), 1n, 11, 55, 84, 99, 279, 318, 325, 334, 450, 466, 470-1, 482, 488, 505, 506n, 507n, 508, 522, 556, 602, 609, 652, 656, 689, 696, 729, 797n, 798n. 801-2; Allies plan assault on, 3, 8, 9, 220-1, 284, 444; Japanese bases in, 231; Allied invasion of, 792-4
NEW CALEDONIA (Sketch p. 5), 11, 17, 24, 44, 220
NEWCOMB, Maj S. P., 380, 460, 467, 491, 626, 664
NEW GEORGIA (Sketch p. 224), 7-8, 11, 56; capture of, 220, 223-6, 232, 273
NEW GUINEA (Map p. 28), 1, 7, 12, 17-18, 28, 50, 55, 58-9, 84, 218, 263, 267, 277, 318, 471, 535, 652, 696, 729, 737, 788, 792, 798-9, 813; discussed at Casablanca Conference, 2-3; Allied plans in, 9, 13-14, 220-1, 282n, 444, 790-1; Japanese Army strength and dispositions in, 11n, 20, 231-2, 415, 524n; Allied strength in, 15-16; airfield development, 231; exploration, 232-3; pre-war administration, 246; naming of villages in, 440n; organisation and command of Allied forces in, 504n; visited by Lethbridge Mission, 686n; Japanese policy and tactics in, 762, 788
NEW GUINEA, DUTCH, 3, 11, 57, 231, 260, 280n; Allied advance into, 802-3, 805-6; Merauke Force in, 810-13
NEW GUINEA, NATIVE POPULATION OF, 240n, 246-7, 259-60, 333, 408; in Salus and Duali area, 37; as guides, 54; and Angau, 66; relations with Japanese, 69-70, 89-90, 416, 424, 426-7, 432, 522, 685, 690, 692, 695, 743, 793, with Australians, 89-90, 260, 410-11, 438, 615, 685, 695, 697, 742; in Markham area, 118-19; in Bena Bena area, 233; reliability of information provided by, 386; Japanese atrocities, 474; in Huon Peninsula area, 517; in Sepik area, 592n, 809-10; in Bogadjim area, 783-4
NEW HEBRIDES (Map p. 814), 654
NEW IRELAND (Sketch p. 793), 3, 57, 566n, 792
NEWMAN, Captain, 96-8, 100, 102, 124, 127, 147, 149, 166
NEWMAN, Maj C. E., 112, 171-2, 207n, 208, 288, 317, 777; commands 58/59 Bn, 772
NEWMAN'S JUNCTION (Sketch p. 109), 203, 208
NEW SOUTH WALES, 265; army dispositions in, 14
NEWTON, Lt T. E., 40
NEW ZEALAND (Sketch p. 5), 11, 24n, 220, 795

NEW ZEALAND AIR FORCE, 11, 226, 795
NEW ZEALAND ARMY, 16n; 2nd Div, 795; 3rd Div, 11, 220, 226, 794-5; 8th Bde, 653; 14th Bde, 794
NGAFIR CREEK (Sketch p. 394), 385, 399-400, 404, 408, 433n
NGARONENO, MOUNT (Map p. 32), 53, 277, 340
NGASAWAPUM (Sketch p. 68), 69
NIALL, Maj H. L. R., 240
NICHOLAS, Maj W. P., 465, 510
NICHOLLS, Col N. A. M., 787
NIELSON, Lt R. H., 375
NIMITZ, Fleet Admiral Chester W., 8-9, 12, 226, 653, 798-800, 813; commands Central Pacific Area, 7; CCOS instructions to, 220; sets dates for invasion of Marshalls, Marianas and Palaus, 791-2
NISBET, Brig T. G., 243, 245, 251, 440, 564, 776
NISHIKAWA, Major, 50
NISSAN ISLAND (Sketch p. 793), 794
NOBLE, Capt Marvin B., 124
NOEMFOOR ISLAND (Sketch p. 799), 806
NOKOPO (Sketch p. 765), 763, 769-70
NOLAN, Lt J. C., 678
NONGORA (Map p. 528); Sketch p. 660), 518, 536, 612, 634, 637, 656, 659, 670, 675, 679; captured, 664-5
NORFOLK (Sketch p. 635), 537n, 659
NORFOLK ISLAND (Sketch p. 5), 16n
NORMAN, Brig C. H. B., 352, 354, 356, 372, 521, 534-8, 540, 542, 544-6, 549, 552-3, 659; commands 2/28 Bn, 350; on Busu River crossing, 351
NORMANBY ISLAND (Map p. 28), 271
NORRIE, Lt F. J., 777
NORRIS, Cpl R. C., 475
NORTH, Maj S. F., 638
NORTH AFRICA, 18-19, 219; Allied landings in, 1, 273, 283; American strength in, 2n
NORTHERN TERRITORY, 566n; Australian Army strength in, 15-16
NORTH HILL (Sketches pp. 452, 635), 452, 458, 463, 504, 512, 526, 532, 539-40, 552-5, 557, 607, 615, 626-7, 632, 636-8, 644, 651-2, 656, 661, 669, 732
NORTH PACIFIC AREA, 816
NORTON, Lt F. A., 620-1
NORWAL (Sketch p. 394), 411
NORWAY, 219, 272
NOUMEA (Sketch p. 5), 7, 9
NUGIDU PENINSULA (Sketch p. 485), 499
NUGU (Sketch p. 684), 685
NUK NUK (Sketch p. 290), 199, 286, 295, 304, 312, 316, 318
NUMADA, Captain, 181
NUNN, Sgt C. W., 88n
NUNN'S POST (Map p. 32), 88, 132, 150
NURU RIVER (Map p. 773), 784
NUZEN (Sketch p. 726), 730

OAKHILL, Capt R. S., 710-11
OBA, Major, 106, 135, 145, 216, 391; commands III/102 Bn, 96, 99
O'BRIEN, Cpl J. J., 698
OBSAU (Sketch p. 235), 440
OBSERVATION HILL (Sketch p. 25), 22, 25-6, 29, 34, 38, 40, 47, 50, 71-2, 74-5, 107, 117, 119-22, 125-7, 166
O'CONNOR, Sgt D. E., 584
O'CONNOR, Col J. C. W., 478, 498, 663, 667, 720-2; commands 22 Bn, 467
O'CONNOR, Pte W. S. M., 69
O'DAY, Lt-Col G. O., 441-2, 577
O'DONNELL, Capt G. C., 246, 250
O'DONNELL, Lt J. L., 618, 620-2
OGAWA, Lieutenant, 46, 112
OGDEN, Maj J. W., 269n
OGELBENG, 247
OGURA, MOUNT, see CAMEL RIDGE-ROUGH HILL
O'HARE, Col M. P., 42, 81, 149n, 781n; commands 1 Mtn Bty, 40
OHATA, Private, 106
OHIBE (Sketch p. 48), 49-50
OIVI, 55
OKABA (Sketch p. 811), 812
OKABE, Maj-Gen Teru, 26, 28, 42, 46
OKAMOTO, Captain, 181
O'KEEFE, Chaplain Rev P. G., 82
OKURA, Captain, 46
OLD MARI (Sketch p. 68), 69
OLD MUNKIP (Sketch p. 394), 410

844 INDEX

OLD VICKERS (Map p. 27; Sketches pp. 170, 174), 35, 44-5, 88, 108-10, 112-14, 116, 150, 152-3, 155, 172, 191-2, 205, 209; capture of, 128-9, 169-71; Japanese counter-attack, 173-6
OLIGADU (Sketch p. 467), 471, **474**
OLUM, native guide, 54
O'MALLEY, Pte W. J., 459
ONGA (Sketches pp. 235, 252), 210, 237-8, 241, 256, 416-17, 432
OOMSIS (Sketch p. 68), 70, 118
OONOONBA, Qld, 177
OPEN BAY (Sketch p. 793), 793
ORFORD, CAPE (Sketch p. 793), 792-3
ORGORUNA (Sketches pp. 591, 759), 592, 680, 689, 691, 694, 702, 704, 711, 739, 745, 754, 757, 759-61
ORIENTAL (Sketch p. 635), 537n, 554, 559, 659, 661
ORIN (Sketch p. 394), 406
O'RIORDAN, Sgt J. M., 652
ORO BAY (Map p. 28), 17, 55, 57-9, 230-1, 321n
ORODUBI (Sketches pp. 109, 290), 87-8, 108-11, 114, 116, 128, 134, 145, 150-5, 164-5, 167, 169, 172, 176, 189, 199, 206-7, 286
ORODUBI TRACK, 208
OROMUGE (Map p. 773), 776, 784
ORT (Map p. 773), 787
OSBORNE CREEK (Sketch p. 109), 113, 172, 208
Osprey, launch, 262
OTTO, MOUNT (Sketch p. 235), 237, 245-6, 250-2
OUTRIDGE, Lt-Col L. MacD., 471, 539
OVERLORD OPERATION, 219
OWEN GUN, compared with Thompson, 51n; *see also* MACHINE-GUNS
OWENS, Lt-Col E. S., 398, 577
OWEN STANLEY RANGE (Map p. 28), 20, 55, 57-8, 291, 344, 358-9, 400, 662, 696
OXLEY, Lt-Col P. H. G., 396

PABU, New Guinea native, 615, 627
PABU HILL (Sketch p. 635), 626, 640, 659, 663-4, 670, 675; naming of, 627; operations on, 630-8, 643-4, 650-3, 656-8, 661
PACIFIC THEATRE (Sketch p. 5), 84-5, 228, 272, 682n, 781, 788, 817; Allied plans and strategy, 1-4, 7-9, 217-22, 790-2; American strength and deployment, 2, 12; Australian Army allotted major role in, 12; American offensive in, 273, 798-9, 813-16
PAGAN, Brig J. E., 464-5
PAGE, Pte D. K., 521
PAGE, Rt Hon Sir Earle, 787
PAINE, Lt R., 582, 584, 586
PAIPA (Map p. 773; Sketches pp. 235, 424), 247, 424, 595, 596n, 753, 755-6, 771-2
PAIPA TRACK (Map p. 773), 756
PALANKO (Map p. 545; Sketch p. 660), 518, 527, 544, 547, 608, 610, 614-15, 649, 665
PALAU ISLANDS (Map p. 814; Sketch p. 5), 231, 788, 790-2, 798-9, 813; capture of, 816
PALLIER, Lt N. W. T., 576-9, 585
PALLIER'S HILL (Sketch p. 577), 576, 584-5, 600; attack on, 577-9
PALM, Tpr N., 249
PALMER, Maj A. S., 690n; commands 2/6 Cdo Sqn, 697
PANAWAI, LAKE (Sketch p. 262), 263
PAPUA (Map p. 28), 7, 10, 12-13, 18, 55, 72, 268, 271, 328, 359, 378, 402n, 423, 507, 566, 686n, 817
PAPUA, GULF OF (Map p. 28), 236
PAPUAN CONSTABULARY, ROYAL, 416, 599n, in Los Negros landing, 796
PAPUANS, THE, 54, 233
PARER, Damien, 172
PARER'S BOWL, 172
PARKER, Lt-Col G. E., 269n
PARMITER, Sgt F. J., 142
PARRAMATTA (Sketch p. 15), 16, 279n, 280n
PARRISH, Lt D. J., 261
PARRY ISLAND, 801
PARRY-OKEDEN, Lt-Col W. N., 713, 767, 786-7
PARTEP (Map p. 327), 20, 26, 53, 341
PASCOE, Capt J. C., 10, 312
PASSLOW, Maj V., 776
PATROLS, Lae-Salamaua area, 53-4, 409-12; in Finisterres, 588, 595-9, 680, 684-6, 710-11; rations and equipment of, 597; Finschhafen area, 607-8, 614-15, 678; at Merauke, 812
PATTINGALE, Capt E. J., 285
PATTON, General George S., 283

PAWSON, Maj J. H., 201
PEAK HILL (Sketch p. 660), 666, 671, 673-5
PEARL HARBOUR, 218, 272, 654, 792
PEARSON, Capt J. N., 338, 345-6, 563-4, 707
PECK, Capt D. V., 53, 409-11
PEDDER, Sgt B. W., 636
PEEL RIVER (Sketch p. 765), 765n
PEIRSE, Air Chief Marshal Sir Richard, 220n
PELELIU ISLAND, 816
PEMBERTON, Lt R. G. M., 110
PENGLASE, Maj N., 75
PESEN (Sketch p. 254), 70, 119, 210, 253, 256-7
PETERSEN, Capt N. H. G., 715-16, 718, 724
PETERSON, Capt B. H., 40
PHILIPPINE ISLANDS (Sketches pp. 5, 218), 2, 8, 11, 84, 218, 221, 231, 788, 798n, 799, 817; invasion planned, 790-1
PHILIPPINE SEA (Map p. 814), 792, 815
Phoenix, American cruiser, 12
PHOTOGRAPHS, 450, 740, 743
PICKEN, Lt-Col K. S., 175, 189, 203-5, 300-1, 315; commands 2/27 Bn, 687
PICKEN'S RIDGE (Sketch p. 562), 687
PICKERING, Cpl R. G., 696-7
PIGEONS, 54, 323n
PIKE, Lt-Col P. H., 453-4, 458, 460-3, 477-8, 483, 485, 490, 511-12, 519
PILCHER, Capt K., 781n
PILE, Sgt R. A., 725
PILIMUNG (Map p. 32), 26, 47, 50, 61, 68, 87n, 108
PIMPLE (Bobdubi area; Map p. 27), 207
PIMPLE (Jivevaneng area; Sketch p. 501), 519
PIMPLE (Lokanu Ridge; Map p. 293), 307-8
PIMPLE (Mubo area; Map p. 108; Sketch p. 25), 25-6, 28-31, 33-5, 38-42, 47, 52, 61-2, 66, 71-2, 78, 80-1, 121, 123, 125-6, 129, 148, 166; origin of name, 22
PIMPLE (Shaggy Ridge; Map p. 740; Sketch p. 708), 680, 682, 688-9; capture of, 705-8
PINCOTT, Pte G. A., 52
PINNACE HEAD (Sketch p. 262), 263
PINNEY, Cpl P. P., 36
PINO HILL (Map p. 545; Sketch p. 635), 535, 559, 607, 614-15, 626, 632, 634, 636-7, 643-4, 651, 656-8, 669
PIONEERS RANGE (Map p. 27), 22, 28, 32, 67, 115
PLACE NAMES, in New Guinea, 627, 642
POLA (Map p. 545), 498-9, 552
POMMERN BAY (Map p. 734), 734
PONAPE (Map p. 814), 790
PONG (Sketch p. 635), 632
PONT, Lt-Col G. McA., 26n
POPA, Cpl Stephen, 530-1
POPE, Maj H. W., 463, 493, 496-8
PORTAL, Marshal of the R.A.F. Viscount, 1n, 219
PORTER, Maj-Gen S. H. W. C., 626-7, 636-7, 639, 644, 651, 652n, 656, 659-61, 669; commands 24 Bde, 615
PORT MORESBY (Map p. 28), 14, 16-18, 20, 55, 57-8, 60-1, 70, 73, 84, 87, 104, 129n, 138, 141, 197, 230, 234, 238, 241-3, 254, 267, 269-71, 275, 277, 279, 280n, 281, 337-8, 341, 343-4, 357-9, 376, 378, 385, 391, 401, 404, 414-15, 422, 428, 433, 439, 445, 479-81, 506-7, 535, 555, 558, 561, 567, 569, 594, 599n, 615, 684, 692, 696, 705, 712, 738-9, 771, 781, 810
PORT ROMILLY (Map p. 28), 236
PORT STEPHENS, NSW, 280n
POST 6 (Sketch p. 811), 812-13
POSTERN OPERATION, 62, 78, 281
POTSDAM (Sketch p. 808), 808
POUND, Admiral of the Fleet Sir Dudley, 1n, 219
POWER, Capt K., 270, 271n, 382, 384, 571, 574-5, 579
POWERHOUSE (Map p. 32), 47, 50, 71
POYNTON, L-Sgt J. W., 432, 435
PRENDERGAST, Lt N. F., 474, 669
PRICE, Capt E. W. A., 123-7, 154-5, 164-5, 192-3
PRICE'S KNOLL (Sketch p. 196), 167
PRIGG, Pte J. R., 148-9
PRINGLE, Capt F. B., 25, 28-30
PRIOR, Lt W. N., 762n
PRISONERS OF WAR, 1; *Australian*, number captured to Aug 44, 817; *Indian*, 809; *Japanese*, 10, 407, 520, 732-6, 743, 746, 767-9, 785-6
PROBY, Lt L. S., 169-71
PROCTOR, Capt P. C. R., 305, 307, 316, 318-20, 395
PROTHERO, MOUNT (Map p. 740), 590n, 740-4, 746, 748-9, 751-2, 754, 756, 771-2; captured 747, 750
PROTHEROE, Sgt R. R., 590n
PROVAN, Maj D., 304-5
PRYOR, Sgt T. G., 441

INDEX   845

P.T. Boats, 318, 505-6, 557, 610, 731n, 786; operations of, 278, 449-50, 457, 521-2, 529-30, 609, 616, 658-9, 727, 730, 734
Purami (Sketch p. 262), 263
Purari River (Map p. 28), 236
Purbrick, Lt W. I., 724
Pursehouse, Capt L., 257, 736
Putland, Capt V. M., 346

Quarry (Sketch p. 319), 316
Quebec Conference, 790
Queensland, 220; strength and deployment of Australian forces in, 14-16
Quembung (Map p. 545; Sketch p. 461), 478, 516, 521, 541
Quoja River (Sketch p. 461), 463, 468, 511-12, 516, 551

Rabaul (Map p. 28; Sketch p. 793), 11, 28, 54, 57, 82, 84n, 119, 129n, 181, 220-1, 226, 231-2, 278, 325, 328, 334, 449, 466, 507n, 522, 524, 609, 653, 731n, 762n, 792-4, 797n, 798-9; Allies plan capture, 2-4, 7-8; neutralisation planned, 790
Rackham, Lt A. J., 603-4
Radar, 279, 488, 508, 561, 569, 575, 599, 680, 692, 738-9; in Lae operations, 274, 334; location of installations, 594; Australian detachment lands Long Island, 731n
Radbone, Sgt G. G., 621
Rae, Lt-Col D. F., 769
Ragitsaria (Sketch p. 424), 424, 437
Ragitsuma (Sketch p. 427), 436
Ragitumkiap (Map p. 396), 417
Rai Coast (Map p. 396; Sketch p. 765), 241, 257, 260, 278, 404, 415, 425, 438, 600, 730, 762, 775, 802; Australian advance, 763-7, 771
Raids, on Allied artillery positions, 210-16
Rainbana (Sketch p. 684), 711
Ramm, Lt J. W. L., 202-3, 296, 309
Ramsay, Maj-Gen A. H. (Plate p. 780), 765, 768-9, 771, 788; commands 5 Div, 595; plans Rai Coast advance, 764; plans capture of Madang, 785
Ramshaw, Tpr D. McK., 746
Ramu River (Maps p. 28, 396), 231, 233-6, 238-41, 243-7, 251, 257-8, 260, 416-17, 426n, 430-2, 434-7, 439-40, 443, 558, 562, 564-5, 586-7, 592-3, 597, 600, 685, 694-5, 697-8, 739, 789, 808-9
Ramu Valley, 234, 237-8, 241-2, 325, 414-16, 425, 433, 438-40, 564, 569, 574, 577, 586, 588, 593-4, 596, 600, 680, 682, 686, 689, 691-3, 696-7, 707, 785, 787, 810; described, 277; native population, 426-7; Bena Force operations, 431-6; 7 Div operations, 436-43, 561-7, 702-3, 738; malaria casualties, 681; Japanese account, 762; relief of 7 Div in, 763, 779
Ranken, L-Sgt H. B., 257n
Ranken, Lt J. B., 257n
Rations: American, 255n, 328. Australian, in Salamaua operations, 112-13, 150, 187; in Lae operations, 310-11, 328, 349, 354-5, 362; in Finschhafen operations, 484, 514-15, 552, 650n; in Ramu Valley, 565; on patrols, 597; in advance to Saidor, 767. Japanese, 407, 525, 650n, 651
Ratliff, Captain, 159, 184, 292, 309
Rattray, Lt K. C., 305
Ravenshoe, Qld, 268
Rawlinson Range (Map p. 327), 275
Rayson, Capt M. W., 118-19
Read, Pte L. H., 195
Read, Lt S. (Plate p. 173), 171
Red Beach (Map p. 327; Sketch p. 333), 275, 326, 337, 347, 349, 352n, 357, 362, 364, 366, 446, 450; landing at, 329-35
Reddin, Capt J. W., 576
Reddish, Maj N. G., 242
Redman, Cpl A. V., 643
Red Platypus, 353n, 635n
Red Roof Hut (Sketch p. 639), 642, 646-7
Redu (Map p. 773), 778
Reeve, Capt E. R., 74n, 147
Reeve's O.P. (Sketch p. 76), 74
Refshauge, Maj-Gen W. D., 314; commands 15 Fd Amb, 71
Reid, American destroyer, 279, 334, 451, 466
Reid, Capt R. K., 332
Rein Bay (Map p. 28), 658
Reinforcements, Australian, Salamaua area, 177; Finschhafen area, 480-3, 523; Ramu Valley, 565, 693. Japanese, 523-4

Reiss Point (Sketch p. 734), 616, 734
Rendell, L-Cpl H. J., 592
Rendova Island (Sketch p. 224), 225
Reno III Operation, 790-1
Reno V Operation, 813
Rentz, J. N., 802n
Rereo (Map p. 773), 778
Rhoden, Lt-Col P. E., 706; commands 2/14 Bn, 595; commands 21 Bde, 705
Rice, Capt M. W., 371, 547, 607
Richards, Lt B. W., 365
Richards, Sgt W. H., 373-4
Richardson, Lt F., 670
Richardson, Lt K. E., 502
Richmond, Capt C. R., 502-3, 547, 636, 658, 664, 669
Ricks, Pte E. C. R., 286
Ridley, Cpl V. R., 634
Rigel, American ship, 267, 274
Rimba (Sketch p. 734), 734
Ritchie, Pte J., 635n
River Ambush (Sketch p. 342), 342, 360, 364
Roach, Lt L. S., 75-9, 97
Road Construction, Bulldog-Wau, 20; Nassau Bay area, 103; Bena plateau, 239; Lae-Nadzab, 402-3, 414; Bogadjim Road, 231
Roberts, Lt D. W., 626
Robertson, Maj A. C., 359, 365, 373, 376, 694, 698-702, 740n, 781n
Robertson, Maj B. E. D., 711
Robertson, WO1 C. A., 125
Robertson, L-Cpl D. J., 30-1
Robertson, Lt-Col F. B., 269n
Robertson, Lt-Gen Sir Horace, commands 1 Armd Div, 17-18; commands 3 Div, 780
Robertson, Lt-Col W. T., 269n, 359n, 385, 389, 423, 425, 692, 738
Robilliard, Lt G. H. G., 575, 590
Robino, Sgt P., 657
Robinson, Lt A. L., 796-7
Robinson, Lt B. L., 168
Robinson, Capt B. R., 178, 209, 253-5, 408
Robinson, Capt M., 621
Robson, Lt-Col E. M., 350n, 359, 382, 384, 389, 586; commands 2/31 Bn, 339
Roche, Lt F. J., 109-11
Rockets, 618
Rockhampton, Qld, 17, 84, 182, 280n, 321n
Rodd, Capt C. J., 587
Rofe, Pte B. R., 243
Rogers, Brig J. D., 446
Rogers, Lt W. E., 469, 476
Roi Island, 800
Roinji (Sketch p. 768), 765n, 768
Rolfe, L-Cpl A. J., 494-5
Rolfe, Capt C. B. N., 104, 106
Romba River (Sketch p. 765), 765n, 767
Ronan, Pte R. J., 503
Roodakoff, Lt A., 812
Rooke, Capt A. N., 189, 191, 234, 236-8, 239n, 242-3, 599
Rooke, Capt P. F., 351, 546, 554, 663
Roon, Cape (Sketch p. 85), 86, 91
Roosevelt, Lt-Col Archibald B., 139-42, 145, 159, 180; commands III/162 Bn, 138; replaced, 183
Roosevelt, President Franklin D., 218, 652; at Casablanca Conference, 1, 3; and China, 217; at Quebec Conference, 790
Roosevelt Ridge (Map p. 293; Sketches pp. 141, 290), 143-4, 159-60, 168, 178-81, 187, 192, 201, 216, 285, 292; capture of, 183-5
Rose, Cpl A. D., 65, 306
Rose-Bray, Capt A. E. B., 437; commands 2/6 Indep Coy, 431
Rosemary, Australian launch, 812
Rosevear, Maj H. G. M., 546, 555
Ross, Lt F. E. H., 338, 345
Ross, Maj J. A., 211, 310-11
Rough Hill (Sketches pp. 290, 301), 286-8, 299-300, 303-4, 314-15, 317, 320
Routley, Maj W. V., 715
Row, Capt R., 419
Row, Brig R. A., 653
Rowan, Lt-Col J. G., 718-20; commands 37/52 Bn, 663
Rowe, Pte L. G., 383-4
Rowell, Maj F. A., 208
Rowell, Lt-Gen Sir Sydney, 283

846 INDEX

ROWLEY, L-Cpl E. R., 157
ROYAL PARK, Vic, 280n
RUA (Sketch p. 726), 730-1
RUANGE (Sketch p. 768), 769
RUBBER BOATS, 338n
RUDKIN, Maj R. S., 519, 547
RUMU RIVER (Map p. 327), 277, 433
RUPERTUS, Maj-Gen William H., 794
RUSHTON, Capt R. A., 367
RUSSELL, Maj W. B., 567n, 577n, 579n
RUSSELL, Sgt W. C., 30
RUSSELL ISLANDS (Sketch p. 224), 224
RUSSIA, 10n, 219; Allied aid to, 4; relations with Great Britain, 218
RUSSIAN ARMY, 790; begins offensive, 1
RUTHERFORD, NSW, 280n
RYAN, Lt J. W., 493-6
RYAN, Lt P. A., 70, 89, 256, 378n, 423
RYAN, Pte R. W., 78
RYAN, WO2 V. J., 723
RYLANDS, Capt C. I., 382, 564

SAABY, Pte J. E., 657
SACHEN BAY (Sketch p. 85), 59, 91
SACHS, Lt J., 74, 167
SADDLE (Map p. 32), 23-4, 34, 61, 75, 78-81, 82n, 86, 102, 119, 126
SAEKI, Colonel Joshiro, 728
SAGERAK (Map p. 396; Sketch p. 427), 416-17, 423, 426, 428-9, 433-4; airstrip at, 430, 436
SAIDOR (Maps pp. 28, 396; Sketches pp. 731, 768), 257, 260, 425, 507, 696, 711, 729-30, 733, 736-8, 745, 761-3, 765, 768-9, 771-2, 777-8, 785, 788-9, 797n, 803, 809; Japanese strength at, 20, 764; American landing at, 731-2
SAIGON, 11
SAIPA (Map p. 773; Sketch p. 591), 424, 600-1, 772, 774-5
SAIPAN ISLAND (Map p. 814), 791; American landing on, 813-15
SALAMAUA (Maps pp. 28, 32; Sketch p. 319), 8, 11, 18, 21-4, 26, 32-3, 35-7, 44-6, 53, 61, 66, 75, 84n, 87, 97, 99, 109, 111-13, 115, 117-18, 132-3, 142, 145, 150-1, 156, 159, 173, 177, 181-2, 184, 188-91, 197, 199, 203-4, 207-10, 215-16, 253, 277, 280n, 281, 286-7, 289, 295, 298, 304, 306-7, 309-10, 314-15, 323, 325, 328, 346, 359, 364n, 381, 390, 393, 395, 401, 402n, 412, 415, 444, 492, 507n, 523, 525, 563, 580, 594n, 666, 672n, 729, 738-9, 762, 766, 770, 784-5, 789, 817; plans for operations against, 3, 9, 55-9, 68, 73, 137-8, 142, 221, 291-2; Japanese strength and reinforcement, 20, 28, 43, 54, 57, 71, 101, 231, 276, 291-2, 391-2, 425, 524; Japanese plan to defend, 135-6, 231; Allied strategy at, 163, 166, 179, 281; Allied strength in area, 178, 400; attacked by Allied air and naval forces, 278; capture of, 317-22; unsuitable as Allied base, 324, 400
SALAMAUA O.P., 112
SALAMAUA TRACK, 289, 313
SALAMI PLANTATION, 797
SALANKAUA PLANTATION (Sketches pp. 485, 494), 468, 470-1, 473, 476, 479, 484-5, 489, 491-3, 498-9, 619
SALANKAUA ROAD (Sketch p. 494), 492
SALAWAKET, MOUNT (Sketch p. 394), 409, 517
SALLAWAY, Pte E. L., 305
SALUS (Sketch p. 141), 37, 99, 102n, 117, 134
SALUS, LAKE (Map p. 32; Sketches pp. 141, 212), 118, 134, 141-3, 145, 171, 180, 211-16
SALVATION ARMY, 82n, 88, 354, 489, 755n
SAMANZINO (Sketch p. 394), 378n
SAMAU (Sketch p. 684), 684-6
SAMBANGA (Sketch p. 394), 409, 597
SAMBEANG (Sketch p. 394), 412
SAMOA, 11
SAMOA HARBOUR (Map p. 32), 137
SANA (Sketch p. 759), 760
SANAI (Sketch p. 808), 809
SANANANDA, 17, 55, 84, 264, 580, 804
SANDERS, Pte J. A., 52
SANDY CREEK (Sketch p. 290), 288, 300-1, 303, 317
SANEM RIVER (Sketch p. 394), 378, 406
SANEM VALLEY, 406-9
SANGAN (Map p. 396; Sketch p. 235), 237, 256, 281, 378, 415-17, 419, 421
SANGA RIVER (Map p. 717), 722-4, 732

SANKWEP RIVER (Sketches pp. 369, 394), 350 ,355, 369, 386, 396
SANSAPOR (Sketch p. 799), 806
SANTA CRUZ ISLAND (Sketch p. 5), 1n
SARANUMA, Captain, 479
SARMI (Sketch p. 799), 792; Americans land at, 805
SARUWAGED RANGE (Map p. 396; Sketch p. 394), 241-2, 257, 260, 399, 406, 517, 524
SASAVELE ISLAND, 225
SATTELBERG (Maps pp. 396, 528; Sketches pp. 617, 639), 227n, 412, 458, 466-7, 470, 473, 478, 483-4, 487-8, 490, 505, 513, 516-17, 519-21, 523-6, 529, 547, 553-8, 560, 615, 633-4, 641-2, 656, 658, 665, 667, 672, 675, 726; derivation of name, 447; maps of, 450-1, 512n; Japanese reinforce, 500; plans for capture, 501, 504, 518, 602-3, 604n, 606, 608, 612-16; Japanese supply problems, 522, 609-10, 649-51; bombed by Allied Air Forces, 535; Australian supply problems, 608-9; Japanese account, 612, 652-3; Australians advance on, 616-30, 639-42, 644-8; captured, 649, 652; Australian casualties 650
SATTELBERG ROAD (Map p. 528; Sketches pp. 461, 617), 464-5, 470, 473, 477-9, 483, 485, 490, 501-2, 504, 513, 516, 518-19, 524-5, 527, 541-3, 551-3, 559, 608, 612-14, 616-20, 622-4, 629, 633, 639, 642, 649n; operations on, 602-5; opening of, 606-7
SAUNDERS, Lt R. E., 700
SAUNDERS, Capt R. W., 24
SAUS (Sketch p. 235), 564
SAVIGE, Lt-Gen Sir Stanley (Plates pp. 204, 780), 19, 33, 36, 47, 51-4, 65, 69, 75, 77, 82-3, 97, 106, 112-15, 118, 120, 124, 127-8, 131, 133-4, 142, 154-6, 158, 165-8, 172, 181-4, 186, 201, 206-7, 210-11, 214-15, 254, 271n, 286, 295, 785, 788; commands 3 Div, 17; estimate and career of, 18; role of forces, 20-1, 37-8, 42-3, 50, 58-61, 71-3, 137-8, 145-6, 150, 188-9, 208-9, 253; takes command in Wau-Markham area, 23, 25; orders and instructions of, 26, 31, 46, 66, 90, 101-2, 287-8, 807; strength of forces in Salamaua-Lae area, 57; supply problems, 70-1, 154; relations with Americans, 103-5, 138-41, 143-4, 159-61, 179-81, 185; and air support, 121, 129n; relations with New Guinea Force, 163-4; opens HQ at Guadagasal, 169; visited by General Berryman, 197, 199-200; hands over to 5 Aust Div, 216, 289; commands I Corps, 780
SAVIGE SPUR (Sketch p. 290), 300, 303, 316-17, 320
SAWERS, Cpl S., 374
SAWYER, Lt S. E., 382-3
SAXBY, Col N. H. W., 26n
SAZOMU RIVER (Sketch p. 726), 732
SCANLAN, Cpl M. D., 557
SCARLET BEACH (Map p. 528; Sketches 452, 531), 448, 460, 463-7, 469-71, 473, 477, 480, 482, 490-1, 500, 502, 505n, 508, 510-11, 516-18, 523-4, 526, 537-41, 543, 551-2, 557, 559, 588, 615, 627, 632, 637, 652-3, 656, 732, 735; naming of, and reasons for selection, 446-7; Japanese strength, 446-7, 478; naval and air support at, 449; 20 Bde role at, 450, move to, 451-2, landing at, 453-7; Japanese seaborne attack on, 529-33; counter-attack on, 550-1, 554, 634
SCARLETT, Lt-Col G. Y. D., 158, 193n
SCHARNHORST POINT (Sketch p. 726), 730
SCHRAM, Cpl A., 336, 347
SCHROEDER, Capt Donald W., 144
SCHULZE, Sgt T. H., 195n
SCOTCHMER, Lt S., 377
SCOTT, Cpl A., 384
SCOTT, Cpl A. F., 555
SCOTT, Lt G. A., 371
SCOTT, Lt J., 443, 709
SCOTT, Lt R. T., 420
SCOTT, Brig T. H., 371, 380, 386-7, 508, 651, 656-7 669-70, 672-3, 676; commands 2/32 Bn, 363
SCOTT, Lt T. H., 597-8
SCOTTER, Lt G. K., 192
SCOTT-HOLLAND, WO2 T. H., 509, 511
SCOTT-YOUNG, Capt N. R., 78
SCOUT CAMP (Map p. 293), 142, 297
SCOUT HILL (Sketches pp. 141, 290), 140, 142, 159, 285, 304, 316
SCOUT RIDGE (Map p. 293; Sketches pp. 141, 290), 144, 159, 168, 178-81, 183-4, 187, 194, 199, 201, 216, 285-6, 291, 295-6, 307-8, 316, 321n; Allied attacks on, 292-4, 304-6

INDEX

SCOUT RIDGE TRACK (Map p. 293), 144, 202, 292, 294, 308
SCREW RIVER (Sketch p. 258), 806n
SCRUB TYPHUS, 735
SEALE, Lt H. P., 426, 785
SEARL, Col B. R. W., 267n, 667
SEARLE, Sgt H. H., 583
SEARLE, Capt L. K., 257n
SEARLES, Lt M. G., 695, 700
SEA SHELLS, as payment for native carriers, 234, 438
SECOMBE, Lt-Gen V.C., 65n
SECURITY, 551n, 652n, 682n, 743n; and use of code names, 506n; *Japanese*, 520, 543n, 746
SEDDON, Capt R. J. S., 340, 358, 740
SEEADLER HARBOUR (Sketch p. 796), 796-7
SEGI POINT (Sketch p. 224), 224
SEKINE, Lieut-Colonel, 46
SEL (Sketches pp. 731, 768), 731, 765n, 769
SELEBOB (Map p. 32), 66, 87, 132
SELEBOB RIDGE, 71
SELEPE DISTRICT, 517
SELLHEIM, Qld, 177
SENTANI, LAKE (Sketch p. 799), 802
SEPIK RIVER VALLEY (Map p. 28; Sketch p. 258), 231, 234, 241, 259-60, 789, 817; pre-war exploration, 233; operations in, 261-3, 432, 806n; 5 Div advance to, 807-10
SEPU (Sketch p. 235), 242-3, 246, 251, 431, 440, 564, 586-7, 592n, 593, 597, 684, 739
SEURE (Sketch p. 768), 765n, 769
SEWELL, Brig H. B., 279n
SEYMOUR, Vic, 60
SHADBOLT, Pte L. G., 52, 98
SHAGGY RIDGE (Map p. 740; Sketches pp. 588, 708), 573, 587-9, 591, 596n, 598n, 599, 680, 682, 686-7, 697, 703, 711, 728, 739-41, 743-5, 752-4, 756, 761n, 762, 771: attacks on, 590, 688-9, 704-10, 745-51
SHAMBLER, Sgt L. E. R., 487
SHARP, Tpr W., 250
SHATTOCK, Capt E. J.. 671, 673-4, 677-8
SHAVE, Lt-Col L. K., 279n
SHELDON, Capt T. C., 453-4, 458, 463-4, 491, 499, 511, 515
SHELDON'S CROSSING (Map p. 327), 344
SHEPPARD, Lt R., 384
SHERLOCK, Lt J. H., 54
SHERVEY, L-Sgt E. J., 383-4
SHERWIN, Chaplain Rev V. H. G., 324
SHERWOOD, R. E., 4n
SHIMADA, Lieutenant, 198
SHIMADA, Private, 106
SHIPPING: *Allied*, 20, 224, 230, 813; *Japanese*, 3, 231
SHOBU, Lieut-Colonel, 510, 728
SHORTIS, Pte G., 803
SHORTLAND ISLANDS (Sketch p. 224), 224
SHRAPNEL, Maj G. S., 468
SHWEBO (Sketch p. 5), 6
SIALUM ISLAND (Map p. 396; Sketch p. 726), 522, 524, 609, 616, 658-9; captured, 730
SIBIDA, CAPE (Map p. 717), 723-4
SICILY, 4, 7, 218-19, 273, 283
SIDES, Sgt F. W., 298
SIEKMANN, Capt D. C., 364, 490, 502, 512-13, 529
SIEKMANN, Lt-Col P. E., 464, 510-12, 543, 548, 551-3
SIEWART, Sergeant, 213-14
SIFFLEET, Sgt L. G., 259-60
SIGAWA (Sketch p. 765), 766
SIGOIYA (Sketch p. 235), 243, 245, 599-600
SIKI COVE (Map p. 528; Sketch p. 461), 452-5, 457-9, 539-41, 544, 546, 549, 552
SIKI CREEK (Map p. 528; Sketches pp. 452, 461), 452 459-60, 465-6, 477, 536-44, 547, 549-51, 553, 555-6, 607, 616, 619, 640, 644-6, 648
SILVER, Cpl E. P., 578-9
SIMBANG (Map p. 528; Sketch p. 485), 499, 504, 514, 516, 543, 615
SIMMONS, L-Cpl J. J., 573
SIMMONS, Lt N. W., 603, 605
SIMMONS, Lt T. McC., 399
SIMPSON, Maj-Gen N. W., 334, 336, 457-8, 462, 504, 511-15, 519, 527, 553, 604-7, 612, 665, 670, 727-30: commands 2/17 Bn, 333; commands 24 Bde, 558; commands 20 Bde, 615
SIMS, Lt-Col C. A. W., 563
SINCLAIR, Sgt B. T., 301
SINCLAIR, Lt S. V., 774
SINGAPORE (Map p. 5), 809

SINGARIN (Sketch p. 808), 809-10
SINGAUA PLANTATION (Map p. 327), 334, 336, 349, 391
SINGLETON, NSW (Sketch p. 15), 16
SINGOR (Sketch p. 765), 766-7
SIO (Map p. 396; Sketch p. 726), 242, 378, 386, 396, 404, 406-9, 482, 487, 505-6, 517-18, 522, 524, 530, 555, 602, 609, 659, 676, 679, 727-8, 730, 734, 736-7, 762, 765, 769n; Japanese withdraw from, 732; occupied, 735; Japanese strength at, 764
SIO MISSION (Sketches pp. 726, 765), 736, 765
SIO TRACK, 408-9
SISI (Map p. 528; sketch p. 461), 478, 490, 504, 512-14, 521, 554, 612, 614; occupied, 618
SISI TRACK (Sketch p. 617), 614, 617-18, 630
SITLINGTON, WO2 K. G., 531-2
SKIDWAY (Sketch p. 796), 797
SKINDEWAI (Map p. 32), 43, 47, 86
SKINDEWAI TRACK (Map p. 32), 31
SKINNER, Maj R. I., 793
SKUSE, Cpl E. E. G., 98
SLIM, Field Marshal Rt Hon Viscount, 782
SMELL (Sketch p. 635), 632
SMITH, Cpl A. J., 77-8, 81
SMITH, Cpl D., 34n
SMITH, Lt D. O., 375, 688
SMITH, Lt E. A. G., 638, 658
SMITH, Lt-Col G. F., 53-4, 69, 90, 118-19, 156, 158, 178, 208-9, 277, 322-3, 341-3, 360, 364, 366, 393-4, 395n, 406-7, 757, 785; commands 24 Bn, 37; introduces rigid anti-malarial discipline, 413
SMITH, Capt G. L., 396
SMITH, Cpl G. L., 78, 93-4, 98
SMITH, Col G. N. C., 310-11
SMITH, Cpl J., 161-3
SMITH, Maj N. S., 781n
SMITH, Maj P. S., 269n
SMITH, Capt R. J. H., 76, 78, 80, 92, 101
SMITH, R. R., 799n, 802n
SMITH, Sgt T. J., 320n
SMITH, Capt W. T., 80-1
SMYTH, Sgt R. N., 251
SNAKE RIVER (Map p. 32), 118
SNAKE VALLEY, 21, 28, 135, 178
SNELL, E. M., 2n
SNELL, Maj L., 459-60, 462-3, 468-70, 472-6, 478, 483, 496-7, 670
SNELL'S HILL (Sketch p. 485), 476, 491, 520
SNIPERS, 80-1, 622
SNOOK, Lt E. R., 236, 341, 571-2
SNOOK'S HOUSE (Sketch p. 235), 244, 246
SOA RIVER (Sketch p. 765), 765n
SOLOMON, Maj H. A., 269n
SOLOMON ISLANDS (Map p. 28; Sketch p. 224), 1-2, 8, 11, 13, 55-6, 221, 223, 792, 801; Allied plans for capture, 3, 7, 9, 220; Japanese strength in, 11n, 231-2; American strength in, 220, 816; operations in, 224-6, 653
SOLOMON SEA (Map p. 28), 328, 449, 466
SOLU RIVER (Sketch p. 690), 596n, 681, 689, 691, 694, 697, 702-4, 711, 739
SOMERVILLE, Admiral of the Fleet Sir James, 220n
SONG RIVER (Map p. 528; Sketches pp. 452, 461), 444, 446, 451, 454, 458, 463-4, 477, 490, 502, 504, 510-14, 516, 521, 523, 526-7, 529, 531n, 532-3, 535-40, 542-4, 546, 548, 551, 553-6, 559, 607, 612, 626, 632, 634, 643, 658, 662, 664-6, 671, 728, 771; Japanese counter-attack at, 636-9
SONG VALLEY, 518
SORONG (Sketch p. 799), 806
SOUSE (Sketch p. 394), 410
SOUTH-EAST ASIA COMMAND, 790
SOUTHERN AMBUSH (Sketch p. 342), 342, 360, 364-5
SOUTH PACIFIC AREA (Sketch p. 5), 4, 7-8, 16n, 444, 505, 790, 792, 798, 817; Allied plans, 1n, 55-6, 221 strength of Allied forces in, 2n, 9, 11, 220; not represented at Washington Conference, 220
SOUTH-WEST PACIFIC AREA (Sketch p. 5), 4, 10n, 16, 18, 90, 273, 354, 466, 706, 737, 763, 782, 795, 799, 801; Allied plans and reinforcement, 1n, 8-9, 20, 55-6, 218, 220-1, 444, 790-1; Allied strength in, 2n, 7, 11-12, 57, 220; strength of Japanese forces, 13, 788; not represented at Washington Conference, 220; Australia not represented on GHQ, 222
SOUTHWOOD, Capt E. F., 418, 420-1
SOUVENIRS, 408
SOWI RIVER (Map p. 717), 615, 720, 723

SPENDLOVE, Lt N. J., 758-9
SPENDLOVE SPUR (Sketch p. 757), 757-9
SPIER, Maj P. E., 671
SPRATT, Pte A. L., 458
SPROGG'S RIDGE (Map p. 740), 744, 746
SPRUANCE, Admiral Raymond A., 8
SPRY, Capt A. F., 625, 735
SPRY STREET (Sketch p. 639), 642, 648
SQUIBB, WO2 A. C., 664
STAINES, L-Cpl D. A., 320n
STALEY, F-Lt E. R., 694, 702, 709, 711
STALIN, Marshal Joseph, 218
Stand To, 330n, 455n
STANLEY, Lt-Cdr G. A. V., 259, 261, 806n
STANTON, Capt A. J., 754
STAPLES, Lt W. L., 355, 366
STARK, Lt J. A., 544, 546
STARMER, Lt A. C., 476
STAR MOUNTAINS (Map p. 28), 233
STARR, Lt-Col P. D. S. (Plate p. 157), 88, 107-8, 110-16, 128, 130-1, 134, 151, 169, 172-3; commands 58/59 Bn, 61
STARVATION HILL (Sketch p. 485), 484, 486
STAVERMAN, Sgt H. N., 259-61, 263
Stawell, Australian corvette, 807
STEAK (Sketch p. 290), 288, 300
STEEGE, Gp Capt G. H., 797
STEEL, Lt H. W., 701
STEEPLE TREE HILL (Map p. 528; Sketch p. 617), 614, 616-19, 621-4, 629-30, 633, 639; captured, 628; *see also* Feature 2600
STEINER, Colonel John J. F., 352n; commands 532 EBSR, 265
STEINHEUER, Lt P. E., 297
STENHOUSE, Maj T. R., 530, 536-7, 544, 549-50, 552, 554
STEPHENS, Sgt J. F., 93
STEPHENS, Capt K. H. R., 28, 31-2, 35-6, 45, 50, 111
STEPHENS' HUT, 117
STEPHENSON, Capt E. V., 749
STEPHENS' TRACK (Map p. 27; Sketch p. 194), 28n, 32, 66-7, 88, 117, 131-3, 146, 167, 197, 200
STEVENS, Sgt G. V., 202
STEVENS, Lt K. W., 370, 675
STEVENS, L-Sgt R. J., 343
STEVENSON, Lt J. G., 200-1
STEVENSON, Maj-Gen J. R., 811-12
STEVENSON, Maj W. R. D., 774
STEVE'S TRACK (Sketch p. 190), 191, 203
STEWART, Cpl A., 776n
STEWART, Lt-Col G., 474
STEWART, Lt-Col H. McB., 119-23, 125-6
STEWART, Capt W. D. P., 211, 214
STILWELL, Lt-Gen Joseph W., 6, 220n
STINKER (Sketch p. 635), 632, 634, 637-8, 651
STIRLING, Maj C. H., 747-8
STOKES, Lt W. E., 365, 373
STOLZENFELS SPUR (Sketch p. 726), 733, 735
STONE, Maj R. I., 267n
STONY CREEK (Sketch p. 39), 28-9, 34n, 75, 119, 126
STORES, badly handled, 271, 549
STRANGE, Maj B. D., 665, 670
STRATEGY, *Allied*, 1-4, 219; in Pacific, 217-20, 790-1, 798-9, 801-2. *Japanese*, 792
STRATHPINE, Qld, 280n
STREET, Capt F. N., 35, 67, 287
STRETCH, Lt W. G., 678
STRETCHER BEARERS, 65-6, 383-4, 498
STRINGER BEACH, 271, 326
STROM, Maj G. F., 216
STRUSS, Capt A. L., 305
STUART, Capt D. B., 210, 417, 419, 590n
STUART, Maj M. R., 470, 474-6, 478, 483, 489, 591, 664, 670
STURDEE, Lt-Gen Sir Vernon, 780
STURROCK, Capt A. S., 26n, 140, 144-5, 160
SUARA BAY (Sketch p. 808), 808
SUBLET, Lt-Col F. H., 350n, 423, 427-30, 434, 567, 687; commands 2/16 Bn, 398
SUBMARINES, 3, 227, 793, 801-2; *Japanese*, 12, 278, 325, 473, 522, 548, 557, 649, 734, 801
SUEZ CANAL, 265
"SUEZ" RIVER (Map p. 327; Sketch p. 333), 333
SUGARCANE RIDGE (Sketch p. 196), 153-6, 163-4, 193n; captured, 164-5
SUGARLOAF (Map p. 32; Sketch p. 394), 53, 177, 209, 322-3, 393-5

SUGINO, Lieutenant, 529-30
SULLIVAN, L-Sgt J. A., 572
SUMATRA (Sketch p. 5), 218
SUMMIT (Map p. 32), 22, 61, 74, 85, 104; conference at, 71-3
SUNSHINE (Map p. 32; Sketch p. 254), 50, 61, 90, 253-4, 269-70, 413
SUPPLY, *Allied*, a problem in New Guinea operations, 21, 51; in Salamaua operations, 37, 65-6, 86-7, 103-4, 132, 137-8, 154, 164, 199, 292; in Lae operations, 269, 332-3, 362, 366, 403; in Ramu Valley and Finisterres, 438, 601, 740-42; in coastal pursuit, 667, 671, 673, 675, 727, 764, 766-7. *Japanese*, in Salamaua operations, 185-6; in Finschhafen operations, 518, 522, 557, 658; dumps found in Sio area, 735-6
SUPPLY DROPPING, in Salamaua operations, 71, 292, 300; in Ramu Valley, 566, 593
SURINAM (Sketch p. 424), 424
SURINAM RIVER (Sketches pp. 235, 562), 247, 443, 563-4, 566-7, 571, 585
SURINAM VALLEY, 688, 697
SURPINE VALLEY (Sketch p. 635), 638-9
SUTERS, Lt T. W., 542, 547, 603-4
SUTHERLAND, Pte D., 648
SUTHERLAND, Brig R. B., 164, 279n, 487
SUTHERLAND, Maj-Gen Richard K., 8-9, 182, 281, 798
SUTHERS, Lt-Col R. A., 468-9, 473-5, 664
SUTTON, Lt A. J., 574
SWAN, Sgt R. A., 108
SWAN'S O.P. (Sketch p. 290), 300, 317, 320
SWEANY, Brig-Gen Kenneth S., 58, 60, 71, 140
SWIFT, Maj-Gen Innis P., commands 1 US Cav Div, 795
SWIFT, Capt P. W., 74
SWIFT, Cpl W. D., 354
SYM, WO1 J., 175
SYMINGTON, Maj W. G., 443, 704-5; commands 2/16 Bn, 687
SYMONS, Lt-Col T. A., 26n
SYRIA, 18-19, 359

TABALI CREEK (Sketches pp. 62, 92), 63, 86, 92-3, 97-8, 100, 102-3, 117
TABUT (Map p. 396), 785
TACTICS, American and Australian compared, 321n; in Sattelberg operations, 618; *Japanese*, in Salamaua operations, 179, in Sattelberg operations, 628, in Song River counter-attack, 639
TADJI (Sketches pp. 799, 807), airfield at, 802, 804, 806
TAGUCHI, Sergeant, 106
TAKAGI, Lieut-Colonel, 479, 501, 524
TAKAHASHI, Sergeant, 216
TAKAMURA, Major, 47, 64-5, 96-7; commands III/102 Bn, 43
TAKANO, Private, 106
TAKATA, Private, 106
TAKEHAMA, Major, 543; commands II/79 Bn, 533
TAKEUCHI, Commander, 306, 307, 309, 325
TALASEA (Map p. 28; Sketch p. 793), 221, 792, 798n
TALBOT, Capt L. S., 256n, 417
TALI (Map p. 327), 334, 336
TAMBU, MOUNT (Maps pp. 27, 32; Sketches, pp. 131, 212), 28, 56, 67, 71-2, 84n, 117, 125, 127, 133-4, 143-5, 153-4, 159, 167-8, 178-9, 181, 183, 185-9, 193n, 201-2, 206-7, 211, 215-16, 285, 287, 291-2, 296, 309, 325; area described, 22; attacks on, 146-50, 161-6, 194-200
TAMBU BAY (Map p. 32; Sketches pp. 141, 194), 134, 138, 140, 158-9, 163, 168, 173, 180-2, 192, 197, 199, 201, 211-12, 214-16, 285, 290-2; Allied operations in area, 141-5; US strength at, 160-1
TAMBU SADDLE (Map p. 27; Sketch p. 131), 115-17, 132, 146, 168
TAMIGUDU (Sketch p. 394), 471
TAMI ISLANDS (Sketch p. 508), 447, 505, 557, 594n; occupied, 507-9
TANAHMERAH (Sketch p. 811), 810, 812
TANAHMERAH BAY (Sketch p. 799), 802, 804
TANAKA, Lieut-Colonel, 158, 193n
TANKS, 17, 479, 548; premature release of news of arrival at Finschhafen, 624n
TAPEN (Sketch p. 768), 769-70
TAPIOLI, Lance-Corporal, 86
TAPPER, Sgt D. L., 592
TARAWA ISLAND (Map p. 814), 800; American landing on, 654-5

INDEX 849

TAREKO (Map p. 528; Sketch p. 461), 463-5, 485, 547, 603
TAREKO TRACK (Map p. 528), 473, 509
TARI (Sketch p. 394), 377, 385, 396
TARIKNGAN (Sketch p. 768), 764, 771
Taroona, Australian ship, 269
TART, Cpl R., 468
TASHIRO Major, 669, 676, 728
TATTERSON, Capt L. V., 29, 34, 38-43, 52, 61, 74, 81, 175
TAYLOR, Colonel Harold, 94, 99, 102-4, 106, 122, 126, 145, 160, 163, 165-6, 185, 187, 195, 197, 199-201, 211, 292, 294, 308; commands I/162 US Bn, 84
TAYLOR, Pte J., 32
TAYLOR, Maj J. L., 233-4, 261-2
TAYLOR, Maj R., 750, 753, 755
TEASDALE, Lt C. K., 592, 690-1, 694-7
TED'S POINT (Sketch p. 333), 333
TELEFOMIN (Map p. 28), 233-4
TENNANT, Sgt D. A., 190
TERAMOTO, Lt-Gen Kumaichi, 232
TERAUCHI, Field Marshal Count Hisaichi, 788; commands *Southern Army*, 11
TERRY'S POST (Sketch p. 562), 687
TESHIMA, Lt-Gen Fusataro, 788
TETEREI (Sketch p. 731), 731
TEWAE RIVER (Sketch p. 726), 616, 729
TEWEP (Sketch p. 394), 407
TEWKSBURY, Lt A. R., 396
THIRGOOD, Capt L. R., 305, 308
THIRLWELL, Maj G. McA., 347
THIRTY-MILE STRIP, 339, 344
THOMAS, Lt G. E., 370, 408
THOMAS, Capt J. C., 406-7
THOMAS, Maj J. H., 389
THOMAS, Maj K. B., 748, 750
THOMAS, Lt P. C., 205-6
THOMSON, Capt A. S., 459, 476-7
THOMSON, W Cdr D. F., 812
THORNTON, Capt J. J., 643, 661, 672-3
THORPE, Pte R., 486-7
THREE PIMPLES (Sketch p. 577), 576-7
THURNWALD, Dr, 233
THURSDAY ISLAND (Map p. 28), 280n, 811
THWAITES, Maj G. R., 142, 144, 192, 730
TIDBALL, Ensign James M., 332
TIETYENS, Maj F. W., 645-6, 665, 675
TIGEDU (Sketch p. 467), 474
TIGHE, Sig C. M., 455n
TIKERENG (Sketch p. 350), 349
TILLER, Sgt W. L., 146, 148-9
TILLEY, Lt-Col Q. A., 412, 715-16, 718, 725
TIMBERED KNOLL (Map p. 27; Sketch p. 109), 311; capture of, 171-2
TIMBE RIVER (Sketch p. 765), 765
TIMBULUM PLANTATION (Map p. 528; Sketch p. 485), 498-9, 552, 609
TIMBUNKE (Sketch p. 808), 806n
Time magazine, 506n
TIMMINS, Tpr E., 250
TIMNE (Map p. 327), 341
TIMOR (Sketch p. 5), 2, 11, 17, 229n, 242, 792, 811
TINIAN ISLAND (Map p. 814), 791, 813; capture of, 815
TINKLER, Maj N., 781n
TINSLEY, Brig W. N., 557n
TIRIMORO (Map p. 528; Sketch p. 467), 474, 484, 490, 504, 514, 516, 526, 543, 615; occupied, 521
TIRIMORO TRACK, 476
TOBACCO, 130n, 472
TOBIN, Sgt T., 299
TOBRUK, 264, 266, 330, 349, 816
"TOJO", 25n; see also LAE O.P.
TOKUA, police boy, 435
TOKYO (Sketch p. 5), 18, 231, 256, 315, 791, 816
TOLSON, Lt-Col J. J., 385, 398; commands III/503 Parachute Bn, 339
TOLSON, Maj W. M., 781n
TOMKINS, Sgt A. V., 67, 88
TOMKINS, Maj R. C., 26n
TOMLINS, Cpl M. C., 618, 620
TOMPSON, Lt-Col R. A. J., 269n, 276, 357, 402n, 588
TOMS, Lt-Col S. J., 572, 576, 581, 583-4, 589-90
TOMS' POST (Sketch p. 562), 595n, 598, 687, 703, 739, 744
TOOCOOMWAH (Sketch p. 394), 408
TOOLE, Lt W. R., 242
TOORBUL POINT, Qld, 280n

TOOWOOMBA (Sketch p. 15), 16, 280
TOPOPO (Sketch p. 684), 684, 742, 776, 784
TOROKINA (Sketch p. 793), 653, 792, 794, 801, 816
TOROKINA, CAPE, 653
TORR, Brig A. G., 279n
TORRENT, Sgt A., 368
TORRES STRAIT (Map p. 15), 227-8, 810-11
TORRICELLI MOUNTAINS (Sketch p. 258), 259-60, 806n
TOWNSEND, Major Vernon F., 184
TOWNSVILLE, Qld, 228, 280n
TRAINING, of Australian Army, 228-9, 265-6
TRAINOR, Lt-Col T. G., 267n
TRAVERS, Lt-Col B. H. (Plate p. 157), 68, 88, 152, 155, 207, 745, 785
TREASURY ISLANDS (Sketch p. 224), 224; occupied, 653
TREBILCOCK, Pte T. G., 92, 101
TRELOAR, Capt H. F., 640
TREMELLEN, Sgt H. A., 778
TRENERRY, Capt A. R., 571, 582, 584
TRENOWORTH, Pte J. G., 354
TRETHEWIE, Lt E. C., 122, 165
TREVALDWYN, Capt D. E., 366
TREVOR'S RIDGE (Sketch p. 562), 571-3, 575, 590, 680; defence of, 580-5
TRIANGLE (Sketch p. 485), 486, 489, 491-3, 496, 499
TRIMBLE, Major Homer, 243
TRINITY BEACH, Qld, 266
TRIPLETT, Lt L. C., 362
TROBRIAND ISLANDS (Map p. 28), 222; see also KIRIWINA ISLAND
TROON, Capt J., 37
TROUGHTON, Pte H. J., 307
TRUK ISLAND (Sketch p. 5), 2, 8, 11, 798-9; Allies plan seizure of, 3-4, 790-2
TSILI TSILI (Maps pp. 28, 327; Sketches pp. 252, 254), 119, 166, 253, 257, 270-1, 276, 279, 337, 338n, 340, 344, 357-9, 404, 738; airfield at, 210, 254-6
TUAM ISLAND (Map p. 396), 522
TUCKER, Lt-Col F. A. G., 619, 622-3, 628, 630, 640-1, 645-6, 665-6, 671, 674-5; commands 2/23 Bn, 553
TULAGI (Sketch p. 224), 1n
TUNIS, 1, 7
TUNKAAT RIVER (Sketch p. 427), 439
TUNOM RIVER (Map p. 717), 716, 718-20
TURKEY, 4
TURNBULL, L-Sgt C. P., 125-6
TURNER, Sgt C. A., 388-9
TURNER, Lt R. A., 308
TURN OFF CORNER (Sketch p. 639), 639
TURTON, Maj D. K., 440, 564-5, 587
TWIN SMITHS (Map p. 293), 313
TYE, Maj K. F., 781n
TYRER, Pte W. A., 41
TYRES, Lt B. W. E., 30-1
TYTER, Tpr C. F., 570

UCHIDA, Major, 533
ULAP (Sketch p. 394), 378, 404, 406
ULIAP CREEK (Map p. 27), 23, 109, 134, 150, 154
ULIGAN HARBOUR (Sketch p. 808), 807
ULITHI ATOLL (Map p. 814), 798-9
UMBOI ISLAND (Map p. 28), 522
UMI RIVER (Sketch p. 427), 423, 430, 433, 436-7; advance to, 428-9; crossing of, 434
UNDARIBA, Corporal, 177
UNDERWOOD, Sgt R. V., 583
URAWA RIVER (Sketch p. 394), 70
UREN, M., 430n, 688n
URIA (Sketch p. 684), 684, 711, 739
URIA RIVER (Sketches pp. 235, 562), 247, 431, 561-3, 566, 569, 576, 579-80, 589
URIA VALLEY (Sketch p. 235), 247, 566-7, 570
URIGINA (Sketch p. 684), 243, 440, 564, 592, 684
URQUHART, Capt R. D., 47, 65, 73, 76, 81, 91-4, 95n, 96-8, 100
URQUHART, Cpl P. E., 318
USINI (Sketch p. 235), 243, 424, 440, 564, 587, 592, 684, 698
USUI, Lieutenant, 125, 311-12

VANIMO (Map p. 28), 20
VAN NOY, Pte Nathan, 530-1
VANPRAAG, Capt J. B., 536, 542
VASEY, Maj-Gen G. A. (Plates pp. 348, 460), 282n, 338-40, 357, 359-60, 366, 372, 376-8, 385, 389-91, 398-9, 402n, 403, 419, 421-3, 425, 430, 506, 565-7, 575, 585-7, 589, 599, 687-9, 694-7, 702, 704-5, 709-11, 713, 738-9, 743, 746, 755, 757, 761, 771,

850 INDEX

VASEY, Maj-Gen G. A.—*continued*
  774; commands 7 Div, 166, 268; in Nadzab-Lae operations, 269-70, 276-7, 337, 365; estimate of, 270, 595, 600; relations with Americans, 275; in Markham-Ramu Valley operations, 414-17, 426, 428, 433-4, 436-8, 561, 702-3; and Bena Force, 431, 438-9; on Finschhafen operations, 558; on 7 Div role in Finisterres, 580, 594; asks for 18 Bde, 692-3; considered for appointment to command I Corps, 780
VELLA LAVELLA ISLAND (Sketch p. 224), 226
VERTIGAN, Maj D. H., 66
VIAL, F-Lt L. G., 23*n*, 258
VIAL'S O.P. (Map p. 27; Sketch p. 116), 23, 115-16, 150
VIAL'S TRACK, 120-3
VICKERS RIDGE (Sketch p. 25), 22*n*, 25, 34*n*, 80
VICKERS RIDGE TRACK (Sketch p. 25), 28-9, 80
VICKERY, Lt E. C., 721*n*
VILA (Sketch p. 224), 224, 226
VINCENT, Maj A. L., 781*n*
VINCKE POINT (Sketch p. 765), 659, 765
VITIAZ STRAIT (Maps pp. 28, 396), 8, 55, 277-9, 284, 444-5, 449-50, 506, 556, 729, 731*n*, 794*n*, 798*n*
VOCO POINT (Sketch p. 388), 388
VOGELKOP PENINSULA (Map p. 799), 231, 790-1, 798, 804, 813; Americans land on, 806

WABAG (Sketch p. 258), 261-2
WADE, Pte C. J. A., 663
WAFFAR RIVER (Sketch p. 252), 256-7
WAGAN (Map p. 327; Sketch p. 369), 135, 366, 368, 370-1, 379-80
WAGOL (Map p. 773), 787
WAHGI RANGE (Map p. 28), 233
WAIME (Map p. 327), 270, 340
WAIMERIBA (Sketches pp. 235, 248), 237-8, 240, 244-5, 247, 251, 431, 434, 564
WAIN, 433*n*
WAIPALI (Map p. 32), 24, 26, 31, 34, 38, 82-3
WAKDE ISLAND (Sketch p. 799), 792, 805
WALEBING, WA, 280*n*
WALINGAI (Sketch p. 726), 609-10, 616, 728-9
WALKER, Col A. S., 354*n*, 681*n*
WALKER, Capt B. G. C., 703
WALKER, Pte J. A., 343, 360
WALKER, Capt J. E., 541, 556, 630, 634
WALKER, Maj K. R., 175-6, 189, 191, 320-1
WALKER, Lt L. G., 190
WALKIE TALKIE SETS, 373, 727
WALL, Lt-Col R. E., 332
WALLDER, Lt J. R., 428-9
WALMSLEY, Pte R. G., 320*n*
WALPOLE'S TRACK (Sketch p. 131), 88, 115, 117, 131, 133, 146, 149, 167-8, 187, 200
WALTERS, Lt E. A., 313
WALTERS, Maj V. M., 146-9, 161-2, 167, 200
WALTERS' TRACK (Sketch p. 146), 146, 149
WAMALA CREEK, 259-60
WAMASU (Sketch p. 291), 107, 303
WAMPAGNAN, 406
WAMPIT (Maps pp. 32, 327), 53, 158, 341
WAMPIT RIVER (Map p. 327), 210, 277, 281
WAMPIT VALLEY, 20, 137, 253-4
WAMPUN (Sketch p. 424), 424, 440, 443, 563, 566, 595; action at, 440-2
WAMUKI (Sketch p. 394), 412
WAMUNTI (Sketch p. 235), 684
WANDILUK (Sketch p. 768), 770
WANDOKAI (Sketch p. 726), 609, 726, 728-9
WANGAN (Sketch p. 808), 809-10
WANKON (Sketch p. 427), 423
WANKON HILL (Sketch p. 427), 436
WANTOAT (Map p. 396), 429, 433*n*, 688, 693, 697, 784-5
WANTOAT RIVER, 785
WAR CRIES, of 9 Div, 265, 625, 629, 640
WARD, Pte L., 314*n*
WARD HUNT, CAPE (Map p. 28), 334
WARD'S AIRFIELD, 276, 358
WARD'S VILLAGE (Map p. 773), 774
WAREO (Map p. 396; Sketch p. 660), 510, 513, 518, 520, 522, 526, 536, 547, 554-5, 557, 560, 602, 608-13, 626-7, 631-3, 649-51, 656-9, 667, 670-4, 676-9, 696, 718-19, 726-7; captured, 675
WAREO TRACK, 537, 615, 669, 675; observation post on, 626-7, 632

WARFE, Lt-Col G. R. (Plates pp. 157, 173), 28, 31 33, 35-6, 43-5, 48, 50, 66-7, 88, 107, 115-17, 124, 131-4, 150-5, 171-2, 181*n*, 209, 298, 301, 303, 322; commands 2/3 Indep Coy, 26; commands 58/59 Bn, 203
WARIA RIVER (Sketch p. 85), 84, 241
WARNER, Cpl N. A., 757-8
WASAMBU (Sketch p. 258), 258
WASHBROOK, Cpl W. L., 648
WASHINGTON, DC, 8, 10, 12, 55, 197, 217-18, 222, 790, 798-9; May 1943 conference, 219-20; Australian Military Mission to, 780
WATAM (Sketch p. 808), 810
WATAM LAGOON (Sketch p. 808), 809
WATCH, Lt-Col J. R., 211, 768-9
WATERHOUSE, Capt H. L., 346
WATERHOUSE, Lt S. G. J., 461-2
WATERS, Pte L. J., 41
WATER SUPPLY, 310, 630-1; in Lae operation, 380; in Finschhafen operations, 489; in coastal advance, 727
WATSON, Lt C. J., 656
WATSON, Capt R., 37, 75
WATSON, Capt R. B., 723, 725
WATSON, Capt W. D., 419-20, 690-1, 694-6
WATT, Cpl A. J., 76-7
WATTS, Capt R. D., 439, 591
WATUT RIVER (Map p. 327; Sketch p. 254), 117-18, 252-4, 256, 270-1, 277, 337, 340-1, 344, 346, 590*n*
WATUT VALLEY, 20, 70, 119, 137, 182, 210, 239, 241, 253, 256, 344; airfields in, 231, 254, 269; strength of Allied forces in, 255
WAU (Maps pp. 28, 32), 1, 18-19, 22, 24-6, 28, 31, 34*n*, 42, 47, 51, 55, 61, 87*n*, 90, 156, 210, 231, 234, 236, 238, 252-4, 269, 324, 341, 424, 762. 817; Australian strength and reinforcement, 14, 20, 58; Japanese withdraw from, 23
WAU VALLEY, 42, 281
WAVELL, Field Marshal Rt Hon Earl, 220*n*, 712-13; commands Burma-India theatre, 5-6; becomes Viceroy of India, 713
WEALE, Capt W. T. H. B., 377
WEBB, Capt D. S., 474, 476, 486
WEBBER, Lt R. B., 803
WEBB'S PLANTATION (Sketch p. 388), 381
WEBER POINT (Sketch p. 734), 734, 765*n*, 769, 771
WEBSTER, WO2 J. V., 303
WEDGWOOD, Lt V. C., 537-8, 540, 549
WEGG, Lt C. H., 337, 345
WEI RIVER (Sketch p. 248), 248, 251, 431
WEITEMEYER, Lt H. W., 376
WELLAM, Pte R. K., 314*n*
WELLINGS, Pte C., 151
WELLS, Lt G. R., 681
WELLS, Lt-Gen Sir Henry, 265, 535
WELLS JUNCTION (Sketch p. 116), 116-17, 150, 152-5
WELLS O.P. (Map p. 27; Sketch p. 131), 23*n*, 33, 45, 61-2, 66, 74-5, 134, 152-4, 164, 168, 192, 193*n*
WENGA (Map p. 773), 777-8
WESA (Sketch p. 235), 237-8, 240, 244-6; action at, 247-51
WESA TRACK, 251
WESTENDORF, Lt A. K., 418
WESTERN AUSTRALIA (Sketch p. 15), Australian Army in, 14, 16
WEWAK (Map p. 28; Sketch p. 799), 8, 11, 57, 182, 252, 259, 277-9, 328, 415, 449, 523, 524*n*, 561, 731*n*, 785, 789-92, 797*n*, 799, 801-2, 804, 806*n*, 809; Japanese strength and dispositions, 20, 231, 260, 425; air attacks on, 204; 6 Div casualties in advance to, 807*n*
WHIFF (Sketch p. 635), 632
WHITE, Lt E. K., 753
WHITE, Maj P. F. B., 626
WHITE, Lt R. B., 598
WHITE, Lt S. G., 165, 193
WHITECHURCH, Sgt J. H., 578-9
WHITEHEAD, Brig D. A., 336, 349, 350*n*, 351, 362, 368-9, 379, 548, 552-3, 559, 608, 612, 614, 617, 623-4, 628-9, 633, 640-2, 644-5, 647, 658, 665-6, 671-5; commands 26 Bde, 334; estimate of, 347, 652; on ration scales, 355; plans capture of Sattelberg, 616, 639
WHITEHEAD, Lt-Gen Ennis C., 253, 278, 282*n*, 414, 426; relations with New Guinea Force, 129*n*; Deputy Commander Fifth Air Force, 276
WHITELAW, Maj-Gen J. S., 24*n*

INDEX 851

WHITELAW, Maj S. H., 47, 133, 208, 210, 291, 303, 315, 317, 406-8
WHITE ROCK (Sketch p. 617), 614, 616, 621
WHITE TRUNK TREE (Sketch p. 617), 617-18, 621
WHITLAM, WO M. J., 305
WHITTAKER, Capt G. K., 66
WHITTAKER'S PLANTATION (Sketch p. 375), 365, 372-6
WHYTE, Maj W. A. S., 589, 754
WICKS, Maj S. W., 721
WIDE BAY (Map p. 28; Sketch p. 793), 793
WIDERU (Sketch p. 467), 467, 469
WILHELM, MOUNT, 586n
WILLIAMS, Lieutenant, 126, 297
WILLIAMS, WO2 A. E., 161-2
WILLIAMS, Maj D. E., 781n
WILLIAMS, Capt H. L., 793
WILLIAMS, J. Ward, 233
WILLIAMS, Lt R. G., 502
WILLIAMS, Capt S. M., 515
WILLOUGHBY, Maj-Gen Charles A., 221, 446, 797n
WILLS, Brig Sir Kenneth, 378
WILSON, Lt-Col B. V. (Plate p. 348), 457
WILSON, Capt H., 715-16
WILSON, Cpl J. A., 421
WILSON, Cpl J. M., 416
WILSON, Tpr K. G., 746
WILSON, Maj R. H. M., 105-6
WILSON'S PROMONTORY, Vic, 228-9
WILTON, Maj-Gen J. G. N., 58, 60, 71, 100, 116n, 134, 161, 164, 168, 180, 199-201; GSO1 3 Div, 26; appointed to Aust Military Mission, Washington, 197
WINCHESTER, Lt-Col T. H. F., 279n
WINDEYER, Maj-Gen Sir Victor (Plate p. 348), 326, 334, 380, 445-7, 450-3, 456n, 457, 463, 465, 467-8, 470-1, 473-4, 476-8, 480, 483, 485-6, 489-92, 495-7, 499, 501, 504, 509, 510-11, 512n, 513, 515-16, 519, 522, 525-6, 541, 543-4, 553, 603, 606, 608, 610, 611, 615, 733, 735; commands 20 Bde, 275, 730; estimate of, 330; prepares plans for Scarlet Beach landing, 447-8, 450; orders advance on Finschhafen, 466; seeks reinforcement of Finschhafen, 479, 481-2, 487, 503-4
WINGATE, Maj-Gen O. C., 5-6
WINTER, Lt R. B., 297, 309-11
WINTERFLOOD, Capt J. S., 33, 115, 117, 131-3, 150, 153-5, 203-5
WINTLE, Sgt E. B., 317
WIRELESS, 399; at Lae OP, 25n; at Kaiapit, 421; in Bena Force area, 600; at Shaggy Ridge, 706; No. 208 Set, 249n, 417; No. 11 Set, 419; compared with American, 563-4; see also WALKIE TALKIE SETS
WISSEL LAKES (Sketch p. 811), 810
WITHERS, Lt-Col L. A., 267n
WITHINGTON, Capt E. A., 719-20
WOISAU, native police boy, 244
WOLEAI ATOLL (Map p. 814), 798
WOLFE, Maj C. C., 812
WOMA (Sketch p. 258), 260
WONAM ISLAND (Sketch p. 508), 508
WONDECLA, Qld, 280n
WONGABEL, Qld, 280n
WOOD, Brig F. G. (Plate p. 204), 51, 60, 62, 64, 66, 74-5, 78, 81-2, 86, 120-3, 125, 163-7, 186, 189, 191, 200; commands 2/6 Bn, 26
WOOD, Lt J. N., 515
WOODBURY, Colonel Murray C., 256, 357, 426n
WOODFULL, MOUNT (Sketch p. 427), 431
WOODLARK ISLAND (Map p. 28), 9, 56, 230, 280n, 402n; airfield, 58, 223; occupation of, 221-3, 273
"WOODPECKERS", 40
WOODS, Cpl W. A., 520
WOODY ISLAND (Sketch p. 39), 119, 128

WOOTTEN, Maj-Gen Sir George (Plate p. 508), 166, 270, 282n, 329-30, 333, 348-9, 352n, 357, 363, 368-9, 386, 389-91, 403, 439, 445, 447-8, 451, 466, 479-80, 490, 504, 508, 513, 517, 521, 527, 529-30, 534-5, 540-4, 547, 550, 556-8, 560, 565, 594, 606, 615, 623, 624n, 629, 633-4, 639, 642, 645, 658, 663-4, 670, 724, 726, 730, 740; appointed GOC 9 Div, 264; confers with Americans on amphibious training, 265; plans Lae operations, 267, 269, 274-5, 334, 337, 378-81; orders crossing of Busu, 351; on supply problems, 362, 366, 507; plans Finschhafen operation, 446, 449; seeks reinforcement, 482-3, 488, 522-3, 555; role allotted, 505-6, 518; defence of Finschhafen, 519, 525-6, 551-2, 602; resumes offensive, 536; plans capture of Sattelberg, 602-3, 608; plans advance to Wareo, 626, 656; orders coastal advance, 662, 727; attaches 9 Div troops to 4 Bde, 666-7
WORLE, Lt H. J., 29
WORNER, Capt J. F., 676-7
WOWOS (Sketch p. 254), 253
WRIGHT, Capt D. A., 754
WRIGHT, Capt G. W., 439
WRIGHT, Lt H. J., 632
WRIGHT, Lt-Cdr M. H., 793
WURTSMITH, Maj-Gen Paul B., 255
WURUF (Sketch p. 254), 70, 253
WYCHE, Capt P., 723

YAFATS RIVER (Sketch p. 427), 428-30
YAGOMAI (Sketch p. 768), 765n, 768-9
YAIMAS RIDGE (Sketch p. 731), 731
YALAU PLANTATION (Sketch p. 734), 772
YALI, Sergeant, 803
YALU (Map p. 327), 339, 359, 385, 398, 404, 415
YAMADA, Maj-Gen Eizo, 523
YAMAGUCHI, Major, 135
YANDELL, Sgt T. L., 583-4
YANGA (Sketches pp. 350, 369), 363-4, 366, 368, 380
YANGALUM (Map p. 773), 772, 777-8
YANO, Captain, 761
YASINGLI (Map p. 32), 50
YATES, Capt W. H., 215, 313
YATI RIVER (Sketch p. 427), 428
YAULA (Map p. 773; Sketch p. 684), 600-1, 689, 702, 775-7, 779, 782
YAUT RIVER (Sketch p. 768), 768-9
YEATMAN, Capt J. C., 640
YELLOW BEACH (Map p. 327; Sketch p. 333), 275, 326, 329-31, 333-4, 336, 347
YELLOW RIVER (Sketch p. 262), 262-3
YIMAS, LAKE (Sketch p. 258), 262
YOGIA RIVER (Sketch p. 591), 680-1, 700, 702-3, 739, 745
YOKOPI (Sketches pp. 591, 684), 424, 566, 592, 596, 600, 689, 702, 774-5
YONAPA (Sketch p. 235), 243, 431, 564, 599
YONEKURA, Major, 424
YOSHIKAWA, Captain, 728
YOSHIWARA, Lt-Gen Kane, 817
YOUNG, WO2 J. S., 574
YOUNG, Lt M. J., 342-3
YOUNG, Capt N. H., 589
YOUNG MEN'S CHRISTIAN ASSOCIATION, 88, 489, 611
YOUNG'S O.P. (Sketch p. 562), 574
YOUNG'S POST (Sketch p. 562), 589
YULA RIVER (Sketch p. 258), 259

ZAG (Map p. 528; Sketch p. 461), 460, 465, 473, 483, 490, 509, 511, 516, 553
ZAGAHEMI (Sketch p. 726), 672, 727
ZANANA (Sketch p. 224), 225
Z-DAY, explained, 276n
ZENAG (Maps pp. 32, 327), 20, 61, 341, 343n

www.ingramcontent.com/pod-product-compliance
Lightning Source LLC
Chambersburg PA
CBHW070752300426
44111CB00014B/2378